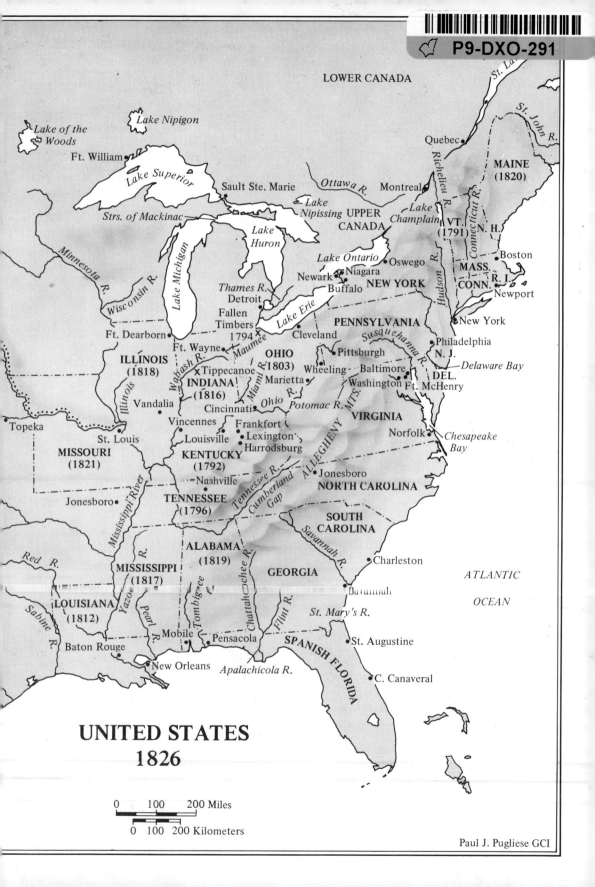

LOWER CANADA

Lake of the Woods

Lake Nipigon

Ft. William

Lake Superior

Sault Ste. Marie

Ottawa R.

Montreal

St. Lawrence

Quebec

St. John R.

MAINE (1820)

Strs. of Mackinac

Lake Nipissing

UPPER CANADA

Lake Champlain

Richelieu R.

VT. (1791)

N. H.

Minnesota R.

Lake Huron

Connecticut R.

Boston

Lake Michigan

Wisconsin R.

Lake Ontario

Oswego

MASS.

R. I.

CONN.

Newport

Newark

Niagara

Buffalo

NEW YORK

Hudson R.

Thames R.

Detroit

Lake Erie

New York

Fallen Timbers 1794

Ft. Dearborn

Cleveland

PENNSYLVANIA

Susquehanna R.

Philadelphia

Ft. Wayne

Maumee R.

Pittsburgh

N. J.

Delaware Bay

ILLINOIS (1818)

Tippecanoe

OHIO (1803)

Wheeling

Baltimore

DEL.

Illinois R.

Wabash R.

INDIANA (1816)

Miami R.

Marietta

Washington

Ft. McHenry

Vandalia

Cincinnati

Ohio R.

Potomac R.

ALLEGHENY MTS.

VIRGINIA

Vincennes

Frankfort

Louisville

Lexington

Harrodsburg

Norfolk

Chesapeake Bay

Topeka

St. Louis

MISSOURI (1821)

KENTUCKY (1792)

Nashville

Tennessee R.

Cumberland Gap

Jonesboro

NORTH CAROLINA

Jonesboro

TENNESSEE (1796)

Mississippi River

SOUTH CAROLINA

Savannah R.

Red R.

ALABAMA (1819)

Chattahoochee R.

GEORGIA

Charleston

ATLANTIC

MISSISSIPPI (1817)

Yazoo R.

Pearl R.

Tombigbee R.

Flint R.

St. Mary's R.

Savannah

OCEAN

LOUISIANA (1812)

Sabine R.

Baton Rouge

Mobile

Pensacola

SPANISH FLORIDA

St. Augustine

New Orleans

Apalachicola R.

C. Canaveral

UNITED STATES
1826

0   100   200 Miles

0   100   200 Kilometers

Paul J. Pugliese GCI

THE
SHAPING
OF
AMERICA

A PEOPLE'S HISTORY OF THE YOUNG REPUBLIC

THE
SHAPING
OF
AMERICA

Page Smith

VOLUME THREE

McGRAW-HILL BOOK COMPANY

New York / St. Louis / San Francisco

Düsseldorf / Mexico / Toronto

1 2 3 4 5 6 7 8 9 D O D O 7 8 3 2 1 0 9

Library of Congress Cataloging in Publication Data

Smith, Page.
The shaping of America.
Includes index.
1. United States—History—1783-1865. I. Title.
E301.S6   973   79-13592
ISBN 0-07-059017-6

For my sons, Carter and Eliot

ALSO BY PAGE SMITH:

James Wilson: Founding Father

John Adams (Two Volumes)

The Historian and History

As a City upon a Hill:
    The Town in American History

Daughters of the Promised Land:
    Women in American History

A New Age Now Begins:
    A People's History of the American
    Revolution (Two Volumes)

The Constitution: A Documentary
    and Narrative History

Contents

VOLUME THREE

	Introduction	*ix*
1.	*The Confederation*	*1*
2.	*"Shays' Rebellion"*	*23*
3.	*Luxury*	*38*
4.	*A New Frame of Government*	*50*
5.	*Ratification*	*95*
6.	*The Grand Procession*	*109*
7.	*The Nation Begins*	*117*
8.	*Assumption and the Capital*	*147*
9.	*Settlers and Indians*	*168*
10.	*The Genêt Affair*	*195*
11.	*The Jay Treaty*	*215*
12.	*The Whiskey Rebellion and Fallen Timbers*	*227*
13.	*The Jay Treaty Again*	*235*
14.	*Transmigration*	*243*
15	*The Quasi War*	*272*
16.	*The Election of 1800*	*285*
17.	*The Protestant Passion*	*309*
18.	*The Spirit of Capitalism*	*326*
19.	*Education*	*352*
20.	*The Family and the Community*	*366*
21.	*Urban Life*	*380*
22.	*The Arts*	*394*
23.	*Republican Medicine*	*426*
24.	*The South*	*434*
25.	*Down the Mississippi*	*454*

26. Marbury versus Madison   472
27. The Louisiana Purchase   484
28. Hamilton and Burr   498
29. To the Pacific   510
30. Homeward Bound   530
31. The Embargo   551
32. War Clouds   579
33. War in the Northwest   591
34. The War at Sea   615
35. Washington and Baltimore   627
36. Andrew Jackson and the Battle of New
     Orleans   644
37. The Election of 1816   654
38. Jackson and Florida   662
39. Hard Times   669
40. The Missouri Compromise   690
41. The Supreme Court   698
42. The Monroe Doctrine   710
43. The Election of 1824   719
44. Migration and Immigration   732
45. The Mission   751
46. American Enterprise   766
47. Class in America   777
48. Whatever Happened to the Founding
     Fathers?   785
49. Lafayette in America   802
50. Jefferson and Adams Correspond   815
51. The Nation Takes Shape   825
     Bibliographic Note   830
     Acknowledgments   832
     Index   833

Introduction

When I undertook my history of the American Revolution, it had been my intention to carry the story of the beginnings of our nation through the debates in the Federal Convention to the ratification of the new Constitution. That plan proved impractical. On grounds of narrative unity, the conclusion of the War for Independence with the Treaty of Paris in 1783 seemed a proper ending for that work. But I was left with a sense of incompleteness. The Revolution had created the possibility, not the reality, of a new nation. It is the Constitution that for all practical purposes is synonymous with our nationhood.

Perhaps as a consequence of this sense of leaving a story unfinished, I undertook to write a documentary and narrative history of the Constitution itself. Fascinating as this exercise proved to be, it also, not surprisingly, left me with a feeling of incompleteness: there were so many other themes and threads to be woven in with the history of the Constitution in order to give the reader a sense of the extraordinary complexity and diverseness of our relatively brief past. I therefore decided to undertake a large-scale history of the United States, carrying on from my volumes on the Revolution. Once I had decided on such a bold course, it seemed somehow to have been inevitable. Indeed, I was surprised that I had not hit upon the notion before. Outside of a number of rather innocuous American history textbooks (the best of which by far is Morison and Commager's *Growth of the American Republic*), no professional historian had undertaken to write an extensive history of the United States for the general reader since the early part of this century. In the nineteenth century the amateur student of American history had George Bancroft's famous *History of the United States* in ten volumes. John Bach McMaster's *History of the People of the United States*, published over a period of thirty years, beginning in 1883, told the story of America's genesis in eight substantial volumes that ended at the Civil War. A ninth volume was subsequently published covering the period of the Civil War and entitled, rather austerely, *The History of the People of the United States During Lincoln's Administration*.

James Ford Rhodes devoted seven volumes to the period from 1850 to 1877 (covering the Civil War years in two-year increments and putting on a final spurt in a belated eighth volume to carry the story to 1896).

With such a spate of general narrative histories in the nineteenth and early twentieth centuries (Woodrow Wilson wrote a multivolume history of the United States and Harvard professor Edward Channing wrote a six-volume history that ended with the Civil War), one is bound to reflect on the absence of comparable works in the last half century. Of course a history written on the scale of McMaster's or Rhodes's mammoth works—in Rhodes's case eight volumes covering forty-five years—would run to more volumes than a modern publisher would dare to publish or a reader, presumably, would care to read. We have accumulated more than a hundred years of additional history since the termination of McMaster's history and, one is tempted to add, far more detailed and intricate history at that. But there are undoubtedly other deterrents more compelling (Allan Nevins and Bruce Catton have, after all, written multivolume works on the Civil War, Nevins's extending to eight volumes).

Perhaps the most obvious inhibition to the writing of large-scale narrative histories of the United States has been the scholarly dictum that a professional historian (which has come to mean, with few exceptions, an academic historian) must be a specialist in some small segment of our history—the early colonial period, let us say, or the Reconstruction era following the Civil War, or the Jacksonian period. The historical pie can be sliced another way, of course—treating labor in American history, diplomacy, constitutional history, the woman's movement in the 1880s, and so on. But the primary dogma of the profession dictates narrow specialization. The penalties invoked against the academic historian who ventures outside his or her field can be severe, especially in the case of young, untenured faculty members. The result of this professional dogma has been that those presumably best suited to write general histories for literate readers are persuaded to confine themselves to monographic (i.e., single, limited) topics. An exception is made for "textbooks," but these are generally (and usually properly) viewed with contempt by the profession. Since some of them have been enormously profitable to their authors, a substantial number have been written, but none has managed to transcend the bland mediocrity of the genre except the aforementioned Morison and Commager.

Moreover, academic historians are only now beginning to struggle out from under the assumption that historical research and writing constitute something called a "social science." That is to say that history should be written in a detached, objective, "scientific" spirit. Hence all the little monographs, analogous to scientific experiments, each one exhausting all the available material in its area (as well as, all too frequently, its readers). The aspiration was to be definitive, to write something so detailed upon such a limited subject that it need never be done again. The fact that the historian was supposed to be detached and objective, to have no strong feelings about his subject, or, if he had such feelings, to rigorously suppress them, was underscored by another dogma: Any proper history should stop well short of the period of the historian's own lifetime; otherwise he might let his own feelings and prejudices compromise his "historical perspective."

It is small wonder that such inhibitions, reinforced by a rigid system of professional advancement based on these canons, discouraged the writing of traditional narrative history. If to venture outside one's field was to invite censure, any effort to revive "old-fashioned" narrative history on a large scale was sure to draw the concentrated fire of all those professional historians whose deity (as well as bread and butter) was monographic history.

These reflections are not, in any sense, novel for me. I have had years to meditate upon the peculiarities of academic history and to develop my own notions of the responsibilities (or, perhaps more simply, the pleasures) of the uninhibited historian. The determination to undertake this work has opened for me a vast new area to reflect upon. When the great narrative historians of the nineteenth and early twentieth centuries composed their interminable tomes (most of which, incidentally, still make excellent reading), they were confident of two things that no longer, it must be said, appear to be anything like the certainties they once were.

First, they believed that "history" could be understood; that is, a historian of reasonable intelligence, armed with the necessary documents, could make sense of the past and give a reasonable account, as Oscar Wilde so wickedly put it, "of what had never taken place." Where for centuries pious Christians had hoped to discern God's intentions for man through revelation or through reason applied to revelation, by the nineteenth century, no longer so pious, they had come to believe they could discern it in history. History thus took on a definitely religious tone, and historians, as a consequence, a quasi-priestly role.

Second, historians of the last century believed that if history could be understood and explained, the history of the United States was the prototype of that explanation. It demonstrated as did no other episode in history the benignness of the Creator. The origin of the United States had been glorious, indeed little short of miraculous (some thought that it was positive proof of God's intervention in history and thus not *short* of a miracle at all). Not only had its birth been miraculous, attended by a figure—George Washington—who some perfervid ministers went so far as to suggest had been sent down by the Almighty for the specific purpose, but its subsequent history had given every indication that its progress was to be "onward and upward," dragging along other peoples of the world willy-nilly. So nineteenth-century historians had two inestimable advantages over their modern-day counterparts. They believed that the past could be understood and, moreover, that they understood it; and they believed that the history of the United States constituted the greatest success story since man had emerged from prehistory.

As the reader may already have suspected, I feel impelled to preface this narrative with the confession that I hold to neither of these convictions. I am by no means certain that I or anyone else can in any real sense understand and/or explain "history," ours or that of any other nation. More important, I am not at all sure how American history is going to come out. It is quite within the realm of God's possibilities that we shall become what the American colonists once thought Great Britain had become, "a reproach and a by-word among the nations." There are abundant signs that we are already perceived by many nations of the world as more benighted than benign.

At the end of my work on the Revolution, of which I conceive this to be a continuation, I quoted Arnold Toynbee's statement in 1961 that we had lost the leadership in our own revolution—that we had become, in the common phrase, "counterrevolutionary," more concerned with wealth and security than with justice and equality. I believe that to be an accurate statement of the case.

I have undertaken this work at a time when there is growing skepticism, not to say cynicism, about most of the claims my historical predecessors once made so boldly in behalf of the United States. From having not long ago been disposed to view our past as an almost unblemished record of progress and "success," we now seem inclined to view it as a series of horror stories, of the mistreatment and exploitation of Indians, blacks, women, Mexicans, and so on. But despite our many sins of commission and omission, the history of the

United States seems to me a great and enthralling story, as remarkable as any in history.

I must also confess that it seems to be a story of decline, which may or may not anticipate "a fall." Thus, if I have to seek a spiritual ancestor in the ranks of historians it would not be from among those amiable and optimistic historians of our own past—Bancroft, Mc-Master, Rhodes, and others of their persuasion. Perhaps the Roman historian Tacitus is a more appropriate model. Tacitus wrote of Imperial Rome, of the decline of private and public morals, of the growth of luxury and ostentation, of the expanding gap between the prosperous and the poor, of the rigidity and inhumanity of an overweening bureaucracy, of the creation of a mercenary army.

Why, the reader may ask at this point, given such "un-American" views, have I undertaken to write the history of the United States at all? We have enough defeatism, negativism, and doom crying as it is. We certainly do not need any more. To this entirely reasonable question I reply somewhat as follows. I believe, as my mentor, the historian Rosenstock-Huessy, said, that "history must be told." History is our collective memory. If we are deprived of our memory we are in danger of becoming a large, dangerous idiot, thrashing blindly about, with only the dimmest understanding of the ideals and principles that formed us as a people, and that we have constantly to reinterpret and affirm if we are to preserve a sense of our own identity.

History must be told because unless we keep our past accessible, we will have great difficulty in creating any decent and humane future. The case is just the opposite from what the "scientific" or positivistic historians would have us believe. Far from hankering after definitive histories that need never be rewritten, the historian should understand that after every great event history requires to be rewritten. So far is history from being scientific that every new event is also a fresh revelation of the past. The upheavals of our own time force us to reassess our history, to mine it for new insights and perspectives.

Since the last of those large-scale popular histories that we have taken note of six cataclysmic events have occurred: two devastating world wars (which closed the door on the nineteenth-century world view), the Russian and the Chinese revolutions, the Great Depression, and the Vietnam War. Can anyone imagine that our view of world history can be the same after these almost incomprehensible crises? The nineteenth century's faith in inevitable progress seems hopelessly naive today. The optimism that was so conspicuous an aspect of the

American character even a generation ago has, in many people, turned to apocalyptic visions of the end of the world brought on by a nuclear holocaust. Privatism, nature worship, religious and secular cults of every description abound in a manner reminiscent of the decadent period of the Roman Empire. And where a new view of the nature of history has asserted itself, it seems more akin to the tragic sense of history that has characterized most historical cultures prior to the modern age.

To put the matter as succinctly as possible, I wish to make our past available as a resource in our struggle to "redeem the time." If there is one motif that I wish to have emerge clearly from this work it is the notion of the United States as a "gathering of nations," as an episode in world history, far more than as a conventional nation. The Old World populated the New. The New World opened a doorway first in the mind of Europe and then for all the other people on the globe. Through that door there appeared tantalizing glimpses of an enchanted if sometimes terrifying garden. The New World revived dreams of edenic innocence, of "natural man" living amid benign nature. Realities begin with dreams, and British North America has always had to bear the burden of those dreams. Dreams lay a heavy charge on reality. Thus, first colonial America and then the United States had always to be both more and less than a nation. It had to cope as best it could with the sometimes radical divergence of the dream and the reality. It had to gloss over things that it was not healthy to gloss over. It had to constantly appear to be better and wiser and kinder and more noble and generous than the world in fact allows. If one small blemish were exposed, it might widen into a chasm too frightful to peer into. Ambiguity could not be endured. Example: Thomas Jefferson, the great expositor of democracy, the prototype of the rational, enlightened man, was in fact a slaveholder, a brilliant and emotional genius whose common-law wife was a slave, his dead wife's half sister. But that could not be endured; the implications were too unmanageable, a symbol of the tragedy and ambiguity of history right at the heart of the democratic ethos.

Thus, while celebrating the glories of our history, we were forced, or we forced ourselves, to pretend that much of it had not happened at all, or had happened in some obscure, unimportant, inconsequential, hardly to be noticed way.

The reason, I suspect, was that we had, from the beginning, to carry the burden of other peoples' illusions, had to appear to be something we were not and could not, in the nature of things, possibly have been. This falsity was not precisely hypocrisy, and it was not the exclusive possession of Americans (or United Staters). It was a mark of the century in which America took form. It was abundantly manifested in Victorian England and bourgeois France. It was probably to a degree the consequence of the rapid decline of the Christian world view and the equally rapid rise of the scientific, rationalistic, romantic civil religion that succeeded it, a religion that defied science, reason, and the national state.

Moreover, in addition to bearing the burden of all the dreams and illusions of the Old World, the United States had to behave like an ordinary, standard, run-of-the-mill nation rather than as an interim event in world history or a kind of holding company for the races of the world on their way to some new and as yet quite unimaginable universal order.

Viewed in this light, it seems to me that the whole history of the United States becomes vague, elusive, problematical, tantalizingly difficult to describe or account for. One becomes conscious at once of two levels of historical reality in the United States: the events themselves, dramatic enough God knows; and behind them, like some vast, dim, almost undecipherable palimpsest, the dreams, the evasions, the buried history, refusing to lie down decently but popping up relentlessly to challenge the myth.

John Locke, the seventeenth-century English philosopher, said, "In the beginning the whole world was America." The earth and the sea lay waiting for the tragic drama of human history to begin, for man to possess it. And at the end America was the world. In 1929 a Japanese visitor to the United States, Murobuse Koshin, wrote, "Know America! We must study that nation before any other, not for its own sake but in order better to understand Japan and the world. . . . To understand the United States is to understand the world, and the end result will be knowledge of our own nation. . . . America is the world, America alone. As American capital began its unrivaled ascendancy, so too did the culture, spirit and way of life of America. In the twentieth century, particularly after the World War, the world is coeval with America. . . . Know America first, whether you worship or despise it, are capitalist or socialist, Westernizer or Pan-Asianist. The world presents us with only one overriding issue—either we worship the United States or we overcome it."

So, first there was the land. So immense that it had never been traversed. Its endless reaches boggled the mind. Its climates and geographies recapitulated those of a dozen diverse nations. It had the mountains of Switzerland; the deserts of Arabia; the rivers of Africa; the interminable plains and forests of the Russian steppes; the rocky shores of Norway; and, with the acquisition of Alaska, the frozen wastes of the Arctic.

The dream must be inhabited. But first it had to be given a form, what was to be called, for want of a better word, a "constitution." So in the beginning, or in the *second* beginning (the first being that of Puritan New England), was the Word. Two thousand years of political theorizing and practical experience crystallized in Philadelphia in the summer of 1787 in the most brilliantly sustained intellectual and oratorical achievement of history. The radical universalism of the Founding Fathers evoked John Winthrop's vision in his "Modell of Christian Charity," written aboard the *Arabella* headed for the inhospitable coast of New England. The colony about to be established was to be, in Winthrop's words, "a praise and a glory that men shall say of succeeding plantations 'the Lord make it like that of NEW ENGLAND.' For we must consider that we shall be as a city upon a hill. The eyes of all people upon us." In words reminiscent of Winthrop's, Gouverneur Morris addressed the delegates at the Federal Convention. "He came here," he declared, "as a Representative of America; he flattered himself he came here in some degree as a Representative of the whole human race; for the whole human race will be affected by the proceedings of this Convention."

The theme was constantly reiterated. James Wilson, who had played a major role in the Federal Convention, told the delegates to the Pennsylvania ratifying convention: "By adopting this system we shall probably lay a foundation for erecting temples of liberty in every part of the earth. It has been thought by many, that on the success of the struggle America has made for freedom, will depend the exertions of the brave and enlightened of other nations." The new constitution, if adopted, "would draw from Europe many worthy characters, who pant for the enjoyment of freedom. It will induce princes, in order to preserve their subjects, to restore to them a portion of that liberty of which they have for some many ages been deprived. It will be subservient to the great designs of providence, with regard to this globe; the multiplication of mankind, their improvement in knowledge, and their advancement in happiness."

It would not be too much to say that the nation was spoken into existence. It was fashioned out of *ideas*. The reality was, in many respects, startlingly difficult to achieve. It was one thing to *declare* a nation; it was something vastly more complex to accomplish it. For seventy years after the ratification of the Constitution and the institution of the new government, the "Union" was precarious in the extreme, constantly threatening to fly apart under the stresses created by slavery on the one hand and commercial and industrial growth on the other. From 1790 to 1865, seventy-five years—almost half the lifetime of the Republic—there was never a decade when the Union did not seem to many Americans to be in the gravest danger of dissolution. It was primarily words that held the nation together. Having been defined by words, it had to be constantly redefined, articulated, spoken, explained.

Then there was the profoundest reality of all, the basic ineradicable schizophrenia—black slavery. All other themes were subservient to that. Slavery in the land of liberty was a paradox no logic could obscure, no plan could remedy, no theology could redeem. In the face of that moral enormity there could be no union, no nation. It ran like an unhealed fracture across the landscape of the American psyche. Everything, in an acute and particular sense, waited on the resolution of that terrible dilemma. The nation could not begin until the slaves were free.

If slavery was the indigestible fact that constantly mocked America's professed devotion to freedom, the story of immigration was *the* story of America. Aside from the aborigines, the native Americans, *everyone else came.* In my history of the American Revolution I described the remarkably heterogeneous collection of peoples of various conditions and nations that made up the original British colonies. But they were just the modest beginning. And, in terms of those who came later, the astonishing diversity of the original settlers appears to have been a conspicuous unity. Almost all came from the British Isles and Western Europe—Holland, Denmark, Sweden, France, and Germany. Dominated by that particular version of the Re-formed consciousness derived from England proper, the first immigrants threw off the yoke of the mother country, declared their devotion to freedom and equality, and ratified a plan of government inherently British in its conception. What followed was the greatest migration in history, a movement of peoples almost incomprehensible in its magnitude. It turned out that Gouverneur Morris, Tom Paine, James Wilson, and the Founding Fathers in general had been right. It did indeed seem that the United States was "subservient to the great designs of providence, with regard to this globe." The geography must be inhabited. The vast empty spaces exerted an attraction beyond resisting.

Man is not a migrating animal. In the history of the race many families have lived five hundred, a thousand years on or near the same piece of land, the same shire or county or province. Now, however, they tore themselves loose from the familiar soil, the familiar sounds, the comfortable customs and festivals, and sailed off into the dream to inhabit landscapes as alien as the moon—from tidy Norwegian farms to the bitter plains of the Dakotas; from the German forests to the scorched earth of Texas or Oklahoma. They thrust westward across deserts and across the cruel mountains to the Pacific. Strange geographies and exotic people. Only the dream held it all together, the endlessly repeated litany: freedom, happiness, promise, fulfillment, riches.

The tensions produced by slavery were replaced by the tensions produced by hordes of alien immigrants. The original immigrants felt themselves in imminent danger of being inundated by the later immigrants. They tried halfheartedly in an age fascinated by genetics to stem the tide. Serious and learned men debated mandatory sterilization of lesser breeds to prevent them from contaminating the gene pool of the superior race. The Statue of Liberty was a statue of irony. Those "huddled masses yearning to breathe free," that "wretched refuse" were in fact a nightmare to the sons and daughters of the original immigrants. The statue was intended simply as a monument to French-American friendship, and more specifically, to the alliance of those nations during the American Revolution. But it got out of hand and was elevated to a universal symbol. "Huddled masses?" "Wretched refuse?" Dross metal refined into gold by the alchemy of Americanization. Recently, patriotic ethnic associations, Polish-Americans, Italo-Americans, Slovakian-Americans have petitioned to have Emma Lazarus's famous lines expunged from the Statue of Liberty on the grounds that they are an insult to the men and women who immigrated to the United States in the last decades of the nineteenth century. Certainly "wretched refuse" does seem a bit strong, even allowing for poetic license. One feels there is a certain ambivalence hidden there. Emma Lazarus was, after all, a woman of aristocratic antecedents, wealthy, privately educated, a disciple of Ralph Waldo Emerson, a proud defender of Judaism, and a champion of the often desperately poor Russian Jews who flocked to New York City in the 1880s. The metamorphosis of the Statue of Liberty from a symbol of the French alliance to the particular representation of the "promise of American life" for immigrants sailing up the Hudson River tells its own story.

As I understand it, each new generation of immigrants, each one "worse" than the one before, at least in the eyes of the originals, brought with them a check drawn on the Declaration of Independence and demanded that it be honored by the descendants of those who had first articulated its unsettling sentiments. As much as prejudice and reactionary politics disposed them not to do so, the "originals" were faced with a serious problem. To have rejected the claims of the immigrants would have been both to deny themselves a much-needed source of cheap labor and at the same time to have flagrantly disavowed one of the crucial Ur-documents—the Declaration. The originals compromised by letting the "wretched refuse" in but making life unpleasant for them once here.

It would be difficult to overstate the primary importance of nineteenth- and early-twentieth-century immigration. Besides the sheer numbers quickly absorbed by the insatiable demands of ceaselessly expanding industrialism, there were incalculable energies released by the efforts of the immigrants to fight their way up from the lower depths of American society. They were like an endlessly working yeast in the great doughy mass of American life. Their fermentation lightened and aerated the mass. They provided the negative (or positive, if you prefer) pole to the white predominantly Anglo-Saxon Protestant ruling class, or Establishment as we say today, a kind of disharmonious counterpoint to the genteel tones of the upper class. They brought with them, as the beleaguered originals had feared, all kinds of aberrant philosophies: socialism, communism, anarchism, syndicalism, not to mention alien religions such as Catholicism. In the end, they battered down or climbed over all the barriers the originals had erected to impede their progress. They completed the *universalization* of the United States the Founding Fathers had dreamed of but not at all, it may be assumed, in a manner the Founders (or anyone else) could have anticipated.

There was also a tradition of native American radicalism. The radicalism of the originals. That was a genuine radicalism, a true revolutionary zeal. From John Winthrop's dream of redeeming Western Christendom with a handful of colonists, through the Revolution itself, to the revolutionary upheavals of nineteenth-century Europe, Americans sought to aid and abet the struggles for freedom and independence they believed to have been inspired by their own struggle against Great Britain. America had a mission. The mission was to redeem the world—first for Protestant Christianity, then for freedom and democracy, and finally for "the American way of life." America had manifestly a destiny: to fill up the continent; to Americanize the world.

One vein of native American radicalism was directed toward the redemption or the conversion of the outside world; the other was directed toward the purification of the United States itself. But it was much more than the reform movement, at least as we commonly use that phrase. It was a powerful, unremitting, initially Protestant Christian impulse to set right everything that seemed to be constantly going wrong with the dream—slavery, drunkenness, repression of women, inequality, injustice, warfare, economic exploitation, and so on, almost beyond enumerating. In virtually all of these movements women were among the leaders, and in many instances they were the leaders. This brings us to another major theme in the history of the United States. The United States is the first modern nation in which women have had a central and, in many instances, a decisive role. Indeed so ubiquitous has been the influence of women that it is safe to say that American history cannot be understood without close attention to their achievements and, perhaps even more important, their psychology. They have been among the most radical critics of our social, political, and economic institutions.

America's homegrown radicals—critics of the system—have been an interesting if largely neglected lot. They run from Tom Paine and the Revolutionary poet Philip Freneau, to William Manning, Josiah Warren, Stephen Pearl Andrews, Victoria Woodhull and her sister, Tennie C., through William Lloyd Garrison to Wendell Phillips, Ignatius Donnelly, Henry George, and more recently, "Big Bill" Haywood, Margaret Sanger, Norman Thomas, and A. J. Muste. They reached their apogee in the Populist movement of the South and Midwest. Again many of them, and certainly populism as a movement, were involved with or derived from radical Christianity.

Regions—a variation on the theme of geography. New England parsons and industrialists, Transcendentalists, Unitarians. Southern planters and yeoman farmers, slaves, and rednecked fundamentalists. Midwestern farmers, corn and grain growers, combine operators, hog butchers. Western cowboys and Indians and miners and lumberjacks. All became part of an inexhaustible mythology. Regions were their own countries, with their own accents, literature, arts and architecture, music, food, traditional attire.

Then there is business enterprise and its related but distinguishable accompaniment, industrialization and technology. The German sociologist Max Weber argued that Protestantism and the "spirit of capitalism" were virtually indistinguishable. He traced, in some detail, the story of how "Puritan asceticism" had prepared the ground for modern capitalism and ended his famous work with a scathing indictment of modern capitalist society made up of "Specialists without spirit, sensualists without heart; this nullity imagines that it has attained a level of civilization never before achieved."

"Capitalism" is not a word I am especially happy with, but since the United States is commonly denominated the world's leading "capitalist nation," we must engage it. It is plainly the case that what the sociologists like to call "entrepreneurial activity" is the most conspicuous feature of American society. After a long struggle business enterprise came to dominate not only the economy but the policies and programs of the federal government as well. It pervades every area of our lives; it has created and controls the media—newspapers, magazines, books, radio, and television. It provides a major part of the money to fund the campaigns of political candidates; it has its representatives in the highest councils of the nation and clearly plays a prominent and often decisive role in the field of foreign policy. It presently claims, in fact, to be virtually synonymous with America, to embody the "American way of life." It wraps about itself the mantle of history, avowing itself the highest expression of the principles of the Founding Fathers. It even professes to find sanction in the doctrines of Protestant Christianity. It has invaded and conquered its traditional adversary—agriculture—and has, beyond question, colored every aspect of American culture from art to sports to food. It has done its best to turn the world into business. If we set out to redeem the world, we seem to have ended up consuming it. But uneasy as intellectuals may be with the problem of business enterprise and, more especially, with the nature and often criminal activities of huge corporations and their modern offshoot, the multinationals, we cannot simply brush it aside or cast it as the villain of the piece. Villainous as it may be in some of its grosser manifestations, it is too deeply entwined with our collective psyche to serve as a satisfactory whipping boy. As Pogo said, "We have met the enemy and he is us." To the degree that the ethic of business enterprise and its most spectacular achievement, the giant corporation, are under a cloud, our whole nation is under a cloud. It does no good to inveigh against capitalism. It was, after all, capitalism that transformed the modern world; that, perhaps more than any of those "good things" we wished to export—liberty, democracy, equality—carried our banner nailed to its masthead. It was capitalism that toppled traditional cultures like ninepins. It seems that a disconcertingly large number of peoples of the world are more attracted to ball-point pens, digital watches, and television sets than to the benefits of democracy.

So, like it or not, we have to put business enterprise in all its various forms in the center of our history.

I would remind the reader at the beginning of this venture of several other major themes. In 1787 when the Constitution was framed, 90 to 95 percent of the population of the states were engaged in farming; 10 percent or less, in business, the crafts, and the professions. The vast majority of Americans worked for a living in the most specific sense of that word. They worked with their hands, plowing, planting, reaping, cutting down trees for firewood and to clear land for new farms. Work meant work done with one's hands— manual labor. Those occupations which did not involve manual labor were not called "work." Work produced a tangible product— something you could pick up and eat like a potato, or drive, like a wagon, or live in, like a house. Today work is whatever is paid for. I even presume, when someone asks me what work I do, to say I write. I do, of course, hit the keys of a typewriter with my fingers, very inexpertly it must be said. But that is no more a claim to honest labor than if I were engaged in selling insurance or filming television commercials.

Today 90 to 95 percent of the population of the United States are engaged in nonagricultural pursuits, and only some 5 or 6 percent in farming, most of these in large-scale "agribusinesses" with heavy capital investments in land and machinery. Such "farmers" could more properly be called agricultural businessmen. So business has conquered everything. Everything is business.

This disparity between those engaged in nonfarming activities and those who are at least technically still described as farmers is by far the largest in the world. The shift from a rural-agricultural to an urban-industrial society in some two hundred years represents the most rapid transformation in the basic economy of any society in any period of history. The overwhelming majority of the American people are completely dependent on a relative handful of individuals about whose problems and methods of earning a livelihood they have very little knowledge or sympathy. The trauma of this transformation is suggested by the fact that the principal proponent of democracy among the Founding Fathers—Thomas Jefferson—believed that the yeoman farmer, the small, independent, self-sustaining farmer, indebted to no one for his livelihood, was the classic citizen of a republic. If ever there was a human type favored by God, Jefferson declared, it was this independent yeoman farmer. Many Americans shared Jefferson's view.

The fact that in the span of little more than a generation small-scale farming with modest capital investment has no longer become an option for Americans is perhaps as significant as any other development in our history.

Another major theme of this work will be the tension between the dogmas and doctrines of Protestant Christianity that made possible, or inevitable, the resistance to Great Britain that brought on the American Revolution, and the novel concepts of man and society that are generally denominated the Enlightenment—what I have chosen to call the Secular-Democratic Consciousness. The Secular-Democratic Consciousness believed in the natural goodness and imminent perfectibility of man, whereas Protestantism believed in original sin and human depravity. Where the Christian Consciousness endeavored to refer all questions to the ultimate authority of God, the Secular-Democratic Consciousness sought to refer them to the will of the majority of the people. Where the Classical-Christian Consciousness clung to the notions of continuity and traditional wisdom, the accumulated experience of the race, the Secular-Democratic Consciousness believed in the power of human reason and its handmaid, science, to reconstruct the world on progressive principles. The Christian Consciousness believed in salvation through faith and grace; the Secular-Democratic Consciousness believed in salvation through scientific education.

It would be wrong to suggest that one group of Americans stubbornly espoused the Protestant Christian view of the world and another subscribed to the Secular-Democratic system. There were, of course, such divisions, often along class lines. But the great majority of Americans held to both views in varying proportions, and did so, in most instances, without the slightest notion that they were completely incompatible.

In any event, this "ultimate" intellectual or moral tension in American history will be a conspicuous element of this work.

Finally, I am tempted to see the American people as a people of astonishing velocity. They have accelerated from the five-mile-an-hour horse-drawn coach of two hundred years ago to the five-thousand-mile-an-hour space vehicle of today. While they have no monopoly on velocity, they have utilized it more fully than any other people. We cannot imagine modern America without the railroads that spanned it in the nineteenth century; or the automobiles that in two generations have transformed both the geographical and the human landscape; or, indeed, the airplanes that have virtually replaced trains as long-distance public transportation. Americans who could never sit still invented the rocking chair so they could be in motion while sitting down. They have hurled themselves through space in every conceivable mode of transportation with a determination that has been the wonder of the world. I used to teach a course on American civilization subtitled "From Plymouth Rock to Moon Rock," and in my mind's eye I was often haunted by John Adams's image of America as a giant plowman, cutting his way across the continent, plowing up the plains, uprooting the trees, leveling mountains, heedless of every obstruction in his path. I added a gloss to Adams. When he reached the Pacific Ocean, the plowman stopped only long enough to fashion his plow into a spacecraft before taking off for the moon.

It would be even more presumptuous of me to speculate on the outcome of this strange story than to undertake to tell it in the first place. In this volume and those that follow, my primary concern will be to try to tell the story of our past as fairly and accurately as possible. To me the history of the United States remains, on one level at least, the story of the world becoming the United States. The peoples of the world bestowed the United States on its inhabitants; they created it by coming to it. And now, it may be said, they want it back. The United States in the world. The world in the United States. It may be a story too vast and complex to be comprehensible. But it is certainly worth a try.

1

The Confederation

With the signing of the Treaty of Paris in 1783, Americans were to discover that creating a nation was, if anything, a more arduous task than winning a revolution. Today, almost two hundred years later, the formation of the new nation has about it a quality of the inevitable. It is difficult for us to imagine that it might not have happened at all.

The "Unitedness" of the states was then more a pious wish than a reality. In the crucible of revolution the basic disparity of the various colonies was overcome, and they were welded together in an incongruous alliance. As soon as peace was concluded that alliance began to exhibit numerous troubling signs of coming apart. First of all, the Articles of Confederation were a striking example of wishful political thinking. Congress could proclaim anything, as one cynical critic expressed it, but could *do* nothing. It was wholly dependent upon the states to comply with its requisitions, or "humble requests."

That the respective states were jealous of their sovereignty and reluctant to yield up the most modest degree of authority to Congress was perhaps best demonstrated by the Articles themselves. The constitutions of the various states had followed to a remarkable degree the constitutional principles laid down by John Adams (they were not, to be sure, Adams's invention; he simply presented them in classic form). But it had apparently occurred to no one that the agreement that bound the states themselves together should be derived from the same model as the state constitutions. Clearly the drafters of the Articles of Confederation had no notion of forming a "state" in the sense in which we use that word today. They intended, as they clearly stated, to form a confederation, or a *federated* republic made up of particular states.

In order to gain any idea of the laboriousness of the process by which the thirteen original states became a single nation, it is necessary to place strong and persistent emphasis on those factors which made the idea of *union* such a precarious one and the struggle to achieve it an enterprise long protracted and arduous in the extreme.

If there was any predominant impression that European visitors to the British North American colonies carried away, it was of their astonishing diversity, often expressed in apparently irreconcilable differences. To the most knowledgeable observers of the American scene, even the successful conclusion of the Revolutionary contest gave no reason to expect that an enduring alliance could be formed among the new states, much less a permanent union. One of the accepted truisms of eighteenth-century political theory was that republican government was possible only among people inhabiting a small and relatively homogeneous geographical area. Laws as strict as the laws governing nature were thought to govern in human affairs. Politics had its own "laws of gravity." Thus, the larger the territory over which a government ruled, the more centralized and authoritarian such a government must be in order to prevent the regions on the periphery from becoming detached from the center and flying off into their own orbits, that is, becoming independent political entities. Theorists could and did point to the experience of Great Britain and her American colonies as proof of the proposition. The British government had been, so the argument ran, too liberal and benign to extend its control over three thousand miles of ocean. How, then, could a single republican government be expected to preside over thirteen (and soon, presumably, many more) states reaching along fifteen hundred miles of coastline from Georgia to Maine and several hundred miles into a thinly settled interior?

Both theory and experience argued against the possibility of such a union. The dean of Gloucester Cathedral (who professed himself a friend of America) declared after the Treaty of Paris: "As to the future grandeur of America, and its being a rising empire under one head, whether republican or monarchical, it is one of the idlest and most visionary notions that was ever conceived even by a writer of romance. . . . The mutual antipathies and clashing interests of the Americans, their difference of government, habitudes, and manners, indicate that they have no centre of union and no common interests. They can never be united into one compact empire under any species of government whatever; a disunited people till the end of time, suspicious and distrustful of each other, they will be divided and subdivided into little commonwealths, or principalities. . . ."

For most of the people who lived in the various states, the ineptness of Congress under the Articles of Confederation was a matter of indifference. They were preoccupied with far more urgent matters. The economies of the states had been devastated by almost seven years of war. The commercial activities of New England had been brought to a virtual halt by the Revolution. Privateering had enriched a few enterprising individuals (indeed there were profiteers everywhere), but the merchants of Massachusetts and Rhode Island were soon keenly aware of the advantages they had enjoyed as participants in the British mercantile system. Now they were outsiders looking in. New York City had been held by the British since 1776. Two disastrous fires during the period of British occupation had burned down some eight hundred houses. In addition, the economy of the city (and, to an extent, of the state) had become geared to the British army of occupation. Stout patriots had, for the most part, fled to the Jerseys or to the interior of the state. With the British evacuation of New York, thousands of Tories departed for Canada or England, carrying away as much of the wealth of the city as could be crammed into the holds of British transports.

Pennsylvania was a state still split by bitter contentions between conservative and radical patriots. In addition, there were numerous Quakers in the eastern part of the state whose loyalty to Congress remained under a cloud.

As for the thousands of slaves in the Southern states who had defected to the British (where many of them fared worse than they had under their masters), the Treaty of Paris provided that as "property," the slaves be returned to their owners. However, the provision was imperfectly observed, to say the least, and this fact provided an excuse for many patriots who had appropriated Tory lands or who owed substantial sums of money in prewar debts to British merchants to refuse to pay.

The resistance of the states to those terms of the Treaty of Paris they found objectionable gave the British grounds, in turn, for holding on to their frontier posts in the Old Northwest; and these posts became rallying points for Indian tribes determined to resist the encroachment of settlers on their lands. Land speculators, whose ranks included George Washington, Patrick Henry, and Benjamin Franklin, bought and sold millions of acres of Western lands and even tried, along the Carolina frontier, to carve new states out of old ones.

Everywhere there seemed to be bones of contention among the states. Some, such as the Wyoming Valley controversy, were old; others, such as the contest between New York and Rhode Island over trade, were the outgrowth of efforts to reestablish maritime commerce.

The Wyoming Valley, which constituted almost a third of the state of Pennsylvania, was claimed by Connecticut on behalf of Connecticut residents who had settled in substantial numbers in the area. The controversy had been settled during the Revolution in favor of Pennsylvania by a court of Congressional Commissioners. But now Connecticut wished to press the issue of possession. Trying perhaps to compensate for its rank as the smallest state after Rhode Island in the Confederation, Connecticut also claimed a "Western Reserve" in the Ohio country. Pennsylvania in turn disputed with Virginia the ownership of an area claimed by the land speculators of the Illinois-Wabash Company.

In the Carolinas, the warfare between Loyalists and patriots had been so terrible and relentless that any Tory who ventured to reclaim his property in that region did so at the risk of his life.

The problem of the Loyalists went, of course, far beyond the issue of their attempts to reclaim their property. The best estimates of the number of Loyalists who fled from the Confederated States vary from sixty thousand to one hundred thousand. The majority of those who departed with the British were members of the colonial upper class, men and women of substance, of wealth and education. If we assume that some seventy thousand left (averaging the estimates), they would constitute almost 20 percent of the free white population. And if we consider, additionally, that a disproportionate number of the refugees fled from New York and Pennsylvania, we may get an idea of the effect on the economy as well as the politics of those states.

Since the Loyalists were represented disproportionately in mercantile and commercial communities in the New England and Middle states, their flight deprived their home states of considerable business experience and capital while at the same time opening the way for ambitious newcomers, "new men" emerging in considerable numbers from the middle class. Since Loyalist entrepreneurs were rapidly replaced, the political effects of their departure were of much greater significance than the economic effects.

If the Loyalists can be assumed to have included the most conservative and tradition-bound elements in the colonial population, it would follow that their removal eliminated much of the "Tory," or conservative, political sentiment in the country. The result was undoubtedly a shift in virtually every state toward the more radical democratic end of the political spectrum. As revolutions commonly create "counterrevolutions," or at least impulses thereto, it seems reasonable to argue that the failure of the new American states to move in any substantial degree toward a counterrevolution may be attributed, at least in part, to the absence of many of those individuals who would have been the natural leaders of such a movement.

Of course, more Loyalists stayed than fled if only because the opportunities for flight were limited, by and large, to those lucky enough to be in Boston; Philadelphia; New York; or Charleston, South Carolina, when those cities were evacuated by the British.

In addition to those who could not flee, a not inconsequential number simply decided to stay and take their lumps. The fate of these bold souls varied according to the degree of their complicity with the British; the region they lived in; their own financial and social status (including, of course, their friends among powerful patriots); and a dozen other less tangible matters, not least their own characters. Even under the best of circumstances the lot of the Loyalists who stayed or tried to return was an unhappy one. While Benjamin Chew, who had been exiled to Virginia, returned to Philadelphia to be in time, elected mayor of that city, Chew was rather an exception. He had been chief justice of the Pennsylvania Superior Court prior to the Revolution. Wealthy and able, he had close friends among prominent patriots.

When someone as moderate as Washington could declare of the Loyalists, "there never existed a more miserable set of Beings than these wretched creatures," and recommend the most draconian measures against them, and Franklin could refer to them as "mongrels" and "fratricides," it is not surprising that the majority of them encountered bitter resentment and frequently open persecution. Although the Loyalists had their advocates among the more compassionate patriots, such advocacy was of little avail. The *Massachusetts*

Chronicle of May, 1783, called on "every Whig" (i.e.,patriot) to "swear, by his abhorrence of slavery, by liberty and religion, by the shades of departed friends who have fallen in battle, by the ghosts of those of our brethren who have been destroyed on board of prison-ships and in loathsome dungeons, never to be at peace with those fiends, the refugees, whose thefts, murders and treason have filled the cup of woe. . . ." The patriots of South Carolina presumably needed no such exhortations to retribution. When twelve notorious Loyalists who had participated in ferocious fighting in the area of Fishing Creek tried to return to the area and reclaim their abandoned plantations, their former neighbors gave them twenty days to leave. When the Loyalists stubbornly refused to decamp, they were attacked; eight were killed, and the remaining four were forced to flee to Charleston.

As human beings, as men and women of decency and devotion to principles, as parents, husbands, wives, friends and ofttimes good Christians, the Loyalists undoubtedly ranked with the patriots. Their dogged adherence to the dictates of their consciences—loyalty to their monarch—was, it might be argued, no less admirable than their countrymen's devotion to liberty. While England had been defeated, or, more accurately, had failed to suppress the Revolution, the weight of that failure fell relatively lightly on the mother country but with crushing weight upon the Loyalists themselves. They were, to put the matter as simply as possible, the tragic victims of one of the great upheavals of modern times. However notable their personal virtues, history is, by and large, unforgiving to those unlucky enough to have been on the losing side.

The tragedy of the Loyalists lies far beyond the scope of this work; in its full dimensions, beyond any historical or literary work. Certainly it can only be hinted at here. But its importance to our story is threefold. Contention over the fate of the Loyalists was one of the divisive issues that plagued the states after the Treaty of Paris. The resentment in the states over the provisions in the treaty designed to protect the rights of the Loyalists encouraged hostility to an already weak and discredited Congress, which was blamed for the unpopular articles. If Congress had had the presumption to lay such an unwelcome burden on the states, in what other ways might it abuse its power and harass honest patriots?

Finally, the plight of the Loyalists has, for our purposes, a symbolic significance. Although perhaps as much as a quarter of the free population of the American states was involved directly or indirectly in the tragedy of the Loyalists, constituting a human disaster on a much larger scale proportionally than the French Revolution, we have, for the most part, suppressed or expunged from our collective historical memory any sense of guilt over our treatment of those unfortunate people.

The Loyalists were, as we have said, only one, and not the most serious, of the many bones of contention over which the states snapped and snarled. Since, as one historian has written, the Revolution was both about "home rule"—that is, the powers and authority of Parliament over the colonies—and about "who should rule at home," the end of the Revolution as an armed conflict and the consequent independence of the states left still unresolved the question of "who should rule at home"—in other words, how literally the propositions stated so boldly in the Declaration of Independence were to be taken. There were of course many American patriots who gave little credit to the radical sentiments of the Declaration, which they regarded as useful propaganda but hardly as the basis of any rational political order. Conservative patriots like Carter Braxton of Virginia deplored the addiction of the New England states to their "darling Democracy."

While patriots of all sections and all stations were virtually unanimous in declaring that former Loyalists should not rule, they were by no means of one mind about who should. The prosperous lawyers and planters who predominated as delegates to Congress, led the regiments and divisions of the Continental Army, and ran the affairs of their home states were not disposed to share their power with men of the "lower orders." In their view, the role of the ordinary citizen was to be tolerably well educated—at the very least able to read and write—to be informed of the issues in free and open debate among the candidates for office, and to choose from among the candidates who presented themselves those most to their liking.

It was not thought then, any more than it is today, that men of the "middling" or "lower" ranks of society would make proper candidates for important political offices. Artisans, mechanics, and farmers were expected to tend to business and, aside from voting in elections, leave the running of their state governments (and the Confederation, weak as it was) to their betters. Even the most ardent advocate of "democracy," Thomas Jefferson, spoke of a "natural aristocracy," envisioning a social and political system accessible to anyone of unusual intelligence and ambition, regardless of social class or financial status.

But it was by no means evident that less privileged Americans shared such views; a substantial number of them were ready to declare boldly that one man was as good as another, regardless of education or social standing. Just as the obstreperous Baptists and the less obstreperous Methodists declared that the simple faith of the ordinary man or woman was a better path to salvation than the sophisticated reason of the theologian, many "fundamentalist" democrats insisted that Harvard graduates were not necessarily better qualified to sit in the seats of power than relatively uneducated farmers or teamsters or honest shoemakers.

If the Declaration of Independence meant what it said, all men were created equal; and it followed, at least to staunch democrats, that they remained equal, if not in wealth and education, certainly in common sense (which had been very popular in America ever since Tom Paine's pamphlet of that name), and perhaps even more important, in the perception of where their own best interests lay. So there was a conspicuous democratic fever evident in the states. "New men," as they were disparagingly called, appeared in many places to dispute the leadership of their towns and states.

They were commonly described by those who had become accustomed to running things and who, on the whole, had run them astonishingly well, as greedy and ambitious men, demagogues who played upon the fears and prejudices of the mass of people. At the time of the Stamp Act, leaders of unruly gangs of sailors and ruffians had hurried moderate middle-class patriots like James Otis and Sam Adams along faster than they wished by taking direct and violent action, action that the more responsible Sons of Liberty were eager to disclaim. It was from the ranks of such men as these that the soldiers of the Continental Army had been recruited; hard-grained, independent individuals who wished not only to be out from under the authority of the British Parliament but to be free of the domination of any class of men whatsoever. These, and men much like them, were the men who had led or participated in the mutiny of the Pennsylvania Line in the darkest days of the Revolution, who had formed their own disciplined brigades and conducted their affairs with as much order and skill as ever evidenced under their appointed officers. It was their breed who had debated forming their own state to the west if justice were not done them by Congress. They did not hesitate to characterize the Revolutionary leaders as aristocrats, imperious gentlemen who had little sympathy with the needs and problems of ordinary men and women. It was they who led the clamor for yearly elections so that as many men as possible might share power and no individual or class preempt it. They considered themselves the exemplars of the principles of the Revolution and the ideals of the Declaration of Independence.

Those who had served in the Continental Army or in the state militia nourished an abiding resentment toward Congress. Unpaid and unfed for long periods of time, ill-equipped and often indifferently led, they readily transferred their wartime suspicions of their political leaders to a body—the Confederation Congress—whose existence was already precarious. The Congress that had so often failed them in war now seemed fated to fail them in peace. The modest rewards of land and cash promised them were not forthcoming.

Nevertheless, the men of the Revolutionary army had fought and bled in a common cause and in doing so had overcome, at least to a degree, their innate provincialism. Perhaps more than those among their countrymen who had not borne arms, they had acquired an impulse toward nationhood or, more simply, had come to think of themselves as a single people, the raw material of a nation. If they felt no loyalty to Congress, they loved General Washington. If the dream of "Independence and Liberty" in whose name they had endured such hardships seemed to them tainted by the indifference of the populace at large to their services and sacrifices, Washington, their "father," became more and more the focus of their aspirations with each passing year. He alone contained the possibility of nationhood, of transcending the sectional animosities and ingrained particularism that characterized the states.

Reinforcing the devotion of the Revolutionary veterans to Washington was the camaraderie of the officers of the Revolutionary army. At the emotional parting of Washington and his officers at Fraunces Tavern in New York, in December, 1873, the general, too moved to speak, had silently embraced each officer in turn. "Such a scene of sorrow and weeping I had never before witnessed," one of those present wrote, "the heart seemed so full, that it was ready to burst from its wonted abode." The discharged officers, led by General Henry Knox, formed an organization called, with specific reference to Washington, the Society of the Cincinnati. Cincinnatus had been the great citizen-general of Rome, a farmer who left his plow to lead a demoralized army to victory and then, scorning power or influence for himself, returned to his farm. The impulse on the part of those officers who had served with Washington to form a fraternal order to preserve their fellowship and serve their country in peace as they had in war seems innocent enough to us today, but it raised a storm of protest among Americans sensitive to the dangers of an aristocracy and fearful of the influence of an army, or even an ex-army, on the domestic affairs of the Confederation. Some state legislatures went so far as to pass laws depriving the members of the Society of the rights of citizenship. Jefferson, Adams, and Franklin, agreeing on little else, concurred in viewing the Society with extreme alarm. The officers, in turn, were startled and indignant at the public outcry and the attacks on the Society in the democratic press. Nathanael Greene, himself a citizen of Connecticut, wrote to Washington that "The public of New England seem to want something to quarrel with the officers about. Remove one thing and they will soon find another. It is in the temper of the people, not in the matter complained of." Knox repeated to Washington the charge against the Society of the Cincinnati that "it has been created by a foreign influence, in order to change our form of government."

The two aspects of the Society that its critics found most offensive were the insignia that its members were entitled to wear—blue ribbon and rosette—and the fact that membership was supposed to be hereditary, descending through the eldest son. Franklin wrote an extraordinary letter on the subject, ridiculing the Society and describing it as an "absurd" effort of grown men to play at nobility. But he so far forgot his prejudices as to accept an honorary membership in the Society several years later.

Jefferson was bold enough to write to Washington (who was head of the Society) from his station in Paris as Congressional ambassador to the French court, deploring the hereditary aspect of the Cincinnati. Everyone "in Europe" to whom Jefferson had mentioned the establishment of the Society had considered it "as dishonorable and destructive to our governments" and predicted that it would, in time, "destroy the fabric we have reared" and produce "an hereditary aristocracy which will change the form of our governments from the best to the worst in the world."

What is perhaps most remarkable is that the beleaguered officers should have stood fast in the face of such assaults. The affair of the Society of the Cincinnati (which, incidentally, survives to the present day and has an honorable place among those numerous associations of Americans devoted to the worship of their ancestors, hardly less pious in this regard than the Chinese) may be taken to demonstrate several points germane to this work. There were many Americans, as General Greene said of his fellow New Englanders, ready to quarrel about anything. There was considerable touchiness in all levels of society about the dangers of an American aristocracy, a concern voiced by a number of individuals—like Jefferson and John Adams—who might themselves be charged with belonging to "an American aristocracy." Moreover, for those who participated in it as soldiers and officers, the Revolutionary War was an experience so powerful—one is tempted to say so sacred—that they were determined to resist heavy popular pressure to abandon their newly created association. To the officers, the public clamor seemed simply another example of the obtuseness of civilians. They had suffered throughout the war from that obtuseness. Now they defied it. Let the people howl with rage or mock them if they wished—they would have their ribbons and rosettes and their heredi-tary line of descent.

Social or class frictions and suspicions in the states were reinforced by economic conflicts. Here the classic division was between debtors and creditors. Creditors were, for the most part, well-to-do farmers and, more notably, merchants in such seacoast cities as Boston, New York, and Philadelphia. Foreign trade languished, and many ships were tied up in port where unemployed sailors added to the unrest and dissatisfaction caused by the depressed state of commercial activity.

The situation was aggravated by the fact that some states were clearly faring worse than others. The relative prosperity of New York stood in sharp contrast to the penury of its neighbors, Connecticut and New Jersey. As these states imported goods at lower duties than those charged at the port of New York, their citizens brought these cheaper items into New York, where they competed successfully with the higher-duties goods imported by New York merchants. The New York Assembly reacted by passing a law in 1785 that imposed on all foreign goods brought into New York from neighboring states the same duties that would have been charged had British ships brought them directly to New York. This ordinance was followed by one that, while raising the duties on foreign goods, imposed those same duties on vessels from Connecticut and New Jersey.

Nathaniel Gorham, a Massachusetts delegate to the almost mori-bund Congress, wrote of the desperate efforts of that body to persuade the states to allow Congress to levy an impost or duty on all goods brought into American ports, "more especially as the situation of N. York enables them so to Tax their Neighbours of Connecticut and N. Jersey as to create such a temper in those States as will greatly weaken if not destroy the Union . . . indeed there is nothing but the restraining hand of Congress (weak as it is), that prevents N. Jersey and Connecticut from entering the lists very seriously with N. York and bloodshed would very quickly be the consiquence."

One of the greatest causes of popular discontent was the shortage of money. Debtors, unable to procure money to pay their debts, were threatened with having their property seized and sold, often at a fraction of its real value, to satisfy judgments against them. Thomas Bee of South Carolina had his property attached by the sheriff and sold for a thirteenth of what it was estimated it would have brought by an unforced private sale. In the state of New York, where there were long-standing hostilities between landlords and tenants, the threat of armed clashes hung in the air. Older citizens recalled the rent riots of forty years earlier when the whole colony had been in a turmoil. A radical democrat, writing in a New York newspaper, proposed direct graduated taxes on sixteen categories of income and property, the tax being designed to reduce differences in wealth.

Rhode Island seemed to many to be a horrible example of the dangers of "licentious democracy." In that state the debtors were plainly in the saddle. Controlling the legislature, they ordered the printing of large quantities of paper money, at the same time making it illegal for creditors to refuse to accept it in payment of debts on the pain of losing their political rights. The turn of events in Rhode Island sent a shudder of dismay through the propertied classes in other states. Massachusetts was still in the hands of the more conservative patriots, who were determined to block such measures by any means at their disposal. They tried to assuage popular resentment by broadcasting a detailed accounting of the state's receipts and expenditures, and a number of prosperous Bostonians signed an agreement to abstain from the importation and use of foreign luxuries. Needless to say, such mild palliatives were little consolation to a farmer whose farm was about to be sold at auction to pay his debts. It might be assumed that he would be even more disenchanted if—as was frequently the case—he was a veteran of the Revolution who already nourished a substantial list of grievances against those who disposed of the political affairs of his state.

The friction between debtor and creditor was further exacerbated by the fact that the laws governing debt were draconian in the extreme. Any debtor who refused to sell everything he owed to discharge his debts might be thrown into prison and kept there until he rotted or until relatives or friends paid his indebtedness. There was no relief through bankruptcy proceedings, and the promulgators and enforcers of the law were unmoved by the argument that a man confined to jail and often required to pay for his food or virtually starve to death was a poor bet to discharge his debts. It must be said that no exceptions were made for rank or social position. Robert Morris, the "financier of the Revolution," who more than any other man was responsible for preventing the complete collapse of Congress's credit during the war, spent almost three years in debtors' prison. James Wilson, who would share with Madison the leading roles in the Constitutional Convention and was subsequently appointed to the first Supreme Court by Washington, died in Edenton, North Carolina, in 1798, trying to evade the imprisonment for debt that awaited him if he returned to his home in Philadelphia. Even a sitting justice of the Supreme Court was not exempt from the harsh debtors' laws of the day.

The situation was made worse, if possible, by the conditions in most prisons. Newgate Prison in Connecticut was almost as notorious as its English counterpart. An abandoned copper mine, it could be reached only by a ladder. In its damp and dismal recesses more than a hundred prisoners were chained by their feet and necks. Rats and mice and every kind of pestilential creature lived in this foulness, which reeked of urine and human excrement. Chunks of earth frequently fell from the ceiling, and the prisoners' clothing rotted off their limbs. At Northampton, Massachusetts, prisoners' cells were barely four feet high, in Worcester the cells were four by eleven feet and without heat, light, or ventilation. In Philadelphia the common cells were eighteen by twenty feet and so crowded that each prisoner had a space of only six by two feet to lie down in at night. Men and women shared such grim accommodations, and although upper-class men and women usually had much better quarters, especially if they could pay for them, they were not infrequently subjected to the conditions we have described. Prostitutes were often allowed inside the prisons and were doubtless sometimes encouraged to ply their trade there. Even where they were excluded there was "general intercourse between the criminals of the different sexes in the jail and . . . the indiscriminate mixture of debtors and criminals," according to a grand jury report printed in the *Philadelphia Gazette*. Another report noted that "there is not even the appearance of decency with respect to the scenes of debauchery that naturally arise from such a situation; insomuch so . . . that the gaol has become a desirable place for the most wicked and polluted of both sexes." Whipping, branding, and use of the pillory were still common forms of punishment, although these were not inflicted on those imprisoned for debt.

Given such conditions of incarceration, the debtor was caught between the proverbial rock and hard place. If he refused to concur in the sale of his property, he would almost certainly be clapped in jail and his property sold anyway to discharge his debts. Worse, he might have his property sold at a fraction of its value at public sale and then, if the sum derived from the sale were insufficient, be put in debtors' prison as well. It is hardly to be wondered that debtors were an angry and militant lot in the years immediately following the Revolution. The independence, freedom, and equality for which they had fought and suffered seemed suddenly illusory. The powerful and well-to-do were free to exploit the less fortunate, those without power. Instead of independence, the debtors found themselves dependent on the moneyed classes, who on the one hand made money scarce and on the other insisted on the prompt payment of debts and showed little awareness of the inherent contradiction in their policy and little concern for its human consequences.

Since this tension between creditors and debtors or, more simply, between those who wielded political and financial power in the various states and those who lacked direct access to such power, was, and remains, a persistent theme in American history, it might be well to reflect for a moment on the significance of this conflict in its earliest manifestation. The surprising aspect of the conflict is not so much that it developed into a dangerous confrontation but that popular dissatisfaction was so slow to take the form of outright resistance. The reason, in part, was that the sacredness of obligations, financial or otherwise, was a central element in Protestant doctrine.

The New Testament was also called the New Covenant—in other words, the new contract or agreement between the Lord and his people, the congregation of the "saints." John Winthrop in his "Modell of Christian Charity," written aboard the *Arabella* on the way to establish the Massachusetts Bay Company in 1630, reminded the Puritan adventurers that they had entered into a compact with God to settle. "Thus stands the cause between God and us," Winthrop wrote;

"we are entered into a Covenant with him for this work, we have taken out a Commission, the Lord hath given us leave to drawe our own Articles. . . . Now if the Lord shall please to heare us and bring us in peace to the place we desire, then hath he ratified his Covenant and sealed our Commission and will expect a strickt performance of the Articles contained in it. . . ." If the Puritans failed to adhere to their part of the contract and should pursue "carnal intentions seekeing greate things for our selves and our posterity," the Lord would "surely breake out in wrathe against us and be revenged of such a perjured people and make us knowe the price of the breache of such a Covenant."

Every Puritan community was initially founded on a compact or covenant, derived in spirit if not in substance from Winthrop's "Modell," and signed by all the members of the community or at least by the saints, the true believers and members of the congregation. It followed that even commercial covenants or contracts partook of this "sanctity." So for creditors to insist on the full, faithful, and complete repayment of debts owed them seemed to them more a matter of Christian morality than of a mere financial transaction. This view imparted to words and actions of the creditor class a tone of self-righteousness that was especially galling to the debtors. The clear implication was that creditors were better Christians and that by insisting on the payment of debts they were acting in accord with Christian doctrine—that they were, in a sense, instruments of the Lord in chastising the wicked and indolent. The fact that the civil laws reinforced this "ethic" by punishing the debtor through imprisonment served to underline the relationship between financial failure and sin. To be a debtor who could not fulfill the terms of his "contract" was to be a sinner in the eyes of the Lord.

The absence or relative unimportance of the creditor-debtor conflict in the South did not mean that that region did not have its own particular tensions and conflicts. In Georgia during the Revolution there had been divisions between different factions of patriots that almost erupted into open warfare between the followers of Button Gwinnett (whose signature is now the rarest among the signers of the Declaration of Independence) and Lachlan McIntosh. McIntosh, indeed, accepted Gwinett's challenge to a duel and wounded him fatally (thus contributing substantially to that rarity). In the Carolinas, the bitterness of the long partisan warfare had left deep scars. In addition, the operations there of General Greene, which had virtually concluded the war, had left a trail of devastated farms and plantations. We have already noted the fate of Tories who returned to the Fishing Creek area to try and reclaim their farms. Such problems were accentuated by settlers and land speculators pushing westward amid rumors of plots to create independent states on the borders of North and South Carolina.

Maryland and Virginia had been contending over rights to the Potomac River for more than a hundred years. According to Maryland, any Virginia ship tied up in the Potomac River was legally in Maryland, since Maryland claimed the river to the Virginia shore. Maryland's contentions were especially irksome to Virginians fishing in the waters of the Potomac; and a virtual state of undeclared war existed along its banks, where oysters, shad, and crabs could be found in abundance. A conference of delegates from Virginia and Maryland had met as early as 1778 to try to establish rules governing the navigation of Chesapeake Bay and the Potomac River. Six years later a rising young Virginia politician, James Madison, was appointed chairman of the state assembly committee on commerce. Four of the ablest politicians of both states—George Mason and Edmund Randolph for Virginia and Samuel Chase and Daniel of St. Thomas Jenifer for Maryland—were appointed as commissioners to draw up "such liberal and equitable measures" as would serve the interests of both states. A "treaty" was concluded that provided for similar duties on the imports and exports of the two states and for mutual defense of the waterways common to them. That, it turned out, left hanging the question of Delaware and Pennsylvania, both of whom carried on commerce through Chesapeake Bay. Proposals were made to join with those states in an extended commercial pact. The response of the Virginia Assembly was to invite all the states to send delegates to a conference "to take into consideration the trade of the United States, to examine the relative situations and trade of the said States," and to propose a scheme that could be adopted by Congress to regulate the trade of the Confederated States.

The most potentially divisive issue facing the Confederation was that of slavery. The South, which exceeded in geographical area as well as in population the North, intended to dominate the Confederacy or any government that might succeed it. (More and more people, well aware of the inadequacies of the Confederation, had begun to talk of the need for strengthening it or for forming a new constitution.) That intention to dominate was in part a consequence of a certain lordly and imperious quality in the Southern character and in part a determination to protect the "peculiar institution" on which the social and economic system of the South rested.

To be forced to defend something that one knows in one's heart is indefensible, while at the same time proclaiming one's devotion to a set of political ideas that are thoroughly antithetical to the practical reality within which one lives and that determine the whole context of one's life-style, is bound to produce serious distortions of character. It is a commonplace to say that the South lived in a state of collective schizophrenia. There has indeed always been a considerable degree of schizophrenia in the American psyche, primarily because, as I have suggested in the introduction to this work, Americans have always had to pretend that everything was perfect in the perfect democracy, the model for the world. The South simply demonstrated what we might call the basic American schizophrenia in an acute form. The gap between the professed democratic faith and the cruel reality was wider in the South than in other regions of the country. And it was augmented there by a paranoia that grew decade by decade until the final cataclysm of the Civil War.

I am sensible to the annoyance such psychological terms may cause the reader. While I consider myself in no way a "psychohistorian," that is to say a historian who attempts to explain the workings of history by reference to Freudian (or Jungian) psychology projected onto the larger stage of history, I am at the same time quite aware of the fact that human societies are characterized by forms of collective consciousness, by attitudes and ideologies without attention to which we cannot begin to grasp their inner character.

The fact of the matter is that the terms "schizophrenia" and "paranoia" are useful simply as a kind of shorthand for the particular frame of mind that came to dominate the South and to affect virtually every issue that faced the Republic for eighty years, almost half of our history as a nation.

To summarize, the forces of division and disorder at work in the period immediately following the Revolution were numerous and powerful. To the basic split between the Slave States and the nonslave states—between, for all practical purposes, the North and the South—were added the numerous disputes among states over land and over commerce we have already mentioned; the strains produced in every state by the claims of the Loyalists (especially strong in the South); the almost universal resentment over the terms of the Treaty of 1783 that provided for the recovery of debts owed British merchants; the debtor-creditor conflict; and the tensions that were the product of financial hardship (the commerce of Massachusetts in 1785 was only a fourth of what it had been prior to the Revolution). All of these conflicts were aggravated by the pitiful condition of Congress and by the failure of the Articles of Confederation to provide for a chief executive, for an adequate system of courts and justice, or for any general administration of the affairs of the states collectively.

When Congress was in session it was poorly attended and often unable to muster a quorum. During its periods of adjournment a Committee of the States was supposed to carry on the day-to-day affairs of government, but it was also frequently without a quorum and was thus unable to conduct even routine business. The letters of delegates to Congress written in the fall of 1786 suggest the state of affairs in that body. A few delegates arrived in December when Congress was scheduled to convene and lingered on in New York until January waiting for a quorum of the states to assemble. Some, after waiting for weeks, returned home a few days before the arrival of delegates who would have established the required quorum. At the end of January, a Connecticut delegate, Stephen Mix Mitchell, wrote that it was still not clear whether "we have a Congress or no. The Scituation of Congress is truely deplorable," he added. "I cannot see there remains any necessity for keeping up a Representation in Congress, in our present Scituation, all we can possibly do, is to recommend [to the states], which is an old stale device no better than the wish of a few individuals relative to publick Concerns."

Even before the war was over many delegates to Congress had serious misgivings about the Articles. They had clearly proved inadequate to the exigencies of the war; perhaps in the less stressful conditions of peace their deficiencies would not be so marked. However, as we have seen, it did not take long for the Articles to demonstrate that they were, if anything, less adequate in peace than in war. The depressed economies of the states were, not surprisingly, blamed on Congress; and if it could not be held strictly responsible for the postwar depression, it clearly was powerless to stimulate economic recovery, to discharge the huge debt left over from the Revolution, to regulate commerce for the common benefit, or to do a hundred other things required of any properly functioning government.

At the same time, it must be said that many of the most critical problems of the postwar era derived less from the Articles than from the suspicion and particularism that characterized the relations of the states (and sections) to each other. Fortunately for those who wished to "form a more perfect union," the Articles were blamed for everything that plagued the states.

Men like Washington, Alexander Hamilton, John Jay, and James Madison had been observing the general deterioration of interstate relations with growing apprehension. Jay wrote to Washington in the summer of 1786 deploring the apparent determination of the states to ignore the portions of the Treaty of 1783 that ran counter to their interests. He thought it "better fairly to confess and correct errors than attempt to deceive ourselves and others by fallacious, though plausible, palliations and excuses." It was an unpleasant task to "oppose popular prejudices . . . and expose the improprieties of States," but it must be done. "Our affairs," Jay added, "seem to lead to some, some revolution—something that I cannot foresee or conjecture. I am uneasy and apprehensive; more so than during the war. Then we had a fixed object . . . yet I did firmly believe we should ultimately succeed, because I was convinced that justice was with us. The case is now altered; we are doing wrong and therefore I look forward to evil and calamities. . . ." Jay could not believe that after all America had suffered it would fail to find a way out of the apparent impasse that confronted it. The Confederated States had not been allowed by the Almighty to become a nation "for transient and unimportant purposes. I therefore believe that we are yet to become a great and respectable people." Selfishness and greed—"private rage for property"—had taken precedence over the public good; "personal rather than national interests" seemed everywhere to carry the day.

Then Jay added a revealing sentence: "The mass of men are neither wise nor good, and the virtue like the other resources of a country, can only be drawn to a point and exerted by strong circumstances ably administered." Most of the leaders of the Revolution partook of what, for want of a better term, I have called the Classical-Christian Consciousness. That is to say, they shared a view of human nature that derived directly from the Judeo-Christian doctrine of original sin. In this view, all of mankind were involved in Adam's original sin in the eating of the forbidden apple in the Garden of Eden. However the story of Genesis was understood, literally or metaphorically, its lesson was clear: men and women had an ineradicable tendency to gratify their own selfish desires; that impulse could never be entirely overcome. With God's help it could be moderated. The individual might, through the discipline of the Christian life, transcend, at least partially and fitfully, that original sin he shared with Adam. The reward for a life of faith would be heaven, an eternity of bliss.

The classical view of human nature was more pessimistic, since while accepting man's similitude, in Aristotle's image, to a pig or a wild beast, it did not envision the Christian possibility of redemption through Christ's love. To those Americans who were students of Greece and Rome, it seemed clear that classical civilization represented the highest human achievement prior to Christianity; hence the Classical-Christian Consciousness—a viewpoint expressed clearly in an essay written by William Manning, a Massachusetts farmer, in 1795. "Men," he wrote, "have implanted within them numerous pashions & lusts continually urging them to fraud violence & acts of injustis toards one another. . . . Man is a being made up of Selfe Love seeking his own hapiness in the misery of all around him, who would Damme a world to save himself from temporal or other punishment. . . . From this dispostion of Man or the depravity of the human hart arises not only the advantage but the absolute nesecaty of Sivil government— without it Mankind would be continually at war on their own spetia, stealing roving fighting with & killing one another."

To the Classical-Christian notion of man as a creature of base impulses, the eighteenth century added the Newtonian idea— expressed in James Otis's *Rights of the Colonies Asserted and Proved,* written in 1764 at the time of the Revenue Act—of a universe governed by moral and social as well as physical laws. The same point of view is implicit in Jay's desire for a "strong government ably administered." Only so can we neutralize or ameliorate the human propensity to put self-interest ahead of public good. The framers of governments must balance one interest or class against another so that a kind of equilibrium is created. Different as they were in education and social standing, Manning and Jay shared the Classical-Christian Consciousness.

Jay ended his letter to Washington by expressing his concern that "the better kind of people, by which I mean the people who are orderly and industrious . . . will be led by the insecurity of property, the loss of confidence in their rulers, and the want of public faith and rectitude, to consider the charms of liberty as imaginary and delusive." In such circumstances this class of people may turn to any demagogue or tyrant who promises them "quiet and security."

Washington replied that Jay's views of the crisis accorded with his own. What the cataclysmic event would be that would bring matters to a head, Washington confessed, was "beyond the reach of my fore-sight. . . . I do not conceive we can exist long as a nation without having lodged somewhere a power, which will pervade the whole Union in as energetic a manner as the authority of the State government extends over the several States."

It might be said here that Washington's observation is a clear indication that Americans who shared his political views were begin-ning to think in terms of a federal constitution that would be modeled on the constitutions of the states; they were beginning to think of the United States as a political entity similar to the states themselves, with certain powers paramount to those of the states; in other words, a federal or national system rather than a Confederation. To refuse to give Congress "ample authorities for national purposes" seemed to Washington "the very climax of popular absurdity and madness." Yet it was useless to berate humanity. "We must take human nature as we find it. Perfection falls not to the lot of mortals." Since an ideal government for ideal beings could not be devised in any event, powers should be granted to Congress adequate to its responsibilities. Wash-ington, too, feared that the continuing crisis would prepare the minds of the people "for any revolution whatever. We are apt to run from one extreme in to another. To anticipate and prevent disastrous contingencies would be the part of wisdom."

It was difficult for Washington to quite take in the changes that "a few years are capable of producing. I am told that even respectable characters speak of a monarchical form of government without horror. From thinking proceeds speaking; thence to acting is but a single step. But how irrevocable and tremendous! What a triumph for our enemies to verify their predictions! What a triumph for the advocates of despotism to find that we are incapable of governing ourselves, and that systems founded on the basis of equal liberty are merely ideal and fallacious! Would to God that wise measures may be taken in time to avert the consequences we have but too much reason to apprehend."

At the time of the incipient revolt at Newburgh in 1783, Washington had addressed the states reminding them that Americans seemed "to be peculiarly designated by Providence for the display of human greatness and felicity." Heaven had "crowned its other blessings, by giving a fairer opportunity for political happiness, than any other Nation has ever been favored with." If the winning of

"absolute freedom and Independency" were capped by the establishment of a sound government, "free circulation of Letters, and the
unbound extension of Commerce, the progressive refinement of
Manners, the growing liberality of sentiment, and, above all, the pure
and benign light of Revelation," the result must be a nation which
would have "a meliorating influence on all mankind" and increase "the
blessings of Society" for people everywhere. Those words had been
written scarcely four years earlier. Washington had reaffirmed them in
his brief remarks to Congress on surrendering his commission. Now
they seemed like ancient history. His exhortations had been neglected,
"though given as a last legacy in the most solemn manner. I had then
perhaps some claim to public attention," he added to Jay. "I consider
myself as having none at present."

"Shays' Rebellion"

As it turned out, the area of the most dangerous economic pressure proved to be in Massachusetts, where there were troubling indications of the incipient cataclysm Washington and Jay feared. There farmers, threatened by foreclosure proceedings against their farms, framed a petition to the Great and General Court of the State, expressing, with uncertain literacy but considerable eloquence, the plight in which they and their families found themselves.

"In the time of the late war," they noted, "being desirous to defend secure and promote the wrights and liberties of the people, we spared no pains but freely granted all that aid and assistance of every kind that our civel fathers required of us." They were still as willing to bear a fair share of the "great debt" caused by the war "as we are to injoy our shars in independancy and constatutional priviledges in the Commonwealth, if itt was in our power." If "prudent mesuers" were taken to create a sufficient supply of money, then they could discharge their debts. If nothing was done for their relief, "in a little time att least, one half of our inhabitants . . . will become banckerupt."

After a review of the depressed prices for farm produce, the petitioners added, "Surely your honours are not strangers to the distresses of the people but doe know that many of our good inhabiitants are now confined in gole for det and for taxes: maney have fled."

The petition closed with a reminder that despite the depressed conditions in the state they had noticed no reduction in the "sallerys and grants" to the governor and "other gentlemen." They could not "reconsile these sallerys . . . with the principles of our Constatution (viz.) piaty, justice, moderate, temperance, etc." The signatures of the petitioners read like an Old Testament roster, with Jeremiah Powers, Nehemiah Stebbins, and Zebedee Osborne leading off the list of fifty-seven names.

The fiscal conservatives in control of the Massachusetts government turned a deaf ear to all such entreaties. Indeed the Massachusetts Great and General Court so far forgot itself as to pass an act imposing duties on paper and vellum used for bonds, deeds, notes, writs, newspapers, bills of lading, and the like. Such documents had to be on sheets stamped by the commissioners of taxes. A stamp tax!

Ten months later a convention of "embattled farmers," from forty-one towns in Worcester County, joined together this time against their own leaders and the state legal system, drew up a similar petition. After enumerating the distress of the "good people" of the county, the petitioners called for a convention to draft a new state constitution that would provide machinery for the relief of debtors and a reform of the financial practices of the state.

Alarmed at the turn of events, James Warren reported to John Adams, emissary of Congress to the Court of St. James's, "We are now in a State of Anarchy and Confusion bordering on a Civil War. . . . The three upper Counties . . . have refused submission to the Government established by the Constitution . . . and are in a State of Rebellion, while the three Eastern Counties are petitioning to be separated from us and formed into a new Government of their own Construction. These are very singular Events. . . . I have long been mortified by the Imbecility and Inattention with which our public Affairs have been Conducted. . . . My small Efforts were Joined with yours and others for many Years in raising a glorious Fabrick on Foundations that should have been as permanent as Time, but suffered to fall into ruin in less than half the Time it took to build it."

The western and southern counties of Massachusetts had been meeting together in conventions since early in 1784 to discuss means of obtaining relief from state taxes and private creditors. The towns of Medway and Wrentham in Suffolk County sent out calls to their neighboring communities for a convention, and Sutton, in Worcester County, followed suit. In August, 1786, delegates from fifty towns gathered at Hatfield and presented a list of twenty-five proposals for the relief of debtors. Particular resentment was expressed against lawyers for fattening on the distress of the poor.

A few days later the Court of Common Pleas was scheduled to sit at Northampton, but some fifteen hundred farmers clustered around the courthouse and prevented the judges from taking their seats. Worcester, Middlesex, Bristol, and Berkshire counties proved ready to follow the example of Northampton. In Worcester County a paper was circulated to gather signatures of farmers who vowed not to permit the courts to conduct their business in that county. The signers of the same document pledged their "lives and fortunes" to prevent all public sales of goods taken by foreclosure.

On September 5 several hundred armed men at Worcester refused entrance to the court to the judge appointed to hear foreclosure cases. The episode was the more striking by virtue of the fact that the judge in question was Artemas Ward, the old Revolutionary War hero, who had commanded the American forces at Bunker Hill. Ward expostulated with the men guarding the courthouse door, but they remained obdurate. His request to address the crowd, among whom were doubtless men who had served under him in the Continental Army, was refused. Finally, his notoriously short temper flared, and he began cursing and swearing. "He did not give a damn for their bayonets. They might, if they liked, plunge them into his heart." Finally, he was allowed to speak. For two hours the old general exhorted the crowd; he was frequently interrupted by yells and jeers and the cry "Adjourn without day"—adjourn indefinitely. It was an extraordinary and disturbing spectacle. Scarcely three years after the end of the war a mob of rebellious farmers threatened violence against one of the heroes of that conflict who was now an officer of the state. Barred from the courthouse, the stubborn old man marched off to the United States Arms Tavern and convened the court there, meanwhile calling on the militia to provide protection. The militia, not surprisingly, were sympathetic to the crowd, which was made up largely of neighbors and friends. Stymied, Ward adjourned the court and decamped, bearing word of the insurrection to Boston.

The Court of Sessions was scheduled to sit at Concord on the very edge of "enemy territory," Boston. Orders were issued for the militia of Middlesex and Bristol to turn out to insure the opening of the court, but when the citizens of Concord assured the authorities that there would be no resistance, officials rescinded the call.

Hardly had the rescinding order gone out when farmers under the command of Job Shattuck began descending on the town. Since fall was coming on and the air was sharp, the newcomers threw together a cluster of improvised shelters, which quickly took on the appearance of a military encampment. On the day scheduled for the convening of the court, the little army turned out in good order, marched to the courthouse, and posted guards at strategic points around it. Hostile observers reported that their muskets, clubs, and swords were generously supplemented by rum. When the judges of the Sessions Court failed to appear, some of the company set out to find them. The judges were discovered at a tavern on the Boston road, doubtless exchanging gloomy reflections on the spirit of rebellion abroad in the land. The search force deployed around the tavern in a thoroughly menacing manner, upon which the judges sent word that they had no intention of trying to hold court. At this news a "sergeant" of the insurgents marched off to Concord accompanied by a fife and two drums to report to the main body.

It was not long before some ninety armed men descended on the tavern where the justices were eating dinner. The leader of the insurgents then addressed the crowd of curious locals who had gathered to gawk. With a considerable sprinkling of oaths, he declared that they must cast their lot with the rebels. All those who refused would, he assured them, be driven out of town at the points of bayonets: "As Christ laid down his life to save the world, so will I lay down my life to suppress the Government from all tyrannical oppression, and you who are willing to join us in this here affair may fall into our ranks. Those who do not shall, after two hours, stand as monuments of God's living mercy." While the leaders of the militant farmers argued with the clerk of the court about a written statement from the judges affirming the suspension of the court, the beleaguered justices slipped away in the darkness.

At Great Barrington, in Berkshire County, eight hundred farmers prevented the sitting of the Court of Common Pleas and then freed all those imprisoned for debt. The next scene of action was Springfield, where the state's supreme court was to convene. It was anticipated that the court would hand down indictments of all those who had been implicated in blocking the sessions of the various courts. The leaders therefore announced that they were determined to prevent the court from convening. Governor James Bowdoin was equally determined to see that the court should sit. He ordered six hundred militia under the command of General William Shepard, who had commanded the Massachusetts 4th Regiment of the Continental Line during much of the Revolution, to secure the courthouse and assure the sitting of the justices.

The next morning some five or six hundred farmers appeared at the Springfield courthouse, armed and in good order. At their head was the man who was, rather undeservedly, to give his name to the whole insurrection, Captain Daniel Shays. "Shays' Rebellion," as it became known, was obviously much more than that. He simply appeared as its leader in the latter and most critical phase of the movement and became, in effect, its spokesman. Perhaps there was a feeling among the moderate elements in the state that to call the farmers' insurrection Shays' Rebellion might suggest that it was the work of one dangerous demagogue and not a popular uprising.

Whatever others might call them, the militant farmers denominated themselves "Regulators" and wore in their hats sprigs of evergreen, as many of them had done ten years earlier when they gathered around Boston to besiege the British. Shays, like Artemas Ward and General Shepard, had fought at Bunker Hill. He had later been commissioned a captain and seems to have been a capable if not outstanding officer, though, like many other company-grade officers, he resigned his commission before the end of the war. Now, as doubtless the highest ranking among the numerous veterans who made up his little army, he assumed or, more likely, was voted command of the motley band. The fact that the farmers marched with more or less military precision and executed their various maneuvers with some flair indicated that they had been preparing for the occasion and that they were far from being the "mob" they were described as being by the champions of law and order.

When Shays' farmers (simply calling them what the great majority of them were—farmers—gives their story an entirely different character than denominating them "the mob," as most nineteenth-century historians writing of the episode did) saw the militia drawn up outside the courthouse, they cursed and jeered them for taking arms against their fellows. Shays finally quieted his men and dispatched a message to the judges warning them not to return any indictments against his force. The judges replied that they were obliged to do as the law and their consciences dictated. Meanwhile the situation between Shays' men and the militia remained highly volatile. It was by no means clear that Shays himself could control the angry farmers. Seemingly determined to bring the militia to an open engagement or drive them from the field, the farmers formed into a line of battle with drums beating and muskets at the ready and advanced as though making an attack. When Shays had, with considerable effort, deflected them, they paraded through the streets of Springfield taunting the militia and daring them to open fire. It was not surprising that the court, in the face of such demonstrations, accompanied as they were with wild shouts, the noise of drums, and a general atmosphere of crisis, could accomplish little. For one thing not enough prospective jurors had appeared to enable them to empanel a jury. The court thus adjourned after a day of vainly trying to do its business. During all this time Shays and Shepard carried out extensive negotiations designed to keep the lid on the explosive situation. When the militia withdrew from the courthouse yard, the area was immediately occupied by Shays' irregulars, who conducted themselves like a conquering army.

At the end of the month the Great and General Court convened in Boston and, under the threat of a general uprising, attempted to accommodate some of the demands that came in from the various county conventions. Soon after the state legislature adjourned, Worcester County called a convention to review its actions and determine to what degree its members had responded to the grievances of the people. The verdict was decidedly unfavorable to the Great and General Court. The problem, as the delegates at the Worcester convention saw it, was that a majority of the delegates to the state legislature were men "in very easy circumstances" who had little idea of what it meant to go hungry, have one's property and livelihood in peril, and be hounded by lawyers and tax collectors more ravenous than "savage beasts of prey."

At the end of November the Court of General Sessions tried to convene in Worcester, only to find the courtroom occupied by armed men from surrounding towns and the yard outside crowded with spectators whose sympathies were clearly with the rebels. When the sheriff, Colonel Greenleaf, read the riot act and ordered the crowd to disperse, he was greeted with good-natured jibes but not obedience. When he attempted to lecture the company, he was interrupted and denounced for the size of his fees, especially those charged for carrying out executions. Whereupon the indignant official declared with more boldness than prudence: "If you think the fees for executions excessive, you need no longer seek for redress, for I will hang you all for nothing with the greatest of pleasure." This sally brought a laugh and a cheer from his auditors, and one was bold enough to stick the symbol of the Regulators—a spring of ever-green—in his hat. The indignant Greenleaf conducted the judges to the United States Arms Tavern where Artemas Ward had earlier tried to hold court, and from there they made their way back to Boston as best they could.

After the encounter at Worcester, Governor Bowdoin ordered the sheriff of Middlesex County to raise a posse of cavalry with the mission of hunting down and arresting those men who, like Job Shattuck and Shays himself, had been most prominent among the Regulators. A cavalry militia unit overtook the fleeing Shattuck, cornered him in the woods behind his house, and finally captured him, badly wounded.

On hearing that a large force was being recruited in Boston to hunt down his ragged and hungry band, Shays ordered a retreat from Worcester, which had become the command headquarters of the Regulators. The mercury had dropped below zero when the retreat began, and a number of men died of the cold or suffered crippling frostbite.

Meanwhile Bowdoin, realizing by this time that local militia could not be counted on because of their ties to the rebels, undertook to recruit an independent force of over four thousand men. These were to be enlisted for thirty days and receive the same pay the Continental Army had received (or, more accurately, was supposed to have received) during the war. The force was to be drawn primarily from those counties around Boston where the populace was least sympathet-ic with the Regulator cause. Thus it was made up of a disproportionate number of those who had been characterized by the Worcester convention as being "in very easy circumstances." General Benjamin Lincoln was placed in command of the volunteer army. When it turned out that there was no money in the treasury to pay the recruits, "a number of wealthy gentlemen made an offer of a loan of the necessary funds." Powder was almost as hard to find as money, but by January 21 the little army was ready to march for Worcester.

While the anti-Regulator army was being gathered at Roxbury, near Boston, Shays, responding to pressure from his own "army" and to their desperate need for arms and powder, planned a foray against an arsenal of the Confederation Congress at Springfield. Bowdoin, hearing of Shays' intention, ordered Shepard to garrison the town and protect the congressional arsenal. The Regulators, undeterred by Shepard's force, swollen now to some twelve hundred militia of uncertain temper, planned to attack and rout them before they could join with the forces assembling at Roxbury. At four o'clock in the afternoon of January 25, Shays began a coordinated attack in which one of his lieutenants, Day, was to move on Shepard's force from the rear while Shays advanced frontally. As Shays's men ascended the long low hill where Shepard had taken up defensive positions, the captain was unaware that the message he had sent to Day had been intercepted.

Shepard first ordered his men to fire over the heads of the advancing farmers, hoping they would panic, but the volley failed to halt them and they came on in good order like veteran soldiers. Shepard then ordered the militia to fire to kill. Another volley rang out and 4 farmers fell. This time panic did spread, and despite Shays' courageous efforts, the Regulators broke and fled, not stopping until they reached the town of Ludlow some ten miles away.

The next day Lincoln's force, which had suffered from the cold almost as much as the Regulators had, reached Springfield. From there he deployed his men in pursuit of the demoralized Regulators. Shays gathered together what was left of his army and fortified two adjacent hills near the town of Pelham. Lincoln, coming up with his army, saw at once that the deep snow would make an attack difficult and costly. Making his own headquarters at Hadley, Lincoln entered into a kind of psychological warfare with Shays, attempting to persuade him that his cause was hopeless and that he should surrender in order to prevent the decimation of his men. Shays was discouraged to hear that a force of Regulators who had surrounded Shepard's militia had been captured, but he was determined to avoid surrender. Appealing for a parley several days hence, Shays led his men on a dash for the town of Petersham. It was a forced march of thirty miles through snow and cold, but the army found warm quarters in the town. The Regulators, confident that Lincoln would not pursue them through such a bitter night, were sleeping an exhausted sleep when Lincoln's advance guard hit the town. In a manner reminiscent of the surprise of the Hessians at Trenton, the dismayed Regulators escaped in small bands as best they could. Two miles outside the town Lincoln's cavalry captured several hundred thoroughly demoralized insurgents.

Many others were hunted down and captured the next day, while a number escaped north to New Hampshire and Vermont and some west to New York.

Small wonder that Lincoln, confident that he had broken the back of the rebellion, sent home most of his recruits, whose thirty-day enlistment periods had, in any event, almost run out. He was, as it turned out, too sanguine. Word arrived a few days later that another Regulator force under a leader named Hubbard had appeared near West Stockbridge. There was also news that several small Regulator units that had been scattered by Lincoln's men had re-formed, been once more dispersed, and re-formed again, each time apparently with an increase in numbers. Another leader, Eli Parsons, had made his way across the Massachusetts–New York border with a group of followers. From there he circulated a letter urging all those who sympathized with the cause, who were opposed to tyranny and oppression, to stand fast. He was confident that he could recruit sympathizers in New York and Vermont. With them he would return, make contact with his Massachusetts friends at Berkshire, and renew the struggle. He was as good as his word. At the end of February a force of Regulators marched from a camp in New York State to Stockbridge, seized supplies there, and carried off prisoners to the vicinity of Springfield. There the militia came up with them. After a fierce clash the outnumbered Regulators fled, leaving 2 dead and 30 wounded to testify to the bitterness of the fighting. Once more they took refuge across the New York line.

Now came a long and laborious effort of rounding up Regulators who had fled to other states. New Hampshire and Connecticut agreed to apprehend all refugees and return them to Massachusetts for punishment. To no one's surprise, Rhode Island welcomed them and Vermont equivocated, as did New York and Pennsylvania. The rebellion was broken by early spring. The democratically inclined John Hancock succeeded the conservative James Bowdoin as governor. The captured insurgents were eventually pardoned, and in time even Shays was permitted to return to Massachusetts. Thus, the state could take some satisfaction from the fact that if it had been stubbornly indifferent to the plight of the debtor-farmers, it had ultimately tempered justice with mercy.

Such a policy was not entirely the consequence of altruism, however. As Bowdoin's defeat indicated, there was much sympathy in the state for the militants. It had been an extremely traumatic experience for Massachusetts, leader with Virginia in the fight for independence, to be seen first ignoring the distress of its people and then taking up arms to suppress an uprising that had been undertaken in the name of liberty and justice.

One of the revealing by-products of the uprising of the Massachusetts farmers was the publication by a trio of young Yale graduates of a series called *The Anarchiad.* Joel Barlow, John Trumbull, and David Humphreys were the authors and editors. *The Anarchiad* contained a mixture of satiric poems, odes, songs, and bits of doggerel all dealing with the dangers of anarchy. The rebellious farmers were cast as bears, owls, frogs, and other animals.

> See the jails open, and the thieves arise.
> Thy constitution, Chaos, is restor'd;
> Law sinks before thy uncreating word;
> Thy hand unbars th' unfathom'd gulf of fate,
> And deep in darkness 'whelms the new-born state.

The Anarchiad, which ran for twelve issues and was widely reprinted in Federalist newspapers, never suggested that the farmers might have any claim to sympathy, or that there was anything paradoxical about the spirit of chaos and anarchy usually associated with fetid cities of Europe manifesting itself in the sunny fields and among the lowing flocks of Massachusetts.

James Madison and Abigail Adams were among those who kept Jefferson and John Adams, resident in Paris and London, respectively, informed of the progress of the uprising of the Massachusetts farmers. Abigail plainly had no sympathy with the rebels. In her opinion, they were "ignorant, wrestless desperadoes, without conscience or principles who led a deluded multitude to follow their standard under a pretence of grievances which have no existence but in their imagination . . . the mobbish insurgents are for sapping the foundation and destroying the whole fabric at once."

The responses of the two friends to the news from Massachusetts were in sharp contrast. Adams was inspired to resume work on a treatise he was writing in defense of the constitutions of the various American states, constitutions the character of which he had to a degree influenced by his *Thoughts on Government,* written ten years earlier. Jefferson, with the detachment consequent on three thousand miles of ocean, took a "long view." While the acts of the Massachusetts farmers were "absolutely unjustifiable," Jefferson hoped that the state authorities would deal mildly with the insurgents. "I hold it," he added, in a letter to Madison, "that a little rebellion now and then is a good thing, and as necessary in the political world as storms in the physical. Unsuccessful rebellions indeed generally establish the incroachments on the rights of the people which have produced them. An observation of this truth should render honest republican governments so mild in their punishment of rebellions, as not to discourage them too much. It is a medicine necessary for the sound health of government. . . ."

This astonishing doctrine evoked a protest even from the liberal Madison. The notion that governments were to be kept in line by a series of "little rebellions" comported so ill with any known theory of government as to constitute a kind of political non sequitur. In Massachusetts, where the suffering and despair of the farmers were beyond calculation and the dismay of the authorities considerable, Jefferson's remark would have seemed merely frivolous, but it has cheered revolutionaries in subsequent generations.

Washington's reaction, by contrast, was a sober one. Responding to Henry Lee's account of the Massachusetts rebellion, Washington once more expressed his anxiety over the question of whether "mankind, when left to themselves, are unfit for their own government. . . . I am lost in amazement when I behold what intrigue, the interested views of desperate characters, ignorance, and jealousy of the minor part, are capable of effecting, as a scourge on the major part of our fellow citizens of the Union. [Some remedy must be soon found or the country would soon be in a state of anarchy.] My humble opinion is, that there is a call for decision. Know precisely what the insurgents aim at. If they have *real* grievances, redress them if possible, or acknowledge the justice of them, and your inability to do it in the present moment. If they have not, employ the force of government against them at once. . . . To be more exposed to the eyes of the world, and more contemptible than we already are, is hardly possible." Every violation of the Constitution must be "reprehended." If the Constitution itself was defective, "let it be amended, but not suffered to be trampled on whilst it has an existence."

If the Massachusetts Farmers' Revolt was the most dangerous challenge that the Confederation faced, its relatively successful resolution was the most encouraging development of the "critical period" between 1783 and 1789. There can be no question that the Massachusetts state elections, which brought the more liberally inclined Hancock and his supporters to power, did much to relieve the social pressures that had led to the uprising. A general economic recovery in the state was undoubtedly an important factor as well.

The Farmers' Revolt was cited by many of those who wished to form a strong federal government as an example of the inadequacies of the Confederation. It is hard to see, however, how the federal Constitution, had it been in existence, could have materially affected the revolt unless it would have been by enabling the president to send federal troops to suppress it. As it turned out, Benjamin Lincoln was probably the best man for the job, and one suspects it was much better to have employed a force recruited by the state than one dispatched by the federal government.

Nevertheless, various factions made what use they could of the revolt. To those whose greatest anxiety was that an excess of democracy would lead to anarchy and in turn to tyranny—a tyranny necessary to restore order—the revolt of the Massachusetts farmers seemed like the reenactment of a lesson from the classical historians Thucydides or Polybius. To those who believed that the ideals of the Revolution were rapidly being subverted by an "aristocracy" of the prosperous and wellborn, the Farmers' Revolt was a confirmation of their darkest fears.

In the nineteenth century, when idealization of the United States reached its apogee, American historians dealt most unsympathetically with Shays' Rebellion. They held that Shays was a "demagogue" (which he plainly was not) and that the militant farmers were "rebels" and "malcontents," who, whenever they assembled (even under the strictest discipline) were a "mob." In recent times historians have been more sympathetic, but the true dimensions of the Farmers' Revolt have seldom been adequately described. The Massachusetts farmers took up arms only after all other avenues for relief had been tried and found completely inadequate. Although those who fought for justice numbered only a few thousand men, they were tacitly supported by tens of thousands of other farmers who shared their feelings to a substantial degree and who affirmed that fact by ballots rather than bullets. Moreover, rather than behaving like an unruly mob, when they took the field the Regulators fought with considerable courage and remarkable tenacity, thereby making evident the depth of their commitment to the cause. Indeed, we may be confident that if their cause had triumphed and a second "revolution" had taken place in confirmation of the first, they and their leaders would have been celebrated as courageous fighters for liberty and justice.

(A) ——— The farmers who took up arms against the state of Massachusetts, for which they had so recently fought, were desperate and embittered men who, just as surely as they had ten years earlier, risked "their lives, their fortunes and their sacred honor." They had experienced social injustice of the most galling kind, and they suffered extremely for their temerity in questioning their rulers. Most of them lost their farms; some lost their lives; many carried to their graves physical and psychological wounds more bitter than those they had received in the Revolution.

The pardoned Shays moved to Schoharie County, New York. There he prospered and became a staunch Federalist. On July 4, 1803, he was a prominent figure at a patriotic celebration where one of the toasts was to "Alexander Hamilton and the Constitution." After the toasts had been consumed, there was a discharge of "musquetry" from a company of volunteers under the command of the Revolutionary veteran "Gen. Daniel Shays." Time had erased the opprobrium if not the memory, and had elevated the rank.

Despite a political and social situation verging on anarchy, Americans did not abate their claim to redeem the rest of mankind from tyranny and oppression.

John Winthrop, with all his dreams of establishing model Christian communities in New England, had no illusions about the limits of all human aspirations. Heaven was still heaven and earth was earth. Earth was, at its best, simply a preparation for heaven. The best that earth could offer was but a preliminary to a future state of eternal bliss among celestial beings, angels, and the souls of men and women made perfect.

The philosophers of the Enlightenment, most conspicuously such French theorists as Voltaire, Diderot, and Condorcet, had, however, attacked the notion that life on earth should be directed toward some (to them) illusory notion of future rewards and punishments. Heaven existed only in the minds of the superstitious, they maintained. The notion of life after death served primarily to reconcile the miserable and oppressed to their situation in this world. Stripped of the illusion that there would be a better life hereafter, they might stir themselves out of their centuries-long lethargy, overthrow their oppressors, and demand some happiness in this life, leaving the hereafter to take care of itself. It was, of course, this new spirit of Enlightenment that had animated the American Revolutionaries and had received its ultimate expression in the Declaration of Independence. And it was this spirit, in its American manifestation, which we have chosen to call the Secular-Democratic Consciousness.

Because no ideas are entirely purely and consistently held, the spirit of the Enlightenment in America retained very substantial elements of the Re-formed Protestant Christian Consciousness, as we shall see throughout this work. But if Americans, for the most part, rejected the antireligious bias of the French philosophers, they enthusiastically embraced the utopian elements in Enlightenment thought. They believed that it was possible to establish a more or less perfect human society in which freedom, justice, and equality would prevail and everyone would be happy according to his or her deserts. John Winthrop had hoped to redeem Western Christianity by creating the model of a Christian community for all other believers to emulate. Now Americans intended to redeem the rest of humanity from "tyranny and oppression" by providing a model political community, a nation, which must inspire all the other peoples of the world to emulation. Moreover, a great many Americans were convinced that this was a mission assigned especially to the United States by God. The most influential nineteenth-century American historian, George Bancroft, did not hesitate to state as much as the underlying theme of his great history.

So even in the midst of a situation verging on anarchy Americans continued to proclaim their redemptive mission. The poet laureate of the Revolution, Philip Freneau, wrote a dialogue on "The Rising Glory of America" to be "pronounced on a public occasion." The actors in the dialogue were the classical figures of Acasto and Leander. Acasto concludes the dialogue:

> And when a train of rolling years are past . . .
> A new Jerusalem, sent down from heaven,
> Shall grace our happy earth,—perhaps this land,
> Whose ample bosom shall receive, though late,
> Myriads of saints, with their immortal king,
> To live and reign on earth a thousand years,
> Thence called Millennium. Paradise anew
> Shall flourish, by no second Adam lost,
> No dangerous tree with deadly fruit shall grow,
> No tempting serpent to allure the soul
> From native innocence.—A Canaan here,

Another Canaan shall excel the old,
. . . the lion and the lamb
In mutual friendship linked, shall browse the shrub. . . .
The happy people, free from toils and death,
Shall find secure repose. No fierce disease,
No fevers, slow consumption, ghastly plague,
(Fate's ancient ministers) again proclaim
Perpetual war with man; fair fruits shall bloom. . . .
The fiercer passions of the human breast
Shall kindle up to deeds of death no more,
But all subside in universal peace.—
—Such days the world,
And such America at last shall have
When ages, yet to come, have run their round,
And future years of bliss alone remain.

We find in Freneau major themes of the new American consciousness—the utopian vision, a democratic fervor religious in its intensity, and a worship of nature as the visible evidence of God's glory. Freneau's poem also gives classic expression to the millennial aspects of Christianity—the promise in Revelation that Christ will come again to reign for a thousand years on earth before taking the saints with him to heaven—thereby allowing Americans to combine earthly utopian expectations with Christian dogma. It was thus often unclear whether the "new Jerusalem" was a secular city inhabited by mortal men and women or the earthly paradise reconstituted under Christ's rule that so many Americans anticipated. But it is plain enough that with each passing decade the inclination to conceive of it as a thoroughly secular or worldly city, a utopia created with a minimum of assistance from the Almighty, grew stronger.

In much the same spirit as Freneau, Timothy Matlack, delivering a lecture before the American Philosophical Society in 1780, eulogized agriculture and noted: "Mankind have talked of a Millennium—a Thousand Years of perfect Peace and Happiness—and some have looked for it to happen about this Time. Whenever the Prophecies of this great Event shall be fulfilled, and the whole Earth become one fruitful *Eden*, the benign Sun of that happy Day will rise upon a perfect Knowledge of Agriculture, a sober, persevering industry, a virtuous, chaste Enjoyment of the Fruits of the Field. . . . To do good is delightful:—And that Country whose Citizens make its Welfare not only the Object of their Business, but of their Pleasure, cannot fail to become wise and happy, and must rise to a Height of Riches, Strength and Glory, which the fondest Imagination cannot readily conceive."

Luxury

Demoralizing as Shays' Rebellion was, there was a very different and, for many of the leaders of the Revolution, even more troubling issue—the moral fiber of the American people. With the war over, ordinary Americans showed a distressing tendency to concern themselves with material matters to the exclusion of their civic duties. The code word here was "luxury." Americans, it seemed, were little inclined to display those virtues of frugality and austerity that were thought to be the essential qualities of true republicans. Instead they appeared disconcertingly preoccupied by the pursuit of luxury.

James Warren wrote a gloomy report to John Adams on conditions in Massachusetts in early 1785. Warren noted: "In this place, the System of Politics remains much as it has been; the same Imbecility, the same servility and the same Inattention still prevail and are likely to continue. Money is the only object attended to, and the only acquisition that commands respect. Patriotism is ridiculed; Integrity and Ability are of little Consequence. Foreign Commerce has extended itself beyond its natural supports, and by its Extravagant Imports greatly Exceeding the Exports, drained off all the Money. . . ." Warren's wife, Mercy, writing a few months later, dwelt on the same theme. She had once cherished the hope that the citizens of the American states, and especially those of her beloved Massachusetts, might be distinguished "for the Simplicity, Magnanimity and Vigour" of their character. She added: "But alas! the Weakness of Human Nature. I fear we are already too far advanced in every species of Luxury to Recede, though much more than our political salvation depended on the Reform. The avidity for Pleasure [the pursuit of happiness?] has increased with our Freedom and a thirst of acquisition for its support pushes to the most dangerous Experiments. . . . It is owing to the Perversion of Reason, a Corruption of Taste and the Cravings of Artificial Necessity which causes the Restless pursuit of objects seldom attainable. . . ." It seemed to Mercy Warren that neither "the Reasonings of the Philosopher nor the maxims of Religion" could persuade Americans to be less single-minded in their pursuit of material things.

The passage, which could be duplicated in letters of many different correspondents, has a curiously modern ring. It was a tenet of the Congregational-Calvinist creed that had shaped the conscious-ness of New England that thrift and restraint were the essential foundations of the God-fearing community as well as of republican government. A constant theme of anxiety thus runs through the letters and correspondence of the Revolutionary leaders concerning the human inclination to luxury and self-indulgence. History taught that only nations capable of stimulating the "civic virtue" of their citizens could long escape tyranny and despotism.

The crucial question therefore was: Would the American people have sufficient strength of character and spirit of self-denial to sustain that most demanding form of government—a republic? Or, once the immediate pressures of the war were over, would they become like other peoples, obsessed with the pursuit of "luxuries," of material rather than spiritual rewards? When Jefferson, abandoning Congress in the darkest days of the Revolution to work on his revision of the statutes of Virginia, was chided by his friends, he defended himself by arguing that the laws of Virginia might never be reformed if they were not liberalized in an era of patriotic fervor. After the war the people of the state would be too preoccupied with selfish concerns to pay much attention to such a recondite subject.

Many, if not virtually all, of the leaders of the Revolution believed that their worst apprehensions were being confirmed. With one voice they deplored the precipitous decline in patriotism and the general infatuation with material things. Yet there was an ambivalence here, too. In order for the country to prosper and grow, it was necessary that the great mass of its citizens be preoccupied with making money. Making money required energy, initiative, enterprise, and hard work; and these were all positive values according to the Calvinistic ethic. When Benjamin Vaughn, Franklin's physician friend, wrote him in Paris that English travelers had commented unfavorably on the "growing Luxury" of America and appealed to Franklin for a "Remedy," Franklin replied with unusual asperity. What the Englishmen identified as luxury was probably no more than an effort by their American hosts to put their best foot forward. Franklin added: "I have not indeed yet thought of a Remedy for Luxury. I am not sure, that in a great State it is capable of a remedy. Nor that the Evil is in itself always so great as it is represented. Suppose we include in the Definition of Luxury all unnecessary Expense, and then let us consider whether Laws to prevent such Expense are possible to be executed in a great Country, and whether, if they could be executed, our People generally would be happier, or even richer." The desire for luxury was the spur to "Labour and Industry," wrote Franklin, who here inserted one of his inimitable stories.

When the skipper of a boat that had carried Franklin and his wife from Cape May to Philadelphia refused pay for his trouble, Franklin's wife sent the skipper's daughter "a new-fashioned Cap." Three years later when Franklin encountered the skipper again, the latter mentioned how much his daughter had enjoyed the cap. "But," the skipper added, "it proved a dear Cap to our Congregation."

"How so?"

"When my Daughter appeared in it at Meeting, it was so much admired, that all the Girls resolved to get such Caps from Philadelphia; and my wife and I computed, that the whole could not have cost less than a hundred Pounds."

At this a friend of the skipper interjected, "True but you do not tell all the Story. I think the Cap was nevertheless an Advantage to us, for it was the first thing that put our Girls upon Knitting worsted Mittens for Sale at Philadelphia, that they might have wherewithal to buy Caps and Ribbands there; and you know that Industry has continued, and is likely to continue and increase to a much greater Value, and answer better Purposes."

While a "vain, silly Fellow" builds "a fine House, furnishes it richly, lives in it expensively, and in a few years ruins himself . . . ," Franklin told Vaughn, "the Masons, Carpenters, Smiths, and other honest Tradesmen have by his Employ assisted in maintaining and raising their Families." Furthermore, Franklin contended that it was primarily in the seaport towns that luxury was in evidence. "The People of the Trading Towns may be rich and luxurious, while the Country [the farming regions] possesses all the Virtues, that tend to private Happiness and publick Prosperity." He himself derived comfort from the thought that "upon the whole, the Quantity of Industry and Prudence among Mankind exceeds the Quantity of Idleness and Folly." (There is considerable evidence, however, that the obsession of Americans with "luxury" was by no means confined to the "Trading Towns." Anna Schweizer, a Swiss immigrant, wrote home, "About American luxury, display, and the sumptuousness of clothing, I could, dear parents, write you volumes. The serving-maid of a farmer living in a desolate farmhouse is scarcely to be distinguished from the daughter of a wealthy city merchant.")

John Adams shared Franklin's opinion to an extent. While he thought a republic could survive only if its people were inculcated with "the principles of humanity and general benevolence, public and private charity, industry, frugality, honesty, and punctuality in their dealings," he accepted the fact that Americans "never were Spartans in their contempt of wealth." "I will go farther," he added, "and say they ought not to be. Such a Trait in their Character would render them lazy Drones, unfit for the Agriculture, Manufactures, Fisheries, and Commerce, and Population of their Country; and fit only for War." The argument of Franklin and Adams appeared to be that some luxury was inevitable in every society—that within reason it was an important stimulus to useful activity and that it was, to a large degree, its own corrective, since those who indulged themselves excessively, besides providing work for others, must squander their fortunes and soon end up destitute.

The dubiousness of the proposition reflects the ambivalent feelings of those who held it. How was one to strike the right balance between the utility of luxury as an incentive to industry and the danger of it as a corrupter of morals? It is hardly necessary to point out that Americans have never resolved that dilemma. The tensions it has caused in our society will be one of the major themes of this work. It appears to be no closer to being solved today than it was in the 1780s. Americans have become the greatest consumers of nonessentials in the history of the world, without, it would seem, being any the happier for it. But if men like Adams and Franklin had ambivalent feelings about the public display of "luxury" as an incentive, they were virtually unanimous in the view that excessive preoccupation with material things—luxury—must in the end destroy the moral fiber of every nation and ultimately bring about its ruin. Many years later Adams wrote to Jefferson: "Will you tell me how to prevent riches from becoming the effects of temperance and industry? Will you tell me how to prevent riches from producing luxury? Will you tell me how to prevent luxury from producing effeminacy intoxication extravagance vice and folly?"

Whatever Adams' feelings, he continued to receive a litany of disaster from his friend, James Warren, who had no doubt that "The foolish Extravagance of this Country has involved us in Confusion and Distress." It was by no means only New Englanders who were alarmed at their fellow citizens' preoccupation with making money. Alexander Graydon of Philadelphia, writing of the postwar era, noted that "pelf . . . was better than liberty; and at no time in my recollection, was the worship of Mammon more widely spread, more sordid and disgusting. Those who had fought the battles of their country, at least in the humbler grades, had . . . earned nothing but poverty and contempt; while their wiser fellow-citizens who had attended to their interests, were men of mark and consideration."

Warren and others who deplored the preoccupation of Americans with material things seem to have made no clear distinction between the single-minded desire of most Americans to make money and a passion for "luxury." One suspects that in the minds of the critics of materialism the desire of a tradesman or artisan for a coach or a handsome home that would be considered appropriate for a gentleman of means and position is taken as evidence of the cancer of luxury. There is undoubtedly a class bias in such judgments. What men like Warren were witnessing was the establishment of a new relationship between people and money. When the leaders and theoreticians of the Revolution spoke so enthusiastically about "equality," they meant it in largely a metaphorical sense. They meant equality before the law, equality in political rights (excluding women, of course, and those without property), and equality of opportunity for middle-class white Christian males over twenty-one who held at least a moderate degree of property. While today that seems a very limited kind of equality, we must keep in mind that it was a radical and startling change in the commonly held notions of how a society should be structured. In every civilized nation of the world there were clearly defined classes. People were born into those classes and, by and large, stayed there all their lives. Their privileges were hereditary. There was very little of what we call today upward mobility in such societies. The lower classes, the powerless, were exploited, cruelly or benignly as the case might be, but they did all the drudgery and all the laborious work so that the upper class might live in idleness and luxury. Indeed the distinction between the upper class and those beneath them was that *members of the upper class did no work.* They were warriors or priests or courtiers. They hunted and gambled and, in England at least, took time from their pleasures to run the country.

The consequence of all such systems was that the best-educated and presumably most intelligent segment of society contributed least in terms of productivity. The real business of society was conducted by a middle class, which in the Western world grew in wealth and importance with each generation. To these energetic, enterprising people the hereditary privileges of the upper class were most onerous. Conscious of their own superior capacities and values, they very much resented any system that held them in subordination. It was essentially this class, transported to America, that had fought and won the American Revolution. Their allies in the struggle had been the ordinary folk, the "common and middling ranks," the farmers, artisans, and mechanics who made up the Revolutionary army. When Mason and Jefferson wrote that all men were created equal, they meant primarily that they, the leaders of the Revolution, were equal to any men anywhere without regard to hereditary rank or ancient privilege. They did not entirely mean that the yeoman farmer with his modest acres was equal to them. Created equal, yes. Equal? Not quite. And the black slave they did not even include in the category of "all men." Nor did they include women.

Be all that as it may, whatever they said and believed about equality and however limited an interpretation they gave to the word, the implications of it were enormous and appeared so to the rest of the world. What those who used the word, doubtless with a twinge of uneasiness, could not have anticipated was that it was to have vast economic consequences. Where they had meant equality to cover political and legal rights, the mass of their fellow Americans interpreted it perhaps above all as *the right to make money.* The Revolution was scarcely over before ordinary Americans realized that the disappearance of the last vestiges of a structured hierarchical society meant that one man had as much right to make money as another. And money, it turned out, in the absence of any clearly defined established social and economic classes, determined a man's rank and importance in society. The son of a farmer or a teamster or a common sailor could become a wealthy merchant or a successful sea captain. It is not surprising that this proved an intoxicating discovery for energetic and enterprising members of the lower classes. For all practical purposes, the "pursuit of happiness" was the pursuit of money.

If one were a prosperous young gentleman with the advantages of a Harvard education and a yearly income sufficient to his needs, it was easy enough to be contemptuous of the pushy, hustling tradesman's son determined to make his fortune and thereby capture "happiness." In an unstructured society (unstructured according to the standards of the day), it became increasingly evident that money created the only structure. There were the poor and the rich and "the middling." Since theoretically everyone had as much chance as his neighbor to grow wealthy, those who failed to do so were failures by definition. They might be, and usually were, perfectly decent, hardworking, honest fellows. They simply lacked the nose and talent for making money. In a highly structured society they would have gone on doing some perfectly respectable and useful task with reasonable skill or competence and, however modest their circumstances, would have been valued for the quality of their work and the piety of their character. In the new Confederated States of America they were more apt to be judged by the house they lived in, the clothes they wore (and, more important, the clothes their wives and daughters wore), and the carriage they drove. One consequence of this alarmingly open situation, where everyone was challenged to get ahead in the world, was an extraordinary degree of anxiety among those anxious to get ahead and among those who were plainly failing to do so.

Not surprisingly, the least "materialistic" members of society were those with the inside track, so to speak, on wealth and social position. For the last two hundred years, they have been among the principal critics of American materialism. It must be said in behalf of these persistent and high-minded critics that there are indeed many negative aspects to a society structured primarily on the basis of money.

In the present day, the conservative theorist Ayn Rand has raised the American obsession for making money into a kind of religion. In all previous societies, she has argued, money was something possessed largely by the upper classes, who inherited it, protected it, hoarded it, or expended it. The notion that money was something an ordinary man could "make" was a brilliant American invention.

In short, the alarmed reactions of James Warren and his peers to their countrymen's love of luxury were the initial manifestations of a force that was perhaps more than any other destined to determine the nature of American society. By offering an entire people the opportunity to make money and thereby define themselves—as successful or unsuccessful—the leaders of the Revolution, to a degree that they could never have anticipated, released extraordinary new energies, energies requisite to the creation of a powerful nation out of a raw and, it seemed, almost limitless wilderness. In a traditional society, the most one can ask of an aristocracy is that it embody and protect the best of ancient custom, that it act as a constant check on monarchs with tyrannical tendencies, and that it have an attitude of enlightened paternalism—noblesse oblige—toward those beneath them. In terms of productivity, of contribution to what we now term the gross national product, they are a nullity. What is more, they inhibit the entrepreneurial activities of the ambitious members of the middle class, since they see them as rivals and wish to protect their own interests against the growth and expansion of the class immediately below them. As for the lower orders, they are perpetually frustrated by constraints of every kind, primarily by a kind of economic bondage to the classes above them. Thus, we might say that in a traditional society only 20 percent of the available human energy (and intelligence) is utilized. If one destroys all distinctions of class and dangles before the dazzled eyes of the entire population the prize of happiness, money—and moreover persuades the multitude that any one of them who fails to enter the contest is a mean-spirited and disreputable fellow—one multiplies the human energy potential incalculably. That is clearly what happened as a consequence of the American Revolution. Small wonder that the Founding Fathers were nonplussed or indignant. They had meant to set off a skyrocket and discovered they had detonated an atomic bomb. They did not realize the consequences of what they had done, and to the ends of their lives most of them continued to deplore the obsession of their countrymen with making money, not realizing that for most of them money-making was the best way they knew to be good Americans.

The sensitivity of Americans on matters of equality was illustrated by Charles Janson, a visiting Englishman, with a revealing story. He had called at the house of an acquaintance and when the door had been opened by a "servant-maid" whom he had not seen before, he inquired: "Is your master at home?"—"I have no master."—"Don't you live here?"—"I *stay* here."—"And who are you then?"—"Why, I am Mr. _____'s *help*. I'd have you to know, *man*, that I am no *sarvant;* none but *negers* are *sarvants*."

There is another part of the equation that cannot, in fairness, be omitted. If the acquisition of luxury-materialism-money was the primary way by which most Americans verified their equality, "expressed" and "authenticated" themselves, made their visible mark in the world, the partakers of the Protestant passion were well aware that "love of money is the root of all evil." So there was a profound ambivalence on the subject. Not only were Americans divided, roughly, into those who sought salvation in modest and humble obedience to the Lord and those who sought it in the feverish accumulation of worldly goods, but the latter group gave more than a little attention to the persistent question of how to take the curse off money. The solution, if not wholly satisfying and if not by any means universally practiced, was to *give money away*. Americans were almost as ingenious in discovering new ways of giving money away as they were in making it. Giving it away was called philanthropy. And in time, Americans became better at doing that than any other people in the world. Rather like the potlatch of the Northwest Indians, giving money away became an even more prestigious activity than making it. Philanthropy was described in Noah Webster's dictionary as: "The Love of mankind; benevolence toward the whole human race; universal good will," and the philanthropist was "A person of general benevolence . . . who exerts himself in doing good."

The model was Stephen Girard, a Philadelphia financier who made the greatest fortune of the day and whose contributions to charity took up nine pages of his will. Prominent among them were large benefactions to the Pennsylvania Hospital; to an institution for the deaf and dumb; to the city of Philadelphia to purchase fuel for the poor; and, finally, two million dollars for the establishment of a free school for orphans, an institution still surviving.

So there was, after all, a way to reconcile making money and serving the Lord or, in the secular, democratic spirit, of combining "science" and self-interest.

Of course the dismay expressed by men like James Warren and John Adams over the obsession with "luxury" that most Americans displayed the instant the Revolution was over had far more than class roots. Adams and Warren were, after all, representatives of that new consciousness shaped by Protestant Christianity, a consciousness whose principal prophet was the Geneva theologian John Calvin. Calvinism preached abstemiousness, austerity, thrift, the dominance of spiritual over worldly concerns. Above all, Protestant Christianity, with its passion for redeeming the world, proclaimed the primacy of the community over the individual. In a sense the individual existed only as a member of a faithful community. John Winthrop had spelled it all out in his "Modell of Christian Charity" written on the *Arabella* on the way to New England. In the "Modell" Winthrop reminded his fellow voyagers that "JUSTICE and MERCY" were the paramount rules of the Christian community. The community must be "knitt together by [the] bond of love . . . the care of the publique must oversway all private respects . . . for it is a true rule that perticuler estates cannot subsist in the ruine of the publique." Thus there may be occasions "when a christian must sell all and give to the poor as they did in the Apostles' times." The little band of settlers "must be knitt together in this worke as one man, wee must entertaine each other in brotherly Affeccion, wee must be willing to abridge our selves of our superfluities for the supply of other necessities, . . . wee must . . . make others Condicions our owne, rejoyce together, mourne together, labour and suffer together. . . ."

It was this power to found communities that enabled the American colonists to assert what they believed to be their rights against the greatest nation in the world. As we shall see, this community-making power was to be an essential element in the growth of the United States into a great nation in its own right. But from the beginning the ethic of the community of the faithful was at war with the ethic of equality proclaimed in the Declaration of Independence. The fact that the only practical interpretation of "equality" was the opportunity to make as much money as anyone else or, ideally, more, meant a rupture of the community. Even Franklin, the apostle of "getting ahead" and "doing good" and the defender of "luxury" as incentive, believed that whatever the individual made beyond what was needed for a modest subsistence for himself and his family could be taken from him and used for the good of the community as a whole. In this respect he was the lineal descendant of John Winthrop. At the same time, Franklin, the most famous American advocate of *thrift* ("a penny saved is a penny earned," etc.), was mildly notorious for his addiction to high living.

Jefferson's indignation at his countrymen's money-grubbing and luxurious ways had a somewhat different origin—the traditions of a landed aristocracy that held business activity in general in contempt.

Added to this essentially snobbish attitude was the inherent suspicion of an agricultural society toward a commercially oriented society or toward those in the society whose concern was with the manipulation of money rather than with the production of food. Bankers were the symbol, of course, of "money manipulation." They made money, not by honest productive labor, but by using money itself to make money, often by excessive charges for the use of money by those who were hard-pressed financially; by confusing immaterial things like bills of exchange and letters of credit with "real" things like land; by special knowledge rather than hard work; by exploiting the sometimes desperate needs of others. There was, it could be argued, no place for them in John Winthrop's model community of Christian charity; they were not notorious for selling their goods to relieve the distress of the poor.

So Jefferson, the wealthy, extravagant, aristocratic Southern plantation owner, and John Adams, the Puritan lawyer-farmer of comparatively modest means, could agree on the inherent wickedness of banks and bankers and mutually deplore the tendency of many of their countrymen to put personal gain ahead of public good.

Here again we have tried to trace what was to be, in many ways, the most profound and enduring split in the collective American psyche: *equality* (the single-minded pursuit of happiness-money), which also called itself by other names such as individualism, free enterprise, and so on; and *community*, which denigrated materialism and struggled valiantly to establish or reestablish true communities. In a sense, there could be no genuine reconciliation between those two "American dreams." They haunt us as much today as they did our ancestors in the first years of the Republic. We experience the tension between them every day of our lives, in every political decision made in the local community, in our state capitals, and perhaps preeminently in our national capital. That, of course, is not remarkable, nor is it unique to the United States. What is important to this particular story is that the tension between these two classic human aspirations has manifested itself in our history in quite novel ways, and since Americans have very little tolerance for ambiguity, for the most part we have been disposed to gloss over this basic schizophrenia.

We might put it this way: in the pre-Reformation period the impulse of a rising middle class to escape from the dominance of the Roman Catholic church—closely allied to monarchs and aristocracies who thwarted the ambitions of the bourgeoisie—created the Protestant

Reformation, a new antithesis to the old synthesis, the Roman Catholic church. Similarly, Protestantism, which began as the quintessence of community, developed its own antithesis, individualism. Individualism proclaimed that the individual was preeminent. Everything existed for the happiness and well-being of the individual rather than for the betterment of the community. The individual was lord of the universe, the final, best, and most successful achievement of human evolution. Although thesis and antithesis—community and individual—were not to be reconciled, not to become synthesis—they were each to make remarkable and indispensable contributions to the unfolding of the nation.

Charles Jared Ingersol, a Pennsylvania Federalist, may have been the first American to state unequivocally the material mission of "this mighty continental nation." It was "commercial liberty; not mere political liberty, but positive freedom." Freedom "from all but the slightest restraints." The real meaning of the Revolution was that the American people "followed the manifest order of nature, when they adoped a free, republican, commercial federation."

A New Frame of Government

Although the events in Massachusetts added considerably to the alarm felt by the Revolutionary leaders (and others as well), we have already noted that the machinery for reforming or replacing the Articles of Confederation had been set in motion by Virginia and Maryland in 1785 when they called for a convention to meet at Annapolis. There can be little doubt that as serious as the deficiencies and as inadequate to the requirements of a unified nation as the Articles were, it was upon the incapacity of Congress to manage the commercial affairs of the Confederation that the movement to reorganize the government rested. In the absence of the problem of commerce (which, we must remember, affected relatively few Americans), there would have been no Federal Convention and no Constitution. The states would almost certainly have formed regional confederations or muddled along until the Confederation dissolved in a nightmare of mutual suspicion and recrimination.

Benjamin Rush, a devout democrat and follower of Jefferson, wrote to his English friend Richard Price to inform him of the impending convention at Annapolis "for the purpose of agreeing upon certain commercial regulations and of suggesting such alterations in the Confederation as will give more extensive and coercive powers to Congress." Rush was hopeful that the convention would have positive consequences, "especially as an opinion seems to have pervaded all classes of people that an increase of power in Congress is absolutely necessary for our safety and independence." Many of the problems that Congress was struggling with, Rush wrote, arose from "a belief that the American Revolution is *over*. This is so far from being the case that we have only finished the first act of the great drama. We have changed our forms of government, but it remains yet to effect a revolution in our principles, opinions, and manners so as to accommodate them to the forms of government we have adopted. This is the most difficult part of the business of the patriots and legislators of our country. It requires more wisdom and fortitude than to expel or reduce armies into captivity."

From Paris, Jefferson wrote to James Madison in February, 1786, expressing his pleasure at the news that the Virginia Assembly "have come to the resolution of giving the regulations of commerce to the federal head" and had joined with Maryland in calling a convention to effect this end. Jefferson added: "The politics of Europe render it indispensably necessary that with respect to every thing external we be one nation, firmly hooped together. . . . If it could be seen in Europe that all our states could be brought to concur in what the Virginia assembly has done, it would produce a total revolution in their opinion of us, and respect for us."

There was one cynical observer of the Annapolis meeting who believed it to be the kingpin in a plan to correct the ills caused by an excess of democracy. Louis-Guillaume Otto was the French chargé d'affaires stationed in New York, the meeting place of Congress. He wrote to the French foreign minister describing the concerns of the delegates with such matters as the fishing rights on the Potomac, the issue of navigating the Mississippi River, and control over the commerce of the maritime states. Otto suspected that the real purpose of the delegates was to strengthen the Articles of Confederation. However, they had emphasized their commercial concerns, in Otto's opinion, because they were well aware that the lower orders were inclined to have as little government as possible—"complete and limitless liberty," as Otto put it. The call to the convention had been framed, he wrote, with "deliberate obscurity, . . . an obscurity which the ordinary citizens could not understand but which the powerful and enlightened portion of the population would have no difficulty understanding."

Only five states attended the Annapolis Convention, too few to take any decisive action. Indeed, the principal accomplishment of the convention was to issue a call for a convention to be held in Philadelphia the following spring "to take into consideration a general plan of commerce and the powers relative thereto." The Annapolis delegates had found that they could do little in regard to commerce "without touching at the same time on other matters intimately connected with the prosperity and national importance of the United States."

It indeed turned out that the apprehensions of the Annapolis delegates over arousing the fears of many of their constituents by any talk of altering the Articles were well founded. Determined opponents of the projected Philadelphia convention appeared in almost every state legislature. Despite the virtual collapse of Congress, there was little support in that body for a constitutional convention. Henry Lee, a delegate from Virginia, wrote to a friend: "With difficulty the friends to the system adopted by the [Annapolis] convention induced Congress to commit your report, altho' all were truly sensible of the respect manifested by the convention to this body, and all zealous to accomplish the objects proposed by the authors of the commercial convention. Indeed their conviction of the inadequacy of the present federal government renders them particularly zealous to amend and strengthen it. But different opinions prevail as to the mode; some think with the Annapolis meeting, others consider Congress not only the constitutional but the most eligible body to originate and propose amendments to the confederation, and others prefer state conventions for the express purpose, and a congress of deputies, appointed by those conventions with plenipotentiary powers. . . ."

The date set by the Annapolis Convention for the convening of the convention to strengthen the Articles of Confederation was the second Monday in May, the fourteenth. But on that day hardly a dozen delegates met in the Long Room of the Pennsylvania State House. It was by no means clear that there would be any convention. Eleven uneasy days followed while additional delegates trickled in. Finally, on May 25, seven states, a bare majority, were represented and the convention was officially convened. It was a discouraging start. Vermont, New Hampshire, Connecticut, and Maryland were not represented until later, and Rhode Island never did attend. Massachusetts at first had only one delegate, Rufus King.

George Washington was chosen chairman of the convention, and while that role precluded his participation in the debates, his majestic presence kept the convention from flying apart on more than one occasion. Two incidents suggest the moral suasion Washington exercised over the delegates. It had been determined at the beginning of the debates that they should be secret, the notion being that only by keeping their deliberations private could the delegates feel completely free to speak their minds and, perhaps more important, change them if they wished. The rule of secrecy was strictly enforced, and while minutes of the proceedings were printed periodically so that the delegates would have a record available of their resolutions, and thus of their progress, they were solemnly enjoined by their chairman not to let the minutes out of their possession.

At the beginning of one session, a delegate brought Washington a set of minutes he had picked up in the hall outside the Long Room. When the delegates had taken their seats, Washington mentioned the errant minutes and delivered an admonitory lecture on the importance of secrecy. The careless delegate might come forward during a recess to reclaim his minutes. But that abashed individual lacked the courage to do so under the general's reproachful eye. The minutes thus lay on the chairman's desk, like an unshriven sin, a reminder to the careless.

On another occasion, Madison was discussing with friends Washington's awesomeness. Gouverneur Morris, the exotic New Yorker, pooh-poohed the notion that Washington was such a formidable figure. Certainly he, Morris, did not stand in awe of him or any other man. Very well, Madison replied, if Morris, on the next social occasion where Washington was present, would go up to him, give him a friendly and familiar clap on the back and a casual salutation, Madison would treat the group to a handsome dinner. Morris accepted the challenge. At the next opportunity he greeted Washington in just such a familiar manner. The general's response to this liberty was so chilling that the usually unflappable Morris withdrew, shaken and thoroughly abashed. At the dinner, he confessed that although he claimed the wager he could never be persuaded to repeat the experiment. If it is difficult to imagine the Revolution without Washington, it is equally difficult to imagine that the Federal Convention could have accomplished its objective without the authority lent to its deliberations by Washington's presence.

Much has been written about this remarkable event, the Federal Convention, which, through the long, humid summer of 1787, from the end of May to the middle of September, debated the classic principles of government and in doing so created a nation. But the event nonetheless remains both mysterious and inexhaustibly instructive. It was the most brilliantly sustained intellectual and oratorical achievement of which history has preserved a record, the fruit of more than two thousand years of political and theological reflection and experience. It was the consummate accomplishment of what I have called the Classical-Christian Consciousness, and it came in the last instant in which that consciousness still retained its authority. (Within a decade, the Secular-Democratic Consciousness, so profoundly different in its view of the nature of man and society, would become preeminent.) We will see that, like most of the momentous accomplishments of history, the Constitution was brought off by a breathtakingly narrow margin.

Certainly the actors in the unfolding drama at Philadelphia were intensely conscious of the historic importance of their gathering. Many of them shared Morris's conviction that they came to Philadelphia, not merely as the representatives of particular states, or even simply of America, but, in Morris's words, "in some degree as a Representative of the whole human race," for "the whole human race will be affected by the proceedings of this Convention."

Doubtless it was such a conviction that caused several delegates to try to keep a record of the actual debates, interminable as they were, and another delegate, Major William Pierce of Georgia, to sketch out the personae of the drama, shrewd portraits of the delegates. Alexander Hamilton of New York, Pierce wrote, "is deservedly celebrated for his talents. . . . To a clear and strong judgment he unites the ornaments of fancy, and whilst he is able, convincing, and engaging in his eloquence the Heart and Head sympathize in approving him. Yet there is something too feeble in his voice to be equal to the strains of oratory;—it is my opinion he is rather a convincing Speaker than a blazing orator. Colonel Hamilton requires time to think,—he enquires into every part of his subject with the searchings of philosophy, and when he comes forward he comes highly charged with interesting matter, there is no skimming over the surface of a subject with him, he must sink to the bottom to see what foundation it rests on. . . . He is about 33 years old, of small stature, and lean. His manners are tinctured with stiffness, and sometimes with a degree of vanity that is highly disagreeable."

Dean of the Pennsylvania delegation of course was Benjamin Franklin, "well known to be the greatest phylosopher of the present age;—all the operations of nature he seems to understand,—the very heavens obey him, and the Clouds yield up their Lightning to be imprisoned in his rod. But what claim he has to the politician, posterity must determine. It is certain that he does not shine much in public Council. He is no Speaker, nor does he seem to let politics engage his attention. He is, however, a most extraordinary Man, and tells a story in a style more engaging than anything I ever heard. . . . He is 82 years old, and possesses an activity of mind equal to a youth of 25 years of age."

Franklin's Pennsylvania colleague, James Wilson, who had joined him to bring Pennsylvania into line in the vote for independence ten years earlier, was to have far more influence in the debates than Franklin. Pierce described him as "among the foremost in legal and political knowledge. He has joined to a fine genius all that can set him off and show him to advantage. He is well acquainted with Man, and understands all the passions that influence him. Government seems to have been his peculiar Study, all the political institutions of the World he knows in detail, and can trace the causes and effects of every revolution from the earliest stages of the Grecian commonwealth down to the present time. No man is more clear, copious, and comprehensive than Mr. Wilson, and yet he is no great Orator. He draws attention not by the charm of his eloquence, but by the force of his reasoning. He is about 45 years old."

Gouverneur Morris, in contrast, was "one of those Genius's in whom every species of talents combine to render him conspicuous and flourishing in public debate:—He winds through all the mazes of rhetoric, and throws around him such a glare that he charms, captivates, and leads away the senses of all who hear him. With an infinite stretch of fancy he brings to view things when he is engaged in deep argumentation, that render all the labor of reasoning easy and pleasing. But with all these powers he is fickle and inconstant,—never pursuing one train of thinking,—nor ever regular. . . . This Gentleman is about 38 years old, he has been unfortunate in losing one of his Legs, and getting all the flesh taken off his right arm by a scald, when a youth."

Among the Virginia delegates were George Mason, author of the Virginia Constitution and Bill of Rights, the Preamble to which had served as the model for Jefferson's Declaration of Independence, and one of the most respected members of the great Virginia bar, and James Madison, perhaps the single most influential member of the convention. Of him Pierce wrote: "Mr. Madison is a character who has long been in public life; and what is very remarkable every Person seems to acknowledge his greatness. He blends together the profound politician, with the Scholar. In the management of every great question he evidently took the lead in the Convention, and tho' he cannot be called an Orator, he is a most agreeable, eloquent, and convincing Speaker. From a spirit of industry and application which he possesses in a most eminent degree, he always comes forward the best informed Man of any point in debate. The affairs of the United States, he perhaps, has the most correct knowledge of, of any Man in the Union. . . . Mr. Madison is about 37 years of age, a Gentleman of great modesty,—with a remarkable sweet temper. He is easy and unreserved among his acquaintance, and has a most agreeable style of conversation."

After giving similar sketches of the remaining fifty-four delegates to the Convention, Pierce added, disarmingly, that he must leave his own character to "those who may choose to speculate on it." He was conscious of having done his duty as a soldier in the Revolution. "I possess ambition," he added, "and it was that, and the flattering opinion which some of my Friends had of me, that gave me a seat in the wisest Council in the World."

Great as the obligation of posterity to Madison for his crucial role in the Convention, we perhaps owe him even more for having kept the most complete notes of the debates, a truly remarkable achievement when we consider how actively involved he was. His carefully guarded notes were not published until 1840, after his death, when they at once revealed the extraordinary intellectual exchange that had taken place.

It is difficult for a reader, almost two hundred years after the event, to grasp the implications of the Federal debates. Cicero wrote, "History at its highest is Oratory," a statement that falls rather strangely on the modern ear but one that provides us with an important clue to the nature of the event that took place in Philadelphia in the summer of 1787. Clearly, there are times when the spoken word—oratory—has a unique power to shape history. Such moments (exceedingly rare) come when speakers and listeners share a substantial number of fairly clearly defined ideas and concepts; when they share, to a degree, a common world of intellect and experience. They come, most typically, during or immediately after cataclysmic political events that have sharpened perceptions and created fields of discourse that can be explored with great precision.

The delegates who met in Philadelphia in May, 1787, filled with the consciousness of being participants in a unique historical drama, had the intoxicating experience of articulating almost three thousand years of Classical-Christian experience. The Word became flesh: a nation was *talked into existence*. That marvelous and mysterious achievement was accomplished by oratory, that is to say, by words spoken with an extraordinary combination of intellect and passion.

It was immediately evident that the larger states—especially Virginia, Massachusetts, and Pennsylvania, which had chafed for years under the one-state, one-vote rule of the Articles of Confederation—were determined to draft a new plan of government that would give them representation in proportion to their wealth and population. It seemed to them intolerable that little Rhode Island or Connecticut should have as much weight in the councils of the Union as Virginia or Pennsylvania. Thus, the delegates had hardly settled in their seats before Edmund Randolph, recently governor of Virginia and one of the most powerful figures in the state, presented them with the so-called Virginia Plan, which seems to have been, in large part, the work of James Madison.

The most notable feature of the Virginia Plan was that it provided for proportional representation. That issue aside, it was, in its general outline, remarkably like the document that was to emerge from the convention almost four months later. Under the Virginia Plan, there were to be two branches of the national legislature—Senate and House. The members of the House were to be elected "by the people of the several States" for terms to be set by the delegates and were to be ineligible for any other state or federal office during that time.

Members of the upper house were to be elected by the lower house from candidates proposed by the states. This national legislature should have all the rights of legislation formerly vested in Congress plus the right to legislate "in all cases to which the separate States are incompetent, or in which the harmony of the United States may be interrupted by the exercise of individual Legislation." Furthermore, the national legislature was to have the right "to negative all laws passed by the several States, contravening in the opinion of the National Legislature the articles of Union; and to call forth the force of the Union against any member of the Union failing to fulfill its duty under the articles thereof."

This was strong medicine for delegates who believed the states were sovereign, and it was to be reinforced by a "Council of Revision" made up of "the Executive and a convenient number of the National Judiciary" and invested "with authority to examine every act of the National Legislature before it shall operate, and every act of a particular [state] Legislature before a Negative thereon shall be final." It was well that the deliberations of the delegates were secret. If word had spread through the states of a plan giving such power to the central government, a clamor would have arisen from the champions of state sovereignty that might well have sunk the convention before it was fairly launched.

The Virginia Plan made plain how far the "nationalists"—the advocates of a strong central government—were willing to go to check the powers of the states. The proposal for a council of revision, somewhat reminiscent of the Council of Censors in the Pennsylvania Constitution of 1776, demonstrated the inherent skepticism of the drafters of the Virginia Plan about the capacity of the national legislature to remain within constitutional bounds.

Under the Virginia Plan, the national judiciary was to consist of "one or more supreme tribunals, and of inferior tribunals to be chosen by the National Legislature, to hold their offices during good behaviour." The courts were given jurisdiction over "all piracies and felonies on the high seas, captures from an enemy; cases in which foreigners or citizens of other States" were concerned; impeachments of "national officers"; and, finally, a very broad category—"questions which may involve the national peace and harmony."

One of the most important provisions of the Virginia Plan provided for the admission of new states, "States lawfully arising within the limits of the United States." Such states should also be guaranteed "a Republican Government."

In 1785 Congress had passed an ordinance specifying the manner in which lands ceded by the states—particularly Virginia—were to be organized. Surveyors were "to divide said territory into townships of six miles square." These, in turn, were to be divided into "subdivisions" of 1 square mile or 640 acres and numbered from 1 to 36. The townships were to be sold alternately entire and by lots at no less than a dollar an acre. Lot number 16 in every township was to be reserved "for the maintenance of public schools."

Two years later Congress extended the ordinance to apply to the territory of the Northwest acquired by terms of the Treaty of Paris (assuming always that the Indians' claims to the area could be extinguished). The Northwest Ordinance did more than simply specify the township plan for land division. It incorporated a kind of mini-bill of rights for settlers in the area. Primogeniture (the passing of land to the eldest male heir on intestate deaths) was forbidden in the territory. Provisions were included for a governor to serve for a term of three years and for three judges, who would have "common law jurisdiction." Governor and judges together could "adopt and publish . . . such laws of the original States, criminal or civil, as may be necessary and best suited to the circumstances of the district, and report them to Congress from time to time." As soon as there were five thousand "free male inhabitants of full age" in the territory, they would be entitled to organize a territorial legislature or general assembly. To sit in the assembly a representative had to own two hundred acres of land. To vote a resident had to have fifty acres.

Moreover, the territorial legislature had the right to send a "delegate to Congress," who would have a seat but no voting rights. Freedom of religion was guaranteed, and Article II consisted of a comprehensive bill of rights. The territory should be formed into "not less than three or more than five states." When any of the tentatively defined states had sixty thousand free inhabitants, such a state was to be admitted "into the Congress of the United States, on an equal footing with the original States in all respects whatever." Finally, there was to be "neither slavery nor involuntary servitude in the said territory. . . ."

One clause declared: "The utmost good faith shall always be observed towards the Indians; their land and property shall never be taken from them without their consent; and in their property, rights, and liberty, they shall never be invaded or disturbed, unless in just and lawful wars authorized by Congress; but laws founded in justice and humanity, shall from time to time be made for preventing wrongs being done to them, and for preserving peace and friendship with them." The Ordinance, not surprisingly, did not make clear how this high-minded sentiment was to be reconciled with the manifest intention of the Ordinance as a whole to turn a region inhabited by Indians into states occupied by large numbers of white settlers.

The Northwest Ordinance was a remarkably enlightened piece of legislation. There were a number of Americans in Congress and out who believed that it would be folly to admit to the Union new states made up of crude and untutored frontier settlers in no way qualified (at least in the opinion of the residents of the original states) for the exacting responsibilities of self-government. The disposition to impose inhibitions or limitations on new states was not a surprising one. It was, after all, the original states that had fought and suffered through the Revolution, created the Confederation, and borne its burdens. Why should new states expect to simply fall heir to such a splendid inheritance without having undergone the heroic labors required to create it? Many individuals shared Gouverneur Morris's conviction that "the busy haunts of men, not the remote wilderness, was the proper school of political talents." They were convinced that if the Westerners got power they would "ruin the Atlantic interests." It was no secret that certain Western settlements were inclined toward independence of Congress itself. More generous sentiments prevailed, in part because some members of Congress and many of their constituents were speculators in Western lands and therefore wished to make the settlement of them as attractive as possible.

After Randolph had presented the Virginia Plan, which included a provision for "the amendment of the Articles of Union whensoever it shall seem necessary" without "the assent of the National Legislature," the house declared itself a committee of the whole so that the plan might be debated with the greatest freedom and informality. The Virginia Plan had not, of course, been drawn from the clouds of theoretical speculation. The reader familiar with the state constitutions and with John Adams's *Thoughts on Government* will recognize classic elements considered by all knowledgeable students of constitutions to be essential to the formation of any sound republican government. These were principles as old, in some instances, as those of the Greek philosophers and historians.

The ancients agreed that there were three types of government— monarchy, aristocracy, and democracy—the rule of the one, the few, and the many, respectively. Each had its traditional strengths and weaknesses. Each tended, in time, to its degenerate form. Most nations went through each form successively until the cycle was complete, at which point it began again. Monarchy declined into tyranny as a constitutional monarch, tempted by the prospect of absolute power, rode roughshod over the law that set limits to all human institutions. A tyrant would fall victim to aristocrats fighting to preserve their traditional rights. Aristocrats, appearing initially as liberators of the people from arbitrary rule, would form an alliance with the democratic element and exercise, for a time, a responsible and enlightened authority. But aristocracy, like monarchy, had its own degenerate form—oligarchy, the rule of the few for their own interests, rule that selfishly exploited the people. Finally, the people, the popular party, would overthrow the corrupt oligarchy and establish democracy, the rule by all the people in public council. But democracy was notoriously unstable; the people were passionate, volatile, and easily misled by demagogues. The corrupt form of democracy was anarchy. The cure for anarchy was a dictatorship proclaiming law and order as the paramount virtues. The dictator would then be legitimated as a constitutional monarch, and the cycle would begin again. (It was, of course, familiarity with this classical formula—democracy tends rapidly and inevitably toward anarchy—that had caused so much alarm among the Revolutionary leaders at the spectacle of Shays' Rebellion. A number of them agreed with Elbridge Gerry, a Massachusetts delegate, that the country's ills resulted from an "excess of democracy.")

While the ancients were reconciled, at least on the theoretical level, to a cyclical view of history whose most distinctive features were the political transformations we have described, in the Christian Era it was considered the role of the statesman and the philosopher to try to find the means of forestalling or, at the very least, impeding the progress of "revolutions" in government. For a century or more political theorists had been suggesting that the only reliable way to introduce any real stability into governments was to "mix" them; to have represented in every government—monarchical, aristocratic or, democratic—sufficient elements of the other classic types to give it a degree of permanence. In this system, the monarchical element must be represented by a king or, in a republican government, a chief executive or president, the limits to whose powers were explicitly stated in a "constitution," written or unwritten. The aristocratic principle (and interest) was represented by an upper house, in England the House of Lords, in most American state constitutions, the Senate. By placing the landed and moneyed classes in a single legislative body, it was thought they could protect their own legitimate interests while being prevented by constitutional "checks and balances" from exploiting the people at large. By the same token, the lower house—in England the House of Commons, in the American states perhaps most typically the Assembly—protected the common people's interests.

Although Americans rejected the notion of any formal hereditary aristocracy, they recognized that there would be a class of people in the United States of superior wealth and social standing (which is not strange, since they considered themselves part of just such a group— what Jefferson called "a natural aristocracy"). It was believed that by incorporating the three traditional forms of government in a single government, the weaknesses of each particular form might, in large part, be overcome and the *inevitable* degeneration long delayed. The government of England seemed to provide living proof of such a theory. Hailed even by such foreign scholars as the great French political theorist Montesquieu as the most enlightened government in the world, a constitutional monarchy in which all the interests of the realm were properly "balanced," the English government served as a model for the republican constitution-makers at Philadelphia. It seemed to some of them, at least, that all that was needed to adapt the British constitution to the soil of the New World was to substitute an elected executive for a king, to prevent the formation of a hereditary aristocracy, and to add a national judiciary that would act as a check upon the legislative and executive branches of the government as well as exercise jurisdiction in disputes between states.

The problem turned out, of course, to be considerably more complicated, most conspicuously in the "federal" aspect. England had no quasi-independent political entities (if we except Ireland, Scotland, and Wales) comparable to the states that formed the Confederation. Nonetheless, British models and precedents were very much in the minds of the delegates to the Federal Convention. In addition, most of the delegates had been actively involved in forming the constitutions of their respective states, and all of them had had a decade of experience in the strengths and weaknesses of their own state governments.

In any event, the Virginia Plan was a comprehensive and well thought out document that caught the champions of "equal" (as opposed to proportional) representation completely by surprise. These were essentially the small-state men, who were determined not to give ground on the question of equal representation. Confronted with the matured Virginia Plan, they suppressed their misgivings, and for several weeks the delegates made deceptively rapid progress in refining the proposal Randolph had submitted to them.

The discussions of these early weeks developed some points of particular interest. A number of delegates expressed serious doubts that the convention had the authority to, in effect, replace the Articles of Confederation by a wholly new constitution. They doubted the people of the states were ready for such a radical change. From the beginning, one of the stickiest points among those delegates who supported the principle of proportional representation was how such proportions should be calculated. Here a split appeared at once between the Free States of the North and the slaveholding states of the South. If a state were to be represented proportionally according to its wealth, the Southerners wished to have their slaves count as property, an idea offensive to Northerners. If representation were to be based on population, surely slaves should not be counted as part of the population. Yet not to count them was to concede that they were property, not people. It was a curious dilemma, one not to be resolved for seventy-five years.

Inevitably the debate came to focus more and more sharply on the issue of suffrage, whether representation was to be equal or proportional. The discussions grew increasingly acrimonious. When William Read of Delaware asked that the question be postponed on the grounds that delegates from his state were forbidden by their instructions "to assenting to any change in the rule of suffrage" and that if the matter were pressed "it might become their duty to retire from the Convention," Gouverneur Morris replied that however much the small-state delegates might threaten, the principle was too important to be abandoned.

When the delegates came to the clause specifying that the members of the first branch of the national legislature "be elected by the people of the several States," Roger Sherman of Connecticut, who had started out as a shoemaker, expressed his opinion that election ought to be accomplished by the state legislatures: "The people immediately should have as little to do as may be about the Government. They want information and are constantly liable to be misled."

Elbridge Gerry supported Sherman and expressed his view that "the evils we experience flow from the excess of democracy. The people do not want virtue but are the dupes of pretended patriots. . . . "He had he said been too republican heretofore; he was still however republican, but he had been taught to experience the danger of the levilling spirit." In other words, like most of the upper class in Massachusetts, he had been traumatized by Shays' Rebellion.

When Sherman and Gerry from democratic New England had spoken their minds, George Mason, the slaveholding Virginia aristocrat, took up the defense of the people. The lower house "was to be the grand depository of the democratic principle of government." To have a "mixed" government, it was essential to have a genuinely democratic component. The lower house "was, so to speak, to be our House of Commons—It ought to know & sympathise with every part of the community; and ought therefore to be taken not only from different parts of the whole republic, but also from different districts of the larger members of it . . . different interests and views arising from difference of produce, of habits, etc., etc."

Mason was ready to admit that "we had been too democratic but was afraid we should incautiously run into the opposite extreme. We ought to attend to the rights of every class of the people. He had often wondered at the indifference of the superior classes of society to this dictate of humanity & policy; considering that however affluent their circumstances, or elevated their situations, might be, [in] the course of a few years, they not only might but certainly would, distribute their posterity throughout the lowest classes of Society. Every selfish motive therefore, every family attachment, ought to recommend such a system of policy as would provide no less carefully for the rights and happiness of the lowest than of the highest orders of citizens." These were enlightened sentiments based, in Mason's view, on scientific reasoning, that is, on the inevitable downward as well as upward mobility that must characterize any society where a particular class was not protected by rigid class barriers. It is worth noting that Mason advanced the same argument used by Franklin in his defense of luxury as providing the incentive in a democratic society.

James Wilson supported Mason. "He was for raising the federal pyramid to a considerable altitude, and for that reason wished to give it as broad a basis as possible." Here again we note a scientific or mechanical metaphor. Wilson continued: "No government could long subsist without the confidence of the people. In a republican Government this confidence was peculiarly essential. . . ." Madison also spoke in support of "the popular election of one branch of the National Legislature as essential to every plan of free Government. . . . He was an advocate for the policy of refining the popular appointments by successive filterations, but he thought it might be pushed too far. . . . He thought too that the great fabric to be raised should be more stable and durable, if it should rest on the solid foundation of the people themselves, than if it should stand merely on the pillars of the Legislature."

There was an additional, unmentioned reason for having the members of the first branch elected by the people of the states rather than by the state legislatures. The champions of a strong national government believed that popular election would help bind the people of the states to the central government and counteract what appeared to them to be the excessive influence of the states. A vote showed 6 states in favor of election "by the people," 2 opposed, with Delaware divided.

The delegates then proceeded to debate Randolph's proposal that "the second branch . . . ought to be chosen by the first branch out of persons nominated by the State Legislatures." There were immediate objections that such a procedure would place too much power in the lower house and would thus tend "to destroy all that balance and security of interests among the States which it was necessary to preserve." Randolph, in a rather halfhearted defense of the clause, stated his belief that the second branch "ought to be much smaller than the first; so small as to be exempt from the passionate proceedings to which numerous assemblies are liable. [The intention was to] provide a cure for the evils under which the U.S. laboured; that in tracing these evils to their origin every man had found it to be in the turbulence and follies of democracy; that some check therefore was to be sought for against this tendency of our Governments: and that a good Senate seemed most likely to answer the purpose." But here the supporters of a strong central government—the nationalists—were caught in a dilemma from which they never extricated themselves and that, in time, was to prove their undoing. If the first branch—the House of Representatives, as it was to be called—represented the people in general and was thus inevitably large and, like large democratic bodies, somewhat unruly and inclined to be carried away by the passions of the moment, and if the second branch was to be a smaller and more select body, disposed by reason of superior fortunes to be especially jealous for the rights of property and by virtue of its smaller size more suitable for cool deliberation; *and* if both were to be chosen, as the nationalists insisted, on a proportional basis, could there be any substantial difference in the size of the two legislative chambers? As Rufus King was quick to point out, "there must be 80 or 100 members [in the upper house] to entitle Delaware to the choice of one of them"—far too many, certainly, for any "cool deliberations."

Wilson, ignoring the dilemma, argued the radical view that both branches "ought to be chosen by the people," though he had no specific proposition as to how this might be done—perhaps by including several states in one electoral district.

The motion to give the national legislature power to legislate in all cases for which the individual states were "incompetent" was agreed to with little debate, but the question of the nature of the national executive was the occasion for a lengthy discussion. When Wilson proposed that the "Executive consist of a single person," there were immediate objections. Roger Sherman took the position that the executive had no other function but to put into effect "the will of the Legislature" and that it should therefore be left to the legislature to appoint any number of executives to carry out its wishes "as experience might dictate."

Elbridge Gerry wished to "annex" a cabinet or council to the executive "in order to give weight & inspire confidence." Randolph was "strenuously opposed" to "a unity in the Executive magistracy. He regarded it as the foetus of monarchy." It smacked too much of the British monarch for his taste. Indeed, he found in the delegates too much of a disposition to imitate the British constitution. Whereas he did not mean "to throw censure on that excellent fabric . . . the fixt genius of the people of America required a different form of Government. . . . The Executive ought to be independent. It ought therefore in order to support its independence to consist of more than one." His recommendation was for three.

Wilson, defending his motion, denied that he was influenced "by the British Model which was inapplicable to the situation of this Country; the extent of which was so great, and the manners so republican, that nothing but a great confederated Republic would do for it."

On the question of how the executive magistrate was to be chosen, Wilson, apologizing for the novelty of the notion, declared that "at least . . . in theory he was for an election by the people." This was an idea much too radical for most of the delegates. Sherman, in fact, wished the executive to be appointed by the legislature. He was "for making him absolutely dependent on that body. . . . An independence of the Executive from the supreme Legislature, was in his opinion the very essence of tyranny if there was any such thing."

As for the chief executive's term of office, suggestions ranged from three years with the right of reelection, to seven years "without re-eligibility." Gunning Bedford of Delaware urged a three-year term with the executive twice eligible for reelection, a possible total of nine years in office. One seven-year term was approved by a narrow margin. Wilson, challenged to propose a mode for the "popular" election of the executive, came up with the idea of electoral districts in which the people of each state would vote for "electors," who in turn would cast their ballots for the executive office. Wilson's motion was soundly defeated, but it was later to reappear in the form of the electoral college.

Franklin then moved that a clause be inserted to the effect that the executive "shall receive no salary, stipend fee or reward whatsoever" for his services. He had prepared a lengthy defense of his motion, which, because of the infirmities of age, he requested Wilson to read for him. It was one of Franklin's few interventions, an interesting if eccentric document. The Doctor was convinced that there were "two passions which have a powerful influence on the affairs of men. These are ambition and avarice; the love of power, and the love of money. Separately each of these has great force in prompting men to action; but when united in view of the same object, they have in many minds the most violent effects. Place before the eyes of such men, a post of *honour* that shall be at the same time a place of *profit*, and they will move heaven and earth to obtain it." Who, Franklin asked, would enter the lists for the office of chief executive under the new government? "It will not be the wise and moderate; the lovers of peace and good order, the men fittest for the trust. It will be the bold and violent, the men of strong passions and indefatigable activity in their selfish pursuits. These will thrust themselves into your Government and be your rulers." While the chief executive might start out with a moderate salary, he would soon be busy to augment it. Franklin continued: "All history informs us [that] there has been in every State & Kingdom a constant kind of warfare between the governing & the governed: the one striving to obtain more for its support, and the other to pay less. And this has occasioned great convulsions, actual civil wars . . . or enslaving of the people. . . . There is scarce a king in a hundred who would not, if he could, follow the example of Pharaoh, get first all the peoples money, then all their lands, and then make them and their children servants for ever. It will be said, that we don't propose to establish Kings. I know it. But there is a natural inclination in mankind to kingly Government. . . . I am apprehensive therefore, perhaps too apprehensive, that the Government of these States, may in future times, end in a Monarchy. But this catastrophe I think may be long delayed, if in our proposed System we do not sow the seeds of contention, faction & tumult, by making our posts of honor, places of profit." Franklin then mentioned Washington as an example of a patriot who had served his country without pay through seven long years of war.

Although Franklin's proposal was virtually ignored by the delegates, it has been quoted here at some length because it demonstrates so well that basic view of human nature and of historical process we have already ascribed to most of the delegates—the Classical-Christian Consciousness that saw man as inherently selfish and greedy and all governments and institutions as doomed to eventual corruption and decay. It is startling to hear Franklin, the confirmed enemy of kings, assuming that Americans would in time, like the rest of humanity, come to yearn for the power and trappings of monarchy. Certainly Franklin's prediction that the combination of power and money would always threaten the liberties of the people was one with which the delegates were not disposed to argue.

Pennsylvania's John Dickinson then made a motion that "the Executive be made removeable by the National Legislature on the request of a majority of the Legislatures of individual States." This was eventually modified to provide that the Senate would have the power to impeach the executive on the indictment of the lower house. In defense of his motion, Dickinson cited the tendency of nations throughout history to become centralized dictatorships. "A limited monarchy he considered as *one* of the best Governments in the world. He was not *certain* that the same blessings were derivable from any other form. It was certain that equal blessings had never yet been derived from any of the republican form. A limited Monarchy however was out of the question. The spirit of the times—the state of our affairs, forbade the experiment, if it were desirable. . . . A House of Nobles was essential to such a Government could these be created by a breath, or by a stroke of the pen? No. They were the growth of ages, and could only arise under a complication of circumstances none of which existed in this Country." But Americans should not despair simply because they did not have the raw materials to create a constitutional monarchy. "If ancient republics have been found to flourish for a moment only & then vanish for ever, it only proves that they were badly constituted; and that we ought to seek for every remedy for their diseases. One of these remedies he conceived to be the accidental lucky division of this Country into distinct States; a division which some seemed desirous to abolish altogether. . . . He hoped that each State would retain an equal voice at least in one branch of the National Legislature. . . . " Dickinson's suggestion of equal representation of the states in one branch was the first time that notion had been put forth. The small-state delegates fastened on it with avidity.

There was a sharp debate over Gerry's motion to give the chief executive an absolute veto over legislative enactments. George Mason expressed the fear that such authority lodged in the executive would lead to an excessive concentration of power. He declared: "We are not constituting a British Government, but a more dangerous monarchy, an elective one. . . . Do gentlemen mean to pave the way to hereditary Monarchy? Do they flatter themselves that the people will ever consent to such an innovation? If they do I venture to tell them they are mistaken. The people never will consent. . . . Notwithstanding the oppressions & injustice experienced among us from democracy; the genius of the people is in favor of it, and the genius of the people must be consulted." He would go no further than to allow the executive the power to suspend bad laws, "till they shall be coolly revised, and the objections to them overruled by a greater majority than was required in the first instance." This was to be a two-thirds majority, as it was to turn out.

Day after day the Randolph resolutions were debated: the jurisdiction of the Supreme Court and its relation to the state courts; the means of amending the Constitution; the proper method of ratifying; whether all states must ratify before the Constitution could go into effect and the new government begin to function; the proper procedures for admitting new states into the Union; and a number of other interesting and important questions.

At this point an almost euphoric atmosphere pervaded the debates. The nationalists were of course most encouraged by the rapid progress that was being made. Not surprisingly, certain thorny problems refused to be laid to rest but kept bobbing up again and again. Among these was the issue of how the members of the first branch of the national legislature were to be chosen—by the state legislatures or by the people directly. On this point Elbridge Gerry once more expressed his uneasiness. "In Massachusetts," he declared, "the worst men get into the Legislature. Several members of that body had lately been convicted of infamous crimes. Men of indigence, ignorance & baseness, spare no pains, however dirty to carry their point against men who are superior to the artifices practiced." On the other hand, although he had recanted his infatuation with democracy, "he was as much principled as ever against aristocracy and monarchy."

Wilson rebutted him. "He wished for vigor in the Government but he wished that vigorous authority to flow immediately from the legitimate source of all authority"—the people. "The Government ought to possess not only first the *force*, but secondly the *mind or sense* of the people at large. The Legislature ought to be the most exact transcript of the whole Society." Mason agreed with Gerry that there were dangers in "democratic elections." The fact was that no form of government "was free from imperfections & evils; . . . improper elections in many instances were inseparable from Republican Governments. But compare these with the advantage of this form in favor of the rights of the people, in favor of human nature."

Madison rose to add his support for popular election. The Virginian, in developing his arguments, not only gave the delegates a lesson in political sociology, he also described the nature of social groups in a manner thoroughly compatible with the views of most of his fellows. He declared: "All civilized Societies would be divided into different Sects, Factions, & interests, as they happened to consist of rich & poor, debtors & creditors, the landed, the manufacturing, the commercial interests, the inhabitants of this district or that district, the followers of this political leader or that political leader, the disciples of this religious Sect or that religious Sect. In all cases where a majority are united by a common interest or passion, the rights of the minority are in danger. What motives are to restrain them [the majority]? A prudent regard to the maxim that honesty is the best policy is found by experience to be as little regarded by bodies of men as by individuals. . . . Conscience, the only remaining tie, is known to be inadequate in individuals: In large numbers, little is to be expected from it. Besides, Religion itself may become a motive to persecution & oppression.— These observations are verified by the Histories of every Country ancient & modern. In Greece & Rome the rich & poor, the creditors & debtors, as well as the patricians & plebians alternately oppressed each other with equal unmercifulness. . . . Why was America so justly apprehensive of Parliamentary injustice? Because G. Britain had a separate interest real or supposed, & if her authority had been admitted, could have pursued that interest at our expense. We have seen the mere distinction of colour made in the most enlightened period of time, a ground of the most oppressive dominion ever exercised by man over man [a reference to slavery in America]." "What," Madison asked, "has been the source of those unjust laws complained of among ourselves? Has it not been the real or supposed interest of the major number? Debtors have defrauded their creditors. The landed interest has borne hard on the mercantile interest. The holders of one species of property have thrown a disproportion of taxes on the holders of another species. The lesson we are to draw from the whole is that where a majority are united by a common sentiment, and have an opportunity, the rights of the minor party become insecure. In a Republican Government the Majority if united have always an opportunity. The only remedy is to enlarge the sphere, & thereby divide the community into so great a number of interests & parties, that in the first place a majority will not be likely at the same moment to have a common interest separate from that of the whole or of the minority; and in the second place, that in case they should have such an interest, they may not be able to unite in the pursuit of it."

Madison's view of society was compatible with Franklin's as stated in the latter's argument against paying a salary to the chief executive. It could be stated plainly enough. Since greed and ambition (or "self-love") was an inherent part of man's fallen nature, it must be assumed that all those who had power would abuse it if not constrained by proper laws. The science of government was thus the almost mechanical art of arranging matters so that no one set of interests or combination of interests could exploit any other group in the society. The solution to this political conundrum must first be sought in the various branches of the government itself, since experience showed that each one would seek to steal power away from the other. What is conspicuous in Madison's exegesis is his view of the extreme precariousness of all political arrangements. While none could be perfect, the best must somehow provide a kind of antidote to human selfishness, to what the eighteenth century called self-aggrandizement. This was the Classical-Christian Consciousness stated in classic form; not a particularly bright perspective, to be sure, but enough to go on. It has been extensively quoted here because it was the clearest and most explicit social analysis delivered during the debates. The principal ideas were later restated in Madison's famous tenth *Federalist* paper.

Much time was given to speeches expressing support for the states vis-à-vis the national government and vice versa. Dickinson was for "a strong National Government but for leaving the States a considerable agency in the System." William Read of Delaware stated with equal conviction that "too much attachment" had been expressed for the states: "We must look beyond their continuance. A national Government must soon of necessity swallow all of them up. They will soon be reduced to the mere office of electing the National Senate. . . . The confederation was founded on temporary principles. It cannot last: it cannot be amended. If we do not establish a good Government on new principles, we must either go to ruin, or have the work to do over again. The people at large are wrongly suspected of being adverse to a General Government. The aversion lies among interested men who possess their confidence."

Wilson objected to Read's offhand abandonment of the states. He wanted to make clear that he "saw no incompatibility between the National & State Governments provided the latter were restrained to certain local purposes; nor any probability of their being devoured by the former."

Wilson and Madison displayed a dogged determination to have some "revisionary" process in the new government, that is to say, a review of all laws passed by the national legislature by a board or council *before* they could go into effect. Madison saw the function of such a body as being that of restraining "the Legislature from encroaching on the other co-ordinate Departments, or on the rights of the people at large, or from passing laws unwise in their principle, or incorrect in their form. . . ." Despite the support of Madison, Wilson, Mason, and other heavyweights among the delegates, the proposed council of revision was rejected by a vote of 8 states to 3.

One issue that clearly troubled the delegates was that of paper money. The principal charge cited against democracy was that where the people had gained control of the state legislatures they had issued large amounts of cheap paper money. In the earliest years of the nation, democracy and cheap money were thus linked and were to remain so through most of the country's subsequent history. The delegates to the Federal Convention were, without a dissenting voice, for "hard" money. It was their expectation that a wealthy and conservative Senate would check the appetite of the democratic lower house for "a depreciating paper."

Strong support was also expressed initially for giving the national legislature "a negative on such laws of the States as might be contrary to the articles of Union, or Treaties with foreign nations." Madison argued that "experience had evinced a constant tendency in the States to encroach on the federal authority; to violate national Treaties; to infringe on the rights & interests of each other; to oppress the weaker party within their respective jurisdictions. A negative [by the legislature] was the mildest expedient that could be devised for preventing these mischiefs. . . . But in order to give the negative . . . efficacy, it must extend to all cases. . . . This prerogative of the General Government is the greatest pervading principle that must control the centrifugal tendency of the States; which, without it, will continually fly out of their proper orbits and destroy the order & harmony of the political System."

When we consider the future of state-federal relationships, it is clear that a legislative veto over state laws would have aroused bitter opposition. What is surprising is that Madison and the other nationalists were ready to go so far in subordinating the states to the "general government." Fortunately for the Constitution's chances of ratification, the majority of delegates were unwilling to travel with them. Gunning Bedford of Delaware pointed out the practical problems involved in such authority. He asked: "Are the laws of the States to be suspended in the most urgent cases until they can be sent seven or eight hundred miles, and undergo the deliberations of a body who may be incapable of Judging of them? Is the National Legislature too to sit continually in order to revise the laws of the States?"

After the Constitution had become the law of the land, a number of states claimed that, primarily through decisions of the Supreme Court, the federal government was being given far more authority over the states than the framers of the Constitution had intended. The debates themselves of course were not available for reference. Had they been so, it would have been clear enough that a substantial number if not a plain majority of the delegates would have wished, ideally, for the general government to have had more power than they dared or could find a practical way to give it.

Despite the striking progress that was being made in the deliberations of the convention, there were certain danger signals that warned of stormy waters ahead. On June 9, William Paterson, a delegate from New Jersey and an able spokesman for the small states, gave a long speech describing the difference between a "national" and a "federal" government and arguing that the delegates had no authority to change the federal system existing under the confederation to a national one. The federal system was one in which each state was represented in the national legislature by one vote. A national system was one resting on proportional representation and assigning to the states a subordinate role. Wilson had "hinted" that if the small states would not come along in a national system, the large states "might be reduced [to the necessity] of confederating among themselves, by a refusal of the others to concur. Let them unite, if they please," Paterson declared, "but let them remember that they have no authority to compel the others to unite. N. Jersey will never confederate on the plan before the Committee. She would be swallowed up. He had rather submit to a monarch, to a despot, than to such a fate. He would not only oppose the plan here but on his return home do every thing in his power to defeat it there."

The nationalists, confident that things were going their way, showed no disposition to compromise. They steamrollered their way along, discussing the basis for proportional representation in both branches of the legislature; discussing the length of the terms for members of both houses; and deciding, after considerable debate, that two years was appropriate for the first branch and seven for the second. Several members objected to two-year terms for the "popular" branch. The people were accustomed to yearly elections and would put up with no less. This argument was successfully countered by the argument that if there were to be yearly elections, members of the first branch who came from states remote from the capital would spend most of their terms traveling to and from the center of government.

On June 11, Roger Sherman's motion that "each State have one vote in the second branch [the Senate]" was defeated 6 states no, 5 states aye. The nationalists pushed on. By the middle of the week nineteen resolutions defining the nature and the powers of the new government had been at least tentatively agreed on. Two days later, however, Paterson requested an early adjournment to give the small states time to prepare an alternative, "purely federal" plan. When the so-called New Jersey Plan was submitted on Friday, June 15, it was seen to differ most conspicuously from the Virginia Plan: first, in stating that "the articles of Confederation ought to be so revised, corrected & enlarged, as to render the federal Constitution adequate to the exigencies of Government, & the preservation of the Union"; and second, in omitting all mention of a "national legislature," referring instead to an augmentation of the powers of the existing Congress and adding a provision for an executive officer elected by Congress.

The New Jersey Plan brought a rude awakening to the nationalists. Paterson defended it warmly, laying his principal stress on the argument that the convention had no authority to do more than strengthen the Articles. Wilson and others replied with long and learned disquisitions on government and the already much reiterated shortcomings of Congress, but young Charles Pinckney of South Carolina put the matter with disconcerting bluntness. "The whole comes to this. . . . Give N. Jersey an equal vote, and she will dismiss her scruples, and concur in our National system." But the large-state men were not yet ready to concede themselves outmaneuvered. Randolph had another go at it; and on Monday, Alexander Hamilton, who "had been hitherto silent on the business before the Convention, partly from respect to others whose superior abilities, age & experience rendered him unwilling to bring forward ideas dissimilar to theirs, and partly from his delicate situation with respect to his own State [New York] to whose sentiments as expressed by his Colleagues, he could by no means accede." He felt that he must now speak out, and speak out he did in one of the longest and ablest speeches given at the convention.

It *was* somewhat presumptuous of Hamilton to lecture the delegates on political history since the Greeks. He went back to the earliest confederacies, associations of "independent Communities into one." He compared the German Diet with the "Amphyctionic Council" of Greek states, the Swiss cantons with the Delian Confederacy, the implications of "national" as opposed to "federal." The Paterson plan was hopelessly faulty in that it undertook to divide sovereignty between the old Confederation Congress and the states. "Two Sovereignties can not co-exist within the same limits. Giving powers to Congress must eventuate in a bad Government or no Government. The plan of N. Jersey therefore will not do. What then was to be done. Here he was embarrassed. The extent of the Country to be governed, discouraged him." His own inclination would be to simply abolish the state governments. They were "not necessary for any of the great purposes of commerce, revenue, or agriculture." There must be subordinate jurisdictions, to be sure, but these had best be established by, and subordinate to, the national government. The difficulty of simply assembling the representatives of the states at the place designated as the capital "almost led him to despair that a Republican Government could be established over so great an extent. . . . In his private opinion he had no scruple in declaring, supported as he was by the opinions of so many of the wise & good, that the British Government was the best in the world: and that he doubted much whether anything short of it would do in America." He had observed, indeed, that more and more of his fellow delegates seemed to be coming to the same conclusion, however reluctantly. "The members most tenacious of republicanism . . . were as loud as any in declaring against the vices of democracy. This progress of the public mind led him to anticipate the time, when others as well as himself would join in the praise bestowed by Mr. Neckar [Necker was the French director of finances and political theorist] on the British Constitution, namely, that it is the only Government in the world which unites public strength with individual security."

Hamilton then echoed Madison's observations on the inclination of those with power to oppress those without. "Give all power to the many," he declared, "and they will oppress the few. Give power to the few, they will oppress the many. Both therefore ought to have power, that each may defend itself against the other." In Great Britain, the House of Lords was "a permanent barrier against every pernicious innovation. . . . No temporary Senate will have firmness enough to answer the purpose." The delegates were naive if they supposed seven-year terms for senators "a sufficient period to give the senate an adequate firmness [against] the amazing violence & turbulence of the democratic spirit. When a great object of Government is pursued, which seizes the popular passions, they spread like wild fire, and become irresistible. He appealed to the gentlemen from the New England States whether experience had not there verified the remark." The only rational solution, Hamilton declared, was to "let one branch of the Legislature hold their place for life or at least during good behaviour. Let the Executive also be for life."

Hamilton then went on to offer his own plan of government, a scheme modeled, not surprisingly, on the British constitution, at least as Hamilton understood that nonexistent document. So far as the minutes and Madison's notes indicate, Hamilton's plan was simply ignored. There is no indication of a reply. In its unabashed conservatism it was too far out for the delegates. They resumed their discussion of the New Jersey Plan, with the nationalists still unwilling to accept the accuracy of Charles Pinckney's statement: Give the small states equal representation in one branch of the national legislature and they will forget their scruples and support the new Constitution. Stubbornly Madison labored on, refuting Paterson point by point as though he might overbear him by superior logic.

Now the delegates voted specifically on their preference as between the Virginia and the New Jersey plans. The tally was 7 to 3 for the Virginia Plan, with Maryland divided. The nationalists undoubtedly heaved a collective sigh of relief. A learned debate then ensued over whether the states had become individually or collectively independent when they broke off from Great Britain. The delegates fretted over the powers to be assigned to the national government and those to be reserved to the states, going over the same ground again and again as though they might at last resolve the question by simple repetition. And they constantly worried about what the people of the states would accept. Under pressure from the supporters of the Confederation Congress, the nationalists gave repeated assurances that they respected the role of the states and wished to preserve, not destroy them. As late as June 20 the motion of Robert Lansing, a newly arrived delegate from New York, simply to augment the existing legislative powers of the Confederation Congress failed by the margin of only two states. It was all very unsettling to the nationalists. Their carefully wrought Constitution suddenly appeared in danger of coming apart before their eyes, and the convention itself seemed on the verge of dissolution.

On June 25, when the delegates once again took up the question of the "method of election, terms, etc., of the Senate," Charles Pinckney rose to give an analysis of American society and the political institutions most appropriate to it. He pointed out that "The people of the U. States are perhaps the most singular of any we are acquainted with. Among them are fewer distinctions of fortune & less of rank, than among the inhabitants of any other nation. Every freeman has a right to the same protection & security; and a very moderate share of property entitles them to the possession of all the honors and privileges the public can bestow: hence arises a greater equality, than is to be found among the people of any other country, and an equality which is more likely to continue—I say this equality is more likely to continue, because in a new Country, possessing immense tracts of uncultivated lands, where every temptation is offered to emigration & where industry must be rewarded with competency, there will be few poor, and few dependent—Every member of the Society almost, will enjoy an equal power of arriving at the supreme offices & consequently of directing the strength & sentiments of the whole Community. None will be excluded by birth, & few by fortune . . . the whole community will enjoy in the fullest sense that kind of political liberty which consists in the power the members of the State reserve to themselves, of arriving at the public offices, or at least, of having votes in the nomination of those who will fill them."

It was thus clear to Pinckney that the constitution of Great Britain would have little relevance for the United States. The social conditions were so different that it would be folly to try to erect in America a system that might be ideally suited to a very different kind of society. It would be generations before such a situation could exist in the United States. "To illustrate this I have remarked that the people of the United States are more equal in their circumstances than the people of any other Country—that they have very few rich men among them,—by rich men I mean those whose riches may have a dangerous influence, or such as are esteemed rich in Europe—perhaps there are not one hundred such on the Continent; that it is not probable this number will be greatly increased: that the genius of the people, their mediocrity of situation & the prospects which are afforded their industry in a Country which must be a new one for centuries are unfavorable to the rapid distinctions of ranks. . . . That vast extent of unpeopled territory which opens to the frugal & industrious a sure road to competency & independence will effectually prevent for a considerable time the increase of the poor or discontented, and be the means of preserving that equality of condition which so eminently distinguishes us."

In Pinckney's view, the debates of the convention had been misled by false analogies in the minds of the delegates to old and settled countries "full of people & manufactures & established in credit. . . . Our true situation appears to me to be this.—A new extensive Country containing within itself the materials for forming a Government capable of extending to its citizens all the blessings of civil & religious liberty—capable of making them happy at home. This is the great end of Republican Establishments. We mistake the object of our Government, if we hope or wish that it is to make us respectable abroad. Conquest or superiority among other powers is not or ought not ever to be the object of republican systems. If they are sufficiently active & energetic to rescue us from contempt & preserve our domestic happiness & security, it is all we can expect from them,—it is more than almost any other Government ensures to its citizens. [It seemed clear that] no two people are so exactly alike in their situation or circumstances as to admit the exercise of the same Government with equal benefit: that a system must be suited to the habits & genius of the people it is to govern, and must grow out of them."

Pinckney's speech is emphasized because it is the most explicit statement by any delegate of the generally accepted notion that an "equality of rank" was the distinguishing feature of American society. Pinckney also placed a unique emphasis on the role the unsettled regions of the West would have in preserving that equality. Furthermore, whereas most of the delegates thought in terms of models and archetypes—the notion that there was some classic constitutional form that needed only to be discovered and emulated—Pinckney disavowed such an idea. Governments must be adapted to the character of the people they are intended to govern. Although Pinckney did not suggest that Americans would be exempt from the processes by which, in other societies, some had grown rich and others poor until oppressive and unjust divisions existed, he did conjecture that in the United States such a stratification would be long delayed by the opportunities for the "frugal and industrious" to remain "independent" by seeking their fortunes in the West.

When the issue of a proper mode of electing the second branch of the national legislature reasserted itself later in the same session, James Wilson confessed his perplexity. "When he considered the amazing extent of the Country—the immense population which is to fill it, the influence which the Government we are to form will have, not only on the present generation of our people & their multiplied posterity, but on the whole Globe, he was lost in the magnitude of the object." The project of Henry IV of France to establish a confederated nation of Europe was a modest undertaking by comparison. He thought it essential that the members of the second branch represent the people and not the states.

Still the small-state, large-state conflict—equal versus proportional representation—overshadowed all discussions. It came most conspicuously to the fore in discussions about the number of members the Senate was to have and their method of selection. This was plainly the Achilles' heel of the nationalists. They were unable to come up with a persuasive solution. Roger Sherman argued that since the delegates agreed on the principle of equality—a rich man, for instance, would have no more weight at the polls than a poor one, one vote—they must accept the fact that a small, "poor" state should have as much weight in the councils of the nation as a large, "rich" one. The point seemed well taken by some delegates, certainly by those from small states.

At this point Dr. Franklin produced another of his "papers," addressed, this time, to Washington. He reminded the delegates that in the most trying days of the Revolutionary conflict, the members of the Continental Congress, meeting in this very room, had offered daily prayers "for the divine protection.—Our prayers, Sir, were heard, & they were graciously answered." Franklin was convinced that without divine help they would do no better "than the Builders of Babel: We shall be divided by our little partial local interests; our projects will be confounded, and we ourselves shall become a reproach and bye word down to future ages. And what is worse, mankind may hereafter from this unfortunate instance, despair of establishing Governments by Human wisdom and leave it to chance, war and conquest." He proposed that all sessions of the convention be opened with prayer.

Franklin's remarks are of interest, especially in view of his reputation as somewhat of a freethinker and agnostic. Certainly it was not long after the convention had concluded its deliberations that many Americans were claiming that such a remarkable document as it had produced could have been framed only with the assistance of the Almighty and offering this proposition as proof that the United States was His special instrument for the redemption of a fallen world. Again we hear echoes in Franklin of John Winthrop's "Modell of Christian Charity," written one hundred and fifty years earlier.

Hugh Williamson replied that the reason the convention had not opened with prayer was that it had no funds to hire a chaplain. Other delegates objected on the grounds that the public might become alarmed if word got about that the deliberations of the convention had reached such a desperate pass that it was necessary to make an appeal for outside assistance. After some desultory and rather awkward debate, the Doctor's proposal was allowed to expire for want of a vote.

Yet there was no overestimating the seriousness of the situation. It was reflected in the increasing number of references by the delegates to the consequences of a failure to agree on a new frame of government. The representatives of Delaware, New Jersey, and Maryland spoke openly of returning home to report that the convention had reached an impasse. It was a tactic particularly unnerving to the nationalists, who had once seemed so close to their goal. Hamilton stated his conviction that this was "the critical moment for forming . . . a Government. . . . We are weak and sensible of our weakness. Henceforth the motives will become feebler, and the difficulties greater. It is a miracle that we are here now exercising our tranquil & free deliberations on the subject. It would be madness to trust to future miracles."

At this point Roger Sherman came back to his earlier proposal—

proportional representation in the first branch, equal representation in the second. "We were partly national and partly federal. The proportional representation in the first branch was conformable to the national principle & would secure the large States against the small. An equality of voices was conformable to the federal principle and was necessary to secure the Small states against the large. He trusted that on this middle ground a compromise could take place. He did not see that it could on any other. And if no compromise should take place, our meeting would not only be in vain but worse than in vain." To deny the states equal representation would be tantamount to "at once cutting the body of America in two."

But the nationalists remained adamant. Wilson and Madison took up the cudgels again, going over familiar ground at great length. The discussions grew more and more acrimonious, and that tranquillity of mind of which Hamilton had spoken was less and less in evidence. Gunning Bedford of Delaware "contended that there was no middle way between a perfect consolidation, and a mere confederacy of the States. . . . If political Societies possess ambition, avarice, and all the other passions which render them formidable to each other, ought we not to view them in this light here? Will not the same motives operate in America as elsewhere? If any gentleman doubt it let him look at the votes. Have they not been dictated by interest, by ambition? Are not the large States evidently seeking to aggrandize themselves at the expense of the small? They think no doubt that they have right on their side, but interest has blinded their eyes. Look at Georgia. Though a small State at present, she is actuated by the prospect of soon being a great one. . . . North Carolina has the same motives of present & future interest. Virginia follows. . . . Will it be said that an inequality of power will not result from an inequality of votes? Give the opportunity, and ambition will not fail to abuse it. The whole History of mankind proves it. . . . The large States dared not dissolve the Confederation. If they do the small ones will find some foreign ally of more honor and good faith, who will take them by the hand and do them justice."

A Massachusetts delegate, Rufus King, objected to Bedford's "dictatorial language." It was not King who had spoken "with a vehemence unprecedented . . . had declared himself ready to turn his hopes from our common Country, and court the protection of some foreign hand. . . . He . . . grieved that such a thought had entered into his heart. He was more grieved that such an expression had dropped from his lips. The gentleman could only excuse it to himself on the score of passion. For himself whatever might be his distress, he would never court relief from a foreign power." At this, cooler heads prevailed and the house adjourned.

When the debates were resumed on Monday, July 2, the eleventh anniversary of the resolution of Congress declaring the American colonies independent of Great Britain, Gouverneur Morris rose to explain why he could not accept a compromise that would give the states equal representation in the Senate. Morris, who shared Hamilton's conservative views and had opposed the admission of new states to the Union on the basis of equality with the old, protested that the proposed compromise would undermine the theoretical function of the Senate. It was intended, after all, "to check the precipitation, changeableness, and excesses" of the first branch whose counterparts in the state legislatures had already displayed indifference if not hostility "against personal liberty, private property & personal safety." It had been said that if the Senate were to be the stronghold of the affluent, it would try to abuse its power. For his part, "he believed so: He hoped so. The Rich will strive to establish their dominion & enslave the rest. They always did. They always will. The proper security against them is to form them into a separate interest. The two forces [the rich and the poor] will then control each other. Let the rich mix with the poor in a Commercial Country, they will establish an oligarchy. Take away commerce, and the democracy will triumph. Thus it has been the world over. So it will be among us. Reason tells us we are but men: and we are not to expect any particular interference of Heaven in our favor. By thus combining & setting apart, the aristocratic interest, the popular interest will be combined against it. There will be a mutual check and mutual security." Above all, Morris professed to fear "the influence of the rich. . . . We should remember that the people never act from reason alone. The Rich will take advantage of their passions & make these the instruments for oppressing them. The Result of the Contest will be a violent aristocracy, or a more violent despotism. The schemes of the Rich will be favored by the extent of the Country. The people in such distant parts cannot communicate & act in concert. They will be the dupes of those who have more knowledge & intercourse."

Morris's speech suggests what may be the likeliest explanation of the stubborn resistance of men like Madison and Wilson. To make the second branch the repository of the principle of equality would vitiate the whole notion of a balance in the legislature between the people as a whole and the commercial and landed "interests"—thus, presumably, leaving "the interests" of the "rich," or aristocratic element, at the mercy of the democracy.

A committee appointed to recommend a compromise (and strongly opposed by the nationalists) brought in on July 5 a report that, as anticipated, proposed proportional representation in the first branch and equal representation by states in the second. One would have thought that would have ended the matter, but the irreconcilables argued on. Gouverneur Morris summoned up all the horrors of a civil war. The Constitution must be established on proper principles, or "the Gallows & Halter will finish the work of the sword." The small-state delegates had taken to hinting of forming foreign alliances should they be refused equality of representation; the spokesmen of the large states, in turn, seemed to be suggesting that they might have to take up arms against their smaller neighbors to keep them from forming such alliances. At this point, there were important defections in the ranks of the delegates of the larger states. Gerry of Massachusetts spoke for the compromise, and George Mason lent it his considerable prestige. He personally found it in the greatest degree inconvenient to be so long away from his own affairs, "but he would bury his bones in this City rather than expose his Country to the Consequences of a dissolution of the Convention without any thing being done."

Still deadlocked, the delegates put down the issue of representation in the second branch to take up the basis for proportional representation in the first branch. Here the most basic conflict of all came to the surface: the division between North and South, between the Slave States and those states where slavery was illegal or of no economic consequence. The South feared that if the Northern states were to have a majority of the members in the first branch, they would conspire against the agricultural interests of the South and even imperil the existence of the institution of slavery. The debate over the number of representatives from each state grew especially bitter, leading Morris to observe that he found many advocates for particular states but few "representatives of America." Pierce Butler and General Charles Cotesworth Pinckney "insisted that blacks be included in the rule of Representation, *equally* with Whites." But the delegates from the Northern states balked. They would go no further than three fifths, and that with the greatest reluctance. Even George Mason, a slaveholder himself, opposed the South Carolinians.

The mercurial Morris now declared himself opposed to counting any slaves for the purpose of representation. To do so would surely be to encourage the slave trade, and he could never agree to that. "A distinction had been set up & urged, between the Northern & Southern States. He had hitherto considered this doctrine as heretical. He still thought the distinction groundless. He sees however that it is persisted in, and that the Southern Gentlemen will not be satisfied unless they see the way open to their gaining a majority in the public Councils. The consequence of such a transfer of power from the maritime to the interior & landed interest will he foresees be such an oppression of commerce, that he shall be obliged to vote for the vicious principle of equality in the 2nd branch in order to provide some defence for the Northern States against it."

Butler replied that "the security the Southern States want is that their negroes may not be taken from them, which some gentlemen within or without doors, have a very good mind to do." As for majorities and minorities, "the people & strength of America" were plainly "bearing Southwardly & Southwestwardly," however the North might deplore the fact.

Elbridge Gerry, still fretting over the possibility that the Western states might in time outnumber and thus dominate the original states, "thought it necessary to limit the number of new States to be admitted into the Union, in such a manner, that they should never be able to outnumber the Atlantic States." But Roger Sherman replied that "there was no probability that the number of future States would exceed that of the Existing States. If the event should ever happen, it was too remote to be taken into consideration at this time. Besides, we are providing for our posterity, for our children & our grand Children, who would be as likely to be citizens of new Western States, as of the old States. On this consideration alone, we ought to make no such discrimination as was proposed."

Gerry persisted. "There was a rage for emigration from the Eastern States to the Western Country, and he did not wish those remaining behind to be at the mercy of the Emigrants. Besides foreigners are resorting to that country, and it is uncertain what turn things may take there." But Gerry's motion to limit representation was narrowly defeated, 5 states to 4, with Pennsylvania divided. The vote was a sectional one. All the New England states voted in support. Pennsylvania was divided; Virginia, North and South Carolina, and Georgia were opposed. North of the Mason–Dixon line only New

Jersey voted to admit new states on the basis of equality with the old. Clearly the unanimity of the Southern states was based, in large part, on the expectation that most of the new states would be in the Southern sphere and accordingly would be slaveholding states; the New England opposition was based on the same assumption. Thus was foreshadowed the bitterest issue that was to face the new nation in the first seventy-five years of its history—the balance of power between North and South.

On Monday, July 16, the delegates resolved to vote on the report brought in by a Committee of the States, "including the equality of votes in the 2nd branch." The vote was recorded as 5 to 5, with Massachusetts divided. North Carolina broke the Solid South by voting aye. Although the vote was recorded by Madison as a tie, he added that "it passed in the Affirmative."

Randolph was still irreconcilable. It would, in his opinion, "be in vain to come to any final decision with a bare majority on either side. For these reasons he wished the Convention might adjourn, that the large States might consider the steps proper to be taken in the present solemn crisis of the business, and that the small States might also deliberate on the means of conciliation."

Paterson was up at once to support the notion of adjourning. He believed that "the rule of secrecy ought to be rescinded, and that our Constituents should be consulted. No conciliation could be admissible on the part of the smaller States on any other ground that that of an equality of votes in the 2nd branch." He would support the indefinite adjournment of the convention "with all his heart."

General Pinckney asked if Randolph meant to adjourn indefinitely or only for the day. If Randolph intended an indefinite adjournment, he was opposed. "He could not think of going to South Carolina and returning again to this place. Besides it was chimerical to suppose that the States if consulted would ever accord separately and beforehand."

Randolph, alarmed at Paterson's response, disclaimed any intention to suggest that the convention adjourn indefinitely. He was "sorry that his meaning had been so readily & strangely misinterpreted." He wished simply for an adjournment until the following day so that the larger states "might . . . take a measure, he would not say what, as might be necessary." John Rutledge of South Carolina saw no need for an adjournment. The case was plain enough. "The little States were fixt. They had repeatedly & solemnly declared themselves to be so. All that the larger States then had to do, was to decide whether they would yield or not. For his part he conceived that although we could not do what we thought best, in itself, we ought to do something. Had we not better keep the Government up a little longer, hoping that another Convention will supply our omissions, than abandon every thing to hazard."

Word got about "out-of-doors" that the delegates were deadlocked and occasioned much uneasiness among the friends of a strong national government. Even Lafayette in Paris heard that the convention was stalled on the issue of representation. He wrote an anxious letter to Washington: "Upon the success of this convention depends perhaps the very existence of the United States. . . . Good Lord! The American people, so enlightened, so wise, so noble, after having so successfully scaled the steep cliffs, now stumble on the easy path."

The adjournment of July 16 was the large states' last expedient. When the delegates from those states met the next morning, they appeared to be a demoralized group. Madison noted that "the time was wasted in vague conversation on the subject, without any specific proposition or agreement." Some of the delegates proved willing to abandon the enterprise, arguing that since "no good Government could or would be built on that foundation, and that as a division of the Convention into two opinions was unavoidable," it would be better for the large states to "propose a scheme of Government" on the basis of which they could form their own Union and leave it to the smaller states to join or not as they wished. "Others seemed inclined to yield to the smaller States, and to concur in such an act however imperfect & exceptional . . . though decided by a bare majority of the States and by a minority of the people of the U. States." The result of the "consultation" was to demonstrate that the large states were unable to agree on a common course of action and that, as a consequence, the victory of the small states was assured.

What is perhaps most intriguing about the long and bitter struggle of the small states for equal representation in the Senate was that what became perhaps the most admired and certainly the most widely copied feature of the Constitution was no one's deliberate choice, conformed to no existing political theory, had no antecedents, and was accepted with reluctance by all parties but by none so much as by the leading figures in the convention—Madison, Wilson, and Morris. What is also worth pondering is that the whole large-state, small-state split may well not have been a real issue. The tensions in American political life have never been of that nature. While this may be, in part, because the small states clearly got the better part of the bargain, it may equally well be that the large states were right in maintaining that the small states' fears of being exploited by the large states were, in fact, quite groundless—chimerical. In other words, the most notable feature of the Constitution (with the possible exception of the Supreme Court) may well have been the consequence far more of illusion than of reality. A good case can also be made for the argument that the essentially meaningless conflict between the large and small states served the highly useful purpose of distracting the delegates from the real division: that between the slaveholding South and the commercial North, a split that underlay most of the debates and came increasingly to the fore after the large-state, small-state controversy had been resolved. As a final irony, consider the fact that at least three of the so-called large states—North Carolina, South Carolina, and Georgia—were, for the most part, simply anticipating that they would become large states. If there were any reality to the large-state, small-state division, Georgia would more realistically have been in the small-state column. For example, in a decade or so the "small state" of Connecticut would have a far larger white population than the "large state" of Georgia. Indeed, at the time of the convention the population of Connecticut was some 232,000 whites versus 53,000 whites (and 30,000 blacks) in Georgia, while tiny Delaware had only 8,000 fewer inhabitants than the Southern state that consistently voted "large." New Jersey, leader of the small states, had a white population of 170,000 in contrast to "large" South Carolina's 140,000 whites (with 109,000 slaves). We can thus say with some confidence that the entire contest between "large" and "small" states, which consumed so much of the time, energy, fervor, and intellect of the delegates for the greater part of the convention, was based on illusion.

Charles Pinckney's prediction weeks earlier that if the small states were given equal representation they would "forget their scruples" and go along with a "national" government proved correct. Indeed, they became the principal advocates of the Constitution as it finally emerged from the convention and its earliest and most eager ratifiers.

After the climax of July 16, much of what followed in the convention had about it an air of anticlimax, which was doubtless an atmosphere far more congenial to the delegates. A great deal certainly remained to be done. Much that appeared to have been settled earlier was now reopened on the grounds that the agreement on equal representation in the second branch required a general reconsideration of the function and responsibilities of the legislative branch. Much debate centered on the mode of electing the chief executive, and there was considerable support for having him appointed by the legislature. There was also sentiment for having him ineligible for reelection so that "he should not be left under a temptation to court a reappointment." Wilson, who had first introduced the idea, noted with satisfaction that more and more delegates seemed inclined "to an election mediately or immediately by the people."

When the issue of impeachment came up again, George Mason declared: "No point is of more importance than that the right of impeachment should be continued. Shall any man be above justice? Above all shall that man be above it, who can commit the most extensive injustice?" Franklin spoke to the same effect. What, he asked, would be the alternative? Formerly the only means of removing a corrupt leader was by assassination, "in which he was not only deprived of his life but of the opportunity of vindicating his character." Madison likewise "thought it indispensable that some provision should be made for defending the Community against the incapacity, negligence or perfidy of the chief Magistrate. . . . He might pervert his administration into a scheme of peculation or oppression. He might betray his trust to foreign powers."

Although many of the following days of debate were taken up with tedious retracing of already well covered ground, they nonetheless have their own fascination, since through them one can trace the slow and difficult process of forming and re-forming ideas until they take shape as political actualities, as specific clauses and articles in a particular document. Moreover, the intellectual level of the discussions remained so high that the debates can be read at almost any point with instruction, though the dramatic impact is never again as striking as in the days of the large-state, small-state battle. In addition, since one reads the debates with hindsight, they are given a heightened effect by the fact that the reader is aware, as in the debate about impeachment, of what the historic consequences of various articles would be.

By the last week of July, the delegates were ready to turn over to the Committee of Detail the responsibility for putting all the various resolutions of the convention in the form of a specific document—the new Constitution. The committee labored at this very exacting task for two weeks. When it was presented to the delegates on Monday, August

6, it was, in most respects, near its final form. It did not contain, as General Pinckney had insisted it must, "security to the Southern States against an emancipation of slaves and taxes on exports," although it did provide that "no navigation act shall be passed without the assent of two-thirds of the members present in each House," a provision later dropped. The delegates went over the draft painstakingly, article by article. An effort by General Pinckney to have the representation of South Carolina increased on the basis of the state's large slave population brought a bitter protest from Rufus King. The fact that the draft gave even the shadow of legitimation to slaveholding was "a most grating circumstance to his mind & he believed would be so to a great part of the people of America. He had not made a strenuous opposition to it heretofore because he had hoped that this concession would have produced a readiness which had not been manifested, to strengthen the General Government and to mark a full confidence in it. The Report under consideration had by the tenor of it, put an end to all those hopes. In two great points the hands of the Legislature were absolutely tied. The importation of slaves could not be prohibited—exports could not be taxed. Is this reasonable? . . . There is so much inequality & unreasonableness in all this, that the people of the Northern States could never be reconciled to it. No candid man could undertake to justify it to them. . . . At all events, either slaves should not be represented, or exports should be taxable."

Gouverneur Morris joined King in attacking slavery. "He never would concur in upholding domestic slavery. It was a nefarious institution. It was the curse of heaven on the States where it prevailed. Compare the free regions of the Middle States, where a rich & noble cultivation marks the prosperity & happiness of the people, with the misery & poverty which overspread the barren wastes of Virginia, Maryland and the other States having slaves. [In the South] every step you take through the great region of slaves presents a desert increasing, with the increasing proportion of those wretched beings. . . . The admission of slaves into the representation comes to this: that the inhabitant of Georgia and South Carolina who goes to the Coast of Africa, and in defiance of the most sacred laws of humanity tears away his fellow creatures from their dearest connections & damns them to the most cruel bondage, shall have more votes in a Government instituted for protection of the rights of mankind, than the Citizen of Pennsylvania or New Jersey who views with a laudable horror, so nefarious a practice. . . . The vassalage of the poor has ever been the favorite offspring of Aristocracy. . . . He would sooner submit himself to a tax for paying for all the negroes in the United States, than saddle posterity with such a Constitution. . . ."

The Southern delegates must have been stunned and furious at this belated tirade by Morris. Estimable as these sentiments were, they came very late in the day and could serve little purpose but to exacerbate tempers already on edge.

The next day, Morris, so liberal on slaves, expressed his suspicion of foreigners and proposed a motion that would deny them citizenship until they had lived fourteen years in their adopted country. James Wilson pointed out that if Morris's motion passed, he himself, a Scottish immigrant, would be barred "from holding a place under the very Constitution which he had shared in the trust of making. He remarked the illiberal complexion which the motion would give to the [Constitution], & the effect which a good system would have in inviting meritorious foreigners among us." Franklin also joined in the opposition to Morris's motion, reminding the delegates that "in the course of the Revolution . . . many strangers served us faithfully. . . . When foreigners after looking about for some other Country in which they can obtain more happiness, give a preference to ours it is proof of attachment which ought to excite our confidence & affection." Morris's motion was defeated.

When the delegates took up the matter of import and export duties, the issue of slavery reasserted itself. This time the antislavery forces found an unexpected ally in George Mason, himself a Virginia slaveholder. Mason declared: "The present question concerns not the importing States alone but the whole Union. . . . Slavery discourages arts & manufactures. The poor despise labor when performed by slaves. They prevent the immigration of Whites, who really enrich & strengthen a Country. They produce a most pernicious effect on manners. Every master is born a petty tyrant. They bring the judgment of heaven on a Country. As nations cannot be rewarded or punished in the next world they must be in this. By an inevitable chain of causes & effects providence punishes national sins, by national calamities. . . . As to the States being in possession of the Right to import, this was the case with many other rights, now to be properly given up. He held it essential in every point of view that the General Government should have the power to prevent the increase of slavery."

Charles Pinckney defended slavery warmly. "In all ages one-half of mankind have been slaves." The South would resist any effort to stop their importation. John Rutledge seconded Pinckney. North and South Carolina and Georgia would never agree to the new government "unless their right to import slaves be untouched. . . . The people of those States will never be such fools as give up so important an interest."

Randolph expressed his own unhappiness with the importation of slaves. "He would sooner risk the constitution. . . . By agreeing to the clause [protecting the importation of slaves], it would revolt the Quakers, the Methodists, and many others in the States having no slaves." To reject the clause might mean losing South Carolina and Georgia to the Union. After much anguish a compromise was agreed to, forbidding the importation of slaves after 1808.

As the deliberations of the delegates drew to a close, George Mason urged the inclusion of a bill of rights in the Constitution. It could be quickly done, and "it would give great quiet to the people." Roger Sherman countered by observing that since all the states had their own bills of rights and these were "not repealed by this Constitution," there was no need for a national bill of rights. On the question of whether a committee should be charged with preparing a bill of rights, the weary delegates voted unanimously in the negative. Since the absence of a bill of rights became the principal charge against the Constitution and, indeed, imperiled its ratification in several states, it might be well to reflect on the delegates' reasons for turning down Mason's suggestion. Although it was undoubtedly true that the delegates were, in varying degrees, worn out by their long stint in Philadelphia and missed their homes and families, it is also true that they simply did not consider the issue an important one. As far as laws passed by the national legislature were concerned, the delegates expected the Supreme Court to declare void those laws that in any way impaired the Constitution or were against "natural equity," in James Otis's phrase. Laws against natural equity included all laws that might infringe on the rights of citizens as defined in the bills of rights adopted by the various states. Since the strongest advocates of a national or federal bill of rights never conceived that it would be invoked by the Supreme Court against statutes passed by the state legislatures, it seemed to the majority of delegates to be superfluous. It was clearly the intention of the framers of the Constitution that violations of articles in the state bills of rights would be handled by the state courts.

On September 15, with the Constitution awaiting final approval and signing, Edmund Randolph and George Mason announced that they could not, in good conscience, place their names on the document or support it in their home state of Virginia.

The final draft of the Constitution, with the exception of equal representation in the Senate, was strikingly close to the proposal with which Randolph had opened the debates. Mason had seen most of his suggestions adopted by the convention, and he and Randolph had played crucial roles in the debates themselves. So these were serious and troubling defections. They were joined by Elbridge Gerry, delegate from Massachusetts. Certainly Gerry, one of the most conservative delegates, and Mason, perhaps the most liberal, made an odd pair. Lansing of New York had already departed for New York to do his best there to prevent ratification and Luther Martin of Maryland emphatically expressed his dissatisfaction. The rumor was circulated that Mason had declared he would rather chop off his right hand than sign his name to such a dangerous document.

Three of the most prominent apostates were from the two largest and most important states in the Union—Virginia and Massachusetts. On Monday, September 17, when the delegates met to sign the engrossed copy of the Constitution, Franklin made a final plea for conciliation, read by James Wilson. There were parts of the Constitution he himself did not approve, but "having lived long, I have experienced many instances of being obliged by . . . fuller consideration, to change opinions even on important subjects. . . . It is therefore that the older I grow, the more apt I am to doubt my own judgment, and to pay more respect to the judgment of others." He thought the Constitution, "if well administered," would prove adequate to the exigencies of the time. It could end in despotism only, "as other forms have done before it, when the people shall become so corrupted as to need despotic Government." Franklin doubted if "any other Convention we can obtain, may be able to make a better Constitution. For when you assemble a number of men to have the advantage of their joint wisdom, you inevitably assemble with those men, all their prejudices, their passions, their local interests, and their selfish views. From such an assembly can a perfect production be expected? It therefore astonishes me . . . to find this system approaching so near perfection as it does; and I think it will astonish our enemies, who are waiting with confidence to hear that our councils are confounded like those of the Builders of Babel; and that our States are on the point of separation, only to meet hereafter for the purpose of cutting one another's throats. Thus I consent to this Constitution because I expect no better, and because I am not sure, that it is not the best. The opinions I have had of its errors, I sacrifice to the public good. . . . If every one of us on returning to our Constituents were to report the objections he has had to it, and endeavor to gain partisans in support of them, we might prevent it being generally received, and thereby lose all the salutary effects & great advantages resulting naturally in our favor among foreign Nations as well as among ourselves, from our real or apparent unanimity."

The appeal was made in vain. Randolph, Mason, and Gerry remained adamant. Gerry predicted there would be "Civil war" in Massachusetts if the Constitution were ratified. Others, acquiescing, were less than enthusiastic. Hamilton declared that "no man's ideas were more remote from the plan than his own were known to be; but it is possible to deliberate between anarchy and Convulsion on one side, and the chance of good to be expected from the plan on the other."

Rufus King then proposed that the Journals of the Convention "be either destroyed, or deposited in the custody of, the President. He thought if suffered to be made public a bad use would be made of them by those who wished to prevent the adoption of the Constitution." It was decided, with only Maryland dissenting, to place them in Washington's hands for safekeeping. Madison's extensive notes, of course, remained in his possession.

While the delegates were signing, Franklin, "looking towards the President's chair at the back of which a rising sun happened to be painted, observed to a few members near him, that Painters had found it difficult to distinguish in their art a rising from a setting sun. I have, said he, often and often in the course of the Session, and the vicissitudes of my hopes and fears as to its issue, looked at that behind the President without being able to tell whether it was rising or setting: But now at length I have the happiness to know that it is a rising and not a setting Sun."

So was concluded one of the most impressive political achievements in history: the beginning of a new political age. In the next two hundred years, at first dozens, and then hundreds of peoples set themselves up as independent nations. All were indebted, to a greater or lesser degree, to the work of the men who had created the first written Constitution of modern times. Perhaps the most widely copied feature of the United States Constitution was, ironically, the federal "system," the most "accidental" part of the Constitution, the portion most bitterly resisted by the principal architects of that document. The Supreme Court, in one form or another, appeared in most subsequent constitutions, and so indeed did many other particular parts and pieces of the Constitution. Least copied was the notion of a single executive who must be both symbolic head of state and administrator of the government. Most new nations preferred the British parliamentary system which provided for a nominal head of the state with primarily formal duties—often called "president"—and a "political" chief executive, usually called "prime minister." But whatever modifications various nations made in the Constitution of the United States to suit their own particular needs and circumstances, it has remained the original, the Ur-document, both a model and a challenge. It is, indubitably, the oldest and most successful written Constitution, and it has been the wonder and the envy of practical politicians and political theorists since it was drafted. Lafayette wrote to Washington, "The new constitution has been carefully studied and much admired by the philosophers of Europe." The *Journal politique de Bruxelles* described it as a "monument of political legislation . . . a product of all the study which ancient and modern republics, the English, Montesquieu and Rousseau have given to this prime concern of public welfare"; and William Gladstone, the great British prime minister, called it "the most wonderful work ever struck off at a given time by the brain and purpose of man."

By now the reader will be conscious of the degree to which the Constitution was the result, to a substantial degree of luck, chance— or Providence, as the delegates themselves preferred to put it. It had been erected on the assumption of most of the delegates that there was a "natural" political order, an almost mechanical system similar to Newton's law of gravity, a system ordained and, in a sense, "underwritten" by the Almighty. They believed that just as the devout Christian could, by means of reason and revelation, discern God's will for him or her as an individual believer, a conclave of Christian politicians could, by applying reason to human experience, deduce the proper form of government. The generation to which the framers of the Constitution belonged was, I think it is safe to say, the last generation of Americans to subscribe to such a doctrine. In any event, it should be evident by now that, philosophical and theological considerations aside, the Constitution as a practical political document was achieved by the narrowest of margins.

5

Ratification

If the delegates to the Constitutional Convention had any notion that their handiwork would be readily accepted by their countrymen, they were soon disabused. Since "national" had a bad connotation for most Americans, suggesting a "grand consolidated government" virtually obliterating the states, the supporters of the Constitution shrewdly termed themselves "Federalists," a word that implied a federation of more or less sovereign states. In reaction the enemies of the Constitution called themselves Anti-Federalists.

At this distance in time, it is difficult to identify the Anti-Federalists by class or political persuasion. Some historians have argued that conservatives (or reactionaries) favored the Constitution, while the democratically inclined were opposed to it. By this reading, the Declaration of Independence marked the high tide of democratic idealism; and the political form that expressed the principles of the Declaration was the Articles of Confederation. The Constitution was a conservative reaction to both the Declaration and the Articles.

While it is true that a number of delegates, prominent among them Elbridge Gerry and Roger Sherman, had expressed disillusionment with the "excess of democracy" they associated directly or indirectly with the Articles, the popular election of the House of

Representatives and, through the electoral college, of the president, gave the ordinary citizen far more of a role in the federal government under the Constitution than he had had under the Articles. Moreover, many of the individuals who signed their names to the Declaration were also prominent in the drafting of the Constitution. Counterrevolutionary activity is typically carried out by a different group or class from the one that perpetrates a revolution.

What we can say with confidence is that the Declaration of Independence was the first and most striking manifestation in America of the Secular-Democratic Consciousness, the American version of the Enlightenment. The Constitution, on the other hand, was the culmination, or final expression, of the Classical-Christian Consciousness. The fact that both consciousnesses existed in the same persons will not surprise any careful student of human nature. As the English historian R. H. Tawney put it, "The heart of man holds mysteries of contradiction which live together in vigorous incompatibility."

Certainly there is no sound historical evidence to support the doctrine of the Constitution as counterrevolutionary. Indeed, one historian has characterized the opponents of the Constitution as "men of little faith," who clung, out of a combination of fear and nostalgia, to what was clearly an awkward and inadequate frame of government. The democratic Benjamin Rush, like many others, saw the Constitution as the completion of the Revolution, a necessary and essential step. Nonetheless, there was loud and determined and, for the Federalists, unnerving opposition.

Much of the opposition to the Constitution was expressed before its critics had read it. The Constitution was (and is) a difficult and complex document (although it is lucidity itself compared with some of its successors). Thus, we may assume that the percentage of those who opposed it based on a close analysis of the text was small. The opposition was on other, largely emotional grounds. One suspects that it contained a good deal of social animus. The framers were, virtually without exception, men of position and power in their own states. They were also, for the most part, prosperous or even wealthy: they were classic members of what Jefferson called "a natural aristocracy." As such, in the burgeoning democratic spirit of America, they were suspect. The convention was attacked by one newspaper as a "dark conclave" of aristocrats, of the wealthy and "well-born" engaged in a conspiracy against the liberties of the people. The harassed Federalists offered "a Receipt for an Antifederal Essay." The ingredients were "*well-born*, nine times—*Aristocracy*, eighteen times—*Liberty of Conscience*, once—*Negro slavery*, once mentioned—*Trial by Jury*, seven times—*Great Men*, six times repeated . . . and lastly, GEORGE MASON's Right Hand in a Cutting-Box nineteen times—put them all together, and dish them up at pleasure. . . . These *words* . . . will bear being served, after being once used, a dozen times to the same table and palate." If we may take the "Receipt" as a rough guide to the objections of the Anti-Federalists, it would appear that class feeling was predominant, followed by alarm at the absence of a bill of rights.

On the other hand, it must be said that the Anti-Federalist attack was often led by individuals such as George Mason and Elbridge Gerry, who were every bit as aristocratic as the Federalists. In Virginia, Richard Henry Lee, a leader of the great Lee clan, placed himself at the head of the opposition, whereas his cousin, "Light-Horse" Harry Lee, the brilliant cavalry officer, fought for ratification. Richard Henry Lee, a delegate to the virtually defunct Confederation Congress, undertook to organize opposition there, his plan being to prevent Congress from sending the Constitution forward to the respective states for ratification. The New York delegates in Congress aided and abetted Lee's efforts. Madison, weary from his labors in Philadelphia, longed to return to his Virginia plantation, but he felt obliged to hurry on to New York, where Congress was sitting, to try to counteract his fellow Virginian.

Lee's strategy, adopted subsequently by most of the Anti-Federalists, was to concentrate his fire on the absence of a bill of rights and to make up a long list of amendments to the Constitution. He proposed, among other things, a "Privy Council" to check the powers of the president. On October 1 he wrote to George Mason: "Your prediction of what would happen in Congress was exactly verified. It was with us, as with you, this or nothing; and this urged with the most extreme intemperance. The greatness of the powers given, the multitude of places to be created produce a coalition of monarchy men, military men, aristocrats and drones whose noise, impudence and zeal exceeds all belief. . . . In this state of things the patriot voice is raised in vain for such changes and securities as reason and experience prove to be necessary against the encroachments of power upon the indispensable rights of human nature."

Patrick Henry, who had refused to be a delegate to the Philadelphia convention because of his attachment to the Articles of Confederation, helped Mason rally opposition to the Constitution in the Old Dominion. In Congress the Federalists could muster at least enough votes to send the Constitution to the states, but they were forced to send it without specific endorsement. They disguised this fact by declaring in their resolution that "Congress had voted *unanimously to transmit* . . . the resolves of the Convention," hoping that it would appear to the hasty reader that Congress had unanimously endorsed it.

One thing was clear enough. The small states were delighted with their bargain—equal representation in the Senate. Delaware's convention unanimously ratified the Constitution on December 7, the first state to do so. Pennsylvania, by no means a small state, followed suit on December 12 by a 2-to-1 margin. It was in his final speech to Pennsylvania's convention that James Wilson referred to the fact that by ratifying the Constitution the United States would "probably lay a foundation for erecting temples of liberty in every part of the earth." Many of its supporters believed with Wilson that "on the success of the struggle America has made for freedom, will depend the exertions of the brave and enlightened of other nations. . . . It will be subservient to the great designs of providence, with regard to this globe; the multiplication of mankind, their improvement in knowledge, and their advancement in happiness."

New Jersey ratified the Constitution unanimously on December 18. If democracy versus aristocracy was the real issue, one must assume there were few democrats in Delaware, Pennsylvania, and New Jersey.

The Federalists counted on the Carolinas, Georgia, and Connecticut to ratify without strong opposition. If Maryland, New Hampshire, and Vermont fell into line, the nine states needed to launch the Constitution would be complete. But Massachusetts, New York, and Virginia were all critically important states. If one of them remained outside, the Union would be seriously compromised. If all three refused to ratify, the prospects for the success of the new government would be dim indeed.

Attention focused first on Massachusetts. There the scars of Shays' Rebellion were still raw. The state was deeply and bitterly divided. Those sympathetic to the grievances of the rebels if not to their tactics were disposed to identify the Constitution with the faction they considered as their oppressor. Some members of the upper class, like Elbridge Gerry, were opposed to the Constitution on the grounds that it was too democratic and would give encouragement to the turbulent and unruly.

As we have noted, John Hancock had succeeded the conservative James Bowdoin as governor of the state. Although in bad health,

Hancock, who had the confidence of the "popular" party, was persuaded to preside over the ratifying convention and lend his reluctant support to the Constitution. Samuel Adams, another democratic hero, kept his peace and finally voted for the Constitution. Nathaniel Gorham and Rufus King, who had been delegates to the Philadelphia convention, carried the principal burden of defending the Constitution. It proved to be an extremely arduous task. The opposition concentrated its fire on biannual elections (old General Thompson kept crying out, "O my country, never give up your annual elections! young men, never give up your jewel!"), on the failure of the Constitution to outlaw slavery, and on the absence of a requirement that every public officeholder be a Christian. The *Boston Gazette*, taking up the Anti-Federal cause, proclaimed: "Bribery and Corruption!!!!" There was, it charged, "The most diabolical plan . . . on foot to corrupt the members of the Convention, who oppose the adoption of the new Constitution. . . . Large sums of money have been brought in from a neighboring state for that purpose, contributed by the wealthy."

As with the Federal debates, we have a record of the debates in the Massachusetts ratifying convention. A delegate from Plymouth County despaired of forming any proper government: "I think that the operation of paper money, and the practice of privateering, have produced a gradual decay of morals; introduced pride, ambition, envy, lust of power; produced a decay of patriotism, and the love of commutative justice; and I am apprehensive these are the invariable concomitants of luxury in which we are unblessedly involved, almost to our total destruction. . . . As people become more luxurious, they become more incapacitated for governing themselves."

Amos Singletary of Worcester County, in the heart of the region of Shays' Rebellion, demonstrated the class animus that lay behind much of the opposition to the Constitution. He was suspicious of "these fine lawyers, and men of learning, and moneyed men, that talk so finely, and gloss over matters so smoothly, to make us poor illiterate people swallow down the pill." In his opinion, these men were simply trying to create offices for themselves so that they might live off the taxes exacted from the people. "They expect to be the managers of this Constitution and get all the power and all the money into their own hands, and then they will swallow up all us little folks, like the great *Leviathan* . . . yes, just as the whale swallowed up Jonah."

Josiah Smith, also of Plymouth County, answered his colleague.

He wished to say a few words "to my brother ploughjoggers in this house. I have lived in a part of the country where I have known the worth of good government by the want of it. There was a black cloud that rose in the east last winter, and spread over the west [a reference to Shays' Rebellion]. . . . The cloud rose there, and burst upon us, and produced a dreadful effect. It brought on a state of anarchy, and that to tyranny. . . . People that used to live peaceably, and were before good neighbors, got distracted, and took up arms against government. . . . People I say took up arms; and then, if you want to speak to them, you had the musket of death presented to your breast. They would rob you of your property; threaten to burn your houses; oblige you to be on your guard night and day. . . . Our distress was so great we should have been content to snatch at any thing that looked like a government . . . even if it had been a monarch; and that monarch might have proved a tyrant;—so that you see anarchy leads to tyranny, and better have one tyrant than so many at once."

Smith ended with a rural metaphor: "Take things in time; gather fruit when it is ripe. There is a time to sow and a time to reap; we sowed our seed when we sent men to the federal Convention; now is the harvest, now is the time to reap the fruit of our labor; and if we don't do it now, I am afraid we shall never have another opportunity."

After weeks of debates, many of the delegates remained resolutely opposed to ratification. When a vote was finally taken, it was alarmingly close. The northern and western counties voted overwhelmingly against the Constitution; the seacoast counties, generally in its favor. Without the support of Suffolk and Essex counties (Boston and the heavily populated north coast), the Constitution would have been defeated. The final tally was 187 yeas and 168 nays. Ten votes decided the issue.

The ratification by Massachusetts was crucially important for several reasons. First, as we have said, it would have been difficult to have initiated a new government without the fourth most populous state, where a large part of the commercial activity of the country was concentrated. If Massachusetts had failed to ratify, it is almost certain that Virginia and New York would also have refused. As it was, word of the Massachusetts ratification reached Virginia at a time in that state's convention debates when the chances for ratification appeared slight.

The Virginia ratifying convention had already been in session for several weeks. The Virginia debates constituted a clash of titans.

Supporting the Constitution were Edmund Randolph (who had experienced a change of heart), John Marshall, Washington, and Madison. Opposing it were George Mason, Patrick Henry, and George Wythe, the revered leader of the Virginia bar and Thomas Jefferson's mentor at the College of William and Mary. Jefferson, the Congressional Commissioner in Paris, was one of the few Virginia luminaries absent from the convention.

Patrick Henry dominated the Anti-Federalist side of the question. Exhausting himself and his listeners with warnings of the horrors that awaited them if the Constitution were ratified, he may, in the end, have done his cause more harm than good through hyperbole and exaggeration. As with the Massachusetts debates, we have a remarkably complete record of the speeches of the delegates. It must be said that one exhausted scribe, after recording page upon page of Henry's oratorical flights, gave up and wrote, "Here Mr. Henry strongly and pathetically expatiated on the probability of the President's enslaving America, and the horrid consequences that must result." Jonathan Elliott's *Debates in the State Ratifying Conventions* includes 663 pages of the Virginia debates, and I suspect Patrick Henry's speeches account for at least a quarter of them. He was particularly indignant at the presumption of the drafters of the Constitution in prefacing the document with "We, the People . . ." rather than "We the States. . . ." Henry declared that "The people gave them no power to use their name. That they exceeded their power is perfectly clear."

Mason, rather oddly, directed his attack to the notion that a republican government such as that provided for by the Constitution, which he had played such a notable role in drafting, could govern a large territory. "Is it to be supposed that one national government will suit so extensive a country, embracing so many different climates, and containing inhabitants so very different in manners, habits and customs? . . . There never was government over a very extensive country without destroying the liberties of the people: history also, supported by the opinions of the best writers, shows us that monarchy may suit a large territory but that popular governments can only exist in small territories." One would have thought the idea might have presented itself to Mason somewhat earlier in the day. It was not clear what his solution was. Sovereign states?

It must be said in behalf of Henry that he spoke, much as Tom Paine had in *Common Sense*, for innocence and simplicity, important ingredients in the American dream and more especially in the

Secular-Democratic Consciousness. He reminded the delegates that "most of the human race" was presently groaning under tyrannical and oppressive governments and that "those nations who have gone in search of grandeur, power . . . and splendor, have also fallen a sacrifice, and been the victims of their own folly. While they have acquired those visionary blessings, they have lost their freedom." That power and freedom were uneasy companions was good Classical-Christian doctrine. Men like Paine and Henry and Jefferson put a quite different gloss on it. The Secular-Utopian spirit in America clung to the dream of innocence and nourished the suspicion of "consolidated" government—"the badge," as Paine had put it, "of lost innocence." Henry expressed the hope of the idyllic, uncorrupted land, the New Jerusalem populated by a redeemed, sanctified people, washed clean of sin, of greed, ambition, luxury, and power. "We are not feared by foreigners," Henry declared, "we do not make nations tremble. Would this . . . constitute happiness, or secure liberty? I trust . . . our political hemisphere will ever direct their operations to the security of those objects, liberty and happiness."

To Henry's dream was opposed Alexander Hamilton's reality. Almost as though answering Henry, Hamilton had declared: "It has been said that respectability in the eyes of foreign Nations was not the object at which we aimed; that the proper object of republican Government was domestic tranquility and happiness. This was an ideal [i.e., theoretical, not real] distinction. No Government could give us tranquillity and happiness at home, which did not possess sufficient stability and strength to make us respectable abroad."

Hamilton was contemptuous of the notion that war and pillage were the consequences of monarchy. "There have been, if I may so express it, about as many popular as royal wars. The cries of the nation and the importunities of their representatives have, upon various occasions, dragged their monarchs into war, or continued them in it, contrary to their inclination, and sometimes contrary to the real interests of the state." He posed a final question to his critics: "Have we not already seen enough of the fallacy and extravagance of those idle theories which have amused us with promises of an exemption from the imperfections, weaknesses, and evils, incident to society in every shape? Is it not time to awake from the deceitful dream of a golden age, and to adopt as a practical maxim for the direction of our political conduct that we, as well as the other inhabitants of the globe, are yet remote from the happy empire of perfect wisdom and perfect virtue?"

While Henry was, in the end, overborne, his dream of innocence would appear as a conspicuous, perhaps even dominant strain in the American consciousness.

Randolph replied to Henry in the Virginia convention by calling the Constitution "the rock of our salvation. . . . I believe that, as sure as there is a God in heaven, our safety, our political happiness and existence, depend on the union of the states; and that without this union, the people of this and the other states will undergo the unspeakable calamities which discord, faction, turbulence, war, and blood, have produced in other countries. . . . Let it not be recorded of Americans, that, after having overcome the most astonishing difficulties, and after having gained the admiration of the world by their incomparable valor and policy, they lost their acquired reputation, their national consequence and happiness by their own indiscretion. . . . Catch the present moment . . . for it may be lost, never to be regained!"

As the debates dragged on, covering the same ground time and again, the tempers of the delegates grew short, and bitter words were exchanged. The issue of slavery came up, as it had in the Federal Convention and in Massachusetts. Mason once more inveighed against the slave trade as "diabolical in itself, and disgraceful to mankind. . . . As much as I value the union of all the states, I would not admit the Southern States into the Union unless they agree to discontinuance of this disgraceful trade." Then, revealing the incurable schizophrenia of the South on the subject of slavery, this most enlightened of slaveowners went on to complain that the Constitution gave the South "no security for the property of that kind [black slaves] which we have already." Another Virginian, John Tyler, "warmly enlarged on the impolicy, [and] iniquity . . . of this wicked trade." And Henry, declaring that "it would rejoice my very soul that everyone of my fellowbeings was emancipated," added, "But is it practicable, by any means, to liberate them without producing the most dreadful and ruinous consequences?" Like Mason, he fretted over the possibility that Congress, under the general welfare clause of the Constitution, might "call for the abolition of slavery? May they not pronounce all slaves free . . . ? They have the power in clear unequivocal terms, and they will clearly and certainly exercise it."

There it was: the schizophrenia produced the paranoia. Even before the Constitution was ratified, three of the most liberal Southerners had made the malady explicit. Only the most traumatic treatment could effect a cure.

When the discussion passed on to the powers of the Supreme Court and the possible abuse of those powers, the opponents of the Constitution charged that the Court might even go so far as to call a state before it and render a judgment that would make a mockery of its sovereignty. John Marshall undertook to defend the Court. In the course of his argument, he reassured the delegates that "no state will be called to the bar of the federal court." Later, when Marshal became chief justice, the Court under his leadership did not hesitate to call states before it. Marshall, keenly aware of his statement in the Virginia convention, felt it hanging over him like a Sword of Damocles decade after decade.

Mason and Henry seemed to imply that if the Constitution were ratified they would resist it however they could. When Mason spoke of fearing "popular resistance to its operations . . . and the *dreadful effects* which must ensue, should the people resist," Henry Lee replied, "I respect the honorable gentleman and never believed I should live to hear opinions so injurious to our country, and so opposite to the dignity of this assembly." Was not Mason, by such threats or intimations, encouraging the very resistance he was deploring? "Such speeches, within these walls, from a character so venerable and estimable, easily progress into overt acts among the less thinking and the vicious." Henry replied with equal vehemence that if the amendments he recommended were not agreed to, "every movement and operation of government will cease; and how long that baneful thing, civil discord, will stay from this country, God alone knows. . . . The interval between this and bloodshed is but a moment."

But Henry proved a gracious loser. Undoubtedly aware that the Federalist leaders in the convention had made a careful tabulation of the ayes and the nays, he begged "pardon to this house for having taken up more time than came to my share. . . . If I shall be in the minority, I shall have those painful sensations which arise from a conviction of *being overpowered in a good cause.* Yet I will be a peaceable citizen. My head, my hand, and my heart shall be at liberty to retrieve the loss of liberty, and remove the defects of this system in a constitutional way. I wish not to go to violence. . . . I shall therefore patiently wait in expectation of seeing that government changed, so as to be compatible with the safety, liberty, and happiness of the people."

On the vote to ratify the Constitution, the ayes were 89, the nays 79—a difference of six votes. Word of the Massachusetts ratification, which came during the Virginia debates and was given much emphasis by the proponents of the Constitution, almost certainly provided the winning margin. New Hampshire had also ratified, though by a close vote. Virginia was thus the tenth state to ratify.

Attention now shifted to New York, a state that had been the object of an intense Federalist campaign to overcome the deep-seated opposition to the Constitution. The most notable weapon of the Federalists had been the so-called *Federalist Papers*, eighty-five essays written by John Jay, Hamilton, and Madison, and appearing initially in the *New York Independent Journal* between October, 1787, and April, 1788, and signed "Publius." The essays were almost as important as the Constitution itself. Because Madison and Hamilton had been delegates to the Federal Convention, the *Papers*, a detailed exegesis of the Constitution, at once took on a quasi-official character. In all arguments about the meaning or interpretation of that sometimes obscure document, they have been quoted by political scientists, judges, and lawyers as authoritative.

The first paper reiterated a now familiar theme. What was at issue was no less than the question of whether "societies of men are really capable or not of establishing good government from reflection and choice, or whether they are to be forever destined to depend for their political constitutions on accident and force. If there be any truth in the remark, the crisis at which we are arrived may with propriety be regarded as the era in which that decision is to be made; and a wrong election of the part we shall act may, in this view, deserve to be considered as the general misfortune of mankind." Again we see the notion that America had the opportunity to inaugurate a "new age" for humanity by giving a practical demonstration of the superiority of reason over force.

The *Papers* are, of course, a product of the same consciousness that created the Constitution and are remarkable for the brilliantly sustained intellectual power they reveal. The tenth paper, written by Madison, is perhaps the most famous; in it Madison expands the analysis of the relationship among the social forces in a society—religion, the various "interests" (agricultural, commercial, industrial)—and the political institutions necessary to create and preserve a degree of harmony and justice among those interests, which he had made in the convention itself.

It is impossible to determine how many minds *The Federalist Papers* may have changed in the state of New York (they were, of course, widely reprinted by other papers with Federalist sympathies in the various states). The political waters of New York were muddied by political rivalries that reached as far back as the late seventeenth century. In the present generation the Clintons and the Livingstons contended for control of the state. What the Livingstons were for the Clintons were against and vice versa. Since the anti-Clinton faction, in which Hamilton was a leader, supported the Constitution, it was almost a foregone conclusion that the Clinton party would oppose it.

At the beginning of the New York ratifying convention, which convened on June 17—nine days before the Virginia convention adjourned—the Anti-Federalists seemed to have a clear majority. Yates and Lansing, who had been delegates to the convention at Philadelphia, were both opposed to its ratification. Hamilton was its principal advocate. Interestingly enough, in New York, the most "aristocratic" of the Northern states, the specter of an aristocracy exploiting the Constitution to rivet chains upon the people was most frequently invoked. Robert Livingston, scion of one of the great families of New York, replied testily to a charge by Melancton Smith. He had always considered the cry of aristocracy to be "the bugbear of party." "We are told that, in every country, there is a natural aristocracy, and that this aristocracy consists of the rich and the great; nay, the gentleman goes further, and ranks in this class of men the wise, the learned, and those eminent for their talents or great virtue. Does a man possess the confidence of his fellow citizens for having done them important services? He is an *aristocrat*. Has he great integrity? Such a man will be greatly trusted: he is an *aristocrat*. Indeed, to determine that one is an aristocrat, we need only be assured that he is a man of merit. But I hope we have many such. I hope, sir, we are all aristocrats."

Smith, who had raised "the phantom of aristocracy," replied that Livingston was trying to make the argument appear ridiculous by carrying it to an extreme. He had meant to say only "that mankind were influenced, in a great degree, by interests and prejudices; that men in different ranks of life, were opposed to different temptations, and that ambition was more peculiarly the passion of the rich and great. . . . My argument was, that, in order to have a true and genuine representation, you must receive the middling class of people into your government. . . ."

The principal argument of the Federalists was that, with the ratification by Massachusetts and Virginia, New York would be left in the company of Vermont and Rhode Island, two states for which most

New Yorkers had only contempt. It was probably the growing awareness of the consequences of such isolation that finally swung the crucial votes to the side of ratification. After more than five weeks of debate during the course of which Hamilton, already in bad health, was often too exhausted to continue, the Federalists were able to count a majority of 2—31 to 29 in favor of ratification. Thus, in the three most important states—Massachusetts, Virginia, and New York—the Federalists marshaled a mere 31 votes more than the opponents of the Constitution. It is hard to see how the margin could have been much narrower.

Historians may speculate in vain about whether a majority of Americans in the various states favored the Constitution. Certainly in many instances delegates were elected to the various state conventions on the basis of whether they had declared themselves in favor of, or opposed to, the Constitution. It seems safe to assume, however, that a number of delegates to the state conventions were elected because their constitutents trusted their judgment in regard to a document too complex for most people to understand. The motives of those who supported or attacked the Constitution obviously varied from state to state and region to region. In Massachusetts everything was colored by Shays' Rebellion, so that one must believe that the vote on ratification there was a kind of plebiscite on the rebellion itself. When all that is said, there was a kind of psychological difference between the adherents and the enemies of the recently drafted document. Those Americans most sensitive to the currents of the so-called Enlightenment, those who believed in the natural goodness of man, in reason, science, and in a minimum of government were, except where other considerations (such as state size) were paramount, in the ranks of the opposition. They would soon denominate themselves Jeffersonian Democrats or Republicans. Those who favored the Constitution were, by and large, those who believed in the "natural badness" of man as opposed to the natural goodness, who believed that all men and women were tainted by the original sin of Adam. They believed in reason and revelation (paired); in the accumulated experience of the race (called history); in the necessity of government as arising out a human greed and "self-aggrandizement," the general human impulse to profit at the expense of others.

The narrowness of the victory of the Constitution cannot, of course, be attributed solely to this division. As we have seen, many factors entered it. But the fact is that the Secular-Democratic tide was rising so rapidly that it would soon become the new orthodoxy and almost wholly inundate the older ethos. Thus, it seems safe to say that the Constitution was accomplished at the last possible moment. Even a year or two later it would have been far more difficult to frame such a government and virtually impossible to have secured its acceptance by the states. First, the processes of disintegration working between state and state, the reciprocal rivalries and jealousies we have already described, would undoubtedly have advanced too far. The South's paranoia about slavery would have been more feverish and Secular-Democratic Consciousness too dominant.

It is not surprising that proponents of the Constitution, considering the odds against it and the hair-raisingly narrow margin by which it was finally adopted, believed that its ratification had been the will of the Almighty. What is almost as astonishing as the fact that it was done at all was the fact that as soon as it had been ratified, far from being the occasion of riots and civil tumults, it became an object of universal veneration. It acquired a magical or quasi-religious character comparable to that accorded by the Children of Israel to the tablets of the Law that Moses brought down from Sinai. Indeed, the analogy was widely remarked. Not only that, the interpretation of the Constitution became the primary preoccupation of the best legal minds in the land for some three quarters of a century. To call the Constitution a sacred document is to overstate the case only slightly. Scripture tells us, "In the beginning was the Word." That was the Genesis. So it was in the United States. Here, too, in the beginning was the Word and the Word was the Constitution. The critical question was how that Word would become flesh, how it would be enacted in history. As it turned out, that question was almost unfathomably complex. The nation could not become a nation in any fundamental sense until that question had been resolved, at least in some reasonable degree. The nation could not, one might say, really *start*. To be sure, it had certain similarities to a nation. People spoke confidently of "the Union," a kind of mystical entity, and the Constitution plainly worked very well on certain practical levels. But roughly one half of the nation could not agree with the other half about what the words in the Constitution really meant. It turned out that reason could not, as the Founders had so devoutly hoped, settle the matter. Ultimately, like so many other knotty problems in history, it had to be settled by force.

6

The Grand Procession

In Philadelphia, when word came that the crucial state of Virginia had ratified on June 26, immeasurably brightening the prospects for the new government, it was decided to combine the celebration of the passage of the Declaration of Independence on July 4 with a celebration of the new Constitution. There must be a splendid parade—a Grand Procession with a series of floats symbolizing the new Union soon to be given practical effect. Francis Hopkinson, poet, essayist, and civic leader, was appointed marshal, and the collective energies of the city were mustered to make the occasion a smashing success. The carpenters, wheelwrights, cabinetmakers and ship joiners were recruited to build floats, aided by ordinary citizens handy with a hammer and saw. An ecstatic Benjamin Rush wrote to Elias Boudinot, one of the presidents of Congress during the Revolution, that the procession "was not to celebrate a victory obtained in blood over any part of our fellow creatures. No city reduced to ashes—no army conquered by capitulation—no news of slaughtered thousands brought the citizens of Philadelphia together. It was to celebrate a triumph of knowledge over ignorance, of virtue over vice, of liberty over slavery. It was to celebrate the birth of a free government, the objects of which were to lessen the number of widows and orphans by preventing the effusion of human blood, to save human nature from the disgraces and desolations of war, and to establish and extend the blessings of peace through the continent of America."

The morning of the Fourth the whole city hummed with excitement. The procession began to form at eight o'clock in the morning as the bells of Christ Church pealed out. In the harbor, the ship *Rising Sun,* rechristened to commemorate Dr. Franklin's already famous comment at the signing of the Constitution and decorated with the flags of friendly nations, fired a cannon salute. Ten vessels, in honor of the ten states that had ratified the Constitution, were anchored the length of the harbor, each flying a white flag with the name of a ratifying state in gold letters.

The superintendents of the parade, with white plumes in their hats, hurried about assigning the floats and marchers their proper places. By nine-thirty the procession had begun to move down Third Street. Certain prominent patriots led the way carrying a sign identifying them as the Declaration of Independence. After them came Thomas Fitzsimmons, "an enlightened merchant and able politician," in Rush's words, riding General Rochambeau's old horse decorated with three fleur-de-lis and thirteen stars representing the French Alliance of 1778, and behind him came one of the prominent lawyers of the city, bearing a staff adorned with olive and laurel and the insignia "The Definitive Treaty of Peace."

The chief justice of the state supreme court, Thomas McKean, was next, mounted on "a lofty ornamented car" in the form of a large eagle, drawn by six horses. He supported a pole surmounted with the cap of liberty. Below the cap was a framed copy of the Constitution and on the shaft were the words "THE PEOPLE." The carriage was twenty feet long; the eagle itself was thirteen feet high and thirteen feet long, with a shield on its breast emblazoned with thirteen stars and thirteen alternate red and white stripes.

Behind the eagle came ten men representing the ten states that had ratified. Each bore a flag with the name of the state in gold letters, their arms linked to symbolize unity.

Next came a handsomely decorated cart carrying the consuls and representatives of friendly nations, each holding his nation's flag—France, Sweden, Prussia, the United Netherlands, and Morocco—certainly an odd bag.

After them came one of the most conspicuous floats of the procession—"The New Roof of the Grand Federal Edifice." The New Roof had been erected on a carriage drawn by ten white horses.

Supporting the roof were thirteen Corinthian columns, three of them unfinished. Above the round dome the figure of Plenty bore her inexhaustible cornucopia. The whole rose to the awesome height of thirty-six feet. Around the base were inscribed the words "In Union the Fabric stands firm."

The builders of this magnificent structure, the carpenters of the city, marched behind it, followed by some 450 apprentices. The sawmakers and file cutters were next. Behind them came the Agricultural Society; the Society of the Cincinnati; veterans of the Revolution; and a group of farmers with hoes, shovels, and forks on their shoulders.

The Society for the Encouragement of Manufacturers followed the farmers with three floats demonstrating the processes of spinning and weaving. A carding machine on the leading float was worked by two people who turned raw cotton into thread with bewildering speed. Another float carried a spinning machine with eighty spindles worked by a single woman. A lace loom followed and, finally, Mr. and Mrs. Hewson and their pretty daughters, printing gay patterns on chintz and calico and attired in becoming dresses of their own manufacture. On a staff at the rear of the Hewsons' wagon flew a flag with the words "May the Union Government protect the Manufacturers of America."

Then came the Light Infantry and eighty-nine members of the Marine Society, carrying spyglasses, sextants, charts, and various other nautical items.

After the amateur sailors came the federal ship *Union*, thirty-three feet long with a crew of twenty-five. Twenty small cannon were mounted at the miniature gunports, and ten horses drew the landgoing ship, which, perfect in every detail, had been built in only eight days. The sails were trimmed along the line of march in response to orders from the bridge, and around the waterline, covering the wheels, was tacked a broad sheet of canvas painted to represent the sea, "so, that nothing incongruous appeared to offend the eye." Following the *Union* came the pilots, shipwrights, joiners, sailmakers, and all those who plied any of the naval trades.

Next in the procession were the trades and professions, the brickmakers and glazers, the cordwainers and coach painters, all in neat frocks with the tools of their trade in their hands. The cabinetmakers had a large horse-drawn platform on which a master carpenter and his apprentice worked at their trade. Even the apprentices had their place, marching six abreast in leather aprons with bucktails in their hats. The painters carried gilded brushes and golden hammers. The bricklayers, with their aprons and trowels, carried a large banner depicting a federal city rising out of a forest with the rays of the setting sun illuminating it. It bore the inscription "Both Buildings and Rulers are the Works of our Hands"—a notably democratic sentiment.

On and on it went: the victualers, the food suppliers of the city, with their motto "The death of Anarchy and Confusion shall feed the poor and Hungry"; the bookbinders, the printers, saddlers, distillers, candlemakers, wheelwrights, coopers, blacksmiths, tanners, engravers, watchmakers, brushmakers—a living inventory of the crafts and skills of the greatest city in America, a metropolis with a population of nearly twenty-five thousand.

Lawyers, doctors, and ministers marched likewise. Leading the clergymen were a Presbyterian minister, a "Rabbi of the Jews," and a Congregational minister, their arms linked to symbolize the close relationship of Judaism and Christianity.

Most striking of all was the silence in which the Grand Procession moved past the crowds of spectators. Scaffolds had been erected at vantage points, and these were dangerously packed. The "foot-ways," the windows, even the rooftops and fences were lined with spectators. But aside from the excited cries of small children at the sight of a father or brother, or some spectacle of special splendor, the procession moved almost in silence, so that the principal sound was the scraping of rough shoes on stone, the clatter of the ironshod wheels of the carriages, and the lively music of a band. As the marchers moved along there were frequent halts. The front of the column moved too fast at first, and then, as it suddenly slowed, the rear ran, accordionlike, against it. Even the breakdown of a carriage was given a symbolic significance: it represented "the obstructions and difficulties the Constitution had met with in its establishment from the arts of bad and the ignorance of weak men."

Benjamin Rush tried to describe for his friend, Elias Boudinot, the emotions raised in patriotic breasts by the marvelous scene. "Never upon any occasion during the late war," he wrote, "did I see such deep-seated joy in every countenance." Foreign spectators declared themselves astonished and impressed, "and many of them who have seen the splendid processions of coronations in Europe declare that they all yield in the effect of pleasure to our hasty exhibition instituted in honor of our Federal Government." All the triumphs and tribulations of the Revolutionary conflict rose up with overwhelming force "to produce such a tide of joy as has seldom been felt in any age or country. Political joy is one of the strongest emotions of the human mind. Think then, my friend, from the objects of it which have been mentioned, how powerful must have been its action upon the mind on this occasion." Every predilection and every disposition was appealed to. "The patriot enjoyed a complete triumph, whether the objects of his patriotism were the security of liberty, the establishment of law, the protection of manufacturers, or the extension of science in his country. The benevolent man saw a precedent established for forming free governments in every part of the world. The man of humanity contemplated the end of the distresses of his fellow citizens in the revival of commerce and agriculture. Even the selfish passions were not idle. The ambitious man beheld with pleasure the honors that were to be disposed of by the new government, and the man of wealth realized once more the safety of his bonds and rents against the inroads of paper money and tender laws. Every person felt one of these passions, many more than one, and some all of them during the procession. . . . Even the *senses* partook of the entertainment, for the variety of colors displayed in the various ornaments of the machines and flags and in the dresses of the citizens, together with an excellent band of music, at once charmed the eyes and ears of the spectators and thereby introduced the body to partake, in a certain degree, of the feast of the mind. . . . It forced open every heart, insomuch that many people provided cooling liquors with which they regaled their fellow citizens as they walked in the procession. . . . Rank for a while forgot all its claims, and Agriculture, Commerce, and Manufactures, together with the learned and mechanical Professions, seemed to acknowledge by their harmony and respect for each other that they were necessary to each other and all useful in cultivated society."

Rush went on to rhapsodize about the symbolism of all those harmonies represented in the procession: "This mixture of the mechanical and learned professions [carpenters and lawyers, for example] in a public exhibition is calculated to render trades of all kinds respectable in our country. . . . It would seem as if heaven stamped a peculiar value upon agriculture and mechanical arts in America by selecting WASHINGTON and FRANKLIN to be two of the principal agents in the later Revolution."

The marchers gathered at Bush Hill for a picnic lunch, or "cold collation," washed down with "American porter, American beer and American cider," as the newspapers reported, and there heard an address by James Wilson that played upon many of the themes in Rush's letter. The Constitution had been drafted and then it had been "laid before the people. It was discussed . . . in the freest, fullest and severest manner—by speaking, by writing and by printing—by individuals and by public bodies—by its friends and by its enemies . . . [and then adopted]. Only in Liberty will a nation flourish . . . the industrious village, the busy city, the crowded port—these are the gift of Liberty; and without good government Liberty cannot exist."

Even before Wilson's speech was over the ships in the harbor began to fire a cannon salute, and when he had finished, the Light Infantry companies on a nearby hill fired three volleys. The picnic was interrupted periodically for patriotic toasts announced by a trumpet blast and concluded by a round of artillery. The thirteen toasts began with "the People of the United States" and ended with "the Whole Family of Mankind."

That night the *Rising Sun* was illuminated as it rode in the harbor, and nature completed her cooperation (the day had been unseasonably mild) by festooning the evening sky with an aurora borealis. Small wonder that Rush was moved to observe that "in the course of the formation and establishment of this government there were ample signs of heaven having favored the federal side of the question. The union of twelve states in the *form*, and of ten states in the *adoption*, of the Constitution in less than ten months, under the influence of local prejudices, opposite interests, popular arts, and even the threat of bold and desperate men, is a solitary event in the history of mankind. I do not believe that the Constitution was the offspring of inspiration, but I am perfectly satisfied that the Union of the States, in its *form* and *adoption*, is as much the work of Divine Providence as any of the miracles recorded in the Old and New Testament were the effects of a divine power." The sentence suggests the general euphoria induced in the citizens of Philadelphia by the Grand Procession.

To Rush, and doubtless to most of those who participated in or witnessed the Grand Procession, it had, in some magical way, created or verified the new government. What before had seemed dim and unsubstantial was now visible. The procession had *enacted* the Constitution, amalgamated it with the deepest levels of common memory—the Declaration of Independence and the Revolution. At the close of his letter to Boudinot Rush wrote: "Tis done. We have become a nation. [Order and justice had] descended from heaven to dwell in our land, and ample restitution has at last been made to human nature by our new Constitution for all the injuries she has sustained in the old world from arbitrary government, false religions, and unlawful commerce." The time of the redemption of humanity was at hand; the instrument of that redemption was the new federal Constitution.

It might also be noted that Rush was America's most prominent temperance advocate. It seemed to him an odd and discomforting anomaly that the citizens of this blessed and enlightened land should be excessively addicted to "spirituous liquors," primarily grain alcohol and West Indian rum. Indeed, drunkenness had been from earliest colonial times the besetting sin of Americans. Rush thus could not forbear to boast to Boudinot that on the day of the Grand Procession, "out of seventeen thousand people who appeared on the green and partook of collation, there was scarcely one person intoxicated. All was order, all was harmony and joy." This, in Rush's opinion, was due primarily to the fact that spirituous liquors were banned and only beer and cider were permitted. (He later felt obliged to add a postscript noting his discovery that "two or three persons" had been intoxicated and that "several quarrels" had taken place.)

Optimistic as Rush was, he was not disposed to venture beyond the hope "that our republican forms of government will be more safe and durable than formerly. . . . A hundred years hence, absolute monarchy will probably be rendered necessary in our country by the corruption of our people." Arguing against John Adams's preference for political and social forms associated with monarchical governments, Rush pointed out, as a clinching point, that "Republican forms of government are more calculated to promote Christianity than monarchies. The precepts of the Gospel and the maxims of republics in many instances agree with each other."

Finally, we might note another aspect of the Grand Procession that revealed what was perhaps the most distinguishing characteristic of the new age. This was the astonishing fact that it had all been put together in eight days. More closely examined, this meant that all the resources of the city had been instantly mobilized by appealing to the talents and energies of the citizens as a whole. All the identifiable groups—trades, professions, societies—were self-activating, so to speak. The Grand Procession was thus a demonstration and a forecast of the way in which, in this new society, human energies could be utilized for almost any desired private or public purpose. People of various classes or occupations could come together, with a minimum of the preliminaries or frictions that distinguished more traditional societies, to accomplish a particular task, do it usually with skill and dispatch, and return as readily to their normal occupations.

The counterpart to this "social spontaneity" was an impulse of Americans, which we shall find evidence of throughout this work, to "associate," to form protective or philanthropic societies in which fraternal and ritual forms were highly important. It seems clear that this tendency, which is so marked in present-day American society, was, from the beginning of the Republic, a form of compensation for the fact that we had few if any identifiable marks or distinctions (outside, perhaps, regional peculiarities of speech) to place us in a particular group or clan or class. Americans have thus suffered as well as profited from being "free-floating," generally unattached to some reassuring social rock. Hence our disposition to drift together— Masons (virtually every American president prior to Dwight Eisenhower was a Mason), Elks, Lions, Moose, and so on.

Philadelphia was already rich in such associations, from the Hand-in-Hand Fire Company to the American Philosophical Society to be Held in Philadelphia for Promoting Useful Knowledge; the Hibernian Society (for those of Irish origin); the St. Andrews Society (for Scottish immigrants); and the aforementioned Society for the Promotion of Manufacturers, which of course had its counterpart in an Agricultural Society. There were, in addition, a bar association, a medical association, and a chamber of commerce to advance the interests of the business community.

In any event, the Grand Procession (which had its counterparts in Boston and New York) was a moment of hope and innocence, profoundly and uniquely American, thoroughly captivating in its naivete, the primal ritual of the new Secular-Democratic Consciousness celebrating the ultimate achievement of the Classical-Christian Consciousness. All that was dark and unharmonious, all strife and ambiguity, all clouds and shadows were banished. I suspect that a people cannot survive or a nation preserve its health and sanity without such dramatic representations of what they conceive themselves to stand for at their best. Art is, among other things, catharsis. But does the drama have to include the ambiguity? Is that perhaps its most basic function? To reconcile its audience to truths often too painful to hold in the consciousness—the ironies and tragic paradoxes of history?

We turn reluctantly from the Grand Procession, convinced that it provides us with important clues to all that follows.

7

The Nation Begins

Following the ratifications of New Hampshire and New York, Congress designated the first Wednesday in January, 1789, as the date for choosing the presidential electors, the first Wednesday in February for them to meet and cast their ballots, and the first Wednesday in March for the new House of Representatives and Senate to convene. The question of where the new government should be established proved to be a bone of contention immediately. Trenton, Baltimore, Philadelphia, and Princeton each had its advocates. Since Congress had been meeting in New York, that city became the capital more by default than intention.

The balloting for senators and representatives went smoothly enough in every state except New York. There the assembly was Anti-Federalist and the senate Federalist. Neither branch would yield to the other on the procedure to be followed in selecting congressmen, senators or presidential electors. In consequence, New York neither voted for president nor sent a senator to the first session of the First Congress.

In those states where presidential electors were chosen by popular vote, the Federalist candidates' announcement that they would vote for Washington as president was enough to assure their election. Although it was never specifically stated, the assumption that Washington would be president undoubtedly underlay all the discussions in the Federal Convention about the nature of the office of president. By the same token, the delegates to the state ratifying conventions assumed that the first president could be no other than Washington. Since the powers granted to the president under the Constitution constituted one of the principal sources of Anti-Federalist opposition and were a matter of concern even to many who supported the Constitution, it seems safe to say that without the widespread conviction that Washington would be the first president the Constitution would never have been ratified.

Pierce Butler, delegate to the Federal Convention from South Carolina, wrote later that the powers granted to the president would have not "been so great had not many of the members cast their eyes toward General Washington as President; and shaped their Ideas of the Powers to be given to a President, by their opinions of his Virtue." David Humphreys of Connecticut, one of Washington's staff officers during the Revolution, wrote to the general, "What will tend, perhaps more than anything to the adoption of the new system will be an universal opinion of your being elected President of the United States and an expectation that you will accept it for a while." Lafayette wrote from Paris, "You cannot refuse being elected President." Yet Washington had demurred. He considered himself to be too old (he was fifty-six) and in poor health. He complained that his hearing was failing and that his plantation, so long neglected, needed all his care.

But the pressure had mounted through all the months following the drafting of the Constitution. A favorite Fourth of July toast in the summer of 1788 saluted "Farmer Washington—may he like a second Cincinnatus, be called from the plow to rule a great people," and predicted that "Great Washington shall rule the land / While Franklin's counsel aids his hand."

Jefferson and Hamilton took the lead in trying to overcome Washington's "vast reluctance" to take on the burdens of the presidency. One of Washington's concerns was that he would be caught in the bitter controversy between Federalists and Anti-Federalists. Would it not be the case, he asked Hamilton, that the adversaries of the Constitution would concentrate their fire on him? "Their plan of opposition [to the new government] is systemized," he wrote, "and a regular intercourse, I have much reason to believe between the Leaders of it in the several States, is formed to render it more effectual."

We must, I think, give principal credit to Hamilton for overcoming Washington's misgivings. The ties of personal attachment were especially strong between the two men. Washington felt a fatherly affection for the younger man and trusted his judgment implicitly. Hamilton replied patiently to each of the general's objections. In August, at the conclusion of the New York ratifying convention, Hamilton had written, "I take it for granted, Sir, you have concluded to comply with what will no doubt be the general call of your country in relation to the new government. You will permit me to say that it is indispensable that you should lend yourself to its first operations—It is to little purpose to have *introduced* a system, if the weightiest influence is not given to its firm *establishment* in the outset."

Washington continued to resist and Hamilton to court him. Even after the electors had cast their ballots and it was widely though unofficially known that Washington had been the overwhelming if not unanimous choice, he refused to say plainly that he would accept the office, although his failure to say no was assumed by his countrymen to constitute consent.

The real question was who should be vice-president. John Adams was the name most frequently mentioned. If a Virginian were to be president, it seemed appropriate, especially to New Englanders, that someone from that region be vice-president, and no one was more eligible than Adams. Adams himself, just back from ten years abroad, first as a Congressional Commissioner and a member of the team that negotiated the Treaty of Paris ending the Revolution, and then as the first American ambassador at the Court of St. James's, took a dim view of his prospects. He wrote his daughter that he did "not stand very high in the esteem, admiration, or respect of his country, or any part of it." This was typical of Adams's self pity. He had made himself somewhat of a controversial figure by writing *A Defence of the Constitutions of Government of the United States of America*. These volumes were, to a large degree, an expansion of his earlier *Thoughts on Government*, which had considerable influence on the formation of several of the state constitutions. The *Defence* reviewed the state constitutions and, not surprisingly, defended them to the degree that they conformed to Adams's own constitutional theories. His arguments were substantially those of the delegates to the Federal Convention. He placed particular emphasis, for example, on combining elements of monarchy (the chief executive), aristocracy (the Senate), and democracy (the popular branch); and on the separation of the executive, legislative, and judicial branches of the government.

So much was unexceptional, but Adams had the temerity to attack the notion that people were "born equal." That they were equal before the law and in the eyes of God he would not deny, but that they were equal in talents or capacities he could not concede. Mankind was manifestly unequal in size, beauty, talents, fortune. "These sources of inequality which are common to every people can never be altered by any because they are founded in the constitution of nature; this natural aristocracy among mankind . . . is a fact essential to be considered in the institution of government."

In the ten years that Adams had been out of the country, there had been a substantial change in the consciousness of Americans, a marked shift to the dogma of equality—a dogma that held, in its simplest terms, that one man was as good as another. Thus, Adams's qualifications of the notion of equality grated on the ears of many of his countrymen. He made two other errors. He praised the British constitution and expressed it as his opinion that the Confederation Congress was "in every way adequate to the management of all . . . Federal concerns." It was a mistake to judge it by the criteria that Adams had established for a good constitution. Congress was "not a legislative assembly or a representative assembly, but only a diplomatic assembly like the States-General of the Netherlands, a group of states meeting to resolve certain problems dealing with international affairs, problems of trade and commerce, of debts and foreign treaties."

It is interesting to note that when Adams sent a copy of his *Defence* to Jefferson, the latter's principal criticism was directed to Adams's defense of the Confederation. The Virginian argued that it exercised both legislative and executive functions and was thus subject to the shortcomings "of all simple, unicameral bodies where the three powers of government were lodged in one branch."

In any event, the *Defence* was attacked in democratic quarters for "a squinting toward monarchy" and was suspected in Federalist circles for its endorsement of the Confederation. Nonetheless, Adams appeared as the strongest candidate for vice-president on the basis of his services to his country and the region of the country he represented. Benjamin Rush, writing to welcome him back to the United States, praised the *Defence* extravagantly and promised that Pennsylvania would certainly support him for the vice-presidency if he, in turn, would commit himself to back Philadelphia as the new seat of government. "This," Rush added, "must be the compensation for their placing a citizen of Virginia in the President's chair and a citizen of

New England in the chair of the senate" (a reference to the fact that the vice-president was to preside over that body).

Adams had an important, if largely passive, enemy in James Madison, who noted that he had "made himself obnoxious to many, particularly in the southern states, by the political principles avowed in his book. Others, recollecting his cabal during the war against General Washington, knowing his extravagant self-importance, and considering his preference of an unprofitable dignity [the vice-presidency] to some place of emolument . . . as proof of his having an eye to the presidency, conclude that he would not be a very cordial second to the General, and that an impatient ambition might even intrigue for a premature advancement."

But Adams's most serious adversary was Alexander Hamilton. Although both men shared an admiration for the British consitution, they could not have been more different in character. Hamilton was small, vain, dapper, brilliant, devious, a born intriguer and political boss, a friend of business and commercial enterprise; Adams was stout, introspective, reserved, scrupulous in his personal and political dealings, much older than the New Yorker, and had a farmer's suspicion of banks and "money-men." It is not clear to this day why Hamilton set himself to block Adams's election as vice-president, or at least to compromise it by deflecting votes to other candidates who in fact had no chance to win. His maneuvers against Adams were conducted under the cover of a desire to be sure there was not a tie between Washington and Adams in the electoral college voting. Since the Constitution provided that the candidate with the largest number of votes be president and the runner-up vice-president, it might have turned out that while it was evident to everyone that the electors clearly intended Washington to be president and Adams vice-president, a tie vote would throw the election into the House of Representatives and thereby create some embarrassment. The remedy, Hamilton argued, was for the electors from some states to throw a vote or two away from Adams to some other candidate, thus assuring Washington of a majority. Well and good. But Hamilton undertook to make this proposal to the electors of four or five states, apparently hoping to deprive Adams of enough votes, if not to defeat him (since he had no serious rival), at least to tarnish his victory. The only motive that can be ascribed to Hamilton is that of ambition. Although ineligible for election to the presidency as a consequence of having been born in the West Indies, Hamilton intended to dominate the Federalist party and was jealous of any possible rival. It thus seemed expedient to him to do what he could to whittle away Adams's prestige.

Adams was subsequently informed of Hamilton's "plot" against him, and it marked the beginning of a hostility between the two men that had profound consequences for the Federalist party. (Adams referred to Hamilton as "the bastard brat of a Scottish peddler" and as "a proud-spirited, aspiring mortal, always pretending to morality, with as debauched morals as old Franklin.") In any event, Hamilton's intrigues were successful. When the votes of the electoral college were counted, Washington had 69 and Adams 34. Not yet informed of Hamilton's campaign against him, Adams was indignant. "Is not my election to this office, in the scurvy manner in which it was done, a curse rather than a blessing?" he asked Rush. "Is this justice? Is there common sense or decency in this business?" He seriously considered resigning but was dissuaded by his friends on the grounds that such an act would cast a shadow over the beginning of the new government.

March 4, 1789, was the day appointed by the Confederation Congress for the inauguration of the new government. Congress had been meeting in a room in the New York City Hall. Larger and more extensive chambers were required for the "National Legislature," but there were no federal funds to provide them. A group of merchants, doubtless anxious to do all they could to insure that the new capital would remain in New York, raised $32,500 and commissioned Major Pierre L'Enfant, who had designed the insignia of the Society of the Cincinnati, to rehabilitate City Hall, which was renamed Federal Hall. On March 4 carpenters and plasterers were still at work. The night before, at sunset, cannon on the Battery saluted the expiring Confederation with a volley, and on the fourth the bells of all the churches in the city pealed throughout the day to mark the beginning of the new government. Unfortunately, only eight senators and thirteen representatives were present. The Anti-Federalists took heart. Perhaps the Constitution would die aborning.

After all the rhetoric, all the extravagant hopes, the colorful parades and celebrations, it was disconcerting to see day after day pass without a quorum. Those legislators who had arrived wondered if they should return home. The *New York Packet* reported at the end of March that uncertainty about whether there would be any government at all had seriously discouraged business. Finally, on March 30, thirty representatives (out of fifty-nine) were counted, a bare quorum, and the House convened in Federal Hall. The Senate was still without a quorum, and it was another week before that body was able to begin its proceedings. The first official act of the two branches was to open and read the ballots of the electoral college. Messengers were dispatched to officially inform Washington and Adams of their election, and the House at once turned its attention to measures designed to limit the importation of British luxuries into the United States.

Adams arrived in New York a few days after he received official word of his election. He was greeted by "a great number of members of Congress . . . and private citizens" in carriages and on horseback and escorted to the home of John Jay, where he received a stream of visitors, many of them old friends from early days of the Continental Congress. The next day he was conducted to the Senate to be sworn in as vice-president. John Langdon, president of the Senate *pro tempore*, met him at the door of the chamber and extended the formal greeting of that body: "Sir, I have it in charge from the Senate to introduce you on your appointment to the office of Vice-President of the United States of America."

Apologizing in advance for whatever might be his shortcomings as a presiding officer, Adams begged the indulgence of his colleagues. Perhaps having in mind his reputation for contentiousness and obduracy, he assured them in his first address that he would do his best "to behave towards every member . . . with all that consideration, delicacy, and decorum which becomes the dignity [of his office]. A trust of the greatest magnitude is committed to this legislature, and the eyes of the world are upon you. May God Almighty's providence assist you to answer their just expectations."

Adams's "delicacy and decorum" were soon to be sorely tried by one of the senators who stood outside the circle of Revolutionary veterans. William Maclay was a Pennsylvania senator; a "new man"; an Anti-Federalist representing the western part of the state and "the democracy," those Pennsylvanians who viewed the Eastern Establishment with considerable suspicion. Maclay, a large, rough bear of a man, rapidly became John Adams's nemesis. To him the new Constitution was "the vilest of all traps that ever was set to ensnare the freedom of an unsuspecting people."

Adams's immediate concern was with setting the proper protocol in addressing various officers of the new administration and in sending and receiving messages from the House of Representatives. His study of government had convinced him that such matters were of great importance. He believed that in order to be effective, a government must have the respect and loyalty of the people. It must therefore have an air of dignity and order. Appropriate forms must be established. Thus, the secretary of the Senate, when taking bills to the House, should bow twice on entering the chamber, again on delivering it to the Speaker, and twice more on withdrawing. Such rigamarole seemed absurd to Maclay and, as it turned out, to the House as well, which rejected it. When Adams proposed that the Speaker of the House be addressed as "Honorable," Maclay led the successful opposition and noted in his journal, "From this omen, I think our President [Adams] may go and dream about titles, for he will get none." Several days later Maclay wrote contemptuously: "Attended the House, ceremonies, endless ceremonies, the whole business of the day. . . . Sorry I am to say it but no people in the Union dwell more on trivial distinctions and matters of mere form [than the New Englanders]. They really seem to show a readiness to stand on punctilio and ceremony."

Washington left Mount Vernon on April 16 and traveled north through Baltimore and Philadelphia. The inhabitants of every town on his route turned out to welcome him and express their devotion. At Philadelphia two triumphal arches had been constructed at the south entrance to the city. As Washington rode under them a laurel wreath "was let fall upon his head" (just how that was accomplished is not at all clear). The city's mounted militia met him and conducted him to the home of Governor Thomas Mifflin, who had been one of his aides during the war. Crowds packed the streets and the church bells rang. There were fireworks, a profusion of flags and bunting, and a splendid feast at the City Tavern. The next day, proceeding on to Trenton, the general passed through another triumphal arch erected by the women of the city in the form of a Federal dome supported by thirteen columns and adorned by a giant sunflower with the cryptic words "To thee alone." On the other side of the arch a company of women, young and old, sang songs and scattered flowers on the road as Washington approached.

On April 23 the general reached Elizabethtown, where a large barge awaited him. It was manned by thirteen master pilots in white uniforms and carried Governor George Clinton, leader of the New York Anti-Federalists, and committees of both houses of Congress. Warships in the river fired volleys as the barge cast off, propelled by "a propitious gale," and one passenger noted that "the very water seemed to rejoice in bearing the precious burden over its placid bosom."

The East River was filled with colorfully decorated boats come out to welcome the hero. They fell in behind the official barge, forming a brilliant aquatic procession, and off Bedloe's Island a sloop came upon the starboard bow and twenty ladies and gentlemen sang "an elegant ode prepared for the purpose, to the tune of 'God Save the King.'" After them another boat swung alongside, and an ode to Washington was sung in parts by a male choir. The New York shoreline was packed with people as far as the eye could see.

As on the occasion of the Grand Procession in Philadelphia, when nature had festooned the sky with a dazzling aurora borealis, the elements were now equally complaisant. The breeze, the sun, the waters, and even the fish conspired to enhance the great event: Elias Bourdinot noted the porpoises, "playing amongst us as if they had risen up to know the cause of all this happiness."

The barge approached the Spanish warship *Galveston*, anchored in the river, which, it had been noted with disapproval, displayed no flags or bunting. But as the presidential vessel drew abreast, the *Galveston*'s captain gave a command and she ran up twenty-eight flags of different nations and fired a thirteen-gun salute.

The barge was to land at Murray's Wharf, where a number of Washington's former officers were gathered as part of the reception committee. The steps were covered with crimson carpeting and the rails hung with crimson cloth. As Washington stepped from the barge, volleys of cannon fire, cheers of the waiting crowds, and the music of bands greeted him in a great diapason of joy and love. It was an ecstatic moment! The hero of the Revolution was transmuted into the reluctant leader of the politically re-formed nation. Six years earlier Washington had taken leave of his officers at Fraunces Tavern in an emotional scene. Now he was back, the father had come back to his children, and it seemed to many that day that no harm could come to a people under his care.

The general's guard had difficulty forcing a path through the crowd to the line of parade where the procession had formed to escort Washington to the presidential mansion, most appropriately in Franklin Square. Every window and walkway was jammed with spectators. Newspaper editor John Fenno heard old people remark that they could now die contented; "they had clung to life for no other purpose than to get a glimpse of the savior of their country."

April 30 was the day set for Washington's inauguration. The Senate assembled at ten o'clock to receive him. Adams took advantage of the interval before his arrival to ask for the "direction of the Senate" on how to address the president. "How shall I behave? . . . Shall I be standing or sitting?" Richard Henry Lee, in reply, began, as Maclay noted, "with the House of Commons, as is usual with him, then the House of Lords; then the King, and then back again. The result of this information was that the Lords sat and the Commons stood on the delivery of the King's speech." Charles Carroll said, a bit rudely, that he thought it was of no consequence how it was done in Great Britain. But before the debate could be carried further the secretary of the Senate appeared and whispered to Adams that representatives were waiting at the door to join the senators in receiving the president. How were *they* to be received? Confusion ensued. Everyone tried to talk at once. Senators left their chairs and clustered around Adams's desk to give their opinions. Adams finally gaveled the senators to order, and the representatives were admitted in one way or another and given seats to await Washington's arrival.

It was an hour before the general appeared, dressed in a dark brown suit with silver buttons, white stockings, black shoes with square silver buckles, and a sword. Adams met him at the door and conducted him to the presidential chair. He then bowed and informed the president that it was time for him to take the oath of office. Adams had prepared a brief speech, but in the strain and tension of the moment he could not remember a word of it. There was an embarrassed silence, and then Adams bowed again, indicated to the president with a gesture that he should arise, and, followed by the train of legislators, conducted him to the balcony of the Federal Hall, where a large crowd waited below to hear Washington take the oath of office from Chancellor Robert Livingston, chief justice of the New York judiciary.

At the conclusion of the ceremony the crowd gave three cheers, and Washington returned to the hall to deliver his inaugural address. His face was grave and sad, and his hands shook so that at times he had trouble reading his speech. His voice was low and tremulous, and those in the rear of the room could hardly hear him. No event could have filled him with greater anxieties, Washington declared, than the news that he had been elected president. His "fondest predilection" and "immutable decision" had been to remain at Mount Vernon, "the asylum of my declining years." The magnitude of the task that faced him "could not but overwhelm with despondence one who (inheriting inferior endowments and unpracticed in the duties of civil administration) ought to be peculiarly conscious of his own deficiencies. [He thus offered his] fervent supplications to that Almighty Being who rules over the universe, who presides in the councils of nations, and whose provident aids can supply every human defect. . . . In tendering this homage to the Great Author of every public and private good, I assure myself that it expresses your sentiments not less than my own. . . . No people can be bound to acknowledge and adore the Invisible Hand which conducts the affairs of men more than those of the United States. Every step by which they have advanced to the character of an independent nation seems to have been distinguished by some token of providential agency; and in the important revolution just accomplished in the system of their united government the tranquil deliberations and voluntary consent of so many distinct communities from which the event has resulted cannot be compared with the means by which most governments have been established without some return of pious gratitude." Here Washington expressed once more the now familiar theme that America's unique achievement could not have been accomplished without the assistance of a divine Providence. It is easy to see how this conviction of the miraculous origins of the United States, shared by Franklin, Benjamin Rush, and a substantial number of their countrymen, came in time to constitute a "civil religion"—the belief, first, that the United States was to be, throughout its history, the specially chosen vessel of the Lord, and then that the United States had become a kind of substitute for God, that is to say, all-wise, all-powerful, eternal, good, and just.

As we have noted from time to time, the Founders were saying something quite different. They were saying that nothing of enduring worth could be created without divine assistance and that even with such assistance all human creations were mortal and tended to decadence and corruption, that the United States could not expect to be immune from the laws of history and nature but that by attention to the lessons of history (a form of divine revelation), by the use of reason, and through the favorable workings of Providence they might create a government that would afford its citizens a degree of happiness and prosperity the world had not yet seen and Americans might enjoy for a longer period of time than that allotted to previous nations.

Washington went on to express his hope that "no local prejudices or attachments, no separate views or party animosities, will misdirect the comprehensive and equal eye which ought to watch over this great assemblage of communities and interests . . . the propitious smiles of

Heaven can never be expected on a nation that disregards the eternal rules of order and right which Heaven itself has ordained. . . ." Public virtue and republican government were indissolubly associated. The Republic could last no longer than the honesty and virtue of its citizens. Moreover, "the destiny of the republican model of government" rested "*deeply*," perhaps "*finally*" on the success or failure of the American experiment.

The moment was a profoundly moving one for his listeners. Many of them wept unabashedly. From the hall the members of Congress formed in procession to walk to St. Paul's Church, where the Episcopal bishop of New York said prayers for the peace and good order of the government. Reconvening, the senators appointed a committee to reply, in Adams's words, to the president's "most gracious speech." The afternoon and evening were given over to celebrations of all kinds, to fireworks, and to viewing the splendid transparent paintings hung outside the homes of the French and Spanish emissaries to the United States.

When the minutes were read the next morning, Maclay arose to object to the phrase "his most gracious speech." He declared: "Mr. President, we have lately had a hard struggle for our liberty against kingly authority. The minds of men are still heated. Everything related to that species of government is odious to the people. . . . I know they will give offence. I consider them as improper. I therefore move that it be struck out."

Adams defended the phrase. It seemed to him captious to object to it simply because of "its being taken from the practice of that government under which we have lived so long and so happily formerly." Maclay persisted. However Americans may have once felt about the government of Great Britain, they now felt very differently, so that "even the modes of it were now abhorred." The enemies of the new government already suspected it of monarchical tendencies. They would be sure to object to such a phrase, "as the first step of the ladder to the ascent to royalty."

George Read of Delaware supported Adams. If Americans were going to object to words "because they had been used in the same sense in Britain, we should soon be at a loss to do business." That might be, Maclay replied, but "at present there is no loss for words. The words 'speech' or 'address,' without any addition, will suit us well enough." On a call for the question, the senators voted to strike out the words. It was a revealing exchange. Americans continued to demonstrate a marked hostility toward the mildest social distinctions expressed in titles or salutations—a hostility recognized even today.

After the Senate had adjourned, Adams sought out Maclay with the intention of giving the frontier senator a short lesson in political science. Respect for authority rested on the observance of proper forms and ceremonies, Adams insisted, but he found the Pennsylvanian a recalcitrant pupil. Maclay would yield to no man in his respect for the president, or for Adams himself, for that matter, but he knew the temper of his constituents. They were not in the mood for such trappings. Adams "got upon the subject of checks to government and the balances of power," Maclay recalled. "His tale was long—he seemed to expect some answer. I caught at the last word and said, undoubtedly without a balance there could be no equilibrium, and so left him hanging in geometry."

The reply to the president's speech continued to be a bone of contention among the senators. The drafters of the reply had referred to the "anarchy and confusion" from which the new government had rescued the country. Some objected to the phrase on the grounds that it would needlessly offend the adherents of the Articles of Confederation. Another phrase that caused dispute was a reference to the "dignity and splendor" of the new Republic. Maclay and others preferred "respectability." Let monarchies lust after "splendor." The word, "when applied to government," Maclay argued, "brought into . . . mind, instead of the highest perfection, all the faulty finery, brilliant scenes, and expensive trappings of royal government . . . quite the reverse of . . . firm and prudent councils, frugality, and economy."

This time Maclay was defeated, and the reply was approved and sent to the president.

Washington's plea for harmony and cooperation was given practical effect in the men he appointed to what came to be called his Cabinet, an institution nowhere provided for in the Constitution but one that developed quite naturally when Washington undertook to consult the heads of the various departments of government. That the choice of Alexander Hamilton as secretary of the treasury was inevitable did not make the appointment of the New Yorker any less important. For secretary of state, Washington intended to appoint Thomas Jefferson, Hamilton's enemy.

In 1785, Jefferson had succeeded Franklin as the emissary of

Congress to the French court. In Paris, he had luxuriated in French culture—art, architecture, the theater, the whole style of French life—while deploring the depressed condition of the poor. He had had a passionate love affair with a beautiful young English artist, Maria Cosway, whose dissolute husband was more interested in the young men of his circle than in his wife. In France he had followed events in America as best he could through his American correspondents, especially James Madison, his young protégé. (We have already taken note of his reaction to the news of Shays' Rebellion.)

Washington wanted Jefferson home so that he might appoint him secretary of state, but first someone had to be appointed to replace him. The nomination of William Short as interim minister provoked a heated debate over the right of the president to make such appointments and the meaning of the words, "with the advice and consent of the Senate." How much advice? How much consent? The Anti-Federalists expressed bitter opposition to a generous interpretation of the clause. Some went so far as to argue that the nominations should originate in the Senate or at least that the president should confer with the Senate prior to announcing his nominations for positions in the executive branch. Senators of this disposition, Maclay not unnaturally among them, were even more adamant about the president's right to remove his own appointees from office, arguing that since the Constitution did not specifically give him such a right, it lay with the Senate. Oliver Ellsworth, who spoke so frequently that Maclay dubbed him "Endless Ellsworth," gave an emotional defense of the president's right of removal, declaring, "It is a sacrilege to touch a *hair of his head . . . we may as well lay the President's head on the block and strike it off with one blow*" as try to deny him the right to remove his own appointees. At this point, Maclay noted, "he paused, put his handkerchief to his face, and either shed tears or affected to do so."

The question continued to be the subject of angry harangues by members on both sides. William Grayson went so far as to declare that the events had proved Patrick Henry right—"consolidation is the object of the new government, and the first attempt will be to destroy the Senate, as they are the representatives of the State Legislatures."

When Jefferson arrived home the new government was scarcely six months old, and he found that Washington had reserved the office of secretary of state for him. He was, as we have noted, well disposed toward the new Constitution, having already defended it against

Adams's criticisms, but he yearned to be back at Monticello and wrote to Washington begging to be excused. Washington would not accept his refusal, however, and in March, 1790, almost a year after Washington's inauguration, Jefferson took up his duties as secretary of state.

Genial Henry Knox, Washington's commander of artillery, was appointed secretary of war; and Edmund Randolph, who had performed such valiant labors in the Virginia ratifying convention, was selected for the office of attorney general.

Washington's apprehensions about factions turned out to be well founded. The dream of peace and harmony that had imparted such a rosy glow to Washington's arrival and inauguration was quickly dissipated by partisan wrangles and bitterness. The two houses of Congress had hardly assembled before their members fell to bickering and quarreling in the most rancorous spirit. It seemed that no issue could be taken up without at once revealing hostile camps. While both houses had a substantial Federalist majority, there were a number of strong Anti-Federalists to dispute every question, men who, like Maclay, thought the Constitution "a vicious trap to ensnare the liberties of the people." Moreover, there were numerous rifts among the Federalists themselves, the principal divisions being, not surprisingly, regional. New England Federalists showed little disposition to trust Federalists of the Middle or Southern states, and the feeling was warmly reciprocated.

It was Maclay's conviction that the supporters of the Constitution were "every one ill at ease in his finances; every one out at the elbows in his circumstances; every ambitious man, every one desirous of a short-cut to wealth and honors. [All such men] cast their eyes on the new Constitution as the machine which could be wrought to their purposes, either in the funds of speculation it would afford, the offices it would create, or the jobs to be obtained under it."

Every effort to give "weight and dignity" to the new government was denounced by the Anti-Federalists as an effort to establish a monarchical form of government. The question of how to sign bills passed by the Senate resulted in days of angry disputation. William Maclay is not, to be sure, an entirely reliable guide to all this turmoil, since he was more disposed than most to see conspiracy and collusion all about him, but his journal makes abundantly clear the anguish of the birth of the Congress of the United States. Maclay blamed his chronic ill-health on the stresses produced by the tensions and hostilities that were so manifest in the Senate chambers. The Pennsylvania senator began to speak of "a court party," by which he meant those senators and representatives who supported the powers of the president. He was convinced that they "were aiming with all their force to establish a splendid court with all the pomp of majesty." The president was their dupe. "Alas! poor Washington," he exclaimed, "if you are taken in this snare! How will the gold become dim! . . . How will your glory fade!"

Maclay was distressed that so many of the legislators in both houses of Congress were lawyers and merchants. "It seems as difficult to restrain a merchant from striking at gain," he noted, "as to prevent the keen spaniel from springing at game that he has been trained to pursue. Habit with them has become a second nature." As for the lawyers, their principal defect was that they never tired of talking; "wrangling is their business." Maclay also observed that every means was used by those with special interests to prevail on their colleagues to fall in line—"Influence, Treats, dinners, attentions, etc." "Candor and integrity" were found "seldom in professional men"; often in the "plain and sober countrymen," presumably like himself. It seemed to him that the way to get ahead in Congress was "to be clean shaven, shirted, and powdered, to make your bows with grace, and to be master of the small chat on the weather, play, or newspaper anecdote of the day."

Congress and the president were defining the relationship between the executive and legislative branches by a process of trial and error. The business of both branches proceeded slowly. Maclay, in the absence of Robert Morris, the other Pennsylvania senator, felt himself "a bird alone." He had had "to bear the chilling cold of the North and the intemperate warmth of the South, neither of which is favorable to the middle State from which I come. " Richard Henry Lee of Virginia and Ralph Izard, "hot as the burning sands of Carolina, hate us. Adams with all his frigid friends, cool and wary, bear us no good-will." Hours were spent debating what were, to Maclay, "all the fooleries, fopperies, fineries and pomp of royal etiquette."

Adams, seeing the tide run against the idea of a title for the president, could not restrain himself from the impropriety of lecturing the senators from the chair. If Washington was to be called no more than "'President of the United States,'" people would "despise him *to all eternity.* This is all nonsense to the philosopher," Adams added, "but so is all government whatever." Maclay then rose and read from the

Constitution: "No title of nobility shall be granted by the United States." To give the president a title such as some members seemed bent upon would plainly be unconstitutional. Not only were such notions nonsense to philosophers, but Maclay was ready to admit "that every high-sounding, pompous appellation . . . must appear bombastic nonsense in the eye of every wise man." Frederick Muhlenberg, a Pennsylvania representative, hearing of Maclay's battle in the Senate against titles, teasingly addressed him as "Your Highness of the Senate."

One of the first tasks of Congress was that of setting import duties on foreign goods. The primary motivation behind the framing of the Constitution was, as we have seen, the inability of the Confederation Congress to control the commercial activities of the states. But the members of the House dillied and dallied. Maclay was indignant. According to him, a number of merchants, knowing that an impost— an import tax—would soon be passed by Congress, had already added the anticipated tax to the price of their imported goods, thus passing on the cost to their customers. The delay in passing a tax allowed the merchants in question to pocket the additional sum. Maclay was convinced that the foot-dragging in Congress was the result of collusion between certain congressmen and their merchant friends. Already the "commercial influence" was corrupting pliant legislators. The Pennsylvania senator busied himself rallying support for a prompt revenue measure.

Another sore point concerned the passage of a bill of rights, which had been promised by the Federalists in a number of states. Those congressmen most concerned with the control of commerce seemed willing to delay a bill of rights (there were also a large number of other proposed amendments to be considered). Finally, all deliberations in both houses were shadowed by a behind-the-scenes struggle over where the capital was to be permanently located. Benjamin Rush bombarded Adams and legislators he considered sympathetic to Philadelphia's claims with demands that the capital be located in the City of Brotherly Love, and Maclay suspected Richard Henry Lee of currying favor with the New Englanders in hopes of having the capital located on the Potomac.

Maclay, who was so critical of the plots and schemes of his colleagues, did not scruple to confide to his journal that he and Rush had pushed John Adams for vice-president with the expectation that he would support Philadelphia as the capital of the new government. In Maclay's words, "We knew his vanity, and hoped by laying hold of it to render him useful among the New England men in our scheme of bringing Congress to Philadelphia." But Adams was unwilling to cooperate, and Maclay added bitterly, "his pride, obstinacy, and folly are equal to his vanity."

Perhaps nothing better demonstrated the depth of sectional difference than the debate on import duties or tariffs. The New Englanders, who imported several million gallons of molasses a year from the West Indies for the manufacture of New England rum, the principal spirituous liquor of the common man, wanted no tax at all or, failing that, the lowest possible one. Members from other states who viewed rum as the devil's potion wished a high tax both to produce revenue and to discourage the trade. Pennsylvania, which had an infant iron industry, had already imposed a stiff "protective tariff" on all imports of iron or steel. It would not be fair, Maclay and Morris argued, for Pennsylvania (and consequently all the other states) to have a lower tariff under the new government than it had had prior to it. That would be, in effect, a breach of faith. Pennsylvanians, encouraged by their state's protective tariff, had invested heavily in the industry. If the importation of cheaper iron from England were not discouraged, the investors would stand to lose. But citizens of Virginia and the Carolinas wished to buy iron products at the lowest possible price. A tariff that kept the price of nails and hinges high for the benefit of Pennsylvania's iron manufacturers was, they claimed with some justice, a tax on them. They, even more than the British, were paying to maintain the infant iron industry of Pennsylvania and to insure handsome dividends for its stockholders. Similarly with the nascent paper industry of the state and with cables and cordage and rope products, on which the Pennsylvania tariff stood at seventy-five cents, again to encourage and protect native industry.

The Senate, after lengthy debate, set the tariff on molasses at four cents, but the New England senators refused to accept a tax they considered too high and tried every subterfuge to have it reduced. "Till quarter after three did the New England members beat this ground," Maclay wrote wearily, "even to baiting the hook that caught the fish that went to buy the molasses" (a reference to the New England trade with the Indies, where fish was exchanged for molasses).

Madeira wine, the favorite drink of the well-to-do, was taxed at eighteen cents a cask with little debate. Loaf sugar was another matter.

Here again sectional interests were much in evidence. Richard Henry Lee opposed "every article, especially the protecting duties," and his Virginia colleague, Grayson, declared himself "against all impost as the most unjust and oppressive form of taxation." The notion of protecting American loaf sugar offended him. According to Maclay, Grayson declared: "It was lime and other vile compositions. He had broken a spoon trying to dissolve and separate it, and so I must go on breaking my spoons and three millions of people must be taxed to support half a dozen people in Philadelphia." The house divided evenly on taxing sugar, and Adams cast the deciding vote in favor of the tariff. The question of an impost on salt brought out a division between seacoast and frontier. Richard Henry Lee supported a high tax on the grounds that "the interior parts of the country with their new lands could much better afford to pay high taxes than the settlers of exhausted lands." Maclay replied that the settlers on the frontier "were the real benefactors to the community, and deserved exemption if any." Maclay became convinced that the unpredictable Lee, "this Ishmael, really wished to destroy the new Constitution."

If Maclay was annoyed by "Ishmael Lee," the belated arrival of Pierce Butler from South Carolina provided him with a new target for his displeasure and a fresh example of Southern intransigence. Maclay wrote that Butler had hardly taken his seat before he "flamed like a meteor. He arraigned the whole Impost law, and then charged [indirectly] the whole Congress with the design of oppressing South Carolina. . . . Until four o'clock it was a battle with less order, less sense, less decency, too, than any question I have ever yet heard debated in the Senate." Two days later Butler was at it again; "he threatened a dissolution of the Union, with regard to his state *as sure as God was in the firmament!* [This first public threat of secession, made, ironically, by a representative of the state that would lead the way in seceding from the Union seventy years later.] He scattered his remarks over the whole impost bill, calling it partial, oppressive, etc., and solely calculated to oppress South Carolina; and yet ever and anon declaring how clear of local views, how candid and dispassionate he was!"

During the debate in the House, Josiah Parker of Virginia proposed a tax of ten dollars a head on every slave imported into the United States. He regretted that the Constitution had not outlawed the trade: "It was great defect in the instrument to suffer such a business to go on. It was contrary to revolutionary principles."

James Jackson of Georgia replied with asperity. It was well for

Virginia to speak so. She had all the slaves she needed and indeed was glad to export her surplus to more southerly states. But the slave trade was the lifeblood of the lower South. "It had become the fashion of the day to talk of emancipation. He would not go into a discussion of the subject. But he would venture to express the belief that it could be shown that the blacks were best off in slavery. Suppose they were set free. What would they do? Work for a living? Maryland had freed her slaves, and did they betake themselves to work for a living? Far from it. They turned common pick-pockets and petit-larceny villains. If Virginia thought slavery an evil, let her begin by setting her slaves free." There were more speeches denouncing and praising slavery, but the matter went no further.

The angry debate over import duties and protective tariffs served to define what, slavery aside, was to be the most persistent conflict in the U.S. Congress—the issue of protective tariffs unceasingly contended for by American manufacturers and opposed by agricultural interests most strongly represented by the Southern states.

The Constitution specified that the national legislature was to establish federal courts "inferior" to the Supreme Court. Thus, one of the early tasks taken up by Congress was the drafting of a judiciary bill to extend the federal court system to the states. The judiciary bill of 1789 provided that this be done through a system of circuit courts, sitting in various judicial districts and presided over by the justices of the Supreme Court, whose number was not stipulated in the Constitution. The bill appeared to Maclay to be "the gunpowder-plot of the Constitution. So confused and so obscure, it will not fail to give a general alarm." He was also annoyed at the constant reference, in the debates on the bill, to British examples and precedents. Oliver Ellsworth and William Paterson were the authors of the bill. Ellsworth, well aware of the importance of the task assigned him, wrote: "I consider a proper arrangement of the Judiciary, however difficult to establish, among the best securities the government will have, and question much if any will be found more economical, systematic and efficient than the one under consideration. Its fate in the House of Representatives, or in the opinion of the public, I cannot determine." The Constitution, as it issued from the Federal Convention, might indeed be likened to a building lacking a crucial beam, in this case the specifics of the federal judicial system; the number of justices; the nature and jurisdiction of the inferior courts; and, most important of all, the relationship of the state courts to the federal courts. James Monroe made an accurate analysis of the situation in a letter to his fellow Virginian, James Madison: "That [the bill] to embrace the Judiciary will occasion more difficulty, I apprehend, than any other, as it will form an exposition of the powers of the Government itself, and show in the opinion of those who organized it, how far it can discharge its own functions, or must depend for that purpose on the aid of those of the States. Whatever arrangement shall now be made in that respect will be of some duration, which shows the propriety of a wise provision in the commencement."

The "exposition of the powers of government" was contained primarily in what came to be the most controversial section of the bill, section 25, which authorized "writs of error" or appeals to the Supreme Court from decisions of the state courts. To the champions of state sovereignty, this section seemed the grossest infringement of the rights of the states. William Smith of South Carolina noted: "It is much to be apprehended that this constant control of the Supreme Federal Court over the adjudication of the State Courts would dissatisfy the people and weaken the importance and authority of the State Judges." Even though both houses counted a comfortable majority of Federalists, the passage of the Judiciary Act of 1789 was very close. A year later, when state versus federal lines were more distinctly drawn, it could not have passed. As it was, it took all the skill and influence of the leading Federalists—Madison, Fisher Ames, and Roger Sherman in the House and Ellsworth and Paterson in the Senate—to get it through. One of the arguments used by the bill's supporters was that is should be passed "as an experimental law . . . in the confidence that a short experience will make manifest the proper alterations," as Fisher Ames put it

Hardly a Congress met for the next thirty-five years without efforts to alter or amend the Judiciary Act of 1789, especially section 25, so obnoxious to states' righters. Before long Madison and Monroe were enticed into the ranks of the Jeffersonian Republicans, and Jefferson himself became one of the bitterest enemies of the act. Section 25 was particularly vulnerable to attack because it established by statute a crucial federal right vis-à-vis the states that had not been stipulated by the Constitution itself, although anyone familiar with the federal debates could be sure that it was entirely consistent with the "national" thinking of the most of the delegates. Moreover, enemies of the federal court system declared, with considerable justice, that had such a provision (allowing appeals from state courts to federal courts) been included in the Constitution, it would never have been ratified. For the truth of this allegation one has only to recall John Marshall's assurances in the Virginia ratifying convention that a state would never be called before the bar of the Supreme Court.

The Judiciary Act that was finally passed in the last week of the first session of Congress provided for a Supreme Court with a chief justice and five associate judges. There were to be, in addition, thirteen district courts and three circuit courts, with two justices assigned to a circuit. Grayson of Virginia, who had fought the bill with all his resources, wrote to Patrick Henry: "The Judicial Bill has passed but wears so monstrous an appearance that I think it will be *felo-de-se* in the execution. . . . Whenever the Federal Judiciary comes into operation, I think the pride of the States will take alarm which, added . . . to a thousand other circumstances,.will in the end procure its destruction." Another Congressman wrote: "This Department, I dread as an awful Tribunal . . . by its institution, the Judges are completely independent, being secure of their salaries, and removable only by impeachment, not being subject to discharge on address of both Houses as is the case in Great Britain."

Perhaps the most decisive point in the passage of the act was the fact that there was little or no notion among most members of Congress or in the country at large of the extraordinary influence the Court was to exert. The senators and representatives were far more preoccupied with the relations between the legislative and executive branches of the government. Both parties, the court party and the Anti-Federalists, believed that the future fate of the country depended on how that relationship was defined. Hence, they had little time or energy to expend on the judicial branch of the new government.

Washington, well aware of the importance of the Supreme Court, took considerable pains in the selection of the justices. He wanted reliable nationalists or Federalists, men of distinction in the law and representative of the various sections of the country. James Wilson had already written indicating that he wished to be a candidate for the chief justiceship, but Washington passed over him to choose John Jay, one of the authors of *The Federalist Papers* and a highly respected lawyer, who, pending Jefferson's acceptance of the post, was acting as secretary of foreign affairs. Jay was forty-four. Virginia must, of course, be represented, and Washington settled on John Blair, who had served as chief justice of the state court of appeals. From

Massachusetts, Washington chose William Cushing, chief justice of the state's Supreme Judicial Court. Wilson, a key member of the Federal Convention and one of the most learned legal theorists in the country, was the obvious choice from Pennsylvania. From the Deep South, Washington chose John Rutledge of South Carolina, former governor of the state and a judge in the state Court of Chancery. His final appointment went to James Iredell of North Carolina, at thirty-eight the youngest justice. All were Federalists. Wilson and Rutledge, members of the Federal Convention, had firsthand knowledge of the formation of the Constitution and were thus, presumably, ideally suited to interpret it.

At the end of July, Maclay, tormented by rheumatism and convinced that the new government was rapidly being turned into a monarchy in all but name, had asked for a three-week sick leave, which was granted by his colleagues, a number of whom were delighted to see him depart. Maclay's experience of the last few months had half convinced him that "Republican theories [were] well enough in times of public commotion or at elections; but all sensible men once in power know that force is the only effectual means to secure obedience. Hence it has flowed, and forever will flow, the failure of republican government. Oligarchies and aristocracies follow till monarchy tops the system, and will continue till some unskilled driver overloads the ass, and then the restive beast throws both itself and the rider in the mire, and the old process will begin again." All his efforts to stem the tide of monarchy had been in vain. One land speculator with a single dinner for pliant legislators would "procure ten votes," where Maclay's "disinterestedness has not procured . . . one." Among his enemies was there "a single one . . . who will not belie, defraud, deceive you for the smallest interest? Health is too great a sacrifice for such a herd." Maclay was convinced that the New Englanders "will cabal against and endeavor to subvert any government which they have not the management of." The Southerners would, of course, do likewise. Consequently, the prospects for the country's future were far from bright.

When Maclay returned to New York in the middle of August, Ralph Izard, a fellow Anti-Federalist, reported that the "court party . . . is gaining ground." Maclay was persuaded that the president himself was only the tool of ambitious men who "would place a crown on his head, that they may have the handling of its jewels." Shortly after Maclay's arrival, the senators were notified that the president intended to visit their chamber with General Knox to obtain their "advice and consent" in regard to a treaty with the Southern Indians. Having been received with considerable ceremony, the president turned to Knox and asked him to read the document in question. Carriages rattling past the open windows made it difficult to hear Knox, but after he had finished Adams read the first article of the treaty and asked for the approval of the senators. There was a long pause, and then, as Adams was about to call for a vote, Maclay stood up to protest the procedure. "The business is new to the Senate," he said. "It is of importance. It is our duty to inform ourselves as well as possible on the subject. I therefore call for a reading of the treaties and other documents alluded to in the paper before us."

Maclay later noted in his journal, "I cast an eye at the President of the United States. I saw he wore an aspect of stern displeasure." Morris and Maclay, in a hasty conference, decided to ask the president to turn over all the relevant papers to a committee of the Senate to study and make recommendations to the whole body. Maclay "saw no chance of a fair investigation of the subjects while the President of the United States sat there, with his Secretary of War, to support his opinions and overawe the timid and neutral part of the Senate."

When Maclay sat down after proposing that the matter be referred to a committee, "the President of the United States started up in a violent fret. *'This defeats every purpose of my coming here,'* were the first words that he said. . . . He cooled, however, by degrees. . . . We waited for him to withdraw. He did so with a discontented air. Had it been any other man than the man whom I wish to regard as the first character in the world, I would have said, with sullen dignity."

The incident confirmed Maclay's fears that the president and the court party intended to make the Senate their tool; in the Pennsylvanian's words, "to tread on the necks of the Senate. . . . He wishes us to see with the eyes and hear with the ears of his Secretary only. The Secretary to advance the premises, the President to draw the conclusions, and to bear down our deliberations with his personal authority and presence. Form only will be left to us. This will not do with Americans. But let the matter work; it will soon cure itself."

When the president invited Maclay to dinner, the senator was convinced that an effort would be made to sway him in the direction of the court party, but he took careful note of the evening and was clearly impressed despite his republican principles. "First," he noted, "was the soup, fish roasted and boiled; meats, gammon, fowls, etc. This was the dinner. The middle of the table was garnished in the usual tasty way, with small images, flowers (artificial), etc. The dessert was, first apple-pies, pudding, etc.; then iced creams, jellies, etc.; then water-melons, musk-melons, apples, peaches, nuts.

"It was the most solemn dinner ever I sat at. Not a health drank; scarce a word said until the cloth was taken away. Then the President, filling a glass of wine, with great formality drank the health of every individual by name round the table. Everybody imitated him, charged glasses, and such a buzz of 'health, sir,' and 'health, madam,' and 'thank you, sir,' and 'thank you, madam,' never had I heard before. Indeed I had like to have been thrown out in the hurry; but I got a little wine in my glass, and passed the ceremony. The ladies sat a good while, and the bottles passed about; but there was a dead silence almost."

When Mrs. Washington withdrew with the ladies, there was hardly more animation. "The President told of a New England clergyman who had lost a hat and wig in passing a river called the Brunks. He smiled and everybody else laughed. . . . The President kept a fork in his hand, when the cloth was taken away, I thought for the purpose of picking nuts. He ate no nuts, however, but played with the fork, striking on the edge of the table with it."

The discussion of the proper pay for the senators and representatives again divided the Senate into the champions of "dignity" and the advocates of democratic simplicity. Should senators receive higher pay than representatives? The court party said yes; the democrats said no. Certain spendthrifts pushed for eight dollars a day for senators and five for representatives. But Maclay was "totally against all discrimination; . . . we were all equally servants of the public." Six dollars was finally agreed upon, but Maclay took such a verbal beating from his colleagues that he noted morosely in his journal: "I came here expecting every man to act the part of a god; that the most delicate honor, the most exalted wisdom, the most refined generosity was to govern every act and be seeing every deed. What must be my feelings on finding rude and rough manners, glaring folly, and the basest selfishness apparent in almost every public transaction!"

But the most agonizing issue, at least for the Pennsylvanians in both houses of Congress, was that of the location of the new capital. Fearing that they could not carry Philadelphia, the legislators from the

Quaker state agitated for a place on the Susquehanna River, but Robert Morris undermined their solidarity by maneuvering for the falls of the Delaware where, it turned out, he had extensive landholdings. Week after week the debate dragged on with more being done "out-of-doors" than in the Senate chamber. Finally, at the end of September the rumor was spread that a majority of the senators had agreed informally on Germantown. And so the first session of the Congress of the United States ended on that rather anticlimactic note.

There was little encouragement to be found in its proceedings for supporters of republican government. Wounds had been opened that would be a long time healing. Differences had been exacerbated rather than reconciled. Days had been wasted in recriminations, and little of a positive nature had been accomplished. In retrospect, it all appears to have been inevitable. The Constitution had been ratified by only the narrowest of margins. The long-standing antagonisms between states, between regions, between classes could not be wished away. The national legislature must become a kind of collecting station for them, a microcosm, a stage on which were acted out all the issues that divided Americans. The powerlessness of the Confederation Congress had given its intermittent deliberations a deceptive blandness. Now it would be seen whether a piece of paper, however artfully contrived, could counteract the centrifugal force of the states. As the first session indicated, it was to prove a nerve-wracking and always uncertain experiment.

Despite the petty squabbles and insistent provincialism, the legislators of the first session of the First Congress had two substantial achievements to their credit. They had brought some economic order out of commercial chaos by passing the impost bill (that, after all, was why they had junked the Articles of Confederation and drafted the Constitution); and they had passed the critically important judiciary bill, which enabled the president to appoint a Supreme Court and formally establish a national judicial system.

During the last weeks of the session news had arrived of an event that was to have an effect on domestic politics second only to the American Revolution. The opening act of the French Revolution had occurred the preceding June when the Estates-General had denominated itself the National Assembly and declared its intention to take control of finances and reform the government. When the indignant king ordered the Assembly to disband, Count Mirabeau, a defector from the order of nobles, called out: "Go tell those who sent you that we are here by the will of the people and that we shall not leave except at the point of a bayonet." A few weeks later a mob of Parisians had stormed the Bastille prison, killing the superintendent and freeing the prisoners. As in the early stages of the American Revolution popular feeling outran the moderate leaders who wished for reform, not revolution. A provisional government was established in Paris, and Lafayette took command of the hastily created National Guard, charged with restoring order. So began the second of the "Democratic Revolutions" that were to usher in more than a century of political upheaval as the new age, so confidently hailed by the leaders of the American Revolution, disclosed itself in the Old World as it had in the New.

When word of the beginning of the Revolution reached America, it was greeted with varying degrees of enthusiasm. Many of the Revolutionary leaders, especially those of a more conservative bent, while approving the movement for more representative government, were disturbed by the violence and bloodshed that accompanied it. Jefferson, observing the headlong course of the Revolution, found himself with very mixed feelings. He had written to Madison questioning "whether one generation of men had a right to bind another. . . . I set out on this ground, which I suppose to be self-evident, '*that the earth belongs in usufruct to the living*: that the dead have neither powers nor rights over it. The portion occupied by any individual ceases to be his when he himself ceases to be and reverts to the society.' If his heirs are allowed to retain it it is at the pleasure of the society not as a natural right." By the same token, a society had no right to incur debts that could not be paid off in a generation, thirty-four years by Jefferson's calculation (later he decided that nineteen years was the proper span). "On similar ground," he continued, "it may be proved that no society can make a perpetual constitution, or even a perpetual law. The earth always belongs to the living generation; they may manage it, then, and what proceeds from it, as they please. . . . Every constitution then, and every law, naturally expires at the end of nineteen years."

Jefferson's notion that a person's right to property, typically land, lapsed with his death and might then be distributed by the society (the living) as it wished has in it echoes of Franklin's doctrine that since everything that a man made beyond a "modest competence" to feed and support his family adequately and to educate his children was made by virtue of the order created by the society, that same society had a right to claim any surplus and dispose of it as it wished. It appeared also to follow from Jefferson's earlier observation that a "little rebellion now and then" was essential to the health of a republic and that "the tree of liberty must be refreshed from time to time with the blood of patriots & tyrants." Jefferson apparently felt (since he does not specifically say, we can only conjecture) that the only way that a major cataclysm such as the French Revolution could be avoided was by a series of "little rebellions," which would make needed social adjustments at intervals and thus prevent the accumulation of injustices and inequities that must finally lead to a terrible upheaval.

On the one hand, Jefferson envisioned the new age as an epoch ruled by reason where human beings and their institutions would be progressively refined through the application of scientific principles, until something like perfection was achieved. On the other hand, from his study of history he saw all great movements of reform in the past starting out with high ideals and gradually degenerating into rigid and exploitive societies, "with the governments preying on the people and the rich on the poor." In other words, what was to prevent the French Revolution from being reenacted in the United States when it, in time, had become as unjust and tyrannical as the Old Regime in France? It must have been reflections such as these that inspired Jefferson's notion of starting everything over every nineteen years, a thought guaranteed to make any orthodox Federalist purple with indignation. Eccentric as Jefferson's notion seems—certainly it was quite counter to the optimistic spirit of the French Enlightenment—it was based on an observation that Jefferson alone among the members of his generation seems to have reflected on: that revolutions move very rapidly toward what we would call today "bureaucratization" and reaction. He had written in his *Notes on the State of Virginia* in a passage not much noticed that "from the conclusion of this war we shall be going down hill"—that is to say, getting further and further away from the principles of the Revolution.

Certainly the idea that "the earth belonged to the living" was characteristic of the Enlightenment (what I have chosen to call in its American manifestation the Secular-Democratic Consciousness). The Classical-Christian Consciousness was incapable of articulating such a notion. All traditional societies were characterized by a respect, if not a veneration, for the past, for ancestors and antecedents. The earth, for example, was the earth of the ancestors; the "living" held it with reverence for them and in trust for their children. Although Jefferson surely did not mean it so, his own remarks could have been interpreted as giving the living generation the right to exploit and despoil the land without regard for future generations. It was ironic that Jefferson, in expressing the view that the past was an irrelevance, or worse, a burden to be discarded, anticipated an American attitude toward the land that was to have unhappy consequences in the mid-twentieth century.

In August, 1789, hardly a month after the storming of the Bastille, the National Assembly adopted the Declaration of the Rights of Man, a bill of rights fashioned out of English and American precedents with an overlay of French philosophy. When copies of it reached America, they vastly increased the enthusiasm of the republicans for the French revolutionaries.

The response of William Maclay, sweating out the last weeks of Congress in New York, was unequivocal. "By this and yesterday's papers," he wrote, "France seems travailing in the birth of freedom. Her throes and pangs of labor are violent. God give her a happy delivery! Royalty, nobility and vile pageantry, by which a few of the human race lord it over and tread on the necks of their fellow-mortals, seem likely to be demolished with their kindred Bastille, which is said to be laid in ashes. Ye gods, with what indignation do I review the late attempt of some creatures among us to revive the vile machinery."

The French Revolution was to become, before the end of Washington's first term of office, a kind of litmus paper by which to test the political orthodoxy or heterodoxy of Federalists and republicans. The Anti-Federalists, who soon began to denominate themselves "Republicans" and sometimes "Democrats" (as distinguished from their "monarchist" opponents), fastened on the Revolution with fanatical enthusiasm. They excused its excesses and praised its triumphs. Best of all, it proved a convenient club with which to belabor the Federalists. The simple if rather strange fact was that to those Americans who might be said to have entered wholeheartedly into the Secular-Democratic Consciousness, the French Revolution was more to their taste than the American. The motto of the French Revolution was so splendid: "Liberty, Equality, Fraternity!" Although the Declaration of Independence had stated that "all men are created equal," it had said nothing about whether they remained so, and there was little or nothing remarked on the subject in the political theorizing of the Revolutionary leaders—certainly nothing in *The Federalist Papers*. John Adams had aroused the antagonism of many of his countrymen by boldly asserting that people were not equal in wealth or talents or physical beauty or almost anything else and suggesting that anyone who held the contrary view was a romantic numbskull with very little knowledge of the world.

Assumption and the Capital

When Congress reassembled for its second session on January 5, 1790, rumors were already circulating of Alexander Hamilton's plan to place the finances of the Republic on a sound footing. The kingpins of the "Hamilton system" were the assumption of state debts by the federal government and the redemption at par of the depreciated certificates issued as money by the Confederation Congress.

The foreign debt at the time was $11,710,387, and the domestic debt inherited from the Confederation Congress was $42,414,085. It was Hamilton's plan to consolidate these obligations with the state debts of roughly $21 million, for a total of some $75 million. Since this was far beyond the resources of the new government, all creditors would receive interest-bearing certificates and the debt would be funded—paid off—as the accumulation of federal revenues, primarily from import duties, permitted. It was, of course, Hamilton's intention to tie all public creditors to the new government with strong economic bonds. The Anti-Federalists or, more broadly, all those who feared the growth of federal power at the expense of the states, were prompt to denounce the "system." The stage was thus set for a prolonged and bitter battle.

The question of assumption, thorny though it was, was far less explosive an issue than the redemption of the old Congress's certificates. The assumption issue divided the states quite simply between those states that still had large debts and were glad to be relieved of them and those states that, through their own frugality and good management (or so they felt), had discharged most of their debts and saw no reason to be charged for those of their less provident neighbors. This division turned out to be manageable. But the rumors of redemption were accompanied by reports of wild speculation, with the moneyed men buying certificates up at a fraction of their face value in anticipation of making a killing when they were redeemed. Stories circulated that many members of Congress, being on the inside, had been speculating in certificates. Those to whom the certificates had originally been issued—the largest and most deserving class, of course, being veterans of the Revolution—would get nothing, having, for the most part, sold them at greatly discounted prices.

Word arrived soon after Congress convened that North Carolina had finally ratified and was now a bona fide member of the Union. The president delivered his First Annual Address to Congress on January 8, recommending that its members give attention in the coming session to "providing for the common defense. . . . To be prepared for war is one of the most effective means of preserving peace. A free people ought not only to be well armed, but disciplined." Despite efforts to effect treaties with "certain hostile tribes of Indians," the "Southern and Western frontiers" remained exposed to Indian depredations, and a military force might have to be dispatched to protect the settlers in those regions.

Conditions of naturalization, salaries for officers of the government, a uniform system of weights and measures, the improvement of roads, and the establishment of a postal system were all matters that required the attention of Congress. Finally, the president hoped the legislators would consider the best way to promote science and literature, since "knowledge is in every country the surest basis of public happiness." He left it to their discretion whether this end would be best accomplished "by affording aids to seminaries of learning already established" or "by the institution of a national university."

Again Maclay was indignant at the reply of the Senate—"The most servile echo I ever heard"—and at the appearance of General Knox with a proposal to raise an army of 5,040 men and officers at a cost of $1,152,000 to go to war with the Creek Indians. Maclay was also critical of the members of Congress going to the president's mansion to deliver their reply to his speech. The whole procedure smacked too much of British practice. The president was "but a man, but really a good one, and we can have nothing to fear from him," Maclay noted, "but much from the precedents he may establish."

The rumors of Hamilton's financial plans were verified when the secretary of the treasury sent the budget to the House of Representatives. "A committee of speculators in certificates could not have formed it more for their advantage," Maclay wrote. "It has occasioned many serious faces." Indeed, the talk in and out of Congress was of little else. Maclay noted, "Hamilton, literally speaking, is moving heaven and earth in favor of his system. . . . The Cincinnati is another of his machines and the whole city of New York." Since the principal objection centered on the injustice of allowing speculators to make excessive profits, Madison proposed a scheme by which certificates would be bought up from speculators, not at their face value, but at the market price, and the difference between the market price and the original value would be paid to those who had first received the certificates. The practical difficulties of this method were soon evident. It seemed to Maclay that the members of both houses revealed a "spirit of uncertainty . . . a want of confidence either in the Secretary's scheme or in Madison's proposal. Like a flight of land-fowl at sea, they seem bewildered and wish for a resting-place, but distrust every object that offers."

Maclay was indignant at what he considered to be the improper use of "influence." In his journal he constantly complained about those among his allies in the Senate who were seduced from their principles by the flattering attentions of "interested parties." "Alas," he wrote, "what poor, supple things men are, bending down before every dinner and floated away with every cask of liquor! He even hinted at out-and-out bribery, though he confessed he had no clear evidence of it.

On the issue of naturalization, the New Englanders were for the most severe requirement, the Pennsylvanians for the most liberal. Again Maclay indulged himself in some reflections not very flattering to the "Eastern men." He wrote in his journal: "We Pennsylvanians act as if we believed that God made of one blood all families of the earth; but the Eastern people seem to think that he made none but New England folks. It is strange that men born and educated under republican forms of government should be so contracted on the subject of general philanthropy." Pennsylvania had been for a hundred years or more a haven for "strangers." The New Englanders were, in Maclay's opinion, "the worst characters of any people who offer themselves for citizens. Yet these are the men who affect the greatest fear of being contaminated with foreign manners, customs, or vices."

While the passage doubtless contained some truth, it was a notable example of the persistence of those sectional prejudices that were so conspicuous during the Revolution. It might also be noted that Thomas Jefferson, soon to be the *beau ideal* of the Pennsylvania democrat, was, if anything, more fearful of the corrupting influence of immigrants than the New Englanders that Maclay castigated.

It was Maclay's view that immigration—"the adoption of strangers," as he put it—had "set Pennsylvania far ahead of her sister states. They are spiteful and envious, and wish to deprive her of this source of population." The Carolinas and Georgia were equally desirous of increasing their populations through immigration but fearful "of importing people who may be averse to slavery."

If the Pennsylvania senator was ill-disposed toward New Englanders, he was hardly more tolerant of "Yorkers." "They were all the creatures of fashion and ostentation, monarchists and tools of the British interests," he wrote. "The men put on airs and dressed foppishly." The women were as bad. They were padded, fore and aft, "with a bunch of bosom and bulk of cotton that never was warranted by any feminine appearance in nature." They walked "bent forward at the middle . . . as if some disagreeable disorder prevented them from standing erect."

The assumption bill and Hamilton's relentless promotion of it, along with an interminable and inconclusive debate on naturalization, exacerbated feelings among the senators. Maclay wrote of his colleagues' use of "base, invective, indecorous language"; three or four were up at a time demanding the floor, "manifesting signs of passion." There was, in his view, "a general discontent among the members and many of them do not hesitate to declare that the Union must fall to pieces at the rate we go on. Indeed, many seem to wish it."

Maclay himself, with all his talk about disinterestedness, was a speculator in Western lands and thus had a vested interest in a generous immigration policy and especially in allowing immigrants to buy and hold land before they became naturalized citizens. Robert Morris, his fellow senator, the "Financier of the Revolution" whose genius in money matters had prevented complete collapse of the Continental economy during the Revolution, and who was already deep in the speculative morass that would eventually land him in a debtor's prison, came to Maclay with a scheme to sell Maclay's Western lands to European investors at a dollar or more an acre and so help to bail Morris out of his financial difficulties as well as return a tidy profit to Maclay.

On the subject of the Western lands generally there was a sharp division in Congress between the speculators, who wished to do everything they could to encourage westward migration, and those members whose interests were attached, through commerce or farming, to the seacoast. The latter wished to do all they could to discourage movement to the west on the grounds that it would drain off many of the more energetic and ambitious characters from the settled regions of the original states, all anxious to increase their own populations and thus their relative weight in the House of Representatives.

Part of the motive of those members of both houses who had supported high tariffs on imported goods was that the resultant high prices might drive people to the frontier in search of cheaper living. Finally, in the contradictory feelings that clustered around the "Western problem," there was anxiety that the frontier regions might detach themselves from the United States and form an alliance with Spain, since the right to the use of the Mississippi River, the critical artery of the Louisiana Territory, owned by Spain and controlled from New Orleans, was essential to any economic development in that part of the West whose tributaries flowed into the Mississippi (most of the trans-Allegheny region).

Land companies claimed huge portions of the Mississippi Basin— the Ohio Company, which had interests in a considerable portion of what was later to become the state of Ohio; the Vandalia Company, which dated to before the Revolution and had attempted to establish the state of Transylvania in the Tennessee-Kentucky area; and many similar land ventures. In addition to Robert Morris, Washington, Patrick Henry, James Wilson, Franklin, and a number of other leading figures of the Revolutionary era were investors in land companies. The Pennsylvania delegation to Congress was itself split over the issue of naturalization and the right of aliens to hold land. Scott told Maclay that George Clymer was "dreadfully afraid all the people [of Pennsylvania] would fly to the Western world." To which Maclay replied, "Scott, I told you some time ago that all this would happen if you taxed the Atlantic States too high, and you gave me a great Monongahela laugh in answer," Maclay's reference apparently being to Scott's own landholdings in the region of the Monongahela River.

Maclay had frequent occasion to reflect on the comment of John Henry of Maryland that "All great [large] governments resolve themselves into cabals." "Ours," Maclay added, "is a mere system of jockeying opinions. Vote this way for me, and I will vote that way for you." Maclay found himself on the negative side of virtually every issue, whether it was pay for ministers to foreign countries—"I wished no political connection whatever with any country whatever"—or funds for a "standing army" of twelve hundred soldiers to protect the frontier—"the first error seems to have been the appointing of a Secretary of War when we were at peace, and now we must find troops lest his office should run out of employment." If a standing army (unconstitutional in his view) were approved, the next demand would be for a navy. All such proposals were part of a plot to rob the people of their liberties, destroy the independence of the states, and form a "consolidated" government. The plan of the court party or monarchy men was "to overwhelm us with debt . . . for fear, as there is likely to be no war, that if there should be no debt to be provided for there would be no business for the general government with all their train of officers. . . . The first thing done under our new government was the creation of a vast number of offices and officers. . . . A Secretary of War with a host of clerks; and above all a Secretary of State. . . . Hence we must have a mass of national debt to employ the Treasury, and army for fear the Department of War should lack employment. Foreign engagements, too, must be attended to to keep up the consequences of that Secretary. . . . Give Knox an army, and he will soon have a war on hand."

It took a visit by the new secretary of state, Thomas Jefferson, to persuade Maclay to vote any funds for the salaries and expenses of American consuls and ambassadors—an early manifestation of what might be called the striped-pants, pointy-head syndrome of American populism. It was Maclay's first direct contact with the democratic hero. He described Jefferson as "a slender man; has rather the air of stiffness in his manner; his clothes seem too small for him; he sits in a lounging manner, on one hip commonly, and with one of his shoulders elevated much above the other; his face has a sunny aspect; his whole figure has a loose, shackling air. He had a rambling, vacant look, and nothing of the firm, collected deportment which I expected would dignify the presence of a secretary or minister. I looked for gravity, but a laxity of manner seemed shed about him. He spoke almost without ceasing. It was loose and rambling and yet he scattered information wherever he went, and some brilliant sentiments sparkled from him."

Jefferson charmed the Senate committee, which agreed without further debate to leave the setting of salaries for diplomats in different countries to the discretion of the president. The episode was a revealing one, demonstrating Jefferson's informality and his skill in getting his way. Where every ploy of Hamilton's aroused resentment and hostility, Jefferson was to prevail through ingratiation.

The president had insisted that Jefferson serve as his secretary of state. In that role the Virginian found himself aligned against Hamilton in every meeting of the Cabinet. In Jefferson's words, "Hamilton and myself were daily pitted in the cabinet like two cocks." In political and, so far as Hamilton indulged in theorizing, philosophical beliefs, in dress, manner, temperament, height—indeed by almost every conceivable measure—they were the antithesis of each other. Hamilton was small, aggressive, dapper; Jefferson tall, somewhat diffident, untidy. Hamilton was an ardent admirer of the British government and everything British; Jefferson a lover of all things French, with a cordial dislike of the British. Hamilton was spokesman for the financial interests of the new nation, the moneyed men, a promoter of infant industry, an advocate of "protection" for American manufacturers; Jefferson an aristocrat by birth and manner, champion of democracy, proclaimer of the superior virtues of rural life, opponent of immigration, suspicious of business and businessmen, and of none more than bankers. Each in his own way anticipated America, and in their mutual distrust—more accurately, hatred—they represented a number of the major polarities in American life: farm versus factory, rural versus urban, democracy versus a moneyed elite (Hamilton had been quoted as saying, "Your people, sir, is a great beast"; Jefferson as echoing Rousseau's declaration that "The voice of the people is the voice of God"), slavery versus emancipation (Hamilton was an outspoken opponent of slavery; Jefferson, while critical of the South's "peculiar institution," was a slaveholder). One could go on and on.

Their dissimilarities seem almost beyond enumerating. Yet Washington kept his two cocks in the Cabinet pit. Why? It could not have been an edifying spectacle. The hostility of the two men must have imparted to every meeting of that body a disagreeable tension.

Jefferson clearly had no stomach for it and tried repeatedly to escape. We can only conjecture that Washington used the two men to demonstrate his determination to transcend factionalism. In another sense, Jefferson was a hostage for good behavior of the more zealous Republicans. Perhaps Washington reasoned that as long as Jefferson remained a leading member of his administration, his enemies would not give full vent to their animosity. On one occastion when Jefferson tried to beg off from his post on the grounds that the differences between himself and Hamilton were so acute as to compromise the proper functioning of the government, Washington wrote to him, "I believe the views of both of you to be pure and well-meant. . . . I have a great, a sincere esteem and regard for you both, and ardently wish that some line could be marked out by which both [of] you could walk."

Jefferson, frustrated at not being able to take the lead publicly in opposition to the policies of the administration of which he was so conspicuous a part, appointed poet Philip Freneau to the position of a translating clerk in the State Department and helped him start an antiadministration newspaper, the *National Gazette*. The Federalists already had a semiofficial newspaper, John Fenno's *Gazette of the United States*. Now it was Fenno against Freneau. Rumor had it that Jefferson himself was the author of many of the articles attacking the administration; and Jefferson recorded in his journal that at a Cabinet meeting Washington had attacked "that rascal Freneau" for sending him three copies of his paper. "He could see in this nothing but an impudent design to insult him; he ended in a high tone," Jefferson wrote.

On another day, Jefferson noted that Washington spoke of "a piece in Freneau's paper . . . ; he said he despised all such attacks on him personally, but that there had never been an act of the Government, not meaning in the executive line only, but in any line, which that paper had not abused. He was evidently sore and warm, and I took his intention to be that I should interpose in some way with Freneau, perhaps withdraw his appointment. . . . But I will not do it," Jefferson added. It was, by any measure, an odd situation.

Through the whole spring of 1790, Congress worried over the matter of assumption. Finally, after months of wrangling, the Federalists hit on a bargain: Massachusetts and South Carolina, the states that had most to gain by assumption, would give their votes for a permanent seat of government on the Potomac River in return for the votes for assumption from those states that wished the capital to be situated in the South.

James Jackson, one of the president's aides, made a "florid harangue" to the Pennsylvania delegation on the advantages of such an arrangement (the Pennsylvania payoff was that the seat of government for the next session of Congress should be moved from New York to Philadelphia). Maclay refused to be party to any such scheme, and its immediate result was to make the atmosphere in Congress even more tense. Maclay noted that Hamilton's supporters in the Senate appeared "drooping . . . turbid and forlorn." Rufus King "looked like a boy that had been whipped, and General Schuyler's hair stood on end as if the Indians had fired at him." Yet they had soon redoubled their efforts. The issue was brought to a vote in the House, and many senators were present to listen to the debate. When the vote was taken, assumption was defeated. Theodore Sedgwick, a Boston Federalist, arose to pronounce "a funeral oration over it." Called to order, he broke down and fled the House. When he returned, "his face Bore the visible marks of weeping." Fitzsimmons, a Pennsylvania representative, flushed bright red, and tears trickled down his cheeks. George Clymer's face turned "deadly white, his lips quivered, and his nether jaw shook with convulsive motions." Fisher Ames "sat torpid, as if his faculties had been benumbed." Elbridge Gerry, interrupted by "consumptive coughs," declared that the Massachusetts delegates would take no further part in the deliberations of the House until they had received new instructions from their state.

In the midst of the crisis over assumption word reached New York of the death of Benjamin Franklin. Maclay was at Ralph Izard's lodgings with a number of congressmen who seemed to him to vie with each other in denigrating the deceased—he had been vain, ambitious, devious, self-indulgent. "I could hardly find it in my heart," Maclay wrote, "to paint the devil so bad."

After several more weeks of behind-the-scenes maneuvering, "Hamilton's gladiators" were ready to try again for the first part of the "capital bargain"—the interim location of the capital at Philadelphia. The full Federalist array was mustered. Butler and Izard "actually went out and brought Governor Johnston [of North Carolina] with his night-cap on, out of bed, and a bed with him." The bed was deposited in the committee room. William Few, also home ill, was sent for. There was a half-hour wait until he arrived, looking weak and pale. The vote was taken, and Philadelphia triumphed 13 to 11. The gladiators, anxious to improve the moment, forced a vote on the Potomac as the ultimate site for the capital. The vote this time was 15 to 9 against.

More confusion! Amid the clamor a call was made and carried for adjournment. "So ended the uproar of the day," Maclay noted.

The plotting continued. Word came to Robert Morris that Hamilton wished a clandestine meeting with him. Morris replied that he would take a walk the next morning on the Battery and the secretary might join him there if he wished. Hamilton was there. He needed one vote in the Senate and five in the House for assumption, he told Morris. If Morris could help him procure the votes, he would instruct his men to support "the permanent residence of Congress at Germantown or the Falls of the Delaware." When Morris informed Maclay of his conversation with the secretary, the latter replied stiffly, "You need not consult me," yet in the next breath he urged Morris to make "the temporary residence of Congress in Philadelphia the price."

Suddenly Baltimore entered the lists for the capital, and all was once more uncertainty. On June 16, with funding, assumption, and the location of the capital all still up in the air, Morris drew Maclay aside and informed him that none other than Jefferson had proposed a compromise: Philadelphia to be the capital for fifteen years, thereafter Georgetown on the Potomac. New lines were drawn and new alliances were formed. Again nothing was concluded. The business of the nation was at a standstill. But there was another element in the plot. Rhode Island finally applied and was admitted to the Union on June 16. Her congressional delegation arrived nine days later and was seated. The question was: How would they vote on the critical issues before Congress?

In July the issue of the capital was finally decided: it would be in Philadelphia for ten years and would then have a permanent seat on the Potomac. Even after the final vote Rufus King proved irreconcilable. "He sobbed, wiped his eyes, scolded and railed, and accused, first everybody and then nobody, of bargaining, contracting arrangements and engagements that would dissolve the Union."

Maclay came reluctantly to the conclusion that the machinations of the Hamilton gladiators had the support of the president himself, who had become, in the hands of his secretary of the treasury, "the dishclout of every dirty speculation, as his name goes to wipe away blame and silence all murmuring." A conspiracy of interested politicians and speculators had taken control of the new government. "Everything, even to the naming of a committee, is prearranged by Hamilton," Maclay wrote in his journal. "I cannot find even a single member to condole in sincerity with me over the calamities of my country. . . . I believe the sun never shone on a more abandoned composition of political characters." The whole country was engaged in speculation on the funding bill, "and, of course, engaged in influencing the measures of Congress. Nor have the members themselves kept their hands clean from this dirty work. . . . The unexampled success has obliterated every mark of reproach, and from henceforth we may consider speculation as a congressional employment." Maclay finally confided to his journal that he wished the president dead—"would to God this same General Washington were in heaven! We could not then have him brought forward as the constant cover to every unconstitutional and irrepublican act."

Vote after vote on assumption and funding found the Senate split 13 to 13, with Adams frequently casting the deciding vote. At the end of July, funding and assumption at last carried the day and Maclay noted in his journal: "A majority are sold, and Hamilton has bought them."

The next item on Hamilton's legislative agenda called for the establishment of a national bank to be called the Bank of the United States. The vote in Congress on the bank was an overwhelmingly sectional one. Thirty-four out of 35 Northern congressmen and 5 out of 25 Southern representatives voted aye. Yet many plain citizens in the Northern and Middle states and a majority of those who called themselves Democrats were suspicious of the bank or openly opposed to it as an instrument of the moneyed classes for the exploitation of their fellows. John Adams, as we have seen, shared Jefferson's hostility toward banks and bankers. But on the Fourth of July, 1791— the day the Bank of the United States opened for business—a crowd of investors was pressing against its doors eager to buy the twenty thousand shares of stock (each share cost two hundred dollars) that were to constitute its capital. Every share was sold within the first half hour. The disappointed would-be investors set up a howl, and one man who had bought a share was offered twice what he had paid for it before he left the building. Madison wrote to Jefferson, "stock-jobbing drowns every other subject. The coffee-house is in an eternal buzz with the gamblers. . . . Of all the shameful circumstances of this business, it is among the greatest to see members of the legislature, who were most active in pushing this job, openly grasping its emoluments." Jefferson wrote to Monroe, "The land office, the Federal town, certain schemes of manufacture likely to be converted into aliment [food] for that rage [speculation]."

The sale of bank stock added fire to the speculative mania created by the funding of the certificates of the Confederation Congress. "For the whole summer scarce anything else was bought or sold or talked of. The stock-jobbers . . . were the only men having anything to do, and if a man had not stock he might as well shut himself up in his cellar," according to the *American Daily Advertiser*. Here again we see evidence of that preoccupation—one might almost say obsession—with making money by one means or another that was, from the first moment of the Republic, so conspicuous an aspect of the American character. To make money, as we have said, was to enjoy the intoxicating experience of altering one's relationship to everything around one. It was a means of asserting oneself, of affirming one's worth, of transcending the present or "given" situation for another, more alluring one. Most important, any number could play. That fiercely directed will, formed by the protestant Reformation, which had been used to establish communities in the wilderness in the face of staggering obstacles and difficulties, might now be used for "self-aggrandizement" by means of money. Money became an extension and a validation of the self. Stocks and stock-jobbing, feverish speculation, and the pursuit of wealth were not invented by Americans; but America was to offer the most fertile field in the world for "making money"; and the character and quality of money—hard or soft, gold or silver, paper or metal—was to become one of the principal vectors of the "American experience." Americans not only "democratized" money by creating a society in which everyone was encouraged to make it, they vastly extended the power of money to work transformations on the environment, natural and artifactual. Money became an extension of human energy or a multiplier of it. It encouraged ingenuity and invention; at the beginning of the Republic, Americans began devising ways to make their fortunes and have never stopped.

The mania for banking clearly could not be satisfied only by the Bank of the United States. That institution was rather the stimulus. If, a month after its establishment, its shares sold for $100 above their par value, that fact served to suggest the desirability of founding other banks. The Bank of the State of New York opened on August 10 and its stock, with a face value of $200, was subscribed in five minutes and a week later sold for $280 in New York and $320 in Philadelphia. But in two weeks the stock had fallen to $100 a share, and the Republican papers were filled with the charges that it had been manipulated by insiders. The *New York Journal* declared it "all the work of the

certificate men, the tools of the ministry, the aristocrats, the conspirators against liberty, the workers of that 'aristocratical engine' which was
to squirt money into the pockets of the people as plentifully as dirt."
Those speculators who had lost their shirts in the drop of the market
were ridiculed as victims of "scriptomania" and "scriptophobia." The
symptoms, according to Benjamin Franklin Bache's *Aurora*, were "a
long face, a pale complexion, deep silence, a light purse, and a heavy
heart."

Maclay was outraged at the speculative mania. He had done his
best, a lonely fighter, in his view at least, against monarchy and
corruption. There was nothing more that he could do to stem the tide.
He would go home to the family he missed so keenly. He asked his
Pennsylvania colleagues if they objected. They made no effort to
prevail on him to stay. So he shook the dust of New York off his feet,
expunged, so far as he could, the memory of the "vile Yorkers," and
made his way back to his wife and children. Many members of
Congress, it seems fair to assume, heaved a sigh of relief. But they had
not seen the last of him. He was back in December for the third session
of Congress, this time in Philadelphia, with his now familiar suspicions
and aspersions. He observed that military operations had been
undertaken against the Wabash Indians "without any authority of
Congress." Surprisingly, he had supported Hamilton's proposal for a
national bank, although he viewed banks in general "as operating like a
tax in favor of the rich against the poor, tending to the assimulation [of
money] in a few hands; and under this view opposed to republicanism."

Maclay also met the famous Dr. George Logan, as stubborn a
democrat as himself, whose motto was Rousseau's *vox populi, vox Dei*
(the voice of the people is the voice of God), which, of course, the
framers of the Constitution were very far from believing, as we have
seen. It was perhaps the most characteristic expression of the nascent
Secular-Democratic Consciousness. Given particular emphasis by the
theorists of the French Revolution, it became the major article of faith
in the new democratic creed.

Maclay, who had the two-year term as senator, was defeated in the
elections of the fall of 1790 by the radical William Findley, largely
through the efforts of his fellow Anti-Federalists. Even they found him
too obdurate and uncompromising. But we take leave of him with
reluctance. He has certainly been a lively guide through the shoals and
rocks of the First Congress. Self-righteous, paranoid, hopelessly biased

against all who differed with him in his notions of republicanism, he was nonetheless a shrewd observer of people and events and a master of invective. Through his remarkable journal he gives us an insight into the mind and psychology of an Anti-Federalist Republican democrat. If Maclay was not as noble as he professed to be, it was equally the case that his enemies were by no means as wicked.

Further, Maclay serves to remind us of how precarious the triumph of the Federalists was. The Constitution had providentially survived a half-dozen close calls. All the labors of the Federalists would have come to nothing if its enemies had been able to emasculate it in its infancy by interpreting it in so constricted and narrow a fashion that it would have been little better than the discredited Articles of Confederation. It is plain from Maclay's journal that he and his allies wished to have virtually no national government. They wanted no regular army or navy, secretaries of state or war, virtually no central administration, only the most restricted power in the presidency, and a powerless federal judiciary. They completely rejected the concept of government to which the framers themselves were committed. The striking thing is that the Anti-Federalists, having lost in the state ratifying conventions (by the slimmest of margins in the three most crucial states), came disconcertingly close to snatching victory from defeat in the First Congress. It took the enormous prestige of Washington (which, as we have seen, gradually eroded under the pressure of partisan politics); the indefatigable machinations of Hamilton and his gladiators; the persistent lobbying of speculators in congressional certificates and a substantial amount of plain "logrolling," as it came to be called (the trading of favors between congressmen); and, finally, a rather dubious bargain to get the Federalist program through Congress. That is to say, to make the new government function as the framers of it intended it should—and all this in the face of what were believed to be substantial Federalist majorities in both houses. As it turned out, the Federalist majorities were more apparent than real. Put another way, in many instances sectional interests turned out to be more important than party alignments.

We will not be able to follow in nearly such detail the deliberations of Congress throughout the balance of this work, but it seemed important both to take advantage of William Maclay's conducted tour and to give the reader a picture of the real, and often rather sordid, workings of our national legislature from its inception, lest he or she think that the politicians of the early Republic were free from the vices and failings that mark, if they do not distinguish, their present-day counterparts.

It was all there in the first moment—the sectional jealousies, the "cabals" or secret agreements, the ubiquitousness of business or commercial "interest," the speculators, the power brokers, the deals and dealers.

As for William Maclay, he returned to his farm near Harrisburg in western Pennsylvania and built himself a fine stone mansion that became the nucleus of the little town of Maclayville. Politics was an addiction. He served in the Pennsylvania House of Representatives for two terms and was an associate judge in his county's court. Fifty-two at the time of his election to the U.S. Senate, he died in 1804 at the then rather ripe old age of sixty-seven. A young neighbor recalled seeing him "wearing a suit of white flannel, with lace ruffles, walking up and down the river bank in Maclayville. He thought he had never seen such a dignified, majestic old gentleman."

Scriptomania was confined initially to the larger cities of the seacoast—New York, Philadelphia, and Boston. But trouble was brewing in the western counties, especially in western Pennsylvania. The excise bill, passed early in 1791, provided for a tax of from twenty-five to forty cents a gallon on imported liquor, according to its strength. On domestic liquors the tax ran from nine to twenty-five cents. The Republicans in and out of Congress had raised a strong resistance to the excise bill, summoning up the specter of parliamentary taxation and denouncing the bill as another barefaced attempt to create a "consolidated monarchical government" determined to generate vast revenues for the purpose of overbearing the states and enslaving the people.

Hamilton's reply to such charges, of course, was that the generation of income was essential if the national debt were to be funded. Although the legislatures of Maryland, North Carolina, and Virginia protested the tax as unconstitutional, it bore hardest on a group least disposed to accept the edicts of the new government—the farmers of the Pennsylvania frontier. Maclay represented these men so far as anyone did. They raised wheat and rye, converting these crops into raw whiskey, which they sent to the eastern towns by pack horse and wagon. The means of transportation were too crude and their cost too great to make the shipment of grain itself practical. Thus, the reduction of the grain to whiskey provided these western farmers with their cash crop. Since these farmers almost monopolized this trade, the excise tax seemed to them discriminatory and they made clear at once that they had no intention of paying it.

The law went into effect on August 1, but in western Pennsylvania no one stepped forward to apply for the job of tax collector and the farmers with stills called a meeting for July 27 at Redstone Old Fort to make plans for general resistance. There delegates issued a call for two conventions, one to meet at the town of Washington at the end of August, the other at Pittsburgh a few weeks later. The Washington convention denounced the law and urged the farmers of the region to treat anyone who undertook to enforce it with hostility and contempt. The Pittsburgh meeting went further and attacked the interest rate on the national debt, the pay scales of federal officials, and the funding system.

The tax collector for Washington and Allegheny counties was intercepted at Pigeon Creek, had his hair cut off, was tarred and feathered, and was set afoot to make his way home as best he could. The abused collector recognized three of his tormentors and swore out warrants against them, but the deputy marshal who was sent to serve them found the people in such an angry and rebellious mood that he deemed it more discreet to refrain. He picked out a local half-wit to carry the message to the officers of the U.S. court at Philadelphia. Somehow word of the poor man's mission got out. He too was seized and was whipped, tarred and feathered, blindfolded, and left in the woods bound to a tree.

A deranged man named Wilson declared himself a tax collector and visited various stills announcing that he was gathering information for the government. Anti-excise men came to Wilson's house at night and burned his clothing, branded him with a hot iron, and tarred and feathered him, leaving him, in the words of an observer, "a sight to make human nature shudder." There the matter rested for the time being. No sustained effort was made to collect the tax. It seemed that the western counties had triumphed in their resistance to the government.

The Federalists profited greatly from the fact that under the new Constitution the postwar depression came rapidly to an end and a period of prosperity buoyed up everyone's spirits. Historians have argued over whether the wave of prosperity was the consequence of a feeling of confidence in the country at large at the inauguration of the new government, or whether the two events were merely coincidental.

It is a difficult question to answer, and evidence can be adduced for both sides. The important thing is that by and large the new government got the credit for it and was thereby immeasurably strengthened. Conversely, if bad times had persisted it would certainly have been blamed on the Federalists by their enemies, and that fact along with the bitter sectional feelings and the profound provincialism of the states would almost certainly have brought the new government down in ruins before it had had a fair chance to prove itself. In any event, the inherent optimism that seems to be such a conspicuous element of the American character asserted itself. Commerce flourished and new industries sprang up like mushrooms in the Eastern and Middle states. Iron mills and textile factories were specially favored by prosperous city dwellers looking for enterprises in which to invest. Lotteries became an infatuation in many states, a quick and relatively easy way to raise money for public improvements.

In the long view, perhaps the most significant episode in the second session of Congress was the appearance of a delegation of Quakers with a memorial calling for the abolition of slavery. It was presented to the House, and on March 17 a bitter debate took place in the course of which Southern congressmen "could not contain their wrath and when arguments failed them, fell to abusing the Quakers, their religion, their morals, and their memorial." They were "denounced as enemies of freedom, spics during the late war, and the guides and conductors of the British armies." Fisher Ames wrote to a Boston friend: "The Quakers have been abused, the eastern States inveighed against, the chairman rudely charged with partiality. Language low, indecent, and profane has been used; wit equally stale and wretched has been attempted." The House had sunk below the most disorderly state legislature. The motion that "Congress have no authority to interfere in the emancipation of slaves, or in the treatment of them within any of the States," passed (on a primarily sectional vote) by the slim margin of 29 to 25, thus increasing, if possible, the paranoia of the South. Indeed, the vote seemed to indicate that almost half of the representatives thought that Congress *did* have authority to emancipate the slaves, or at least ameliorate their condition.

During the recess that followed the first session of Congress, Washington took a tour through New England. The reasons were doubtless both personal and political. It had been noted by visitors that the president looked sad and pensive. Maclay observed that he tapped abstractedly with his fork against the side of the table. The endless entertaining, frequently of people he knew to be opposed to the policies of his infant administration, was clearly a strain and a burden. He made no small talk. He felt ill-at-ease in such company, and his guests were usually equally constrained. He was well aware of the bitterness of the debates in Congress, of the increasing frequency of thinly veiled attacks on him, and of the gradual erosion of his popularity among the Anti-Federalists. He was subject to periods of profound depression, as he had been during low points of the Revolution. But with the same dogged persistence that had marked his conduct throughout the war, he carried the weight of the new Republic on his shoulders, knowing that he was the essential pin that kept the whole rickety structure from flying apart.

He felt old far beyond his years. His hearing was failing, and this contributed to his sense of declining powers. As thin-skinned as most men, he winced at the constant sniping of the Anti-Federalists' newspapers. It seemed as though a political hurricane swirled around him and that he stood in its eye, imperturbable. Actually, he was far from that; he suffered excruciatingly, but he kept his suffering largely to himself. Occasionally it broke out in one of those famous rages that terrified those around him. All he had wanted was to be left alone to live out his few remaining years at his beloved Mount Vernon, and now he was attacked for wanting to be a king. It touched him on his most sensitive nerve. His deepest pride was that he had put power from him; that when the devil had tempted him to place himself at the head of his army and secure justice for his men and order to the Union, he had firmly and unhesitatingly rebuffed the notion. It had been widely said that history could not produce another example of such rectitude. It seemed to Washington as though he had placed all his dearly won fame and honor on the scale; the only question that remained to be answered was whether they would be worn away by those partisan animosities so vividly displayed in Congress. How much of Washington's enormous prestige must be expended to preserve his country? It was as though every week saw a little more of it used up. There might thus be a time when none was left. Although the enemies of the Constitution, of a federal or "consolidated" government, did not yet dare attack him directly, they nibbled away at him with sly references and cutting allusions.

So Washington's New England journey served two purposes. It got him away from New York, the scene of incessant intrigue, and it refreshed him by demonstrating anew the firm hold he had on the affections of ordinary men and women. In every town and village the inhabitants turned out to express their love with joyful celebrations and grateful remembrances—with innumerable bad poems, lavish feasts, and displays of fireworks. He paid special attention to Revolutionary veterans in the crowds that flocked to see the savior of the Confederacy and the Father of the country. The wavering Federalists of New England were vastly encouraged by the journey. It also served as a sobering demonstration to the Anti-Federalists of the president's popular support. Only at Boston did the president receive something of a cold shoulder. John Hancock, who had lent his name so reluctantly to the ratification of the Constitution, was the left-wing governor elected in the aftermath of Shays' Rebellion. He obviously thought it politically expedient not to make any official fuss over the president's visit. He thus remained churlishly at home on the apparent grounds that as the head of the independent state of Massachusetts he owed no homage to Washington, who was only the chief administrative officer of the federation of such independent states. Perhaps surprised by the degree of enthusiasm displayed by the citizens of Boston for the hero of the Revolution, Hancock tried to made amends the next day.

When Congress assembled in the fall, a major piece of unfinished (or unbegun) congressional business was that of amendments to the Constitution, especially a bill of rights. Ratification of the Constitution had been possible in at least four states only by solemn assurances that the first order of business of the Congress would be the adoption of a bill of rights and the consideration of a number of amendments proposed in the various state conventions. Elbridge Gerry, who had opposed the Constitution in part because of the absence of a bill of rights, now argued that "the salvation of America depends on the establishment of the Government whether amended or not." Another senator, supporting Gerry, stated that the new government was a government in name only. "And how long it will remain in such a situation, God only knows. . . . We are not content with two revolutions in less than fourteen years; we must enter upon a third, without necessity or propriety."

There was good reason for such apprehensions. Richard Henry Lee and William Grayson, the two Virginia senators, plainly intended to try to amend the Constitution to make it conform to their strong states' rights bias. They had made no bones of their plan in declaring themselves candidates. Madison had almost been defeated for the House of Representatives on the basis of a rumor that he was opposed to amendments. At the insistence of Madison the matter was referred to a committee made up of a representative from each state. When the committee reported to the House, the next question was whether the amendments should be interwoven with the Constitution or simply appended to it in a block. The Anti-Federalists wished to go through the Constitution article by article and clause by clause. That way they might alter any number of articles under the pretense of incorporating the individual articles of the debated Bill of Rights. The Federalists were of course horrified at such a suggestion. It would be tantamount to holding a new constitutional convention.

In the words of a Federalist member: "He had seen an act entitled 'an act to amend a supplement to an act entitled an act for altering part of an act entitled an act for certain purposes therein mentioned.' If the gentlemen were disposed to run into such jargon in amending and altering the Constitution, he could not help it," but he clearly deplored it. Nonetheless, the members decided to open that Pandora's box. All kinds of alarming things fell out at once, such as a motion to alter the Preamble to include the sentence: "Government being intended for the benefit of the people, and . . . derived from their authority alone." Next it was proposed to change the representation in the House from thirty-six to two hundred (passed by the House, this amendment died when the states refused to ratify it).

Finally, baffled by the problems attendant on trying to revise the whole Constitution, the congressmen decided to confine their attention, at least initially, to the Bill of Rights per se. Perhaps the most significant exchange on the Bill of Rights took place as a consequence of Madison's suggestion that it should apply to the states as well as to the federal government. The House voted down the Virginian's motion by a substantial margin.

After considerable debate the House agreed on sixteen amendments and sent them to the Senate, which cut them down to fourteen. In a House–Senate conference they were reduced to twelve. The states refused to ratify two—the change in the ratio of representation and a provision concerning pay for congressmen. The remaining ten became the first ten amendments of the Constitution.

Although we often speak of the first ten amendments to the Constitution as though they constituted the Bill of Rights, in practical fact it was only the first eight that involved the points of traditional bills of rights. The Ninth Amendment stated: "The enumeration in the Constitution, of certain rights, shall not be construed to deny or disparage others retained by the people." And the Tenth declared that "The powers not delegated to the United States by the Constitution, nor prohibited by it to the States, are reserved to the States respectively, or to the people." In fact, the Ninth Amendment had uncertain meaning and little significance. So far as its meaning was decipherable, it belonged to the realm of pious platitudes. The Tenth Amendment, only slightly less opaque, became a rallying point for "strict constructionists" and states' righters.

Settlers and Indians

While Congress struggled to give substance to the new Constitution, events of some moment took place on the vast and poorly defined frontier. The Treaty of Paris (1783) that concluded the Revolution had provided for compensation to the Loyalists for confiscated property and, among other things, the British abandonment of the posts they had held in the Old Northwest. In defiance of the treaty, the British had held on to the posts, giving as their excuse the fact that the American states had refused to honor their treaty obligations in regard to the Loyalists. British retention of the posts encouraged Indian tribes in the region to take a hard line with congressional negotiators who tried to buy up their lands and conclude treaties with them.

From the moment the earliest settlers had established themselves on the continent there had been serious clashes with the Indians. Initially the whites simply fought for survival. On the defensive, they had no place to which to retreat unless they were to plunge into the ocean. But having made good their foothold in the coastal settlements, settlers began to press inexorably into the interior. The move westward was to be, in some ways, the major theme of American history. Pamphleteers, theorists, and politicians spoke confidently of occupying the continent, although they assumed that would occur in the distant future. Centuries must pass, they assumed, before this vast land, thinly populated by aborigines, would be covered with farms, towns, and great cities. The notion that it might happen in a few generations, even decades, seems to have occurred to no one but a few half-mad visionaries.

In fact, the persistent and relentless pressure of westward migration was one of the most remarkable phenomena in history. It was already very much in evidence before the Revolution. It continued during the Revolution, most notably in the South and in the Wautauga settlements, and did so in the face of devastating Indian raids. After the war it increased very substantially in volume, doubtless encouraged by the illusion that the Indians had been intimidated by the defeat of their British supporters.

There was about the westward movement a quality of the instinctual that put the thoughtful observer in mind of the migration of lemmings into the sea. It involved legendary hardships and dangers, and mortality rates that would turn an actuarian pale. It was the most striking manifestation of the new man that Hector St. John de Crèvecoeur had speculated about in his *Letters from an American Farmer*. The "American experience," that odd mixture of Calvinist dogma and frontier living, had created a human type that the Revolution confirmed or "set," an individual to whom it seemed as natural as breathing to start a new community, carrying with him— "internalized," as we say today—all the values and institutions needed to set up stable communities in the wilderness.

From the beginning, the movement had its fascinated observers, amateur sociologists and anthropologists who studied it, described it, and pondered its significance. They perceived it as having successive stages. Benjamin Rush wrote to an English doctor friend giving a detailed analysis of "the manner of settling a new country," based on his own observations. "The *first* settler in the woods is generally a man who has outlived his credit or fortune in the cultivated parts of the state. His time for migrating is in the month of April. His first object is to build a small cabin of rough logs for himself and family. The floor of his cabin is of earth, the roof of split logs; the light is received through the door and, in some instances, through a small window made of greased paper. A coarser building adjoining this cabin affords a shelter to a cow and a pair of poor horses. The labor of erecting these buildings is succeeded by killing the trees on a few acres of ground near his cabin; this is done by cutting a circle around the trees two or three feet from the ground." Corn is then planted and the lone settler lives during the summer on fish and wild game—squirrels, rabbits, partridge and turkeys. His animals feed in the woods, and "for the first year he endures a great deal of distress from hunger, cold and a variety of accidental causes, but he seldom complains or sinks under them. As he lives in the neighborhood of Indians, he soon acquires a strong tincture of their manners. His exertions, while they continue, are violent, but they are succeeded by long intervals of rest. His pleasures consist chiefly of fishing and hunting. He loves spirituous liquors, and he eats, drinks, and sleeps in dirt and rags in his little cabin."

Such a settler remains two or three years on the crude farm he has hacked out of the wilderness. Then, "in proportion as population increases around him, he becomes uneasy and dissatisfied. Formerly his cattle ranged at large, but now his neighbors call on him to confine them within fences to prevent their trespassing upon their fields of grain." The arrival of other settlers drives off the game. "Above all, he revolts against the operation of laws. He cannot surrender up a single natural right for all the benefits of government, and therefore he abandons his little settlement, and seeks a retreat in the woods, where he again submits to all the toils which have been mentioned."

Sometimes the original tenant simply abandoned his crude farm and moved westward. More often he sold it with its "small improvements . . . to a *second* species of settler." This was "generally a man of some property." He would pay down a third or fourth of the cost of three or four hundred acres of land, twenty-five or fifty dollars, and the rest in installments. His first object would be to enlarge the cabin and make it more comfortable, and he would typically do this with planks instead of logs, "as sawmills generally follow settlements." His roof would be clapboards—coarse shingles split out of short oak logs. He would have "a board floor as well, a second floor or sleeping loft and a cellar, an orchard of fruit trees, and, in a year or so, a stout log barn." The trees his predecessor killed and left standing he would cut down and burn or root out the stumps. He would diversify his crops, adding rye to wheat. He would distill the rye into whiskey, which would be his cash crop. Although he would be more stable and industrious than the first settler, "his house as well as his farms bears many marks of a weak tone of mind." While he has windows in his house, they are "unglazed, or, if they have had glass in them, the ruins of it are supplied by old hats or pillows. He has little use for the institutions of civilized life, schools or churches, and he is equally indisposed to support civil government; with high ideas of liberty, he refuses to bear his proportion of the debt contracted by its establishment in our country. He delights chiefly in company—sometimes drinks spirituous liquors to excess—will spend a day or two in attending political meetings; and thus he contracts debts which (if he cannot discharge in depreciated currency) compel him to sell his plantation . . . to the *third* and last species of settler."

This last type is clearly Rush's ideal: he is a substantial man of "good character" not addicted to "spirituous liquors." A neat, tidy man with a strong sense of social responsibility, a churchgoer and school supporter, pious, hardworking, ingenious in building up his farm. He ditches water from a stream or river, builds a solid stone barn "100 feet in front and 40 in depth." He has sturdy fences, a house garden for vegetables. He improves his stock by careful breeding. He builds a smokehouse. His wife weaves, tends the garden, and milks the cows. His sons work with him in the fields. He builds a house large, convenient, and filled with useful and substantial furniture. "We do not," Rush wrote, "pretend to offer immigrants the pleasures of Arcadia. It is enough if affluence, independence, and happiness are ensured to patience, industry, and labor." The cheapness of land, Rush added, "render[s] the blessings which I have described objects within the reach of every man."

Having described the process, Rush could not forbear from adding some reflections upon it. "This passion for migration . . . will appear strange to a European. To see men turn their backs upon the houses in which they drew their first breath—upon the churches in which they were dedicated to God . . . upon the friends and companions of their youth—and upon all the pleasures of cultivated society . . . must strike a philosopher on your side of the water as a picture of human nature that runs counter to the usual habits and principles of action in man. But this passion, strange and new as it appears, is wisely calculated for the extension of population in America."

Timothy Dwight, former president of Yale College, took a tour through New England almost a generation later and described the states of settlement in words that echoed Rush's. He, too, was moved and awed by the westward migration. He saw it as "a novelty in the history of man," of the implications of which his countrymen were only dimly aware. "The colonization of a wilderness by civilized men, where a regular government, mild manners, arts, learning, science, and Christianity have been interwoven from the beginning, is a state of things of which the eastern continent and the records of past ages furnish neither an example, nor a resemblance."

Like Rush, Dwight described this new class of "the more restless, idle, roving inhabitants, who, as the state of society in these countries [Western territories] advance[s] toward order and stability, will leave them for the same reasons which induced them to quit the places of their nativity. Such men cannot continue in any regular society, but quit it, of course, for places where they may indulge their own idle and licentious dispositions. Like a company of pioneers, they always go forward in the front of regular settlers and seem to be of no other use than to remove the difficulties which might discourage the attempts of better and more quiet men. Accordingly, they have constantly preceded the real, substantial farmers in every course of emigration and will probably precede them until the New England colonization shall be stopped by the Pacific Ocean." These would be the plainsmen, the hunters and trappers and guides of the midcontinent and the mountainmen of the Rockies, a classic American breed whom we shall encounter throughout every stage of this history.

In truth, both their detractors—men like Gouverneur Morris who believed that "the Busy haunts of men and not the remote wilderness, was the proper school of political talents"—and their defenders, Madison, James Wilson, and George Mason among them, had only the vaguest notion of the character, needs, or motives of the men and women who pushed westward like an irresistible tide. They and the land they inhabited had the dimmest reality to the vast majority of those who guided the affairs of the new Republic. A few of the more enterprising had traveled to the western boundaries of their own states, but that was their farthest range.

The handful of Easterners who traveled to the frontier found that life there had a very different character from that in the seacoast states. Young William Preston, a South Carolinian whose father sent him off on a three-thousand-mile tour of the frontier, noted that in nearby Kentucky even aristocratic families that had migrated from Virginia "had lost a portion of Virginia caste and assumed something of Kentucky esteem, an absence of reticence and a presence of presumptuousness." (It is perhaps worth noting that in London, Washington Irving, a New Yorker with whom Preston became close friends, chided the young South Carolinian for being too informal and open.)

Preston wrote: "Amongst persons my own age . . . there was a self-dependence not to say self-assertion, and ostentatious suppression of the smaller courtesies of life and minute observances of convention, which was not pleasant. When emigration to a new country takes place even in masses, civilization is not transported or preserved. New physical circumstances induce new developments, and a fermentation of society must take place. An old state of society cannot be propagated in a new country. A certain loss of civilization is inevitable. Stranger and hardier qualities may be superinduced, but they supplant the gentler and more refined."

Talleyrand, a French refugee visiting a colony of his countrymen in Ohio Territory, took a dim view of the frontiersman. He wrote: "He is interested in nothing. Every sentimental idea is banished from him. Those branches so elegantly thrown by nature—a fine foliage, a brilliant hue which marks one part of the forest, a deeper green which darkens another—all these are nothing in his eye. He has no recollections associated with anything around him. His only thought is the number of strokes which are necessary to level this or that tree. He has never planted [a tree]; he is a stranger to the pleasure of that process. Were he to plant a tree, it never would become an object of gratification to him, because he could not live to cut it down. He lives only to destroy. He is surrounded by destruction. He does not watch the destiny of what he produces. He does not love the field where he has expended his labor, because his labor is merely fatigue, and has no pleasurable sentiment attached to it."

Henry Tuckerman, an indefatigable traveler, wrote of the frontier as an area completely lacking "that vital and vivid connection between the past and present," having instead "the painful sense of newness; the savage triumph, as it were, of nature, however beautiful, over humanity."

Among the most vivid accounts we have of frontier life is that of the Reverend Doctor Joseph Doddridge, whose family had moved from Maryland to the western border of Pennsylvania when he was four years old. Doddridge, an Episcopal minister who had studied medicine under Benjamin Rush, entitled his account, modestly enough, *Notes on the Early Settlement and Indian Wars, of the Western Part of Virginia & Pennsylvania, from the Year 1763 until the Year 1783 Inclusive.*

When he composed his recollections in the early 1820s he was in his fifties, but it seemed to him that he must have lived at least a hundred years to have witnessed the remarkable changes recorded in his *Notes*. Like many other pioneers, he felt that the "rising generation" had already forgotten the hardships and sacrifices of their fathers and grandfathers and that it was his task to revive those memories. Doddridge wrote: "The task of making new establishments in a remote wilderness in a time of profound peace is sufficiently difficult; but when, in addition to all the unavoidable hardships attendant on this business, those resulting from an extensive and furious warfare with savages are superadded, toil, privations and suffering are then carried to the full extent of the capacity of men to endure them."

After Doddridge's father brought his family over the mountains to the western borders of Pennsylvania, their supply of the Indian meal from which corn bread was made was used up six weeks before their crop of corn was ready to be harvested. Wild turkey and bear meat had to take its place, but they were poor substitutes and the children were "tormented with a sense of hunger." Doddridge remembered how eagerly he and his brothers and sisters "watched the growth of the potato tops, pumpkin and squash vines, hoping from day to day to get something to answer in place of bread. How delicious was the taste of young potatoes when we got them. What a jubilee when we were permitted to pull the young corn for roasting ears. . . . We then became wealthy, vigorous and contented with our situation, poor as it was."

Doddridge enumerated the "indigenous fruits" of the Pennsylvania and Ohio frontier that were such an important part of the food supply of the earliest settlers. The first fruit in the spring was the wild strawberry. The "service trees" were next. They filled the woods with their delicate blooms in April, and the berries were ripe in June, sweet, "with a very slight mixture of acidity." On Sundays, with the men well armed against marauding Indians, the settlers collected the berries, sometimes chopping down the trees to get them, since ladders were too awkward to carry. Blackberries grew abundantly where there were wind-felled trees. The children gathered these in the fall, again accompanied by armed and watchful adults. Wild raspberries and gooseberries were less plentiful but a welcome treat when they were found. Wild plums were excellent and numerous in bottomlands along streams. In the fall wild grapes made delicious wine. Black, red, and sugar haws grew on large bushes along watercourses. Their big berries were a special favorite of the children. Wild cherries were also abundant, along with small sour crab apples that made delicious jelly.

Pawpaws were to be found along the banks of most streams. Thick-shelled hickory nuts, with their sweet meat well protected, were scattered through the forests, along with white and black walnuts, hazel nuts, and chestnuts.

Most frontiersmen dressed in a kind of modified Indian garb. The hunting shirt was universal, a "kind of loose frock" usually made of linsey (a coarse linen), "reaching halfway down the thighs, with large sleeves, open before and so wide as to lap over a foot or more when belted." A jacket or poncholike cape covered the shirt and was sometimes fringed or embroidered with colored thread. The bosom of the belted shirt served as a pouch "to hold a chunk of bread, cakes, jerk [dried beef], tow for wiping the barrel of the rifle." The belt was tied behind and hung with further necessaries: mittens, a bullet bag, a tomahawk, and a scalping knife in a leather sheath. Breeches or leggings covered the legs. Sometimes they ran only to the upper thighs, just above the bottom of the shirt or frock, and many of the younger men affected the Indian breechclout, a width of cloth run through the front and back of the belt and around the loins.

The shoes were moccasins that reached up to, and were tied around, the ankles. In cold weather they were stuffed with deer's hair or dry leaves to keep the feet warm, but the leather was so permeable by water that the common remark was that when the ground was wet moccasins were simply "a decent way of going barefooted." As a consequence of traveling much of the time in wet moccasins, the commonest complaint of frontiersmen was rheumatism. The women dressed in linsey petticoats and bed gowns, went barefoot in dry weather, and in winter they wore moccasins or shoepacks, shapeless creations of cloth and leather. Cabins were without closets or ward-robes, and the clothes of the occupants hung on pegs along the walls.

Domestic utensils were simple and few. Bowls, cups, and plates and spoons were usually made of wood. Sometimes gourds and hard-shell squashes served. Iron pots, knives, and forks were among the few precious possessions that could be carried on a packhorse or ox over the mountains. Salt and sugar were scarce and expensive. A bushel of salt was worth a good cow and a calf. Fractions of a bushel were commonly measured by the handful. Sugar could be made from the sap of maple trees in the early spring, but salt had to be bought from a trader. "Hog and hominy," or various portions of the pig and bleached corn, were culinary staples, along with johnnycake (cornmeal and milk, baked in the ashes of the fire) and corn pone. Supper was commonly milk and corn mush, supplemented when possible with venison, squirrel, or bear. Indian corn was the essential ingredient in all frontier diets—ground, leavened, bleached, in a half-dozen forms and combinations. Doddridge was eight years old before he tasted a cup of tea or coffee; and it was a wonder to him to have it in a porcelain cup with a saucer.

In the economy of the family there was a crude division of labor—a skilled mason might work in exchange for woven cloth—but most families did their own weaving; tanned their own leather; and made their own moccasins, belts, and so forth. Doddridge's father built a loom and wove cloth on it for the family's garments and made the thread for the moccasins and shoepacks. Of necessity, the men of the family were blacksmiths, carpenters, tanners, coopers, masons, and inventors.

Most families lived within hailing or running distance of a crude fort, to which they could repair, if lucky, at the first sign of an Indian raid. When any sign of hostile Indians was noted, the swiftest young men were sent from cabin to cabin in the dark to summon the families to the fort. As Doddridge recalled such a scene from his childhood, the messenger "came softly to the door, or back window, and by a gentle tapping waked the family. . . . The whole family were instantly in motion. My father seized his gun and other implements of war. My stepmother waked up and dressed the children as well as she could. . . . Besides the little children, we caught up what articles of clothing and provisions we could get hold of in the dark, for we durst not light a candle or even stir the fire. All this was done with the utmost dispatch and the silence of death. To the rest it was enough to say *Indian* and not a whimper was heard afterwards." Collected in the fort, the settlers next had to decide how long to wait there. The Indians would seldom attack such a fort, but after filling the adjacent woods with howls of fury and frustration would depart—or at least pretend to. Often they would burn the abandoned cabins and destroy what crops they could. There were times when some of the more foolhardy families, concerned about their gardens, possessions, and domestic animals, would return to their cabins before it was certain that the coast was clear (a situation usually determined by scouting parties). These posed a hazard to everyone, because if they were trapped by Indians still lurking in the vicinity a general effort must be made to save them and a number of lives thereby imperiled.

As Doddridge put it: "The early settlers on the frontiers of this country were like the Arabs of the deserts of Africa, in at least two respects: every man was a soldier, and from early in the spring, till late in the fall, was almost continually in arms. Their work was often carried on by parties, each one of whom had his rifle and everything else belonging to his war dress. They were deposited in some central place in the field. A sentinel was stationed on the outside of the fence, so that on the least alarm the whole company repaired to their arms, and were ready for combat in a moment." In addition to the Indians, there were a thousand natural hazards. A falling tree might smash a rail fence and horses and cattle would then get into a field and destroy a crop. Raccoons would kill the chickens. An early frost might burn the corn, a flood destroy, or a drought parch it. Bugs and rodents, birds, deer, squirrels, and every creature that crawled or flew competed with the farmer for his meager crops.

Disease, accident, and illness were the constant companions of the settlers. Without doctors, everyone must be his or her own physician, so there were numerous practical treatments, many of them traditional folk remedies, and others borrowed from the Indians. A burn or a cut could easily become infected in an environment never characterized by cleanliness and often by squalor. For burns a poultice of the inevitable Indian meal was often applied, or roasted turnips. Many children died of croup, whose cure was taken to be the juice of roasted onions. Sweating was the remedy for fevers, and there were numerous antidotes for rattlesnake and copperhead bites. Those who suffered from rheumatism used the oil of rattlesnakes, wolves, geese, bears, and skunks and warmed their aching joints in front of the fire. Coughs, consumption, pleurisy, hepatitis, and diarrhea were common and often fatal. Doddridge's mother died in her thirties from an abrasion made by a horse's stepping on her foot; a poultice was applied but the wound became infected. His father died at forty-six from hepatitis.

If we except drinking, dancing was the principal diversion on the frontier. Every settlement had a fiddler or two, and no opportunity was missed to hold a dance. Singing was another entertainment. Doddridge recalled that many songs were about Robin Hood, and most of the others were "tragical . . . love songs about murder." Young men hunted, shot at targets, and held contests with bow and arrows and tomahawks. But weddings were the greatest occasions for festivities, which usually lasted for days.

Without the normal apparatus of crime enforcement—courts, lawyers, judges, and jails—the people of the frontier "were a law unto themselves." The qualities most valued were "industry in working and hunting, bravery in war, candor, honesty, hospitality and steadiness of deportment. . . . The punishment for idleness, dishonesty, and ill fame generally, was that of 'hating the offender,' " a kind of ostracism which in small communities usually had the effect of reforming the culprit or driving him or her away. The person who did not do a proper share of the common work at house-raisings, logrollings, and "harvest parties" was described as a "Lawrence," and when the idler needed help it was refused. A special anathema was pronounced against the man who shirked his duties in defending the settlement. He was "hated out as a coward."

So community sanctions and pressures took the place of the law, and took it, on the whole, very effectively, if often cruelly. Punishment for conventional crimes as opposed to social dereliction were harsh in the extreme, brutal whippings being the most common form. The theft of "some small article" was punished by thirteen stripes on the back (for the thirteen stripes on the flag of the United States) and then exile. A "convict-servant," that is, someone who had been sentenced to a period of servitude for a prior offense, or a slave in those frontier regions where slavery was permitted, was subjected to whippings so severe that he was often days recovering. Some were whipped each day for a series of days. Doddridge saw more than one man whipped so brutally that "in a little time the whole of his shoulders had the appearance of a mass of blood, streams of which soon began to flow down his back and sides. . . . His trousers were then unbuttoned and suffered to fall down about his feet, two new hickories were selected from the bundle, and so applied that in a short time his posteriors, like his shoulders, exhibited nothing but lacerations and blood."

Doddridge was sent by his father to lodge with a relative in Baltimore so that he might have an education, but he returned gratefully to the frontier when his stint was up, revolted by what he had seen of slavery. "From this afflicting state of society," he wrote, "I returned to the backwoods, a republican, without knowing the meaning of the term, that, is an utter detestation of an arbitrary power of one man over another."

The frontier was to Doddridge preeminently the region where the true meaning of freedom and independence was understood. "The patriot of the western region finds his love of country and national pride augmented to the highest grade when he compares the political, moral and religious character of his people, with that of inhabitants of many large divisions of the old world. . . . [In the United States] instead of a blind or superstitious imitation of the manners and customs of our forefathers, we have thought and acted for ourselves, and we have changed ourselves and everything around us." As critical as he was of luxury and the accumulation of material things, Doddridge was quick to acknowledge that "the early introduction of commerce was among the first means of changing, in some degree, the exterior aspect of the population of the country, and giving a new current to public feeling and individual pursuit." Without the remarkable growth of commerce, Doddridge declared, "our progress towards science and civilization would have been much slower."

Doddridge, like Rush and Dwight, depicted the frontiersman as someone who wanted "*elbow room*," and therefore as soon as he felt himself crowded, "fled to the forest of frontier settlements, choosing rather to encounter the toil of turning the wilderness into fruitful fields, a second time, and even risk an Indian war, rather than endure the inconveniences of a crowded settlement. Kentucky first offered a resting place for these pioneers, then Indiana and now the Missouri and it cannot be long before the Pacific Ocean will put a final stop to the westward march of those lovers of the wilderness."

It is clear that Doddridge's own feelings about the frontier were mixed ones. While he hailed the progress of "science and civilization," he regretted the disappearance of the solidarity and sharing of hardship that characterized the frontier he had known, and he understood very well that life on the frontier was often "nasty, brutish and short." Trying to sum up his feelings, he wrote, "The truth is, the western country is the region of adventure. If we have derived some advantage from the importation of science, arts and wealth, we have on the other hand been much annoyed and endangered, as to our moral and political state, by an immense importation of vice, associated with a high grade of science and the most consummate art, in the pursuit of wealth by every description of unlawful means." It was only a strict adherence to the law, in Doddridge's opinion, that had saved "our infant country . . . from destruction by the pestilential influence of so great an amount of moral depravity." Here is the agonizing question once more: how to use "greed," or the commercial spirit, for the useful progress of society without suffering from the "moral depravity" that wealth and luxury bring with them. All the ambivalence and ambiguity was there. The central schizophrenia: the hope for, and fear of, progress; the faith that law could control the unjust, the exploiter; the dream of innocence and the desire to be thought "civilized" by the world. We could hardly find a passage more expressive of the ambiguity of our consciousness. One way to look at the mystery of frontier settlement is to reflect upon the fact that those men and women who ventured out to the frontier, wherever that frontier was at the moment, deliberately subjected themselves to the physical and psychological hardships that characterized the most depressed peasant societies of Europe. Far from seeking wealth or ease, *they sought hardship.* Did we not know they were there by their own free will we might have thought them exiled to suffering more cruel than Devil's Island or Siberia.

If the towns and cities of the Eastern seacoast represented American "culture," the frontier was the "counterculture." To the rural frontier, Easterners were tenderfoots, or later, dudes or city folk or city "slickers" whose ways and manners seemed excessively refined or effeminate. To the Easterners, the frontier settlers were picturesque and colorful but part of a crude and violent world that was infinitely remote and somewhat of an embarrassment. Frontiersmen's language was rude and rough, their clothes hardly distinguishable from the garb of Indians, their houses huts and hovels. Easterners were, at best, patronizing toward the frontier, at worst hostile or indifferent. The closest we could come today to the atmosphere of many early-nineteenth-century frontier settlements would be a present-day agricultural commune made up of urban and suburban young men and women, barefoot, wearing tattered and dirty clothes, living in abandoned shacks or crude if colorful habitations of their own construction, proudly reproducing the conditions of hardship, dirt, and discomfort that characterized our original frontier counterculture.

If it had not been for Easterners' speculations in Western lands and their desire to find settlers for them, it is doubtful that the West would ever have been granted political parity with the East. So it might be said that the history of the country took place on two levels. One was the level of conscious political actions; of negotiations with foreign countries; of commercial regulations, laws, and statutes designed to effect particular purposes. The other was simply what ordinary people did, usually with little attention to what was transpiring in the seats of government—most of all, those people who went west. They not uncommonly felt suspicion and hostility toward the politicians in New York, Philadelphia, and later Washington, D. C., who professed to be acting in their interest. Their attachment to the Republic was often less strong than their attachment to the piece of stony or stump-cursed land they had carved out of the forest.

The most remarkable thing of all about their infatuation with the intractable forest—and something that neither Rush nor Dwight commented on—was that it existed in the face, not simply of hardships that would make a strong man blanch, but of the constant danger to life itself. As Doddridge reminds us, *worse* than disease or crippling accident, hunger, or cold, was the constant presence of the Indians. Any isolated frontier cabin or small settlement lived with the nightmare of an Indian raid hanging over it like the proverbial sword. And death itself was, of course, not the worst that could happen. There was excruciating torture for men captured alive or merely wounded and rape of the women and young girls or living in captivity in an Indian tribe. On occasion whole villages were wiped out, and there was hardly a frontier settler who had not had a relative or friend fall victim to Indians on the warpath. The Indian combination of stealth, ferocity, and shattering sound made him as frightening a figure as could well be conceived. And yet, in the face of that constant and for us today almost inconceivable terror, the settlers pushed inexorably westward onto Indian lands. Meanwhile the federal government did its best to create a buffer between the advancing settlers and the beleaguered Indians by carrying on virtually continuous treaty negotiations to buy Indian lands—or perhaps more accurately, since the Indians had no notion of landownership—to bribe them to move farther west and thus avoid confrontation with the migrating whites.

The alternative to treaty agreements with the Indians was open warfare, in which, however reluctantly, the federal government must support the settlers, fight and drive off the Indians against whose hunting grounds the settlers pressed so relentlessly, and establish forts to keep some kind of order in the frontier territories. The conclusion of a new treaty opening up Indian lands for settlement did not necessarily mean security from Indian raids. There were often dissident factions within tribes that refused to honor the treaty or tribes that claimed hunting rights on lands that had been bargained away by rivals. Moreover, it seemed as though vast new regions had hardly been ceded by tribes of Indians before word came of settlers pressing on into territory into which the Indians had been driven and which they were determined to defend against further white intrusions. And so the process must begin again, interrupted, when friction between settlers and Indians became severe, by Indian "wars." The federal government has often been depicted as the oppressor of the Indians. The fact is that it was, with certain notable exceptions, the Indians' best friend, in the sense that it had a vested interest in dealing fairly with the aborigines, restraining white advances into their territories, setting aside adequate "reservations," and generally attempting to impose some degree of order on a situation that was inherently chaotic.

Perhaps the strongest influence on the Indian tribes of the East was trade with whites. The whole story of white-Indian relations from the time of the earliest settlements in New England and Virginia was dominated by trading, and much of what was most negative in its effect on Indian culture was the consequence of the fact that for many tribes their principal contact with white civilization was through a human type hardly representative of the more positive aspects of that culture. Furs were the Indian commodity most desired by whites, and in the fierce competition among both whites and Indians to control the fur trade much blood was shed and the way of life of many tribes radically altered. For one thing, the fur trade disposed tribes to move away from the seacoast to river and forest areas where furbearing animals, particularly the beaver, were to be found in abundance. It also engendered warfare between tribes anxious to make good their claims to areas rich in beaver. As beaver were "mined out" of one river watershed, a tribe was forced, or felt itself forced, to seek new hunting grounds. In the words of one historian, "In its most destructive form, the trading activity of the white caused starvation. In its least destructive it reshaped the social organization of the tribes and altered their economic subsistence patterns." Put another way, the white man exploited the Indian desire for the trinkets and artifacts of a more sophisticated culture. The corruption of the Indian began with beads and mirrors, gold-laced jackets, knives, guns, and plumed hats.

More devastating even than European-American artifacts were the diseases the white men brought with them. Anthropologists have estimated that in a ten-year period the Huron and Iroquois confederacies lost over half their numbers to epidemics, particularly smallpox epidemics, to which the Indians were especially vulnerable.

The white-Indian conflict could not have been avoided unless Americans had been content to remain strung along a thin stretch of the Atlantic coast (indeed, strictly speaking, unless the whole of continental North America had been preserved as an Indian reservation). Paradoxically, the westward movement was a demonstration of the vices and virtues of "democracy." American enterprise, sometimes rather confusingly called "free" enterprise (as though there were also nonfree enterprise), was nowhere more dramatically revealed than in that movement. The American brand of individualism with its unshakable confidence in its ability to overcome any obstacle, human or natural, was the basic ingredient. To neutral observers, it often appeared as a kind of disease, the congenital madness of a whole people. Rush and Dwight were right; it was without precedent in the long history of the race. Each lonely settler in his remote cabin, and each band of settlers, obviously felt capable of subduing a whole wild continent. The Indians, fierce and terrifying as they might be in their particular materializations, were primarily an impediment to be swept aside. The Indian culture, Indian art and lore, the Indians' close and reciprocal relationship with nature, which in the present age of "loving the land" we so admire, meant nothing to a frontiersman or settler in danger of having his brains bashed out by an artistically decorated tomahawk or his horses driven off by a magnificently accoutered band of young braves.

Frontier attitudes toward the Indian covered a wide range, to be sure. As Rush indicated, the frontiersmen and settlers were most closely associated with Indians and Indian culture. They dressed similarly, adopted Indian tactics and practices, ate Indian food, smoked Indian tobacco, took Indian women for their wives or mistresses. Their lives depended on their achieving a minimum of rapport with the Indians. Initially, they were a handful against thousands. Their successors, the more settled and stable types, by and large feared and hated the Indians. To them the Indians were savages to be rooted up and exterminated. It must be said in their defense that they saw the Indians at their worst, as simple destroyers, wild creatures, hardly human, who set their painstakingly built cabins and barns to the torch, killed their stock, and raped their wives.

The members of the new Congress had to deal with the problem of white-Indian relations in the first months of the new nation. The complexity of the issue was pointed up by the difference in the two problems that confronted them. In one, the Wabash Indians and their allies in the Old Northwest were killing settlers who infringed on their territory. That was a relatively simple problem. It required a military expedition to drive off the Indians and secure the new settlements. The other involved a treaty negotiated between the United States and the Creek Indians, whose traditional homelands were in southwestern Georgia. The treaty was designed to secure the rights of the Indians to their lands. It brought forth bitter declamations from the Georgia representatives in Congress. James Jackson, a Georgia member, declared: "That treaty has spread alarm among the people of Georgia. It has ceded away, without any compensation whatever, three millions of acres of land guaranteed to Georgia by the Constitution. . . . Has the Government recognized the rights of Georgia? No. It has given away her land, invited a savage of the Creek nation to the seat of Government, caressed him in a most extraordinary manner, and sent him home loaded with favors." It was widely reported that the Creek Treaty contained secret clauses inimical to Georgia. "Good God! are there to be secret articles between the United States and any nation under heaven? . . . Will Congress suffer the laws of the United States . . . to be placed where no man can read them, and then punish the people for disobeying them? The people, sir, will never submit to be bound by secret articles." Jackson's outburst suggests the difficulties of the matter. Not surprisingly, the treaty was to have an unhappy aftermath.

The most immediate issue involved the Indians of the Northwest, who, as we have noted, were emboldened by the British retention of the posts in the region north of the Ohio. The Delaware, the Shawnee, the Miami, the Wyandot, and the Ottawa tribes made common cause against the frontier. The Confederation Congress had taken the attitude that all these tribes had forfeited their rights to the land by their support of the British during the war. Nonetheless, Congress went to considerable pains to placate the Indians with treaties and presents. The Fort Stanwix Treaty in 1784 was designed to extinguish the claims of the Iroquois to the area of present-day Ohio, Illinois, and Indiana. The Wyandot, Chippewa, and Delaware accepted similar terms, and the Shawnee fell in line a year later. But the Miami, the Kickapoo, and the Potowatomi refused to enter treaty negotiations. It was a familiar problem in dealing with the Indians. The Potowatomi belonged to the Algonquian language group. They had been traditional enemies of the Iroquois and had cast their lot with the French. The very fact that the Iroquois had concluded a treaty with Congress disposed the Potowatomi to hold out.

The situation was much the same with the Miami. They had been at war intermittently with the Iroquois for a hundred years and had lost many braves to them and to the Sioux. Now they prepared to go on the warpath against any white settlers north of the Ohio: some thousand at the old French settlement of Vincennes, thirteen hundred on what was known as Symmes's Purchase, and another thousand on land claimed by the Ohio Company. The rest were scattered in small settlements, the most prominent of which were Clarkesville and Kaskaskia.

All during the spring and summer reports came in of Indian attacks. In the revealing words of a nineteenth-century historian, "At first they were supposed to be merely accounts of such barbarities as the Indians had always perpetrated on the settlers of a new country from the days of John Smith and Miles Standish on down," casual massacres, the interception of a boatload of emigrants on the Ohio, burned-out cabins, kidnapped women and children. Arthur St. Clair, the Revolutionary veteran who was more of a politician than a general, had been appointed governor of the Northwest Territory. He fixed the seat of his administration in Cincinnati, which he named after the Society of the Cincinnati of which he was then president, an act that brought bitter criticism from the enemies of the fraternal order. St. Clair dispatched Major John Hamtramck to discover the intentions of the Indians, and Hamtramck in turn engaged a French trader at Vincennes to visit the tribes and report on their mood.

The trader's account was alarming. There was no doubt in his mind that at least three of the tribes were preparing for war. St. Clair immediately began to gather a ragtag force to strike at the Indian strongholds along the Wabash River. The expedition he scraped together was placed under the command of Colonels John Hardin and James Trotter. A hint of the fate of the little force of 1,453 men might have been read in the fact that although Hardin was the senior officer, he was disliked for his strict discipline. The men thus refused to accept him as a commander, and he was forced to give way to the more amiable Trotter. The clashes with the British-allied Indians during the Revolution had made it clear that in no military operations was march discipline more important than in campaigns against the Indians. Silence, mobility, and speed were essential if an enemy were to be taken by surprise.

The march to the Wabash turned out to be as close to low comedy as the ill-fated Sandusky expedition nine years earlier. The invading force was made up of a tatterdemalion militia band composed largely of old men and boys, since few husbands and fathers could be spared from their frontier farms. These gathered with a motley collection of arms, some with broken muskets and others with nothing better than a rusty sword. Quarrels broke out immediately between the untrained militia and the regulars, who were little better prepared for such an expedition. Their first objective was a cluster of Miami villages some thirty miles away. Hardin was given command of the strike force, whose mission was to suprise the Indians in their wigwams and prevent their escape until the main body of troops arrived. He and his men spent a day and a half crashing through the forest to reach the village. Not surprisingly, they found it deserted. It was another two days before Trotter arrived with the main body, and four days were then consumed destroying the villages and burning the fields. At night, security was so slipshod that Indians were able to steal into the American camp and drive off most of the pack and artillery horses, thus making further pursuit impossible.

Hoping to salvage something from the ill-fated foray, General Josiah Harmar, who was military commander of the territory under St. Clair's jurisdiction, dispatched Trotter with three hundred men to round up any Indians in the vicinity. One Indian was chased and killed; another was sighted at a distance, and the four officers in Trotter's command, including the colonel himself, set off in pursuit and were gone for half an hour while their troops roamed about leaderless.

With Trotter in disgrace, Hardin was given his turn. Dispatched on a similar raid, he and his force discovered the remains of a recently abandoned Indian campground. Hardin deployed his men in a line of advance and pressed farther into the forest. One of the companies, failing to receive orders to move, remained at the point of departure. Without scouts to his front or outriders to protect his flanks, Hardin stumbled into an ambush. Finding themselves under fire, the militia abandoned their arms and ran, with their commander in the lead. The officer commanding the little detachment of regulars swore later that he and his men had stood their ground until all but himself were killed and that he had then made his escape. Whatever the particular circumstances, the operation was a fiasco. When the militia and the humiliated Hardin found their way back to the destroyed Indian villages, Harmar ordered a general withdrawal to Cincinnati.

Hardin, anxious to redeem himself, persuaded Harmar to place him in command of 350 men to trap the Indians when they returned to their villages. He set out on a night march, hoping to surprise the Indians at dawn, but the sun was well up before the little party reached the villages. Scouts reported that the Indians had returned and might still be surprised. Hardin deployed his force in three divisions. Two were to advance directly on the villages, and the third was to circle behind the villages to cut off the savages' retreat. The maneuver proceeded smoothly enough until the troops flushed an Indian and fired at him, thus alerting the rest, who fled with the militia in pursuit. When the Indians finally turned on their pursuers, the militia once more panicked and fled back to the general's main force. Harmar now adopted a strategy not unknown to generals dispatched against the Indians. He announced that the expedition had been a great success: the Indians had been scattered and demoralized, and five Indian villages and winter supplies of corn in the amount of twenty thousand bushels had been destroyed. He then set out on a triumphal return to Fort Washington. In fact, the expedition had, like other such ventures, exactly the opposite of its intended effect. The inept conduct of the Americans had emboldened the Indians, and the destruction of their villages had infuriated them. Wavering clans were encouraged to take the warpath. Meanwhile settlers, heartened by Harmar's account of his success, pressed farther into the Ohio country. Marietta grew to eighty houses and a small stockade. Belle Prairie, at the juncture of the Kanawha and Ohio rivers, was another busy settlement. Sawmills and a mill for grinding corn were built on convenient streams, Duck Creek and Wolf Creek.

The most exposed settlement was at Big Bottom, forty miles farther upriver. There twelve families had begun the process described by Rush of carving their primitive farms out of the uncongenial forest. On January 2, 1791, Indians attacked at dusk, killed all the settlers—men, women, and children—and burned their houses and barns to the ground.

The news of the Big Bottom Massacre sent rumors flying along the frontier from one isolated settlement to another. The most alarming rumor was that the great Joseph Brant was at the head of a large force made up of Miami and Wabash Indians, bent on driving the whites out of the whole Northwest Territory. Settlements too small to think of defending themselves successfully packed up what they could carry and, driving their animals ahead of them, headed for the fort at Marietta, which was manned by twenty regulars.

Rufus Putnam, son of General Israel Putnam who had commanded the American forces at the Battle of Bunker Hill, had founded, or refounded, the town of Marietta where he served as territorial judge.

He wrote imploringly to General Washington, his father's old commander in chief, describing the Big Bottom Massacre, the exposed situation of the Americans, and the desperate need for help, adding, "Unless Government speedily sends a body of troops for our protection, we are a ruined people."

The Big Bottom Massacre called for a strong government response. Washington appointed St. Clair commander of a force with the task of pacifying the Indians by seeking them out and defeating them in battle and then building a chain of forts from Cincinnati to the confluence of the St. Mary and St. Joseph rivers. St. Clair set about accumulating men and supplies for his expedition. The summer months, best suited for campaigning, were lost as the general painstakingly collected and equipped his army. Finally, late in September, he set out for Indian territory with twenty-three hundred regulars and a number of militia. On the banks of the Great Miami River where it entered the Ohio he built Fort Hamilton. From there he advanced forty-four miles down the Ohio and constructed Fort Jefferson. Leaving Fort Jefferson, a crude and hastily constructed palisade, he and his army resumed their tortuous progress west and south along the river. The fall air was sharp, and the mists that hung over the water gave the soldiers chills and fevers. The militia were poorly prepared for an extended campaign. Many of them fell ill; food supplies ran short; and it was forbidden to kill game along the line of march for fear of alerting the Indians. St. Clair himself fell ill and had to be carried for miles on a stretcher. The commander's sickness further undermined morale, and the militia began to desert, fifty or sixty at a time.

After a ten-day march, during the course of which St. Clair lost more than half of his force through attrition, fourteen hundred thoroughly demoralized men reached what St. Clair thought was the western terminus of his expedition, the St. Mary. Actually it was a branch of the Wabash, a creek some fifty feet wide. St. Clair placed his troops in two lines along the creek. He situated the militia encampment on the far side of the creek a quarter of a mile away. A mile beyond the militia, a force of regulars formed an advance guard whose mission was to search the woods for Indians. They soon realized that the woods around them were alive with the enemy, and they hastily withdrew to the main body to alert St. Clair.

St. Clair took no action to warn the members of his command, and at dawn the Indians attacked and routed the militia, apparently taking them by surprise. Those who were not killed in the first encounter fled across the creek with the Indians in pursuit. A handful of regulars lined the bank to cover their crossing. St. Clair then formed the remainder into a square around the artillery. It was a strange formation to take up in the face of an Indian attack.

During the Revolution it had taken almost five years to train soldiers of the Continental Army to stand and fire in close formation rather than in the extended skirmish lines they had learned from the Indians, taking advantage of every tree and fold in the terrain for protection and concealment. The British, meanwhile, had learned to employ the tactics the Americans had abandoned; and at the Battle of Green Spring, a few months before Yorktown, American soldiers, advancing through the woods in close formation, had encountered the British spread out and fighting Indian fashion. Now St. Clair behaved as though he were fighting a conventional European war. Standing in line, firing, and dropping back, exposed to the musket fire of Indians hidden behind tree trunks and rocks, the Americans suffered heavy casualties. The regulars demonstrated their superior discipline by making bayonet charges, but they might as well have been chasing shadows; the savages slipped away with hoots of derision, and when the soldiers returned to their lines the Indians renewed their fire. Those regulars who fell in the bayonet charges were scalped in sight of their comrades.

The fight continued for four hours with the Americans getting the worst of it. The officers in their bright uniforms were the special targets of the Indians, as British officers had so often been of American marksmen. Five officers were killed and scalped, and five more were severely wounded. St. Clair decided to make a desperate effort to break through to the trail over which he and his men had traveled. Another bayonet charge drove the Indians back long enough for the panic-stricken militia to gain the path. They threw away their guns and packs, stripped off their heavy boots, and fled for their lives. The regulars followed in hardly better order, leaving wagons, artillery, horses, tents, and supplies behind and abandoning the wounded to the scalping knife and torture by fire. Some six hundred regulars and perhaps half as many militia made their way to Fort Jefferson, a distance of twenty-nine miles that had just taken them ten days to traverse. Spurred on by terror, they returned in less than ten hours.

As was almost invariably the case, the triumphant Indians, filling the woods with their wild cries, fell on the plunder, fighting and squabbling among themselves as to the apportionment of the loot. Distracted by the spoils of war, they failed to pursue St. Clair's shattered force. Although Little Turtle, a Miami chieftain famous for his skill in battle and wisdom in council, was in command (it had been Little Turtle who had been most instrumental in the defeat of Harmar's expedition a year earlier) and apparently responsible for the tenacity with which the Indians fought, he could not control his warriors after the Americans had fled. They entered enthusiastically into the postbattle ritual of torture. Wounded soldiers had their arms and legs torn off. Others were disemboweled or castrated. Women who had accompanied the army and were abandoned in the rout had stakes driven through their bodies.

At the beginning of the battle the American force had outnumbered the Indians, who, it has been estimated, brought less than a thousand warriors to the fray. The brilliant victory of Little Turtle and his braves sent shock waves along the entire frontier. Had the Indians had the capacity for concerted and coordinated action, they might have followed up their success with forays that would have devastated the frontier settlements as far east as Pittsburgh and killed or driven out most of the white settlers in the Northwest Territory. But such a massive rollback of white settlement would, at best, have offered the Indians only a temporary respite. Indian councils were seriously divided. While many of Little Turtle's braves wished to wage a war of extermination against the frontier settlements, the chieftain felt that persistent warlike acts on their part would lead to their own extermination. He therefore counseled negotiations for peace.

When word was brought to Washington of St. Clair's defeat by the Miami, he was at the dining table, as he had been when the news arrived of Arnold's betrayal of West Point. At the insistence of the officer who brought the message, Washington's secretary, Tobias Lear, whispered the news to him. Washington's face never changed expression. When the meal was over and the guests had departed, Washington abandoned himself to one of his terrible rages, cursing St. Clair and railing against the cowardice of the soldiers.

The Anti-Federalists showed considerable ingenuity in laying the blame for the debacle on the Federalists. It was, they argued, Federalist speculators, intent on robbing the Indians of their lands to fatten their own purses, who had promoted settlement in the Northwest and thereby provoked the Indians into defending their homes. Now they would reap a political dividend by calling for a large and expensive army to put down the Indians and save the settlers. To supply the army they would impose more ruinous taxes and then doubtless employ the army to collect them. Finally, the army would be used to suppress all honest Republicans.

General St. Clair bore the brunt of popular displeasure, and as he made his way eastward to give an accounting to his commander in chief people lined the streets of the towns through which he passed to jeer and hoot at him.

Having discussed the frontier settlers in some detail, it may be appropriate to add further reflections on their savage adversaries. The most irresolvable conflict in the relationship between the white man and the Indian was that the Indian lived in a world before the Fall—a world of primal innocence before, in Christian terms, man acquired the knowledge of good and evil. There was about everything the Indian did, therefore, this innocence, this "good conscience." When he killed and mutilated his enemies, stole their horses, killed or carried off their women, he had no concept by which such action could be judged bad nor could he be easily made to feel guilt concerning it. His shamans and many of his talismanic animals were "tricksters." What the white man called deceit the Indians admired as splendid cunning. The Indian tribes lived in a vast and beautiful and terrible Garden of Eden. It was only the white Christian's notion that killing and violence had been absent from the original Garden. Killing and violence were there, but they were not understood to be "sinful," since there was no notion of sin. (I might note, parenthetically, that I use the notion of sin or self-consciousness—consciousness of the nature of good and evil—as much in an anthropological as in a theological sense.) Anthropologists now understand that primitive tribal consciousness is compatible with the Christian notion of a state of innocence before the Fall. The story of Adam and Eve, seen in these terms, is simply a parable about the burden of taking on a new kind of self-consciousness, the abstract knowledge that certain acts were good and others bad. Adam's shame at perceiving himself to be naked is the story of the beginning of the modern consciousness of self as separated from, or as over against, nature. There is an unfathomable poignance about a letter from Narissa Whitman, the missionary wife of the missionary Marcus Whitman, who wrote to her sister, "Some among the Indians feel almost to blame us for telling them about eternal realities. One said it was good when they knew nothing but to hunt, eat, drink and sleep; now it is bad." That she herself felt the ambiguity of her mission is evident. She wrote: "Of late my heart yearns over them more than usual. They feel so bad, disappointed, and some of them angry because my husband tells them that none of them are Christians; that they are all of them in the broad road to destruction. . . . They try to persuade him not to talk such bad talk to them, as they say, but talk good talk, or tell some story, or history. . . ."

Self-consciousness, with its attendant shame and guilt, began the process out of which the modern consciousness emerged. Postprimitive consciousness produced abstract thought, science, the great "world religions," and all of the appurtenances of "civilization." But civilized man has never ceased to yearn for his lost tribal innocence when *everything* was done with a good conscience. If "shame" was known and used as a method of social control in the tribe, "guilt" was as yet to be discovered. To argue that whites who wished to see the Indian "redeemed," like the rest of the world, should have understood that to destroy the Indian consciousness was, in effect, to destroy the Indian quite misses the point. To have understood that would have been to ask the great majority of whites to reject their whole notion of civilization and, indeed, of the power of Christianity to re-form the world. A few, it turned out, were willing to do just that. They used an idealized version of Indian culture to denounce the shortcomings of an increasingly alienating urbanized industrial world.

The secular apostles of reason did no better than the evangelical Christians. While the latter wished to force the Indians to eat the fruit of knowledge of good and evil, the rationalists were equally ruthless in their determination to make Indians "reasonable" members of white society; they had, if anything, less patience than the Christians with the richly imaginative symbolic life of the Indian. To them it was little better than the collection of superstitions by means of which orthodox Christianity enslaved the minds of its adherents.

The Anglo-Indian philosopher Raimundo Panikkar speaks of the nature of the tribal consciousness or, as he calls it, the *"ecstatic moment"* in the development of human consciousness when "Man simply knows. He knows the mountains and rivers. . . . Man knows Nature. Knows also his God and the Gods. He stumbles and he errs, but he allows himself to be corrected by the things themselves. Man learns above all by obedience, i.e. by listening . . . to the rest of reality which speaks to him." That was, in essence, the state of the consciousness of the American Indians. In the earthly Paradise, "Man's approach is straightforward. He does not desire something 'else' or something 'more' than what is; indeed, there is no room for anything else. . . . When man sees in the apple something 'other' than the apple, he is on the verge of losing his innocence." The universal, cosmic tragedy of man, incorporated by Christians and Jews in the story of Adam's fall, was that lost innocence and, in place of it, what Gerald Heard, the English theologian, called "wrong appetency," imagining and wanting "something 'else' or something 'more' than what is." The initial corruption of the red man by the white was just this introduction of something else and something more—of beads and mirrors, blankets and plumed hats. Innocence was destroyed. The white man was the serpent in the Garden, and his trading junk was the apple. But there was no stopping this process, then or in retrospect; there was no conceivable way of avoiding the corruption of innocence, the terrible Fall into self-consciousness, into guilt, into "feeling bad," as the Cayuse Indians complained Marcus Whitman made them feel and for which they finally killed him, his wife and child. The tragedy was that what had been for civilized man from the times of ancient Sumeria and Egypt a millennia-long process was forced instantly on the American aborigine *from outside*. It was as though all the complex tragedies and remarkable achievements of civilized man had to be experienced by the original American instantly.

The sense in which the aborigine saw the apple as an integral part of the whole web of nature on which he depended for the perpetuation of his life can be substantiated a hundred different ways. To the Western mind, one of the most striking ways is to be found in the numerous Indian legends where men and women have intercourse with animals and produce alternately human or animal offspring. The point that must be kept in mind is that charming as such tales may appear to the romantic modern secular imagination, the separation of man—or one might better say, the *escape* of man—from nature was a great emancipation. As enmeshed in nature as he was, the attitude of the American aborigine toward the natural world was light-years away from that of the modern nature lover or conservationist who so idealizes him. The Indian hunter killed a hundred or a thousand buffalo to butcher fifty. The rest were left for the wolves and vultures. He was completely prodigal, a stranger to deferred gratification. His appetites had to be sated instantly. That was, indeed, the clue to his vulnerability to liquor as well as to the lure of trading goods. That was not "good" or "bad" in any way that the Indian could possibly grasp, and thus the white man's world and values seemed to him hopelessly rigid and arbitrary. By the same token, it was inconceivable that the white man should ever accept (except in the most superficial way) the world of the Indian. He could hardly begin to penetrate it. He could observe and describe it, find features in it that were profoundly appealing to him, romanticize and sentimentalize it, but he was as incapable of understanding it, except in glimmering little bits or pieces, as the Indian was of understanding his world.

The final, inescapable reality of the world of the so-called Indian was that there were tribes, almost beyond numbering or recording, roaming the wilderness and, less often, farming the cleared fields of the North American continent, most of them in a constant state of transformation. They spoke over a thousand languages or variations of languages, so that it is small wonder that the white settlers were constantly tempted to believe that they were the remnants of the lost tribes of Israel whose tongues God had "confused" at the Tower of Babel. In the long development of man, transcending tribalism had meant the opening up of vast new kinds of human energy and imagination. It was one of the great liberations that the human spirit has experienced. It postulated "one world," a common human race, an abstract idea that could be imagined only when man was separated from nature and from his primitive tribal consciousness. In the New World, civilized man confronted the tribal consciousness from which he had escaped thousands of years earlier. So the white man's encounter with the Indians was, in essence, an encounter with his own primitive self; and it was, of course, dimly perceived as such.

A special irony of the white-Indian confrontation lay in the fact that the ideal type of the new age—the inner-directed, Reformed Protestant democrat on the frontier—was the classic adversary of the Indian. For every enlightened upper-class Bostonian or New Yorker who loved the Indians as brothers and sought to do good for them, there were nine, or perhaps ninety-nine, frontier settlers for whom the only good Indian was a dead Indian. John Holmes, who grew up in the staunchly abolitionist town of Mastersville, Ohio, where copies of William Lloyd Garrison's *Liberator* were treasured keepsakes, recalled that the Mastersville Literary and Debating Society seriously debated the question: "Should the uncivilized Indians be exterminated." Many less liberal towns would have considered it subversive even to take the negative side of such a topic.

10

The Genêt Affair

When the Second Congress assembled in October, 1791, most of the senators and representatives had been reelected, but there were some notable newcomers. Anthony Wayne had replaced the bitter Georgia Anti-Federalist James Jackson in a disputed election that evidently involved some fraud. Jackson protested the election so convincingly that Wayne was unseated by a unanimous vote of the House, but a motion to give Jackson his seat was lost in a tie vote when the acting chairman cast his ballot for Wayne. William Findley, the Anti-Federalist enemy of William Maclay, won a seat in the House, as did old General Artemas Ward. Roger Sherman replaced Oliver Ellsworth in the Senate (Ellsworth having been appointed a justice of the Supreme Court), and a brilliant newcomer appeared from New York: Aaron Burr, grandson of the famous theologian Jonathan Edwards, son of a well-known minister, graduate of Yale at the age of seventeen. Burr had been on Benedict Arnold's heroic march to Quebec and had been one of the most notable of the brilliant young officers on Washington's staff during the Revolution.

The new Congress was addressed by Washington the day after it had convened. It was significant that the president laid his principal stress on the prosperity of the country. Like his successors down to the present day, he was anxious to claim credit for a flourishing economy.

195

He congratulated the legislators on "the progessive state of agricul-ture, manufacture, commerce, and navigation." These, he pointed out, were quite unmistakably the consequence of "that revival of confi-dence, public as well as private, to which the Constitution and laws of the United States have so eminently contributed." A good portion of the president's address dealt with the problem of the Indians in the Northwest. He spoke optimistically of St. Clair's expedition, designed to persuade "the deluded tribes" to make a speedy peace. "It is sincerely to be desired," Washington said, "that all need of coercion in the future may cease and that an intimate intercourse may succeed, calculated to advance the happiness of the Indians and to attach them firmly to the United States."

The remarks were not hypocritical. Throughout his administra-tion Washington negotiated with the Indians as though they were composed of independent nations. His policies were aimed at protect-ing them so far as possible from the repacity of speculators working through the agency of particular states.

Washington strongly emphasized the importance of a fair "mode of alienating their lands, the main source of discontent and war." To Washington and those Americans who gave serious thought to the "Indian problem"—that is to say, those who believed that the solution was not to be found in simply killing the Indians—accommodation with the aborigines seemed eminently possible if patience, tact, and humanity were employed. Little, if anything, was known about the Indian tribes of the interior and Western country, but the immensity of the continent seemed to insure ample land for white settlement with areas reserved for the Indians. It was well known that many tribes were nomadic and ranged over vast areas without any specifically defined "homeland." It thus seemed reasonable to believe that such tribes might be persuaded to move to more remote regions. Some in fact had already shifted their grounds several times in response to the pressure from settlers or, in many instances, voluntarily in search of undis-turbed hunting ranges or to preempt the territory of defeated or tributary tribes. Many had shown an astonishing adaptability to new geographical environments. McGillvray, the handsome and able half-breed chief of the Creek Nation, had visited Philadelphia and had been received by Washington with the honors appropriate to the head of an independent nation, the action that had so infuriated James Jackson.

The president urged Congress to pass laws relating to commerce with the Indians that would "secure an equitable deportment toward them" and to undertake "such rational experiments" as might impart to them "the blessings of civilization."

It might be noted that two of the "experiments" that had already been tried on the Indians (many, many more were to follow) were conversion to Christianity and education. Dartmouth College had its origin in Eleazar Wheelock's Indian school. That divine, according to song and legend, ventured into the New Hampshire wilderness with a *"Gradus ad Parnassum* and a Bible and a drum and five hundred gallons of New England rum." His principal convert was Samson Occom, who traveled to England with the Reverend Whitaker and there gave several hundred sermons to raise money for an expanded version of the Indian school. It is worth noting that Whitaker and Occom collected ten thousand pounds, a very considerable sum for those days, and secured the patronage of Lord Dartmouth; hence the name Dartmouth College. Occom must be counted one of the first successful college fund raisers. The English were obviously charmed to hear a former savage preaching the Gospel. After his return to America, Occom became a missionary to the Montauk and Mohegan Indians.

Education and conversion usually went hand in hand. One was supposed to insure the other, although the order was unimportant. The difficulty with the experiment of converting the Indians was that they then fell between two stools. They were not fully accepted by the whites, and they were scorned and reviled by other tribes and not infrequently attacked and slaughtered.

Finally, Washington asked Congress for a system of "adequate penalties upon all those who, by violating the Indians' rights, shall infringe the treaties and endanger the peace of the Union" and he concluded his comments on the Indian situation by urging Congress to adopt regulations that would reflect "the mild principles of religion and philanthropy toward an unenlightened race of men whose happiness materially depends on the conduct of the United States."

From the Indians, Washington went on to speak of the "duties on distilled spirits." These had, on the whole, been paid, with some inevitable grumbling. There was still, he confessed, "some degree of discontent." This was a reference to the western counties of Pennsylvania where the tax was, in the main, still uncollected. Washington recommended a policy of firmness and restraint.

Then there was the matter of a permanent residence for the

government. Pursuant to the acts of Congress, a district comprising ten square miles on the banks of the Potomac adjacent to the towns of Georgetown and Alexandria had been "fixed" and a "city . . . laid out agreeably to a plan which will be placed before Congress."

The first census had been completed, and Washington gave his auditors "the pleasing assurance that the present population of the United States borders on 4,000,000 people."

The most serious problem that confronted Washington, aside from the growing barrage of criticism from the Republicans, was the problem of the Indians. Washington was reluctant to adopt a policy based on punishment of the Indians for St. Clair's defeat. The problem was complicated by the fact that the Miami were the only tribe involved in the defeat. To dispatch a punitive force to humble the Miami might well bring in the Delaware, Shawnee, Ottowa, Potawatomi, Wyandot, and Chippawa. Washington thus decided to send a peace mission, headed by General James Wilkinson, to try negotiation once more. Wilkinson carried with him an offer to impart to the Indians those "blessings" of which the president had spoken in his address to Congress, "of teaching you to cultivate the earth and raise corn [many tribes were excellent farmers; it was, after all, to them that Americans owed potatoes, squash, corn, melons, and, unhappily, tobacco]; to raise oxen, sheep, and other domestic animals, and to educate your children, so as ever to dwell upon the land." Wilkinson spoke less tactfully of the power at the command of the government: "The warriors of the United States number like the Trees in the woods, their meat & their bread grow in their fields and upon their farms, and they make arms and ammunition for their own use." The Indians, in contrast, were "scattered over a Country many hundred miles in extent" and depended "on the forests and the casualities of the hunt for their subsistence and procure their arms and ammunition from a distant nation [Great Britain]." Ironically, the group dispatched to carry the president's and Wilkinson's messages to the more distant tribes was ambushed and most of the party were killed or captured.

With the Indians nothing succeeded like success. The victory of the Miami over St. Clair, Washington feared, might encourage the Southern Indians, the Choctaw, Cherokee, and the warlike Creek, to join in common warfare on the frontier settlements. Such a united Indian front would place a severe strain on the human and material resources of the new nation. Washington therefore dispatched agents to the Southern tribes to try to dissuade them from taking to the warpath. The fate of Wilkinson's mission foreshadowed the futility of Washington's efforts at further negotiation. Stories of Indian atrocities against isolated settlements continued to filter back from the frontier, and the pressure on Washington to take action mounted. His response was a bill for the protection of the frontiers. This bill, which looked to the raising and equipping of three thousand soldiers, thereby bringing the number of regulars to near six thousand, occasioned heated discussions. One of the opponents of the bill asked, "Do these natives hold a land we have an indubitable right to claim? Are we so contracted in territory that we stand in immediate need of immeasurable tracts of wilderness? We are told we have purchased it! Is a keg or two of whiskey, a couple of bundles of laced coats, and a few packages of blankets, an equivalent for a region as great as a kingdom? Is a treaty signed by the scratches of the drunken chiefs of two tribes to be binding on the sober chiefs of a hundred tribes? No. They have as much right to their hunting-grounds as we have to our cities or our farms."

To the Republicans it was clear that the bill was the consequence "of a capricious ministerial resentment" against the innocent Indians and an effort to puff up the Department of War. The census had revealed that there were too many people in the country. The secretary of the treasury had discovered he had too much money. A campaign against the Indians was an ideal way to get rid of both surpluses at once.

The government's reply was that "our fellow-citizens, our friends, our dearest connections" were daily "exposed to all the rage of savage barbarity. They cry to us for help." Between 1783 and 1790 more than fifteen hundred settlers had been killed or taken captive, two thousand horses run off, and fifty thousand dollars' worth of property destroyed. When a treaty had been offered to the Miami in 1790, they had asked for thirty days to consider it and in that time "killed one hundred and twenty whites, roasted several more alive at the stake," and ultimately refused to treat further. It was too late for debate about the origins of the war. "We are involved in it. We cannot go back." On the vote to raise the necessary force the tally was 34 to 18.

With the bill for the protection of the frontier passed and the secretary of the treasury authorized to raise the necessary funds, the next question was who should command the army. Washington had a marked preference for Henry "Light-Horse Harry" Lee, whose brilliant cavalry operations had so aided Greene in the Southern campaigns, but there were senior officers with stronger claims, among them Anthony Wayne. As it turned out, Wayne's reprieve in the matter of the disputed seat from Georgia was short-lived. The House had ordered a new election, but Wayne had refused to be a candidate. He was thus available and anxious to command the expedition against the Northwest Indians. Washington gave the command to Wayne, and the victor of Stony Point threw himself energetically into the work of assembling and equipping his army. It proved a lengthy and exacting task.

Washington, who had undertaken the presidency with the greatest reluctance, looked forward to the end of his term in 1792 as a release from an irksome prison, but even the rumors of his retirement spread alarm in the Federalist ranks. Many Republicans were almost equally disturbed at the prospect, fearing that the "succession" might make John Adams—in their view, an open advocate of monarchy and, what was perhaps worse, a New Englander—president. Jefferson, who was now completely alienated from his old friend and had joined in the general and quite uninformed allegations that he was a monarchist, allied himself with Madison and others in trying to prevail on Washington to accept a second term. If the Federalists needed the shield of Washington's enormous prestige, the Republicans feared that his withdrawal might lead to the dissolution of the new government. Few of them wished for that. Their aim, rather, was to gain control of it and shape it to what they persisted in maintaining was the design of its drafters. Edmund Randolph, the attorney general, began a letter to Hamilton with the words "Persuaded as I am, that the last effort for the happiness of the United States must perish with the loss of the present Government. . . ."

In May Madison reported to Jefferson that Washington had requested him to help prepare a farewell address to be delivered on the occasion of his leaving the presidency. One of the arguments Randolph, Jefferson, and Hamilton put forward was that if Washington accepted another term he might be able to retire in two years rather than serve out the full four. Randolph compared the crisis of the country with a civil war. If there were a war, Washington could not "stay at home." How much easier would it be "to disperse the factions, which are rushing to this catastrophe, than to subdue them after they shall appear in arms?" Washington must not leave the field with the new system still "incomplete." Such entreaties finally overbore Washington's personal inclinations, and he let it be known that he was willing at least to begin another term. The Republicans thereupon turned their attention to defeating Adams for the vice-presidency. For this purpose they gave their support to George Clinton, the New York political boss who had narrowly defeated John Jay for governor a few months before. Aaron Burr was also described as being willing to "support the measure of removing Mr. A."

On the Federalist side, Hamilton, who had no fondness for Adams, could turn up no better candidate. He was bitterly opposed to Clinton. An effort to float Burr as a candidate for the vice-presidency alarmed Hamilton, who described his fellow New Yorker as a man "whose only political principle is, to *mount at all events* to the highest legal honors of the Nation and as much further as circumstances will carry him," an ambition not dissimilar to Hamilton's own.

By October it was evident that Adams had a comfortable margin over Clinton. The New Yorker had gotten the 12 votes each of New York and North Carolina and the 21 of Virginia, which with Pennsylvania's 1 and Georgia's 4 gave him 50 to Adams's 77. Washington had all 132 electoral votes.

Although Washington's new term would not begin until March, 1793, when he delivered his Fourth Annual Address to Congress in November, 1792, the continuation of his administration was taken for granted. Once more the president's emphasis was on the Indian situation. The resistance of the Northwest tribes to all efforts at negotiations had forced him to proceed, Washington declared, with plans for Wayne's campaign. The emissaries that had been sent to spread word of the government's desire for peace had been massacred. In the South, too, there had been depredations by the Chickamauga Indians of the Cherokee tribe. The recruitment of Wayne's force had gone forward expeditiously, but Washington again reminded the legislature that plans for military operations must be accompanied by laws that would restrain the commission of outrages upon the Indians, "without which all pacific plans must prove nugatory." Washington proposed to have "qualified and trusty persons" reside with the various major tribes to act as liaison between the Indians and the federal government and to protect the Indians from white intrusions.

The president had also to report to Congress that some communities continued to resist "the collection of the duties on spirits distilled within the United States," although on the whole "contentment with the law [appeared] to be progressive." Defiance could not be con-doned, and Congress could be sure "that nothing within constitutional and legal limits which may depend on me shall be wanting to assert and maintain the just authority of the laws."

The post office had gotten started, but the complaint had been made that the rates were discriminatory against newspapers. Since papers were of great importance in "facilitating the circulation of political information," Washington trusted Congress would provide some remedy. Finally, Kentucky had drawn up a constitution and qualified itself to be admitted to the Union as the fifteenth state (Vermont having been the fourteenth).

Pursuant to an act of Congress, a mint had been established with the assistance of "some artists from abroad," engaged to design the money. When the proposal was made to have on the obverse side of gold and silver coins an eagle with the words "United States of America" and on the reverse side the head of the incumbent president, an outcry came from the Republicans that to put the president's head on a coin would be confirmation of their charge that the new government was a monarchy in everything but name. One member warned his colleagues "against the cabals, the corruptions, the animosi-ties which in times to come might be excited by men eager to see their faces and their names go down to a remote posterity on the coin."

Overshadowing all domestic issues at the beginning of Washington's second term were the convulsions of the French Revolu-tion, which proceeded at such a breakneck pace that every packet of dispatches and papers from France announced some dramatic (and usually bloody) new development. Prussia and Austria, alarmed lest the infection of the Revolution spread, and urged on by French nobles who had taken refuge in their countries, had formed an alliance against Revolutionary France. In April, 1792, France declared war against Austria and deployed almost 150,000 soldiers in three armies, two of them led by Rochambeau and Lafayette. When their armies failed to rout the Austrians, Rochambeau and Lafayette were called before the Revolutionary government, tried, convicted of dereliction of duty, and proscribed. Lafayette was forced to flee and was captured and imprisoned by the Austrians for four years, a misadventure that doubtless saved his life.

In September the French forces had defeated the Prussians at the Battle of Valmy. When word of this victory reached Philadelphia, a few weeks after Washington's annual message to Congress, the Republicans of the city indulged themselves in a delirious celebration. Church bells were rung, guns discharged, and rum consumed in substantial quantities.

Happy Republicans sang the French Revolutionary song, "Ca Ira," which was credited to Benjamin Franklin, the story being that when Franklin in Paris received word of the American defeats at Brandywine and Germantown, he said, "This is indeed bad news, but ça ira, ça ira, it will come out all right in the end." The story was widely told, printed in the newspapers, and retrieved in 1789 to become a slogan of the French Revolution.

In Boston, the Republicans set January 24, 1793, as the day for festivities celebrating Valmy, announcing that "as rank, the invidious progeny of aristocratic zealots, was abolished by the title citizen, the joy of the metropolis would show itself that day in cordial hilarity." The friends of France were urged to wear the red, white, and blue cockade of the French Revolution in their hats, and on the festival day the sunrise was greeted by a discharge of cannon. A barbecued ox was placed on a wagon and accompanied by "twelve citizens in white frocks and armed with cleavers, made its way through the streets of Boston. Behind it came 800 loaves of bread followed by hogsheads of rum punch. The celebrators set themselves up on State Street and distributed their Republican bounty to the citizens of the city. The ox on which the crowd fed was Aristocracy being offered up on the altar of Democracy in praise of Liberty, Equality and the Rights of Man. The remnants of the feast were sent to the almshouse. Some of the crowd marched off and released the prisoners in jail for debts. Schoolchildren were lined up on State Street and presented with sweet biscuits stamped with the words 'Liberty and Equality,'" Two balloons were released over the city with the same insignia. Everyone called one another by "the social and soul-warming term 'Citizen' or 'Citzeness'" after the French model (the ladies were as Republican as the men) and abjured even such modest titles as "Reverend," "Sir," and "Madam."

The lieutenant governor and the French consul were guests of the Republicans at Faneuil Hall, the scene of so many memorable meetings in the period of Revolutionary agitation. The room was decorated with broken crowns and scepters, French and American flags, and a "great eye of Providence" that looked down "benignly . . . on the scene of Love and Unity."

The mechanics had an especially lavish repast and sang "God save Great Washington," the plain implication being that the general was the prisoner of monarchists and aristocrats.

When night fell a large lantern was hoisted to the top of the liberty pole. On one side was the ruins of the Bastille, on the other a wounded British lion. Toasts were drunk to the French and American revolutions, to the French leaders, to Tom Paine, and to the ladies—"the American Fair, who, it was hoped, would ever keep their favors for the Republican brave." Use of the term "citizen" (and "citess") became such a fad that "it was used in the notices of deaths and marriages, Tradesmen put it on their bills. It fell from the lips of judges as they sat upon the bench."

The infatuation was of course by no means universal. If many Federalists had at first welcomed the news of the French Revolution, they were soon alarmed by its wild and bloody course, so different in spirit from their own Revolution. They also suspected that their political enemies were embracing the Revolution with such fanatical enthusiasm at least in part as a means of discomforting them. In all the hoopla about the comparatively modest French victory at Valmy, little was said about the fact that the greatest friend of America, Lafayette, had been forced to flee for his life from the Revolutionary government. Doubtless that fact alone would have been enough to make Washington and his former officers disenchanted with the Revolution. The British, with all their faults, seemed eminently just and sensible in contrast to the wild disorders that wracked their cross-Channel neighbor.

Small wonder the fervent celebrations of the Francophiles—the victims of a form of madness that their opponents called "Gallomania"—gave the Federalists cause for anxiety. The leveling spirit might, indeed, swallow them up. But beyond that it was simply a puzzle. What did it mean? The American Revolution was not yet a decade old. The new government had been designed to extend its blessings to all Americans. The country was prosperous and flourishing beyond the most sanguine expectations of the men who had framed the Constitution. Three thousand miles away a very different kind of revolution was going on. It shared with the American Revolution little more than the name and the dream of a better human order. At best, it was an enormously complex, almost incomprehensible event. The Republicans acted as though it could be summed up by a few catchwords and slogans. What was more, they implied that it was the *true* Revolution, the real emancipation of mankind, while the administration of President Washington was hardly to be distinguished from the tyrannical and oppressive government of George III.

All of this seemed extraordinarily perverse to most Federalists. They could not make it out. To see sober mechanics and tradesmen, solemn judges and pretty girls going about with cockades in their hats prattling of "fraternity and equality," calling each other "Citizen" and "Citess," and building toy guillotines as reminders of the execution of the French nobles was to cause the most serious doubts about the credentials of the Goddess of Reason at whose shrine the Republicans professed to worship. The Federalists' suspicions of democracy were substantially strengthened by the behavior of their adversaries.

Moreover, Gallomania was not to be a passing fancy. It rapidly became one of the determining factors in American politics. Every political figure must take a stand and be measured on the French question. While the divisions were roughly class divisions in the Northern and Middle states, they became largely sectional in the South where yeoman farmers and plantation owners alike cast their lot with the French cause. Yet even in the North the lines could not be drawn simply according to class. Often there were divisions within families. This was notoriously the case in the Ames family, where Dr. Nathaniel Ames was an ardent Francophile while his brother, Fisher, a Massachusetts representative in Congress, was a "high" Federalist.

Every excess of the French Revolution was pointed to by the Federalists as evidence of its corrupt and violent character and excused by the Republicans as necessary to secure the rights of man. Democratic Societies, or as they came to be called by the Federalists after their French counterpart, "Jacobin Clubs," were started in most of the larger towns and cities. The first of these, founded in Philadelphia in 1793 by a lawyer, Peter Duponceau, stated its purpose quite plainly. It was established to support the French Revolution by all the means at its disposal on the grounds that "should the glorious efforts of France be eventually defeated, we have reason to presume that, for the consummation of monarchical ambition . . . [this] country, the only remaining repository of liberty, will not long be permitted to enjoy in peace the honors of an independent, and the happiness of a republican government. . . . The seeds of luxury appear to have taken root in our domestic soil; and the jealous eye of patriotism already regards the spirit of freedom and equality as eclipsed by the pride of wealth and the arrogance of power."

When the Massachusetts Constitutional Society was formed a few months later the Reverend Jedidiah Morse of Charlestown wrote to Oliver Wolcott, controller of the treasury, that the group considered "themselves as the guardians of the rights of men, and overseers of the President, Congress, and you gentlemen, the heads of the principal departments of State, to see that you don't infringe on the Constitution."

The Federalists were certainly not far behind in the matter of invective. A Federalist poet described the Jacobins as:

> A strange, unlettered, multifarious band—
> Some with weak heads, but well-intentioned hearts,
> Are simple dupes to Anti-Federal arts;
> Who, viewing tyrant acts in useful laws,
> Mistake foul Faction's, for fair Freedom's cause.
> The rest are genuine progeny of dirt,
> Who, for a pint of rum, would sell their shirt! . . .
> An envious, restless, swearing, drinking crew,
> Whom sense ne'er guided, virtue never knew;
> Some foreign ruffians, hireling tools no doubt,
> French, Irish, Scotch, complete the "rabble route."

A writer in the *Independent Chronicle*, a Boston newspaper, replied in kind: "What a continual yelping and barking are our swindlers, Aristocrats, Refugees [a reference to refugees from the French Revolution], and British Agents making at the Constitutional Societies!"

The enticing question is: What lay beneath the rhetoric? How are we to translate the Republican paranoia about monarchy into understandable political terms? One must conclude, I believe, that class antagonisms in the United States ran much deeper than we have been inclined to recognize— *and that this class feeling was more bitter in the first decades of the Republic than it ever was again.* Many Americans who lived through the Revolution had come to believe quite genuinely that in the new age the Revolution was presumed to usher in there would be no distinctions of social position or wealth. Everyone would in fact be equal. This view, it seems reasonable to conjecture, was most commonly held by those Americans who were least "equal." Thus the resistance by a substantial part of the population—especially those living in towns and cities—to all forms and institutions of the old order. If the mass of these individuals were to be found among "the lower orders," their leaders were, for the most part, those democratic idealists of the higher classes who have been evident in every period of our history. In this struggle between what I suppose we might call the Revolutionary Establishment versus the Counterculture, the French Revolution was simply a convenient kind of reference point or, in Jedediah Morse's phrase, "a sort of political thermometer." The perfervid celebrations of Valmy were really messages to the Establishment. The louder and clearer these messages sounded, the gloomier the Federalists (called Tories by their opponents) became.

Since there was never any serious danger that the United States would become a monarchy, the question is: How should we understand the Anti-Federalists' obsession with the notion that it was the Federalists' settled determination to impose that form of government on the country? Was it simple politics or simple delusion? It was probably a combination of both. After all, it had been only fifteen years or less since Tom Paine's *Common Sense* had attributed all the evils of the world to monarchy. Paine had written at the end of his tirade against kings: "In short, monarchy and hereditary succession have laid (not this or that kingdom only) but the World in blood and ashes. . . . 'Tis a form of government which the word of God bears testimony against, and blood will attend it." Since in 1790 there were few Americans of mature years who had not felt the intellectual and emotional impact of Paine's pamphlet, it seems reasonable to assume that the Anti-Federalists' horror of monarchy derived in large measure from that work. But it is clear that "monarchy" was also a convenient code word that was taken to stand for a wide range of political sins; for a strong central government most of all; for rule by an "aristocracy" of the moneyed and the wellborn; and for almost anything else pushed by the Federalists, from salaries for legislators and judges to banks and taxes. Paine had also written that "government is the badge of lost innocence," and this aphorism struck a responsive chord in the hearts of most Americans. The statement that "the best government was the least government" was to become the motto of the Jeffersonian Republicans. And it would be piously reiterated generation after generation as the government grew even larger. That was another of our basic schizophrenias. We longed for innocence, for the dream expressed by Patrick Henry in the Virginia convention that no nation should fear us and no citizen be oppressed while another part of us wished to be rich and powerful. The Anti-Federalists made themselves spokesmen for the dream of innocence.

In April, 1793, word reached America that the king had been beheaded and that France had declared war against England, Holland, and Spain. The less zealous Francophiles had second thoughts. To assist the French would mean to be involved in a war with Great Britain and with two of America's allies in the Revolution, Spain and Holland. Spain, in possession of the Louisiana area and in control of the Mississippi, was in an excellent position to stir up the Southern Indians, who needed, as we have noted, very little encouragement. War with England would make it far more difficult to bring the Indians of the Ohio country to terms. Moreover, aid to France would expose American shipping to seizure by British naval vessels. Altogether it was a disheartening prospect. Yet the United States had an alliance with France under the terms of which the French were free to use American ports in time of war.

When Washington received word of the French declaration of war, he called together his Cabinet for advice. The crucial question was whether the treaties made with France when she was a monarchy were binding in view of the complete change in government brought about by the Revolution. Washington believed that the wisest and safest course would be to declare American neutrality, but he was well aware that such a policy would bring a democratic storm around his ears. He put a series of such questions to Jefferson, Hamilton, Randolph, and Knox. Included was the question of whether the United States should receive a minister from the French Republic.

The answer to the last question had in fact been rendered moot by the arrival at Charleston, South Carolina, of the French frigate *L'Ambuscade,* carrying the new French minister to the United States, "Citizen Genêt," Edmond Charles Édouard Genêt, a novice diplomat who had most recently served in Russia. Washington and his Cabinet decided on a policy of neutrality, and a proclamation to that effect was printed in the Philadelphia papers the day Genêt landed at Charleston, South Carolina. Any persons violating the Proclamation of Neutrality by aiding either of the belligerents would be prosecuted.

Before he had been received by the president or accredited as the representative of the French Republic, Genêt began a series of actions that were, after considerable storm and stress, to prove his undoing. He immediately dispatched orders to French consuls that they were to act as admiralty courts for judging all prizes brought into American ports by French privateers. His next step was to commission two American vessels, renamed the *Citizen Genêt* and the *Sans-Culottes* (the nickname for the kneebritchless ones, thus the lower class, the proletariat), and dispatch them to intercept British merchant vessels. Within days the instant French navy was bringing ships into Charleston to be condemned as prizes of war under the terms of the French-American Treaty of Commerce, and in a few weeks the pro-French secretary of state, Thomas Jefferson, was receiving complaints from the British of violations of Washington's Proclamation of Neutrality. A British merchant ship, the *Grange*, had been seized in Delaware Bay and sent to Philadelphia as a prize of war.

Meanwhile Genêt made his way from Charleston toward Philadelphia in what was far more of a triumphal procession than an ordinary journey. He was wined and dined in every town he passed through. Speeches, fireworks, lavish feasts, and innumerable toasts marked his progress northward. At Philadelphia, *L'Ambuscade* announced his impending arrival with a cannon salvo, and a throng of people collected at the state house and went from there to Gray's Ferry to escort him into the city.

At Oeller's Tavern he was the guest of the Democratic Society. Duponceau, as president, read a poem in French, praising Genêt as an apostle of democracy, at which there were delirious shouts and cheers. A party of sailors from *L'Ambuscade* arrived and exchanged Gallic embraces with the company. They entertained the group with the *Marseillaise*, and Genêt sang selections from a new Revolutionary opera.

> Should France from her lofty station,
> From the throne of fair Freedom, be hurl'd,
> 'Tis done with every other nation,
> And Liberty's lost to the world.

Washington felt obliged to receive Genêt and acknowledge him as minister of the French Republic, but he was furious with the Frenchman for his behavior and it was evident in his chilly demeanor; he was barely civil and Genêt was indignant. Perhaps as the representative of the French Revolution he had expected to exchange a "fraternal hug" with the leader of the American Revolution. He was especially angry to see a painting of King Louis in the room where Washington received him. He believed it an intentional rebuke.

Despite his cold reception by Washington, Genêt was intoxicated by the popular acclaim that had greeted him everywhere. He proceeded to dispatch a series of imperious letters to Jefferson. The United States still owed France $2,300,000 of "war debt," French loans to America during the Revolution. Although the debt was not yet due, Genêt urged that it be paid immediately, since the Republic was sorely in need of money. In addition, he proposed a new treaty, "a true family compact" on a "liberal and fraternal basis."

To the request for a new treaty Jefferson replied that no treaty could be concluded without the consent of the Senate, which would not convene until fall. Hamilton declared that the government had no money to pay off the French loan, and to pay it off before it fell due might, in any event, be interpreted as a hostile act by Great Britain. Genêt was not to be deterred. He threatened to incur debts for military supplies and charge them against the loan. Washington was stubbornly determined to maintain the principle and practice of neutrality, and when the *Citizen Genêt* tied up at a wharf in the Delaware River, Washington ordered two American sailors on board arrested and charged with violating the neutrality proclamation. He then directed Genêt to order the *Citizen Genêt* out of American waters. This threw the Frenchman into a passion. "The crime," he wrote, "laid to their charge, the crime which my mind cannot conceive and which my pen almost refuses to state, is the serving of France, and the defending with her children the common and glorious cause of liberty."

The Philadelphia Republicans were almost as indignant as Genêt over Washington's policy. There were public demonstrations in different quarters of the city that featured denunciations of Washington and threats to force the government to take up arms against Great Britain. John Adams had muskets brought into his house to defend it, if necessary, against assault. Another grand feast was planned for the French minister. Again Oeller's Tavern was the site. Two hundred Republicans attended, paying four dollars apiece, and many others were turned away for lack of space. There were fifteen toasts; a liberty cap of red silk was placed at Genêt's seat; and any number of patriotic songs were sung, including, of course, the *Marseillaise*. All this under Washington's nose.

L'Ambuscade sailed on to New York where scenes similar to those in the Quaker City were repeated. A red liberty cap was placed in the Tontine Coffee-House by the Republicans, and the Federalists were challenged to try to tear it down. Meanwhile, word was brought to Governor Clinton that an American vessel, the *Polly*, had been renamed the *Republican* and was being refitted as a French privateer. To the surprise of many and the anger of his Republican supporters, Clinton responded by ordering a company of militia to seize the ship.

The prospects of combining devotion to the cause of liberty with the allure of profits to be made from privateering proved too tempting for many Republicans. The *Roland* sailed from Boston, the *Carmagniol* from the Delaware, the *Cincinnatus* from Charleston, where Governor Moultrie connived at the sailing of another privateer, the *Vanqueur de la Bastille*. More disturbing was that the courts conspired on occasion with the privateers; Republican judges refused to order prizes returned to their owners, and a jury freed Gideon Henfield, one of the sailors on the *Citizen Genêt* whom Washington had ordered arrested.

Benjamin Franklin Bache's *Aurora,* a relentlessly Republican newspaper, rivaled Freneau's *National Gazette* in its attacks on Washington.

An atmosphere of crisis hung over Philadelphia. To some it seemed that Genêt rather than Washington was running the country. A group of embattled merchants collected six thousand dollars "for the defence of the city."

In this situation things were brought to a head by the issue of the British brig *Little Sally,* which had been captured by the *Citizen Genêt* and was being converted into a privateer with fourteen cannon under the new name of *La Petite Démocrate*. Washington was at Mount Vernon, and when word was carried to Jefferson of the plans for *La Petite Démocrate* the secretary of state promised that it would not be allowed to sail until the president had returned to the city. Preparations nonetheless went ahead rapidly, and Governor Mifflin was informed that the ship would sail within a few days. He immediately sent secret word to Genêt urging him to keep the ship in port. Genêt sent back the defiant message that he was determined to have the vessel sail at the earliest moment. Her crew would forcibly resist any effort to delay her departure. Mifflin thereupon mustered 120 militiamen, but before they could be dispatched, *La Petite Démocrate* was gone from her berth. Washington thus returned to find a *fait accompli*. It was clear to the president that his secretary of state had failed to act with firmness. What he did not know was that Jefferson had written to Madison urging him to do all he could to refute the notion that the president had the constitutional right to issue the Proclamation of Neutrality. The result was a pamphlet warfare between Hamilton as "Pacificus," defending the president's authority, and Madison as "Helvidius," denying it. The issue now became not the justice or injustice of the Proclamation of Neutrality but whether Washington had exceeded his constitutional authority in issuing it. The tension was heightened in the port cities by clashes between French and British sailors.

At the end of July word reached New York that a French vessel had anchored off Sandy Hook. Citizen-Captain Bompard of *L'Ambuscade* sent one of his officers and some sailors to welcome her, but it turned out she was a British frigate, the *Boston*, commanded by Captain Courtney. Courtney then proceeded to "call out" Bompard and *L'Ambuscade,* challenging him to combat. Bompard as promptly accepted, and hundreds of New Yorkers set out in boats to witness the engagement while it was estimated that ten thousand lined the shores. When *L'Ambuscade* came up with the *Boston,* Bompard, wearing a red liberty cap, called out to Courtney, who replied with a broadside. For two hours the ships exchanged fire until, with Courtney dead and the main-topmast carried away, the *Boston* broke off the engagement and fled. When the victorious *L'Ambuscade* reached the East River, she was greeted by the ecstatic cheers of throngs who lined the banks and crowded onto the docks.

As serious as Genêt's efforts to use American ports for outfitting and commissioning privateers were his efforts to stir up trouble on the sensitive boundary with Spain along the Mississippi River. The independent frontiersmen bitterly resented Spain's high-handed behavior in imposing tariffs on goods that passed by barge through New Orleans. They were thus only too ready to listen to propositions aimed at driving the Spanish out of the territory. Genêt apparently intended to use the French loan that he pressed Hamilton to pay off or, barring that, the proceeds from privateering activities, to recruit and equip an army of frontier settlers to launch an attack on the Spanish posts in the Louisiana Territory. This would of course have precipitated war with Spain, and when rumors of such a plan reached Jefferson it further disenchanted him with Genêt.

It is commonly said in history textbooks that Genêt overreached himself by publicly appealing to the American people to reject Washington's policy of neutrality. The truth is somewhat more complicated. It might better be said that he was the victim of a Federalist strategem. Rufus King and John Jay vowed that Genêt had been heard to declare that he *would* so appeal. The remark had been repeated by Alexander Dallas, a member of the Pennsylvania Democratic Society, to Hamilton and Knox. They told Jay and King, who in turn reported it as a fact, and it was widely stated to be so in all Federalist newspapers.

The Republicans replied in vain that there was a vast difference between making such a threat in an impassioned moment and actually putting it into effect. But Genêt and the Republicans found themselves on the defensive, a dangerous situation politically. Governor Moultrie of South Carolina, Genêt's first sponsor, wrote him that his behavior had lost him the support of many who were friends to the French cause, and Madison observed gloomily to Monroe that "his conduct has been that of a madman. He is abandoned by his votaries even in Philadelphia. Hutchinson declares that he has ruined the Republican interest in that place."

Genêt compounded his difficulties by writing to Washington demanding "an explicit denial, a statement 'That I have never intimated to you an intention of appealing to the people.'" That such a letter was a serious breach of diplomatic protocol Genêt must have known. Jefferson, who felt his own position had been seriously undermined by Genêt, sent him a cool response telling him as much. Genêt then appealed to Randolph as attorney general to charge King and Jay with libel, and when Randolph refused he declared he would take his case to the Supreme Court.

Washington had already requested Genêt's recall, and in February, 1794, a new minister appeared to take his place. Meanwhile, the Girondist party, to which Genêt belonged, had fallen from power and had been replaced by the more extreme Mountain party. Since it was already evident that the French Republic punished failure with death, Genêt wisely declined to return to France. Instead he courted and married a daughter of George Clinton and became as enthusiastic a farmer as he had been a revolutionary propagandist. His extravagant behavior may be laid to his youth. He was only twenty-eight when he arrived in the United States; he died forty years later in Dutchess County, New York, at the comparatively ripe old age of sixty-nine, presumably a good deal wiser.

Before we leave Citizen Genêt, we might reflect briefly on the probable consequences had Washington decided to honor the French treaties and give aid and support to the Republic. Such a decision, while it would have been enormously popular with the Anti-Federalists (who perhaps made up between a quarter and a third of the population), would have been greeted with dismay by all those who depended on seagoing commerce for their livelihood (privateers commissioned by Genêt aside, of course). Certainly the country was in no condition, politically or economically, to become involved in a war with Britain. At the very least, such a conflict would have imposed a severe setback to the general prosperity that had done so much to create confidence in the new government. Beyond that, it would have greatly increased the debt and thereby imperiled Hamilton's financial system. The account is all on the debit side. Given the bitter factionalism that already existed, it is hard to believe that the new federal government could have survived. Indeed, a more skilled and tactful diplomat than Genêt would surely have created enormous problems for Washington's administration. As it turned out, the Genêt affair, by leaving the opposition abashed and demoralized, unquestionably gave the government a new lease on life.

Although, as we have seen, Jefferson had not allowed his position as a member of Washington's Cabinet to inhibit him in trying to arouse opposition to his chief's policies, he chafed at the constraints of his office. He had no taste or aptitude for routine labors, felt himself overborne in the Cabinet by Hamilton, and yearned for his beloved Monticello. The Genêt affair had been a purgatory for him and he finally prevailed on Washington to release him from his duties as secretary of state. Washington, determined to maintain some degree of Republican-Federalist balance in the Cabinet, asked attorney general Edmund Randolph to replace Jefferson. Hamilton, having completed his financial system, followed Jefferson into "retirement." But while Jefferson made a considerable show of abjuring politics, Hamilton took on the role of *de facto* leader of the Federalists. His continuing influence in Washington's administration was guaranteed by the appointment of one of his principal lieutenants, Oliver Wolcott, as his successor, and another loyal supporter, Timothy Pickering, as the successor of Henry Knox, who had also resigned, as secretary of war.

11

The Jay Treaty

The respite afforded Washington by the discrediting of Genêt proved a brief one. Encouraged by an edict of the French National Convention giving all neutral vessels the rights of French ships, hundreds of American merchantmen set sail for the French West Indian islands loaded with dried fish, flour, hides, and timber, the traditional items of West Indian trade. But Great Britain, it developed, had no intention of respecting American neutrality. British cruisers seized American ships by the dozens in the Caribbean, and vessels flying the flag of the United States that put into ports in the Indies such as St. Kitts or Martinique found their cargoes confiscated as contraband and their crews thrown in the brig. Horrendous stories were carried to Philadelphia by every ship that arrived from the Caribbean. One hundred thirty American vessels had been condemned as prizes in St. Eustacia alone. When the British took Martinique in February, 1794, every American ship in the harbor was boarded by British marines, who tore down the American colors, stripped the sails from the masts, and clapped 250 sailors in a foul prison ship.

The British, although the chief offenders, were by no means the only ones. French, Spanish, and Dutch privateers and warships also preyed freely on American shipping. But the principal American anger centered on the British. They had an imperious and arrogant way of doing things that was especially galling. The truth was that they viewed the Americans with contempt as an irredeemably lower-class lot whom it was a pleasure if not a duty to put in their proper place.

The cry for war against Great Britain was once again raised. American commerce languished. Shipowners were afraid to send their vessels to sea. Idle sailors clogged the seaport towns and added their ire to the already combustible human mass. At Gloucester, Massachusetts, two hundred sailors marched to the town fort, ran up the flag, and stated their intention of defending it against any English attackers. At Marblehead three thousand militia drilled on the common and called for war on Britain. Congress responded by passing a bill on March 4 appropriating money to repair the fortifications of all seacoast harbors, and in New York Baron Friedrich von Steuben directed the building and repair of earthworks at strategic points. Columbia students turned out to work alongside members of the Democratic Society, the Tammany Society, the grocers, the bakers, schoolmasters and their charges, lawyers, and carpenters.

A few days after the passage of the bill on harbor defense, Congress authorized the beginnings of a navy. Six frigates were to be built. The talk everywhere was of war. But President Washington was determined to do all in his power to avoid the conflict. He knew better than his countrymen how ill-prepared the nation was. England would doubtless have been delighted by a declaration of war, which would have done little except to make a universal display of American impotence. A handful of British frigates could have blockaded every American port. One of the most galling aspects of the situation was that while American ships lay idle at their wharfs, foreign ships, predominantly British, sailed off with their holds full of American produce. Some newspapers called for an embargo. The *American Daily Advertiser* declaimed, "Lay on an embargo. Let it be general, and cover every ship in our ports save those of our good allies, the French. . . . Then shall we cease to feed those who insult us. Then shall we fairly meet the question, Are our sailors to be maltreated, our ships plundered and our flag defied with impunity?"

Embargo was the course upon which Washington's Cabinet and the leaders in Congress decided. Short of war, it was all that could be done. Washington's proclamation on March 29 of a thirty-day embargo was greeted enthusiastically. Ports were promptly shut and before the month was out Congress extended it another month. When it expired a great clamor was raised, especially by the Democratic Societies, and a violent storm was hailed as divine punishment for the cowardice of Congress. Anti-British feeling reached new heights. In Charleston, South Carolina, a statue of the elder Pitt, Lord Chatham, a hero to Americans for his defense of their cause in the years prior to the Revolution, was pulled down. The front of Christ Church in Philadelphia bore a bas-relief of George II, king of England when the church was constructed. It was torn off the facade of the church by angry Democrats. The Democrats were especially active in Charleston where effigies of Fisher Ames, William Pitt, and Benedict Arnold were paraded through the streets and then burned.

In all these matters Hamilton played an important role as Washington's most trusted adviser, as an enemy of France, and as a strong advocate of closer ties with England. From George Hammond, the British minister in the United States, he conveyed to Washington hints that Great Britain was ready to alter her policy of settled hostility to the United States. Hamilton had done everything in his power to prevent Congress from passing legislation that would retaliate against Great Britain through commercial regulations. The British, meanwhile, shutting the United States out of trade with their West Indies possessions, instructed the commanders in their Western posts to encourage the Indians of that region to fend off all incursions of settlers into the area north and west of the Ohio River. In addition, British agents kept in contact with the dissident elements in Kentucky and Vermont, apparently toying with the idea of trying to draw them into an alliance of some kind.

The Federalists in Congress led the fight to raise an army of twenty-five thousand regulars and eighty thousand militia in anticipation of war. This measure put the Republicans, who had been clamoring for war but who were resolutely opposed to a large standing army, in a dilemma.

The Federalists, having taken steps to provide for war, now urged Washington to send a special envoy to England to make a last attempt to resolve the principal differences between the two countries in hopes of preventing an armed conflict. Washington was reluctant to take such a step. He was convinced that Great Britain was set on a war policy and that a mission such as that proposed by certain leading Federalists could do nothing to deflect her.

Word that Britain had lifted some of the more onerous restrictions on American trade induced Washginton to send an envoy to undertake negotiations. Hamilton was his preference, as he was of most of the Federalist leaders, but rumors of his appointment brought such a strong reaction from Republicans that Hamilton withdrew his name rather than imperil the mission and Washington appointed John Jay, chief justice of the Supreme Court. To sweeten the dose for Republicans, he also sent to the Senate the nomination of James Monroe as minister to France and successor to Gouverneur Morris, whose hostility to the French revolutionaries was well known. Washington wrote to his new secretary of state, Edmund Randolph, that his policy was "to prevent a war, if justice can be obtained by fair and strong representations (to be made by a special Envoy) of the injuries which this country has sustained from Great Britain . . . ; to put it into a complete state of military defence, and to provide *eventually*, such measures as seem to be pending in Congress . . . if negotiation in a reasonable time proves unsuccessful."

Despite Washington's hope that Congress would take no steps to irritate Britain and compromise Jay's efforts, in June, 1794, the House passed a nonintercourse bill designed to stop all trade with that country, and it was blocked in the Senate only when Adams, as presiding officer, broke a tie vote. "We the old Sachems," he wrote to Abigail, "have enough to do to restrain the Ardour of our young Warriors.—We shall Succeed however, I still hope, in preventing any very rash Steps from being taken." Whatever the temper of the Democratic Societies may have been, Republican leaders denied any desire for war with England. Most of them agreed with the author of a letter to Monroe: "If there is any reason to apprehend a rupture between Great Britain & America it will . . . very much affect prices in general. . . . War certainly should be avoided if with any degree of propriety it can be done." Madison insisted that measures of retribution, far from bringing on war, would cause the British to back off. She would "push her aggressions just so far and no farther, than she imagines we will tolerate."

Underlying the dispute in Congress about the best method of forcing concessions from the British was the classic split between the commercial North and the agricultural South, of which we have already taken note. The Republican strength was in the South. The Southern Republicans were quite willing to try the experiment of closing American ports to the British or passing a nonintercourse measure, since it would be the Northern merchants, shipowners, and sailors who would have to pay the cost of such policies. The harder the Southern Republicans pushed for such restrictions on trade, the more lukewarm Northern Republicans became. The Federalists, for their part, were convinced that war would split the country along regional lines. Timothy Dwight wrote to Oliver Wolcott, "A war with Great Britain, we at least, in New England, will not enter into. Sooner would ninety-nine out of hundred of our inhabitants separate than plunge themselves into such an abyss of misery." And Fisher Ames wrote a friend that he dreaded "anarchy more than great guns."

The Federalist program must be, in Dwight's view, "Peace, peace, to the last day it can be maintained; and war, when it must come, to be thrown upon [the Republican] faction, as their act and deed." The Republicans characterized the Federalists as irredeemable Anglo-philes; but in fact, the latter were almost as disenchanted with the British ministry as were their opponents. Adams blamed British ill-treatment on "a national insolence against us," and Theodore Sedgwick, a high Federalist, wrote, "Such indeed are the injuries which we have received from Great Britain that I believe I should not much hesitate on going to war, but that we must in that be allied to France, which would be an alliance with principles which would prostrate liberty and destroy every species of security." Even Fisher Ames declared: "The English are absolutely madmen."

The prospects for the success of Jay's mission were not good. As Hamilton pointed out to the chief justice, Britain had all the cards. It was vain to believe that the British, "fortified by the alliances of the greatest part of Europe, will submit to our demands, urged with the face of coercion, and preceded by acts of reprisal. . . . A proper estimate of the operation of human passions, must satisfy us that she would be less disposed to receive the law from us than from any other nation." Despite such a gloomy analysis, Jay was enjoined to try to get indemnification for the seizure of American ships and a settlement of the portions of the peace treaty that England had heretofore refused to honor, including compensation for the slaves the British had carried off at the end of the war. In addition, he was to try to negotiate a commercial treaty that would allow American ships to trade with the British West Indies. That Washington's expectations were not extrava-gant is indicated by a letter from Adams to Jefferson in which he noted, "The President has sent Mr. Jay to try if he can to find any way to reconcile our honour with Peace. I have no great Faith in very brilliant Success; but hope he may have enough to keep us out of war."

The Republicans did manage to block the move to increase the army to twenty-five thousand men. In a compromise move funds were voted for ten gunboats to protect the coast, a favorite project of Jefferson's and Madison's.

When the session ended, the Federalists were pleased with the results. Hamilton wrote to Jay: "All mischievous measures have been prevented, and several good ones have been established. . . . Men's minds have gotten over the irritation by which they were some time since possessed, and if Great Britain is disposed to justice, peace, and conciliation, the two countries may still arrive at a better understanding than has for some time subsisted between them." But Great Britain, as things developed, was not so disposed.

From the moment Jay arrived in England he was wined and dined by the British, who had been told by Hammond that Jay was vain and disposed to be pro-British. It was said that "Mr. Jay's weakness was Mr. Jay." At the same time, Jay's attitude was one of moderation and accommodation. "No strong declarations should be made," he wrote, "unless there be ability and disposition to follow them with strong measures." What he finally got from the British may well have been all anyone could have gotten in the circumstances. Certainly threatening and blustering could have accomplished nothing. What little Jay did get, or rather what he failed to get, aroused such a storm in the United States that it is difficult, even at this date, to make a fair judgment on the treaty itself.

By its terms the British agreed to give up the troublesome frontier posts by June, 1796, and to refer the claims against them for destruction of American shipping to a mixed commission for adjudication. In additon, the right of American vessels of under seventy tons to trade with the West Indies was granted, as well as open trade with the British East Indies. The treaty also ruled out the sequestering of debts owed by American to British citizens, a policy pushed by the Republicans as retribution for the seizure of American ships and cargoes. Under the terms of the treaty Americans were obliged to accept the principle that trade not allowed in peacetime would be illegal in war and also consent not to impose special tonnage duties on British vessels in American ports for a period of twelve years. This had been another weapon with which Madison and the Republicans had hoped to force concessions from the British. Jay also accepted a stipulation that the United States would prohibit the exportation of molasses, sugar, coffee, cocoa, and cotton, all of which had traditionally been brought from the West Indies on American vessels and then shipped to European ports. The restriction on cotton was especially objectionable to Southerners, who hoped, with the benefit of a ginning machine recently invented by a visiting Yankee, to make cotton an important item of export. Jay dropped all references to compensation for the slaves taken away at the end of the war. He himself was an ardent antislavery man and was not personally disposed to press the issue. Finally, he failed to obtain a clause giving up the right of impressment, a human and moral issue that aroused the strongest emotions in Americans of every class and section. Such a provision had not been included in his instructions, but it had appeared in an early version of the treaty and its absence in the final draft was made much of by critics of the agreement. All in all, it might be said that there was something in the treaty to offend everyone and precious little to cheer about.

Jay himself had no illusions about the treaty, but he defended it as the best that could be obtained under the circumstances. He knew very well, as did all the Federalists, that the Republicans were lying in wait for him and his treaty. Their mood can be judged by a letter to Madison from Monroe (who, incidentally, had angered Federalists by giving an emotional speech to the National Convention, praising the Revolution and proclaiming American support for it) in which the U.S. minister to France expressed his hope that Washington could be made aware of "the principles and crooked policy of the man [Jay], disguised under the appearance of great sanctity and decorum." Another leading Republican had expressed his opinion, before Jay concluded the treaty, that since Britain was on "the Verge of Bankruptcy, Humility and disgrace Mr. Jay has nothing to do but exhibit the *sine qua non* of the House of Representatives last Session [the nonintercourse bill] to the British Minister to acquire all he has a right to ask " And Madison was equally confident that he would accomplish "much if not all he aims at."

Well before the treaty arrived at Philadelphia rumors were circulating that the allegedly pro-British Federalist negotiator had betrayed the interests of his country. John Adams, hearing such stories, wrote to Abigail, "I am very much afraid of this Treaty! but this is in confidence." One story was spread about that when Jay had been presented to the queen he had kissed her hand. This desperate deed prompted an editor to write: "John Jay, ah! the arch traitor—seize him, drown him, hang him, burn him, flay him alive! Men of America, he betrayed you with a kiss! As soon as he set foot on the soil of England he kissed the Queen's hand . . . and with this kiss betrayed away the rights of man and the liberty of America."

One ship bearing two copies of the treaty was overtaken by a French privateer, and the copies were thrown overboard to prevent their capture. Another copy took three months to make the Atlantic crossing. When Washington received the treaty on the morning of March 5, 1795, Congress had been adjourned for three days. Both the president and Randolph were dismayed when they read its terms. They believed that a rejection of it would be tantamount to war, but to make it public before ratification would be to invite bitter attacks on it from all quarters. Although it would be four months before Congress would convene again, the president and secretary of state decided to keep the terms of the treaty secret until then.

When Congress convened on July 8, the treaty was submitted to the Senate. There it was debated briefly under a bond of secrecy. Washington and Randolph had decided that Article XII, forbidding the export from the United States of products from the Caribbean islands (among them cotton) was too much to stomach, and they proposed that the Senate ratify the treaty minus this provision. The first vote on amending the treaty was defeated 20 to 10, revealing that the Federalists, quite miraculously, had exactly the two-thirds vote needed to ratify. Still the terms of the treaty remained secret, and all the fulminations of the Republican press were rebuffed by the Federalist assertion that they did not know whereof they spoke. Finally, Pierce Butler, senator from South Carolina, sent a copy of the treaty to Madison, who leaked it to Bache's *Aurora*. Having printed the text of the treaty, Bache headed for New England, scattering copies of it with an appended critique as he went. As soon as the terms were generally known, it was plain that the fat was in the fire. The flames of Democratic Republicanism (or however we designate the pro-French, anti-British faction), dampened by the outcome of the Genêt affair, now rose higher than ever. In Boston a mob seized a British ship that was rumored to be a privateer that had preyed on American shipping in the Indies and burned it to the waterline. In New York when Hamilton tried to speak in favor of the treaty he was stoned from the platform, which occasioned a Federalist wit to note that by knocking out Hamilton's brains the Republicans would "reduce him to an equality with themselves."

A few days later when Hamilton, encountering some Republican acquaintances, was goaded by them, blows were exchanged, and

Hamilton offered to duel all the Republicans, one at a time. The challenge was accepted, but since Hamilton already had a duel pending nothing more came of the encounter.

A favorite pastime of the Democratic Societies came to be burning Jay in effigy. There was hardly a town or hamlet from Vermont to Gerogia that did not have a go at it. Partisan politics even invaded the churches. At the Hingham, Massachusetts, meetinghouse after morning communion a Republican took his seat in the front of the gallery, wearing a French cockade in his hat. At the end of the service, "to the consternation of the pastor before he was able to leave the pulpit, the hat fell from the gallery and the Federalists over benches, pews, etc., ran and caught it, from which they dismounted the [cock]ade. This was followed by clinching, swearing, and even by blows. The screechings of old women heightened the scene. Here was in view justices, lawyers, and even grand juries, all clinched by collars, hair, and cheeks, until at last the Jacobins were thrust out of the house, some with no hats, others with bloody cheeks, and nearly all with dishevelled polls."

A similar scene took place at the Quincy meetinghouse in the vice-president's hometown and at nearby Milton. To the French cockade, Federalists responded with an "American cockade," bringing pressure on all those who "supported General Washington" to proclaim the fact by wearing the emblem in their hats. Members of Congress wore it. General William Hull, in command of the army, ordered it worn by officers and men. It was described as "a pledge of friendship among Federalists and of attachment to our Constitution and Government, while at the same time it proves an eyesore to Jacobins. Let it then be worn by all federalists and the lye will at once be given to those lying dogs, the Jacobins, who have dared to assert that we are a divided people!"

Fisher Ames was moved to wish for the suppression of the Jacobin Clubs, of one of which his brother was a member, describing them as "born in sin, the impure offspring of Genêt. They are the few against the many, the sons of darkness (for their meetings are secret) against those of the light; and above all it is a town cabal attempting to rule the *country*."

Fifteen hundred "citizens of Boston" voted unanimously against ratification of the treaty, and groups of furious Republicans roamed the streets breaking the windows of known supporters of the hated document. In the somewhat overheated words of a Federalist newspaper, the *Centinel,* "The laws prostrate—magistrates literally trampled under foot—women and children frightened—bonfires made in the centre of the town—oaths and imprecations united with threats to tear the hearts of magistrates from their breasts and roast them at a fire."

When Governor Samuel Adams was appealed to to restore order, he dismissed the disturbances as "a mere watermelon frolic, the harmless amusement of young persons." To George Cabot, a wealthy Boston Federalist, the popular response to the treaty suggested the weakness of the Constitution itself: "After all," he wrote, "where is the boasted advantage of a representative government over the turbulent mobocracy of Athens, if the resort to popular meeting is necessary? Faction, and especially the faction of great towns always the most powerful, will be too strong for our mild and feeble government."

A popular toast among Republicans was: "A perpetual harvest to America; but clip't wings, lame legs, the pip, and an empty crop to all Jays." Another expressed the hope that "the cage constructed to coop up the American Eagle" would "prove to be a trap for Kingbirds and Jays."

At Charleston, South Carolina, a person dressed as a hangman burned copies of the treaty, and an English flag was dragged through the streets and burned in front of the home of the British consul. The only man who tried to defend the treaty was dragged to the town pump and dowsed until he almost drowned. The citizens of the city were called upon to assemble in a town meeting to condemn the treaty. "Are the People the Legitimate Fountain of Government?" the handbill announcing the meeting asked. "There is creeping into your Constitution an insidious Serpent, whose venom, once infused, will exterminate every remaining spark of Gratitude and National Faith. . . . *Great Britain* is the universal Foe of *Liberty*; and you, from your Regeneration to the present moment, have been the guiltless victims of her Infernal malice."

The attacks on Washington became more and more virulent. One writer compared him with Caesar and Cromwell; another declared he had taken on "the seclusion of a monk and the supercilious distance of a tyrant" and presumed to ride in a carriage where he had once appeared on horseback. He was denounced as "a political hypocrite" and "a man in his political dotage." By his oppressive and tyrannical acts he had forfeited the affection and respect of the people. "To be an opposer of the President," one writer noted, "will soon be the passport to popular favor."

Underlying much of the Republican clamor over the treaty was the fact that the Secular-Democratic Consciousness, the "American Enlightenment," call it what we will, believed (and believes), as Felix Gilbert put it, that there "should be no difference between the 'moral principles' which rule the relations among individuals and 'moral principles' which rule the relations among states. . . . Diplomacy should be 'frank and open.' Formal treaties would [then] be unnecessary. . . . Foreign policy and diplomacy . . . owed their importance to the fact that rulers followed false ideals and egoistic passions instead of reason. The logical consequence was that in a reformed world, based on reason, foreign policy and diplomacy would become unnecessary, . . . the new world would be a world without diplomats."

Before Washington could sign the treaty word reached the United States that the British were again seizing American ships carrying noncontraband—in this instance, grain. Washington left Philadelphia for a respite at Mount Vernon, apparently determined not to put his name to the treaty until he had received some assurance from the British that they would desist from any more such acts. While he was at Mount Vernon, a British frigate intercepted a French packet carrying letters from Fauchet, Genêt's successor, which strongly implied that he had been involved in private dealing with Secretary of State Edmund Randolph and had received secret information from him concerning policies of Washington's administration. There were even hints of money being paid to Randolph. The British minister forwarded the dispatches to George Hammond, minister to the United States, with instructions to him to see that they got into those hands where they would do the most harm to the French cause. Hammond turned the papers over to Wolcott and Pickering. They were, of course, delighted with the windfall. Without informing him of the captured dispatches, they tricked the unsuspecting Randolph into urging Washington to return to Philadelphia because of a crisis in regard to the treaty. When Washington returned, they sprang the trap, turning the documents over to the president. He reacted rather as he had when Arnold had betrayed him. Barely suppressing his fury, he put the worst interpretation on the dispatches and confronted Randolph with the damaging evidence. Randolph defended himself as best he could against the vague and unsubstantiated charges and resigned his office. Washington, apparently primarily as a result of his indignation over what he considered Randolph's betrayal, suppressed his misgivings about the renewed acts of British aggression and signed the treaty on August 14, 1795. Nathaniel Ames noted in his diary: "Washington now defies the whole Sovereign that made him what he is—and can unmake him again. Better his hand had been cut off when his glory was at its height, before he blasted all his laurels." And Bache declared, with perhaps more accuracy than marked most of his assertions, that the president had signed the treaty "in a fit of bad humor occasioned by an enigmatical intercepted letter."

Miss Rachel Bradford, a staunch Federalist, wrote to a friend that the signing of the treaty seemed to have brought a lull in Republican agitation, adding, "what the Demoniaks of Congress may bring forward to excite new commotions on the subject we shall soon know." While the Senate was, as we have seen, safely Federalist, the House was another matter. In order for the treaty to be given effect, money had to be appropriated. This was the responsibility of the House. And here the Republicans intended to make their last stand.

12

The Whiskey Rebellion
and Fallen Timbers

While our attention has been fixed to the eastward—on the plight
of American commerce caught between the belligerent powers
of Europe, on the French Revolution, and on Jay's negotiations in
England—two important events were taking place to the west. The
first was what came to be called the Whiskey Rebellion; the second was
the victory by General "Mad Anthony" Wayne over the Northwest
Indians at Fallen Timbers.

As we have already noted, the whiskey "still" had been boiling
away since the excise tax on spirituous liquors was passed by Congress
in 1791. The western counties of Pennsylvania, whose economies were
based on the distilling of rye liquor, had taken the lead in resistance to
the tax, intimidating tax collectors and defying court orders. In February, 1794, Congress took steps to alleviate some of the most burden-
some aspects of the act, especially the requirement that farmers charged
with violating the law answer to indictments at Philadelphia, more
than a hundred miles from their homes. Congress also took steps to
enforce the act in a bill passed on June 5, 1794. A writ was promptly
issued naming seventy-five distillers who were alleged to be in defiance
of the law and a federal marshal was dispatched to serve them. He
encountered no resistance until he came to the last offender, a man

named Miller whose farm was fifteen miles west of Pittsburgh. Miller was at work in his wheat field, reaping the harvest that would be converted into whiskey. After the marshal left, the harvesters gathered at a nearby village and spread the word that "the Federal Sheriff is taking away men to Philadelphia." Some thirty-seven men, most of them militiamen, took their muskets and marched off to the house of the revenue inspector on the outskirts of Pittsburgh. The inspector, warned of their coming, had posted a band of armed blacks in a nearby house.

The farmers appeared in the early morning, and when the inspector challenged them and they refused to reveal the purpose of their visit or disband, he ordered his small force to open fire. Six of the farmers were wounded and one was killed. The rest scattered to spread the word, and by nightfall five hundred men had assembled at Couche's Fort. A Revolutionary veteran was voted commanding officer, and the band set off for the inspector's house. He had wisely departed, but eleven regulars and a major from Fort Pitt were occupying the premises. When the farmers demanded to see the papers of the inspector and search the house, they were refused and firing broke out. One of the leaders who tried to stop the shooting was killed by a soldier's bullet, and the farmers reacted by setting fire to the barn and outbuildings. The fire spread to the house, and the soldiers were smoked out, disarmed, and marched away as prisoners. Alarmed at their own temerity, the farmers allowed the squad of regulars to escape but, steadfast in their determination to resist the collection of the tax, made plans for a larger gathering at Mingo Creek a few weeks later.

At the Mingo Creek meeting one of the bolder spirits, David Bradford, proposed to take some illegal action that would force all the farmers to support the dissidents. Two days later he and his companions robbed the mail on the post road from Pittsburgh and opened letters to try to determine what word had been sent to Philadelphia. Bradford and his band decided to call out the militia to render "a service to your country," without stating the specific purpose. Once the militia had been mustered, an all-out effort would be made to persuade them to remain under arms and resist all efforts to collect the tax.

Four men were sent to Pittsburgh to inform its inhabitants that if the male residents failed to turn out with the militia the next day to form a united front with the Washington County farmers, every house would be burned to the ground. The terrified inhabitants knuckled under promptly. As one of them wrote, "I believe most of the Women in town were in tears; the people appeared (by the lights) to be all stirring, and I believe the most of them hiding property. I also began to hide or bury property." The next morning at ten o'clock the residents of Pittsburgh assembled at Braddock's Field, the place appointed for the militia muster. "We entered the field," John Wilkins wrote later to a friend, "and marched about one mile through a crowd of people, scarce a face known to me—a constant fire of small arms was kept up, equal to almost any battle, some loading and firing for their diversion, others blazing away at the trees." As the rebellious farmers in Massachusetts had done eight years earlier, the militia units formed up under their elected officers; a semblance of order was established, supplies were requisitioned, liquor was forbidden, and boats were requisitioned to carry the army across the Monongahela River. It was estimated that six thousand men and a considerable number of women marched through Pittsburgh in a line that extended for two miles. By nightfall they were across the river.

When word of the uprising reached Philadelphia, the Federalists urged Governor Mifflin to call up the eastern militia to suppress the rebels, but the governor, probably wisely, demurred. He doubted, he said, that the militia would "pay passive obedience to the mandates of the Government." President Washington then acted without hesitation. He secured a statement from one of the justices of the Supreme Court to the effect that Washington and Allegheny counties were in defiance of the law and fixed September 1 as the date for a special muster of twelve thousand militia from New Jersey, Pennsylvania, Maryland, and Virginia.

Trouble was at once encountered in western Maryland, which, like Pennsylvania, was deeply involved in the manufacture and sale of rye whiskey. At Frederick efforts to call out the militia were frustrated by Pennsylvania visitors who told a large crowd that the government was determined to tax them all into poverty. At this someone cried out, "God save King George!" referring to the president. This was going too far. He was tarred and feathered for his pains.

At Hagerstown, Maryland, when the draft for the militia began, the officers were beaten and driven out of town. A liberty pole, the symbol of no taxation without representation, was erected during the night; when supporters of the government cut it down, another was erected in its place, defended this time by militant Democrats. Liberty poles soon became symbols of defiance. Every town sympathetic to the "Whiskey Boys" set up one bearing such legends as "Liberty and No Excise, O Whiskey!"; "Liberty and Equality"; and "Liberty or Death."

In Virginia any impulse to resist the president's call was disarmed by the appearance of Daniel Morgan, victor at Cowpens and hero of the frontier. Governor Mifflin placed himself at the head of the Pennsylvania militia. Richard Howell, governor of New Jersey and veteran of the Revolution, commanded the famous New Jersey Blues. By the end of September thirteen thousand men were on the march. Some were veterans, but many were hardly more than boys who soon missed the comforts and conveniences of home as they straggled westward in the growing chill of fall. They were accompanied by a corps of newspaper reporters who kept their readers informed of the progress of the army and sent back a stream of human-interest stories about the young recruits and the country through which they were marching. Rain fell by the buckets, and the supply wagons carrying their tents and baggage fell behind, so that the soldiers were forced to sleep where they could on the cold, damp ground. A reporter for the *American Daily Advertiser* informed his readers that Hannibal's trip across the Alps could not have been more arduous.

When Washington and Hamilton joined the troops at Carlisle, Pennsylvania, six weeks had been consumed in collecting and moving the militia to their confrontation with the insurgents. The intention was to give the Whiskey Boys ample time to reflect on the consequences of their intransigence.

At Parkinson's Ferry on the Monongahela a meeting of delegates from the communities where the insurgents were strongest took place. The issue was armed resistance to the last or accommodation. Bradford spoke for the radical faction; a young Swiss, Albert Gallatin, who had immigrated to America when he was nineteen, urged moderation. While the debate went on, commissioners arrived from the president to arrange for capitulation and offer terms. A committee of twelve was appointed by the insurgents to hear the government's conditions. When they acceded, they were renounced by their fellows and accused of having accepted bribes. Several days later a committee of sixty insurgents assembled at Redstone Old Fort to renew the debate. When Gallatin again spoke for accepting the commissioner's terms, some of the crowd pointed their muskets at him. Afraid that the extremists would intimidate the more moderate, Gallatin called for a secret ballot. The tally was 34 to 23 in favor of compliance.

Under the terms proposed by Washington the inhabitants of every town in the region were to register their willingness to abide by the law. Allegheny, Westmoreland, Washington, and Fayette counties refused to fall in line, and while Washington returned to Philadelphia for the opening of the fall session of Congress, Hamilton and his amateur army pressed on to Parkinson's Ferry where a number of the reputed ringleaders of the insurrection were rounded up.

In the corralling of rebels at Parkinson's Ferry much violence and abuse was vented on the captives by the ill-disciplined militia. Stories of people dragged from their beds, reviled, and beaten were numerous, as were tales of the hardships suffered by those who had to march back to Philadelphia as prisoners to be tried for treason in federal courts. When the prisoners arrived in the city, they were paraded through the streets with the word "insurgent" on their hats and were hooted and jeered at. After lengthy hearings charges were dismissed against most of the men for want of evidence. Only two were found guilty of treason, and these were subsequently pardoned. So, on the whole, the episode was viewed by most Americans as salutary. The new government had displayed both its resolution and its capacity for mercy. The bustling and conspicuous role Hamilton had played and his obvious pleasure at being Washington's right-hand man was widely and unfavorably noted by Republicans, but what was perhaps most significant about the whole episode was that the Republicans, if we except Mifflin's initial waffling, avoided the cause of the Whiskey Boys like the plague. The principal Republican newspapers condemned them, and the Democratic Societies outside western Pennsylvania and Maryland laid low. Apparently both Washington and Randolph had feared that the temper of the insurgents might prove contagious, but their fears were unwarranted.

The other significant event of 1794 was Anthony Wayne's expedition against the Northwest Indians. Wayne, a meticulous planner and organizer, had completed the recruitment of his force by late autumn of 1793. He then marched his men, under the strictest discipline, into Indian Territory and went into winter camp at Greenville, not far from where St. Clair had suffered his crushing defeat. There he engaged his men in rigorous training exercises and toughened them by sending them on scouting forays through the surrounding forests. He built Fort Recovery on the site, garrisoned it, and, as soon as the snows of winter had melted, pushed on to the

Maumee River where it met the Au Glaize, and constructed Fort Defiance. At St. Mary's River his soldiers erected Fort Adams. It was August before Wayne had penetrated, with some three thousand men, to the heart of Indian country near the British post of Fort Miami on the Maumee. There he sent scouts under a flag of parley to offer to negotiate with the Indians. Encouraged by their victory over St. Clair and by the support of the British who provided them with arms and ammunition, the Indian spokesmen asked for ten days to consider Wayne's proposal. "If you advance," they declared, "we will give you battle." Wayne, convinced that the tribes were determined to fight and simply wanted the ten days to augment their forces, refused and ordered his troops to move forward in battle order.

The area where the Indians had chosen to make their stand had suffered from the effects of a hurricane. Thousands of trees had been blown down—fallen timbers—and formed an almost impenetrable tangle, ideally suited for the Indian style of fighting. It was into this natural defensive position that Wayne's tough, disciplined soldiers forced their way. Wayne had deployed them in two extended skirmish lines, the first to advance and engage the Indians behind stumps and fallen trees, the second to remain in reserve and attack through the forward line as the battle developed. The second line was never committed. Faced with the skillful and determined attack of the first line, the Indians broke and fled after less than an hour's engagement, leaving the field to Wayne. The Battle of Fallen Timbers demonstrated dramatically the weakness of Indians in any extended military campaign against the whites. Usually fighting individually, without any overall plan or battle leadership, they could seldom sustain a protracted engagement, especially if the tide of battle appeared to be going against them. Under such circumstances, they could not effect that most difficult of military maneuvers, a retreat. They were brave and agile and demonstrated remarkable stamina, but they lacked any order or cohesiveness.

Little Turtle, who had led the Indians in the attack on St. Clair, was present at Fallen Timbers and understood quite well the respective strengths and weaknesses of the two opposing forces. He knew Indians had little chance against white soldiers properly led. In defense, or in warfare of position or maneuver, the Indians were almost invariably routed. From the news that Indian scouts brought of Wayne's painstaking preparations, Little Turtle concluded that the Indian cause was doomed. He had urged his fellows to negotiate the best terms they could with the "General-Who-Never-Sleeps." The appellation was the greatest compliment he could have paid to Wayne. With characteristic Indian economy of language he had epitomized the general's most essential quality and anticipated the outcome of the battle.

After the Indians were routed, Wayne destroyed their villages, cut down their crops in the fields, and carried off or destroyed their corn, the precious staple of the Indian diet, leaving them largely dependent on the charity of the British. What was most demoralizing to the impressionable savages was that Wayne carried out his "scorched-earth" policy almost within sight of the British fort to which the Indians looked for protection. The message was unmistakable: "Your avowed friends, the English, are the agents of your misfortune. They have equipped you with arms and encouraged you to resist the advance of our settlers into your country, but now you see they are quite powerless to protect you from the consequences of your mistaken deeds."

Wayne now moved unimpeded up the Maumee to the juncture of the St. Mary's and St. Joseph's, where he built a stout fortification he named Fort Wayne. The army then returned to Greenville and went once more into winter quarters.

The next summer the warriors and chiefs of tribes of the Northwest began to collect at Greenville to negotiate with the U.S. commissioners. For weeks they came in, a few dozen or a few hundred at a time—Kickapoo, Miami, Chippewa, Ottowa, Potawatomi, Wyandot, and Shawnee. They had, collectively, a vast amount of experience with the white man. They had roamed over a wide extent of territory, the Kickapoo being undoubtedly the most peripatetic, moving from the Tennessee River in the South through the present states of Wisconsin, Illinois, Indiana, Ohio, Pennsylvania, and New York. They would go as far again before they were assigned a "home." The same was true in varying degrees of the other tribes. Their great chiefs were present, including Little Turtle and an as yet unknown young Shawnee warrior, Tecumseh, who had fought well at Fallen Timbers, and other warriors who had led their braves in notable victories over the whites.

While they waited for the treaty negotiations to begin, the Indians entertained themselves with games and feasts. Yet the occasion had about it an inescapable atmosphere of gloom. The tribes were aware that their efforts to check the encroachment of whites had failed. They were meeting to acknowledge and seal that failure. They could not know what was ahead for them, but they were keenly aware that their life was no longer to be what it had been.

At the end of several weeks of negotiations, marked by the well-established formalities that characterized treaty meetings, an agreement was reached by which the Indians surrendered their claim to some twenty-five thousand square miles of territory, an enormous expanse of land. In return they received twenty thousand dollars in presents and were promised an allowance of ten thousand dollars a year to be distributed among the tribes who accepted the treaty, a kind of annual prize for good behavior.

At the end of the council, General Wayne addressed the Indians: "Brothers, I now fervently pray to the Great Spirit that the peace now established may be permanent, and that it will hold us together in the bonds of friendship until time shall be no more. I also pray that the Great Spirit above may enlighten your minds, and open your eyes to your true happiness, that your children may learn to cultivate the earth and enjoy the fruits of peace and industry."

The tide of westering emigrants, whose pressure had precipitated the "Indian troubles" resolved by Fallen Timbers and the Treaty of Greenville and whose progress west had been only slightly interrupted by the "war," now resumed their irresistible movement, for the most part following the rivers flowing toward the Mississippi.

13

The Jay Treaty Again

When Washington addressed Congress on December 8, 1795, he was very well aware of the troubled and unhappy state of the country and the bitter factional quarrels that filled the newspapers daily. He chose, however, as all presidents have done since his day, to accentuate the positive. He congratulated the Congress on "the numerous and extraordinary blessings we enjoy." The Indians had been pacified. There were hopeful signs that the pirates of the Mediterranean might cease to prey on American ships in that sea. The Jay treaty had secured "amicably very essential interests of the United States" while laying "the foundation of lasting harmony with a power whose friendship we have uniformly and sincerely desired to cultivate."

If foreign affairs were encouraging, in domestic matters Washington discovered "equal cause for contentment and satisfaction." While European nations were devastated by wars and civil discord, "our favored [country] in happy contrast, has enjoyed general tranquility. . . . Our agriculture, commerce, and manufacturers prosper beyond former example. . . . Every part of the Union displays indications of rapid and various improvement. . . . Is it too much to say that our country exhibits a spectacle of national happiness never surpassed, if ever before equalled?"

The implication was clear enough. If Americans were embroiled in angry disputes with each other, it was because of their own folly. Considering the burdens and "accumulated evils" the people of most traditional societies labored under, Americans were, by comparison, greatly blessed.

The president had scarcely left the chambers of Congress before a bitter wrangle broke out in the House that belied his optimistic words. A number of members did not wish to present a reply to the president's message. A "reply" smacked of monarchy. The objection had been raised before; now it was more strongly sustained. An unpleasant contention arose over the phrase "undiminished confidence" in a draft of the reply. The Republicans argued that confidence in the president was greatly diminished. To state otherwise would be hypocritical. And so the matter dragged on from day to day, demonstrating, as loud as the angry words exchanged, how little trust or comity was left in the House.

Washington's birthday, which had been celebrated since the end of the Revolution, was now in the offing, and there were objections to observing it. In the words of one member, "In place of reminding Mr. Washington that he was the servant of the people, he was . . . treated like a king. Had any more been done for King George?" Republican papers not infrequently referred to Washington as "King George" and as the evil stepfather of his country rather than as the benign father. The *Aurora* offered its readers a poem for the president's birthday:

> Excisemen, Senators, and army Hectors,
> All hail the day in clear or squalid notes,
> Place-hunters, too, with lordly Bank directors,
> Loud in the general concert swell their throats.
> The splendid Levee, too, in some degree,
> Must Caesar's dignity and power display;
> *There* Courtiers smooth approach with bended knee,
> And Hoary Senators their homage pay.

Those honest Americans who criticized such pompous charades, the *Aurora* continued, had been denounced as "scum."

> Dare you (ye swinish herd of infamy)
> Against your *country's father* thus transgress

> Who for his Wisdom and Integrity
> Doth "undiminished confidence possess?"

It was March, 1796, before the president sent the Jay treaty to the House to be implemented by the appropriation of funds. There was a strong faction in the House that wished to make the treaty the occasion to insist that that body had a right equal with the Senate of passing on all treaties. They argued that the treaty had been unconstitutionally made in the first place.

The leader of the Federalists in the House was Fisher Ames, a brilliant pamphleteer and speaker and an able manager. The Federalists in and out of Congress believed that the fate of the treaty lay in his hands. But Ames had been ill for weeks, and Washington felt it unwise to delay sending the treaty to the House until the Federalist champion had recovered, especially since he was being publicly accused of doing precisely that.

One of the ablest Republican debaters was the same Albert Gallatin we encountered at Parkinson's Ferry trying to prevail on the Whiskey Boys to accept the authority of the federal government. He supported the right of the House "to share in the treaty-making power which the President and the Senate enjoy." A treaty was a law; the Constitution gave the House the right to participate in the making of all laws. The Federalists were not slow to attack Gallatin. In the words of one newspaper, the question was: "Will you prostrate your General in war and your President in peace, the laws of your country, and the authority of your Senate at the feet of an itinerate Genevan, the prime minister of the Western insurrection, the assuming foreigner whose machinations have cost the country twelve hundred thousand dollars [the estimated cost of suppressing the insurrection]? Or will you support the Man and the Senate?" Madison, who surely knew better, took the same tack on Gallatin, and a number of days were consumed in reviewing the Constitution itself, *The Federalist Papers,* and the debates in the state ratifying conventions. Much of the discussion revolved around the right of the House to call for the documents in the hands of the president relating to the treaty. For two weeks the House engaged in an absorbing and learned if often repetitious debate. Finally the members voted 61 to 38 to ask the president for all papers relating to the treaty.

Washington took a week to consider the matter and compose an answer. The papers in question had already been submitted to the

Senate and were available to the House through that channel. The request for the president to deliver them was, in effect, the assertion of a claim by the House to be included in the ratification of all treaties, and Washington understood it to be so. His reply was temperate but explicit. It did not, he stated, appear to him "that the inspection of the papers asked for can be relative to any purpose under the cognizance of the House of Representatives, except that of an impeachment, which the resolution had not expressed." He reminded the representatives that, far from hiding anything, he had submitted the papers in question to the Senate. After reviewing the constitutional questions, he added, ". . . it is perfectly clear to my understanding, that the assent of the House of Representatives is not necessary to the validity of [a] treaty . . . and as it is essential to the due administration of the government, that the boundaries, fixed by the constitution between the different departments, should be preserved; a just regard to the constitution and to the duty of my office . . . forbids a compliance with your request."

Washington's response, as he had surely anticipated, provoked angry declamations in the House and two defiant resolutions. The issue was debated for fourteen days more, while the Republicans gloried in a majority of 6 against appropriating the funds to give the treaty effect. Finally, on April 26, Fisher Ames, pale and ill, asked for and was given the floor. Word that he was to speak on behalf of the treaty had spread, and the House chamber was jammed with spectators, many of them senators and officers of the government. The vice-president was among those who listened enthralled to a speech given dramatic emphasis by the physical condition of the speaker. Ames was listened to, John Adams wrote Abigail, "with a silence and interest never before known, and made an impression that terrified the hardiest [of his opponents] and will never be forgotten." Adams sat beside Supreme Court Justice James Iredell, and the two exchanged whispered exclamations. "My God! how great he is!" the justice murmured. "He is delightful," Adams replied. Iredell: "Gracious God how great he has been!" Adams: "He has been noble." Iredell: "Bless my stars, I never heard anything so great since I was born!" Adams: "It is divine." And so they went on with their "interjections, not to say tears, till the end."

Many of those who listened were convinced that the future of the Republic hung in the balance with the Jay treaty. Without it, they thought, there would be war and with war inevitable dissolution of the Union.

In a different time and place and with none of that feeling of crisis that obsessed Ames's listeners and intensified their response to his words, the modern reader will nonetheless hardly fail to be moved by the eloquence Ames displayed. He could not profess, he admitted, to being disinterested: "It would be strange that a subject, which has aroused in turn all the passions of the country, should be discussed without the interference of any of our own. We are men, and therefore not exempt from those passions; as citizens and representatives, we feel the interest that must excite them. The hazards of great interests cannot fail to agitate strong passions; we are not dispassionate; it is impossible we should be dispassionate. The warmth of such feelings may becloud the judgment, and, for a time, pervert the understanding. But the public sensibility and our own, has sharpened the spirit of inquiry, and given animation to the debate. . . . The only constant agents in the political affairs are the passions of men. Shall we complain of our nature? shall we say that man ought to have been made otherwise? It is right already, because He, from whom we derive our nature, ordained it so; and because, thus made and thus acting, the cause of truth and the public good is the more surely promoted."

Ames then went on to separate the issue of the authority of the House from the question of the treaty itself. It would be a fatal error, he declared, to reject the treaty to prove the power of the Congress. Why, then, if it was not intolerably bad, had it aroused such opposition throughout the country? The answer was to be found in the infatuation of Americans with the French Revolution. "In our newspapers, in our feasts, and some of our elections, enthusiasm was admitted a merit, a test of patriotism; and that made it contagious. In the opinion of party we could not love or hate enough. I dare say . . . we were extravagant in both." Such passionate attachments to the fortunes of other countries had produced a kind of psychological dependence that often interfered with people perceiving the best interests of their own country. Every treaty was thus "as sure to disappoint extravagant expectations as to disarm extravagant passions. . . . Hatred is one that takes no bribes."

Ames placed special emphasis on the consequences of the British retaining the Western posts in the event the treaty failed. All the frontier settlements would then be constantly ravaged by the Indians.

And finally, there was the real danger of war if no accommodation could be made with Great Britain.

"Let us not hesitate, then, to agree to the appropriation to carry [the treaty] into faithful execution. Thus shall we save the faith of our nation, secure its peace, and diffuse the spirit of confidence and enterprise that will augment its prosperity. The progress of wealth and improvement is wonderful, and some will think, too rapid. The field for exertion is fruitful and vast, and if peace and good government should be preserved, the acquisitions of our citizens are not so pleasing as the proofs of their industry [which will be] the instruments of their future success." Ames was convinced that if the appropriations were not voted and the treaty thereby permitted to take effect, "I, slender and almost broken as my hold upon life is, may outlive the government and constitution of my country."

Adams noted that while some Republicans affected amused contempt, "their visages grimaced horrible ghastly smiles." Many of those present, Adams among them, wept unabashedly. Joseph Priestley, the great English radical who was visiting America and was present in the audience, compared Ames's speech with those of the elder Pitt and the great parliamentary orators. Before it the Republicans had counted a majority of 6. Even though they forestalled a vote when Ames had finished speaking, fearing that some waverers might have been persuaded by it to support the treaty, when a vote was finally taken to refer the treaty from the House sitting as Committee of the Whole to the House in formal session, the vote was 49 to 49. Frederick Muhlenberg, as Speaker, cast the deciding vote to report it out. For his pains he was attacked and slashed with a knife by his brother-in-law, a fanatical Republican.

Two days later when the House voted on the appropriation itself, the vote was 51 to 48 and markedly sectional. Most of the Northern Republicans accepted it; the Southerners remained adamant. Undoubtedly as influential as Ames's eloquence was the fact that in the uncertainty about the fate of the treaty, business and commerce languished. Ships were held in port, stocks declined, and produce prices dropped sharply. The House was flooded with memorials urging that the treaty, whatever its faults, be allowed to take effect before all commerce came to a halt.

Ames's speech was a classic expression of the Federalist creed. In his assertion that men were ruled by their passions, he echoed Madison, Gouverneur Morris, and others in the Federal Convention.

But men might transcend prejudice, provincialism, and self-interest through the process of discussion and debate. Larger views might prevail if a degree of mutual trust obtained and opinions were given a chance to "ripen." Indeed that was perhaps the most that could be hoped for from the best of political systems. Ames's analysis of the origins of the Republicans' irrational attachment to the French Revolution was, again, characteristic of Federalist thinking. It displayed that detachment from the passions of the moment that the Federalists prided themselves on; that was the fruit of the perspective only history, with its record of the follies and triumphs of the race, could give. That the Age of Reason should reach its climax in such an utterly unreasonable event as the French Revolution and, moreover, that it should drive a portion of their fellow citizens quite mad could be encompassed by the "philosophy" of the Federalists, though it must be said their philosophy often provided them with cold comfort in the face of the excruciating reality.

It is also worth noting that many of Ames's listeners wept unabashedly. We have seen the Founding Fathers individually and collectively weep on occasions that moved them deeply. Washington wept at moments of despair during the Revolution; when he parted with his officers at Fraunces Tavern at the end of the Revolution; when he surrendered his commission to Congress. Again, there were tears at Washington's inaugural; and now, perhaps most surprisingly to the modern consciousness, when Ames spoke so brilliantly in behalf of the Jay treaty. The point is that it had not yet become unmanly for American males to weep when they were deeply moved. We will talk more, in the course of this work, about the ways in which most American men came in the course of the next century to rigorously suppress any display of emotion. Ironically, it was that most emotional of men, George Washington, given to rages and tears, who came to be the model and ideal of masculine self-restraint.

Finally, it is agreeable to report that Fisher Ames, who quite sincerely anticipated his own imminent demise, lived another twelve years and, although plagued by ill-health, turned out a stream of trenchant critiques of the French Revolution and the philosophical assumptions behind it. All of them were rich in learning and in historical allusions, thoroughly Federalist and increasingly archaic.

Of the treaty to whose acceptance his brother had contributed so greatly, Nathanial Ames, a Republican, wrote in his diary: "The Treaty fish swallowed, tail foremost, by Congress. The President is a rebel against General Washington and the United States. . . . The Federal Government become as near as arbitrary as any European; the worst Tories and Conspirators with English [are] caressed."

The *Aurora*, blaming Washington for the treaty's acceptance, declared: "If ever a nation was debauched by a man, the American Nation has been debauched by Washington. . . . If ever a Nation has been deceived by a man, the American Nation has been deceived by Washington. . . . Let the history of the Federal Government instruct mankind, that the masque of patriots may be worn to conceal the foulest designs against the liberties of a people." It was certainly ironic that the grandson of Benjamin Franklin should become the most scurrilous detractor of the president, the only American more revered than the author of *Poor Richard's Almanack*.

14 Transmigration

The Jay treaty finally consummated, the nation had another crisis to face, a crisis occasioned by Washington's retirement and the question of succession. Eugen Rosenstock-Huessy has said that every new age begins with a new experience of time. It was the inspiration of the framers of the Constitution to limit the presidential term to four years, although, as the reader will recall, this was a decision not readily or by any means unanimously reached. The future has always been a source of anxiety to human beings, whatever their stage of cultural and social development. All human groups have devised various ways of robbing the future of its oppressiveness, among early cultures perhaps most commonly by what has been called the "myth of eternal return," the periodic return of a hero or demigod or, as in Christianity, a final return.

The framers stumbled on the idea of dividing the future into four-year segments. Every four years a new leader would be confirmed or an old one reconfirmed. In political terms, this had the effect of robbing the future of at least a portion of its potentially threatening character. Today we take our four-year presidential elections so much for granted that it seems a kind of a natural law of politics. But it was once as difficult to imagine as it is for us to imagine otherwise.

That Washington was determined not to be a candidate again was no secret. The urgent question was who his successor was to be. To most Federalists it seemed proper and indeed highly desirable that the vice-president should succeed the president. Moreover, the president was a Southerner. It was important that he be followed by a Northerner, preferably a New Englander. Adams was far from a popular figure. He had no personal coterie as Hamilton had. As vice-president his very inconspicuousness had proved an asset, since it had protected him, in the main, from Republican attacks.

The most enthusiastic Democrats, who had once denounced Adams for his presumed defense of monarchy and addiction to pomp and ceremony, viewed him as a lesser evil than Washington. He had no "great name" under the cover of which the Federalists could plot the destruction of their country. Although those Federalists like Hamilton who couldn't abide Adams's stiff New England ways, his pompousness and irascibility, his constant display of personal rectitude, and his tendency to lecture those who differed from him, tried to turn up an alternative, the only serious rival was Thomas Jefferson, the generally acknowledged leader of the Anti-Federalist Republican-Democrats. Although Adams was unwilling to give any public indication or take any actions that could be interpreted as what we today would call running for office, he felt he was the proper heir to Washington and that the presidency was rightfully his.

Jay was the only other Federalist mentioned as a presidential candidate, and if the New Yorker had not had the millstone of the treaty about his neck he might very well have been the choice of a majority of Federalists.

Adams took Jefferson's candidacy seriously enough to sound out his once close friend. He wrote to the Virginian deploring the excesses of the French Revolution. "Passion, prejudice, interest, necessity has governed," he noted, "and a century must roll away before any permanent and quiet system will be established." Jefferson, replying, disavowed any active interest in politics. His experience as secretary of state had cured him. It was "a subject I never loved and now hate." He made no direct response to Adams's strictures on the French Revolution. "I am sure from the honesty of your heart you will join me in detestation of the corruption of the English government."

One possibility Adams had to consider was that Jefferson might edge him out for the presidency, leaving Adams, as runner-up, still stuck in the vice-presidency. He was determined not to serve under his

former friend. They were so opposed in their views of government—
"in different boxes," as Adams put it—that such an outcome would
produce "a dangerous crisis in public affairs." Most Federalists regarded the possibility of Jefferson's becoming president with horror,
since they were convinced that he would immediately begin to
dismantle the "system" that Washington had shaped so laboriously.
Adams had a different opinion. If either Jay or Jefferson became
president, "government will go on as ever," he wrote. "Jefferson would
not stir a step in any other system than that which is begun. Jay would
not wish it."

Adams thought the electors might settle on him on the grounds
that he was "so old that they all know they can make me miserable
enough to be glad to get out of it as soon as Washington, if not in half
the time." The comment is revealing. It reminds us that with no
constitutional limit on the number of terms a president might serve,
Adams at least viewed two terms as a comparatively modest tenure.

Federalists and Republicans alike were full of anxieties about the
coming election and even about the capacity of the Union to survive.
One Federalist reflected that if, under the leadership of the revered
Washington, in the midst of general prosperity and peace, "such a
crisis could be produced" as seemed continually on the verge of tearing
the country apart on purely ideological issues, what must happen
"when adversity, disturbance, and panic shall prevail; when the hated
head of one party shall, as all ruling parties will, abuse its power
sometimes and commit blunders at others?"

Oliver Wolcott, Hamilton's successor as secretary of the treasury,
wrote to Jonathan Dayton informing him that Washington would
"decline a reelection," adding, "I fear the country is not sufficiently
united to make a choice by the electors." The summer of 1796 was
filled with such conjectures.

It was September before Washington publicly announced his
determination to retire. Four years earlier, when he had first attempted
to retire, Madison had prepared a Farewell Address at the president's
request. Washington intended to update this document and use it as
the basis for his last offical message to his countrymen. In May, 1796,
he sent a draft of it to Hamilton for his comments and suggestions.
Hamilton spent almost three months working on his own version. He
may well have delayed to give Washington less time to write, or to
solicit an alternative draft from Madison. In any event, the document
Hamilton sent to Washington was substantially the one that Washing-

ton used. Since, in the words of the most perceptive student of the Farewell Address, "of all the Political Testaments of the eighteenth century [it] alone succeeded in achieving practical political significance," we should pay close attention to it.

It was, in fact, not an address but an essay prepared with the thought that it would be reprinted in newspapers and read by Washington's countrymen in every part of the Union. Now that the time had come when he must retire, Washington wished to give an accounting of the trust he had held. "Not unconscious at the outset of the inferiority of my qualifications, experience in my own eyes, perhaps still more in the eyes of others, has strengthened the motives of diffidence to myself; and every day the increasing weight of years admonishes me more and more that the shade of retirement is as necessary to me as it will be welcome." Unity of hearts and spirits was essential if the country were to prosper. "With slight shades of difference, you have the same religion, manners, habits and political principles. You have in a common cause fought and triumphed together. The independence and liberty you possess are the work of joint councils and joint efforts, of common dangers, sufferings, and successes."

Washington warned especially against "geographical discriminations" and "the baneful effects of the spirit of party generally." Evident in all governments, it was most apparent and most dangerous in "those of the popular form. . . . It agitates the community with ill-founded jealousies and false alarms; kindles the animosity of one part against another; foments occasionally riot and insurrection. It opens the door to foreign influence and corruption. . . ."

The president's words bespoke the political travail of the past four years. "Excessive partiality for one foreign nation and excessive dislike of another, cause those who they actuate to see danger only on one side, and serve to veil and even second the arts of influence on the other. . . . The great rule of conduct for us, in regard to foreign Nations is in extending our commercial relations to have as little *political* connection as possible." Europe had her own interests and concerns, which had little to do with those of America. Time would make the United States too strong to be dallied with by foreign powers. "If we remain one People, under an efficient government, the period is not too far off, when we may defy material injury from external annoyance . . . when we may choose peace or war, as our interest guided by justice shall counsel."

"Why forego the advantages of so peculiar a situation? Why quit our own to stand upon foreign ground? Why, by interweaving our destiny with that of any part of Europe, entangle our peace and prosperity in the toils of European ambition, Rivalship, Interest, Humour or Caprice?

"'Tis our true policy to steer clear of permanent alliances, with any portion of the foreign world. [Washington reminded his readers that it was] folly in one nation to look for disinterested favors from another. . . . There can be no greater error than to expect, or calculate upon real favours from Nation to Nation.—'Tis an illusion which experience must cure, which a just pride ought to discard. [Such were the counsels of] an old and affectionate friend. [He hoped] that they may now and then recur to moderate the fury of party spirit, to warn against the mischiefs of foreign Intrigue, to guard against the Impostures of pretended patriotism. . . ."

Though it was bitterly attacked by the Republicans as anti-French, the Farewell Address became in time a touchstone for American foreign policy.

Colored as it was by Hamilton's and Washington's "realism," the address nonetheless contained an element of that very utopianism that Hamilton so derided—the notion that the New World was somehow purer and better, more blessed, than the Old World, above its ambitions, ancient rivalries and "caprice." If only the United States could remain unentangled, the implication was, all its promise might be fulfilled.

There were two problems inherent in the Washington-Hamilton formulation, one immediate, one long-range. The address did not even attempt to rebut the Republican claim that the true mission of the American Revolution was the political and social redemption of the world and that France was carrying on that mission by acting as an agent of the new age. The long-range consequence was that by setting the United States off from the spoiled Old World it encouraged what came to be called isolationism, the antithesis of that spirit of "revolutionary universalism" so conspicuous at the height of the struggle for independence. It thus established another of America's schizophrenias: the yearning to redeem humanity versus the desire to remain uncontaminated.

For the moment, the Farewell Address was hardly more than a drop of oil on the troubled waters. In the words of Fisher Ames, it was "a signal, like dropping a hat, for the party racers to start" (while of course appearing to be out for no more than a casual stroll). To draw strength away from Jefferson in the South (where Adams was unpopular), the Federalists prevailed upon Thomas Pinckney of South Carolina (Pinckneys were as ubiquitous in South Carolina as were the Lees in Virginia), who had just negotiated a favorable treaty with Spain, to allow his name to be placed on the ballot as the Federalists' unofficial candidate for the vice-presidency.

New York Republicans threw their support behind Aaron Burr, and the campaign was given added drama by the efforts of Fauchet's successor as French minister to the United States, Pierre Auguste Adêt, to swing votes to Jefferson. He published a catalogue of charges against the government in November, going so far as to threaten action by the Directory if Washington's policy were not reversed by a new administration.

In Pennsylvania handbills circulated urging the voters to support Thomas Jefferson, "the uniform advocate of equal rights among citizens," over Adams, "the champion of rank, titles, and hereditary distinctions." The Republicans were indeed more enterprising in "taking their case to the people," as we say today. They printed thousands of posters and handbills and nailed them on fences and gateposts. Aaron Burr alone campaigned actively, taking a six-week tour through New England to try to round up votes.

By the end of November the electors had all been chosen. In ten states—Tennessee, Vermont, Rhode Island, Connecticut, New York, New Jersey, Delaware, South Carolina, Georgia, and Kentucky—the legislatures chose the electors. Each elector was to vote "for two persons." Six states held popular elections for electors: New Hampshire, Massachusetts, Pennsylvania, Maryland, Virginia, and North Carolina. Meanwhile, Alexander Hamilton, with his penchant for deviousness and manipulation, set afoot a plot to divert the presidential election to Pinckney as a more orthodox Federalist than Adams (and more under Hamilton's influence). Hamilton's scheme called for each of the electors in Pinckney's home state of South Carolina to give one of his votes to Pinckney but to throw away a few Adams votes and thus give the presidency to Pinckney.

Despite an accumulation of evidence, Adams was reluctant to believe that Hamilton was plotting against him. He professed to consider him a friend, but when he was finally convinced of the New Yorker's complicity, he wrote Abigail that he knew Hamilton "to be a proud-spirited, conceited, aspiring mortal, always pretending to morality, with as debauched morals as old Franklin. . . . As great a hypocrite as any in the U.S. . . . That he has 'talents' I admit, but I dread none of them . . . I shall take no notice of his puppyhood but . . . maintain the same conduct towards him that I always did—that is, to keep him at a distance."

Had Hamilton's plan succeeded, its most notable consequence would have been to hasten the demise of the Federalist party. Adams would certainly have refused to serve as vice-president, leaving the office to Jefferson or Burr. Word of the plot leaked out at the last moment, however, and a number of New England electors protected Adams by scratching Pinckney's name from their ballots. From November to January, when the ballots were officially counted, rumors circulated continually. Samuel Otis, younger brother of James and secretary of the Senate, wrote to Adams that "By lies, abuse, and bribery" the Republicans would carry Pennsylvania. But Adams would get 51 votes from New England and 17 south of the Mason-Dixon line. A scattering of votes in other states should give Adams more than the 70 needed for election, and those would "contain ⅞'s of the honesty and property, and ⅘'s of the good sense of the nation."

Fisher Ames made his own calculations, and they indicated an uncomfortably close race. "Accident, whim, intrigue, not to say corruption, may change or prevent a vote or two. . . . Who can foresee the issue of this momentous election? Perhaps the Jeffs, foreseeing a defeat, may vote for Mr. Pinckney, in which case he might come in with two-thirds of all the votes." In the more likely event that Adams was elected president and Jefferson vice-president, the two men would, "like two suns in the meridian . . . meet and jostle for four years, and then the Vice would be first."

On February 8 the votes were counted, and Adams, with a bare margin of 3 votes (71 to 68 for Jefferson), was president. His reaction to the news was like that of all successful aspirants to the office. It confirmed his confidence "in the sense, spirit, and resources of this country, which few other men in the world know so well [and] have for so long tried and found solid." Pinckney was third with 59 votes.

The response of the country was heartening. The "transmigration" had been successfully made, and people everywhere seemed disposed to give the new president the benefit of whatever doubts they may have had. One Republican newspaper hailed the day when the country would be governed by "talents and science" rather than "the mysterious influence of a man." Adams's great services to the Revolution were recalled, and his stubborn integrity was praised. Jefferson symbolized the mood of reconciliation by visiting Adams and pledging his support.

Adams's old friend, Chief Justice Oliver Ellsworth, administered the oath of office to Adams, and he delivered his inaugural address, appearing, as Washington had before him, often close to tears. He reviewed the history of America's struggle for independence, the trying years of the Confederacy, the drafting of the Constitution. If he had ever had any reservations about the Constitution, they had long since been dissipated. "From an habitual attention to it, satisfaction in its administration, and delight in its effects upon the peace, order, prosperity, and happiness of the nation—I have acquired an habitual attachment to it and veneration for it." No badges of office could be more respectable than the authority that sprang "fresh from the hearts and judgments of an honest and enlightened people. . . . It is their power and majesty that is reflected, and only for their good, in every legitimate government."

Adams praised Washington and reiterated the former president's warning about involvements with foreign nations. He would, he assured his audience, give proper regard to the "rights, interest, honor, and happiness of all the states in the Union without preference or regard to a Northern or Southern, an Eastern or Western, position." Further, he would support every rational effort to encourage schools, colleges, universities, academies, and "every institution for propagating knowledge, virtue, and religion among all classes of the people, not only for their benign influence on the happiness of life in all its stages and classes and of society in all its forms, but as the only means for preserving our Constitution from its natural enemies, the spirit of sophistry, the spirit of party, the spirit of intrigue, the profligacy of corruption, and the pestilence of foreign influence which is the angel of destruction to elective governments. . . ."

Adams took pains to express his "personal esteem for the French nation, formed in a residence of seven years chiefly among them, and a sincere desire to preserve the friendship which has been so much for the honor and interest of both nations. . . . [He had] an unshaken confidence in the honor, spirit, and resources of the American people . . . and a veneration for the religion of a people who call themselves Christians. . . ."

The Republicans were even more enthusiastic about Adams's inaugural than his fellow Federalists. George Mason was reported to have said that the country would lose nothing by the change in administrations, "for he had never heard such a speech in public in his life." Bache hailed it as a model of wisdom and moderation, and Adams as a man "of incorruptible integrity," a "friend of France, of peace, an admirer of Republicanism, the enemy of party. . . . How characteristic of a patriot!" Adams was delighted with the reception accorded him. The inauguration, he wrote Abigail, was, "taken together . . . the sublimist thing ever exhibited in America. . . . The sight of the sun setting full-orbed, and another rising (though less splendid) was a novelty."

Washington returned to the joys of Mount Vernon, his long purgatory over at last. His elevation to the rank of a demigod has often obscured the real character of that extraordinary man. Perhaps it is ultimately impenetrable. Certainly he was not the man that successive generations of pious Americans turned him into. That he was passionate and ambitious and somewhat vain is clear enough. It is equally clear that he usually kept his emotions in close check—the quality John Adams most admired in him was his "self-command"—and that he was able to sustain extraordinary labors and to persevere in the face of setbacks and discouragements. Great as were his services as wartime military leader, the term of his presidency was, if anything, more crucial to the survival of the nation. Considering the strains and stresses to which the new nation was subject, we cannot doubt that without him it would have run on the rocks of factionalism and foundered. Above all, he decisively shaped the office of which he was the first occupant. When Abigail Adams met Washington just after his inauguration, she wrote to her sister, "it is my firm opinion that no other man could rule over this great people and consolidate them into one mighty empire but he who is set over us."

The impulse of many of his contemporaries to turn Washington into a deity is understandable. His attributes were godlike. His magnificent presence was so intertwined with our origins as a nation that he must invariably command our awe and admiration whenever we take sufficient time to contemplate him. Quite simply, *he was the father.* More surely than any other historical figure, he shaped a people by his intelligence and character, by his determination to reconcile and absorb all factions. Nothing could be wider of the mark than to see him, as his enemies came to depict him, as an impassive, rather simple man manipulated by his subordinates. Though he listened attentively to his aides and advisers, the crucial decisions were always his. He commanded.

The man who succeeded him was a very different person. Most of what was good in the heritage and traditions of New England was in John Adams, along with a good deal of what was narrow, cramped, and provincial. He was as true an intellectual as his rival Jefferson. Books and ideas were food and drink to him. He prided himself on being a student of man as both a social and a political animal. Where Jefferson was fertile in brilliant insights and unforgettable aphorisms, Adams was "systematic." His *Defence of the Constitutions of Government of the United States of America*, marred as it was by its hasty composition, was the most ambitious work of political and social theory written by any of the members of the Revolutionary generation. As a classic product of the Classical-Christian Consciousness, its basic assumptions rested on a not particularly flattering view of human nature, and it kept Adams in continual hot water with those doctrinaire democrats who were indignant at any suggestion that the voice of the people was not indeed the voice of God.

Eccentric and cranky as Adams was, *his* character was almost as well suited for the exigencies of his administration as Washington's had been for his, most strikingly in his independence. Failing in his dangerous gamble to replace Adams with a more pliant Pinckney, Hamilton clearly intended to guide Adams's administration of the government through the agency of his staff, specifically Timothy Pickering, Washington's secretary of war, and Oliver Wolcott, secretary of the treasury. These were Hamilton men who gave their unquestioning loyalty to the New Yorker and looked on him as the real leader of the Federalist party. Adams, in consequence, soon found himself beset on two sides—by the Republicans who before long renewed their partisan attacks, and by members of his own party who expected him to be the instrument of their wills.

Adams's first crisis as president grew into the most controversial event of his term of office. Shortly before his retirement, Washington had recalled James Monroe as ambassador to France. The reports that filtered back of Monroe's actions in Paris, his alleged subserviency to the thoroughly corrupt and despotic Directory, and his criticisms of his own government's policy toward France had induced Washington to summon him home. (Barras, one of the members of the Directory, bade Monroe farewell with these words: "Assure the good people of America, Citizen Monroe, that, like them, we adore liberty, that they will always have our esteem, and that they will find in the French people that Republican generosity which knows how to grant peace as well as cause its sovereignty to be respected.")

Having recalled Monroe, Washington tried to persuade Madison to replace him, but Madison refused. Washington turned to Charles Cotesworth Pinckney, Revolutionary general, delegate to the Federal Convention, and a strong South Carolina Federalist. Pinckney accepted, but when he tried to present his credentials to the Directory he was rudely rebuffed. Its members were indignant with Washington for replacing Republican Monroe with Federalist Pinckney. In addition, they were apparently convinced that the French party was so strong in the United States that in the event of open hostilities with France the friends of the Revolution would take control of the government. Pinckney was, in any event, treated scandalously and told to leave the country. When word of the ambassador's reception or, more accurately, nonreception reached Adams, he reacted in a way that revealed his feelings toward the Directory far more accurately than the conciliatory words of his inaugural address. He at once sent a note to the members of his Cabinet soliciting their views as to the proper response to the Directory's calculated insult. The questions he asked indicated the temper of his mind. What preparations should be made for war? In the absence of a navy, should American privateers be commissioned to prey on French shipping? Should new frigates be commissioned? And, finally, should a fresh mission be undertaken to Paris, or would such a mission be "too great a humiliation of the American people in their own sense and that of the world"?

Several Cabinet members turned to Hamilton for instructions, and he told them they must support further negotiation in order to disarm the suspicion that "the *actual* administration is not much averse from war with France. . . . How very important to obviate this!" he added.

Guided by Hamilton, the Cabinet urged caution and conciliation in the French negotiations. That fact is significant in the face of the Republican charge that the Federalists wished for nothing so much as war with France. James McHenry clearly spoke for his fellow Cabinet members (and for Hamilton) when he urged Adams "to obviate causes of discontent and restore and confirm cordial harmony; to discuss and settle amicably the topics of mutual complaints, and thereby to obtain a revocation of those acts on the part of France . . . which have oppressed our trade and injured our citizens."

Adams, in his headlong way, had already called for a special session of Congress in May to consider what action might be appropriate. The effect was to inflate the episode and infuriate the Republicans.

All the suspicions and antagonisms that Adams's inaugural had allayed came flooding back. The new president was no better than the old. He was mad—in his dotage, Bache declared. A particular object of Democratic scorn was the president's proclamation calling for a day of fasting, humiliation, and prayer. The *Aurora*, which invariably referred to Adams as "the President by three votes," accused him of having become president "by tricks, by frauds, by finesse," and of now trying to rush the country into war because of some breach of diplomatic protocol. A few weeks later when Bache went to view and doubtless to deride the new frigate the *United States*, which was near completion, Clement Humphreys, the son of the builder, gave him a pummeling that was widely applauded by the Federalists.

Adams, meanwhile, set about selecting members for a special mission to the Directory. He sounded out Jefferson, but Jefferson, holed up in Monticello and suffering from ill-health and depression, refused. Adams then asked Jefferson to try to prevail on Madison to be one of the special envoys, but Madison likewise declined, which was, as it turned out, just as well, since the Cabinet, hearing that Adams had approached Madison, threatened to resign *en masse* if the Virginian were appointed.

Even before Congress assembled, the Directory added fuel to the fire by issuing an order that any American sailors taken from English warships would be hanged as pirates. This edict was especially cruel, since the French knew as well as the Americans that the British policy of impressment meant that there were many unwilling Americans serving on British warships.

When Congress assembled on May 13, Adams recounted for the members the events surrounding the Pinckney affair. Such behavior, he declared, "ought to be repelled with a decision which shall convince France and the world that we are not a degraded people, humiliated under a colonial spirit of fear and a sense of inferiority, fitted to be the miserable instruments of foreign influence, and regardless of national honor, character, and interest." He called not only for negotiations but for a general strengthening of America's defenses—and above all for the establishment of a respectable navy.

The vice-president was among those who deplored the militant tone of the address. He feared that the House and the Senate might "raise their tone to that of the executive, and embark in all measures indicative of war and, by taking a threatening posture, provoke hostilities from the opposite party." As Abigail Adams put it, "The

Antis. want to qualify. They dare not openly countenance the conduct of France, but they want to court and coax her." To Bache all such talk was mere braggadocio. Even the launching of the *United States* at Southwark, witnessed by twenty thousand enthusiastic spectators, was ridiculed by the *Aurora*, which quoted Talleyrand's comment that France need fear nothing from a nation of debaters who had been trying for three years to build three frigates.

The Senate commended the president for his "vigilance, firmness, and promptitude." "Effectual measures of defense" were the best means "to check aggression and prevent war." The House likewise assured Adams of its "zealous cooperation in those measures which may appear necessary for our security or peace," but there was much more debate there than in the Senate, and Matthew Lyon, the radical democrat from Vermont, refused to accompany his colleagues to deliver the reply to the president. Let the "gentlemen of blood" and good breeding go. He was too simple and democratic. He did not spring from "the bastards of Oliver Cromwell" or "from the witch-hunting Puritans of New England who persecuted the Quakers and despised all joy."

On the last day of the month Adams submitted to the Senate the names of Pinckney, Francis Dana, and John Marshall as "envoys extraordinary and ministers plenipotentiary to the French Republic ... to dissipate umbrages, to remove prejudices, to rectify error and adjust all differences by a treaty between the two powers." When Dana declined to serve, Adams went back to his old friend Elbridge Gerry. Gerry had been one of his original choices, but when the Cabinet had balked Adams yielded. Now he nominated him to take Dana's place.

Before Gerry and the other commissioners departed a revealing exchange took place between the president and his envoy. Gerry had complained in a letter to Adams of the existence in America of an anti-Gallican faction. To this Adams replied that there were indeed Americans who believed that France had tried to exercise undue influence in the United States. Some of these were anti-French because they considered the French "a false, deceitful, treacherous people"; others because they hated "atheism, deism, and debauchery." The notion that Americans hated the French because they were good republicans Adams dismissed as absurd; the French were no more capable of republican government "than a snowball can exist a whole week in the streets of Philadelphia under a burning sun." The dangers to America came, not from British influence or any trend toward

monarchical government, but from "the universal avarice and ambition of the people" who could think of nothing but making money and
had even turned elections into "a species of lucrative speculation, and
consequently scenes of turbulence, corruption, and confusion."

Two other episodes might be mentioned here that added, if
possible, to the intensity of partisan feelings. Thomas Paine, champion
of the rights of man and citizen of the world, had arrived in France in
the early stages of the Revolution and contributed a pamphlet
advocating the abolition of kings. In 1791 he published in England the
first part of his *Rights of Man*, returned to France to be hailed as a hero,
and was made a member of the National Convention. He soon made
himself unpopular with the more extreme Jacobins by speaking out
against beheading Louis XVI (Paine proposed banishing him to
America). During the Reign of Terror Robespierre had him thrown
into the Luxembourg prison, usually the last step before the guillotine.
Paine had written from prison exhorting Washington to bring
pressure on the French government, or whatever group at the
moment constituted the government, to free him. Washington,
doubtless believing that Paine had gotten no better than he deserved
for meddling in the Revolution, and unwilling to appear as supplicator
before men who constantly denounced him, did nothing. Monroe
finally secured his release. Paine resumed his seat in the National
Convention and, embittered by his months in prison and by what he
viewed as the president's rejection of him, wrote him a furious letter in
the form of a response to his Farewell Address, accusing him of "a sort
of non-describable, chameleon-colored thing called prudence," so
closely allied with hypocrisy that he "easily slid into it." Paine ended his
letter with a sentence that did more to becloud his reputation than any
other act of commission or omission in his long and remarkable career.
"As for you, sir, treacherous in private friendship (for so you have
been to me, and that in the day of danger), and a hypocrite in public
life, the world will be puzzled to decide whether you are an apostate or
an impostor; whether you have abandoned good principles or ever
had any." To make sure his attack on Washington was well read, Paine
printed it as a pamphlet.

The Paine letter had, as a kind of companion piece, a letter written
by Jefferson to his Italian friend and sometime Virginia neighbor,
Philip Mazzei. After telling Mazzei that his health was so bad he
despaired of living much longer, Jefferson went on to comment on the
political scene. The government had been taken over by "timid men

who prefer the calm of despotism to the boisterous sea of liberty. . . . It would give you a fever were I to name the apostates who have gone over to these heresies, men who were Samsons in the field and Solomons in the council, but who have had their heads shorn by the harlot England." Then Jefferson added a curious and ambiguous sentence. "We have only to awake and snap the Lilliputian cords with which they have been entangling us during the first sleep which succeeded our labors." Mazzei translated the letter into Italian and sent it to a newspaper in Florence. From there it found its way into the hands of the editor of the *Moniteur*, the official organ of the Directory, who published it in a French translation, and from there it made its way to the United States where it was re-translated into English and published in the *New York Minerva* and subsequently in most other Federalist papers as evidence of Jefferson's duplicity.

Meanwhile, Jefferson's adversary, Alexander Hamilton, had a contretemps of his own. Though he could be cold as ice in a crisis, deliberate and cautious in planning political strategies, there was a streak of recklessness in him, a willful disposition to play with fire that was to prove, ultimately, a fatal flaw. It was manifest in his relations with women as well as in the political area. In the case of Maria Reynolds it gave rise to the most painful scandal of his career. A Pennsylvanian named Clingman had been jailed for making fraudulent claims against the government. Friends of Clingman persuaded Frederick Muhlenberg, Speaker of the House, to visit him in jail, and there Clingman and a partner in crime named Reynolds hinted that they had incriminating evidence against Hamilton. Muhlenberg, delighted at the opportunity to destroy Hamilton's public reputation, told a colleague in the House, Abraham Venable, and Senator James Monroe. The three men returned to the jail, and Reynolds and Clingman repeated their story that they had evidence of improper speculations in public securities on Hamilton's part. Reynolds would say no more until he was bailed out, but as soon as he was free he left for parts unknown. The three self-appointed sleuths then went to Mrs. Reynolds, who told them that she had received letters and money from Hamilton, but again she implied that the letters related to his alleged speculations and that the money was in payment for her and her husband's silence.

The woman's appearance and manner spoke more eloquently of her character than her words, but the Republican bloodhounds were too excited by the chase to exercise their critical faculties. They collected all the material from Maria Reynolds she would give them, made a memorandum of their conversations that they all signed, and then went to Hamilton and confronted him with the "evidence." Hamilton admitted at once that Maria Reynolds had entrapped him. She had come to him with a plea for help in the affair of her husband, seduced him (presumably not a difficult accomplishment), become his mistress, and then, with the complicity of her husband, blackmailed him. To prove his case, Hamilton read some of the correspondence with Mrs. Reynolds. At this point his accusers apologized, promised to preserve his secret, and departed.

But the opportunity to discredit Hamilton proved to be too much for Monroe, a future president of the United States, to resist. He was determined to do what he could to undermine the leader of the Federalists. When he departed from the United States to become ambassador to France in 1794, he left the ambiguous letters the triumvirate had gotten from Maria Reynolds "with a respectable character in Virginia" (most likely Jefferson), from whose hands they passed into the possession of James Thomas Callender, one of the most rancorous and unscrupulous journalists in our history, who at the moment had placed his services at the disposal of the Republicans. Callender's relations with Jefferson were close, and Jefferson's support encouraged him to bring out a yearly "history" directed against the policies and actions of the government.

In 1797, Callender published his *History of the United States for 1796,* and in it he included the Monroe documents. Since, ambiguous as they were, they suggested sexual, not financial, irregularities, Callender charged that Hamilton had forged them to cover up his illegal speculations. To preserve his public reputation Hamilton sacrificed his private honor and, it might be said, humiliated his devoted wife by publishing his correspondence with Maria Reynolds and acknowledging that she had been his mistress and his blackmailer. He quite justifiably blamed the affair on political animus, indeed on "the spirit of jacobinism," which, in his view, "threatened more extensive and complicated mischiefs to the world than have hitherto flowed from the three great scourges of mankind, WAR, PESTILENCE and FAMINE. . . . Incessantly busied in undermining all the props of public security and private happiness, it seems to threaten the political and moral world with a complete overthrow." Hamilton told the whole sordid story in some detail, the moral of the tale being the lengths to which the "jacobean" infatuation could carry men who presumably coveted the name of gentlemen and who had been entrusted with important public offices. While Jefferson's role in the whole affair is obscure, what can be said with confidence, I think, is that he could easily have squelched the entire matter. Ten years later he may have keenly regretted that he had not done so.

President Adams's envoys extraordinary arrived in Paris on October 4, 1797. They presented their credentials and received the cards of hospitality that every foreigner was required to carry. Negotiations, they were told, would begin in ten days, but instead of formal negotiations on that day a Major Montlorence called on Pinckney. He had word from a private secretary of Talleyrand's that the Directory was annoyed by certain expressions in Washington's Farewell Address. These would have to be publicly repudiated before serious negotiations could begin. In addition, a bribe must be paid to individual members of the Directory, say, fifty thousand dollars, and a substantial loan promised to France.

The demands for bribes and public apologies were reinforced with threats of arrest if the American envoys remained recalcitrant. An additional demand was added several days later. Adams, in addressing Congress, had, by implication, made some objectionable references to the Directory. These must also be retracted. "But gentlemen," added the go-between, designated as Monsieur Y, "I will not disguise from you that, this satisfaction being made, the essential part of the treaty remains to be adjusted. You must pay money; you must pay a great deal of money." The envoys sent an account of their reception to Pickering on October 22. They then settled down to await instructions.

It was ironic that the negotiations with the Directory were to take place through Talleyrand, who, having fled to America to escape the guillotine, had returned to France in the aftermath of the so-called Thermidorian Reaction, where the Directory, with the support of Napoleon Bonaparte, was doing its best to check the excesses of the Revolution.

On March 5, 1798, the president informed Congress that official word had been received of the progress of the French negotiations. As soon as the dispatches had been decoded, Congress would be told of their purport. Two weeks later he sent word to Congress that the mission had been a failure. The insults to Pinckney had been compounded. The honor of the United States had been mocked. The country must prepare for war. When Adams read the dispatches, he was furious. His first impulse was to declare war on France. "Every effort and every resource should be called into action which cannot be done unless there is a formal declaration of war," he wrote. "To me there appears no alternative between actual hostilities on our part and national ruin." Again the advice of his Cabinet was on the side of caution and restraint. Wolcott recommended strong measures "for the protection of the persons and property of our seagoing and commercial citizens," and McHenry advised "a qualified hostility," whatever that might be.

Adams wanted to send to Congress the deciphered dispatches, describing in detail the humiliation of the envoys, but again his Cabinet dissuaded him. Such an act might indeed precipitate war and expose the envoys to some form of retribution (Abigail compared them with the three men in the fiery furnace—Shadrach, Meshach, and Abednego). In Abigail's words, it was "a very painful thing" for Adams to hold back the dispatches. Without them people could hardly realize the enormity of the French behavior, but second thoughts convinced him that the country needed time to get itself collectively in a frame of mind that would accept war. A step at a time was better than a headlong rush.

When Adams, on March 19, sent a mild message to Congress drafted by Wolcott that simply stated that the commissioners' correspondence offered "no ground of expectation that the objects of their mission can be accomplished on terms compatible with the safety, honor or essential interests of the nation," the Republicans launched a barrage of invective at the president. Jefferson referred to it as "an insane message" and admitted that the Republicans were "petrified with astonishment." Their strategy was to contend that the dispatches in fact revealed quite the opposite of what the president implied—that was why he had refused to make them available to the Senate. It was another Federalist plot to push the country into war with its natural ally, France. Jefferson proposed that, to gain time, Congress should adjourn on the grounds that its members had to "go home and consult their constitutents on the great crisis of American affairs now existing." He was convinced that the real purpose of the Federalists was to split the Union into North and South.

The Republicans were so enterprising in rallying opposition to the president's message in the form of memorials and petitions questioning the president's authority to order the arming of merchant vessels that Adams soon felt himself in a state of siege. To his intense indignation, a number of town meetings in Adams's home state sent him such memorials. He was soon sorry he had not run the risk of sending the actual dispatches to Congress and hoped the Republicans in Congress would call for them. On April 2 the Republicans obliged, although the shrewder among them suspected a trap. Gallatin—"the sly, the artful, the insidious Gallatin," as Abigail Adams called him—refused to join in the call, and William Giles was overheard to say to friends, "You are doing wrong to call for those dispatches. They will injure us." Even with a number of Federalists joining in requesting the papers, the Republicans failed to comprehend their danger.

When the papers were received and disseminated through the newspapers, the results were all that the most vindictive Federalist would have wished. Panic and dismay swept through the Republican ranks! Bache and the *Aurora* immediately denounced the president for releasing them; it was no less than a betrayal of the American people. "The Jacobins in Senate and House were struck dumb," Abigail wrote to her sister, "and opened not their mouths, not having their cue, not having received their lessons" from Jefferson and Madison. Jefferson admitted that the dispatches had "produced such a shock in the Republican mind as had never been seen since our independence," but his tactic was to try to shift the blame to the envoys and their "artful misrepresentations." The Directory was made of high-minded men who could never be suspected of bribery. Adams had gone too far in criticizing the French. He should apologize. Such was Jefferson's view, but the country reacted quite differently. Fisher Ames wrote that "The Jacobins were confounded, and the trimmers dropt off the tree like windfalls from an apple tree in September." Theodore Sedgwick wrote from Boston that the effect of the publication of the dispatches "on the people . . . has been prodigious. The leaders of the opposition . . . were astonished and confounded at the profligacy of their beloved friends, the French."

John Adams had the intoxicating experience of being hailed as a popular hero. The merchants of Philadelphia sent him a letter thanking him "for his firm and steady conduct." It was reported to him that "the common people" were saying that if Jefferson "had been our President, and Madison and Burr our negotiators, we should all have been sold to the French." Congress, displaying "a degree of spirit which has not before appeared," proceeded to pass legislation looking to the defense of the country.

Addresses of support for Adams's policy poured in from all over the country. French tunes were replaced by patriotic American songs, and Joseph Hopkinson, son of Adams's old friend Francis Hopkinson, provided the lyrics for a song entitled "Adams and Liberty" and wrote "Hail, Columbia!"—both of which became favorites to be sung on every public occasion. At a performance of a popular play, *The Italian Monk*, the actor Gilbert Fox led the audience in singing "Adams and Liberty." "At every chorus," Abigail wrote her sister, "the most unbounded applause ensued . . . it was enough to stun one." The letters and addresses of support continued to pour in. "They breathe one spirit," Abigail wrote, "they speak one language—that of independent freemen—approving the measures of government and expressive of full confidence in the wisdom, virtue, and integrity of the Chief Magistrate," her husband. The students of Princeton and Dartmouth sent pledges of loyalty to Adams and the United States. Harvard students wrote: "Our lives are our only property, and we were not the sons of those who sealed our liberties with their blood if we would not defend with these lives that soil which now affords a peaceful grave to the moldering bones of our forefathers."

"Yankee Doodle," which had proved infinitely adaptable, was once again employed for political purposes:

> Tho' X. and Y., and Madam Sly,
>   They made demand for money;
> For, as we're told, the French love gold
>   As stinging bees love honey.
> Yankee Doodle (mind the tune)
>   Yankee Doodle dandy, etc. . . .
>
> Bold Adams did in '76
>   Our Independence sign, sir,
> And he will not give up a job,
>   Tho' all the world combine, sir.
>
> Americans, then fly to arms,
>   And learn the way to use 'em:
> If each man fight to 'fend 'is rights,
>   The French can't long abuse 'em.

In reply to the addresses that flooded in, Adams could not forbear from making observations unflattering to France and to Republicans. Hamilton wrote to Wolcott deploring the "intemperate and revolutionary" quality of some of the letters, which had been widely reprinted in

Federalist newspapers, and urging Wolcott to do his best to persuade Adams to moderate his tone. He noted "It is not for us, particularly for the government, to breathe an irregular or violent spirit. . . . There are limits which must not be passed, and from my knowledge of the ardor of the President's mind . . . I begin to be apprehensive that he may run into indiscretion. . . . Some hint must be given, for we must make no mistakes."

When Adams set May 9 as a day of "Public Humiliation, Fasting, and Prayer Throughout the United States," rumors circulated that there was a French plot "to set fire to several different parts of [Philadelphia] . . . to massacre man, woman, and child," but the only incident to mar the day was an attack by a group of some thirty young Republicans on a patriotic gathering in the State House Yard. They tried to tear the Federalists' black cockades from their hats. One was arrested, the light-horse troop was called out to patrol the streets in case of further disorder, and a guard was posted in front of the president's house.

Preparations went on everywhere for war with France. Congress voted to build twelve new frigates and raise ten thousand men. Newburyport, Massachusetts, undertook a campaign to raise money to build a twenty-gun ship and loan it to the government, and Abigail Adams wrote her son John Quincy that "This city . . . has become *one* military school, and every morning the sound of the drum and the fife lead forth."

Bache's *Aurora* and Matthew Cary's *Independent Chronicle* lost readers at such a rate that Jefferson feared they must expire. "If these papers fall," he wrote Madison, "republicanism will be entirely browbeaten." He detected hopeful signs of open insurrection against the government in Pennsylvania and of "inquietude" in New Hampshire and New York.

Still, appearances were deceptive. The Republicans were subdued but by no means routed. There was an alarming movement in Philadelphia to recruit a special militia force of Republicans, since the volunteer corps of the city was dominated by Federalists. Adams himself inclined strongly to an open declaration of war on the grounds that only by doing so could the full resources of the country be mustered. He was dismayed to hear that despite the fact that the envoys had been ordered home, Gerry had lingered on in Paris at the urging of Talleyrand, who had hinted that if all the envoys departed the Directory would declare war against the United States. The

Federalists themselves were divided. Many of them were aware that the unity of the country was more apparent than real. The longer the period without actual outbreak of war, the more people would have second thoughts about the expense of building a navy and recruiting an army. Stephen Higginson wrote that "nothing but an open war can save us, and the more inveterate and deadly it shall be, the better shall be our chance for security in the future"; and Fisher Ames noted that "Though I do not wish Congress to declare *war*, I long to see them wage it."

On June 18 John Marshall arrived in Philadelphia, and the city turned out to greet him with the greatest fanfare in its history. An escort of carriages, hundreds of horsemen, and three cavalry companies rode to meet him at the city line. As he entered the city church bells were rung and people lined the streets cheering and waving handkerchiefs.

Marshall was convinced that the French leaders did not want war with the United States but simply thought they could browbeat and bully it into complying with the wishes of the Directory. In this it was, as we have seen, encouraged by a steady stream of reports from Adêt and friends of France in America assuring them of the predominance of pro-French sentiment in all parts of the Union. Marshall's arrival was fortuitous. Adams had been seriously considering asking Congress to declare war before it adjourned. Now he decided to wait and see if word of the American reaction to the XYZ affair might persuade the Directory to pull in its horns.

Before Marshall left for his home in Virginia, the Federalists gave a grand dinner "as evidence of their affection for his person and their gratified approbation of the patriotic firmness with which he sustained the dignity of his country during his important mission." The justices of the Supreme Court, the army field officers, the Episcopal and Catholic bishops, and many members of Congress attended. Sixteen toasts were drunk, "with unbounded plaudits," to the United States; "to the people and the government—'one and indivisible!'"—to the heroes of the Revolution; and finally to the stirring slogan, "Millions for defense but not a cent for tribute!"

Since Adams was determined to have an army, the question was who should command it. Washington was the obvious and inevitable choice, but he wished to have Hamilton as his second in command. It was clear that Washington would not be an active commander in chief and that the responsibility must fall on the second in command. Such pressure was brought to bear on Adams to appoint Hamilton to the post that Abigail confided to a friend, "that man [Hamilton] . . . would become a second Buonaparty if he was possessed of equal power. . . . You can hardly conceive what a powerful interest is made for Hamilton." Hamilton had, after all, made it clear that one of his favorite historical figures was Julius Caesar. The thought of Hamilton at the head of the military forces of the United States considerably dampened Adams's desire for war with France, and as it became clear that he could not avoid Hamilton's claims without a serious split in the Federalist ranks, he sounded more and more conciliatory. In addition, the letters of John Quincy Adams writing from London, where he was serving as U.S. ambassador to Great Britain, provided the president with a brilliant analysis of the situation on the other side of the Atlantic. It seemed evident to John Quincy that European feudalism was breaking up. "The opinions upon the theory of government," he wrote to his father, "are wild, discordant and absurd, but the republican spirit is diffused everywhere." The future course of France seemed plain enough. "All the nations of the earth must be prepared to see France, under a military government, by turns anarchical and despotic, and, perhaps with all the democratical forms; with a country ruined, desolated, incapable of supporting a large part of its population; with an immense army inured to every danger, habituated to consider life as the cheapest of all human possessions, at once poor and prodigal, rapacious and dissolute, elated by extraordinary victories, and considering itself as the champion for the liberties of the human race. . . . [He was convinced that] nothing in Europe will stand before them; it is a grapple for life and death between all the ancient establishments, and a new single military government of which France is to be the head. . . ,"

On July 6 an encounter took place between a sloop of war, the *Delaware*—with Stephen Decatur, the elder, in command—and a French privateer of twenty guns that had plundered an American merchant-man, the *Alexander Hamilton*. Decatur pursued the privateer and came up with four vessels. In order to identify the privateer, he pretended to be a merchant vessel and made as though to flee. When the privateer closed on him, Decatur turned, opened fire, and captured his pursuer. When he brought his prize to Philadelphia, he was greeted by enthusiastic crowds and acclaimed a hero.

The threat of war had given greater impetus to the building of a navy. By the spring of 1799, nine naval vessels under the command of Captain John Barry of the *United States* cruised in the area of the Lesser Antilles to protect American shipping. Captain Thomas Truxtun with a little fleet of five operated in the region of St. Kitts. Other vessels patrolled the Windward Passage, and a fourth division was stationed off Cuba. In addition, it was estimated that 365 privateers, manned by 6,874 sailors, were on the prowl. Patriotic hearts were exalted by news of a victory by Truxtun and the *Constellation* over the French frigate *L'Insurgente*. After an engagement of an hour and a half off the island of St. Kitts, the French ship struck her colors to the American frigate.

It is not surprising that the Federalists were intoxicated by the public acclaim that showered down upon them in the aftermath of the XYZ affair, or that they should have been tempted to so seriously misread it as to believe that they could take virtually whatever measures as they chose to consolidate their power. The more reflective of them knew well that popularity was a fickle mistress. Perhaps it was that very uneasiness that led them into a series of what were to prove to be fatal errors.

The Federalists had long chafed under the virulent attacks of the Republican press. It was not only the personal abuse that Washington and Adams had to endure that was particularly offensive to the Federalists; they were convinced that no government could long survive if public confidence in the honor and integrity of its leaders were systematically undermined by lies and billingsgate. It thus seemed to some Federalists that the undeclared war with France, or the "quasi war" as it came to be called, provided an opportunity to check the "lying tongues" of the more extreme Republican editors. Hamilton had warned, "we must make no mistakes," but the admonition fell on deaf ears.

On June 18, Congress passed a naturalization bill extending the period of residence required for citizenship to fourteen years. The rationale behind this change was that foreigners, principally Irishmen, were leaders in the opposition to the government. A week later a companion piece, "an act concerning aliens," was passed; and on July 14 a statute was enacted providing punishment for seditious writings against the government or its leaders. Under the provisions of the Alien Act, the president was authorized in war or at the threat of war to seize, secure, or ship out of the country all aliens who were natives of the enemy nation. The treason and sedition bill introduced by Senator

James Lloyd of Maryland stipulated a fine of not more than five thousand dollars and imprisonment for up to five years for any person, alien or citizen, who should attempt to oppose or defeat the operation of any law of the United States, "or shall threaten any officer of the United States Government with any damage to his character, person, or property, or attempt to procure any insurrection, plot, or unlawful assembly or unlawful combination." Similar penalties were provided for those found guilty "of printing, writing, or speaking in a scandalous or malicious way against the government of the United States, either House of Congress, or the President, with the purpose of bringing them into contempt, stirring up sedition, or aiding, or abetting a foreign nation in hostile designs against the United States." Truth was admissible in defense, and the duration of the act was limited to two years.

Matthew Cary's *Independent Chronicle* promptly declared that under "the execrable law, . . . to laugh at the cut of a congressman's coat, to give a dinner to a Frenchman, to let him sleep in your bed, will be treason. . . . The independent citizens of America will never be deterred from a manly censure on their servants. May the hand be palsied and the voice grow dumb that shrinks from such a task, let the threats of the servants of the people be ever so loud. . . . [As for Lloyd, he should] have that kind of immortality which has fallen to the lot of the ruffian who burned down the Temple of Diana. Give the name of this Vandal, this Goth, this Ostrogoth, this Hun, to be a byword among the nations!"

Since the Alien and Sedition Acts were to contribute very substantially to the downfall of the Federalists, it may be well to consider them briefly. In every major conflict in which the United States has been involved, most notably in the Civil War and in two "world wars," Congress has passed similar legislation severely infringing on the First Amendment's guarantee of freedom of speech. Such statutes have had little political consequence because the vast majority of the citizens affected by them have supported the war and enthusiastically endorsed the suppression and persecution of the small minority who opposed it. With the Alien and Sedition Acts the case was quite different. A very substantial portion of the American populace identified with the French cause. Their leaders included men like Jefferson and Madison. They clearly predominated in a geographical area—the South—which made up half the nation. They had the resources—the "media outlets," as we would call them today—the numbers and the resolution to extract every possible iota of political advantage from the Federalists' mistake. The Federalists aided and abetted their enemies by initiating prosecutions against Republican editors that were clearly punitive in intent.

The first man to feel the effect of the law was Matthew Lyon, the Vermont congressman who had refused to go with the rest of the House to reply to Adams's address. Later, when he was mocked by Roger Griswold, a Connecticut Federalist, Lyon spit in his face. The House was at once in an uproar, and for a moment it appeared as though Federalists and Republicans might mix in a general brawl. Order was restored and a committee was appointed to recommend what action should be taken against Lyon. The committee's report was for expulsion. Lyon apologized, and on the vote of the whole House the tally was 52 to 44 against Lyon. Since three fourths of the votes were needed for expulsion, Lyon's political hide was saved. But the Federalists promptly nicknamed him the "Beast of Vermont," and Griswold, furious at the failure of Congress to expel Lyon, attacked him several days later in the House chamber and beat him badly with a heavy stick. The two were parted, someone brought Lyon a cane, and he in turn attacked Griswold. The episode provided more fuel for the party press. Federalists denounced Lyon as a "coarse-grained, half-educated Irish clown," "the spitting Lyon," an indentured servant who had turned on his betters.

When the sedition bill was passed, Lyon wrote a letter denouncing it. The letter was printed in the *Vermont Gazette*, and as soon as Lyon returned from Philadelphia he was arrested and indicted for libel under three counts. The charges against him: the letter to the *Gazette*; the statement in a private letter that the response of the House to Adams's speech on the subject of the Directory should have been "an order to send him to a mad-house"; and Lyon's denunciation of Adams's fast-day proclamation for using the "sacred name of religion as a state engine to make mankind hate and persecute each other," adding that every consideration of public good had been, in Adams's administration, "swallowed up in a continual grasp for power, and unbounded thirst for ridiculous pomp, foolish adulation, and selfish avarice."

The judge's verdict was guilty and the sentence was a one-thousand-dollar fine and four months in jail. Thus did the Federalists provide the Republicans with a martyr. His son promptly issued a series of pamphlets under the title *The Scourge of Aristocracy and*

Repository of Important Political Truths. To keep the country informed of the efforts of the Federalists to suppress free speech, Republicans sang a song at their political rallies that went:

> Come take a glass in hand to drink his health,
>   Who is a friend to Lyon,
> First martyr under Federal law
>   The junto dared to try on.

A favorite pastime of young activists on both sides was the erection and cutting down of liberty poles. The French faction would erect a pole surmounted by a French liberty cap, and the Federalists would chop it down. Albert Gallatin, the Republican leader in the House who had opposed all measures of preparedness, was hooted and reviled at Reading, Pennsylvania, and burned in effigy outside the tavern where he was lodging. In New York a riot broke out after a Federalist march up Broadway, and in the state legislature Brockholst Livingston, a Republican and presiding officer, refused to entertain motions from James Jones, an elderly Federalist. Jones later intercepted Livingston, cursed him, and beat him with his cane. Livingston challenged Jones to a duel and shot him dead.

As the months passed, it became increasingly apparent that the Federalists had let prosperity go to their heads and had made a serious mistake in attaching their cause to the imminence of a war with France. An unpopular stamp and house tax did almost as much as the Alien and Sedition Acts to arouse resentment and suspicion in the country at large.

Gerry, lingering in Paris after the other envoys had been recalled, defying the president and enraging the Federalists, nonetheless served the cause of peace by serving as a conduit through which Talleyrand continued to send assurances of the Directory's desire for peace with the United States. The naturalization bill stuck in the craw of many Americans who had no sympathy with the French Revolution. The patriotic hysteria that followed the revelations of the XYZ affair could not be sustained indefinitely. As it subsided, a reaction set in that was not favorable to the Federalists. At town meetings, at militia musters, and on every public occasion or holiday, Republicans encouraged petitions and memorials declaring the Alien and Sedition Acts unconstitutional, a gross infringement on the First Amendment. When Congress convened, the senators and representatives were disconcerted to find hundreds of petitions containing thousands of names awaiting them.

Republicans who deplored what they considered the usurpation of the rights of the states by the federal government took an even more serious view of the implications of the acts. They were concerned, not so much with the argument that the acts were unconstitutional because they were contrary to the First Amendment (and they did not seek to have the Supreme Court declare them to be so), but rather with the argument that they were an unconstitutional encroachment upon the states, each of which had its own bill of rights with its own articles protecting freedom of speech and the press.

The vice-president of the United States was the leader in a movement to encourage the states to declare such bills null and void. At Monticello, Jefferson began to shape his doctrine of nullification. His thesis was that "whensoever the general government assumes undelegated powers, its acts are unauthoritative, void, and of no force" and, even more mischievous, that each party, or state, "has an equal right to judge for itself, as well of infractions as of the mode and measure of redress."

Jefferson did not stop there. He went on to state, in uncompromising terms, the doctrine that the states were sovereign over Congress. The states, he argued, had created Congress. It was, therefore, "merely the creature of the compact, as subject as to its assumptions of power to the final judgment of those by whom, and for whose use itself and its powers were created and modified." If the tendency of the federal government to encroach on the rights of the states were not promptly checked, it would "necessarily drive these States into revolution and blood." Taken literally, Jefferson's doctrines would have meant the dissolution of the Union. As it was, they were to have a most unhappy history. They became in time the rationale for the doctrine of secession—that any state had a right to secede from the Union if, in its judgment, the national government overstepped its constitutional authority.

Jefferson was well aware that he was expounding "revolutionary" doctrine, and the modern reader must wonder to what degree the Virginian's "resolutions" were influenced by the views he had expressed in his letter to Madison, written from Paris in the early stages of the French Revolution—that all laws and constitutions should be rewritten every fifteen or nineteen years; that a "little rebellion now and then" was salutary; and that the "tree of liberty" must be periodically watered "by the blood of patriots."

George Nicholas, a political ally of Jefferson's in Kentucky, wrote that if Jefferson would draw up his arguments in the form of resolutions, he would introduce them in the legislature of that state. Jefferson agreed on the condition that the authorship be kept a strict secret. John Breckinridge, leader of the Kentucky legislature, was a hot Republican, but Jefferson's resolutions were too strong for him. They passed through the legislature of that state in a more moderate form. Madison likewise steered a milder set of resolutions through the Virginia Assembly. The Kentucky Resolutions called on Congress to reconsider and repeal the Alien and Sedition Acts, whereas Jefferson's resolutions had contained a simple declaration of defiance. Breckinridge wrote to a friend that he hoped his modifications of Jefferson's original resolutions would "silence all calumnies, with respect to our disposition towards disorganization or disunion, I think the ground we have taken cannot be shaken; that no exception can be made to the firm but decent language in which we have expressed ourselves. I assure you with confidence, we have but one object, & that is, to preserve the constitution inviolate, & that by constitutional efforts."

Most of the states north of the Mason-Dixon line specifically rejected the resolutions. The other Southern states did not endorse them. It was clear that the revolutionary sentiment that Jefferson had tried to evoke did not exist, torn and troubled as the country was. Jefferson's only recourse was "to work within the system." Madison and Monroe, his most active lieutenants, therefore directed their energies to securing the presidency for him in the forthcoming election.

15

The Quasi War

The taxes the Federalists had imposed in order to pay for the construction of the fleet and augmentation of the army became in time the principal cause of resentment against the Adams administration. The direct property tax on land, buildings, and slaves was especially onerous. The tax on houses was calculated by counting the number and size of the windows. This meant a visit by a tax assessor, enough to alarm and irritate any honest householder. Alexander Graydon, a shrewd observer of the political scene, wrote: "A provisional army was voted, volunteer corps invited, ships of war equipped, and as a part of the system of defense, the Alien and Sedition Acts were enacted. But the most volcanic ground of all was yet to be trodden. . . . The simple, well-meaning Federalists . . . with no small degree of self-complacency . . . passed a law for a direct tax. . . . This tax on real property was the fatal blow to Federalism in Pennsylvania." And elsewhere.

Often the first a prospective taxpayer knew of the impending tax was the sight of an assessor walking around his house counting and measuring his windows. The excise tax had aroused the Whiskey Boys of western Pennsylvania. The property tax infuriated the farmers of Bucks County, a Republican stronghold in eastern Pennsylvania, who found a leader in young John Fries. When efforts were made at various meeting places to explain the nature and purposes of the tax, groups of angry farmers shouted down the assessors and threatened to tar and feather them. Assessors bold enough to try to carry out their jobs had dogs set on them and scalding water poured on their heads. When the assessors combined their forces at the town of Milford, the local militia were called out and John Fries was chosen to command them. Fries intercepted the assessors at a local tavern and ordered them out of the county. When they persisted in "taking the rates," two of them were seized by the militia at Quakertown and imprisoned.

In Pennsylvania's Lehigh County efforts to arrest those who refused to allow their property to be assessed were forcibly resisted. Finally a federal marshal succeeded in arresting half a dozen of the resisters, and they were sent under guard to Bethlehem where the less militant were released on parole and the rest were confined at the Sun Tavern. Word of the arrests aroused the country roundabout, and a company of several hundred farmers proceeded to Bethlehem to free the prisoners. There they ordered the marshal to release his charges on the threat of burning down the town; when he delayed, the crowd freed the men to the accompaniment of exultant cheers.

When news of the episode at Bethlehem reached Governor Mifflin, he called out the Philadelphia militia, who marched into the rebellious counties, notified the tax resisters that they were guilty of treason, and began making arrests in what was often an unnecessarily harsh and brutal manner. Fries was tracked down, and many of his principal followers were also rounded up. Reports were widely published in Republican papers recounting the brutality of the troops, who had taken it upon themselves to cut down liberty poles in a number of towns through which they passed. Some were accused of whipping children and assaulting women. So, at least, were the charges published in the *Reading Adler*. Certain militia, indignant at the accusations, returned to Reading, bore the editor off to the town square, and there, before the people of the town, proceeded to whip him. In the midst of this impromptu discipline, a calvary troop rode up and rescued the editor. The militiamen involved were arrested and immediately bailed out.

All these accounts were printed in the *Aurora* and embellished by William Duane, who had succeeded Bache as editor. One afternoon a body of militiamen visited Duane in the office of the *Aurora* and demanded an apology. When he refused, they dragged him into the street and whipped him. It was a time when "whipping editors" was what one might call a common practice, a hazard of the profession, but such actions did nothing to sweeten the disposition of the Republicans and, indeed, won to their cause many citizens who didn't give a fig for the French Revolution but disliked intensely the high-handed behavior and condescending attitudes of the Philadelphia Federalists. All of this, as the elections of 1800 approached, worked to the disadvantage of John Adams and to the advantage of Thomas Jefferson. The result of the whipping was to make Duane more remorseless than ever in his attacks on the Federalists.

Duane was an able man with a colorful background. Born in America, he had been an employee of the East India Company in India. Forcibly ejected from that country by the British governor for troublemaking, he had studied law in England; become a parliamentary reporter; served as editor of the *General Advertiser*, the seedling of the famous *London Times*; and had come back to America in 1795. He landed in Philadelphia where, finding the journalistic style of Bache's *Aurora* to his liking, he became a major contributor to the paper and, on Bache's death, its editor.

As for John Fries, he was twice tried and convicted of treason. A date was set for his hanging, but a presidential pardon saved his life. Fries' pardon by Adams was denounced by the Federalists and taken by them as another proof of the president's weakness. A Massachusetts constituent wrote, "Our people in this state are perfectly astonished. . . . I am fatigued and mortified that our government, which is weak at best, would withhold any of its strength when all its energies should be doubled."

The gubernatorial campaign of 1798 in Pennsylvania was closely followed by Federalists and Republicans alike. The two parties were almost equally divided in the state. Since Mifflin was ineligible for reelection, the Republicans ran Thomas McKean, chief justice of the state and a moderate Republican. The Federalist candidate was James Ross, an able lawyer but a man without a popular following. If the Republicans could retain their hold on the state, the chances of electing Thomas Jefferson president in place of John Adams would be greatly strengthened.

Pennsylvania was the home of two of the most rancorous Republican newspapers in the country, the *Aurora* and the *Independent Chronicle*. It had also been the scene of the Whiskey Rebellion and, more recently, of Fries' rebellion. With Philadelphia as the nation's interim capital, Pennsylvania was perhaps the most politically conscious and involved of all the states. By October 12 the election returns made it clear that McKean had won the state handily. Pennsylvania thus remained securely in Republican hands.

A curious reversal now took place in the respective Hamilton and Adams wings of the Federalist party. As we have seen, it had been Hamilton who, at the beginning of the crisis with France produced by the refusal of the Directory to accept Thomas Pinckney as American ambassador, had cautioned against rushing into war with France; and it was Adams whose immediate reaction had been to call for a declaration of war. Now it was Adams who had second thoughts. The reports from Gerry, galling as his behavior had been in terms of proper diplomatic protocol, had at least raised the serious possibility that the Directory, so far as it could be said to have a common mind on anything, wished to remain at peace with the United States. Its strange tergiversations were thus to be interpreted less as the result of warlike policy than of ineptitude, misinformation, and casual malice.

More influential than Elbridge Gerry's messages from Paris were the letters Adams continued to receive from John Quincy. In his son's opinion, France was anxious to avoid an armed conflict with the United States and had been disconcerted by the preparations for war that had followed the XYZ affair.

It had also become increasingly evident to Adams that Hamilton was doing his best to control the policy of the administration through his influence on the Cabinet. Shortly after Adams returned to Philadelphia from Braintree, Massachusetts, for the opening of the fall session of Congress, he decided to send yet another emissary to France to test the question of whether the Directory was finally ready for serious negotiations.

A series of communications had passed between Talleyrand and young William Vans Murray, American minister to The Hague, assuring Murray that any minister the United States sent would be received "with the respect due to the representative of a free and independent nation."

With Murray confirming the reports from Gerry and John Quincy, Adams called his Cabinet together and announced that he felt the time had arrived to dispatch a new mission to France. He had, he informed them, received the assurances that he had requested from the Directory. The Cabinet objected and, under the sway of Hamilton, urged Adams to delay. Things were in such an uncertain state in France that the Directory might fall before the envoys could cross the ocean.

There was certainly more than a little truth in the secretaries' description of the situation in France. The Directory had become largely the creature of Napoleon, who had begun that remarkable string of victories that, without precedent in the history of modern warfare, were to change the map of Europe. Defeating the Austrians at Millesimo, he had marched about Italy tearing up ancient political entities and erecting republics much as a precocious child might build villages out of paper blocks—the Lombard Republic; the Cisalpine Republic (Milan, Modena, Bologna, Ferrara); and the Ligurian Republic. Needless to say, the news of the almost instant creation of so many republics filled American Francophilies with ecstasy; even Federalist Protestants were charmed to hear that he had bullied the pope and occupied Rome.

With Italy exposed to the rights of man and to liberty, equality, and fraternity, all secured by republican governments (which began to topple almost before Napoleon had departed for more exotic lands), the French commander sailed for Egypt in the spring of 1798 with thirty-five thousand troops, capturing Malta on the way.

The Egyptian campaign was marked by splendid initial victories and ultimate defeat. Abandoning his army, Napoleon had hurried back to France to meet the Second Coalition, an alliance between Russia and England directed against him, which Austria and Portugal promptly joined. A series of allied victories in Germany and Italy were offset by a severe defeat in the Netherlands, all of which led to the coup d'état of 18th Brumaire (under the new rational Revolutionary calendar; November 9 under that observed by the rest of the world) in which Napoleon deposed the Directory and assumed the powers of a dictator, calling himself first consul (his term was to last ten years). The first consul had two assistant consuls, and his new regime was known as the Consulate. A new constitution was drafted, the Constitution of the Year VIII, the year eight of the new era. The Constitution was a thoroughly reactionary document that provided for a senate of eighty persons appointed for life. The Tribunate of one hundred could debate but not vote (the Legislative Assembly of three hundred persons could vote but not debate). The people at large voted for the Notables of the Commune who, in turn, elected one tenth of their number as the Notables of the Department, of whom one tenth again became Notables of France. From this select group came the members of various legislative bodies. All real power was retained by Napoleon. It was just such a constitution as critics like John Adams predicted must be produced by philosophers and theorists.

Ignoring the advice of his Cabinet, Adams sent the name of William Vans Murray to the Senate as the new French minister. The Federalists in the Senate tried to dissuade Adams from reopening negotiations and then, when he remained adamant, declared they would vote against the mission on the grounds that Murray was too young and inexperienced for such an important assignment. Adams responded by naming three envoys: Murray; Patrick Henry; and Oliver Ellsworth, chief justice of the Supreme Court. When Henry declined, Adams nominated William Davie of North Carolina in his place.

The president soon felt the wrath of the Hamiltonian Federalists. William Cobbett, editor of *Peter Porcupine's Gazette* and long a Federalist war-horse, denounced him as a traitor to his party. It was reported that Hamilton had described him as "a mere old woman and unfit for a President." George Cabot spoke of "the surprise, indignation, grief, and disgust" that had "followed each other in quick succession in the breasts of all true friends of our country"; and Fisher Ames wrote to Pickering that Adams had encouraged the Jacobins "to raise their heads from the mire of contempt." Adams was "too much the creature of impulse or freakish humor. He is a revolutionist from temperament, habit, and, lately, what he thinks policy. He is too much irritated against many, if not most, of the sound men of the country [the right-wing Federalists, needless to say] even to bestow on them his confidence. . . ."

Uriah Tracy, newly elected to the Senate from Connecticut, expressed his intention of resigning. He had devoted much of his public career to rooting out "democracy and French principles. . . . I can and will resign if all must be given up to France." Abigail wrote her husband that his decision had "universally electrified the public. . . . It comes so sudden, was a measure so unexpected, that the whole community were like a flock of frightened pigeons; nobody had their story ready; some called it a hasty measure; others condemned it as an inconsistent one; some swore, some cursed." It was "a master stroke of policy."

Despite the bitterness of the Hamilton faction, the short-term political consequence of Adams's determination to send a new mission to France was an immediate gain in strength for the Federalists throughout the country. For the first time in six years Georgia elected a Federalist congressman, and in Virginia John Marshall defeated an incumbent Republican. William Heth, a Virginia Federalist, wrote to Hamilton, "We have obtained such an accession of numbers [in the

Virginia congressional delegation] as well as of talents that I think we may consider Jacobinism as completely overthrown in this state."

In the long run, however, Adams's decision to dispatch the envoys probably cost him the presidential election of 1800. While it caused general rejoicing among Republicans and gave Adams a brief popularity with the radical democrats, it must be doubted that it lured many of them into the Federalist ranks. One thing it plainly did was split the Federalists irrevocably. From the time of the departure of the envoys, the Hamiltonians were as remorseless in their assaults on Adams as the Francophiles had ever been. They thus revealed themselves as irreconcilables—men who, in their attachment to the British and their hatred of the French, were willing to hazard everything.

One feels that the Hamiltonian Federalists might have redeemed all their errors and transcended all their shortcomings if they had not been so obsessively and unremittingly hostile to everything that the French Revolution stood for, and—what turned out to be far more serious—if they had not allowed that hostility to govern all their actions. No one could have taken a dimmer view of the French Revolution, once its true colors were revealed, than Washington and, after him, Adams. But both men eschewed what we might call the politics of irreconcilability. The Hamiltonian Federalists did exactly what Washington had warned his countrymen against in his Farewell Address and what the Hamiltonians had been so contemptuous of when they observed it in their opponents: they had indulged themselves in "excessive partiality for one foreign nation and excessive dislike of another." To be sure, the Republicans had done and continued to do the same thing, but the difference was that important ideological offshoots of the French Revolution were to become grafted on the American tree. Some of its basic assumptions about the nature of man and society, however naive or superficial, were in the process of becoming articles of faith in the American political creed. And one cannot even say that the imposition of the French Revolution on the American Revolution was without certain positive consequences. In their preoccupation with creating a "favorable business climate," as we would say today; in their affection for things British, especially British trade and commerce; in their suspicion and hostility toward "the mass of the people," the Federalists squandered the greater part of that capital of respect and gratitude to which they had fallen heir as a result of the ratification of the Constitution. If the impulse that lay behind the passage of the Alien and Sedition Acts was understandable and the actual persecutions under the acts few in number, they nonetheless constituted an act of political folly against which the more sagacious Federalists had warned.

In the midst of excitement created by Adams's dispatching of the envoys and the assembling of Congress, Washington died on December 14, having apparently caught pneumonia from a ride in the rain. Benjamin Rush, who was called to his bedside, bled him copiously, which could hardly have helped, and after an illness of only a few days he expired. He was in his sixty-eighth year, a proud, stern, passionate man. For most Americans, he was the greatest man in all of history, greater than an Alexander, a Caesar, a Cromwell. Abigail Adams, hearing of his death, echoed the sentiments of a great majority of her countrymen and women when she wrote: "Possessed of power, possessed of an extensive influence, he never used it but for the benefit of his country. . . . When assailed by faction, when reviled by party, he suffered with dignity. . . . If we look through the whole tenor of his life, history will not produce us a parallel."

His deification, as we have noted, had begun before his death. His death simply accelerated the process. A New England minister, pronouncing an elegy, declared: "Liberty's temple is rent in twain. Her spotless high priest hath retired to rest, through the portals of everlasting fame. . . . Though they said he was a god, he died as a man; let us not murmur, but rather wonder, that his great and immortal soul should be contented to reside in a human form so long."

On Washington's death all the controversy and criticism that had surrounded his terms as president disappeared without a trace. He became immaculate, irreproachable, more (and less) than human. The ingenuous Parson Weems sketched the ideal Washington that Americans clearly preferred to the real one. Historians have noted that the surest path to historical oblivion for Washington's contemporaries was to have criticized him during his lifetime. I believe that the reason for this blind adulation (as opposed to a "sighted" and proper adulation) is that with the decline of the Classical-Christian Consciousness, with its essentially tragic view of history, and its replacement by the Secular-Democratic Consciousness, with its determinedly optimistic view of history, Americans became unable (or unwilling) to cope with ambiguity. In the same spirit that American history had to become an unblemished record of splendor and "goodness," so our heroes had to be perceived as being without blemish. To allow even the most modest share of human frailties and failings to us as a people or to our heroes as individuals was to call into question the most fundamental tenets of the American faith. And to do *that* was to risk gazing into the bottomless pit. What Americans could not face in Washington (and lesser heroes) was what we could not face in ourselves—the fact that we were much like other human beings the world over. To have faced that would have been to imperil our "civil religion," the worship of America, that came in time largely to replace Christian religion as the dominant element in the consciousness of most Americans.

The country abandoned itself to mourning. The House and the Senate visited President Adams to express the grief of their members. The Senate: "Permit us, sir, to mingle our tears with yours. On this occasion it is manly to weep. To lose such a man at such a crisis is no common calamity to the world. Our country mourns her father. The Almighty has taken from us our greatest benefactor and ornament. . . . Washington yet lives on earth in his spotless example; his spirit is in heaven. Let his countrymen consecrate the memory of the heroic general, the patriotic statesman, and the virtuous sage. Let them teach their children never to forget that the fruit of his labors and his example are their inheritance."

Gouverneur Morris, hearing of Washington's death, wrote: "Few men of such steady, persevering industry ever existed, and perhaps no one who so completely commanded himself. Thousands have learned to restrain their passions, though few among them had to contend with passions so violent. . . . He could, at the dictate of reason, control his will and command himself to act." Dr. Nathaniel Ames confined himself to a dry entry in his diary: "All the Gazettes still crowded with accounts of the Parade and Pomp of Woe at Washington's Death and celebrating his Apotheosis! In preference to that of Christ in N. Jersey." It remained for John Marshall to pronounce the most succinct and memorable elegy—"first in war, first in peace, first in the hearts of his countrymen."

Newspapers were printed with black borders. Shops shut up. Theaters closed. Church bells tolled all day long in many towns as though grief could not be adequately expressed in words. Many people wore mourning clothes. Perhaps most notably, weeks later when word of Washington's death reached Torbay in Newfoundland, the British ships in the harbor flew their flags at half-mast. It was a reminder that the dead general was a universal hero.

The most important addition to the new Congress at its convening in October, 1799, was a Virginia representative, John Randolph of Roanoke. He was twenty-seven, destined in time to be one of the most exotic and powerful political figures in our history. His most conspicuous characteristic was a temper so extreme as to verge on the insane. The story was told that as a small child he had fainted from rage and could only "with difficulty be restored." In the House, although notorious for the bitterness of his invective and his merciless castigation of those with whom he differed, he became the leader of the Southern states' rights faction. Randolph, who—it was said—had been castrated in a childhood accident, had indeed a high-pitched voice and an effeminate appearance. Abigail Adams wrote of him, "This stripling comes full to the brim with his own conceit and all Virginia democracy. He chatters away like a magpie." But soon he ruled.

With Congress assembled, an effort was made to repeal the Sedition Law, but it was turned back by the Federalists and a series of persecutions was initiated against Republican editors, including William Duane; Anthony Haswell of the *Vermont Gazette*; and Charles Holt, editor of the *New London Bee*. As we have noted, James Callender, encouraged by Jefferson, had published an attack on Adams's administration under the title *The Prospect Before Us*. It was a venomous tract, which the vice-president described as producing "the best effect." It served to inform the "thinking part of the nation; and these again . . . set the people to rights." The degree of mutual paranoia is suggested by a letter of Jefferson to his nephew observing that "the enemies of our constitution are preparing a fearful operation." Among other informative items in the *Prospect* was Callender's observation that Washington had been "twice a traitor" and "the rancor and tardiness and timidity of Mr. Washington were succeeded by the insolence of Mr. Adams." Adams had labored "with melancholy success to break up the bounds of social affection and under the ruins of confidence and friendship to extinguish the only beam of happiness that glimmers through the dark and displicable farce of life —the French Revolution. France was the proper model for the United States. "The French," Callender concluded, "are cheerful and powerful"; their churches were flourishing; and "internal improvements are advancing faster in the Republic than in any part of the United States."

Among the stories printed by Republican newspapers to discredit Adams was the tale that he planned to marry his daughter Nabby to one of the sons of George III and thus start an American dynasty that would reunite the United States with Great Britain. Washington, before his death, had supposedly heard of the plan and had gone to Adams dressed in a white uniform to plead with him to abandon the scheme. Adams had refused and Washington had visited him a second time in a black costume to remonstrate with him again. Adams remaining adamant, Washington had donned his old uniform as commander in chief of the Continental Army, gone to Adams, and threatened to run him through with his sword if he did not give up the notion.

Another story claimed that Adams had sent General Pinckney to England in a U.S. frigate to procure four pretty girls as mistresses— two for the general, two for himself. When the tale was repeated to Adams, he wrote to his nephew, "I do declare upon my honor if this be true General Pinckney has kept them all himself and cheated me out of my two."

Another weapon with which the Republicans belabored the president involved the case of an English sailor, Thomas Nash, accused of murder and mutiny aboard a British warship. Nash escaped and was caught in Charleston, South Carolina. He claimed to be an American sailor, Jonathan Robbins, of Danbury, Connecticut. Under Article 27 of the Jay treaty, Nash was jailed and turned over to the British consul for extradition to the West Indies to be tried for his crimes. The Republicans insisted that Nash was Robbins, an innocent man, and charged that Adams's intervention in the case was an example of his toadying to the British. Jefferson encouraged the effort to make political hay of the episode, writing, "No circumstance since the establishment of our government has affected the popular mind more. I hear that in Pennsylvania it had a great effect."

Republican rallies were held in every state. That in Fayette, Kentucky, was typical. There sixteen toasts were proposed, one to "Thomas Jefferson, the pride of the Republicans and the terror of aristocrats; may he soon be raised to the seat to which his unfortunate country has been too long in elevating him." Another was to "The President of the U. States; may he soon retire to Quincy by general consent, accompanied by his *Defence of the American Constitutions!*"

The Hamiltonians were almost as busy as their opponents. They toyed with the possibility of substituting Oliver Ellsworth or General Charles Cotesworth Pinckney for Adams as a presidential candidate (Hamilton seemed determined to make it a practice to try to oust Adams with one Pinckney or another). Adams knew that members of his own Cabinet were involved in the plotting against him. He had apparently decided to put up with them rather than stir up more intraparty rancor by sacking them, but his temper betrayed him. He got into an unpleasant exchange with McHenry, accused him of taking orders from Hamilton, and then launched into a tirade against

Hamilton. McHenry, indignant at Adams's attack on him, offered his resignation and Adams accepted. Four days later he requested Pickering's resignation and, when he was refused, fired him. The resignation and firing meant that the Federalist fat was in the fire. The party rupture was visible for all to see. Years later Pickering, attempting to vindicate himself, wrote that in his opinion Cabinet officers were not bound by any rule of *"implicit obedience*. . . . On the contrary, I should think it their duty to prevent, as far as practicable, the mischievous measures of a wrongheaded President."

Adams offered McHenry's post as secretary of war to John Marshall, who refused it. The president then appointed Samuel Dexter, a Massachusetts senator, to the office and prevailed on Marshall to accept Pickering's job as secretary of state.

As the election drew near, Adams's supporters deserted him one by one. In John Quincy's words, these men directed their "personal abuse and deadly animosity against the President," men who had "known him in public and private life for thirty or forty years; who have acted with him in a variety of public capacities, and with some of whom he has been for many years in habits of friendship."

Oliver Wolcott, who remained as secretary of the treasury after McHenry and Pickering had departed, wrote to Fisher Ames comparing Adams and Jefferson. He found little to choose between them. "However dangerous the election of Mr. Jefferson may prove to the community I do not perceive that any portion of the mischief could be avoided by the election of Mr. Adams. We know the temper of his mind to be revolutionary, violent and vindictive. . . . His passions and selfishness would continually gain strength; his pride and interest would concur in rendering his administration favorable to the views of democrats and Jacobins. . . ." Above all, Adams had little understanding of, or sympathy with, the business and mercantile interests.

George Cabot, another Boston Federalist, took a more realistic view of the situation. He did not see how it would "be practicable to discard Mr. Adams as a candidate at this period without confounding us in this quarter, and consequently exposing the whole party to a defeat." Indeed a kind of fatalism seemed to possess many of the Federalist leaders. Like Wolcott, they couldn't bear Adams or Jefferson, and they despaired of the future of the Republic. Even Abigail Adams, usually so resolute, wrote to John Quincy Adams that the Republicans of Massachusetts were "so gratified to see the Federalists split to pieces that they enjoy in silence the game. . . . So much for elective government; if we pass the ordeal this time, I am satisfied from what I have seen and heard that it is the last time. God save the United States of America."

Thomas Boylston Adams, another of the president's sons, echoed the same theme: "It seems to me that nobody cares for the constitution—the framers of it are apparently in many instances disgusted with it—and all its original enemies . . . and all the Virginia tribe, as also the small folks *here* and in other parts of the Union, when they carry the day, will assuredly try to set up something else."

Even Wolcott was disturbed by Hamilton's implacable campaign against Adams. When the latter tried to get him to leak confidential material, Wolcott answered that it would be pointed out if he did so that "the President has not injured me; that he has borne with my open disapprobation of his measures; and that I ought not to oppose his re-election by disclosing what some will term personal or official secrets."

On September 26 Hamilton sent Wolcott a copy of his "letter" attacking Adams, much of it based on material supplied by Wolcott, McHenry, and Pickering. "I hope from it two advantages," Hamilton wrote, "the promoting of Mr. Pinckney's election, and the vindication of ourselves."

After defending himself against the charge of being pro-British and anti-French (he confessed that "Revolutionary France, after her early beginnings, has been always to me an object of horror"), he attacked Adams's "ill humors and jealousies" and "unfounded accusations." At the same time Hamilton had, he declared, "Finally resolved not to advise the withholding from [Adams] of a single vote," since "the body of Federalists, for want of sufficient knowledge of facts, are not convinced of the expediency of relinquishing him." But as for himself, he would not support Adams even if it meant the election of Jefferson. "If we must have an *enemy* at the head of the government," he wrote, "let it be one we can oppose, and for whom we are not responsible, who will not involve our party in the disgrace of his foolish and bad measures."

If there was any political capital to be made from a treaty with France, it came too late to be of any aid to the beleaguered John Adams. A "Convention of Peace, Commerce and Navigation . . ." was signed on September 30, 1800, a little more than a month before the presidential elections. It provided for the return of ships seized by both nations in what had come to be called the quasi war, enumerated wartime contraband, and left the matter of indemnities to future negotiation.

16

The Election of 1800

While Jefferson did not engage in public campaigning, he worked hard behind the scenes, planning strategy and encouraging beleaguered Republican newspaper editors with contributions of money to keep them in business. In a letter to Elbridge Gerry, he laid out his principles, or what would later come to be called "platform." He strongly supported the Constitution, but it was clearly a Constitution that he interpreted in the strictest and narrowest sense. He was, he declared, "for a government rigorously frugal and simple . . . and not for a multiplication of officers and salaries merely to make partisans," or "for increasing, by every device, the public debt, on the principle of its being a public blessing." He was opposed to a standing army and preferred to rely on the militia "for internal defense . . . till actual invasion, and for such a naval force only as may protect our coasts and harbors." Finally, he was against "linking ourselves by new treaties with the quarrels of Europe," and he was most emphatically for freedom of religion and freedom of the press.

The Federalists of course were not behindhand in attacking Jefferson, most commonly for infidelity and un-Americanism, that is, French ideas. Perhaps the most frequently quoted denunciation of Jefferson on religious grounds was that of "A Christian Federalist" of

Delaware who asked: "Can serious and reflecting men look about them and doubt, that if Jefferson is elected, and the Jacobins get into authority, that those morals which protect our lives from the knife of the assassin—which guard the chastity of our wives and daughters from seduction and violence—defend our property from plunder and devastation, and shield our religion from contempt and profanation, will not be trampled upon and exploded. . . . Let these men get into power, put the reins of government into their hands, and what security have you against the occurrence of the scenes which have rendered France a cemetery, and moistened her soil with the tears and blood of her inhabitants."

The Reverend Jedediah Morse, the renowned minister of the First Congregational Church of Charlestown, Massachusetts, "the father of American geography," and an indefatigable champion of the remnants of Calvinism, became perhaps the most notable and articulate adversary of the philosophical doctrines of the French Revolution and thus, by implication, of Jefferson. To Morse, whose remarkable son, Samuel F. B. Morse, was to invent the telegraph, the new "religion" of reason and science, whose political manifestation was the French Revolution, was an outright assault on traditional Christianity.

It is necessary to pay some attention to the Reverend Morse because he introduced and popularized what we might call the doctrine of the Illuminati. Essentially it was the notion of an international conspiracy of deists, atheists, skeptics, and freethinkers to undermine the Christian religion, to destroy the basic institutions derived from it—most particularly, though by no means exclusively, the church and the family—and to absorb the United States into an international network of rationalism and irreligion. The forerunners of the Illuminati had been the Freemasons who wished to establish a worldwide fraternal order and were themselves clearly a product of the eighteenth-century Enlightenment. If the notion of the conspiracy of the Illuminati was preceded by the Freemasons, it had an extraordinary progeny. Almost from the founding of the Republic many Americans have given evidence of a curious kind of collective paranoia based on the belief that the United States has been the object of a series of conspiracies. As soon as a set of political ideas that could be defined as "socialism" appeared (in the early nineteenth century), there were a substantial number of Americans who were convinced that international Socialists were plotting to subvert American institutions.

The Socialists were followed by the Marxian Communists, and

they, in turn, by a mysterious and mythical company of international Jews who scared the daylights out of Henry Ford with the fabricated Protocols of Zion, a purported plan for conquest of the world through the control of international banking, news media, and so on. Common to all these conspiracies has been the threat to the Christian churches, the threat of "godless atheism," in one form or another, to a heretofore devout Christian people. The paranoia had, of course, a basis in fact. The Classical-Christian Consciousness was rapidly being eroded by its Secular-Democratic rival. There was every reason for the older orthodoxy to fear the new, which, of course, proclaimed itself as the truth and denounced the old orthodoxy as false.

The Reverend Morse's identification of the Illuminati conspiracy was widely circulated. He had in his hand, he claimed, "the names, the ages, the places of birth of a hundred members of a Society of the Illuminati . . . founded in Virginia by the Grand Orient of France."

The *Aurora* and the *Independent Chronicle* replied to Morse's charges with derision. Having tried every other bugaboo in vain, the Federalists were now reduced to creating a new hobgoblin to frighten ninnies. This time the French "were about to cut off every Christian's head, turn the Old South into a riding school, set Charlestown meeting-house on fire. . . . This done, the clergy were to be turned out . . . to graze."

Morse's sermon on the Illuminati, delivered on the day set by the president for prayer and fasting and published as a pamphlet, was answered by an attack on the clergy of New England as conspirators for Federalism. *A View of the New England Illuminati, who are indefatigably engaged in destroying the Religion and Government of the United States, under a feigned Regard for their Safety, and under an impious Abuse of True Religion* (long titles were the style) accused the New England clergy of having formed their own society dedicated to obsolete aristocratic notions, to attacks on the French, on the rights of man, on liberty of thought and speech. "In New England were the true Illuminati, destroying the principles of free government, and overturning the altars of every church but their own."

Republicans played on the theme of the New England clergy as the true Illuminati in a satirical poem:

> Sage Demo's and Tories, I pray you take heed,
> And I'll give you a sketch of my time-serving creed—
> For my creed it is cash, and my stipend salvation,

For which I'll destroy all the hopes of the nation,
In my black gown and cravat so white.

Jefferson's reflections on religion were "odious" to those Americans, most commonly to be found in New England, who shared Jedediah Morse's convictions. After Jefferson's resignation from his unhappy interlude as governor of Virginia, he sat down to reply to a series of questions that François Marbois, secretary of the French legation at Philadelphia, had circulated among members of Congress about the various American states. While he completed his reply in 1781 (under the heading *Notes on the State of Virginia*), he continued to add to the original manuscript, and when he departed for France in 1784 he carried it with him. He had it published in Paris in 1785 for private distribution among his friends. Two years later he authorized a British printer to publish a commercial edition, and it was this, which promptly found its way to America, that provided the basis for attacks on Jefferson's religious beliefs. In the *Notes* Jefferson was critical of all constraints on religious freedom. Men and women were answerable only to God for their religious beliefs, Jefferson declared. "The legitimate powers of government extend to such acts only as are injurious to others. But it does me no injury for my neighbour to say there are twenty gods, or no god. It neither picks my pocket nor breaks my leg. . . . Reason and free inquiry are the only effectual agents against error. Give a loose to them, they will support the true religion, by bringing every false one to their tribunal, to the test of their investigation. They are the natural enemies of error, and of error only." The principal error of orthodox Christians was to believe that religious uniformity could be forced on the pious. But it was unattainable. "Millions of innocent men, women, and children, since the introduction of Christianity have been burnt, tortured, fined, imprisoned; yet we have not advanced one inch towards uniformity. What has been the effects of coercion? To make one half of the world fools, and the other half hypocrites. To support roguery and error all over the earth."

Jefferson had written in condemnation of the Virginia statute of 1705 that made the Church of England the established church of the dominion of the Virginia. Largely through his influence the Virginia Statute of Religious Liberty, giving political effect to Jefferson's eloquent words, was passed in 1786. But his indictment of religious establishments was a red flag to New England Congregationalists in those states where that church was "established," that is to say, the only denomination officially recognized by the state. While the establishment meant little in practical terms and all denominations were in fact accepted as legitimate, Jefferson's attack on ecclesiastical authority and his substitution of the individual conscience as the final measure in all matters concerning religion was thoroughly alarming to the orthodox. Moreover, his confident assertion that "reason" could infallibly discern the truth appeared to men like Morse to be direct assault on the "faith" Christians believed to be the rock on which Christianity rested.

In addition, Jefferson seemed to imply that rather as all men were equal, all religions were equal. There were even rumors that Jefferson questioned the divinity of Jesus Christ, and it is unquestionably true that not a few ministers warned their congregations of the dangers of having an infidel for president. Thus, to many devout Americans the approaching election of 1800 appeared to be a contest between Christianity and atheism.

One theme that the New England Federalists professed to find particularly objectionable was the Southern evocation of "liberty." The *Connecticut Courant* declared that the citizens of Connecticut were not disposed "to learn the principles of liberty [from] the slave-holders of Virginia," and a reader agreed: "We want no *Southern lights* in these parts: We have northern lights,—we have gospel light, and political light, sufficient to exterminate Jacobinism."

The Republicans were especially adept at appealing to the particular interests of individual states. Thus, in New England where in most states the Congregational church was the established church and such sects as the Quakers and Baptists were viewed as upstarts, Jefferson's pronouncements on religious liberty were played down; but in Pennsylvania, the state originally founded on principles of religious liberty, they were loudly advertised. "To religious men," one Pennsylvania Republican wrote, "Mr. Jefferson has indisputably been the most useful character since William Penn." As president he would encourage "the sound practical *Equality* of the Quaker; the *equal Brotherhood* of the Moravian, the Mennonist, and the Dunker."

Perhaps in the last analysis, the most effective Republican tactic was the cry that it was time for a change. "*Is it not high time for a CHANGE?*" a Republican leaflet asked. A similarly seductive cry was to echo in American politics through successive party struggles.

In Pennsylvania, where McKean had defeated James Ross, the Federalists controlled the upper house of the state legislature and the

Republicans the lower. Since neither house could agree on a method of determining the choice of electors after weeks of hopeless wrangling, a compromise was accepted by both parties that gave 8 votes to the Jefferson-Burr ticket and 7 to Adams-Pinckney (each elector voting for two candidates, one assumed to be president and one vice-president).

The real hinge of the election, as it turned out, was New York City. The Federalists in 1796 had attained a strong majority in the legislature of that state and had elected that symbol of Federalism, John Jay, governor. They thus looked forward, initially with considerable confidence, to carrying the state for the Federalist ticket, despite the fact that the most serious split in the Federalist ranks was manifest there. The outcome of the New York elections of 1798 turned primarily on the efforts of one man, Aaron Burr. Burr came of distinguished New England lineage. His maternal grandfather, Jonathan Edwards, leader of the Great Awakening in the 1740s, was America's most famous theologian and philosopher. His father, Aaron Burr, had been, in practical fact, the founder of the College of New Jersey, later Princeton College, and one of the foremost preachers of his day. He had married Jonathan Edwards's beautiful and talented daughter, Esther, child of a mother equally gifted. Burr's father and mother had both died when he was in his infancy, and he was raised by an uncle. Young Aaron showed the same precociousness that had distinguished his father and grandfather. Tapping Reeve, a brilliant young lawyer, was private tutor to Burr, who qualified to enter Yale when he was eleven years old, although Yale delayed his admission on the undoubtedly legitimate grounds that he was too young. When he was finally admitted to Yale, he proved an apt but not brilliant student and, in the custom of the day, "sowed his wild oats" with more than ordinary ingenuity. After an intense experience of religious conversion had run its course, Burr decided to devote himself to purely worldly concerns on the model of Lord Chesterfield. He had been a member of Washington's staff, but some conflict arose and Burr resigned and received a combat command as lieutenant colonel. By the end of the war he had made a reputation for personal bravery and fierce ambition, married the widow of a British officer, and begun the study of law. After the war he rose rapidly to the top of his profession and, as Federalists and Republicans began to define themselves, Burr cast his political lot with the Clintons.

His principal rival, both professionally and politically, was Alexander Hamilton. Burr had had every advantage of birth and family fortune; Hamilton was one of America's first self-made men. Yet in almost every other way they were startlingly alike. Burr, born in February, 1756, was a year older than Hamilton (born January 11, 1757). Both were strikingly handsome, Hamilton with light brown or reddish hair and blue eyes, Burr dark. Both were short in stature, meticulous dressers, brilliant lawyers, and relentlessly ambitious. Both were political to their fingertips. Both were voracious womanizers. An acquaintance of Burr's wrote: "His intrigues were without number. His conduct most licentious. The sacred bonds of friendship were unhesitatingly violated when they operated as barriers to the indulgence of his passions. For a long period of time he seemed to be gathering, and carefully preserving, every line written to him by any female, with or without reputation; and, when obtained, they were cast into one common receptacle—the profligate and corrupt, by the side of the thoughtless and betrayed victim. All were held as trophies of victory—all esteemed alike valuable."

With Governor George Clinton as his sponsor, Burr's rise in New York politics had been rapid. He had served for two years as attorney general of the state. His handsome estate, Richmond Hill, was one of the finest mansions in New York, a kind of general headquarters for New York Republicans. From it Burr plotted the strategy that enabled him to defeat General Philip Schuyler, Revolutionary veteran and the father-in-law of Alexander Hamilton, for the U.S. Senate in 1791. In the Senate he increased his reputation as a brilliant political manager and made himself the leader of the Republicans in that branch. Schuyler had ousted Burr in the Federalist sweep of 1796, and Burr returned to the New York legislature. With the assembly as his political base, he began planning to regain Republican control of the state in time for the election of 1800.

His wife, whom he adored, had died in 1794, and after her death the only child of that marriage, Theodosia, became his ruling passion. She was a child with the striking beauty and intelligence that seemed a genetic legacy of the women in the Edwards-Burr family, and her father devoted himself to her education with a zeal rivaled only by that for his political intrigues. When she was ten years old she had read Horace and Terence in Latin, spoke and read French fluently, and was studying Greek. After her mother's death she became her father's hostess, presiding over the active social life at Richmond Hill with the grace and wit of a mature woman. I have spoken elsewhere of America as the "land of daughterhood," a country in which the unique relationship between fathers and daughters gave rise to the movement for women's rights that was so conspicuous an aspect of nineteenth-century America. We shall encounter many more of these relationships during the course of this work, but none was as intense and dramatic as that between Aaron Burr and Theodosia.

It was this man, now in his forty-fourth year and at the height of his personal powers and political reputation, who undertook to reverse the fortunes of the New York Republicans and, in so doing, advance his own. It must be said that brilliant and successful as he was, people sensed in Aaron Burr a desperate will that verged on madness, a kind of suppressed rage, the feeling that he was always on hairtrigger, sinuous, volatile, high-strung, and at the same time remorselessly calculating. Even those allied with him and eager to avail themselves of his remarkable energy and intelligence did not wholly trust him.

Rural New York was predominantly Federalist. It was, therefore, the city that had to be brought overwhelmingly into the Republican fold if the party of Jefferson and Democracy were to triumph. If Aaron Burr did not invent "machine politics," he certainly raised the practice of politics to a new stage of efficiency and sophistication. It was his inspiration to prevail on men well known throughout the state to let their names be placed in nomination as electors while, as Abigail Adams wrote, the Federalists chose men of "no note, wholly unfit for the purpose." In addition, he developed a system of committees to work on the ward level and organized political rallies in every section of the city. One of his lieutenants noted, "Never have I observed such a union of sentiment; so much zeal and so general a determination to be active." Another Republican worker wrote to Albert Gallatin, "If we carry this election it may be ascribed principally to Col. Burr's management and perseverance."

Voting lasted for three days, and Burr was everywhere rounding up stray votes, doing last-minute campaigning, and encouraging his cohorts. In the Seventh Ward, he stayed at his post for ten hours, and one of his aides was so busy about the polls that he went without food for fifteen hours. Even the Federalists, outnumbered and outmaneuvered as they were, were inspired to emulation, and one reported, "I have not eaten dinner for three days and have been constantly on my legs from 7 in the morning till 7 in the afternoon."

When the votes were counted, the Republicans had won a notable victory. One of them wrote to Gallatin, who, with Madison, was the principal coordinator of the Republican national campaign, that the election "has been conducted and brought to issue in so miraculous a manner that I cannot account for it but from the intervention of a Supreme Power and our friend Burr the agent. . . . His generalship, perseverance, industry, and execution exceeds all description, so that I think I can say he deserves anything and everything of his country."

What he clearly deserved in the eyes of most Republicans was the party's nomination for vice-president, and that is what he got—much to his misfortune, as it turned out. In any event, there is no gainsaying that it was Burr who brought New York into the Republican fold, thereby guaranteeing that the state's 12 electoral votes would be cast for Jefferson.

Hamilton was dismayed at the outcome and tried to prevail upon his old friend, Governor Jay, to call a special meeting of the legislature while it was still in the control of the Federalists to pass an election law that would nullify the Republican victory. Hamilton wrote: "In times like this in which we live, it will not do to be overscrupulous. It is easy to sacrifice the substantial interest of society by a strict adherence to ordinary rules. . . . They ought not to hinder the taking of a legal and *constitutional* step, to prevent an atheist in Religion, and a *fanatic* in politics [Jefferson] from getting possession of the helm of State." Jay, to his credit, refused.

When Adams addressed a joint session of the House and Senate in November, 1800, meeting for the first time in the new Capitol, the outcome of the presidential election was still unknown. "May this territory be the residence of virtue and happiness!" he declared. "In this city, may that piety and virtue, that wisdom and magnanimity, that constancy and self-government which adorned the great character whose name it bears be forever held in veneration!"

The election of 1800 was complicated by the fact that three different procedures for choosing electors were employed in the various states. One was by general popular election; one was by election through districts; and one was by the state legislature. By the end of November it was evident that the Federalists had carried all the New England states. New York, as we have seen, was in the Republican column. New Jersey and Rhode Island were Federalist; Pennsylvania divided, 8 and 7. Maryland was split. To the south, Jefferson and Burr had carried every state except North Carolina, where 4 out of 12 electors were Federalists, and South Carolina, which still had not voted. No vote was "thrown away," so that the final tally showed Jefferson and Burr with 73 votes apiece to 65 for Adams. In the two most closely contested states, New York and South Carolina, the shift of relatively few votes would have given them to Adams, or, conversely, if the voting in those states had been by districts, thus splitting the vote, Adams would have triumphed.

When the news of the outcome in South Carolina reached the other states, making it clear beyond doubt that the Jefferson-Burr ticket had won, the Republicans abandoned themselves to delirious celebrations. The country had been rescued from monarchy and aristocracy, from the moneymen, the bankers, and the "interests," and made safe for democracy and the people.

Nathaniel Ames, noting the election of Jefferson and Burr in his diary, added, "It is hoped treason will not be so triumphant as in the last [four years], that the reign of terror is over, and that free discussion will cause terror only to traitors."

At the Green Tree Tavern in Philadelphia there were toasts and speeches and the singing of "Jefferson and Liberty" and other songs composed for the occasion. At Pittsfield, Massachusetts, the church bell was employed so strenuously in celebrating Jefferson's victory that it broke. But such festivities were soon dampened by the realization that Jefferson was not in fact the new president, whatever the clear intention of the voters had been, but that, because he and Burr had an equal number of votes, the matter must now be decided by the House of Representatives. There Jefferson needed a majority of nine states to be officially declared president. The new House, chosen in the same elections that had chosen the electors, would be heavily Republican, but the old House, which under the Constitution had to decide the election, was so closely divided that the Federalists were in a position to deny Jefferson the presidency.

Ironically, the outgoing Federalist administration met for the last weeks of its life in the new capital, Washington. A crude, unfinished town with inadequate lodgings even for Congress, it had about it both an unfinished and a somewhat ramshackle air. The presidential mansion was a most impressive structure, and although the plaster was still damp on the walls, John Adams moved in and then sat down to write his beloved Abigail, who had stopped off in New York. He had been enthusiastically welcomed in his progress south, he told her, and now, "Before I end my letter," he added, "I pray Heaven to bestow the best of blessings on this house and all that shall hereafter inhabit it. May none but wise and honest men ever rule under this roof."

There was not much indication of either quality among the

congressmen who assembled at the end of February to decide the election. The diehard Federalists in that body were determined to rob Jefferson of the presidency if they could get away with it. Their strategy was to block Jefferson's election and then appeal to the Senate to appoint an interim president, perhaps Chief Justice of the Supreme Court Oliver Ellsworth or Secretary of State John Marshall, until new elections could be held. It was the politics of desperation, of irreconcilability that they had so often accused their opponents of. Rumors of the scheme brought down a swarm of angry Republicans on the already overcrowded town of Washington. Threats of an armed invasion were bandied about if Congress attempted to frustrate the will of the voters. There were reports of militia drilling in Virginia, preparatory to a raid on Washington, that prompted a Federalist newspaper to warn that seventy thousand regulars could be recruited in Massachusetts to suppress any such rebellion.

Meantime in the overcrowded town—in one boardinghouse fifty men slept on the floor with no beds or blankets—rumors chased each other in a bewildering roundabout. When the balloting began, eight states supported Jefferson while six cast their votes for Burr. Maryland and Vermont were divided. Eight more ballots were taken, and then another eight without any change. At midnight the balloting resumed. Some members of the House had sent for bedding and caught what sleep they could while others dozed in their chairs. At one, two, and then four o'clock, new ballots were taken. By noon of the next day twenty-nine ballots had been completed and the vote was as it had been on the first.

After the thirty-third ballot on Friday the thirteenth, the House adjourned until Monday. Efforts had been made to persuade Burr to withdraw. While he did declare that he was not seeking the presidency, he refused to say that he would not serve or make any public or private move that might have settled the issue in Jefferson's favor. Although he refused to bargain with the Federalists to gain votes, his silent acquiescence in the attempt to rob Jefferson of the presidency cost all the influence he had acquired by his brilliant management of the Federalist campaign in New York. Jefferson would never forgive him, nor would the rank and file of Republicans. If the election of 1800 did nothing else, it marked the end of Burr's extraordinary political career. It revealed to the world what had earlier been only dimly perceived—his dangerous and insatiable ambition.

Over the weekend certain Federalists, led by James Bayard of

Delaware, had apparently received assurances from Jefferson in regard to preserving the navy and not turning Federalists out of their jobs wholesale. Thereupon on the thirty-sixth ballot, Federalist members from Maryland and Delaware cast blank ballots, thus putting those states in Jefferson's column and assuring him of the election. Now, indeed, the Republicans gave themselves over to celebration. Cannons were fired, bells rung, toasts once more drunk to "Jefferson, the Mammoth of Democracy" and all the gods and heroes in the Republican shrine. A favorite song went:

> Hark! the echoes of Joy, how they ring through the land!
> Avaunt, ye pale tyrants, 'tis Freedom's strong voice.
> On the hills of Columbia she fixes her stand
> And proclaims the glad tidings, and this is her choice:
>   Lo! Jefferson bright;
>   Fill up the bumper—that's right—
>   Here's his health, we'll support him, if needful we'll fight;
> But in Union and Harmony we *wish* to *combine*,
> And kneel with devotion at Liberty's shrine.

Jefferson was to be inaugurated on March 4. On February 13, Congress had interrupted its efforts to choose a president in order to pass the judiciary bill, which formed the three existing judicial districts into six with their own federal judges and relieved the justices of the Supreme Court of the arduous task of attending circuit court in addition to fulfilling their primary function as judges of the supreme tribunal of the land. Twenty-three new judgeships resulted from the bill, which might well be called the last classic Federalist piece of legislation passed by Congress.

Adams immediately began to appoint loyal Federalists to the new positions. Oliver Ellsworth, in failing health, resigned as chief justice, and Adams was left with another plum to award to a deserving Federalist. His first thought was of Jay. When Jay declined, Adams intended to offer the chief justiceship to Associate Justices Cushing and then Paterson, in that order. Friends of both men began at once to lobby for their respective candidates, but Adams decided Cushing was too old and infirm for the job. Paterson, author of the New Jersey Plan in the Federal Convention, was too closely associated with the Hamiltonians for Adams's taste. The president then decided to nominate John Marshall, and on January 20 sent Marshall's name to the Senate. Even among the Federalists there was substantial opposition to the appointment. Jonathan Dayton, senator from New Jersey, wrote to Paterson that it was "with grief, astonishment and almost indignation" that he sent him news of Marshall's nomination, "contrary to the hopes and expectations of us all." Nevertheless, Marshall's appointment was confirmed.

The morning of his rival's inauguration Adams departed for Quincy without attending the simple ceremony. He rode back to Massachusetts to die, embittered and angry at his defeat. He blamed it on Hamilton and was understandably bitter. "Seventy-three for Mr. Jefferson and seventy-three for Mr. Burr; May the peace and welfare of the country be promoted by this result!" he wrote Elbridge Gerry. "But I see not the way as yet." To his son John Quincy he noted, "Mr. Hamilton has carried his eggs to a fine market. The very two men of the world that he was most jealous of are now placed over him." He then went on to make a penetrating analysis of the cause of his defeat. "No party that ever existed knew itself so little or so vainly overrated its own influence and popularity as ours. None ever understood so ill the causes of its own power, or so wantonly destroyed them. If it had been blessed with common sense, we should not have been overthrown by Philip Freneau, Duane, Callender, Cooper, and Lyon, or their great patron and protector [Jefferson]. A group of foreign liars, encouraged by a few ambitious native gentlemen, have discomforted the education, the talents, the virtues and the property of the country. The reason is, we have no Americans in America. The Federalists have been no more Americans than the Antis." Adams concluded that Great Britain and France had dominated American politics for more than a decade.

Gouverneur Morris had his own analysis of the Adams defeat. "Virginia was almost in open revolt against the national authority during Mr. Adams's reign," he wrote, "because a Yankee, and not a Virginian, was President . . . by downright demonstration, it is shown that the republican party were not dissatisfied because the power of the Government was too great, but because it was not in their hands . . . to lead honest men by slow but sure degrees to abjure the principles of our Constitution, and co-operate in their own subjugation to the aristocracies of Virginia and New York."

Perhaps the most consoling words were those of John Quincy, who wrote: "By sending the late mission you restored an honorable peace to the nation without tribute, without bribes, without violating any previous engagement. . . . You have, therefore, given the most decisive proof that in your administration you were not the man of any party, but of the whole nation, and if the eyes of faction will shut themselves against the value of such a character, if even the legal and constitutional judgment of your country . . . will be insensible to it, you can safely and confidently appeal from the voice of heated and unjust passions, to that of cool and equitable reason, from the prejudices of the present to the sober decision of posterity."

Jefferson, for his part, was convinced that the election was a bloodless revolution. "The Revolution of 1800 was as real a revolution in the principles of our government as that of 1776 was in its form," he wrote, "not effected by the sword, as that, but by the rational and peaceable instrument of reform, the suffrage of the people." That will doubtless seem rather an overstatement to the modern reader. In any event, it is a proposition to be subsequently tested.

What is most significant about the election of 1800 is that power was transferred from one party to another under conditions of rivalry so bitter that many thoughtful Americans doubted that the Constitution could survive and that bloodshed could be avoided, whatever the outcome. Before the election, John Quincy Adams had written to his brother, Thomas Boylston, "It is impossible for me to avoid the supposition that the ultimate necessary consequence, if not the *ultimate object of both the extreme* parties which divide us will be a dissolution of the Union and *a civil war*." And Christopher Gadsden of South Carolina wrote, "'tis impossible that the union can much longer exist . . . our government must prove *an abortion*, or smothered in its earliest infancy, [and] will afford to anti-republicans and future historians the strongest example ever heard of, of the instability and short duration of such kind of government." When such men held such opinions, the mere fact that a peaceful "transmigration" of power took place was, in itself, of enormous significance. The fact was that it was the first time, in modern history certainly, that such an event had taken place. The election of 1800 would thus be notable for that if for no other reason.

It would be a mistake also to underrate the importance of the fact that it took place exactly at the opening of the new century. The ends of centuries seem to be invariably accompanied by certain psychological phenomena. Man, being a time-bound creature, is ruled, to a degree, by his consciousness of the character of the times. The *fin de siècle* spirit is typically one of weariness and anxiety, and even, in a certain sense, of approaching death (suicide rates increase, for example); there is often a feeling of slackness, of time running down, of disappointed hopes and defeated dreams. Conversely, the new century (often depicted as a robust infant) is seen as a time of renewal, of new enterprises and fresh energies. The classic drama of a century's end and beginning was severely modified in the late eighteenth century by the commencement of the new Republic of the United States and even more, of course, by the French Revolution. To those who saw the French Revolution as the hope of the world it was as though the new century had begun a decade early. To its enemies, of course, it marked the death knell of everything they cherished: order, the rule of law, decency, privilege, tradition, religion, civilized values generally.

The Federalists certainly behaved as though Jefferson's victory marked the beginning of the descent into chaos, while the Republicans acclaimed it as the completion of the "Revolution of 1776," the emancipation of America from monarchy and tyranny. Yet it remains, to a substantial degree, a puzzle. The fantasies of both parties seem so bizarre that one gropes in vain for an entirely satisfactory explanation. Surely it does not lie in the realm of rationality. Difficult as it is to believe that the Republicans really thought that Washington and Adams intended to turn the United States into a monarchy, reunite it with England, or create an American aristocracy, we must, I think, take them at their feverish word. By the same token, it is clearly the case that the Federalists were convinced that the Republicans, especially the more rabid Republican press, were bent on importing the French Revolution and murdering pious Christians in their beds. So we are obviously witnessing a psychosociological phenomenon that is only distantly related to the political and ideological forms in which it presents itself.

The French Revolution is almost certainly the key. To give a reasonably accurate account of its various stages would take a volume the size of this one. But it is important to keep in mind that we are talking about the most awesome and cataclysmic event of modern history. The influence of the American Revolution was felt in every modern and ultimately in every ancient nation, but it was experienced as a set of ideas and principles. The relative powerlessness of America made its ideas all the more potent, but the French Revolution was an explosion of human energy too vast to be fully comprehensible. Customs and institutions hundreds of years old disappeared in the smoke of Napoleon's cannon. The rise and fall of the guillotine was like a metronome. Tens of thousands perished under its merciless blade. Thousands of others were drowned, burned, or murdered in their beds. Hundreds of thousands of Austrian, British, German, Italian, Portuguese, Spanish, Egyptian, Turkish, Syrian, Russian, and French soldiers were killed or maimed or died of disease and malnutrition. It was a convulsion more dreadful than any in nature, an upheaval that, in its protracted agony, changed the course of history.

To the great majority of Americans, Europe was as remote as the moon, and their notions of it were a kind of ragbag of clichés and stereotypes—senile kings, corrupt aristocrats, downtrodden peasants, and so on. A hundred years or more would pass before the consequences of the French Revolution could be properly assessed. It was as though the old order, in breaking open, had revealed, even as the new order was struggling to be born, glimpses of hell. The Anti-Federalist Republican-Democrats had, in their fanatical attachment to the French Revolution, hitched their wagon to a very erratic star whose every wild gyration they felt obliged to explain and excuse. In this they demonstrated another conspicuous American trait—the espousal of the causes of all those in other parts of the globe who, downtrodden and oppressed, sought to unburden themselves of their oppressors. This was part of what a modern English critic has called "the radical universalism" of the American Revolution.

While, as we have seen, the framers of the Constitution purported to act on behalf of all mankind, it seems clear that the ranks of the Federalists in general contained more practical businessmen and enterprising land speculators than idealists. The Revolutionary leaders had, in the latter days of the war when the Confederation so often seemed ready to come apart at the seams, expressed the conviction that the hope for freedom everywhere in the world depended on the success or failure of the American Revolution. By this reading, the French Revolution was the first sign of that revolutionary ardor, which, it had been hoped, would sweep away all citadels of unjust and oppressive authority. The fate of the French Revolution was thus intimately associated with that of the American Revolution. Peter Duponceau, the Philadelphia lawyer, argued that if the French Revolution were aborted, the reactionary forces in the United States would take heart from its defeat and fasten a strict and repressive regime on the United States. They thus, in a manner of speaking, *superimposed the French Revolution on the American Revolution.* By melding the two, they committed themselves to justifying the unjustifiable. In this they remind us of the liberal intellectuals of the United States (and a number of Western European countries) in the 1930s who, having embraced the cause of Soviet communism, were forced to justify every horror of the Stalin regime.

It could also be argued that the Anti-Federalist Republican-Democrats were instinctively combating a phenomenon that had not yet been given a name—what came to be known as counterrev-olution—the tendency of all revolutions to move rapidly toward authoritarian forms of government and excessive bureaucratization. It was this possibility that had so troubled Jefferson and led to his eccentric proposal that property be redistributed and laws junked every nineteen years. In view of all this, it may not be unreasonable to assume that under the general looniness of more fanatical Franco-philes there was forming a kind of bedrock democratic consciousness, what we might term today "a lower-middle-class and working-class ego support system," by means of which groups in the society that had never had any substantial voice in their own affairs manifested their determination to force their leaders to take seriously that stirring blasphemy, *Vox populi, vox Dei.*

Such an explanation of Gallomania is reinforced by a remarkable exercise in political theory entitled "The Key of Liberty," written by a semiliterate farmer of Billerica, Massachusetts, William Manning. We have encountered Manning earlier as a spokesman for the doctrine of original sin, who described man as having "so strongly implanted in him a desire of Selfe Seporte, Selfe Defence, Selfe Love, Self Conceit, Selfe Importance, & Selfe agrandisement, that it Ingroses all his care and attention so that he can see nothing beyond Selfe. . . . Give a man honour & he wants more. Give him power & he wants more. Give him money & he wants more. In short he is never easy, but the more he has the more he wants."

In "The Key of Liberty" Manning described himself as someone who had "Never had the advantage of six months schooling in my life." Nor had he been more than "50 miles from where I was born in no direction." Yet he had always felt it his obligation "to search into & see for my selfe in all matters that consarned me as a member of society. . . . [Since the Revolution he had] bin a Constant Reader of public Newspapers & closely attended to men & measures ever since . . . through framing Constitutions, makeing & constructing laws, & seeing what selfish & contracted ideayes of interests would influence the best picked men & bodyes of men."

After an analysis of the origin and nature of republican government and the functions of its various branches, Manning added, "a free government is one in which all the laws are made & executed according to the will & interest of a majority of the hole peopel and not by the craft cunning & arts of the few." In order for the majority to be properly informed, "it is absolutely nesecary to have a larger degree or better means of knowledge amongue the peopel." Manning gave a detailed account of the way that those who had power—"the few"— used it to further their own interests at the expense of "the many."

The "grate shuffel"—the sharp differences between the few and the many—centers on the control and use of money. "As the interests & incomes of the few lays chiefly in money at interest, rents, salaryes, & fees that are fixed on the nominal value of money, they are interested in haveing money scarce & the price of labour & produce as low as possable. For instance if the prices of labour & produce should fall one halfe it would be just the same to the few as if their rents fees & salleryes were doubled." If the many, on the other hand, could raise the price of labor by a half and "have the mony circulate freely they could pay their debts, eat & drink & injoy the good of their labour with out being dependant on the few for assistance."

Manning was convinced that the new federal Constitution provided the political means for the many to defend themselves against the exploitative tendencies of the few, but the problem was that the few were more mobile, more articulate, better able to concert their interests. They controlled, in large part, the means of communication and the avenues to power. In Manning's words, the few, "to gain the power they cant constitutionally obtain, Always indevour to git it by cunning & corruption. . . . To efect this no cost or pains is spared, but they first unite their plans & sheems by asotiations, conventions, & coraspondances with each other. The Marchents asotiate by themselves in Chambers of Commerce, the Phitisians by themselves, The Ministers by themselves, the Juditial & Executive Officers are by their professions often called together & know each others minds, & all letirary men & the over grown rich, that can live without labouring, can spare time for consultation. All being bound together by common interest . . . join . . . to counteract the interests of the many & pick their pockets, which is effected ondly for want of the meens of knowledge amongue them."

Manning's principal villains were the land speculators and stock-jobbers, who "not ondly swindle honest individuals out of their property, but by their bribery & corruption have grate influence in our elections, & agitate our publick Counsels."

Doctors had established "Meditial Societyes" and, under the name of eliminating "Quacary of all kinds," had so far raised their own fees "that a poor man can git so grate cures of them now for a ginna [a guinea, ten dollars], as he could fifty years ago of an old Squaw for halfe a pint of Rhum." The delivery of a baby, which fifty years earlier would be done by a midwife for "halfe a doller," had been monopolized by doctors and now "costs a poor man 5 hole [dollars]."

"Marchents," ministers of the gospel, and lawyers were all part of the network of the few. Teachers and scholars were hardly better, "for if we apply for a preacher or a School Master, we are told the price So Much, & they cant go under, for it is agreed upon & they shall be disgrased if they take less."

The remedy, in Manning's judgment, for the constant encroachments of the few upon the rights of the many, was the organization of the "many" into societies for the advancement of their own best interests. The few were, after all, simply acting as all men were disposed to do. Manning was not opposed to "the asotiations of any ordirs of men, for to hinder it would hinder their improvements in their professions, & hinder them for being servisable to the Many." He simply wanted the many to emulate the few. He proposed a "Society of Republicans & Labourers" to be "divided into mctings like the ordir of Cincinaty, viz.—Class—Town—County—State & Continental Meetings." Most important of all, it would have its own newspaper to keep its members informed on all matters that affected their interests as laborers.

Manning was an enthusiastic supporter of the "Democraticle" societies "made up of men of Republican prinsaples & grate abilityes who did all in their power to inliten the peopel into their true Interests," and for their pains were constantly attacked by the Federalists—"their eyes would sparkel, their chins quiver, & they would call them Jacobins, Shasites, Disorganizers & Enemyes to all government."

What makes Manning's essay so important (it was never published and was not discovered among family papers until the 1950s) is that however much historians wish to recapture the feelings and attitudes of ordinary men and women, particularly those of what Manning calls "the labouring classes"—those who make their living by working with their hands—most of the written material available to them is the product of the few, the educated and articulate upper classes who, however intelligent and even humane they may be, view society quite differently from those whose existential situation is entirely different. It is interesting, in this respect, to compare Madison's statements in the Federal Convention and in the tenth *Federalist* paper about the opposing interests in a society with Manning's. Both men reasoned from the same premises: people were inherently selfish and disposed to promote their own best interests. Madison believed that a government could be so skillfully fashioned that the legitimate interests of every group could be protected; Manning saw the flaw in that proposition. No matter how cleverly a government was constructed, it could not protect the powerless from the powerful. Only they could protect themselves. The proper arrangement of the government was thus only the first step. The critical issue was whether the many could convert their technical majority into genuine power.

The decade of the 1790s tested this proposition with rather inconclusive results. The historian is often tempted to pass judgments. It is human to prefer one side over another. At the same time, the historian has a responsibility for doing justice to all parties. Thus, a dialectical method is perhaps the soundest. The Federalists had to their credit the most impressive accomplishment in political history—the federal Constitution. That was the thesis. Since they were only human, it was perhaps inevitable, in the very nature of the political process itself, that they should be insensitive to the demands of the many and be alarmed at the formation of a democratic "temper" among ordinary citizens of the Republic. This is especially so when we consider how repugnant to sober, thoughtful Americans were the excesses of the French Revolution. The Republicans were the antithesis. Their suspicions of the few, of the money manipulators, stockjobbers, speculators, bankers, and their allies—the officers of the government, the ministers, lawyers, scholars, and doctors—were an essential corrective. Each side, in the manner of political opponents generally, if not universally, painted the other in the most extreme and exaggerated colors—veritable caricatures.

Under the circumstances it is not surprising that many Americans of various political persuasions felt little hope that the Republic could long survive. Ironically, it may have been the fact that the political polarization caused by the French Revolution was entangled with sectional jealousies and divisions that prevented the country from splitting irretrievably over events in a nation three thousand miles away—that and the fact that every new report of atrocities caused some falling off from the French faction.

The real issues could not be faced; they were only hinted at, alluded to. On the deepest level, they were sectional differences, and the sectional differences ultimately revolved around the insoluble problem of slavery. In the seven Southern states, John Adams garnered 9 electoral votes, 5 in Maryland and 4 in North Carolina, out of a total of 56. It was the same in New England. The 49 votes of those states all went to Adams, not one to Jefferson.

So, in essence, the election of 1800 was less a contest between Republican and Federalist principles and policies than between North and South, slavery and nonslavery, though that issue was seldom referred to. It was also, of course, more than that. It was a manifestation of the new Secular-Democratic Consciousness and of the particular quality of American democracy with its innate and ineradicable suspicion of power and wealth and social pretension.

Thus, the principal significance of the election may be said to have been symbolic. On the practical political level, things went on much as before, but the election registered a kind of sea change in the temper of the American people, a slight but highly significant shift in attitudes and perceptions. We now know that the makers of revolutions invariably show considerable ingenuity in turning them to their own advantage, usually through the creation of bureaucracies that they control. It is not unreasonable to assume that the makers of the American Revolution were involved in this same "natural law of revolutions." They were consolidating their own power and doing their best to insure privileged positions for themselves. Their opponents had no language to describe this process. They had to use old words like "monarchy" and "aristocracy" to describe new institutions and interests like "bureaucracy" and "financial oligarchy."

However, when all is said and done, there remains a quantum of Republican and Federalist rage difficult to account for. It found its expression in the press in an outpouring of vituperation never again equaled by partisan newspapers in the United States. Of course Americans of both political persuasions quite seriously feared for the existence of the Republic. If the Republic expired in the agonies of its birth, monarchy, tyranny, oppression, and exploitation would take heart and reassert themselves with renewed confidence everywhere.

There was thus a kind of escalation of invective. One attack provoked another. The Federalists insisted that the rancor and bitternesses, the libelousness of the attacks on the government stemmed from the fact that the editors of many of the Republican newspapers were aliens. There were a striking number of foreign editors (most of them Irish) among the ranks of the Republican journalists—Thomas Cooper, Callender, Duane, and, on the Federalist side, William Cobbett. But there were also many native Americans, and the model, Bache, was after all the grandson of Benjamin Franklin.

In addition to the fact that it was generally believed that the times were desperate, one suspects there was another very potent element in the equation. The newspapers of the young Republic may be accounted the first free press in history. It was as though all the subterranean words and feelings that had been bottled up for centuries—all the suppressed suspicion and hostility toward *all* forms of authority—suddenly came bubbling up out of the darker recesses of the psyche like molten lava from an erupting volcano. A new form of human expression was suddenly available. (There had of course been newspapers in England and America for over a century, but they suffered numerous constraints and inhibitions.) The temptation to explore it to its limits was irresistible. What we might call "verbal types" were attracted to American journalism as bees are to sugar or vultures to carrion. A modern analogy suggests itself. The disappearance in the present age of constraints on sexual matters has been followed by a compulsive effort to break every taboo and push verbal and visual representations of sexuality to their ultimate limits.

But whatever the explanation for the excesses of journalists like Bache or Cobbett, the essential fact the student of our history must grasp firmly is that our earliest years as a nation were characterized by an almost pathological rage and bitterness, reflected in, and undoubtedly accentuated by, our newly free press; and that that rage and bitterness are very much at odds with our image of ourselves as a happy and united people from the moment of our birth. Furthermore, that rage and bitterness were not soon or easily dissipated.

It is not so much that we have concealed these facts as that we have failed to contemplate their meaning. The contemplation of the facts raises troubling ambiguities, and Americans have no theoretical apparatus for dealing with ambiguity; that is to say, Americans have no tradition, no "philosophy," no "symbol system," no psychology, no religion, no political science—in short, no conception of man and his relation to the world that enables them to deal with the tragic and ambiguous nature of that human history of which the history of the United States is merely a subdivision, although a fascinating and important one.

Viewing the election of 1800 in retrospect, we can say with considerable confidence that however much sympathy we may feel for John Adams, who was a reasonably good president and plainly deserved the second term that he so strongly desired (that sympathy may of course, be more strongly felt in the breast of the writer than of the reader), it was most fortunate that Jefferson and the Republicans triumphed. Despite their fanatical and ill-informed devotion to the French Revolution and their naive notions of the nature of government, the country very much needed to have them accede to power. To have been excluded for another four years simply to do justice to the incumbent president would almost certainly have driven them mad (they were verging on that state). Power—at least properly limited constitutional power—has been observed to have a sobering effect on those who achieve it. It brought the great majority of Republicans to their senses, just as the loss of it drove a good many Federalists out of theirs.

Finally, as we have suggested, it may very well have prevented the accumulation of power in the hands of what we might call "the Revolutionary elite," the able and ambitious men who provided the leadership in the Revolution itself and assumed, quite naturally, that they were best qualified to continue to exercise it in peace as they had in war.

Having said all that, we must pause a moment to give credit to the Federalists for their remarkable achievements. If this sounds like a requiem, it is of course. The Federalists, while they clung to small corners of power and influence and enjoyed a few revivals sparked by unpopular Jeffersonian measures, were, for all practical purposes, ushered off the stage of history with the election of 1800. Before their timely demise, however, they had created a Constitution and initiated a government. We persist in our argument that only their consciousness could have created just and efficient agencies of self-government. The radical democratic consciousness that brought them down might have the capacity to identify and check dangerous concentrations of power and function as a jealous watchdog of American "liberties," but it was totally devoid of even the beginnings of a notion of how a government might be created. It demonstrated that fact quite amply by its muddleheaded devotion to the French Revolution, which is not, of course, to say that the French Revolution did not have much about it that could be viewed with awe, astonishment, and a mild degree of hope. It was, after all, the catalyst for a new social and political order, the second of the great revolutions that have transformed the modern world. With the election of 1800 much of its ideological superstructure became engrafted on the American consciousness, and that, ironically, at the moment when it was in the process of becoming a classic military dictatorship.

The Federalists' most representative men were Washington and, to a more modest degree, Hamilton and Adams, and their epitaph the Constitution. One need say no more for them.

17

The Protestant Passion

On December 31, 1800, Dr. Nathaniel Ames noted in his diary: "Here ends the 18th Century. The 19th begins with a fine clear morning wind at S.W.; and the political horizon affords as fine a prospect under Jefferson's administration, with returning harmony with France—with the irresistible propagation of the Rights of Man, the eradication of hierarchy, oppression, superstition and tyranny over the world, by means of that soul-improving genius-polisher; the palladium of all our national joys—the printing press, whose value tho' unknown by the vulgar slave, cannot be sufficiently appreciated by those who would distain to better the image of God." These fine, enlightened sentiments could be taken as a manifesto of the Secular-Democratic Consciousness. The new age had just experienced a miraculous revival. To Ames, the entwined principles of the American and French revolutions seemed triumphant everywhere. The printing press was the means for the universal dissemination of their truths; and these, once absorbed by the virtuous citizen, would insure the advance of civilization to ever greater heights of prosperity and rational bliss.

A Republican Congress, enchanted by the prospect of the new century opening before it and mindful of the remarkable transformations affected in the century past, commissioned the Reverend Samuel Miller to prepare *A Brief Retrospect of the Eighteenth Century* for general distribution. We too may well take the occasion to look at Americans at the turn of the century in a broader perspective. We are all aware that men and women do not live by politics alone. Indeed politics is primarily an "end product," the particular practical form certain ideas and aspirations take when they are ready to enter history. Culture precedes and largely determines politics.

If the practical activities of Americans in the first decade of the new nation were in large part dictated by the need to domesticate the geography and carry forward the task of inhabiting a limitless landscape, an inner landscape, the landscape of ideas, determined how that task would be accomplished. The most prominent element in that inner landscape was Protestant Christianity. Just as the Revolution itself is unimaginable without the particular consciousness created by Re-formed Christianity, the subsequent history of the United States must be inscrutable without close attention to it. This statement may seem to the reader to contain an obvious contradiction. I have been at some pains to describe the manner in which the Classical-Christian Consciousness was being eroded and, in many ways, largely supplanted by the Secular-Democratic Consciousness; transmuted into the Secular-Democratic Conscionsness might be a more accurate way to put it. In the wake of Max Weber's study of the Protestant ethic and the spirit of capitalism, historians have generally acknowledged the decisive influence of Protestantism on a wide range of American characteristics and attitudes that persisted long after the *total* Calvinist system had been discarded. The residues that remained or that were grafted on the Enlightenment view of man and the world were of great importance. While, in the social and political realm, the new consciousness dominated, transferring to the United States, as we have noted before, many of the attributes of God, and reading American history as though we had escaped collectively from the "tragedy of history," on the level of individual personal faith, and even on the level of social motivation, most Americans both considered themselves Christians and clung to important elements of Christian doctrine, specifically the divinity of Christ and the Trinitarian creed. Since man is not, except fitfully, a rational animal, the vast majority of Americans did not trouble themselves excessively over the fact that they held fast to two basically contradictory intellectual and/or religious systems or explanations of reality. We were, after all, destined to be a schizophrenic people.

We have already seen religion mixed into politics, most conspicuously in the election of 1800 with the charges of atheism leveled against Jefferson. The fact that such charges had little if any effect on the outcome of the election can be, I think, taken as indication of two things. First, in the upsurge of zeal for the French Revolution many Americans found themselves attached to traditional religious denominations more through formality than piety. Second, they were no longer sophisticated enough religiously to make much sense of the charges against Jefferson or to take them very seriously. Those who took the trouble to find out what he had said discovered that they, in large part, agreed with him.

Calvin, as the reader will recall, propounded the doctrine of predestination. God had, from the beginning of time, determined which souls were to be saved and which damned, and there was no escape from this destiny. Good or bad, pious or heretical though the individual Christian might be, he or she could do nothing to change what was predestined. Faithful Christians might observe every commandment, attend church punctiliously, be dutiful servants of the Lord, and still have no assurance of gaining heaven. To be sure, they searched untiringly for a sign that they were among the elect, the saints, and when they received the "sign" they worried for fear it was a false sign, the result of their yearning for a sign. They were constantly tempted by Arminianism, the doctrine that one could earn salvation by faith and good works. Orthodox Calvinists resisted Arminianism, seductive as it was, because it transferred power from God to man. If the individual could earn salvation, he or she was in that sense a rival of the Almighty and God's omnipotence was diminished.

If God were omnipotent, part of his omnipotence must be that he had foreknowledge of everything that would happen in human history from the beginning to the end of time. Thus, he had to know who was to be saved and who damned. It was too rigorous a doctrine for ordinary mortals, and time softened its harsh outlines. The notion crept in that those who were demonstrably pious, full of good works, and fortunate in their worldly concerns had, in effect, received marks of divine favor. The children of the saints were assumed to be saints also, even in the absence of a clear sign. Enlightenment ideas, a growing faith in the reasonable and rational powers of human beings, gnawed away at the roots of the tree of Calvinism. As the Congregationalists (the Puritans) grew more worldly and successful, their attention to the basic tenets of their faith became more and more formal observances lacking in the almost fanatical piety of the original settlers.

The Great Awakening of the 1740s had been an effort to rekindle the emotional fires of the Puritan forebears. It had split the church into New Lights—those who sought to recover the charismatic, emotional character of their faith— and the Old Lights, who objected to "ranting sermons" and irrational utterances; and it had greatly encouraged the growth of the Baptists and later the Methodists, who made no bones of their emotional, "evangelical" predisposition.

What had in fact happened to the Congregationalists was what was to happen to virtually every Protestant denomination throughout American history. Starting with an intensely emotional religious experience that emphasized faith, piety, and austerity, it had grown more rational and more worldly as its members prospered. Increasingly it became the religious badge of the New England ruling class, the establishment. And when it was no longer in touch with the needs of the more marginal members of the society who required some theological response to the often hard and bitter realities of life in America, a new religious group or denomination appeared to cater to those needs.

The story was much the same with the Quakers, who had, in their infancy, startled conventional churchgoers by stripping off their clothes and running naked through the "steeple houses," as they termed the churches, to dramatize the coldness and spiritual corruption of the established church, and had literally quaked with emotion. Now, like the Congregationalists, they were less emotional and more rational. They stressed meditation and the "inner light" and combined simplicity with worldliness in their own neat amalgam.

It was much the same with the Presbyterians, who considered themselves, if anything, more Calvinistic than the Congregationalists and differed from them in church organization.

The Anglicans, who turned into the Episcopalians when the Revolution forced them to cast off their subordination to the Church of England, maintained a comfortably relaxed form of the Catholic liturgy and, by emphasizing ritual over dogma and reason over emotion, sailed quite placidly along, more or less immune to the ups and downs of the other denominations. In every state of the Union the Protestant Episcopal church tended to be preeminently the church of the well-to-do and the wellborn. It made no great demands on its members and was notably genteel. It rested quite splendidly on the

Book of Common Prayer, perhaps the most notable accomplishment of the English Reformation and one of the great devotional works in the history of religion.

The strength of the respective denominations in 1800 (the country contained some 3,105 congregations and religious groups) is estimated roughly as follows: Congregationalists, some 600,000; Episcopalians, 530,000; Presbyterians, 450,000; Quakers, 50,000; Baptists, 40,000; Roman Catholics, 25,000; Methodists, 5,000. There were, in addition, some 2,000 Jews. Perhaps another 100,000 Americans belonged to a variety of smaller Protestant sects like the German Pietists.

The Protestant denominations were subject, as we have noted, to both class and geographical categorization. The Episcopalians were concentrated in the South, especially in the planter aristocracy of that section. The Baptists were concentrated in the Southern frontier, though they were by no means limited to that region. The Presbyterians were also well represented by frontier missionary efforts, as was the infant Methodist church, which more than any other denomination was to be identified with the frontier, largely through the efforts of its famous circuit riders.

The Catholics were overwhelmingly Irish and were found predominantly in Pennsylvania. In that state the Dutch and German Reformed and Lutheran churches, all deriving from European Calvinism, numbered some 200,000 members between them. In addition there were three pietist churches, descending in large part from the German pre-Reformation reformer John Huss—Moravians, Mennonites, and Dunkards. All were from the Germanic principalities. The Moravians were distinguished by their devotion to the religious music of the Bach family.

The Baptists, as the Reverend Charles Woodmason had put it, "by their Address & Assiduity . . . wormed the Presbyterians out of all their strong Holds," making them "the most numerous and formidable Body of people . . . in the Interior and Back parts of the Province [North Carolina]." A Congregational minister, Noah Worcester, attributed their success to the "confident manner, and affecting tone, with which they address the passions of their hearers." Worcester added: "Many people are so ignorant, as to be more charmed with sound than sense. And to them, the want of knowledge in a teacher . . . may easily be made up, and overbalanced, by great zeal, an affecting tone of voice, and a perpetual motion of the tongue. If a speaker can keep his tongue running, in an unremitting manner . . . and can quote . . . a large number of texts from within the covers of the Bible, it matters not, to many of his hearers whether he speaks sense or nonsense."

Reason might rule in Boston, but religious emotionalism carried the day on the frontier. We sometimes think of the frontier as made up of sober, solid men and women (or reckless cowboys), but the fact is that the frontier was characterized by often desperately hard and depressing conditions—disease, death, psychological breakdown, and, not infrequently, suicide. Under such intense pressures, only wild outpourings of emotion preserved people's sanity. The religious revival was the most characteristic expression of the frontier settlement. Richard McNemar was a frontier preacher in Kentucky who described the revival of 1800 in that state. "It first began," he wrote, "in individuals who had been under deep convictions of sin, and great trouble about their souls." As they came to a conviction of their salvation, "they were constrained to cry out, with tears and trembling, and . . . to warn their fellow creatures of the danger of continuing in sin. . . . Under such exhortations, the people began to be affected in a very strange manner. At first they were taken with an inward throbbing of heart; then with weeping and trembling: from that to crying out, in apparent agony of soul; falling down and swooning away till every appearance of animal life was suspended, and the person appeared to be in a trance."

From these "small beginnings" the revival spirit spread, "and these strange exercises still increasing, and having no respect to any stated hours of worship, it was found expedient to encamp on the ground, and continue the meeting day and night. To these encampments the people flooded in hundreds and thousands, on foot, on horseback, and in wagons and other carriages. [The meetings] exhibited . . . a scene of confusion that would scarce be put into human language. . . . No sex or color, class or description, were exempted from the pervading influence of the spirit; . . . from the age of eight months to sixty years, there were evident subjects of this marvelous operation."

The climactic meeting, attended by more than 4,000 persons, lasted five days. McNemar wrote: "How persons, so different in their education, manners and natural dispositions, without any visible commander, could enter upon such a scene, and continue in it for days and nights in perfect harmony, has been one of the greatest wonders that ever the world beheld." Other observers of frontier revivals noted that some of the participants fainted, while others were seized by the "barks," barking like dogs and running about on all fours, and some jerked spasmodically as though possessed. Such phenomena disgusted respectable churchgoers and confirmed them in their opinion that the majority of frontier settlers were little better than the savages whose right to the land they contested.

If we were to take three essential dogmas as representing Christian orthodoxy, we might list the doctrine of Christ's divinity (that he was both God and man); his death on the cross and the resurrection; and the doctrine of the Trinity (that the Godhead consists of three persons or manifestations of the divine: God the Father, God the Son, and God the Holy Ghost or Holy Spirit). Of these three dogmas, or essential beliefs, the last is undoubtedly the most important. Without going into a historical-theological account of the origin of the Trinity, it is sufficient to say that the practical effect of the doctrine is to preserve the notion of a "living God" who remains actively concerned with every soul on earth. If God is, in some increasingly difficult to imagine heaven, His Holy Spirit "dwells among us" and is constantly accessible. We might call this view theistic, or theism. The rational skepticism of the Enlightenment, summarized in Descartes' "I think, therefore I am," had particular difficulty with the doctrine of the Trinity, which appeared to the enlightened consciousness to be blatantly illogical. How could one be three?

Almost as hard to swallow was the illogical proposition that Jesus Christ was both human and divine. There were problems as well with the crucifixion of Jesus and his resurrection, but the Trinity was the major stumbling block. The effect of the Enlightenment on Christians was somewhat as follows (allowing always, of course, for infinite variations). The notion of a God was almost universally accepted; hence, deism. Christ was thought of as a wise and good man, the greatest of the prophets of Christianity, the supreme moral teacher. Whether God was an active principle in the universe or had simply created it to run by certain "natural laws" without His active intervention was a moot point with those who considered themselves rational Christians.

Benjamin Franklin, Benjamin Rush, and John Adams are helpful in measuring the changes in Christian doctrine that characterized the period we are discussing. As a young man, Franklin had tried to achieve moral perfection by making a list of twelve virtues (to which he subsequently added humility) and trying to achieve perfection in each of them in turn by a week of concentrated effort.

The Enlightenment had adapted the Christian notion of perfection achieved in the afterlife and applied it to man's earthly existence. The Christian sought to do God's will but, knowing himself or herself sunk in original sin, did not aspire to perfection in this world. The young Franklin, who was what we might call an Enlightenment Christian, having dismissed the notion of original sin, apparently did not think it presumptuous to try to achieve perfection.

In his twenty-first year he stated his "First Principles" of religion. "I believe there is one supreme, most perfect Being, Author and Father of the Gods themselves. . . . Also, when I stretch my Imagination thro' and beyond our System of Planets, beyond the visible fix'd Stars themselves, into that Space that is every Way infinite, and conceive it fill'd with Suns like ours, each with a Chorus of Worlds forever moving round him, then this little Ball on which we move, seems, even in my narrow Imagination, to be almost Nothing, and myself less than nothing, and of no sort of Consequence." Under such circumstances, Franklin could not imagine that the "Supremely Perfect" could deign to pay any attention to "such an inconsiderable Nothing as Man" and believed it was even less likely that He should require "Worship or Praise from us."

Nonetheless, since all men had in them a "natural principle, which inclines them to DEVOTION, or the Worship of some unseen Power . . . I think it seems required of me, and my Duty as a Man, to pay Divine Regards to *something*." Assuming that under the one Supreme God there were a number of lesser gods each responsible for his own particular planetary system, it was to the God of this universe that Franklin intended to offer his "praise and adoration." He was anxious to have this God as his friend, and he believed that He would be most pleased with him if he, Franklin, was first virtuous and then happy, "since without Virtue Man can have no Happiness in this World."

Since it seemed clear to Franklin that this God wished him to be without "Passion or Perturbation" but rather "elevated with Rational Joy and Pleasure," he would pray regularly to Him, "O Creator, O Father! I believe that thou art Good, and that thou art pleas'd with the pleasure of thy children. Praised be thy name for Ever!"

While Franklin thought it undignified and inappropriate to pray for worldly things, he nonetheless mentioned, in passing as it were, his hopes that his "Father will not withold from me a suitable share of Temporal Blessings, if by a Virtuous and holy Life I conciliate his Favour and Kindness." He also hoped that his Father would preserve him "from Atheism & Infidelity, Impiety, and Profaneness" and assist him in avoiding "Irreverence and ostentation, Formality and Odious Hypocrisy." Franklin then proceeded to list all the human failings he wished his Father's aid in overcoming.

A number of things might be said about this appealing document. While it is, in many ways, very much the work of a young man, there is no reason to believe that Franklin changed his mind substantially during his long lifetime. His "First Principles" were consistent with an effort to describe the basis of a "rational" Christianity, what science knew of the universe. He wished for "Rational Joy" and to avoid "Passion and Perturbation." But his "Adorations" and "Petitions" are adapted from the liturgies of the medieval church. There is no mention of Christ, the Son, or of the Holy Spirit. Underlying Franklin's theology is the notion that anyone can pretty much make up his own religion to suit himself. In addition, there is a strong emphasis on the importance of "pleasure." Franklin reiterates his conviction that the "Father" wishes His children to be happy. He is here undoubtedly reacting to his childhood experience of New England Puritanism-Congregationalism with its suspicion of worldly pleasures. When the positive injunctions of the Puritans to redeem the world had lost their force, only the negative injunctions remained, and these had clearly pressed hard on the young Franklin, who, like the old Franklin, had an enormous capacity for the sensuous delights with which life abounded.

The other, much younger Philadelphia Benjamin—Rush—had an intellectual biography that was similar in many ways to that of Franklin. It must be said that while Franklin had mapped out his course in religious matters at an early age with a thoroughness typical of him, Rush was all his life "a seeker," never resting long in one opinion and constantly reexamining and often modifying his beliefs.

Starting out as a Presbyterian, Rush parted company with that denomination because he became convinced that while "doing good" was the main object of the Christian, "The clergy and their faithful followers . . . are *too good* to *do good*." Thereafter he attended Episcopalian, Baptist, and Presbyterian churches and, for a time, considered himself an Episcopalian. In his later years he wrote to John Adams that his creed was "a compound of the orthodoxy and heterodoxy of most of our Christian churches."

As a young man, Rush, like Franklin, occupied himself with "the sublime study of Divinity" and wrote to a friend that to have been a minister "would be my most delightful employment," since "to spend and be spent for the Good of Mankind is what I chiefly aim at." He had decided, reluctantly, that he was not suited for the ministry and must give his attention to "the study of Physic," that is, medicine. That, he felt, was a field almost as important as the ministry, since it dealt with "the weakness and mortality of human nature."

Rush's early correspondence with his friend Ebenezer Hazard is full of piety and lamentations over the "low ebb" of religion and the terrors of death, "so much the King of Terrors that even pious men shrink from it," and gloomy reflections about the shortness of life and the vanity of human endeavors.

Some twenty years later, his letters began once more to contain numerous reflections on religion. While Rush seems never to have seriously engaged himself in theological problems as such, his correspondence is full of expressions of conventional piety. The extent of his theological naivete is suggested by a letter to British radical Richard Price in which Rush declares that he has "embraced the doctrines of universal salvation and final restitution," adding that his belief in these doctrines "is founded wholly upon the Calvinistical account (and which I believe to be the *tenor* of Scripture) of the person, power, goodness, mercy, and other divine attributes of the Saviour of the World. These principles . . . have bound me to the whole human race; these are the principles which animate me in all my labors for the interests of my fellow creatures. No particle of benevolence, no wish for the liberty of a slave or the reformation of a criminal, will be lost. They must all be finally made effectual, for they all flow from the great Author of goodness, who implants no principles of action in man in vain."

Rush noted with pleasure "the progress of reason and liberty in Europe." He saw them "as preludes to a glorious manifestation of [the power and influence of the Gospel] upon the hearts of men." What had begun as a movement designed to bring "liberty to the whole world" would, in time, bring something even better, "the salvation of all mankind."

To Jeremy Belknap, Rush wrote: "It is the Spirit of the Gospel (though unacknowledged) which is now rooting monarchy out of the world. . . . How truly worthy of God who styles himself LOVE is that religion which is opposed to everything which disturbs or violates the order and happiness of society. . . . Yes, my friend, I anticipate with a joy which I cannot describe the speedy end of the misery of Africans, of the tyranny of kings, of the pride of ecclesiastical institutions. . . . I anticipate the end of war and such a superlative tenderness for human life as will exterminate capital punishments from all our systems of legislation. . . . It is possible we may not live to witness the approaching regeneration of our world, but the more active we are in bringing it about, the more fitted we shall be for that world where justice and benevolence eternally prevail."

Writing again to Belknap, Rush observed: "A belief in God's universal love to all his creatures, and that he will finally restore all those of them that are miserable to happiness is a *polar* truth. It leads to all truths upon all subjects, more especially upon the subjects of government. It establishes the equality of mankind—it abolishes the punishment of death for any crime—and converts jails into houses of repentance and reformation. All truths are related, or rather there is but one truth. Republicanism is a part of the truth of Christianity."

Rush's theology was as strongly influenced by Enlightenment notions as Franklin's more specifically deistic principles. Calvin did not, of course, preach the doctrine of universal salvation—far from it. He insisted on the predestined salvation of only a handful of saints. He did not exhort the faithful to do good but to make faith the foundation of their lives. Rush's conviction that nothing good was lost and all would, in the end, work for the best is far from the tragic sense of history that I have argued was an essential component of the Classical Christian Consciousness. Beneath Rush's expressions of piety one can plainly discern the general American faith in "progress on and up." An enemy of capital punishment, Rush wrote to Jeremy Belknap, that "The Son of Man came not to destroy men's *lives*, but to *save* them [is] a passage that at once refutes all the arguments that ever were offered in favor of slavery, war, and capital punishments."

Rush is also important as a prototype of the American reformer. Perhaps the most crucial element of the Enlightenment to enter the mainstream of American Protestantism was the notion that human society could be perfected, not by reason alone (as the theorists of the French Revolution argued), but by reason informed and guided by the teachings of Christ and applied vigorously wherever human deficiencies appeared.

Devoted as he was to science, Rush was convinced that reason alone could not improve the human condition. He wrote to Noah Webster, who was compiling his dictionary and who had been, in Rush's view, excessive in his reliance on human reason in a Fourth of July oration: "Alas! my friend, I fear all our attempts to produce political happiness by the solitary use of human reason will be as fruitless as the search for the philosopher's stone. . . . It seems reserved to Christianity alone to produce universal, moral, political, and physical happiness. Reason produces, it is true, great and popular truths, but it affords *motives* too feeble to induce mankind to act agreeably to them. . . . I anticipate nothing but suffering to the human race while the present systems of paganism, deism, and atheism prevail in the world."

To do good was man's highest calling, in Rush's view, and to him there could be no end to it. When John Dickinson, old and ailing, wrote to Rush that he wished only "rest," Rush replied: "Remember, my dear friend, that 'none liveth to himself.' Even our old age is not our own property. All its fruits of wisdom and experience belong to the public. 'To do good' is the business of *life*. 'To enjoy *rest*' is the happiness of heaven. We pluck premature or forbidden fruit when we grasp at *rest* on this side of the grave."

One has the feeling that Rush's God was very much like Rush himself—devoted to doing good, intelligent, reasonable, humane, and reform-minded.

Rush's friend, John Adams, gives us still another reading on the permutations of Calvinism produced by the so-called Age of Reason. Adams, of course, considered himself the eternal enemy of those Enlightenment ideas that found their most striking expression in the French philosophers—men such as Diderot, Condorcet, Rousseau, and Voltaire—and he filled his copies of their works with contemptuous exclamations. His special scorn was reserved for the notion of human perfectibility. Firmly committed to the doctrine of original sin (or inherent human depravity), he viewed such utopian doctrines as "mischievous nonsense."

Where Rush simply ignored the doctrine of original sin, Adams made it the center of his social and political system. He considered himself a Christian, and when reading a history of philosophy by the French author Depuis, who argued against revealed religion, Adams noted indignantly: "If you neither love, honor, admire, or fear this, your own universe, you are an idiot and deserve no conversation or correspondence with rational beings!" If Depuis did love and honor the world, what was that but worship? To those who maintained that the sin and suffering in the world argued against the existence of a merciful and omnipotent God (who surely could right these wrongs), Adams replied with the conventional Christian argument that God did not "interpose His power to prevent [evil] because this would destroy that liberty without which there would be no moral good or evil in the universe." What then would be left but "a mere chemical process, a mere mechanical engine to produce nothing but pleasure?" Granted that the world was composed of atoms, as the "physicalists" argued, "the question remains, who and what moves them."

When Joseph Priestley talked of human perfectibility, Adams asked Rush, did he and his followers mean that "chemical processes may be invented by which the human body may be rendered immortal and incapable of disease upon earth?" He considered the philosophers of the Enlightenment to be "honest enthusiasts carried away by the popular contagion of the times." The fact was, however, that "moral and political hysterics are at least as infectious as the smallpox or yellow fever."

But Adams himself was certainly a child of the Enlightenment and an ally of Rush in his belief that it was the duty of the Christian citizen to do his or her utmost "to amend and improve others and in every way ameliorate the lot of humanity; invent new medicines, construct new machines, write new books, build better houses and ships, institute better governments, discountenance false religions, propagate the only true one, diminish the vices, and increase the virtues of all men and women wherever we can."

Like Rush, Adams believed that the Bible contained "the most perfect philosophy, the most perfect morality, and the most refined policy" to be found and, above all, that it was "the most republican book in the world for in the observance of its commandments were to be found the only preservative of republics." If the commandments against fornication and adultery were widely and generally broken, a republic could not survive because its moral fibre would be eroded, the duties of citizenship would be subordinated to private lusts and pleasures.

As Adams understood it, "The Christian religion is the brightness of the glory and express portrait of the eternal, self-existent, independent, benevolent, all-powerful and all-merciful Creator, Preserver and Father of the Universe. Neither savage nor civilized man without a revelation could ever have discovered or invented it. Ask me not then whether I am a Catholic or Protestant, Calvinist or Arminian. As far as they are Christians, I wish to be a fellow disciple with them all."

Adams, like Rush, was concerned with the question of whether a nation could get along without religion. He sensed a growing spirit of skepticism, largely a product of the French Revolution, and it made him profoundly uneasy, but he comforted himself with the thought that people in general would "insist upon the risk of being damned rather than give up the hope of being saved in a future state. The people will have a life to come," he noted, "and so will I."

This latter remark sounds orthodox enough, but Adams, as did many of his fellow Congregationalists, found he could not accept certain Calvinist doctrines such as predestination and certain Christian dogmas such as the divinity of Christ, his death and resurrection, and the concept of the Trinity. To Adams, the notion that the "greatest man in history" should have ended his life nailed to a cross seemed blasphemous, the doctrine of the Trinity a theological puzzle of no importance.

Adams wrote to Jefferson when the two old men had resumed their correspondence: "It has been long, very long a settled opinion in my Mind that there is not now, never will be and never was but one being who can Understand the Universe. And that it is not only vain but wicked for insects to pretend to comprehend it. . . . No Mind, but one, can see through, the immeasurable System. It would be presumption and Impiety in me to dogmatize, on such Subjects. My duties, in my little infinitesimal Circle, I can understand and feel. The Duties of a Son, a Brother, a Father, a Neighbour, a Citizen, I can see and feel: But I trust the Ruler with his Skies."

The millennial impulse in more or less orthodox Christianity was perhaps best expressed by Samuel Hopkins in a widely reprinted sermon delivered in 1793 entitled "A Treatise on the Millennium." "The Millennium will be a time of great enjoyment, happiness and universal joy. . . . And this great increase of happiness and joy on earth will be the natural and even necessary consequence of the great degree and universality of knowledge and holiness, which all will then profess. The knowledge of God, and the Redeemer, and love to Him, will be source of unspeakable pleasure and joy in His character government and kingdom. . . . All outwardly worldly circumstances will then be agreeable and prosperous, and there will be for all, a sufficiency and fulness of every thing needed for the body, and for the comfort and convenience of every one. . . . [There would be no war] to impoverish, lay waste and destroy, [no extravagance or intemperance] in food and raiment and the use of the things of life. . . . Every thing . . . will be used with great prudence and economy. . . . Nothing will be sought to gratify pride or inordinate, sensual appetite or lust: So that there will be no waste of the things of life. Nothing will be lost."

The land itself would be far more productive, producing "twenty, thirty, sixty, and perhaps a hundred fold more. And that which is now esteemed barren, and not capable of producing any thing, by cultivation, will then yield much more, for the sustenance of man and beast, than that which is most productive now. . . . And in this way, the curse which has hitherto been upon the ground, for the rebellion of man, will be in a great measure removed. . . . Then, in a literal sense, the vallies shall be filled, and the mountains and the hills shall be low, and the crooked shall be made straight, and the rough ways shall be made smooth, to render traveling more convenient and easy, and the earth more productive and fertile."

That curious mixture of piety and millennial utopianism that developed in the United States was expressed by Samuel Adams, writing to congratulate Jefferson on "peace" (as it turned out, it was an extremely short interval). Adams assured the president that "the principles of Democratic Republicanism are already better understood than they were before; and that by the continued efforts of Men of Science and Virtue, they will extend more and more till the turbulent and destructive Spirit of War shall cease—The proud oppressors over the Earth shall be totally broken down and those classes of Men who have hitherto been the victims of their rage and cruelty shall perpetually enjoy perfect Peace and Safety till time shall be no more."

The principal spokesman for the view expressed by Rush that all men and women were to be "equally" or "universally" saved was the Reverend Charles Chauncy. For a time the Universalists appeared primarily as dissenting members of the Congregational and Presbyterian churches. Eventually a portion separated themselves and formed a denomination by that name. Perhaps as many simply held to their views and brought about, particularly among the Congregationalists, a kind of universalist temper.

A more dangerous challenge came from a liberal faction, which called itself Unitarian, that is to say accepting God as the Ruler of the Universe while formally rejecting Trinitarian Christianity. Against those who insisted that the Bible must be understood as the literal Word of God, Unitarian minister William Ellery Channing declared, "Our leading principle in interpreting Scripture is this, that the Bible is a book written for men, in the language of men, and its meaning is to be sought in the same manner, as that of other books." It thus requires "the constant exercise of reason on the part of the reader. . . . We, therefore, distrust every interpretation which, after deliberate attention, seems repugnant to any established truth. We reason about the Bible precisely as civilians do about the constitution under which we live." Among the conclusions drawn from the Bible was the conviction of "GOD'S UNITY, or that there is one God, and one only. To this truth we give infinite importance." While only God Himself was divine, "Unitarian Christianity" acknowledged "the greatness of the work of Jesus . . . and the sufferings which he bore for our salvation, we feel to be strong claims on our gratitude and veneration."

Many New Englanders felt as did Abigail Adams, who chafed at listening to sermons "that I cannot possibly believe." Such ministers' idea of eloquence seemed to her to consist "in foaming, loud speaking, working themselves up in such an enthusiasm as to cry, which has no other effect upon me than to raise my pity." She wished to hear "liberal good sense . . . true piety without enthusiasm, devotion without grimace, and religion upon a rational system."

So John and Abigail Adams became Unitarians. Hundreds and then thousands of their fellow New England intellectuals followed them into the new denomination, which soon became the established church of "rational Christianity." The Protestant passion for reform, although of a rather rarefied and high-minded variety, found its focus in New England Unitarianism.

The Baptists stood at one end of the theological spectrum and the Unitarians at the other, with every sort of variation in between. As the cases of Franklin, Rush, and Adams make clear, the breakup of Calvinism (we must also emphasize again that a very substantial residue of Calvinism remained) resulted in a remarkable range of individual and collective responses.

We speak of this fragmentation (which was to go on and on) as American religious pluralism. John Adams viewed it, in its infancy, as a salutary development. What it meant sociologically was that it was always possible to devise a new variation of the Christian faith to meet the needs of every group and every condition, so that the disintegrative effects of American life were mitigated to some extent. Indeed, it soon appeared that one of the "rights" of Americans was to establish new religions whenever the spirit moved them.

We have argued that the Reformation re-formed the consciousness of those men and women caught up in it; that it invented something called "an individual," responsible for his or her own salvation, who could "establish not only new religious sects, and new congregations, but also new businesses, new financial enterprises, entire new communities, and even new ways of conceiving of the relation of individuals to one another—new ways, that is, of designing political and constitutional arrangements." So, in addition to a mental landscape made up, in large part—or at its deepest level—of religious or quasi-religious concepts, there was on the subconscious level a set of psychological imperatives, of "internalized values" that were as important as the "ideas" that reinforced them, or were sometimes in conflict with them. The result was a person who had "learned to live, to a remarkable and perhaps unprecedented degree, by his own will." He proved capable of forming endless new combinations and permutations, political, social, and religious. Like recombinant DNA, he went on mutating with bewildering speed and facility. In one lifetime such an "individual" might encompass half a dozen careers or occupations and move twice as many times to new locations, changing his religion as often as his occupation.

18

The Spirit of Capitalism

The geography of eighteenth-century America was extraordinarily diverse. Tillable land was the clue to it all for a nation of farmers.

The granitic soil of New England, which every spring yielded up a harvest of frost-heaved rocks bigger than a man's head, rocks that were good for fencing fields but hard on the plow and plowman, was said to have penetrated the physiology of those who tried to wrest a living from it. Dartmouth men at least have celebrated themselves as having "the granite of New Hampshire in their muscles and their brains." But it was the forests and the innumerable small and large streams of New England that determined its future, that and the character and culture of its citizens.

The Middle States were far better suited to diversified farming. As we already observed, the rich crops of grain in western Pennsylvania determined the "whiskey" economy of that region and much of the political attitudes of its inhabitants.

The South, with its mild climate and rich soil, was an odd combination of a quasi-feudal landed aristocracy, resting on the mass production of cash crops by servile and degraded workers, and Thomas Jefferson's beloved yeoman farmer (found most typically in Virginia and North Carolina).

326

The most striking fact about the geography of the country besides its variety was the difficulty of traversing it. For the individual traveler to find his way across it was arduous enough; to transport a heavy load any distance was so time-consuming and expensive as to be generally impractical. Navigable bodies of water were the lifelines of the country's infant economy. The word "tidewater" bespoke the economy of Virginia. The plantations that lined the James and York rivers were situated where the movement of the tides allowed oceangoing vessels to load cargoes from the plantation docks. Frontier settlements were strung along the Ohio and its major tributaries like beads on a string. Their cash crops must move down the Mississippi River system to New Orleans if they were to find a market.

Americans' view of the land itself was ambivalent. In the Old World, land had been inextricably bound up with wealth and power. The rich owned the land; the poor worked it. To own a few precious acres of land was to achieve a degree of dearly prized independence yearned for by many but attained by very few. In America there was more land than anyone could measure or comprehend. It was like man's ancient dream of picking up money in the streets. It *was* money, as good as money, better than money. It was money at interest because every year it increased in value, often by very substantial increments. And one could, almost literally, pick it up. If, by the constant and inexorable process of augmentation, it had grown to be expensive, one had only to move somewhat farther west; how far west depended on a fairly precise equation of how much money (or credit) one had available and how much land he wished to purchase. Someone might sell his town lot, go fifty miles west and purchase a neat farm, another fifty miles and buy a small forest, another hundred and procure an empire. And one could, as Benjamin Rush and Timothy Dwight described it, do all three successively. So from the beginning land was money. Whereas in virtually every other culture arable land was a rare, treasured, and lovingly cared-for space, full of sacred powers and potencies (for it produced that which made life possible), in America it was primarily a form of currency.

The Old World spoke of ares (approximately one fiftieth of an acre) or hectares (some two and a half acres). They measured land out in plots not much larger than a good-sized rug. Americans talked about hundreds and thousands and millions of acres. For a land speculator a profit of a cent an acre was a delightful gain, if he held title to a hundred thousand acres along, let us say, the lower Wabash

River. A profit of five or ten cents per acre was beyond dreams of avarice. In such transactions the fiscal imagination of American entrepreneurs was shaped; the whole notion of mass production— large quantities at small per unit profit—was born out of the fever of land speculation that possessed the country long before its official birth as a nation. There was thus little of the sentimental or romantic (or reverent) in the average American's view of the land. Things in plentiful supply are not commonly highly valued. Land was too cheap and too available to evoke those feelings toward it that are characteristic of long-settled and traditional cultures. Moreover, the land—that is to say, the almost impenetrable virgin forests, the deep and often turbulent rivers, the swamps, the mountains so difficult to find one's way across—was perceived as fearsome and menacing. It was, after all, filled with hostile Indians. The Indians were almost like an extension and epitome of the oppressive wilderness. A tree might (and often did) conceal a painted savage. The swamps and forests were full of deadly miasmas, which were described as "noxious exhalations from putrescent matter" and "poisonous vapors floating in the atmosphere." They made strong men ill and carried off a terrible crop of newborn infants. It was simply a fact that the forests of that day were more deadly to the health of those who lived in them than our modern cities are. Much as we perceive our cities as dangerously polluted environments, their air filled with cancer-producing chemicals, asphalt jungles where savage marauders roam the streets, our forefathers saw the forests as decidedly uncongenial to their health and safety. If the only good Indian was a dead one, the only good tree was a felled one.

Since geography is land and water, geography was determinative. It was the stage on which all the action took place, the scenery, and the setting. The stage set became an integral part of the play. Americans were as much the captives of geography as its conquerors. The slowness and difficulty of travel and communication, plus the extreme variations in topography and climate, condemned them to a thoroughgoing provincialism. The Revolution partially and briefly overcame that provincialism, but the country lapsed back into it. Every foreign and domestic crisis revealed the precariousness of the Union. The provincialism of individual states was reinforced by sectional animosities and prejudices, and these in turn were reinforced by a specific political proscription that held that in all essential matters the states were superior to the federal government—the doctrine of the Virginia and Kentucky Resolutions.

The first efforts to transcend the geography were, not surprising-ly, generated by economic need, by the desire to make money by transporting goods to market. Since the movement of boats and barges on rivers and inland waterways was the cheapest and most practical form of transportation, it was natural if not inevitable that ways should be sought to extend this method by the building of canals.

In this first major capitalistic venture, there were demonstrated the dominant characteristics of most subsequent business enterprises in the United States down to the present time. First, there was the question of expertise, of an effective technology. In instances where the practical problems were especially complex, this involved import-ing foreign experts. More often it inspired a process of trial and error, where imagination and a native gift for improvisation were substituted for professional skill—sometimes, it must be said, with disastrous results. Then there was the matter of raising capital to carry the project through. Canals were costly undertakings. To finance them strained the modest resources of the regions where they were built.

In addition to developing an adequate technology and raising the necessary funds, an engineer must supervise the labors of a large work force, whose food and living quarters must be provided during the digging of the canal. Most canals involved the construction of locks, by means of which boats and barges could be raised and lowered, often over considerable gradients. Once built, a canal had to be maintained against erosion or damage to its banks. It was especially vulnerable to floods, and the farmers through whose lands most canals passed were quite prepared to sue the canal company if a canal overflowed and destroyed their crops.

Canals were of three basic types: those designed to connect two separate waterways, say the Schuylkill and Susquehanna rivers; those built to make an existing river navigable by building detours around shallows or rapids; and those providing feeder lines into navigable rivers or major canals. Building canals soon became, like so many subsequent undertakings in America, a craze. By 1790 thirty canal companies had been incorporated in eight states. The magic words were "internal improvements," and every community with access to a flow of water was convinced that its future prosperity and happiness rested on building a canal. The first ones were modest affairs only a few miles long. Digging a ditch, even a few miles long, deep enough to float a good-sized boat was, with the technology available—primarily plows and shovels—a major undertaking.

The first major canal project was initiated in Massachusetts in 1793 under a charter signed by Governor John Hancock. The Middlesex Canal Company was granted permission "to construct a canal from Boston Harbor to Chelmsford on the Merrimac River, collect tolls and sell stock in the company." Hancock's famous signature should, in itself, have encouraged subscribers to the company's stock. The purpose of the canal was to bring timber, granite, firewood, and other products from New Hampshire to the Boston market.

The task of supervising the building of the canal was given to a self-educated engineer and veteran of the Revolution named Loammi Baldwin. The intention was to cross the Concord River some twenty miles to the north and cut through from there to the Merrimack. Water from the Concord would fill the canal. Baldwin had read what books he could find on canal building in the Harvard library as an undergraduate, but he had never even seen a lock, that crucial element in a canal. Accompanied by a friend who was a surveyor, Baldwin set off to run a route for his canal. He discovered, among other practical difficulties, that he would have to have a lock system that could raise boats a hundred feet. His surveyor friend's calculations were so crude that he made an error in estimating elevation of forty-one feet in six miles. Baldwin realized that his own knowledge was inadequate to the task and persuaded the company to hire an Englishman, William Weston, who seems to have been the only man in the United States with any experience in building canals.

When stock was offered at $225 a share in 1794 it was quickly snapped up. In the intervening years, while the canal was being built, it was speculated in so heavily that by 1804, when barges began to move along the canal's banks, it had increased in value to $475. This was, of course, a purely speculative value. When the canal was completed it extended for twenty-seven miles. The banks contained towpaths where mules or horses pulled the barges at the speed of a slow amble. There were twenty-eight locks on the canal, which raised and lowered boats 107 feet. At Pawtucket, on the Merrimack, a side canal a mile and a half long was built with the expectation that it would be used as the site for a water-powered textile mill.

Between four hundred and five hundred men worked on the canal for nine years at the standard wage of eight dollars a month. In terms of modern undertakings it might be compared with the Alaska pipeline. That such an ambitious enterprise could be carried to completion in the first years of the Republic revealed a great deal about the practical consequences of the American Revolution. I have spoken earlier of the fact that the American interpretation of "equality" as a promise of "every man a capitalist" released an enormous supply of energy and ingenuity. The Middlesex Canal was a manifestation of that energy and ingenuity. It was also typical that the undertaking proved much too ambitious. The cost of the canal was $528,000. Its debts were never discharged, and thousands of investors lost their money. But other thousands who had speculated in the canal stocks during the nine years the canal was being built made small fortunes.

When the company was liquidated in 1860, a share of stock that had had assessments of $740 against it had returned in the history of the company only $559. After the canal was finished a number of small "feeder" canals—the Wicasee, Amoskeag, Hookset, and Union—were built to hook it into a transportation network. In addition, the managers of the canal built sawmills and flour mills along its course and conducted excursions on brightly decorated barges for prospective stockholders. A passenger line with comfortably furnished barges was established between Billerica and Chelmsford.

In 1800 the Union Company was given a charter to improve the navigation of the Connecticut River between Middletown and Hartford, Connecticut. The company did so with notable success and subsequently tied in with a number of short, "homemade" canals built by small farming communities to transport their produce to market. One of the earliest of these was the South Hadley Falls Canal, which was begun in 1793 and completed a year later. The most notable aspect of the South Hadley Falls Canal was that it was built by Yankee ingenuity with local money and labor. In its own way it was as significant as the far more ambitious Middlesex Canal. If the latter was an early example of organizational and entrepreneurial skills, the more modest venture revealed the talents available among the ordinary citizens of rural towns.

In the two miles of the South Hadley Falls Canal there was a fifty-foot rise, and a hundred-yard stretch ran between rock cliffs forty feet high. Since the building of locks was beyond the engineering resources of the adjacent communities, the builders devised an inclined plane, the first in America, where barges were winched up one side of a slope and lowered down the other. A barge entered a wooden "container," a door was secured behind it, and it was raised by two water-driven wheels sixteen feet in diameter. The container-vehicle had wheels of graduated size built to conform to the slope gradient so that the barge would always be level.

The South Hadley Falls Canal was a modest engineering wonder and was copied by other canal builders, but the company, like its Middlesex counterpart, fell on hard times. Fishermen complained bitterly that it prevented the running and spawning of shad and salmon, and farmers charged that it caused flooding in the fields adjacent to it, accompanied by outbreaks of malaria. Its enemies petitioned the Connecticut legislature to order the canal closed, and though the move failed, the key dam was remodeled; two years later it was swept away in a spring flood. Two successive dams were demolished by floods before the project was abandoned. Again we have a kind of parable of American enterprise versus what we call today the environment. The first dam on a major New England river, the Connecticut, immediately produced a sharp conflict between competing and equally legitimate economic interests—the farmers and lumbermen who wished to get their products to the market and the fishermen who found their livelihood imperiled. The dam and canal, eloquent testimony to the imagination, ingenuity, and hard work of their builders, posed the perpetual conflict between nature and human artifice; more specifically, between dams and fish. The flooding and destruction of the South Hadley Falls Dam was only a temporary setback. In America dams were destined to win hands down.

Another canal on the Connecticut was that at Montague Falls. It was built in 1800, and it carried barges three miles through eight locks and two dams and opened up another fifty miles of river to water transportation.

The most important and long-lived of the Connecticut River canals was the so-called Windsor Locks Canal, some twelve miles upriver from Hartford. The principal cargo on the Connecticut canals was timber, and the hard-bitten, blasphemous men who guided the lumber barges down the river were the soulmates to the teamsters who hauled loads over almost impassable roads. At the major locks, where boatmen waited for their barges or log booms to be raised and lowered, taverns sprang up like mushrooms. Drunken brawls were common. Windsor was especially notorious. The word was that a man could get anything he wanted there. A convenient distillery was located at nearby Warehouse Point, and compliant ladies were numerous. The countryside around Windsor was tobacco country, and General Israel

Putnam was credited with starting the cigar industry by importing "three donkey-loads of Havana cigars." A local tobacco grower then sent for a cigar maker from Cuba, and soon Windsor Particulars were a major article of export from the area. A cheaper cigar was the Short Six, or "twofers"—two for a penny.

The most ambitious canal in New England was the Blackstone. It was first proposed in 1796 in the excitement created by the Middlesex Canal, but it was twenty-five years before work was begun on a canal that extended forty-five miles from Narrangansett Bay in Rhode Island to the town of Worcester, Massachusetts. There were forty-eight locks fashioned of granite blocks in the length of the canal, and it was built in four years, an indication of how rapidly canal technology had advanced since ground was broken for the Middlesex Canal.

In Philadelphia the rage for canals was stimulated by an Irishman named Christopher Colles, who lectured on hydrostatics and hydraulics and preached the gospel of canals to enthusiastic audiences. He made a model steam engine, although he did not succeed in making it propel a boat. He spoke with captivating eloquence of the advantages to be gained from building a system of canals to connect the Hudson River with the Great Lakes.

When the Schuylkill and Susquehanna Company offered its stock for sale in 1791, bids were received for thirty-nine thousand more shares of stock than were issued. But it was to be more than twenty years before the first shovelful of earth was turned.

In Virginia the Patowmack (Potomac) Company was formed, with George Washington as its president, to build a series of canals on that river. Washington was given fifty shares of stock for his services as president. He accepted them only on the condition that he could give them to a college. The support of Washington, whose dream was to connect the Potomac with the Ohio, was constantly being sought by inventors and promoters. When an Englishman, Henry Wansey, was visiting Washington, he noted that after breakfast the president went to look at a model of a device "to convey vessels on navigable canals, from one lock to another, without the expense of having flood-gates, by means of a lever, weighted by a quantity of water pumped into a reservoir [large container]." Wansey added: "The President has continual applications from the ingenious, as the patron of every new invention, which, good or bad, he with great patience, listens to, and receives them all in a manner to make them go away satisfied."

In 1786 two hundred laborers, most of them indentured servants

and slaves, began work on a canal around the Great Falls of the
Potomac near Georgetown. After initial setbacks, the company hired
James Rumsey as engineer. Rumsey was a Marylander, a machinist by
trade and a tinkerer and inventor by inclination, who had turned his
attention first to improving the machinery of mills. In 1784 he had
demonstrated for Washington a boat with steam-driven poles or oars,
and in March, 1785, he was granted a charter "to navigate and build
boats calculated to work with greater ease and rapidity against rapid
rivers." A year later he launched a boat on the Potomac that was driven
by a water jet forced out the rear of the boat by steam, and in
December, 1787, he demonstrated his jet-driven craft before an
enthralled audience of prospective investors. The following year the
Rumseian Society was formed in Philadelphia, with Benjamin Franklin
as a member, to help finance his experiments.

The Patowmack Company persuaded Rumsey to interrupt his
steamboat venture in order to direct the building of the canal. He soon
had nearly a thousand men working under his direction, the majority
of them recently arrived Irish immigrants who tried to allay their sense
of alienation and the arduousness of their labors by drinking and
fighting and running away; in the latter case, since they worked on a
labor contract, they were hunted down, brought back, and had their
heads and eyebrows shaved (and were sometimes beaten) as punishment.

In all, five canals were built by the Patowmack Company, the most
famous the five-lock canal at Great Falls. The cost of water transportation was half of that by land. In the first year of operation forty-five
thousand barrels of flour "together with much whiskey, iron, wheat
and tobacco was locked through, the tolls amounting to somewhat
more than $10,000." But efforts to extend navigation farther upriver
turned out to be excessively expensive, and the principal accomplishment of the Patowmack Company was to pave the way for the famous
Chesapeake and Ohio Canal Company, some twenty-five years later.

A companion company to the Patowmack was the James River
Company, which was given a charter to make that river navigable as far
upstream as possible. A seven-mile canal around the falls at Richmond
was completed in 1789, opening up almost two hundred miles of river,
and a flood of goods—flour, tobacco, whiskey, wheat, flax, barley,
smoked hams, and salt pork—poured into Richmond. The city experienced a boom, and land values rose for the farms and plantations
along the river.

It was not enough that canals should facilitate transportation. They had also to advance civilization and promote public happiness. Robert Fulton painted a glowing word picture of the benefits to be expected from his proposed network of canals: twelve canals, fifteen hundred miles long, fifty miles apart, running from New England to Georgia, eighteen thousand miles in all, and thirty canals running six hundred miles into the interior. With no inhabitant more than twenty-five miles from a canal, the network would sustain a population of 108 million, according to Fulton's calculations. He presented his plan as a substitute for an army and navy. "Such communications would facilitate every species of industry. Canals bending around hills, would irrigate the grounds beneath, and convert them into luxuriant pasturage. They would bind a hundred millions of people in one inseparable compact—alike in habits, in language, and in interest; one homogeneous brotherhood, the most invulnerable, powerful and respectable on earth." The "genius and resources" of the country should be directed to "useful improvements, to the sciences, the arts, education, the amendment of the public mind and morals . . . such are the labours of the enlightened republicans—those who labour for the public good. Every order of things, which has a tendency to remove oppression and ameliorate the condition of man, by directing his ambition to useful industry is, in effect, republican."

The great canal boom was still ahead. It reached its apex in the 1820s and 1830s, given added stimulus by the completion of the Erie Canal, the greatest engineering feat of the first half century. Here we have only had an introduction to the remarkable network of waterways that provided the principal means of transportation for freight prior to the railroads. Without the canal system, which left no major river flowing to the Atlantic unaffected, the extraordinary growth of the Old Northwest would have been impossible. It was the states formed out of that region that provided a staging area for the migration into the trans-Mississippi West.

Toll roads, built by private corporations that paid their investors out of the fees collected from users, supplemented the canal system. Like the canals, they were a typically American solution to the challenge posed by the great distances that had to be traversed in a country where states were almost the size of nations. While they did not present the engineering problems associated with canal building, they did require both financial and technical skill and ingenuity, especially in the construction of bridges. Often the funds raised by stock subscription were augmented by lotteries approved by the state legislatures, so the natural acquisitive instinct of Americans was harnessed on several levels.

A lottery ticket was often a much better risk than a share of stock because through inexperience, mismanagement, bad luck, or corruption, the majority of stock companies organized to carry out "internal improvements" failed. But Americans turned out to be more or less inured to failure. In fact, it has often been observed that as a people we are better able to cope with failure than with success. Both as individuals and as a nation, we seem to have been perpetually sustained by the faith that all the small failures must, ultimately, add up to a smashing success. And success indeed crowned such efforts often enough to provide an incentive for future efforts. There was a resilience in the American character that seemed able to survive repeated fiscal shocks and disappointments. Part of this quality may have derived from the fact that the great majority of Americans began life in comparatively modest circumstances, and all had the expectation of improving them. Thus, disasters were perceived as temporary setbacks. Men and women knew they could always survive at a subsistence level. If they were defeated in the East, they could move west. If they were defeated in the town, they could try their luck in the country. Since the great majority had begun their lives as farmers, they lived with the assurance that they could, at any time, take up that relatively unspecialized calling and at least feed their families. Moreover, even though this or that canal company or toll road company might eventually fail, it would not hesitate in its salad days to distribute dividends of 12, 15, and even 20 percent. And if it failed ("when" might be more accurate), the canal or the road remained and continued to serve people's needs.

Finally, even a canal company that failed created innumerable jobs beyond those involved in the actual building of the canal—work for boatbuilders, boatmen, tavernkeepers, prostitutes, lock operators—not to mention the economic stimulus it gave to the regions that were opened up to water transportation. So failure did, after all, mean success. Highly irrational as the process was, it worked. It was the means by which the geography was organized. The first great American entrepreneurial activity was directed at altering the landscape. The South Hadley Falls story was repeated innumerable times in the first decades of the nation's existence.

It must also be said that the canal-building era produced the most delightful means of transportation known to modern times. To move quietly through a rural landscape with only the sounds of lapping water, the creak of the tiller, the leisurely clop of mule hoofs on the towpath, and the songs of birds was bliss. Aquatic animals—muskrats and otters, frogs and turtles—had their habitats along the banks, and fish found their way into the canals, so that a line trailed behind a barge often produced a tasty dinner. So, in the beginning, water was everything; all solutions were aqueous.

If the construction of canals and toll roads required major outlays of capital, the principal business activity of the seacoast cities remained foreign commerce. The seas and oceans of the world corresponded, in a sense, to the rivers and canals that tied the rather tentatively united states together. Some historians have gone so far as to maintain that the American Revolution was brought on by the desire of colonial merchants to protect their trading privileges. However that may be, oceangoing commerce with England and the West Indies had been the most essential element in American prosperity. Many merchants had a rude awakening after the Revolution when they lost the advantages American ships had enjoyed as part of the British trading empire. Now they had to go it on their own.

The loss of the markets they had enjoyed as colonists of Great Britain, and the chronic uncertainty about the policies of the belligerent powers in Europe, forced American merchants to seek new trading areas, often in remote and exotic parts of the globe. One such area was the Pacific Coast; another was the Far East.

The first ship to reach Canton, China, was the *Empress of China*, sailing out of New York in February, 1784. While Americans were infatuated with the art and artifacts of China, little was produced in the United States that was needed or desired by the Chinese. The one exception was the ginseng root, which was highly prized for its medicinal properties and grew wild in the woods of New England. Boston soon became the center of the China trade. Vessels from her ports would sail for the Orient with a load of New England ginseng and return with tea, embroidered silks, and porcelains. Since there was a limit to the Chinese consumption of ginseng, Boston merchants soon found a means of extending their trade with Canton.

In 1780 the merchant ship *Columbia*, under the command of Captain Robert Gray, returned to Boston after a three-year voyage around the globe. In its hold was a cargo of tea from Canton. With him, Gray brought Owyhee, a native of the Sandwich Islands, wearing a cloak of scarlet feathers with golden suns and a striking feather helmet shaped like that of a Greek warrior.

After rounding Cape Horn, Gray had sailed up the Pacific coast trading with the Indians and collecting furs. These furs, he discovered when he reached Canton, were highly prized by Chinese traders. They thus seemed the perfect complement to the already diminishing ginseng trade. The voyage was so successful that the investors dispatched Gray six weeks later on another voyage to the northwest and hence to China. This time, coasting the shores of what would become the Oregon Territory, Gray had come upon a wide outflow of fresh water that indicated a large river. The river's current was so strong that Gray could not enter its mouth.

Finally, with a strong following wind, the *Columbia* made her way through the surf at the entrance of the river on April 29, 1792. Gray's fifth mate gave a simple enough account of the historic occasion. "Saw an appearance of a spacious harbour abreast the Ship, haul'd our wind for . . . undershort sail . . . and when over the bar had . . . water, quite fresh. . . . We directed our course up this noble *River* in search of a Village. The beach was lin'd with Natives, who ran along shore following the Ship Soon after, above 20 Canoes came off, and brought a good lot of Furs, and Salmon, which last they sold two for a board nail. The furs we likewise bought cheap, for Copper and Cloth. They appeared to view the Ship with great astonishment and no doubt we was the first civilized people that they ever saw. . . . Capt. Gray named this river *Columbia*'s. . . . This River in my opinion, wou'd be a fine place for to set up a Factory. . . . The river abounds with excellent *Salmon*."

Gray had been advised by a fellow ship's captain to "treet the Natives with Respect where Ever you go. Cultivate friendship with them as much as possible and take Nothing from them But what you pay them for according to a fair agreement, and not suffer your peopel to affront them or treet them Ill." The advice proved not always easy to follow. The Indians of the Columbia River region were cousins of the Tlingit and Haida tribal groups, whose range extended north into Canada and along the Gulf of Alaska as far as the Alaska Peninsula. They constituted one of the most advanced and warlike tribes on the continent, with a splendid iconography—expressive animal masks, totem poles of rich and intricate design. From redwood logs they fashioned canoes fifty feet long that could hold thirty men or more. Military triumphs, the torture of prisoners, and the capture of slaves were the central concerns of most tribes; white traders, commonly called "Boston men" by the Indians, often found them dangerously mercurial. The principal families of the tribe were identified by different totems, to whose protection they pledged themselves. Among the clans were the Killer Whale clan or family, and the Salmon, Beaver, Cannibal Spirit, and Bear clans. Each family wore an emblem of its animal spirit. A visitor from another village always sought out the members of his own totemic group, who he knew would welcome him.

The catching and smoking of salmon constituted the main hunting and food-gathering activity of these tribes, and warfare was their principal recreation. In war any trick or stratagem that could defeat the enemy was admired. Members of defeated tribes were often taken as slaves by the victors. The most famous of their rituals was the potlatch, where the wealthier members of the tribe gave much of their wealth away to enhance their prestige. The most powerful member of the tribe was the one who could give most away, and many of the handsomest artifacts of the tribes were made to be given away at the potlatches. Sometimes, as an especially extravagant gesture, a slave would be clubbed to death.

For the Northwest Indians, the world was full of "spirits," most importantly the spirits of animals. A Chief of the Sky People corresponded to a kind of principal deity, and the trickster-creator Raven was the central animal spirit. An archetypal Old Woman lived under the sea and kept the sun in her house, releasing it each day to travel across the sky.

Gray sailed some thirty miles up the river, traded with the Indians, took on water, and sailed out nine days later, having, among other things, established the basis for a subsequent American claim to the region. More important to his financial principals, he had laid the foundation for the Boston-Canton trade based on sea-otter and seal pelts. To the Northwest Indians the Boston ship captains brought the usual articles of Indian trade: ribbons, looking glasses, beads, pocket-knives, plumed hats, razors, cloth, pots and pans, needles. In exchange they received the furs that were so much in demand in Canton.

The ships were often the better part of two years making the long and dangerous round trip, but the profits were enormous and a whole group of Boston families—the Perkinses, Sturgises, Cushings, and Forbeses most prominent among them— laid the basis of fortunes that survived for generations. Robert Bennet Forbes had shipped out at the age of thirteen on a China trader with nothing but a Bible and a sea chest. He was captain of his own ship at twenty, owned it by the time he was twenty-six, and in time became the most prosperous merchant in Boston. One example of the profits to be made will perhaps suffice. The standard price for an otter skin in Indian trade was an inexpensive chisel that was worth about fifty cents. The pelt could then be sold in Canton for fifty dollars. Soon Boston merchants were ordering particular items—gowns, furniture, sets of china—to be made to their specifications by Chinese craftsmen. Many of these are still to be found in Boston homes and in the museums of port towns such as Salem and Marblehead.

The China trade that centered in Boston and carried sealskins and beaver and sea-otter pelts to Canton and Hong Kong continued to grow in the early decades of the nineteenth century. Chinese and Boston merchants had, it turned out, a natural affinity for each other. Samuel Eliot Morison, the historian of Boston's maritime past, paints a vivid picture of "Yankee seamen, fresh from the savage wilderness of the Northwest," encountering the exotic culture of Canton. "Against a background of terraced hongs with their great go-downs or warehouses, which screened the forbidden city of Rams from foreign devils' gaze, flowed the river, bearing a city of boats the like of which the American seaman had never dreamed. Moored to the shore were flower-boats, their upper works cunningly carved into the shape of flowers and birds, and strange sounds issuing from their painted windows. Mandarin boats decorated with gay silk pennants, and propelled by double-banks of oars, moved up and down in stately cadence. Great tea-deckers, with brightly lacquered topsides and square sails of brown matting, brought the Souchong, Young Hyson, and Bohea from upriver. In and out darted thousands of little sampans, housing entire families who plied their humble trades aboard. Provision dealers cried their wares from boats heaped high with colorful and deadly produce. Barber's skiffs announced their coming by the twanging of tweezers. . . . Twilight brought the boat people to their moorings, a bamboo pole thrust in oozy bottom, and paper lanterns diffused a soft light over the river. For color and exotic flavor there was no trade like the old China trade, no port like Canton."

By 1806 the fur trade between Boston and Canton was valued at over $5 million and included 17,445 sea-otter skins, 140,297 sealskins, and 34,460 beaver skins. American vessels brought back with them ten million pounds of tea. The Sandwich Islands were soon incorporated into the Boston-China trade as a stopping-off point for weary crews and as a source of sandalwood. The Sandwich Islanders, or Kanakas (Hawaiians), proved to be excellent sailors and were promptly recruited as crew members and fur collectors.

If the Boston–Northwest Coast–Canton trade was the most spectacular, it had many counterparts. Salem, after trying the Canton trade, switched to the Dutch East Indies, Manila, and the coast of Africa, but the ports made by its captains in 1790 also included Cadiz, Spain (lemons, feathers, raisins, oil, and salt); Lisbon (wine, lemons, and figs); St. Eustatia in the West Indies (sugar, rum, and gin); Martinique (molasses, raisins, and limes). When the *Henry,* captained by twenty-one-year-old Jacob Crowninshield, sailed in 1791 from Salem for Mauritius, the French colony on the North African coast near the Cape Verde Islands, it carried a cargo of "pottery and ale, iron and salt fish, soap and gin, hams and flints, whale oil and candles, saddles and bridles, lard and tobacco, chocolate and flour, tables and desks."

When France restricted this trade, Salem established commercial ties in India. Benjamin Joy acted as an agent for Salem merchants in Calcutta, and Thomas Lechmere became an alderman of Bombay. American merchant vessels often engaged in a kind of circular trade between Ceylon, Bombay, Calcutta, Madras, Rangoon, Bengal, and the Coromandel Coast. Indian cottons were much prized, among them Beerboom gurrahs, a white sheeting, and Pulicat handkerchiefs, camel's-hair shawls, spices, pepper, ginger, and a hundred other exotic articles.

In 1805 over seven million pounds of pepper were imported into the United States, most of it to Salem. That same year Salem merchants imported two million pounds of coffee from Arabia. That there were hazards in such trade is indicated by the fate of the *Essex.* In the Red Sea the ship added to its crew some Arabs who were actually pirates and slaughtered every American on board. When the news reached the owner of the *Essex,* he is reported to have said, "Well, the ship is insured!"

In addition to the trade with Sumatra and Surinam, Salem merchants and captains developed trade with Calcutta. The ship *George* made twenty-one trips to Calcutta and back in a period of twenty-two years. Joseph Peabody's brig, *Leander,* made twenty-six voyages to the Far East, Africa, Asia Minor, and Europe in twenty-three years.

New York grew even more rapidly as a port than Boston and Salem, and ships whose home ports were Philadelphia and Baltimore also carried on an extensive trade with Europe and the West Indies. Foreign markets were opened up, such as the pepper trade with Sumatra, exploited vigorously for a decade or so, and then replaced by new markets.

Marblehead concentrated her trading activities in the Baltic, the West Indies, and countries of the South American mainland. New York was heavily involved in the West Indian trade, and Baltimore, Philadelphia, and Charleston, South Carolina, dispatched their merchant vessels to Brazil, the Azores, Ostend, Calais, Manila, or wherever a fast profit was to be made. The risks were high but the profits were great.

Much of the success of such ventures was the consequence of the ability of the ship's captain or the factor to take advantage of new opportunities that presented themselves in the course of a cruise that might last a year or two. The capacity to take initiative in making difficult and potentially costly decisions was very largely the consequence of the character of American society where such qualities, uninhibited by any class distinctions, were sought out and rewarded. The American merchant, by virtue of the flexibility that resulted from this devolution of responsibility, had an important edge over his Dutch or English rival. Another advantage of American merchants was their willingness to take substantial risks. This was, in large part, also the result of certain American character traits and social attitudes. In England and to an even greater degree in France, much money was "family money," money needed to sustain a particular family in a certain style. Thus the emphasis was, inevitably, on caution rather than on boldness. The pioneering spirit, the lust of the hunt, or excitement of "adventure" had its monetary as well as its geographic expression. American "individualism" implied that a man's money was his own and what he did with it was his own business. An individual with the bravado to stake everything on a single turn of the wheel of fortune was more apt to be admired for his boldness than censured for his recklessness. Timothy Dwight, referring to the Bostonians' mercantile bent, wrote that they were "distinguished by a lively imagination. . . . Their enterprises are sudden, bold, and sometimes rash. A general spirit of adventure prevails." From rags to riches and back to rags again in three generations was a notably American drama. The American notion of money as something to be made and used rather than saved or cautiously augmented often gave American merchants a crucial competitive edge.

Sailors constituted an almost invisible subculture in American society. They had their own folklore, songs, superstitions, and language. They were the frontiersmen of the world's oceans. As the land frontiersmen moved south and west, the sea frontiersmen moved south and east. What the Mississippi River Valley was for land frontiersmen the numerous harbors and ports of the Atlantic seacoast were to the sailors. As many farmboys dreamed of going west, many others dreamed of the romantic life of a sailor. Thus, land and sea frontiersmen shared many character traits. They were both capable of enduring extreme physical hardship; they had an insatiable appetite for novelty and adventure and a distaste for conventional society. They were both intensely democratic in their politics and highly political. There were, however, also significant differences. The frontiersman (as distinguished from the trapper) was, almost of necessity, a family man, the sailor a rover. The frontier settler was the classic independent man, the sailor was the employee of a merchant and a ship's captain and lived a life of the most exacting discipline. As we have noted, the crew of a sailing ship was like the nerves and muscles of a well-articulated body, a kind of living organism in which every portion must work as smoothly and integrally with the others as the most finely tuned machine. When the sailing ship reached its apogee in the early decades of the nineteenth century, it was one of the most refined and exquisite creations of human art and ingenuity. In the intricate multitude of ropes, spars, masts, blocks, and sails lay a beauty and power that could be unfurled only by arms, hands, and fingers as skilled and graceful as those of a dancer. So once a sailor had become an agent of that beauty, grace, and power, had moved in unison with his fellows to let out the innumerable sails and see them catch the wind, it was not surprising that he became an addict. It seems safe to say that man has known no more satisfying cooperative effort than that required to maneuver a great sailing ship. Samuel Eliot Morison makes the point that for Americans sailoring was a young man's avocation. We produced no marine proletariat in part because the great majority of sailors were boys who "ran away to sea" for three, four, five, or six years and then returned to the farms from which they had come, or joined the stream of settlers moving westward if they did not become the masters of ships themselves. Captain Zachary Lamson of Beverly, Massachusetts, sailed on one voyage with a crew of thirteen, every one of whom became master of his own ship.

With the rapid expansion of American commerce, young sailors of ability who wished to make the sea their calling often rose meteorically. Besides the adventure, there was money to be made. Wages were good. In 1799 boys were paid eight to ten dollars a month, ordinary seamen fourteen to seventeen dollars, able seamen eighteen dollars, and petty officers as much as twenty-four dollars a month. Such wages compared favorably with those of farmhands or laborers, who in 1800 were usually paid no more than a dollar a day, out of which they had to provide their own keep.

The difficulty the historian has with the marvelous and inexhaustibly compelling story of the sailors is that they left no tracks on the trackless oceans they traversed. They built no towns as monuments to their skill and courage, wrote few letters or diaries to tell us how they felt rounding the Horn or Cape or venturing into the Indian Ocean or among the islands of the South Pacific. They liked to think of themselves as the finest sailors in the world, and they doubtless were—only the British could challenge them—but for the most part they vanished as unmarked as the winds that propelled them on their grand voyages. We will, nonetheless, try to keep them in mind. They were fortunate enough to have two splendid spokesmen, one in America's greatest novelist, Herman Melville, and another in a fine "amateur" of the sea, Richard Henry Dana. Beyond that, they and the merchants who dispatched them tied the United States both practically and symbolically to the rest of humanity in every exotic land around the globe. So I would hope the reader will continually think of American history as lines of force radiating outward—eastward across the oceans and westward across the forests and plains and mountains, each voyage and each migration a line or thread of life.

Much more modest were the initial efforts to establish manufacturing enterprises—manufactories, as they were called. The first such undertakings, little more ambitious than a village workshop, were iron manufactories and powder mills, the latter stimulated by the demand for powder to blast rocks to make canals and toll roads. Iron foundries had existed for more than a hundred years. The move now was to expand existing foundries and build new ones.

James Wilson of Pennsylvania, a framer of the Constitution and justice of the Supreme Court, had been one of the directors of the Birdsborough Iron Works founded by his brother-in-law in the 1790s. He also bought land on the Wallenpaupack River that he thought would make a good site for an industrial center. Just as water provided the cheapest form of transportation, it was the only source of power to run the machines of a manufactory. The heart of Wilson's venture was to be a mill for making cloth, and he contracted with a Danish immigrant, John Davenport, who had worked as a weaver in Copenhagen, to make sixty-four looms, "for the purpose of weaving sail, duck and other cloth by means of machinery to be impelled by water."

By Wilson's calculations the manufactory could turn out almost ten thousand "pieces" of duck at $11.50 per piece. The gross return was estimated at $110,400 a year, an immense sum when one considers that the Middlesex Canal returned only $17,000 a year to its owners. As construction was beginning on the cloth mill, Wilson contracted for the building of two sawmills below Wallenpaupack Falls. Both projects proved to be financial disasters.

But Wilson had many counterparts, especially in the Middle and Eastern states; where one entrepreneur fell, two seemed to spring up in his place.

The beginnings of manufactories were accompanied by a rash of inventions. We have already mentioned Laommi Baldwin, Christopher Colles, and James Rumsey, the latter two experimenting with steam engines. They were members of a considerable company, for inventing was, like acquisitiveness, a consequence of the new age when every man might aspire to fame and riches. Benjamin Franklin was, of course, the prototype. The third president of the United States was also an inspired tinkerer who was never so happy as when devising some ingenious solution to running a clock, opening a door, conveying wine from the cellar, or inventing an indoor toilet. As secretary of state, Jefferson had prevailed on Congress to pass the necessary patent legislation and then, with General Knox and a board of patent commissioners, had decided which inventions were worthy of being patented. Only three patents were issued in 1790, and there was soon a general outcry by inventors who were indignant when their inventions were refused patents. Such a procedure, they claimed, was undemocratic. They raised such a row that the law was revised in 1793, and the secretary of state was instructed not to reject any application unless it were shown to be potentially harmful in its effects. Inventing became as much of a fad as canal building. Far more important, it revealed itself as a kind of innate characteristic of a people who were constantly challenged by their environment and by their attitude toward physical labor (respectful of it but anxious to minimize it) to develop cheaper and easier ways to perform traditional tasks. In the first decade of the new Republic, Leonard Harbah, a Baltimore mechanic, patented a machine to reap grain and a workable threshing machine. Benjamin Folger invented a device to make candles from the refuse of right whales. Henry Voight claimed to have invented a process for turning iron into steel.

Inventions should, it was felt, have social as well as practical utility. Robert Fulton, pressing for the adoption by the infant American navy of his torpedo, argued that it would promote peace. Only civilized nations with advanced technology would have the money or the science to build them, and these nations had a common interest in avoiding war. Men, "without reflecting . . . exclaim that it is barbarous to blow up a ship with all her crew. This I admit . . . but all wars are barbarous, especially offensive wars." If torpedoes, by discouraging unjustified attacks, would "prevent such acts of violence, the invention must be humane. . . . If science and energy should sweep military marines from the ocean, America will be the garden of the world—an example for Europe to imitate."

The most famous of this first generation of inventors was young Eli Whitney, a native of Westborough, Massachusetts. While still a boy, Whitney had found a way to make nails more quickly than by the laborious hand method then prevailing. From nails he went on to manufacturing pins for ladies' bonnets, and then men's canes. At the age of twenty-four he interrupted his budding career as a manufacturer to enter Yale College. When he graduated he decided to study law. Through the Yale placement office he learned that there was an opening in Georgia for a boy's tutor. Whitney's notion was to work as a tutor and study law, but when he got to Savannah he found that the position had been filled.

In this crisis Mrs. Nathanael Greene, widow of the Revolutionary general, offered to take him in at Mulberry Grove, her home on the Savannah River, while he studied law. There Whitney was a fascinated observer of the economy of a cotton plantation. Cotton grew profusely in the rich alluvial soil along the river, but removing the seeds from the bolls was the bottleneck to large-scale cotton production. A slave could clean only a few pounds of cotton a day, and at that rate it was almost impossible to make any profit from a cotton crop. Whitney had already charmed Mrs. Greene by devising a dozen modest laborsaving devices for her plantation. The culture of the South was one that put a low value on manual dexterity, indeed on any kind of physical labor, the vast portion of which was relegated to slaves, so a young man with a degree from Yale who constructed things with his hands was a seven-day wonder among the plantations that stretched along the languorous waters of the Savannah near Mulberry Grove. When Mrs. Greene heard her neighbors bemoaning the tediousness of the process of deseeding cotton, she boasted of her young houseguest, who "could make anything."

Whitney found the challenge irresistible, although he had to make his own tools and even his wire. None could be bought in Savannah, which seemed as strange to the New Englander as his determined tinkering seemed to the Southerners who met him.

The "gin" that Whitney built consisted of a four-foot-long drum or cylinder some five inches in diameter, with a series of circular saws two inches high and half an inch apart. The cotton was drawn through a steel grating that stripped the cotton from the seeds. Another drum, armed with bristles and revolving in the opposite direction, brushed the cotton from the sawteeth, while a fan blew away the lint. It is surprising that the machine, so simple in its principle and in its operation, was not invented before—which is not to take anything away from Whitney, whose genius was to be demonstrated repeatedly.

The story of the invention had its grim symbolic overtones. Word that a Yankee was building a machine to gin cotton soon spread throughout the region. To the greedy and unscrupulous it was like hearing that gold had been discovered nearby. Before the gin was even completed thieves broke into the building where Whitney worked and stole it. Whitney went back to Connecticut to raise money to build an additional machine, get his invention patented, and arrange for its manufacture. Before he got home a claim for a patent had been filed for a machine that was clearly copied after his. It took sixty lawsuits, a vast amount of money, and considerable time before Whitney got approximate justice. South Carolina paid him fifty thousand dollars, and North Carolina allowed him a percentage of the use of each gin for five years. Tennessee accepted a similar arrangement but reneged.

There was all the irony that one could wish in the fact that a Yankee built the machine that brought spectacular prosperity to the

Deep South and made slavekeeping in that region so profitable that if there had ever been any hope for voluntary emancipation of the slaves it was lost with the appearance of the gin. Perhaps no invention in history has brought with it such a rapid and dramatic transformation in an established mode of production. Whitney's machine could gin 1,000 pounds of cotton a day—the output of almost a thousand slaves working by hand. In 1791, 189,500 pounds of cotton was all that could be exported from the South. *Ten years later the amount had risen to 41 million pounds.*

The great English historian Thomas Babington Macaulay wrote much later in the century: "What Peter the Great did to make Russia dominant, Eli Whitney's invention of the cotton-gin has more than equalled in its relation to the power and progress of the United States." The praise may seem excessive. It certainly places more emphasis on cotton as the critical element in American history than is justified. But it does give us a reading on the value sober and rational men placed on the invention of the gin.

Of Whitney's devotion to litigation, we might say that in his stubborn determination to get everything that was coming to him he displayed a native characteristic of his countrymen, and perhaps more particularly of his region, as surely as by his gift for invention. Moreover, his interminable lawsuits did not seriously inhibit his capacity for innovation. In 1798, he began an arms factory near New Haven, Connecticut. Here he displayed his genius much more strikingly than in the invention of the relatively simple cotton gin. The factory was set up on the principle of division of labor. Each worker was assigned to perform one or two simple operations. All the parts of the guns were interchangeable. Whitney's arms factory at New Haven was the forerunner of the modern assembly line. To be sure, there had been precedents in earlier factories, but Whitney went further than any of his predecessors in rationalizing the process of production, and he proved the practicality of the idea of interchangeable parts.

Today we live in what we might call an "interchangeable society." We eat interchangeable food, drive interchangeable cars, live in interchangeable houses. We ourselves often seem disconcertingly interchangeable. Modern wisdom has it that "no man is indispensable," where we once thought all were indispensable or, at the very least, irreplaceable. Eli Whitney started all that by separating the product from its fabricator in a manner that is vaguely suggestive of the tendency of nineteenth-century industrial society to separate man from his Maker. That intervention, brilliant as it was, was the beginning of the alienation of man from his work that is such a conspicuous aspect of modern society. We can more or less calculate the effects of the cotton gin in terms of acres of cotton planted, tons exported, yards woven into cloth, and so on. On the level of work, of simple manual labor, its effect was wholly benign. It is to be doubted that anyone was ever made wiser or better by picking the seeds out of a pound of cotton. That was unmitigated laboriousness. But a gun was another matter. Cruel and deadly though it might be, it was also a thing of beauty, often of exquisite craftsmanship, approaching in many instances the beauty of a samurai sword or a Toledo sword blade. The product of a fine gunsmith was easily distinguishable from that of the less skilled and was eagerly sought for and known by the name of its maker. If Americans have been an inventive people, we have also been a gun-toting people. We are told the West was won with the Colt revolver and Winchester repeating rifle. We have always been armed to the teeth, bristling with large and small artillery, the only people in the world whose Constitution guarantees them the right to "bear arms." We can only contemplate the symbolic significance of the fact that the division-of-labor, interchangeable-parts innovation was first applied to the manufacture of guns, thus in time making guns so cheap that it was possible for every American to exercise his constitutional right to "bear" one.

Karl Marx said that the nature of a society is determined by the processes of production. If this is even more or less true, Eli Whitney may have done more to determine the character of modern America than any man in our history.

Whitney's invention of the cotton gin meant an almost unlimited supply of relatively cheap, long-fibered cotton. At first virtually all of this was cotton exported to England, much of whose wealth was based on its early exploitation of the power looms and spinning jennies of Richard Arkwright. Arkwright's technology was so far ahead of that of any competitors that England enjoyed a virtual monopoly on the manufacture of cotton cloth. Determined to protect the country's privileged position, Parliament passed laws prohibiting, under pain of severe punishment, any machines or plans from leaving England.

Samuel Slater, an ambitious young Englishman, three years younger than Whitney, had been privy to the Arkwright secrets through an apprenticeship with Arkwright's partner, Jedediah Strutt. Hearing that Congress had passed an act for the encouragement of manufactures and that the Pennsylvania legislature had offered a bounty to anyone who could introduce the Arkwright process into that state, Slater set off for America. Landing in New York, he heard that a Rhode Island Quaker, Moses Brown, had started a cotton mill at Pawtucket. Brown, who had invested a considerable sum of money in a highly inefficient mill, replied to an inquiry from Slater by writing, "If thou canst do this thing, I invite thee to come to Rhode Island and have the credit of introducing cotton-manufacture into America."

For the twenty-one-year-old Englishman the invitation was irresistible. When he reached Pawtucket, Slater declared the existing mill hopeless. A fresh start must be made. The young man spent eleven months re-creating from memory the complex Arkwright loom. When he was finished, a mill with seventy-two spindles powered by water was ready to begin operation. By the end of the century seven mills with over two thousand spindles had been built, and the New England textile industry had been established through the cooperation of a Yankee entrepreneur and an Englishman with a remarkable memory. Moses Brown, who lived to be ninety-eight, became the prototype of the New England industrialist and financier and, true to his breed, left his state much the richer for his philanthropies, most conspicuous among them the university that bears his name.

The great age of American industrialization lay half a century or more ahead, but these early ventures demonstrated the American proclivity for business enterprise, indeed for a kind of reckless, headlong plunge into whatever ventures seemed most likely to bring a windfall of profits. They thereby anticipated all that was to be done. For the most part, manufacturing was on a modest scale. Almost every town in New England and the Middle States had its incipient capitalists, but the odds were heavily against their achieving their dreams. Their manufactories, usually employing no more than a half-dozen lads or girls, were, as we would say today, badly undercapitalized. As important was the fact that a system of distribution was virtually nonexistent. Their marketing area was, for the most part, limited to the distance a man could drive a wagon in a day. Those manufacturers who lived near a city like Boston or Philadelphia or within its environs had, of course, a larger market, but when we recall that Philadelphia, the largest city in America, had a population of only forty thousand and was thus smaller than many American towns today, it is evident that even "city" demand was modest.

Another inhibition to industrial growth was the fact that available capital was urgently needed to develop the transportation systems of the states. Commerce rather than manufacturing was the characteristic economic activity of the early years of the Republic. Agricultural products by far outweighed the output of the manufactories. The transportation and domestic distribution and foreign export of agricultural staples, timber, and fish had first priority.

19

Education

If there was an area of American life that was to rival religion in its influence on the American mind and character, it was education.

The earliest grammar schools of New England had been established to insure that Christian children would learn to read so that they could study the holy Scriptures and have an intelligent understanding of God's Word. *"In the beginning was the Word, And the Word was with God, And the Word was God."* In the priesthood of all believers there was no room for illiterates. Calvin had declared that "Faith consists not in ignorance, but in knowledge." The reader will perhaps recall John Adams's statement that the founders of New England "had left among their posterity so universal an affection and veneration for . . . liberal education, that the meanest of the people contribute cheerfully to the support and maintenance of them every year. . . . So that the education of all ranks of people was made the care and expense of the public in a manner that I believe has been unknown to any other people ancient or modern."

Harvard and Yale had been founded to provide an educated ministry. As an early history of the Massachusetts Bay Colony put it: "One of the things we longed for, and looked after was to advance *Learning* and perpetuate it to Posterity; dreading to leave an illiterate

352

Ministery to the Churches, when our present Ministers shall lie in the Dust." The statutes of Harvard specified that students "dilligently attend the Lectures without any disturbance by word or gesture . . . be slow to speak, and eschew not only all oaths, lies, and uncertain rumors, but likewise all idle, foolish, bitter scoffing, frothy wanton words and offensive gestures," while the Yale statutes, a few years later, condemned "Disobedient or Contumacious or Refractory Carriage towards his Superiors, Fighting, Striking, Quarreling, Challenging, Turbulent Words or Behaviour, Drunkenness, Uncleaness, Lacivious Words or Actions, wearing woman's Apparel."

The Great Awakening had given a fresh stimulus to the founding of Christian colleges. Dartmouth had been started to educate and convert the Indians, and the Baptists had established Rhode Island College (later Brown University) in 1764 to train their own ministers.

By the end of the century Harvard, Yale, and William and Mary in Virginia, which had been chartered in 1693 and opened its doors several years later, were far less preoccupied with producing ministers than with giving a higher education to the scions of those families in whose hands lay effective political and financial power. It was this fact that caused William Manning to complain of those who "cried up costly collages" as a bulwark of their special privileges. His remedy was "For every state to maintain as many Coledges in conveniant parts thereof as would be attended upon to give the highest Degrees of Larning, [and for every county to do the same for] Grammar Schools or Acadimies . . . & no student or scholar to pay anything for tuition . . . & every person be obliged to send his children to school, for the publick are as much interested in the Larning of one child as an other."

Manning's comments make it clear that education on the elementary and secondary-school level was far from being as common even in New England as John Adams would have had us believe. Those Founding Fathers who discussed education (and most of them did) were agreed on one basic tenet: a republican form of government could not survive without an educated citizenry. The primary purpose of an education was to enable a citizen to properly discharge his responsibilities as a member of a free society. There was very little agreement, however, on the actual content of such an education beyond the rudiments of reading and writing. Benjamin Rush believed that religion was an essential component of education. As he put it: "Religion is necessary to correct the effects of learning. Without religion I believe learning does real mischief to the morals and principles of mankind." Rush was thus pleased that the various denominations had taken the responsibility for maintaining schools and colleges for their members. But Rush wanted a strictly practical education, while his friend Adams wished to preserve classical learning (the arguments have a familiar ring). Greek and Latin were, to Rush, subjects that stressed and perpetuated class distinctions, that had about them a thoroughly aristocratic or elitist character. To Adams they were simply the basis of a genuinely humane education.

Rush devised his own educational scheme, which had interesting similarities to that of Manning. "Let our common people be compelled by law to give their children (what is commonly called) a good English education. Let schoolmasters of every description be supported in part by the public, and let their principles and morals be subject to examination before we employ them. Let us have colleges in each of the states, and one federal university under the patronage of Congress, where the youth of all the states may be melted (as it were) together into one mass of citizens after they have acquired the first principles of knowledge in the colleges of their respective states."

Rush would have the "law of nature and nations, the common law of our country, the different systems of government, history and everything else connected with the advancement of republican knowledge and principles . . . taught. . . . This plan of general education alone will render the American Revolution a blessing to mankind."

Benjamin Franklin also emphasized the practical side of education. He advocated the establishment of an academy where the pupils should be treated with "familiarity and affection." When they had completed their studies, the trustees of the school should take an active part in trying to "establish them whether in business, offices, marriages, or any other thing for their advantage." The school should have a library "with maps of all countries, globes, some mathematical instruments, an apparatus for experiments in natural philosophy and for mechanics; prints of all kinds, prospects, buildings, machines, etc." Franklin put great emphasis on physical training. The students should be "frequently exercised in running, leaping, wrestling, and swimming." As to their studies, "it would be well if they could be taught everything that is useful and everything that is ornamental. But since art is long and their time is short," they could learn only the "most useful and most ornamental." They should be taught to write well and to draw, for "drawing is a kind of universal language, understood by all nations." English grammar should be taught by reading the best authors of liberal politics, the "styles principally to be cultivated being the clear and concise."

Like Rush, Franklin placed great weight on history. "Indeed, the natural tendency of reading good history must be to fix in the minds of youth deep impressions of the beauty and usefulness of virtue of all kinds, public spirit, fortitude, etc." Histories of nature and commerce should be read along with those "of the invention of arts, rise of manufactures, progress of trade . . . with the reasons, causes, etc." This would lead to a curiosity about "mechanics" or, as we would put it, technology, "by which weak men perform such wonders, labour is saved, manufactures expedited, etc." Gardening and agriculture should also be taught, and "with the whole should be constantly inculcated and cultivated that benignity of mind which shows itself in searching for and seizing every opportunity to serve and oblige." A school based on Franklin's description of the ideal academy was actually started in 1749, and Franklin served as its "president" for seven years. It must certainly have been the most progressive school of its time.

Noah Webster, an ardent nationalist who wished to transform English into American by simplifying spelling in a republican spirit, primarily by dropping the *u* in such words as "labour" and omitting the final *e* in words like "give," had strong views on education. He agreed with Rush that it should be practically oriented. The dead languages—Latin and Greek—should be dropped from the studies of all but future scholars. Since business and agriculture were the concerns of most Americans, schools should place a strong emphasis on subjects related to those occupations. An education should be planned "which may not only diffuse a knowledge of the sciences, but may implant in the minds of the American youth, the principles of virtue and liberty; and inspire them with just and liberal ideas of government." Like Rush, Webster believed that the inculcation of "virtue" was as important as practical learning. The geography of America and the history of the Revolution as well as "a compendium of the principles of the federal and provincial governments, should be the principal school book in the United States." It appeared to Webster that "what is now called a *liberal Education,* disqualified a man for business. . . . The method pursued on our colleges is better calculated to fit youth for the learned professions than for business." Like Rush, Webster believed that "the *virtues* of men are of more consequence to society than their *abilities,* and, for this reason, the *heart* should be cultivated with more assiduity than the *head*."

Noah Webster reinforced his notions about the moral aspects of education by writing a spelling book that became the standard work for most schoolchildren. (He once estimated that it had sold seven million copies.) Each lesson was illustrated by a story that had a moral. For Webster two things were essential to "the continuance of Republican governments." These were "1. Such a distribution of lands and such principles of descent . . . as shall give every citizen a power of acquiring what his industry merits. 2. Such a system of education as gives every citizen an opportunity of acquiring knowledge and fitting himself for places of trust. These are fundamental articles; the *sine qua non* of the existence of the American republics." All of this meant that education must be "public," publicly supported and available to every American.

On the subject of education of women, Webster was only moderately enlightened. "Female education should have for its object what is *useful*." Useful meant primarily what a girl needed to know to be a companionable wife and instructive mother—English, arithmetic, geography, and poetry, but no novels, since they were on the whole "pernicious" and "trifling." Webster also revealed his class bias in his concern over the fact that many women were overeducated in comparison with men. "A mechanic or shopkeeper in town, or a farmer in the country, whose sons get their living by their father's employments, will send their daughters to a boarding school, where their ideas are elevated, and their views carried above a connexion with men in those occupations. . . . This fatal mistake is illustrated in every large town in America. In the country, the number of males and females, is nearly equal; but in towns, the number of genteely bred women is greater than of men, and in some towns, the proportion is, as three to one."

We might say two things about Webster's observation. First and most important, it points up one of the most striking and unique characteristics of American society—the father's special solicitude for the education of his daughters. The direct result of this was the Woman's Rights movement of the 1830s and 1840s.

Second, it was to remain a fact of American life that when only a few upper-class males went to college, American women were, by and large, better educated than their middle-class masculine counterparts and became thereby the "culture bearers" of the society, whether in New York City or Missoula, Montana.

Jefferson had, if anything, an even more comprehensive plan than Webster's "to diffuse knowledge more generally through the mass of the people." He advocated dividing every county into districts of five or six square miles "and in each of them to establish a school for teaching reading, writing and arithmetic." The teacher would be supported by the school district, "and every person in it entitled to send their children three years gratis, and as much longer as they pleased, paying for it." Every year the brightest boy "whose parents are too poor to give further education" would be chosen to go to one of the grammar schools, of which there were to be twenty in the state. In these schools the pupils would learn "Greek, Latin, Geography, and the higher branches of numerical arithmetic." After two years in grammar school the "best genius of the whole [would be] selected, and continued six years, and the residue dismissed. By this means twenty of the best geniuses will be raked from the rubbish annually, and be instructed, at the public expense." At the end of six years, one half would again be dismissed, and the rest, "chosen for the superiority of their parts and disposition," were to be sent on to the College of William and Mary to spend three years in the study "of such sciences as they shall chuse."

As Jefferson later wrote to Adams about his plan: "Worth and genius would thus have been sought out from every condition of life, and compleatly prepared by education for defeating the competition of wealth and birth for public trust." The ultimate aim of the whole scheme of education would be "the teaching of all children of the state reading, writing, and common arithmetic" and the "geniuses" as much more as they could absorb. The object would be to increase "the freedom and happiness" of the "mass of the people" with, of course, obvious benefits to the state, since "the principal foundations of future order will be laid here."

Jefferson was opposed to "putting the Bible and Testament into the hands of the children at an age when their judgments are not sufficiently matured for religious enquiries." Instead, their "memories should be stored with the most useful facts of Grecian, Roman, European and American history." They should also be taught "the first elements of morality" in order to learn that happiness "does not depend on the condition of life in which chance has placed them, but is always the result of good conscience, good health, occupation, and freedom in all just pursuits." Jefferson's plan was to select "the youths of genius from among the classes of the poor," who should benefit the state by developing "those talents which nature has sown as liberally among the poor as the rich, but which perish without use, if not sought for and cultivated." Above all, such a plan would make "the people . . . safe, as they are the ultimate guardians of their own liberty."

Jefferson wished the elementary curriculum to be "chiefly historical," because he believed that "history by apprising [the pupils] of the past will enable them to judge of the future; it will avail them of the experience of other times and other nations; it will qualify them as judges of the actions and designs of man; it will enable them to know ambition under every disguise it may assume; and knowing it, to defeat its views." In every government there was "some germ of corruption and degeneracy." All governments degenerated when entrusted to the "rulers of the people alone." People as citizens must be properly informed of the workings of their governments and actively involved on every level. They were the "only safe depositories" of the powers of government. "And to render them safe their minds must be improved to a certain degree." Finally, in his plan of education reform, Jefferson wished to begin "a public library and gallery, by laying out a certain sum annually in books, paintings and statues."

Jefferson's comprehensive scheme for public education constitutes an excellent explication of Enlightenment ideas and its author's notion of the importance in a republic of "a natural aristocracy of talents." It was consistent with the principle of equality, and it advanced the notion of releasing a vast new pool of human energy and intelligence that in traditional societies had been suppressed and lost. At the same time, it was cruel in its ruthless selectivity and intellectually arrogant in its assumption that the ultimate test of the value of human beings was academic. In its faith in reason (especially in its faith in the study of history), it was typical of the Age of Reason (the French revolutionaries worshiped the Goddess of Reason). Whereas Rush insisted that religion was an essential corrective to secular "learning," Jefferson plainly wished to dispense with it.

John Adams had no such comprehensive plan as Jefferson's, but during the American Revolution he had sketched briefly in a letter to Abigail what might be called his generational plan of education. He had written: "I must study politics and war that my sons may have the liberty to study mathematics and philosophy. My sons ought to study mathematics and philosophy, geography, natural history and naval architecture, navigation, commerce and agriculture, in order to give their children a right to study painting, poetry, music, architecture, statuary, tapestry and porcelain."

Later, when, at Rush's urging, Adams and Jefferson renewed their friendship in a series of remarkable letters, Jefferson chided Adams for his outmoded ideas about the aims of education. Jefferson declared that he belonged to the school "who advocated the reform of institutions . . . with the progress of science" and firmly believed that "no definite limits could be assigned to that progress." Adams, on the other hand, had been quoted as advocating "steady adherence to the principles, practices and institutions of our fathers," and speaking as though they represented "the consummation of wisdom, and akme of excellence, beyond which the human mind could never advance." Although Adams had disclaimed "the wish to influence the freedom of enquiry," he had also been quoted as saying that it would "produce nothing more worthy of transmission to posterity, than the principles, institutions, and systems of education received from their ancestors." This seemed to Jefferson such an obscurantist view that he could not consider it Adams's "deliberate opinion." "You possess, yourself, too much science," Jefferson added, "not to see how much is still ahead of you, unexplained and unexplored."

Adams replied, "Checks and Ballances, Jefferson . . . are, our only security, for the progress of Mind, as well as the Security of Body." The *"general principles* of Christianity; and the general Principles of English and American Liberty" were the principles received from the ancestors that Adams believed must be preserved in any proper system of education. Learning had an intellectual or, if Jefferson preferred, a scientific, that is to say a detached, objective, rational element, rigorous in its pursuit of the truth and "progressive" in its nature; but it was also anchored in a world of "general principles" or moral values that were the result of a slow accumulation of human wisdom, and these must balance "scientific" learning.

The future was on Jefferson's side, of course. With each passing decade, education in America came more and more to replace religion as the path to at least worldly salvation. The educational enterprises of religious denominations were gradually supplemented and finally, in large part, replaced on the primary and secondary level by public education; and with the development of state universities and community colleges, even William Manning's democratic reforms were realized.

The Protestant emphasis on education as a means of making God's Word accessible to every Christian merged with the republican notion of education for citizenship and the Enlightenment idea that education would result in the refinement of the individual's rational faculties, the development of science, and the progressive improvement of the race. The result was another curiously American amalgam. Education became a quasi-sacred activity. If its efficacy could not be demonstrated, it had to be believed in. It was an article of the American secular faith that education per se was good. It turned immigrant children into Americans. It was visible tangible evidence that the United States *was* the land of opportunity ruled by Jefferson's aristocracy of talents drawn from all walks of life. Wherever there was a glaring deficiency in American society, there was faith that education would mend it. Education was not, therefore, viewed as a way of transmitting a particular body of knowledge and set of beliefs (although of course it was that in part at least) but as a kind of sacred rite that could overcome evil, heal class and ethnic divisions, reform domestic life, moderate greed, and, finally, insure its subjects of a head start in their "pursuit of happiness."

There was something both touching and admirable in such illusions. Remote from reality as such dreams were, the simple fact is that the American "educational system" was a wonder, and if it necessarily fell far short of the aspirations Americans had for it (since it was, after all, a human and not a divine institution), American history is unimaginable without it.

John Adams was one of the relatively few Americans who believed that "there is no necessary connection between knowledge and virtue. Simple intelligence has no association with morality. What connection is there between the mechanism of a clock or watch and the feeling of moral good and evil, right or wrong?"

Washington, as we have noted, was a supporter of a national university, and Rush was one of its principal promoters. As soon as the Federal Convention had completed its work on the Constitution, Rush drew up a plan entitled "To Friends of the Federal Government: A Plan for a Federal University." Graduates of various colleges would be admitted to the national university for what we would call today postgraduate work. The purpose would be "to prepare our youth for civil and public life." Primary emphasis should be on "the principles and forms of government, applied in a particular manner to the explanation of every part of the Constitution and laws of the United States, together with the laws of nature and nations." Ancient and modern history should be taught, as well as agriculture "in all its numerous and extensive branches"; the "principles and practice of manufactures"; and "the history, principles, objects, and channels of commerce."

Also to be included were natural history and philology, the latter being devoted especially to "the cultivation and perfection of our language." The new age was "the age of simplicity in writing in America," and the refinement of American speech was considered important, as it would "probably be spoken by more people in the course of two or three centuries than ever spoke one language at one time since the creation of the world." French and German should also be taught in the Federal University, as well as "all those athletic and manly exercises . . . which are calculated to impart health, strength, and elegance to the human body." Four young men should be sent abroad to collect and bring back the most advanced knowledge available in Europe in the fields of "agriculture, manufactures, and commerce, and in the art of war and practical government." Two more young men "of suitable capacities should be employed at the public expense in exploring the vegetable, mineral, and animal productions of our country, in procuring histories and samples of each of them, and in transmitting them to the professor of natural history."

"Should this plan of a federal university or one like it be adopted," Rush wrote, "then will begin the golden age of the United States." While European universities were preoccupied with scholarly minutiae "disputes about Hebrew points, Greek particles, or the accent and quantity of the Roman language"—young Americans would be mastering "those branches of knowledge which increase the conveniences of life, lessen human misery, improve our country, promote population, exalt the human understanding, and establish domestic, social and political happiness."

People like Rush and Jefferson were not, of course, satisfied to theorize about education. They worked indefatigably to help create a system of public education, and when conservative legislators dragged their feet they often took matters into their own hands. One of the problems that concerned Rush and others was that while the children of members of Christian denominations, whether Baptist, Congregationalist, or Quaker, had reasonable assurance of receiving at least a rudimentary education in parochial schools, the children of the unchurched, who were presumed to be in the greatest need of practical and moral instruction, had nowhere to go.

In New York, the legislature granted a charter to De Witt Clinton and some other prominent citizens of the city to establish "a Free School in the City of New York for the Education of Such Poor Children as Do Not Belong To or Are Not Provided For, by any Religious Society." The school was intended to provide for children who were "wandering about the streets exposed to the influence of corrupt example" and "destitute of all moral and mental culture." The trustees of the school declared they wished to be "gleaners in the wide field of benevolence." The error of European societies, Clinton wrote, had been to "confide the light of knowledge to the wealthy and the great," while America was, or should be, committed to "dispensing, without distinction, the blessings of education." A decade later fifty women "of distinguished consideration in society and belonging to the different religious denominations" volunteered to be teachers.

When Benjamin Rush's "Plan for Establishing Public Schools" failed to pass the Pennsylvania legislature, Rush helped to establish the Philadelphia Society for the Free Instruction of Indigent Boys.

On the level of primary and secondary education, advocates of free schools and pauper schools contended over public responsibility for education. The free-school champions fought for free public education for all youths. The promoters of pauper schools concentrated their efforts in maintaining schools for the indigent on the grounds that such schools were the only practical antidote to lives of lawlessness and crime. Thus, New York City had five schools for poor black children but none for whites.

One of the motives behind the establishment of schools for poor boys was undoubtedly philanthropic. But another was that every city was troubled by gangs of boys who roamed the city, fought with each other, and committed constant acts of vandalism. The problem became so acute in Philadelphia in the summer of 1795 that Mayor Matthew Clarkson issued a lengthy proclamation deploring "the disorders resulting from the bad conduct and intractableness of . . . children, apprentices and domestics."

Whether the schools were for the sons (and less frequently the daughters) of the prosperous middle and upper classes or for "indigent boys," whether the curriculum was classical or merely practical, the education dispensed to the pupils was saturated with strict moral imperatives and accompanied by an inordinate amount of physical chastisement—whippings, canings, floggings, slappings. Such constant corporal punishment seems to have been a relatively new development. It had not characterized the schools of New England in the early colonial period, and we can only guess at its psychological origins. It may, of course, in part have been the consequence of the generally permissive attitude of many parents toward their children that was so often commented upon by foreign travelers. Indulged at home, they were perhaps unruly in school, and their teachers may have felt obliged to apply the rod vigorously to maintain any kind of order.

Or perhaps such persistent chastisement was simply a by-product of the crudity and roughness of American life. In any event, such an emphasis on physical punishment can hardly have had a salutary effect on its victims. Richard Henry Dana's autobiographical sketch is filled with incidents of being mercilessly thrashed by sadistic masters, and when he visited Japan in later years he marveled, reflecting upon the atmosphere of the Boston schools of his youth, at the happy faces of Japanese schoolchildren who were never subjected to beatings.

To reading, writing, and arithmetic were added, in the more advanced grades, geography, history, and, increasingly, rhetoric, as well as "a little Latin and less Greek" for young scholars who intended to go on to college. Much of the teaching was in the form of simple moral precepts and stories, each of which made an improving point. The tone had been set generations earlier by the famous *New England Primer,* which began with *A* for Adam and solemnly observed, "In Adam's fall we sinned all." Especially favored were stories about the patriots who had won American independence. Washington was the most prominent, and Parson Mason Weems' biography was the favorite, with its shamelessly invented story of priggish young George and the cherry tree ("I cannot tell a lie. I did it with my little hatchet"); but there were numerous other brief lives intended primarily for schoolchildren.

Jedediah Morse, the father of American geography, wrote a *Universal Geography,* the greater part of which was devoted to the geography of America but which in its title indicated its author's determination to place the United States in a proper relation to the rest of the globe. Indeed a good deal of the "radical universalism" of the Revolutionary era survived well into the new century. David Ramsey, who had written an excellent history of the American Revolution, used it as the basis for a "Universal History" that he did not live to complete. His plan, as his literary executor wrote, was to call his work "Universal History Americanized, or, an Historical View of the World, from the earliest records to the 19th century, with a particular reference to the state of society, literature, religion, and form of government in the United States of America."

One widely used history by Samuel Wilson stated propositions common to its species. "The American Revolution had been the offspring of a state of society, rapidly advancing, under circumstances, moral and physical, peculiarly favourable to general improvement." The "consolidation of liberty" in America had set an example for the world. "Astonishment and admiration and sympathy soon ripened into zeal to imitate, as the success of the American example in self-government tested the doctrines of the American Revolution, and proved their soundness. . . . Vast changes in principles and frameworks of governments have already been silently or violently effected; still more extensive and important [ones] are plainly at hand . . . substantial reforms are in progress every where throughout the civilized globe; and all are parts of a stupendous series of organic changes, of which the American Revolution marks the first era."

Wilson was a prophet of progress on "mechanical principles." He wrote: "The co-operation of knowledge and civilization with fortune or Providence, in this work of human regeneration, may not unaptly be compared to that of physical phenomena, which, by the agency of independent laws, without apparent concert, produce the finest and noblest results. Intellectual and moral improvement, the soil from which public virtue and liberty spring as the natural growth is formed, gradually, from a thousand indirect and direct sources, as the earth is formed for the benevolent purposes of vegetation, upon a barren rock."

Many Americans considered such notions dangerously close to heresy. Frederick Butler, who had already written *Sketches of Universal History*, began his *Complete History of the United States . . . down to 1820* with the declaration that his purpose was "To shew that one supreme eternal God created the universe, and by His mighty fiat, spake all worlds into existence, with all the beings that inhabit them . . . that His wisdom regulates and controuls all events, that the smallest as well as the largest are equally the objects of His care. . . . To shew the same superintending power, wisdom, and government of God, in planting his church in this wilderness of the west, and thus laying the foundation of a great nation, which has grown up and taken its rank amongst the free and enlightened nations of the earth, is also the great design of this work."

Thomas Low Nichols, an American journalist whose radical notions were so inhospitably received by his fellow Americans that he emigrated to England, wrote of his schooldays in America: "We were taught every day and in every way that ours was the freest, the happiest, and soon to be the greatest and most powerful country in the world. . . . Our education was adapted to intensify our self-esteem, and to make us believe that we were the most intelligent, the most enlightened, the freest, most Christian, and greatest people the sun ever shone upon. Ours was the model Government of the world; our institutions were the model institutions, our country the model Republic. I do not in the least exaggerate. We read it in our books and newspapers, heard it in sermons, speeches, and orations, thanked God for it in our prayers, and devoutly believed it always."

What is worth noting in the reiteration of America's virtues is that as the century wore on the schoolbooks more and more clearly credited the United States with the attributes of the divine—justice, wisdom, benevolence, power, and glory—and, at least by implication, eternal life.

With each passing decade the notion of universal free public education was pushed as the answer to all the failures and inadequacies in American society. It was, for example, only through education that the poor could be imbued with the proper Christian morality and thereby saved from being charges on society, that middle-class youth might be inspired to emulate the patriots and taught the essentials of citizenship, and that scions of the upper class could be prepared for roles of leadership. It was education that would enable free blacks or the runaway slaves to take their proper place in the larger white society. While Jefferson's ideal of a rational, scientific education made rapid progress, especially in the colleges, it was indistinguishable from more traditional Christian training in its emphasis on the existence of a basic moral order in the universe, which it was the duty of teacher and student to discover and affirm, and in its exaltation of the United States as the consummation of world history.

20

The Family and the Community

If an "individual" inhabits a portion of geography and reacts to that geography in terms of an internal landscape of ideas and, more subtly, of unconscious responses that are often the residue of outmoded and forgotten ideas, he or she lives in a family, the primary and perhaps dominant institution in most societies. Americans were no different. Indeed, if anything, they lived more intensely in families than most peoples. The family had taken on a new importance with the Reformation because certain priestly functions had devolved on the father of the family. In the absence of a number of traditional institutions—a powerful centralized church, a rigid social hierarchy with clearly defined classes—the family became the nucleus of all social groups. Communities were not formed of individuals but of families. So with congregations. Communities were typically congregations of families.

The family, in rural areas, and even to a large degree in the towns, was the basic economic unit. All its members were productively employed sowing and reaping, sewing and weaving, milking and mulching. In this respect, the new Republic was little different from the old colonies. In farming communities like those of western Pennsylvania, the women were almost as active in political matters as

366

the men. In the larger towns middle-class values and attitudes were more evident, and the role of women was apt to be more circumscribed. The town concerned itself more with fashion and fashionable behavior, though, as we have noted, the country was by no means immune to such allurements.

The relationship of father and son was a close one but, again in contrast with traditional societies, the mother-son relationship was also a close one and destined to become far closer, while the father-daughter relationship—the prototype here being Aaron Burr's relationship with his daughter Theodosia—was unique. Indeed, children were often spoiled to a degree that occasioned the comment of foreign visitors. Moreau de St. Mery, a French refugee, complained that American children were "very willful," adding, "in general they are naughty." They demonstrated their naughtiness "in hitting little Negroes" and in throwing snowballs at passers-by, including Moreau; and a Swiss immigrant, Johannes Schweizer, noted that "parental authority is now, and continues to be, in a miserable state. In truth in the nursing child there can already be seen the selfish, bullheaded adult."

An Englishman named Charles Janson had similar observations. He wrote that "most parents make it a principle never to check those ungovernable passions which are born with us, or to correct the growing vices of their children. Often have I, with horror, seen boys, whose dress indicated wealthy parents, intoxicated, shouting and swearing in the public streets. In the use of that stupefying weed, tobacco, apeing their fathers, they smoke segars to [an] immoderate . . . degree."

The family was, typically, a network of relationships that included aunts and uncles, grandparents, great-aunts and great uncles, and numerous cousins. Because the age of mobility had not yet arrived, the majority of the members of an "extended" family lived in the same community and had done so for several generations. The extended family constituted an elaborate social security system that took care of its members in crises of all kinds—illness, old age, death, impoverishment, accidents, birth. Most social life was, by the same token, family life: visiting relatives and observing special days such as birthdays, anniversaries, and Thanksgivings, as well as numerous Sabbaths together. There were, moreover, tasks to be done by all members of a family that were adapted to the age and capacities of the individual from the child of four or five to an ancient aunt.

Grandparents had a central role in the training and education of grandchildren. Their experience was valued as something to be transmitted to the younger generation. (John Adams especially regretted the death of his mother-in-law because her beneficent influence in the rearing of his children would be missed.) At the same time, it should be said that the new age was increasingly youth-oriented. The fact that the Americans were a young people and the United States a young nation was much emphasized as a positive quality, suggesting fresh energies and a boundless future. The Old World was perceived to be tyrannical and corrupt, exercising a discredited authority. The Old Regime in France had been over-thrown by the revolutionary ardor of the young. Revolutions were, after all, the work of young men and women. The old had little taste for revolutionary upheaval.

The American Revolution, like the French, had been the work of comparatively young men; in many instances during that conflict fathers remained loyal to the British Crown while their sons and daughters were patriots. So while old people in the persons of grandparents and elders continued to be honored and respected within the family, their authority was gradually eroded. We thus find disparaging comments on age, especially in the Republican press, where the word "old" was more and more frequently used in a pejorative sense. The Enlightenment faith in progress through science and reason clearly favored the new over the old and, by an inevitable projection, the young over the old. The experience of the old, once treasured and conceived of as an inheritance to be passed on to the young, now often seemed obsolete and out of date. Religion is the area in which, traditionally, the role of elder in passing on the wisdom of the fathers was crucial. But here, too, innovation was the order of the day, and the old religion often appeared to be as irrelevant as the old science.

This negative attitude toward age manifested itself in the new constitutions of Connecticut and New York, which set maximum ages of 70 and 60, respectively, for judges in the higher courts, causing John Adams to write to Jefferson that he could "never forgive New York, Connecticut, or Maine for turning out Venerable Men of sixty or seventy from the seats of Judgement, when their judgement is often the best."

If Americans repressed sex, they gave close, and to the modern imagination, morbid attention to death. Every detail of a loved one's death throes was observed and often recorded in letters or diaries. Death was a common subject of conversation, with much attention to the fashion in which friends and relatives died, what their last words had been, their gestures and expressions, their expectations of a happier life to come. The rites of death were usually extensive, and those who attended the funerals wore mourning clothes.

The family had to perform a number of functions in 1800 that today are taken care of by a variety of public and private agencies and institutions. While formal schooling on the elementary level took place in "reading schools" and "dame schools," and on a more advanced level in grammar schools and, especially in the South, with private tutors, a vast amount of education took place in the family. A father taught his son to harness a horse, plow, milk the cow, hunt deer and wild turkey, fish, and perform an infinite number of practical tasks. A mother taught her daughter to sew and cook, tend a garden, and care for the chickens. All of this training had moral overtones. The good workman praised the Lord by his work. There was no work degrading in itself. As the Puritan poet George Herrick had written, "Who sweeps a room as by Thy laws/Makes that and the action fine." This was the essence of the so-called work ethic. Good work, however humble, was a form of celebration.

Today when monotonous and brutalizing work seems to predominate in our society we hear much repining over the disappearance of the work ethic. Small wonder. As jobs have become more and more dehumanizing, we have lost the sense that they have another dimension—the Protestant notion that "to work is to pray."

The family was a supplementary if not essential school for its children. By the same token, it was the entertainment center. Playing games, singing, playing musical instruments (often homemade), and reading aloud were all common family diversions. Prayers and Bible readings were part of the life of every devout household. In the South, where slave labor permitted extensive leisure activities, play was far more highly developed than in the Middle and Eastern states. Lawn bowling, archery, gambling, horseracing, cockfighting, fencing, billiards, and a wide variety of games such as chess and piquet were all, in a sense, family activities.

In addition to the wide variety of "services" families supplied to their own members, certain families performed a larger social function by supplying, generation after generation, the leaders of their local communities, of their states and, not infrequently, of the nation. This was a phenomenon most readily observed in the larger towns and cities. In Boston, subsequent generations of Adamses, Lowells, Cabots, Ameses, Hollowells, Prescotts, and Warrens were conspicuous in, if they did not dominate, the social and political scene. Connecticut produced successive generations of gifted and energetic Trumbulls, Wolcotts, and Ellsworths. In New York City it often seemed as though the Clintons and the Livingstons divided up the political plums between themselves and their political adherents, with the Jays always pressing them. Philadelphia had the Shippens, Rushes, Chews, Morrises, Drinkwaters, Graydons, and a dozen others; Baltimore, the Carrols, Tilghmans, Bordleys, O'Donovans; Charleston, the Gadsdens, Ravenals, Butlers, and innumerable Pinckneys. Such "old families" (all families are, presumably, equally old, and "old" here refers to families that, through a number of generations, had held on to money and power) constituted the "aristocracy" the Republicans were constantly inveighing against, but it must be noted that there were numerous "old families" in the Republican, as well as in the Federalist, ranks. The Randolph family of Virginia, to which that rabid Republican John Randolph of Roanoke belonged and to which Jefferson was connected, was about as old as an American family could get. The point is that family, in the sense of an inherited and carefully maintained social position, was a major element in the political life of the early Republic.

The modern reader is sensitive to the affectional character of family life. Was it warm and intimate in the eighteenth century? Did members of the family kiss, embrace, touch, laugh, and play together? Or was it cold and formal? Of course families are as different as the individuals who compose them. We have many accounts of family frolics, "romps," expressions of youthful high spirits, and, as Moreau de St. Mery put it, "naughtiness." At the same time, we are chilled to read in a letter from Abigail Adams to John, praising the accomplishments of their remarkable son, John Quincy, that he "laughs too much." The phrase reminds us of a basic repressiveness in the Puritan character. Moderation and reserve were the most valued attributes. (Abigail and John Adams most admired Washington's self-control.)

In the South family relations were more open and expressive, but there the presence of large numbers of household slaves before whom certain appearances must be maintained was also inhibiting. In addition, a subtle but profoundly important change was taking place in the relationships between husbands and wives. The Puritans, as we have seen, recognized sex as a central fact of life and accepted premarital sex as, to a degree, inevitable. The courtship of John and Abigail Adams was one in which mutual sexual attraction was obviously a major element. Yet seventy-five years later Charles Francis Adams, John's grandson, boasted in his diary that he had never had any sexual feelings for his wife-to-be. It appears that sometime in the three quarters of a century between the marriage of John and Abigail Adams and the marriage of their grandson, sexual mores in the United States changed profoundly in the direction of repressiveness. Several things seem clear (though much is certainly obscure). The Revolution brought with it a widely commented on loosening of moral standards. Money became, for example, a kind of free-floating element to be pursued and obtained as best one could (without excessive regard for moral scruple). Sex, which is so commonly related to money, attained a somewhat similar status. Rumors had circulated during the Revolution about a mistress or mistresses of Washington. Hamilton had publicly acknowledged his sordid affair with Maria Reynolds without seriously impairing his standing with his fellow Federalists. There was soon to be a sex scandal involving Jefferson, widely circulated in the Federalist press. A curious document exists purporting to be a record of the sexual exploits of James Wilson. A typical entry reads: "Lay . . . all night with a black wench in the Inn. Dank in oder, but in the breach much the same as the white. Her parts were small, she saying that she had never before enjoyed a man; she shrieked some and shrieked more but I made entry in due form and time, and did most vigorously attend to her."

The purported diary has all the marks of a forgery, but if it is a forgery (it may indeed be the diary of quite another, more obscure James Wilson), it is odd that someone should have taken the trouble to compose it. The intention must have been to circulate it in printed form to damage Wilson politically.

Benjamin Franklin, of course, was much preoccupied with sex. He had at least one illegitimate child and numerous affairs that were by no means dark secrets. Trying to account to his son William Franklin for the latter's illegitimacy, he confessed that the "hard-to-be-governed passion of youth hurried me frequently into intrigues with low women that fell in my way." Indeed, no one has ever discovered who William Franklin's mother was. Franklin's son, in turn, had an illegitimate child by an unknown Englishwoman in London and became in time the Tory governor of New Jersey.

Franklin had seen marriage as a better way to relieve sexual tensions or "licentiousness" than furtive and dangerous encounters with women who might infect a man with disease or claim him to be the parent of her children. But now marriage came to be increasingly separated from sexuality.

The wife was not perceived to be a sexual partner but a housekeeper, homemaker, mother, advancer of her husband's career, and so on. She was fashionable, refined, and genteel—a lady. A lady was not supposed to have strong sexual appetites. That was unladylike. This change in attitude was, of course, a gradual process, and its psychological roots are both complex and obscure.

So far as one can judge, two or three sets of ideas contributed to it. The emphasis on reason and the downgrading of passion may well have played a part. Sexual behavior was "unreasonable," difficult to control and uncertain in its consequences. In addition, in the American psyche, there was an increasing preoccupation with "control," control of one's self, of the environment, of the historical process. Control was, in the main, the child of reason and science. The notion gradually gained currency that semen, like money, should be saved and not spent recklessly. It should be saved, ideally, for the production of children. It was a kind of physical "capital"; if a man spent it foolishly, he would become bankrupt, that is, physically weak and debilitated. Finally, as Protestant Christianity became less and less ardent in its mission of redeeming the world, its negative injunctions were stressed far more than its positive ones. The "Thou shalt not" superseded the "Thou shalt." Moralism gradually replaced piety. Sexuality was an ideal target for a repressive morality.

In the South the institution of slavery affected sexuality as it did all other aspects of life. While it is difficult to tell which came first, the exploitation by white masters of the sexuality of black women or the sexual gentility of their wives, it is clear enough that the identification of slavewomen with uninhibited sexuality reinforced the sexual reserve of white women. Sexual responsiveness was seen by the wives of slaveholding masters as "black" and odious. Mary Chesnut, wife of a planter, wrote bitterly of "the hideous black harem" that slaveowners maintained and added, "Those beastly Negress beauties are only animals," an undoubted reference to their sexual attributes.

So, North and South, sexuality was feared by properly brought up ladies, but, as always, it intruded itself. By the 1820s the romantic movement, in large part a by-product of the French Revolution, had done its bit to cloud the picture by creating a particularly sticky and saccharine ideal of the relationship between the sexes.

That is not to say that no husbands and wives had mutually satisfying sexual relations within their marriages. The situation certainly varied from section to section and, more important, from class to class and from rural to urban environments. Perhaps most important, it varied from individual to individual. Yet overall, it was much as we have described it, and the fact that much sex, in the respectable middle-class world to which a great many Americans belonged, had to be bootlegged, so to speak, had its effect on many other facets of our national life. It might be said to be another of our national schizophrenias—perhaps the prototype of all the others. In any event, it is a theme to which we will be returning throughout this work. Certainly, the character of family life was strongly influenced by the division of women into wives on the one hand, and uninhibited sexual partners on the other.

A classic example of the awkwardness of Americans in regard to sexual matters can be found in William Preston, a young South Carolinian. Preston saw a statue of Venus in Florence that much offended him. He wrote: "The countenance has a bad expression—it is not that of purity and trust. It is not that of a virtuous woman. The nudity of the figure is not pleasant. . . . We can well conceive a grand naked man when wild in the woods . . . but a naked woman is positively unpleasant. I doubt whether her configuration is so conformable to the lines of beauty as that of the male. . . . Modesty is an essential element of female beauty, at least it is to the civilized and Christian mind. Woman is picturesque but not statuesque."

Attitudes toward feminine sexuality had a close relationship to the commonly held views of the proper role of women in American life. The diminished sexual role of the wife was accompanied by a marked loss of status for women generally. The importance and influence they had enjoyed during the colonial and Revolutionary periods unmistakably declined, especially in the larger towns and cities where women lost, along with their "sex appeal," their economic utility.

Even so enlightened a man as Benjamin Rush could write to a young female friend about to be married: "You will be well received in all companies only in proportion as you are inoffensive, polite and agreeable to everybody. . . . Don't be offended when I add that from the day you marry you must have no will of your own. The subordination of your sex to ours is enforced by nature, by reason, and by revelation. . . . In no situation whatever, let the words 'I will' or 'I won't' fall from your lips till you have first found out your husband's inclinations. . . . The happiest marriages I have known have been those when the subordination I have recommended has been most complete. . . . [The ideal wife is] kind, obsequious, uncontradicting."

For those at the lower economic levels of the European nations that provided the greater portion of the population of America, food, shelter, and procreation were the central preoccupations. If the number of Europeans at the bottom of the economic pile who actually starved to death was small, the number who felt the persistent and demoralizing pinch of hunger was large, as were the deaths related to inadequate nutrition. Most poor people lived in wretched dwellings owned by rent-wracking landlords—in bleak rooms that were poorly ventilated, verminous, cold and damp, and cramped with more human beings than the few rooms could accommodate. Space was at a premium. Quaint-looking country cottages were often as crowded and unhealthy as their noisome city counterparts. A farmer or mechanic fortunate enough to procure a tiny piece of land on which to erect a house might well be years in the building of it, taking such time from his regular labors as he could. In such circumstances, with food and space at a premium, a large brood of children was in the nature of a disaster for a workingman and, as a consequence, simple folk methods of birth control were passed on from generation to generation.

In most societies it is observable that the prosperous express their prosperity primarily in terms of those things denied the less fortunate. Thus, in England, enormous feasts and vast manor houses testified to the superior circumstances of the rich. In America the relation of at least the rural poor to food, shelter, and procreation was vastly different.

Whatever else might be lacking, there was usually food in abundance. The immigrant Johannes Schweizer, traveling on the Pennsylvania frontier, was astonished to come upon "the poor hut of a daily laborer who at the time was busy beating flax." Eight half-grown children loitered about the house, enough to sink the hopes of a Swiss farmer, but the wife was quick to buy one of the Bibles Schweizer was peddling and then invited him to dinner. He hesitated, thinking that a large family in such modest circumstances must be strained to feed an extra mouth. "But how amazed I was," Schweizer wrote. "Instead of the meager meal I expected there were sausages, ham, a guinea hen, cabbage and salad, butter, white bread, jam, and an apple pie on the table." White bread was a rare luxury on the table of a European peasant. In Schweizer's homeland such a feast would be the mark of a prosperous man or reserved for a wedding or a funeral. "You must help yourself as best you can when you are poor and have so many children," the wife said to her incredulous guest. When the children were older they planned to go up the Susquehanna River, where cheap land still might be bought. "Here they had only eight acres and this is hardly enough to feed their three cows and eight pigs." To Schweizer, it was a kingdom.

Schweizer's comments were echoed by many other immigrants. An abundance of food, especially beef and white flour, was one of the most conspicuous aspects of American society at every economic level, if we except the urban poor. What in other countries people schemed, fought, robbed for, and hoarded was, in the United States, the bounty of the seemingly inexhaustible land.

At one farm when Schweizer asked the owner how many cows he had, the man replied that he really had not counted them recently. They roamed free in the woods, and he suspected that he may have had several stolen but trusted that his cows had calved and more than covered his losses. In such circumstances food was clearly abundant.

It was much the same with shelter. The American favored a house that could be simply, quickly, and cheaply constructed and often almost as quickly abandoned. The ideal building material was the lumber of trees that, in any event, had to be cut down to make space for fields, pastures, and gardens. We can hardly recapture the delight that an immigrant on the frontier must have felt at the notion that the materials with which to build his house were *free*. If he wished something more elaborate than a log hut, he had to mill the lumber himself or pay a modest fee to the miller. Since expense was "no consideration," the average American was perpetually building, re-building, enlarging, adding on with the increasing size of his family. Schweizer wrote, "Nothing astonishes the Germans [and Swiss] as much as the gorgeous houses of the farmers." Often a farm recapitulated the progress of its owner from poverty to wealth. The original cabin would be preserved and used perhaps as a shelter for pigs or cows or a smokehouse. Near it would be a more pretentious frame house, now perhaps occupied by a son or a hired hand, and finally, a handsome brick or stone mansion in Greek Revival style for the master of the farm.

With plenty of food and space, procreation was an asset rather than a liability, and many Americans took conspicuous advantage of the fact by having very large families, thereby producing, in effect, their own labor force.

If Americans had a new relationship (or a different one) to food, shelter, and procreation, they also must be considered in regard to their attitude toward time. Americans have always stood in a peculiar relationship to time. Hermann Maurer, the German sociologist of religion and disciple of Max Weber, wrote, "Time had to become God's Time before it could become Daylight Savings Time." God required a careful accounting of how one spent his or her time, which was the portion of eternity one was allotted by God. To waste it was, in the American variant of Protestant Christianity, a sin only slightly less grave than pride. In John Adams; his son, John Quincy; and his grandson, Charles Francis, we find this same guilty refrain. "My day was otherwise much wasted"; "I wasted my afternoon, excepting in a walk with Mr. Brooks"; "Having finished Rollin I hardly knew what to do with myself and wasted the time somewhat in doing little or nothing." This litany of lost time is from Charles Francis Adams's diary, but it could as well have been from his father's or grandfather's. It was a common trait of Americans. It was what propelled them into that hurried and harried pace that few foreigners failed to comment upon, which made the men one passed on the street look pale and anxious and, with each generation, increased the incidence of what came to be known as "nerves," a kind of national disease. After several weeks in the United States, Johannes Schweizer wrote, "It is impossible for Europeans to imagine the activity and energy or rather reality and life, of America. It is the dream of a high fever."

If men and women inhabit a space, live perhaps even more intensely in a world of ideas and of unconscious residues of acquired attitudes and assumptions, and reside in families that place their ineradicable stamp upon them, they also live in communities, or certainly did in the United States in 1800. These communities came in two basic sizes—small and smaller. The American cities, or the population centers that deserved that name in 1800, were no more than half a dozen in number, and they were, without exception, seacoast ports—Boston, New York, Philadelphia, Baltimore, and Charleston. These cities ranged in size from Philadelphia's 45,000 to Boston's 20,000 and Baltimore's 15,000. Everybody else lived in towns of a few hundred to a few thousand or, in the South, on scattered farms or plantations. Thus, out of a population of some million no more than 150,000 lived in "cities," all of substantially less than 50,000 people. In other words, not quite 5 percent of the population were city dwellers, and even the city dwellers lived in what we would today call small towns.

As the communities were of two sizes, so were they of two types—what I have chosen to call "cumulative" and "convenanted" communities. The cumulative communities were those where people congregated or accumulated in response to some economic opportunity. The seacoast ports would be the prototype. The covenanted communities were those that were established, usually by a group of families who shared some common religious faith or social vision, as *communities*. Thus a half-dozen families from Salem, Massachusetts, dissatisfied with the liberal tendencies of the local Congregational congregation, might move in a body to Salem, Vermont, or Salem, Ohio. The process by which such towns reproduced themselves might be termed a form of social "cloning," that is to say, a process by means of which the clone was almost indistinguishable from the original, being perhaps only somewhat more conservative. The effect was to create a method of settlement for new communities that preserved a remarkable degree of homogeneity with the parent communities. Each new covenanted community carried with it the social forms and institutions of the old, the character of family life, the basic religious attitudes and racial type. Even the politics of the parent community were usually faithfully reproduced in its offspring. The New England settlers who made up the greater portion of the new settlement in the area north and west of the Ohio River brought with them the classic institutions of the New England town—the church, the school, and the militia muster. They were familiar with the system of land distribution in the Western territories since the Northwest Ordinance had incorporated the township method of land division practiced in New England.

The cumulative towns were settlements that grew up around some trade junction or natural resource that could be readily exploited. River junctions such as the confluence of the Allegheny, Youghiogheny, Monongahela, and Ohio rivers, the site of Pittsburgh, or St. Louis at the conjunction of the Missouri and Mississippi rivers, were ideal locations for such towns; and they often grew rapidly while the covenanted communities, not being oriented primarily toward economic activity, usually remained small. Sometimes, of course, convenanted communities that located, more or less inadvertently, at economically favorable sites enjoyed (or suffered from) expansion as rapid as that of any cumulative community.

The two types of community, in their ideal forms, could be said to represent the two aspects of the American character that we have discussed: the desire to make money quickly and in large amounts; and the desire to redeem the world. Often the founders of the covenanted communities were conspicuously unworldly men and women, dreamers and visionaries, reformers and revivalists. Even when they turned their hands to practical business activities, they often proved too impractical and unstable for such routine ventures.

The speculators, the get-rich-quick, fast-buck artists accumulated in the cumulative communities and gave them a "boom-town" atmosphere from their inception. In the latter part of the century, they were the "wide-open" mining towns, the lumber towns, the cattle towns, familiar from a thousand Hollywood movies. A popular ditty in a particular cumulative town went "Churches and schools/Are for women and fools;/So rally around the saloon, boys."

The majority of towns in the United States in 1800 were much closer to the covenanted than to the cumulative towns, though many were, to be sure, a combination of the two, and the development of canals had given a stimulus to the rise of towns along rivers and canals as trading centers and transfer points.

According to their nature, towns provided their inhabitants with a variety of services and diversions. These ranged from the schools and churches of the covenanted towns to the taverns and bawdy houses of the rawer cumulative communities. For most small towns the church was the center of social as well as religious life. In New England communities, "horse-shedding" was perhaps the most common form of social life. Every church had a horse shed for the protection of the horse carriages that brought their owners to town for Sunday meeting. Between the morning and afternoon services, members of the congregation gathered, weather permitting, in the horse sheds to gossip, argue theology, or simply "visit."

Election day, militia muster day, and Thanksgiving Day were community holidays and times for socializing. There was sledding in the winter, swimming and fishing in the summer, hunting in the fall. I have argued elsewhere that the small town was an especially congenial environment for a boy to grow up in, to gain a sense of confidence in his own powers and, in time, of mastery. An old friend of mine who had grown up in such a town, trying to account for the effect on him of his small-town origin, declared that it had given him the assurance that there was no one so far above him or beneath him that he could not meet him on an equal footing.

The town allowed boys and girls to grow at their own pace. Its social and political life was multigenerational. Moreau de St. Mery, noting the addiction of Americans, especially of women, to dancing, added, "at the same dance you will see a grandfather, his son and his grandson, but more often still the grandmother, her daughter and her granddaughter. If a Frenchman comments upon this with surprise, he is told that each one dances for his own amusement, and not because it's the thing to do."

Religious revivals, or freshenings, were common to towns; they were almost, in fact, an institutionalized part of town life. With all its simple pleasures town life was often narrow, hard, and emotionally constraining. Revivals provided an opportunity for an outpouring of emotions that were generally suppressed. To sing and shout, to weep and pray together periodically was an essential release and a means of reaffirming the solidarity of the town. The pressures for conformity in the town were persistent. Many towns were one-denomination towns—all Congregationalists or Baptists or Quakers—or one-party towns, Federalist or Republican or "reform" towns, antislavery or temperance. Later in the century Mastersville, Ohio, was a Republican, strongly antislavery town. It had only one Democrat—Tex, the town drunk, from Texas, of course. The young men of Mastersville amused themselves by getting Tex drunk on election day (not a difficult task) and tricking him into voting Republican.

Family and community, then, were the essential matrices in which the American character was formed. There were other "characters" of course, but they were, in a sense, deviations from that basic character.

21

Urban Life

A merica's cities were far more cosmopolitan than its towns. They were points of entry, not just for foreign merchandise and immigrants, but for ideas, news, and fashions.

It has been estimated that as many as twenty-five thousand French refugees came to the United States in the decade immediately following the storming of the Bastille. Since most of them congregated in Philadelphia and New York, it seems safe to assume that they made a substantial impact on those cities. Some had been strong supporters of the Revolution until, by some word or act, or by virtue of their class, they had brought on themselves the all too readily evoked wrath of those who momentarily held power. Others, repulsed by the bloody excesses of the Paris Commune, sought asylum in America.

Among the more notable émigrés was Moreau de St. Mery. Born of a wealthy French colonial family in Martinique, Moreau was a scholar of the laws of the West Indies; he settled in Paris in 1784 and at the outbreak of the Revolution threw himself so wholeheartedly into the cause that he was elected president of the provisional governing body of Paris in the spring of 1789. In that capacity, he received the keys of the Bastille after its fall on July 14, and he did his best to bring order to the distracted city. A colleague wrote of him on that memorable night, "his prudence and *sang-froid* grew stronger in the midst of excitement . . . immovable as a rock beaten upon by a storm, he remained at his post while everyone else deserted." The members of the provisional government, upon being superseded by the Commune, ordered a medal awarded to Moreau for "the coolest courage, the most courageous foresight and the most unvarying devotion to the cause." When he opposed the lawlessness and violence of the Paris mobs, he was attacked in the street, beaten badly, and left for dead. After Robespierre seized power, Moreau fled the country just ahead of the guillotine.

In the United States he found or was soon joined by a number of his countrymen, among them the duc d'Orléans, the future ruler of France as Louis Philippe, and Charles Maurice de Talleyrand-Périgord, bishop of Autun, former and future foreign minister of France. Gouverneur Morris, as American minister to France following Jefferson's return home, knew Talleyrand and appears to have shared a mistress with him. Talleyrand, like Moreau, had been a leader in the initial stages of the Revolution. He was appointed to a committee to draft a new constitution for France, but when the massacres broke out in September, 1792, Talleyrand feared his own life was in danger. He escaped to England and, expelled from that country, sailed for America where Moreau encountered him in May, 1794. The thirty months Talleyrand spent in America were not, on the whole, happy ones. He found a kindred spirit in Alexander Hamilton, but the determination of the Republicans to support the Revolution without question or cavil made life difficult for him. Moreau tells in his journal of watching a celebration of the Fourth of July from the windows of Talleyrand's house in New York with a group of exiles, all of whom had been early supporters of the Revolution. He wrote: "The Governor [Mifflin] and the people who accompanied him in this fête were preceded by a long procession of French Jacobins, marching two by two, singing the *Marseillaise* and other republican songs. Both times, going to the fête and bringing the Governor back from it, they interrupted themselves to address invectives to us in the windows where they saw us. . . . The Minister of France to the United States, Genêt . . . was in the procession, and sang and insulted us like all the others. We wept for our country and for him."

It is hard to imagine a scene more charged with irony: seven Frenchmen, who had supported the Revolution and knew it at first hand, abused by Americans celebrating their Independence Day.

To make ends meet, Moreau opened a "printing, stationary and book shop," catering primarily to French refugees in the city. He also added to his stock "certain small contrivances—ingenious things said to have been suggested by the stork"—birth control devices, undoubtedly condoms, of which he carried "a complete assortment" for the four years he remained in business. Though like the books, the condoms were stocked "primarily . . . for the use of French colonials, they were in great demand among Americans, in spite of the false shame so prevalent among them."

In addition to the French refugees, Philadelphia numbered many other foreigners among its inhabitants. They collected in particular parts of the city; the area above Third Street in the Northern Liberties, for instance, was given over almost entirely to Germans. Moreau de St. Mery noted that "Almost all . . . foreigners come from Europe because they are discontented with their governments. . . . They hate cities, and suspect everyone of profiteering, speculation, etc."

A young English scholar and translator, John Davis, attributed to the influence of French émigrés a vast improvement in the way young Philadelphia women walked and carried themselves. They "blushed at their own awkwardness, and each strove to copy that swimming air, that nonchalance, that ease and apparent unconsciousness of being observed, which characterized the French young ladies as they passed through the streets." And while some simply appeared ridiculous in trying to imitate their visitors, "many polished their natural ease into elegance." In the same city, Davis one day observed a group of young men from Charleston "sitting before the door of the Indian Queen [a popular bar] drinking punch cooled with ice, and obscured in volumes of tobacco smoke . . . laughing over their adventures in Mulatto Alley, at Charleston, or recommending to each other the different brothels at Philadelphia." At this juncture (it was a beautiful moonlight night) an American girl threw up the window and sang a song to the company in the room. "When the song was concluded, the lads from Charleston gave it their applause. . . . 'Encore! encore! bravo! bravissimo!'" The ladies responded by continuing "to warble in succession." The incident indicated to Davis a freedom, openness, and "simplicity of manners" in social matters that was uniquely American.

Moreau de St. Mery, as befitted a Frenchman, made extensive observations about American sexuality. "Bastards," he noted, "are extremely common in Philadelphia." The reason, he believed, was that when a child was twelve months old, his mother could "farm him out for twenty-one years. This makes it possible for her to commit the same sin for a second time." While Moreau found American women uncommonly pretty, he was startled at the freedom they enjoyed. Everything seemed concentrated in their youth: "while charming and adorable at fifteen, they are faded at twenty-three, old at thirty-five, decrepit at forty or forty-five." He wrote that what astonished him more was that "they invariably make their own choice of a suitor, and the parents raise no objection because that's the custom of the country. The suitor comes into the house when he wishes; goes on walks with his loved one whenever he desires. On Sunday he often takes her out in a cabriolet, and brings her back in the evening without anyone wanting to know where they went." But such freedom ended with marriage. "When one considers the unlimited liberty which young ladies enjoy," Moreau wrote, "one is astonished by their universal eagerness to be married, to become wives who will for the most part be nothing but housekeepers of their husbands' homes." It appeared to Moreau that the desire to marry was "inspired by the fear that she who does not marry will be thought to have some fault that disgusted her suitors."

The Frenchman then goes on to "say something that is almost unbelievable." Upper-class Philadelphia women, he wrote, "without real love and without passions, give themselves up at an early age to the enjoyment of themselves; and they are not at all strangers to being willing to seek unnatural pleasures with persons of their own sex." Just how Moreau penetrated into such a dark territory is not explained.

Accompanying the remarkable freedom allowed young women was an equally remarkable prudery. He noted: "The American women divide their whole body into two parts; from the top to the waist is stomach; from there to the foot is ankles. This poses a dilemma for doctors who must penetrate this extreme delicacy to discover the nature of a patient's ailment. He is forbidden the slightest touch; his patient, even at the risk of her life, leaves him in the vaguest doubt." One young woman of his acquaintance who had a sore on her breast could bring herself only to describe it to her doctor as a pain in her stomach.

The Frenchman also noted that Quaker youths were "visitors in the houses of ill fame, which have multiplied in Philadelphia and are frequented at all hours. . . . The street walkers are of every color." The latter had become surprisingly bold. They were "very young and very pretty girls, elegantly dressed, who promenade two by two, arm in arm and walking very rapidly at an hour which indicates that they aren't just out for a stroll. . . . Anyone who accosts them is taken to their home. They pretend to be small dressmakers. They fulfill every desire for two dollars."

There was another class of women in Philadelphia who acted as procuresses. "A man who wished a sexual partner was introduced to them and they arranged for an assignation at their own homes, sending for a girl to meet their customer's specifications." According to Moreau, "if a man desired a beautiful person of high rank, or one more difficult to persuade, or supposed to be a virgin, higher prices [than the normal three dollars] had to be paid, either in money or in gifts." Sometimes a young man who met a woman under such circumstances was startled and embarrassed to find that she was someone he knew socially.

Moreau's observations on the sexual behavior of Philadelphians are so at odds with our commonplace notions of sexual mores in the early period of our history that one can hardly avoid speculating on their accuracy, especially since they are not supported by other contemporary accounts. Here it can be said only that sex has been for some time an area of French expertise. Moreau de St. Mery obviously felt none of the inhibitions in discussing it that constrained Americans and visiting Englishmen. Moreover, at almost every point where his journal can be checked on other matters, Moreau appears to have been a perceptive and accurate observer.

If I am correct in my speculation that sex became, like money, "an independent variable," detached from its primary locus in the family marriage bed, it clearly came in consequence to be more and more specifically attached to particular women who "sold" it or provided it for money. Prostitutes were no recent phenomenon in America, to be sure. They were evident in every port town of the colonial era. What was far more novel was the appearance of mistresses, the "kept women" of those men who could afford them. To resort occasionally to prostitutes, serving girls, or "low women" (it is interesting to note that uninhibited sexuality came, increasingly, to be associated with "lower-class" women) was one thing; to keep a mistress before or after marriage was quite another matter.

For the city dweller there were plays, exhibitions, circuses, concerts, balloon ascensions, bookstores, newspapers, museums, and, in Philadelphia, a planetarium. In Philadelphia, New York, and

Baltimore, street vendors sold oysters from large tubs, as one visitor reported, "by the dozens and hundreds up to ten o'clock at night . . . where they are peddled on barrows to the accompaniment of mournful cries."

There was much social life and "entertaining" among the upper class, lavish dinners and interminable teas on the British model. Moreau reported that his hosts in Philadelphia commonly had a breakfast at nine of ham, herring, toast, and coffee or tea. Roast beef and potatoes was a popular dinner dish, but there was always an egg and a fish course as well, boiled green peàs and "thinly sliced cabbage," and a quantity of sweets, to which Americans were "excessively partial and which are insufficiently cooked." For dessert there was, typically, fruit, cheese, and pudding, all of which were washed down with hard cider, beer, and white wine. The main course was accompanied by Bordeaux or Madeira. After dessert the women, again following the English mode, which seemed barbaric to the Frenchman, withdrew and left the men to smoke their cigars and drink an interminable round of toasts. "Sometimes," Moreau added, "dinner is prolonged in this manner far into the night, but finally the dinner table is deserted because of boredom, fatigue or drunkenness." The whole family was united at tea, "to which friends, acquaintances and even strangers are invited."

Moreau and a number of other visitors commented on the extremes of temperature to be experienced in American cities— "atmospheric inconsistency," as he called it. The cities were stifling in summer, and the cold was "glacial" in winter. Moreau also noted, quite shrewdly and accurately, that Americans, "in spite of their pretended detestation of the English . . . really love them, even though they fear them. In spite of their conceit, they subconsciously feel themselves to be inferior to the English. . . . Their tastes, their customs and above all their habits are really the same as those of the English."

Philadelphia was the foremost city of the United States, the capital *pro tem* and the scene of innumerable reforms and improvements characteristic of the new age. Like its sister cities, it was a commercial center, and the making of money and the talk of it were the constant preoccupations of most of its inhabitants. While European cities were also trading and manufacturing centers, the commercial spirit was leavened by the dominance of a more or less parasitic aristocracy that lived on inherited wealth from great estates or royal patronage of various kinds. To such a class, talking of money was boring and in bad taste. To many Americans, especially those who lived in the cities, it was the most important and absorbing topic imaginable. Moreau de St. Mery and numerous other foreign visitors often took caustic note of this unattractive obsession. Brissot de Warville, a French traveler, wrote of the people of Boston: "Commerce occupies all their thought, turns all their heads, and absorbs all their speculations. Thus you find few estimable works, and few authors." Moreau wrote: "Love of money sometimes even stifles delicacy." Americans of Dutch descent seemed to the Frenchman especially penny-pinching: "They carry niggardliness so far it couldn't possibly go farther. They almost starve themselves, and treat their slaves miserably."

Since money was the essence, everything was for sale. "Americans cling to nothing, attach themselves to nothing. . . . Four times running they will break ground for a new home, abandoning without a thought the house in which they were born, the church where they learned about God, the tombs of their fathers, the friends of their childhood, the companions of their youth, and all the pleasures of their first society. . . . Everywhere, even in Philadelphia, which is America's outstanding city, everything is for sale, provided the owner is offered a tempting price. He will part with his house, his carriage, his horse, his dog—anything at all."

The two theaters of Philadelphia were conveniently known as the Old and the New Hall. The New Hall could accommodate 750 persons in the pit, the boxes, and the balcony. Blacks and the lower orders of women were admitted only to the balcony. Moreau de St. Mery wrote that the plays were acted with considerable gusto and that the entr'actes were frequently bawdy, with "such words as Goddamn, Bastard, Rascal, Son of a Bitch. Women turn their backs to the performance during these interludes."

Theatergoers had the pleasure of seeing the English comedian John Bernard, who had been lured to Philadelphia by the extravagant salary of one thousand pounds a year. He was popular as Shylock, Hotspur, Falstaff, Bottom, and played in a number of light comedies. Bernard, who was also a shrewd social critic, traveled widely and left an account of a typical tavern breakfast of "eggs and bacon," noting that it was not uncommon for the guest to have to prepare his own and wait upon himself. He wrote: "No sooner were you seated than the house dog (of the large wolf-breed) would arrange himself beside you, and lift his lank, hungry jaws expressively to your face, [while] the young children, never less than a dozen (the women seeming to bear them in litters in those regions), at the sight and smell of the victuals would set up yell enough to frighten the wolves. . . ."

The city had also constructed one of the first and certainly the handsomest public waterworks in the country. Charles Willson Peale's museum, on the ground floor of the American Philosophical Society, was a remarkable repository of stuffed birds and animals, dinosaur bones and fossils, and Indian artifacts. The city prison was the largest in the United States, the best designed and most up to date. Work was provided for the inmates, and the sexes were segregated—an important new reform—as was the practice of separating the common criminals from those imprisoned for debt. The emphasis was on rehabilitation rather than on punishment. Capital punishment was limited to treason and egregious murders, and some reformers like Rush wished it abolished.

Moreau de St. Mery was told that of 4,860 debtors and 4,000 criminals confined in the prison in a ten-year period, only ten had died, "and no criminal who was released has been convicted again." Credit for the reforms was given to the Philadelphia Society for Alleviating the Miseries of Public Prisons.

The larger cities, built for the most part of wooden frame houses that were heated by fireplaces and lit by candles and oil lamps, were constantly threatened by devastating fires, and had, in consequence, developed highly efficiently volunteer fire departments whose training and equipment were the wonder of foreign visitors. Hardly a night passed in New York, for example, during which the fire bell was not rung and one or more of the insurance company fire-fighting teams did not turn out to combat a dangerous conflagration. New York City had 1,347 firemen with 42 hand-drawn or horse-drawn engines and thousands of feet of hose.

Philadelphia's College of Physicians, "formed to encourage knowledge in medicine, anatomy, chemistry, and in order to render the practice of medicine more uniform," was the first of its kind in the United States. At the Pennsylvania Hospital, Rush had made the insane patients his special concern. They had been confined in damp cells in the basement of the hospital building until Rush urged the "managers" to change their accommodations. The cells, he wrote, were "dishonorable both to the science and humanity of the city of Philadelphia." Rush was especially unhappy over the practice of confining the insane in straitjackets, also called "mad shirts." He had seen patients in such devices lying in their own excrement. To supplant the straitjacket, Rush designed a less oppressive chair to which patients might be bound.

Habits to which city dwellers were addicted were incessant smoking and, what was even more objectionable, chewing tobacco and spitting "promiscuously." Moreau was also convinced that Americans ruined their digestive systems by drinking liquids that were much too hot in the winter and too cold in the summer, so that their stomachs were constantly subjected to thermal shock and doused with "liquors, rum, brandy, whiskey." Drunkenness was, in consequence, a very common phenomenon.

Philadelphia was called the City of Brotherly Love, but Moreau de St. Mery observed that this love was not extended to "colored people." Although, through the efforts of the Quakers, there were few slaves, black people were usually servants and were generally treated with contempt and hostility. Workmen would not accept them as fellow laborers or apprentices and, Moreau noted, "when it snows, any colored man who passes is sure to be showered with snowballs by white children." Blacks of course had their own society and their own life. They could not be buried in white cemeteries or attend white churches. The African Methodist Episcopal Church was the church of upper-class blacks. On Sunday, black women dressed in all their finery with "chignons of white people's false hair, white kid gloves and parasols." Young black women commonly dressed in pink.

"For the shocking contempt with which they are treated in Philadelphia, black women had some revenge," according to Moreau, by seducing "young white girls and sell[ing] them to houses used for corrupt practices. The price for such a transaction is ordinarily thirty dollars, of which the purveyor keeps the better part." Such houses were among the "snare[s] to betray unwary youths" that Rush deplored.

In the same city the Pennsylvania Abolition Society, having little hope of abolition, did its futile best to improve the condition of "free people of color in the United States." At a convention in Philadelphia in 1796 the society issued an address to free blacks urging them to "turn to the various religions, learn reading, writing and arithmetic, bring up their children properly; . . . study the Holy Scripture, that monument to the fundamental equality and parenthood of the human race which has only one father; that they encourage their children to learn useful trades, to be faithful to their duties as fathers, mothers, husbands and wives; that they abstain from strong liquor, avoid intemperance and dangerous pleasures, enter only into legal marriages." In these injunctions one discovered common themes that were to recur in all white admonitions to blacks down to the present moment. Free black life, with its looseness and spontaneity, its extravagant and expressive emotional life, its deep springs of sadness and laughter, was a perpetual source of uneasiness to white society, and even those whites who labored most valiantly to free the slaves and improve the status of free blacks were disconcerted to discover that free blacks did not necessarily turn into whites with black skins but often preserved a life and consciousness of their own that whites could not penetrate. Like the free and (by white standards) indolent life of the Indian, who seemed to spend his time in those yearned-for and fantasied masculine pursuits of hunting, fishing, fighting, and making love, the secret life of blacks was both alluring and disquieting, and the identification of blacks with sexuality made it especially so. The more anxious and repressive white society became in matters of sex, the more black sexuality troubled whites.

Since one of the ways by which we express our social (and sometimes our political) views is in our dress (today we have articles of clothing that carry messages in words and pictures), it is not surprising that the post-Revolutionary–period Federalists and Republicans expressed themselves as emphatically through their attire as by their words and writings. Federalists, by and large, clung to the old-style costume, with powdered hair for younger men, wigs for the older, kneebreeches, silk stockings and buckled shoes, long coats of wool (silk or velvet for more formal occasions), and flowered vests. Their enemies affected the styles popular in Revolutionary France. Perhaps the most striking innovation was trousers, earlier known as "skilts" and "tongs," and worn by farmers and European peasants.

Democrats scorned wigs and powdered hair, and instead of holding the hair back in a peruke or tying it with a ribbon, they allowed it to hang more or less naturally and cut it to a length slightly above the collar. More important, it was encouraged to "flow" and curl gracefully over the forehead and around the face, or, as a critic put, it must be worn "as if you had been fighting a hurricane backward." Sideburns were popular. Tricornered hats were replaced by high-crowned round hats.

Rush noted, among his inventory of improvements in life-style, that "umbrellas, which were formerly a part of female attire only, are now used in warm and wet weather, by men of all ranks in society." Republicans nonetheless attacked them as symbols of luxury and effeminacy. The wearing of underwear had become common and was considered a health measure in a time when baths were infrequent and considered by many to be unhealthy.

Women's dress was "looser," as became a more open and free society. Older women were offended at the abandonment of stays and the emphasis placed on female breasts. Abigail Adams noted at a presidential party that when some of the women present curtesied, their breasts almost escaped from unsubstantial moorings.

Women began to wear trousers, as they were called, almost as soon as men did. They were of many cuts and shapes, from beguilingly tight to remarkably loose. Pantaloons that came down the calf were also popular, and buckles on shoes were replaced by more democratic laces. Even hats grew more democratic. A young Connecticut woman took out a patent for a straw material for bonnets and won a prize of twenty pounds from the London Society of Arts for her design. Women's hats had "scarce any rim" and were "turned up at each side and worn very much on the side of the head," a contemporary observer tells us.

The world of fashion, which was thoroughly though not exclusively Federalist, caused offense to critics by what seemed to them a frivolous and excessive concern with the latest and most extreme modes. The French traveler Brissot de Warville noted with regret that seven or eight women at a party were "all dressed in great hats, plumes, etc. . . . Two among them had their bosoms very naked. I was scandalized at this indecency among republicans." "Detached curls" were popular in women's hair.

The fact was that even among staunch Republicans high fashion competed constantly with democratic simplicity. Dogskin shoes were in great demand among beaus and fops and again denounced by democrats as symbols of Federalist decadence. Special attention indeed came to focus on the shoe. The year 1800 was the year that right and left shoes were invented; heretofore they had been interchangeable. Their inventor, William Young of Philadelphia, who may be one of the more notable if obscure benefactors of the race, advertised shoes in "Plover and snipe toes, goose and gander toes, gosling toes, hog and bear snouts, ox and cow mouths. . . . Suwarrows, Cossacks, hussars, Carrios, double-tongues, Bonapartes . . . Swiss hunting, fulldress, walking, York." Shoe polish was invented the same year. Indeed, one has the impression that all the variety and elegance that had formerly been expressed in wigs, velvet coats, embroidered vests, and lace cuffs had descended to the shoe, that most utilitarian article of clothing!

Thomas Carlyle has demonstrated that the garments we wrap our poor bones in are as eloquent a record of our inner selves as the pictures we paint or the buildings we build. From William Young to Brooks Brothers the clothes worn by American men and women provide a revealing index to manners and attitudes far beyond the merely sartorial.

Perhaps as revealing as dress were the names Americans gave to the communities they founded with such bewildering rapidity. Name-giving is one of the primary and most mysterious attributes of man. Strange powers inhere in names, and in giving them we reveal much of ourselves. Citizens of the United States, by founding, in a few generations, thousands upon thousands of communities, had the opportunity to exercise this name-giving capacity as no other people in history. They drew on eight basic categories of names: (1) heroes of the Revolution—Washington, Franklin, Madison, and so on; (2) cities of classical times—Athens, Rome, Corinth, Troy; (3) Indian names—Coosawhatchie, Chickahominy, Allagash; (4) cities mentioned in the Bible—Bethlehem, Shiloh, Bethesda; (5) names of a founder—Jonesville, Henry, Mastersville; (6) literary allusions—Ivanhoe, Byron, Hiawatha; (7) names taken from an event—Bloody Mountain, Cripple Creek, Stray Horse Gulch; (8) mocking names—Hardscrabble, Cash and Carry, Hell-for-Sartin.

We can tell a good deal about the aspirations (or lack of them) of the settlers of a community by the name they gave it. Thus, religious names—Bethel or Mount Hermon—almost invariably indicate that the town was started by settlers with strong religious convictions, often in the aftermath of a religious revival.

In the period following the establishment of the new government, when the country was very conscious of analogies to the Greek democracies and the Roman Republic, there was a rash of Romes (New York, 1786), Athenses (Georgia, 1801; New York, 1805; Pennsylvania, 1786), Uticas, Syracuses, Troys, and so on. Foreign visitors who came upon an Athens or a Paris in the forest—a huddle of log cabins, clapboard buildings, and muddy streets—were invariably given to reflections on human folly and presumption. None of those communities so boldly named turned out to be serious rivals of the originals, although some grew to be respectable metropolises. Syracuse and Memphis thrived, but the Athenses and Romes serve largely to remind us of the extraordinary pretensions of our ancestors. There is a naivete in all such evocations of antiquity that invites ridicule, but a destiny has to be dreamed before it can be achieved, and it must be said that an essential part of America was fashioned out of such extravagant dreams.

Americans have, from the very beginning, had a deep ambivalence about cities. There have probably been few cities in modern times more compelling than Philadelphia at the turn of the eighteenth century. It was the archetypal city with all the pleasures and delights of urban life, prosperous, enlightened, the home of the best science, the liveliest politics, the most civic-minded citizens, the most progressive public institutions, with a constantly growing and fascinatingly heterogeneous population—an American microcosm. Yet more than 90 percent of all Americans were farmers. The great majority of these had never even visited a city, but "the city" nevertheless existed in their imaginations as an unholy place where bankers, land speculators, stockbrokers, and various other money manipulators lived; where people put on airs (Moreau de St. Mery, the French aristocrat and scholar, was told that he couldn't have a ticket to George Washington's birthday ball because he was a shopkeeper!), wore fancy clothes, and spent the money they had extracted from gullible countrymen on balls, fancy carriages, and imported luxuries.

The city was, above all, the place where sin abounded in the form of illicit sex and its constant companion, venereal disease. Thomas Jefferson was the spokesman for the rural ethic. He wrote: "Those who labour in the earth are the chosen people of God, if ever He had a chosen people, whose breasts He has made His particular deposit for substantial and genuine virtue. . . . Corruption of morals in the mass of cultivators is a phenomenon of which no age nor nation has furnished an example . . . generally speaking, the proportion which the aggregate of the other classes of citizens bears in any state to that of its husbandmen, is the proportion of its unsound to its healthy parts, and a good enough barometer whereby to measure its degree of corruption."

Manufacturing, in Jefferson's view, was best left to Europe and its depressed masses. "The mobs of great cities," he concluded, "add just so much to the support of pure government, as sores do to the strength of the human body." Cities were "the unsound" parts of the body politic, unhealthy "sores," the source of corruption. These were the words of the prophet of democracy, who had adored his years in Paris and was eager to return. In any event, in this, as in so many other matters, he spoke the American mind, or a substantial portion of it. The fact was, however, that the United States was unimaginable without its cities, modest as they were by present-day standards. They were collecting stations for the capital that made the great canal-building era possible; they were ports of entry for the hundreds of thousands of immigrants who came to the United States each year; they were communication points, the seedbeds of new ideas, and patrons of a developing native cultural and intellectual life.

With each passing generation the balance swung more and more to the urban side of the scale until today we are the most urbanized people in the world, 95 percent urban, 5 percent rural. Yet all through that transformation, the most radical and far-reaching in history, we clung to the image of ourselves as an essentially rural people and cherished the Jeffersonian image of farmers as the chosen people of God, another instance of our collective split personality.

The cities of the United States in 1800, of which we have taken Philadelphia to be the prototype, were still communities, that is, they were aggregations of individuals who encountered each other in a sufficient number of face-to-face relationships to form genuine communities. A visitor could walk about any of them in an hour or so, see the principal sights, and in the course of a day meet a number of leading citizens and many of no particular distinction but odd and interesting enough in their own way. In this respect, the cities were more different in degree than in kind from the smaller communities of which we have spoken. The cultural, intellectual, and commercial opportunities they afforded were far greater, but the human types that made up the population and the sense of a social order that, however diverse, somehow cohered, were consonant with the towns and villages that stretched from Vermont to Georgia.

22

The Arts

The art, architecture, and literature of the new Republic sought to give expression to what the artists and writers conceived to be the inner spirit of the nation. The model was a combination of republican Rome and democratic Athens. A preoccupation with antiquity was not new. Classical authors and antiquities were in great vogue in England as well as America long before the Revolution. Colonial polemicists had used such pen names as Cicero, Cato, Caesar, and Cassius. But the establishment of the Republic gave fresh impetus to the classical ideal. Such notions as that of civic virtue were borrowed from the Romans, while American democrats exalted the Greeks. When sculptors began to make statues of Washington, they not infrequently depicted him in Roman costume. Popular engravings of the president followed suit.

Jefferson's own home, Monticello, of which he was architect, incorporated classical motifs, and his plan for the Virginia capitol at Richmond was adapted from the Maison Carrée at Nimes, a building Jefferson had described as "one of the most beautiful, if not the most beautiful and precious morsel of architecture left to us by antiquity." In a letter to Madison on the subject of the Virginia capitol, Jefferson wrote, "You see I am an enthusiast on the subject of the arts. But it is an enthusiasm of which I am not ashamed, as its object is to improve the

394

taste of my countrymen, to increase their reputation, to reconcile to them the respect of the world, and procure them its praise." The austere but graceful facade of the capitol, which looked indeed like a Roman temple, did much to encourage the development of a school of architecture generally denominated the Classical Revival.

If Jefferson was its principal proponent in the South, a brilliant young Boston architect named Charles Bulfinch helped to develop a New England variant, the Federal style, featuring direct brick facades with large, evenly spaced windows and classical ornamentation. After graduating from Harvard, Bulfinch had departed on the grand tour that was so often an essential part of the education of an upper-class American male. He spent seven months in England and then continued on to the Continent where he met Jefferson in Paris and was given a guided tour of the architectural splendors of the city. He journeyed on to Marseilles, Rome, Florence, and Milan and then returned to Boston to take up a business career and help plan the first trading expedition from Boston to Canton, China, by way of the Columbia River. When the Massachusetts legislature announced its intention of erecting a capitol on the crest of Beacon Hill, Bulfinch, then twenty-four, decided to submit a plan. In four months he had completed a design, with cost estimates, that was accepted by the Great and General Court. On the Fourth of July, 1795, the cornerstone was drawn up the hill by fifteen white horses, one for each state in the Union, and in a ceremony presided over by Governor Samuel Adams and Paul Revere as Master of the Grand Lodge of Masons, put in place. After this triumph Bulfinch was sought after by the most prosperous and influential men in Boston, and in addition to a number of handsome private homes he built numerous churches and banks, which, with quite unconscious symbolism, were often not easily distinguished from each other.

Most characteristic of an emerging popular culture in America were the building manuals published by Asher Benjamin, of which perhaps the best known was *The American Builder's Companion* (1806). In these works Benjamin gave easy-to-follow directions for the amateur architect-builder, along with examples of classical detail meant to add a touch of elegance even to simple houses. His manuals were early examples of the classic American genre of "how-to" books. Benjamin wrote: "Those carpenters in country villages who aspire to eminence in this business, having no Architect to consult, are under the necessity of studying the science thoroughly and without a master.

To them, therefore, this book is peculiarly adapted; it contains the principles of many expensive folios condensed into a narrow space and applied to modern practice." Many of the handsome early-nineteenth-century houses that still line the commons of New England towns derived from Benjamin's popular work.

In the realm of painting, the three most successful "American painters" did most of their work in England. Benjamin West had begun his excursions into painting while still a boy, using earth colors given him by neighboring Indians and making his own brushes with badger hair. He soon found sponsors, and in 1760 he was sent by them to Italy to study the old masters. Taught by several of the leading Italian painters of the day, West spent three years in Rome and then opened a studio in London. Painting in the mannered style of the late baroque on such classical themes as *The Parting of Hector and Andromache*, he attracted the attention of George III and with the patronage of the king began a series of flamboyant historical paintings that made him the most famous painter in England. His *Death of General Wolfe on the Plains of Abraham* was universally admired and imitated. The revolutionary aspect of his *Death of Wolfe* was that instead of following the convention of depicting Wolfe in Roman garb, West painted him and the other figures in their British uniforms.

West was one of the founders of the Royal Academy, and after the death of Sir Joshua Reynolds he became its president. Son of a poor Quaker, West powdered his hair, wore side curls and silk stockings, and was very much a man of the world; his studio was often filled with fashionable ladies and gentlemen, lovers and patrons of the arts. Nevertheless, West retained a strong feeling of attachment to his native country and befriended every young American painter able to find his way to London.

John Singleton Copley was the first and most gifted American artist to be encouraged by West. Copley had shipped his marvelous portrait of young Henry Pelham playing with his pet squirrel to West, and West had praised it warmly. Reynolds, the most fashionable portraitist in England, had, West reported, called it *"very wonderful,"* and had expressed the opinion that proper instruction would make Copley "one of the first Painters in the World." Copley wrote to West in reply: "I think myself peculiarly unlucky in Liveing in a place [Boston] into which there has not been one portrait brought that is worthy to be call'd a Picture within my memory, which leaves me at a great loss to gess the stile that you, Mr. Reynolds, and the other Artists practice."

Charles Willson Peale, an aspiring artist from Maryland, had gone to Boston to meet Copley and be instructed by him, although he was only three years younger; then, sponsored by a Maryland judge who paid his debts and underwrote the trip, Peale set sail for England, armed with letters of introduction to Benjamin West. Peale found his compatriot "truly affectionate." West, three years older than Peale, took great pains with the young American, who wrote home: "I have great Hopes of Returning Home a tolerable proficient and give Some Satisfaction to my Benefactors." Peale also visited Benjamin Franklin, then in London serving as a colonial agent, and found the Doctor with a handsome young woman on his knee.

After two years of working under West's tutelage, the homesick Peale returned to America and his wife, not much more refined in his technique than when he had left. The elaborate historical and allegorical paintings that had made West's reputation had little attraction for Peale. He preferred portraits and domestic scenes.

It took Copley another nine years to find his way to England. A far more gifted painter than Peale, and tied by his family to the Loyalist cause, Copley encountered the hostility of Boston patriots for his association with notorious Tories. When a Tory friend visited him, a crowd collected outside his house and "desired to know how I came to entertain such a Rogue and Villin." Copley appeased the crowd by assuring them that his friend had left, but had he been there, Copley reflected, "I must either have given up a friend to the insult of a Mob or had my house pulled down and perhaps my family murthered." He determined to leave for England on the next ship.

The situation of Copley on his departure in 1774 was far different from that of Peale. He was not only at the height of his powers as an artist; he was incomparably the finest artist America had produced. If we consider that Benjamin West had done all his work in England, it might be said that Copley was the first American artist deserving of the name. In the space of a decade his work had far outstripped the accomplishments of his predecessors and contemporaries. English critics had compared him with Van Dyck and Rubens. In America, he had more commissions than he could accept and was, by colonial standards, a wealthy man.

In England, Copley was impressed by the neat, orderly appearance of the country, which contrasted so strikingly with the rawness and disorder of the American landscape. He commented especially on the fact that "not a spire of Grass Grain or Beans" was trampled in the unfenced fields that stretched along country roads. In America even stout fences failed to intercept intruders, who seemed to feel it was their right to venture where they pleased. He wrote to his wife that a patriot friend "was greatly mistaken when he said we were Saints & Angels in America to those that inhabit this Country," adding, "we Americans seem not halfway remov'd from a state of Nature."

West was as friendly and helpful a host for Copley as he had been for Peale. He took him to the Royal Academy, introduced him to Reynolds, and gave him a view of students painting from a naked model, which much impressed Copley. West advised him to take a tour through France and Italy, which Copley dutifully did. But he knew his own powers had developed fully in America, as he wrote his half brother, "I have got through the Dificulty of the Art, I trust, and shall reap a continual Source of pleasure from my past Industry."

An English artist, George Carter, who accompanied Copley on his journey to Rome, described him as "very thin, pale, a little pock-marked, prominent eyebrows, small eyes, which after fatigue seemed a days march in his head." With a woman's white French bonnet to shade his face from the sun, a yellow-and-red silk kerchief trailing down his back, a cinnamon-colored greatcoat, and "a friar's cap hanging down to his heels," Copley appeared the very image of an eccentric artist. Carter found him excessively touchy on the subject of America. Copley, he noted, had "laboured near an hour to prove that a huckaback towel" was softer than a Spanish silk handkerchief and gave "a long-winded discourse upon the merits of an American wood-fire, in preference to one of our coal." If Americans continued to advance for the next hundred years at the rate they had in the past, he told Carter, "they shall have an independent government; the woods will be cleared, and, lying in the same latitude, they shall have the same air as the south of France; art would then be encouraged there, and great artists would arise." Yet Copley confessed that by comparison with the architectural and artistic wonders he had seen, Boston appeared "a collection of wren boxes."

When word reached Copley of the beginning of hostilities in America, he decided to send for his wife and make his home in England until things were settled. He wrote: "Poor America, I hope the best but I fear the worst. yet certain I am She will finially Imerge from her present Callamity and become a Mighty Empire. and it is a pleasing reflection that I shall stand amongst the first of the Artists that shall have led that Country to the Knowledge and cultivation of the fine arts."

Copley began a series of historical paintings somewhat in the manner of West but superior in execution. We cannot follow his subsequent career in detail. It is perhaps sufficient to say that while his work became more and more popular, so that people paid to visit exhibitions of his latest works, he never surpassed and seldom equaled the best paintings he had done in America.

Regardless of the fact that West and Copley resided in England, Americans claimed them as their own and constantly put them forward as evidence that the United States excelled in art as well as politics. The editor of the *Massachusetts Centinel* declared: "While we boast a *Washington*, as the great master of the art of war—a *Franklin* the chief of Philosophers—an *Adams*, and an infinitude of others, as statesmen and politicians whose abilities have been acknowledged throughout the civilized world; America may pride herself in giving birth to the most celebrated Artists of the present age."

Ralph Earle was another notable young artist, whose Loyalist activities almost resulted in his being shot for treason. Before the Revolution he had painted a marvelous portrait of Roger Sherman, revealing the ex-shoemaker turned lawyer and patriot leader in a classic pose, lantern-jawed and craggy as Connecticut granite. In England, as a refugee from the Revolution, Earle, according to a contemporary, "destroyed himself by habitual drinking."

Gilbert Stuart, born in 1755 in North Kingstown, Rhode Island, was the son of a Scottish Presbyterian minister who was also involved in the manufacture of snuff. Stuart, as a child, had a good ear for music, played several instruments, and liked to draw. It was said that he got his first instruction from a slave who drew on the heads of tobacco casks. He attended a painting and drawing school in Newport run by a Scottish portrait painter named Cosmo Alexander, and when Alexander returned to Scotland, Stuart accompanied him. After Alexander's death Stuart returned to Newport, where he received several portrait commissions from the wealthy Jewish merchants. Feeling the limitations of the provincial setting, he returned to England, where he lived in what is usually called "dire" poverty, eking out a living playing the organ at a church and getting a few modest commissions.

After a year of barely making ends meet he wrote to West,

"takeing this liberty" because of his "poverty and ignorance," without "bussiness or Freinds, without the necessarys of life so far that for some time I have been reduced to one miserable meal a day & frequently not even that." West gave him lodging and work as his assistant, and for five years young Stuart worked at his craft under the older man's tutelage. Although like Copley a Tory in his political sympathies, Stuart was equally touchy about his American origins. It was said that when Dr. Samuel Johnson congratulated him on speaking such good English and asked him where he had learned it, Stuart replied impertinently: "Sir, I can better tell you where I did not learn it—it was not from your dictionary." Stuart liked to play the part of a savage American for his British hosts and, when asked where he was from, would reply, "Six miles from Pottawoone, and ten miles from Poppasquash, and about four miles west of Connonicut."

Stuart's apprenticeship with West was apparently based more on material than on artistic need. The younger man had a keen sense of his own capacities and was bored at being put to work doing backgrounds for West's "*ten-acre* pictures," as he put it. In 1782, however, Stuart painted a full-length portrait of an ice-skater, William Grant, that caused a minor sensation in the British art world because of the novelty of the theme and composition; the young American was established as an important artist in his own right. When he set up in business for himself, he received numerous commissions despite his lack of reliability (he became notorious for accepting down payments for portraits, starting them, and then failing to finish them).

Stuart toured the British Isles painting portraits. He did a likeness of William Temple Franklin, Benjamin's Tory son, in 1784, and Franklin called him "the first Portrait Painter now living," adding, "he is moreover an American. . . . He is astonishing for likeness. I heard West say—'that he *nails* the face to the Canvass.'" Stuart's genius lay, to a considerable degree, in the quality of life and vitality that he conveyed through his treatment of flesh. "Flesh," he said, "is like no other substance under heaven. It has all the gaiety of a silk mercers shop without the gaudiness or glare and all the soberness of old mahogany without its deadness or sadness."

Courted and dined by titled lords and ladies, Stuart replied in kind, spending money with an openhanded extravagance that kept him constantly in debt. In 1793 he returned to the United States, where he painted portraits of a number of prominent politicians and then established himself in Boston. For the next twenty-five years he dominated the art scene in that city. His wit, his fame as a conversation-alist, and his brilliance as a painter overshadowed his eccentric habits, his unreliability, and his periodic fits of depression. When Stuart, old and ailing himself, painted John Adams in his ninetieth year, Adams wrote to a friend, "Speaking generally no penance is like having one's picture done. . . . But I should like to sit to Stuart from the first of January to the last of December, for he lets me do as I please and keeps me constantly amused by his conversation."

What is perhaps most notable about the "first generation" of American artists who found their way to Benjamin West's atelier was that the three most gifted of them—Copley, Stuart, and Earle—were Tories. Moreover, their great talent was for portraiture and beyond that for the direct and faithful representation of character. The eighteenth century was preeminently the age of portraiture. The reasons were twofold. First, especially in America, portraits were what the more prosperous patrons wanted and were willing to pay for. Thus, an aspiring artist who wished to earn a living by his craft was obliged to paint portraits in order to survive. But equally important, the artists, critics, and philosophers of the eighteenth century were intensely interested in "physiognomy," which a dictionary defines as "the art of judging character and disposition from the features of the face. . . . The foretelling of destiny from the features and lines of the face. . . . The face viewed as an index to the mind and character." This was precisely what the painter and the viewer (and perhaps less frequently, the subject) wished to see in the finished portrait—not simply a face but the revelation of character. The astonishing rise of American artists to the front rank of portrait painters was therefore not purely fortuitous but was in some way related to the nature of American society and the way in which the heirs of the Protestant Reformation looked at the world and, more particularly, the way they looked at each other. American painters like Copley and Stuart showed the same capacity for "invention" in painting—for the original and imaginative treatment of traditional subjects—that their compatriots demonstrated in the invention of steamboats and reapers. It was the "originality" of the Americans more than their technical competence that caught the attention of connoisseurs.

Charles Willson Peale, a lesser painter than Copley and Stuart but a better patriot, and a more "representative" man, might be taken as the exemplar of the democratic artist of the new age. Peale had joined the Pennsylvania militia as a "Common Soldier" at the beginning of the Revolution. Soon afterward he was elected first lieutenant by his men, and since there is much more waiting than fighting in any military unit, Peale continued to paint and, as did his fellow painter John Greenwood, earn extra money by making false teeth. He described himself unflatteringly as somewhat eroded by the rigors of army life, "a thin, spare pale faced man, in appearance totally unfit to endure the fatigues of long marches, and lying on the cold, wet ground, sometimes covered with snow. Yet by temperance and a forethought of providing for the worst that might happen, he endured his campaign better than many others whose appearance was more robust."

In his care for his men, Peale was an ideal officer. He was attentive to their needs, wrote reassuring letters to their families, made moccasins for their bare feet, and conscientiously put their welfare before his own.

If Peale felt duty-bound to do all in his power for the soldiers in his company, he was even more solicitous for his family; in his constant alternation between camp and home to assure himself that his wife and children were not starving to death, he was typical of the average Continental soldier. Often Peale slept in the snow-filled woods with only his gun and his dog. On one occasion he awoke to find his right hand "senseless" and, he feared, frozen; he sat up all night rubbing it with water, afraid of the "loss of a hand to a Person who had his living to get by his labours."

At Valley Forge, Peale occupied the long hours painting miniatures on ivory, and it was there that he began what became in time a kind of artistic industry for him and other aspiring artists—painting pictures of Washington. Although there is no record of the precise number of such portraits he turned out, it was the beginning of what was to prove his mainstay as an artist for the rest of his life.

After the war, bad eyesight forced Peale to give up the painting of miniatures. He now concentrated on full-length portraits of Washington, one such being commissioned by the trustees of Princeton College to commemorate Washington's modest victory there. Meanwhile he continued to produce almost as many children as paintings (giving them such names as Raphael, Rembrandt, Titian) and, deep in debt, constructed a sixty-six-foot building adjacent to his house as a gallery, where the portraits of thirty notable Americans were exhibited.

Several years later Peale built at one end of his gallery an "Exhibition of Moving Pictures." The "moving-picture" show lasted some two hours and was described by Peale as "NATURE DELINEATED, and in Motion." The viewer saw a series of changing scenes: the dawn breaking with the singing of birds and crowing of cocks; Market Street at nightfall with the streetlights coming on; a landscape with cloudy sky followed by rain and lightning and then a rainbow; and a scene from Milton's *Paradise Lost* featuring smoke, flames, and the Devil. The grand finale was a representation of the battle between the *Serapis* and the *Bonhomme Richard* under the command of John Paul Jones. Between scene changes there were readings from Milton and Shakespeare and music by a quartet.

When the gallery and moving pictures proved a financial disaster—it has "injured my health and straightened my circumstances," he wrote—he decided to open a museum devoted to "American curiosities," especially to those of the natural world. He thus set out on "a new, but no less arduous undertaking, that is the preserving of Birds & Beasts etc."

Peale was a deist, a democrat, an admirer of the French Revolution, and a worshiper of nature. He had been collecting dinosaur bones and skins of birds and animals for some years and a natural history museum was the almost inevitable consequence of his interest in the natural world. The gallery was converted into a museum, with the moving-picture room becoming a rock grotto for the exhibition of alligators, snakes, and reptiles. The museum itself was a strange polyglot collection of stuffed birds, portraits of eminent Americans, and geological specimens.

In 1800 Peale gave a series of lectures on "The Science of Nature" in his museum. In his view, "the comfort, happiness, and support of all ranks, depend on their knowledge of nature. . . . In short it is a source from which man is taught to know himself." As ardent a pacifist as a naturalist, he argued that "If one hundredth part of the sums lavished on war, were applied to the encouragment of science . . . the condition of millions of inhabitants [of the globe would] be ameliorated, and the world then be a Paradise compared to its present situation." Even the animals did not war against their kind: "so foul an infamy is found alone on man!" The fault, in Peale's view, was "want of education." "The mind of man is ever active, it must be employed continually, and the greater number of inlets that can be opened for him to receive instruction, with rational amusements, the more effectually will he be drawn from vicious habits."

Peale is certainly one of the most ingratiating figures in American history. He was a classic self-made man, an attentive and devoted husband and father, a courageous soldier and officer who took a paternal care for his men, a firm democrat, an ingenious inventor and craftsman, an amateur scientist, and the very model of the virtuous and enlightened citizen.

One of the most interesting American painters was John Trumbull, son of the governor of Connecticut and a cousin of the poet John Trumbull. Trumbull had early felt the ambition to be a painter and, headed for Harvard, he stopped off to visit Copley, who had yet to depart for England. He found "an elegant looking man, dressed in fine maroon cloth, with gilt buttons." Copley's paintings were the first Trumbull "had ever seen deserving the name." In his words, they "riveted, absorbed my attention, and renewed all my desire to enter upon such a pursuit."

At Harvard, Trumbull completed his undergraduate work in a year and a half, spending more time studying his Piranesi prints and Copley's portraits than the prescribed curriculum. Like Peale, Trumbull was an ardent patriot and was determined to put his talent as a painter at the service of his political principles. He therefore chose as subjects heroes from the days of republican Rome, men whose "devoted patriotism [was] always before my eye." Governor Trumbull, like innumerable fathers of artistically inclined sons, noted, "I am sensible of his Natural Genius & inclination for Limning and Art I have frequently told him, will be of no use to him."

Trumbull abandoned his classical paintings long enough to organize a militia unit, drill them, and march off to join the Continental Army surrounding Boston. There he was made an aide-de-camp to Washington, but he was touchy and sensitive and unhappy at his failure to be promoted as rapidly as he felt he deserved to be. Frustrated further by the knowledge that at best he was marking time in his ambition to become a renowned painter, he resigned his commission and devoted his full time to his brush and palette, selling tea and rum on the side to make a living. Later he hastened to London where he presented a letter of introduction to West from Benjamin Franklin.

West received the newcomer with characteristic hospitality and put him to work. But Trumbull did not try to conceal his strong American sympathies and in consequence was soon clapped in jail as an agent of Congress. (He had expressed contempt for the British and had written to his father of the Carlisle Commission: "'Tis the sword

The Death of General Wolfe. Painting by Benjamin West. *(The Bettmann Archive)*

The Death of General Montgomery. Painting by John Trumbull.
(The Bettmann Archive)

John Quincy Adams. Painting by John Singleton Copley. *(Courtesy Museum of Fine Arts, Boston. Gift of Mrs. Charles Francis Adams.)*

Boy with a Squirrel, by John Singleton Copley
(*Museum of Fine Arts, Boston*)

Roger Sherman. Member of the Continental Congress and Signer of Declaration of Independence. Painting by Ralph Earle. *(The Bettmann Archive)*

The Skater. Portrait of William Grant by Gilbert Stuart. *(National Gallery of Art, Washington. Andrew W. Mellon Collection.)*

The Artist in His Museum. Painting by Charles Willson Peale. *(Pennsylvania Academy of Fine Arts. Joseph and Sarah Harrison Collection.)*

The Battle of Bunker Hill. Painting by John Trumbull. *(The Bettmann Archive)*

he Surrender of Cornwallis at Yorktown. Painting by John Trumbull. *(The Bettmann Archive)*

Mrs. Sara Trumbull on Her Deathbed. Painting by John Trumbull
(Courtesy of Joseph Lauman Richards)

only that can give us such a peace as our past glorious Struggles have merited.—The sword must finish what it has so well begun.")

Trumbull was convinced that he had been arrested as retribution for the execution of Major André. West interceded with the king for his pupil, insisting that Trumbull had been "so entirely devoted to the study of . . . [his] profession as to have left no time for political intrigue." Trumbull nonetheless remained in prison for eight months; he had comfortable quarters, however, and was allowed to paint and to walk in an adjacent garden. Gilbert Stuart, who was familiar with prison through periodic incarceration for debt, painted the confined Trumbull. All efforts by the American artist to gain his freedom through legal channels came to nothing until Edmund Burke took up his cause, promising that if "peaceable & rational methods" came to nothing he would introduce a bill in Parliament.

Trumbull returned to America in 1782. There he determined to follow West's footsteps by concentrating on historical paintings, more especially on paintings depicting the great events of the American Revolution. The particular event the artist typically focused on in the midst of the historical scene was the death of the hero. Death, in heroic or melodramatic form, was to be a major preoccupation of the nineteenth-century historical painter as it was of the nineteenth-century consciousness.

To support himself, Trumbull conceived the notion of painting historical and patriotic subjects, such as the signing of the Declaration of Independence, and then having engravings made, which could be sold relatively inexpensively. As he put it, "the great object of my wishes . . . is to take up the History of Our Country, and paint the principal Events particularly of the late War:—but this is a work which to execute with any degree of honour or profit, will require very great powers." Those powers could be attained only by studying with West and being exposed to the work of European masters. Trumbull finally persuaded his father to underwrite two more years of study with West, and he arrived in England in 1784. West received him with "the same boundless liberality and the same friendship which I had experienced from him formerly."

If the eighteenth century might be characterized as a century devoted to exploring and proclaiming the rational nature of man, and if portraiture is seen as representing an aspect of that exploration, the nineteenth century was to be the century of historical consciousness. It was to history that men and women of the century were to turn most commonly for explanation and encouragement, for clues to the nature of man and society. But it was to a particular kind of "progressive" history that they turned, a history in which, as we have seen, error and superstition were to be overcome by science and reason. The American Revolution was, at least for Americans, the preeminent *historical event* (of which the French Revolution was a consequence of almost equal significance). The Revolution brought into human discourse both a new perspective and *a new way of looking* at the past and the future. Previously the past of a society had been represented primarily in symbols, in facades, in costumes, in ceremonials and rituals. The future had been conceived of as essentially a continuation of the status quo or the reestablishment of some dimly rumored earlier and better time.

The American Revolution, which began as an ostensible effort to recapture an earlier and better England, went on to offer the radical vision of a better human destiny, *different* from anything that had taken place or had even been imagined in the past. The Revolution thus produced a new category for thinking about man and his fate. Every state in the Union soon established a historical society and began the assiduous collection of materials relating to its history. *Historical painting* was the immediate and inevitable consequence of this new category of thinking, and John Trumbull was its first and most conspicuous practitioner in America.

This was the motivation that drove Trumbull incessantly. He began his study of anatomy at five or six in the morning and then painted all day. He had no ambition to be a fashionable and wealthy painter. He thought the English frivolous and corrupt.

When he at last felt himself ready to begin his great task, he made a series of ink sketches for his *Death of Montgomery* and *The Battle of Bunker Hill*. As *The Battle of Bunker Hill* took form, Reynolds, Copley, and other artists came to watch and encourage the young American. West was especially encouraging. When the painting was finished, he called it "the *best picture* of a modern Battle that has been painted. . . . *No Man* living can paint such another picture of that Scene."

In the center of the painting, General Joseph Warren is dying, pierced by a British bullet in the final charge at the American emplacement. West's *Death of Wolfe on the Plains of Abraham* was of course the prototype of all such paintings. Now, it was said, the pupil rivaled the master. Trumbull also drew freely from Copley's brilliant *Death of Major Peirson*, but the final result says more than words can about the way in which the Revolution was to be "remembered" by Americans. The romantic vision was already taking root. "Grandeur," "nobility," "melancholy," "pain and suffering," and, perhaps above all, "sacrifice" were the dominant themes. While Trumbull took great pains to represent particular historical figures accurately, the scene itself was a very substantial distance from the chilling reality of suffering and death that pervades the field of battle.

In *The Death of Montgomery* and *The Battle of Bunker Hill* Trumbull had begun the work that was to occupy him until his death—the creation of America's "memory" of the Revolution. It seems safe to say that for millions of Americans Trumbull's paintings have indeed constituted their "image" of the Revolution.

Like Peale, Trumbull found that portraits of George Washington helped to put meat on his table. In 1790 the president sat twelve times for Trumbull, who presumably painted more than one portrait in those sittings. (Stuart, like Peale and Trumbull, also painted innumerable Washingtons. He had a flat charge of $100 for a Washington portrait and referred to the copies he made of his Athenaeum portrait as his "hundred dollar bills.") Trumbull's standard price for a head of Washington (or anyone else) was $100. Head with hands was $150; half length, $250; full figure, $500. In the course of a long life Trumbull painted countless portraits of political figures. The vision that we have of many members of the generation of Founders is a kind of montage of Stuart and Trumbull, with a touch of Peale.

Trumbull fully realized his ambition to record the high points of the Revolution. Four huge historical paintings by Trumbull now hang in the Rotunda of the Capitol in Washington, D.C.: *The Declaration of Independence* (the most famous and most "useful" of his works); *The Surrender of General Burgoyne at Saratoga, The Surrender of Cornwallis at Yorktown*; and *The Resignation of General Washington, at Annapolis, Maryland, 3 December, 1783.*

Trumbull was at his best in a half dozen of his large-scale battle scenes and in his miniatures and sketches. Since he had only one eye, perspective gave him trouble and of all the artists of the new Republic his work was most uneven. A few of his best canvases rank only below Copley's. The religious paintings and the classical scenes he turned out during his long life are most often an embarrassment. Strongly drawn to architecture, he designed several buildings in the Classical style, the best known being the Meetinghouse at Lebanon, Connecticut, and the First Presbyterian Church in Philadelphia. In his old age Trumbull's powers diminished sharply, but he himself became a kind of work of art, erect and handsome, a notable relic of an earlier era; his portrait was painted numerous times by younger artists who considered him quite rightly as one of the founding fathers of American painting.

Displaying that preoccupation with death that was to be such a conspicuous feature of the nineteenth-century consciousness, Trumbull painted a picture of his wife, Sarah, on her deathbed at the instant of expiring and built his own sepulcher beneath a gallery that held his paintings. Copies of the historical paintings in the Rotunda and his paintings of religious subjects hung there as well. Admission was twenty-five cents, and all profits, after the cost of maintaining the gallery had been met, were to be "forever applied towards the education of needy and meritorious students in Yale College."

When Trumbull died in 1843, the tombstone, for which he had written the text, read in part: "Col. John Trumbull, Patriot and Artist, Friend and Aid of Washington. . . . To his Country he gave his SWORD and his PENCIL." It was a fitting epitaph.

It must be said that the artists of the new Republic had to struggle under the handicap that painting was often associated in the popular mind with monarchy and aristocracy. Science was a more appropriate study for republics, while the arts were encouraged by "civilized monarchy." Certainly patronage was a bread-and-butter issue for artists. The historian Charles Rollin had warned that "a taste for statues, pictures and other rare curiosities of art, may be commendable in a prince . . . but when a person abandons himself to it entirely, it degenerates into a dangerous temptation, and frequently prompts him to notorious injustice and violence." There was something in the Protestant suspicion of icons and sacred images that was also uncongenial to the visual arts. If Rome had emphasized the Image, Calvin had emphasized the Word. Art in America thus had to face a double hazard: its association, for the fervent democrat, with monarchy, aristocracy, and luxury; and the separate but related feeling on the part of fervent Christians that it was tainted with vanity and worldliness.

The Word, ironically, proved far less adaptable to the requirements of the new age than the pen or brush.

Just as Peale and Trumbull gave their attention to celebrating the glory of the Republic, young gentlemen of a literary bent undertook to

produce poems and essays in praise of liberty and republican government. Their literary models were, like Jefferson's architectural models,
classical. Virgil was the favorite poet. The potential of the novel had
yet to be developed. Poetry, and to a lesser degree drama, were the
obvious modes in which to commemorate the grandeur of the
Revolution and the "Rising Glory" of the Union.

Timothy Dwight, whose descriptions of Western settlements we
have quoted, set out to become a modern Virgil by writing a heroic
poem. His coadjutor in establishing American letters was John
Trumbull, cousin of John Trumbull the painter. Trumbull was a
collateral descendant of Jonathan Edwards, who was Dwight's great-
grandfather. Showing the same astonishing precociousness as his
famous ancestor, Trumbull had read the Bible through by the age of
four and mastered the rudiments of Latin by six. At eight he passed
the entrance examinations for Yale but wisely waited until he was a
mature thirteen before matriculating.

Dwight had learned the entire alphabet at one sitting and by the
age of four was preaching to the Indians. Like Trumbull, he was ready
to enter Yale at the age of eight but also delayed until he was thirteen.
By the time they were twenty, the two young men were lecturing on
rhetoric and literature to Yale students, and Trumbull had given a
commencement address on the "Use and Advantages of the Fine
Arts." He declared: "I appeal to all persons of judgment, whether
they can rise from reading a fine Poem, viewing any masterly work of
Genius, or hearing an harmonious concert of Music, without feeling an
openness of heart and an elevation of mind, without being more
sensible of the dignity of human nature, and despising whatever tends
to debase or degrade it?" To Trumbull, Yale seemed hopelessly out of
date, and he had written a long satirical poem entitled *The Progress of
Dulness*, which resulted in his being criticized for undertaking to
"ridicule religion, disgrace morality, sneer at the present methods of
education, and, in short, write a satire upon Yale-College and the ten
commandments."

A major theme in Trumbull's and Dwight's work became the
pretensions of the lower orders of society to adopt the airs and
manners of their betters—luxury, in short. It seemed to them that the
movement to increase the number of colleges would simply encourage
"our lowest Mechanics" to put on the airs of gentlemen until there
would be "no such Thing as common People among us." Trumbull

satirized Dick Hairbrain, the simpleminded son of a newly prosperous farmer whose awkwardness and vulgarity mocked his attempts to follow the latest fashions.

If there was an American aristocracy, Dwight and Trumbull were certainly members of it, and their attacks on the democratic tendencies in American life are revealing. If we may take Trumbull's and Dwight's attitudes to be reasonably representative of their fellows at Yale, Harvard, and Princeton, it is not surprising that William Manning was so critical of the Federalists for "crying up the advantages of costly collages" that were strongholds of "monorcal prinsaples."

Two recruits to the ranks of Federalist poets were also Yale graduates, David Humphreys and Joel Barlow. (Barlow transferred from rustic Dartmouth to the more sophisticated Yale.) Humphreys wrote, "No sooner had we seen each other at the place of our education, than . . . a certain similarity of genius, and congeniality of soul, connected us by the ties of an indissoluble friendship."

Timothy Dwight took the first shot at composing the "heroic poem" on America that John Adams hoped for. It was entitled *The Conquest of Canaan* and was dedicated to Washington, "The Saviour of his Country, The Supporter of Freedom, And the Benefactor of Mankind." While purporting to be an account of the Exodus of the Hebrews from Egypt, the poem was understood to be an allegory of the American fight for independence. Widely praised by Americans— John Adams wrote "Excepting Paradise Lost I know of nothing Superiour in any modern Language"—it was dismissed by British critics as bombastic and overblown.

Dwight's most serious rival was Barlow, whose long narrative poem, *The Vision of Columbus*, was intended to vindicate the United States "from those despicable aspersions which have long been thrown upon us and echoed from one ignorant Scribbler to another in all the languages of Europe." In the poem, Columbus is in prison, accused of mistreating the Indians of the Caribbean islands and misusing his power. A Seraph visits Columbus to comfort him in his misery and disillusionment by foretelling the future glory of America. In Barlow's *Vision of Columbus* Philip Freneau's theme of the coming millennium was vastly elaborated.

While tedious and overblown as a poem, Barlow's epic is important as a kind of map of the American consciousness, more particularly that of the Federalists, in the era of the 1780s and 1790s. The original edition listed 769 subscribers, among them Louis XVI, who ordered twenty-five copies. In the poem Barlow took up the question of whether Columbus's discovery of America had been an event of tragic rather than hopeful implications.

Barlow compared this ambiguity in the birth of the Americas with the uncertainty and anxiety of the period from the end of the Revolution to the inauguration of Washington as president. Barlow promised his readers that the United States through a "Source" of "creative Power" would become in time a great nation spreading its beneficent influence over the entire globe until the world was "one great empire" connected by commercial ties, common ideals (American), and a common language, and governed by a "general council" of the "fathers of all empires." Universal love would then be the order of the day.

> See, thro' the whole, the same progressive plan,
> That draws, for mutual succour, man to man,
> From friends to tribes, from tribes to realms ascend,
> Their powers, their interests and their passions blend;
> Adorn their manners, social virtues spread,
> . . . .
> Till each remotest realm, by friendship join'd,
> Links in the chain that binds all human kind,
> The union'd banners rise at last unfurl'd
> And wave triumphant round the accordant world.

To Barlow, the United States was to be seen primarily as a stage in man's progress toward "one world." While he foresaw tribulations and warfare, he was convinced that ultimately the refinement of human nature and social institutions by reason and science must make the new age a prelude to the millennium. He thus epitomized in his long, turgid, and today almost unreadable poem the major themes of Secular-Democratic Consciousness. But he went further. In his "trans-nationalism" he anticipated such enterprises as the League of Nations and the United Nations, and in his strong emphasis on commerce as the means of binding nations together he anticipated the rise of multinational corporations in the late twentieth century and the opportunities thereby created for the organization of an international economy. So if Barlow's *Vision* was a failure as a poem (in the sense that no one reads it anymore, although we still look at Trumbull's or Peale's pictures), it is compelling as a guide to the new consciousness and as a prophecy of the new age.

Barlow, moreover, accomplished what many of his compatriots attempted on a less epic scale. He consoled Americans for the tumult and disorder of the immediate present by assuring them that it was working for the future glory of the United States (and of course, for the rest of mankind as well). The "future orientation" of Americans was to be perhaps our most constant consolation for the often desperately hard and bitter facts of daily existence. The classic expression of that poignant faith has been the expectation that the children must "do better" than the parents, be better educated, make more money, have an easier life.

Barlow demonstrated his own commitment to free enterprise by persuading a group of French tradesmen to settle on lands he claimed to own on the Ohio River. When Barlow failed to hold up his part of the bargain, the unhappy immigrants suffered severely.

The best-known Federalist editor was Joseph Dennie, a Bostonian and a Harvard graduate, who edited a literary magazine called *The Port Folio*, which was devoted to belles letters, poems, essays, reviews, and "the arts and sciences." An English visitor declared that it "would do credit to the most polished nation in Europe." Dennie, in any event, was an outspoken enemy of democracy. He declared in his journal: "Its omens are always sinister, and its powers are unpropitious. It was weak and wicked in Athens. It was bad in Sparta, and worse in Rome. It has been tried in France, and has termined in despotism. . . . It is on trial here, and the issue will be civil war, desolation and anarchy. . . . The institution of a scheme of polity, so radically contemptible and vicious, is a memorable example of what the villainy of some men can devise." For this impertinence, Dennie was indicted and tried in a case that caused as much indignation in Federalist ranks as the earlier prosecutions of Callender and Austin had caused among Republicans. Dennie was acquitted and became, if possible, even more relentless in his denunciation of democrats and democracy.

As we have already noted, the end of the Revolution witnessed a surge of "new men and new principles" into the ranks of business and political leaders. It was against these upstarts—the Dick Hairbrains— that Hugh Henry Brackenridge wrote his "novel," *Modern Chivalry*. The leaders of the Revolution—the Founders—accepted, with only modest reservations, the notion that in the new United States individuals from the "lower orders" would make their way by diligence, energy, and talent into the ranks of those who directed the affairs of the nation. This was Jefferson's natural aristocracy. What they did not anticipate and what, as we have seen, they viewed with undisguised dismay was that the new age gave opportunities to many men to advance themselves without going through the "socializing" process that would have enabled the upper class to have absorbed them without stress or strain. Without waiting to smooth off their rough edges, they reached boldly and directly for power. And when they succeeded in grasping it, they showed contempt and hostility toward their betters rather than deference and gratitude.

Brackenridge, himself the son of poor Scottish immigrants, had done things the right way. Through natural intelligence and industry he had gotten into and through the College of New Jersey at Princeton. Thus he was in a position to join the viewers-with-dismay. When he was ousted from his seat as a Pennsylvania legislator by the radical leader William Findley, an ex-weaver (who, the reader may recall, was later to defeat William Maclay for his U.S. Senate seat), Brackenridge's antipathy to the new men was confirmed, and he began his satire on those "climbers" who took advantage of the new order to scramble over those superior to them.

The principal characters of *Modern Chivalry* are the Captain and his Irish servant, Teague. In one typical scene the Captain comes upon an election campaign where the rivals are "a man of education" and a weaver. The Captain addresses the multitude: "It is very astonishing to me that this weaver should conceive himself qualified for the trust. . . . The mechanical business which he pursues, must necessarily take up so much of his time, that he cannot apply himself to political studies. I should therefore think it would be more answerable to your dignity and conducive to your interest, to be represented by a man of at least some letters, than by an illiterate handicraftsman like this. . . . There is no analogy between knotting threads and framing laws. It would be a reversion of the order of things." While the Captain was speaking thus, his servant, Teague, "hearing so much about elections and serving the government, took it into his head, that he would be a legislator himself." The crowd responded enthusiastically to the notion, "owing . . . to the fluctuations of the popular mind, and a disposition to what is new and ignoble." When the Captain expostulated with them for exerting "the democratic prerogative" in such an eccentric manner, he was told that although Teague "may not be yet skilled in the matter" there was "a good day a-coming. We will empower him; and it is better to trust a plain man like him, than one of your high flyers, that will make laws to suit their own purposes."

The Captain takes Teague aside and persuades him to withdraw, and the disappointed crowd has to settle for the weaver. Brackenridge then steps forward to deliver a lecture on democracy to his readers. He does not mean to imply that only the wealthy should be legislators. Some of them, especially those who have inherited their money, are little better than the weaver or Teague. "Genius and virtue are independent of rank and fortune; and it is neither the opulent nor the indigent, but the man of ability and integrity [Brackenridge himself, in other words] that ought to be called forth to serve his country."

If we except the work of Copley, Stuart, and West, the area of the arts in which the young Republic made its most notable contributions may have well been in the most practical of the arts—architecture. Handsome Georgian and Neoclassical buildings were built in all the states, and many remain as reminders of the age. But there were no great poems or novels, no brilliant literary essays (*The Federalist Papers* were certainly great political essays), no enduring dramas, no memorable statuary. With very few exceptions the arts in the early Republic are valuable primarily for the insights they offer into the hopes and aspirations of Americans.

Sophisticated European visitors were amused and often contemptuous of the tendency of Americans to talk as though the United States were a great nation, especially favored by the Almighty, whose destiny was to reform the corrupt Old World by its example.

Looking about them they saw a raw, polyglot people, crude and presumptuous in their manners, with only the rudiments of civilization, a people without an art or literature, without stately manor houses or châteaux, splendid boulevards or handsome public buildings, a people who, as Moreau de St. Mery put it, were an odd amalgam of Indians and Europeans. While conceding that they had advanced very notably to the European end of the scale, the mere fact that Moreau used the Indian analogy was revealing. It *was* extraordinary—the conviction of Americans from the earliest days of the Republic that the United States was the proper model for the rest of the world and that its destiny was to dominate that world, not through force of arms as other nations had attempted to do, but through the superiority of its institutions and the irresistible power of moral suasion. Bitterly divided along sectional lines, hopelessly compromised in their democratic professions by slavery, challenged by the almost incomprehensibly arduous task of populating a vast continent, Americans took it as a simple matter of fact, as well as an article of their faith, that they were the chosen of God and that the future belonged to them.

In the face of such astonishing presumption more than one visitor went home half persuaded—both repelled and attracted by this strange new episode in human history. Typical were the comments of Baron Hyde de Neuville, a French royalist who visited the United States and who wrote: "A new wind is blowing across the world, at once the cause and product of our Revolution. The precise consequences are difficult to predict and will be slow in developing, but I am beginning to think that America has discovered the secret and anticipated the hour."

23

Republican Medicine

M edicine is the most practical of the sciences, and its practitioners in the United States, the doctors of medicine, enjoyed an importance and a prestige much superior to that of their colleagues in other countries. Physicians had rivaled lawyers in patriotic zeal, and like the lawyers they had benefited directly from the growth of professionalism. They had formed medical associations, analogous to the bar associations, to discourage "quackery," improve training, and establish professional standards. With the lawyers, they had become the most visible representatives of the new "natural aristocracy" of talents.

Most of the leading physicians belonged to the magic circle of upper-class families. If they had not all been born with silver scalpels in their mouths, most had at least teethed on respectable pewter. William Shippen, Phillip Physic, and Benjamin Rush were the leading physicians of Philadelphia, a city that, as in so many other matters, prided itself on being the exemplar of science and progress.

The Shippens were one of the oldest and most respected Quaker families in Pennsylvania. William's grandfather and father were both doctors. He studied in England under two well-known physicians and received a degree from the University of Edinburgh. Back in Philadelphia he gave the first lectures on anatomy in America and organized the medical school of the College of Philadelphia. There he served successively as professor of anatomy, surgery, and midwifery. During the Revolution, he was director general of the Military Hospitals for the Armies of the United States. In that post he found himself under attack by Benjamin Rush for the deplorable conditions that existed in the army hospitals. Shippen and Rush became bitter enemies, differing in medical as well as political matters.

Phillip Physic was the youngest and most gifted of the triumvirate. He, like Shippen and Rush, had studied in England and had been licensed by the Royal College of Physicians; he returned to America in time to assist in the yellow fever epidemic of 1793.

It is now evident that the fever was brought to Philadelphia with the influx of French refugees who had escaped Toussaint L'Ouverture's massacre in Haiti. The citizens of the city displayed their best qualities in the aid they extended to the refugees. Food, clothes, money, and shelter were provided. Many received "farms . . . free transportation, ploughs, tools and five months' provisions" to establish them in a new life. Fourteen thousand dollars, a large sum in those days, was raised by public subscription for their relief. Their unwitting reward to their benefactors was the yellow fever that broke out a few weeks after their arrival. Soon the whole city was in a state of panic over the spreading contagion.

The first symptoms were fever, inflamed eyes, and headache; the victim would, in the course of three or four days, begin to bleed from the nose and vomit blood. The accepted remedies were bleeding, fasting, and purgation. Each day the death rate mounted until thousands of inhabitants of the city began to flee to country towns. Church bells tolled constantly in mourning for the dead. Bonfires were lit in various parts of the city to purify the air. Every conceivable remedy was tried in turn—garlic, tobacco, mud baths, vinegar, camphor. Meanwhile the anopheles mosquito made its deadly unperceived way about a city where window screens were unknown. The more prosperous doused themselves with all the remedies they could afford; the less fortunate consoled themselves with rum and rye, and it was reported that a number of people drank themselves to death out of fear of the disease. Since the stagnant water that served as breeding grounds for the mosquitoes was less prevalent in upper-class neighborhoods than it was in the poorer sections, the mortality rate was highest among the laborers and mechanics. Most shops and businesses closed, and many people found themselves out of work.

John Davis, the young English scholar and translator, had walked from New York to Philadelphia, arriving at the height of the yellow fever epidemic. On the last leg of his journey he hitched a ride in a coach that had picked up three "Quaker girls" who were actually prostitutes in disguise and gave Davis the address of their "house" in Philadelphia. Davis found the city half-abandoned. "The courts of law were shut . . . the door of the tavern was closed . . . no theatre invited the idle . . . the dice lay neglected on the gaming table. . . . The hospital cart moved slowly on where the chariot before had rolled its rapid wheels; and the coffin-makers were either nailing up the coffins of the dead or giving dreadful preparation by framing others for the dying. . . . In this scene of consternation, the negroes were the only people who could be prevailed upon to assist the dying, and inter those who were no more. Their motives were obvious; they plundered the dead of their effects, and adorned themselves in the spoils of the King of Terrors. Nothing was heard but either the groans of the dying, the lamentations of the survivors . . . or the howling of domestic animals which those who fled the pestilence had left behind."

Stephen Girard, perhaps the wealthiest Philadelphian, undertook to superintend an emergency hospital that was set up at Bush-Hill. The only nurses that could be recruited were prostitutes. Patients died by the score, and it was impossible to persuade anyone with the power to resist to enter the hospital.

Children whose parents had died in the plague roamed the streets in search of scraps of food. Finally the city made some provision for 190 of them. In New York and Baltimore the situation was almost as bad. By November, when the temperature had dropped enough to kill the mosquitoes, the death toll was estimated at over four thousand in the afflicted cities.

In the summers of 1795 and 1796 yellow fever claimed hundreds more lives, but in 1797 it recurred with a terrifying virulence. In an effort to control the spread of the fever in Philadelphia, streets were barricaded and sections of the city quarantined. All houses that contained stricken persons were required under the pain of a fine of five hundred dollars to display a yellow flag.

There was no general agreement as to the cause of the fever. Some doctors and many citizens were convinced it was contagious.

Others denied it. The followers of Dr. William Currie contended that it was imported (which was correct) and that it was contagious, which, strictly speaking, was incorrect. Nonetheless if one were near stricken people one's chances of being bitten by an infected mosquito were considerably increased.

Benjamin Rush, on the other hand, believed that the fever was caused by the dirt that accumulated in city streets, especially in the poorer sections of town, and his adherents directed their efforts to draining pools of foul water and removing garbage. But Rush also bled and purged, while Currie followed more conservative procedures and declared with more than a little truth that Rush's remedies were more dangerous than the disease.

Testimony was gathered from the survivors of both methods of treatment, and the newspapers were filled with charges and counter-charges. As the death toll mounted in the city, trade and commerce once more came to a halt. Sunday services were no longer held in the churches. Courts were closed and the offices of government scattered from Trenton to Richmond. Tents lined the Schuylkill, where food and shelter were given to the indigent.

It is probably not going too far to say that only the fact that the fever was limited to the summer months saved New York, Philadelphia, and Charleston, where the disease was most devastating, from being abandoned. America had, since the first settlers reached its shores, experienced various epidemics—of typhoid, influenza, smallpox—in which many people had lost their lives, but nothing had approached the severity of the recurrent yellow fever that began in the summer of 1793.

At the very moment when poets and preachers were prophesying a future free of the ancient curses of war and disease, the end of pain and suffering, and hailing science as the savior of mankind, the most terrifying plague in the country's history disrupted the life of its major cities and fell with particular force on the capital of the nation.

Many devout Christians (especially those who lived in rural areas) believed the fever to be God's judgment on a wayward people. Philadelphia was notorious as a place where theatrical performances took place, where men and women revealed their vanity by affecting the most modern and decadent styles imported from England and France, where cardplaying and gambling were condoned, where luxury was rampant, where prostitutes walked the streets and vice of every kind could be bought. One New England Federalist pointed out that the fever had been most virulent in those cities from which the envoys to France had departed—New York, Philadelphia, and Charleston. It was God's judgment for entering into negotiations with the godless Directory, admitted champions of atheism.

At the same time, the epidemic demonstrated as nothing else could the impotence of the doctors who tried to save the lives of its victims, as well as the primitive state of what passed for medicine. The best-trained doctors had no notion of the bacterial causes of infection. There was no antiseptic or concept of antisepsis, no anesthetic except enough rum or rye to render a patient more or less insensible. The most common remedies were folk remedies, herbs and potions as old as the Greeks. It was not far off the mark to say that the practice of medicine was much as it had been for two or three thousand years. Doctors could sew up wounds (and hope they would not become fatally infected), set broken limbs (and saw off those too badly smashed for setting), preside over births (which, on the whole, they probably did less well than the midwives whom they forced out of practice), dispense purgatives, and bleed their patients (often to death).

What is perhaps most striking about the medical profession in 1800 is that the social status of doctors was far greater than their professional accomplishments warranted. Paradoxically, the yellow fever epidemics, which demonstrate to a modern mind the hopeless inadequacy of the medical theories and practices of the time, vastly enhanced the reputation of the doctors themselves. Most of them responded heroically to the crisis. At daily risk of their own lives, they tended the ill and dying, working until they dropped from exhaustion, comforting where they could not cure. Disillusioning as it was to have the profession itself so bitterly divided (Benjamin Rush's son, John, beat with a cane a rival doctor who had disparaged his father, whereupon the doctor challenged young Rush to a duel), the controversy focused attention on the "science" of medicine in a most dramatic fashion.

The fact that the prestige of doctors, their status, and their social role far exceeded their professional attainments had important consequences for the development of American medicine. It meant, among other things, that able and ambitious men were attracted to the profession in substantial numbers and that many of these men worked indefatigably to advance medical knowledge. While the study and practice of medicine in England and Europe at the beginning of the nineteenth century were far advanced over that of the United States, before the century was out American medicine would be preeminent.

Here Benjamin Rush serves as our prototype. His axiom was "The science of medicine is related to everything." He was thus a pioneer in psychiatry, and his interests extended to animal behavior, chemistry, botany, steam engines, crime and punishment, forestry, religion, philosophy, and, as we have seen, education. He wished to see medicine democratized and, to use a popular modern word, demystified. In Rush's visionary future men and women would be their own doctors. Properly instructed in the rudiments of good health and good living, they could avoid most ills and prescribe for the rest. Appropriate dress and diet, for example, were two areas most obviously under the control of the individual (as was abstention from spirituous liquors).

In the period prior to the Revolution, Rush contended that from the "general use of distilled and fermented liquors, drunkenness was a common vice in all the different ranks of society." Due to excessive drinking, stays and tight clothes for the women, wigs and other sartorial encumbrances for men, poor heating, and the bad air of crowded rooms, disease was frequent. Cholera, dysentery, "intermitting fever," a "slow chronic fever" also called "the nervous fever" were common, along with the "billious fever. . . . Pneumonies, rheumatisms, inflammatory sore throats, and catarrhs."

The "malignant sore throat" rivaled scarlet fever in its danger to children. In Rush's words: "Death was common between the 50th and 60th years of life from gout, apoplexy, palsy, obstructed livers and dropsies. Fifteen or twenty deaths occurred, every summer, from drinking cold pump water, when the body was in a highly excitable state from great heat and labour." Smallpox and "pulmonary consumption" took numerous lives. Since dentistry was yet unknown, "Pain and disease from decayed teeth were very common."

The most modern theory of disease attributed it to "morbid acrimonies and other matters in the blood." Thus, one of the most common remedies was "diet drinks" to "thin and incrassate the blood." "Great reliance was placed upon the powers in nature" and rest and quiet and a bland diet were usually prescribed for patients. When blood was drawn, it was "often drawn from the feet, in order to excite a revulsion of disease from the superior parts of the body." Sweating, purges, and vomits were also much in use. "The use of opium was confined chiefly to ease pain, to compose a cough, and to restrain prenatural discharges from the body. Such were the prejudices against it, that it was often necessary to conceal it in other medicines," Rush added.

Digitalis, lead zinc, and arsenic were all common remedies along with "cold air, cold water, and ice," and "opium and bark," which "occupy a shelf in the closets of many families." Most unpleasant of all, leeches were used in "diseases which are removed, by their seat or local nature, beyond the . . . lancet."

Dr. Thomas Bond, a well-known Philadelphia physician, was given credit for the "introduction of mercury into general use. . . . He called it emphatically 'a revolutionary remedy,' and prescribed it in all diseases which resisted the common modes of practice." Blisters, warm and cold baths, "vapour baths," wine, and "riding on horseback, the fresh air of the seashore, and long journies" were among the prescriptions for "invalids." Of all the remedies Rush so proudly enumerates as evidence of the scientific advances in medicine, the latter were perhaps the most efficacious, since they had the effect of removing the patient from the reach of the doctor.

At the time when Rush wrote his treatise on the progress of medicine, he was convinced that the rapid strides made in overcoming disease were the result of better "life-styles" (more comfortable and healthy clothes, less drinking, better insulation) as well as of notable advances in medicine. Above all, improvement was to be attributed, in his view, to "the diffusion of medical knowledge among all classes of our citizens, by means of medical publications and controversies." Many people had thus been "taught so much of the principles and practice of physic, as to be able to prescribe for themselves in the forming state of acute diseases. . . . It is to this self-acquired knowledge . . . that physicians are in part indebted for not being called out of their beds so frequently as in former years." Equally important, "sick people are now instructed in the nature of their diseases, and informed of the names and design of their medicines, by which means faith and reason are made to co-operate in adding efficacy to them. . . . By thus disputing every inch of ground with death, many persons have been rescued from the grave, and lived, years afterwards—monuments of the power of the healing art."

The treatment of which Rush was the principal advocate— bloodletting—was, he reported proudly, "now used in nearly all diseases of violent excitement . . . nor is it forbidden, as formerly, in infancy, in extreme old age, in the summer months, nor in the period of menstruation."

The fact was that the progress in medicine of which Rush boasted was almost entirely illusory. Indeed, the proliferation of doctors and remedies, most particularly the spread of the practice of bleeding, represented a marked decline from those "powers of nature" so much trusted in more primitive times.

Significantly, Rush ended his treatise on the progress of medicine with a plea to the Almighty for relief from the "pestilential calamity" of yellow fever: "Dear cradle of liberty of conscience in the western world! nurse of industry and arts! and patron of pious and benevolent institutions! May this cease to be thy melancholy destiny!"

When all is said and done, Rush and his fellow physicians, so devoted to the public weal, so remarkable for their civic virtue, so confident in the efficacy of their "scientific" remedies, and above all so confident that the future must bring great improvements in the treatment of disease and traumatic accidents, were most appropriate "founding fathers" for American medicine.

24

The South

We have talked, in this intermezzo, of various aspects of the life of Americans in, roughly, the year 1800. But of the South we have said comparatively little, and the South is, in many ways, an entirely different story. The most pervasive reality of the South was of course slavery. Every aspect of Southern life was affected and infected by it. Every visitor commented on it. It lay at the heart of the profound ambiguity, the essential schizophrenia of American life. For while slavery was confined, with increasingly few exceptions, to the South, its poisonous consequences were felt in all corners of the country. It touched every political issue; it divided religious denominations; it cast its dark shadow westward. It produced an almost universal paranoia in the South and that least attractive of traits, self-righteousness, in the North. As we have seen in Philadelphia (and the same was true of other Northern cities), most whites, especially those of "the lower orders," disliked or perhaps more accurately despised blacks, assigned them the most menial tasks, and kept them, by and large, in a degraded and demeaning condition. But the general contempt for blacks by whites who lived north of the Mason-Dixon line did not prevent Northerners from continuously denouncing slavery and abusing the South for perpetuating it.

If we attempt the rather difficult task of viewing the matter from the perspective of the Southerner, we begin to understand the depth of the Southern dilemma. By the time of the Revolution slavery had become, by a slow process of accretion, a central fact of the economy of the South. At this stage it is futile to try to assign blame for that basic and inescapable fact. The slave population in certain areas of the South exceeded the white population, and even enslaved, slaves posed a constant threat to their masters. To have emancipated the slaves would have impoverished thousands of the most powerful and influential citizens of the South and left the entire economy of the region in a shambles. The vast majority of the slaves were without the most basic skills needed to make their way in a highly competitive white society. The abolition of slavery would have produced social dislocations verging on chaos.

In the strictest sense, black slavery was a problem without a solution. Its incongruity, staggering in a nation that constantly and even tiresomely proclaimed its devotion to freedom, was certainly not lost on even the most charitably disposed observers of the American scene. It is well to keep in mind that there is no crueler burden to bear than to be forced to justify constantly and continually that which you know in your heart is unjustifiable. That was the unremitting tragedy of the South.

John Davis, the Englishman who had made a modest name for himself by translating Napoleon's account of his Italian campaign into English for a New York publisher and whose comments on the yellow fever in Philadelphia we have already noted, decided to look for a position as a children's tutor in Charleston, South Carolina. His first prospective employer was an arrogant and imperious planter who quizzed Davis mercilessly if ignorantly. The Englishman declined the job when he concluded that his predecessor had been dismissed for getting the mistress's slave girl, Prudence, with child when in fact the culprit had been the master himself.

After an interlude as professor of English at Charleston College, Davis took a job as tutor in the home of a member of the wealthy and powerful Drayton family. There he had an opportunity to observe Southern plantation life at first hand. Setting out from Charleston on foot, he walked through the flat pine forests to the Drayton cotton plantation at Coosawhatchie, a distance of more than fifty miles. At Ashepoo, a "hamlet . . . of three or more log houses," he found "the inhabitants of every sex and age had collected round a huge elephant, which was journeying with its master to Savannah." A chattering monkey made up the third member of the company. Since the log cabin that served as an inn had only one bed, Davis perforce shared it with the elephant driver.

The next day, Davis "dined at a solitary log house in the woods upon exquisite venison." His host was the owner of a small plantation, who cultivated a little rice, Davis noted, "and maintained a wife and four children with his rifle." He owned half a dozen Negroes, but four of them, he told Davis, "had absconded." Coosawhatchie consisted of "a blacksmith's shop, a courthouse and jail." There were half a dozen rice and cotton plantations in the vicinity, and one of these was the Drayton plantation. The house itself, which was simply a large log cabin, was approached by an avenue several miles long. On the right of the house were a "kitchen and other offices: on the left, a stable and coach-house: a little further a row of negro huts, a barn and yard." Davis found the surrounding woods "rather dreary," but the comfort and conveniences of the house and plantation charmed him. The Drayton cuisine was "sumptuous, and an elegance of manners presided." Davis had his own room with a fireplace "that might have vied with the highest circles of polished Europe," a horse at his disposal, and the services of a black man. Everywhere about him he discovered a curious combination of elegance and crudity. The master who was so courteous to his guests cursed and abused his black servants unmercifully in the presence of those same guests. Household slaves went about their duties in tattered clothes that exposed much of their bodies, but at the approach of visitors they rushed to don handsome livery.

Davis had three young charges, the Drayton son, William Henry, named after his uncle, the Revolutionary leader, and two girls, Maria and Sally. William Henry, raised like a young prince, studied no more than he wished.

Mockingbirds and whippoorwills filled the woods with their haunting music. Eagles vied with fish hawks for the river's shad and perch. Hunting was the most common diversion for all ages of males; and Davis's pupil, William Henry, was always in the forefront. "He galloped through the woods, however thick or intricate; summoned his beagles [Sweetlips, Music, and Smoker], after the toil of the chase, with his horn; caressed the dog that had been the most eager in pursuit of the deer, and expressed the hope that there would be good weather to hunt again the following Saturday." Deer hunting was only the beginning. Young William Henry seemed "determined . . . to make havoc among birds and beasts of every description." There were doves to hunt in the cornfields, wild geese in the ponds, squirrels "on the tops of the highest trees."

Underneath the elegance-crudity of plantation life was the ever present reality of slavery. To Davis, "Whatever may be urged upon the subject of negroes, as the voice of millions could lend no support to falsehood, so no casuistry can justify the keeping of slaves . . . no one from being a person can become a thing." The Englishman found it "incredible . . . that the children of the most distinguished families in Carolina are suckled by negro women. Each child has its momma, whose gestures and accent it will necessarily copy. . . . It is not unusual to hear an elegant lady say, 'Richard always grieves when Quasheehaw is whipped, because she suckled him.'" White masters had "a very mean opinion" of "the understanding of negroes," but it was obvious to Davis "that the sentiments of black Cuffey who waits at table, are often not less just or elevated than those of his white ruler." The lines of William Cowper came to Davis's mind: "Slaves cannot breathe in England;/ . . . They touch our country, and their shackles fall."

The paradoxes of Southern life lay all about the young tutor. The master of the plantation appeared to rule like a tyrant, yet "the legislative and executive powers of the house belonged to the mistress. The master has little or nothing to do with the administration; he is a monument of uxoriousness and passive endurance. The negroes are not without the discernment to perceive this; and when the husband resolves to flog them they often throw themselves at the feet of the wife and supplicate her mediation."

So the mistress was, in effect, the master. She managed the essential affairs of the plantation, kept track of the finances, and controlled the fate of a large retinue of household slaves. At the same time, she affected the most languorous pose and reclined for hours on the ubiquitous sofas that were a prominent feature of every Southern house, sipping cooling drinks and attended by a young slave girl who fanned her with a spray of peacock feathers. This elegant lady, "if she lets fall her pocket-handkerchief, has not the strength to pick it up, but calls to one of her black girls who is all life and vigour." And whose sexual favors, it might be added, were more often enjoyed by the master than those of his languid and elegant lady.

Such ladies did not hesitate to send their slaves of either sex to privately run "sugar houses" that existed simply to chastise slaves.

There slaves were punished for minor offenses by whipping—twelve lashes for twenty-five cents. The victims of such wanton cruelty frequently ran away, although the punishments for flight were terrible, often mutilation, the cutting off of a hand or foot or ear. Davis extracted from a Charleston newspaper a typical ad for a runaway: "Fifty dollars reward! Whereas my waiting-fellow, Will, having eloped from me last Saturday, without any provocation, (it being known that I am a humane master), the above reward will be paid to any one who will lodge the aforesaid slave in some jail, or deliver him to me on my plantation at Liberty Hall. Will may be known by the incisions of the whip on his back; and I suspect has taken the road to Coosawhatchie, where he has a wife and five children whom I sold last week to Mr. Gillespie."

Charles Janson, a fellow countryman of Davis's, gives a classic account of a slave market, usually held the first week of the New Year. "At these times slave-dealers attend from a distant part of the country, making a trade of their fellow-men. Husbands forever separated from their wives; mothers torn from their children; brothers and sisters exchanging a last embrace, are subjects of mirth to the surrounding crowd of bidders. Indulgent nature equally formed this sable group; yet, it would seem that while the exterior of the Ethiopian is tinged with the darkest hue, the heart of the white man is rendered callous to all the finer feelings. . . . Often I have witnessed negroes dragged, without regard to age or sex, to the public whipping post, or tied up to the limb of a tree, at the will of the owner, and flogged with a cow-skin, without pity or remorse, till the ground beneath is dyed with the blood of the miserable sufferer."

Another English traveler, J. F. D. Smyth, wrote of the typical field hand, "He is called up in the morning at day break, and is seldom allowed time enough to swallow three mouthfuls of hominy, or hoecake, but is driven out immediately to the field to hard labor, at which he continues, without intermission, until noon. . . . About noon is the time he eats his dinner, and he is seldom allowed an hour for that purpose. . . . They then return to severe labour, which continues in the field until dusk in the evening, when they repair to the tobacco houses, where each has his task in stripping alotted him, that employs him for some hours."

Ocean Plantation, the Coosawhatchie plantation of the Draytons, was considered too unhealthy in the summer for any but slaves and an overseer, so in May the family departed for their mansion on the

Ashley River near Charleston, a splendid brick house with a facade as handsome as that of the plantation house was crude. In Charleston, the summer residents vied with each other in the sumptuousness of their parties. It seemed to Davis that they "strive to exceed each other in the vanities of life."

To walk the streets of the town was to brand oneself as a person of inferior rank. Every gentleman rode a fine horse or drove a carriage. As Davis put it, "He who is without horses and slaves incurs always contempt. . . . Even the negroes are infected with this idea; and Cuffey shall be heard to exclaim, 'He great blackguard that; he got no negur. Where his horse? He always walk.'"

For Davis the lavishness of the entertainments failed to compensate for the tedium of the conversation, which was of nothing but cotton. Faced with another winter in the isolation of Coosawhatchie, Davis decided to turn north and resume his career as a translator in New Jersey and New York.

John Bernard, English comic actor and manager for some years of the Federal Street Theatre in Philadelphia, traveled widely in the South. He observed: "In nine cases out of ten the supporters of the system [of slavery] have been its greatest victims. I do not hesitate to say they have been its sincerest detesters. It certainly is no enviable lot when a man happening to be born on a particular spot which is cursed by an indisposable legacy, can be put in the pillory by every enthusiast who makes feeling, not fact, his rule of reasoning. I do not remember a single instance of a planter defending the origin of his possessions, or one who defended the continuance of slavery by other than this single argument; that human agency is required in the cultivation of the Southern soil."

Yet Bernard's description of the day of a Southern planter is a classic one: "During the summer he [the master] used to rise about nine, when he exerted himself to walk as far as his stables to look at the stud which he kept for the races; at ten he breakfasted on coffee, eggs, and hoe-cake, concluding it with the commencement of his diurnal potions—a stiff glass of mint-sling [i.e., julep]—a disorder peculiar to the South. He then sought the coolest room and stretched himself on a pallet in his shirt and trousers, with a negress at his head and another at his feet to keep off the flies and promote reflection. Between twelve and one . . . he would sip half a pint of some mystery termed bumbo, apple-toddy, or pumpkin flip. He then mounted a pony, and with an umbrella over his head, rode gently around his estate to converse with his overseers. At three he dined, and drank everything—brandy, claret, cider, Madeira, punch, and sangaree, then resumed his pallet with his negresses, and meditated until teatime."

Bernard's planter varied this regimen by going in a wagon well supplied with guns, ammunition, fishing rods and tackle, and all the equipment needed to make juleps, "attended by a train of blacks," to a nearby pond where he would immerse himself under a canvas awning. One black man would set his fishing line and stand by it to warn him of a bite while another loaded his gun and placed it near him so "that he might pop at the first bird that offered. . . . Thus combining the four stable enjoyments of bathing, drinking, shooting and fishing." But the master of the plantation still yearned for company. "If at length the form of a stranger appeared, he sprang from his plank and shouted an invitation to alight and take a drop of something sociable."

While Bernard's sketch is clearly a parody, it does give us a vivid picture of plantation life, above all, perhaps, of its essential boringness. Bernard's host apparently lived in the hope of visitors to relieve the tedium of an unfulfilling leisure.

The South was not, of course, composed of vast plantations like that of the Drayton family. The great majority of the population was made up of the yeoman farmers that Jefferson celebrated. But strong and subtle ties—in addition to the negative tie of slavery—bound together the small farmer and the lordly plantation owner, who, despite his aristocratic way of life, was actually more democratic than his Northern counterpart. Both the small farmer and the great planter made their living from the land. Even if small-scale farmers owned only a few acres and a slave or two or three, they did not hesitate to dignify their modest farms with the name "plantation" (in much the same spirit that a present-day Westerner will call any piece of land larger than an acre a "ranch"). A common devotion to hunting and its corollary, horsemanship, also proved an enduring tie between the plantation owner and the farmers. Richard Henry Lee had been able to recruit his cavalry legions from among such men. John Davis tells of his young charge's obsession with hunting. In that he was like every young Southerner regardless of class. It is almost impossible to overstate the social importance of hunting in the South or, perhaps, of sport, since horseracing and cockfighting were ancillary to hunting. A Southerner was judged, not by where he had gone to school or how much money his daddy had or what profession he pursued, but by his skill as a hunter and how he sat his horse. Hunting and horses, horses and hunting, with some cockfighting thrown in—that was the cement that bound Southern classes together. That, of course, was typical of the English aristocracy as well. It was upper class and lower class—farmers and hunters all—against the pious, money-oriented, commercial middle class. The Yankee Federalist who so scorned slavery would not think of socializing with the poor farmer, the artisan or mechanic of the city; but the Southern gentleman, with his easy, open ways, could lapse quite readily into the jawing lingo of his slaves or the drawling blasphemies of his farmer neighbor.

John Bernard described a typical Virginia horserace in which "a low, long-backed shaggy plebian [horse], undressed and dirty, his legs pillars and his monstrous head set upon a short, straight neck" outran a field of "sleek, proud, well-trained elegant-limbed English thoroughbreds." The horses were ridden by their owners, whether the masters of great plantations or hardscrabble farmers, and at the quarter-horse races the sides of the quarter-mile straightaway were "generally lined by a motley multitude of negroes, Dutchmen, Yankee pedlars, and backwoodsmen, among whom, with long whips in their hands to clear the ground, moved the proprietors and bettors, riding or leading their horses. The event was always proclaimed by a tornado of applause from the winner's party, the niggers in particular hallooing, jumping and clapping their hands in a frenzy of delight." Bernard witnessed as many as twenty quarter-horse races in a day followed by "trials at rifle-shooting, cock-fighting, and boxing." He observed: "What with the wrangling of the owners, the slang of the grooms, the fun of the niggers, and the diversities of other characters upon the ground," the "muscular backswoodmen" among them, the scene "was one of the most animated and primitive I had the fortune to stumble on." Slaves who were involved in training horses or caring for the hunting dogs, the hounds, or fighting cocks enjoyed a special status with their masters. Like Chicken George in Alex Haley's historical novel, *Roots*, they entered the charmed Southern circle of men of whatever color or class whose lives were dominated by their passion for sport.

John Davis told of dining with an indifferent farmer, four of whose six slaves had run off, who kept his family supplied with food by his rifle.

The Southerners who migrated west carried their life-style with them. A visitor to a frontier town dominated by Southerners wrote: "They mount their horses . . . drinking and trading horses until late in the evening." Such a man "'reckons' they should know how to write their names, and 'allows' it's a right smart thing to be able to read when you want to . . . but he don't 'calculate' that books and the sciences will do as much good for a man . . . as the handy use of a rifle." The New Englanders in the area were smart enough, "But they can't hold a rifle nor ride at a wolf hunt . . . and he reckons, after all, these are the great tests of merit."

In any discussion of slave life it is essential to keep in mind the fact that there were two distinct classes of slaves—household slaves and field hands. On the Green Spring plantation of Philip Ludwell in Virginia, the division of field and household slaves was listed as fifty-nine "crop Negroes," twelve house servants, four carpenters, one wheelwright, two shoemakers, and three gardeners.

The crucial thing with the field hands was that they were *together*, dozens or hundreds of them. As distinguished from the slaves who functioned as personal or household servants and thus were constantly in the presence of whites and inevitably absorbed many of their attitudes, the field hands lived on the periphery of the white world.

Most visitors to plantations took astonished note of the fact that the "crop" slaves, after laboring from dawn to dusk in the fields, sat up far into the night over the large fires, even in the heat of summer. Around the fires the rich vibrato of their voices rang in the night air. Often they played homemade musical instruments and sang haunting songs of work and travail and weariness and pain. Praising the Lord and talking and singing alike were punctuated by that dark, uninhibited laughter that no white man could imitate. Even when they dared not plot to achieve it by armed insurrection, they dreamed of freedom. The bolder talked about it cautiously, and the boldest or most desperate ran away in search of it. The white master dreamed of black freedom too, but his dreams were nightmares. There is no way of knowing how many Southern whites have waked in their beds in a cold sweat of fear at the dream of black insurrection, but it is safe to assume that it must have been a considerable number over the years.

By virtue of their numbers and the brutalizing conditions of their lives the field hands formed a plantation subculture. They developed their own rituals of which the nighttime bonfire was the symbol. Around that fire in summer and winter, they preserved themselves from despair. In the process they created what we call today "black consciousness." Out of suffering they created joy. And the uncomprehending white man who caught tantalizing bits of that joy-out-of-suffering fastened on it as evidence that they were happy childlike characters who loved their masters and were, with the exception of a few malcontents and "bad niggers," content with their lot. At the end of his autobiographical novel, *Portrait of the Artist as a Young Man*, James Joyce wrote with youthful grandiloquence, "I go forth . . . to forge in the smithy of my soul the uncreated conscience of my race." That is what the black field hands who sat around their eternal midnight fires did—they forged the uncreated conscience of their race by songs and stories.

The laws relating to slaves tell their own somber story. The "black code" of one Southern state provided that "if more than seven slaves are found in any road without a white person, twenty lashes apiece; for visiting a plantation without a pass, ten lashes; for letting loose a boat from where it is made fast, thirty-nine lashes; for having any article for sale without a ticket from his master, ten lashes; for traveling in any other than the most usual and accustomed road, when going alone to any place, forty lashes; for traveling in the night without a pass, forty lashes; for being found in another person's Negro quarters, forty lashes; for hunting with dogs in the woods, thirty lashes; for being on horseback without the written permission of their master, twenty-five lashes; for riding or going abroad in the night or riding horses in the daytime, without leave, a slave may be whipped, cropped, or branded in the cheek with the letter R, or otherwise punished, such punishment not extending to life, or so as to render him unfit for labor." In "enlightened" Virginia there were seventy-one "crimes" for which a black man could be executed as opposed to three for whites.

In the words of a fugitive slave: "So galling was our bondage, that to escape from it, we suffered the loss of all things, and braved every peril, and endured every hardship. Some of us left parents, some wives, some children. Some of us were wounded with guns and dogs, as we fled. Some of us secreted ourselves in the suffocating holds of ships. Nothing was so dreadful to us as slavery."

The relationships between white masters and mistresses and their black slaves were too subtle and complex to be readily described. But it is safe to say that the effect of the slaves on their masters was as striking as that of white culture on the slaves. The relationship might best be described as a classic love-hate or love-fear relationship.

In the plantation house the master and mistress and their children "loved" the black men and women who attended to their daily needs, and there are innumerable accounts of devoted slaves who ran out, weeping and crying out with joy, to greet master or mistress on their return from a long absence. On such occasions there were embraces and all the signs of genuine affection. Black and white were, after all, involved over their lifetimes in the most intimate human scenes—birth, illness, death. They shared moments of happiness and times of hardship or disaster. And yet in the depths of the relationship hate and fear were as strong as love. When she heard that her cousin, Betsey Witherspoon, had been murdered in her bed by her slaves, Mary Chesnut wrote: "I broke down; horror and amazement were too much for me. . . . She did not die peacefully in her bed, as we supposed, but was murdered by her own people, her Negroes. . . . Horrible beyond words! Hitherto I have never thought of being afraid of Negroes. I have never injured any of them; why should they want to hurt me? Two-thirds of my religion consists of trying to be good to Negroes, because they are in our power, and it would be so easy to be the other thing. Somehow today I feel that the ground is cut away from under my feet. Why should they treat me any better than they have done cousin Betsey Witherspoon? . . . Mrs. Witherspoon's death has clearly driven us all wild."

So there it was, in the very heart of the household, Betsey Witherspoon's "own people," part of her "family." Perhaps she had been murdered by the woman who had suckled her children. Fear and loathing; love and affection and trust. Horror and terror. In the center.

More remote but equally terrifying was the perpetual threat of general slave insurrection. In 1800 Virginia was thrown into a turmoil by the rumor of a slave uprising. Governor James Monroe called the general assembly into session to inform them that a plot had been discovered by slaves on several plantations near Richmond to kill their masters, join slaves in the city, seize arms and ammunition from the penitentiary where they were stored, and "take possession of the town." The plan had been revealed by two slaves on one of the plantations marked for destruction. Monroe reported to the legislators that guards had been placed at strategic points in the city and horsemen dispatched to patrol the roads leading to Richmond. Mounted militia had been sent to arrest the leaders of the conspiracy, and some twenty blacks had been rounded up and placed in jail, although the leaders had escaped.

Gradually more and more details came to light. Plans had been made for the formation of a black cavalry unit as well as infantry. Men had been assigned to units, a "general" had been chosen, and tactics devised that called for the lower end of the city to be set afire while the armory was attacked. Apparently the plan "embraced most of the slaves in this city and neighborhood," Monroe told the assembly, "and . . . extended to several of the adjacent counties . . . if not the whole of the State." To Monroe, "it seemed strange that the slaves should embark in this novel and unexampled enterprise of their own accord." He hinted at outside agitators.

According to the testimony of one of the conspirators, the intention was to kill all whites except "Quakers, Methodists and Frenchmen," who were to be spared as "being friendly to liberty"; also to be spared were "all the poor white women who had no slaves." The leader was a black named Gabriel who had told his followers that before he would bear any longer what he had borne, "he would turn out and fight with a stick." Five hundred bullets had been collected, spears made from old bayonets bound to poles, crossbows fashioned, a few ancient pistols rounded up, and a flag made with the words "death or liberty" on it.

The consequences of what was called Gabriel's insurrection, although no white man was killed or wounded or a shot fired, were far-reaching. The Virginia legislature, conscious that it could not slaughter the hundreds of slaves presumably implicated in the plot, spent interminable hours debating what action to take. Ten slaves were executed, and Monroe asked Jefferson to try to procure some Western territory to which free blacks might be sent. The president replied by suggesting the West Indies or Africa.

Gabriel's plan for an insurrection, bizarre and impractical as it was, frightened slaveholders far beyond the borders of Virginia. The notion of gradual emancipation, which although always remote had at least been discussed, now became unmentionable. The *Virginia Herald* expressed the opinion of many Southerners when it denounced all talk of "liberty and equality" as "dangerous and extremely wicked in this country where every white man is a master and every black man a slave. . . . There can be no compromise between liberty and slavery. The man who thinks so is a fool. . . . There is no middle course. We must either abolish slavery or continue it. . . . If we will keep a ferocious monster within our country, we must keep him in chains, no one would turn a lion or a tiger out in the streets.—Slavery is a monster,—most horrible of all monsters, tyranny excepted. Democracy, therefore, in Virginia is like virtue in Hell. The Ethiopian can never be washed white. The slaveholder can never be a Democrat." Any slaveholder who professed to be was telling "a damnable diabolical lie."

As it turned out, a substantial majority of those Southerners who held slaves were determined to call themselves Democrats however Federalist editors might rage; and to live as best they could with that "most horrible of all monsters."

Jefferson, like George Mason in the Federal Convention, had gloomy forebodings about a slave insurrection, and he wracked his brain for a solution, going so far as to draft a bill for the Virginia legislature to consider. The bill provided that all slave children should be kept with their parents until they were eighteen and twenty-one, for females and males, respectively. "They were then to be brought up at public expense, to tillage, arts, or sciences, according to their geniuses" and finally "colonized to such place as the circumstances of the time should render most proper, sending them out with arms, implements of household and of the handicraft arts, seeds, pairs of useful domestic animals, etc., to declare them a free and independent people, and extend to them our alliance and protection, till they shall have acquired strength."

The reason for "sending them out" was that "deep rooted prejudices entertained by the whites; ten thousand recollections, by the blacks of the injuries they have sustained; new provocations; the real distinction which nature has made; and many other circumstances, will divide us into parties, and produce convulsions, which will probably never end but in the extermination of one or the other race."

Jefferson was equally eloquent on the corrupting effect of slavery on white masters. "There must doubtless be an unhappy influence on the manners of our people produced by the existence of slavery among us," he wrote. "The whole commerce between master and slave is a perpetual exercise of the most boisterous passions, the most unremitting despotism on the one part, and degrading submission on the other. Our children see this, and learn to imitate it. . . . If a parent could find no motive either in his philanthropy or his self-love, for restraining the intemperance of passion towards his slave, it should always be a sufficient one that his child is present. But generally it is not sufficient. The parent storms, the child looks on, catches the lineaments of wrath, puts on the same airs in the circle of smaller slaves, gives a loose to his worst passions, and thus nursed, educated, and daily exercised in tyranny, cannot but be stamped by it with odious peculiarities. A man must be a prodigy who can retain his manners and morals undepraved by such circumstances."

Jefferson, at least, had no notion that the slave was a happy, carefree child of nature, content to be the ward of a kind master. He must prefer any other fate "to that in which he is born to live and labour for another: in which he must lock up the faculties of his nature [and] . . . entail his own miserable condition on the endless generations proceeding from him. With the morals of the people their industry is also destroyed. For in a warm climate, no man will labour for himself who can make another labour for him. . . . And can the liberties of a nation be thought secure when we have removed their only firm basis, a conviction in the minds of the people that they are of the gift of God? Indeed I tremble for my countrymen when I reflect that God is just; that his justice cannot sleep forever: that considering numbers, nature and natural means only, a revolution of the wheel of fortune, an exchange of situations is among possible events: that it may become probable by supernatural interference. The Almighty has no attribute which can take side with us in such a contest." Jefferson wrote these words in the closing months of the Revolution, and he added his hopes for "a total emancipation," and "with the consent of the masters, rather than by their extirpation."

Miscegenation, most typically between white men and black women, and the consequent mixed offspring of such unions, was one of the most bizarre aspects of American slavery. The sexual exploitation by white masters of their female slaves was a conspicuous part of Southern life. Mary Chesnut inveighed against "a [master] who runs a hideous black harem with its consequences under the same roof with his lovely white wife, and his beautiful and accomplished daughters. He holds his head as high and poses as the model of all human virtues to these poor women whom God and the laws have given him."

Josiah Quincy, visiting in Charleston, noted that "the enjoyment of a negro or mulatto woman is spoken of as quite a common thing; no reluctance, delicacy or shame is made about the matter. It is far from uncommon to see a gentleman at dinner and his reputed offspring a slave to the master of the table. I myself saw two instances of this, and the company very facetiously would trace the lines, lineaments and features of the father and mother in the child, and very accurately point out the characteristic resemblance. The fathers, neither of them, blushed or seemed disconcerted. They were called men of worth, politeness and humanity."

In the course of telling his autobiography to John Davis, a slave named Dick described his "young master" calling for a julep as soon as he got out of bed in the morning. "So charged, he was always upon the scent after game, and mighty ficious [vicious?] when he got among the negur wenches. He used to say that a likely negur wench was fit to be a queen; and I forgot how many queens he had among the girls on the two plantations." The young squire did not live long, Dick continued. "He was killed by a drunken negur man who found him overficious with his wife. The negur man was hanged upon a gibbet" and was three days in dying.

So there was more than a measure of collective madness in the South. Small wonder that attacks upon slavery infuriated Southerners. They were victims, too, as Mason and Jefferson had pointed out. They had not created the system whose benefits they enjoyed and whose horrors they endured. They were men and women of human clay with presumably the same incongruous mixture of good and bad qualities as the rest of the race; but the circumstances in which they lived encouraged them each day to exercise the least admirable of human qualities.

Many whites were, of course, kind to slaves. In the North some devoted their lives to their emancipation. But the "system" was intolerable by any measure. Under the weight of it, under the largely unrecorded and incalculable suffering that was its accompaniment, a rich and intricate subterranean life took shape.

In a society that increasingly suppressed its emotions, the emotions of blacks were exuberantly expressed in singing, dancing, music, in the rhythms of clapping hands, in shouting and wailing, in primitive Christian hope and joy. What could not be endured the slaves turned into the endurable through forms of common expression that were armor for their souls. Among a dominating race that doubted their capacity for the more sensitive human feelings, they far "outfelt" their masters. They tempered the required deference with mockery. They laughed at the white man's ways until they cried; they cried until they laughed again. When they could not bear the pain, they sang. No stranger or, in its own way, more noble sight is vouchsafed the historian than the techniques of survival developed by black slaves in republican United States; and no stranger juxtaposition than that of white and black in the American South, loving and hating, despising and mocking, an unending epiphany of violence and fear; of exploitation on the one side and infinitely subtle forms of revenge on the other.

Even today it amuses Northern liberals to hear Southern whites say that they love and understand blacks. Condescending and presumptuous as such a statement is, there is a grain of truth in it. By now, Southern whites and blacks have a long common history, of which all these tangled elements we have mentioned form the fabric. One does not easily escape from such a web of history, as many black people who have gone north have discovered. A love-hate relationship, excruciating as it may often be, is still far better than no relationship at all.

Count Segur, formerly French ambassador to Russia, traveled in America and found it delightful. He wrote, "Every individual displayed the modest and tranquil pride of an independent man, who feels that he has nothing above him but the laws, and who is a stranger alike to the vanity, to the prejudices, and to the servility of European society. No useful profession is ever ridiculed or dispised." The only dangers that could "menace, in the future, this happy republic . . . [are] the excessive wealth which is promised by its commerce, and the corrupting luxury which may follow it," and the situation of two classes of whites in the South—one, "a very large class of poor whites, and another of enormously wealthy proprietors" sustained "by the labor of blacks, slaves, which increases largely every year, and may and must be frequently driven to despair and revolt by the contrast of their servitude with the entire liberty enjoyed by men of the same color in other States of the Union." Count Segur, like the chevalier de Chastellux, could see no outcome but a "separation which would enfeeble and perhaps break this unhappy confederation, which can preserve its power only in being firmly locked and united together."

A symbol of the crudity and brutality of American life, especially in the South, was the practice of "gouging" and biting. A traveler tells us: "When two boxers had wearied of pummeling each other, they came to close quarters and wrapping the opponents hair around their forefingers, they pressed their thumbs into the sockets of their eyes, trying thereby to gouge out an eye. The victor, for his expertness, receives shouts of applause from the sportive throng, while his poor eyeless antagonist is laughed at for his misfortune."

Americans whose embarrassed attention was called to this barbaric custom insisted that it was an archaic mode of fighting, but the

Englishman Charles Janson maintained that "this more than savage custom is daily practised among the lower classes in the southern states." Janson had witnessed such a contest in Georgia where, "after a brief and violent skirmish," one of the combatants had "sprung up with his antagonist's eye in his hand!!! The savage crowd applauded. . . . The eye is not the only feature which suffers on these occasions. Like dogs and bears, they use their teeth and feet . . . upon each other." John Stanley of Bertie County, North Carolina, was said to file his teeth in preparation for such a contest; Thomas Penrise, of the same state, caught cheating at cards, and attacked by his fellow players, snuffed out the candle, "gouged out three eyes, bit off an ear, tore a few cheeks, and made good his escape." Butting and kicking were also favored modes of assault. "A fellow named *Michie*" boasted to Janson "that he could kick any man, six feet high, under the chin, and break his jaws."

Thomas Ashe, an English novelist and adventurer, traveling in the region, was told that such matches were a common feature of the spring and fall race meetings in Kentucky, each of which lasted "fourteen days without interruption, aided by the licentious and profligate of all the neighbouring states."

Gouging was the lower-class equivalent in the South to the upper-class habit of dueling. Personal honor and its accompaniment, personal combat, were features of Southern life. Gouging reflected the cruel realities of frontier life much as revivals did. A man had to constantly prove himself to be rougher, tougher, more tenacious and enduring than a potential rival. The boundless cruelty of slavery doubtless had something to do with such barbarous contests. When slaves fought among themselves, they fought with the same kind of ferocity. Dick, the slave who told his life story to John Davis, boasted of having bitten off and swallowed the toe of a rival suitor. He was praised for his spunk by his master and fellow slaves, since his opponent was a much larger and stronger man who was "tromping" him.

Janson admitted that such encounters were most typically to be found in the settlements on the Carolina and Kentucky frontier, where the inhabitants "live in the woods and deserts, and many of them cultivate no more land than will raise them corn and cabbages, which, with fish, and occasionally a piece of pickled pork or bacon, are their constant food. . . . Their habitations are more wretched than can be conceived of; the huts of the poor of Ireland, or even the meanest Indian wig-wam, displaying more ingenuity and greater industry. . . .

Amid these accumulated miseries, the inhabitants of log-houses are extremely tenacious of the rights and liberties of republicanism. They consider themselves on an equal footing with the best educated people of the country, and upon the principles of equality they intrude themselves into every company." In the country taverns judges, lawyers, plantation owners, and tbe governor himself "must associate with their fellow-citizens of every degree."

Thomas Ashe left us a lively description of a "ball" in a Kentucky tavern. The room was "filled with persons at cards, drinking, smoking, dancing, etc. The *music* consisted of two bangies—crude drums played by negroes nearly in a state of nudity, and a lute, through which a Chickasaw breathed with much occasional exertion and violent gesticulations. The dancing accorded with the harmony of these instruments. . . , This ball, considered a violent, vulgar uproar by me, afforded the utmost delight to the assembly." However, it came to a sudden conclusion when a "drunken politician seized a friend by the throat, and threatened to annihilate him, if he did not drink 'Damnation to Thomas Jefferson.'" At this the tavern keeper hastily adjourned the meeting before the fight could spread, and the disgruntled revelers straggled off.

Southern society has often been characterized as feudal in character and the plantation with its slaves compared with the medieval fief with its serfs. The analogy, which the South, infatuated with the romantic novels of Sir Walter Scott, came to cherish, was in most ways a misleading one. The medieval serf was protected by an elaborate structure of customary law that defined the duties of the lord to his serf as well as those of the serf to his master. Thus, the basic harshness of the feudal system was mitigated by a network of reciprocal obligations and responsibilities, which at the height of the feudal period ran both up and down and were ratified and superintended by the Roman Catholic church. In the slaveholding states of the American South there were no such well-established protections for the rights of slaves; they were largely at the mercy of their masters. Those with kind and considerate masters clearly fared better than those whose owners were "slave drivers." If there was a touch of the feudal about the South it was to be found in the mystique that bound the farmer of modest means, with a slave or two, to the plantation capitalist who numbered his slaves by the dozen or, in some instances, by the hundreds; that, and a kind of personal honor. It proved almost impossible, despite decades of effort by more enlightened Southern politicians, to wean Southerners from their devotion to duels. The Southerner displayed a touchiness in matters that he conceived of as involving his "honor" that astonished visitors and provided the basic ingredients of the Western gunfighter almost a century later.

It must also be kept in mind that scattered throughout the Southern states were a number of communities that condemned slaveholding and refused to participate in it. Such were the Quaker communities and the settlements of Moravians in North Carolina.

Taking one thing with another, Northerners and Southerners were about as different as two divisions of the same race inhabiting the same continent could be. John Davis, having left South Carolina to seek his fortune as a translator in New York, returned to Virginia to teach school. There the visit of a peddler provided him with an occasion to contrast the native Virginians with some "Yankee immigrants" from New Jersey. "The New Jersey man puts his hand to the plough," he wrote; "the Virginian only inspects the work of his farm. The New Jersey man lives with the strictest economy, and very seldom visits or receive visits; the Virginian exceeds his income, loves to go abroad, and welcomes his guests with the smiles of hospitality. The New Jersey man turns every horse out to labour, and walks whither he has to go on business; the Virginian, thinking it degrading to be seen on foot, has always his riding-hag saddled and fastened to the fence. The New Jersey man . . . seldom enlarges his mind or transfers his attention to others; the Virginian is remarkable for his colloquial happiness, loses no opportunity of knowledge, and delights to show his wit at the expense of his neighbor. Neither a dancing-master, a pedlar, or a maker of air-balloons was ever encouraged by a New Jersey man; but on a Virginian they never fail to levy contributions. . . . The treasury of the pedlar is in vain laid open to the eyes of the New Jersey man; neither the brilliant water of the diamond, . . . nor the lustre of the topaz has charms to allure him; but the Virginian, enamoured of ornament, cannot gaze on them with impunity. He empties his coffers of every dollar to adorn the apparel of his wife and daughters."

It was thus not without reason that the states were tempted to feel themselves sovereign. Their citizens were far more aware of the uniqueness of their particular states than most Americans are today. The states *were* different—which is, of course, simply to say that their inhabitants were different. The section that demonstrated the greatest homogeneity was undoubtedly New England, but even there Vermont was an outpost of radical democratic ideas and freethinking, existing in uneasy alliance with old-style Calvinism. Maine considered itself another matter entirely from Massachusetts, of which she had been the restless northern wing for so long. Connecticut, from having been the most liberal, had become the most conservative of all the New England states. As for Rhode Island, that "nest of vipers," as a Bostonian had earlier called it, remained out of step with its neighbors.

Of the so-called Middle States, New York differed vastly from Pennsylvania, where remnants of the Quaker tradition were conspicuous, and the generally conservative eastern part of the state was constantly at odds with the democratic frontier. The Southern states were even more sharply distinguished one from the other. Their only common bond was slavery. Aristocratic Virginia was as unlike crude and unpolished Georgia as two states could be. Some of Georgia's convict-colony character lingered on, and La Rochefoucauld-Liancourt, a refugee from the French Revolution, described the citizens of the state as "the most barbarous drunken disorderly and reckless people in America." A New Yorker visiting Georgia in 1818 wrote of the state legislature, "Their conduct was beneath that of any crew of sailors that was ever seen. Cursing, quarreling, hollowing, drinking and getting drunk." Whenever Congress passed a law or the Supreme Court handed down a decision uncongenial to Georgians, their usual reaction was to threaten summary destruction to anyone who might attempt to enforce the objectionable statute or decision.

To South Carolinians, who had the highest pretensions to elegance and culture, Georgians seemed hardly removed from the savages they were constantly fighting. North Carolina, sandwiched between nouveau riche South Carolina and Virginia, the grande dame of the Southern states, had its own clearly distinguished character, more practical, more down-to-earth, an unabashed plebeian rubbing shoulders with its aristocratic neighbors. Much the same could be said of the new frontier states. Those of the Southern frontier were typically cruder versions of the states from which they had drawn most of their settlers, but they shared certain frontier characteristics—a determined democracy, a suspicion of Eastern bankers and money-men, a punitive attitude toward the Indians, an emphasis on "equality" as an ideal.

The point is that the persistence of a states' rights psychology simply reflected that in many ways the "united states" were far more like small individual nations than like one homogeneous national state.

25

Down the Mississippi

The vast river system that constituted the Mississippi River Valley tied the country together, as well as setting its distant limits. The rivers that rose on the western side of the Alleghenies flowed westward to the Mississippi while a corresponding series of rivers rising in the Rocky Mountain region flowed eastward to empty into the same river. The Old Northwest, as we have frequently had occasion to note, was bound to the South by the Ohio River, which was both water highway and boundary. It was a means of access to the Illinois and Indiana country. Flowing into the Mississippi, the Ohio also enabled travelers to float down to New Orleans and the territory of Louisiana.

The Allegheny and Monongahela rivers flowed into the Ohio at Pittsburgh, the starting point for most river-borne journeys west and south. North of the Ohio, settlements were characterized by the attitudes and institutions of New England and the Middle States; South was slave territory. For hundreds of miles the Ohio defined the northern and western borders of Virginia and Kentucky; all along its banks were farms (on the Ohio and Indiana side), plantations (on the Virginia and Kentucky banks), and small settlements. At Cairo the Mississippi and the Ohio joined forces and moved majestically through lowland country past New Orleans to the Gulf of Mexico.

454

So essential a part of the experience of those men and women who emigrated west and southwest was that great river system of which the Mississippi was the spine that we must try as best we can to join them in their watery progress. Our guide will be Francis Baily, a twenty-one-year-old Englishman, son of a London banker, who set out down the Ohio from Pittsburgh in the fall of 1796.

River transportation, though often extremely hazardous, was at its benign best the most entrancing mode of travel. In silence, save for the creak of oars in oarlocks and the gentle lapping of water against the sides of the boat, the river carried its passengers along at an average rate of three to six miles an hour, depending on the swiftness of the water's flow. The sensation of floating was in marked contrast to the bone-rattling jolts of the crude roads and traces over which horses and wagons must travel in the only alternative mode of transportation. River travelers often had the feeling of being motionless while the landscape wound past them. The river and its banks offered unending panoramas of new vistas and changing terrain.

Francis Baily had the good fortune to join up with a fellow Englishman named Heighway who was setting out with two artisans and their wives to start a little settlement on the Miami River. After waiting several days for rains to raise the river sufficiently to float the boat, Baily embarked with Heighway and his party on a flat-bottomed Kentucky barge. Dry weather had "prevented all navigation for some time," Baily noted, "and the vast body of emigrants and shopkeepers who were bound to Kentucky" took advantage of the opportunity to head down the swollen river. Many of the boats in the small armada were "most miserably supplied, with scarcely a covering to the boat or a blanket to lie down on, and barely a pot or a kettle to dress what provisions they might chance to meet with," for many of them counted on stopping and hunting or fishing to feed themselves during their journey. Baily and his companions were, by comparison, well supplied with "beef, mutton, flour, bacons . . . three or four good feather beds and plenty of bedding." They planned to stop at farms along the river for milk, eggs, and butter. Above the first rapids they took on an old man as a pilot to guide them through the "riffle" and paid him a half dollar for his trouble. Many dangerous stretches of the river had such a service available for the cautious (and prosperous) traveler. Others took their chances, often with disastrous and sometimes fatal results.

Baily's barge had to lay to for several days as did most of the other boats on the river because of ice floes that threatened to overturn it.

Resuming their journey, they ran aground on a sandbar and had to slip into the icy water to lighten the boat's load; their efforts were unavailing, and all night long chunks of ice smashed against the stern of the boat threatening at every moment to stave in the sides and end their trip before it had well begun. The next morning they hailed a flatboat coming down the river with a load of flour, and its crew helped them drag the barge off the bar.

A hundred miles down the river they reached Wheeling, Virginia, a recent settlement of some fifty log cabins and a stone house belonging to the town's founder, a Mr. Lane. Lane had an Indian wife, and some of his in-laws were visiting when Baily arrived. After replenishing their supplies in Wheeling, Baily and his companions pushed on, or rather floated on, in the company of a Kentucky merchant who joined them. That night they tied their barge to a tree and made the acquaintance of an Irishman, who "was forming himself a plantation; he had made himself a miserable hut, and was erecting some kind of shelter for the few cattle he had brought with him."

At that point, the ice effectively closed the river, and the travelers were obliged to make camp as best they could. On both sides of the river, other boats were tied up waiting for the ice to melt and the river to rise. Soon there were fifteen or sixteen travelers who had joined Baily and his friends. Every day some of the more experienced hunters in the party scoured the adjacent woods for deer, turkey, bear, "or any other animals fit for food." The technique for killing bears was to tree them and then cut down the tree. The tree down, one man would fire at the bear while the others covered him in case the animal was only wounded and disposed to charge.

During the enforced stop Baily took the opportunity to visit nearby Indian burial mounds, the awesome remains of some long-vanished Indian race. There were three such mounds, each a hundred feet or more in height and fifty or sixty feet in diameter at the top. On one of them, Baily found a tree with the initials of earlier visitors carved into its trunk.

After ten days the travelers were finally set free when the ice began to break up, "with a noise like thunder." Now the danger was that their barge would be crushed like an eggshell by tons of ice. Baily's powers of description failed him at the sight of "this vast body of ice . . . grating with a most tremendous noise against the sides of the river, and bearing down everything which opposed its progress!—the tallest and stoutest trees [were] obliged to submit to its destructive fury." Baily, Heighway, and the artisans began to unload their barge, hoping to save what they could before it was crushed or swept away. By laboring in frigid water up to their waists for three hours with little rest, they rescued the better part of what Baily estimated to be a cargo of eleven tons, much of it seeds and farm equipment intended to stock the plantation; then ice stove in the boat and carried away the shattered hull. That night the temperature dropped to seventeen degrees below zero. The next morning "the river was one floating wreck. Nothing could be discerned amidst the vast bodies of floating ice (some of which were as big as a moderate-sized house) but trees which had been torn up from the banks, and the boats of many a family who had scarcely time to escape unhurt . . . and whose whole property . . . was now floating down. . . . Canoes, skiffs, flatts, in fact, everything which was opposed to its fury, was hurried along to one general ruin."

Baily and the members of his party erected a kind of tent made out of clothes and blankets to protect themselves and the cargo they had managed to rescue from the barge. Finding an abandoned log building nearby, which had apparently once sheltered cattle, they chinked up the cracks, lined the interior with blankets, and built a rough chimney. There, as Baily put it, they commenced "*housekeeping.*"

On Christmas Day, Baily reflected, "Here I am in the wilds of America, away from the society of men, amidst the haunts of wild beasts and savages, just escaped from the perils of a wreck, in want not only of the comforts, but of the necessaries of life, housed in a hovel . . . not good enough for a pigstye." This, while his father and mother, sisters and relatives were in a fine, warm house enjoying the day's good cheer. Some apples had been rescued from the boats, and along with some Indian meal a "rough kind of apple pudding" was made as the entire Christmas feast of the marooned travelers. Yet all this time, Baily wrote, "we were very happy. . . . We were strangers to all those artificial wants which man in a civilized state has brought upon himself. . . . Whether it were the novelty of the thing which attracted us, or the scenery of the country, and the sublimity of its views, so very different from what we had been used to in the *old* country, I know not; but certain it is, there is something so very attractive in a life spent in this manner, that were I disposed to become a hermit, and seclude myself from the world, the woods of America should be my retreat; there should I, with my dog and my gun, and the hollow of a rock for my habitation, enjoy undisturbed all that fancied bliss attendant on a state of nature."

Baily, a true child of the romantic age, went on to speculate on the Indian or woodsman who, "ignorant of all the deceits and artifices attendant on a state of civilization, and unpracticed in the vices and dissipation of degraded humanity and unconscious of artificial and unnecessary wants," had only the trees and wild animals for his companions. He was moved to reflect upon "whether human happiness has kept pace with the progress that has been made in civilization." It plainly seemed doubtful to the young Englishman, stranded in the frigid forests of the Kentucky frontier.

Heighway's artisans were experienced boatbuilders who had constructed the original barge that had carried the party this far, and they set to work to build another so that the journey could be completed. While they worked the rest of the party learned how to tap maple trees, and they had soon collected and boiled down the sap to twenty pounds of sugar, a very welcome addition to their meager larder. Finally, when the spring floods had raised the river almost twenty feet, the barge was completed and the little party was ready to resume its journey. The new boat was thirteen feet wide and forty feet long with a covered cabin and an open space in the bow for horses. After laboriously loading the boat with the cargo rescued from its predecessor, they set off.

Baily was once more entranced by the scenery. The long reach down which the barge now floated was a straight stretch of the river fifteen miles in length, interspersed with numerous islands. The setting sun reflected on the water, and "the river looked like a little sea of fire before us . . . by the rapidity and smoothness of its current . . . silently hurrying us on towards it."

An important aspect of the Ohio River and the rivers that flowed into it was that at periods of high flow, primarily in the spring when the snows melted, a "back current" was created. The Ohio itself would rise so far above the level of the rivers entering it that water from the Ohio would flow back up such rivers as the Licking and Miami, thus enabling settlers and tradesmen to float up the rivers for fifty or even a hundred miles rather than having to buck the current.

Baily's party floated on, past the Muskingum River on the right, the Little Kanawha and the Great Kanaway on the left. The current was so rapid and the banks of the river so inundated that the voyagers were afraid to put to shore for the night for fear of having the barge dashed against the trees that lined the flooded shallows. Obliged to spend the night on the river, they had the unnerving experience of a severe storm with lightning and thunder playing about them and the expectation that they might at any time run upon a snag, or "sawyer" as it was called; be dashed against an island; or run aground on a sandbar.

At the height of the storm, the barge being swept along by the river, Baily saw a light ahead and then, above the noise of the storm, heard wild cries. As they came closer he could see half-naked human figures with firebrands in their hands moving in strange gyrations around a fire. Finally the mystery resolved itself. The wild scene "proved to be nothing more than a few Indians, who, disturbed by the inclemency of the weather, could not sleep, and were innocently diverting themselves with singing and dancing round their fire." More likely they were preparing to go on the warpath.

Past Gallipolis, where Joel Barlow had left his colony of desperate Frenchmen stranded a few years earlier, past the Guyandot River to the Big Sandy that marked the boundary line between western Virginia and Kentucky, the barge sped. Kentucky was already a romantic legend. This was Daniel Boone country. Twenty-five years earlier Boone had led settlers through the Cumberland Gap to a spot where, he declared, "nature was . . . a series of wonders and a fund of delight."

Baily and Heighway had been three months on the Ohio River (including, of course, the delay forced by the freezing of the river). They calculated they had come some three hundred miles. The Licking River, the Kentucky, the Rolling, and the Green were passed on their left; the Little Miami, the Miami, the Silver, the Anderson, and the Little, far less consequential streams, on their right. Saltlick Creek was one of the best-known salt springs to which deer, buffalo, and other animals beat paths through the woods. The settlement of Limestone, nineteen miles from the Little Sciota River, was, Baily noted, "the resort of all emigrants who are bound to the interior of this state. Here they land their goods and their domestic implements . . . and transport them to their distant settlements, in waggons which they either bring with them, or hire at this place." At Limestone the banks of the Ohio on the Kentucky side began to "assume here a settled appearance." From Limestone to Louisville, a distance of some two hundred miles, Baily saw an "agreeable mixture of woods and plantations" forming "a number of most enchanting views."

Columbia on the Little Miami was the end of the line for Heighway. He had purchased thirty or forty thousand acres of land along that river for $1.25 an acre, half down and the rest to be paid in installments. Heighway's projected metropolis was some thirty miles from the river. A few settlers, it turned out, had already arrived and were awaiting Heighway at Columbia, and he sold land to them at $2.00 an acre. Town lots were $6.00 an acre. Purchasers of town lots were required to build a house within a specified time or forfeit their lots. The first twenty families received a free lot in town and four acres outside with the provision that they build a house on the town lot and cultivate their four acres. Heighway anticipated his profits from the rise in land values as more settlers arrived; thus he held back substantial portions of his purchase in anticipation of such an increase.

Baily accompanied Heighway and his little band of settlers to the site of their new town. Heighway, Baily noted, "seemed to eye the ground and the country about, with that degree of secret pleasure which a man may be conceived to take in viewing a spot which, in point of cultivation, was to be the work of his own hand. He seemed to anticipate his labours, and fancied he saw fruitful cornfields and blushing orchards in every object he beheld, and expressed a secret satisfaction in thinking he should end his days in this delightful country." While the settlers set to with their axes cutting down trees to clear fields and build houses, Baily went exploring the uplands and the bottoms that ran along the Little Miami. Grass, he noted, grew in the woods to the height of three or four feet, so cattle could simply be turned out to graze under the trees. Among the wild fruit trees of the region were gooseberry, plum, cherry, and apple. The forest was composed primarily of hardwoods—oak, maple, buttonwood, dogwood, buckeye, walnut, and hickory. Oaks four feet in diameter without an intervening limb to their crest seventy feet high were not uncommon. Baily saw such trees cut down to kill a bear or set on fire to smoke out a raccoon.

Heighway pointed out to Baily where he intended to erect the courthouse, and the spot intended for the state legislature, "for he had already fallen into that flattering idea which every founder of a new settlement entertains, that his town will at some future time be the seat of government." In a few days cabins began to rise and gardens were laid out, and Baily felt a "secret inclination to stay and cultivate the ground with them." He imagined himself, "when the first class of settlers had moved off, and a more civilized race had succeeded," telling his children "how we raised this flourishing settlement from the howling wilderness."

But Baily was headed for New Orleans (he has, after all, still to conduct us down the Ohio to the Mississippi and hence to Louisiana), so early in April he parted with Heighway and his settlers, collected provisions for several months at Columbia—biscuits, flour, brandy, beef, bacon—and a trunk or two of articles to trade with the Indians, and caught an "Orleans boat" headed south. Baily estimated he had come a thousand miles from New York City and had three thousand miles ahead of him.

Cincinnati, on the Ohio side of the river opposite the Licking, was the most considerable town on the Ohio, containing three or four hundred frame houses. It was, as Baily put it, "the grand depot for the stores which come down from the forts established on the frontiers." It was also the seat of the government of the territory. There were Indian mounds nearby, and the town was full of manufacturers (workmen), making "mechanical necessaries, such as tubs, kegs, fire-arms, etc.," for the frontier forts.

The Orleans boat set off with four passengers, who also constituted the cook and crew. Each person took a two-hour shift, his responsibility being to hold the boat near the center of the river and keep it clear of snags or sandbars by a pull on the steering oar. One day ran gently into the next as the four men performed the modest routines required to keep them on their course. Near Louisville a canoe drew alongside them, and Baily discovered to his delight that the old man paddling it was Colonel Daniel Boone, the discoverer of the state along whose boundary they were floating. Boone came aboard and entertained the passengers with accounts of his life as a scout and trapper. Did he not, Baily asked, take pride in the growth and prosperity of the state of Kentucky, which had, in so short a time, risen from "a desert wilderness . . . to flourish in arts and sciences and the conveniences of life"? "No," Boone replied, with a shake of his head, "they were got too proud." No longer content with simple things, they lusted after luxury and grew soft and dissipated. Boone was, Baily observed, "one of that class of men who, from nature and habit, was nearly allied in disposition and manners to an Indian." He had received a large parcel of land from a grateful state, but "when societies began to form around him, he moved off . . . unwilling to live among men who were shackled in their habits, and would not enjoy uncontrolled the free blessings which nature had bestowed upon them." He was on his way to trap beaver where he could "enjoy the pleasures arising from a secluded and solitary life."

Louisville was a smaller version of Cincinnati and the last town of any consequence on the Ohio before it merged with the Mississippi. There were rapids there that had to be negotiated with great caution, and travelers usually put up in town before tackling the last stretch of the river. From Louisville, it was on past the Green River and Pigeon Creek, founded by the French and still maintaining a decidedly French character. At Pigeon Creek the inhabitants were engaged primarily in trade with the Indians.

The Wabash, on the Ohio side, was a hundred miles beyond Pigeon Creek. There Baily and his companions saw a number of Indians camped on the shore, but they were unsuccessful in their efforts to make contact with them. Fort Massac, near the mouth of the Tennessee, was the next settlement at which the travelers stopped. Founded by the French in the 1760s, it had been occupied by a contingent of U.S. regulars, ordered to check any move by Frenchmen in the region to attack Spanish Louisiana. In command was the hospitable Captain Zebulon Pike.

Indians lived around the fort, and Baily and his companions "bartered a number of things with them for skins, etc." When a violent storm blew up and their boat was about to be dashed on the rocks, Indians standing on the bank came to their rescue. Baily was much impressed with "the undaunted perseverance and laborious efforts of this race of men." The Indians, having noticed that the boat contained a cask of brandy, indicated that some drafts from it might be an appropriate reward for their labors. "Accordingly, having seated them on some barrels round a fire we had in the boat, we drew them a cup, which after going around once or twice, was soon emptied. They then wished for some more. We at first refused; but, on their promising to leave the boat as soon as it was finished, we at last consented. By the time this had gone round, the liquor had begun to take effect . . . ; they were then only in the first stage of intoxication—a state where the faculties are fully preserved, but the spirit somewhat enlivened. We endeavored, then, to get rid of them before they got any worse; but they (now grown familiar with us) liked our company (or rather the company of the whiskey barrel) too well to part; and one of them, taking hold of me, made me sit down by him, and began to teach me his language, telling me what he called the different objects which happened to present themselves."

As the Indians grew inebriated, "they were very vociferous for more" and refused to leave the boat. The alarmed travelers sent for soldiers to remove them, but Captain Pike, "who understood the management of them," came down instead and "after expostulating with them, told them that there was but one more cup in the barrel and if they would drink it ashore they might have it . . . so, rather than lose the last dear drop, they consented." When they were safely on the shore, Baily and his friends pulled up the gangplank and cast off. Pike assured them they were fortunate to escape, "for had they been suffered to have gone on as they wished, they would have committed the most atrocious crimes without compunction or remorse." The incident moved Baily to reflect as so many whites had done before him (and were to do after him) on the Indian as a symbolic figure—"man in a state of nature," content "with those gifts which so bountiful a parent has bestowed; . . . his days as spent in the delightful pleasures of the chase . . . ; when this is over he returns to his family, and they each, with thankful hearts partake of the delicious repast; his wants are few; his cares are less; and at night he lies down with his family with an undisturbed mind to enjoy the sweet comforts of refreshing sleep, and to awake in the morning to new pleasures." This was the lot of the Indian before the white men corrupted him, "for the sake of oppression and plunder" with that "sweet destroyer of all human cares—the distilled juice of the wine." (Baily told of hearing the "half savage" white men of the frontier tell of killing an Indian "with the same unconcern . . . as of killing a deer or a turkey, and . . . would mimic him in his dying agonies.")

The Indians' disastrous and sometimes fatal addiction to liquor is only one of the unsolved mysteries that continue to enshroud them. It is even hard to determine whether the problem lies in the province of the physiologist, psychologist, or anthropologist, though recent evidence seems to point toward physiology. Baily's encounter reminds us once again of how central a place those tribes of aborigines, included in the general denomination "Indian," had in the white imagination.

On April 25 Baily and his little party had the "happiness of seeing . . . the majestic current of the Mississippi, which flowing along with all the apparent insolence of pride, seemed to distain any connexion with so paltry a stream as the Ohio." The "two noble rivers" made a striking contrast, the Ohio "in the turbidness and ebullition of its current," the Mississippi "in its limpid, gliding stream." It had been five months since Baily had set off from Pittsburgh.

Baily could not part with the river that had been his home for the better part of five months without some observations on the "delightful scenery which it was continually presenting to us. If we put ashore to gather herbs and vegetables for our subsistence, we saw the works of nature profusely lavished throughout an uninhabited country. If we possessed the water, our attention was continually attracted by the flight of immense flocks of wild fowl, and other birds, who, undisturbed, preserved their course through the air . . . or we might behold the nimble deer browsing on the banks, or the fierce bear darting through the thicket."

The landscape of the Mississippi was strikingly different. The river was far wider, full of sawyers and islands, with the banks low and so crowded with cottonwoods and willows as to obscure the country beyond. Whereas on the Ohio the traveler had a strong sense of being carried swiftly along through luxuriant forests that crowded the riverbanks, on the Mississippi there was much more a feeling of vast spaces—the river itself, so wide and deceptively gentle, and beyond its banks, level floodplain intermittently glimpsed. One consequence was that the river frequently meandered and changed its course, forming islands where mainland had been before. When the river was high, it overflowed its banks and spread so far that it was often difficult to find its main channel. The low land along the river was interrupted by bluffs that were the preferred sites for the little settlements strung along the banks of the river like crude beads.

The first town the travelers came to on the Mississippi was New Madrid on the west bank. It had been founded in 1789 by a Spanish officer from New Orleans, and its population numbered around six hundred. New Madrid was the northern outpost of Spanish Louisiana. Since the Spanish claimed jurisdiction over the Mississippi River to its mouth, they required all travelers to put ashore, describe their cargoes, and receive Spanish passports. As Spain was at war with Britain, Baily was careful to conceal his identity as an Englishman, "well knowing what an inquisitorial and tyrannical race of mortals I had to pass through." Baily and his companions had to appear before the Spanish commandant and through an interpreter satisfy him "that we were not come to plunder the country."

The Spanish had attracted American settlers to New Madrid by offering them from 240 to 400 acres of land free. Baily took advantage of the stop to reconnoiter the land around the town. The uninterrupted expanse of grassland was the beginning of the Great Plains, miles of land "without a tree or shrub upon it; and affording a striking contrast to the dark and shady woods from which I had just emerged." Baily traded with Indians who lived in the vicinity. He got deer, beaver, and bear, otter and raccoon skins for his trading trinkets, and he discovered that skins were used as money; a beaver was equal to four dollars and a raccoon to twenty-five cents. A mile below the town they visited a Dr. Waters, an American surgeon employed by the Spanish, who was also a merchant and a farmer. Baily noted that he "lived in a most miserable tent" and carried on his business as a tradesman "in a little room which served him for a kitchen, shop, . . . and every other purpose for which he might have occasion." Waters had a number of slaves "lodged in hovels, as is the custom in this country." The whole scene disgusted Baily. It might be added that when Waters died seven years later his estate was valued at sixty thousand dollars, the equivalent of perhaps half a million dollars today. Clearly there was money to be made by enterprising individuals indifferent to hardship.

From New Madrid to New Orleans, Baily and his boatmates traveled in the company of four other Orleans boats, which put up every night together along the banks of the river and proceeded by day, a small flotilla, borne on the breast of the river. It was a romantic idyll interrupted only by stops to have their passports checked by Spanish officials at Natchez and Pointe Coupée. Flocks of duck and geese were interspersed by pelicans; eagles and vultures perched in the upper limbs of river-drowned cottonwoods watching for floating carrion or fish, and enormous alligators basked on the riverbanks or on sawyers in the river, splashing into the water at the approach of the boats. Occasionally they passed a keelboat being rowed upriver by fifteen or twenty straining oarsmen, most often slaves.

As they approached the town of Chickasaw Bluffs, the travelers saw a number of Indians standing on the banks, "enjoying the mildness of the evening and the beauty of the setting sun." They stood immobile, dressed in printed calico shirts and breechclouts, watching the boatmen tie up their barges; when the white men approached them they produced peace pipes, and after a few solemn puffs with the visitors they began to trade enthusiastically. The half-dozen white families who lived in the town could hardly be distinguished in their dress or manners from the Indians. The Chickasaw, a warlike tribe, were kept in a state of relative amiability by presents from the federal government; when Baily encountered them they were in a touchy and disgruntled mood because their yearly supply of gifts had been late arriving. At the appearance of a boat in the distance, they hurried down to the riverbank in the hope that it was bringing the long-delayed presents. According to the Chickasaw tradition, the tribe had originally lived west of the Mississippi but had crossed the river under the guardianship of a great dog, with a pole for a guide. Each night they stuck a pole into the ground and the next day they traveled in the direction toward which the pole leaned. By this uncertain mode they had come to a region between the Choctaw, the Cherokee, and the Shawnee in what is today Alabama. When the Spanish explorer of the Mississippi, Hernando de Soto, spent a winter with them in 1540, he estimated their numbers at ten thousand warriors. They had allied themselves with the British against the French and the Creek, having originally been part of the Creek Confederacy. At the onset of the American Revolution they could count no more than a thousand warriors; they remained loyal to the British and raided the Southern frontier settlements. When Baily encountered them, they had been reduced in numbers by warfare and disease to perhaps five hundred warriors; and these, the Englishman was informed, were about to take the warpath against the Creek in retaliation for the murder of several young braves. Baily reported that "one of their chiefs (who spoke tolerable English) told me it was a proposition of some of the young warriors, and that the old men had scarcely given their approbation."

From Chickasaw Bluffs, Baily and his party floated down to the mouth of the Arkansas River, which flowed westward, parallel to the more southerly Red River, as far as Santa Fe in the Spanish province of New Mexico at the foot of the Rocky Mountain range. Although the Arkansas was said to be navigable for seven or eight hundred miles of its more than thousand-mile length, that was largely conjecture; the Spanish jealously guarded the river and the trade with the Indian tribes who lived along it by means of a fort some ten miles upriver from the juncture with the Mississippi.

Three days later the party passed the Yazoo River on the left bank, a river that ran into Georgia and Cherokee country and that the Spaniards claimed as the northern boundary of West Florida. Baily estimated the Yazoo to be some 160 miles south of the Arkansas. They had thus traveled roughly 50 miles a day—far more, certainly, than they could have made traveling overland. At Walnut Hills near the mouth of the Yazoo there was an imposing Spanish fort, and here the travelers were supposed to show the passports they had been given at New Madrid. Annoyed at the overbearing manner of the Spanish officials they had already encountered, they decided to make a run for it. Ignoring signals to land and a cannon fired at them, they drifted past and the next day prepared to pass the Grand Gulf, a vortex or series of whirlpools, reputed to be the most dangerous spot on the river. Holding the boat to the center of the river by energetic rowing, Baily and his companions got safely through and were soon at Natchez.

Natchez, a town of some five thousand inhabitants, thoroughly Southern in its style, was still firmly in the hands of the Spanish, although Spain had presumably surrendered it to the United States under the terms of a recently negotiated treaty, and an American flag flew above the town. Baily therefore had to submit his passport. Here slaves were very much in evidence. Indians came and went, and river traffic north and south filled the town with boatmen, travelers, and traders. On the riverbank an Indian demonstrated his mode of catching alligators to a fascinated audience. With one hand he held a piece of raw meat in front of the beast; in the other, a stick sharpened at both ends. As the alligator opened his "enormous mouth" to seize the food, the Indian swiftly exchanged it for the sharpened stake so that the animal impaled itself and was towed ashore, "admidst the applause and acclamation of the spectators who stand by admiring the daring act."

It was at Natchez that Baily sold the remainder of the goods that he had brought with him from Cincinnati. All he got in exchange from the Spaniard to whom he sold them was a "certificate." When he protested to the Spanish governor, he was told that it was "legal tender" and that he must accept it. Baily then asked to see the law to that effect, and the commandant informed him that he, himself, was the law and that more protests would land him in jail. At Baily's incredulous laugh, the commandant became enraged and once more threatened him with prison, thus leaving the Englishman to some grim reflections on Spanish as opposed to Anglo-American justice.

The owners of the boat on which Baily had traveled from Cincinnati sold their flour in Natchez and prepared for the long, slow trip back up the river, while Baily looked for another vessel to carry him the remaining three hundred miles to New Orleans. At a tavern where travelers put up he met a Mr. Douglass who was preparing to carry cotton to New Orleans. The cotton was packed in bags that held from 150 to 250 pounds. The barge would carry two or three hundred such sacks to New Orleans for a charge of a dollar and half to two dollars per sack. Baily went aboard and the freight barge set off. Below Natchez the mosquitoes made life miserable for Baily and the crew of the boat.

The following day they passed the mouth of the Red River, which emptied its reddish waters into the Mississippi. It was at the juncture of the Red and Black rivers that de Soto had died and been buried 250 years earlier. (The Red River, like the Arkansas, rose in New Mexico.) Fifty miles upstream was the French town of Natchitoches.

The country between the Red River and the Gulf of Mexico was "a high, rich and beautiful country, skirted with clumps of flourishing trees, and interspersed with fine, rich prairies, which produce corn and cotton in great perfection," a traveler named John Sibley wrote in 1802. "The immense flocks of cattle with which they are covered, are almost incredible; ten thousand head may be seen in one view." In Sibley's opinion, "The lands of Red River alone are capable of producing more tobacco than is now made in all the United States, and at less than one fourth part of the labour; and in all Louisiana, I think more than ten times as much cotton might be made as in the United States." The bottomlands were five or six miles wide, "the soil twenty feet deep, and like a bed of manure." Frenchmen had lived along the river for more than a hundred years but had taken little advantage of the extraordinary richness of the soil. The town of Natchitoches had an air of general dilapidation, having declined in population from several hundred to some forty families. Farther upriver was a settlement of some five hundred persons, many of them discharged French soldiers, living in squalor and sustaining themselves by hunting bear and deer.

From Baton Rouge to New Orleans, Baily traveled past "one uninterrupted chain of plantations." The plantations were protected against the ravages of the river by slave-built levees so high that from the barge he could look down on the handsome manor houses and luxuriant fields of cotton and sugarcane. Now, no longer threatened by sawyers and sandbars, the party traveled at night under a full moon accompanied by the sounds of bullfrogs and the "howl" of alligators. Baily wrote: "This noble river, whose bosom, smooth and unruffled, reflected the . . . beams of the goddess of night, contributed itself, in a great measure, to the majesty and magnificence of the whole.

Everywhere I cast my eyes I beheld marks of the industry of man, which formed a happy and striking constrast of the works of art to those of nature."

On June 6, Baily at last arrived in New Orleans, the goal of his seven-month journey, the southern axis of the American empire. He found New Orleans a delightful refreshment to his weary spirit. The most cosmopolitan city in North America, its predominantly French character was everywhere in evidence. Creoles were all those native-born inhabitants of French or Spanish blood, including a number of mixed bloods, mulattoes, quadroons, and octaroons. The streets of the town were laid out at right angles and named after princes of the French royal family—Bourbon, Toulouse, Orleans. Along them were houses that were far more reminiscent of a Mediterranean culture than of the New World, shaded arcades, wrought-iron festooned balconies, and interior courtyards filled with palm and bougainvillea, hibiscus, bird-of-paradise, and camellia plants. It was a city Catholic in its religion and catholic in its racial composition. It had its own distinctive cuisine, featuring shrimp and fish and spicy sauces. Oranges, lemons, melons, bananas, pineapples, and nuts of various kinds were "vended about the streets by the negroes."

A great seaport, it was the collecting station for all the produce that poured down the Mississippi. The docks were lined with bales of cotton, casks of bacon and hams, molasses, sugar, tobacco from the lower reaches of the river, and barrels of flour.

The coffeehouses were the center of the lively social life of the city. Cards and billiards were played there all day long and far into the night. The administration of the city was in the hands of the cabildo, or city council, a hereditary body. The law was civil law rather than common law, a mixture of French and Spanish.

There were six gates to the city, which were shut at night, and the Spanish authorities imposed a nine o'clock curfew on the inhabitants. Levees lined the riverbanks for a distance of fifty miles and protected the city from inundations by the river. The tops of the levees were covered with fine gravel and shaded by orange trees; in the summertime the tops of the levees served as malls where, as Francis Baily reported, there was "always a fashionable resort for the beaux and belles of the place." The inhabitants were predominantly Irish, English, Scotch, American, French, and Spanish, with the latter very much in the minority. Baily found the city full of "adventurers," men "who leave their own country for the sake of profit and advantage to themselves," men "of a speculative and enterprising turn" who formed friendships readily on the basis of "interest or immediate pleasure" but abandoned them as quickly as they had formed them. The clothes worn by the residents of New Orleans demonstrated "by their variety, the variety of the inhabitants themselves; the short linen jacket of the Americans . . . the long flowing gown, or the cloak of the Spaniards . . . the open trousers and naked collar of the more casually attired." Others wore "the more modern dress of light pantaloons and large cravats." Some wore "the black or white chip hat; others . . . the beaver and *feathers.*"

Sunday in New Orleans was a day given over to "hilarity and cheerfulness." Hardly had the Sabbath services ended "when the violin or fife struck up . . . and the lower classes of the people indulged themselves in all the gaiety and mirth of juvenile occasions. Singing, dancing, and all kinds of sports were seen in every street." The slaves, "let loose from the hand of their master . . . would meet together on the green, and spend the day in mirth and festivity. Here they would appear," Baily wrote, "with countenances illuminated and beaming with happiness, as if . . . they had never been snatched from their own country by the cruel hands of the Christian."

Here we take reluctant leave of Francis Baily. He was certainly what Americans were to come to call "a good sport." He cheerfully endured the hardships and dangers that were an inevitable part of such an expedition. What he saw, by and large, charmed him. He had a splendid capacity, doubtless partly the consequence of his youth, to enter into often disconcertingly new experiences, to observe the human and natural landscape around him, and to convey to his readers a sense of the boundless drama and romance of the Western country. I hope it will cheer the reader to know that he returned home and, after a successful career as a stockbroker, retired to become a distinguished amateur astronomer and president of the Royal Astronomical Society. He died in 1844, full of honors, his account of his travels in the United States as yet unpublished. It was issued twelve years later by his heirs. A portrait of him that survives shows a bold, strong-featured face with a prominent nose, a generous mouth, and dark eyes.

In our abbreviated version of Baily's trip we have, I trust, introduced the reader to the vast Mississippi Valley and to the river system that made possible the "opening of the West."

It seemed to the Reverend Joseph Doddridge that the Mississippi

Valley had "been designed by Divine Providence for the last resort of oppressed humanity. A fruitful soil, under a variety of climates, supplies abundantly all the wants of life, while our geographical situation renders us unconquerable. From this place of refuge we may hear, as harmless thunder, the military convulsions of other quarters of the globe. . . . Vice and folly may conquer; the world never can. Happy region! large and fertile enough for the abode of many millions. Here the hungry may find bread, and conscience the full possession of its native rights."

One hardly knows the proper metaphor for the Mississippi and its tributaries. They were both the circulatory and the nervous systems of the great body of the continent. Hopefully they will never be far from our consciousness in this work. Until the day when the iron tracks of the railroads replaced their ceaseless currents (and to a degree obliterated them from our collective memory) they were the lifeblood of the Republic.

The traveler, trader, or settler who proceeded north and west on the Mississippi River, past the point where the Ohio joined it, came to St. Louis, where the Missouri enters the Mississippi. About that we shall have more to say, for the Missouri was the river that carried Meriwether Lewis and William Clark almost to the Oregon Territory.

26

Marbury versus Madison

We will let our English friend, John Davis, give a vivid if not entirely accurate account of Thomas Jefferson's inauguration as the third president of the United States in March, 1801. Davis wrote: "The politeness of a member of the Senate from Virginia had procured me a convenient seat in the Capitol; and an hour after, Mr. Jefferson entered the House, when the august Assembly of American Senators rose to receive him. He came, however, to the House without ostentation. His dress was of plain cloth, and he rode on horseback to the Capitol without a single guard or even servant in his train, dismounted without assistance and hitched the bridle of his horse to the palisades. The Senate Chamber was filled with citizens from the remotest places of the Union. The planter, the farmer, the mechanic and the merchant, all seemed to catch one common transport of enthusiasm, and welcome the approach of the man to the chair of the sovereign authority, who had served his country in various offices of dignity. . . ." Jefferson, "having taken the oaths to the Constitution, with a dignified mien, addressed the august Assembly of Senators and Representatives."

The address was one of Jefferson's happiest efforts. If he often

472

faltered as a politician, he seldom did as a writer. When he contemplated "a rising nation, spread over a wide and fruitful land, traversing all the seas with rich productions of their industry, engaged in commerce with nations who feel power and forget right, advancing rapidly to destinies beyond the reach of mortal eye," when he reflected on "these transcendent objects" and saw "the honor, the happiness, and the hopes of this beloved country committed to the auspices of this day," he confessed himself overwhelmed by the magnitude of the task before him. The past election had stirred up such strong emotions, he reminded his listeners, that "strangers unused to think freely and to speak and to write what they think" might believe anarchy could be its only outcome; but the election, "being now decided by the voice of the nation, according to the rules of the Constitution, all will, of course, arrange themselves under the will of the law, and unite in common efforts for the common good. All, too, will bear in mind this sacred principle, that though the will of the majority is in all cases to prevail, that will to be rightful must be reasonable; that the minority possess their equal rights, which equal law must protect, and to violate would be oppression. Let us, then fellow-citizens, unite with one heart and one mind. Let us restore to social intercourse that harmony and affection without which liberty and even life itself are but dreary things. . . . We have called by different names brethren of the same principle. We are all Republicans, we are all Federalists. If there are any among us who would wish to dissolve this Union or to change its republican form, let them stand undisturbed as monuments of the safety with which error of opinion may be tolerated where reason is left free to combat it."

Some Americans and many Europeans had expressed the conviction that a republican government was too weak to maintain itself, but Jefferson believed "this, on the contrary, the strongest Government on earth." If men could not be trusted to govern themselves, who indeed would govern them, "angels in the form of kings?"

Americans were "kindly separated by nature and a wide ocean from the exterminating havoc of one quarter of the globe . . . possessing a chosen country, with room enough for our descendants to the thousandth and thousandth generation; entertaining a due sense of our equal right to the use of our own faculties, to the acquisitions of our own industry, to honor and confidence from our fellow-citizens, resulting not from birth but from our actions and their sense of them; enlightened by a benign religion" that in all its various forms taught "truth, temperance, gratitude, and the love of man." The only thing needed to complete the happiness of Americans was "a wise and frugal government which shall restrain men from injuring one another, shall leave them otherwise free to regulate their own pursuits of industry and improvement, and shall not take from the mouth of labour the bread it has earned. This is the sum of good government, and this is necessary to close the circle of our felicities." (It is interesting to note that when John Davis, armed with a letter from Vice-President Burr, sought a job in the Treasury Department under Albert Gallatin, he was told by the secretary that not only would no new appointments be made but that, in an effort to cut down the inflated government bureacracy, a number of those presently employed would be fired.)

Jefferson's inaugural address instantly became one of America's sacred texts, along with Washington's Farewell Address. His reference to "an overruling Providence" and "Infinite Power" encouraged those Christians who considered Jefferson a howling atheist but did not offend his deistically inclined supporters. Altogether it was a masterly accomplishment and was hailed ecstatically by the Republican press and cautiously by the Federalists.

Among the other consequences of the election of 1800 was the discrediting of Burr, who turned to the bizarre schemes that were to prove his undoing. Alexander Hamilton, whose maladroit maneuvers had contributed substantially to the defeat of the Federalists, returned to New York to resume the private practice of law. The death of Washington, whom Hamilton considered "an aegis very essential to me," had been a serious setback. Washington's advocacy of Hamilton had always been the New Yorker's political ace in the hole. The victory of his bitterest rival, at least in part as a consequence of his own mistakes, seemed to complete the ruin of his own political career. Never notably stable, Hamilton was now given to fits of profound depression.

In November his eldest son, Philip, a handsome and promising young man of twenty, and a friend named Price found themselves sharing a box at the theater with George Eaker, a strong Burr partisan. In a Fourth of July speech, Eaker had praised Burr—excessively, Philip Hamilton thought—and had disparaged the elder Hamilton. Philip thus made "in levity" references to the speech which Eaker overheard. The latter invited young Hamilton outside. There was a scuffle; Eaker called Hamilton and Price "damned rascals"; Hamilton demanded an apology, and as they parted Eaker said, "I expect to hear from you."

A challenge was sent by both Price and Hamilton. Eaker and Price met, fired unsuccessfully at each other four times, and then were parted by their seconds, honor presumably satisfied. It remained for Eaker and Philip Hamilton to meet. The young man's friends said that Philip, feeling that he had precipitated the quarrel by his injudicious remarks, decided he would "reserve his fire, receive that of his antagonist, and then discharge his pistol in the air." The two young men met at a dueling ground in Weehawken, New Jersey, on November 23, 1801. Philip Hamilton held his fire and was fatally wounded. He was carried across the river on a ferry, taken to his father's house, and died the next morning. It must have seemed to Alexander Hamilton almost as though Burr's finger had been on the trigger.

Somehow Hamilton's personal tragedy epitomized the tragedy of a nation that a brief seventeen years before had begun its existence with such fair prospects and had rapidly degenerated into a degree of partisan bitterness that could kill the son of one of the principal founders of the Republic.

Hamilton wrote to a friend that he was glad that his son was "out of the reach of the seductions and calamities of a world full of folly, full of vice, full of danger, and of least value in proportion as it is best known." In 1802, not long after his son's death, he wrote: "Perhaps no man in the United States has sacrificed or done more for the present Constitution than myself; and contrary to all my anticipations of its fate . . . I am still laboring to prop the frail and worthless fabric. Yet I have the murmurs of its friends no less than the curses of its foes for my reward. . . . Every day proves to me more and more, that this American world was not made for me."

Gouverneur Morris noted in his diary that he had dined with "Gen. Hamilton and [Rufus] King" and added: "They are both alarmed at the conduct of our rulers, and think the Constitution is about to be overturned; I think it is already overturned. They apprehend a bloody anarchy; I apprehend an anarchy in which property, not lives, will be sacrificed. That it is the intention of those gentlemen who have engaged themselves in the notable business of pulling down the Constitution to rear a monarchy on its ruins, I do not believe; that such is the natural effect of their measures, I am perfectly convinced."

The Federalists had left behind a guardian of their constitutional principles in the person of John Marshall, the new chief justice of the Supreme Court and the principal thorn in the side of the new president. Marshall himself was apprehensive over what the change in administration might mean. On the day of Jefferson's inauguration he wrote: "Today the new political year commences. The new order of things begins. . . . There are some appearances which surprize me. I wish however more than I hope that the public prosperity & happiness may sustain no diminution under democratic guidance. The democrats are divided into speculative theorists & absolute terrorists. With the latter I am not disposed to class Mr. Jefferson. If he arranges himself with them it is not difficult to foresee that much calamity is in store for our country—if he does not they will soon become his enemies & calumniators."

Jefferson moved into the still unfinished White House recently vacated by the Adamses, bringing with him his garden implements and carpentry tools, his beloved maps and books, his plants and his mockingbird. Soon the White House was as untidy as Monticello. In everything he did Jefferson was determined to reflect republican simplicity in contrast to Federalist formality. He walked around the White House in carpet slippers and the comfortable and often eccentric attire that were as much a mark of his "style" as his neat signature and often uncombed hair.

The president had hardly settled in his new quarters before a journalistic chicken came home to roost. Jefferson had issued a pardon to the execrable James T. Callender, who had served nine months in prison at Richmond under the Sedition Act, and had ordered the federal marshal there to rebate Callender's two-hundred-dollar fine. When the marshal was slow to comply, Jefferson sent Callender fifty dollars on his own account. But Callender wanted more. He had unearthed the story of Jefferson's relationship with Sally Hemings and determined to use it to blackmail Jefferson into giving him a job as postmaster. As Jefferson put it in a letter to James Monroe, Callender "intimated that he was in possession of things which he could and would use in a certain case." Callender failed to get the job, and there matters rested for almost a year.

Initially Jefferson had indicated that he would refrain from turning out federal officeholders simply because they had been appointed to their positions during the Federalist era, but as the pressure from members of his own party grew more and more intense, he gave way and one Federalist after another was pried loose and replaced by a Republican. Jefferson promptly sent the Senate the names of Levi Lincoln, Albert Gallatin, James Madison, and Henry Dearborn to be attorney general, secretary of the treasury, secretary of state, and secretary of war, respectively.

The Republican Congress meanwhile set to work to nullify the effect of John Adams's "midnight judges" by passing legislation designed to negate the Judiciary Act of 1789, which had decreased the number of Supreme Court justices to five, relieved them of their exhausting circuit duties, and established twenty-nine districts. The prospect of the repeal of the Judiciary Act dismayed the Federalists, who rightly saw it as the beginning of an attack on the integrity of the Court. A Federalist congressman wrote: "The passage of the bill to destroy the judiciary may be much obstructed but it will pass. Mr. Jefferson has set his heart upon the measure. 'Tis his favorite measure and his party will (whatever scruples some of them may feel about the constitutionality of it) make this desired offering to his revengeful spirit." John Breckinridge, the Kentucky senator, wrote that no Republican legislator should leave his post "till the Federal Courts and the Excise Law are both laid low in the grave with old Johnny Adams."

While the debate on the repeal of the Judiciary Act was going on, John Marshall and Thomas Jefferson squared off for the first of a series of contests that were to have major consequences for American constitutional history. Whereas much of the drama of the Hamilton-Jefferson confrontation might be found in the striking physical and temperamental differences between the two men—Hamilton small, dapper, and intense; Jefferson tall, thin, and rather languid in manner—Marshall and Jefferson were cast in much the same mold. They were both members of the Virginia ruling class; both were untidy in their dress. We have already noted Jefferson's almost ostentatious informality. Marshall let his hair grow too long and often forgot to comb it. His boots were old and sometimes muddy, and the knee buckles of his britches were commonly loose. He was frequently to be seen doing menial tasks—carrying firewood or shopping for food on his way home from a session of the Court.

William Wirt, one of the foremost lawyers of the day, wrote, "In his whole appearance, and demeanor, dress, attitudes, gestures, sitting, standing, or walking, he is as far removed from idolized grace of Lord Chesterfield, as any other gentleman on earth."

There is an engaging story about John Marshall's absentmindedness. Marshall and some friends, riding out to Mount Vernon to visit Washington, stopped for lunch at a a tavern on the way. When the travelers were within a mile of Mount Vernon, they got off their horses to get "their coats, vests & cravats" out of their saddlebags for their arrival. "Marshall drew out two long squashes, a pumpkin & some ears of corn." At the tavern, he had absentmindedly picked up a farmer's saddlebags instead of his own. Just at this moment, Washington rode up and, seeing them all laughing, asked "the cause of the sport." When the party told him, "in broken language, interrupted with bursts of laughter, pointing to Marshall & his bags, Washington got off his horse & leaned up against him, hardly able to stand for laughter."

If Marshall and Jefferson were strikingly alike in appearance, they were very different in temperament. Jefferson was passionate and headlong, quick to take offense, and relentless in pursuit of an enemy, emotional, intuitive, a man of impulse. Marshall was firm but conciliatory, methodical, patient, political to his fingertips. Benjamin Latrobe, the architect, wrote that Marshall left something to be desired as an orator, "but for talent, he substitutes genius, and instead of talking *about* his subject, he talks upon it . . . he is superior to every other orator at the Bar of Virginia, in closeness of argument, in his most surprising talent of placing his case in that point of light suited to the purpose he aims at, throwing a blaze of light upon it, and of keeping the attention of his hearers fixed upon the object to which he originally directed it. He speaks like a plain man of common sense, while he informs and delights the acute."

Everyone who knew Marshall commented on his sweetness of temper, his thoughtfulness, his equanimity, his courtesy. We have already noted his gloomy forebodings about the consequences of Jefferson's election. In a letter to Madison, Jefferson had criticized Marshall's "lax, lounging manners," which had "made him popular with the bulk of the people of Richmond. . . ." Jefferson also denounced his "profound hypocrisy."

The occasion of the first Marshall-Jefferson confrontation involved William Marbury, a Federalist whom Adams had appointed as a justice of the peace in his last days in office. Marbury's commission had been approved by the Senate and signed by Adams. It had then gone to Secretary of State John Marshall, but before it could be registered, Adams's term of office expired and Jefferson ordered all appointments made and commissions issued by Adams to be withheld—he called them "an outrage on decency." Marbury thereupon brought a suit to force Jefferson to release the commissions. The suit requested the Court to issue a mandamus directing the new secretary of state, James Madison, to surrender the commission.

Just the fact that the Court had been willing to consider Marbury's plea made Republicans uneasy. Breckinridge wrote to Monroe, "What think you of the rule entered upon by the Federal Court last week against the Secretary of State to show cause? . . . I think it the most daring attack which the annals of Federalism have yet exhibited. I wish the subject of the Courts to be brought forward in the Senate next week." Another Republican wrote that "the conduct of the Judges on this occasion has excited a very general indignation and will ensure the repeal of the Judiciary Law of the last session, about the propriety of which some of our Republican friends were hesitating."

John Randolph made the animus of Republicans to the Court explicit. To him, the ambitions of the justices "extend only to a complete exemption from Legislative control; to the exercise of an inquisitorial authority over the Cabinet of the Executive. . . . In their inquisitorial capacity, the Supreme Court . . . may easily direct the Executive by mandamus in what mode it is their pleasure that he should execute his functions."

Several things need to be said here. For the framers of the Constitution and all orthodox Federalists, the Supreme Court was the linchpin of the Constitution. It was the duty of the Court to declare the law and of the people of the United States, and their elected officials, up to and including the president himself, to obey the Court's decisions. That was what was meant by a government of laws, not of men. If the president or any of his Cabinet members or any of the representatives or senators of the United States were beyond the jurisdiction of the Court, they were, by definition, above the law, and the result must be a government of *men*, not of *laws*. The basic perception of the Classical-Christian Consciousness that underlay such a theory of the functioning of the Court related to the view of human nature as "fallen." Power, unless checked by wise laws, would be abused.

To the Secular-Democratic Consciousness, such notions were absurd and undemocratic. What the people wanted the people were entitled to have. Elections registered their wishes, and those elected were charged with carrying them out. The Supreme Court was an undemocratic institution, not elected but appointed, not susceptible to the wishes of the people because not removable by them. Therefore, whenever it intervened to check the "democratic" branches, it was thwarting the wishes of the people. From this it followed that the Court, since it was imbedded in the Constitution and could not very well be abolished, must be so limited and curtailed in its powers that it could not interfere with the will of the people.

The election of Jefferson had registered the will of the people. The Supreme Court had no right to impose the mildest check on that will so registered. That, at least, was the view of Jefferson and the leaders of the Republican party. Marshall was well aware that an order to Madison—in effect an order to Jefferson—to register Marbury's commission would be defied, thereby making a public demonstration of the limited powers of the Court and weakening its authority. Jefferson doubtless hoped the Court would follow such a line. Another consequence would be similar suits by other commissioners. On the other hand, if the Court simply rejected Marbury's suit, many people would interpret the action (or inaction) as evidence of weakness on the part of the Court; its friends would be disheartened and its enemies encouraged.

The Republican Congress, perhaps with the view to delaying a decision on *Marbury* v. *Madison*, abolished the June and December terms of the Court so that fourteen months necessarily intervened before the Court could render its decision. Meanwhile, Republican politicians lost no opportunity to attack the Court. William Plumer, from New Hampshire, wrote: "The Judges of the Supreme Court must fall; they are denounced by the Executive, as well as the House, and why should they remain to awe and embarrass the Administration? Men of more flexible nerves can be found to succeed them."

While the *Marbury* v. *Madison* case hung in the balance, the Republicans in Congress zeroed in on the Judiciary Act of 1789. After weeks of acrimonious debate a bill to repeal it passed the Senate by a party vote of 16 to 15; 59 to 32 in the House.

Federalist dismay over the repeal of the Judiciary Act was widespread. A Federalist editor wrote that "the Constitution has received a wound it cannot long survive. The Jacobins exult; the Federalists mourn; our country will weep, perhaps bleed." The repeal was seen "as part of a systematic plan for the total subversion of the law itself . . . operating in its consequence a complete destruction of the independence of an integral part of the Government, and introducing a system of corruption into the sanctuary of the Constitution." It was, said another, "the death warrant of the Constitution." Gouverneur Morris, who had written the final draft of the Constitution, wrote that "the repeal of the Judiciary Bill battered down the great outwork of the Constitution. The Judiciary has been overthrown," because the judges would, it was foreseen, resist assaults on the Constitution by acts of the legislature. "The Constitution is, therefore, in my opinion, gone." Another framer of the Constitution, Charles Cotesworth Pinckney, declared that it was clear that the Republicans were determined "to destroy a work whose adoption they opposed and whose execution they have constantly counteracted. . . . I do not imagine they will stop there, they will proceed in their mad and wicked career and the people's eyes will be opened."

Accentuating the bitterness of the controversy over the repeal was the anxious anticipation of the Republicans that the Supreme Court would declare the repeal unconstitutional, thus precipitating a potentially revolutionary situation. Caesar Rodney of Delaware, whose principal claim to fame was that he had ridden all night in order to arrive in Philadelphia in time to swing the vote of his state in support of the resolution declaring the colonies independent, wrote to a friend that if the Court dared to "assert unconstitutional powers [such as issuing a mandamus to Madison or declaring the repeal of the Judiciary Act unconstitutional], I confidently trust there will be wisdom and energy enough in the Legislative and Executive branches . . . to arraign them for the abuse of their authority at the proper tribunal. . . . They should remember . . . that there is a boundary which they cannot pass with impunity. If they [the justices] cross the Rubicon, they may repent when it shall be late to return. . . . We shall discover who is master of the ship."

When the Court assembled after its mandated recess to deliver its decision in the case of *Marbury* v. *Madison*, "most gentlemen of the Bar" were present to hear what was widely believed to be the most crucial decision yet rendered by the Court.

In the words of the chief justice: "The following questions have been considered and decided.

"1st. Has the applicant a right to the commission he demands?

"2dly. If he has a right and that right has been violated, do the laws of his country afford him a remedy?

"3dly. If they afford him a remedy is it a *mandamus* issuing from this court?"

First, the appointment was "not revocable, and cannot be annuled . . . . The right to the office is then in the person appointed, and he has the absolute, unconditional power of accepting or rejecting it." It followed that "to withhold his commission . . . is an act deemed by the Court not warranted by law, but violative of a vested legal right."

Marshall seemed to be throwing down the gauntlet to the president. But he had devised an ingenious way out. If Marbury had a right and the right had been violated, did he then have a remedy at law? Section 13 of the Judiciary Act of 1789 had apparently conferred such a right. But, Marshall declared, that section of the act had been unconstitutional. It was "therefore absolutely incapable of conferring the authority and assigning the duties which its words purport to confer and assign." Marbury, it turned out, had no remedy under law. The Supreme Court had original jurisdiction, under the Constitution, only in cases "affecting ambassadors, other public ministers and consuls, and those in which a state shall be a party. In all other cases the Supreme Court shall have appellate jurisdiction." It was "a proposition too plain to be contested, that the constitution controls any legislative act repugnant to it; or, that the legislature may not alter the Constitution by an ordinary act. . . . The constitution is either a superior, paramount law, unchangeable by ordinary means or it is on a level with ordinary legislative acts. . . . The particular phraseology of the Constitution of the United States confirms and strengthens the principle . . . that a law repugnant to the Constitution is void, and that *courts*, as well as other departments, are bound by that instrument."

By the decision, of which Marshall was the principal architect, the Court asserted: (1) that the president had acted illegally; (2) that Congress had acted unconstitutionally; (3) that the Court, like the executive and legislature, was bound by the Constitution; (4) that it was the business of the Court to declare what the Constitution in fact meant. Finally, in declaring the authority of the Court, Marshall had left the co-ordinate branches without any ready weapon to attack it.

The Court had already declared in the *Hayburn* case that laws passed by Congress contravening, in the opinion of the justices, the Constitution were invalid, but the particular circumstances of *Marbury* v. *Madison* dramatized the issue in a wholly novel way. Marshall's ingenuity had succeeded in strengthening the Court at the moment when it seemed in serious peril.

The Federalists were delighted by the decision, with the exception, presumably, of poor Marbury, and the Republicans were enraged. Jefferson was furious and twenty years later described it as "very irregular and very censurable." The fact that more bitterness did not result from the decision was due, in part, to the fact that a few weeks later the Court handed down a decision declaring that the repeal of the Judiciary Act of 1789 was constitutional.

At this decision, Republicans were perhaps more disappointed than Federalists, because many of them had counted on using a decision declaring repeal unconstitutional as a weapon to destroy the Court. Again it is hard not to feel that the Court, well aware of the Republican animus against it, was anxious to avoid a contest in which all the advantages lay with Congress. From the point of view of the justices, far more important than overthrowing an objectionable statute was confirming the power of the Court to judge the issue of constitutionality.

The justices must have noted with some amusement the Republican delight with their decision in *Stuart* v. *Laird* upholding the constitutionality of what came to be known as the Judiciary Act. The decision, Duane declared in the *Aurora*, "stands as a living reproach to such as can believe . . . that you [the justices] would surrender the chastity of the Court to the lust of envy. . . . The weight of your authority then calmed the tumult of action, and you stood, as you must continue to stand, a star of the first magnitude."

27

The Louisiana Purchase

The reader will have caught me grumbling more than once over the fact that in history many things happen simultaneously but the historian can only treat them sequentially. While the furor over the Judiciary Act and *Marbury* v. *Madison* went on, Jefferson was faced by a series of knotty problems. The move to decommission the ships of the infant federal navy was delayed by persistent problems with the Barbary pirates. These brigands, operating out of Tunis, Algiers, and Tripoli, exacted an onerous toll on all shipping in the Mediterranean. They had, in effect, blackmailed England and the United States, among other seagoing nations, into paying them large yearly sums to refrain from seizing their merchant vessels. Delay in paying meant depredations against American ships and the loss of American lives. Congress had gone along meekly enough, paying blackmail, but Jefferson now nudged them toward naval action to chastise the pashas and beys who fattened on the tribute, proposing that what was left of the much-maligned "Adams" navy be employed for that purpose.

Word had reached the President soon after his inauguration that Spain had arbitrarily closed New Orleans to Mississippi River shipping, thus applying a severe economic squeeze to the American settlements along the Mississippi and its eastern tributaries, down which they were accustomed to send their wheat and pork. There was an immediate clamor for armed action against the Spanish at New Orleans.

The Kentucky frontier, West Florida, the District of New Orleans, the crude settlements along the Mississippi, and even the area west of the Mississippi, along the Red River and the Arkansas, made up a region, without clear social or political definition, which proved a constant temptation to ambitious intriguers. To the independent frontiersmen who were drawn, as by an enormous magnet, to the Mississippi River and who mingled along its banks with Spaniards, Frenchmen, and Indians, Spanish rule was especially irksome. Spanish officials viewed the frontiersmen as little better than savages and made no effort to conceal their contempt. The laws were written in a foreign language and were often no more than what the Spanish commandant at Natchez or New Orleans declared them to be. Trials in civil and most criminal cases were held without juries, by indifferent if not hostile judges.

The Spaniards exercised their control over the navigation of the lower Mississippi in a heavy-handed and unpredictable manner. It took months for letters from Americans in New Orleans or western Kentucky, describing some intolerable Spanish abuse of authority, to reach the center of government in Philadelphia or, subsequently, Washington. When it did, it was often ignored. Gentlemen in Philadelphia could not be persuaded to take seriously the needs and aspirations of some thousands of Americans who, in their view, would have done better to stay in their original states rather than create problems by pushing themselves into areas where they did not belong. The whole matter was complicated by the fact that the Spanish actively encouraged Americans to migrate to the Louisiana Territory because they wanted it settled. What the settlers and traders of the frontier wanted, of course, was to persuade the federal government to send a military force to wrest the region from the Spanish and then turn it over to the administration of its inhabitants, as had been done with the Northwest Territory.

The closing of New Orleans to American river commerce brought matters to a head. While Jefferson was resisting the call for a military expedition, he learned that Spain, by the Treaty of San Ildefonso, had pledged to return to France the territory of Louisiana that France had given to Spain in 1762, at the end of the French and Indian Wars, in compensation for Spain's loss of Gibraltar.

Jefferson knew that France, ruled by the aggressive first consul,

Napoleon Bonaparte, would be a much more formidable neighbor than Spain. He immediately named James Monroe as minister extraordinary and plenipotentiary to both France and Spain, since Spain had not yet formally turned Louisiana over to the French. The Senate approved Monroe's appointment, and the House allocated $2 million to be used to purchase New Orleans, thus assuring the Western states of a port of deposit for their goods.

Robert Livingston, the U.S. ambassador to France, was, pending Monroe's arrival, instructed to do his best to persuade Napoleon to agree to pay the debts owed for the seizure by French warships of American merchantmen and either to sell the United States an area at the mouth of the Mississippi or to provide some guarantee of the free use of the river. Talleyrand, who envisioned a great future for France in Louisiana, intercepted Livingston's correspondence, and it was not until the latter found a way to bypass the French foreign minister and get to the first consul directly that he received any encouragment.

Whatever impulse Napoleon may have had to exploit Louisiana for the glory of France was considerably dampened by the events on Santo Domingo (Haiti), where Toussaint L'Ouverture in 1795 had led some four hundred thousand slaves in an insurrection against their white masters and, after an interval of bitter fighting, had declared Santo Domingo an independent nation. The United States had accepted L'Ouverture's invitation to resume trade during the period of the "Quasi War" with France. When the Treaty of 1800 ended the state of undeclared war with France, a combined fleet of French and Spanish ships with ten thousand sailors, soldiers, and marines arrived at the island, captured L'Ouverture, and reestablished French control over the island. Slavery was reinstituted, and a number of black leaders were executed. But in 1803 when England and France were again at war, the blacks of Santo Domingo once more rose up and threw off the French yoke. The consequence of these upheavals was that Santo Domingo, which might well have served as a staging area for French soldiers and settlers headed for Louisiana, was, because of its internal turmoil, rendered useless to Bonaparte. A French Louisiana, moreover, would be a constant temptation to England, which had already attacked Santo Domingo. Rather than have it fall into British hands, Napoleon preferred to sell it to the United States. He thus instructed Talleyrand to offer Jefferson the entire Louisiana Territory. Livingston responded that he had been instructed to buy only the island of New Orleans and such a portion of West Florida as France might also have reclaimed from Spain. Napoleon's reply was, in effect, buy all or nothing.

Meanwhile Monroe arrived in Paris and received the astonishing news. The price for all of Louisiana was 100 million francs and the assumption by the United States of the debts claimed from France, roughly $20 million. The purchase price was reduced after some negotiating to a total, for land and debts, of 80 million francs—11 million down and the rest to be paid in installments over twenty years.

The agreement presented Jefferson with a dilemma. In the matter of the Constitution he was a strict constructionist who had staked his political career on the proposition that no powers could be exercised by the federal government that were not specifically stipulated in that document. The Federalists, of course, argued that there were numerous powers available to the federal government that were "implied" by the Constitution, that is to say, that were the logical and proper extension of those powers specifically granted. But not Jefferson. The Constitution said nothing about the power of the president and/or Congress to acquire what amounted to a whole new country. On the other hand, Jefferson had always been infatuated with the West. He had supported the campaigns of George Rogers Clark in the Old Northwest during the Revolution; he had been a close student of Indian life and culture; and even before Louisiana had dropped into his lap, he had prevailed on Congress to approve a surveying and exploring expedition into the region south of the Great Lakes where large areas were unmapped.

Jefferson proceeded to sound out leaders in Congress on the possibility of rushing through an amendment that would authorize the government to acquire such a purchase as that of Louisiana, but he was advised unanimously that he could do so under the treaty-making powers of the Constitution and that he must swallow his scruples or lose his prize. Napoleon had made him an offer he could not refuse. Not only would the purchase put an end to the perpetually troublesome problem of the control of the mouth of the Mississippi, it would almost double the land area of the United States.

The New England Federalists, a number of whom had been pressing for military action against Spain to open up the Mississippi River, now came forward to oppose the Louisiana Purchase. They had seen the Republicans abolish the excise tax, lower the national debt by some five million dollars, reduce the army to a handful of regulars, dismantle a large part of the navy, allow the Alien and Sedition Acts to expire, repeal the Judiciary Act of 1789, and proclaim their intention of sharply curtailing the powers of the Supreme Court. It seemed to them that the country was firmly in the hands of the South, led by Virginia, and that the purpose of the South was to reduce the North to a condition of political and economic bondage.

By adding the Louisiana Territory to the United States, Jefferson and the Republican majority were paving the way for addition to the Union of Slave States that would forever destroy any hope of parity between Slave and Free States and leave the North permanently and irredeemably under the domination of the South. Rather disunion than such a fate, the irreconcilable Federalists declared. The champions of implied powers now became strict constructionists and attacked Jefferson bitterly for his unconstitutional action in acquiring Louisiana. The American impulse toward aggrandizement, toward acquiring vast new increments of land, was already well set as a quality of mind. We had lusted after Canada during the Revolution and were to lust after it again. Indeed, many Americans professed to believe that it was God's intention that the United States should fill up the whole continent of North America on the principle of neatness and symmetry, thereby bringing civilization to the savages and the benefits of enlightened political institutions to the Mexicans and the Canadians. The Federalists, by their rancorous opposition to the Louisiana Purchase far more than by the loss of the election of 1800, placed themselves athwart a mainstream of American history and doomed themselves to the status of a minority party.

The Federalist newspapers and their diminishing number of readers entertained themselves by emphasizing the enormous sum of money involved in the purchase. If the $15 million involved were stacked up one upon the other in silver dollars they would make a pile three miles high; it would take twenty-five ships to carry it; and so forth. Such statistics seem to have been the first instance of what was to become a minor American infatuation—visualizing money piled up to dramatize the cost of a public improvement, the national debt, an unpopular war, and so forth—one more manifestation, a cynic might have said, of the American obsession with money. There were reports by supporters of the purchase that it included a mountain of pure salt 180 miles long and 40 miles wide, white and shining and treeless, worth the whole purchase price in itself. Streams of salt water cascaded down its glistening slopes. Bushels of it had been brought to St. Louis by traders in the interior of the country. The Federalists replied to these reports with derision. There was also, doubtless, a lake of pure Irish whiskey and a valley of hasty pudding.

The opposition of the Federalist diehards was easily overridden, and on December 20, 1803, the vast Louisiana Territory became part of the United States.

Gouverneur Morris was one of the few Federalists to express support for the purchase. It was his view that the expansionist impulses of Americans were, in the long run, irresistible. He was indifferent to the question of whether the purchase was constitutional or not, "for, at the rate things go on, the Constitution cannot last, and an unbalanced monarchy will be established on its ruins. . . . I have made up my mind to float along as gently as I may." When someone wrote to ask what the intentions of the framers of the Constitution had been in regard to such acquisitions of territory, Morris replied, "I am certain that the country between Mississippi and the Atlantic exceeds by far the limits which prudence would assign if, in effect, any limitation be required." He himself would not have supported a clause limiting the territory of the United States to the region east of the Mississippi because, much as he had opposed granting political parity to Western states, he "knew as well then as I do now that all North America must at length be annexed to us—happy, indeed, if the lust of dominion stop there. It would therefore have been perfectly utopian to oppose a paper restriction to the violence of popular sentiment in a popular government." This was a backhanded endorsement, to say the least!

New Orleans, the capital of the territory, was delivered to the American commissioners—William Claiborne and General James Wilkinson—by the turning over, quite literally, of the keys to its six gates. Claiborne welcomed the residents, who had gathered in the town square, as citizens of the United States and assured them that "their liberty, their property, their religion, were safe" and that "their commerce should flourish, . . . their agriculture . . . be protected, and that they should never again be transferred." The French tricolor, which had been raised over the city only twenty days before, was lowered and the American flag raised in its place.

The bill passed by Congress to establish a government for the newly acquired territory was anything but democratic. It provided for a governor to be appointed by the president for a three-year term and for a legislative council of thirteen members similarly appointed. Wilkinson had been made military commander, and Claiborne governor. Both, as it turned out, were unfitted for their jobs. There was unrest in the new territory from the instant of its birth. A petition was drawn up and brought to Washington by three representatives of the territory claiming that the territorial government was unconstitutional and that it violated the terms of the treaty by which France had sold the territory to the United States. The inhabitants were taxed without representation and were obliged to obey laws they had had no choice in making. When their petitions received short shrift from Congress and the president, residents of the territory began to talk of open rebellion.

Meanwhile, Jefferson felt the barbs of the free press he had so extolled. On July 10 Joseph Dennie's *Port Folio*, which had survived a legal action brought against it for denigrating democracy, published a poem that made reference to the increasingly widely circulated story of the president's slave mistress, Sally Hemings. Written in the supposed dialect of a black named Quashee, it read in part:

> For make all like, let blackee hab
> De white woman . . . dat be de track!
> Den Quashee de white wife will hab
> And massa *Jefferson shall hab de black.*
> Huzza! me say, and make de noise!
> Huzza for Quashee! Quashee will
> Huzza for massa Jefferson!

The racial hostility and contempt in the poem bespoke an attitude toward black people far more venomous than that evinced by most Southerners. It was followed by a series of articles by Callender in the *Richmond Recorder,* a Federalist paper, abusing Jefferson and revealing, for the first time, that Jefferson had encouraged Callender in his scurrilous attacks on Washington and Adams. There was, in addition, the unnerving sense that someone close to Jefferson was in touch with the "opposition," for Callender reported that when Jefferson read the attacks on him, he flew into "a violent passion" and declared, "I did give the dam'd rascal the hundred dollars, but it was mere charity."

If it was possible to increase Federalist bitterness against Jefferson, the Callender revelations certainly did it. Abigail Adams wrote him that the news of his support for Callender was "the Sword that cut asunder the Gordian knot"—her feelings of friendship for Jefferson—which had hitherto survived "all the efforts of party Spirit . . . rivalship by Jealousy or any other malignant fiend."

Republicans denounced Callender, who retaliated by publishing in the *Recorder* of September, 1802, his account of Jefferson's relationship with Sally Hemings. "It is well known," he wrote, "that the man, *whom it delighteth the people to honor*, keeps and for many years has kept, as his concubine, one of his slaves. Her name is SALLY. The name of her eldest son is Tom. His features are said to bear a striking resemblance to those of the president himself. . . . By this wench Sally, our president has had several children. There is not an individual in the neighbourhood of Charlottesville who does not believe the story, and not a few who know it."

Once out, the story was repeated by many Federalist newspapers, some of which added cautious disclaimers like that of the *Gazette of the United States*, which referred to the reports in the *Recorder* and then added, "We have heard the same subject freely spoken of in Virginia, and by Virginia Gentlemen; but as we possess no positive vouchers for the truth of the narrative, we do not choose to admit it into the "Gazette," while there remains the possibility of a calumny." The Republican newspapers had to satisfy themselves by attacking Callender, who was certainly an object worthy of their disapprobation. The defense of Jefferson was made more difficult by his refusal to speak a word on the subject. Madison was reported to have called the story "incredible," and Henry Lee and other Virginians rallied to scoff at Callender's charges. Two Virginia newspapers, the *Frederick Town Herald* and the *Virginia Gazette*, professed to have made their own investigations that confirmed Callender's story. John Adams, who had known Sally Hemings when she stopped in England with Jefferson's daughter on her way to Paris, accepted the story as an almost unavoidable matter of course, writing that it was "a natural consequence of that foul contagion in the human character—Negro slavery." Abigail's reaction to the ill-fortune of the man who had encouraged Callender's attacks on her husband was that he had gotten no better than he deserved: "The serpent you cherished and warmed," she wrote Jefferson, "bit the hand that nourished it, and gave you sufficient specimens of his talents, his gratitude, his justice, and his truth."

Chief Justice Marshall was too human to suppress his pleasure at seeing his enemy get his comeuppance and went so far as to congratulate Callender on his articles in the *Recorder*. Callender at once announced that "Mr. Marshall says that this is the best conducted paper in America, that such an editor must be supported, and that he never before saw such a variety of subjects so correctly handled." At which the rival *Richmond Examiner* hinted that "upon this point [miscegenation] his [Marshall's] character is not invulnerable."

Beyond the partisan political clamor was a human tragedy not unlike thousands of other such tragedies except in the prominence of the white master involved—the president of the United States. It must be said to Jefferson's credit that he seemed genuinely fond of, or perhaps even devoted to, Sally Hemings. Their relationship was as long as most marriages—from sometime in 1787 to Jefferson's death in 1826, thirty-nine years. Her children were set free on Jefferson's death. Their son, Madison Hemings, noted in his recollections that Jefferson had made that promise in order to persuade Sally Hemings to return to the United States with him. So far as we know, Jefferson was not involved in the casual rutting with black women that characterized the relationships of so many white masters with the black women on their plantations. The tragedy is made more poignant by the depths of Jefferson's own feelings about the evils of slavery, feelings that were expressed well before Sally Hemings became his mistress. That he should, at the same time, have been the apostle of democracy, the enunciator of the dream of human equality, is simply another of those profound ironies so common to history.

Beyond that, we may take the episode as symbolic of that ambiguity or schizophrenia evident in almost every aspect of our particular history as a people. American historians of the Secular-Democratic persuasion for whom Jefferson is a perfect and unblemished hero have done their very considerable best to disprove the story that Sally Hemings was Jefferson's mistress (common-law wife might be a more appropriate term) and the mother of a number of his children. That these intelligent and high-minded men have expended so much time and energy in such a futile enterprise is more of a credit to their hearts than to their heads. But far beyond that, it is a mark of our general incapacity to deal with history as tragedy. It is simply inconceivable to Jefferson's admirers that he could have done something so "disreputable" as take a "half black female slave" to his bed. But after all she was handsome, intelligent, the half sister of his dead wife. It is hard not to conclude that a strange combination of classic American attitudes toward both sexuality and blackness lies beneath their almost fanatical denials of what Jefferson never denied himself.

The crux of the matter is not that Jefferson had extramarital relations (although it must be said that the same historians have, for the most part, denied that Jefferson's love affair with Maria Cosway was anything more than platonic), but rather that his partner was a half-black slave. Hamilton had revealed his own sexual dalliance, a far more degrading relationship in strictly human terms than Jefferson's, without apparent damage to his political influence. During the Revolutionary War, rumors had circulated widely about Washington's affairs with women who were little better than camp followers. The revelations about Sally Hemings had no discernible effect on Jefferson's reelection as president two years later. The ridicule of the Federalist press was directed less at the sexual than the racial aspects of the relationship. While it is unquestionably true that attitudes toward sexuality were growing more rigid and repressive in the last decades of the eighteenth century (and would grow far more so as the nineteenth century ran its course), deviations from strict sexual mores were clearly not yet a serious political liability. The whole Sally Hemings incident might thus be said to reveal more about the racial than the sexual attitudes of Jefferson's countrymen.

Not satisfied with the Hemings story, the indefatigable Callender (who made it a practice to reprint the ferocious Republican attacks upon him in the *Recorder*) dug up an old scandal involving Betsy Walker, the wife of a friend of Jefferson's. Thirty-five years earlier, during the absence of her husband, John Walker, Jefferson had allegedly tried to seduce the young woman left in his charge. There was apparently enough truth in the story to persuade Walker that, despite the passage of years, he had to challenge Jefferson to a duel to vindicate his honor.

The Federalists found another bone to gnaw on in the matter of Tom Paine, who had been reluctant to return to the United States for fear of his ship's being intercepted by the British. Jefferson arranged for Paine to return on a U.S. frigate. As though it were not bad enough to aid and abet the return to America of this notorious atheist and defamer of Washington, the President invited him to stay at the White House. Paine's *Age of Reason* had become the target of orthodox Calvinist preachers everywhere. It was denounced as "too blasphemous to meet the public eye," and Dennie's *Port Folio* described Paine as "*the greatest infidel on earth.*" His visit with Jefferson encouraged the Federalists to link sexual license with atheism. A poem appeared, again in the *Port Folio*, in which Paine, with Jefferson absent, is engaged in seducing Sally Hemings when "Tall Tom" returns like a specter and tears out Sally's tongue for betraying him.

In the exercise of his duties as president, Jefferson, as we have seen, was somewhat inhibited by his theory that the powers of the chief executive were severely limited by the Constitution. He had criticized Washington and Adams for constantly exceeding their constitutional authority; he did not wish to seem to be meddling in matters that he had insisted were the exclusive province of Congress. But the fact was that Jefferson was a strong-minded and sometimes willful president who was determined to do all in his power to make Congress the instrument of his will. Since he felt constrained, by his often stated political principles, from doing this openly, he had to do it convertly by encouraging a leadership in Congress that was amenable to his wishes. By the same token he solicited and, more important, followed the advice of his Cabinet far less frequently than his predecessors. Nonetheless he never missed an opportunity to emphasize the "democratic decision-making process," as we would call it today, which he professed to believe took place in his administration.

In a letter to his friend William Short, Jefferson described the process in these words: "Our government, altho', in theory, subject to be directed by the unadvised will of the President is, and from its origin has been, a very different thing in practice. . . . All matters of importance or difficulty are submitted to all the heads of departments comprising the cabinet; sometimes by the President's consulting them separately & successively as they happen to call on him; but in the gravest cases by calling them together, discussing the subject maturely, and finally taking the vote, on which the President counts himself as but one: so that in all important cases the Executive is, in fact, a Directory, which certainly the President might control, but of this there was never an example either in the first or the present administration. I have heard indeed that my predecessor [Adams] sometimes decided things against his council by dashing & trampling his wig on the floor."

All that we know about Jefferson's administration and, indeed, about his personality speaks to the contrary. He sometimes acted without consulting his Cabinet officers at all; he often consulted them in the most casual, desultory way, and he not infrequently acted in opposition to their advice. But Jefferson had considerable capacity for self-delusion, and there is no reason to doubt that he believed his words even if his actions belied them.

While it was clearly the case that the Supreme Court was perceived by Jefferson and the Republicans as the stronghold of Federalism, unreachable by the electorate and the only obstacle to the complete triumph of Republican principles, it must be said that some justices gave the Republicans ample cause for displeasure. It was the practice of judges in many courts to deliver addresses to grand juries that went considerably beyond points of law into far wider political issues. Certain judges took advantage of such occasions to lecture the jurors on proper constitutional principles and, in doing so, to attack the actions and policies of the Republican administration. The most notorious justice in this regard was Samuel Chase of Maryland, an old Federalist who had for some years shown signs of instability. Following passage of the new Judiciary Act of 1789, which swept away the sixteen circuit court judges and returned the justices to the arduous labor of the circuit, Chase, addressing a grand jury at Baltimore, launched into a tirade against the Republicans and against the new state constitution of Maryland, which had offended Chase by providing for universal suffrage and thus, in his view, opening the door to "a mobocracy."

When Jefferson read Chase's address, he felt confident that he now had in hand an instrument with which he might clip the Court's wings. "Ought this seditious and official attack on the principles of our Constitution and on the proceedings of the State . . . go unpunished?" Jefferson asked a Republican Congressman. Chase's offenses included strong evidence of bias in the cases of Fries and Callender.

Prodded by the president, the House brought in a bill of impeachment against Chase early in 1804, and the Senate began his trial in February. Fisher Ames despaired of seeing justice done in the atmosphere of partisan politics that prevailed. "You may broil Judge Chase and eat him, or eat him raw," he wrote, "it shall stir up less anger or pity than the Six Nations would show if Cornplanter or Red Jacket was refused a belt of wampum."

The Republicans, counting noses in the Senate, had the uneasy feeling that they might have misjudged their colleagues when they pressed so confidently for Chase's impeachment. They held a 25 to 9 majority, and only 23 votes were needed for impeachment, but Aaron Burr presided over the Senate and was still the implacable enemy of

Jefferson. Several other Republican senators had expressed strong misgivings about the impeachment. Jefferson gave special attention to wooing Burr, who was invited to dine at the White House. In July, 1804, while the impeachment of Chase was still pending, Burr killed Alexander Hamilton in a duel. Virginia senator William Giles, one of the leaders in the impeachment, drafted a petition to the governor of New Jersey requesting that the murder indictment against Burr be quashed, and public offices were found for the relatives of a man to whom Jefferson had previously refused any mark of favor.

John Randolph concluded the case against Chase in March, 1805, in an extraordinary performance, sobbing, bursting into tears, and ranting in his high-pitched voice until he collapsed from exhaustion. The voting on impeachment was dramatic. The Senate chamber was crowded with spectators. Aaron Burr ordered the eight articles of impeachment read, one at a time, and then voted on. The clerk called the roll on Article 1. Only 16 senators voted for conviction. Chase was unanimously acquitted of the second article, and so it went. Only on the eighth, which dealt with his address to the Baltimore grand jury, were as many as 19 votes recorded for impeachment. Burr then rose, turned toward Chase, and declared him acquitted. Returning to the House of Representatives, the enraged Randolph proposed an amendment to the Constitution providing that the justices could be removed by the president on the joint request of a majority of both houses of Congress. It passed by a strictly party vote. The errant justices might yet be brought to heel.

The Federalist press, jubilant over Chase's acquittal, acclaimed it as a "triumph of reason and justice over the spirit of party." Henry St. George Tucker, a Virginia Republican, wrote to a friend: "I regard the acquittal as a foul disgrace upon our country. . . . It really seems as if the People were afraid to touch this golden calf they have formed— this talisman, the fancied charm which is to preserve us through every danger."

Tucker's comments were significant. It was true that the Court had, in a remarkably short time, acquired a kind of aura that was to make it impregnable to Republican attacks. In a quite mysterious and inexplicable way it had come to embody the essence of the Constitution. But to the Jeffersonians it appeared as no more than the agency by means of which the popular will as expressed at the ballot box was frustrated. The Republican position was stated by William Giles during the Chase impeachment proceedings. It was his view that "all the

Judges of the Supreme Court . . . must be impeached and removed . . . and if the Judges of the Supreme Court should dare, as they have done, to declare an Act of Congress unconstitutional, or to send a mandamus to the Secretary of State, as they had done, it was the undoubted right of the House of Representatives to impeach them, and of the Senate to remove them, for giving such opinions, however honest or sincere they may have been in entertaining them. . . . A removal by impeachment was nothing more than a declaration by Congress to this effect: you hold dangerous opinions, and if you are suffered to carry them into effect, you will work the destruction of the Union. We want your offices for the purpose of giving them to men who will fill them better."

It is hard to know quite what to say in response to such a view of constitutional government. It is, of course, based most clearly on the assumption that the people can do no wrong, that "the voice of the people is the voice of God," and that they can be trusted never to oppress or persecute those whose opinions differ from their own; in short, that there is no system of natural law or public morality that can set limits to the use of power, provided always that the majority support such power. This was clearly Giles's opinion and, it seems safe to assume, Jefferson's.

28

Hamilton and Burr

A t the same time Jefferson was negotiating the purchase of Louisiana, Vice-President Aaron Burr, ostracized by the Republicans and snubbed by Jefferson for his role in the election of 1800, was busy forming an alliance with the most reactionary Federalists in and out of Congress. Timothy Pickering, Roger Griswold, Uriah Tracy, and William Plumer later conceived the notion of winning New York for the Federalists by supporting the apostate Republican, Burr, in the gubernatorial contest of 1804, thereby paving the way for the secession of the Northern states from the Union. In the view of the New England secessionists, New York was the key state in such a plan. Burr was an eager accomplice. More orthodox Federalists, or those who drew the line at such desperation politics, met in an Albany tavern to plan measures to block Burr's election. Two friends of Burr's eavesdropped on the meeting and reported it to the papers, which announced that Hamilton had roused himself from his political retirement long enough to direct the campaign to thwart his longtime rival's bid for the governorship.

Pickering and other New England members of Congress were active in Burr's behalf, and toasts at a dinner given by his New England supporters in Boston gave clues to their expectations: "To the Virginia Dominion—may it be bounded by the Constitution or by the Dela-

498

ware." "The Federal virtues are obliged to swarm from the seat of Government—may they find a hive in the North." "Aaron's Rod—may it blossom in New York . . ."—a reference to Aaron, the brother of Moses, leading the chosen people of Israel out of the land of Egypt.

The election was the bitterest in New York City's history. Charges were made that Burr's supporters wished to split the Union (which some of them certainly did) and that they intended to send agents to the South to stir up slaves to murder their masters. There were fights and riots in the final days before the election; shops closed and gangs of political partisans roamed the streets armed with staves and rocks.

Defeated at the polls, Burr blamed Hamilton for his loss and decided to murder him. The pretext was the report by a man named Charles Cooper that Hamilton had said in the course of a private conversation that Burr "was a dangerous man and ought not to be trusted with the reins of government." Cooper had repeated the conversation in letters that had been reprinted in several newspapers. Burr cut one such report out of a paper and sent it to Hamilton with demands for a denial. A curious correspondence followed, with Hamilton evasive and Burr persistent.

On June 27, 1804, Hamilton received a formal challenge from Burr and accepted it, although he considered dueling as "in the highest degree criminal." We can only guess at the state of mind that led Hamilton to accept Burr's challenge. He certainly had no illusions about the motive behind it or its probable outcome. His own political career lay in ruins. His bitterest rival, Thomas Jefferson, had triumphed and seemed bent on undoing all that Hamilton had labored to build; his own party seemed determined to complete the wreck of the Union by plotting to secede. He had besmirched his name and humiliated his wife in his revelation about his affair with Maria Reynolds, all to no substantial effect. Most terrible of all, his brilliant and promising son, Philip, had died in a politically motivated duel, and his daughter had gone mad with grief over her brother's death. Philip Burr, who had died in his father's arms professing his Christian faith, undoubtedly provided both an incentive to his father to embrace a similar end and a model for the elder Hamilton to emulate in his refusal to fire at his adversary. His deadly enemy may have thus done him a better service than he intended. To a man whose religious beliefs precluded suicide, Burr's implacable hostility may have offered a welcome way out of a life that had become intolerable. Hamilton was, after all, a comparatively young man, forty-seven at the time of his duel with Burr. But life for him had lost its savor.

The night before the duel was to take place, a few of his oldest and closest friends gave him a party over which, not surprisingly, there hung a morbid and funereal air. Hamilton, so often lively and gay, was quiet and withdrawn. At the end of the evening he rose to sing the mournful song that Wolfe had sung in anticipation of his death on the Plains of Abraham in the conclusive battle of the French and Indian Wars.

The next morning, Hamilton, carrying the pistols his son had used in his fatal duel, rowed across the Hudson River to the field in Weehawken, New Jersey, where Philip had received a mortal wound three years earlier. Hamilton fired his own pistol into the air. Burr's bullet passed through his liver and lodged in his spine. Like his son, he was carried back across the river to his home; and like his son he lived some twenty-four hours in great pain before dying in the afternoon of July 12.

Proud, ambitious, vain, intriguing, conservative, he is an enormously compelling figure who defined and embodied one half of that divided American consciousness to which we must pay such close attention. Hamilton had written two years earlier to his friend, Gouverneur Morris: "Mine has been an odd destiny." And so, indeed, it had. Rising from the obscurity of an illegitimate birth to become one of the two or three most powerful and influential men of the new age, he was the father of American capitalism and, as such, suffered "bad press" in subsequent generations, since Americans have felt obliged, while making business the essence of the American ethos, endlessly to proclaim their allegiance to democratic principles. Hamilton has thus been a victim of one striking manifestation of our schizophrenia: we were to become the most powerful capitalist industrial power in the world under the banner of Jeffersonian agrarian democracy. Hamilton had, undoubtedly, an authoritarian streak in him, but he was a financial genius who held steady in his conviction that the destiny of America was to be most strikingly and essentially expressed through business enterprise.

John Adams, both a more attractive figure and a more systematic exponent of the Classical-Christian Consciousness, was quite blind to the implications of the business ethic that Hamilton championed. He shared with Jefferson a devotion to the agricultural life and a profound suspicion of banks, bankers, and all manipulators of money. So Hamilton is essential to complete our triad, which then looks something like this:

Hamilton {
business-financial bias
original sin—natural
depravity
authoritarian inclinations
entrepreneurial
consciousness
}

Adams {
agricultural bias
original sin—natural
depravity
Classical-Christian
Consciousness
}

Jefferson {
agricultural bias
human perfectibility
reason and science
Secular-Democratic
Consciousness
}

It remained for Daniel Webster to pronounce Hamilton's most famous epitaph: "He smote the rock of the national resources and abundant streams of revenue gushed forth; he touched the dead corpse of the Public Credit, and it sprang upon its feet. The fabled birth of Minerva, from the brain of Jove, was hardly more sudden or more perfect than the financial system of the United States, as it burst forth from the conceptions of Alexander Hamilton."

If that is a bit orotund for the modern taste, it nonetheless puts the case well enough; and the ambivalence of our feelings about Alexander Hamilton simply measures our ambivalence about ourselves and our past. There were a number of human qualities of Thomas Jefferson that no more deserve our approbation than the less appealing aspects of Hamilton's character, but there is a good deal of truth in the complaint of a recent Hamilton biographer that Jefferson's failings have been as carefully obscured by his admiring biographers as Hamilton's have been stressed. The prime example, of course, would be Jefferson's relationship with Sally Hemings.

The denigration of Hamilton and the glorifying of Jefferson can best be seen as simply two more strategies in our determined effort to avoid the meaning of our history, or to tidy it up so that it conforms to the requirements of the Secular-Democratic Consciousness. Hamilton's life is classic tragedy. But then so, of course, is Jefferson's. Since we have no way of coping with the tragic dimensions of history, it is easier to cast it in terms of heroes and villains. By this system Jefferson comes out the hero, Hamilton the villain.

The day of Hamilton's funeral the church bells of New York tolled from six to seven in the morning and seven to eight in the evening. The English and French warships in the harbor fired their guns in a salute to the dead statesman, and thousands of New Yorkers lined the streets as the funeral procession made its way to Trinity Church. Only Washington's death had evoked such an outpouring of public grief.

Burr, who had escaped to Philadelphia, was indicted for murder, and on August 2, a coroner's jury found him guilty. In Philadelphia, Burr entered into negotiations with the British minister to the United States, Anthony Merry, apparently with a view to breaking off the Louisiana Territory from the United States and forming a separate confederacy with himself at its head under the sponsorship of Great Britain. Merry wrote to the British foreign secretary that Burr, "the actual Vice-President of the United States," had offered "to lend his assistance to His Majesty's Government in any manner in which they may think fit to employ him, particularly in endeavouring to effect a separation of the western part of the United States from that which lies between the Atlantic and the mountains, in its whole extent."

Having contacted Merry, Burr then began plotting with the commanding general of the army of the United States, which, to be sure, consisted of only thirty-five hundred men. Like Burr, James Wilkinson is certainly one of the genuine villains in American history. He was already involved in treasonable correspondence with the French and Spanish. He knew Burr of old and he first encouraged him and then, as we shall see, betrayed him. With Wilkinson's assistance Burr contacted a number of discontented politicians from western Kentucky and Louisiana. Once more Burr approached Merry to try to get some assurance of British help. He needed a loan of half a million dollars to equip an expeditionary force that would seize New Orleans and establish the new "nation." There was further wild talk of invading Washington and hanging Jefferson.

Having sown such seed, Burr went to Pittsburgh and began the journey down the Ohio that we have already traveled with Francis Baily. Below Parkersburg, near the mouth of the Little Kanawha, he stopped off at an island owned by an Irishman named Herman Blennerhasset. Blennerhasset had graduated from Trinity College, Dublin, had been trained as a lawyer at King's Inn, had inherited a fortune, and had set out for the United States with a substantial library and apparatus for scientific experiments. Like Baily's friend Heighway, he had been entirely captivated by the country through which the Ohio River ran, had bought his island, and had begun the labor of building an English estate, complete with lawns and greenhouses. Blennerhasset and his wife were fascinated by Burr and intrigued by his grandiose schemes. In Blennerhasset, Burr found the man to bankroll his fantasies. From Parkersburg he floated on down the Ohio to Cincinnati and thence to Nashville, Tennessee, everywhere along his route sounding out sentiment for a separation of the Western country from the Union.

At Nashville, Burr found that the way had been prepared for him by a showman who had passed through displaying a wax statue of the vice-president after his duel with Hamilton. Now Burr was the toast of the town. Andrew Jackson, commander of the Tennessee militia, who had recently resigned as a judge in the state supreme court to devote full time to trying to get his own personal affairs in order, was especially cordial. He had nothing against duels. He had already fought two, killed one opponent, and threatened the life of a rival Tennessee politician, the famous Nolachucky Jack Sevier. Jackson provided Burr with a handsome barge to carry him to New Orleans.

At Fort Massac the vice-president spent four days with General Wilkinson discussing plans for the rebellion. On the way down the river Burr had encountered numerous Americans who, indignant with the federal government for not ousting the Spanish from their posts on the river, uttered rebellious sentiments. In New Orleans it was the Creoles and Spanish residents who expressed their displeasure with an autocratic American regime that allowed them no representation and imposed American law and the English language on them in defiance of the provisions of the purchase treaty. Perhaps the most significant barometer of the frontier mood was the fact that the killing of Hamilton, which in the East had caused shock and dismay even in Republican ranks, was praised and applauded. The West lived by the gun, and the Federalists were as much hated as the Spanish.

At New Orleans, Burr fell in with a group of some three hundred Americans who were planning to drive the Spanish out of the Red River region and indeed out of all of Mexico. Burr tried, without success, to enlist them in his plans to form a Western republic. By September, 1805, he was back in St. Louis conferring with Wilkinson, convinced the Western country was ripe for revolt. Wilkinson, for his part, had been doing his best to foment discontent in the army, even going so far as to sound out the officers under his command. He had been so firmly rebuffed that he apparently lost his nerve, and when Burr described the rebellious spirit in the Southwest, Wilkinson replied that "The Western people . . . are bigoted to Jefferson and Democracy."

Meanwhile, rumors of Burr's plotting began to circulate in

Washington. Stories appeared in the *Aurora* and elsewhere and rapidly became a subject of public gossip. Now Burr discovered that he could expect no help from the British. Indeed, the British foreign office, dismayed at Merry's inclination to fish in troubled waters, recalled him. Burr then turned, with breathtaking effrontery, to the Spanish minister to the United States, Marquis Casa Yrujo, and, through Jonathan Dayton, tried to prevail on the Spanish government to bankroll his venture. After a largely fruitless winter and summer trying to recruit men and raise money, Burr, his daughter Theodosia, and a handful of conspirators, among them Peter Ogden, a nephew of Jonathan Dayton's, and Samuel Swartwout, set out to initiate the rebellion and establish the new republic in the Mississippi Valley.

Again Burr stopped off at Blennerhasset's island. The poor, addled Irishman, charmed by the beautiful Theodosia and completely taken in by Burr's mad visions, readily agreed to the use of his island as a kind of staging area for the liberation of the West. He contributed money, supplies, boats, and his own considerable energies to what appeared to him a glorious and inevitably successful venture.

In the face of growing evidence of Burr's conspiracy, Jefferson seemed curiously unconcerned. Word reached him of boats being built at Marietta and other points along the Ohio and Mississippi. Men were being enlisted and supplies accumulated at strategic points. Finally, the district attorney of Kentucky, prodded by Joseph Daveiss, a newspaper editor, began proceedings against Burr in the district court at Frankfort. When Burr appeared on the day appointed for a hearing on the charge of treason with Henry Clay as his lawyer, the whole town was filled with his supporters, who jammed the courtroom and cheered loudly when the case was postponed because of the absence of an important witness. A few weeks later a grand jury was again impaneled, heard the testimony of witnesses, and exonerated Burr. That night a ball was given in his honor.

Meanwhile, Burr's lieutenant, Samuel Swartwout, had tracked Wilkinson down at Natchitoches on the Red River and delivered a letter from Burr informing the general that everything was in readiness for the military expedition. Five hundred men would leave the Ohio in November and rendezvous with Wilkinson at Natchez three weeks later. At this point the general decided to inform Jefferson of Burr's plans, hoping thereby to extricate himself. He sent a dispatch to the president describing Burr's plot in terms most likely to conceal his own involvement. When the dispatches reached Jefferson a month later, he finally took action, sending orders to army officers in

command at Pittsburgh, Fort Massac, and Chickasaw Bluffs to apprehend any men they had reason to believe might be involved in a
projected expedition against New Orleans. The governors of Ohio and
Kentucky were also alerted, as was Andrew Jackson.

William Henry Harrison, governor of the Ohio Territory, acted
promptly, calling out the militia and seizing the boats that were being
built at Marietta. Blennerhasset and some thirty of his supporters
escaped down the Ohio. Burr, arriving in Nashville, on the Cumberland River, found his friend Jackson in charge. Jackson himself was
between the devil and the deep. If he failed to apprehend Burr, his
own ties with the conspirator might come to light. If he arrested him,
Burr might try to implicate him in the conspiracy. Word was sent to
Burr that he had best get out of town as quickly as possible, and he
decamped for New Orleans with a nephew of Mrs. Jackson's in his
party.

At the juncture of the Ohio and the Cumberland, Burr joined
forces with Blennerhasset, and the combined party of some hundred
men continued on down the river. Jefferson's order had meanwhile
reached Wilkinson at Natchitoches, and he had proceeded to New
Orleans, where he took command of the city, commandeered merchant
vessels, and arrested Swartwout and Ogden without warrants or
charges. In a struggle over Wilkinson's authority to arrest and hold
Ogden, the judge of the court resigned and Wilkinson was left in
complete control of the city. Hearing of his betrayal by Wilkinson
and the arrest of Ogden and Swartwout, Burr landed his party on the
west bank of the Mississippi and established a kind of military camp
there.

The acting governor of Mississippi sent three militia officers across
the river to persuade Burr to give himself up. Burr did so. After he
was indicted and released on his own recognizance, he went into
hiding, and a reward of two thousand dollars was posted for his arrest.

Disguised as a boatman, Burr headed for Spanish territory. He
was recognized at Wakefield, Alabama, however, and after three weeks
in jail there he was sent on to Richmond, Virginia. There on March 30,
1807, he was brought before John Marshall. Ogden and Swartwout had
already been released on the grounds that Wilkinson had acted
illegally in arresting them. Jefferson had tried to prevail upon
Congress to validate Wilkinson's actions retroactively, but the Republican Congress had balked. The charges against Burr were treason and
misdemeanor. Since the charge of treason required the testimony of
two witnesses to an overt act, Marshall dismissed that charge but placed

Burr under bond to reply to the misdemeanor charge in the circuit court that would open its session on May 22.

The attorney general, constantly pressed by Jefferson, persisted in trying the treason charge. Jefferson's role in the prosecution of Burr is an enduring mystery. After ignoring for months the rumors of Burr's conspiratorial activities (failing, indeed, even to respond to letters informing him of the moves of the plotters, playing down and even misrepresenting to Congress the facts known to him), he suddenly threw himself into the Burr prosecution with a remarkable intensity. Although warned that the case against Burr was a weak one because of the strictness of the requirements for proving treason (Burr had committed to the time of his arrest no "overt" act), Jefferson insisted on pressing it. Certainly Jefferson knew that the disgraced Burr presented no political threat to him. Indeed the president expressed his conviction that Burr was at least somewhat mad in a letter to Du Pont de Nemours in which he noted that anyone who could have expected such a conspiracy to succeed "must be perfectly ripe for Bedlam." (Bedlam was the notorious London insane asylum, a symbol of madness.) John Adams wrote in a similar vein to Benjamin Rush that Burr "must be an Idiot or a Lunatick," and William Plumer, who knew Burr well, wrote, "Burr is capable of much wickedness, but not so much folly."

Why, if Burr was a ruined man, unstable to the point of insanity, was Jefferson so relentless in his pursuit of him? In any event, the consequence was another confrontation between Jefferson and Marshall. The trial, which lasted five months, attracted hundreds of onlookers of every political denomination to Richmond and occupied the attention of the country for the better part of the summer and fall of 1807.

Whatever the president's motives in pressing the prosecution of Burr, he must have been galled at the sight of the defendant going to court each morning attended by several hundred of his supporters. Even the impaneling of the jury to hear the charges and decide on the indictment was attended by intense drama when Burr challenged the method of selection and pointed out that two close supporters of the president had been placed on the jury illegally. Marshall upheld Burr's complaint. New members were chosen, and John Randolph of Roanoke was selected as a foreman. The defense requested the appearance and testimony of the president. Marshall considered the request and then read his opinion that since the president was a citizen of the United States, like every other American, he had no grounds on which to plead an exemption if his testimony were required. The court issued a subpoena to Jefferson, which he refused. However, the papers that the subpoena requested were delivered to the court. The counts returned against Burr by the grand jury charged him with having waged war against the United States and having undertaken an expedition to capture New Orleans.

The lawyers for the defense argued that the prosecution must prove that Burr had been present on Blennerhasset's island when the men there were assembled for the purported expedition. No argument that attempted to link Burr to them could be entertained by the court until it had been proved that they had been engaged in treason. Similar points of law were raised. Marshall considered the arguments of the defense lawyers and agreed: the overt act must be proved by the testimony of two witnesses. The prosecution had given no evidence that it could produce such evidence; in its absence everything else was hearsay. The testimony of the government witnesses was therefore inadmissible.

Marshall's decision effectively demolished the case against Burr, and it went promptly to the jury, which returned a verdict of not guilty. The charge of high misdemeanor remained, and a new jury was chosen to hear that charge. The federal statute concerning treason stated that for any person "within the jurisdiction of the United States, [to] begin, or set on foot, or provide, or prepare the means for any military expedition against the territory of any foreign prince or State, shall be guilty of a high misdemeanor." Again the indictment was found faulty, since Burr had not been present at the time specified in the indictment, and the jury once more returned a verdict of not guilty.

Now the government tried to switch the trial to the court of the territory of Mississippi. Marshall refused to do so, but he did consent to hear additional testimony as to Burr's treasonable acts, so for five weeks such testimony was given. Marshall then indicted Burr and Blennerhasset for preparing and initiating a military expedition against a friendly nation—Spain—and ordered them to appear at the next session of the U.S. circuit court at Chillicothe, Ohio.

Burr and Blennerhasset failed to appear at the appointed time and place, and that was the end of the affair. Burr slipped aboard a ship on the Delaware River and escaped to England. A few months later, he was expelled as an "embarrassing" person and found a temporary refuge in Sweden. Then he went to Paris, where he was constantly under police surveillance. He finally returned to England, where he lived in poverty for a year before finding his way back to the United States at the beginning of the War of 1812 disguised under a wig and with the assumed name of Arnot. In New York, he resumed his own identity and tried to take up his law practice, although he was still subject to prosecution by the government.

Theodosia's eleven-year-old son died not long after Burr's arrival in the United States, and the next year Theodosia herself died at sea on a trip from Charleston to New York to be reunited with her father. Her death was the most terrible blow of all. Burr was destined to live another twenty-three years, ostracized from the company of most of his old friends and eking out the barest living. At the age of seventy-three he married a rich widow and squandered her money.

Every year that passed made it plainer that Hamilton had been the victor in their fateful encounter at Weehawken. The kindest (and truest) thing to say about Burr, I believe, is that he was quite mad—all his brilliant talents, his family name, his fortune were wasted through his insatiable appetite for fame.

Jefferson, in his determination to see Burr hanged for treason, befriended every unsavory character who promised to help him achieve that end; the worst of all was Wilkinson, who managed to ingratiate himself with the president and escape the snare in which the other conspirators were trapped. Historians, by and large, have taken sides in regard to Burr's trial, depending on whether they were pro- or anti-Jefferson. The pro-Jeffersonians have emphasized the fact that Burr was undoubtedly guilty and suggested that Marshall bent the law to free Burr and embarrass Jefferson. The anti-Jeffersonians have stressed the president's sponsorship of the wretched Wilkinson, his apparent vindictiveness, and the clumsiness of the indictments, which, they argued, left Marshall no choice but to rule against the prosecution. The feeling persists that Jefferson, by acting promptly when evidence of Burr's plans were first brought to his attention, could have nipped the plot in the bud. His dilatoriness raises the possibility that he was determined to wait until Burr had thrust his neck so far into the noose of treason that there could be no escape from it. Such a supposition would explain his anger when Burr managed to elude his revenge. As for Marshall's role, he would have been less than human if he had not been pleased to be the source, once more, of embarrassment to his enemy. His decisions to exclude evidence were nonetheless perfectly defensible in strictly legal terms.

Perhaps the most plausible explanation of Jefferson's avidity in the Burr case was that he hoped to strike at Marshall through Burr. If Burr were set free, Jefferson was confident that the public reaction would be so strong that an amendment could be passed curtailing the authority of the Supreme Court. He wrote in this vein to the villainous Wilkinson: "The scenes which have been acted at Richmond are such as have never before been exhibited in any country where all regard to public character has not yet been thrown off. . . . However, they will produce an amendment of the Constitution which, keeping the judges independent of the Executive, will not leave them so, of the nation."

The most significant aspect of the entire Burr affair is what it revealed about the temperament of the frontier. Farfetched as Burr's scheme may have been, he could not have even conceived it if there had not been a very considerable amount of "separatist" (and expansionist) sentiment all up and down the Mississippi Valley. The principal lesson Jefferson and his Cabinet might have deduced from the episode was that the bonds that held East and West together were extremely tenuous ones.

29

To the Pacific

Having traveled down the Ohio River to the Mississippi and thence to New Orleans with Francis Baily, we are ready for a far more dramatic journey. Dispatched by Jefferson to seal the greatest achievement of his administration, the Louisiana Purchase, the Lewis and Clark Expedition ranks as one of the greatest explorations in history.

From his days as minister to France, Jefferson had dreamed of sending an expedition up the Mississippi to the Missouri, and then west to the "Stony" (Rocky) Mountains, and down some westward-flowing river to the Pacific. He had first tried to enlist John Ledyard, the indefatigible adventurer and explorer, to attempt such a journey from the West Coast eastward, but that venture required the permission of Catherine the Great of Russia, who claimed most of present-day Alaska as far south as California. Catherine gave her assent but then withdrew it and hustled Ledyard back to Poland. An effort in 1792, supported by the American Philosophical Society, had also proved abortive when the French minister denied passage through the Louisiana Territory to Meriwether Lewis and the French naturalist André Michaux.

In 1803, when Congress was debating the renewal of an act governing the establishment and supervision of trading houses dealing with Indian tribes of the Northwest, Jefferson saw another opportunity to further his pet project and persuaded Congress to authorize an expedition to contact other tribes that might become involved in trade. The real purpose—to explore a route to the Pacific—was concealed.

Jefferson's personal secretary, Meriwether Lewis, was afire to go, and Jefferson considered him an ideal leader, "intimate with the Indian character, customs and principles; habituated to the hunting life . . . honest, disinterested, liberal, of sound understanding, and a fidelity to the truth so scrupulous, that what ever he should report would be as certain as if seen by ourselves." Lewis chose his friend, William Clark, to accompany him, and Jefferson had both men commissioned as captains of infantry. They were issued detailed instructions and ample supplies: "Instruments for ascertaining, by celestial observations, the geography of the country through which you will pass, have been already provided. Light articles for barter and presents among the Indians [including handsome silver "peace medals" designed by John Trumbull for distribution to important Indian chiefs], arms for your attendants, say for ten to twelve men, boats, tents, and other travelling apparatus, with ammunition, medicine, surgical instruments and provisions."

"The object of your mission," Jefferson wrote, "is to explore the Missouri River, and such principal streams of it, as . . . may offer the most direct and practicable water-communication across the continent, for the purposes of commerce." It was to the Indian tribes that Jefferson wished the explorers to give particular attention: "The extent and limits of their possessions; Their relations with other tribes or nations; Their language, traditions, monuments; Their ordinary occupations in agriculture, fishing, hunting, war, arts, and the implements for these; Their food, clothing, and domestic accommodations; The diseases prevalent among them, and the remedies they use; Moral and physical circumstances which distinguish them from the tribes we know; Peculiarities in their laws, customs, and dispositions; And articles of commerce they may need or furnish, and to what extent."

Finally, since every nation had an interest "in extending and strengthening the authority of reason and justice among the people around them, it will be useful to acquire what knowledge you can of the state of morality, religion, and information among them; as it may better enable those who may endeavor to civilize and instruct them, to adapt their measures to the existing notions and practices of those on whom they are to operate."

In their dealings with the Indians they were to "treat them in the most friendly and conciliatory manner . . . allay all jealousies as to the object of your journey; satisfy them of its innocence; make them acquainted with the position, extent, character, peaceable and commercial dispositions of the United States; of our wish to be neighbourly, friendly, and useful to them, and of our dispositions to a commercial intercourse with them." The most prominent chiefs should be invited to visit Jefferson in Washington at the expense of the government. By the same token, if any chiefs wished to have their sons "brought up with us, and taught such arts as may be useful to them," the expedition should care for them and bring them back with them. They were also to teach the Indians how to inoculate themselves against smallpox.

Lewis and Clark were also instructed to pay close attention to "the soil and face of the country," to the plants, trees, animals, evidences of volcanic action, minerals, climate. Their observations were to be written on "paper-birch, as less liable to injury from damp than common paper."

Jefferson's instructions reveal him at his fascinating best. He had already made the trip a hundred times in his imagination, viewed the endless reaches of the Missouri, seen the "Stony" Mountains and, finally, the gleaming waters of the Pacific. Lewis and Clark were to be his eyes and ears. He was their brain and nervous system. The passing references to commerce are vastly outweighed by the "scientific" instructions, especially in regard to the Indians. It was the Indians who obsessed Jefferson. He was greedy for every detail of their lives, and, typically, he wished to bring to them as rapidly as possible the benefits of civilization, of "science" and "reason" and "justice," not to mention inoculation against smallpox, the most terrible killer of the aborigines. No doubt clouded his mind that all this must be beneficent. The Indians must be as susceptible to progress as the whites. Like Doddridge, and the vast majority of his countrymen, Jefferson simply could not imagine that the Indians might resist the advantages of white civilization, including eventual amalgamation with whites.

We fly over the country so casually today in jet airliners that it is difficult for a modern man or woman to conceive the spell its vast, unmapped spaces cast over on the minds of Americans early in the nineteenth century. Those almost limitless spaces contained, in addition to such rumored natural wonders as mountains of pure salt, the most exotic peoples on the face of the earth, the aboriginal tribes of America, perhaps the lost tribes of Israel. The expedition of Lewis and Clark was, of course, no secret to the American people. "Never,"

Jefferson wrote, "did a similar event excite more joy through the United States. The humblest of its citizens had taken a lively interest in the issue of this journey, and looked forward with impatience to the information it would furnish."

Lewis left Washington on July 5, 1803. At Pittsburgh, he picked up supplies for his journey and selected the soldiers to accompany him. The expedition floated down the Ohio much as Francis Baily had a few years earlier. Where the Cumberland joined the Ohio, the group was joined by William Clark. Various delays forced them to spend the winter months in a camp on the eastern bank of the Mississippi not far from St. Louis. On May 14, 1804, after the ice on the Missouri had broken up, they began their ascent of the river.

The group consisted of nine young Kentuckians recruited by Clark, fourteen soldiers from the Pittsburgh military post who had volunteered for the expedition, two Frenchmen—one a hunter, the other an interpreter—and York, a slave belonging to Clark. A corporal, six privates, and nine experienced rivermen were also engaged to help get the expedition over the first leg of its journey. A large part of the baggage contained bales of presents for the Indians—handsome silver- and gold-laced coats and plumed hats for principal chiefs plus the usual glasses, beads, paints, and knives valued by all the tribes.

Three boats carried the party and its equipment. The main boat was fifty-five feet long, drawing three feet of water with a forecastle and cabin and locks for twenty-two oars. Two other open boats of six and seven oars completed the little fleet. Two horses were led along the banks of the Missouri "for the purpose of bringing home game, or hunting in case of scarcity."

It was hard going from the first. The party had to fight its way upstream against the current, its way impeded by innumerable sawyers lying just below the surface. The river, swollen by spring freshets, was icy cold, and a chilly May rain frequently soaked the members of the expedition to the skin. Headwinds further slowed their progress to sometimes no more than three or four miles a day.

Twenty miles from the Mississippi, the party came to St. Charles, a French settlement of some hundred cabins and a Catholic chapel. The inhabitants, Clark noted, "unite all the careless gaiety, and the amiable hospitality of the best times of France. . . . they posses much natural genius and vivacity" and were capable of "long, laborious and hazardous . . . hunting excursions." But their exertions were "all

desultory; their industry . . . without system, and without perseverance." They were content to hunt and fish when they were hungry and
to cultivate luxuriant house gardens for their own table, but of trade,
growth, and progress they had no notion.

Another twenty miles up the river the party passed a small
settlement of "emigrants from the United States," and they encountered Kickapoo Indians who traded four deer for two quarts of
whiskey. The home territory of the Kickapoo was the headwaters of
the Kaskaskia and Illinois rivers, east of the Mississippi, but they
occasionally hunted along the Missouri. The Kickapoo were a minor
Algonquian tribe, consisting of no more than a hundred warriors and
perhaps five times that number of women, children, and old people.
They had joined forces with George Rogers Clark in his attack on
Vincennes and after the war fought alongside their traditional allies,
the Miami, against the incursions of white settlers into the Ohio
country. After Wayne's victory at Fallen Timbers, they had ceded a
substantial part of their land in return for a yearly annuity from the
government.

Making their way west and increasingly northward, the expedition
passed the last white settlement on the Missouri, and the next day two
canoes loaded with furs were encountered coming downriver from the
region of the Omaha Nation, and a large Pawnee raft from the Platte
as well as three others from the Grand Osage. At the Osage River, the
expedition entered the territory of the Osage Nation; like the Omaha,
the Osage were part of the Siouan family apparently located originally
in the region of Virginia and the Carolinas and pushed westward by
the more numerous and powerful Iroquois. The Osage divided their
time between hunting and agriculture, living in semipermanent
villages of oven-shaped houses fashioned of saplings and mud. They
raised corn, pumpkins, and beans. The nearby village of the Great
Osage numbered some five hundred warriors. An additional thousand
warriors inhabited two other villages. The warriors were large,
handsome men, "said to possess fine military capacities"; but because
their neighbors had secured rifles from white traders, the Osage
found themselves at a marked disadvantage in their encounters with
the Dakota.

The Osage myth of creation held that the founder of the nation
was a snail who lived a simple life on the banks of the river until a flood
swept him away and left him high and dry on the shore where the sun
"ripened him into a man." Tired and hungry, he was rescued by the

Great Spirit, who gave him a bow and arrow and taught him how to kill and skin deer. Returning to his home as a snail, he found a beaver ready to challenge him for control of the river, but the beaver's daughter prevented bloodshed by offering to marry him and share the river. The Osage had, therefore, always abstained from killing their brother the beaver, until the high prices offered by white traders for beaver pelts had made them less considerate of their relatives.

Now the travelers were well into Indian country where only fur traders ventured. From here on they were at the mercy of the numerous tribes, many of them warlike, who roamed the Plains and for whom the Missouri and its tributaries served both as rough dividing lines between tribal ranges and as a means of transportation for furs carried to St. Louis. The success of their mission depended on the skill and tact of the two leaders in dealing with the tribes they must encounter and on their own hardihood and perseverance in persisting in the face of increasingly difficult conditions.

Two French traders, their canoes bound together and loaded with the skins of beavers they had trapped at the headwaters of the Kansas River, informed them that the Kansas Nation was hunting buffalo on the Plains. Soon there were frequent signs of Indians, although they were seldom seen. Empty campsites, the hoofprints of Indian ponies, and the impressions of moccasins revealed their proximity. The riverbanks were a constantly changing panorama of open plain and cliffs. The party passed a series of salt licks and crumbling sandy banks and then limestone rocks inlaid with multicolored flints depicting various animals. While the main party took turns laboring at the oars, the hunters fanned out on horseback looking for game—deer and then bear.

As they approached the territory of the Sioux, the party felt considerable uneasiness. The Sioux were one of the dominant tribes of the Plains. They controlled much of the fur trade in the region and had the reputation of being warlike and unpredictable. On June 12, a French trapper named Durion was intercepted on his way to St. Louis with a raft of furs and buffalo tallow. Durion had lived as a trader with the Sioux for twenty years, and Lewis persuaded him to travel upriver with them to act as their intermediary and interpreter.

The next day the expedition came to the site of the ancient village of the Missouri Indians, members of the Siouan family, who had been virtually wiped out years before by the Sac and Fox Indians, Algonquian tribes who were traditional enemies of the Sioux. From that point on, the river was full of shifting sandbars that impeded the progress of the boats. Oars and sails did little to help. Ropes were attached to the boats, and they were towed from the banks or from the shallows along the shore.

The hunters ranged ahead shooting bear, deer, and an occasional raccoon or beaver, the tail of which was a prized delicacy. But mosquitoes made life miserable, and ticks constantly attached themselves to those who ventured into the river. Oars broke on hidden snags, and new ones had to be fashioned. In time, the labor of dragging the heavy boats upstream created a morale problem. As one exhausting day followed another, the members of the party were increasingly conscious of the fact that they were moving farther and farther from civilization and deeper into the endless plains and forests where they had nothing to depend upon but their own energy and resourcefulness. Seeing abandoned Indian campsites along the river was a reminder of the perpetual state of warfare among the tribes of the region and the danger of becoming caught in a net of inveterate hatreds that characterized the relations between various Indian nations.

At every stage of their trip Clark or Lewis recorded the data that Jefferson had instructed them to observe—temperature; character of the soil, flora, and fauna; indications of mineral deposits. Occasionally the explorers' basic diet of bear and deer meat was relieved by wild plums, raspberries, crabapples, and mulberries. They saw pelicans and flocks of brightly colored parakeets. At the juncture with the Kansas, the Missouri was five hundred yards wide, slow and turbid. Three hundred braves of the Kansas Tribe lived in several villages near the river. Like the Missouri, they had been greatly reduced in numbers by the Iowa, who, though they belonged also to the Siouan family, had thrown in their lot with the Algonquian Sac. The Sac and Iowa, armed with rifles, had inflicted heavy casualties on the Kansas villages.

The Fourth of July, 1804, was observed by the firing of a gun and the distribution of an extra gill (about four ounces) of whiskey to all hands. Wild grapes and roses grew along the riverbanks; geese and a wolf were sighted. One of the party was bitten by a rattlesnake and treated with a poultice. And so they struggled on, day after day, burned brown by the relentless summer sun, drenched by thunderstorms; fourteen bitter miles, three, eighteen on a good day; past creeks and rivers, grassland, wooded hills, limestone, redstone, clay, and sand; the river always mercurial, unpredictable, rising and falling with sudden storms or the entry of substantial rivers into its bed.

The river Platte was one of the principal reference points for the expedition. When they reached it on July 22 they had come some two hundred arduous miles. Wide and shallow, the Platte was the region of the Oto and the Pawnee. The Pawnee, the principal tribe of the Caddoan family, had originally occupied the region directly east of the Mississippi and south of the Ohio into Louisiana. By the seventeenth century, perhaps under pressure from the Iroquois, they had moved west to the area of present-day Nebraska. A more northerly group came to be known as the Arikara, or Ree, Indians. The Pawnee were the astronomers of the North American Indians. They believed certain stars such as the Morning Star and the Evening Star were gods, and the rituals celebrating them are among the most poetic of all those of the Indian peoples. The Arikara also referred to the stars for the best time to plant and to hold their religious celebrations. They believed corn had come into the world as a maiden, and to them its germination represented the life force. They worshiped a single, remote, all-powerful deity and the Mother Earth. It was to be their boast that they had never fought the white man; they were also hospitable to the remnants of other tribes who sought their protection, among them the Oto and the Missouri. The Pawnee, split into four small bands, were basically an agricultural people who supplemented their supplies of corn by hunting buffalo. In recent years the Osage, pushed westward by the Sac, had substantially reduced their numbers by constant warfare.

Past the Platte, the Missouri meandered through prairie and meadow, the banks lined with cottonwood, oak, black walnut, hickory, and elm trees. Now there were ample bags of geese, turkey, and deer for the hunters, and the river swarmed with catfish.

On July 31 scouts encountered and brought back to the river fourteen Oto and Missouri Indians—six of them chiefs—accompanied by a French trader who acted as interpreter. This was the first formal contact with Indians of the interior country, and Clark and Lewis rode out to meet them and give them presents of roasted meat, pork, and flour and meal. In return the Indians sent them watermelons.

Next morning a canopy made of a sail was raised for the visiting Indians to assemble under, and the members of the expedition formed up and paraded for their guests. Meriwether Lewis then addressed them, telling them that the territory was no longer under the jurisdiction of France but had been bought by the United States. The six chiefs replied in turn, expressing "their joy at the change in government; their hopes that we would recommend them to their great father (the president), that they might obtain trade and necessaries." They wished, above all, for arms and ammunition, since they were at war with the Omaha. As the "grand chief" was not present, a flag, a peace medal, and some silver ornaments were sent to him. The lesser chiefs received smaller medals, along with paint, garters, a canister of powder, and a bottle of whiskey, "which appeared to make them perfectly satisfied."

The absent grand chief had the impressive name of Weahrush-hah, which, as Clark noted, when translated into English, "degenerates into Little Thief." The spot was named Council Bluffs by the two leaders. They considered it an ideal place for "a fort and a trading factory," being a day's ride to the Oto, one and half to "the great Pawnees," two days from the Omaha, two and half from the Wolfe Pawnee, and not far from the hunting grounds of the Sioux.

Something must be said here about the Indian and the horse. Until the Spanish conquest of Mexico and the explorations of Ponce de León in Florida, no American Indian had ever seen a horse. In less than two hundred years, the ancient cultures of the Plains Indians had adapted to the horse in spectacular fashion. The horse was now the center of their tribal life. A warrior's or chief's standing with his fellows rested in large part on his skill as a horseman and on the number of ponies he owned or, more important, the number he could steal. The stealing of ponies thus became, next to hunting, the principal preoccupation of many tribes. Cunning, stealth, daring, and hardihood, the most admired qualities among the Indians, all were required to carry out a successful raid. The stealing of ponies had the advantage of being less hazardous than outright warfare while at the same time increasing the wealth and prestige of the successful raiders. Of course if the raiders were discovered by those they robbed from, they would be killed and scalped; in any event, as soon as their depredations were discovered, they were sure to be relentlessly pursued and if overtaken either killed on the spot or tortured to death.

The main Indian method of killing buffalo, by which, as William Clark said, "vast herds are destroyed in a moment," was to drive the herd off a precipice above the Missouri River. A young brave, disguised under a buffalo skin with the head and horns over his own head, would station himself near the herd. Other hunters on horse-

back would then raise a cry to start a stampede. The Indian in buffalo garb would then try to decoy the herd toward the cliffs, running
ahead of them, passing over the rim, and concealing himself on a
ledge below it. As Lewis and Clark noted, among the hundreds of dead
and injured buffalo, the Indians "select as much meat as they wish,
and the rest is then abandoned to the wolves, and creates a most
dreadful stench."

Many of the abandoned villages that Lewis and Clark passed on
their laborious progress upriver were reminders of the devasting
smallpox epidemics that had wiped out the great majority of their
inhabitants. Some once powerful tribes had been virtually destroyed. A
deserted Omaha village contained the burned ruins of over three
hundred cabins where three years earlier more than four hundred
men and the greater part of the women and children in the village had
died of the terrible disease. In Clark's words: "They had been a
powerful and military people but when these warriors saw their
strength wasting before a malady which they could not resist, their
frenzy was extreme, they burnt their village, and many of them put to
death their wives and children, to save them from so cruel an affliction,
and that all might go together to a better country."

As the party approached the country of the Mandan Indians, Clark
and Lewis undertook to act as peacemakers between the remnants of
the Omaha and the Oto. At the same time, in order to attract "any
neighbouring tribes," they set fire to the surrounding prairies. This
was "the customary signal made by traders to apprise the Indians of
their arrival." Chiefs of the Oto and Omaha came in, and Lewis,
through an interpreter, inquired about the reason for their hostility. It
began, he was told, when two of the Missouri who had found refuge
with the Oto had gone on a horse-stealing raid against the Omaha but
had been detected and killed. The Missouri had then felt compelled to
avenge the deaths. The assembled chiefs were given the usual gifts by
Lewis and Clark and were urged to reconcile their differences without
fighting.

In August there were two desertions, and one of the sergeants,
Charles Lloyd, died of "bilious colic." It was the first casualty of the trip
and temporarily dampened the spirits of the little party.

At the end of the month three of the men, hunting game, had
their first contact with a party of Yankton Sioux, who treated them to a
fat dog, "of which they partook heartily, and found it well-flavored."
The Yankton Sioux were part of the great Siouan family, which, in its

various branches and clans, dominated the Plains. The Sioux, or Dakota, became, indeed, the archetypal Indians. They were the buffalo-hunting "horse Indians" whose great chiefs were to be figures like Sitting Bull and Crazy Horse. It was they who wore the headdresses of eagle feathers and the soft-fringed and bead-decorated shirts that the average person today identifies as the costume of the Indians but that in fact was characteristic of only the Dakota, or Sioux. They lived in tepees made of buffalo hides, "painted with various figures and colors."

In physique, they were tall with broad shoulders and muscular bodies, high cheekbones and aquiline, or Roman, noses. Their traditional enemies were the tribes of the Algonquian family, who pressed on them from the southwest and north through southern Canada. Clark described the Yankton Sioux as having "a certain air of dignity and boldness" and noted that they were fond of decorations and used "paint, and porcupine quills, and feathers . . . with necklaces of white [grizzly] bear claws three inches long." The tribe had a group of young braves who had pledged never to retreat or avoid danger and who constituted a "shock force." "These young men," Clark wrote, "sit, and encamp, and dance together, distinct from the rest of the nation." They were so fanatic that once, when crossing the Missouri on the ice and coming upon a stretch of open water, they walked straight on; a number died before the remainder could be forced to stop by the rest of the tribe.

Another council was held. After Lewis had made his speech, he and Clark smoked the pipe of peace, distributed presents, and ate a substantial feast. Clark noted: "The young people exercised their bows and arrows in shooting at marks for beads . . . and in the evening the whole party danced until a late hour. . . . Their musical instruments were the drum, and a sort of little bag made of buffalo hide . . . with small shot or pebbles in it, and a bunch of hair tied to it. This produces a sort of rattling music."

The next morning the first chief, having consulted the others, replied in this fashion: "I see before me my great father's [the president of the United States's] two sons. You see me, and the rest of our chiefs and warriors. We are very poor! we have neither powder or ball, nor knives; and our women and children at the village have no clothes. . . . I wish, brothers, you would give us something for our squaws." The other chiefs spoke to much the same effect; "all the harangues," Clark wrote, "concluded by describing the distress of the nation; they begged us to have pity on them; to send them traders: that they wanted powder and ball; and seemed anxious that we should supply them with some of their great father's milk," by which they meant whiskey.

Pushing on, the expedition came upon their first prairie dogs, called *petit chien* by the French, living in villages by the thousands, and found nearby a forty-five-foot-long dinosaur skeleton "in a perfect state of petrification." They broke off some portions to send back to the president. They also saw large herds of buffalo and the swift and beautiful antelope (which they called goats), as many as three thousand at a time, dotting the plains and shadowed by numerous coyote, which Clark termed "small wolves."

At the end of September the expedition entered the territory of the Teton Sioux, the most numerous and powerful of that family. Protected from the Algonquian by Dakotan tribes to the east, the Teton Sioux grew at the expense of their neighbors. They specialized in horse-stealing raids against the Mandan, whose numbers had been greatly reduced by smallpox, often killing and scalping women and children while they worked in the cornfields. Taking to the horse culture with a vengeance, they had virtually given up agriculture and had stopped making the pottery for which they had been famous. They befriended the Algonquian Cheyenne, refugees from the east; but Pawnee, Mandan, Crow, and all the lesser tribes of the region lived in perpetual fear of their forays.

It was therefore crucial for the expedition to ingratiate themselves with the Tetons. Under the protection of the Teton Sioux, Lewis and Clark could proceed with relative safety as far as the foothills of the Rocky Mountains. The numerous Teton chiefs were given presents of the first class—laced uniform coats and cocked hats with plumes, medals, and tobacco. The principal chiefs were invited aboard the party's flagship and were even urged to spend the night. The most delicate diplomacy was involved, since the chiefs, fascinated by the white men and, above all, by the boats and the supplies they carried, were obviously reluctant to allow them to proceed up the river, holding on to the rope and clinging to the mast of the boat when they were asked to go ashore by Clark. They wanted whiskey and more presents, one chief announced. To this Clark replied that "we were not squaws, but warriors; that we were sent by our great father, who could in a moment exterminate them; the chief replied that he too had warriors, and was proceeding to offer personal violence to Captain Clark, who immediately drew his sword." The Indians responded by notching their arrows and forming a circle around Clark. The swivel gun on the bow of the boat was aimed at the Indians, and twelve men formed up behind Clark. It was perhaps the most dangerous moment of an expedition that had faced and would face innumerable hazards, but it passed when the chief ordered his warriors to drop back and then, having refused to shake Clark's hand in a gesture of amity, changed his mind and climbed back in the boat to accompany them to his village up the river.

At the village, Clark and Lewis were conducted to a council room formed of saplings covered with skins. There some seventy men sat in a circle around the chief. Four hundred pounds of buffalo meat were piled in the center of the circle as a gift for the whites. Near the chief, supported by two forked sticks, was the pipe of peace, the bowl made of red clay, the three-foot-long stem of ash, the whole decorated with feathers, hair, and porcupine quills. An old chief spoke of the tribe's need for the protection of the Great Father, and Lewis assured him of it. Then the old man sacrificed "the most delicate parts of the dog . . . held up the pipe of peace, first pointed it towards the heavens, then to the four quarters of the globe, then to the earth, made a short speech, lighted the pipe," and presented it in turn to Clark and Lewis. At the feast that followed the leaders of the expedition had their first taste of dog meat and of pemmican, dried and jerked buffalo meat mixed with grease and "a kind of ground potato."

The meal was followed by a dance, the music for which was provided by ten men who played a kind of tambourine of skin stretched across a hoop and a rattle with "five or six young men for the vocal part." The women, fantastically adorned and carrying poles decorated with the scalps and tokens of war taken by their husbands, danced alone in a "shuffle." Some of the scalps were fresh ones taken in a raid on their cousins, the Omaha, during which they had destroyed forty lodges, killed 75 warriors, and taken 25 squaws and children prisoners. The latter were a dejected and miserable-looking lot, and the American captains gave them awls and needles and interceded on their behalf with the chief. The Great Father, they told him, would wish them returned to their people.

The Sioux women were handsome, and both sexes appeared "cheerful and sprightly" but proved, on further acquaintance, "cunning and vicious." The warriors had their heads shaved except for a "small tuft on the top," which they allowed to grow long and wore in plaits decorated with an eagle feather. In ceremonies and on the warpath, they smeared their bodies with a mixture of grease and coal and wore over their shoulders a loose buffalo robe adorned with porcupine quills. The enlisted men of the party were at first disconcerted by the Indian custom of pressing their wives on them as bedmates, but they soon accommodated themselves to the practice.

When the expedition was ready to push on up the river, the Tetons again appeared determined to stop them, but the two captains faced them down and cast off. Now Indians rode along the shore following the boats and providing an unwelcome escort. The whites had the distinct impression that the Sioux were simply waiting for a convenient opportunity to attack them.

The next tribe the explorers encountered were the Arikara, members of the Caddoan family and cousins of the Pawnee. The Arikara women paddled out to the boats in canoes made of skins stretched over a basketlike frame and were astonished at the sight of Clark's slave, York, "a remarkably stout strong negro." York responded to their curiosity by telling them that he had once been an animal, but had been caught and tamed by his master, and he proudly displayed his strength.

Again there was a council and gifts and speeches. The Arikara were "tall and well proportioned, the women handsome and lively," but the tribe was plainly a poor one. They had little in the way of personal adornment but were "kind and generous" and did not beg as the Sioux had. The women were "disposed to be amorous, and our men found no difficulty in procuring companions for the night. . . . The black man York participated largely in these favours; for instead of inspiring any prejudice, his color seemed to procure him additional advantages from the Indians, who," in Clark's words, "desired to preserve among them some memorial of this wonderful stranger." In contrast to the Teton Sioux who had abandoned agriculture for the hunt and raid, the Arikara lived in semipermanent villages of lodges constructed of willow branches interwoven with grass, the whole coated with clay (which of course made them vulnerable to raids by more aggressive and nomadic tribes), and cultivated corn, beans, pumpkins, watermelons, squash, and their own kind of tobacco.

Beyond the Arikara lay the Mandan, who, before smallpox and the Sioux had decimated them, had occupied nine large villages along the Missouri where they pursued an agricultural and hunting life. It was with the Mandan, or near the Mandan, that Clark and Lewis decided to spend the winter. The river would soon start to freeze over, and it was essential to find a sheltered spot, hopefully adjacent to friendly Indians. Parties of Iowa and Minitari, the latter also known as the Hidatsa, Big Bellies, or Gros Ventres, who were allied with the Mandan and at war with the distant Shoshone, joined the expedition as it approached the principal Mandan villages. The ritual of the council was repeated. Lewis took the occasion to urge the Mandan to make peace with the Arikara. Presents were distributed with proper attention to the rank of the chiefs. The most popular proved to be an iron mill to grind corn, what we today would call "appropriate technology." Since the expedition wished to spend the winter with the Mandan, special pains were taken to establish cordial relations. Again York was an object of fascination for the Indians, and they were delighted when the white men danced with each other. Such dances, indeed, became the principal form of entertainment for the Indians.

The members of the expedition now began to build houses to store their supplies and huts to live in. When finished, the little complex consisted of two rows of four huts, each room fourteen feet square with a slanting roof. In addition, two large rooms were built for stores and provisions. Even before the structures were completed Indians came in a steady stream to observe what was going on and to receive gifts. One chief returned half a dozen times, bringing large sides of buffalo and deer, which were carried by his wife, who on another occasion brought a boat on her back for her husband to use in the river. Some uneasiness was created among the Indians by agents of the Hudson's Bay Company, who, anxious to discourage competition, circulated rumors that the white men intended to join the Teton Sioux in an attack on the Mandan. Clark helped to allay suspicion by offering to help the Mandan avenge the death of a young brave at the hands of Sioux raiders.

The religion of the Mandans centered on the notion of good medicine. Each member of the tribe selected a spirit or animal that became his "medicine," his intercessor with the Great Spirit. A Mandan whom Clark met boasted that he had offered up seventeen horses "to my medicine." The origin myth of the Mandan held that the nation had once resided in an underground village near a lake where a grapevine grew. Some of the bolder individuals climbed the vine and emerged above the earth, "which they found covered with buffalo and rich with every kind of fruits." They returned and told of the wonders of the world above, and the members of the tribe began climbing the grapevine to this marvelous land. When half of the tribe had ascended by this means, a fat woman broke the vine by her weight and the rest of the nation was forced to remain below, where the good Mandan would return after death.

Now the weather grew bitterly cold and much of the party's energy went into keeping warm and hunting deer and buffalo, which, thin and tough as they had become with the onset of winter, provided the group's principal food. Temperatures were often below zero, and frostbite was a constant danger. The blacksmith of the party became a major asset because he was able to fashion iron weapons for the Indians in return for corn.

Early in January, with the river frozen deep and buffalo scarce, the Indians held a buffalo dance designed to attract buffalo to the vicinity. According to Clark, it was devised by the old men of the tribe, and it is easy to understand why. When the elders had assembled around a fire, "with the image of a doll dressed as a woman before them, the young men of the village bring their wives along with food and tobacco." The women wear nothing but a robe or mantle "loosely thrown round the body." Each husband then goes to one of the old men and begs him to have intercourse with his wife. "The girl then takes the old man (who very often can scarcely walk) and leads him to a convenient place for the business. . . . If the old man (or a white man) returns to the lodge without gratifying the . . . wife, [the husband] offers her again and again. . . . We sent a man to this Medicine Dance last night," Clark added; "they gave him four girls."

The party suffered a serious setback in February when raiding Sioux intercepted hunters bringing back meat to the encampment, threatened their lives, and made off with the horses and sleds piled high with meat. At the Arikara villages the Sioux left word that "in the future they would put to death any of us they could, as we were bad medicine."

By April the ice on the river had broken up, and the expedition prepared to push on. Before leaving they packed boxes to be sent back to Jefferson with a cooperative trader. Included were a stuffed antelope with its skeleton, a weasel, three squirrels, a prairie dog, the horns of a mountain goat, elkhorns, a buffalo skin, and a number of Indian articles, all sure to appeal to the president's scientific instincts.

At the Mandan village, they acquired two interpreters, George Drewyer and Toussaint Charbonneau, a French trapper, whose wife, Sacagawea, was a Snake Indian captured by the Minitari in a raid and sold to Charbonneau. Sacagawea had her infant child with her.

The party of thirty-two, filling six canoes and two large barges, set off on April 6. Now the landscape changed. There were frequent hills, and the river often cut between banks so high that the travelers were unable to scale them. "Large irregular masses of rocks and stones" towered above them, black and yellow and red. By the end of the month they reached the Yellowstone River, wide and clear and shallow, flowing over a sandy bed uninterrupted by stones or rocks. On into May they inched their way north and west. The days were warm and sunny, but the nights were cold and there were occasional flurries of snow. The Mussellshell River, which rose in the Rockies, was an important landmark. There, they calculated, they had come 2,270 miles from the point where the Missouri emptied into the Mississippi.

The expedition reached the Black Hills late in May, and from their summit Lewis got the first glimpse of the Rocky Mountains, "the object of all our hopes, and the reward of all our ambition." Now the country was barren, treeless; the earth, pumice stone and black-weathered rock looking burned and desolate. Only elk, bighorn sheep, and jackrabbits were to be seen.

Near the headwaters of the Missouri the riverbed became more difficult to traverse. Clark noted: "The banks are so slippery in some places and the mud so adhesive that they are unable to wear their moccasins; one fourth of the time they are obliged to be up to their armpits in the cold water and sometimes walk for several yards over the sharp fragments of rock . . . all this added to the burden of dragging the heavy canoes is very painful, yet the men bear it with great patience and good humor."

As summer came on the familiar companions of the party returned; mosquitoes made their lives miserable. At the falls of the Missouri (in what is now central Montana), which they reached in the middle of June, they had to unpack the canoes and find a portage where they could carry their boats and equipment a distance of eighteen miles. Wheels were built to facilitate moving the boats, and the entire company had to make several trips to convey their supplies above the falls.

Pushing on up the river, the expedition was increasingly harassed by grizzly and brown bears who invaded their camps and stole unguarded food. Clark and Lewis took turns leading a small advance party ahead of the main body to scout the country ahead, find suitable campsites, and kill game for the evening meal. A succession of scenic wonders unrolled continually before their eyes.

In what is today southwestern Montana, perpendicular black

granite cliffs rose some twelve hundred feet above them, "a most sublime and extraordinary spectacle. . . . Nothing can be imagined more tremendous than the frowning darkness of these rocks, which project over the river and menace us with destruction." They called the range of rocks the "Gates of the Rocky mountains." Now the country grew familiar to Sacagawea. She recognized White Paint Creek and informed Lewis that they were approaching the three forks of the Missouri. A sharp lookout was kept for signs of the Snake (or Shoshone) Indians from whose tribe Sacagawea had been kidnapped. The success of the expedition depended on securing horses from them to carry the party over the Rockies to a point where the Columbia River or its tributaries would become navigable. Deer and elk grew scarce and buffalo were no longer to be seen, but geese, cranes, pheasants, and an abundance of gooseberries and purple currants helped to supplement the deer and antelope. Progress on land was impeded by the ubiquitous prickly pear, which was as much a torment to the men's feet as the mosquitoes to their heads, piercing their moccasins and having to be extracted from the soles of their feet.

When the expedition came, at last, to the forks of the Missouri, the two leaders named the southwest branch the Jefferson, "in honor of . . . the projector of the enterprise, and the middle branch Madison" (a river destined to become one of the great trout streams of the United States). A third river was named the Gallatin, and Sacagawea announced that they were encamped "on the precise spot" where she had beem camped when the Minitari (or Hidatsa) raiding party first came upon them. They had killed 12 men, women, and young boys and made the rest of the women prisoners, she told the two captains without any sign of emotion.

Proceeding up what they took to be the Missouri (of the three forks), they passed another substantial river, which Lewis named Philosophy, again in honor of his patron, Thomas Jefferson, the philosopher of democracy. (Unfortunately, the name was later changed to Stinking Water because of the river's strong mineral taste.) The next day Lewis named a river that the party passed Wisdom and another that, symbolically, emptied into the Jefferson, he called Philanthropy, the noblest of civic virtues. So Philosophy, Wisdom, and Philanthropy flowed into Jefferson, a conceit that must have pleased Lewis.

Sacagawea identified the Beaver's-head River as a spot where her tribe often made its summer camp. Now the search for her tribe became more urgent. Lewis, taking some of the hardiest members of the party with him, ranged far ahead and south of the river, resolved "to meet some nation of Indians before they returned, however long they might be separated from the party." Finally Lewis, searching the terrain with his field glasses, saw some two miles away a single mounted Indian whom he took to be a Shoshone. The task was to approach him without frightening him off. If he took alarm he might return to his tribe with word that Sioux were in the area, whereupon the whole band would decamp. When he came within hailing distance, Lewis took a blanket from his pack, and placing his rifle on the ground some distance away, he waved the blanket and placed it on the ground, the traditional signal that one came in peace and wished to parley, "a universal sign of friendship among the Indians on the Missouri and the Rocky Mountains." He then took off his shirt to try to indicate that he was a white and not a Sioux or Minitari warrior, calling out "*tabba bine*," or white man. Despite all his blandishments, the Indian turned his horse and dashed off through the willow bushes when Lewis was some hundred yards away.

Two days later Lewis and his companions came upon three Indian women. One fled but the others, seeing their escape cut off, sat down and bowed their heads, a classic gesture of an Indian inviting his or her enemy to strike the death blow. Lewis induced the women to stand, assured them by signs that they had only peaceful intent; he gave them some needles, beads, and two mirrors; and he daubed some red paint on their cheeks, "a ceremony which among the Shoshonees is emblematic of peace."

Lewis conveyed that he wished the women to lead them to the camp of their people, but they had only gone a short distance when sixty mounted braves came rushing toward them. Lewis put down his gun and walked toward the braves with the women who, when the Indians had reined in, explained that Lewis and his companions were white men and showed them the presents they had received. At this, three warriors jumped from their horses and embraced Lewis. "The whole body of warriors now came forward," Lewis noted, "and our men received the caresses, and no small share of the grease and paint of their new friends." The Indians then pulled off their moccasins as a sign of friendship and indicated to the whites that they should do the same. As he did so, Lewis could not help reflecting that Moses had likewise been admonished to remove his shoes when he stood on holy ground. The peace pipe was smoked, presents were distributed—blue beads and red paint were especially popular—and the entire party headed gaily for the Indian village.

There Lewis and the men with him were the center of fascinated attention. They were conducted to a lodge of willow and leather construction, and there was more smoking and distribution of trinkets. Food was scarce in the village, but the Shoshone were so relieved to find that their visitors were friendly white men rather than hostile Indians that the night was spent in dancing and singing.

The next day, Lewis undertook to try to persuade the Indians to accompany him to the forks of the Jefferson to meet Clark and the rest of the expedition and to enter into negotiations over the purchase of horses. The Indians, suspecting a plot to deliver them to their enemies, became instantly sullen and suspicious, and it took all of Lewis's diplomatic skill to persuade their chief, Cameahwait, to accompany him. White men, he told the chief, believed it dishonorable to "lie or entrap even an enemy by falsehood." If the Indians persisted in their suspicions, no white men would ever come to trade with them and bring them the guns by means of which they might fight their enemies on equal terms. If the Indians did not have the courage to go with him, he must go alone. Cameahwait at once replied that he was not afraid to die. Eight warriors joined him, and the rest of the village set up a cry of lamentation at what they conceived to be the imminent destruction of the bold ones; but the party had gone only a short distance before twelve more warriors joined them and finally all the men of the village and most of the women were trooping happily along, their fears forgotten.

As no one had had anything to eat for almost a day, Lewis sent two of his men ahead as hunters. As soon as this movement was observed a number of the Indians became uneasy and turned back to the village. Fortunately the hunters shot a deer, and when word reached the Shoshone they dashed ahead as fast as their ponies would carry them. When they reached the spot where Drewyer was skinning and cleaning the deer, "they all dismounted in confusion and ran tumbling over each other like famished dogs; each tore away whatever part he could and instantly began to eat it; some had the liver, some the kidneys . . . one of them . . . seized about nine feet of the entrails . . . yet though suffering with hunger they did not attempt as they might have done to take by force the whole deer." When the deer had been dressed, Lewis kept a quarter for himself and his men and gave the rest to the Indians, who ate it raw. Two more deer were shot, and the Indians, their appetites sated, were soon in excellent spirits.

When Indians and whites arrived at the river there was another awkward period because the boats under Clark's command had not reached the rendezvous, and the Indians once more suspected treachery. But Clark, leaving the boats to come on behind, had started walking along the bank with Charbonneau and Sacagawea. They had covered only a mile or so before Sacagawea began "to dance and show every mark of the most extravagant joy . . . pointing to several Indians . . . advancing on horseback, sucking her fingers at the same time to indicate that they were of her native tribe." As Sacagawea, her husband, and Clark approached the rendezvous point where Lewis and the Indians awaited them, "a woman made her way through the crowd towards Sacagawea, and recognizing each other, they embraced with the most tender affection." They had both been captured and had shared the rigors of captivity, but Sacagawea's friend had escaped and made her way back to her tribe. A few minutes later Sacagawea saw Cameahwait, one of two brothers who had survived the Minitari raid. In Clark's words, "She instantly jumped up, and ran and embraced him, throwing over him her blanket and weeping profusely."

With the expedition reunited and contact made with the Shoshone, Clark and Lewis were impatient to be on their way. They needed a guide and a number of horses. From all accounts of the Indians, the most difficult and dangerous part of their journey lay ahead of them—from the headwaters of the Missouri, or as far as it was navigable, up the steep and flinty eastern slopes of the Rockies, across the Continental Divide to the point where the rivers flowed west to the Pacific. They were told that game was scarce and that the paths, such as they were, were so strewn with sharp stones that even the tough Indian ponies came up lame or slipped from the narrow ledges with their packs. Nonetheless, there was no thought of turning back.

It was decided that Clark should set off with eleven men to search for the Columbia River and, when he found it, begin the construction of boats to carry the party down the thousand miles or so to the ocean. Meantime, bargaining for horses went on with the Shoshone. Three excellent horses were exchanged for a uniform coat, a pair of leggings, three handkerchiefs, and three knives. Another was traded for an old checkered shirt and a pair of canvas leggings.

At the edge of the Continental Divide, with two thirds of the epic journey behind him, Lewis took note in his journal of his thirtieth birthday—August 18, 1805. "I reflected," he wrote, "that I had as yet done but little, indeed, to further the happiness of the human race or to advance the information of the succeeding generation. I viewed with regret the many hours I have spent in indolence . . . but since they are past and cannot be recalled, I dash from me the gloomy thought, and resolved in the future, to redouble my exertions and at least endeavour to promote those two primary objects of human existence by giving them the aid of that portion of talents which nature and fortune have bestowed on me; or in the future, to live for *mankind,* as I have heretofore lived *for myself.*"

Clark's party made slow progress along the steep slopes and deep ravines that marked the rocky spine of the continent. On the second day out they encountered a small band of Shoshone who had built weirs to trap salmon. The Indians shared some of their catch with the white men. It was their first taste of Pacific salmon, sure evidence that their course now lay downhill. They had indeed entered into a new realm. As the life and economy of the Plains Indians revolved around the buffalo, the Indians of the western slope depended primarily on salmon—dried, smoked, pulverized, and made into a kind of paste and supplemented, in the seasons when salmon no longer ran up the rivers, by river fish, berries, and roots of various kinds.

The Indians who lived along the Snake and Columbia rivers were far less prepossessing than the horse Indians of the Plains. The "Pierced Noses," or Nez Percé, as the French had named them, were the most prominent tribe on the western slope of the Rockies. They had squat, stout bodies and broad faces. The Flathead Indians were disfigured by their practice of binding boards on the faces of their infants to flatten and elongate their foreheads. They were obviously pleased with the effect, but it did not enhance their appearance in the eyes of the whites.

The Shoshone, in a manner of speaking, straddled the Rockies. They were essentially Plains Indians, but they had been pushed back to the Rockies in a process by which the Iroquois, the most powerful and warlike family, had pushed the Algonquian—originally a family that had shared the Eastern hunting lands with them—into the Old Northwest and then west of the Mississippi.

The Algonquian, pressed by the white settlers and chastised by Wayne at Fallen Timbers, pushed on the Caddoan family, the Pawnee and Arikara and the Siouan family, and they, in turn, bore on the

Snake, the principal tribes of which were the Kiowa, the Comanche, and the Shoshone. As we have already noted, some of the antagonisms within families were as bitter as those between tribes of different families (the family being not a confederacy but a group of tribes related by similarities in language and culture). Thus, the Teton Sioux were death to the Mandan, also members of the Siouan group; and the Sioux took under their wing the Cheyenne, an Algonquian tribe. An additional irony was that the more remote tribes suffered severely in warfare with Eastern tribes from the fact that the closer the contact Indians had with the whites, the more commonly they were armed with the feared musket or rifle. Hence the hope of the Mandan, Arikara, and the Shoshone for trade with whites that they might procure guns and ammunition and thus have a better chance in battle against their traditional enemies.

The Shoshone, always fearful of encountering the Sioux who had inflicted dreadful casualties on them, suffered acutely each year between the end of the salmon runs and the time when they dared to venture back to the western rim of the buffalo country to hunt. The members of the expedition found the Shoshone the most appealing of the many tribes of Indians they encountered. In the words of Clark: "Such is their terror [of the Minitari or Hidatsa Sioux] that as long as they can obtain the scantiest subsistence, they do not leave the interior of the mountains; and as soon as they collect a large stock of dried [buffalo] meat, they again retreat, and thus alternately obtaining their food at the hazard of their lives, and hiding themselves to consume it." Nonetheless, they were "not only cheerful but even gay," and to Clark their character had in it "much of the dignity of misfortune." They did not beg as the Teton Sioux did nor steal as did the Arikara. "With their liveliness of temper," Clark noted, "they are fond of gaudy dresses, and of all sorts of amusements, particularly to games of hazard; and like most Indians fond of boasting of their own warlike exploits, whether real or fictitious."

The Shoshone were short in stature, "with thick flat feet and crooked legs." The most popular adornment of the men was a collar or cape of otter skin decorated with several hundred little rolls of ermine skin and a fringe of black ermine tails and appliquéd with shells of the pearl oyster. The seams of their leggings were sometimes fringed with "tufts of hair taken from enemies . . . they have slain." The killing of an enemy counted for nothing without the scalp to prove it. There were few old men in evidence and those the explorers saw did not appear "to be treated with much tenderness or respect." A warrior might have two or three different names in his lifetime. Each new achievement entitled him to a new name—"the stealing of horses, the scalping an enemy, or killing a brown bear."

Their government was "perfectly free from any restraint. Each individual is his own master, and the only control to which his conduct is subjected, is the advice of a chief supported by his influence over the opinions of the rest of the tribe." The man, as with most Indian tribes, was the complete master of his wives and daughters and could barter them away, "or dispose of them in any manner he may think proper. . . . The husband will for a trifling present lend his wife for a night to a stranger." Any sexual liaison not authorized by the husband might, however, be punished by death. Clark wrote that the women of the tribe were condemned "to the lowest and most laborious drudgery . . . they collect the roots, and cook; they build the huts, dress the skins and make clothing; collect the wood, and assist in taking care of the horses on the route. . . . The only business of the man is to fight; he therefore takes on himself the care of his horse, the companion of his warfare; but he will descend to no other labour than to hunt and fish." The shield of the Shoshone was a sacred object decorated by magic symbols that deflected arrows and bullets. In addition, many of the warriors wore suits of armor made of folds of antelope skins glued together until they were stiff and hard. Favorite horses were often painted, their ears cut in various shapes, and their manes and tails trimmed with bright feathers.

By the end of August, Clark and his party were back from reconnoitering a route through the mountains; and the whole party, provided with pack horses by the Shoshone, set forth on the last leg of the journey. Their path lay along narrow mountain trails where even the surefooted horses on several occasions slipped and fell down talus-covered slopes. When that happened the party had to halt and recover the baggage carried by the animal. It alternately rained and snowed, and game was so scarce that the men had to dip into the meager food supplies they were carrying with them. It was only the Indians they encountered along their route, fishing in the streams and river and drying their catches on the bank, who saved them from acute hunger and perhaps starvation. The aborigines sold them salmon, roots of various kinds, and, most important of all, large numbers of dogs. If the members of the expedition had felt an initial squeamishness about eating man's best friend, they soon got over it, and from the

Rockies to the ocean, roots, salmon, and dogs were the staples of their daily fare.

The Indians now encountered belonged to the general language group anthropologists have termed the Penutian family, made up of "California tribes" such as the Yokut, Klamath, Modoc, Cayuse, and Chinook. In present-day Washington, a number of so-called Shahaptin tribes were scattered along the Columbia River and its tributaries, the Nez Percé being the best known. The Klikitat, Umatilla, and Yakima were among the more prominent, but there were innumerable other smaller tribes with unpronounceable names: the Eneeshurs, "inhospitable and parsimonious, faithless to their engagements," who "in the midst of poverty and filth, retain a degree of pride and arrogance which renders our numbers our only protection," Clark noted; the Wallawalla, the most honest and dependable of all the tribes the party encountered; the Skeetsomish, Towahnnahiook, and Smackshop; the Multnoman, the dominant tribe on the middle Columbia; the Chilluckittequaw, Weocksockwillacum, Nehuh, Wahclellah, Clahclellah, Neerchokioo, and others too numerous to mention. The chief of the Chilluckittequaw startled Lewis by producing a medicine bag from which he proudly drew "fourteen forefingers" that he had cut off the hands of his dead enemies, apparently Indians of the Snake tribes. Tattooing was not uncommon, especially among the women; a Chinook woman had "Jonathan Bowman" tattooed on her leg.

The Nez Percé, or Chopunnish, were, as we have noted, one of the larger tribes and the first substantial one contacted by the expedition after it left the Shoshone villages. It was with the Nez Percé that the horses that had brought the party from the Shoshone to the headwaters of the Snake (Clark named it the "Lewis" but the name failed to take) were left against the day of the white men's return, and it was the Nez Percé who provided guides and food.

The Indians of the Columbia River region were all part of what might be called a root and salmon culture. They were short and bowlegged, in the opinion of Clark, from squatting on their haunches. Most were flatheaded. They lived in long lodges—sometimes over two hundred feet long, built of cedar and bark, sunk as much as six feet underground. Fires were made in pits in the center of these dwellings, often occupied by a dozen or more families. The men and women slept on shelves or bunks built along the sides of the lodge. Their dead were commonly wrapped in skins and stacked up like firewood in special structures.

The salmon and the bear were sacred, and the tribes had various rituals to propitiate their spirits. The first run of salmon in May was eagerly awaited and celebrated with joy, since it brought an end to their winter diet of roots and "pounded" salmon.

The river and coast Indians were as dependent on the canoe as the Plains Indians were on the horse. The canoes ran in size from small one- or two-man models to forty-footers that could carry twenty people or more and were handsomely carved fore and aft. All were made of redwood, and the white men marveled at the skill with which they were maneuvered even in the heavy seas of the Pacific. The status of the coast Indian women was much higher than that of the women of Plains Indians, which led Clark to make the shrewd observation that the condition of women rested, not on the degree of "civilization" of the Indian, but upon the economic utility of the women. "Where the women can aid in procuring subsistence for the tribe," he noted, "they are treated with more equality, and their importance is proportioned to the share which they take in that labour." The river and especially the coast women shared the fishing chores with the men and were the principal root gatherers. They also took their turns in paddling and steering the canoes. "They were permitted to speak freely before the men, to whom indeed they sometimes address themselves in a tone of authority," a liberty unthinkable among the horse Indians of the Plains. When a great feast was prepared the food was cooked and served by the men. The particular province of the women was basketry—the weaving and decorating of baskets, some of which were so tightly woven they could hold water.

Like the Sioux and virtually all other Indian tribes, husbands pressed their wives on their white visitors whenever they were camped near Indian villages. At the mouth of the Columbia an old Chinook woman brought six unmarried girls to the expedition's camp. She had a regular scale of prices according to her opinion of "the beauty of each female." To decline a husband's offer of his wife or daughter "for a fish-hook or a strand of beads" was "to disparage the charms of the lady, and therefore gives such offense, that although we had occasionally to treat the Indians with rigour, nothing seemed to irritate both sexes more than our refusal to accept the favours of the females."

Among the hunting tribes such as the Sioux and Assiniboin, the old were usually abandoned when they became a burden to the tribe in its constant movement and interminable warfare. In Clark's words, "As they [the Sioux] are setting out for some new excursion, where the old man is unable to follow, his children or nearest relations, place before him a piece of meat and some water, telling him that he has lived long enough, that it is now time for him to go home to his relations, who could take better care of him than his friends on earth, leave him, without remorse, to perish, when his little supply is exhausted." The more settled tribes of the West Coast seldom left their old to die but were attentive to their needs and showed deference at least to the old chiefs.

Gambling was a major preoccupation of many of the tribes, a pastime they pursued "with a strange and ruinous avidity," often gambling away their most precious possessions—their wives, canoes, and weapons.

One custom common to the tribes of the Columbia Basin was the use of the sweathouse. It was not unique to these tribes by any means, but it was especially favored by them. Such a facility was formed by damming a creek outlet, digging it out, and making a hollow square six or eight feet deep, covered over with a conical roof of woven branches and mud. "The bathers descended by [a hole in the top] taking with them a number of heated stones and jugs of water; and after being seated round the room, throw the water on the stones till the steam becomes of a temperature sufficiently high for their purposes." This was followed by a plunge in the icy waters of the river. One Indian they met varied the routine by washing himself down with his urine afterward. The steam baths were "so essentially a social amusement, that to decline going in to bathe when invited by a friend is one of the highest indignities which can be offered to him." Sometimes the baths developed into a good-natured contest to see who could endure the hottest steam without fleeing.

On their passage down the river the members of the expedition passed countless fish weirs and small groups of Indians fishing with raised spears, or gigs, and occasionally with hooks. The fish were spread on raised wooden racks to dry, and the air was pungent with the odor of burning hickory limbs. The Snake and Columbia rivers and their tributaries were the highways of the Indians who passed "in great numbers up and down the river," Clark noted.

The practical hazards of the descent of the river centered on the numerous rapids that constantly threatened to overturn the expedition's six canoes. Frequent stops had to be made for repairs and to dry clothing and supplies soaked by the turbulent waters.

By November, the expedition had reached the lower waters of the

Columbia. Here the river widened out to more than a mile across. Covered with flocks of duck and geese, the water was saline, indicating that the explorers had entered a tidal area. Here the Indians Clark called the Clatsop predominated, with the Chinook, Tillamook, and Kalamath. These tribes considered themselves the guardians of the river mouth and largely controlled the trade with the British and American trading vessels that anchored there, usually in May, and spent the summer trading. Many of the Indians wore sailors' clothes and hats. But like all the river Indians they went barefoot, because moccasins were ill-suited to their primarily aqueous environment.

In addition to such tribes as the Clatsop and Chinook, there were the Luckton, Youitt, Cookoose (these are all Clark's improvised phonetic spellings), the Ulseah, Kickawi, Kahunkle, Shiastuckle, Chilt, Clamoitomish, Killaxthokle, Quinult, and Calasthorte, most of the latter numbering no more than a hundred or so members.

Now the party suffered a new inconvenience, the perpetual rainfall of the region. For ten days rain fell almost continuously until the travelers and all their belongings were thoroughly soaked. Many of the men were stricken with bad colds and fever. Under such conditions it was almost impossible to hunt game, and hunger added to the misery of being cold and wet. Winter was coming on, and it was imperative to find a convenient and healthy spot to establish quarters. As Clark put it, the rain had "completely wet all our merchandise, spoiled some of our fish, destroyed the robes, and rotted nearly half of our few remaining articles of clothing, particularly the leather dresses."

On the alluvial lands stretching back from the river a tuberous root the Indians called "wappatoo" grew wild. These roots, traded for with the Indians, quickly became a staple of the party's diet.

On December 8, after several weeks of searching, the two leaders settled on a site for a fort, on which the men immediately began work, it was named Fort Clatsop after the nearby Indian tribe. Despite the constant rain, work went ahead on the huts and the buildings to be used to hold the dwindling supplies of the expedition. Hunters scoured the hills above the bay for deer and elk, and day after day a procession of Indians of various local tribes appeared to trade, talk, or merely look. Clark or Lewis inquired the names of each of them, their points of origin and their customs, noted their dress and weapons, and, so far as they could, their languages and dialects.

Once the huts were completed and those members of the party who were ill or in bad health were provided for, the two captains devoted much of their time to describing in detail the flora and fauna of the region. The routine of camp life was interrupted in January by news of a great event. A whale had beached on the shore near the mouth of the Columbia River, and Indians came from miles away to strip it to the bones, carrying away all the meat and blubber, fighting over every morsel with other voracious scavengers—gulls and vultures, foxes and wolves.

30

Homeward Bound

As the winter months passed, the Lewis and Clark company impatiently awaited the coming of spring and their homeward journey. The principal difficulty that faced them on the return trip was the scarcity of game along their route up the Columbia and Snake to the Missouri. The salmon had not yet begun to run, and the expedition's supply of trading goods, by means of which they might procure roots and dogs from the Indians, was much diminished. Indeed, the Indians themselves were often so short of food they could spare nothing for the white men. Elk and deer were scarce, difficult to hunt in the forest, and almost inedible from the rigors of the winter, so the members of the party had to make heroic efforts to lay in a sufficient supply of dried elk and venison, along with roots and smoked fish, to serve as a basic ration for at least the initial stage of their return trip.

On March 23, 1806, the party loaded their canoes and left Fort Clatsop. The progress was slow once the canoes had passed the lower river basin. Water was high and the rapids were far more difficult to ascend than descend. Portages were frequently necessary with all the tedious effort of unloading, carrying, and reloading. Canoes could not be towed successfully because of a lack of ropes, the irregular nature of the riverbanks, and the force of the current. Finally the captains decided to trade their canoes (and whatever else they could spare from their supplies) for enough horses to continue by land. Once they reached the area of the Nez Percé, they expected to reclaim their horses, proceed to the Shoshone, retrieve the canoes and barges that had brought them up the Missouri, and float downriver to St. Louis.

The negotiations for horses proved to be protracted and tiresome. Although the river Indians had little use for horses, they were symbols of wealth and status, and the Indians were reluctant to part with them for the increasingly modest articles left to the expedition. Finally, the combined efforts of Clark and Lewis managed to secure enough sore-backed horses to enable the party to push on. The fame of Lewis and Clark as doctors—men who made powerful medicine—preceded them, and when they reached Nez Percé territory they had nearly fifty patients awaiting them. Short of food, the two captains established a rough fee schedule: for a dose of sulfur and cream of tartar, a dog; for a major operation such as lancing and dressing an abscess, a plump colt.

The difficulties of communication are indicated by Clark's account of a council with Nez Percé chiefs. Captain Lewis spoke in English to one of the men in the party who knew French. He translated the captain's speech into French to Charbonneau, who translated it into Minitari for Sacagawea, who in turn translated what was said into Shoshone; finally a young Shoshone prisoner of the Nez Percé, who understood their language, translated the speech for them.

The most frustrating part of the trip home came when the party reached the entrance to the Rockies in May and found the snow still too deep for them to pass over to the headwaters of the Missouri. The delay occasioned by the condition of the trails through the area was made more debilitating by the bad health of a number of members of the expedition and the difficulty of obtaining food. It was primarily by trading Lewis's medical skills, modest as they were, for horses and dogs that a meager supply of meat was obtained.

In the middle of June the impatient travelers decided to set off once more. Although the snow was ten feet deep in some places, a crust had formed over which horses were able to walk without breaking through. So again, with infinite labor, the party advanced toward the Continental Divide, the hunters ranging ahead in desperate search of game. Three Indians were finally engaged for the extravagant price of two guns to lead the expedition to the headwaters of the Missouri. On the trail the explorers found the cache of supplies that they had left on the way west and gratefully loaded it onto their horses. For almost two weeks the party proceeded, their pace determined in large part by the availability of grass for their horses. Where they encountered meadows free of snow, they halted to let the animals graze. At Traveler's-rest, a luxuriant valley with grass for the horses and game for the men, the party split into two groups. Lewis, with nine men and an Indian guide, headed north for Marias River to see if it offered better access westward than the path they had followed. He would then descend it to the point where it joined the Missouri.

Clark traveled with the rest of the company to the Jefferson River. There they retrieved a cache of supplies along the riverbank, the most welcome portion of which for the men was plugs of chewing tobacco. Everything was in good order, and the canoes they had sunk and weighted with stones were repaired and refloated. Half of the party then started down the Jefferson in canoes, while Clark and half a dozen others rode on to the Yellowstone, built two canoes, and headed for a rendezvous at the juncture of the Yellowstone and the Missouri.

Coming down the Marias, Lewis and the men with him had the first serious clash with the Indians, a party of Minitari braves who tried to steal their horses and guns. In the fighting that followed, the Indians were routed and Lewis shot one brave in the stomach. The horses were recovered, and the men hurried on to their planned meeting at the forks, aware that they would probably soon be pursued by a Minitari war party. Pushing their horses as much as they dared, Lewis and his men traveled almost seventy miles down the Marias before stopping for a brief rest. Arriving at the conjunction of the Jefferson and the Missouri, they were overjoyed to meet the men who had arrived there. Now they had five canoes and a barge. The current, swollen by freshets and creeks carrying the runoff from the hills, was swift; and aided by the oars of the men the boats made a dazzling seven or eight miles an hour, the land rushing past them as they entered the last leg of their journey. Game was plentiful and plump from the spring grasses. Hunters sent ahead to replenish the larder brought in twenty-nine deer. Eager to be home, the party was early to bed under improvised mosquito nets and was on the river again at four or five in the morning. At the mouth of Yellowstone they found a note from Clark telling them that he and his men would meet them farther down the river.

It was August 12 before the two parties—Lewis's group and the men with Clark—were reunited on the Missouri near the mouth of the Little Missouri. Here they got the unwelcome word from two trappers that the Minitari, Mandan, Arikara, and Blackfoot Indians were all at war. This seemed to preclude the possibility of any of the chiefs' returning to Washington with the expedition; but Clark finally persuaded Big White, a Mandan chief, to accompany them farther. Now, however, they parted company with Sacagawea, of whom Clark wrote: "She has borne with a patience, truly admirable, the fatigues of so long a route, incumbered with the charge of an infant, who is even now only nineteen months old."

At the Arikara village, farther down the river, Clark heard that seven hundred Sioux warriors were on the warpath against the Mandan and Minitari. There he and Lewis renewed their friendships with the chiefs and urged them not to go to war with the Sioux.

Through the waning days of September the canoes and barges sped along down the river, often making fifty miles or more a day. On September 23, the expedition reached its immediate haven, St. Louis, where, in Clark's words, "we arrived at twelve o'clock, and having fired a salute went on shore and received the heartiest and most hospitable welcome from the whole village." They had been gone two years and four months. They had traversed nearly eight thousand miles across the most beautiful and terrible landscape in the world, parted from all that was familiar, all that was "civilized."

So ended one of the most remarkable odysseys in history, all of which—the endless journey up the mighty, eternal rivers, across the fearful mountains—was a projection of the imagination of Thomas Jefferson. It was his good medicine that sent them off and his spirit that accompanied them every step of the way across the continent and back. Man has been called a "reasoning animal," a "believing animal," and the like, but surely he is equally and perhaps preeminently a searching, exploring, journeying animal with an apparently insatiable appetite for traversing new landscapes. If, in America, that ancient impulse manifested itself as a national characteristic, the Lewis and Clark Expedition was the most powerful expression of it.

If the reader wonders why I have carried him or her on such a lengthy excursion, I must answer somewhat as follows. First, it is an adventure story of inexhaustible drama. Second, it serves to carry us across the whole staggering expanse of the country as it was experienced by all Americans who traversed it prior to the coming of the railroads and thereby gives us at least a fragmentary sense of our geography on the east-west axis. Third, it has introduced us to many of the Indian tribes who inhabited the country at that time and, I trust, conveyed an idea of the remarkable variety of those tribes as well as something of their customs and manner of life.

The expedition could have been accomplished only by men of the new breed. In it one can discern such themes as the relationship between democracy and leadership. Meriwether Lewis and William Clark were remarkable leaders. They did everything they expected their men to do; they undertook the most arduous tasks—trailblazing, hunting, negotiating with the Indians. They led the men of their party with consummate skill, inspiring and encouraging them, doctoring and caring for them; and they kept their voluminous notes and journals. In the face of every human and natural hazard, they patiently, heroically recorded *everything*. The expedition thus symbolized the scientific spirit of the new age, which initially was most occupied with observing and recording. Reading their account today, thrilling and absorbing as it is, we can hardly imagine the discipline of will that lay behind it, or the imaginative anticipation of almost every hazard and difficulty. How were the abilities and capacities of the odd lot of men who made up the expedition to be best utilized? Obviously and necessarily only by trusting each one of them with all the responsibility he could bear.

Certain members were constantly being detached on their own, often for days at a time, to procure game, round up stray horses, or search for companions slow in returning from a particular mission. What a happy inspiration it was to name rivers and mountains after them! There could hardly have been a better way to make them feel that they were engaged in an epic venture.

It was a joint venture in another way as well. It could not have been accomplished without the active assistance of many individual Indians and the cooperation of numerous tribes. Although the skill of Clark and Lewis in securing that cooperation was remarkable, at the hands of a large number of Indians the party received acts of kindness and generosity that were simple human responses that flowed naturally and spontaneously across the considerable chasm of racial and cultural differences. There is no more decent and humane account of white-Indian relations than the expedition's story, an idyllic tale in the midst of so many less happy encounters. That the leaders respected the Indians and were endlessly intrigued by them and their ways and, more important, managed to import much of that feeling to their men is abundantly evident.

Today when we lack even an adequate concept of the heroic, when our heroes are athletes, rock singers, and actors (a Gary Cooper and a John Wayne, make-believe heroes), it is difficult to conceive of the heroic dimensions of that marvelous journey. As much as we know, there is much more that we wish to know. In the relationship of the two leaders to each other, we are reminded of those classic masculine bonds, Damon and Pythias, David and Jonathan, who were "lovely in life and in death they were not divided." It was the prototype of a masculine relationship that is to be found only in war or on the American frontier when men's lives depend on each other.

Jefferson's genius was manifested in the sure instinct of an antimilitary man that the best "mode" for the expedition was an at least residually military one. It is easy to forget in reading the narrative that Lewis and Clark were both captains, so little does the conventionally military enter into their relations with the men of the expedition, but one senses it was nonetheless crucial to the success of the expedition. It made the right mix of authority and democracy possible.

Then there is the question of what came later. What was it like for Clark and Lewis and the other men of the expedition to live with the American continent in their heads, to return to the mundane considerations of daily life, conscious that they possessed knowledge, exclusive to them, of the vast, incomprehensible, uncommunicable strangeness and mystery of the continent and its aboriginal inhabitants?

There was about the whole adventure a primal innocence—white men and their red brothers unspoiled in Eden, a moment of purity, of grace, when man and landscape interacted in a continuous enthralling drama. Clearly the travelers were sustained by a kind of ecstasy, a continual euphoria that armored them against all hardships and perils. Luck, the handmaid of intelligent energy, was constantly with them, so that like characters in a fairy tale or folk myth they seemed invulnerable.

It was the middle of February, 1807, before the two captains reached Washington. There they were given heroes' welcomes. Congress voted them and their men "donations of land." Lewis was appointed governor of Louisiana and Clark brigadier general, in command of the territorial militia.

But there was a worm even at the heart of this splendid apple. The reader will recall Meriwether Lewis's gloomy reflections on his thirtieth birthday. Halfway through one of the epic adventures in history he deplored the fact that he had "yet done but little, very little, indeed, to further the happiness of the human race or to *advance the information of the succeeding generation* [author's italics]." This was the Protestant passion for redeeming the world with a vengeance.

Lewis found his new job as governor of the Louisiana Territory a thoroughly demoralizing one. The Burr conspiracy had left a dark cloud of discontent, and the threat of rebellion hung over the region. French, Spanish, and American settlers were hostile to one another and angry with the high-handed and arbitrary government imposed on them by Jefferson's administration. Lewis, surrounded by anger and suspicion, much of it the consequence of the fact that he was Jefferson's appointee, struggled to bring a degree of order out of chaos. But it was a shattering experience for someone of his tender sensibilities. How could it be that his idol and patron, the president of the United States, the hero of democracy and champion of the West, could have aroused such bitter resentment? Lewis lapsed into a depressive state. Clark and others who knew of his condition were alarmed. Jefferson called him back from St. Louis to Washington. On the way he stopped at Chickasaw Bluffs where the Indian agent, one Neely, found him so apprehensive and distraught that he decided to accompany him on the remainder of his trip. Delayed by the need to search for two lost horses, Neely remained behind while Lewis went on and found lodging in a house owned by a man named Grinders, a day's travel beyond the Tennessee River. Grinders was away and his wife was so disconcerted by Lewis's odd behavior that she moved into an outbuilding and left the house to Lewis. There, at three in the morning, he shot himself, or as Jefferson put it, "did the deed which plunged his friends into affliction, and deprived his country of one of her most valued citizens."

For Jefferson it was another of those grievous losses of which he could hardly bring himself to speak. Lewis had been like a son to him. He was thirty-four at the time of his death, handsome, brilliant, gifted, it seemed, with every splendid human trait, master of a continent, truly one who had gone to the mountains.

Speculation is vain but well-nigh irresistible. Was Lewis overwhelmed by the disparity between that generous and heroic world he had encompassed and the political antagonisms and bitterness that confronted him in his new role? Or was there, more simply, some secret wound or some genetic curse that had left him with nerves strong enough to endure the most formidable hazards of the wilderness but not the terrors of civilization? The symbolism is almost too pat. America was a land that could drive its best to madness, the greatest achievements shadowed by tragedy.

Clark must have been deeply affected by the fate of Meriwether Lewis and of his brother, George Rogers Clark, whose daring raids against the English posts in the Ohio country during the Revolution had made him a national hero. In his later years the older Clark lived crippled and impoverished in a crude hut on Corn Island in the Cumberland River. When, in response to his request for a military pension, he was sent a ceremonial sword by the Virginia legislature, he was reported to have said, "When Virginia needed a sword, I gave her one. Now she sends me a toy. I want bread!" thereupon snapping the sword in two with his crutch.

Having declined a command in the War of 1812, Clark accepted the post of governor of the Missouri Territory with his headquarters at St. Louis. There he reigned, at the entrance to the West, the most colorful and influential figure in the territory.

Next to Clark and Lewis in fame was the Indian woman, Sacagawea. She became a legendary figure. There were innumerable stories of her sudden appearance like a materialized myth to help a floundering party of emigrants find their way through trackless territory, to give help and encouragement in some desperate moment. Baptiste, the infant she had carried to the Pacific and back, with the encouragement of Clark, became a well-known guide.

On our travels with Francis Baily, we have already met Lieutenant Zebulon Pike in command of Fort Massac on the Mississippi. In the summer of 1805, before Lewis and Clark had returned from their expedition, General James Wilkinson, Pike's patron, dispatched him with several squads of soldiers to explore the headwaters of the Mississippi.

Pike departed from St. Louis on August 9, 1805, with a sergeant, two corporals, and seventeen privates in a keelboat some seventy feet long, provisioned for four months, with orders, as Pike put it, "to explore the source of the Mississippi making a general survey of the river and its boundaries, and its productions, both in the animal, vegetable and mineral creation: also to include observations on the savage inhabitants of its Banks."

The story of what followed was very similar, in many ways, to the experience of Lewis and Clark: laborious progress up the river against the current and sometimes against the wind, portaging around rapids, snagged by sawyers and caught on sandbars. Rowing, towing from the banks, and the use of sails carried them up the river. Hunters moved ahead shooting game and keeping the crew supplied. There were frequent contacts with Indians, primarily the Sac and Fox tribes. Past the Illinois, the Rock River, the Wisconsin, the Black, the Chippewa, and the St. Croix to Leech Lake where the Mississippi rose, the party made its way. They encountered numerous French traders who were alternately suspicious and helpful. They met William Ewing, an "Agent appointed to reside with the Sacs to teach them the science of Agriculture," and apparently a disastrous choice. Again the Indians were helpful. At the Des Moines rapids the Sac toted the heaviest loads. Tobacco, knives, whiskey, and peace medals were distributed and speeches exchanged pledging peace. At the Falls of St. Anthony, Pike enlisted a French halfbreed, Pierre Rousseau, as an interpreter and exchanged the cumbersome keelboat for smaller barges. Relations with the Sioux were sensitive, and Pike paid particular attention to their chiefs. The principal chief of the Sioux smoked the peace pipe with Pike and spoke pointedly of his *"New Father,"* a reference to the Louisiana Purchase. "He was happy to see one who knew the Great Spirit was the Father of all; both the White and the Red people; and if one died the other could not live long:—that he had never been at War with their new father, and hoped always to preserve the same good understanding that now existed." Afterward there was a feast of wild rice and venison and a dance, "attended by many curious maneuvres—Men and Women danced indiscriminately," Pike noted. "They all were dressed in the gayest manner, and each had in their hand a small skin of some description."

At the Racine River, Pike and his men watched several hundred Sioux warriors play a game called Le Crosse (now known as lacrosse), hurling a small ball and catching it skillfully with sticks having a leather webbing at their end. When his men had built a little settlement of huts, similar to those that the Lewis and Clark expedition had wintered in on the Missouri, Pike found himself "powerfully attacked with the fantastic's of the Brain. . . . I was like a person entranced, and then, could easily account why so many persons who had been confined to remote places, acquired the habit of drinking to excess; and many other vicious habits, which, have at first been adopted merely to pass time."

It was an exacting journey and Pike noted in his journal several days before Christmas: "Never did I undergo more fatigue performing the duties of Hunter, Spy, Guide, Commanding officer, etc, etc. Sometimes in front, sometimes in the Rear—frequently in advance of my party, 10 or 15 miles; that at night I was scarcely able to make my notes intelligible."

Near the headwaters of the Mississippi, north of Red Cedar Lake, was a trading post of the North West Company. This was Chippewa country, a tribe traditionally hostile to Americans. Again Pike and his men were on the alert, but an Indian Pike encountered told his interpreter that the Chippewa had greater admiration for Americans than for the English, Spanish, or French, "alluding to Warlike Atchievements . . . they [Americans] are White Indians."

Pike picked up a young Chippewa near the Savannah River and made him his special companion, though the two could converse only by hand signals. Pike became so attached to his Indian friend that when the Chippewa departed he "felt the curse of solitude," which induced him to reflect on the desolation of such a life. "The wealth of Nations would not be an inducement for me to remain secluded from the Society of Mankind, surrounded by a savage and unproductive Wilderness, without Books, or other sources of Intellectual enjoyment, or ever being blest with society of the cultivated and feeling mind of a civilized fair." It could only be the attachment that the traders felt for the Indian women, he concluded, that could reconcile them to ten, fifteen, or twenty years in the wilderness.

His legs and arms swollen with rheumatism and chilblains, Pike reached Leech Lake—which he took to be the Mississippi headwaters— on February 1 and spent the following day reading Volney's account of his travels in Syria and Egypt and perhaps reflecting on how much more arduous his own expedition had been. At Leech Lake, Pike mustered his little company of soldiers who had endured such hardships, put them through the manual of arms for the edification of the Sauk Indians, and issued them new clothes. They then went back down the river; and on April 30, eight months after they had set out, they were back in St. Louis.

Overshadowed as it was by Lewis and Clark's expedition, Pike's exploration was nonetheless worthy of comparison. His journal is a fascinating record of human ingenuity and endurance, and he added very substantially to the knowledge of a part of the Louisiana Territory about which little was known to Americans.

Pike had hardly had time to get his notes and journal in order before Wilkinson dispatched him on another expedition, this time to return some Osage chiefs to their tribe, to make contact with the warlike Comanche, to explore the Arkansas River to its source, and then to make his way to the headwaters of the Red River and down it to the Mississippi. Wilkinson wrote: "In the course of your tour, you are to remark particularly upon the Geographical structure; the natural History; and population . . . taking particular care to collect & preserve, specimens of every thing curious in the mineral or botanical Worlds, which can be preserved & are portable. [He was also charged with bringing back a number] of the most respectable Cammanches."

On July 15, 1806, three months after his return from the Mississippi expedition, Pike was off again, this time with two junior officers, a surgeon, sixteen privates, and two interpreters, plus chiefs of the Pawnee and Osage and their wives and children, to the number of fifty-one, who had been rescued from the Potawatomi and were being returned to their native village as a gesture of goodwill by the U.S. government. Pike's plan was to make his way up the Kansas River in boats to a point several hundred miles west of St. Louis and then strike across country to pick up the Arkansas near the middle of present-day Kansas. The Indian males walked along the banks of the Kansas with a number of the soldiers as protection, while the rest of the party pushed upriver with the boats carrying the baggage of the expedition and the Indian women. A month out from St. Louis, Pike and his company arrived at the Osage village, and the return of the chiefs and their families was an occasion for general rejoicing.

At the end of November, Pike sighted and tried to reach the peak that bears his name. He failed to climb it, but his description of what he called the "Grand Peak" resulted in its being named for him, the only substantial public reminder of his expedition. Turning south from the Grand Peak, Pike and his party made their way into present-day New Mexico. This was Spanish territory, and Pike and his men were apprehended and taken prisoner by the Spanish authorities. Pike's papers were confiscated, and the Americans were carried off to Santa Fe. When they were finally released, the party made their way down the Red River to Natchitoches, arriving there almost a year after they had set out. The fact that Pike never received the attention and acclaim that he felt the magnitude of his accomplishment merited was due at least in part to political considerations. He returned in the midst of the Burr conspiracy to find Wilkinson under a cloud that affected everyone in any way connected with him. Lewis had been Jefferson's special protégé, and Clark a member of an important Kentucky family. While Jefferson was much interested in the results of Pike's expedition, which his interest in Western exploration had certainly helped to stimulate, he not unnaturally gave first priority to the expedition he himself had dispatched. So Pike's great achievements have never found their proper place in our national folklore.

31

The Embargo

As the presidential election of 1804 approached, the Republicans chose George Clinton as their candidate to replace Burr. The Federalists ran General Charles Cotesworth Pinckney for president and Rufus King for vice-president, but they had little enthusiasm for the ticket, which was certainly a pedestrian one. Pinckney was an able and intelligent man who had performed valuable services for his country, but no one could confuse him with a political figure of force and energy who would be capable of drawing the shattered Federalists together or making any appeal to popular feelings. The Pinckney-King ticket seems to have come about as much by inadvertence as by choice. Now that Hamilton was dead, John Adams, stiff and austere as his public manner was, was the last Federalist with any hold on the popular imagination, and he had eschewed politics. The absence of appealing candidates was a measure of the decline of the party itself. Outside the literary circles dominated by the Hartford Wits and Joseph Dennie's *Port Folio*, it was difficult to find any up-and-coming young Federalists.

These were Federalist minuses. On the Republican plus side was Jefferson's charisma. He was the first president to impart a personal style to the office. Good Democrats were delighted at the stories of his presidential receptions where all formality was abandoned and everyone was treated alike without regard for rank or station. As the president had put it himself, he wished to bury "levees, birthdays, royal parades, and the arrogation of precedence in society. . . . In social circles," he declared, "all are equal, whether in or out of office, foreign or domestic; & the same equality exists among ladies as among gentlemen. . . . 'pell-mell' and 'next the door' form the basis of etiquette in the societies of this country."

All events seemed to conspire to enhance Jefferson's popularity. When the Louisiana Purchase was ready to fall into his lap, he stretched his principles to catch it. He got credit for dismantling the better part of an expensive navy and for using what was left to teach the brigands of Algiers and Tripoli a lesson they would not forget. Unwilling to take responsiblity for declaring war himself on the ground that he had no power under the Constitution to do so, Jefferson secured from Congress a bill authorizing him to take all necessary steps to protect American shipping in the Mediterranean.

William Bainbridge, commanding the *Philadelphia*, the first of the squadron to arrive in the Mediterranean, captured a Moorish ship that had recently captured a Boston merchantman. When he threatened the captain with death as a pirate, that gentleman produced an order from the governor of Tangiers authorizing the seizure of American ships. When Commodore Edward Preble arrived, he sailed to Tangiers, rescued a number of prisoners, and forced the governor to sign a new treaty guaranteeing the rights of American vessels in the Mediterranean. Word then reached Preble that the *Philadelphia* had run aground off Tripoli and been captured along with the captain and crew. Preble decided to blow up the ship in the harbor of Tripoli. On February 16, 1804, young Stephen Decatur and a raiding party slipped into the heavily guarded harbor, boarded the frigate, and set it afire. The famous British admiral Horatio Nelson called it "the most daring act of the age."

When news of the capture of the *Philadelphia* reached Jefferson, he asked for and received permission from Congress to build four more frigates to sail as soon as possible under the command of James Barron. Meanwhile, Preble borrowed eight gunboats from the king of Naples and bombarded Tripoli on five different occasions. Thrilling reports reached the United States of boarding parties engaged in hand-to-hand combat with Turkish sailors and marines. Decatur again distinguished himself in the fighting.

News of the American forays and victories redounded to the

further glory of Jefferson and the Republicans, and the election of 1804 became a landslide with 162 electoral votes for Jefferson and Clinton and 14 for the Federalists. Only Connecticut and Delaware went for Pinckney and King. The defeat of Federalism seemed complete.

A large part of the reason for Jefferson's success was that the Republicans had embraced Federalist principles. Federal power had grown spectacularly under Jefferson by virture of the Louisiana Purchase, which placed at the administration's disposal millions of acres of public lands. Jefferson had instituted a highly arbitrary government in the newly acquired region. He had built additional frigates to carry on a four-year-long war against the Barbary potentates three thousand miles away, and in his purchase of Louisiana and in the Barbary Wars he had increased the national debt enormously. As the historian John Bach McMaster put it: "The fusion of the two parties which so justly delighted Jefferson was due, therefore, not merely to the republicanizing of the Federalists, but to the Federalizing of the Republicans."

In his second inaugural address Jefferson pointed with pride to the achievements of his administration. The costs of government had been reduced by "the suppression of unnecessary offices, of useless establishments and expenses," and in consequence the unpopular excise taxes had been abolished and the charges of government met by import duties; it had become "the pride and pleasure of an American to ask, what farmer, what mechanic, what laborer, ever sees a tax gatherer of the United States?" The revenues from trade would in time be more than sufficient to discharge the public debt as well. Then any surplus might be used to improve "rivers, canals, roads, arts, manufactures, education, and other great objects within each state." If surplus funds were used for such public improvements and war was then forced on the United States, its expenses might be met by a temporary "suspension of useful works"; then, the war concluded (presumably by an American victory), such funds would "return to the progress of improvement."

Jefferson defended the Louisiana Purchase on the novel grounds that "the larger our association, the less will it be shaken by local passions." He added, "In any view, is it not better that the opposite bank of the Mississippi should be settled by our own brethren and children, than by strangers of another family?"

The president had a special word to say about "the aboriginal inhabitants of these countries." He had regarded them "with the commiseration their history inspires. Endowed with the faculties and rights of men, breathing an ardent love of liberty and independence, and occupying a country which left them no desire but to be undisturbed," they were "now reduced within limits too narrow for the hunter's state." Humanity therefore dictated that they be taught agriculture "and domestic arts" and encouraged "to that industry which alone can enable them to maintain their place, in existence, and to prepare them in time for that state of society, which to bodily comforts adds the improvement of mind and morals." To that end the government had "liberally furnished them with the implements of husbandry and household use" and extended to them "the protection of the laws."

Unfortunately, these "endeavors to enlighten them on the fate which awaits their present course of life" and, above all, to induce them to exercise that quality in which their white conquerors so excelled—reason—had encountered "powerful obstacles," most prominent among them the Indians' preference for their own customs and culture, "the habits of their bodies, prejudice of their minds, ignorance, pride, and the influence of interested and crafty individuals among them." Such people as these tried to inculcate in them "a sanctimonious reverence for the customs of their ancestors; that whatever they did must be done through all time; that reason is a false guide . . . that their duty is to remain as their Creator made them, ignorance being safety, and knowledge full of danger."

Much could be said about this passage in Jefferson's inaugural. It might be difficult, I suspect, to show that Jefferson was more "reasonable" than the aborigines for whom he expressed solicitude, but in the Age of Reason and in the Secular-Democratic Consciousness for which he was the spokesman, the notion of reason must rule, however unreasonable in fact. The Enlightenment understood all human beings to be essentially reasonable; that was their *nature*. To the mind that deplored the traditional forms of Western Christianity as remnants of superstition and bigotry, the mysteries and rituals of the Indians seemed hardly more enlightened. Jefferson was, after all, exemplary in his interest in the Indians. He had been a student of their culture, a defender of their rights, an admirer of their oratory. Like his fellow rationalists, Jefferson was quite ready to celebrate the Indians' many "noble" characteristics and to make comparisons between decadent white civilization and the happy innocence of the "lords of the forest." But when push came to shove, he expected them, as virtually all his fellow citizens did, to adopt the manners, values, and way of life of a more "rational" social order. There were indeed only two basic points of view held by Americans toward their aboriginal neighbors. One took the position that Indians were a brutal, treacherous, barbarous lot and should be exterminated; the other was fascinated by the Indian cultures, felt a deep attraction to them, studied them with devoted attention, recorded all that could be discovered about them, mourned their passing, and wished to assist the Indians themselves in acquiring the benefits of civilization, for clearly they could not remain as they were.

It is helpful to recall in this regard that one of Joseph Doddridge's motives in writing his history of the Indian wars was to preserve an accurate picture of the American aborigines for posterity. "The Indian nations," he wrote in 1824, "are now a subjugated people, and every feature of their former state of society must soon pass away." As a race they must inevitably become amalgamated with whites. That had been the fate of many conquered people before—the Assyrians, the Chaldeans, the Romans. "And yet the English, French, and Italians are, in part, the descendants of the ancient Romans. Such will be the fate of the aborigines of our country. They will perish, or lose their national character and existence, by admixtures with their conquerors." That was reason enough to preserve their history. It would become more fascinating and extraordinary, the further Americans were in time from the original events. The Secular-Democratic Consciousness, with its simple, optimistic view of human nature, could not imagine that there might be a "consciousness" utterly unlike its own and quite incapable of being transformed into something else by "reason" and "education." What was missing from all relations between white man and red man, or between "native Americans," as we prefer to say today, and all the immigrants who came to their land, was any adequate notion on the part of the immigrants of the mental world of primitive people or, more broadly, of human personality. If the immigrants had had such a notion, it would probably have done little in the final analysis to prevent the destruction of the Indian cultures, but many lesser tragedies might have been avoided or ameliorated. When the president of the United States, the admiring student of their cultures and their avowed champion, could express such impatience at their desire to preserve their old customs, it is small wonder that only tragedy lay ahead.

Jefferson's feelings toward Federalist newspapers were evident in his comments in his inaugural address on "the artillery of the press," which had been "levelled against us, charged with whatsoever its licentiousness could devise or dare." Such abuses "of an institution so important to freedom and science, are deeply to be regretted . . . they might, indeed, have been corrected by the wholesome punishments reserved and provided by the laws of the several states against falsehood and defamation." But other public duties were too pressing. Jefferson had, of course, encouraged the most libelous newspaper attacks on the Federalists, on Washington, and on Adams; he had sponsored Freneau, subvented Callender, and applauded Bache and Duane. Now he was getting some of his own medicine, and it was bitter to swallow. Joseph Dennie had been prosecuted and other Federalist editors had been threatened with legal action. There was, indeed, a threat in Jefferson's reference to "wholesome punishments" that had not been administered because the responsible officials were too busy. They might soon find time.

But the railings of the Federalist press had been in vain. The government, "conducting itself in the true spirit of the Constitution, with zeal and purity," had been vindicated. Jefferson's fellow citizens had pronounced the verdict by their votes. "Truth and reason have maintained their ground against false opinions in league with false facts, the press, confined to truth, needs no other legal restraints; the public judgment will correct false reasonings and opinions, on a full hearing of all parties." The fact that Jefferson devoted almost a sixth of his inaugural address to a discussion of the press reveals the depth of his bitterness against the Federalist newspapers.

As for the Federalists, Jefferson prayed that even they in time might see the light, that the scales might fall from their eyes, and let them perceive the "facts . . . piercing through the veil drawn over them." Then they would realize that their aspirations and those of the Republicans were in truth the same: "that the public efforts may be directed honestly to the public good, that peace may be cultivated, civil and religious liberty unassailed, law and order preserved, equality of rights maintained, and that state of property, equal or unequal, which results to every man from his own industry, or that of his fathers." Meanwhile the right-thinking Republicans must "cherish the Federalists with patient affection," do them "more than justice, in all competitions of interest," confident that in time "truth, reason, and their own interest would at length prevail" and "gather them into the fold of their country," completing thereby an "entire union of opinion."

This last was doubtless the unkindest cut of all to the Federalists. The implication was clear enough. The Republicans were the party of truth, reason, and patriotism; the Federalists, the party of falsity, unreason, and something that verged on treason. They must, eventually, be reconciled with truth and reason. Then there would be "union of opinion," no more party faction, and no more Federalists. Jefferson believed that true policy was discoverable by reason, that he had discovered it, and that those who dissented from his views were "unreasonable" or malicious. He yearned for "a union of opinion" when all should be "harmony." The union of opinion he yearned for was *his* opinion. With such a unity there would be no need for courts or parties.

Jefferson was not the first or last American politician to hold to such notions. The Federalists thought themselves the exponents of reason and truth and saw the Republicans as fanatics swept away by their irrational attachment to the French Revolution. The point is that under Jefferson's libertarian rhetoric there lay an ultimately authoritarian rationale. It was experience, not theory, that would teach Americans better. They did not yet understand the practical implications of the political principles they espoused. Real political democracy is only possible, I suspect, when we are willing to act as though our opponents have hold of some important portion of the truth, however much in our hearts we may doubt it. When we are determined to combine our conviction of the truth of our own ideas and the rectitude of our motives with overt political action, we have launched ourselves on the path of the dictator and tyrant. Both Federalists and Republicans were often as close to that fatal step as the Constitution would allow them to go. The Federalists had at least a theoretical edge in their awareness of the compromised and contingent nature of all human undertakings. Such an understanding adhered to in practice as well as in theory was an antidote to fanaticism.

At the end of his address, doubtless to reassure once more those who considered him an enemy of religion, Jefferson again invoked the support of "that Being in whose hands we are, who led our forefathers, as Israel of old, from their native land, and planted them in a country flowing with all the necessaries and comforts of life."

As his new term of office opened, Jefferson was faced with an issue that would overshadow every other aspect of his administration. The perpetually troublesome question of the trading rights of a nonbelligerent in wartime inhibited the commercial activity of the United States and vastly complicated the governing of the nation. The reader will recall the prophecy in Joel Barlow's *Vision of Columbus* that the development of international commerce would pave the way for the brotherhood of peoples of the world. We have talked about the enormous energy and capital resources that were channeled into the building of canals and the development of inland waterways, but these efforts paled in comparison with the ocean commerce of the Middle and Northern states.

The most potent expression of the emerging democratic-capitalist ethos was the trading empire of the United States, which reached from China to Africa to Argentina. Such was the enterprise of American merchants, the ability of her sailors and sea captains, and the ingenuity of her shipbuilders that with every passing decade her ships carried a larger portion of the world's sea traffic. In addition, the almost constant state of warfare among the major European powers, which subjected their ships to the perpetual threat of seizure by their enemies, offered an unparalleled opportunity for neutral American ships to carry often desperately needed supplies to the belligerents. At the same time, each warring nation went as far as it dared in restraining neutral trade with its enemies. Thus, a stream of "orders in council," of various proclamations and edicts, were issued by the various belligerents designed to gain advantages for themselves and deny aid to the enemy. Often such orders were issued and enforced without warning to vessels already at sea. Sometimes they were obscure in their language and subject to a variety of interpretations. Some were in defiance of accepted principles of international law or of existing treaties. The situation could hardly have been more chaotic. American ships, sailors, and cargoes were being constantly intercepted at sea, carried into the ports of one belligerent or another, and condemned as prizes of war. How could commerce flourish under such conditions? Enormous profits were to be made, profits that, in the judgment of those venturing their capital, made all the risks worth taking. There was a compensatory factor at work. The more ships seized, the greater the profits of those who slipped through blockades.

American ships found an especially lucrative trade in transporting the produce of the West Indian and South American colonies of Spain, France, and Holland to the mother countries. Silver bullion was carried from Mexico and Peru to Spain in American vessels. Sugar, coffee, indigo, and hides were all staples of the Caribbean and Latin American trade. Ships carrying the flag of the United States journeyed to La Plata, Vera Cruz, the Antilles, Dutch Guiana, and as far as Manila in the Philippines.

While the fleets of Great Britain controlled the seas, the trade of neutrals, and primarily that of the United States, provided her enemies with the supplies they needed to sustain the conflict. Thus, in January, 1804, Britain declared a "paper blockade" of certain West Indian ports. A paper blockade was one that could not be maintained by cruising war vessels but that, in effect, authorized privateers to seize any vessels sailing in defiance of it. In the following months the blockade was extended to the ports of England's continental enemies—to Dieppe, Calais, Dunkirk, and Ostend, among others. The blockade, reinforced by a decision in the British Admiralty Court, put an end to the highly profitable American trade with England's enemies. Henceforth only goods bought in the United States could be carried in American ships to an unblockaded belligerent port. For example, sugar loaded in Cuba, carried to Philadelphia and thence to Spain, a trade once permitted, was now proscribed. The result was to wipe out a major part of the maritime trade of the United States and produce a kind of panic in the ports whose prosperity depended on foreign commerce. Insurance companies refused to underwrite voyages made in defiance of the Admiralty Court ruling. Of the ships that defied the British edict, over a hundred were captured and their cargoes confiscated. The Caribbean was soon swarming with privateers that were little more than pirates operating under the sanction of the British definition of contraband. The boldest of these lay off the mouth of Charleston Harbor, captured American ships and crews, and subjected them to various outrages, often stripping them of their clothes and putting them in longboats to make their way to shore as best they could.

When Congress convened in the autumn, it was faced with a pile of petitions from seaport towns complaining of the new British policy and, in some instances, urging the government to take military action if necessary to protect American ships. The matter was refered to John Randolph's Committee of Ways and Means. Randolph, who had little sympathy with mercantile enterprise, let months pass without taking any action. Finally a resolution of nonimportation was offered, declaring that since the British seemed determined to act in an arbitrary and high-handed fashion, making their own rules concerning neutral trade and impressing American sailors, "no goods, no wares, no merchandise grown or made in England or any English colony or dependency should be imported into the United States."

The proposal for nonimportation of British goods was opposed by those Southerners who depended on the sale of cotton to Great Britain and on British products in return. The secretary of the ·treasury produced figures that showed that in the previous year the United States had imported some $36 million worth of British goods, creating a customs revenue of $5.5 million;. the balance of American commerce had come to only $6 million. Such a measure would do little, it was argued, except embarrass the United States financially and ruin the cotton planters.

A compromise was reached in the passage of a bill submitted by Joseph Nicholson of Maryland, who proposed a list of specific goods the importation of which was to be forbidden. By and large, they were things that no one stood in particular need of; the bill as passed appeared as more of an irritant to Great Britain than an act with any power to compel.

In April, 1806, Jefferson signed the bill into law. The same month a coastal sloop, the *Richard*, was fired upon without warning by a British warship, the *Leander*, whose captain had an evil reputation for stopping and bullying American merchant vessels and impressing American seamen. The shot was apparently intended as a warning to the *Richard* to heave to to be boarded, but it killed John Pierce, who was at the ship's wheel. The *Richard* escaped and made its way to New York, where the headless body of Pierce was laid out at the Tontine Coffee-House and viewed by thousands of New Yorkers as evidence of British brutality. Pierce was given a public funeral, flags in the city were lowered to half-mast, and church bells tolled.

The Tammany Society took the lead in mourning Pierce's death. The headquarters of the Society, known as the Great Wig Wam, flew a flag at half-mast, and the members of the Society were urged to wear black bands on their hats and coatsleeves and carry their bows and arrows with them in the funeral procession. The Federalists were quick to use the incident to create sentiment for war with Great Britain. New York sailors signed a petition accusing the government of cowardice in failing to protect their rights. The president, the petition declared, would do much better to spend more time attending to the defenses of the country and less to skinning and stuffing raccoons.

The Pierce episode provided an occasion for sailors and captains to launch a vigorous campaign against impressment. For years the British had been stopping American merchant ships, searching them, and carrying off any sailors that they determined, often by the most arbitrary means, to be British subjects. Impressment was, indeed, the most inflammatory policy of the British in the years following the end of the Revolution. A hundred merchant ships seized and condemned in English ports did not cause American blood pressure to rise as much as the story of a single American impressed by a British frigate. For Americans, this act was a symbol of the arrogance of the English. It mocked American pride and emphasized the powerlessness of the vestigial American navy. Washington had repeatedly condemned impressment and called for a halt to the practice. Adams and Jefferson had protested in turn, all to no avail. Now a flood of bitterness poured out. There was, in fact, little that Americans could do but rail. Even a navy ten times as large could not have protected the thousands of merchant vessels that covered the seven seas.

It was estimated that two thousand American sailors had been impressed between 1796 and 1801. Their names were painstakingly collected and efforts were made to secure their release, but the British naval officers put every possible obstacle in the way of their rescue. The situation was aggravated by the poor pay and brutal conditions of service on British ships and the high wages offered by American shipowners, which encouraged British sailors to desert at the slightest opportunity. So great was the exodus that the British navy and merchant marine were faced with the necessity of laying up ships for lack of crews to man them. At Norfolk, Virginia, the entire crew of a British vessel signed on an American warship. Thus, the British became more assiduous than ever in impressing sailors and more heedless of their true nationality.

The Americans, it must be said, encouraged the desertion of British sailors. Most Americans could see no reason why a man sensible enough to prefer the free life and high wages of a citizen of the United States should not be encouraged and harbored. The Virginia legislature with unconscious irony went so far as to pass a law making it a felony for any one to "deliver up, for transportation beyond the sea, any free person."

James Monroe, now ambassador to Great Britain, sought a change of British policy on neutral trade and impressment of American sailors from a series of short-lived governments. He had been instructed by

Madison to try to use the Non-Importation Act of 1806 as a means of securing concessions from the British. Before Madison's instructions could reach Monroe, he received word from Charles James Fox, head of the newest British government, that further restrictions were to be placed on neutral trade, including, of course, that of the United States. The European coast from Ostend to the Seine was already blockaded. All other ports were now closed to neutral ships that had come from, or intended to go to, any port of an enemy of Great Britain. While Monroe pressed for negotiations on the points so offensive to Americans, Fox became ill of the gout and died a few weeks later.

It was the end of August, 1806, before serious discussions between Monroe and William Pinckney, who had been sent to join him, and the British foreign secretary began. After four months of negotiations an agreement that did little more than reaffirm the much-abused Jay treaty was ready to be signed when Napoleon, having defeated the Prussians at Jena and having entered Berlin, thereby confirming his domination of the Continent, issued his Berlin Decree, which charged England with having violated the law of nations by "working paper" blockades. In retaliation, he declared the British Isles to be in a state of blockade and banned all trade with that country. Thus, while American merchants and sailors were still reeling from the effects of the British orders in council, Napoleon struck them another blow that threatened to wipe out what trade was left. The British commissioners, who in their view had made substantial concessions to Monroe and Pinckney, announced that things could go no further until it was apparent what the reaction of the United States would be to Napoleon's decree. Unless the U.S. government gave clear evidence of its determination to resist the Berlin Decree, the British must adopt equally draconian measures.

When Monroe and Pinckney protested such a condition as a form of blackmail designed to involve the United States in a war with France, the British negotiators signed the treaty. Before it was clear what the policy of the United States would be toward France, however, the king issued new orders in council that went substantially further than the earlier ones to which the U.S. commissioners had so strongly objected. Trade by neutrals between any ports of France or its colonies or allies was prohibited. Any ships involved in such trade would be subject to capture and confiscation.

The treaty negotiated by Monroe and Pinckney was rejected by Jefferson and Madison without being referred to the Senate. The two commissioners were told to await further instructions, but before they could be drafted, George Canning succeeded to power as the prime minister, became the foreign minister of a new government in which he exercised the principal power, and the British frigate *Leopard* fired on an American warship, the *Chesapeake*, commanded by James Barron.

During the tedious months of negotiation, British warships had performed fresh acts of provocation. Captain William Love of the *Driver* had been forbidden to enter any American port as a consequence of his high-handed and illegal actions. Ignoring the president's orders, he sailed into Hampton Roads, Virginia, and when warned to leave wrote an insolent letter comparing Jefferson with Robespierre and the United States to the Barbary States. In Passamaquoddy, Maine, the *Pogge*, Lieutenant Flintoph in command, searched shipping in the harbor; fired on the town, endangering the lives of children playing on the green; impressed some sailors; and shot away the rigging of a schooner at anchor.

In February, 1807, while a British cruiser was anchored at Hampton Roads, five British sailors escaped in a longboat and made their way to Norfolk where three of them enlisted on the U.S. frigate *Chesapeake*. A protest was made by the British consul at Norfolk and sent on to the secretary of the navy, who inquired of Barron whether the men were in fact British sailors. Barron replied that they were not. Two were free blacks, one from Maryland and one from Virginia. The other had been born on the Eastern Shore of Maryland. All had been impressed. A few weeks later five more British sailors deserted from the *Halifax*, also claiming to have been impressed.

American authorities refused to return these men, and one of them joined the crew of the *Chesapeake*. When this news reached Admiral George Cranfield Berkeley, commander of British war vessels in American waters, he ordered all ships to keep watch for the *Chesapeake* and, when encountered, to stop her and make a search for the deserters. The *Chesapeake* had recently been commissioned. Her crew had not yet received its training, and her guns were not unlimbered. On June 22, 1807, the ship left the waters of Hampton Roads and headed out to sea to replace the *Constitution* on patrol duty in the Mediterranean. The British frigate *Leopard*, waiting at the mouth of Hampton Roads, crowded on sail and pursued her. Overtaking the *Chesapeake*, the captain of the *Leopard* sent Barron a copy of Berkeley's order and expressed his intention of coming aboard to search for the deserters. Barron replied that none was on board and that none but the commanding officers could muster the men on an American warship. When this word delivered to the captain of the *Leopard*, he put his ship alongside the *Chesapeake* and delivered a broadside into the American vessel.

The *Chesapeake* was completely unprepared for the assault, and it was twenty minutes before a gun could be fired. Meantime the *Leopard*'s fire had killed 3 men and wounded 18 others, the *Chesapeake*'s hull had been pierced, and much of the rigging had been shot away. Barron struck his colors. The British came aboard, called up the crew of 375, took the 3 impressed Americans and a British deserter, one Ratford, from the *Halifax*, and returned to Hampton Roads. The next day the battered *Chesapeake* made anchor off Norfolk, and soon word of the attack had spread through the town, confirmed by the arrival of a longboat with eleven badly injured seamen in it.

The British consul wisely barricaded himself in his house, and British officers and sailors ashore hurried back to their ships. The citizens of the town met and passed resolutions forbidding any intercourse with British ships in the harbor and urging the wearing of black for ten days in mourning for the dead sailors and for the affront to the people of the United States. Preparations were made to defend the town, and when a British naval officer sent an imperious note demanding that food and water be supplied to British ships, the mayor reminding him that his demands had arrived on the Fourth of July, informed him that the decision not to supply British ships was one taken by the people of the town themselves and that he had no authority in the matter.

In port towns and cities from Charleston, South Carolina, northward, angry crowds met to express their indignation and call for strong measures against British warships in American waters. A proud and free people could no longer ignore such insolent flaunting of their honor, they asserted. Jefferson, under considerable pressure to declare war, issued a proclamation ordering all British ships to leave American waters immediately, barring them from procuring food or water in American ports. A message was dispatched to Monroe and Pinckney in London instructing them to demand from the British government the release of the sailors taken from the *Chesapeake*, the disavowal of the attack itself, the recall of Berkeley, and the abandonment of impressment. Congress was in recess, or it might have been difficult to avoid a declaration of war. When word reached Monroe of the *Chesapeake* affair, he presented Jefferson's demands to the new head of the British foreign ministry, George Canning. Canning replied that Berkeley would be recalled, renounced the idea of boarding or searching American warships, and agreed to send a special minister to the United States to explain the British position on neutral trade and determine appropriate reparations. But he would yield nothing on impressment, and Monroe broke off negotiations. As for the British public and press, they were as belligerent as their American counterparts. The *London Times* denounced Americans as insolent upstarts and urged a naval bombardment of seacoast towns to bring them to their senses.

In the United States a spate of pamphlets both for and against war were rushed off the presses. The Federalists blamed the crisis on the Republican policy of short and easy naturalization. Democrats had called the United States "the asylum of oppressed humanity," which was simply another name for "the vagabonds and wandering felons of the universe. Hordes of vulgar Irish scarcely advanced to the threshold of civilization, all the outcast villains, all the excrescences of gouty Europe" had landed in America and been thereby transformed from "slaves to citizens." These aliens introduced into American politics "the savage hatred" they felt toward England. The Republicans, of course, blamed the situation on the prior Federalist administrations for encouraging the British in their depredations and for alienating the French, America's true allies.

American commerce suffered an additional blow when the king of Spain followed Napoleon's lead and put out his own version of the Berlin Decree. When the American ambassador to France asked that U.S. vessels be exempted from the Berlin Decree because it conflicted with the French–U.S. Treaty of 1800, Napoleon, now emperor, replied that since Americans allowed the British to search their ships, she adopts the principle that the flag does not cover the goods, and that as she submits to the orders in council of England, so she must submit to the Berlin decree of France."

Napoleon, having defeated the Poles and destroyed the Russian army at Friedland in June, 1807, concluded the Treaty of Tilsit and then ordered neutral Denmark to join in the war against England or be invaded. The British, getting wind of Napoleon's plans, struck first. They demanded that the Danes surrender their navy to Great Britain for safekeeping until the contest with France was over. If the Danes refused, the British would level Copenhagen. When the king demurred, the British began a naval bombardment that destroyed half of Copenhagen and killed over 2,000 of its citizens. Every Danish merchant ship in an English port was subsequently seized and its cargo confiscated. Holland, under Napoleon's brother Louis Bonaparte, seized all neutral ships in the harbor at Amsterdam. As if all this were not enough, the British retaliated with a new order in council, forbidding neutral trade with France or her allies and requiring that all neutral trade enter some port of the United Kingdom or Gibraltar or Malta, pay a specified duty, and secure a license to trade. When word of Napoleon's policy and the new British orders in council reached Jefferson, he responded by pressing for an embargo on all American shipping. No vessel should leave any American port lest it become a hostage in the terrible game of war between Napoleon and Great Britain. Such an embargo, Jefferson was convinced, would soon bring the warring nations to a more tractable mood.

The most sensible and well-thought-out opposition to Jefferson's plan was expressed by Gallatin, who warned that such interference with the rights of individuals must produce a strong reaction and smack of the arbitrary and dictatorial. If Jefferson was determined to impose an embargo, Gallatin urged that it be for a specified period. Jefferson ignored Gallatin's suggestions, and his domination of the rest of the Cabinet was so complete that the members suppressed their misgivings and concurred in his scheme.

When a draft of the bill was presented to the Senate, that body suspended the requirement for three readings of a bill, and four hours later the Republican majority passed it in the form that Madison proposed it. In the House, after all attempts at amendment had failed, it was approved 82 to 44 and on December 22, 1807, became law.

Of all the responses that the administration might have taken, the embargo was the worst. Granted, the United States found itself in an impossible situation, challenged by both France and England; but the embargo, which fell on a particular section and class of people—the seaport towns of the North and Middle states, and merchants, sea captains, and sailors—could cause only bitter divisions and much actual suffering. Whereas the country needed to be united, the embargo split it. Whereas the maritime arm needed to be strengthened, it was seriously weakened as ships lay idle at their berths.

When news of the embargo reached the port cities, they erupted into a fever of activity that told more of what was to be the reaction of merchants and sailors than volumes of exposition could have done.

Every ship that could sail was rushed to sea. Anyone who could haul a sheet was recruited off the street to man such vessels. Ships that had anchored in the harbors prior to unloading their cargoes sailed off, preferring to take their chances of finding a purchaser elsewhere than be tied up by the closing of the ports. Since the Embargo Act did not apply to ships engaged in coastal trade, many merchants and ship's masters presented false bills of lading and shipping papers so that they could evade the embargo. This strategem soon became so common that Congress was forced to respond with a law requiring all coastal vessels to post a bond of double the value of the cargo—the bond to be forfeited if the ships sailed to a foreign port, almost invariably the West Indies.

Enforcing the embargo was comparable to attempting to plug a leaky dike. Heavy penalties were specified, and the practice of bonding was extended to riverboats and small vessels whose normal routes were limited to strictly local traffic—bays, sounds, and harbors—as well as to fishing boats and whaling vessels.

George Henry Rose, Canning's special emissary to deal with the *Chesapeake*, had meanwhile arrived and presented to Jefferson the demand that his order of July, 1807, following the assault on the *Chesapeake*, be publicly rescinded before any serious discussion could take place. To this calculated insolence Jefferson replied evasively, assuring Rose that the United States would not declare war against Great Britain in any event and asking, in effect, that Rose allow Jefferson to save face. Rose responded by suggesting that Jefferson draw up a statement along the lines indicated by Rose, postdate it, and deliver it to him with the understanding that he would then make known the British reparations for the attack on the *Chesapeake*. Jefferson complied, but when it turned out that the British required a disavowal from Barron for acts he had not done, negotiations collapsed once more and Rose prepared to return home.

Before Rose could leave, Timothy Pickering, secretary of state under Washington and Adams, wrote to him urging that Great Britain ease up on its measures against the United States. If England would allow time for the effects of the embargo to be more deeply felt, the country would vote the Republicans out of office, the Federalists would return to power, and they would be responsive to the plight of Great Britain in its life-or-death struggle with Napoleon. It is remarkable that Pickering was willing to run the risk of prosecution under the so-called Logan Act, which he had initially prompted when Dr. George Logan had meddled in diplomatic matters with France by entering into an intrigue with the British emissary aimed at defeating the official policy of the government.

The hope for a separate union of New England states, which had surfaced three years earlier at the time of Burr's campaign for governor of New York, was revived. Initially, New England separatists, or disunionists, had been convinced that the adherence of New York was essential to their scheme. This time men like Rufus King and Pickering seemed willing to have New England go it alone rather than remain part of a Union that included Virginia. Much of the animus of the diehard Federalists concentrated on John Quincy Adams, whom, because he refused to identify himself with their politics of desperation, they viewed as a traitor and whom they were determined to turn out of his seat as a senator from Massachusetts for voting for the embargo. In this they succeeded at the next election.

John Quincy Adams, for his part, felt that he was reenacting his father's defeat as president. He wrote in his diary: "The country is so totally given up to the spirit of party that not to follow blindfold the one or the other is an inexpiable offence. The worst of these parties had the popular torrent in its favor, and uses its triumph with all the unprincipled fury of a faction; whilst the other gnashes its teeth, and is waiting with all the impatience of revenge for the time when its turn may come to oppress and punish by the people's favor. Between both, I see the impossibility of pursuing the dictates of my own conscience without sacrificing every prospect . . . of retaining that character and reputation I have enjoyed."

Gouverneur Morris had similarily gloomy reflections on the embargo and the consequences of party spirit. The Republicans, he wrote to a friend, "thrive by sacrificing permanent public interest to a fleeting popularity. Their opponents therefore cannot expect favor from the people until the mischiefs that result from misconduct shall be felt."

Certainly the effects of the embargo were much as Gallatin had predicted. Seaports took on something of the aspect of deserted cities, at least in the areas of the docks, usually such a scene of bustle and activity. An English traveler in New York wrote: "The port indeed was full of shipping, but they were dismantled and laid up; their decks were cleared, and scarcely a sailor was to be seen on board. Not a box, bale, cask, barrel, or package was to be seen upon the wharves. Many of the counting houses were shut up, or advertized to be let; and the few solitary merchants, clerks, porters and laborers that were to be seen were walking about with their hands in their pockets. The coffee-houses were almost empty; the streets, near the water-side, were almost deserted; the grass had begun to grow upon the wharves."

Many unemployed sailors returned to their home farms, but there was a residue in every port city who were threatened by starvation. In New York a proposal was made to employ them on public works such as grading the streets and filling in boggy spots around the city; but, perhaps considering that sailors had little taste for such work, it was decided to enlist them in U.S. service and give them various "made" jobs at naval installations in the city. In Philadelphia the chamber of commerce provided funds to put them to work making rope, oakum, gaskets, and such maritime articles as they were competent to manufacture.

New England newspapers were filled with bitter attacks on the "Dambargo." They pointed out that Embargo spelt backward read "O-grab-me." There were innumerable satires and "squibs." "Why is the Embargo like hydrophobia?" "Because it makes us dread the water." A popular cartoon showed John Bull holding the head of a cow and Napoleon holding the tail while Jefferson milked it without a bucket. Smuggling, especially of flour, became endemic. Coastal ships carried flour south to the border of Georgia and Spanish Florida. There it was transferred in five-ton loaders, exempt from the embargo, to ships that carried it to the Indies. The same procedure was followed to the north at Halifax. In addition, much produce in Vermont and Maine was smuggled into Canada on sleds in the wintertime and by wagons in the spring.

When Congress began a debate on the best course to be followed in stopping such trade, a representative from New York named Gardenier rose to denounce the embargo in unsparing terms and accuse the Congress of conspiring to fasten the country "to the car of the imperial conqueror"—Napoleon. The charge threw the House into an uproar. An attack on Gardenier was answered by a challenge to a duel; Gardenier accepted it and was seriously wounded. Congress proceeded to include five-ton boats in its restrictive legislation and then went on to extend it to carts, wagons, and sleds.

To the indignation of Jefferson and the Republicans, smuggling flourished from Detroit to Buffalo and on to Lake Champlain. The president issued a proclamation stating that the country around Lake Champlain was involved in a conspiracy to defeat the laws of the United States and that its inhabitants were insurgents.

When Congress adjourned in April, it left Jefferson with authority to end the embargo. But at the insistence of the administration it had also passed a third supplementary embargo bill, designed once more to plug up a leak in the three earlier bills as well as authorizing measures for defense of the country and the building of a new quota of Jefferson's beloved gunboats. The effect of the original bill and its successors was to enmesh the most innocent supplier of Boston or New York City in a maze of regulations, paperwork, and bonds that had to be posted guaranteeing that no leg of lamb or crate of chickens would find its way to a European market. Jefferson, the apostle of minimum government, had imposed on the country such restrictions as it was not to experience again until the twentieth century. Regardless of how wise the embargo may have been in strictly philosophical terms, in practical terms it was a disaster. Any statute so obnoxious to a substantial portion of the population that normally law-abiding citizens will not observe it except by force is a bad statute in a democratic country. But the greater the public clamor against the embargo, the more determined Jefferson was to enforce it by whatever means required, even to calling out U.S. Army soldiers if necessary.

Jefferson would doubtless have been more than human if his punitive state of mind had not been, to a degree at least, related to the fact that his political enemies were concentrated in New England; to punish New England for its stubborn and "unreasonable" resistance was too good an opportunity to ignore. In his second inaugural address he had called on the Federalists to follow the rule of reason and be gathered once more "into the fold of their country," completing an "entire union of opinion." Now, however, the Federalists were once again acting defiantly and unreasonably, not to say treasonably and disloyally, thereby remaining outside "the fold." Conscious of his own rectitude, the president was determined to force compliance. So the strange game went on.

Someone had been discovered shipping flaxseed and pot ashes which might find their way to a European port. Very well, flaxseed and potash were placed under the ban. Flour should no longer be shipped from one port on the Chesapeake Bay to another, lest some illegal scheme was at work. Tighter and tighter the net was drawn, and more and more bitterly it was resented and ingeniously evaded. It all had little to do with England and France by this time. It had to do with Thomas Jefferson's obsession that he must be obeyed and his enemies punished. When the complaint was made that the government's restrictions were so inhibiting that the citizens of larger cities were in danger of starving, he directed the state governors to grant permits to individuals of unimpeachable character to bring in enough flour to prevent famine. The Federalists called such permits "Presidential Bulls and Indulgences," and the recipients of them "O-grab-me Pets." When James Sullivan, Republican governor of Massachusetts, protested against one of Jefferson's edicts that had been declared illegal by a Republican justice of the Supreme Court on circuit, the champion of states' rights and author of the Virginia and Kentucky Resolutions ordered him to comply and instructed General Henry Dearborn, secretary of war, to prepare to put down an insurrection in Massachusetts or elsewhere.

In the words of John Bach McMaster, Jefferson "made himself commissary for the nation, and declared what and how much people should eat." He proscribed the shipment of New Orleans flour to the bakers of New York lest it go astray at sea, and he made his wishes felt in the smallest towns as well as in the cities. A dramatist determined to write a play on the vanity of human pretensions and on the delusions of power and the irony of history could hardly have found better material for his pen. When a ship's captain at Buckstown, Maine, applied to Gallatin, who had the unhappy task of enforcing a law he had had serious misgivings about from the first, for a permit to sail, Jefferson ordered that before permission be granted in such a case, the character of the entire area must be taken into account. If it was "tainted with a general spirit of disobedience," then the person concerned must give proof that he had "never said or done anything himself to countenance that spirit."

At Sackett's Harbor in Jefferson County, New York, on the Canadian border, smugglers fought skirmishes with federal troops, and revenue cutters were fired upon by smugglers disguised as Indians. In another town a high-handed government agent and his crew were jailed by indignant citizens. Reports of such open defiance of the law and the government poured into the offices of the Treasury Department in Washington, and Jefferson gave them an inordinate amount of time and attention.

Jefferson's basic lack of sympathy with New England's commercial activity is revealed in a letter to a friend, Thomas Leiper, in which he deplored the "absurd hue and cry" that had been raised by those merchants who, in Jefferson's view, wished to sacrifice "agriculture and manufactures to commerce . . . and to convert this great agricultural country into a city of Amsterdam." It was "New England commerce," he wrote, "which has kept us in hot water from the commencement of our government, and is now engaging us in war."

Some of Jefferson's closest supporters were dismayed at the consequences of the embargo. Pennsylvania Democrat Dr. George Logan, always officious, wrote: "Your errors in conducting the exterior relations of our country oppress the minds of your best friends with the most anxious solicitude—you may yet retrieve your character and preserve the confidence of your fellow citizens. Call together your too long neglected Council [Cabinet], take the state of the Union into consideration, submit every subject with frankness to discussion, and, united with them, determine on such measures as may preserve the peace and honour of your country. Your own reputation imperiously demands that you should recede from pretensions and projects, which are demonstrably groundless and unjust." Robert Smith, secretary of the navy, followed Gallatin into muted opposition to the embargo. But Jefferson remained adamant. Subject since his mother's death to intermittent migraine headaches, he now suffered from them acutely.

In England, Parliament debated the orders in council, with Lord Grenville and Lord Erskine denouncing them as unconstitutional, against the laws of nations and even the Magna Charta. Petitions came to the House of Commons from a number of mercantile cities, but the opposition move to repeal the orders was overwhelmingly defeated.

On the Continent, Napoleon turned on his ally Spain; seized the country and Portugal along with it; and ordered all ships, including American vessels in the ports of Spain, Italy, and France, to be seized. When the U.S. ambassador asked why, Napoleon replied that he was simply assisting in enforcing the embargo. Some ships, sailing under U.S. colors, had evaded the embargo and were engaged in carrying on trade between European ports. These Napoleon would detain to assist in forcing compliance to the laws of Congress. By this stratagem Napoleon acquired over 250 American ships and their cargoes. He had crowned his brother Joseph king of Spain, but the Spanish people promptly rose up and turned him out, capturing an army of 20,000 French soldiers in the process. Thus, Napoleon came a cropper by virtue of a mass uprising of the Spanish under circumstances that recalled the uprising of French peasants and workers against their masters.

December 22, 1808, marked a year since the embargo had been imposed. The day was observed with demonstrations throughout New

England. Sailors at Salem assembled at sunrise at the North Bridge where a British reconnoitering party had been turned back in the days before the battles of Lexington and Concord and fired guns for half an hour. In other port towns, sailors and shipbuilders marched to funeral music, and ships in the harbors flew their flags at half-mast.

A young poet named William Cullen Bryant wrote "a satire" on the embargo:

> Go wretch! resign the Presidential chair,
> Disclose thy secret measures, foul or fair;
> Go, search with curious eye for horned frogs
> 'Mid the wild wastes of Louisiana bogs:
> Or where Ohio rolls his turbid stream
> Dig for huge bones, thy glory and thy theme.

If it was not clear how much England and France had suffered from the embargo, there was no question of the disastrous economic effects it had had in the United States. Federal revenues from duties collected on American shipping fell from sixteen million to a few hundred thousand dollars. There were estimates that as many as 50,000 sailors were unemployed and that a total of 100,000 men had been out of work since the beginning of the embargo. Many businesses failed, and thousands of individuals were imprisoned for debt. In New York City alone in 1809 1,300 individuals were thrown into debtors' prisons, and a year later 1,150 were still jailed for debts of less than twenty-five dollars. In the South, where many plantation owners were deeply in debt, "stay laws" were passed forbidding or limiting the collection of debts during the period of the embargo. Such laws were patently unconstitutional, but their proponents argued that the crisis made them necessary.

The greater the resistance to the embargo and its subsequent extensions, the more determined Jefferson was to enforce it. The Force Act, as it came to be called, was the unhappy culmination of Jefferson's abortive policies. Violating a number of the provisions of the Bill of Rights, most particularly the provisions against unlawful search and seizure and due process, the Force Act made the port collectors dictators with virtually unlimited power over every boat or ship that sailed, from a boy's skiff to a merchantman. The Federalists did not fail to comment on the fact that Jefferson, who had been unwilling to create a navy to defend American ships and sailors against

France or England, now ordered the employment of twelve new revenue cutters and the outfitting of all available naval vessels to enforce the embargo against his countrymen.

A handbill entitled "The Constitution Gone" declared that the Force Act made a mockery of all the principles the American Revolution had been fought for and left aggrieved citizens with no choice but "civil war or slavery." In various ports along the New England coast, the federal government's revenue agents were openly opposed. Sailors armed themselves and their ships and defied Coast Guard cutters to stop them. When General Dearborn, commander of the modest regular army, ordered governors to take action to see that the provisions of the Force Act were observed, Governor Jonathan Trumbull of Connecticut, father of the artist John Trumbull, refused, quoting the words of the Virginia and Kentucky Resolutions and stating that when Congress acted unconstitutionally the states were absolved from obeying. At Plymouth, Massachusetts, when a ship loaded with dry codfish put out to sea in defiance of the collector, she was captured and returned to Provincetown on Cape Cod. There forty "Indians" boarded her and sent her off to sea again. When the governor called out the militia, they declared that they would do nothing in support of the Force Act.

In the midst of the crisis over the enforcement of the embargo, the presidential elections of 1808 approached. Jefferson, following the example of Washington, made clear that he would not be a candidate. His heir apparent was his secretary of state, James Madison, and Madison was agreeable to the majority of Republicans. When a Republican caucus met in Washington to choose a candidate, Madison won out over Monroe, and Clinton was again selected as candidate for the vice-presidency. In the state elections, the Federalists appeared to be making a strong comeback. Massachusetts and New York were recaptured; Vermont and New Hampshire returned to the fold. But in the matter of selecting presidential electors, the Federalists showed little energy or imagination. Charles Cotesworth Pinckney and Rufus King were again put up in New York and were again defeated. An effort was made to rally Federalist voters behind George Clinton for president, but there was no clear leadership or intelligent plan.

A minor irony in the campaign was an article by Citizen Genêt, now married to George Clinton's daughter and an avowed enemy of the Republicans, who wrote in the *New York Register* denouncing Madison and Jefferson as "Gallo-Americans," tools of Bonaparte. The embargo, Genêt charged, "was dexterously contrived to comply, as much as possible with [Napoleon's] imperious wishes." Its secondary purpose was to "compel our merchants to turn to the plough and their wives to the care of a dairy, and the labor of the loom. . . . What a glory it will be to have accomplished such a useful and moral revolution without scaffolds, without bloodshed, and with the help alone of a few messages and letters. The maritime states humbled and empoverished, Virginia, resting on the arm of slavery, ruling the union in peace, Philosophy triumphant, and the sage of Monticello, having modestly thrown his mantle on his devoted servant [Madison], proclaimed by his disciples far superior to Confucius the legislator of China."

Madison and Clinton won over their lackluster opponents by a large margin, 122 to 46, with 6 votes for Clinton as president, but the Federalists made substantial gains in both the House and Senate, and the country remained in a state bordering on civil war.

Jefferson, in the final months of his term, refused to take any action in regard to the embargo on the grounds that his successor must be given free rein to deal with matters as he saw fit.

The results of the election were not officially known until January 4, 1809. For the next two months, until Madison's inauguration, the country was, in effect, without executive leadership. Jefferson looked forward, he wrote his French friend, Du Pont de Nemours, to retiring "to my family, my books and farms. . . . Never did a prisoner, released from his chains, feel such relief as I shall on shaking off the shackles of power. Nature intended me," he added, "for the tranquil pursuits of science, by rendering them my supreme delight. But the enormities of the times in which I have lived, have forced me to take a part in resisting them, and to commit myself to the boisterous ocean of political passions. I thank God for the opportunity of retiring from them without censure, and carrying with me the most consoling proofs of public approbation."

Despite Jefferson's inactivity, Congress, flooded with petitions from the state legislatures and pressed most urgently by members from the commercial states, voted in February, 1809, to raise the embargo and replace it by a nonintercourse bill, forbidding trade with either of the belligerents until they had revoked their oppressive orders in council against American shipping.

Four years earlier Jefferson had started his second term under the most favorable auspices. In the interim his actions and policies had produced economic disaster and political chaos in the states north of the Mason-Dixon line and considerable unrest in the Mississippi Valley. The assaults on the Supreme Court in the cases of Chase and, in a different manner, of Burr, had failed, but they had helped to make the Court a focus of Republican hostility. In enforcing the embargo, arbitrariness had replaced persuasion and force had been substituted for reason. Jefferson was well aware that he had left an unholy brew for his successor. Madison inherited a war that was at least in part a consequence of Jefferson's ill-conceived embargo.

But with Jefferson mythology always outstrips reality. In the long run, Jefferson's personal rancor, his deviousness, his authoritarian inclinations—what he *did*—mattered far less than what he represented. While it is true that his rank in the hierarchy of American heroes has risen and fallen in response to changes in the ideals and aspirations of his countrymen, he has always had a secure place in the "top ten." Through most of the history of the Republic, Washington clearly outranked him; and Hamilton, on occasion, has briefly superseded him. But Franklin Delano Roosevelt, by claiming him as the patron saint of the New Deal Democrats, assured his modern preeminence. He now ranks well above Washington in the minds of many Americans, especially those of a liberal persuasion.

But the basic schizophrenia remains, the unfathomable ambiguity. The author of the magic phrase, "pursuit of happiness," was dogged by personal tragedy all his life in the premature deaths of many of those closest to him. His father died when he was fourteen. One of his sisters, Elizabeth, was apparently mentally retarded; another died at the age of twenty-five. His closest friend and brother-in-law, Dabney Carr, died in his late twenties and was buried at Monticello where he and Jefferson had entered into a boyhood oath that the first to die should be buried there by the survivor. It was a devastating loss. Then came the unhappy episode with the wife of his friend, Jack Walker, that led to Walker's challenging Jefferson to a duel at the time of the Callender revelations.

Martha Wayles Jefferson bore her husband six children in ten years, four of whom died. In addition, she had several miscarriages. When she died in childbirth in the tenth year of her marriage, Jefferson collapsed and did not leave his room for ten days. His daughter, Martha, married Thomas Mann Randolph, a wild young man who eventually went mad and threatened his wife's life. His law teacher, George Wythe, was poisoned by a stepnephew along with

Wythe's black housekeeper and a young mulatto slave, who was apparently the son of Wythe and the housekeeper. Two of Jefferson's nephews brutally murdered and dismembered a slave who broke a pitcher that had belonged to their mother. One of his favorite granddaughters, Anne, married Charles Bankhead, a "worthless . . . malignant drunkard" who stabbed her brother, Thomas Jefferson Randolph, so severely that he almost died. Later when Bankhead, in a drunken rage, cursed his father-in-law, Thomas Mann Randolph, the latter struck him over the head with an iron poker.

Jefferson acknowleged the tragedy in his own life, if his admirers refused to. To a visiting Dutch nobleman who had commented "I pitied your situation for I thought you unhappy," Jefferson replied, "I have known what it is to lose every species of connection which is dear to the human heart: friends, brethren, parents, children . . . "; and in his correspondence with John Adams toward the end of their lives, he wrote poignantly, "I have often wondered for what good end the sensations of Grief could be intended. All our other passions, within proper bounds, have an useful object. . . . I wish the pathologists then would tell us what is the use of grief in the economy, and of what good is it the cause, proximate or remote." It was a rationalist's question that was not very satisfactorily answered by Adams's comment that grief "drives men into habits of serious Reflection sharpens the Understanding and softens the Heart . . . [serves] in short to make them Stoiks and Christians."

Most tragic of all was Jefferson's relationship with Sally Hemings. He feared and hated slavery—his dreams were haunted by visions of vengeful blacks—and loved a slavewoman. In his will five slaves were set free. Two of them—Burwell and Joe Fossett—were the sons of Sally Hemings's sisters. Another was John Hemings, half brother of Sally, the other two were Sally and Jefferson's sons. Madison and Easton Hemings, twenty-one and eighteen, respectively. Two of Sally Hemings and Jefferson's other children had "escaped," apparently with the tacit consent of their father. Sally herself, then fifty-four, was not freed in the settlement of the estate and was listed on the slave register as worth fifty dollars. Perhaps Jefferson's decision not to free her was due to the fact that under the laws of Virginia, a freed slave must leave the state at once. Monticello was as much the home of Sally Hemings as it was of Jefferson. To free her would have been to turn her out of her home. The historian Fawn Brody speculates that Jefferson did not free Sally because to have done so would have inevitably revived the old scandal by drawing attention to her. Jefferson's daughter, Martha, freed her two years later when the estate was sold and could no longer provide a home for Sally.

When the census of 1830 was taken, Easton Hemings, living near Monticello, was listed as white, as was an older woman living with him—Sally Hemings. After her death in 1835 her sons went to Ohio, and in 1873 Madison Hemings, then a man of sixty-eight, wrote in the *Pike County Republican* a detailed reminiscence of his life at Monticello, of the role of his mother as Jefferson's "concubine," and of his own descent from the third president of the United States.

We cannot treat the personal tragedies that haunted Jefferson's life as incidental or irrelevant to his political career. The fact that the final and irredeemable tragedy of his relationship with Sally Hemings lay at the very center of his domestic life symbolizes the tragedy at the heart of American democracy.

32

War Clouds

The small, neat, unassuming, and somewhat indecisive man who now became the chief executive of the United States was a classic intellectual. We have seen him in the Federal Convention giving his stamp to the Constitution of the United States to a greater degree than any other delegate. We have read his cogent arguments for that document in *The Federalist Papers*. We have heard him (rather indistinctly, to be sure, since he spoke in such a low voice) in the Virginia debates of the ratifying convention, patiently and brilliantly rebutting the flamboyant Patrick Henry.

Now James Madison was president, not by virtue of his own practical political skills (though he certainly had those) or as a consequence of wide popularity among the voters in general, but because the charismatic Jefferson had cast his cloak over him and made him his heir apparent. The situation was full of ironies. The most skillful expositor in the Federal debates of the Classical-Christian Consciousness, the philosopher of Federalism, had succumbed completely to Jefferson's magical evocation of the new Secular-Democratic spirit. Rigorously suppressing whatever misgivings he may have felt at Jefferson's attacks upon the Supreme Court and the Republican espousal of a notion of states' rights thoroughly antithetical to the views he had expressed in the Constitutional Convention as well as in *The Federalist Papers* themselves, Madison had become the dutiful lieutenant of the prophet of democracy and thereby the fourth president of the Republic. He ascended to that precarious eminence at a moment when the Union was more seriously threatened than at any time since its inception twenty years earlier. The separatist doctrines of the Virginia and Kentucky Resolutions that his leader had drafted ten years earlier and that he himself had espoused were now being hurled in his face by mutinous New Englanders. The Monroe faction of his own party was ready to pounce upon him; John Randolph's vengeful attitude toward Jefferson had been transferred to his successor.

Madison was one of the last of what were now coming to be called "the Fathers"—the great figures of the Revolution—left in active politics. Perhaps at the insistence of his handsome and vivacious wife, Dolley, his inauguration was attended by all the pomp that Jefferson had so conspicuously disavowed as representing the trappings of monarchy. A company of uniformed militia escorted him to the Capitol. Ten thousand people, it was said, attended the inauguration ceremony.

As the new president began his inaugural address, he appeared "extremely pale and trembled excessively . . . but soon gained confidence and spoke audibly," for Madison something of a triumph. Most of his speech was taken up, not surprisingly, with "the injustice and violence of the belligerent powers"—France and England—and the efforts of the United States to fulfill its "neutral obligations with the most scrupulous impartiality." He assured his audience that he would do his best to maintain peace while preserving the honor of the United States, "to promote . . . improvements friendly to agriculture, to manufactures, and to external as well as internal commerce." Like Jefferson before him, he promised "to carry on the benevolent plans which have been so meritoriously applied to the conversion of our aboriginal neighbors from the degradation and wretchedness of savage life to a participation in the improvements of which the human mind and manners are susceptible in a civilized state."

Margaret Bayard Smith, a devoted Republican whose husband, Samuel, had edited the *National Intelligencer*, the semiofficial newspaper of the Republican administration, wrote in her diary: "To-day after the inauguration, we all went to Mrs. Madison's. The street was full of carriages and people, and we had to wait near half an hour, before we could get in. . . . Near the door of the drawing room Mr. and Mrs. Madison stood to receive their company. She looked extremely beautiful . . . all dignity, grace and affability . . . thousands and thousands of people thronged the avenue. . . . Every inch of space at the Capitol was crowded and there being as many ladies as gentlemen, all in full dress, it gave rather a gay than a solemn appearance."

When seats were sought for the Democratic ladies and gentlemen, it was discovered that "the sovereign people would not resign their privileges and the high and low were promiscuously blended on the floor and in the galleries." That night at the inaugural ball, with the hall so crowded windows had to be broken to allow in some air, Dolley Madison shone "like a Queen while her husband looked exhausted." At Margaret Smith's comment that she wished she could offer him a chair, the new president replied wanly, " 'I wish so too,' . . . looking as if he could hardly stand."

So began Madison's administration. Under pressure from the radical wing of his party to dismiss Albert Gallatin as secretary of the treasury, he clung doggedly to the brilliant and independent Swiss immigrant, but as a sop to the left faction he nominated Robert Smith, a party stalwart, but a pompous and ineffective man, as secretary of state. Smith proved so inept that Madison had in effect to act as his own secretary of state. As secretary of the navy he chose Paul Hamilton, former governor of South Carolina; and for the Department of War, William Eustis, a surgeon during the Revolution.

Tentative and unsure of himself, Madison was confronted by the two most astute and devious political figures of the day, George Canning, head of the British foreign ministry, and Emperor Napoleon Bonaparte. It was Madison's hope, by holding out the promise of renewed trade with the United States, to persuade both belligerents to revoke their orders in council. It was the game of Canning and Napoleon to so play on the hopes of the American president that he would be deceived into resuming trade with one nation while maintaining its ban on trade with its enemy. So Canning and Napoleon proceeded to whipsaw Madison back and forth between them. David Erskine, the British minister, encouraged Madison to believe that if he withdrew the U.S. restrictions against trade with Great Britain while leaving them in effect against France, Britain would revoke her orders in council of January and November, 1807. To this gambit Napoleon replied through his foreign minister, Caldore, that he would lift his

Berlin and Milan decrees so far as they applied to the United States if the United States would then insist that Britain observe the principle that the ships of neutral nations could carry on in war all trade that had been permitted in peace.

A few weeks after Madison had taken office, Erskine assured him that the orders in council would be suspended on June 10, 1809. Madison replied by issuing a proclamation declaring that American ships would be free to trade once more with Great Britain on that date. At this news there was frantic activity in every seaport up and down the coast as ships long idle were prepared to sail, crews were recruited, and cargoes were assembled. In the space of three weeks more than 670 vessels were made "shipshape." The militia were dismissed; the gunboats pulled ashore.

But Erskine was recalled, the orders in council reaffirmed; and a notorious enemy to the United States, Francis Jackson, was dispatched by Canning to take over the negotiations. Jackson arrived with instructions that Canning knew Madison could not accept and began an insolent exchange of letters with Madison charging him, in effect, with deceit. Madison reimposed nonintercourse with the British, requested Canning to recall his minister, and once again began preparations for war. After months of debate Congress passed a bill to take the place of the Nonintercourse Act of 1809. Known as Macon's Bill No. 2, it restored free trade with France and England until March, 1811. If in the meantime either power lifted its restrictions on American trade, the president was to announce the fact by proclamation, wait three months, and then, if the other belligerent had not followed suit, the provisions of the earlier Nonintercourse Act would go into effect against the obdurate power. That Congress should have been reduced to such an awkward, not to say inane, piece of legislation is a measure of the intractability of the problem and the confusion and lack of leadership that existed in that body as well as in the executive branch of the government. Napoleon had already issued another decree—the Rambouillet Decree. Under its terms, no ship of France could enter any American port, and any American vessel in any port of France or any country under her domination would be seized and confiscated. By the time the edict was publicly known, 150 American ships had been seized and their cargoes put up for sale.

At this point two events not directly related to the hopelessly entangled state of American commerce must be noted. When Napoleon placed his brother Joseph Bonaparte on the Spanish throne, revolts against Spain broke out in most of that country's colonial possessions. Mexico, Venezula, and Argentina threw out the Spanish viceroys who ruled over them. West Florida, which extended from the Mississippi to the Pearl River, likewise took note of the fall of the Spanish throne, and a movement was soon afoot to declare it independent. The region had a motley population of Spaniards, Englishmen, and Americans, many of them the dregs of the Southern frontier. While a portion of these wished to set up in business for themselves, the majority preferred to be annexed to the United States, and to make their views known they issued a declaration of independence, adopted a constitution and a flag with a single star, and recruited an army of 104 men. The army, reinforced by rivermen and sailors, seized Baton Rouge on September 23, 1810. The convention that had undertaken these measures now declared West Florida to be independent of Spain and instructed its president to seek annexation to the Union as a state.

Madison's response was to declare West Florida annexed, but rather than granting it statehood he directed that it should fall under the administration of the governor of the Louisiana Territory, William Claiborne. For a brief time it appeared that some Floridians would resist annexation under such terms but the appearance of Claiborne at Baton Rouge, reinforced by gunboats and militia from New Orleans, discouraged resistance, and the Baton Rouge portion of West Florida was peacefully integrated into the District of Orleans.

The example of Baton Rouge was followed by Americans in settlements near what is now Mobile, Alabama. An armed foray against the Spanish garrison of that town was driven off, but the Spanish governor of the Floridas, Vincente Folch, despairing of any support from his homeland and not wanting to see the Floridas become part of a French empire or fall into the hands of brigands, wrote to Madison offering to surrender both Floridas to the United States. Madison at once asked Congress to pass a resolution declaring that the United States was unwilling to have the Floridas pass into the hands of any other power and requested authority to accept them with the concurrence of the Spanish officials there. The debate in Congress was secret, but it was evident that the Northern states were, in the main, strongly opposed to adding more territory in the South that would in time be made into new Slave States, thereby further diminishing the power of the Free States. The authority Madison requested was granted by the Republican majority, with the statement that the United States could not acquiesce in the Floridas' passing under the control of another power, specifically France or England (though neither of course was mentioned), and the additional stipulation that their acquisition was to be temporary, subject to future negotiation should Spain throw off the Napoleonic yoke.

Congress then moved on to the question of whether to accept the petition of the District of Orleans to be admitted to the Union as a state. Here again, Northern senators and representatives opposed the measure as in the highest degree unconstitutional. Josiah Quincy, a representative of Massachusetts, was perhaps the bitterest opponent of statehood. He was, he declared, devoted to the Union, but he was convinced that if Orleans was admitted as a state, "the bonds of the Union were dissolved" and each state was free to go its own way or form a new alliance with other states.

The argument revolved around the point that while the Constitution provided for the admission of new states they must be states that were within the boundaries of the United States at the time of the ratification of the Union. After protracted debate, Congress voted 77 to 36 to admit the district as a state, and the Senate concurred. The misgivings of men like Josiah Quincy were not without foundation. During the period of Spanish control, thirty-nine thousand slaves passed through Mobile and New Orleans to be employed on the plantations that stretched along the Mississippi, the Mobile, the Tombigbee, and the Alabama rivers. Thousands more were smuggled in, and some six thousand Cuban refugees brought two thousand slaves with them. Whatever might be said about ameliorating circumstances in the old Slave States (and that was little enough) could not be said about conditions in the Louisiana Territory, where slaves worked under foremen usually recruited from the dregs of white society. The region soon had merciless "black codes" that forbade slaves to congregate, ride horseback, carry arms, or buy liquor.

Having paved the way for the admission of the new Slave State of Louisiana, Congress went on to debate the rechartering of the Bank of the United States. This had been a classic Federalist-Republican conflict. The Republicans professed to fear banks as the engines by means of which the moneyed classes exploited the farmer and the artisan. Hostility to banks was an article of faith with most Southerners and the majority of farmers. The Republicans had been especially hostile to a "national" bank, which might be used by an unscrupulous administration for the advantage of its friends. In addition, the frantic commercial and speculative activity of the early decades of the

Republic had led to the establishment of dozens of banks, many of them very shaky and undercapitalized ventures, over which the Bank of the United States attempted to exercise a much-resented control. By the time the question of renewing its charter came up, over a hundred banks had been chartered in various states.

The debate over rechartering was long and bitter, with its advocates warning that its demise would bring financial chaos. But the outcome was foreordained. What was perhaps most striking about the debate was that in the Senate it pitted two "new" men against each other. William Crawford had begun life as a poor boy in Virginia. There, like many another young man in modest circumstances before and since, he taught school and studied law on the side. He helped to compile the first digest of the laws of Georgia; he was a state legislator by the age of thirty; and five years later, in 1807, he was appointed by the Georgia legislature to fill out an unexpired term in the U.S. Senate.

True to the type of the hotheaded Southern legislator, always touchy on the subject of his honor, he had fought two duels rising out of political quarrels, wounding his opponent seriously in the first and being wounded himself in his second set-to. Crawford was handsome, brilliant, eloquent in debate, and, perhaps most significant, young—the model of the new self-made man.

To the surprise of his friends, Crawford took the side of the bank. His principal opponent was Henry Clay, whose origins were, if possible, even humbler than Crawford's. Clay, five years Crawford's junior, had been born in an area known as "the Slashes" on the Pamunkey River in Virginia in 1777. His father, a Baptist minister, had died when Henry was four years old. He received the rudiments of an education in a "log school." His mother remarried and moved to Kentucky, but with the help of relatives Henry made his way back to Richmond when he was fourteen and found a job as a clerk in a dry-goods store. Young Clay had the same fierce ambition that characterized Crawford, and he found a sponsor in George Wythe, Jefferson's law teacher and the dean of the Virginia bar. His relationship with Wythe was the classic one of a brilliant and ambitious young man with a wise and experienced mentor. Clay learned much more than law from George Wythe. Indeed, it was the attorney general of Virginia who, through Wythe's advocacy, taught Clay the rather modest amount of law he needed to receive his law license. Clay moved back to Kentucky, became an ardent Republican, and soon made himself conspicuous as the most gifted young man in that frontier state. Clay's long suits were charm and eloquence. His speeches often moved his auditors alternately to laughter and to tears. In Kentucky he advanced his political fortunes by marrying Lucretia Hart, daughter of one of the most prominent men of the state. When Aaron Burr had passed through Kentucky in the later stages of his strange venture and been arrested, young Clay had secured his release.

In 1806, at the age of twenty-nine, Clay had been appointed, like Crawford, to fill out a U.S. Senate term that expired at the end of that year. In the few months that he served, the young man made a strong impression on his Senate colleagues. In the state legislature he emerged as the leader and a strong supporter of Jefferson's embargo. Like Crawford, Clay dueled with a political opponent, and both he and his rival were slightly wounded. Thus equipped with the credentials needed by a Southern politician, Clay was once more appointed to fill out the term of a Kentucky senator. He was then thirty-two, and he at once established himself as one of the most powerful and lucid speakers in the Senate, a champion of home industries, an advocate of expansion, an enemy of the bank. Where Crawford was handsome, Clay's long, narrow face was agreeably homely, and his manners, in contrast to those of the Georgian's, were simple and informal.

Elected to the House of Representatives in the midterm election of 1810 was another C, John Caldwell Calhoun, the grandson of a Northern Ireland Presbyterian who had emigrated to Pennsylvania from Donegal in the 1730s. Calhoun's father had moved to the South Carolina frontier, Cherokee country, and had been involved in many fierce encounters with those formidable warriors. He was also prominent in South Carolina politics all his life and preached to his son the doctrine that "government was best which allowed the largest amount of individual liberty compatible with social order." A radical philosophical anarchist of a type that would become familiar in the United States in subsequent generations, the senior Calhoun looked forward to a time when "the improvements in political science would consist in throwing off many constraints deemed necessary to an organized society." Though he died when Calhoun was only thirteen, he had a profound influence on his son.

John Calhoun, born in 1782, was the youngest of the three C's by five years. He had been tutored by his brother-in-law, a staunch Calvinist minister, and graduated from Yale in 1804. From Yale he went to Judge Tapping Reeve's famous law school at Litchfield, Connecticut. Calhoun's piercing, deep-set eyes, his high forehead and prominent nose gave him a formidable presence, the impression of which was heightened by his personal austerity and a somewhat disconcerting intensity of manner. Where Clay was all easy affability, Calhoun had about him a quality that suggested an Old Testament prophet.

There was another brilliant young man of the same generation who, while not yet a member of Congress (he would be elected for the first time two years later), would so soon share with Clay and Calhoun the leadership of Congress that it is appropriate to introduce him here. Daniel Webster, born in Salisbury, New Hampshire, in 1782, had a typical small-town New England boyhood. He helped to earn his way through Dartmouth by teaching, and after his graduation, he, like Clay, continued teaching school while he studied law. He was admitted to the New Hampshire bar in 1807 and almost at once became one of the most sought-after lawyers in the state. His appearance was somewhat similar to Calhoun's—compelling eyes under dark, bushy eyebrows, a high forehead, and a wide, rather fierce mouth.

Webster, in contrast to Calhoun, was self-indulgent and loved good living. He was to become the hero and *beau ideal* of New England as Calhoun was of the South and Clay of the West.

Different as Clay, Calhoun, and Webster were in many ways, the three men had much in common. They were all consummate orators able to sway and bewitch their listeners. Each of them defined, in exhaustive detail, a set of ideals and principles to which a substantial portion of his constitutents subscribed. They dramatized and embodied these ideas and principles in a way unique in our history, and in doing so they made Congress the center stage for the political history of the next thirty or forty years (Calhoun died in 1850, Webster and Clay in 1852). A succession of presidents was to come and go, but these three extraordinary men, never presidents themselves (each of them was too strongly defined and too closely identified with sectional interests to be acceptable as a national candidate), loomed far larger than all the presidents elected during their congressional years with the exception of Andrew Jackson. What is more striking is the fact that their preeminence was achieved primarily through the power of speech—by oratory.

The Constitution, splendid as it was, was only a set of political propositions declared to be law. It was already clear that opinions about its meaning varied widely. The collective states were still very far from forming a genuine union. Hostility and suspicion between states and sections was much more common than trust. Every new crisis threatened to tear the country apart. It was not even clear what the mysterious and constantly evoked "Union" meant—a loose confederation of states or a traditional nation? Where other modern nations had centuries of what might be called prehistory, the gradual accretion of forms and customs that lay deeper than memory and that bound their people together by intricately woven bonds, the United States was a kind of "synthetic," one might even say "hypothetical," nation that had just started yesterday, so to speak. It was a new phenomenon in the world. Who would have thought before that one could simply declare a nation to be; that one could produce it by an act of the conscious will and intelligence, and that, having produced it, could keep it together by that same "will," rather precariously reinforced by a set of political "ideas"? But this is, in fact, what was happening and what was to continue to happen down to the ultimate crisis—the Civil War. The "Union" was to be perpetually (and usually contradictorily) defined and redefined and thereby held together by *words*. So far as it existed as more than simply geography, the United States was to be talked into existence as other countries were fought into existence, or as they simply accumulated, over long periods of time, such a store of common experiences that made them, finally, a nation. This being "talked into existence" was to happen most conspicuously in that ultimate forum, the Supreme Court, and in the Congress of the United States; and it followed quite naturally that the greatest talkers—the most brilliant orators—would, in consequence, dominate the minds and imaginations of the American people for almost half a century.

In any event, Henry Clay and his adherents bested Clay's fellow Republican, William Crawford, and the Bank of the United States was allowed to expire, though it cannot be said it went quietly to its grave. The bank issue must, in any event, have been a welcome interruption to the unresolvable dilemma of what to do about the aggressive and insolent behavior of France and Britain, who appeared to be vying with each other to see which nation could impose the more grievous humiliations on the United States.

On the flimsiest of evidence, Madison declared that France had suspended its Berlin and Milan decrees and on that basis he recommended nonintercourse with Great Britain. A debate ensued in the House that grew so exceedingly bitter that when John Eppes, Jefferson's son-in-law, accused John Randolph, a cousin of Jefferson's, of deliberately delaying the vote, Randolph called him a liar and Eppes challenged him to a duel. Jefferson had narrowly averted a duel between another son-in-law, Thomas Mann Randolph, and John Randolph five years earlier. This time friends intervened, and the duel was prevented. The bill was passed, but word soon came that Napoleon, far from having relaxed the hated decrees, had ordered that American ships captured at sea carrying contraband under the definition of the decrees be burned, and two ships had indeed been destroyed.

Madison (who had been much under the influence of William Duane of the *Aurora*; the Smith brothers—Robert Smith, his hopeless secretary of state, and Samuel Smith, a senator from Maryland; and William Giles, the manager of Republican politics in Virginia) now divested himself of Robert Smith at the urging of Gallatin, the only outstanding member of his Cabinet, and persuaded James Monroe to take his place.

Monroe was faced with a deteriorating situation. George III, periodically insane, had passed beyond the pale, and a regency had been established. William Pinckney, despairing of any concessions on the part of Great Britain, had left England. Augustus Foster, the successor to the impudent Jackson, was about to depart for home. British-American relations, which could hardly have been worse, were in fact worsened by an encounter between the forty-four-gun American frigate *President*, under the command of John Rodgers, and a smaller British warship, the corvette *Little Belt*. Madison's proclamation renewing trade with France, on the mistaken notion that the Berlin and Milan decrees had been suspended, had brought a blockade of British warships to the American coast where their commanders behaved with characteristic insolence, stopping and boarding American coastal vessels as well as those headed for European waters and impressing American seamen. Madison had ordered the *President* to protect American shipping, and Rodgers had hardly passed out of the Chesapeake Bay when he sighted what he assumed to be a naval vessel. The two ships approached each other as darkness came on until Rodgers was close enough to hail the other ship. Rodgers, unable to distinguish the ship, called out, "What ship is that?" His query was rebuffed, and, according to the crew of the American ship, a cannon-ball was fired from the strange vessel, striking the mainmast of the *President*. Third Lieutenant Alexander James Dallas, whose father was the prominent Pennsylvania Republican of the same name, thereupon fired one of the *President*'s guns without orders and a general engagement began; it lasted some fifteen minutes and left the *Little Belt* riddled by cannonballs and 32 British dead or wounded.

The *President* sailed on to New York where report of the unequal contest caused an effusion of patriotic pride that spread through the country. Foster lodged a strong protest and insisted that the *President* had attacked *Little Belt* without provocation.

Through all this, sentiment for war with Britain was growing in the country. The younger Republicans like Clay and Crawford became increasingly the open advocates of war. An animus against Great Britain, by no means confined to the Republicans, grew by the month. It was not so much that the policies of Napoleon were less insufferable than those of Canning; it was more that most Americans felt a historical antipathy to England: England was arrogant and overbearing in its contacts with the American government, while France, for the most part, was polite and devious. Only Jefferson's determination to preserve the peace at almost any price had kept many of his followers from openly pressing for war against Great Britain. Now that deterrent was removed, and the agitation for a declaration of war became more intense.

Underlying much of the pressure for a declaration of war against Great Britain was the desire of the "War Hawks" to invade and seize Canada. As though the United States had not enough real estate already, many of its citizens yearned to add that interminable dominion, some on the grounds that it was America's destiny to rule the entire continent of North America. Others argued that the inclusion of Canada would make the United States more symmetrical.

33

War in the Northwest

The year 1811 was full of dire portents. The winter had been one of the severest in memory, and the spring rains caused many of the great rivers in the midcontinent river system to overflow their banks. In some areas the country for a mile or more on either side of the Mississippi flooded. "Unprecedented sickness followed," in the words of a contemporary traveler. Squirrels, "obeying some great and universal impulse," moved south by the tens of thousands, covering the countryside. When they came to the Ohio they plunged in, and many drowned crossing the river. A comet lit the night sky for months on end, and in the fall a series of earthquakes shook the Mississippi Valley from one end to the other. The epicenter of the ultimate quake was the frontier town of New Madrid, which was totally destroyed. In Richmond, Virginia, a terrible fire broke out on Christmas Night in a theater, killing more than thirty people, among them the governor and his wife. To the superstitious or devout, the events, in their particular conjunction—especially the squirrels, the earthquakes, and the comet—seemed to be warning of worse disasters to come or, perhaps, punishments for vanity, materialism, and divided councils. Pious Federalist ministers hinted such omens indicated God's wrath with a Republican administration.

Certainly one of the strangest and most terrible events of 1811 was the murder by Jefferson's nephews, Lilburn and Isham Lewis, who had moved to the Kentucky frontier, of a young slave who had broken a pitcher belonging to their mother.

The Lewis brothers tortured the slave and then hacked the mutilated body to pieces in front of other slaves. They tried to burn the remains in the fireplace, but the great earthquake interrupted their grisly work and toppled the chimney before the portions of the body were consumed. The brothers then buried the dismembered corpse under the reconstructed fireplace, which was once more demolished by another earthquake tremor. Meanwhile a dog carried off part of the skull, a neighboring planter found it, and the crime was exposed.

The millennial impulse that was never far below the surface of the Protestant evangelical mind surfaced with a widely broadcast prophecy that the world was coming to an end on June 4. In many country districts work was suspended, and corn was not sown in the expectation that no one would be around to reap it.

Meanwhile the country drifted toward war. When Congress debated a bill authorizing the president to raise an army of fifty thousand volunteers, the question of whether such a force could be ordered into Canada was heatedly debated. Allied with it was the question of whether to break with Jefferson's policy of only building war vessels suitable for the defense of the ports and harbors of the United States—the notorious gunboats—or whether to build a navy capable of engaging enemy vessels at sea. The "new" Republicans, men like Clay and Calhoun, had no difficulty changing ships in midstream. They wanted well-built and well-manned frigates that could hold their own or outsail the naval vessels of either of the belligerents. To the old Republicans, a vote for a substantial navy was a betrayal of the faith. A large navy must inevitably be an instrument to impoverish and oppress the people. Despite the imminence of war and the best efforts of the new Republicans, Congress voted down all proposals to build more frigates, to substantially increase the regular army, or, barring that, to raise a provisional army of twenty thousand men. Nonetheless, there were substantial costs in repairing seaport defenses and increasing the number and armament of Jefferson's gunboats, and Congress reluctantly turned its attention to the question of where money was to be found to pay for the war the country was drifting into. The hated internal duties that had led to the Whiskey Rebellion were revived. These were, primarily, a tax on salt, on licenses for the distilling of liquor from molasses, on refined sugar, on pleasure carriages, and on various categories of stamps. Included in the bill were greatly increased tonnage duties on imported goods. In addition, provisions were made to raise eleven million dollars through the sale of government bonds redeemable in twelve years.

Clay and his fellow War Hawks continued to bring pressure on Madison to request a declaration of war. The rumor went about that Clay had made his support for Madison's reelection in 1812 conditional on the president's assurance that he would support such a declaration. Clay's proposal was that an embargo be imposed for thirty days, and if at the end of that time Great Britain had not made substantial concessions, war be declared.

In April a bill was brought to the House in which a sixty-day embargo was specified prior to a declaration of war. The Senate extended the interval to ninety days, but the House resisted, and both chambers agreed on sixty days as the period of grace. Since the political situation in England was changing rapidly and a more conciliatory spirit was manifesting itself in that country as a consequence, in large part, of the economic hardships caused by nonintercourse, the ninety-day period would, by allowing time for word of British concessions to reach the United States, have avoided a war altogether or, at the very least, postponed it indefinitely. Although the debates in Congress had been secret, word of the impending embargo leaked out, and a number of ships were rushed to sea before the official word closing all American ports reached the Treasury Department officials in charge of enforcing the act. When no word had reached the government of any amelioration in the British position by June 1, Madison sent a "warning message" to the Senate. After retracing the various indignities that the country had suffered at the hands of Great Britain, Madison concluded: "Whether the United States shall continue passive under these progressive usurpations and these accumulating wrongs, or, opposing force to force in defense of their national rights, shall commit a just cause into the hands of the Almighty Disposer of Events . . . is a solemn question which the Constitution wisely confides to the legislative department of the Government."

In the House, John Calhoun, chairman of the Committee on Foreign Relations, recommended war. The vote was 79 ayes and 49 nays. From Ohio to Georgia all the representatives voted for war with the exception of 5 Virginians (out of 19) and 3 out of 9 North

Carolinians. The antiwar vote was concentrated in New England states, New York, and New Jersey, but even here there were 17 votes for war. The Senate concluded its deliberations on June 18, also voting for war. On the following day Madison issued a proclamation declaring the United States to be at war with Great Britain and then rode over to the War Department, "stimulating everything," one observer noted, "in a manner worthy of a little commander-in-chief, with his little round hat and huge cockade."

So began America's strangest war. The theater of operations extended from Montreal, through the region of the Great Lakes, to New Orleans and along the Atlantic coast from Halifax to Maine, and thence down to the tip of Florida and around the rim of the Gulf of Mexico to Mobile and Pensacola. It extended from the West Indies to the English Channel and the Irish Sea. All the odds favored the British, as they had done, indeed, at the beginning of the American Revolution. England was the greatest commercial and naval power in the world. While it is true that she had been engaged on and off for more than a decade in a life-and-death struggle with Napoleon Bonaparte, in which virtually the whole Continent of Europe was arrayed against her, she had fought the most brilliant general of the age to a standstill and would soon topple him from his imperial chair.

Great Britain had naval vessels without number (the United States had five serviceable frigates to more than a hundred for England), seasoned officers, and battle-tested troops. Against all of her apparent advantages, she still had the overwhelming disadvantage that in the last analysis had cost her her American colonies—a contemptuous attitude toward all things American. To the British, the American navy was a joke: its ships were cockleshells that would turn turtle if they fired a broadside; its sailors, British deserters excepted, were farmboys and bumpkins commanded by amateurs; its army, of course, was nonexistent. If Americans had proved surprisingly tenacious enemies in the Revolution, their single-minded devotion to money-making had, since that time, undermined their moral fiber and rendered them totally unfit for the hazards and hardships of war.

Americans, for their part, viewed the British as bullies and cowards and were confident that their privateers would drive British merchant shipping from the seas while their courageous militia took Canada. Few Americans realized how vulnerable their port towns were to British raids or sufficiently considered the fact that Canada, which they expected to pick like a ripe plum, could also serve as a staging area and line of departure for British and Indian attacks on western New York, Ohio, and indeed, the whole Mississippi Valley frontier.

It is necessary here to give some attention to the situation of the Indian tribes of the upper and lower Mississippi Valley. For several years a Shawnee Indian named Crouching Panther, or Tecumseh, had been visiting tribes as far south as Tennessee and Georgia preaching the gospel of Indian unity. He was convinced that if the tribes of the Mississippi Valley could be drawn together in a military alliance, they could check the inroads of the whites into Indian territory. Tecumseh's vision was of a great Indian nation, occupying its own wild region, supported by the British in Canada and strong enough to repel all white attacks.

Tecumseh was one of a set of triplets born to a Shawnee woman. A brother of Tecumseh, the Open Door, Tenskwatawa, was a one-eyed seer, mystic, and shaman, the maker of powerful medicine. Tecumseh, who had fought against Wayne at Fallen Timbers, was a fearless and brilliant leader, an orator and tireless organizer. Together the two men made a formidable combination. Tenskwatawa, also known as the Prophet, assured the tribes that his brother was trying to unite that he could make medicine that would repel bullets. Tecumseh's plan was to recruit the young braves of every tribe, and, ignoring the chiefs—often older men who, in his view, had been corrupted by the whites— assemble them in a great congress, and there concert plans to check the advance of the settlers.

It was into this volatile situation that William Henry Harrison, the governor of the Indiana Territory, insinuated himself. Harrison, a Virginian, had made himself anathema to most of the settlers in the territory by his efforts to have the provision in the Northwest Ordinance prohibiting slavery repealed by Congress. In an effort to recoup his popularity, he requested the secretary of war to give him permission to enter into treaty negotiations with the Indian tribes of the region—the Miami, the Potawatomi, the Delaware, and the Kickapoo—with a view toward purchasing substantial portions of the lands secured to them by the Treaty of 1796 that had followed General Anthony Wayne's victory at Fallen Timbers. The chiefs who assembled at Fort Wayne were the older and more moderate leaders who had been worn down by years of fighting and negotiating, in both of which they invariably lost. Harrison both bribed and intimidated them, pointing out the consequences of obduracy of their part and the advantages to them of cooperation. The deal was consummated after the appropriate speeches pledging peace and brotherhood, and some three million more acres of Indian land thereby became available for settlement by whites.

Tecumseh, who had established a base of operations at the juncture of Tippecanoe Creek and the Wabash, was infuriated when he learned of the treaty. The Wyandot came in and together the warriors gathered at Tippecanoe issued a proclamation declaring the treaty to be of no effect. The lands would not be surrendered. Harrison arranged a meeting with Tecumseh at which the Indian leader assured the governor that he did not wish war. If the treaty were voided and the U.S. government agreed not to purchase any further lands without the express consent of the warriors of the tribes involved, he would promise that his followers would commit no aggressive acts against the United States.

Harrison rebuffed him, and Tecumseh left for the South to try to persuade the powerful Creek Nation to join his confederation. Rumors constantly circulated on the frontier that the Indians were preparing to fall on all white settlements from Ohio south, and pressure mounted on Harrison to make a preemptive raid on the Indian stronghold on the Wabash. Harrison complied and began to muster troops and militia levies on the upper Wabash to be in a position to launch an attack on Tippecanoe. When a soldier working on a fort was shot, presumably by an Indian, Harrison marched to a point some twelve miles from Tippecanoe. Choosing a campsite on open ground, surrounded by woods and underbrush, Harrison prepared to parley the next day with the Prophet who, in the absence of Tecumseh, was the principal chief. An hour before dawn the Indians caught the sleeping soldiers in a surprise attack. By the light of the campfires they inflicted heavy casualties on the sleepy and demoralized whites, but by dawn the soldiers had rallied, formed up into units, and finally charged the Indians and forced them into a swamp, where many were killed.

Harrison's casualties were 188 men killed or wounded, among them 34 officers. The battle made Harrison a hero and ultimately president of the United States. It was thought, briefly, to have broken the back of the Indian confederation, but that hope turned out to be premature. As soon as Tecumseh returned from his mission to the southern Indians, where he had sowed the seeds of an uprising, raids began on white settlers and settlements. British agents had assured Tecumseh that war between that country and the United States was inevitable. When that war came, the British would join him in attacking the frontier settlements from the Canadian border to the Ohio. Thus, when Congress declared war in June several thousand warriors under the leadership of Tecumseh and the Prophet were waiting to wreak havoc on the Ohio frontier.

Prior to declaring war, Congress had authorized an increase in the regular army to thirty-two thousand men, called for fifty thousand volunteers for a provisional army, and provided for mustering one hundred thousand militia into federal service. Recruits were slow in signing up, despite an enlistment bounty of sixteen dollars, for a war in which they could perceive no immediate threat from the enemy. Various expedients were resorted to, to persuade the reluctant. Many New England towns offered to augment the regular pay of recruits by as much as double their official pay, but the governors of three New England states resisted the secretary of war's request for militia. Governor Roger Griswold of Connecticut stated that the call-up of militia was unconstitutional, since there was no threat of invasion or domestic insurrection.

The generals on whom Madison relied to command a virtually nonexistent army were, for the most part, survivors of the Revolutionary conflict. Henry Dearborn, senior major general, had fought at the Battle of Bunker Hill, had accompanied Benedict Arnold on his famous march to Quebec, and had served as a major at Saratoga and Monmouth, but he was vain and unimaginative and in poor health. Thomas Pinckney, more notable as a diplomat than as a soldier, had been an aide-de-camp to Benjamin Lincoln during the Revolution and had been wounded at Camden. James Wilkinson, the master plotter and betrayer of Burr, was the senior brigadier general. Wade Hampton, a South Carolina aristocrat who had served with Francis Marion and Thomas Sumter in the Southern campaigns of the Revolution, was another senior officer. William Hull, governor of the Michigan Territory, had been with Washington at Cambridge and Trenton and had led a division at the famous Battle of Stony Point; but he, like Dearborn, was well past his prime. Young Winfield Scott believed most of the general officers had been ruined by excessive drinking. Certainly they were to demonstrate the axiom that it is a gross error to fight a new war with the heroes of an older one.

The navy, modest as it was, was a shining contrast to the army. The war with the Barbary states had brought forward a new generation of brilliant young naval officers—superior, it would prove, to those in the service of any other nation. It had also made it possible to separate the sheep from the goats and to bring the officers and sailors to a high state of efficiency and morale. When war was declared there were sixteen warships of all classes (gunboats excepted) on the navy's rolls: three of forty-four guns—the *United States*, the *Constitution*, and the *President*; three of thirty-eight—the *Constellation*, the *Congress*, and the *Chesapeake*; and ten others ranging down to the twelve-gun *Viper* and *Enterprise*. There were no American ships to match the huge British seventy-four-gun frigates. When U.S. warships encountered such vessels, they simply crowded on sail and made their escape.

The war was highly unpopular in New England. It was New England that stood to lose the most, at least in the view of the Federalists. Its seaports would be blockaded, its merchant ships and fishing boats shut up, its seaport towns bombarded and burned, its across-the-border trade with Canada interrupted, its commerce ruined. Town after town in Massachusetts and Connecticut expressed its opposition to the war and, as we have seen, raising soldiers proved difficult in the extreme. Newburyport, Massachusetts, was typical in its reaction. A substantial majority of its citizens fired off a proclamation denouncing the war as the "death-blow to liberty" and the end of the Union. Ministers inveighed against it from their pulpits. On the Fourth of July in Dedham, Massachusetts, Jefferson was described as Jeroboam, "who made Israel to walk in sin." Attempts were made to form a third party, the Friends of Peace and Commerce.

Gouverneur Morris wrote to a friend: "Men without talents, administering the powers of a conventional government over communities which boast of freedom, exercise a tyranny which would drive the slaves of Asia to despair, and no man is hardy enough to raise a finger. Am I awake, or do I dream? It seems to me I was once a member of Congress during a revolutionary war; but is it certain there was such a thing as Congress? Was there a revolutionary war? If I venture to groan aloud, I am told to be patient—to wait. And what are we to wait for? Must we wait till the claws of a human tiger tear us to pieces to look for a heart? We once had hearts—hearts that beat high with the love of liberty. But 'tis over. Adieu! I will not plague my friends with the expression of my anguish."

South of New York, sentiment was strong in favor of the war. In Baltimore, when a newspaper, the *Federal Republican*, denounced the war, its offices were sacked by a mob, its type scattered, the press destroyed, and the building that housed it demolished. The editor, determined to assert the principle of free speech even in wartime, secured a new press, barricaded his house, collected some friends to garrison it, and printed another edition of his paper. Again a mob attacked, and this time they were fired upon from the house; one man was killed and several others wounded. The mayor and the captain of militia intervened. At this point, the mob agreed that the house would be spared if its defenders went to prison. Among those in the house were General Henry "Light-Horse Harry" Lee, the brilliant cavalry leader of the Revolution, and General James Lingan, another Revolutionary veteran. As soon as the editor and his friends were in jail, the mob destroyed the house and then turned its attention to the jail itself. It was broken into with the connivance of the jailors, and the prisoners were beaten insensible by a butcher armed with a club. The crowd then battered the unconscious bodies with sticks and clubs for two hours, sticking penknives through their cheeks and pouring hot wax into their eyes. Lingan was killed, and Lee was so badly wounded that he never fully recovered. The leaders of the mob were arrested, tried, and acquitted.

There is a kind of symbolic horror in the incident. That one of the genuine heroes of the Revolution should have perished in such a fashion tells volumes about the violence of party feeling in the United States in the initial phase of the war. The incident certainly did not go unnoticed. Federalist newspapers and even some Republican journals deplored the attack on the freedom of the press and "mobbing" in any form. The more irreconcilable Republicans replied that the Federalists had set an example by their defiance of the embargo, their attacks on customs officials and recruiting officers, and their talk of disunion. It was, after all, a Federalist paper that carried on its masthead the words "To tell you the truth, Southern brethren, we do not intend to live another year under the present national administration."

The first efforts of the American forces that gathered along the Ohio frontier under the command of General William Hull were directed to securing Detroit as a base of operations against Canada. Hull arrived in that town on July 5 and, yielding to the importunings of his officers and men, crossed the straits that separated Michigan Territory from the lower extremity of the province of Ontario. There, instead of attacking Fort Malden, Hull lingered with his ill-clad and poorly equipped troops at Sandwich, issuing a pompous call for its defenders to surrender.

Fort Malden controlled the entrance to the straits through which all vessels passed on their way from Lake Erie to Lake St. Clair and Lake Huron. While Hull waited for the local farmers to flock to his standard, his opposing number, English Brigadier General Isaac Brock, hastened to reinforce Fort Malden, collecting Indian allies on the way. Hearing from all sides that the British were coming, Hull withdrew to Detroit and there surrendered to Brock on August 15, 1812, without firing a gun. So much for the invasion of Canada. It was a poor beginning, but worse was to follow. Hull was court-martialed and sentenced to be shot, but Madison pardoned him. The fault was certainly far more the president's and his secretary of war's than Hull's. Hull's troops were such as to dishearten any commander, and he had no confidence in the support of Henry Dearborn.

Dearborn had been immobilized by an armistice proposal from Sir George Prevost, the governor general of Canada, who had just received news that the British ministry had repealed the obnoxious orders in council. Dearborn accepted Prevost's offer and sent off to Washington for instructions.

The British action had been prompted by a growing revolt against the orders on the part of British merchants, manufacturers, and workingmen. Prior to the orders in council, England had shipped each year to the United States goods valued at more than sixty million dollars; a major part of her foreign trade was with her former colonies. The orders in council had caused a sharp rise in the cost of such necessary commodities as flour, potatoes, and sugar. Even as prices rose, workers were laid off in factories until it was alleged that seventy thousand skilled workers were without employment. In Liverpool alone sixteen thousand unemployed were on relief. Petitions from the manufacturing towns poured into Parliament. Finally, yielding to mounting pressure, Lord Castlereagh announced on June 23 that the orders were lifted. The day was a week before Madison's war message to Congress and almost a month before the final American proclamation announcing the commencement of hostilities.

While Dearborn waited for instructions, Hull was captured and Brock and Prevost made good use of the time to strengthen the defenses of the British posts along the border.

The Niagara River runs from Lake Ontario to Lake Erie; Buffalo, a town of a few dozen houses founded only ten years earlier, stood at the point where the river runs into Lake Erie. The southern rim of Lake Ontario constitutes the northern boundary of both the state of New York and the United States. At the northeastern end of that southern shoreline, near the entrance to the St. Lawrence, was Sackett's Harbor, a busy center for trade both up the St. Lawrence to Montreal and down the river to the lower posts and to Detroit.

The commanding general of the region from Niagara to Sackett's Harbor was Stephen Van Rensselaer, head of the great patroonship on the upper Hudson. He had been a Federalist candidate for governor of New York and was now major general of the New York militia. An able politician, but lacking in any real military experience, Van Rensselaer, on arriving at Lewiston on the Niagara River above the falls, found himself in command of an incredibly motley collection of ragged and inadequately armed men, some of whom, with the winter coming on, lacked even shoes. Their pay was in arrears, and there was little or no ammunition. Reading accounts of these frontier recruits, one is reminded that the various frontiers teemed with drifters, fugitives from the law, idle and dissolute men, as well as sober and industrious settlers. Whenever there was a campaign against the Indians, a number of these former types appeared, and there is little doubt that Van Rensselaer had his share of them. In any event, he did his best. Waiting in the American camp at Black Rock for supplies and arms to arrive, he drilled his little force of some thousand men and tried to create, at least on the parade ground, some semblance of a military order and discipline.

Van Rensselaer's instructions from Secretary of War Eustis were to invade Canada, and with the untrained troops clamoring for action and Republicans accusing him of hanging back because of his Federalist sympathies, Van Rensselaer determined to cross the river and seize Queenston on the Canadian side. While he was planning the crossing and assault, he received encouraging news that Brigadier General Alexander Smyth was on his way with 1,650 regular troops. Smyth was an Irishman who had made his home in Virginia, been admitted to the bar, secured a commission in the army four years earlier, and done some service in the Louisiana Territory. With war imminent the rapid expansion of the army had made him a general, perhaps one of the least qualified in the army's history. When Smyth reached Buffalo, Van Rensselaer solicited his support for the attack on Queenston, but Smyth had his own plans and refused to cooperate.

The Canadian town had had a garrison of some 350 British regulars and militia. Brock, the captor of Hull, commanded a regiment at nearby Fort George. Van Rensselaer decided on a night attack, one of the most difficult military maneuvers to execute with inexperienced men. The first boat to push off from the American side of the river carried with it the oars for all the other boats. That marked the end of the first attack.

The next night the assault troops were placed under the command of a cousin of General Van Rensselaer's, Colonel Solomon Van Rensselaer, a competent officer; and thirteen boats, each carrying twenty-five men, crossed the river under the cover of darkness, drove back the British defenders along the shoreline, and seemed to have the situation well in hand. But the British counterattacked and Van Rensselaer was wounded. Meanwhile, a few regulars under a Captain Wool climbed the steep bluff above Queenston and seized a battery of cannon that commanded the town. Two attacks on the hill were beaten off by the Americans, and Brock was killed. The capture of the town now seemed assured, but the main body of the Americans—almost a thousand men—was still at Black Rock on the other side of the Niagara, and they refused to join the assault troops. The wounded Van Rensselaer returned to plead with them, but the militia stood on their constitutional rights and insisted that the limit of their duty was "to repel invasion," and the regulars refused to move without them.

Thus secure in their rights, the militia watched while their countrymen were driven off the hill above Queenston. Since no one would row boats across to pick them up on the shore, the Americans finally surrendered. General Van Rensselaer, unable to impose any discipline on his troops, asked Dearborn to relieve him of his command, and Dearborn replaced him with Smyth.

At the Black Rock camp, Smyth began his duties by issuing a handbill that told as much about the issuer as anyone needed to know. "Our first army has been disgracefully surrendered and lost," it proclaimed. "Another, led on by popular men, destitute alike of theory and experience in the art of war, has been sacrificed in an attempt to cross the river where the enemy is strongest. But in a few days the troops under my command will plant the American standard in Canada. They are men used to obedience, silence, and steadiness. They will conquer or they will die." Then followed an exordium to volunteers to join his standard: "Are you not related to the men who fought at Bennington and Saratoga? Has the race degenerated? . . . Shame where is thy blush! No! where I command, the peaceful man, the child, the maid, the matron shall be secure from wrong. Men of New York, the present is the hour of renown. Advance, then, to our aid."

One of the strongest appeals to farmer-volunteers was that of destroying once and for all the Indian allies of the British. So appeals were broadcast to "the independent and high-minded yeomanry" of the western counties to reinforce Smyth at Niagara. They were assured that a quick campaign would "palsy the savage hand" then "wielding the scalping knife." Some thousand men did in fact troop into his camp, and they found it far from the disciplined and experienced force that had been advertised. The so-called Irish Greens, volunteers from New York, became involved in a racial brawl with troops from Pennsylvania, and the regulars had to be called out to quell it. Word had been spread that any militiamen or volunteers who set foot on Canadian soil would thereby be obliged to serve for five years in the regular army. At this rumor the Baltimore volunteers, known as the "mob-boys," apparently a reference to the killing of General Lingan and the fatal wounding of General Lee in the Federal-Republican riot, the "Drafted Militia" from Pennsylvania, and most of the Irish Greens announced their unwillingness to cross the river.

The Seneca and Cayuga Indians, members of the Six Nations and traditional enemies of the Algonquian family over whom Tecumseh had exercised so much influence, contributed five hundred warriors; by the end of November, Smyth had forty-five hundred regulars and volunteers, a number of whom had, to be sure, stated their unwilling-ness to cross the river. Prior to his attack, the general produced another bit of overblown rhetoric. "Come on, my heroes, and when you attack the enemy's batteries let your rallying word be 'The cannon lost at Detroit—or death.'"

On the night of November 27, Smyth dispatched an advance party of soldiers and sailors to spike the Canadian guns. This accomplished, the sailors returned, abandoning the soldiers, who were promptly captured. After this inauspicious start, mistake followed mistake. Just as the leading echelons were entering their boats, word came to halt the operation. Smyth had heard a bugle blow on the Canadian side and, assuming that the enemy was alerted, had ordered the attack halted. There was an uproar throughout the army. Some of the militia expressed their indignation by smashing their muskets; others de-clared their intention of leaving for home. Someone remarked that the sailors should have spiked the British bugles instead of the guns, and Smyth was nicknamed "Van Bladder."

Another crossing was planned. The men were called to their posts and several of the boats were loaded, but Smyth once more canceled the attack. One of Smyth's senior officers then called him a coward. Smyth challenged him to a duel, and the whole army was edified by the sight of the two senior generals firing at each other and missing.

Smyth's situation was soon untenable. His own men hooted at him when he appeared, and a militiaman fired a blank charge from his musket at the discomfited commander. When he was challenged to account for his behavior, Smyth blamed his troops. They were too undisciplined and inexperienced to carry out such a demanding operation, he claimed. He certainly had a point, but he would have been on stronger ground had he issued no proclamations.

Dearborn, who had his headquarters at Plattsburgh on Lake Champlain, had been ordered by Eustis to advance into Canada and capture Montreal, but he had the same problem with his volunteers and militia that Van Rensselaer and Smyth had had. They refused to budge, and Dearborn had no choice but to go into winter camp without having accomplished anything in the military line.

Hull's surrender at Detroit had left the frontier as far south as Georgia exposed to the depredations of Tecumseh and the Prophet who, anxious to revenge Tippecanoe, began a campaign of murderous raids. Kentucky took the lead in mustering an army to defend the frontier. Henry Clay recruited citizen-soldiers, and two congressmen signed up to fight. It was said that fifteen thousand men volunteered, and of these some ten thousand were signed up. Harrison, the hero of Tippecanoe, was still governor of Indiana Territory, but Kentucky made him major general of its militia. He took command of the Kentucky contingent and headed for Fort Wayne, which was under an intermittent siege by Tecumseh's Indians. There he received word of his appointment as commander in chief of the regular army in the Northwest. The command he took over was, in the highest degree, demoralized. It was without food, clothing, and proper arms and ammunition; the men were dressed in tattered clothes minus coats and in many instances blankets, and they were often without shoes. Sending urgent requests to Washington for supplies, Harrison pushed north toward the Maumee in three columns, one composed of Ohio volunteers and militia; a second made up of the Kentuckians he had commanded, now led by Brigadier General James Winchester; and a third of Virginians and Pennsylvanians. The wagons that were bringing supplies to the Maumee in anticipation of the rendevous there of the three columns were stuck in the mud and abandoned and boats carrying provisions and winter clothing were blocked by the freezing of the St. Marys River. Many horses died for want of forage, but the troops pushed on to the rapids of the Maumee. At the rapids two Frenchmen appeared to urge Winchester to drive a force of some three hundred British and Indians out of a village called Frenchtown on the Raisin River near the point where the Maumee flowed into the southern end of Lake Erie.

Since Winchester had 1,300 soldiers under his command, it was determined to send 650 of the best men under Colonels William Lewis and John Allen to rout the British and their Indian allies. At two o'clock in the afternoon, the Kentucky volunteers encountered some 200 of the enemy, and a sharp firefight ensued. Finally the British and Indians were driven back, and Frenchtown was occupied. The danger to the Americans was much more serious than they apparently realized. Only eighteen miles away across the straits that connected Lake Erie with Lake St. Clair and separated Michigan Territory from Canada was Fort Malden, where Hull had lingered too indecisively before withdrawing to Detroit. There Proctor, the British commander, had 4,000 men—British regulars, Canadian militia, and Tecumseh's Indians.

The day after the engagement at Frenchtown, Winchester came on with the rest of his command, and the troops found quarters for themselves wherever they wished. Some located in the town and some outside it; a large part of the force was on one side of the Raisin River, and Winchester was on the other. No adequate security was posted; no regular patrols were sent out; and only the most casual defenses were erected. Proctor, with 1,000 Indians and Canadians, set out two days later from Malden for Frenchtown and arrived undetected in front of the American force on January 22, 1813. He brought up cannon and began to bombard the town while Kentucky marksmen picked off 185 of his men. The U.S. 17th Infantry Regiment was meanwhile attacked in their bivouac area by a mixed party of Indians and Canadian militia, who pushed them back to and then across the frozen river until the Americans panicked and fled. Colonel Allen was killed, and almost 100 of his men fell with him and were scalped by the Indians. The remaining Americans surrendered, among them Winchester, who then advised those Americans who still held out behind a picket fence to give themselves up.

An observer noted how wretched and dirty the Americans appeared, their clothes in tatters, while from beneath their dilapidated hats "their long hair fell matted and uncombed over their cheeks."

Proctor had promised Winchester that the private property of the prisoners would be left to them once they had laid down their arms, that the wounded would be cared for and the prisoners protected from the vengeance of the Indians. In fact, as soon as the Americans had surrendered their rifles and muskets, the Indians began to pillage the camp. When Proctor, unable to control them, withdrew, the Indians turned their attention to the wounded. Some were dragged from their beds, and other perished when the Indians set fire to the house that was being used as a hospital. In all, some 30 wounded Americans were killed and mutilated.

When news of the disaster at the Raisin River reached Harrison, he burned the precious stores that had been so painstakingly collected at the rapids of the Maumee and withdrew to the Portage River. There he assembled a force of several thousand, returned to the rapids and built Fort Meigs, which he garrisoned with some five hundred Virginia militia, most of whom, when their period of enlistment expired in March, departed for home, leaving only a handful of defenders. Harrison, learning of their untimely departure, returned with three hundred men, arriving shortly before the fort was besieged by Proctor, with almost a thousand Canadians plus twelve hundred of Tecumseh's Indians, artillery, and several gunboats. A Kentucky brigade coming down the Au Glaize River and hearing of the attack on Fort Meigs hurried up to try to raise the siege but were surrounded; 700 were killed, wounded, or captured.

Proctor, unable to breach the fort or persuade his volatile Indian allies to continue the siege, withdrew. But the situation in the Detroit-Malden-Sandusky region along the southern rim of Lake Erie remained a dangerous one. The Americans, with all their grand ideas of invading and annexing Canada, had suffered a series of humiliating defeats. Almost without exception, the military and civilian leadership had been deplorable; the so-called soldiers little better than undisciplined and ill-equipped mobs; the supplies hopelessly inadequate; and the overall strategy, devised by Eustis and Dearborn, completely unrealistic. So far were the Americans from seizing Canada that the real question was whether they could defend the Ohio and Indiana country from the Canadians and Indians.

In this string of military debacles, there now appeared one bright spot. Proctor, having been forced to abandon his investment of Fort Meigs, decided to hunt down Harrison at his post on the upper Sandusky where the American commander had assembled a large store of supplies. Between the mouth of the Sandusky and Harrison was a dilapidated stockade known as Fort Stephenson, which was defended by 160 men under the command of a young regular army officer, George Croghan. His uncle had been a famous Indian fighter, his father had been an officer in the Continental Army, and his mother was a sister of George Rogers Clark (and, of course, of William Clark as well). When Proctor began his progress up the Sandusky, with 500 regulars and 700 Indians, Harrison ordered Croghan to abandon Fort Stephenson, but Croghan persuaded Harrison to allow him to defend it. "We are determined to maintain this place, and by Heaven we will," he declared, in one of those trenchant but happy phrases that successful leaders seem disposed to utter. (Perhaps the similar remarks of unsuccessful leaders are mercifully forgotten.)

Proctor first bombarded the fort and then ordered a simultaneous attack by three teams of 120 men, the Indians to attack from the rear. While Harrison, ten miles away, made no effort to come to its support, the little garrison fired so coolly and accurately that all of the officers and a fifth of the men in the attacking echelons were killed or wounded, and Proctor, never notable for tenacity, withdrew.

To a country starved for news of some triumph of American arms, however modest, word of George Croghan's courageous defense of Fort Stephenson was hailed with as much enthusiasm as if it had been the rout of ten thousand British regulars. He was promptly promoted to the rank of lieutenant colonel and was given a gold medal by Congress.

While the conduct of the land war was the occasion for nothing but gloom, things went much better on the water. In the long run, the control of Lakes Erie, Ontario, and Champlain were of more strategic consequence than any number of forts. With the lakes in British hands, the United States was vulnerable to raids or invasion along an arc that ran from Detroit to Vermont. Moreover, the lakes and rivers that emptied into them constituted a critically important transportation network. Commodore Isaac Chauncey was given command of such a navy as there was on Lakes Erie and Ontario. The Lake Erie "navy" consisted of a brig named the *Adams*, which was captured by the British when Hull surrendered Detroit. It was thus necessary to start from scratch, and work was begun on two brigs.

Oliver Hazard Perry was a young naval officer from Rhode Island who had been tempered by service in the wars with the Barbary pirates. He applied for duty with Chauncey and arrived in Erie just at the moment when a small fleet was being constructed. Perry found the boats almost completed but unguarded and without cannon. He showed great enterprise in securing the necessary materials and fittings to complete the vessels, and when Dearborn captured Fort George five armed merchant vessels that had been blocked from access to Erie by the fort became available to Perry. He now had under his command four small schooners with one gun apiece; two with two guns; one with three and one with four; and the *Niagara* and the *Lawrence*, which mounted twenty guns. All that was lacking were the crews to man them. "The enemy's fleet of six sail," he wrote Chauncey, "are now off the bar of his harbor. . . . Give me men, sir, and I will gain both for you and myself honor and glory on this lake, or perish in the attempt." He enlisted some men to serve at ten dollars a month until there should be a battle. Slowly he accumulated and trained crews to man and fight his ships.

The British fleet on the lake, under the command of Captain Robert Heriot Barclay, was made up of six ships, the largest of which were the *Detroit* with nineteen guns, and the *Queen Charlotte* with seventeen. Perry's fleet had an edge both in number of ships and of the sailors and marines aboard them. He chose the *Lawrence* as his flagship and flew a pennant from her with the words "Don't give up the ship."

On September 15 the two fleets formed a line of battle with the *Lawrence* engaging the *Detroit*, the *Queen Charlotte*, and several of the smaller British vessels, while the captain of the *Niagara* stood off from the center of the engagement. The *Detroit* and the *Queen Charlotte* were heavily damaged, but the *Lawrence*, receiving the concentrated fire of the two largest British brigs and unsupported by the *Niagara*, was virtually demolished. All her guns but one were silenced, and 83 of her crew of 103 were killed or wounded. The scene on board was reminiscent of the *Bonhomme Richard* under John Paul Jones in its terrible engagement with the *Serapis* during the Revolution. Naval engagements in the age of sail were the bloodiest and most desperate of human encounters. In no land battles could the opponents have fought on in the face of such a high rate of casualties. Severed limbs, decapitated bodies, rivulets of blood and fragments of flesh, the screams and cries of the wounded were commonplaces of naval warfare, everything made more ghastly by the confined quarters of the ship. Under such circumstances it took more than human resolution to fight on; each battle, whatever the size of the ships involved, was a kind of epic of courage and endurance, possessed of a hideous drama seldom if ever realized in land battles. Naval officers bore a unique responsibility, the captain most of all of course, for it was his decision and his alone (or that of the officer who replaced him if he was killed) to decide when wood and flesh could endure no more. On land soldiers might run away or hide behind trees or rocks or surrender as individuals or in small groups. Sailors had no such option. While the soldier often had a choice—"to fight or flee"—his seagoing counterpart commonly had to fight until he died or triumphed.

Now Perry, his ship an unmanageable wreck filled with dead and dying men, had to decide whether to strike his colors or continue the battle from the deck of another ship. Here the odd reluctance of the *Niagara* to become engaged worked to the advantage of the American fleet. With the chaplain and the purser as his aides, Perry fired the one operable cannon on the *Lawrence*; and then, with his brother and four sailors, he rowed to the *Niagara*, took command, and headed for the battered British vessels. Coming up on them, he performed the classic maneuver of sailing between two lines of British ships, firing port broadsides at one line of enemy ships and a starboard broadside at the other. The *Lawrence*, with only fourteen uninjured men aboard, at this point struck her colors. She was followed not much later by the *Queen Charlotte*, dead in the water. The *Detroit* was already out of action, and the rest of the fleet followed the lead of the *Queen Charlotte*.

Perry had in fact "given up the ship," but he had won so notable a victory that no one noticed. Now he sat down and wrote one of the most famous battle communiqués in history (he was almost as gifted a writer as a fighter): "We have met the enemy and they are ours. Two ships, two brigs, one schooner, and one sloop."

The victory gave the Americans control of Lake Erie, made the British positions at Malden and Detroit untenable, and opened the door for an invasion of Canada. Equally important, it gave an enormous boost to American morale. A nation so starved for victory that it had lionized Major Croghan for his defense of Fort Stephenson now gave itself over to an orgy of exultation. Perry's name was on every tongue, and towns and cities vied with each other to shower praise and gifts on the young hero. The fact that Perry was a New Englander undoubtedly helped to reconcile many of that region to an unpopular war. Young Washington Irving, struggling to make a living as a writer, pondered on the nature of Perry's victory and the public reaction to it. "We behold Perry," he wrote, "following up his daring movement with sustained energy,—dashing into the squadron of the enemy,—breaking their line,—raking starboard and larboard,—and in this brilliant style achieving a consummate victory." Irving described Perry as the ideal American hero, young, "of a manly and prepossessing appearance; mild and unassuming in his address, amiable in his disposition, and of great firmness and decision." Contemplating the splendor of his triumph, Irving ended his sketch with a flourish: "In future times, when the shores of Erie shall hum with busy population; when towns and cities shall brighten where now extend the dark and tangled forest; when ports shall spread their arms, and lofty barks shall ride where now the canoe is fastened . . . ; when the present age shall have grown into venerable antiquity," then will the story of the battle "stand first on the page of . . . local legends, and in the marvelous tales of the borders."

Harrison now bestirred himself and appealed for fresh troops. The new secretary of war, John Armstrong, who was only a mild improvement over his incompetent predecessor, sent him twenty-six hundred regulars. Kentucky, which seemed to have an inexhaustible supply of fighting men, mustered four thousand, one thousand of whom were mounted. The governor of Kentucky, Isaac Shelby, a veteran Indian fighter and hero of the Revolution, now sixty-three years old, led the Kentucky contingent. The Kentucky infantry floated north down the Sandusky to Lake Erie where Perry transported them to the Ontario peninsula a few miles from Malden.

Proctor, alarmed by Perry's victory, had already abandoned the fort there and Detroit as well and begun a retreat up the peninsula toward York. Harrison took command of the combined force of the regulars and the Kentuckians and pushed hard after Proctor. On the afternoon of October 5, the American general overtook the British force deployed on the north side of the Thames River at the edge of a forest. The British right flank was covered by a swamp held by Tecumseh's Indians. Their left rested on the river. The officer in command of the Kentucky cavalry, Richard Johnson, persuaded Harrison to let him charge the British positions. He divided his men into two units, ordering one to seize the British cannon while he himself led the attack on the Indians. We have often had occasion to note that the Indians, while devastating in the attack, had neither the organization nor the temperament to withstand a sustained assault by American troops. The Battle of the Thames was no exception. The Kentucky volunteers dismounted and flushed the Indians out of the swamp where Shelby's riflemen cut them down mercilessly. Many

Canadians and Indians escaped, but Tecumseh and 33 of his warriors were killed. Some of the Kentucky soldiers cut strips of flesh from the thighs of the dead leader to use for razor strops—a custom, it must be said, that was not uncommon on the frontier.

The victories of Perry on the lake and Harrison on the ground secured the region of Michigan and the western end of the frontier (a far cry, it might be noted, from the grand plans for invading Canada). It now remained to secure Lake Ontario and drive the British from Niagara. Harrison's regulars were sent to Sackett's Harbor with the mission of capturing Lewiston at the entrance to the St. Lawrence, and Chauncey collected a fleet of fourteen vessels with 980 sailors.

The commander of the small British fleet on the lake was Sir James Yeo, who commanded six ships with ninety-two guns. Although much smaller in numbers, the British boats were much better suited for naval warfare. On April 22 the American fleet attacked York (now Toronto), the capital of Upper Canada, on the southwest shore of Lake Ontario. The fight was a sharp one before the garrison of some 600 regulars and militia surrendered. Young Zebulon Pike, who had discovered the peak that bears his name, was among the Americans killed. A good deal of wanton destruction went on. The two houses of the provincial assembly were burned, and a number of houses were looted by the poorly disciplined soldiers.

The next objective was Fort Niagara, and here a well-coordinated amphibious attack drove the British out. The way now seemed open at long last for an invasion of Canada, but Dearborn was too ill to push the campaign aggressively. He was replaced by the execrable James Wilkinson, who squabbled constantly with his second in command, Wade Hampton. The British rallied under the able leadership of Prevost, and the Americans soon found themselves on the defensive again. A British attack on Sackett's Harbor was rebuffed with very heavy casualties. An American force of 540 men surrendered to 260 British near Fort George. Yeo and Chauncey fought several inconclusive naval battles. By the end of the year the British had retaken Fort George and Canadian Niagara and had seized and burned Black Rock and Buffalo. After Wilkinson's blunders had resulted in a court-martial (which exonerated him) and he was succeeded by George Izard, who had been an aide-de-camp to Alexander Hamilton, things began to take on a happier aspect. Izard was one of the new generation of officers like his able brigadier, Jacob Brown, and Winfield Scott, and, on the naval side, Perry. The American forces were organized under

Jacob Brown into three brigades, which included a number of Indians of the Six Nations. One was commanded by Scott; one by Peter Porter; and the third by Eleazar Wheelock Ripley, who had graduated from Dartmouth in 1800, practiced law, and become Speaker of the Massachusetts legislature. At the beginning of the war Ripley had enlisted in the 21st Infantry as a lieutenant and been so rapidly promoted that he was now a colonel.

The American force was directed to attack the British under the command of Major General Sir Phineas Riall, whose troops were scattered in posts at Chippawa, Queenston, York, and Fort Erie. Erie was easily captured, and the Americans pressed on to Chippawa. There, Scott's brigade in the van became engaged in close fighting with the British, who finally dropped back to Queenston. Knowing that the enemy forces outnumbered his own, Brown made his camp at Chippawa and sent out Scott to intercept a force of British marching from Lewiston. Riall meanwhile had advanced to Lundy's Lane, not far from Brown's camp, to reinforce Riall. Scott missed the force from Lewiston (which had been recalled by the British commander, General Drummond) but ran unexpectedly into Riall's troops. Scott instantly attacked; and Riall, assuming from the boldness of Scott's initial assault that the American main force was in front of him, prepared to retreat. Drummond, coming up, countermanded the order, however, and the British and Americans were heavily engaged.

The Americans launched a bayonet attack on the hill where the British artillery was situated and took the British guns. A regiment of Americans then attacked the British flank and forced the whole main line to withdraw from the high ground they had occupied. Three times the British counterattacked the hill, to be met each time by heavy fire from their own recently captured artillery. Finally, Brown, having suffered heavy casualties and being wounded himself, was forced to withdraw. Scott had also been wounded, and the command devolved on Ripley, who dropped back to Fort Erie on the Canadian side of the Niagara River and began to extend and strengthen its works. This was what American soldiers did best; they were excellent diggers, and in several days the fort's defenses were greatly improved, with entrenchments totaling almost three thousand feet encircling the palisades.

Drummond now moved to the attack and began a bombardment with heavy cannon. The British, attacking in three columns, after many hours of shelling, managed to penetrate the northeast breastwork. American reinforcements rushed into the breach and there the fighting became intense. Again and again the British returned to the assault, but each time were thrown back with heavy casualties. Finally Drummond abandoned the attack. If the Americans were often unreliable in the attack, they were, unlike the Indians, stubborn and dangerous in defense. The reasons were that it was much more difficult to flee from a fortified position than in the open field, and the superiority of American marksmanship counted for far more in defense than in attack. The British casualties were, indeed, appalling and give the best evidence of the discipline and courage of the troops. They counted 905 men killed, wounded, and captured, against 84 Americans.

Frustrated in the attack, Drummond laid siege to the American positions and continued his bombardment, but bad weather dampened his powder and the spirits of his troops, and, low on supplies and ammunition, the British commander made plans to withdraw. Before he could do so, Brown, somewhat recovered from his wound, ordered an attack on the British lines. Porter, with sixteen hundred men, made a surprise assault, spiked the enemy guns, and blew up two of their redoubts.

While the Americans maintained control of Lake Erie and Lake Ontario, Lake Champlain became the preserve of a British fleet that destroyed an American supply depot at Plattsburgh and immobilized the U.S. forces in the area by intermittent raids. Izard was alarmed to learn that eleven thousand of Wellington's veterans had been sent from England and were camped on the Sorel River, which pointed like a dagger at the heart of New England. A substantial number of British were soon on the move. At Plattsburgh, on the New York side of the river, they stopped in front of strong defenses to allow time for Captain George Downie's fleet to come down the lake to join in the attack.

Chauncey had meanwhile scraped together an ill-assorted little fleet of ten gunboats and four small ships, the *Eagle*, the *Saratoga*, the *Ticonderoga*, and the *Preble*. The British ships, the *Confidiance*, of thirty-seven guns and a crew of three hundred—by far the most formidable ship of either fleet—the *Chubb*, the *Linnet*, and the *Finch*, were supplemented by twelve gunboats. When Downie reached the harbor at Plattsburgh, he found the American fleet drawn up to block his entrance. It was under the command of thirty-year-old Thomas Macdonough, who had, like Perry, won his naval spurs in the Tripolitan War, serving under Preble and Decatur. The British had an overall advantage of some ten guns and two hundred men. Macdonough, anchored on "springs," had taken the precaution of kedging his flagship, preparing to swing her around to bring his offside batteries into action.

The *Eagle* was engaged by the *Chubb* and the *Linnet* and soon disabled the *Chubb* and forced it to strike. The *Ticonderoga* battered the *Finch* into submission. But the real contest involved the heavily gunned *Confidiance* and the *Saratoga*. The *Confidiance* opened fire at a range of three hundred yards and in its first fire killed or wounded a quarter of the crew of the *Saratoga*. After an hour of broadside exchange, the starboard batteries of the *Saratoga* were so badly smashed as to be virtually useless. Downie had been killed, and the *Confidiance* had been almost as battered as the *Saratoga*. Macdonough then kedged his ship and brought his port batteries to bear on the British flagship, firing, as he had throughout the engagement, the principal, or "pointing gun," despite the fact that he was twice knocked unconscious by a nearby explosion and a falling spar. The *Confidiance* tried and failed to kedge and, after being engaged for two and a half hours, struck her colors. The British had lost 75 of their 95 guns and 200 sailors and marines killed or wounded, exclusive of prisoners. The American loss was also heavy.

Again euphoria greeted the news of Macdonough's victory. Prevost, disheartened, made no further attempt to employ Wellington's veterans. The military situation on the Canadian–U.S. border from Detroit to Sackett's Harbor remained much as it had throughout the war. On the American side it was a grim tale of ineptitude, timidity, lack of discipline, and mismanagement that extended from the secretaries of war down to the commanders in the field, a tale redeemed by three or four modest American "victories" and two brilliant naval exploits—those of Perry on Lake Erie and Macdonough on Champlain. As always in war, leadership was the key to success or failure.

34

The War at Sea

While the news from the Northwest was almost all bad, the spirits of Americans were sustained by a series of victories at sea by ships of the minuscule American navy.

When war was declared, only five naval vessels out of fifteen were ready to put out to sea. These were dispatched by the secretary of the navy with the mission of intercepting any of the British cruisers that had been blockading the port of New York and seizing any British merchant ships that they might encounter. Finding no cruisers, the commander of the fleet, John Rodgers, set off in pursuit of a fleet of eighty-five British merchant vessels in convoy from Jamaica. On June 23, Rodgers came up with the fleet and a British frigate, the *Belvidera*, under the command of Captain Richard Byron. Rodgers gave chase, overtook the *Belvidera*, and opened fire. A gun on the *President*, Rodgers's flagship, exploded, wounding or killing 16 men, Rodgers among them. In the confusion caused by the explosion, the British ship escaped to Halifax with news of the commencement of the war.

From Halifax, the British commander of the American fleet dispatched five warships to intercept Rodgers—the *Shannon*, the *Africa*, the *Aeolus*, the *Belvidera*, and the *Guerrière*. The *Guerrière*, separated from the rest of the fleet, encountered the *Constitution*, which had recently left Annapolis under the command of Isaac Hull after being refitted and taking on supplies. Hull immediately prepared for action and came alongside the *Guerrière*, Captain James Dacres commanding. But it was dark, and the American captain was unable to be absolutely sure of the ship's nationality. Before an engagement could start the rest of the British fleet appeared on the horizon, and Hull had to run for his life. The wind died down, and Hull sent out his longboats to tow the *Constitution*. The *Shannon* followed suit and was gaining when the wind freshened and the *Constitution* drew ahead. Then the wind died again and the process was repeated, with the *Shannon*, towed by many more boats, coming close enough to fire a shot at the *Constitution*. Hull now sent out longboats carrying anchors on long ropes. The anchors were dropped, and the crew of the *Constitution* hauled away until they brought the ship up to the anchors. In this fashion the chase continued hour after hour, through the day and the night and the next day, the men growing more and more exhausted.

At six in the evening of the second day, Hull saw a strong wind sweeping toward him. He reefed his mainsails as if a hurricane were approaching. The captain of the *Shannon* followed suit and bore up into the wind. As the wind struck Hull's ship, he shook out his sails and made off before the *Shannon* and the ships strung out behind her could get under way. The freshening wind was followed by rain squalls that hid the *Constitution* from her pursuers, and she made good her escape after a pursuit of thirty-six hours.

Hull found a refuge in Boston Harbor, where his weary crew had a chance to rest and the ship could take on water and supplies. The *Constitution* then put to sea in early August and, cruising the waters off Newfoundland, came up with the *Guerrière* once more. Dacres had issued a challenge to fight any U.S. frigate, and Hull was anxious to erase the memory of his flight from the British squadron. So began one of those classic naval encounters in which the eighteenth and early nineteenth centuries so delighted. They were like medieval jousts, ship against ship, captain against captain. Surrounded by a courtly protocol, where victor received the surrender of the vanquished with all the honors of war, exchanges of courtesies and compliments, they were often preceded by some notable exchange via speaking trumpet between the captains of the rival vessels, and they continued in their bloody course until one ship or the other was virtually demolished.

For several hours the two ships maneuvered for the most favorable position, seeking the windward side. These preliminaries often determined, between two closely matched frigates, the final outcome, so they were themselves full of drama, exacting tests of the skill of the captains and their crews and the sailing qualities of their ships.

Finally, when the two ships were within pistol range, Dacres bore off to port, indicating that he was ready to engage the *Constitution* at extremely close range. This was the ultimate challenge and the ultimate test. Here boats and men were locked, as it were, in mortal combat. Guns were fired at close range, and grape and canister swept the decks in a terrible hail of destruction. Musketeers in the crow's nest and tied to the rigging looked plainly into the faces of their adversaries and fired at each other scarcely thirty yards apart. Hull, accepting Dacres's challenge, brought his ship closer and closer to the *Guerrière*. While the British frigate continued to fire, battering the *Constitution* severely, Hull, his cannon loaded with grapeshot and round shot (antipersonnel charges), held his fire until he was hardly fifty feet away. Finally, his impatient men heard the command to fire, and a devastating storm of shrapnel left the decks of the *Guerrière* covered with dead and wounded men. In *ten minutes*, according to accounts of the battle, the contest had reached its climax. At that point the mizzenmast of the *Guerrière* fell into the sea, forcing her into the wind. Hull then came about and tried to close with the *Guerrière* with the intention of boarding her. In attempting this maneuver, the bowsprit of the *Guerrière* came into contact with the offwind side of the *Constitution*, providing Dacres with an opportunity to board the *Constitution*. With marines and sailors from both frigates prepared to board but restrained because of the rough seas, the struggle now turned into an exchange of musket fire between men clustered in the forecastle of the *Guerrière* and their counter parts on the quarterdeck of the *Constitution*.

Finally, finding boarding impossible, the two ships wore off, and as they did the foremast of the *Guerrière* toppled, pulling down the mainmast with it. The English frigate was now helpless, and in a few minutes Dacres ordered her colors lowered. The *Constitution* was the victor. The *Guerrière's* hull had been pierced by thirty balls. Seventy-nine of her crew were dead or wounded. The British prisoners and the wounded were brought on board the *Constitution*, and the dead of both sides were buried at sea. The hulk of the *Guerrière* was set afire, and the *Constitution*, badly battered herself, made for Boston where she arrived on Sunday, August 30.

Although many Bostonians decried the war as a Republican conflict, they could not deny themselves an orgy of celebration. Hull moved up the bay past ships hung with flags and pennants, to the sound of guns, the ringing of church bells, and the distant cheers of entranced spectators. Feasts followed with endless toasts; ceremonial swords were voted for Hull and his officers, bonuses for the sailors and marines. Joy was universal. As word of the victory spread, one town and city after another abandoned itself to similar festivities.

The famous victory of the *Constitution* was followed by a series of less spectacular but nonetheless delicious naval triumphs. The *Wasp* of eighteen guns defeated the *Frolic*, of the same armament; of a crew of 110 men on the *Frolic*, there were, at the end of the battle, only 20 not dead or wounded. The Americans lost 5 killed, and 5 were wounded. The victory was clouded by the fact that while the *Wasp* was occupied with the aftermath of the battle, the seventy-four-gun British frigate *Poictière* came up and forced her to surrender. Still it was a notable demonstration of superior American seamanship and was understood as such by Americans and British alike.

Two weeks later, the *United States*, a forty-four-gun frigate under the command of Stephen Decatur, engaged the British vessel *Macedonia* off the Azores. The *Macedonia* had been built to carry thirty-four guns but had forty-nine when she encountered the *United States*. The *Macedonia* came down on the weather gage, slightly in advance of the *United States*. In the long-range exchange of cannon fire as the frigates approached each other, the American vessel had a decided advantage, which it maintained at closer quarters. Decatur crossed the stern of the *Macedonia*, raking her badly, came about and repeated the maneuver, coming up on the lee side, where he delivered a final broadside that forced the battered *Macedonia* to strike.

In a contest lasting an hour and a half, the guns of the *United States* had shot away the mizzenmast of the *Macedonia* and had killed 43 and wounded 61 of her crew. On the *United States* 12 men were killed or wounded. Again when word reached the United States, ecstatic celebrations followed. The city of New York ordered a life-sized portrait of Decatur painted to hang in the city hall.

The next month William Bainbridge, commanding the *Constitution* and accompanied by the *Hornet*, was cruising off the coast of South America when he discovered, in the port of San Salvador, the British sloop of war *Bonne Citoyenne*, of eighteen guns. Bainbridge challenged the captain of the *Bonne Citoyenne* to fight the *Hornet*, also of eighteen guns, with himself commanding, promising that the *Constitution* would stay out of the fight whatever its consequences. The captain of the *Bonne Citoyenne* declined, perhaps mindful of the half-million pounds in specie he had on board.

Leaving the *Hornet* to blockade the harbor, Bainbridge continued his cruise and on December 23 came up with the *Java*, a frigate of forty-nine guns and four hundred sailors and marines. The *Java* outgunned the *Constitution* by a narrow margin and carried more men. In the first exchange of broadsides, the wheel of the *Constitution* was carried away, making it difficult to maneuver the ship. Bainbridge decided that his only chance of victory was to come to close quarters with the *Java*. There the fire of the U.S. ship was so intense and accurate that the *Java* lost its bowsprit and jibboom. Under the cover of the smoke from the cannonading and the smoke from fires on both vessels, Bainbridge came about, bringing his starboard batteries to bear, and then bore in once more, again raking the *Java* and shooting away her masts, one by one, until the ship lay dead in the water. The crew fought on, however, in the fashion of the times, with their captain badly injured. Finally, with 48 dead and 102 wounded (almost half of her total complement of men), she struck her colors. The United States had another hero to place alongside Hull and Decatur.

Before another month was out, the *Hornet*, James Lawrence in command, engaged and defeated the *Peacock*. This time it took only fifteen minutes for the American ship to reduce its opponent to a shattered hulk.

The naval victories had, of course, no particular effect on the outcome of the war. They were like fleabites to the British naval establishment, but they were fleabites that itched and festered. George Canning had referred contemptuously to the American navy as "a few fir-built things with bits of striped bunting at their mast heads." Now the British newspapers were filled with gloomy accounts of the American victories. The fact that their implications were exclusively psychological made the pills of defeat more bitter to swallow. They touched Britain on her most sensitive nerve. Of all things cherished by that proud country, none occasioned more pride than the prowess of her sea captains and sailors. The country of Drake and Nelson had to endure having her nose tweaked almost monthly in the opening phases of the war by an upstart nation for whom she felt primarily contempt. The surrender of Detroit and the victories of Brock and Prevost on the Northwest frontier were small consolation to the people of England for the American naval victories that were so overwhelming that they proved beyond reasonable doubt that Britannia's "rule of the waves" rested on sheer tonnage rather than on the storied dominance of her seamen.

The *London Times* spoke its magisterial mind on the defeat of the *Guerrière*, little guessing what was to come: "The loss of a single frigate by us when we consider how other navies of the world have been treated, is but a small matter. When viewed as part of the British navy it is nothing; yet it has cast a gloom over the city which it is painful to see. . . . People look only at the triumph of the Americans—a triumph small enough and of no importance, save for a rigorous scrutiny of the behavior of those responsible for it."

As word of new American triumphs reached England, the gloom thickened, and the "explanations" for the defeats flowed faster. The masts of the *Guerrière* were rotten; the *Macedonia* was not fully manned. But the editor of the *Courier* had to confess of the *Java* that "nobody ever supposed that one of our best frigates would not be a match for the American."

An article in one British journal, the *Pilot*, stated: "Any man who foretold such disasters this day last year would have been treated as a madman or a traitor. He would have been told that ere seven months had gone by the American flag would have been swept from the ocean, the American navy destroyed, and the maritime arsenals of the United States reduced to ashes. Yet not one of the American frigates has struck. They leave their ports when they choose and return when it suits them their convenience. They cross the Atlantic, they visit the West Indies, they come to the chops of the channel, they parade along the coast of South America. Nothing chases them; nothing intercepts them—nay, nothing engages them but to yield. . . ."

Sweet as the American victories were, they proved ephemeral. Within another year, the American navy had been virtually eliminated by the vastly larger and more heavily armed British squadrons. The *United States* was captured, the ill-fated *Chesapeake* sunk, the *Constitution* and the *President* shut up in Boston Harbor by seventy-four-gun frigates. But the point had been made, nonetheless; and as in the Revolution, American privateers continued to prove a terror to British shipping.

It may be pertinent to reflect here upon the reasons for the striking contrast between the performance of Americans on water and on land. As we have noted earlier, sailing a ship required a high degree of discipline. A vessel could not even raise sails and make for the open sea until a number of men had performed a number of fairly demanding and closely coordinated tasks. The ship was thus, in a sense, itself the disciplinarian. Certainly leadership was also important. There were ill-kept ships and poorly disciplined crews, but on the whole these were the exception, and most soon fell victim to the relentless requirements of the sea.

The process by which a promising midshipman ascended to the command of his own vessel was a very rigorous one; few incompetents slipped through. Certainly we cannot underrate the importance of the extended war with the Barbary States as a school for the navy, but I believe that equal weight must be given to the new human type who manned the ships of the U.S. Navy and the multitude of privateers that ranged the oceans of the world. The farmboys who made up the greater part of such crews were ideal raw material. That they were a far cry from the depressed classes from which the British navy drew its fighting men is demonstrated by the fact that the more enterprising British sailors deserted whenever they had the opprotunity.

When one took an independent and self-reliant New England farmboy and subjected him to the discipline of a warship under a captain who had gained his epaulettes, not by virtue of his social class, but under highly competitive circumstances, and who came, essentially, from the same origins as the men he commanded, one had a winning combination. Moreover, American naval technology, stimulated by the inclination of officers and men to take personal initiative, soon outstripped that of Great Britain. If two thirds of the outcome of a battle rested on the skill and courage of those who aimed and fired the cannon that constituted the principal armament of a frigate, the remaining third might be said to rest on the marksmanship of marines and sailors armed with muskets who fired at the gunners and officers of the enemy vessel. In this the Americans, most of whom had shot guns since they were young boys, were clearly superior.

The naval engagement, in addition to having a degree of finality and conclusiveness rare in human experience, was an ultimate testing of the disciplined will. Americans, as we have seen, had opted for, or had had thrust upon them, the necessity to live by "will" rather than by custom or tradition (what might be called "forms of social instinct"). Once *will* had assumed control, the crucial question came to be whether that will, so vulnerable to the darker instincts, could be disciplined by the individual. The question was especially crucial, since the forces of American life were cruelly disintegrative. When the will was disciplined, often at great psychic cost, the results were often spectacular. The classic naval engagement was, then, a kind of demonstration of the powers of the new, disciplined will. It was a drama enacted between two human types: the Englishman, the model of the old type; the American, the archetype of the new consciousness. The superiority of American naval gunnery, the most decisive element in these contests, is sometimes accounted for on the grounds that the Americans had had training since childhood in firing muskets and rifles. There may well be some truth in that notion, but the fact is that there is only the most casual technical relationship between the aiming of a musket and the aiming of a cannon. More to the point, in the aiming of the gun there was an emphatic assertion of the self. So I believe we must conclude that the social and cultural differences between Great Britain and the United States expressed themselves in some final way in the flight of cannonballs between their respective frigates.

The very qualities that made for superior sailors tended to have a negative effect in land warfare. The same type of young man who went off to sea to become an exemplary sailor marched off to fight as an infantryman and not infrequently took to his heels at the first sign of the enemy or the first thump of musket fire. The often poor performance of the American foot soldier as contrasted with the sailor was the result, in large part, of lack of discipline and poor leadership. As we have said, the ship *required* discipline if it were to sail. An infantry company had no such "shaping environment." The independent and self-assertive young man who turned out for a militia muster was little inclined to take orders, and those he took, he subjected to critical scrutiny and did not, in many instances, hesitate to disobey if he thought them stupid or ill-advised. Just as he had not been trained to obey, he was commanded by officers who had not been trained to command, such training being in civil life primarily the consequence of a clearly defined aristocratic class.

If the navy had been "blooded" in the Barbary Wars, it was true that many of the officers and men who took up arms to invade Canada were veterans of forays against the Indians. But the Indians were even less disciplined than the Americans, and fighting them was poor preparation for engaging well-trained troops. Most important, perhaps, was the fact that many army officers held their rank by virtue of being prominent Republican politicians rather than because they had demonstrated qualities of leadership. The Battle of New Orleans was to prove, as numerous battles of the Revolution had done, that properly led, the American soldier could give a good account of himself.

With the U.S. Navy, never much more than a symbolic navy, effectively neutralized, it remained to American privateers to make Great Britain feel the effects of the war. Without the depredations of the privateers, England would have had little incentive to make peace. Things were more or less stalemated along the Canadian border, which was in fact a triumph for British arms, since that was the only region where the American forces could hope to inflict any substantial damage on British interests. So it remained to the privateers to torment the British lion.

Within a month after the declaration of war, sixty-five privateers had put out from American ports. Within six months almost five hundred British merchantmen had fallen prey to them and those that followed them. Merchant ships from the Indies almost always traveled in convoys protected by several British frigates. Since such convoys covered miles of ocean, American privateers lurked on the edges like wolves around a flock of sheep, cutting off and capturing stragglers before British warships could intercept them. These American vessels carried a relatively light armament and depended on speed and maneuverability to escape from enemy warships. The effect of the privateers was that of a large, unofficial navy, since the more heavily armed did not hesitate to engage British warships of comparable armament and, in the vast majority of cases, defeat them.

Most infuriating to the British was the fact that the sea-lanes around the British Isles swarmed with these daring intruders. So many ships were seized by them in the waters of the Irish Sea that British merchants could not get insurance for crossing from Ireland to the English coast. The Liverpool merchants, protesting to the Admiralty over its inability to protect British shipping in its own waters, referred quite accurately to the depredations of the privateers as "a new system of warfare."

Lloyd's of London, the famous insurer of maritime voyages, on June 3, 1814, listed thirty-seven merchant vessels taken by privateers in the period of a few weeks. The *Perry*, out of Baltimore, captured twenty-two British ships in a two-month cruise, while the *Governor Tompkin* seized and burned fourteen ships in a sweep through the

English Channel. Thomas Boyle, captain of the privateer *Chasseur*, dispatched a handbill to Lloyd's declaring a blockade of "all the ports, harbors, bays, creeks, rivers, inlets, outlets, islands and sea-coast of the United Kingdom." That was really twisting the lion's tail!

The most famous engagement of a privateer—and one that demonstrated the degree to which they constituted a kind of auxiliary navy—involved the schooner *General Armstrong* under the command of Samuel Reid. Reid was the son of a British naval officer who had been captured by Americans during the Revolution, resigned his commission, and become a citizen of the United States. Young Reid had gone to sea at the age of eleven as a cabin boy, and had served as a midshipman under Thomas Truxton in the West Indies. He was thirty-one when he slipped through the British blockade of New York and sailed for the Portuguese Azores. In the harbor of the neutral port of Fayal, three British warships cornered him—the *Plantagenet* of seventy-four guns, the *Rota* of forty-four, and the *Carnation* of eighteen. Their combined crews numbered over two thousand men. The *Armstrong* had seven guns and ninety men.

Reid pulled the *General Armstrong* so close to shore that the British warships dared not venture within cannon range. However, their commander dispatched four barges filled with sailors and marines to seize the schooner in defiance of the port's neutrality. Reid warned the barges off, but when they came on he ordered his men to open fire, and the British were soon driven off with heavy casualties. An Englishman, visiting Fayal, described the second attack. "At midnight, it being about full moon, fourteen large launches [some accounts say seven] containing about forty men each, were discovered to becoming in rotation for a second attack. When they got to within gun-shot a tremendous and effectual discharge was made from the privateer, which threw the boats into confusion. They now returned a spirited fire, but the privateer kept up so continual a discharge it was almost impossible for the boats to make any progress. They finally succeeded, after immense loss, to get alongside of her and attempt to board at every quarter, cheered by the officers with a shout of 'No quarter!' which we could distinctly hear as well as their shrieks and cries. The termination was near about a total massacre. Three of the boats were sunk, and but one poor solitary officer escaped death in a boat that contained fifty souls; he was wounded. . . . Some of the boats were left without a single man to row them; others with three and four."

The governor of Fayal, appealed to by the American consul, had sent a note to the commander of the British squadron, asking him to respect the neutrality of Fayal and desist in his attacks on the privateer. In return he got a characteristically British response. Captain Lloyd "was now determined to have the privateer at the risk of knocking down the whole town; and if the governor suffered the Americans to injure the privateer in any manner, he would consider the place an enemy's port, and treat it accordingly." "Finding this to be the case," Reid wrote in his account of the engagement, "I considered all hope of saving our vessel to be at an end. I therefore went on board and ordered all our wounded and dead to be taken on shore and the crew to save their effects as fast as possible."

At daylight the *Carnation*, of eighteen guns, with the shallowest draft of the British squadron, pulled within range and began to bombard the *General Armstrong*, which answered so effectively that the British brig was forced "to cease firing and to haul off to repair." At this point, our English observer noted, "We may well say 'God deliver us from our enemies' if this is the way the Americans fight."

Reid scuttled the *General Armstrong* to avoid having it fall into enemy hands and rowed to shore with his crew, convinced that further resistance would be futile and result only in the needless loss of American lives. Captain Lloyd, since he could do nothing else, fired on the innocent town, destroying a number of houses and wounding some of the inhabitants. The British casualties were estimated at 250. On the American side, 2 men were killed and 7 wounded. The engagement had an important side effect. The British ships were on their way to Jamaica to reinforce the fleet there under the command of Sir Edward Pakenham, who was headed for New Orleans. The delay occasioned by their ill-fated encounter with the *General Armstrong* gave Andrew Jackson a few more precious days to strengthen the defenses of that city.

Reid, carried back to Savannah by a Portuguese ship, became the toast of that town and a number of other cities. The New York legislature gave him the inevitable sword, and the governor appointed him harbor master and warden of the port of New York. His final contribution to American history was to propose that another star be added to the flag with the addition of each new state.

The British Admiralty tried, as most bureaucracies would, to keep the facts of Fayal from the public, but it was a classic instance of what might be called "the Bunker Hill mentality" of the British military: undertake a suicidal mission based on a contemptuous misreading of the enemy; persist in it to the point of disaster; and then, furious and spiteful, punish some innocent bystanders. The English are a great people with many noble attributes, but the episode at Fayal revealed them at their worst.

Despite the naval triumphs, many Americans agreed with Gouverneur Morris that "in every point of view the nation is openly and deeply disgraced." Morris spoke for many of his fellow Federalists when he observed: "I think I can perceive a storm gathering in the East which may blow our Union flag from the mast-head. If during the gale it be proposed to New York that she be the frontier of a southern or a northern section, she would, I believe, adopt the latter alternative, in which case New Jersey could not but join the State by whose arms she is embraced." Pennsylvania, on the other hand, might well cast its lot with the South and "cover with her broad shield the slave-holding States; which, so protected, may for a dozen or fifteen years exercise the privilege of strangling commerce, whipping negroes, and brawling about the inborn inalienable rights of man. It seems to me almost certain that, if peace be not immediately made with England, the question of negro votes must divide this Union."

35

Washington and Baltimore

Undoubtedly the most demoralizing news received by Americans during the War of 1812 was word that Napoleon had been defeated and toppled from his imperial throne and that France had, at long last, made peace with England, freeing thousands of veterans of General Arthur Wellington's army for service in America.

Napoleon's downfall had begun with his invasion of Russia in the fall of 1812. The Russians had burned Moscow rather than see it occupied by the French, and in his retreat through the bitter winter the emperor's army had virtually disintegrated. The countries conquered by Napoleon—his "allies"—lost no time in taking steps to regain their independence. Prussia was first; German principalities followed. Austria declared war on France in August, 1813. Spain was next, aided by Wellington's army. The Dutch and the Allied armies invaded France on January 1, 1814. For a moment, at the Battle of La Rothière, Napoleon seemed about to regain the upper hand, but starting with the Battle of Laon in March he suffered a series of setbacks. At the end of the month the Allies entered Paris. Napoleon abdicated and was exiled to the island of Elba.

With Napoleon out of the way, the British yearned to properly chastise the Americans. The *London Times* declared on April 15, 1814:

"There is no public feeling in this country stronger than that of indignation against the Americans." In the British view, the Americans with all their ranting about freedom and liberty had given aid and comfort to the most notorious tyrant in modern history, and while a beleaguered England had been fighting both for her life and the freedom of Europe, the United States had stabbed her in the back by declaring war on her. The *Times* fulminated: "That a republic boasting of its freedom should have stooped to become the tool of the Monster's ambition; that it should have attempted to plunge the parricidal weapon into the heart of that country from whence its own origin was derived; that it should have chosen the precise moment when it fancied Russia was overwhelmed, to attempt to consummate the ruin of Britain—all this is conduct so black, so loathsome, so hateful, that it naturally stirs up the indignation that we have described."

Indeed, the newspaper went so far as to suggest that Madison had been in the pay of Napoleon; "or it is possible he may have performed the Monster's bidding out of pure rancour towards England." The words "punish" and "chastise" appeared frequently in the editorial pages of newspapers and on the tongues of politicians. "Government have turned their views toward the *chastisement of America*," a friend wrote to Sir Henry Clinton, who knew a good deal about the problems involved in "chastising Americans." The *Times* was anxious that no American desire for peace be allowed to interfere with the impending punishment: "May no false liberality, no mistaken lenity, no weak or cowardly policy interpose to save them from the blow. . . . Strike. Chastise the savages."

Humiliated on the Englishman's native element, the sea, and under heavy fire at home from the opposition benches, Canning and his ministers decided to undertake a series of punitive blows against the United States. A series of raids was planned and launched against American coastal towns and cities.

Lewiston, Pennsylvania, on the Delaware, was bombarded for twenty-four hours after its inhabitants refused an imperious demand for food by the captain of the British squadron blockading the capes. Little damage was inflicted, however, because the ships were unable to get well within range of town.

A raid was threatened at Annapolis and Baltimore where Rear Admiral Sir George Cockburn sailed a fleet of seven ships as far as the mouth of the Susquehannah. Cockburn then took possession of Spesutia Island near Havre de Grace, from which point forays were made into the Maryland countryside. A raid was mounted against

Frenchtown, where five ships were burned and a large stock of military supplies destroyed.

At Havre de Grace, Cockburn's men seized the batteries and burned four boats, several taverns, a number of private homes, two ferryboats, a sawmill, stables, a bridge, and innumerable stacks of hay without encountering any substantial resistance. The burning of the houses, Cockburn declared, was to teach their owners "what they were liable to bring upon themselves by building forts and acting towards us with so much useless rancor." Georgetown and Fredericktown were next raided, and a number of buildings were burned. Cockburn then withdrew to the British station off Lynnhaven at the Roads. From there the little town of Hampton, Virginia, was attacked; after a sharp battle the militia were driven off, and the town, in which the British lost some 50 men, was pillaged under the direction of Cockburn. Women were molested by British soldiers, and several were apparently raped. These forays spread panic through the whole region of the Chesapeake Bay and the Potomac River as the residents of the area realized how vulnerable they were to British attacks.

To the north, Wareham, Massachusetts, was visited by British frigates, and ships in the harbor were burned. Maine was invaded and declared to be part of New Brunswick. Castine and Moose Island, Maine, and Nantucket, Massachusetts, were likewise occupied and claimed as British territory. Vice Admiral Sir Alexander Cochrane, in command of the British navy in American waters, gave orders on July 18, 1814, calling for the ships under his command to destroy all the towns and villages on the Atlantic coast that were vulnerable to attack.

In an effort to draw American troops from the Canadian border, Major General Robert Ross was ordered to make a major diversionary attack on an American city. The principal question was whether to launch an attack on Baltimore, a major seaport, or on Washington. Cochrane, Ross, and Cockburn agreed to make an initial attack on Washington and then, if successful, push on to Baltimore.

An alarmed Madison called for the muster of ninety-three thousand additional militia, although there was no money in the treasury to pay them and no adequate supply depots to equip them. Much was proposed and numerous orders were issued, but little was done to strengthen the defenses of the capital or muster an adequate force for its protection. Thus, when Cochrane's fleet of fifty-one ships appeared in Chesapeake Bay, everything was still at sixes and sevens. The British plan called for land-and-sea envelopment of Washington. British soldiers would land at the head of the Patuxent River and march along its banks to Bladensburg where they would turn southwest toward the city. The British fleet would sail up the Potomac, past the inadequate defenses of Fort Washington and past Alexandria to the capital.

Commodore Joshua Barney, in command of Jefferson's gunboats, was ordered to destroy them before they fell into the hands of the British. Washington was turned upside down in an effort to muster some similitude of an adequate defense. The president, who had been described unflatteringly by Washington Irving as "a withered little applejohn," was at his best in the crisis, dashing about to supervise and encourage the belated efforts to repulse the British. General William Winder, who had been defeated and captured by the British in Canada, was in command of the defense of the city and issued a proclamation declaring that thousands of volunteers would soon arrive to "teach our haughty foe that freemen are never unprepared to expel from their soil the insolent foot of the invader."

Meantime the "haughty foe" came on by land and water unopposed. A thousand ill-equipped and poorly trained Maryland militia were rounded up, but only two hundred flints could be found for their muskets. James Monroe, the secretary of state, rode out to act as a scout for Madison and those members of his Cabinet who were trying to collect an army. He came back with word that six thousand soldiers were advancing along the Patuxent. In Washington the most important government papers were collected and removed to safety, among them Washington's commission as general of the Continental Army, the journals of Congress, and the Declaration of Independence. Everywhere people were collecting prized possessions, rounding up transportation where they could, and fleeing from the city. "The distress here and in Georgetown is beyond description," an observer wrote; "women and children [are] running in every direction." Added to the alarm over the approach of the British was the rumor of a slave uprising.

Madison, leaving Dolley to care for the presidential mansion, headed for Winder's encampment some eight miles east of the city. Including the sailors from Barney's demolished gunboats, Winder by now had three thousand men, a respectable force to oppose the British, especially if deployed behind strong defense works. Within twenty miles there were another three thousand men. At Bladensburg, Colonel Stansbury had fourteen hundred men, and Winder ordered him to march toward Upper Marlboro. Doing so, he encountered the

British advancing in force toward Bladensburg. Immediately, all American plans were changed, and such units as could be located were ordered to gather at Bladensburg to try to check the British army there. But Winder, afraid of being cut off from Washington, ordered his forces to retreat to the city. There Madison and his Cabinet, taking matters out of Winder's incompetent hands, decided to engage the British at Bladensburg and ordered every man who was able to carry arms to join the army; the president himself set out with a number of his aides and Cabinet, including Monroe, to reinforce those Americans who had been left at Bladensburg when Winder fell back to Washington.

When the British regulars attacked, the Americans fought back briefly and then fled, leaving Barney and his sailors with five pieces of artillery to fight on with until Barney was wounded and his gunners were driven off by a bayonet charge. That was the last organized resistance to the British advance on the nation's capital. Once in the city, the British set fire to the Capitol itself. The president's house, already called by some the White House, was next burned, then the Navy Yard and the Treasury Building. The following day, August 25, the War Department, some private houses, and the office of the *National Intelligencer* were put to the torch.

Amid the destruction Admiral Cockburn, mounted on a "liberated" horse, was much in evidence, joking and showing objects he had taken from the president's house. At the offices of the *National Intelligencer*, he called out to the soldiers who were smashing the presses and scattering the type, "Be sure that all the C's are destroyed, so that the rascals can no longer abuse my name!" Two patriotic thunderstorms limited the damage from the fires and saved the greater part of the White House from destruction.

Margaret Bayard Smith, who had fled with her family to Brookville, Maryland, there received "the sad news that our city was taken, the bridges and public buildings burnt, our troops flying in every direction. Our little army totally dispersed. Good God," she added, "what will be the event!" Soon the remnants of the defeated army passed "pale and feeble . . . more with fright than fatigue—they had thrown away their muskets and blankets." She wept tears of anguish over "the state of our country." "We are naturally a brave people and it was not so much fear, as prudence which caused our retreat. . . . The enemy were 3 to 1. Their army composed of conquering veterans, ours of young mechanics and farmers, many of whom had never before carried a musket. But we shall learn the dreadful, horrid trade of war. And they will make us a martial people for never, never will Americans give up their liberty." Comparatively safe in Brookville, Mrs. Smith thought of the "poor soldiers, lying on every part, sinking under fatigue and pain and hunger, dying alone and unknown, scattered in woods and fields."

Returning to Washington, Margaret Smith visited the Capitol and the president's house, of which nothing remained "but its cracked and blacken'd walls. . . . That scene, which when I last visited it, was so splendid, throng'd with the great, the gay, the ambitious placemen, and patriotic Heroes was now nothing but ashes. . . . Who would have thought that this mass so solid, so magnificent, so grand which seemed built for generations to come, should by the hands of a few men and in the space of a few hours, be thus irreparably destroy'd." Dolley Madison, who had assured herself immortality by carrying off Gilbert Stuart's portrait of Washington, was in tears at the loss of her possessions. The wine cellar, which had escaped the attentions of British soldiers, was consumed by American militia after the British had left the city.

With the British ships arriving at the mouth of the Patuxent, the troops who had pillaged Washington boarded their transports and dropped down the river. Admiral Cochrane, who commanded the fleet, had been extremely uneasy about the entire operation. He could not believe that an army the size of that commanded by Ross could proceed almost fifty miles into enemy territory, pillage its capital, and return unscathed. Ross was almost equally skeptical. Cockburn had been the only enthusiast. By dint of much arguing, he had prevailed on the reluctant Ross, and whatever credit is due for the spectacular success of the raid belongs to Cockburn.

When news of the burning of the U.S. capital reached Britain, it was received with considerable satisfaction. The "chastising" of the American savages had begun, under conditions that revealed on the part of the Americans a "pusillanimity hitherto unknown in the long course of ages." Now it was evident "how dangerous and fatal it is to rouse the sleeping lion of the British Isles." Certainly, the British press assumed, it marked the end of Madison, who had reportedly shot himself in humiliation. The *Public Ledger* predicted that within a year Boston, Philadelphia, New York, and Baltimore would be "heaps of smoldering rubbish."

The British paid a heavy price, however, for the pillaging of

Washington in that often elusive area called world, or in this instance, European, opinion. Great Britain's arrogance left her with few genuine friends on the Continent. The French sounded a common note when the Paris papers called Ross and Cockburn pirates. The *Journal de Paris* asked: "How could a nation eminently civilized, conduct itself at Washington with as much barbarity as the old banditti of Attila? . . . Is not this act of atrocious vengeance a crime against all humanity?"

In their eagerness to get in their licks against their ancient enemies, French writers indulged in a bit of exaggeration describing Washington as "one of the finest capitals of the world" and "a city whose riches and beauty formed one of the most valuable monuments of the progress of the arts and of human industry."

Their anxieties quieted by the ease of the investment of Washington, Ross and Cochrane allowed Cockburn to persuade them to attack Baltimore. Again the plan was for a joint land-water attack. The British regulars under Ross were to land at North Point on the peninsula formed by the Patapsco and Back rivers where they entered the bay. Cochrane and the fleet would reduce Fort McHenry, guarding the inner harbor, and bombard the city while Ross made an assault from the east.

The defense of Baltimore was placed in the hands of Samuel Smith, brother to the Robert Smith whom Madison had forced out of his Cabinet. If Samuel Smith was not the most ingratiating of men, he was a capable and energetic officer who soon had most of the inhabitants of the city laboring on its fortifications. Over ten thousand men were scraped together to man the strong positions on Hampstead Hill, where Ross intended to make his attack after marching up the peninsula. The defenses of the fort were substantially strengthened, and a number of boats were sunk below the fort at the entrance to the inner harbor to block the passage of Cochrane's fleet. Commodore John Rodgers was a great asset. He organized a brigade of almost one thousand sailors and did much to quiet the panic of the citizens of Baltimore.

One of Smith's principal tasks was to try to reassemble the militia that had been scattered at Bladensburg. A want ad was placed in the local papers urging them to gather at Baltimore. Another ad called on "Elderly men, who are able to carry a firelock, and willing to render a last service to their Country." Most important of all, militia from the neighboring state of Virginia poured into Baltimore to aid in its defense. The 38th U.S. Infantry Regiment pitched their tents on Hampstead Hill and were joined by five companies of volunteers from Pennsylvania.

On Sunday, September 11, word reached Baltimore that the British were on their way up the bay with the manifest intention of attacking the city. The Sabbath services were interrupted by the news, and the Reverend John Gruber dismissed his congregation with the prayer: "May the Lord bless King George, convert him, and take him to heaven, as we want no more of him."

Smith, as concerned about a possible British movement by land as by water, dispatched General John Stricker with some thirty-two hundred men for North Point to guard the peninsula. Fort McHenry was under the command of young Major George Armistead whose wife expected their first child at any hour.

Here two other incidents must be mentioned. Francis Scott Key, a young Georgetown lawyer, had gone with a friend to try to arrange for the release of an elderly American doctor captured by the British. He and his friend were politely received by Admiral Cochrane but detained lest they carry back some word of the British plan of attack. A year earlier, when Fort McHenry was being refurbished, Armistead had appealed to Samuel Smith for a "suitable ensign to display over Star Fort . . . a flag so large that the British will have no difficulty in seeing it from a distance." Mary Young Pickersgill, a widow whose specialty was making flags, was given the task. The fifteen stars were each two feet across, and the alternate red and white stripes—fifteen of those as well—were two feet in width; four hundred yards of cloth were required to make the huge flag, which, when raised on its towering pole, could indeed be seen miles away.

Ross, with forty-seven hundred men and accompanied by the irrepressible Cockburn, looking for more action, landed at North Point at seven o'clock on the morning of September 12 and headed up the peninsula for Baltimore. Stopping for a leisurely breakfast at the Gorsuch farm, Ross's advance guard encountered a patrol of Americans from General Stricker's detachment. There was an exchange of fire, and Ross came forward with his staff to assess the situation. When turning his horse to ride back and bring up the main body, Ross was struck by a sharpshooter's bullet and was fatally injured. The command devolved on Colonel Arthur Brooke, a relatively inexperienced officer, who pushed his soldiers on until they encountered Stricker's hastily laid out defensive line across their path, the right flank on Bear Creek, the left on Bread and Cheese Creek. Stricker had made excellent disposition of his troops to meet the British attack. As the British advanced, the American artillery, loaded with every kind of scrap metal that could be collected, opened fire with considerable effect. Soon afterward the infantry fired. When Brooke maneuvered to Stricker's left, the militia there gave way and ran for their lives, spreading panic as they went. For a time the center held, and the militia, protected by a heavy rail fence, kept up a scattered fire. Private Uriah Prosser, a Revolutionary veteran, was killed fighting beside his son, and many others fell with him. Finally Stricker, imperiled by the flight of the militia that exposed his flank and rear, managed to extricate the main body of his troops and withdraw in some kind of order, avoiding the shameless rout of Bladensburg. One hundred sixty-three Americans had been killed or wounded and 50 taken prisoner. The British had also suffered substantial casualties, over 300 men. The troops were weary from marching and fighting and demoralized by the death of their commanding general.

Meanwhile, Cochrane was attempting to reduce Fort McHenry to rubble with bombs discharged from boats that were little more than floating platforms. The mortars and cannon were designed to lob shells into forts that could not be safely engaged by warships. Thus, Cochrane's frigates could lie well out of range of the batteries in Fort McHenry while the fort was bombarded by shot and shell as well as by Congreve rockets intended to set fire to anything combustible.

The time of flight of a bomb was calculated by the officer in charge of firing, and a fuse was cut with the intention of having the bomb burst just before impact, throwing its deadly shrapnel far and wide. Fortunately, it was a crude method; many bombs burst too soon, others after impact, and some not at all; hence, "bombs bursting in air" was an accurate description of the destiny of many such shells.

That the intention of the British was to leave Baltimore in ruins is indicated by a letter from one of the British officers to his wife the evening of the attack: "I do not like to contemplate scenes of blood and destruction, but my heart is deeply interested in the coercion of these Baltimore heroes, who are perhaps the most inveterate against us of all the Yankees, and I hope they will be chastized even until they excite my pity, by which time they will be sufficiently humbled."

At seven o'clock on the morning of September 12 the five British bomb boats, safely out of range of the fort two miles away, began their bombardment. Since each bomb boat could fire some forty shells an hour, Cochrane was confident that the fort would be destroyed long before sunup. After futile efforts to reach the British boats, Armistead had no alternative except to order his men to hunker down and protect themselves as best they could, leaving them, as one officer put it, "like pigeons tied by the legs to be shot at."

Hour after hour the bomb boats continued their erratic fire without any sign that the fort was being substantially weakened. At two o'clock in the afternoon a bomb did land on the southwest bastion, dismounting a cannon and killing its crew, a somber indication of the potency of the shells when they landed on target. One subsequently landed in the powder magazine. If it had exploded, all of the occupants of the fort would have been blown sky-high, but someone quickly doused the fuse with water. In the midst of the bombardment, the defenders of Fort McHenry were enormously encouraged by the appearance on the parapet of a cock that crowed loudly and defiantly.

In midafternoon, Armistead noticed that three bomb boats and the rocket ships were moving closer to the fort, apparently confident that its guns had been silenced. As soon as they were within range, Armistead ordered his guns to open fire. Two of the boats were hit in the first volley, and Cochrane ordered them to withdraw. There matters rested until evening, with the bomb boats continuing their intermittent shelling. It was clear to Cochrane by this time that the reduction of the fort was a vain hope. Although he had cautioned the already cautious Brooke against attacking Baltimore, Cochrane had also promised to continue the bombardment as a cover to an attack were Brooke determined to carry it out, so at eight o'clock in the evening his bomb boats and the rocket ship increased their rate of fire. But Brooke had decided against an attack on Hampstead Hill. He had been informed that fifteen thousand Americans were dug in, support-ed by 120 guns, and his own observations revealed that the defenses were very well constructed. Fifteen thousand Americans seemed rather a large number for forty-five hundred British soldiers to engage, even if they were Wellington's "Invincibles." So Brooke, despite the urging of Cockburn—less insistent now that Ross was dead—decided that discretion was the better part of valor and prepared to withdraw to North Point.

The bombardment of the night of September 12–13 was thus somewhat in the nature of a "parting shot," although there were a considerable number of them. But it made a splendid display with bombs bursting in air and the Congreve rockets casting a red glare over the fort and harbor and the British ships. Francis Scott Key had Federalist inclinations and was by no means a supporter of Madison's war; he also deplored Baltimore's reputation as a "mob city." But his encounter with the British officers, extending now over four days, had been disillusioning. He found them "illiberal, ignorant and vulgar . . . filled with a spirit of malignity against everything American," so he watched the spectacular bombardment through "the perilous night" with considerable anxiety and when dawn revealed Mrs. Pickersgill's enormous flag still flying, he sat down and wrote a poem for the occasion on the back of a letter he found in his pocket.

As the British fleet began to drop down the river, Commodore Rodgers wrote to the secretary of the navy: "The enemy has been severely drubbed [a justifiable exaggeration under the circumstances] —as well his Army as his Navy—and is retiring down the river after expending many tons of shot, from 1800–2000 shells, and at least 700–800 rockets." Major Armistead received an immediate promotion to lieutenant colonel from Madison and a commemorative punch bowl the size of a British bomb, while Mrs. Armistead gave him a baby daughter. "So you see, my dear wife," he wrote, "all is well, at least your husband has got a name and standing that nothing but divine providence could have given him, and I pray to my Heavenly Father that we may long live to enjoy." Sad to say, he died four years later at the age of thirty-eight.

Francis Scott Key completed the poem he had begun the morning after the final bombardment of Fort McHenry. He planned to have it sung to the tune of "Adams and Liberty," which, in turn, had been borrowed from an English drinking song. He showed it to several friends, one of whom took it to the *American and Commercial Daily Advertiser* and had it printed as a handbill to be distributed around town. It was an immediate success and a few weeks later, when it was reprinted in a newspaper, someone added a title—"The Star-Spangled Banner."

As word of the defense of Baltimore spread through other states, patriots gave themselves over to celebrations—bells, the firing of cannon, flags, bunting, feasts, dancing in the streets, music, and much singing of the new song. The illusion of British invincibility was shattered. One newspaper proclaimed "Ten thousand victories cannot give them their former hopes, and the spell is lost forever."

On the other side of the Atlantic the *Morning Chronicle* passed on to its readers the titillating news that Baltimore had not only surrendered to Cochrane but had "seceded from the Union and proclaimed itself neutral." The *Morning Post* hailed the abortive attack as "another brilliant victory. . . . All the victories of Alexander, Caesar, Scipio, and Hannibal are dimmed by the resplendent glories of the heroes of our isle . . . it is indeed distressing that their immediate duty requires them to contend with a set of creatures who take the field only to disgrace the musket."

News of the indignities suffered by the nation's capital complicated the already difficult task of the team of American peace negotiators who had been meeting with their British counterparts in Ghent. The Americans were rather a mixed bag—John Quincy Adams, Albert Gallatin, Henry Clay, James A. Bayard, and Jonathan Russell. John Quincy Adams was all New England stiffness and rectitude. Henry Clay, representative of the Southwest, was a model of amiability and informality but a tough bargainer. Gallatin, who had resigned his position as secretary of the treasury, was a man who had overcome the prejudices created by his foreign accent and manner to become the most essential member of Madison's administration. At forty-seven Bayard was the same age as Adams and the commissioner most strongly identified with the Federalists. He had opposed the declaration of war, but he was a moderate and judicious man who had steered a sound course between the shoals of party rivalries. Russell, four years younger than Adams and Bayard, was included primarily because he was a New England Democrat and a supporter of Madison's administration. The most active British negotiator, though not the head of the mission, was Henry Goulburn, an Englishman of no great distinction who took a conspicuously hard line from the first. His position strengthened by the raid on Washington, he sent news of the burning to Clay, suggesting that it might relieve him of any boredom he might feel in Brussels where the American commissioner had gone for an interlude of sightseeing after months of deadlocked talks.

The initial demands of the British had seemed hardly credible to the Americans: the creation of an Indian buffer region between Canada and the United States in the Ohio Territory; the exclusion of any naval or military forces on the Great Lakes; the redrawing of the American Canadian boundary along the line from Sackett's Harbor to Lake Champlain in such a fashion as to place that area on the Canadian side; and, finally, a substantial part of Maine.

Lord Liverpool and the earl of Bathurst, who directed negotiations from London, seemed to fluctuate between wishing to prolong the war in order to complete the chastisement of the Americans and desiring to conclude peace because of the ruinous cost of continued fighting and the desire of British merchants to see an end of American privateering.

The American envoys were strengthened by the unsettled state of things on the Continent. Russia had taken Poland, and France appeared to be growing restive. Suddenly England needed peace as badly as the Americans. In its dilemma the ministry turned to Wellington and urged him to "go out with full powers to make peace, or to continue the war." The government was, Liverpool wrote, anxious to bring the war "to an honourable conclusion." Wellington refused and gave Liverpool some plain talk: "I confess that I think you have no right from the state of the war to demand any concession of territory from America." With signs of mutiny in Parliament, the ministry became increasingly conciliatory.

News of the British debacle at Plattsburgh tipped the scale toward the Americans. A British staff officer wrote, "Good God! Is it to be borne that an officer in command of 9,000 British troops shall retreat before a handful of Banditti . . . as if there were no such thing as national honour and professional credit to fight for!" Even before news reached Britain of the reverses to British arms in the Northwest and the repulse of Cochrane at Baltimore, the government was clearly prepared to retreat from its initial positions while at the same time pushing on with plans for an expedition against New Orleans—perhaps with the notion that even if a treaty were concluded, the capture of New Orleans and the resultant control of the Mississippi could bring about a new round of negotiations. The negotiators thus gradually retreated toward the status quo ante bellum—the situation at the time of the beginning of the hostilities.

While the defenders of Baltimore were bracing for an attack on the city and the British ministry was mustering troops and transports to capture New Orleans, the most intractable Federalists of New England were plotting secession from the Union. In their view, the War of 1812 was directed as much against New England as Great Britain. Harrison Gray Otis, one of the more moderate Federalist leaders, described it as "the war made upon *us*," and in speaking in the Massachusetts state legislature he spelled out New England's paranoia.

Its most basic anxiety was the extension of the "territorial limits" of the United States. The Louisiana Purchase still rankled. If Congress could take such unconstitutional action, why might it not in time undertake to add states on the northwest coast of the continent? It was evident to any reasonable man "that this multiplication of new States, not parties to the original compact, must soon be regarded as fatal to the rights and liberties of some of the present members of the confederacy, and consequently as an unsupportable grievance." The acquisition of Louisiana had already "excited a spirit of cupidity and speculation," Otis declared, "which is among the causes of our present troubles." The addition of new states had resulted in the loss of influence by the New England states in the "National Councils" and in the imposition of "systems of commercial restriction, of War, and conquest, fatal to their interests and outrageous to their feelings."

Gouverneur Morris was convinced that the only measure that could "rescue the country from her present miserable and ridiculous condition is to appoint a few representatives of both parties to meet other representatives from the States north of the Potomac, and consider the state of the nation; that this body, when met, will readily take the ground no longer to allow a representation of slaves; that this geographical division will terminate the political divisions which now prevail, and give a new object to men's minds; that the Southern States must then either submit to what is just or break up the Union."

The discontent of New England culminated in what is known to history as the Hartford Convention. The suggestion had been several times made of a convention to discuss the common grievances of New England, the implication of course being that the consequence of such a convention might well be a secession of the Northern states from the Union. In sections of Massachusetts where the secession Federalists were strongest, the call for a convention had been one of the Federalist planks in the state elections of 1814; the Federalists had captured the legislature and the governorship by substantial margins. In the fall, the Massachusetts legislature recommended that "a conference should be invited between those states, the affinity of whose interest is closest." The conference was to consider the best means for defense against the foreign enemy—England—and, by implication, against the domestic enemy—the South. The delegates, it was suggested in the call to the convention, might wish to take steps "for procuring a convention of the Delegates from all the United States, in order to revise the Constitution thereof, and more effectually to secure the support and attachment of all the people, by placing all upon the basis of fair representation," a reference, of course, to the fact that the slave population of the South was counted as "three-fifths of all other persons" for the purposes of representation in the House.

Caleb Strong, the governor of Massachusetts, had sent a secret emissary to the British commander in Halifax to sound out that gentleman on the possibilities of a separate peace between the New England states and Great Britain in the event Madison tried to enforce certain federal measures in that state, but none of this penetrated the convention that met at Hartford on December 15.

The *Boston Gazette*, welcoming the call for a convention, declared: "If James Madison is not out of office [by July 4, 1815] a new form of government will be in operation in the eastern section of the Union." The *Columbian Centinel*, the authoritative Federalist paper, reminded the delegates to the convention of how little Holland "threw off the yoke of Spain (our Virginia)."

The general feeling was that the federal government was on the brink of collapse. A Virginian who visited the White House reported that the president looked "miserably shattered and woebegone. In short, he looks broken-hearted." Daniel Webster predicted "a blow-up soon. . . . Everything is in confusion. . . . If Peace does not come this winter, the Govt. will die of its own weakness." A few days later he wrote, "The Govt. *cannot last*, under this war, and in the hands of these men another twelve-month. Not that the opposition will break it down, but it will break itself down. It will go out. This is my sober opinion."

News of the Hartford Convention aroused indignation in many quarters, especially, of course, among New England Republicans and those Federalists who put loyalty to the government above partisan politics. Abigail Adams spoke for her husband as well as herself when she wrote of a resolution of the legislature denouncing the war: "The conduct of our own State Government cannot surely meet the approbation of any real American. I should much rather chuse, that the Name of my Family should be blotted from the page of History, than appear upon Record as the proposer of such a Resolution. . . . I do not view this war, as waged for conquest, or ambition, but for our injured Rights, for our freedom, and the security of our Independence, and therefore rejoice when any Naval victory, or military success attend upon our Arms."

In the South the convention was viewed as unmistakable evidence of New England's instinct for treachery. The *Richmond Enquirer* called on Madison to order the U.S. Army to attack New England and declared: "No man, no association of men, no state or set of states *has a right* to withdraw from this Union, of its own accord. The same power which knit us together, can only unknit us. . . . The *majority of states* which form the Union must consent to the withdrawal of *any one* branch of it. Until *that* consent has been obtained, any attempt to dissolve the *Union*, or to obstruct the efficacy of its constitutional laws, is Treason—Treason to all intents and purposes."

The convention, to which the respective states by and large appointed the most moderate Federalists, turned out to be a damp firecracker. There was no talk of secession or a new constitution. Instead, resolves were passed on such issues as the right of the government to call up state militia and the propriety of using "federal revenue for purposes of conquest"—a reference to the attempted invasion of Canada. In addition, the delegates recommended "certain amendments to the Constitution." The final report of the convention conceded that "a sentiment prevails to no inconsiderable extent . . . that the time for a change is at hand. Those who so believe, regard the evils which surround them as intrinsic and incurable defects in the Constitution. . . . This opinion may ultimately prove to be correct. But, as the evidence on which it rests is not yet conclusive," the convention had contented itself with "some general considerations . . . submitted in the hope of reconciling all to a course of moderation and firmness." The Constitution had, it was true, been perverted by a weak and dishonest administration, "But to attempt upon every abuse of power to change the Constitution would be to perpetuate the evils of revolution. . . . Finally, if the Union be destined to dissolution by reason of the multiplied abuses of bad administrations, it should, if possible, be the work of peaceable times and deliberate consent. . . . These are among the principal objections against precipitate measures tending to disunite the States, and when examined in connection with the farewell address of the Father of his country, they must, it is believed, be deemed conclusive."

The handiwork of the Hartford Convention is of interest primarily as an inventory of all the grievances the New England Federalists had accumulated in fifteen years of Republican rule. The report listed such particulars as Jefferson's attack on the federal judiciary, the ruthless turning out of office of Federalists, the admission of new Western states, devotion to France, and "Lastly *and principally*,—A visionary and superficial theory in regard to commerce, accompanied by . . . a ruinous perseverance in efforts to render it an instrument of coercion and war." The last was certainly true. Jefferson had conceived and carried into effect a policy aimed at coercing England by sacrificing the commercial life of New England, the section of the country most favorably disposed toward the former mother country.

The seven amendments to the Consitution proposed by the convention spelled out its resentments in detail. In addition to eliminating slaves as a basis of representation, the delegates wished to effectively block the admission of new states by requiring a concurrent two-thirds vote of both houses; allow no naturalized citizen to hold any appointive or elective office in the federal government (the anti-Gallatin amendment), and no president to serve more than one term or the same state to have two successive presidents. The delegates must have known that any hope of their amendments being accepted by states outside New England were chimerical; yet here they were—in part, at least, a record of the reactionary politics of the diehard Federalists. While the leaders, pleased at having restrained the hotheads and revolutionaries, were congratulating themselves on the moderate temper of the convention, the rest of the country was shaking its collective head at this fresh evidence of New England's waywardness. The fact that the report of the Hartford Convention appeared just at the moment when the news arrived of Jackson's great victory at New Orleans and, a few weeks before news of the peace signified by the Treaty of Ghent reached Washington, made it seem even more carping and archaic. It did have the positive effect of clearing the air in New England, and that, with the conclusion of the war, brought an end to talk of secession. Harrison Gray Otis, the principal architect of both the convention and the report, termed it no more than "a manual of elementary principles—a commentary on WASHINGTON's Farewell address." It was hardly that, but it was no call to arms either.

36

Andrew Jackson and the Battle of New Orleans

The American treaty commissioners and their British counterparts had signed a treaty—the Treaty of Ghent—on Christmas Eve, but it would be weeks before the momentous fact that peace had been concluded would be known in the United States. Meanwhile Sir Edward Pakenham, Wellington's brother-in-law, appointed to replace Ross and direct the British assault on New Orleans, had departed for an invasion rendezvous at Jamaica. We must now go back some months to trace Andrew Jackson's campaign against the Creek Indians, stirred to rebellion by Tecumseh's visit and the dream of driving the white men into the Atlantic Ocean. Little Warrior, an ardent disciple of the Shawnee chief who had participated in the massacre of the wounded American soldiers at Raisin River, turned south to try to persuade the warriors of his tribe to take the warpath. On the way, he and his braves, anticipating the destruction of all whites, murdered a family of white settlers.

When the Creek chiefs heard of the killing of the settlers by Little Warrior and his braves from the Indian agent Benjamin Hawkins, along with a demand to deliver them for justice, the chiefs ordered the offenders killed. This caused even greater excitement among the Southern tribes. The chiefs had to place themselves under Hawkins's protection. Some two thousand "Red Sticks," given that name because of their red war clubs, voted to kill all those Indians involved in the ·death of Little Warrior and his band and to drive the white men out of the Southern states. There was a small and inconclusive engagement at a place called Burnt Corn, in Monroe County, Alabama, but news of that battle and word that the Indian prophets High Head Jim and Josiah Francis were whipping up the Indians in the region to go on the warpath caused panic on the frontier. Hundreds of isolated settlers abandoned their farms and gathered at "forts," usually some agreed-on spot where they could erect rough palisades. On a bend of the Alabama River, at the home of Samuel Mims, a prosperous half-breed, such a fort was built and occupied by settlers fleeing from the aroused Indians. By August, 1813, there were 553 people in the fort, an ill-assorted company that included a few volunteer militia, friendly Indians, men, women, and children. Once gathered and feeling confidence in their numbers, the defenders of the fort became lax. Although warned by slaves that large numbers of hostile Indians were nearby, the settlers dismissed the warnings.

The Red Sticks attacked while the occupants of the fort were at supper. Of the 553 persons in the fort only 15 or 20 escaped. Those not killed in the first attack were tortured to death and horribly mutilated, and over 250 scalps were borne off on scalp poles by the triumphant Creek. Stimulated by their success, the Indians ravaged the region, burning houses and barns and destroying crops in the abandoned fields. Numerous whites were killed, and the country was soon virtually deserted by settlers, who crowded into five or six "forts" like that at Samuel Mims's plantation. Word went out to the governors of Tennessee, Louisiana, and Georgia calling for militia levies to drive off the Indians. Twenty-five hundred men were mustered and put under the command of Andrew Jackson.

Jackson himself was recovering from the effects of a fight with another Tennessee hero, Thomas Hart Benton. Jackson, angry at some remark attributed to Benton, had tried to horsewhip him in a tavern in Nashville. For once the hot-tempered Tennessean seems to have bitten off more than he could chew. In the brawl that followed he was thrown downstairs and shot in the shoulder. Now, the bullet still in his shoulder, Jackson began his campaign against the Creek with a motley collection of tough but poorly trained, undisciplined soldiers. Already known as "Old Hickory" because of his toughness and durability, Jackson was forty-six years old and amply endowed with that fierce tenaciousness that is one of the primary ingredients of a successful military leader. Like George Rogers Clark, Benedict Arnold, John Paul Jones, and Oliver Hazard Perry, Jackson possessed remarkable powers of charismatic leadership and an unflinching determination to succeed in whatever mission he undertook. Where a more conventional commander would have waited for food and supplies for his army, Jackson sent foraging parties out ahead and pushed into the wilderness, establishing Fort Deposit on the Tennessee and Fort Strother at the headwaters of the Coosa. He then pushed on and destroyed a party of Hillabee Creek who were attacking the Indian town of Talladega, occupied by friendly Creek.

Back at Fort Strother, a portion of Jackson's troops, cold, unpaid, and half-starved, mutinied. Jackson prevailed on the volunteer militia to help him suppress the mutiny, but the next day it was the turn of the volunteers to start for home. Now it was the militia who blocked the volunteers. For a few days there was relative calm; then the volunteers, announcing that their terms of enlistment were up, stated their determination to depart on December 12. Jackson, having exhausted his powers of persuasion, called out his small army at eight o'clock in the evening, arrayed the militia supported by cannon against the volunteers, and told them that if they were determined to leave they would have to do so over his dead body.

New recruits arrived the next day and the volunteers were dismissed, but the new men were worse than the old. Jackson nevertheless advanced deep into Red Stick country and fought an inconclusive engagement there with a large body of Creek. The situation was too risky even for Jackson, and he fell back to Fort Strother. Two other armies were no more successful. The Creek remained unchastened. Finally a new muster of four thousand men was called up by the governor of Tennessee, and half of them were assigned to Jackson. Again, there was the perpetual problem of short enlistments and poor discipline. Jackson shot a soldier who refused to obey an order and threatened to treat every man who tried to leave as a deserter.

By the time Jackson had produced some order in his army, many of the men had only a month left of their term of enlistment. He thus decided to float his troops down the Coosa to the Ocfuskee Indian settlement. There the Indians had built a crescent-shaped fort of logs across a bend of the river. Sending part of his force, including a large detachment of Cherokee, to cut off any retreat, Jackson opened artillery fire on the front of the fort. Attacked in the front and rear and suffering heavy casualties, the Indians refused to surrender and fought to the death. Out of over 800 Indians in the fort at the beginning of the battle, 557 were killed in the fighting. More were shot trying to swim to safety. Jackson's losses were 51 killed and 158 wounded, among them Samuel Houston. From the Ocfuskee settlement, known from the bend in the river as the Horseshoe, Jackson marched his force south, destroying abandoned Indian villages on the way until the remaining Red Sticks escaped into Florida.

Upon his return to Tennessee, Jackson was promoted to the rank of major general and was put in command of the military district that took in most of the Southwest frontier. He was ordered to establish his headquarters at Mobile and make a treaty with the vanquished Creek. The problem was that the only Creek around for Jackson to make peace with were those who had refused to join the Red Sticks and who had, in many instances, assisted the whites. Jackson nonetheless drove a cruelly hard bargain with the chiefs at Fort Jackson—a treaty that John Bach McMaster, no champion of the Indians, referred to as "one of the many gross and shameless wrongs on the Indians which disgrace the American people."

Jackson demanded, among other things, that the Creek give up all their ancestral lands between the Chattahoochee and the Coosa rivers as indemnity for the war. When the chiefs refused the treaty, Jackson threatened to declare them enemies and to hunt down and kill them and their followers. Convinced that they had no alternative, the chiefs signed away a large portion of the homeland guaranteed them by earlier treaties.

The pattern was already a familiar one: the younger and more impetuous warriors of tribes at peace with the United States stirred up by their shamans or prophets and enraged by illegal encroachments of whites on their hunting lands, would descend on isolated settlements and kill their inhabitants. A "war" would follow in which militia and regulars would defeat the Indians and then demand as part of the peace agreement another large cession of land.

In September, Jackson received word that the British apparently planned an expedition against New Orleans with a force of some 15,000 of those fabled veterans of Wellington's army. Madison ordered Jackson to take charge of the troops in the region—numbering some 12,500—and to be prepared to defend the city. By the time Jackson received his instructions from Madison, the news of the British intention to seize New Orleans had circulated throughout the country. The New England Federalists assumed that Pakenham's expedition against New Orleans could succeed; indeed they wished it success. A British victory and the capture of the mouth of the Mississippi seemed to the Federalists the only hope of removing the incubus of the Louisiana Purchase. Timothy Pickering, the irreconcilable, wrote: "From the moment that the British possess New Orleans, the Union is severed." The West must then ally itself with Great Britain to assure access to the Mississippi, and the "good old Thirteen States" might finally put their house in order.

Jackson, who was ill, arrived at New Orleans early in December. There he found that Edward Livingston, a lawyer and a member of the great Livingston clan of New York who had been forced to emigrate to New Orleans to escape imprisonment for debt, had organized a Committee of Defense and induced the governor to call a special session of the legislature. But the legislature did nothing, and New Orleans appeared likely to be Britain's for the plucking. A great fleet had rendezvoused in Cuba; Admiral Cochrane's flagship was an eighty-gun frigate, and it was accompanied by fifty British ships of the line—frigates, corvettes, and troopships carrying twenty thousand soldiers, sailors, and marines, among them two black regiments raised in the West Indies and four regiments of the famous Scottish Highlanders.

A week after Jackson arrived with only a small portion of the troops under his command, the British force landed at Chandeleur Island at the southeastern end of Lake Borgne, a part of that complex network of lakes and moraines that characterize the geography of the Mississippi where it enters the Gulf of Mexico. Barges and shallow-draft brigs of war entered the lake, where they encountered six gunboats that were captured and destroyed on December 14. Now the British were within striking distance of New Orleans. Two bayous, Bienvenu and Mazant, ran past plantations within a mile or two of the river, the latter connected to it by a canal. Ten miles up the river lay New Orleans, virtually defenseless.

When word reached Jackson of the destruction of the American gunboats on Lake Borgne, he responded by mobilizing all the resources of the territory, from Pierre and Jean Lafitte and their pirates to the merchants of New Orleans. A proclamation was issued to the citizens of the city declaring that every male resident who failed to appear with a firearm would be considered a friend of the British. Jackson followed this by declaring martial law.

Meanwhile the British were laboriously moving troops across Lake Borgne in launches and barges. On December 22, 1,688 British soldiers made their way along Bayou Mazant to the canal and hence to the Villere plantation, where they captured the whole family. Major Gabriel Villere, whose father, Jacques Villere, was major general of volunteers in New Orleans, escaped and carried word to Jackson. At that point there was nothing between the British detachment and the city. But with Villere's news, Jackson ordered the cathedral bells tolled and drums beat to summon all troops and volunteers to the parade ground. The lateral irrigation canals that ran off the river at each plantation provided natural defense lines, and certain of these were immediately occupied by U.S. regulars and Tennessee volunteers. Jackson, with 2,200 men and two artillery pieces, headed down the east bank of the levee to the Villere plantation while the fourteen-gun *Carolina* dropped down the river and, when Jackson was in position for an attack, opened fire from the river. Dusk and a heavy fog enabled the Americans to penetrate directly into the British camp before they were discovered, and there the veterans of Wellington's army found themselves engaged in furious hand-to-hand fighting with the strangest soldiers they had ever seen—wild-looking men in shabby clothes and hunting shirts. The British withdrew until they found a refuge behind an old levee, and a stand-off occurred.

The psychological effect of the American forces' instant response was enormous. The inclination of most commanders in such circumstances would have been to turn their attention to defensive measures. Jackson's decision to attack was the mark of his brilliance as a military leader.

The disconcerted British commander pushed the movement of his troops, until by Christmas Day six thousand were encamped at the Villere plantation; it proved, however, a slow and arduous task to bring the artillery—nine fieldpieces and three mortars—across the swamps to support the British assault on the American defenses. Jackson meanwhile established his main line on the Rodriguez Canal and put his men to work constructing strong emplacements and breastworks. Jackson's defense works along the canal were made of earth, but where they ran through the woods they were constructed of felled trees, two feet apart, with earth between.

With their guns brought up, British artillery set the *Carolina* afire with hot shot, and thirty British guns were emplaced in eight batteries to support an infantry attack. On January 1 General Pakenham ordered his artillery, supplemented by the Congreve rockets, to open fire on the American lines as the preliminary to an assault. The Americans replied, and their fire was so much heavier and better directed that four hours later the British artillery had been put out of action. Pakenham, his Wellington veterans notwithstanding, now began to have misgivings. He decided to delay the attack until more of his men had made their way from the main camp at the entrance to Lake Borgne. Four days thus passed before Pakenham, now commanding eight thousand redcoats, renewed the assault on the American positions.

Before he could launch his attack on Jackson's line, Pakenham felt he had to put an American battery under the command of General David Morgan out of action. Morgan's battery was situated in a fort on the west bank of the river. The British detachment dispatched on this mission was carried so far downriver by the current that they landed six miles below the American fort. Since Pakenham's attack against Jackson was to be coordinated with the movement against Morgan's battery, Pakenham waited for more than an hour for that operation to begin, and then, knowing only that something had gone awry, he ordered the advance.

Against his veterans was arrayed as variegated an "army" as could be imagined. Most conspicuous were the Louisiana Creoles, many of them young French gentlemen from New Orleans and the adjacent plantations, in gaudy red-and-blue uniforms. There were sailors from the *Carolina* and several other vessels with their cannon; a battalion of free blacks; a battalion of French Santo Domingo refugees; some old French soldiers; Tennessee and Kentucky volunteers; and, scattered along the line to stiffen it, units of the regular army. The scene that followed was reminiscent, in many ways, of the Battle of Bunker Hill.

It seemed to Pakenham that the weakest part of the American line was its east end, which extended into a swamp and so far as his spyglass revealed was defended by what appeared to him to be ununiformed civilians—in other words, the notorious militia who invariably threw down their arms and fled when confronted by the bayonets of British regulars. It was toward the left, or east, of the American line, therefore, that Pakenham dispatched his most trusted assault troops, who floundered forward in a formation sixty men wide and eight deep, in high spirits, loaded down with heavy packs, scaling ladders, and fascines to be used to fill in the irrigation ditches. Whatever might be the deficiencies of the frontier militia in open engagements, when they were ensconced behind almost impregnable works with nothing to do but aim and shoot their muskets and rifles, they were the most dangerous antagonists in the world, and this the pride of the British army discovered at fearful cost. Everywhere the British assault units, advancing in the main across open ground completely exposed to the combined fire of their opponents, suffered terrible casualties. Well before they reached the ditch in front of the American line, they broke and fell back, leaving hundreds of dead and wounded on the field. At their line of departure they were regrouped by General Sir Samuel Gibbs. This time they discarded their packs and came on the double. Gibbs was shot, and Pakenham, waving his hat and cheering his men on, was hit by a cannonball and killed instantly. On the left bank the British had more success. There they drove off the men protecting Morgan's battery, spiked his guns, and moved upriver to the rear of Jackson's line.

The death of Pakenham meant the end of the British attempt to take New Orleans. The officer on whom the command devolved, sickened by the slaughter of his country's finest troops, began his withdrawal. Almost 700 British soldiers had been killed, including 3 generals, 11 colonels, and 75 officers of lower rank. Many more had been wounded—estimates ran as high as 2,000. The American losses were 18 killed and 13 wounded. What had taken place was less a battle than organized carnage. It demonstrated clearly once again that the British military mind, in the grip of irrelevant and outmoded chivalric ideals, was prepared to sacrifice thousands of ordinary Englishmen to sustain the mystique. There was no military logic or excuse for the kind of operation Sir Edward Pakenham launched against Jackson's virtually impregnable lines. He would never have dared to make such an assault against Napoleon's seasoned troops. New Orleans was highly vulnerable to attack from half a dozen directions. Pakenham's task was to deploy his forces so that the Americans would be forced to meet his veterans on open ground. But Pakenham was too contemptuous of the fighting qualities of his enemy to condescend to employ conventional tactics against them. The sternest trial of troops—and thus the greatest glory—was an assault against strong defensive positions. Here all their training and discipline were put to the ultimate test. Here was where colors and banners were to be-earned to grace the dining halls of famous regiments and prove beyond cavil the superiority of British arms.

Poor Pakenham, who was no better or worse than most of his class, paid for his delusions with his life, as well as with the lives of many brave and honorable men. He did so, in the final irony, in a "battle" that took place after peace had actually been concluded but before the news had reached America.

The key to the devastating British losses at the Battle of New Orleans lay, in part at least, in the poignant fact that the ordinary soldier's sense of his own reality or "worth" was directly related to his capacity to advance unflinchingly in the face of almost certain death. Such attitudes are only to be found in a strongly delineated class society where the psychic life of a segment of the lower classes (in this case, the army) is absorbed in, or dominated by, the chivalric ideal of the aristocracy. It is unquestionably true that no American soldiers could have performed so exacting and suicidal a feat. (It may also be doubted that any American officer would have ordered an attack under such circumstances.) In a society lacking any notion of "natural" or traditional subordination—where the individual was, indeed, aggressively determined to make it clear that "he was as good as the next fellow" and perfectly ready to subject any "order" to critical scrutiny and obey or disobey it as he was inclined—dominance over others could be established only on economic grounds. Those who had power in American society were, in essence, those who controlled the economic destinies of others, primarily as employers. Of course, this is true in most if not all societies, but in many other cultures raw economic power was balanced, or supplemented, by other forms of power, class undoubtedly being the most common.

In a democratic society the role of the military leader is a peculiarly exacting one. He has to establish his authority primarily on personal or moral grounds; by virtue of his ability to dominate the usually unruly wills of others. This meant that the successful military leader was, typically, a person of remarkable *intensity*, often verging on a kind of madness. We have argued that men like Benedict Arnold, George Rogers Clark, John Paul Jones, "Mad" Anthony Wayne, and, in the political realm, Alexander Hamilton and Aaron Burr, were possessed by a degree of single-minded intensity of purpose (commonly called ambition) that touched on, and sometimes slipped over into, the realm of madness. Andrew Jackson certainly belonged to the type.

In conventional armies, competence rather than genius is required. Any well-trained military unit should be able to function effectively under adequate leadership. That is the only proper basis for a regular army. In American military units the situation was quite different. In commanding a mixed bag of intractable individualists, a substantial degree of genius was required if any worthwhile results were to be achieved. It had nothing to do with "courage" or "cowardice" but a good deal to do with the new consciousness and Secular-Democratic psyche.

The Battle of New Orleans, which could hardly be said to have been a battle at all in the true sense of that word, may have been a fitting conclusion to a war that need never have been, that settled nothing, and that had threatened to deepen the already deep political and sectional differences in the country.

37

The Election of 1816

What of the War of 1812? In the days when historians thought it
their duty to explain the "causes" of everything, there were a
number of causes put forward—the expansionist spirit or, as it came to
be known, "manifest destiny" (manifest in the desire to add Canada to
the United States); impressment; the British orders in council; and so
forth. I recall one list of twelve causes that I dutifully memorized in
graduate school. As with most important events in history, the causes
of the War of 1812, once one gets past the most simple and obvious
causes (which are rarely enough to satisfy the historian), are complex
in the extreme. Jefferson's policy of peace at any price, his illusion that
the United States could defend its legitimate interests in the world
without an army or a navy, may well have been a major factor in that it
encouraged the notion that the United States would never use force to
defend its rights and if it did that it lacked effective means of doing so;
important too were Madison's indecisiveness and tendency to continue
to defer to Jefferson even after he had become president; the
ambitions of the War Hawks; a residual hostility toward Britain; and
"bad timing."

"Unnecessary" as the war may have been, it nonetheless served its
own curious function. First, and perhaps of greatest importance, it

altered England's perception of Americans. Certainly upper-class Englishmen continued to look upon their transatlantic cousins with a condescension bordering on contempt—a view that, to be sure, they took toward most "lesser breeds"—but after the War of 1812 they perforce took them more seriously. The string of American naval victories at the beginning of the war, fleabites though they may have been, destroyed the illusion of British naval invincibility. The massacre of Wellington's Invincibles at New Orleans, though it proved actually very little about the fighting capacities of the respective armies, forced the British to take American arms seriously and gave that country a much keener sense than it had had before of the power of the United States to injure Great Britain.

Despite the euphoria produced by the defense of Baltimore, Macdonough's victory on Champlain, and the Battle of New Orleans, the war had a sobering effect on Americans as well. As it turned out, there were more than enough humiliating defeats and egregious errors to go around. The attempted invasion of Canada had been a fiasco. The American "fleet," despite its brilliant victories, had been driven from the sea early in the war. The national capital had been sacked; the United States had been forced to face unpleasant realities. Hereafter it felt a strong identity of interests with Great Britain. The impulse to yearn for English admiration, to idolize English institutions and English ways, strongest in New England but never far from the surface even in the South, reasserted itself so emphatically that Jefferson would write to James Monroe in 1823, "[with Great Britain] on our side we need not fear the whole world. With her, then, we should most sedulously cherish a cordial friendship."

So the War of 1812 marked the beginning of a new era in the relations between the United States and England. In a sense, it "ratified" the Revolution. It demonstrated to the British in what was perhaps the only conclusive way that the United States, whatever its failings and shortcoming, was "for real," and in doing that it allowed the natural affinity between the two nations to develop in a normal, and, for the most part, healthy way. It was one thing for a nation as proud as Great Britain to reluctantly abandon, after almost eight years, the effort to bring the United States back into a state of dependence and subordination; it was a change in consciousness of quite another dimension for Great Britain to take the nation that had resulted from that unfortunate misunderstanding seriously as an equal in the arena of international power politics. Much contempt of the United States remained in England as well as at least a modicum of that hatred so stridently expressed in the British newspapers during the war, but other and generally better sentiments soon came to overshadow them. Perhaps, in the long run, one of the most enduring consequences of the war was the fact that it made clear beyond cavil how economically interdependent the two countries were. Both nations suffered severely from the interruption of their trade, and with the war over it sprang forth in a vast outpouring of exports and imports.

Finally, if the war strengthened Americans' always precarious grip on reality, it also gave them a new sense of pride and unity. Despite the dogged efforts of the diehard New England Federalists to use the war as an occasion for pushing for a separate "confederation" and the region's foot-dragging response to calls for volunteers, the average Northerner took great pride in the naval achievements of such heroes as Perry, Decatur, and Macdonough, and of the men and officers who sailed and fought under them. While the war went badly elsewhere, New Englanders and New Yorkers gloried in Yankee naval victories. At the same time, these were "national" victories, celebrated with joy in Charleston, South Carolina, as well as Charlestown, Massachusetts. After the successful defense of Fort McHenry, "The Star-Spangled Banner" was sung with almost as much enthusiasm on the streets of Boston as in Baltimore.

It might be said that a nation, at least a kind of made-up, fabricated nation, is not truly a nation until it has demonstrated to itself and to others that it has the will to take up arms and defend itself. The United States was perilously close to being disunited in 1811. The country had lived through what, in retrospect, was to appear as one of its most critical periods (exceeded only by the Civil War era), a time of rancor, bitter partisanship, and frequent calls for disunion. Wise and moderate men had, time and again, despaired of the future of the Republic. But now they had fought the greatest military power in the world to a standstill, and a sense of nationhood and national unity possessed the country. If the basic differences remained as deep and dangerous and insoluble as ever, there was a new awareness of the reality of the United States as a nation. North, South, and West had each made dramatic contributions to the war.

So this strange, muddled, "unnecessary" war, which solved nothing on the practical level, appears to have resolved much on the psychological level. Indeed I am tempted to argue that it paved the way for the country's acceptance of Henry Clay's great Compromise of

1820, which in turn postponed, most happily, the day of final reckoning on the ultimate question—slavery.

In addition to the heightened sense of nationalism, the end of the war was marked by three or four significant developments. The impulse to democratic economics, or, more specifically, the determination of many small-town financiers to share in the huge profits they assumed the big-city banks were making had led to the refusal by Congress to recharter the Bank of the United States; this, in turn, had led to the rapid proliferation of banks of all degrees of unsoundness, the wild expansion of paper money, a drain of specie into New England due to the balance of trade in favor of that region, and a subsequent refusal of the new banks to redeem paper notes with specie.

In two years the number of banks increased from 88 to 208. The banks had authority to issue bills up to three times or more the amount of specie in their vaults. Not only did banks issue paper currency, but municipal corporations, individuals, factories, tradesmen's associations, and unchartered banks also issued such dubious paper. One result of the shortage of hard money in the form of small coins was the issuing of tens of thousands of one- and two-cent notes. A six-and-quarter-cent note survives issued by "A General Assortment of Groceries in Philadelphia" and redeemable "on demand, in groceries, or Philadelphia bank-notes."

In Zanesville, Ohio, thirty different "banks" issued currency, institutions with such names as Owl Creek Bank, the Perryopolis Bank, the Virginia Saline and the Parkersburg Bank, known also as the Saddlebag because its capital had been brought from Pittsburgh in the promoter's saddlebags.

The paper "coins" were known as shinplasters, and some were issued by tavern keepers, barbers, and blacksmiths. They were in fact rather like the redeemable coupons issued by modern grocery chains or gas stations.

In this chaotic financial situation, everyone suffered—buyers, sellers, investors in banks, and even speculators. Pressure thus mounted to do what had been undone, to reestablish a national bank by means of which some control could be exercised over private banks. Since the war had stimulated "wildcat" banking ventures, it was not surprising that the national feeling generated by the war facilitated the adoption by Congress of a plan for a national bank. The war had dramatized the fact that the states, however much they might dwell on their "sovereignty," were in fact part of a complex national economy, and if this economy were to flourish some order would have to be imposed on the financial activities of the states.

When Congress began its debate on chartering a national bank, two of the great triumvirate of Clay, Calhoun, and Webster were in favor of it. Clay and Calhoun spoke in its favor, and Webster opposed it. It was a revealing reversal of positions. The South was suffering from the constant drain of specie to New England. New England was profiting from the same process and was quite content to continue it. But the argument in Congress revolved around the question of the authority of Congress to charter a national bank. Calhoun, the Republican or Democratic states' rights champion-to-be, argued that the U.S. government was given the right to coin money but that it had in fact surrendered that right to some 260 banks scattered around the country over whom it had no control. It was the responsibility of the government to restore and insure hard money or specie redemption, and the only practical way to do this would be to charter a national bank. Webster based his objection on the grounds that Congress had no right to interfere with the operation of state banks.

After several weeks of debate, the Republican Congress voted to reestablish the national bank. The bank was another step toward enacting the once much denounced program of the Federalists. Indeed, by the time of the election of 1816, traditional party lines had lost all meaning. The Republican party, originally the party of peace and states' rights, had become the war party, the party of centralized power, the party of the Louisiana Purchase, loose construction, internal improvements, a strong army and navy, protective tariffs, and a national bank. The Federalists had become strict constructionists, enemies of internal improvements, advocates of states' rights, opposed to chartering a national bank. As John Adams put it, "Our two great parties have crossed over the valley and taken possession of each other's mountain." The turnabout exhausted irony and moved the acerbic John Randolph to call his party's platform "old Federalism, vamped up into something bearing the superficial appearance of Republicanism." The fact was that while the Federalists had had a sharp resurgence in 1814 and 1815, it was the party's last fling before it quietly expired. The Republicans had appropriated its principles even while denouncing them. The Federalists were left with no principles and no candidates that had any national appeal. The only question to be decided in 1816 was which of several leading Republican candidates should be designated as that party's candidate for the presidency.

James Monroe was Madison's choice for his successor. He, like Madison before him, had served as secretary of state. He was, moreover, looked upon as one of the last prominent figures, although a decidedly minor one, of the Revolutionary generation. His principal challenger was William H. Crawford, the brilliant young Georgian, a representative of the "rising generation" of democratic politicians who had taken control of Congress and who were more practically than ideologically oriented.

The result was a good deal of behind-the-scenes maneuvering. A visitor to Washington from Georgia noted, "Every day dims the ranks of Mr. Monroe's friends. The fact is that an overwhelming majority is in favor of Mr. C. and that he can be the next president if he wishes." But Crawford apparently had misgivings either about his own capacities or about whether the moment was a propitious one to push his candidacy. The tide swung, or was swung by administration forces, back to Monroe, and a caucus of Republican congressmen meeting in March chose him as the party's candidate. But it was by a disconcertingly narrow margin—65 to 54—and it seems clear that if Crawford had been willing to accept the nomination it could have been his.

Much of the opposition to Monroe centered on the fact that it was undesirable to have another Virginia president. The state seemed to have a monopoly on the office. From 1789 to 1816, a period of twenty-seven years, there had been only four years—Adams's term—when the office had not been held by a Virginian. Now there were to be eight more.

Jefferson wrote to Monroe from Monticello: "I shall not waste my time in idle congratulations. You know my joy in the commitment of the helm of our government to your hands." The Federalists, for their part, offered no candidate of their own, although Federalist electors cast thirty-four symbolic votes for the old Federalist war-horse, Rufus King, who had written to a friend shortly before the electoral college met (some of the Federalist electors did not even bother to attend): "It is quite worthy of remark, that in no preceding election, has there been such a calm respecting it; and it is equally so, that the Candidate does not possess the full respect or confidence of either party."

Fifty-nine years of age at the beginning of his term of office, Monroe was one of the least prepossessing of the major political figures of his age. He was not without ability, but he lacked distinction. His office was more the result of his long and dutiful services to his party and its leader, Jefferson, than to any conspicuous talents of his own. At his inauguration he seemed, in his old-fashioned wig, broadcloth tailcoat, kneebritches, and buckled shoes, like an agreeable reminder of an earlier and better age. It must be said in his favor that he was without vanity and without that jealousy of superiority that often characterizes mediocre men in high office. He made Crawford secretary of the treasury, where he distinguished himself; made John Quincy Adams, the ablest and most experienced diplomat of his day, secretary of state; and Calhoun secretary of war. It is interesting to note that Andrew Jackson had written him urging such a course of action: "Now is the time to exterminate the monster called party spirit. By selecting characters most conspicuous for their probity, virtue, capacity and firmness, without any regard to party, you will go far to . . . eradicate those feelings, which, on former occasions, threw so many obstacles in the way of government; and perhaps have the pleasure of uniting a people heretofore divided." Monroe replied that he believed firmly "in the principle, that the Chief Magistrate of the country, ought not to be the head of a party, but of the nation."

In his inaugural address—the first given out-of-doors—delivered to "an immense concourse of officers of the government, foreign officers, strangers (ladies as well as gentlemen) and citizens," Monroe touched all the proper chords: his determination to maintain "adequate land and naval forces," to bind the Union together "by roads and canals," and to give attention to encouraging manufacturers.

The congratulatory tone of his address ("we find abundant cause to felicitate ourselves in the excellence of our institutions . . . our citizens individually have been happy and the nation prosperous") was by now well established. Americans, it seemed, could hardly stand any direct references to difficulties that might prove intractable or disasters beyond redeeming. A disinterested observer might hardly have believed his ears when the president shook out his oratorical sails thus: "And if we look to the condition of individuals what a proud spectacle does it exhibit! On whom has oppression fallen in any quarter of our Union? Who has been deprived of any right of person or property? Who restrained from offering his vows in the mode in which he prefers to the Divine Author of his being?"

The American people constituted "one great family with a common interest." And then there was the familiar evocation of the origins: "Never did a government commence under auspices so favorable, nor ever was success so complete. If we look to the history of other nations, ancient or modern, we find no example of a growth so rapid, so gigantic, of a people so prosperous and happy. In contemplating what we have still to perform, the heart of every citizen must expand with joy when he reflects how near our Government has approached to perfection. . . . If we persevere in the career in which we have advanced so far and in the path already traced, we cannot fail, under the favor of a gracious Providence, to attain the high destiny which seems to await us." Democratic politics was a politics of optimism.

Having sounded the note of national reconciliation, Monroe gave practical effect to his words by touring the Middle and Northern states. He thus became the first president since Washington (if we except John Adams) to visit New York and New England. His trip became a triumphal procession from one city to another with thousands of people lining the streets to cheer him as he passed. Philadelphia, Trenton, New York, New Haven—the story was the same everywhere—tumultuous welcomes, speeches on national unity, the Union, the reconciliation of political and sectional differences. At Hartford, the principal speaker honoring him declared that "the spirit of party, with its concomitant jealousies and misrepresentations, no longer renders alien to each other those who ought to be bound together by fraternal affection."

Rhode Island was not to be outdone by Connecticut; and Massachusetts, the heart of enemy territory, seemed determined to outstrip all other states in welcoming the new president. Monroe was met on the road to Boston by a reception committee, cavalry, the city militia, and thousands of ordinary and extraordinary citizens on horseback and in carriages. The *Chronicle* declared: "The visit of the President seems to have wholly allayed the storms of party. People now meet in the same room who, a short while since, would scarcely pass along the same street." Another paper called his visit "an event which has a more direct tendency than any other to remove prejudices, harmonize feelings, annihilate dissensions, and make us indeed one people, for we have the sweet consolation that the President will be President not of a party, but of a great and powerful nation." The *Boston Centinel* picked up the happy phrase that the president's trip represented the beginning of "the era of good feelings."

38

Jackson and Florida

As soon as the smoke of battle had drifted away, the hero of New Orleans became its scourge. Jackson, at loggerheads with the officials of the city, kept it under martial law well after the British had departed. He also ordered his subordinate officers to refuse to obey any orders from Secretary of War William Crawford that were not channeled through him. John C. Calhoun, who succeeded Crawford, handled his hotheaded general with kid gloves. When it was reported to Jackson that Winfield Scott had characterized his behavior as little short of mutinous, Jackson immediately challenged General Scott to a duel—which Scott very sensibly refused on the grounds that it was a barbarous and unchristian custom.

Jackson's services were soon required in East Florida. That area, never very securely in the hands of the Spanish, had become a refuge for runaway slaves from Georgia and South Carolina, Red Stick Creek who had escaped Jackson's vengeance, and a variety of pirates, freebooters, and filibusters (companies of men who made expeditions in support of Spain's revolting American colonies).

Into this highly volatile brew were stirred the Seminole Indians. The Seminole were members of the Hokan-Siouan stock and the Muskogean family, which included the Choctaw, Chickasaw, and upper and lower Creek—known as the Five Civilized Tribes because of their settled agricultural life. Tall, handsome, stout people with broad faces, they were sun worshipers by tradition. An eccentric Englishman by the name of Colonel Edward Nicholls, declaring that he was acting as an agent of the British government, had negotiated an alliance with the Seminole during the War of 1812 and had built a fort on the Apalachicola, which he stocked with hundreds of barrels of powder. When Nicholls departed for England, escaped slaves established themselves in what came to be called the Negro Fort and from that stronghold raided across the border into southern Georgia, rustling cattle and sheep and terrorizing white settlers. Jackson dispatched General Edmund Gaines and Lieutenant Colonel D. L. Clinch to invade Florida, if necessary, and wipe out the Negro Fort. A small flotilla of boats proceeded upriver toward the fort. When the fire of their cannon failed to batter down the palisades, Clinch decided to try to set the fort ablaze with hot shot. A ball fell on the powder and some seven hundred barrels blew up, killing over 270 men, women, and children. The black leader and a Choctaw chief who survived were accused of having burned alive a party of whites and were summarily executed.

The destruction of the Negro Fort turned out to be only the opening episode in a war with the Seminole, who were increasingly indignant at the intrusion of whites into the region. A Scotsman named Gregor MacGregor, whose declared intention it was to form Florida into an independent republic, placed himself at the head of a motley band and forced the Spanish commander of Amelia Island to surrender to him. He then encouraged the Seminole to take the warpath, and in the spring of 1817 the Indians began to carry out widespread raids, killing settlers, burning cabins, and driving off cattle. When Gaines destroyed a Seminole village in retaliation a full fledged war broke out. A detachment of soldiers, carrying with them seven women and four children, were ambushed on the Apalachicola River, and all were killed and mutilated except four men who swam the river to safety.

This was sufficient incentive for Jackson to launch an attack on Spanish Florida. He sent a message to President Monroe asking for formal authority, rounded up some Tennesseans, and with an armed naval escort commanded by Lieutenant Isaac McKeever, headed for St. Marks on Apalachee Bay. McKeever was given the following instructions: "It is reported to me that Francis and Peter McQueen, the prophets who excited the Red Sticks, are now at work near St. Marks exciting the Seminoles. With them are . . . Arbuthnot, and a motley crew of brigands made up of slaves enticed or stolen from their masters during the last war. They will, as the army approaches, attempt to escape to the sea islands. You will therefore cruise along the coast and seize all sorts of persons—black, white, and red . . . and hold them for adjudication. In eight days I shall be at St. Marks and will communicate with you in the bay."

The Arbuthnot to whom Jackson referred was another Scotsman with a penchant for fishing in troubled waters. He had been a merchant in Caribbean commerce and had moved to Florida to trade with the Indians; he soon became their advocate, a kind of chief without portfolio, writing in their behalf to the British ministry and to Spanish authorities to complain that in the matter of Florida the United States was violating the terms of the Treaty of Ghent.

On his way back from a trading expedition to the Bahamas, Alexander Arbuthnot learned of Jackson's expedition. Hastening to St. Marks, he sent a message at once to his son, who was in charge of the trading post at Billy Bowlegs on the Suwannee River, warning him of the approach of Jackson and McKeever. Jackson meanwhile advanced on St. Marks, encountered and routed a party of Indians, and set fire to an Indian town where he found a thousand head of cattle carrying Georgia brands.

Arriving at St. Marks, the general sent word to the Spanish governor that he intended to occupy the town with American soldiers, and when a detachment of Americans encountered Arbuthnot about to leave the town, they intercepted him and brought him to Jackson. McKeever, entering St. Marks Harbor under a British flag, lured one of the Indian prophets, Francis, on board, trussed him up, and shipped him off to Jackson, who promptly hanged him for the massacre of whites on the Apalachicola.

Jackson's next objective was the town of Billy Bowlegs, center for free Negroes and runaway slaves. (It got its name from the chief there, Billy Bowlegs.) When Jackson, making his way through swamps and across creeks for a hundred miles, arrived at the Suwannee, he found the town deserted, as a result, in part at least, of Arbuthnot's warning. While Jackson's army was busy destroying the town, two blacks and two whites wandered in, not knowing it was in the possession of Americans. One of them carried Arbuthnot's note to his son. Another of the white men was a Scottish trader, Robert Ambrister. With his trap empty, and the Seminole, Creek, and runaway slaves well out of range, Jackson returned to St. Marks and there court-martialed the two Scotsmen for inciting the Indians to go on the warpath, spying, and giving aid and comfort to the enemy. The men were found guilty by a two-thirds majority of the court-martial board, which, it may be assumed, was hardly more than an extension of Jackson's will. Arbuthnot was sentenced to be hanged and Ambrister to be shot.

Jackson ordered the sentences to be carried out and returned with his men to Fort Gadsden, where word reached him that the Spanish governor of Pensacola had taken a large number of Indians under his wing. This news was followed by a letter from the governor himself ordering Jackson to leave West Florida. Jackson's response might have been anticipated. He marched to Pensacola, occupied the town, and captured the governor and such troops as remained after the Indians had fled.

When word of Jackson's actions reached Washington, the Spanish minister, Don Luis de Onis, lodged a vigorous protest with Secretary of State John Quincy Adams: "It seems that under the pretence of chasing and punishing the Seminoles, General Jackson not only violated Spanish soil, but actually possessed himself by force of arms of the bay and fort of St. Marks. . . . Not satisfied with this, he next demanded Pensacola just as if war existed between Spain and the United States. . . . Against these acts of hostility and invasion I protest most solemnly in the name of the King, my master, and I demand . . . the punishment of the general and his officers."

Monroe summoned his Cabinet to consider what action should be taken in response to Onis's dispatch. The Cabinet found itself in a dilemma. Jackson was a popular hero of such stature that any effort to discipline him would be sure to stir up a storm of protest. On the other hand, he had on this and other occasions shown such a high-minded disregard of the authority of his own government that to support him in his latest actions or to pass over them lightly would be to appear to condone his insubordination.

Far more serious, there was the prospect that unless prompt measures were taken to call Jackson to account and disclaim responsibility for his behavior, the United States might find itself at war with Spain, which, of course, was what Jackson and most of the residents of the region bordering the Floridas devoutly wished.

Crawford, the Tennessean, was in favor of a strong disciplinary action against Jackson. Secretary of War Calhoun, citizen of a state that had suffered from the forays of blacks and Indians in East Florida, was likewise in favor of some kind of chastisement of Jackson. John Quincy Adams, the New Englander, a man with, presumably, the least personal or ideological affinity with the frontier hero and the greatest responsibility for preserving peace with Spain, unexpectedly came forward as Jackson's advocate. Adams based his defense of Jackson's actions on the grounds that the Treaty of 1795 between Spain and the United States stipulated that both countries had a responsibility for restraining the Indians from any acts of hostility along their common borders. Spain had been unable to observe this article of the treaty, and the United States was simply helping out. In the course of doing so, certain misunderstandings and confusions had arisen, but these matters could be easily adjusted. Monroe was in agreement with the majority of his Cabinet. It was his view that Jackson had acted contrary to his orders and had engaged in open acts of war.

Jackson was certainly high-handed, arbitrary, given to furious outbursts of temper, and intolerant of authority. But he was a fighting general, the most brilliant general officer in the American army. It is hard not to suspect that Monroe and his Cabinet were, at least subconsciously, glad to find an excuse to clip their insubordinate general's wings.

Adams perhaps had a more objective view of the whole matter. In any event, it provided him an opportunity to write one of his greatest "state papers" to his Spanish counterpart, Don Jose Pizarro. While he was still working on a shatteringly conclusive reply to the indignant protest of the Spanish court, Congress assembled and began its own debate on Jackson's campaign. Now came the most fateful moment in the whole drama. A motion was presented stating: "That the House of Representatives . . . disapproves the proceedings in the trial and execution of Alexander Arbuthnot and Robert C. Ambrister," and for four weeks the resolution and its amendments were debated. At least three careers were profoundly influenced by the outcome. Henry Clay, the *beau ideal* of the new politics and spokesman for the frontier, aligned himself against the military hero of the frontier. The rest of the country turned its fascinated attention on the contest in Congress. Spectators "filled the galleries to suffocation," and newspapers everywhere carried detailed accounts of the speeches of the representatives.

Clay, viewing the office of secretary of state as the stepping-stone to the presidency, had been bitterly disappointed when Monroe chose Adams for the job. His attack on Jackson may have been based in part on his perception of him as a regional rival and in part on the hope of discrediting John Quincy Adams, who had championed the general's cause and who was clearly Clay's most formidable *immediate* competition for the presidency.

Margaret Smith reported that the Senate had adjourned to hear Clay's speech in addition to "all the foreign ministers and many strangers. . . . The gallery was full of ladies gentlemen and men, to a degree that endangered it . . . and yet such a silence prevailed that tho' at a distance I did not lose a word, Mr. Clay was not only eloquent but amusing and more than once made the whole house laugh." During the speech, gallant members of the House passed up to ladies they knew in the galleries oranges and cakes wrapped in napkins and fixed to long poles.

Clay chose to appear as defender of the rights of the Creek, denouncing Jackson for having hanged Francis, the so-called prophet. "When did even conquering and consolidating Rome fail to respect the altars and gods of those whom she subjugated? Let me not be told that these prophets were impostors who deceived the Indians. They were their prophets. The Indians believed and venerated them. . . . We leave to the humane and benevolent efforts of the reverend professors of Christianity to convert these unhappy nations yet immersed in gloom. But spare them their prophets! Spare their delusions! Spare their prejudices and their superstitions! Spare their religion such as it is, from open and cruel violence."

When Jackson read those words they seemed to him to be cynical and hypocritical, and from that day forth he was Clay's implacable enemy. While Clay insisted that he "cheerfully acquitted" Jackson "of any intention to violate the laws of the country and the obligations of humanity," he just as plainly accused him of both. "We are fighting a great moral battle for the benefit not only of ourselves but of all mankind. The eyes of the whole world are fixed upon us. One the larger—part is gazing with contempt, with jealousy, and with envy. The other part with hope, with confidence, and with affection. To us belongs the high privilege of transmitting unimpaired to posterity the fair character and the liberty of our country. Can we expect to execute this high trust by trampling or suffering to be trampled down law, justice, the Constitution, and the rights of other people? Beware how you give a fatal sanction in this infant period of our republic, scarcely two score years old, to military insubordination." To acquit Jackson of all blame would be "a triumph of the spirit of insubordination, a triumph of the military over the civil authority, a triumph over the powers of this House, a triumph over the Constitution of the land. And I pray most devoutly to heaven that it may not prove in its ultimate effects and consequences a triumph over the liberty of the people."

In politics eloquence is a dangerous gift. An opponent's vote may be forgiven, but if it is accompanied by a brilliant oratorical display it is very apt to inflict a wound that will never heal. Clay had, in essence, declared that to vindicate Jackson would be to discredit the United States in the eyes of the world and to take the first step on the road to a military dictatorship. Jackson did not lack for defenders, some of whom compared his executions of Arbuthnot and Ambrister to Washington's execution of Major André during the Revolution. When a vote was finally taken, the motion to rebuke Jackson was defeated.

In the Senate, Jackson's actions were severely criticized and, after several weeks of debate, formally censured. The irony of the whole episode was that it lay beyond the authority of Congress to take action in any event. The issue lay between the president as the commander in chief and his recalcitrant general. If Jackson were to be reprimanded or, what was hardly conceivable, relieved of his duties, only the president had the constitutional right to do so. Congress thus consumed almost a month in debating a question that was, strictly speaking, none of its business. Needless to say, the controversy served to make Jackson, more than ever, the hero of the South and the West, where the surest way to popular preferment was hanging Indians and British citizens.

39

Hard Times

I f the end of the war brought an "era of good feelings," it also brought a flood of British goods—satin and silk, fine muslin, hardware, tea, coffee, molasses, sugar, and innumerable household items. The British commercial invasion soon threatened to be more devastating than the military one. Manufacturers with huge backlogs of goods dumped them on the American market, where they were eagerly snapped up by wholesalers and retailers hungry for merchandise and by customers impatient to buy imported articles once more. A severe depression was soon felt in American cities and towns where manufacturing was carried on. Unemployment became a serious problem. The treaty that concluded the war closed most of the West Indian trade to American ships and seamen, and again ships lay idle in port.

Rhode Island, Massachusetts, and Pennsylvania, where the country's infant manufacturing ventures were concentrated, suffered most. The various embargoes and nonintercourse acts, followed by the war itself, had been a powerful stimulus to American manufacturing, especially to the production of goods utilizing Southern cotton, and of iron products. If Americans still had a long way to go to rival English cloths, in the absence of competition they had made a substantial start. Within thirty miles of Providence, Rhode Island, there were 140 cotton mills turning out 28 million yards of cotton a year to the value of $6 million. Now they were threatened with ruin. Hands were dismissed and many factories simply closed their doors.

In consequence, the demand was raised for tariffs to protect American industry. Were the new factories, built at such cost and with such ingenuity, and their expensive machinery to be allowed to rot away? The question of tariffs had been and would be again a sectional issue. The South, as an agricultural, importing region, argued that tariffs increased the cost of the goods it must import without any compensating advantages. Southern agriculture was thus being taxed for the support of Northern industry. In this instance, however, the Southern argument was muted by the fact that during the war the South had found a partial outlet for its enormously expanding cotton production in Northern manufactories. This made the South susceptible, at least for the moment (and at least as far as tariffs on imported textiles were concerned), to the argument that Congress must promptly pass a schedule of tariffs to protect American manufacturers.

Alexander James Dallas, Madison's secretary of the treasury, thus brought forward a bill that specified high duties on items that could be manufactured in the United States. A tax of 20 percent of the value of the article was imposed on articles the United States manufactured in insufficient quantities to meet the full demand, and a nominal tariff for revenue on all other articles of import. The principal opposition to the bill came, ironically, from New England. The merchants of Boston, Salem, Providence, and the other port towns of the region feared that heavy import duties would seriously inhibit trade. It would not be the last time commerce and industry found themselves on opposite sides of a question.

These same merchants soon found a way around the tariffs by selling British goods at auction—"off the boat," so to speak. A week of auction sales in New York, Philadelphia, and Boston brought in over $1.3 million. One auction advertised the following items for sale: "Yorkshire cloth and Scotch muslins, silk, jaconet muslins, bombazettes, jerseys, saggathys, windsor soap, grantines, and London Duffel blankets, cut nails, salt, bed-covers, tacks, pencil-cases, toy watches, tooth-brushes, pins, grindstones, cast-iron pots, cart-boxes, tea-kettles, iron bolts, axes, broad hoes, spades, ploughshare-moulds, lightning rods, zinc, stoves, jugs, iron, wool, and negro pipes."

An examination of American imports and exports from the early years of the nineteenth century to 1816 suggests the uncertainties of the nation's commerce. In 1807, for example, the American merchants exported goods to the value of $109 million and earned in carrying charges another $53 million. (The 2 to 1 ratio of the value of exports to transportation charges remains remarkably steady.) Imports totaled $146 million. The next year, 1808, the value of U.S. exports dropped to $26 million under the impact of the Berlin and Milan decrees and the British orders in council; not until 1850 would the combined value of American exports and carrying charges again reach the $160 million range.

The low point of American exports was reached in 1814—$8 million. As we have seen, the end of the war brought an enormous surge of commercial activity. Exports rose in 1815 to $55 million and the next year to $84 million, while imports, the vastly greater part from Britain, rose from $16 million to $85 million and the next year to $151 million. But both imports and exports leveled off or fell in the remaining years of the decade and showed little inclination to rise for the next fifteen years, indicating that the commercial activities of the major port cities had reached a point of maximum expansion. Atlantic commerce had in fact become a virtual monopoly of the older "Federalist" aristocracy in the seacoast cities. It was a class as exclusive as the men's clubs that began to develop in the same era. Venture capital went elsewhere in search of investments, most often west in the growing canal and highway systems of "internal improvements."

The postwar recession grew rapidly into a severe depression, the consequences of which were most keenly felt in the seacoast cities where thousands of people were unemployed. With peace on the other side of the Atlantic, the degree to which American prosperity had been based on the almost constant state of war in Europe became increasingly evident. The depressed condition of foreign trade was accompanied by a state approaching chaos in the domestic economy. Wild speculation in lands and in such internal improvements as toll roads and canals had been encouraged by the proliferation of banks issuing their own often worthless currency.

Swiss immigrant Jakob Rütlinger, a teacher, commented on the riskiness of business enterprise in the United States. "The most incredible speculation often goes on in this field," he wrote. "In the port cities, if a man has a large quantity of merchandise, or has just received a large amount, he often auctions it publicly if he thinks that with his money he may make even more through speculation. . . . This is America, which dares to undertake the impossible."

Despite the reestablishment of a national bank, by 1818 there were 392 banks in 23 states and territories, including 59 each in Pennsylvania and Kentucky; Ohio had 28 and Maryland 25. Financial democracy required that the opportunities for profit be "equal." No one group or class of citizens must be allowed to monopolize the management of money and benefit from the profits that were to be realized thereby. In the odd American equation between imagination and money (or avarice and the means of satisfying it), imagination and/or avarice constantly outstripped money or capital.

As we have argued earlier in this work, most Americans felt that access to capital constituted the essence of democracy. They were deeply suspicious of the "order" and "control" that some of their fellow citizens wished to impose on the economy. They suspected, quite rightly, that the order would redound to the substantial benefit of the managers of it, most of whom lived in Boston, New York, and Philadelphia, and who could be readily distinguished by their clothes, their accents, and their manners. Thus, the most democratic states tended to have the largest number of banks, most of them eager to pass out money in the best democratic spirit to anyone who asked for it. One such bank had $27,000 in gold and silver to redeem $395,000 in paper.

But the problem was obviously more complicated. It was the custom for nineteenth-century historians to deplore the hopelessly unsound character of such banks and applaud all efforts to reform or abolish them. Recently there has been considerably more sympathy with the democratic impulse behind the banks. Given the desperate need for capital and for some kind of circulating medium in all parts of the country, the banks undoubtedly performed a necessary function, even if they performed it badly. Striking a balance between meeting an almost universal need and preserving some semblance of financial order was no easy task. The champions of a centralized banking system of course blamed hard times on the proliferation of banks; and they blamed that proliferation, in turn, on the greed of the average man. Such critics felt that greed (or the acquisitive instinct) was more or less the exclusive privilege of the upper classes. Manifested in a discreet and tasteful fashion, it was understood to be simply taking proper care of one's family.

The banks were doubtless no more to blame than a dozen other aspects of the economy. When factories fell idle, the clamor rose for ever higher import duties or tariffs to protect American industries. The Society of Delaware County [Pennsylvania] for the Promotion of National Industry and Economy called for a statewide convention to draft a petition to Congress, and the newspapers carried long columns of arguments pro and con the matter of higher tariffs. The enemies of manufacturing took the opportunity to denounce factories for drawing off capital from farming and internal improvements and attacked them as breeding grounds of immorality.

The depression worsened. Thirty businesses in Philadelphia, which in 1816 had employed 9,672 persons, had fired 7,500 of them by 1818. Stores and factories were abandoned. Of eighty-nine stores on Market Street, forty-nine were empty in 1819. The numerous business failures and bankruptcies caused hardships that can hardly be imagined today, in large part because of the debtors' laws that permitted a person, as we have noted, to be jailed for debt and kept in jail until he or she could pay off the debt or until it was paid by friends or relatives. The situation of the debtor was worse than that of the common criminal.

In Philadelphia and other cities many jailed debtors were prevented from starving only by the intervention of the Humane Society. Moreover, in the period between 1800 and 1819, conditions in prisons had deteriorated markedly. The high hopes held by reformers for the rehabilatory effects of prisons at the beginning of the century had been deflated as drunkenness, prostitution, homosexuality, and crime flourished in the jails. Thus, for many people bankruptcy meant, not simply the loss of their business and their real and personal possessions, but incarceration under the most demoralizing conditions, in filthy and noisome pesthules where disease was often endemic. A petition to Congress from Northumberland County in Pennsylvania bespoke common grievances when it declared that "the larger part of the people, even with the utmost economy, could hardly obtain the very necessaries of life; that debts were unpaid, creditors dissatisfied, and the jails full of honest but unfortunate persons whose wives and children had thereby become a burden on the township."

It is perhaps worth reflecting briefly on the reasons for the savagery of the debtors' laws. Most of them had passed virtually intact from English common law. They reflected an attitude toward property that was imbedded in the Anglo-American theological, political, and legal tradition. Furthermore, we must remember that they were part of a much broader code of laws whose punishments were, almost as a matter of course, cruel and inhuman. When a hungry man could be hanged for killing a deer, it is hardly surprising that he should find himself in jail for a five-dollar debt.

The ownership, the disposal, and the security of property had been the central issue in the centuries-long struggle for power in England between the king and Commons, or, more generally, between the Crown and the landed aristocracy. To protect property, whether in the form of land or of taxes, from appropriation or misuse by the king had been the tenet of Magna Charta, the Declaration of the Rights of Man, the American Revolution, and all the particular bills of rights in the state constitutions. To owe a man a debt was to owe him a portion of his property. It thus touched the most profound level of historical anxiety. The Protestant Reformation, which had reformed the theological and, with it, the psychological world of its adherents, had endowed property and money with a special kind of sanctity. The good Christian was a man or woman faithful in the discharge of worldly as well as otherworldly duties and obligations. It was almost as though Calvin had added an additional commandment: "Thou shalt pay all thy just debts, for property is blessed of the Lord." Because it became apparent in time that such draconian debtors' laws inhibited business enterprise more than they helped it (and because more humane ideas came to prevail), the laws were gradually relaxed. Vermont took the lead by making fifteen dollars the minimum debt for which a person could be imprisoned. But it is critically important to remember that the basic attitude toward debts and, above all, toward property in land or coin of the realm, persisted in the United States down to the present time, so that many Americans still treat "property rights" as a kind of ultimate moral value.

Undoubtedly another element in the harshness of the laws was the feeling that every individual was a member of a family and a community. Thus, if he or she were in debt, family and neighbors had an obligation to free him or her by paying off the indebtedness. In the vast majority of cases of debt in more or less normal times, friends and relatives reclaimed imprisoned debtors in short order. The greatest sufferers were, ironically, those who were friendless or those whose debts were too large for their friends and family to discharge. Thus Robert Morris, called, as we have noted, the financier of the Revolution, and at one time one of the richest men in America, spent almost two years in debtors' prison; and James Wilson, one of the principal figures in the Federal Convention and a justice of the Supreme Court, escaped jail only by fleeing to North Carolina.

At best, imprisonment for debt was a nightmare that hung over every American throughout the course of his life (it was far less of a threat to women directly because of their financially dependent situation). There was hardly a family that had not sacrificed a member to such cruel incarceration. Flight from debt was not an insignificant factor in the population of the frontier.

Quite apart from imprisonment for debt, unemployment, growing month by month, caused such misery and suffering in the cities that the soup kitchens and other charitable organizations, many of which had been established to alleviate the distress of the unemployed during the War of 1812, soon found themselves unable to cope with the thousands of hungry people who were idle.

A Society for the Relief of Widows and Young Children, the Female Hospital Society, the Humane Society, the Female Society of Philadelphia for the Relief and Employment of the Poor, and a Society for Supplying the Poor with Soup all struggled to assist the unemployed in Philadelphia.

In the depressed state of affairs, such organizations found their modest resources strained far beyond their means. The Society for Supplying the Poor with Soup was the one that felt the strongest pressure. It had been accustomed in the winter to ladling out soup to such needy individuals as made their way to its headquarters. From a few dozen persons, it found the numbers of supplicants increasing to the hundreds and then thousands. Unable to cope with such numbers, the Society organized a citywide relief committee by wards and districts to solicit money and distribute food.

New York and Boston followed a similar path. When a soup kitchen was opened in the former city, it fed 1,200 persons in the first twenty-four hours. Plans were made to provide for twice as many the next day, but the number of hungry people was again far greater than anticipated. By March, 6,640 men, women, and children were being fed each day at soup kitchens in various wards of the city. In Philadelphia one kitchen alone distributed twenty-four thousand quarts of soup in a few months. That such grim statistics shook the faith of the more fainthearted in the inevitability of progress in the United States is suggested by a growing debate over public measures that might properly be taken to ameliorate the situation of the unemployed. Much of this discussion centered on the issue of internal improvements. One of the most arresting of the pamphlets produced on the subject was Daniel Raymond's *Thoughts on Political Economy*. Raymond linked the country's need for what he called "public works" with the necessity of doing something to meet the needs of the unemployed. When times were bad, merchants and manufacturers, though their ships might lie idle in port and their factories' doors be closed, managed, for the most part, to maintain comfortable existences. It was the sailors and the factory workers who suffered most. In Raymond's words, "National distress must always be sought for among the labouring poor—Distress among them, is a distress which touches life."

Raymond was especially contemptuous of the argument that employing the unemployed on public works would somehow impose a strain on the private sector. The result would be quite to the contrary. "Suppose the United States," he wrote, "was to employ ten thousand men during the next ten years, at an annual expense of two millions of dollars, in making roads, canals, and other permanent improvements, in the country; is there any reason to suppose, that any portions of labour would be withdrawn from other branches of industry? . . . Fifty thousand men might, no doubt, be employed on public works, without lessening the annual product of labour a single pound. It is, therefore, possible for the nation to expend a large amount of labour and money, on public works, without, in other respects, diminishing public wealth."

The notion of employing the unemployed on public works proved to be somewhat ahead of its time, but the sentiment for internal improvements (public works) supported by public funds allocated to the states was strong except in New England. It had sufficient backing in Congress to produce a bill for internal improvements, which passed and was vetoed by Madison (on the urging of Jefferson) a few hours before the end of his administration.

The depressed economy had numerous side effects. One of the most conspicuous was the increase in crime, especially theft and armed robbery. Gangs of unemployed youths roamed the streets of the cities, mugging and robbing law-abiding citizens. It was noted that a large proportion were young blacks. In Philadelphia innumerable philanthropic societies struggled to provide for the poor—paupers, as they were called—and their efforts plus provisions by the city for assisting the poor resulted in the Quaker City's being referred to critically as an "emporium of beggars." In classic American fashion, committees were appointed or simply sprang up to study the various causes of poverty and crime and to make recommendations on how best to eradicate them. There were committees on pauperism in general and committees preoccupied with such specific causes or consequences of pauperism as Sabbath-breaking, profanity, and intemperance. The statistics they gathered were alarming. The Pennsylvania Society for the Promotion of Public Economy, formed for the purpose of improving the "condition of the poor, and removing or preventing the causes that produce mendicity," produced numerous suggestions for making the improvident more provident by instructing them on how to save fuel and how to prepare inexpensive but wholesome dishes. Committees appointed to deal with the growing problem of alcoholism brought in gloomy reports. In New York City the Society for the Prevention of Pauperism estimated that fifteen thousand persons were living on charity of one kind or another. Some thousand of these were "worthy persons reduced to poverty by the depressed state of commerce." The poverty of another thousand was due to a variety of causes, but the committee estimated that as many as ten or twelve thousand of the indigent had fallen on evil ways as a result of drunkenness, though cause and effect were admittedly hard to distinguish.

Over two thousand shops in the city were licensed to sell intoxicating liquors, primarily rum, not to mention innumerable houses that dispensed drink illegally. It followed that if each "tippling house" sold an average of $2.50 worth of rum each day, the laboring classes would expend almost $2 million annually on liquor, a sum that would supply the entire city with bread for a year.

The Society for the Prevention of Pauperism appointed nine subcommittees to look into lotteries, prostitution (which had become such a serious problem that in several cities societies had been formed to aid poor young girls who might otherwise be drawn into prostitution), pawnbrokers, gambling, intemperance, and the effects on poor youth of inadequate education and training. Other cities took similar measures, none with any conspicuous success.

A serious controversy arose over the form of charitable assistance to the poor. Critics of charitable organizations charged that they had the effect of producing a permanent dependent class of paupers for whom living on private and public handouts became a way of life long after the economic crisis that had impoverished them was over. This was an especially troubling issue in a country obsessed by the work ethic. Idleness was the root of most evil. To feed the idle was to run the risk of encouraging idleness. It was a dilemma that was to continue to plague the Republic. At the heart of the problem lay the issue of whether a democratic government was economically viable. Americans had been promised happiness if they worked hard, saved their money, and were reasonably pious. The presence of increasing numbers of hungry and despairing people, of drunkards, prostitutes, and delinquent children raised troubling questions.

Youth gangs were especially demoralizing to city residents. In addition to theft and robbery, they engaged in wanton acts of vandalism and terrorized decent people on the streets, shouting abuse at them and threatening them with bodily harm. It was suspected that a rash of fires in the Philadelphia wards was the work of young arsonists. The problem was so serious that the mayor called a citywide conference to hear proposals from concerned citizens on steps to be taken to deal with juvenile crime. The mayor alone, acting as a justice of the peace, had in a three-month period sent twenty youths from the ages of ten to eighteen to prison for robbery. The prevalence of juvenile crime gave a strong impetus to the movement for free public education open to all. The simplest way to get gangs of boys off the streets was to put them in school. Pawnshops where thieves disposed of their loot were another major concern of the reformers.

In some areas of the major cities committees were formed to take law enforcement into the hands of the residents themselves. In Philadelphia each ward designated seven young men to encourage residents to take "measures to suppress the alarming nightly depredations on the persons and property of our citizens." Sensitive to the charges that many of the malefactors were black, the African Episcopal Methodist Church offered to assist in trying to "suppress the villainies and vices carried on in this city."

The anxiety and general demoralization produced by the economic situation was reflected in a report by the Congressional Committee of Manufacurers: "In a time of profound peace the country is embarrassed with debts; real estate is shrinking in value; the markets for manufacturers and the yield of the farm are declining; commerce is struggling not to retain the carrying trade of other lands, but of our own. Not one national interest is thriving. Why are these thing so? The sea, the earth, the forest yield their abundance. Pestilence and famine commit no ravages. . . . Plenty blesses the land. Whence, then, this burst of distress? History affords no other example of a people impoverished while in the full enjoyment of health, peace, and plenty."

The questions were unusually candid and could, presumably, be asked only in anticipation of a conclusive remedy, in this case higher tariffs. But of course there were almost as many solutions as there were individuals to propose them. The remedies for the ills of the country could, however, be divided into two major categories: economic and moral. Those proposing economic remedies were divided, in turn, into five major (but not exclusive) divisions—those advocating public works; those urging aid to the farmer; those who wished for aid to the manufacturer; those who were convinced that the encouragement of foreign commerce was the key to renewed prosperity; and those who, attributing the depressed state of affairs to the westward migration of hundred of thousands of the most enterprising citizens of the original states, wished the government to take steps to discourage that vast movement.

The moralists pointed, not surprisingly, to a general decline in private and public morals. They frequently evoked the Revolutionary era as a time when public spirit—civic virtue—predominated over private concerns. It was stated as an irrefutable axiom that the tone of political life had declined disastrously. Even so sophisticated an observer as Albert Gallatin was, in his son's words, convinced that "the whole system of political life in America has undergone a change," a change "most distasteful" to him. The moralists emphasized such matters as the growing disregard for observance of the Sabbath; widespread profanity; sexual license; greed—as manifested in wild speculation in land; the proliferation of banks; the spread of gambling; and, above all, alcoholism (or intemperance), which was so persistent and apparently ineradicable as to constitute a kind of national disease. If juvenile crime and chronic poverty were largely urban problems, drunkenness infected communities of every size from rural towns to seacoast ports. No class and neither sex was spared, although the most baneful effects were felt in big cities and isolated rural communities.

The great majority of the moralists were Christians of one denomination or another, and they thus felt that the underlying cause of America's distressing condition was the widely noted decline in Christian piety. It was from the ranks of moralists that the combat troops of reform were recruited. They made up the membership of the philanthropic societies that struggled so manfully and, soon, womanfully—women came increasingly to play major roles in such societies—with the "social evils" that appeared in such bewildering profusion. It turned out, for example, that even harmless-sounding "oyster-houses" had become dens of iniquity where boys and young men were introduced, not simply to oysters, but to rum and prostitutes and were thereby started on the road to ruin.

The moralists increasingly concentrated their attention on intemperance as the most crucial problem and the one that *seemed* most susceptible of solution, or at least amelioration. After all, drunkards were, from time to time, reformed. Even John Adams was attracted to the idea of prohibition. He confessed himself "grieved to the heart to see the number of idlers, thieves, sots and consumptive patients made for the physicians in those infamous seminaries [taverns]." He wrote to Benjamin Rush that Little Turtle, chief of the Miami Indians, had petitioned him, when he was President, "to prohibit rum to be sold to his nation . . . because he said I had lost three thousand of my Indian children in his nation in one year by it." Adams added: "If I should, in my will, my dying legacy, my posthumous exhortation, recommend heavy, prohibitory taxes upon spirituous liquors, which I believe to be the only remedy against their deleterious qualities in society, every one of your brother Republicans and nine-tenths of the Federalists would say that I was a canting Puritan, a profound hypocrite, setting up standards of morality, frugality, economy, temperance, simplicity, and sobriety, that I knew the age was incapable of."

Drunkenness was, indeed, America's national malady. We have noted throughout this work how from the days of the earliest settlers in colonial America, drunkenness had been a problem. Even in the records of Puritan ministerial associations we find strong expressions of concern over intemperate clergymen. We are never to hear the end of it. Ironically, it was only the Indians who seemed less capable of coping with alcohol than white citizens of what was constantly affirmed to be the happiest and most enlightened nation of the world. So one comes constantly back to the question of why. What are the roots of this national disease?

We have mentioned the anxiety produced by becoming "an individual" rather than being, in essence, a member of a corporate group. The perils and hazards of being an individual were reflected in the fact that Americans disposed to drink excessively were inclined to drink alone, in their own homes or even in their rooms, rather than in common social situations and celebrations where tipsiness was ritualized and acceptable. When they drank in public, they most typically drank in taverns, where individuals collected whose only common denominator was apt to be their affinity for the juice. Drunkenness was also made more difficult for the individual to cope with by virtue of the social stigma that attached to it. The injunctions against drinking created a tension in which drinking became a secret and pleasurable vice, a relief from social pressures.

The "openness" of American society, in which everyone was at least theoretically encouraged to advance in the world and "succeed," meant that failure had particularly devastating consequences in terms of the individual's sense of his own worthiness. Related to the success-failure syndrome was the ruthlessly competitive character of much of American life and what I have spoken of as the disintegrative effects of America. The fact is that each class and section of the United States had its own incentive to drink to excess: the upper classes because of the pressure on them to preserve their privileged status against the efforts of those struggling up from below; the middle classes because they were spurred on by ambition and the yearning for upward mobility; the laboring classes because of the instability, the hardship, the often pinched and dreary quality of their lives; the farmers and frontier settlers because of isolation, boredom, and hardship; New Englanders because they attempted to observe such a rigid moral code; Southerners because they so valued conviviality and lived perpetually with the horror of slave revolt.

To anyone who reflected seriously on the problem, it should have been clear enough that the national disease revealed something of the basic reality of America, that it was, in short, a symptom rather than merely an independent, free-floating fact. But that was another of those unpalatable truths Americans were disinclined to swallow. So we now encounter the beginnings of the "temperance movement" in the United States, one of the most ubiquitous, persistent, poignant, and fruitless reform movements in our history.

Not surprisingly, the voluminous reports on the "distracted" state of the economy and the disastrous social consequences, and the general discussion provoked by them, raised in the minds of many people serious questions about the country's future and, indeed, the world's.

At the Fourth of July celebration in Concord in 1796, the Reverend Samuel Thacher had cried, "All Hail! Approaching Revolutions!" and dared to anticipate "the consequent emancipation of a world." The revolutions had approached and then receded. Reactionary regimes held power in virtually every European nation except England. In the face of such reverses at home and abroad, even American optimism faltered. In the long history of the rise and fall of nations, it might well be that the rise of the United States was no more than an exceptionally transitory event to be followed by a precipitous fall. Were all the hopes for freedom, happiness, and universal peace to prove as ephemeral as a dream? If man was a creature endowed with reason, reason must produce a solution. If he was a child of God, a stricter observance of the divine injunctions must bring a new effusion of grace expressed in progress and prosperity. Many Americans, of course, thought man was both of these and that a combination of both attributes must, in the long run, overcome the most intractable problems.

In 1819 Emma Willard, an early champion of the cause of women, proposed to the legislature of New York "a Plan for Improving Female Education" and took note of the growing disillusionment with the future prospects of the nation. She declared: "An opinion too generally prevails that our present form of government, though good, cannot be permanent. Other republics have failed, and the historian and the philosopher have told us, that nations are like individuals; that at their birth, they receive the seeds of their decline and dissolution." Emma Willard challenged the analogy. Human beings, as distinguished from animals, were able to pass on their ideals and values from generation to generation. There was "no physical cause, to prevent this succession's going on, in a peaceable manner, under a good government, till the end of time."

If there were widespread signs of decadence and dissolution, if the Republic seemed in growing danger, the reason must be sought elsewhere. To her, the causes for the widely commented on "depravation of morals and manners" were not to be found in "the introduction of wealth," which was inevitable in a growing and energetic country, but in faulty education and especially in the inadequate education of women. Willard noted: "Nations, calling themselves polite, have made [women] the fancied idol of ridiculous worship, and we have repaid them with ruin for their folly. But where is that wise and heroic country, which has considered that our rights are sacred, though we cannot defend them? that tho' a weaker, we are an essential part of the body politic, whose corruption or improvement must effect the whole? and which, having thus considered, has sought to give us by education, that rank in the scale of being to which our importance entitles us?"

In her advocacy of female education, Emma Willard touched on a theme that was to characterize virtually all reform movements in the United States. Its basic premise was that the promise of the Republic had dimmed. Luxury, greed, ambition, self-seeking had compromised all the bright hopes of the Founders. But it was premature (and un-American) to despair. The remedy was _____. Here the reformer could fill in the blank with his or her particular reform—temperance, abolition of slavery, improvements in the status of women, free love, cooperative communities, socialism, anarchism, or, in not a few instances, all of them together.

The issue of internal improvements did not end with Madison's veto. Much of the discussion in Congress, which was extensive and often bitter, revolved around the question of whether under the Constitution payments could be made to the states for "improvements"—canals, highways, bridges, public improvements of all kinds. There were both practical and ideological considerations. The capability of the states to raise money by taxation was very limited. The federal government, on the other hand, had wealth beyond calculation in the form of lands to sell (not to mention tariffs and duties on imports). It thus seemed to many Americans that it was only fair for the government to assist with improvements, the effect of which would often be felt far beyond the boundaries of particular states.

What gave special urgency to the issue was the astonishing growth of the West. It was argued that if good roads were not constructed through the Appalachians, if rivers were not improved by locks and connecting canals and those running east and west were not made navigable, Western trade would move down the Mississippi, and its advantages would be lost to the seacoast ports. Not only would there be striking economic disadvantages in such an event, but the social and cultural ties that bound the country together would be weakened. Like virtually every issue, the matter of internal improvements was a sectional one. From New York south there was strong sentiment in support of internal improvements; New England, which had a strong anti-Western bias, in part because so many of her inhabitants were headed in that direction, was resolutely opposed.

In his *Thoughts on Political Economy* Daniel Raymond had declared "The capacity of a nation for acquiring the necessaries and comforts of life, depends on the development of the moral and physical energies of man. . . . Let political economists cease their disputes about productive and unproductive labour, and employ their talents in ascertaining what kinds of labour have a moral, and what an immoral tendency, and then they may render some service to mankind." Manufacturing labor was the most profitable because it required the most skill. A weaver could earn more in a day than a plowman.

To Raymond it was an error to underrate the importance of "the comforts and luxuries of life" as opposed to the "necessaries." The fact was that "the more unnecessary the gratification, the better will labour be paid which produces it.—Hence, stage-players, and mountebanks, are always better paid than cultivators of the soil,—dancing masters and fiddlers, better paid than teachers of sciences." The real index to the economic health of a society, Raymond maintained, was to be found, not in the state of the commercial classes, but "among the labouring poor."

Raymond had the Jeffersonian predilection for farming. "Agriculturists," he wrote, "are a superior class of men to manufacturers. They enjoy more vigorous health, and possess more personal courage. They have more elevated and liberal minds. It is more congenial to man's nature; to be abroad in the fields, breathing a pure air, and admiring the works of creation, and the Beauties of nature, than to be confined in the unwholesome impure air of a workshop."

It did not follow from this, however, that the government should encourage agriculture and neglect manufacturing. "That is the best regulated community, where agriculture and manufacturing labour, bear a due proportion to each other, and when one preponderates in too great a degree . . . it becomes the duty of the government to interpose and restore the equilibrium by encouraging and protecting the other."

The most striking aspect of civilized life, according to Raymond, was its interdependence. The savages "did not desire, or if they desire, they know not how to procure any of those articles which we denominate the comforts of life." With civilized man, even the humblest had so many needs beyond those he could satisfy himself that he was largely dependent on the products of others.

War, Raymond argued, far from depressing national economies, was always a powerful stimulant. It encouraged trade and manufacturing; if it made the former more hazardous, it also made it far more profitable. "The expenditure of public money, in public works, frequently has a not less invigorating influence than war, on national industry. . . . The body-politic like the natural body is liable to fall into a state of comparative lethargy and torpor. It then becomes necessary to arouse its dormant energies, by administering stimulants. The expenditure of public money in public works, will often produce this effect."

What is so striking about Raymond's tract is that it reminds us that there was, more than a hundred years before Roosevelt's New Deal and the so-called welfare state, a large and respectable body of opinion—almost certainly a majority of the country—and a set of closely reasoned arguments that favored government intervention on a large scale to undertake generally useful public works and to use such works to stimulate the economy in slack times.

In the debate in Congress on internal improvements Calhoun appeared as the principal advocate of public works. "What can add more to the wealth, strength, and political prosperity of our country than cheapness of intercourse?" he asked his colleagues. "It gives the interior the advantages of the seaboard. . . . The strength and political prosperity of the republic are concerned in it. No country enjoying freedom ever occupied as great an extent of territory as that possessed by the United States. One hundred years ago the most profound philosopher did not suppose it possible that a pure republic could exist on even so small a scale as Great Britain. Yet what was then considered chimerical we have [achieved], and so happily are the powers of the States and the General Government blended, that much of our political prosperity is drawn from the very extent of our territory. Let it not, however, be forgotten—nay, let it be forever kept in mind—that our vastness exposes us at the same time to the worst of all calamities—dissension. We are great, and rapidly, I was about to say fearfully, growing. This is our pride and our danger, our weakness and our strength. The strongest of all cements, it is true, is the wisdom, the justice, the moderation of this House. Yet good roads and canals will do much to unite us. . . . Let us therefore bind the republic together with roads and canals."

It had been argued against public works that the Constitution, by not specifically authorizing Congress to undertake them, had, in effect, forbidden them; but Calhoun answered that he was "no advocate of refined arguments on the Constitution. That instrument was not intended as a thesis for the logician to exercise his ingenuity on." The guide in interpreting it must be good common sense. Congress was entitled to do anything it considered conducive to the "general welfare." What could be more for the general welfare than measures designed to stimulate the growth and prosperity of the country and to bind its various sections more closely together?

On the Senate vote 34 of the New England representatives voted nay and 6 aye. Delaware, Maryland, and Virginia were opposed 20 to 8. New York, Pennsylvania, and Ohio together gave the bill 51 out of 56 votes. Altogether it got a majority of 2 in the House and 5 in the Senate.

If many of his followers defected, especially Republicans from the frontier states of Kentucky, Tennessee, and Ohio, Jefferson himself kept the faith. He wrote to Virginia Senator William Giles in 1825 deploring the agitation for public works. To him it represented a dangerous concentration of federal power at the expense of the states. Under the authority to establish post roads, the proponents of public works "claim that of cutting down mountains for the construction of roads, of digging canals, and aided by a little sophistry on the words 'general welfare,' a right to do, not only the acts to effect that, which are specifically enumerated and permitted, but whatsoever they shall think, or pretend shall be for the general welfare." Jefferson was also alarmed at the rise of a new dominant class "founded on banking institutions, and moneyed incorporations under the guise and cloak of their favored branches of manufacturers, commerce and navigation, riding and ruling over the plundered ploughman and beggared yeomanry." It revived all his anxieties about monarchy.

In the primarily agricultural communities in which the vast majority of Americans lived, the effects of hard times were generally less severe than in the cities. The advantage of the farmer was that he belonged to a category so broad and inclusive that it took in the hardscrabble farmer with a few barren acres and the prosperous husbandman whose acres were numbered in the hundreds. The thrifty farmer might gradually add to his landholdings until he possessed a barony, but he was under no compulsion to do so, and the fact is that the ethic of colonized or covenanted community was opposed to undue accumulation of property. Rather than being honored or admired, the farmer who by sharp practices and single-minded devotion to material gain profited substantially beyond his neighbors often felt considerable social pressure to mend his ways. This was especially the case if he indulged himself in conspicuous display, built a pretentious house, drove about town in a handsome coach, or in other ways made a show of his wealth.

Most honest farmers professed contempt for the luxury and ostentation manifested by the wealthy city dweller. William Manning in 1796 had written his "Key to Libberty" to rouse his fellow workingmen to the proposition that they were being exploited by the more privileged orders in society—the lawyers, the businessmen, the clergy, the teachers and doctors, and could protect themselves only by organizing and fighting for their own interests. Manning was not bitter about the disposition of the well-to-do who did not have to live by the sweat of their brows to take advantage of those beneath them. That was the way society worked. Since "self-love" and "self-aggrandizement" were the strongest human impulses, such behavior was to be expected, and it was thus all the more necessary to be prepared to counteract it. Manning's essay was never published, and in the early enthusiasm for "equality" it was hardly noticed that republican democracy proved markedly more generous to some than to others.

The average workingman was expected to work from sunrise to sunset, and if he got more for his labor than his counterpart in other countries it was precious little for all that. Signs of prosperity and luxury were all about him, but it was increasingly evident to the workingman that his share of the country's growing prosperity remained modest in the extreme. Immigrants and free blacks, desperate to find work of any kind, threatened him from below. And the avenues for advancement seemed more impenetrable with each passing decade. In the various workingmen's associations that sprang up, a ten-hour day and free public education for all children became the most common demands.

In Philadelphia in 1822 millwrights and machine workers of that city met at a tavern and passed resolutions calling for a 6:00 A.M. to 6:00 P.M. working day, with an hour each for breakfast and dinner. Two years later when Congress was considering a tariff bill that the commercial interests opposed, a group of "operatives" from textile mills around the city disrupted a meeting of merchants at city hall with shouts of "tariff, tariff" and "protection to American goods," broke furniture, and smashed windows. Most cities had schools for children of the poor, but many workingmen refused to send their children to such schools on the grounds that to do so was an admission of poverty.

Workingmen found champions among middle-class reformers who agitated for legislation to "prevent the rich from swallowing up the inheritance of the poor" and warned of "injurious consequences to the community of individuals amassing large landed property." There was increasing talk of the necessity for the reform of a system that distributed its wealth so inequitably. Most civic-minded urbanites plumped for one reform or another as all that was needed to create a just society, but an increasing number of "radicals" questioned the soundness of the system and called for wholesale changes. There were indications that the relentlessly competitive character of some areas of American life was eroding the sense of community that, it was said, had earlier characterized American towns. The most dramatic evidence of such attitudes was to be found in a community started in Pennsylvania in 1824 by the eccentric Welsh industrialist, Robert Owen, and his son, Robert Dale Owen, who had given the workers in his cotton mill at New Lanark, Scotland, a considerable share in the management of the plant and its profits. Owen's dream was of "unrestrained co-operation on the part of all members for every purpose of social life." Where better to preach his doctrines than in the United States?

Margaret Smith met the English reformer in Washington and reported that "Mr. Owen cares not how degraded, vicious or ignorant his new colonists may be, he feels the power of his system to be such, that they can soon be rendered virtuous and educated." In his words: "They want nothing and therefore are without temptation—make a man happy and you make him virtuous—this is the whole of my system, to make him happy, I enlighten his mind and occupy his hands and I have so managed the art of instruction that individuals seek it as amusement. Two of the most moral agents I use, are musick and dancing. . . . Dancing combines both exercise and amusement, and of all pleasures musick is the most innocent and exhilerates the spirits, while it soothes the passions." "Cool and dispassionate in his manner," Margaret Smith wrote, "slow and even difficult in his enunciation—with a face indicative of a strong mind, but no imagination, it is difficult to conceive that Mr. Owen is a visionary and an enthusiast—yet so he is called."

When George Rapp, a German religious visionary who had come to the United States with a number of his followers who practiced plain living and the sharing of all goods, moved farther west to find soil better suited to the growing of grapes, Owen and *his* followers moved into their vacated quarters and named their community, a model for others to emulate, New Harmony.

Owen's cooperative communities were to stress the education of children who were still malleable and could be taught. They were to be taken from their parents, lest they imbibe their outmoded social notions, and taught the proper principles of unselfishness and mutual help. "There were to be no churches, or sects or creeds, no religious worship, but moral lectures, and such a system of public education as would foster in the young a love of justice, morality and truth." Singing and dancing were emphasized, and the children were to be exposed to noble works of art. "Learning should cease to be a task and become a source of wonder and delight."

Soon a thousand men, women, and children had gathered at New Harmony. They were organized into six departments: agriculture, manufacture, mechanics, commerce, general economy, and domestic economy. Everyone was assured of freedom of speech and equality of rights, and there was common ownership of property. From this Owen went on to condemn private ownership of property entirely and to declare that marriage was an archaic institution. Men and women should be "married" without ceremony and be free to dissolve the relationship whenever they wished. Owen was soon being denounced, not surprisingly, as a Socialist and an infidel, and indignant parents descended on New Harmony to rescue the younger members from his clutches.

New Harmony was destined to be short-lived. There was much harmony but little profit, and Owen's money soon began to run out. Perhaps the colony's most important effect was to demonstrate that there were a substantial number of Americans who were less than entranced by the "way things were." People came to New Harmony in such numbers that Owen was forced to take advertisements in newspapers declaring that there was no more room at the commune. Some persistent would-be members built crude cabins on New Harmony land, and Owen had to tear their huts down to drive them off.

New Harmony would have many successors, all dedicated to reestablishing the true community, to overcoming the disintegrative effects of American life—most conspicuously the grinding competition resulting from the desperate struggle to "make it."

40

The Missouri Compromise

In the midst of the economic depression and the moral and mental depression resulting from it, the presidential election of 1820 rolled around. It must be considered the least actively contested election in our history. No serious opposition to Monroe appeared in the ranks of his own party or outside it. It did not occur to anyone to blame him for the state of the economy or to suggest that he had any responsibility to try to do anything to improve it. Out of some 232 votes for president in the electoral college a single symbolic vote was cast by New Hampshire for John Quincy Adams so that Washington's position as the only president elected unanimously might be preserved.

Overshadowing the election and even the state of the economy was the question of the admission of Missouri to the Union. Louisiana had been admitted as a state in 1812, with Indiana, Mississippi, Illinois, and Alabama following between 1816 and 1819. The legislatures of Indiana and Illinois had barred slavery. The territory of Missouri had no barrier to slaveholding and had thus become the refuge for all slaveholding Southerners disposed to migrate westward.

Timothy Flint, a Congregational minister and missionary, observed a stream of settlers, as many as a hundred a day, passing through St. Charles on the north bank of the Missouri River on their way to the territory and described the scene in his journal: "The whole appearance of the train—the cattle with their hundred bells; the negroes with delight in their countenances, for their labors were suspended and their imaginations excited; the wagons, often carrying two or three tons, so loaded that the mistress and the children are strolling carelessly along . . . carried me back to the pastoral pursuits of those ancient races whose home was a tent wherever their flocks found range. Just about nightfall they come to a spring or branch where there is water and wood; the pack of dogs set up a cheerful barking; the cattle lie down to ruminate; the team is unharnessed; the huge wagons are covered so that the roof completely excludes the rain; cooking utensils are brought out; the blacks prepare a supper which the toils of the day render delicious." Boone's Lick was the party's destination.

In three years of such migration the population of the Missouri Territory doubled, and a request for statehood came to Congress. When the request was reported out of committee, an amendment was proposed that would forbid the entry into the new state of any more slaves and provide for the gradual emancipation of those already there. The amendment ignited a blaze of oratory that flamed away for weeks on end, and before it was finished the whole country had become involved. In a letter to John Holmes, an antislavery crusader, Jefferson called the Missouri question "a fire-bell in the night," which "awakened and filled me with terror. I considered it at once as the knell of the Union." It might be put to rest for a time. "But this is a reprieve only, not a final sentence." There was no man on earth, he insisted to Holmes, who would more willingly make any sacrifice to put an end to the system of slavery. "But as it is, we have the wolf by the ears, and we can neither hold him, nor safely let him go. Justice is in one scale and self-preservation in the other."

Jefferson was convinced that "a geographical line, coinciding with a marked principle, moral and political . . . and held up by the angry passions of men, will never be obliterated." He could think of no better solution than leaving the matter to the states to decide as they thought fit. By inflaming popular feelings the Missouri question had, Jefferson believed, made disunion inevitable. "I regret that I am now to die in the belief, that the useless sacrifice of themselves by the generation of 1776, to acquire self-government and happiness to their country, is to be thrown away by the unwise and unworthy passions of their sons, and that my only consolation is that I live not to weep over it." To a friend he wrote, "In the gloomiest moment of the revolutionary war I never had any apprehensions equal to what I feel from this source."

In his correspondence with Adams, Jefferson raised the specter of a slave insurrection. Hopefully the final schism would be delayed. "Surely," he wrote, "they will parley awhile, and give us time to get out of the way. What a Bedlamite is man!" Adams replied: "Slavery in this Country I have seen hanging over it like a black cloud for half a Century. If I were as drunk with enthusiasm as Swedenborg or Wesley, I might probably say I had seen Armies of Negroes marching and counter marching in the air, shining in Armour. I have been so terrified with this Phenomenon that I constantly said in former times to the Southern Gentlemen, I cannot comprehend this object; I must leave it to you. I will vote for forcing no measure against your judgments. What we are to see, *God* knows, and I leave it to him and his agents in posterity. I have none of the genius of Franklin to invent a rod to draw from the clouds its Thunder and lightning."

In Congress the efforts of the antislavery men to exclude slavery from Missouri were defeated, but it soon became apparent that although they could not muster the votes to directly prohibit slavery, they did have enough weight in the House to block the admission of Missouri. Maine had for some years been pressing to be separated from Massachusetts and admitted as a state in its own right. The admission of the two states was now linked by the proponents of slavery, but the antislavery forces rejected the bargain. Finally, it was proposed that Missouri be admitted without mention of slavery but that Congress agree that north of thirty-six degrees and thirty minutes of latitude slavery should be forbidden in any territory of the United States.

While the question was being debated in Congress, antislavery feeling in the North, dormant for a decade or more, instantly revived. (Interestingly enough, the only antislavery newspaper in the country, the *Philanthropist*, was published by a Southerner and was distributed principally in the South.) Now antislavery sentiments were on every Northern tongue. There were angry meetings at Trenton and Boston, at Philadelphia and Baltimore, and in numerous towns throughout the Northern states. The petitions and resolutions drafted by such gatherings of indignant citizens were all to the same effect—slavery was unchristian, immoral, and unconstitutional, an unmitigated evil that must not be allowed to spread beyond its present boundaries. Representatives and senators from the Northern states were instructed to vote against the admission of Missouri as a Slave State. Pennsylvania went so far as to call for the abolition of slavery altogether.

Elias Boudinot, former president of the Continental Congress, wrote his wife: "We have been a good deal agitated here on the dispute relating to once more, (and it should be forever), establishing Slavery in the Missouri, and of consequence, in the United States, and causes great anxiety. It is whispered about by the knowing ones, that there is a wheel within a wheel and that there is some bargaining taking place between the East & Southern Interests. I know not how this is, but this I can pretty clearly guess at, that if it should take place there is an End to the happiness of the United States."

In the South it was a very different matter. In state after state equally indignant citizens declared that Congress had no right to set any conditions for the admission of a new state other than those specified in the Constitution. To do so would be to take a man's property from him without due process of law, and that, surely, was unconstitutional. The Virginia legislature pledged to "support the good people of Missouri in their just rights and admission into the Union on equal terms with the other states, and would cooperate with them in resisting with manly fortitude any attempt which Congress might make to impose restraints or restrictions as the price of admission."

Leaving the Capitol one day with his fellow Cabinet member, Calhoun, John Quincy Adams expressed his anxiety about the Missouri Compromise. Calhoun replied that he did not think it would destroy the Union, but if it did, "the South would be from necessity compelled to form an alliance, offensive and defensive, with Great Britain."

"But would that not be returning to the status of a colony?" Adams asked.

"Yes, pretty much, but it would be forced upon us."

After they parted company, Adams reflected that if there were a dissolution of the Union it would necessarily be followed by "the Universal emancipation of the slaves." "Slavery," he added, "is the great and foul stain upon the North American Union, and it is a contemplation worthy of the most exalted soul whether its total abolition is or is not practicable; if practicable, by what it may be effected, and . . . what means would accomplish it at the smallest cost of human suffering. A dissolution, at least temporary, of the Union, as now constituted, would be certainly necessary, and the dissolution must be upon a point involving the question of slavery and no other. The Union might then be reorganized on the fundamental principle of emancipation. This object is vast in its compass, awful in its prospects, sublime and beautiful in its issue."

When the Sixteenth Congress met in an atmosphere of growing crisis to take up "the Missouri question," it met in the restored and reconstructed chambers that had been burned down five years earlier by the British troops. Out of the 185 members of the House, 84 were new faces and 56 of these came from Northern states. As soon as the new Congress had been organized and Clay chosen as Speaker, John Scott of New York sought to introduce a bill forbidding the extension of slavery in any U.S. territory. Clay began the debate by declaring that he would never vote for the admission of Maine as long as restrictions were imposed on Missouri. "Equality is equality, and if it is right to make the restriction of slavery the condition of the admission of Missouri, it is equally just to make the admission of Missouri the condition of that of Maine."

After days of futile debate, John Taylor of New York submitted an amendment forbidding slavery in Missouri and added what turned out to be a fateful "sweetener" for the Southern states: "Provided, always, that any persons escaping into the same . . . such fugitive may be lawfully reclaimed, and conveyed to the person claiming his or her labor or service." The bill passed the House, but a similar bill failed in the Senate. There the bill to admit Maine was joined to a bill to admit Missouri without restrictions as to slavery. After the antislavery forces failed in an effort to have the two issues considered separately, a senator moved to forbid any more slaves being allowed to enter Missouri after it became a state. This amendment was debated for three long weeks. One of the principal and often reiterated arguments of the Southern senators was that by confining slavery to its present limits such a restriction would result in the black population of existing Slave States so far outnumbering their masters that no white person would be safe in his own home.

The climax of the debates came with the speech of William Pinckney, the Maryland lawyer and diplomat, and one of the famous orators of the day. He was to be answered by Rufus King, a relic of the Revolutionary era and now sixty-five years old. It was another of those oratorical set pieces so dear to American hearts. The scene in the Senate was much like that in the House when Clay castigated Jackson for his actions in the Seminole Wars. Fashionable ladies crowded the galleries and spilled over onto the floor of the chamber. A party of young women who had been invited to attend by Vice-President Daniel Tompkins took seats usually set aside for the foreign diplomatic corps.

Eloquent as they may have been, neither Pinckney nor King added anything new to the already interminable arguments. The Senate remained deadlocked. The amendment to exclude any additional slaves from Missouri was defeated; at this point Jesse Thomas, a senator from Illinois, proposed that Maine and Missouri be admitted to the Union, Missouri without restriction as to slavery, and that in all lands acquired by the Louisiana Purchase above the line thirty-six degrees, thirty minutes of latitude, slavery "shall be and is hereby forever prohibited." This paragraph was followed by a provision for the return of fugitive slaves that might escape into the territory. This compromise the Senate gratefully accepted by a vote of 34 to 10. Now the Senate bill went to the House, which handled it most cruelly. The Thomas amendment was defeated 159 to 18. A Senate-House conference followed, and after considerable wrangling a new compromise was agreed upon. In essence, the House gave way and accepted a slightly modified form of the Senate bill by a vote of 90 to 87, the result of considerable "management." Eighteen of the aye votes came from Northern states, and John Randolph christened these congressmen "doughfaces"—Northern men with Southern principles.

The matter seemed finally resolved, although Clay in his anxiety to prevent any reopening of the question repeatedly ruled John Randolph out of order and thereby incurred the Virginian's unrelenting enmity.

Tortuously hammered out as it was, the compromise failed to satisfy Northerners or Southerners. Congressmen who had voted for the bill were burned in effigy in the North and bitterly denounced in public meetings. For some of the new members it marked the virtual end of their brief careers in the House; they were resoundingly defeated in the next congressional elections. But more trouble was ahead. The Missouri bill, while admitting Maine as a state, had simply authorized Missouri to hold a convention and draft a constitution. Presumably encouraged by the victory of the proslavery forces in Congress, the Missourians pushed their luck by inserting two provisions in their proposed constitution highly objectionable to all antislavery men. One clause specified that the state legislature might never emancipate slaves without the consent of their masters, and the other excluded free blacks or mulattoes from ever entering the state.

With these defiant and inflammatory clauses the issue was once more ignited. The House, by a vote of 93 to 79, refused to admit Missouri to the Union with the offensive articles. Debate went on day after day with no resolution of the impasse in sight. Finally Clay managed to have the issue referred to a Committee of Thirteen of which he was chairman. The committee set as a condition for the admission of Missouri that the state agree to pass no law barring entry to citizens from any other state. But the House rejected the compromise 83 to 80. Meanwhile, the time for the meeting of the electoral college and the official counting of the votes drew closer. Missouri, assuming statehood, had sent in her electoral votes, and a conflict arose over whether her votes should be counted. To count them, the opponents of admission argued, would be to concede that Missouri was already a state. Thus, when the votes were opened and officially counted a wild scene took place at the point when the three votes of Missouri were to be tallied.

A few days later another motion was made to admit Missouri subject to the condition recommended by the Committee of Thirteen. Again it was defeated. At this a Southern member moved to rescind the prohibition against slavery in the Louisiana Purchase territory north of $36° 30'$ on the grounds that it had been linked to the admission of Missouri. Clay once more succeeded in having the motion referred to a committee, this time of twenty-three, which after due deliberation brought in a resolution that was simply a rewording of the earlier resolution proposed by the Committee of Thirteen. By dint of assiduous arm-twisting in the cloakrooms of the House, the Speaker finally lined up a majority of members in favor of the rephrased resolution, and it passed on February 26, 1821, 87 to 81.

In the aftermath of the Compromise, John Quincy Adams had another conversation with Calhoun on the question of slavery. Calhoun insisted that slavery had "many excellent consequences." Adams disagreed firmly but politely, remarking in his diary: "The discussion of this Missouri question has betrayed the secret of their souls. In the abstract they admit slavery is evil, they disclaim all participation of it, and cast it all upon the shoulders of our old Grandam Britain." But when probed, "they show at the bottom of their souls pride and vainglory in their condition of masterdom. They fancy themselves more generous and noble-hearted than the plain freemen who labour for subsistence. They look down upon the simplicity of a Yankee's manners, because he has no habits of overbearing like theirs and cannot treat Negroes like dogs. . . . What can be more false and heartless than this doctrine which makes the first and holiest rights of humanity to depend upon the color of the skin. It perverts human reason, and reduces men endowed with logical powers to maintain that slavery is sanctioned by the Christian religion, that slaves are happy and contented in their condition, that between master and slave there are ties of mutual attachment and affection, that the virtues of the master are refined and exalted by the degradation of the slaves; while at the same time men vent execrations upon the slave-trade, curse Britain for having given them slaves, burn at the stake Negroes convicted of crimes for the terror of the example, and writhe in agonies of fear at the very mention of human rights as applicable to men of color. . . . If the Union must be dissolved, slavery is precisely the question upon which it ought to break. For the present, however, this contest is laid asleep."

41

The Supreme Court

Chief Justice John Marshall and the Supreme Court had infuriated Jefferson and the Republicans by the decision in *Marbury* v. *Madison* and by failing to convict Aaron Burr of treason. While no cases of comparable significance in terms of the relations between the judicial and executive branches came before the Court in the following years, as a bastion of Federalism, it continued to be a thorn in the side of the Republicans. In 1810, in the case known as *Fletcher* v. *Peck*, Marshall had another dramatic opportunity not only to assert both the jurisdiction of the Court over state legislatures and state courts but also to explicate the article in the Constitution concerning the obligation of contracts. Years earlier a thoroughly corrupted Georgia legislature had passed out some some 35 million acres of the so-called Yazoo lands at a cent and a half an acre to cronies (including themselves). subsequent legislature had declared the transaction void, but mea while a number of persons had bought portions of the land in good faith, and one of these sued to preserve his purchase.

Fifteen years after the original fraud, the case of the plaintiff, Fletcher, reached the Supreme Court. In an opinion delivered by Marshall, the Court declared that the original sale by the Georgia legislature constituted a contract that could not be broken by a subsequent legislative enactment. After reviewing the nature of a contract, Marshall stated: "Georgia . . . is part of a large empire; she is a member of the American Union; and that Union has a constitution the supremacy of which all acknowledge, and imposes limits to the legislatures of the several states, which none claim a right to pass. The constitution of the United States declares that no state shall pass any bill of attainder, ex post facto law, or law impairing the obligation of contracts. . . . Whatever respect might have been felt for the state sovereignties, it is not to be disguised that the framers of the constitution viewed, with some apprehension, the violent acts which might [have] grown out of the feelings of the moment, have manifested a determination to shield themselves and their property from the effects of those sudden and strong passions to which men are exposed. The restrictions on the legislative power of the state are obviously founded on this sentiment; and the constitution of the United States contains what may be deemed a bill of rights for the people of each state." In addition, the repeal of the Yazoo Land Act constituted an ex post facto law, since it retroactively penalized those innocent individuals who had bought portions of the land in good faith. "It forfeits the estate of Fletcher for a crime not committed by himself, but by those from whom he purchased."

Georgians were indignant at "this monstrous and abhorrent doctrine," and Republican newspapers denounced it as another instance of the Court's determination to usurp the powers of the states, but the decision attracted relatively little comment elsewhere.

Six years later, Virginia, in the case of *Martin v. Hunter's Lessee*, challenged the right of the Supreme Court to receive cases on writs of error to the state courts; in other words, whether the Court could review a state court decision on the grounds that the state court might have been incorrect in its decision. The Judiciary Act of 1789 had given that authority to the Court, and in the intervening period it had taken such jurisdiction in sixteen cases without strong objection from the states. Now the Virginia Court of Appeals had refused to accept an appeal of its decision to the Supreme Court on the ground that the section of the Judiciary Act giving that authority to the Court was unconstitutional.

This time the decision of the Court was delivered by a new justice, Joseph Story, appointed by Madison. "The object of the constitution," Story declared in 1816, "was to establish three great departments of government: the legislative, the executive and the judicial departments. The first was to pass the laws, the second to approve and execute them, and the third to expound and enforce them. Without the latter it would be impossible to carry into effect some of the express provisions of the constitution. How, otherwise, could crimes against the United States be tried and punished? How could causes between the two states be heard and determined? . . . For the states to suppose that a decision of the Court was not an obligation binding on them, but might, at their pleasure, be omitted or declined, is to suppose that, under the sanction of the constitution they might defeat the constitution itself." The Court was of the opinion that its appellate power was "supported by the letter and the spirit of the constitution."

Jefferson, from Monticello, continued to view the Court with a jaundiced eye. After the *Fletcher* v. *Peck* decision, he referred in a letter to Madison to "the rancorous hatred which Marshall bears to the Government of his country" and noted "the cunning and sophistry within which he is able to enshroud himself. . . . His twistification of the law in the case of Marbury, in that of Burr and the late Yazoo case, show how dexterously he can reconcile law to his personal biases." And to Gallatin, he wrote of Marshall's "inveteracy . . . and his mind of that gloomy malignity which will never let him forego the opportunity of satiating it on a victim." In the 1820s he was still unrelentingly hostile to the Court, writing to a Republican justice: "The great object of my fear is the Federal Judiciary. That body like gravity, ever acting, with noiseless foot, and unalarming advance, gaining ground step by step, and holding what it gains, is ingulphing insidiously the special [state] governments into the jaws which feed them." Jefferson's attitude was essentially that of his party. The fact that the Republicans did not launch a sustained attack on the Court was due to the preoccupation of Congress with more pressing matters rather than to any reconciliation between that party and the federal judiciary.

In 1818 the Court was presented with a case that had far-reaching consequences. Dartmouth College was a small institution in New Hampshire started by Eleazar Wheelock as a school for Indians. Never notably successful with the Indians, it had survived as a regional college whose most famous graduate was Daniel Webster. The New Hampshire legislature undertook to alter the college's original charter to place it more directly under the control of the state. The college brought suit to protect its independence, and the case reached the Supreme Court in 1818 where no less a personage than Daniel Webster undertook to argue it for Dartmouth. The issue was similar to that in *Fletcher* v. *Peck*. The case attracted little attention, and Webster noted that the Court held "a small and unsympathetic" audience. Webster, nonetheless, made a long and learned exposition of the sanctity of contracts, and a reporter for the *Columbian Centinel* wrote, "Our friend Webster never made a happier effort. To a most elaborate and lucid argument he united a dignified and pathetic peroration which charmed and melted his hearers." It charmed and melted future generations of Dartmouth students as well, for in the course of it he referred to the New Hampshire institution in these words: "It is . . . a small college, and yet there are those who love it."

The Court held over its decision until the next term. Even this case had political overtones. The defenders of the college's original charter were, for the most part, Federalist; those who wished to incorporate it into the new state university were Republicans, led by the governor, William Plumer. Jefferson himself took an interest in the case, writing to Plumer that "The idea that institutions established for the use of the Nation cannot be touched or modified, even to make them answer their end, because of rights gratuitously supposed in those employed to manage them in trust for the public, may, perhaps, be a salutary provision against the abuses of a monarch, but it is most absurd against the Nation itself. Yet our lawyers and our priests generally inculcate this doctrine."

Jefferson's comments on the Dartmouth College Case are worth noting if only because of his assumption that while a monarch may abuse the rights of his subjects, it is "absurd" to believe that a republican government is in need of constraints on the popular will.

Isaac Parker, the Federalist chief justice of Massachusetts, had declared that "the people ought to be made to know that, in certain cases, their rights are above the reach of the Legislature." It was this point that Webster dwelt on in his argument. Unless the Court upheld the inviolability of such charters as that under which Dartmouth had operated for more than fifty years, "Colleges will become a theatre for the contention of politics. Party and faction will be cherished in the places consecrated to piety and learning. . . . It will be a most dangerous experiment to hold these institutions subject to the rise and fall of popular parties and the fluctuations of political opinions."

Marshall, who delivered the opinion of the Court, took note of the "magnitude and delicacy of this question. The validity of a legislature is to be examined; and the opinion of the highest law tribunal of a state is to be revised." Marshall then traced the history of the college as a private educational institution and the nature of the contract by which it had been established. Having determined that the charter of the college was a true contract, Marshall then considered the question of whether the New Hampshire legislature could modify it without the concurrence of the college. The act of the legislature, the Court judged, had as its intention "to convert a literary institution . . . under the control of private literary men, into a machine entirely subservient to the will of the government." It followed from this that the act of the legislature was unconstitutional and void.

The *Boston Daily Advertiser* hailed the decision as "calculated to ensure permanency to those numerous valuable institutions, so honorable to [the good people of New England], against the fluctuations of party and the rude attacks of rash innovators."

The "rash innovators" were of course furious, and the Court was denounced for frustrating the will of the people and usurping powers that properly belonged to the states. Happily three of the Republican judges concurred with the two Federalist justices, one Republican alone dissenting. It was especially infuriating to the Republicans to see presumably reliable Republicans appointed to the Court fall under Marshall's sway and vote to uphold the dominance of the Supreme Court over the state courts and state legislatures.

Although the importance of the Court's ruling in the Dartmouth College Case was hardly realized at the time, before many years passed it became one of the Court's most influential decisions, used to protect corporate property interests against the efforts of state legislatures to revoke or modify them in the public interest.

Prior to the Dartmouth College Case few corporations had been chartered because of uncertainty about their permanence. In 1800 only 8 manufacturing corporations had been chartered in the whole country. Only 213 corporations had been chartered in all, most of these banks, bridges, canals, and turnpikes. The Dartmouth College Case was followed by a great increase in the number of corporations.

In the same term that saw the decision in the Dartmouth College Case the Court was severely tried by another case that caused intense popular feeling. We have already noted the waffling of Congress on the issue of a national bank—chartered in 1791, allowed to expire in 1811, and then revived in 1816 when state banking had gotten out of control. The truth was that its effort to impose some constraints on the fiscally irresponsible activities of the state banks caused friction from the moment that the new Bank of the United States was chartered in

1816. The strategy the states developed to clip the wings of the branches of the Bank of the United States was to impose such exorbitant taxes on the branches that the bank had to abandon them.

In Maryland, a Mr. McCulloch brought a suit against the state for having imposed such taxes on the bank. The champions of states' rights rallied in support of Maryland. Three of the greatest lawyers of the day—William Pinckney, William Wirt, and Webster—argued for the plaintiff that the Maryland statute imposing the tax on the branch of the Bank of the United States was unconstitutional. Luther Martin and Joseph Hopkinson carried the main burden of the defense for the state.

Martin, in concluding his argument, stated that he wished to quote one final authority he felt should be conclusive. He then read from Marshall's speech in the Virginia ratifying convention assuring the delegates that the Supreme Court would never call a sovereign state before it. Marshall, at Martin's words, heaved a deep sigh; later, when Story asked him its cause, Marshall confessed that he had long anticipated some enterprising attorney's digging up the quotation and using it against him: "To tell you the truth, I was afraid I had said some foolish things in the debate; but it was not so bad as I expected."

Webster spoke for three days against the right of a state to tax a corporation chartered by Congress. Story wrote to a friend, "I never, in my whole life, heard a greater speech; it was worth a journey from Salem to hear it; his elocution was excessively vehement, but his eloquence was overwhelming. His language, his style, his figures, his arguments were most brilliant and sparkling. He spoke like a great statesman and patriot, and a sound constitutional lawyer. All the cobwebs of sophistry and metaphysics about States rights and State sovereignty he brushed away with a mighty besom."

It took the justices only three days to draft their decision, and Marshall delivered the unanimous verdict of the Court, affirming that "The government of the United States . . . though limited in its powers, is supreme; and its laws, when made in pursuance of the constitution, form the supreme law of the land, 'anything in the constitution or laws of any state to the contrary notwithstanding.'"

Marshall placed strong emphasis on the necessary and proper clause of the Constitution that gave Congress the power to pass laws requisite to give full effect to its stated powers. He dismissed the arguments of those who declared that Congress could exercise no powers not specifically granted it under the Constitution. "The baneful influence of this narrow construction on all the operations of the government, and the absolute impracticability of maintaining it without rendering the whole government incompetent to its great objects," might be easily demonstrated.

Having established the right of Congress to charter the bank, the Court then went on to consider the question of whether the Maryland legislature had the right to tax it. If the states were allowed such a right, it would have the effect of enabling the states to defeat any act of Congress that did not please them and thus at once destroy the national powers of Congress and with it the Union. "The Court," Marshall concluded, "has bestowed on this subject its most deliberate consideration. The result is a conviction that the states have no power, by taxation or otherwise, to retard, impede, burden, or in any manner control the operations of the constitutional laws enacted by Congress to carry into execution the powers vested in the general government."

Virginia was the most vocal state in protesting the decision of the Court. *Niles' Weekly Register*, published in Baltimore, denounced it as a "total prostration of States-Rights and the loss of the liberties of the Nation. . . . The principles established . . . are far more dangerous to the Union and happiness of the people of the United States than anything else that we ever had to fear from invasion." The *General Intelligencer* of Philadelphia declared: "Never was a bad case worse supported by constellated talents, learning and wisdom. . . . It seems as if nature had revolted from 'the debasing task assigned to them' and that their [the attorneys for the bank] reason and judgment had forsaken them for the destructive purposes they were pledged to fulfill, in defiance of all human rights, human joys, and divine commandments. I feel a pang of despair for my country, when I think of the tyrannical purpose for which they pronounced their false judgment upon this subject."

Not all reactions were hostile. Federalist papers acclaimed the verdict, and the *Western Monitor*, a Kentucky paper, commended "the strong, lucid, masterly" arguments, the "strength and fairness of reasoning which we have seldom if ever seen surpassed. . . . At all events—whatever opinions may be entertained—we trust we shall have no forcible resistance to the laws of the United States—no contemptuous violations of judicial decisions—no acts of hostility to the government of the Union."

The Kentucky editor's apprehensions were well founded, as he doubtless knew. Kentucky's neighbor, Ohio, was about to defy the

Bank of the United States, the Congress, and the Court. The state auditor directed his assistant to collect the tax the Ohio legislature had levied on the branch of the Bank of the United States. Armed with a warrant, the assistant entered the bank, carried away $120,475, and, ignoring a federal court injunction, delivered the money to the state treasurer at Columbia. This bold act was sharply criticized by many Republican papers. A Georgia newspaper denounced it as manifesting "a disregard for the union and harmony of the States, and a contemptuous defiance of the supreme constitutional authorities of the Republic." The governor of Ohio repudiated the act, declaring that he viewed "the transaction in the most odious light, and from my very soul I detest it. I am ashamed it happened in Ohio."

A federal marshal finally retrieved the appropriated "tax" money, and the state treasurer was jailed for contempt. But the unrepentant legislature voted to affirm the Virginia and Kentucky Resolutions and outlawed the Bank of the United States in Ohio. Not content with these gestures, the legislators proceeded to draw up a list of federal powers they considered unconstitutional and solicited the support of the other states in defying all federal statutes judged by the states to infringe upon their rights. Only Virginia endorsed the Ohio Resolutions.

It is worth noting that the initial challenge to the Court came not from those Southern states that had been so often identified with the extreme states' rights position but from Maryland, a border state, and Ohio, a Free State with strong ties to New England. Of course, the New England states had been highly vocal on the subject of states' rights and had repeatedly threatened to form a separate confederation in the period of the embargo during Jefferson's presidency and during the War of 1812. It is thus clear that few if any of the states, however much they might declaim about the greatness of the Union, thought of themselves as part of an indissoluble nation whose supreme powers were lodged in the federal government. The notion that the states must yield to a "grand consolidated government" on matters they considered of vital interest was abhorrent to them. *In other words, after almost thirty years of existence as a nation, the great majority of the political leaders of the states, if not of the people themselves, had not accepted the basic assumptions that guided the Founding Fathers in framing the federal Constitution.*

Each Court decision that reaffirmed the powers of the national government over the states brought cries of outrage from various sections of the country. In 1821 Virginia, the Court's most inveterate enemy, challenged it directly. The state legislature passed a series of resolves declaring that the Court had "no rightful authority under the Constitution to examine and correct" the judgments of the state courts. The *Richmond Enquirer* applauded the actions of the legislature, stating that "the principle which it asserts seems to be essential to the existence and preservation of States-Rights, and the true foundation of our political system." The particular case in question was that of *Cohens* v. *Virginia*. Cohens had been found guilty by a Virginia court of selling lottery tickets in defiance of a state law forbidding the practice. He sued on the grounds that since lotteries were permitted in the District of Columbia and he was a citizen of the District, he was free to sell his tickets.

The case was the kind that Marshall relished. Rather like *Marbury* v. *Madison*, it enabled him to enunciate important constitutional principles while, in effect, upholding the verdict of the lower courts. The real issue, to Marshall and his fellow justices, was not so much whether Cohens was a successful plaintiff as whether the Supreme Court could review a criminal case appealed from a state court. The attorney for Virginia, who was to be rewarded by being subsequently appointed to the Court, concluded his argument by declaring: "Nothing can so much endanger [this government] as exciting the hostility of the State governments. With them it is, to determine how long this government shall endure."

In *Cohens* v. *Virginia* the Court upheld its power to hear criminal cases on appeal and then upheld the verdict of the Virginia court on the grounds that Congress had not intended to authorize a lottery in that state. The decision confirmed the *Richmond Enquirer*'s conviction that "The judiciary power, with . . . a spirit as greedy as the grave, is sweeping to their destruction the rights of the States," and the *Cincinnati Gazette* saw the verdict as another blow at the sovereignty of the states and an effort to erect "on their ruins a mightily consolidated empire fitted for the sceptre of a great monarch."

In the next important case to come before the Court, the Court for the first time dealt with the question of the power of the federal government over the internal commerce of the states. For almost twenty-five years the Livingstons and the Fultons had enjoyed a monopoly on steamboat travel on the Hudson River and the waters within the state under a charter from the New York legislature. Connecticut and New Jersey, whose waters mingled with those of New York on the north and south, found the monopoly especially objectionable, since it excluded their steamboats from the lucrative water-borne traffic of the region. Guerrilla warfare threatened to break out between the three states, with gunfire already having been exchanged on occasion. In this atmosphere Aaron Ogden, former governor of New Jersey, brought a test suit.

When the case was argued before the Supreme Court, a dazzling array of legal talent was once again enlisted. Daniel Webster and William Wirt were the principal attorneys for Ogden. Of Wirt, a friend wrote, "His voice is powerful, his tones harmonious, and enunciation clear and distinct. He never speaks without evincing ardor and feeling. . . . He delights and convinces, and no man hears him without understanding his arguments [which are] . . . constantly enlivened by classical allusions and flashes of wit." Urging a friend to come and hear the steamship case argued, Wirt himself wrote: "Oakley [one of the attorneys for the monopoly] is said to be one of the first logicians of the age, as much a Phocion [the great Athenian statesman] as Emmet [another of the monopoly lawyers] is a Themistocles, and Webster is as ambitious as Caesar. He will not be outdone by any man, if it is within the compass of his power to avoid it. It will be a combat worth witnessing."

To the participants and to the spectators these battles were as dramatic and resonant with history as the encounter of Hector and Achilles at Troy. The country, as we have said before, was "talked into existence." Other nations had arisen out of custom and conquest, with the slow accumulation of the myths and traditions that define a historic people. This one—the United States of America—took shape through the intoxicating power of inspired speech.

On Wednesday, February 4, 1824, at eleven o'clock in the morning, the Court convened. Like a warrior preparing for battle, Webster had been up the entire night before. He had never, on any occasion, he told his friend, George Ticknor Curtis, had "so completely the free use of his faculties. . . . At nine A.M. after eleven hours of continuous intellectual effort, his brief was completed. He sent for his barber and was shaved, he took a very slight breakfast of tea and crackers . . . he read the morning journals to amuse and change his thoughts, and then he went into Court and made that grand argument which, as Judge Wayne said . . . twenty years afterward 'released every creek and river, every lake and harbor in our country from the interference of monopolies.'"

When Webster began, the room was "excessively crowded."

Marshall, who still wrote with a quill pen, scorning that "barbarous invention," a steel pen, nibbed his quill with a pocketknife and nodded to Webster to begin. Webster wrote afterward: "I think I never experienced more intellectual pleasure than in arguing that novel question to a great man who could appreciate it, and take it in; and he did take it in, as a baby takes in its mother's milk."

Oakley gave an effective reply. It was one of "the most ingenious and able arguments ever made in this Court," a spectator noted, adding, "You can form no idea what interest this decision excites at Washington." Wirt, concluding the case for the plaintiff, in the opinion of many eclipsed even Webster. The *Richmond Enquirer* called it "the finest effort of human genius ever achieved in a Court of Justice . . . a powerful and splendid effusion, grand, tender, picturesque, and pathetic. The manner was lofty and touching; the fall of his voice towards the conclusion was truly thrilling and affecting."

Two weeks passed before the Court was ready to present its opinion. When it reassembled, the chamber was jammed with lawyers, legislators, and fashionable ladies. The decision of the Court first disposed of the "narrow" versus "broad" interpretation of the Constitution. In the opinion of the justices only a broad interpretation could be justified. The authority of the federal government over commerce must be understood to include navigation; otherwise it would be a dead letter, since commerce was clearly carried on in considerable part by waterborne transportation. It was the opinion of the Court that "The power of Congress . . . comprehends navigation within the limits of every state in the Union; so far as that navigation may be, in any manner, connected with 'commerce with foreign nations, or among the several states, or with the Indian tribes.' . . . The acts of New York must yield to the law of Congress; and the decision sustaining the privilege they confer, against a right given by a law of the Union, must be erroneous." The act chartering the monopoly had been an unconstitutional intrusion of the state into the federal domain, and the monopoly was thus illegal and dissolved. The decision of the Court was generally applauded (although it reaffirmed the supremacy of Congress and the right of the Court to overrule state legislatures and state courts) because monopolies were unpopular, and the general public was pleased to see one of the most conspicuous ones curtailed.

Gibbons v. *Ogden* largely completed the "system" of the Marshall Court by defining and redefining the powers of the federal government vis-à-vis the state. It is evident that what we have called the disintegrative effects of American life were manifest on the political as well as the psychological level. The union was constantly threatening to fly apart under a variety of strains and stresses. The dogma of states' rights or state sovereignty—the doctrine that the states could, in effect, ignore whatever congressional legislation they found un-palatable—was so deep-seated that three decades of Court decisions could not uproot it. Hardly a session of Congress passed without the introduction of bills to curtail the powers of the Court. In the fall session of 1823 Senator Johnson of Kentucky introduced a bill that would have required the concurrence of seven judges in an opinion "involving the validity of State statutes or Acts of Congress. Some remedy," he declared in introducing the bill, "must, ere long, be adopted to preserve the purity of our political institutions."

A few months later, a president-to-be of the United States, Martin Van Buren, senator from New York, brought in a bill requiring the concurrence of five justices in such cases. The debates in Congress that followed on the introduction of such bills provided an opportunity for Webster to emerge as the Court's most eloquent defender, but it was not without other champions, among them Senator William Harper of South Carolina, who declared: "The independence of the Judiciary is at the very basis of our institutions. . . . It is in times of faction, when party spirit runs high, that dissatisfaction is most likely to be occa-sioned by the decisions of the Supreme Court. . . . However high the tempest may blow, individuals may hear the calm and steady voice of the Judiciary warning them of their danger. They will shrink away; they will leave that majority a minority, and that is the security the Constitution intended by the Judiciary."

The continued opposition to the Court reminds us how unconge-nial it was to the democratic temper of the country. As the "original sin" branch of the government, it was an affront to the notion that the people were wise and good and that their will should in all cases prevail. The reader will recall by how narrow a margin the Constitu-tion was approved at all and how quickly the Classical-Christian Consciousness that produced it became archaic. It was true, as its enemies charged, that the Court was a persistent, largely invisible force, immune, to a considerable extent, from the fluctuating political tides. It is not going too far, I think, to call it "an essential anachro-nism," a survival from an earlier age, an age whose true character grew dimmer year by year in the popular mind.

42

The Monroe Doctrine

In 1815, following the return of Louis XVIII to the throne he had so hastily vacated a few months before, Tsar Alexander I of Russia proposed a declaration of Christian principles that he prevailed upon Emperor Francis I of Austria, Frederick William III of Prussia, and most of the monarchs of Europe to sign. The signers thereupon became known as members of the Holy Alliance, which in time became synonymous with reactionary politics.

France was occupied by Allied troops to insure her good behavior. In Spain, Ferdinand VII was restored to the throne after Wellington's armies had completed the rout of the French. Ferdinand was reactionary, inefficient, mercurial, and ruthless in repressing the liberal elements in his country. As we have seen, the unsettled state of things in the homeland had encouraged Spain's American colonies to revolt, and by 1820 most of them had declared their independence.

On the practical level, we have already taken notice of the degree to which the European wars had affected America. It is hard to imagine that the Louisiana Purchase would have dropped into Jefferson's lap if Napoleon had not been anxious to avoid its falling into the hands of England or reverting to Spain. Andrew Jackson's foray into Florida had given John Quincy Adams the opportunity to enter into extensive negotiations with Spain directed at securing Florida for the United States while giving Spain guarantees for the security of Texas. In 1821, the treaty with Spain was concluded. In the Southwest, the adventurers and planters who longed to get their hands on Texas were indignant at what they considered their betrayal by the Monroe administration. For ten years Americans along the Texas border had been meddling in Mexican affairs. An uprising had taken place against Ferdinand VII in 1808, and revolutionary juntas or committees had been established in most Spanish towns. When word of the revolt reached Mexico, the champions of Mexican independence tried to follow suit. A Catholic curate, Hidalgo y Costilla, in the province of Guanajuato, gathered an army of Indians, mestizos, and creoles and seized the local seat of government. Hidalgo, gathering recruits as he went, then marched on Mexico City, but there the viceroy decreed that he and his followers would be excommunicated if they did not lay down their arms. Under this threat Hidalgo's pious legion melted away.

Hidalgo was captured and executed, but one of his lieutenants made his way across Texas and enlisted a group of Americans who were delighted to have any pretext to enter Texas. They invaded Texas, captured San Antonio, and executed the Spanish officials of the town. A few months later Spanish troops drove those who were not killed or captured back across the Sabine River. Such raids and forays went on for the next ten years. When Ferdinand was placed back on the throne of Spain by the Holy Alliance, the Mexican revolutionaries were ruthlessly suppressed.

The reestablishment of Spanish rule did not daunt the Americans who coveted Texas. In the aftermath of the treaty an expedition of Americans and Mexican liberationists—they called themselves "the patriots"—set out, three hundred strong, from Natchez, crossed the Sabine, and issued a proclamation stating that Texas was an independent republic. Once more the invaders were routed by Spanish troops. At this point Moses Austin, a native of Connecticut who had come west to make his fortune at mining, and his son, Stephen Fuller Austin, began exploring the possibilities of establishing a settlement in Texas by purchase rather than by arms. Austin's plan was to buy land from the Spanish authorities on which to settle a colony of three hundred American families. Austin's proposal was accepted by the Spanish governor of Texas. The Americans must all be or become Catholics and pledge allegiance to the Spanish Crown. They could then purchase land for twelve and a half cents an acre.

Moses Austin died before the settlement could be established, and his son took charge. When Stephen Austin arrived in San Antonio to complete the transaction, he discovered that Mexico was in revolt against Ferdinand. Word of the military uprising against Ferdinand in Spain had triggered the revolt, led by an officer named Agustín de Iturbide, who undertook to establish a constitutional monarchy with himself as Emperor Agustín I. Emperor Agustín, to help fill the depleted royal treasury, began at once to sell large allotments of Texas land to American contractors, who promised to promote settlement. Each farmer would be allowed 177 acres and each cattle rancher 4,428 acres. Before the settlers could claim their lands, Emperor Agustín was overthrown and an independent Mexican republic was established; the government, known as the Constitutent Congress, adopted the Constitution of the United States of Mexico. The leaders of the new government, considering that they had acted in the spirit of the American struggle for independence, continued Iturbide's policy of opening Texas to settlers from the other "United States."

The members of the Holy Alliance had a common interest in putting down all movements for independence in any of their colonial possessions. It was, in practical fact, the mustering of an army by Ferdinand VII of Spain to reestablish Spanish control of her colonies in America that had provided the occasion for the revolt against him at home, which, in turn, had encouraged Mexico to declare itself independent. Alarmed at the news from Mexico, the Holy Alliance held another congress, this time at Verona, and authorized France to take military measures to place toppled-down Ferdinand back on his throne once more.

It was clear that once the Spanish rebels had been subdued the Holy Alliance would turn its attention to the revolted colonies of Spain in America, and this both the British and the Americans wished to forestall. Indeed, Albert Gallatin, the U.S. minister at Paris, went so far as to tell the French government that "if France was successful in her attack on Spain, and afterward attempted either to take possession of some of her former colonies or to assist her in reducing them under their former yoke, I was of the opinion that the United States would oppose every undertaking of this kind."

At the same time, John Quincy Adams viewed with considerable skepticism the current infatuation with constitutions so evident in countries that had cast off the yoke of imperialism. "I cannot wholly divest myself of my anxiety for my children, my country, and my species," he wrote. "The possibility is that the fabrication of constitutions will be the occupation or the sport, the tragedy, comedy, or farce, for the entertainment of the world for a century to come." Adams saw "little appearance of the prevalence of correct notions of the indispensable machinery of a free government, in any part of Europe or America."

Monroe, uneasy at the prospect of the Holy Alliance's interfering in the affairs of the Western Hemisphere and prodded by Henry Clay, who pressed resolutions in Congress warning the European powers to stay out of the Americas, began to formulate a statement designed to deter such intervention. The matter of Russian intrusion from Alaska down the northwest coast almost as far as San Francisco, and the traditional interest of the British in that region, gave an added urgency to such a declaration.

In 1820, a congressional committee had brought in a report recommending that the area at the mouth of the Columbia River be formally occupied by the United States and that trade with the Indians be regulated by Congress. The report described the advantages to be derived from the fur trade and placed much emphasis on the fact that the Lewis and Clark Expedition had demonstrated the practicality of establishing a trade route from the Northwest across the Rockies to the Missouri. The House of Representatives showed little interest in the committee's recommendations, and a proposed bill was tabled.

In 1822, the Russian minister inadvertently revived the issue by handing to John Quincy Adams an edict from Emperor Alexander granting Russian citizens trading, fishing and whaling rights in the waters and along the northwest coast as far south as the fifty-first parallel of latitude. Suddenly the whole issue of Oregon presented itself once more, but again, the House refused to consider the matter and Adams began negotiations with the Russian minister on the rights of the United States in the region. In the course of the discussions, Adams stated that the United States was determined to resist the intervention of the European powers in the affairs of the Americas. England meanwhile associated herself with the American protest to Russia on the grounds of her well-established interest in the trade of the Northwest. In Adams's words, "The American continents henceforth will no longer be subjects of colonization. Occupied by civilized independent nations, they will be accessible to Europeans on that footing alone, and the Pacific Ocean and every part of it will remain open to the navigation of all nations, in a like manner with the Atlantic." It was an astonishingly bold assertion of the hegemony of the United States in the Western Hemisphere and could not have succeeded without the support of England, who, for reasons of her own, was anxious to see the imperial schemes of the Holy Alliance checked. Adams instructed Richard Rush, son of Benjamin and ambassador to the Court of St. James's, to propose that the line of 55° be set as the southernmost limit of Russian settlement, 51° as the northernmost line for American settlement, and that the intervening space be assigned to Great Britain.

Both the British and the Russians rejected the American plan. Britain countered with the proposal that a line be drawn from the Rocky Mountains to the Pacific on the line of 49°, a continuation of the boundary separating the United States and Canada. This reasonable solution was, in turn, rejected by Monroe, and there the matter rested for the time being.

John Quincy Adams was as wary of British imperialism as of that of the Russians or the Holy Alliance. In his determination to fend off the interference of foreign powers in the affairs of the New World, he had frequent sharp exchanges with Stratford Canning, the British minister to the United States. When Canning pressed Britain's interest in the Oregon country, Adams replied by asking Canning how Britain would react if the United States showed an interest in the Shetland Islands.

"Have you," Canning asked, "any *claim* to the Shetland Islands?"

"Have you any *claim*," Adams replied, "to the mouth of Columbia River?"

"Why, do you not *know*," replied he, "that we have a claim?"

"I do not *know*," Adams said, "what you claim nor what you do not claim. You claim India; you claim Africa; you claim—"

"Perhaps, a piece of the moon."

"No, I have not heard that you claim exclusively any part of the moon; but there is not a spot on *this* habitable globe that I could affirm you do not claim; and there is none which you may not claim with as much color of right as you have to Columbia River or its mouth."

Pressed by Adams to issue a statement defining the American position, Monroe wrote to Jefferson for advice, and Jefferson replied in a letter dated October 24, 1823: "Our first and fundamental maxim should be, never entangle ourselves in the broils of Europe. Our second, never to suffer Europe to intermeddle with cis-Atlantic affairs. America, North, and South, has a set of interests distinct from those of Europe, and peculiarly her own. She should therefore have a system of her own, separate and apart from that of Europe. While the last is laboring to become the domicil of despotism, our endeavor should surely be, to make our hemisphere that of freedom. . . . Great Britain is the nation which can do us the most harm of any one, or all on earth; and with her on our side we need not fear the whole world. With her then, we should most sedulously cherish a cordial friendship; and nothing would tend more to knit our affections than to be fighting once more, side by side, in the same cause." That Jefferson, the lifelong enemy of Great Britain, could write in such vein was the surest evidence of the effect on Republicans (and Americans generally) of the tangled and indeed nightmarish history of Europe since the rise of Napoleon. The Federalists had lived and died by their devotion to England. Jefferson's conversion to their cause could bring them only more satisfaction. He went on to support a declaration to the effect that "we will oppose, with all our means, the forcible interposition of any other power, as auxiliary, stipendiary, or under any form or pretext, and most especially, their transfer to any [European] power by conquest, cession, or acquisition in any other way."

Thus urged on by Adams and encouraged by Jefferson and Madison, and perhaps most important, by the British, Monroe, never a bold man, issued what was perhaps the boldest declaration ever pronounced by an American president. He chose as the occasion his annual address to Congress on December 2, 1823, at the beginning of his last year in office.

The clearly expansionist intentions of Russia in the Oregon region, Monroe told the senators and representatives, had raised the whole question of the future relationship of the "American conti-nents" to the European powers. To put the matter succinctly, these continents "by the free and independent condition which they have assumed and maintained, are henceforth not to be considered as subjects for future colonization."

Any effort of the European powers "to extend their system to any portion of this hemisphere" would be considered by the United States "as dangerous to our peace and safety." We would not interfere with any of the "existing colonies or dependencies," but "we could not view any interposition for the purpose of oppressing [the newly independent nations of South and Central America], or controlling in any other manner their destiny . . . in any other light than as the manifestation of an unfriendly disposition towards the United States."

What was promptly called the Monroe Doctrine enjoyed instant popularity in both the United States and England. It was almost as though the spirit of the Revolution had been revived—the United States had put herself forward as the friend of all those who struggled for freedom and independence. The triumph of reactionary politics in Europe had, on the one hand, forced Americans to abandon their hopes for the imminent rise of republican governments in that quarter of the globe, and on the other, it had allowed them to come forth as the protector of those new "constitutional republics" that had sprung up like mushrooms right under their noses. Perhaps most ironic of all, this remarkable assertion of American power had been encouraged, if not actually made possible, by Great Britain. And Thomas Jefferson, whose determined anti-British policy had torn the country apart in the period of the embargo, was speaking enthusiastically of knitting "our affections" by "fighting once more, side by side" against the forces of evil!

Hearing the news, Henry Brougham, a liberal British statesman, wrote to a friend that "the question with regard to South America is now disposed of, or nearly so, for an event has recently happened than which no event has dispersed greater joy, exultation, and gratitude over all the freeman of Europe—that event which is decisive of the subject with respect to South America is the message of the President of the United States to the Congress."

The *London Courier* called Monroe's address "a document of more than usual importance. . . . After so clear and explicit a warning there is not one of the Continental powers, we suppose, that will risk a war with the United States—a war in which . . . the good wishes of Great Britain . . . would be all on the side of the United States. . . . Protected by the two nations that possess the institutions and speak the language of freedom," Great Britain and the United States. The independence of the South American countries was "placed beyond the reach of danger."

The members of the Holy Alliance were, needless to say, less taken with the Monroe Doctrine. The official newspaper of the French government ridiculed the message and denounced Monroe as a dictator.

A modern philosopher-psychologist has written of "peak" experiences in the life of an individual. Certainly nations have them as well. The declaration of the Monroe Doctrine, in large part the creation of John Quincy Adams, was such a moment. It announced the arrival of the United States as a full-fledged world power and the beginning of an accord between this country and Great Britain that, with a few rough spots, was to become one of the most enduring, if informal, alliances in the world. "Liberty-loving" and "English-speaking" became phrases commonly used to describe the world's two most durable constitutional governments.

For thirty-five years—since the beginning of the Republic—the domestic politics of the United States had been almost completely dominated by events in Europe, more specifically the rivalry between Great Britain and France. Finally, through the good offices of the Holy Alliance, the United States was free of its strange infatuation with events on the other side of the ocean, events that it always, in any event, understood very imperfectly. The Monroe Doctrine can be read as: (1) the first decisive assertion by the United States of its determination to protect its interests against the imperial ambitions of any European power; (2) an expression of moral and, if necessary, military support for our brave, freedom-loving South American neighbors; and (3) a declaration of global independence. Washington's famous advice in his Farewell Address to avoid involvement in European politics had, in fact, fallen on deaf ears. Now, almost thirty years later, it became the official creed of the United States.

The American conviction that it was our mission to redeem the world had been considerably modified by the course of history. The succession of European wars, which were really one continual war, bore most heavily, as war always does, on the "lower orders," the peasants and workers who were drafted into the armies and dragged off to fight and often to die in complicated dynastic struggles in whose outcome they had little interest.

The rise of industrialism in the Old World brought with it new horrors of poverty and exploitation for the unhappy men, women, and, more and more frequently, children, who worked long hours in unhealthy conditions and lived in squalor. In the face of such conditions, it was perhaps inevitable that the traumas occasioned by life in the United States should have all seemed relatively mild.

Louis XVIII, prompted by Talleyrand and the British, who sponsored the reestablishment of the Bourbons in an attempt to introduce some stability into French politics, issued a constitution and in the first Treaty of Paris recognized the independence of the Netherlands, the German and Italian states, and Switzerland, and promised to abolish the slave trade. The treaty was followed by the Congress of Vienna, a nine-month-long conclave of European royalty and their ambassadors and foreign ministers dominated by the Austrian statesman Prince Klemens Wenzel Nepomuk Lothar von Metternich. Metternich was to give his name to the age of political reaction that lasted from the Congress of Vienna to the revolutionary upheavals of 1848. Through a series of congresses, skillfully managed by him, the monarchs of Europe concerted their common efforts to suppress political or social reform.

The intricate redistribution of powers, titles, thrones, and principalities that resulted from the prolonged deliberations at Vienna fortunately need not detain us. The end of the Congress was hastened, ironically, by the return of Napoleon from his exile at Elba. Bonaparte seized Paris; Louis fled; and at Vienna the new Allies united to dispel, for the last time, their recurrent nightmare, the irrepressible Corsican. The Allied forces were placed under the command of Wellington, who defeated Napoleon at Waterloo. Napoleon was once more forced to abdicate; tried unsuccessfully to escape to America; was captured by the British; and, with the unanimous approval of the Allies, exiled to the island of St. Helena, where he lived until his death six years later.

There is no question that these events had both practical and what we might call philosophical consequences in America. They encouraged America to constantly compare the happy condition of the New World with the chaotic situation in the Old, while raising considerable doubts about whether it was, after all, the destiny of the United States to reform the world. Since the first euphoric moments of the French Revolution, the political currents seemed to be running strongly in the opposite direction (although it took the Republicans an uncommonly long time to acknowledge that Napoleon was not the prophet of a new order). Monarchies appeared to grow stronger by the day. The most notable consequence of all this was to strengthen the conviction of most Americans that the rest of the world was sunk in sin and evil and that the United States was the special vessel of the Almighty. It thus encouraged what we might call a "fortress mentality," the notion of the United States, not as model (since no one seemed inclined to imitate it—rather, the reverse), but as a refuge, a haven, separated by three thousand miles of ocean from the wickedness of Europe.

43

The Election of 1824

Monroe's reelection in 1820 pointed up the virtual collapse of the party system that had prevailed since the adoption of the Constitution. What followed was a period of political disorientation, dominated by sectional politics. Virginia still exercised considerable influence in the Old South, but Calhoun had emerged as the spokesman of the slave interests. The Southwest had its own peculiar concerns and its own idols, paramount among them Clay and Jackson. New England had found its champion in Daniel Webster, who was to tower over other representatives of that region for thirty years. The West north of the Ohio, populated in large part by migrating New Englanders, identified on a number of issues, especially that of slavery, with its home region.

Under these circumstances, the ordinary citizen had both an incentive and an opportunity to make his own views and ambitions felt. The months leading up to the election of 1824 made it clear that he intended to take advantage of the opportunity. While Americans had enjoyed most of the prerogatives of a free and democratic people for a generation or more, they had nonetheless been subject to various constraints and restrictions designed to keep the most essential power in the hands of members of the upper class or what we are disposed today to call, rather loosely, the Establishment. This, on the whole, had been as true of the Republicans, despite all their democratic rhetoric, as of the Federalists. Now there were the stirrings of a revolt against the "old politics." New men and new principles were pushing their way to the fore, the men more important than the principles. For the next thirty-five years there would be only one dominating national political figure—Andrew Jackson; the rest were sectional leaders. Any one of the latter—Webster, Clay, or Calhoun—towered over such presidential nonentities as Millard Fillmore, John Tyler, Zachary Taylor, James Buchanan, or Martin Van Buren, the latter doubtless the best of a poor lot. But all of them were to be denied the office they so coveted by their very prominence as sectional leaders. And American politics, from having been dominated for the first generation of the life of the Republic by foreign politics, was to be dominated for the second generation by the issue of slavery. It was almost as though America's irrational devotion to the French or English was simply an evasion of the real, inescapable fracture—slavery. Once the inscrutable workings of history had demolished European politics as the vector of U.S. politics, slavery came quickly and inevitably to the fore.

But that story lies ahead. The election of 1824 fixes our attention. It is certainly one of the most interesting elections in our history. In a sense, it was the first "modern" election, the first election in which a number of candidates actively "ran" for election. It was replete with every kind of political maneuvering, infighting, and armtwisting. Monroe's second term had hardly commenced before jockeying began for the inside track in the presidential election four years later. Hezekiah Niles, the able editor of *Niles' Weekly Register*, visiting Washington in early 1822, was startled to find "so great a buz about the person who should succeed Mr. Monroe," and wrote a few months later that much of the legislators' time was spent in "electioneering for the next President of the United States."

John Quincy Adams offered his own analysis of the political situation. "The collisions of opinion upon the principles of government had lost all their asperity and much of their ardor," he wrote; "the results of the French Revolution had disappointed the enthusiasts of democracy, and the Republican administration had adopted and practiced upon most of the principles which they had strenuously contested while the government was in Federal hands." With no real issues, the election came to hinge, to a degree quite novel in the history of the Republic, on the personalities of the candidates more than on their political principles.

William Crawford, who had done an excellent job as secretary of the treasury under Madison and Monroe, in addition to occupying a number of important diplomatic posts, was the first choice of the powerful New York–Virginia axis. John C. Calhoun had acquired a considerable reputation for his support of the War of 1812, his advocacy of internal improvements, and the skill and energy he had displayed as secretary of war. Henry Clay had played a central role in the declaration of war against Great Britain in 1812; had made himself the spokesman of the new nationalism, so popular in the West; and had dominated the House for more than a decade as Speaker, introducing a degree of order and discipline to that body it had not previously known. Adams, who knew Clay as well as any man, wrote: "Clay is an eloquent man, with very popular manners and great political management. He is, like almost all the eminent men of this country, only half educated. His school has been the world, and in that he is proficient. His morals, public and private, are loose, but he has all the virtues indispensable to a popular man. . . . Clay's temper is impetuous, and his ambition impatient. He has long since marked me as the principal rival in his way, and has taken no more pains to disguise his hostility than was necessary for decorum and to avoid shocking public opinion. His future fortune, and mine, are in wiser hands than ours. . . . Clay has large and liberal views of public affairs, and that sort of generosity which attaches individuals to his person. As President of the Union, his administration would be a perpetual succession of intrigue and management with the legislature. It would also be sectional in its spirit, and sacrifice all other interests to those of the Western country and the slaveholders."

Since Crawford was the front-runner with support in most sections of the country, the first task of his rivals was to undermine his candidacy. In South Carolina, Calhoun and a powerful rival, William Lowndes, accepted a kind of joint candidacy, both declaring themselves in the race and agreeing to support each other initially. John Quincy Adams, hearing that Calhoun's candidacy was intended primarily to check Crawford, allowed his name to be put forward by supporters.

Andrew Jackson, who had not been considered a candidate, detested Clay for his attack on him at the time of the Seminole Wars and had little use for Crawford. He thus permitted his friends in the

Tennessee legislature to propose him as a candidate to help check the ambitions of Clay and Crawford and to assist his faction in regaining control of the state. Initially, neither he nor his backers considered him as a serious candidate for the presidency. Clay was convinced that Jackson would withdraw as soon as the balance of political power in Tennessee shifted. But as news of the action of the Tennessee legislature spread, a ground swell of popular support for the hero of New Orleans swept through state after state. Although a number of the state legislatures followed suit and put forward the names of one candidate or another—Georgia, her "favorite son," Crawford; Kentucky, Clay; and South Carolina, when Lowndes suddenly died, Calhoun—popular gatherings of citizens in many of the same states registered their enthusiastic support of Jackson. Since the party caucus was Crawford's best hope of securing the nomination, all of those opposed to Crawford were also opposed to the caucus method of nomination whereby the members of the House and Senate had traditionally decided their party's presidential ticket. The caucus was continually denounced by Crawford's opponents on the grounds that it was a blatantly undemocratic process, designed to thwart the will of the people and allow the party managers to control the nomination of presidential candidates. Jackson's supporters, delighted at the popular response to the news of his candidacy, encouraged the formation of "Hickory Clubs" whose members wore black silk vests stamped with Jackson's stern visage. In Sevier County, Tennessee, huge banners bearing the names of the presidential candidates were placed in line, and the voters who had gathered to express their preference were instructed to gather under the banner of the man of their choice. Six hundred and sixteen voters gathered under Jackson's standard, seven under that of Adams, three under Clay's, and one under Crawford's.

Support appeared for an Adams-Jackson ticket with the slogan: "John Quincy Adams/Who can write/And Andrew Jackson/Who can fight." This combination came to be known in some states as the "People's Ticket." In Maryland the voters of Cecil County supported the Adams-Jackson ticket; and a convention of state legislators and citizens in Mississippi, unable to decide on one candidate, endorsed both men. Since no generally accepted procedure existed for nominating candidates (in eleven states candidates were chosen by "general ticket," in six by state legislatures, and in four by electoral districts), groups of supporters of the various candidates, who had no more authority than their own assertion of it, met in a number of states and announced the "support of the voters" of their respective states for the candidates they favored, only to be countered by other rump meetings declaring for other candidates.

Early in 1824 William Crawford suffered a severe stroke that left him partially paralyzed. Every effort was made to keep his condition a secret and, when known, to minimize its seriousness. But his illness, plus the discrediting of the caucus system (which his supporters persisted in and which did, in fact, name him as the official Republican candidate), seriously weakened his position.

Mudslinging and slander, by no means new to American political contests, was freely indulged in by the supporters of the various candidates. Clay was depicted as a gambler and a drunkard. Adams was the victim of an apparently doctored letter designed to depict him as indifferent, during the Treaty of Ghent negotiations, to American rights to the navigation of the Mississippi. Even John Adams was the victim of partisan politics. A letter was exhumed that Adams had written in 1804, when he was still bitter over his defeat by Jefferson four years earlier: "I shudder at the calamities which I fear his [Jefferson's] conduct is preparing for his country from a mean thirst for popularity, an inordinate ambition, and a want of sincerity." The letter was published with the intention of hurting John Quincy, but its incidental effect was to cause some strain in the relationship between Adams and Jefferson. But Jefferson brushed the incident aside. "It would be strange indeed," he wrote to an embarrassed Adams, "if, at our years, we were to go an age back to hunt up imaginary, or forgotten facts, to disturb the repose of affections so sweetening to the evening of our lives."

Clay's denunciation of Jackson's conduct in the Seminole Wars was reprinted and circulated to discredit Clay with Jackson's supporters and to discredit Jackson with Clay's and Adams's supporters. Crawford was charged with having mishandled treasury funds; he was investigated and cleared of any misdoing.

Pennsylvania, considered a Calhoun stronghold, was a crucial state, and Jackson's workers put on a classic campaign there. Western Pennsylvania was known to be a stronghold of pro-Jackson sentiment. The Jacksonians whipped up an enthusiasm for their candidate in that section that soon spread through the state, and at Philadelphia in October, 1823, a convention adopted resolutions supporting Jackson:

"Because, he has always been a uniform and consistent democrat.

"Because, he is eminently qualified, both as a statesman and as a warrior to govern the nation wisely, in peace, and to conduct her triumphantly through war.

"Because, as a patriot, we have full confidence in his moderation, his virtue and his firmness; being a friend to the *rights of man* and *universal suffrage*."

Six months later the state Republican convention at Harrisburg declared its support for Jackson, and Calhoun dropped out of the running for the presidency, content to run almost unchallenged for the office of vice-president. The field was thus narrowed to four: Adams, Jackson, the half-paralyzed Crawford, and Clay, who continued to take an optimistic view of his chances.

John Quincy Adams wrote to his wife: "All the leading members of both houses of Congress, all the editors of accredited printing presses throughout the Union, and all the caucusing managers of the state legislatures, have been engaged, each with his own views, and as retainers to their respective *patrons*, in crying me down and disgracing me in the estimation of the people. Meanwhile I have not a single active partisan in Congress; not a single printing press in pay or in promise; not one member of any one state legislature disposed to caucus for me, or connected with my interest." Perhaps the best one can say about these observations, so tainted with self-pity, or indeed paranoia, is that they were thoroughly inaccurate. John Quincy Adams had many friends and supporters in various parts of the country working assiduously in his behalf. Why, then, the contention that every man's hand was turned against him? Whatever its origin, it was a pose that generation after generation of Adamses seemed positively to revel in.

Despite the discrediting of the caucus, Crawford, ill as he was, still stood an outside chance if he could carry New York. De Witt Clinton had dominated the politics of the state for years. His opponents, led by Martin Van Buren, had ousted the Clinton faction in 1822 and then, in a plainly vindictive act, removed Clinton from the board of the commissioners of the Erie Canal. This had brought such a strong popular reaction that Clinton, an Adams supporter, had been reelected governor in the next election, and the balance of power had shifted to the People's party, which supported Adams and Jackson. After days of balloting and intrigue in the New York legislature, a compromise was reached that gave Adams 25 electors to 7 for Crawford. Had New York remained solid for Crawford, he would have received 67 electoral votes to 99 for Jackson and 58 for Adams in the national tally. While the vote would still have been thrown into the House of Representatives, it would have been virtually impossible for Clay to prevent Jackson from being chosen president by that body.

Meantime, the Jacksonians in Tennessee had elected their man to the Senate, where he arrived just in time to participate in a splendid celebration of the Battle of New Orleans and, by his reserved and dignified demeanor, to reassure those who thought of him as a crude frontiersman.

It was all a strange spectacle, to be sure. In terms of what might not unreasonably be assumed to be proper qualifications for president of the United States, Jackson stood at the bottom of the class. He had fought two duels and had been involved in several incidents that were little better than street brawls. He had been ruthless in his suppression of, and hostility toward, the Indians and high-handed and arrogant in dealing with the Spanish. He was notorious for having a terrible temper. He had no substantial administrative experience and had never run for an important state office prior to his election to the Senate (where he failed to distinguish himself in his brief time there). He had had no diplomatic experience, and he certainly lacked any hint of diplomacy in his temperament. He was a slaveholder and a man of profoundly conservative disposition in many ways. His political principles were not known (which of course was a great advantage, since people were free to ascribe to him any principles they wished). Apparently the most precise thing the convention of Philadelphia Democratic Republicans could find to say about him was that he was "a friend to the rights of man," except of course blacks and Indians.

The man who, in the last stages of the campaign, emerged as his principal rival was without question one of the most gifted figures in American politics, a brilliant writer, a marvelously skillful diplomat, an experienced legislator and administrator, the son of New England's revered John Adams, second president. Indeed, John Quincy was virtually the only political figure of national stature produced by that region between the time of John Adams and the appearance on the political scene of Daniel Webster. He had even been a Harvard professor.

Yet he was stiff and ill at ease with members of his own circle, and many people found his manners repellent. Richard Henry Dana wrote in his diary: "He impresses you as an awkward, selfish, wrong-headed man, obstinate, & capable of being vindictive. You have to call up all you know of his independence, his fearlessness, his vast acquirements, & great public services, to avoid returning the treatment you receive." One of the noblest men in America in public life, John Quincy Adams was one of the least *likable*. He had none of the politician's small arts of ingratiation. He hated the sordid scrambling for votes, the handshakes, the specious compliments to constituents or prospective political allies. Self-righteous, tormented by a classic Puritan conscience that would never let him rest, he was acutely conscious of what it meant to be the son of John Adams, of the almost unbearable burden placed on his shoulders by that heritage. He had seen his father, defeated by Jefferson in the bitterest presidential campaign in the nation's brief history and denied the second term that he felt was his due, retire to die and then live on, year after year, a good part of that life nourished and sustained, especially after Abigail's death, by the accomplishments of his brilliant son.

He had been a charming and lighthearted young man, full of high spirits and fun. John Singleton Copley had painted one of his most captivating portraits of a strikingly handsome young John Quincy. But years later Eastman Johnson painted a picture of a stern, iron-willed old man. The two portraits—Copley's and Johnson's—trace the development of "character" in the strict New England sense of that word, the gradual suppression of the open, the spontaneous, the emotional, for the guarded, the reserved, the formal. Charles Francis Adams wrote of his father, who once laughed too much: "He is the only man I ever saw whose feelings I could not penetrate . . . but I can study his countenance for ever and very seldom can find any sure guide by which to move. This is exactly the manner which I wish to obtain." "He makes enemies," his son added, "by perpetually wearing the Iron Mask."

When the electoral votes were opened and counted, it was evident, as everyone expected, that no candidate had a majority of the electoral votes. Jackson had 99 to 84 for Adams, 41 for Crawford, and 37 for Clay. The Twelfth Amendment to the Constitution, passed in the wake of the disputed Jefferson-Burr election of 1800, provided that if no candidate had a majority of all votes cast in the electoral college, the House of Representatives should choose the president from among three candidates having the largest number of votes, the voting being by states and the votes of a majority of the states being necessary for election.

Clay so dominated the House that the assumption was in many

quarters that if he came in among the top three presidential candidates the representatives would surely vote for him. If this was indeed the case, Clay missed becoming president by three votes. Still, if he had been one of the final three, one may wonder if the House would have dared to give the office of president to a man whose popular vote, as well as electoral vote, fell so far short of that of his two rivals.

In any event, the maneuvering that followed the news of the deadlocked presidential vote was as intense, if briefer, as that which preceded the electoral vote. It was plain to everyone that Clay held the key to the office. It was undoubtedly he who would open the door and admit one candidate or the other. The followers of both Adams and Jackson courted him assiduously; and he, though apparently never disposed toward Jackson, thoroughly enjoyed his role as kingmaker as soon as he had had, as he put it to Adams, "a decent time for his own funeral solemnities as a candidate." "My position in relation to the friends of the three returned candidates is singular enough and often to me very amusing," he wrote a friend. "They all believe that my friends have the power of deciding the question, and that I have the power of controlling my friends. . . . Really the friends of all three gentlemen are so very courteous, and affectionate, that I sometimes almost wish that it was in my power to accommodate each of them."

Much attention has been focused on the point at which Clay decided to throw his weight behind Adams because of the charge of the Jacksonians that Adams had "bought" Clay's votes by offering him the office of secretary of state in his administration. Toward the end of December Clay wrote to a friend in New York that he had "long since decided in favor of Mr. Adams, in case the contest should be between him and General Jackson," noting "unequivocally" that he could not "support a military man." Certainly, Clay had profound misgivings about Jackson, which he had expressed publicly at the time of the debate in Congress on the Florida expedition. He knew Jackson had a strong dislike for him and not only that he could expect no preferment from Jackson were he to become president, but instead all possible obstacles to his own ambitions. So there was every reason for Clay to support Adams, however lukewarm he may have been toward the New Englander. But when word got out that Clay was doing his best to prevail on the Kentucky and Ohio congressional delegations to cast the votes of their states for Adams, one of Jackson's supporters made the aforementioned charge that Adams had bartered away the secretary of stateship for Clay's support. The impetuous Clay immediately denounced the anonymous accuser as "a base and infamous calumniator, a dastard and a liar," and challenged him to a duel. His calumniator proved to be a Pennsylvania congressman named George Kremer, a notorious eccentric. Having promised to produce evidence to support his accusation, Kremer then backed down and refused to appear before the committee appointed to investigate. The Jacksonians nonetheless seized on the incident and raised the cry of "corrupt bargain."

Meanwhile, every possible pressure was brought to bear on wavering representatives to fall in line for one candidate or the other. New York was the critical state and was almost equally split, so rumor had it, between Crawford and Adams. The deciding vote was that of old General Van Rensselaer, who had been bedeviled by the supporters of both men until he was thoroughly distracted and confused. The Crawfordites were convinced that he had committed himself to their man, but somehow Clay's agents got to him, and he cast his vote for Adams at the decisive moment. His detractors insisted he had simply acted out of cowardice—his wife had ordered him to vote for Adams. The poor general attributed his decision to an act of God. As it came his turn to vote, he declared, he closed his eyes in prayer, and when he opened them and glanced down he saw a ballot with Adams's name on it, picked it up, and put it in the ballot box. His punishment was ostracism by his oldest friends and army messmates.

When the roll was called in the House on February 9, Maryland, owing in large part to the influence of Daniel Webster, came into the Adams column along with Kentucky and Ohio. Louisiana and Missouri, which had originally voted for Jackson and Clay, respectively, also came over to the Adams column, along with Illinois and New York, giving the New Englander a majority of 13 states to 7 for Jackson and 4 for Crawford. One of the oddities was that 4 states went for Crawford, a candidate whose health might not have allowed him to hold office—the Georgian polled 54 votes to 71 for Jackson and 87 for Adams.

When the committee carried word to Adams of his election, it was said that sweat rolled down his face—that "he shook from head to foot and was so agitated that he could scarcely stand or speak." One of the committee members said later that from Adams's "hesitation, his manner and his words, he really thought he was going to decline."

If ever a man was qualified by character, practical experience, and intelligence to be president of the United States, it was the man of the

"Iron Mask," to use Charles Francis Adams's phrase. Yet he had barely slipped into the office. He had won only by the kind of behind-the-scenes dealing and maneuvering that he loathed, and he owed his victory indisputably to a political rival who held him in contempt and for whom he felt an equivalent scorn.

In a letter written in 1822, Adams had spoken feelingly of those politicians "who would barter a Presidency for a department or an embassy, or stoop to spread the table of greatness for the promise of the crumbs which may fall from it."

Now many of Adams's fellow citizens believed the worst of him—that this man, to whom his reputation for integrity was more precious than life, had secured the highest office in the land by means of a "corrupt bargain"; that he was a "Clay President," an impostor who had managed to thwart the expressed preference of his countrymen for the hero of New Orleans. Jackson's followers were convinced their candidate had been cheated out of the presidency. He had polled almost half again as many popular votes as Adams and had carried 11 states in the electoral college to 7 for his principal rival. Apparently the only inhabitants of Washington to express uninhibited delight at Adams's election were the city's blacks, "who when they heard of his election . . . expressed their joy by Hurras."

By becoming president of the United States, a quarter century after his father had held that office, John Quincy, in a sense, vindicated the elder Adams. Certainly his triumph cast a warm glow over the last years of his father's life. Hearing of his son's triumph, John Adams wrote: "The multitude of my thoughts, and the intensity of my feelings are too much for a mind like mine, in its ninetieth year."

Agonizing as the campaign had been for a man of John Quincy's rectitude, he and his father had room in their "philosophy" for it. One must never expect much of one's fellows—pride, ambition, "self-love," and "self-aggrandizement" were the basic stuff of human nature. Yet "philosophy" could not assuage the wound, nor obscure the fact that John Quincy was a kind of accidental president, the lucky survivor of a tangled political skein, a man who belonged far more to the old order than to the new. There was a harbinger of troubles to come in the fact that at a White House reception following the final balloting in the House, Jackson was the object, according to Margaret Smith, of more attention than the new president.

In his inaugural address Adams praised the Constitution, which had carried the country through "a most eventful period in the annals of the world" and had not "disappointed the hopes and aspirations of those illustrious benefactors of their age and nation"—its framers. "It has," Adams declared, "promoted the lasting welfare of that country so dear to us all; it has to an extent far beyond the ordinary lot of humanity secured the freedom and happiness of the people. . . . The year of jubilee since the first formation of our Union has just elapsed; that of the declaration of our independence is at hand. The consummation of both was effected by this Constitution.

"In the compass of thirty-six years since this great national covenant was instituted . . . a population of four millions has multiplied to twelve. A territory bounded by the Mississippi has been extended from sea to sea. New states have been admitted to the Union in numbers nearly equal to those of the first Confederation. . . . The people of other nations, inhabitants of regions acquired not by conquest, but by compact, have been united with us in the participation of our rights and duties, of our burdens and blessings. The forest has fallen by the ax of our woodsmen; the soil has been made to teem by the tillage of our farmers; our commerce has whitened every ocean. The domination of man over physical nature has been extended by the invention of our artists. Liberty and law have marched hand in hand. . . . Such is the unexaggerated picture of our condition under a Constitution founded upon the republican principle of equal rights. To admit that this picture has its shades is but to say that it is still the condition of men upon earth. From evil—physical, moral, and political—it is not our claim to be exempt."

Even so mild a reference to the fact that Americans were not immune to the negative aspects of "the condition of men upon earth" marked John Quincy Adams as a man who shared with his father the view of man as a creature burdened by the taint of original sin.

Adams's determination not to be guided by political expediency but to judge every issue on its merits, free of party fanaticism, was expressed in his conciliatory words to members "of the two great political parties which have divided the opinions and the feelings of the country." Both "contributed splendid talents, spotless integrity, ardent patriotism, and disinterested sacrifices to the formation and administration of this Government, and . . . both have required a liberal indulgence for a portion of human infirmity and error."

In his first address to Congress, John Quincy Adams came out strongly in support of internal improvements. "The great object of the institution of civil government," he declared, "is the improvement of the condition of those who are parties to the social compact, and no government, in whatever form constituted, can accomplish the lawful ends of its institution but in proportion as it improves the condition of those over whom it is established. Roads and canals, by multiplying and facilitating the communications and intercourse between distant regions and multitudes of men, are among the most important means of improvement. But moral, political, intellectual improvements are duties assigned by the Author of Our Existence to social no less than to individual man." Such "progressive improvement" was a "sacred and indispensable" duty of governments.

Adams then recommended the establishment of a national university, which, he reminded his auditors, had been a project dear to the heart of Washington. Other countries had been far more enterprising than the United States in the advancement of science, in providing funds for scientific explorations that had added substantially to the general fund of human knowledge. Could the United States, he asked, do less? Vast areas of the United States remained to be mapped and surveyed. The Columbia River and the northwest coast should be further explored.

Adams also recommended "the establishment of a uniform standard of weights and measures" and, along with a university, "an astronomical observatory, with provision for support of an astronomer." As things stood, the United States was now in the awkward position of depending for its knowledge of the heavens on the observations of European astronomers, "which we must fain receive at second hand."

Adams's speech revealed the dilemma of the intellectual as politician in America. There was something of the New England schoolmaster in John Quincy Adams as there had been in his father. He was inclined to lecture legislators as though they were backward schoolboys, and in truth many were backward enough. But, like all congressmen, they had a low tolerance for lectures. Many of them were aware of the contempt their highbrowed president felt for them, and that awareness did not put them in the most amiable of moods. Moreover, he stood before them as a minority president, a president by accident in the minds of many.

44

Migration and Immigration

The census of 1820 revealed that the population of the states numbered 9,638,000, an increase of some 33 percent since the census of 1810. These citizens of the twenty-three states and two territories were distributed as follows: 1,600,000 in New England; 2,700,000 in the Middle Atlantic states; 2,900,000 in the Southern states; and 2,250,000 along the frontier from Canada to New Orleans. Every one of the original states had *lost* population with the exception of minute gains in South Carolina and Connecticut. New York had replaced Virginia as the most populous state, but the most striking change was in the region beyond the Allegheny Mountains. New York City had grown from approximately 45,000 in 1800 to 123,000 and had replaced Philadelphia as the largest city in the Union. Boston had approximately doubled in size, from 20,000 to 43,300, while Baltimore had zoomed past Boston, growing from 15,000 to 62,700.

In the twenty-year period between 1800 and 1820, it was estimated that approximately 184,000 immigrants had entered the United States, the greater proportion of them Irish and English. Since the population had grown in this period by more than 4 million, it was evident that the native population had been paying strict attention to the biblical injunction to be fruitful and multiply.

The most striking phenomenon of the period was, of course, the vast and continuing westward migration that threatened the older states with depopulation. In October, 1811, a resident of a Pennsylvania town on the road to Pittsburgh reported that 236 wagons, each accompanied by a number of men, women, and children, had passed by in one month headed for Ohio. From New York State wagons and sleighs poured west in an unending stream, many of them bearing New Englanders, abandoning rocky and unproductive farms for the rich river valley soil of Ohio and Indiana. New England, in fact, was well on the way to becoming a kind of breeding ground for the West. Year after year fecund husbands and wives produced more children than the land could accommodate, and the most energetic and ambitious of these went to the northern reaches of the Mississippi Valley to make their fortune.

A report from Newburgh, New York, told of sixty wagons with seventy former residents of Massachusetts passing through the town in a single day in June. In six years—1810 to 1816—it was calculated that Ohio's population grew from 230,000 to 400,000, while Indiana's swelled from 24,000 to 70,000. Such an exodus was highly demoralizing for those who stayed behind. It far exceeded the boldest predictions and raised in the Atlantic states the specter of a radical shift in economic and political power to the region of the Mississippi Valley.

Various measures were proposed in the legislatures of Eastern states to stem the flow, which was likened to blood draining from the body politic. Those New Englanders who had strongly opposed the Louisiana Purchase felt that their darkest fears were being realized. In their view, at the moment when the balance of power tilted decisively westward, the Union would be, for all practical purposes, an unsubstantial shadow of its former self and a mockery of the aspirations of its Founders.

One significant feature of the migration was the fact that the great majority of those making their laborious way along the highways, trails, and rivers that ran westward went as groups, as extended families, or, most frequently, as congregations. They were settlers of Rush's and Dwight's third type—community makers. We have tended to romanticize the American town, especially that of New England with its classic institutions of church, school, and town meeting. But the fact was that a town could, and not infrequently did, become a battleground for contending factions in church or state. The dream of John Winthrop's "city on a hill" survived in the hope of the true community where faction, competition, and selfishness were subordinated to the common good. The reality was often quite different.

When most doctrinal issues were believed to involve eternal bliss or damnation, religious disputes took on a particular intensity. The very closeness and intimacy of town life turned simple misunderstandings into bitter vendettas. Generations of inbreeding produced character types susceptible to a variety of psychoses. Every village had its quota of "village idiots," eloquent testimony to the dangers of a limited gene pool; its chronic alcoholics; its sufferers from hypochondria or acute depression; its psychologically and economically marginal personalities. The fact was that the town was a little like the girl with a curl in the middle of her forehead. When it was "good" it was apt to be very very good (a close approximation of the ideal human group), "and when it was bad it was horrid."

Thus, in Clarendon, Vermont, a traveler reported "vice predominant and irreligion almost epidemical Sabbath disregarded profanity debauchery drunkenness, quarreling by words and blows & parting with broken heads and bloody noses."

So, in addition to barren, boulder-strewn fields where every spring the frost heaved up a fresh crop of rocks to break the farmer's plow and children grew far more luxuriantly than wheat or corn, that fiercely independent *will*, of which we have spoken so often, clashed constantly with other wills quite as intractable. All these matters were a powerful incentive to migration. Not infrequently, a dissident group in the town, or a dissident portion of the congregation that felt the town had fallen off from its original principles and ideals, would set off to establish a new, purified, and more orthodox community. Sometimes the migration might be prompted by resentment over the fact that the town was dominated by a few families who had come to constitute a kind of ruling class.

Often towns that had sunk into a kind of moral lethargy were aroused by a religious revival. Inspired by a "freshening of the spirit," a portion of the faithful would sign a "covenant," or agreement, to establish a new community in the West. Such new towns were usually faithful replicas of the originals. The settlers who founded Norwalk, Ohio, wished it to be a refined and purified verson of Norwalk, Connecticut. A historian, discussing the founding of Hudson, Ohio, by colonists from New Haven, wrote that while the town "might in many ways, be more primitive and ruder than New Haven, yet in another way, it was the Connecticut original in purer form, undiluted and undistracted by modern worldliness and the change encroaching on the east." The point can hardly be emphasized enough. A Congregational church in Poultney, Vermont, moved in a body to East Springfield, New York.

Almost invariably the settlers were led by a "founder," a dominant and charismatic figure like David Hudson of Goshen, Connecticut, who had been a godless man until he was caught up in a revival and "born again." He vowed to serve God by founding in the wilderness a community whose members would live according to God's ordinances as understood by Hudson.

When a group from Granville, Massachusetts, decided to migrate, a 24-member Congregational church drew up a covenant and constitution and transplanted pastor, deacons, and church members to Granville, Ohio. The emigrants numbered 176. Their first act in Granville, Ohio, was to hold a church service. One of the band later wrote of how they wept when they heard their voices echoing among the lonely and forbidding trees: "They wept when they remembered Zion."

Oberlin, in Lorain County, Ohio, was another classic transplanted New England community. The colonists were asked to pledge themselves to "a life of simplicity, to special devotion to church and school, and to earnest labor in the missionary cause."

In addition to members of existing, more or less orthodox denominations who went west so they might better serve the Lord, any number of radically unorthodox sects that found themselves out of favor in established communities went west in pursuit of their own brand of redemption. Prominent among these were the Spiritualists. Antioch, Ohio, was started by a colony dedicated to spiritualism, free love, and democracy and was the scandal of every town in the vicinity. Tales of orgies, of wild dances and promiscuous lovemaking, of babies born in the midst of unholy revels, circulated through the country. Finally, a courageous Methodist circuit rider ventured into the town (which had driven every other minister of the Gospel out), and managed to convert the town virtually *en masse* to Methodism. Antioch thereafter became a model of Christian orthodoxy.

The Union Colony got its start in Poultney and Bennington, Vermont, where the Reverend Sylvester Cochrane recruited ten families. The Vermonters signed a covenant before they left home that began:

"*Whereas*, The enjoyment of the ordinances . . . of the Gospel is in a great measure unknown in . . . the Western country; and

"*Whereas*, We believe that a pious and devoted emigration

is . . . one of the most efficient means in the hands of God, in removing the moral darkness which hangs over a great portion of the valley of the Mississippi; and

"*Whereas*, We believe that a removal to the West may be a means of promoting our temporal interest, and we trust [may] be made subservient to the advancement of Christ's kingdom;

"We do therefore, form ourselves into a colony with the design of removing into some parts of the Western country . . . and agree to bind ourselves to . . . the following rules. . . ."

The rules covered codes of behavior. No settler was allowed to own more than "one farm of 160 acres, and one village lot of 10 acres, within the limits of the settlement," to insure a degree of economic equality.

A final injunction to the colonists of Vermontville, as the community came to be called, again recalls John Winthrop's "A Modell of Christian Charity." "As we must necessarily endure many of those trials and privations which are incident to a settlement in a new country . . . we agree we will do all in our power to befriend each other; we will esteem it not only a duty, but our privilege to sympathise with each other under all our trials, to do good and lend, hoping for nothing again, and to assist each other on all necessary occasions."

The impulses to emigrate were doubtless as varied as the individuals who pulled up stakes and moved west, but the two predominant themes were, unquestionably, the desire, as the Vermont migrants wrote, "of promoting our temporal interest," and the hopes of refounding the good community for "the advancement of Christ's kingdom." The cumulative communities were the consequence of ambitious individuals' collecting at a particular spot for the purpose of improving their material condition. The covenanted, or colonized, community was conceived of primarily as a channel of redemption.

Migration in the South was at least as great as in the North. A traveler on the road from Nashville, Tennessee, in 1817 encountered caravans of Carolinians and Georgians headed for Burnt Corn Spring, Alabama. He counted 207 "carts, sleighs, gigs, coaches and wagons," 29 flocks of cattle, 27 droves of pigs, and 3,000 men, women, children, and slaves. The result was wild speculation in Alabama lands. One public auction brought in $3 million and townsites often sold for $300 or more an acre.

The North Carolina legislature estimated that in a period of twenty-five years over 200,000 of its citizens had "removed to the waters of the Ohio and the Tennessee, and it is mortifying to see that thousands of rich and respectable citizens are still moving West each year, to be followed by thousands of poorer citizens who are literally driven away by the prospect of poverty."

In Virginia the assembly's Committee on Roads and Internal Navigation deplored the constant emigration from the state: "How many sad spectacles do her lowlands present of wasted and deserted fields, of dwellings abandoned by their proprietors, of churches in ruins! The fathers of the land are gone to where another outlet to the ocean [the Mississippi] turns their thoughts from the place of their nativity, and their affections from the haunts of their youth."

In addition to groups and congregations, many individual families made the dangerous and exhausting trek west. A blacksmith from Rhode Island walked to Albany in the middle of winter with his wife and eight children, dragging a few possessions in a small cart. Another family—husband and wife and five children—walked to Ohio pushing a wheelbarrow. Such migrants swelled the population of already established frontier settlements. In a thirteen-day period 73 wagons and 450 emigrants passed through Haverhill, Massachusetts, headed for Indiana.

The end of the War of 1812 saw a resumption of the flow of immigration, primarily from England and Ireland. Many of the English were prosperous farmers who were nonetheless tenants and wished to own their own land. Sometimes the better part of whole villages came together to colonize lands in the West.

An Irish paper in New York noted the arrival of four hundred Irishmen at New York in one week in August, and statistics available for the end of that month show that in another week fifteen hundred immigrants from Great Britain reached Boston, New York, and Philadelphia. The arrival of so many immigrants in a time of severe depression caused a good deal of anxiety in the United States, and there were calls for legislation to impose checks on the number of new arrivals; but there was little response in Congress and immigrants continued to clog the seaport cities and impose a severe strain on their capacities. The estimate was that thirty thousand immigrants had arrived in the United States during 1817.

The same kind of alarm we have noted in the original states over Western migration was expressed in England over the exodus of residents of the British Isles. A London newspaper noted in 1816 that "the continued and increasing emigration from this country to America becomes every day more alarming." The country was already suffering from "this serious drain of the most useful part of the population . . . its best hands in arts and manufactures." Another newspaper noted that "several farmers who lately occupied about 4,000 acres of land in Lincolnshire, [have] recently emigrated to America, having sold all their live and dead stock. They were accompanied by the curate of the village." Anti-American propaganda was disseminated to discourage emigration. Finally Parliament did pass legislation limiting the number of persons who could be carried on ships of certain tonnage, which had the effect of causing a sharp rise in transatlantic fares and thereby discouraging the poor from emigrating.

Much the same reaction came from the Swiss cantons and the German principalities. A Geneva paper complained that "a great many Swiss from all the Protestant cantons are going soon to depart from Basle for America."

Niles' Weekly Register noted in August, 1816, that a ship had arrived in New York from Bordeaux with 52 "artists and manufacturers of various descriptions, vine-dressers and husbandmen—232 other persons arrived at New York, in one day from Hull, England, and Waterford, Ireland. Vessels are almost every day reaching some of our ports with passengers from England, Ireland, France, Germany, etc." Niles also reported that English and Swiss were "preparing, in many places, to leave their country by neighborhoods or parishes, as it were, and in the new world to possess and enjoy the friends of their youth, by settling together." Such a settlement was the so-called English Settlement of Edwards County, Illinois. In March, 1818, the *Achilles* sailed from Bristol, England, for Philadelphia. On board were forty-four men, farm laborers and mechanics from Surrey, and one married woman. They were joined by an almost equal number of London mechanics and tradesmen from various parts of England. From Philadelphia "they made their way, some in wagons, some on horse-back, over the mountains to Pittsburgh, then descending the Ohio in flat-boats to Shawneetown," and from there "on foot, in wagons and on horse-back, to . . . Boltenhouse Prairie." Following them came the organizer of the venture, Morris Birkbeck, with some of the choicest breeds of cows, hogs, and sheep and another large contingent of emigrants. "To remove all these people and their luggage, and the animals that I had brought, to our Settlement, nearly a thousand miles inland," Birkbeck wrote, "was no small undertaking, at a time when there was neither turnpike or railroad, and steamboats few. . . . Patience, toil, time, and money were all required and all freely bestowed.

"We had some difficulties, peculiar to ourselves, as a foreign people," Birkbeck noted. "The Americans, by pushing onward and onward for almost two generations, had a training in handling the axe and opening farms, and, from experience, bestowing their labor in the most appropriate manner, which we, from our inexperience, often did not. Fresh from an old country, teeming with the inconveniences of civilized life, at once in a wilderness with all our inexperiences, our losses were large from misplaced labor. Many were discouraged, and some returned, but the mass of the settlers stayed, and, by gradual experience, corrected their first errors, thus overcoming difficulties which had well-nigh overcome them. The future success of the Settlement was obtained by individual toil and industry."

Birkbeck's account of the growth of Albion (England), as the town was called, by the erection of buildings and the accretion of new settlers, is a classic of pioneering. A "log tavern" and a blacksmith's shop, "the two germs of civilization were now planted—one of the useful arts, the other a necessary institution of present civilization. Any man could now get his horse shod and get drunk in Albion, privileges which were soon enjoyed, the latter especially."

Almost every month, individuals or small groups found their way "from all parts of England" to this remote Albion. When Birkbeck asked a Welshman who had landed at Charleston, South Carolina, how he had found his way fifteen hundred miles, he replied, "Oh, I just bought me a horse, sir, and inquired the way."

After an interval of five or ten years, a new wave of English immigrants found its way to Edwards County. They came primarily in response to letters from the first settlers describing how they had prospered in their new home. In Birkbeck's words, "Having done well themselves, and by a few years of hard labor acquired more wealth than they ever expected to obtain, they wrote home to friend or relative an account of their success. These letters handed around in the remote villages of England . . . reached individuals in a class to whom information in book form was wholly inaccessible.

"The writer, known at home as a poor man, . . . telling of the wages he received, his bountiful living, of his own farm and the number of his livestock, produced a greater impression in the limited circle of its readers than a printed publication had the power of doing."

One such letter was written by a John Watson from Aurora, Dearborn County, Indiana. Arriving there with his wife and children, penniless, "a stranger, without friends, acquaintance, utensils of any kind," and stricken by illness, he had within two years "worked it so that I have 2 cows, 2 calves, 9 pigs, and one calf expected in August. . . . Much good land can be bought . . . for one dollar and a quarter per acre . . . indeed, so good is the prospect for a man who must live by industry, that I wish all my friends and acquaintances were here with me. I can safely say, I would not, nor would my Mary, return to England on any account whatever."

The first state of Albion was one of subsistence. In three or four years, the farms, well drained and ditched, began to produce a surplus of corn, pork, and beef, but there was no market and after disposing of their produce to traders for uncertain profits, "the farmers began to build their own flat-boats, load them with the produce of their own growth, and navigate them by their own hands" down the Mississippi to New Orleans. "Thus were the channels of trade opened, and in this way was the chief trade of the country carried on for many years."

To Birkbeck, the change in the situation of the immigrants was "truly wonderful." "Once poor laborers . . . now farmers themselves in another hemisphere, boat-builders, annually taking adventurous trading-voyages of over a thousand miles, and many of them becoming tradesmen and merchants on a large scale, and commanding an amount of wealth they once never dreamed of possessing. And well they deserve their success. They have earned it by perseverance and hard labor, flinching at nothing."

Johannes Schweizer recounted just such a story concerning a young indentured German who got the permission of an indulgent master to marry an indentured girl on a nearby farm. The two masters then "lent" them their freedom and a hundred dollars and sold them five acres of land for six dollars. The girl "spun and knitted"; her husband made shoes and worked as a laborer. In two years their debts were paid; they sold their five acres for one hundred dollars; and they had a cow and six pigs left over. With this nest egg they bought eighty acres of land, cleared the trees, floated them down the Lehigh River to the town of Castor, made enough money to pay for the land, and then sold it in six years for two thousand dollars. Then they bought a plantation of 320 acres that already contained a house and barn and started a small sawmill on the Susquehannah. As people settled in the area, the man who had begun his American career as an indentured servant became the wealthiest man in the county.

Birkbeck attributed the success of the English Settlement to the fact that it had been established on open prairie and the settlers thus "saved a generation of hard and unprofitable labor" in hacking down trees and clearing the land.

For every success such as that of Birkbeck's there were dozens of failures and defeats. In the words of one Englishman, Isaac Holmes, who had settled in the Indiana country, "even if you have escaped from prisons and pauperism," you will "sometimes 'hang your harp on the willow, and weep,' when you remember distant England. Very few emigrants howsoever many have been their disgusts and evils in the old country, or their successes in the new, can forget their 'dear native land' . . . distance only enhances her value, and, as a much-loved, ungrateful mistress, her charms only are remembered and cherished . . . the incurable mania of the British exile."

The advice from Englishmen in America to those at home contemplating seeking a new home across the Atlantic was: Do not come if you are prosperous at home, addicted to the creature comforts, or a professional—a schoolmaster, a lawyer, a clerk. Such are a glut on the market. Do not come if you are a city dweller—the cities are full of unemployed artisans and mechanics; if you are susceptible to extremes of climate, reluctant to do manual labor, or offended by the familiarity of the lower classes. In the words of one Englishman: "That degree of freedom which the servants and lower orders assume in America, is really disagreeable to those who have not been accustomed to it. We may speak in favor of equality; but the fact is, that nearly all who advocate this doctrine 'wish to reduce every one to the equality of themselves'; but they by no means wish to raise those who are below or beneath them to their own level."

Our same informant recounts a revealing discussion with a tailor in a small New Jersey town who had emigrated from England a few years earlier. "I should indeed be foolish," the tailor told him, "to think of returning. Here I can obtain work at a price at least one-third higher than in England; there it was with great difficulty I could get employment. Certainly, the climate and many other things are disagreeable, but that corroding anxiety of not knowing whether I could maintain myself, is removed; and this more than recompenses me for coming hither."

From 1815 to 1830 Switzerland was troubled by a depressed state of business and agriculture and severe social dislocations. Unemployment was widespread, and prices were so high that even the employed poor suffered acutely. Among the Swiss who found their way to the United States were two friends—Johannes Schweizer, who came to America in 1820 with his wife, Anna, and nine-year-old daughter, and Jakob Rütlinger, a teacher, who joined Schweizer three years later in Lancaster, Pennsylvania, a center for Swiss and German immigrants. Both men wrote accounts of their experiences that reinforce and substantially supplement observations by immigrants of other nationalities.

Schweizer, like many other new arrivals, was disconcerted by the contradictions and paradoxes that seemed to abound in America. He warned his readers that "America is the land of contradictions: Want and superabundance, freedom and slavery, unrestrained liberty and coercion, dove-like simplicity and the cunning of the snake, the highest culture and the lowest barbarism—nowhere in the world do they stand so close together." To the Swiss immigrant, "America is still a child, an ill-bred child, but blessed with many fine, enviable gifts. This is why the good and sometimes the bad appears on it. It seems as though a capricious genie had chopped up all possible good and bad together in a concoction and poured it over America."

Like many immigrants who came after him, he and his wife and child were thrilled by their first sight of New York. "What do I see?" Schweizer wrote. "A New World appears before my eyes. . . . We can sail right to the city. The view . . . opens before us and it is enchanting. As in a dream, new things crowd before our eyes and vanish just as quickly."

Johannes's wife, Anna, was also a shrewd observer of American mores. She spoke of the day of their arrival in America as "a holy feast for us all the years of our life." But she found the voyage itself so grueling that she had often felt the wish, "Oh, if only we could *fly* to America!"

We also get from Schweizer a keen sense of the suffering and desolation involved in making a place for oneself in a strange land. He felt that "Americans needn't deny the advantage which America has over many other countries, perhaps over all the countries on earth.

But they must also point out how much the immigrant risks and suffers, how many bitter humiliations he has to tolerate, how many sacrifices he must make before he can enjoy these advantages! How many cannot in their whole lifetime achieve their goals, but must, like Moses, be satisfied if they can only see Canaan and know that their children will achieve the success they wanted. . . . Only he whose miserable bit of bread is made bitter with sorrow and need, who can work and has the strength to do without for a while, will sooner or later feel happy and see sorrow and need vanish, even though he does not acquire any shining kingdoms."

There were already troubling indications of resentment toward immigrants. Schweizer noted that "a great many [Americans] wish that immigration could be restricted to those people [who] would be accepted anywhere, to those with money, or at least to decent people." "What an ungodly mass of people we will have in a hundred years!" Americans were beginning to ask, "Does not the seed of our political disruption lie right here?"

Many of Schweizer's fellow immigrants had brought with them products of their homeland that they hoped to sell in the United States, using the profits to help establish themselves, but like Schweizer, who had been advised to bring a consignment of Bibles, most found that their items were not suited to the American market and were thus virtually worthless.

What perhaps most impressed the Swiss newcomer and later his friend, Rütlinger, was that Americans performed tasks in a hasty and slapdash fashion. But they soon noticed that appearances were deceptive. Under the apparently careless and casual attitudes of Americans toward their work, they displayed "a tremendous dexterity . . . and their tools assist them admirably." The American cared far more about techniques for saving labor and completing a job quickly than about thoroughness. The consequence was that the American did several times the amount of work in a day that his better-trained and more conscientious European counterpart could accomplish. In Schweizer's words, "The drive to complete every job as soon as possible is everywhere evident. It is a general characteristic."

In addition to being impressed by the remarkable output of human energy he observed in the United States, Schweizer was convinced that "the American farmer and worker live much more happily than the German or Swiss" by virtue of being less inhibited by guilds, qualifications for residence, and all the bureaucratic constraints experienced in Europe. In America, "Nothing, absolutely nothing, restricts him from the free and unencumbered use of his strength and ability."

Schweizer was disconcerted by the unkempt appearance of most American farms. He saw, to the dismay of his thrifty Swiss soul, apple trees whose fruit had been allowed to fall from the branches and was being consumed by cows and pigs. But when he asked a German farmer "the reason for the waste of fruit and the careless cultivation of the land," he was told, "Don't reproach the Americans for laziness or carelessness. You will soon discover that we are more industrious than any German people, but we have too much to do." It was harvest time, and no one had time to pick apples. Actually the untidy-looking fields produced bumper crops. "Neatest and cleanest," his newfound friend told him, "isn't always best. If we can produce enough, the appearance is unimportant. . . . The result justifies our methods. And further-more, the yield of our fields has increased for forty years."

Among the deficiencies Schweizer noted and commented on was the lack of feeling on the part of Americans for "beautiful gardens. . . . The reason I believe is not flattering to the popular character. Little genial sympathy, no sense of the poetry of life, only a speculative philosophy of life exists here. That is why painters, poets, musicians are as rare here as the nightingale, but the country swarms with lawyers and jurists as Egypt swarmed with locusts in the days of the Pharaohs."

Schweizer soon became discouraged at the prospects of making a decent living. Prices were high and employment was scarce. Moreover, he was disheartened to encounter strong prejudices against Swiss as well as German immigrants. But again his farmer friend gave him encouragement and advice: "It is certain that many times you will regret the step you made. It will be astonishingly difficult to find suitable employment. . . . But don't be discouraged; you are, after all, in a fortunate land. In five years you would not want to return. . . . So . . . remember what I say, America is a fortunate land!"

There were plenty of people ready to advise any immigrant willing to listen as to how best to make his way in his new country. One Swiss weaver, penniless and abandoned to despair by the side of the road, was given a friendly lecture by a passing Quaker who told him, "Learn to help yourself. Take this thought with you on your way. He who looks back whimpering, in America, may well turn into a pillar of salt"; the Quaker then sweetened the advice with some money.

A group of immigrants recounted to Schweizer their experiences in trying to get established in the United States. For all of them it had been a painful experience of trial and error, but all of them emphasized that America was the land of second chances. No one had to pay for his or her "errors and missteps with deprivation. None of the farmers or artisans who lost their fortunes through speculations in the last two years ate one chicken less," a German farmer told him.

The one lesson that all immigrants who undertook to give advice to their countrymen stressed was the necessity for the newcomer to turn his hand to any task, however humble, that would enable him to get a start in his adopted home. Jakob Rütlinger cited as an example of the flexibility of character necessary to succeed the case of a country-man, N., who was "a distinguished man and an excellent musician." For several years, he wandered from one seaport city to another trying to make a living teaching music. Finally, much discouraged, he took up work as a chimneysweep. "Everyone appreciated him because he was industrious and performed this dirty work very capably." He found he could thus make a decent living and also become acquainted with the more prosperous families in the town. Having discovered which ones had musical inclinations, he appeared incognito, "with white, delicate skin, beautiful clothes, and powdered hair," to offer his services as a music teacher. He was an immediate success, but instead of abandoning chimneysweeping, he swept chimneys by day and taught music by night unrecognized in each role. Having "learned enough from experience to know how uncertain every occupation is . . . he wanted to keep his chimneysweeping in reserve, so that he would not lose his customers if the music instruction should suddenly come to an end."

Resilience and adaptability were essential attributes for those who wished to succeed. A man might be "making a good living one day," Rütlinger noted, "and the next day his business may stand idle. He has to think of something else to do. It is not rare that a man has to struggle through dozens of occupations before he can become a farmer. However, once he has reached this goal, he is in the safest and happiest position in this country. . . . Then he can enjoy the fruits of his own labor."

The contradictions of American life were a constant theme of Johannes Schweizer. "One hour you exult in the good fortune of becoming a citizen of this happy land under such a just and wise constitution and government, being able to live among such unprejudiced, moral, and educated people," he wrote; "the next hour you would like to flee to an uninhabited desert. The principle of eternal anarchy is reflected in the Constitution. The laws seem to benefit only scoundrels. The people seem to be a mob of vagabonds, haphazardly come together, from whom all feeling for tradition, order, and propriety has vanished. You no longer find a pleasing, gentle education, but only materialistic self-interest."

One such contrast was between "a fine, pleasing, well-educated . . . tailor . . . who could indeed pass for a personage in Europe who had completed several schools," and the family of a newly rich millionaire, ensconced in a mansion, who greeted a foreign visitor: "Well, whaddaya think of this country? You got a wife and child?"

To Schweizer the greatest robbers in America were not the thieves and footpads who infested the city streets but the unscrupulous rich who used the law and lawyers to defraud their fellows. Thus, the path of the immigrant was strewn with dangers. He might be cheated by the captain of the ship he sailed on; cheated, upon arrival, out of the modest funds he had brought with him by unscrupulous sharpers whose favorite dodge was to sell him inferior or nonexistent land at inflated prices. Above all, he had to contend with the strangeness of everything—the language, the food, the customs and manners of the people, the currency, the business practices. The lot of indentured servants was especially harsh. They often had to work two or three years under a demanding master to pay off the cost of their ocean crossing.

Perhaps the most demoralizing aspect of American life for the new immigrant was the uncertainty of every venture. The economic situation seemed to put a premium on the gambling instinct, and it was of course notorious that Americans were more addicted to gambling than were any other people. This was one reason why the farm was the symbol of security. "People who have no land of their own or no home of their own, and who must depend on something other than themselves," Jakob Rütlinger wrote, "are in as difficult a position as someone who can't skate and is chased out on the slippery ice. They have no firm base, no secure foundation. If they are very careful and capable of much work, they can make a living, but it must be sought ceaselessly and anxiously. Everything you begin is so uncertain and subject to capricious chance as nowhere else."

The Irish immigrants presented a particular problem. They were often illiterate and impoverished. They crowded into the port cities where the Sons of Tammany did their best to keep them from starving to death. They were disposed to drink to excess and brawl among themselves as well as form gangs to waylay peaceable citizens. Fortunately there were canals to be built, and the Irish, desperate for work, could be recruited in large numbers to work under conditions and at a rate of pay few native Americans would tolerate. Thousands were hustled off to one or another of the canals that were continually under construction, the most famous of course being the Erie Canal.

An Irish-American advised newly arrived immigrants to avoid all contact with their countrymen, who were "always fond of meeting their countrymen on landing, and of encouraging them to take a share of grog or porter." That was the path to perdition. "The best plan would be to engage a year with some opulent farmer, for which period of service you will receive $100, and during that time be found in meat, drink, washing, and lodging. This will be an apprenticeship that will teach you the work of the country, such as cutting timber, splitting fence rails, and other work that is not known in Ireland. Be temperate and frugal, attend worship on Sundays with your employer's family. This will keep you clear of a nest of vipers, who would be urging you to go to tippling-houses with them, to drink whiskey, and talk about Ireland."

After a year's apprenticeship, the immigrant might have learned enough to venture out on his own, go west, work hard, acquire some land, and in time become "rich and independent." That not many Irish immigrants followed such recommendations was readily admitted by the author, who estimated that no more than a fourth of the Irish who immigrated to the United States were ever able "to procure one foot of land." Most, thoroughly demoralized by the strangeness of their surroundings, took to drink or took work on highways or canals where they had for companions "the most abandoned drunken wretches that are in existence."

The Irish were tolerated because they were the earthmovers. Hardly a canal was built in the period covered by this volume—1783 to 1826—that did not employ Irish workmen as its basic labor force. It was work so hazardous and exhausting that few native Americans would undertake it. Tens of thousands of Irishmen did, and thousands died of a variety of diseases that came to be particularly associated with canal-digging. Their principal coadjutors among the immigrants were the Germans; one engineer on the Delaware and Hudson Canal wrote of brawls between Irish and German workers in which dozens of men were injured. "Of course the brawling slows up the work," he told a newspaper reporter. "No canal was ever dug through pleasanter country—no swamps or muck to contend with—no extremes of weather. But that doesn't mean anything to these club-swinging Irishers. I don't know what they've got to fight about. They don't need a reason; they fight just for the hell of fighting."

The Delaware and Hudson Canal, which, incidentally, connected those two rivers, was perhaps second only to the Erie Canal as an engineering feat, including 107 locks, 22 aqueducts (to carry it over streams or rivers), 16 feeder dams, 22 reservoirs, and 136 bridges. It has been estimated that over three thousand Irishmen worked on the Delaware and Hudson Canal, digging and blasting their way through millions of tons of earth and rock with no earthmoving equipment other than shovels, scoops, and wagons. They often worked waist-deep in water, plagued by insects and mosquitoes, decimated by malaria, typhoid, swamp fever, and rheumatism. Their food was the cheapest; their shelter temporary barracks or tents erected along the route of the canal; their pay eight dollars a month. An extra incentive was a dollop of whiskey every two hours. The Irish contractors connected with Tammany Hall brought over thousands of their countrymen on indenture and then rented them out to the canal builders to get their passage money back. Those Irishmen who found their way to the South were given work too dangerous and unhealthy to risk the lives of slaves on. A dead slave represented an investment of hundreds of dollars; a dead Irishman, ten dollars to bury him.

For the most part the Irish congregated in Northern cities where they drowned their despair in rotgut liquor and expressed their rage in wild brawls and riots. Finally, they constituted the flocks of patient and durable priests who ministered the rites of the Roman Catholic church to them. It might be said that in Protestant America, their religion was the most serious charge against the Irish. For many Americans, the pope was still the Antichrist, and all Catholics were a threat to the Reformed faith.

Joseph Priestley, whose experiments with electricity and pioneering work in chemistry had won him membership in the Royal Society and the friendship of Franklin and whose warm espousal of the American cause during the Revolution and later of the French Revolution had made him persona non grata with many of his countrymen, had landed in the United States and joined his sons at

Northumberland on the Susquehannah River in 1794. Several years later he wrote a letter to a friend in Leeds that was widely reprinted in English newspapers and that William Cobbett, a Federalist editor and himself an immigrant, estimated was responsible for attracting thousands of immigrants. "The advantages we enjoy in this country are indeed very great," Priestley declared. "Here we have no poor; we never see a beggar, nor is there a family in want. We have no church establishment, and hardly any taxes. . . . There are very few crimes committed, and we travel without the least apprehension of danger, the press is perfectly free, and I hope we shall always keep out of war. I do not think there ever was any country in a state of such rapid improvement as this at present."

In his caustic comments on the letter, Cobbett was particularly indignant at Priestley's statement that "we have no poor." That, and indeed the letter itself, was "an abominable falsehood." "Of the mischiefs American independence has produced in the world," he added, "that of seducing thousands upon thousands of ignorant Europeans from their homes, to die with hunger and sickness in the woods and swamps of the United States, is not the least. I could fill a volume with the names of the miserable wretches who have been thus ruined in the space of a very few months. I could relate facts that would astonish any European."

The truth, of course, lay somewhere between Priestley's and Cobbett's views. The literature of immigration is filled with such contradictory views of the joys and horrors of becoming an American, and we shall encounter many of them in the course of this work. Perhaps what needs to be said here is that the experience of immigrants was determined by three factors: the amount of money they brought with them to establish themselves in their new home; the demand that existed for their particular skill or talent; and their own outlook on life. For those relatively few who, like Priestley, came as men of well-known public character and accomplishments, with money in their wallets, the United States was usually a happy haven. For those at the bottom of the social pile, whatever the country of their origin, life was often cruelly hard. Moreover, such persons, much less cosmopolitan than those further up the social ladder, and far more deeply rooted in a particular "subculture" with its own particular folkways and simple satisfactions, often suffered severely from being plunged into an alien world where language (or accent), customs, manners, food, and drink were all demoralizingly unfamiliar. Most immigrants of this class, despairing or alienated as they might be, had no way to extricate themselves. They were trapped in the promised land. The unrecorded sufferings of simple people, the pain and even terror of that migration are beyond computing, part of the often devastating human cost of filling up the interminable continent.

45

The Mission

The Protestant passion continued to expand in the period from 1800 to 1826, along the lines suggested by its earlier development. Unitarianism (with Boston as its headquarters) strengthened its hold on the more liberal spirits of New England. The Episcopal church claimed a larger and larger proportion of the successful business and professional upper class in the seaport cities of the Atlantic Coast. Inland, the Baptists, Methodists, and Presbyterians grew apace through assiduous missionary activity. On the frontier and in small towns everywhere the revival meeting became virtually an institution. The temperance movement soon allied itself with the revival, and the two together became the most potent force in moderating the drunkenness that was so conspicuous an aspect of town life. Drunkenness aside, the most eloquent testimony to the psychological pressures of life in the towns and villages that spread westward through the interminable forests to the Mississippi was the raw emotionalism of the revivals themselves. Undoubtedly the most significant extensions of the passion to redeem the world were to be found in the growth of revivalism, the development of the missionary movement, and the appearance of the frontier circuit rider.

Charles Finney was one of the most famous revival preachers of his day, and his description of his own conversion is a classic account of the experience of a born-again Christian in 1821. Walking in the woods near his home, Finney tried to pray but found that the words would not come and that he felt so weak he could hardly hold himself up. In his words, "An overwhelming sense of my wickedness . . . took such powerful possession of me, that I cried at the top of my voice, and exclaimed that I would not leave that place if all the men on earth and all the devils in hell surrounded me." The words of the Scripture came to Finney, "'Then shall ye go and pray unto me, and I will hearken unto you.' . . . I seized hold of them with the grasp of a drowning man."

Returning home in a state of ecstasy, Finney entered his house: "There was no fire, and no light, in the room; nevertheless it appeared to me as if it were perfectly light. As I went in and shut the door after, it seemed as if I met the Lord Jesus Christ face to face. It did not occur to me then, nor did it for sometime afterward, that it was wholly a mental state. On the contrary it seemed to me that I saw him as I would see any other man. He said nothing but looked at me in such a manner as to break me right down at his feet . . . and I fell down . . . and poured out my soul to him. I wept aloud like a child [and] the Holy Spirit descended upon me in a manner that seemed to go through me body and soul. I could feel the impression like a wave of electricity, going through and through me. Indeed it seemed to come in waves and waves of liquid love. . . . It seemed like the very breath of God. . . . No words can express the wonderful love that was shed abroad in my heart. I wept aloud with joy and love. . . . These waves came over me, and over me, and over me, one after another, until I recollect I cried out, 'I shall die if these waves continue to pass over me,' I said, 'Lord, I cannot bear any more'; yet I had no fear of death."

While Timothy Dwight and his protégé, Lyman Beecher, held the Calvinist fort against the Unitarianism of William Ellery Channing, they nonetheless softened the severest aspects of predestinarianism. Sinners were punished by assignment to Hell, they argued, because they had chosen evil of their own free will. The obvious implication was that if one chose good, one might have a reasonable expectation of salvation.

Lyman Beecher was the orphan son of a blacksmith, raised by an uncle and apprenticed as a blacksmith. An interested minister, Thomas Bray, was impressed by the boy's intelligence and prepared him for Yale where he fell under the influence of Timothy Dwight. After a stint as a Presbyterian minister at East Hampton, New York, Beecher found a post in the Congregational church at Litchfield, Connecticut. There he preached the new, modified Calvinism but preached it with such fervor that he became a leader in New England revivals, and his reputation spread throughout the country.

Famous as Lyman Beecher became as one of the champions of embattled Calvinism, he was to be even more famous as a progenitor. He and his remarkable wife produced eight children, four of whom— Henry Ward Beecher, Harriet, Catharine, and Isabella—came to be numbered among the most notable members of their generation. Harriet, the most gifted, wrote a beguiling account of her father preaching in the Litchfield meetinghouse: "In front of the pulpit was a bench on which at noon, between the two long sermons, some members of the congregation who came from afar sat and ate their dinner. Consequently there would be by time of the afternoon service sundry crumbs of cheese and bread on the floor. In the base of the pulpit just above the floor dwelt a number of pious church mice, and in the afternoons, when Father was thundering away in the lofty pulpit, I would see their little bright eyes shining cautiously out of their holes. If father became quiet they would venture out and begin a meal on the crumbs; but suddenly some awful words, like reprobation or foreordination, would come roaring down from above, the mice would run for their lives and not venture out again until they thought the danger past."

Beecher made himself the leader of the temperance movement in his ministerial association. He had gone to visit a young man who had been active in revival activities and found him drunk in bed and his wife in tears. The scene prompted him to write six sermons against drunkenness, which became the first famous temperance tracts of the day. His remedy was "the banishment of ardent spirits from the list of lawful articles of commerce by a correct and efficient public sentiment such as has turned slavery out of half of our land and will yet expel it from the world." Thus began the intimate connection between Christianity and temperance in the United States that has, in one form or another, survived down to the present day.

In 1816 Beecher's wife died, leaving him devastated. Harriet wrote: "The communion between her and my father was a peculiar [unique] one . . . intellectually and morally he regarded her as the better and stronger portion of himself and I remember hearing him say that, after her death, his first sensation was a sort of terror like that of a child suddenly shut out alone in the dark."

But he did not abate his "thundering." "From the time Unitarianism began to show itself in this country," Beecher wrote later, "it was a fire in my bones. . . . My mind had been heating, heating, heating." Now much of his energy was devoted to denouncing its heresies. "You are right in thinking the Unitarians are gaining," he wrote a friend. "Their power of corrupting the youth of the commonwealth by means of Cambridge [by which he meant Harvard, now a stronghold of Unitarianism] is silently putting sentinels in all the churches, legislators in the halls and judges on the bench and scattering elsewhere physicians, lawyers and merchants."

Lyman Beecher married again, a doctor's daughter, "noted for beauty, wit and cultivation," and between revivals, fits of depression, and "dyspepsia," made a delightful father for his talented brood of children and, at last, comfortably established at the Hanover Street Church in Boston, became a famous champion of orthodoxy against all heresies, especially that of Unitarianism, stimulating and leading numerous revivals.

Missionary activity was the response of the Protestant passion for redeeming the world to the fact that the world was full of heathens. Missions to the Indians were as old as the original settlement of the colonies—John Eliot had translated the Bible into an Indian language in the 1660s and had converted thousands of Indians to Christianity. The consequences of conversion, as we have noted, were often that the Christianized Indians, accepting the injunction to give up their warlike ways, became the victims of other Indian tribes who hated them as renegades, or of whites not inclined to make very careful distinctions between one Indian and another.

With the opening up of the West, two new fields of "home" missions emerged. The first was a continuation and extension of earlier efforts to convert the Indians. Better organized and vastly more ambitious, its adherents believed the only solution to the Indian problem was the conversion of the Indians to Christianity. The second was an effort to bring Christianity—Bibles, ministers, and seminaries—to the frontier regions, particularly to the Mississippi River Valley. While many new towns were settled, as we have seen, by congregations of the devout, "cumulative" towns that simply attracted settlers because of the prospect of economic gain were notoriously wild and licentious.

Samuel John Mills, a native of Torrington, Connecticut, and a graduate of Williams College, became the leader of the movement to bring the Gospel to the crude and lawless settlements of the West, especially the wide-open river towns. In New York, Connecticut, Massachusetts, and New Jersey, societies were formed to establish or revive Christianity on the frontier.

Other Williams students joined Mills and soon recruited prospective missionaries from Middlebury College, Dartmouth, and Yale. Mills and a friend, John Schermerhorn, toured the Western states and territories in 1813, distributing Bibles and preaching the Gospel. They brought back alarming reports of the unchurched condition of the regions through which they had traveled. They estimated that some areas containing as many as fifty thousand people were without churches or preachers. In those states settled by New Englanders Christianity was strongest; those settled from the Southern states were more often in "spiritual darkness."

Mills and Schermerhorn also took note of an increasingly common phenomenon, the great diversity of sects and "religions." A people capable of devising a better plow or more efficient wagon proved equally ingenious in inventing new religions. There were New Lights, Universalists (who subscribed to the democratic notion of universal salvation), Swedenborgians, Spiritualists, and Infidels. Everywhere Mills and his companions went they attempted to organize Bible societies to procure and distribute Bibles and encourage family prayers and Bible reading.

A second expedition several years later, financed by combined missionary societies, went armed with seven hundred Bibles, five thousand copies of the New Testament, and thousands of religious tracts in French. It was Mills's estimate that there were seventy-five thousand families between the Alleghenies and the Mississippi without Bibles. The New York Bible Society, dismayed at the news, called a conference of seventy Bible societies to organize a national campaign to combat godlessness in the West. The result was the American Bible Society. In five years it had 239 chapters and had distributed 140,000 Bibles or New Testaments.

Undoubtedly, the roots of the revived interest in the Christian religion lay in part in an ebbing of the utopian expectation that, while closely identified with liberal Christianity, had a pronounced secular bent. The defeated expectations of the French Revolution disposed Americans to consider more seriously the state of their own souls. In the words of a historian of the missionary movement, "The secular causes which had for a time repressed the spirit of missions, were removed. Religion, from which the struggle for national existence and the formation of the national government had partially withdrawn the minds of men, was beginning to recover its former power."

The involvement of American merchants and American ships and sailors in commerce with the remote regions of the world aroused the interest of pious Americans in heathen lands. There was a special incentive to foreign missionary activity in the millennial expectation that so often made itself felt in the various Protestant sects and denominations. If Christ were to return to earth to reign a thousand years, it would happen only after his Word was preached to the unconverted everywhere. Thus, it was logical to assume that foreign missionary work on a vast scale must hasten the millennium.

Again Samuel Mills and his "Williams Band" were central figures. It was said of Mills that his mother had told a friend, "I have consecrated this child to the service of God, as a missionary." Mills's first ambition was to be a missionary, "not to the American Indians, but to the heathen of some foreign land."

The work of foreign missions was already well established in England, where it had followed in the wake of British imperialism. The subject of foreign missions now became a central topic in the councils of the principal Protestant denominations, inspired, in large part, by Samuel Mills and his young friends. In 1810, the American Board of Commissioners for Foreign Missions was formed by a synod of the Presbyterian church, in response to the appeals of Yale divinity students and the injunction of Christ to his followers, "Go ye into all the world, and preach the gospel to every creature." The first meeting of the board closed its sessions with an address "to the Christian Public," which read, in part: "The Lord is shaking the nations—his friends in different parts of christendom are roused from their slumbers; and unprecedented exertions are making for the spread of divine knowledge, and the conversion of nations. In our own country, the missionary spirit is excited, and much has already been done for imparting the gospel to the destitute in our new and frontier settlements." The address went on to appeal for financial support. "When millions are perishing for lack of knowledge, and the young disciples of the Lord are waiting, with ardent desire, to carry the gospel of salvation to them; shall these millions be left to perish, and that ardent desire be disappointed?"

On the grounds that the heathen peoples of the world were as much in need of care for their bodies as their souls, two of the young men who had volunteered for missionary service went to Philadelphia to pursue medical studies in anticipation of the day when funds would be raised to dispatch them to foreign parts. In doing so they initiated a vitally important aspect of Christian missionary activity—the establishment of hospitals and clinics as a high priority (along with schools and colleges) in every missionary field.

In 1811, although adequate funds were still lacking, the commissioners decided to trust to God's Providence and dispatched five young men, three of them married, to Calcutta. "A season of more impressive solemnity," the commissioners reported, "has scarcely been witnessed in our country. The sight of five young men, of highly respectable talents and attainments, and who might reasonably have promised themselves very eligible situations in our churches, forsaking parents and friends and country, and every alluring earthly prospect and devoting themselves to the privations, hardships and perils of a mission for life to a people sitting in darkness in a far distant and unpropitious clime, could not fail deeply to affect every heart not utterly destitute of feeling." Less hardy Christians responded generously to appeals for funds, and in a few weeks over six thousand dollars had been collected, enough to pay the passage to India and support the five young missionaries for a year.

They knew well enough what lay ahead of them. Adoniram Judson, in writing to ask the hand of Ann Hazeltine, had acknowledged the hazards of his chosen career. "I have now to ask, if you can consent to part with your daughter early next spring, to see her no more in this world? Whether you can consent to her exposure to the dangers of the ocean; to the fatal influence of the southern climate of India; to every kind of want and distress; to degradation, insults, persecution, and perhaps a violent death? Can you consent to all this for the sake of Him who left His heavenly home and died for her and for you . . . for the sake of Zion and the glory of God?"

The commissioners provided specific instructions for the missionary band. They were not to mix in politics; they were to form missionary churches. "In teaching the gentiles," their mandate read, "it will be your business, not vehemently to declaim against their superstitions, but in the meekness and gentleness of Christ, to bring them as directly as possible to the knowledge of the truth. . . . So far as truth has access, so as to produce its effects, the errors and superstitions and vices of paganism will fall of course."

The British East India Company, concerned only with the commercial exploitation of the various peoples under its control, ordered the missionaries to return at once to the United States. The intervention of British missionaries won them a reprieve. Two went to Madagascar. The Judsons and Rices converted to the Baptists and helped to start a mission in Burma. After repeated rebuffs, another mission was started in Bombay.

In such modest and unpromising fashion began one of the most extensive and potent manifestations of the Protestant passion. The story of American foreign missions is a moving and dramatic chapter in our history. Never adequately told, it is a tale of remarkable hardihood and perseverance on the part of tens of thousands of dedicated men and women. Before the century was over thousands of schools and medical clinics and hundreds of colleges and universities would be established in virtually all gentile countries, that is to say, in most of the non-Christian countries of the world, and hundreds of thousands of "natives" from China to Syria would be converted to Christianity. Perhaps more important, many hundreds of thousands more were taught in American (and English and German and French) schools; were treated in clinics; and were introduced to Western notions of democracy, justice, and constitutional government. It is common practice today to deplore the effects of Western culture on the non-Western peoples of the world, many of them with cultures far older and aesthetically richer than anything the West could offer. But it must be kept in mind that in many of the cultures into which the missionaries went at such sacrifice the great mass of the people lived in hopeless poverty and degradation. In our newfound respect for other cultures and religions, it is well to recall, for instance, that the status of ordinary women in most such cultures was hopelessly degraded and dependent, that arbitrary authority was the rule rather than the exception, and that rigid caste and class sytems were cruelly exploitative.

The role of missionaries is a complex one that certainly has many unhappy chapters. Missionary activity in such ancient high cultures as Japan, China, and India was certainly very different in its effects than missionary activity in the South Pacific islands, among the headhunters of New Guinea, the Ashanti of Africa, or the Sandwich Islanders.

We have earlier taken note of the fact that in colonial America the "Puritan" form of American Protestantism performed an essential social function by binding primarily (but not exclusively) the New England colonies into tightly knit communities that were, in essence, civil versions of the congregation. The binding or "covenanting" was the heart of the matter. It provided the basic social unit—the township—for the larger society, set its standards, provided its norms, and articulated its values. When the congregation was virtually coterminous with the citizenship, a remarkable degree of unity and homogeneity was achieved. The primary focus of the covenanted communities of colonial America was the Old Testament. It was the imagery of the Old Testament that exerted the most powerful sway over the consciousness of colonists—Exodus, Ezekiel, Micah, and later Jeremiah—the flight from Egypt, the gathering of nations, the independence of those who "sat under their fig tree and under their vine," and the dangers of disobedience to God.

The crisis of the American Revolution meant a dramatic shift in emphasis to what we might call the theological-philosophical-political-historical or "structural" aspects of Christian doctrine, exemplified by the Classical-Christian Consciousness of the men we have called the Founding Fathers. Once the Constitution had been achieved, interest shifted to a new area of Christian dogma—the millennial expectation of which Benjamin Rush was such an ideal exemplar. Christian utopianism—the millennial expectation—could not be sustained indefinitely in the face of the frustrations and disappointments that confronted the new Republic. The shift this time was to the notions of individual salvation, typified by the revival.

In the Puritan town salvation was thought of as something that happened within the community of the faithful. Every individual needed the reinforcement of his or her brothers and sisters. Salvation was, in a sense, a corporate enterprise. When the older covenanted communities began to break down under the pressure of increasing social and religious diversification, the emphasis came to be on the individual's search for salvation. In those covenanted communities that broke off from the older communities and attempted to revive the redeemed community, the corporate character of the religious experience survived. In the older communities, however, the disestablishment of the original denominations—primarily the Congregationalists, the Presbyterians, and in the South the Episcopalians—hastened the shift to what we might call personal Christianity. This also involved a marked shift from the primacy of the Old Testament to the New— from Exodus, Ezekiel, and Micah to Luke, Corinthians, and the

Revelation of St. John. Here Christ assumed a centrality that he had not had in the earlier period. The devout Christian did not merely seek to obey God's commandments, to live a devout and pious life; he or she actively sought suffering and sacrifice. Christ was described in Scripture as "the suffering servant," as one who had taken upon himself the sins and sufferings of the whole world and who had died on the cross in the archetypal redemptive act. In the mystery of Christian dogma, God so loved the world that He gave His only Son as a sacrifice, that all who believed in him should not perish but have everlasting life. It followed from this that the model of the perfect Christian life was one in which one was humble, sacrificing oneself for others, and gladly suffering ridicule and obloquy for the sake of the despised and rejected of the earth. Today we seek "salvation" by "realizing ourselves," "expressing ourselves," "getting what is due us out of life," extracting from the pressures and anxieties produced by the need to achieve and "get ahead" in American society some precious essence of happiness and indulgence.

In the United States in the early decades of the nineteenth century a substantial number of our ancestors sought salvation through service and suffering. To them, the missionary task was made to order; more accurately, it was created by them as an expression of their desire to serve their Lord, Jesus Christ, in spirit analogous to that in which he had served the world.

Increasingly to men and women of such disposition the condition of their enslaved black brothers and sisters in the South offered an ideal opportunity to reenact their Savior's life of service and suffering. Here were the seeds of the abolition movement. The phenomenon of runaway slaves was not a new one. Slaves had been escaping from their masters from the earliest days of slavery. We have already seen them making common cause in the Florida jungles with the Seminole Indians. Even after Jackson's foray, they continued to live in the swamps and tropical forests, launching raids into nearby Georgia to free other slaves. They hid in the bayous of Louisiana, found occasional refuge in Indian villages, occupied the Great Swamp of Virginia where no man ventured to pursue them. A number had always made their way north seeking freedom—some as far as the uncongenial cold of Canada, the boldest and most enterprising westward.

The pursuit and capture of runaway slaves was a flourishing business. Southern and border-state newspapers were filled with advertisements for runaways and the activities of slave-hunting teams with trained dogs and the most disreputable whites were notorious. Runaways were, indeed, one of the principal sources of the South's paranoia. Not only did runaways make a mockery of the South's fantasy of slaves as happy, carefree children who loved their masters and were content with their lot; each was a substantial piece of property. A prime field hand was valued at from five hundred to twelve hundred dollars, which in modern currency might be roughly the equivalent of two thousand to five thousand dollars. Every time a slave escaped, it was as though five or ten acres of land (or more, depending on the region) had vanished, or a barn with five cows had been consumed by fire. Southern slaveowners felt in perpetual danger of having their capital run away, of the possibility that they and their region would bleed to death through the perpetual drain of their human property. It is hard to know whether the psychological or material aspects of the problem were more debilitating to Southerners. It would eventually drive them into a kind of collective insanity.

While it is probably the case that between the beginning of the nineteenth century and the Civil War not more than fifty or sixty thousand slaves escaped out of four million, they added up in value to millions and millions of lost dollars, and they increased in numbers with each passing decade as more and more sympathetic whites undertook to aid and abet them in their escapes. I believe it is not too much to say that the escape of slaves and the frantic efforts of their owners to recapture them virtually monopolized the attention of white Americans, North and South, from the early 1830s, when the abolitionists and their "action arm," the underground railroad, emerged as a full fledged social movement to the outbreak of the Civil War. It is a story of inexhaustible drama, of an infinity of extraordinary tales of heroism, black and white—accounts that, faithfully printed in abolitionist journals, built bit by bit a sentiment among the people of the North hostile to the extension or perpetuation of slavery.

The awakening of the consciences of individuals, both Northern and Southern, to the enormity of slavery as a crime against humanity rather than as merely an unfortunate and deplorable institution, had been itself a slow process. As we have seen, surviving members of the Revolutionary generation, such as Jefferson and Adams, much as they deplored the existence of slavery, could not bring themselves to allow it to become a bone of contention between the North and the South and thereby imperil the Union. While Adams was bitterly opposed to slavery and believed that "every measure of prudence . . . ought to be assumed for the eventual total extirpation of slavery from the United States," he cautioned that a way must be found that "should not inflict severer calamities on the objects of our commiseration [the slaves] than those which they at present endure, by reducing them to despair, or the necessity of robbery, plunder, assassination, and massacre, to preserve their lives." The freed slaves must have "some provision for furnishing them employment, or some means of supplying them with the necessary comforts of life. The same humanity requires that we should not by any rash or violent measures expose the lives and property of those of our fellow-citizens who are so unfortunate as to be surrounded with these fellow-creatures by hereditary descent, or by any other means without their own fault."

But a new generation perceived the matter differently. In Maryland in 1818, the Reverend Mr. Gruber, a Methodist minister, quoted from the Declaration of Independence in attacking slavery and was arrested and charged with inciting to insurrection. His attorney, Roger Taney, defending him, declared: "Slavery is a blot upon our national character, and every real lover of freedom confidentially hopes that it will be effectually wiped away. And until the time shall come when we can point without a blush to the language held in the Declaration of Independence, every friend of humanity will seek to lighten the galling chains of slavery."

The underground railroad took shape slowly. Among its earliest "conductors" were a group of Presbyterian ministers from the South who settled along the northern bank of the Ohio. So situated they were in an ideal position to assist slaves escaping from Virginia and Kentucky across the Ohio. Such escapees they passed along to the few individuals known to be sympathetic enough to slaves and brave enough to run the risk of helping them escape to safer regions. Often a slave would be passed along in this way to Canada until he reached central and western Ohio, where the Ottawa Indians would help him reach the shores of Lake Erie, whence he could cross to Canada.

Another route ran to the region of the Western Reserve in eastern Ohio, which, filled with New Englanders, was a stronghold of antislavery sentiment. In its initial phases the railroad, which was yet to be so named, was simply an informal network, information about which was passed by word of mouth. The slaves who undertook to escape were, of necessity, the boldest, the most enterprising and confident. Often they were of mixed blood—like Frederick Douglass—the sons or daughters of the master of the plantation. Such men and women often had preferred status; knew more of the white world beyond the plantation; and, at least in the early days before the prohibitions against teaching slaves to read or write had become virtually universal throughout the South, might have acquired the rudiments of reading and writing. In addition, they were acutely aware of the injustice of a system that made them, the children of free men, slaves themselves. One other characteristic was common to the great majority of the black runaways—they were devout Christians whose faith taught them that all men were brothers and to whom rumors came that white men with similar convictions were ready to assist them in their efforts to be free. When one considers the hazards involved in running away, the harshness of the slave system is highlighted. Many runaways had never been more than a few miles from the plantation on which they had been born; the world beyond was an unknown land, filled with enemies all ready to return them to slavery. They had no maps, no guides, no compasses or other instruments by which to plot a course. The most terrible chastisements awaited those who were recaptured, perhaps the most common being mutilation, including sometimes the chopping off of a foot or the cropping of ears, noses, and fingers.

As we have noted, trained slave hunters were always ready to pursue them, with the baying of bloodhounds announcing their proximity. The runaways had usually no more food to nourish them than a hastily snatched ham or sack of cornmeal, and they had literally hundreds of miles to cover. First, they had to reach a Free State or territory, where they were still subject to pursuit and recapture by their masters; hundreds of miles farther was the icy and unfamiliar sanctuary of Canada. Every slave who undertook to escape abandoned friends and sometimes spouses and children, parents and grandparents. Often, of course, an entire black family, threatened by separation, undertook to escape together, although the risks of recapture in such cases were vastly increased.

However determined and courageous they were, slaves could not have escaped in any substantial numbers unless there had been, in the South itself, an intricate "support system" made up of free blacks; renegade slaves who often lived off the land in inaccessible swamps or mountainous areas; slaves on plantations along the way; some scattered settlements of friendly Indians; and, finally and not least important, sympathetic whites, some of them "poor whites," who in their own depressed condition identified with the runaways, others nonslaveholding Christians or members of radical Christian sects such as the Mennonites and Quakers.

Two cultures existed in the South: the dominant, slaveholding plantation owners, increasingly feudal, cemented together by the need to protect their black human property against all those who wished to steal it or entice it from them; and the antislave culture, a much looser and less readily definable alliance of all those who had no sympathy for the institution of slavery. The antislave culture, if we include the slaves themselves, outnumbered the slave culture perhaps two or three to one.

In addition to the white "conductors" of the underground railroad, an increasing number of free blacks in the North devoted themselves to helping their enslaved brothers and sisters escape to Canada. Not only did those white Christians who took direct responsibility for assisting slaves to escape see themselves as thereby serving Christ, they saw the blacks who passed through the conduits of the underground railroad as the embodiment of Christian nobility, men and women who, whatever risks their white abettors ran, far exceeded them in the dangers and hardships they endured. Thus, when a white abolitionist reached in the dark of night for the hand of a fleeing slave, it was often an ecstatic moment for black and white alike, a verification of their common Christian faith that had demonstrated its power to overcome every obstacle.

The underground railroad was perceived by those whites increasingly involved in it as perhaps the most critical moment in the history of Western Christendom. What was at stake, in their view, was nothing less than the survival of Christianity in the world. If the abomination of slavery persisted or, infinitely worse, spread, the United States must abandon any pretense to being a Christian nation. It must accept the perpetuation of an enormity too terrible to endure; the American mission to redeem the world must turn into a tragic mockery of Christian expectations. Seen in this light, the beginning of the abolitionist movement was not merely a critical moment in American history; it was a moment of profound significance in world history. Henrietta Buckmaster, in her great account of the movement and the development of the underground railroad, takes the action of a

Quaker woman, Hannah Gibbons, in harboring a fugitive slave as a symbolic episode containing the purest meaning of abolitionism.

Benjamin Lundy, also a Quaker and one of the early organizers of the underground railroad, wrote: "I heard the wail of the captive. I felt his pang of distress, and the iron entered my soul." Thus inspired, he started an abolitionist newspaper, the *Genius of Universal Emancipation*, in 1815, which began with six subscribers in his hometown of Mount Pleasant, Ohio. He took to the road like Johnny Appleseed, scattering his journal wherever he could find a sympathetic reader, and in six months he had over five hundred subscribers. In ten years he traveled twenty-five thousand miles, five thousand on foot, sowing the seed.

46

American Enterprise

Francis Cabot Lowell and Nathan Appleton, two young Bostonians, had begun talking in 1811 about the possibility of building a cotton mill at nearby Waltham. The practicability of such an undertaking rested on being able to reproduce the power loom that had recently been developed in England. Lowell built a reasonable imitation in the back of a store on Broad Street; it was an ingenious modification of a British machine he had seen on a trip to Manchester, England, and soon it was installed in a water-powered factory. Appleton, the principal investor in the new plant, wrote years later: "I well recollect the state of admiration and satisfaction with which I sat by the hour, watching the beautiful movement of this new and wonderful machine, destined as it evidently was, to change the character of all textile industry."

The time was the autumn of 1814, and the moment was every bit as significant as Appleton suggested. As we have noted, cotton manufacturing had been going on in New England—its center had been Rhode Island—for more than a decade, but the machines used were comparatively primitive, and the factories, as it turned out, were economically practical only because of the European war. Now, with

766

the development of the most up-to-date power loom, American capital was ready to make its first notable entry into American industry.

The Lowell loom was the precursor of a vast industrial empire whose products would, in time, flood the world. Initially, the success of the factory meant the cementing of an alliance between the Southern planter with his cotton and the Northerner who commanded capital, an alliance that would dominate American politics for the next half century. Lowell and Appleton were more than shrewd and enterprising businessmen; they were men of conscience—of New England conscience, to be exact. Like many other entrepreneurs, they were troubled by the charges that the growth of manufacturing in the United States must inevitably bring with it the sordid and depressed conditions that characterized the great industrial cities of England, already somewhat of an international scandal. Great numbers of wretched men and women and malnourished children worked long hours there in unhealthy conditions for meager wages and lived in hopeless squalor, drowning their miseries in gin and dying prematurely of disease and overwork.

Lowell and Appleton agreed that such consequences must not follow from the development of industry in the United States. In Appleton's words, "The introduction of the new cotton manufacture in this country, on a large scale, was a new idea. What would be its effect on the character of our population was a matter of deep interest. The operatives in the manufacturing cities of Europe, were notoriously of the lowest character for intelligence and morals. The question therefore arose, and was deeply considered, whether this degradation was the result of the peculiar occupation, or of other and distinct causes. We could not perceive why this peculiar description of labor should vary in its effects upon character from all other occupations."

It occurred to Lowell and Appleton that New England farmgirls, many of whom had been engaged in "cottage industry" or "household manufacture"—spinning and weaving cloth in their own homes—and were now the victims of the technological unemployment that resulted from the introduction of machinery, might be recruited as "operatives." "Here," again in Appleton's words, "was . . . a fund of labor, well educated and virtuous. It was not perceived how a profitable employment has any tendency to deteriorate the character. The most efficient guards were adopted in establishing boarding houses, at the cost of the company, under the charge of respectable women with every provision for religious worship. Under these circumstances, the daughters of respectable farmers were readily induced to come into these mills for a temporary period." Indeed the mills resembled nothing so much as boarding schools for young ladies. Neatly and becomingly attired, the girls were swift and efficient workers whose wages soon were more than double those of their European counterparts. They attended classes in the evening, formed literary societies, and published a magazine that had thousands of subscribers. Called the *Lowell Offering*, it was "written, Edited and Published by Female Operatives Employed in the Mills" and printed by the "Misses Curtis & Farley."

The poems in the *Lowell Offering* were romantic evocations of life: "Like what is life? 'Tis like a vision flying. . . ." "The World, The world! how beautiful and blest it seems/When from the home of childhood, forth we look. . . ." There were humorous essays, one on toothaches; serious essays on such subjects as study ("Man is a being formed by nature for study. The germ of intellect lies folded within his breast, and must be cultivated with care and attention"); international law; Hannah More; Pythagoras, the Greek philosopher. And there were serialized novelettes, often about factory life.

As word spread of the factory girls at Lowell, they became the eighth wonder of the world. A stream of visitors passed through Lowell to marvel at the cleanliness, the good order, the decorum, the cheerful faces, and the attractive appearance of the "operatives." Calhoun visited Lowell in 1818 and went away convinced that the future greatness of the United States lay in an alliance between the mill owners in towns like Lowell and the cotton growers of the South.

Andrew Jackson praised the "Lowell System," and Davy Crockett wrote after a visit: "I could not help reflecting on the difference of conditions between these females, thus employed, and those of other populous countries, where the female character is degraded to abject slavery. Here were thousands, useful to others, and enjoying all the blessings of freedom, with the prospect before them of future comfort and respectability. . . . I regret that more of our southern and western men do not go there, as it would help to do away with their prejudices against these manufactories."

Anthony Trollope came some years later and reported that "everything is beautiful, philanthropic, profitable, and magnificent. . . . Lowell is the realization of a commercial Utopia." To the champions of manufacturing it was a godsend. It seemed to answer all the charges that factories corrupted the morals and degraded the lives of their workers. It confirmed the American conviction that no work was degrading if done in the proper spirit.

Visitors were especially impressed by the pervading atmosphere of piety. There were, they noted, *thirty* churches as well as a free public library and a museum in Lowell. Famous not only in the United States but also in Europe, the Lowell girls proved that in manufacturing as so many other areas of human endeavor American genius could provide models for the rest of the world to emulate. Who would have thought, before Lowell demonstrated it, that manufactories could be institutions not only for profit but for self-improvement and cultivation?

More significant, perhaps, in the long run than the tidy dormitories presided over by respectable matrons, the literary societies, and the sketching classes was the fact that, as Appleton put it, "it was the Americans who first introduced the manufacture of heavy goods by the application of the least amount of labor to the greatest quantity of raw material thus producing a description [type] of goods cheaper to the consumer than any heretofore existing." What was at issue was, quite simply, the democratization of production. Johannes Schweizer and many others had noted how deeply the "labor-saving" instinct was imbedded in the American character. Every American worker, and, by extension, every employer, had a vested interest in discovering the quickest, easiest, and cheapest way to accomplish a particular task. The consequences were, almost literally, beyond calculation.

The New England girls, bright, alert, and well educated; the New England waterpower from the innumerable streams and rivers that veined the region; and the Yankee ingenuity exemplified by men like Lowell, plus the inexhaustible supply of cotton produced by the slave system, had by the 1820s laid the foundation for the rapid development of American industry.

Despite the interest in manufacturing stimulated by the Lowell and Waltham cotton mills and their charming female "operatives," canal building continued to exert the greatest attraction for venture capital and indeed reached its apogee with the building of the Erie Canal. The vision of a great engineering work—a canal almost three hundred miles long—that would connect the Great Lakes with the Hudson River was not by any means unique with De Witt Clinton. Gouverneur Morris, a champion of the canal until his death, had written: "I hope the business may be effected in a proper manner, for it is (I believe) that most extensive theatre for the display of skill and industry which can be found on this globe." Morris feared that "our minds are not yet enlarged to the size of so great an object." But it was Clinton's determined perseverance, that quality he so admired, that made the Erie Canal a reality. Appointed to a commission to survey and determine the practicability of a canal in 1809, he was then deputed to try to enlist the support of Congress. Turned down there and even deposed as mayor of New York by a Republican council, in 1817 Clinton prevailed upon the New York State legislature to support the canal and the same year was elected governor of the state, from which office he was able to push its construction. On July 4, 1817, Clinton himself broke ground for what was to be hailed as the greatest achievement of the new century.

To those who declared that such a canal would take decades to build, Clinton replied, "What has been accomplished elsewhere we shall accomplish here; the day will come in less than ten years when we will see Erie water flowing into the Hudson." It was a staggering undertaking, a canal 363 miles long with a descent of 555 feet from the lake to the river. It would require 83 locks, 27 of them in the first 15 miles.

Clinton assembled a group of brilliant young men who were to become known as the Erie School of Engineering, foremost among them Canvass White. They addressed themselves to the practical problems of the canal. White was sent to Europe to collect the most up-to-date information available. He returned with reams of notes and drawings and the most advanced instruments for surveying.

A crucial question facing Clinton and his aides was whether to construct the locks of wood or stone. Wood deteriorated rapidly; stone would have to be bound by expensive hydraulic cement available only in Europe. White recalled that an English engineer, visiting Massachusetts, had come on a small deposit of trass—volcanic pumice—the main ingredient in hydraulic cement. Believing that trass might be found in New York State, White began canvassing the area near Chittenango, which had a geologic formation similar to that in which the Massachusetts trass had been discovered. His search proved fruitless, and he was about to abandon it when he met two young men who, in answer to his questions, told him they knew of a deposit of porous gray stone nearby. They led White to the area, and he discovered that it was indeed the precious trass. It would be going too far to say that the Erie Canal could not have been completed without Canvass White's trass, but the expense of the repair and upkeep of the canal would certainly have been far greater and the building of the locks far more laborious.

The building of the canal, especially within the period Clinton had promised for its completion—six years—required the assembling of men and materials on an unprecedented scale. The canal was to be started at several points simultaneously. Offices were opened to buy the necessary equipment—principally mules, horses, wagons, stump-pullers, wheelbarrows, and shovels—and the route was divided into three divisions, each under a chief engineer. The engineers in turn contracted out the work to individual contractors, who engaged subcontractors.

The most formidable obstacle was the eleven-hundred-foot-high Niagara escarpment. This was surmounted by the so-called Lockport combines, which consisted of five pairs of double locks cut through solid rock so that boats, traveling in opposite directions along the canal, might ascend and descend the escarpment at the same time. The Lockport locks were the achievement of Nathan Roberts, a largely self-taught engineer.

In order to solidify public sentiment behind the canal, Clinton pressed his engineers to complete the "Long Level" between Syracuse and Herkimer—a distance of sixty-nine and one-half miles—in the first year; and they did so, to the confusion of the canal's opponents and the delight of its supporters. As the canal progressed, hundreds of young farmers along the route signed on for hard money and at once demonstrated that native American capacity of which we have already taken note for discovering easier, laborsaving ways of doing things. Uprooting the stumps of trees in the path of the canal was the most arduous and time-consuming task. The New York farmers soon devised a machine that, with a team of horses and a crew of six, could tear out thirty or forty stumps a day. Next they developed a technique in which a cable was attached to the top of a tree, which was then "wound down," roots and all, by means of an endless screw turned by a single man. The cumulative effect of many such ingenious expedients was undoubtedly an important factor in the remarkable speed with which the work proceeded.

Long before the canal was completed, Clinton turned water into the Long Level between Rome and Utica, and had a sixty-foot-long barge, *Chief Engineer of Rome*, built as a promise of things to come. A boat floating on a major segment of the canal gave an enormous boost to the whole enterprise. "Attended by many respectable gentlemen and ladies," the *Chief* made the trip in a day, and a reporter for the *Genesee Messenger* reported enthusiastically: "The scene was extremely interesting and highly grateful. The embarkation took place amid the ringing of bells, the roaring of cannon and the loud acclamations of thousands of exhilarated spectators, male and female, who lined the banks of the newly created river. The scene was truly sublime."

Although Clinton's political enemies almost succeeded in ousting him from the governorship of the state in 1821, four years after work had started the canal had been opened for 220 miles. Two important aqueducts remained to be built at the Genesee River and at Cohoes on the Mohawk. The canal was carried over those two rivers on two aqueducts, 802 and 1,188 feet long, respectively.

The year 1825 was the year of the official opening of the canal. On October 26, Clinton, in the *Seneca Chief*, gaily decorated with flags and bunting and drawn by a team of four gray horses, started a triumphal procession from Buffalo along the canal and on down the Hudson to New York where thousands of citizens waited to celebrate the event. Not since the end of the Revolution had there been such a moment of exuberant celebration. The canal had become the national symbol of American determination and ingenuity, of the American capacity to turn extravagant visions into practical realities. Carried through in the face of bad times and against a formidable array of human and natural obstacles, it declared that Americans could do whatever they set their minds to. In the words of Colonel William Stone: "They [the builders of the canal] have built the longest canal, in the least time, with the least experience, for the least money and to the greatest public benefit."

All along the route delirious crowds hailed the flotilla. At Albany steamboats waited to tow the barges down the Hudson to New York, where the party arrived on November 4 to a tumultuous welcome, culminating three days later with "a great illumination and fireworks displayed at City Hall."

One of the city's most eminent literary figures described the celebration: "The Aquatic display transcended all anticipations, twenty-nine steamboats, gorgeously dressed, with barges, ships, pilot-boats, canal-boats, and boats of the Whitehall firemen, conveying thousands of ladies and gentlemen, presenting a scene which cannot be described." At Sandy Hook the "Wedding of the Waters," which became a favorite subject for artists, was consummated by pouring two kegs of Lake Erie water into the Atlantic, "to commemorate," in Clinton's words, "the navigable communication which has been established between our Mediterranean Sea and the Atlantic Ocean." Thirty thousand visitors had crowded into the city for the glorious event. The aquatic display was followed by a parade up Broadway, with two hundred floats depicting the building of the canal and exemplifying its symbolic significance. Interspersed with the floats were cultural societies, militia units in colorful uniforms, and bands playing patriotic tunes. Commemorative medals were struck for presentation to President John Quincy Adams and to former presidents John Adams, Jefferson, Madison, and Monroe. All kinds of souvenirs—plates, cravats, bowls, dishes, and silk handkerchiefs bearing portraits of Clinton and the *Seneca Chief*—were sold in great quantities.

One of the principal contractors on the canal was a New York businessman named William James, grandfather of the great American philosopher of the same name and the novelist Henry James. James, one of the orators of the day, began his remarks by noting: "It is the distinguishing attribute of man to be excited by what is grand, beautiful and sublime in nature, or what is great and beneficial in the combinations of intellect and art." The company present had assembled "to celebrate the completion of a work which in grandeur of conception, and benefits to the human family, surpass every national improvement that has been attempted in any country; a work that sheds additional lustre on the United States, bearing the stamp of the enterprising spirit, and resolution which declared our independence, and the intelligence and wisdom that cemented the union of different republics by the adoption of the federal constitution."

The canal was, in short, the concrete and practical fruit of independence, the materialization of the ideas and ideals that had created the nation. It symbolized, as nothing else could, the ties that bound the nation together; it was the perfect democratic artifact, superior in conception and execution to the greatest palaces and monuments of the Old World. James found it difficult to put into words his own feelings of awe at the scale of the canal and its various "philosophical" implications. Contemplating it, he was encouraged to hope that "neither tyrannical aristocracies, or intriguing demagogues" could ever "succeed in corrupting our citizens or blighting our liberties. . . . We therefore rejoice this day for the extension of the population, liberty and happiness of man. . . . At this moment, I feel an indescribable emotion, something like a renewal of life."

The historian has the same difficulty as William James in suggesting the degree to which the canal obsessed and enchanted Americans in the fall of 1825. Involved as it had become in partisan political wrangling, it nonetheless was very much "a renewal of life." Completed while the memory of the disastrous depression of 1819 was still in people's minds, it was taken to be a symbol of the boundless potentialities of the country, its resilience and its hopes.

A popular song, written for the occasion, expressed the feeling of most Americans:

> . . . it is not that Wealth now enriches the scene,
> Where treasures of Art, and of Nature, convene;
> 'Tis not that this union our coffers may fill—
> 'Tis, that Genius has triumph'd—and Science prevail'd
> Tho' Prejudice flouted, and Envy assail'd,
> It is, that the vassals of Europe may see
> The progress of mind, in a land that is free.

The canal was an instant success. It made New York City the center of commercial activity in the United States. Towns along its route became bustling cities, and new towns were established at its numerous junctions and locks. By the end of 1825, tolls in the sum of almost a half-million dollars had been collected, 13,110 boats had passed between Buffalo and Albany, and "40,000 persons had passed Utica on freight and packet boats during the season; a daily average of forty-two boats, arks and cribs."

The success of the Erie Canal led to a new canal mania, and it seemed as though everywhere excavations for canals were being started. A whole system of feeder canals for the Erie was undertaken, the most famous perhaps being the Black River Canal from Rome to Utica. The southern counties of the state agitated for a canal to tie them to the golden network, and the result was the Chenango Canal, ninety-seven miles long, from Binghamton to Utica. In the infatuation for canals a number were built that proved, as in the earlier period, to be financial disasters; but the Erie had more business than it could accommodate, and one observer wrote: "Having taken your position at one of the numerous bridges, it is an impressive sight to gaze up and down the canal. In either direction, as far as the eye can see, long lines of boats can be observed. By night, their flickering head lamps give the impression of swarms of fireflies."

The opening of anthracite coalfields in western Pennsylvania gave a strong impetus to canal building in that already well built state. Anthracite coal, cheap and long-burning, was soon preferred to wood in the eastern towns and in fuel-hungry Philadelphia.

As we have noted earlier, passengers as well as freight moved by the canals, and a number of travelers recorded their impressions. Charles Dickens, riding the Pennsylvania Main Line Canal, noted, "The menu for breakfast and supper offers the traveller tea, coffee, bread, butter, salmon, shad, liver, steaks, potatoes, pickles, ham, chops, black-pudding and sausages. Midday dinner was precisely the same minus tea and coffee." Dickens, who traveled on a number of canal boats during his tour of the United States in the 1840s, described a typical craft: "It resembles a small Noah's Ark—a houseboat whose only deck is the roof of the cabin. In the bow, carefully cut off from the rest of the boat is a tiny cuddy for the crew. Next back of this is a ladies' dressing room and cabin, sometimes a separate room, sometimes cut off from the main cabin only by a red curtain. Next is the main cabin, 36 to 45 feet long, which was saloon and dining room by day and men's dormitory by night. Back of this is the bar, and finally, at the very stern, is the kitchen, almost always presided over by a negro cook, who is usually the bartender also. The other members of the crew are the captain, two drivers, two steersmen, one each for the day and night shifts."

At bedtime, Dickens observed, "two or three members of the crew began carrying adjustable berths, sheets, pillows, curtains, and so forth, into the main cabin. . . . Each berth was a narrow wooden or metal frame with a strip of canvas fastened over it. It was held in position at one side by two projecting iron rods which fitted into two holes in the side of the cabin; and on the other side or front side by two ropes attached to the edge of the frame and suspended by hooks from the ceiling. There were at least three beds in a tier, one above the other . . . all fastened to the rope . . . which thus furnished beds for from thirty-six to forty-two people. It seems incredible that so many people could have lain down in the limited space on one of those boats." The passengers so arranged seemed to Dickens like so many volumes packed together on shelves, and it is small wonder that Nathaniel Hawthorne found "the main cabin . . . a chamber of horrors in which sleep is impossible." The passengers were assigned their berths by drawing numbers, and Dickens described them "gathered around the master at one of the tables, drawing lots with all the anxieties and passions of gamesters depicted in their countenances; while others with small pieces of cardboard in their hands were groping among the shelves [beds] in search of numbers corresponding with those they had drawn. As soon as any gentleman found his number he took possession of it immediately by undressing and crawling into bed. The rapidity with which an agitated gambler subsided into a snoring slumberer was one of the most singular effects I have ever witnessed."

Frances Trollope, mother of the novelist Anthony Trollope, having experienced such accommodations, wrote tartly: "I can hardly imagine any motive of convenience powerful enough to induce me again to imprison myself in a canal boat under ordinary circumstances."

"Painless" dentists with traveling offices were soon a familiar sight on the Erie Canal. Extractions were fifty cents and were usually accompanied by banjo playing to muffle the groans of the patient. Traveling medicine shows were a popular diversion. One side of the cabin would typically fold out to make a stage, and black boys would often sing and dance to attract a crowd to hear the pitchman's commercial for the new, improved, giant-size all-purpose elixir.

The literary young ladies of the Lowell factories would become before long as extinct as the dodo, but the Erie Canal remained in business until 1882, by which time it had taken in tolls of $121,461,871 in uninflated dollars, with substantial profits to its investors and the state of New York. Converted into the New York State Barge Canal, it still carries almost 5 million tons of freight a year over essentially the same route that De Witt Clinton and his engineers laid out in 1816.

47

Class in America

The question of the role of an aristocracy in a democratic society was one to which John Adams and Thomas Jefferson devoted much thought. Adams (and most of the delegates to the Federal Convention) believed there was an irresistible tendency in every society to arrange itself into classes of some kind, however defined. Jefferson was addicted to the notion of "a natural aristocracy," an aristocracy of talents rather than of hereditary class. Both men recognized that a "democratic aristocracy" had certain leadership functions to perform in a healthy society. The trick was to prevent such exceptional men from hardening into a class; from using the power granted them by the people for their own interests rather than for the interests of their constituents. On the other hand, a "natural" and therefore rapidly changing "aristocracy" would not embody any particular set of ideals and values suitable for emulation by the population, or those portions of it that wished to secure recognition and have access to power.

In a fairly rigidly defined class society like that of Great Britain, the aristocracy represented, ideally at least, a code of manners and behavior that, by serving as a model or standard, had a generally beneficent influence far beyond the boundaries of the class that embodied them. These values might be taken to include civic virtue or unselfish service to the state (or Crown); honor (fairness, decency, and

777

justice in dealing with others); an indifference to purely material or mercenary considerations; an adherence to principle rather than expediency; a compassion for the unfortunate; and, perhaps above all, a willingness to assume the responsibility for a leadership based on moral imperatives.

In the United States, where there were no official classes, those who exercised power might or might not be figures worthy of emulation. The American counterpart of the British aristocrat coveted no more exalted title than that of "gentleman." But he usually treasured that and, typically, prefixed it, at least in his own mind, by "Christian." In the older Atlantic coastal cities—Boston, New York, Philadelphia, Baltimore, and Charleston—there were clear and unmistakable "class lines." All those cities (and many smaller ones) had families who had dominated the financial, political, and social life for generations. They jealously guarded access to their ranks, and while they formed numerous political alliances with other groups or classes, they did so, by and large, on their own terms and almost invariably for the purpose of strengthening their hold on the levers of power. While these local elites were bound together, in many instances, by the ties of consanguinity as well as by mutual business, political, and professional interests, they did not appear to constitute a "national" class; and as we have seen, they were not accorded the deference that a traditional aristocratic class could demand. They were not perceived as "models" or ideal types. Their aristocratic inclinations were scoffed at and mocked.

In the absence of a clearly defined upper class whose privileges were acknowledged and ideals imitated, Americans, in need of standards of behavior, relied heavily on an idealized Christian "type." The Bible took the place, in a sense, of an upper class. This was not, of course, a new development. As we have noted, the Bible, particularly the Old Testament, had had a central place in the mental world of the American colonists long before the Revolution. But even in an increasingly secularized post-Revolutionary society it provided an important set of social norms. The journals, diaries, and letters of a substantial number of nineteenth-century Americans make it clear that they wished to be "good Christians." To whatever one of the extraordinary and constantly proliferating sects or denominations they belonged (and many of course belonged to none), they tried to measure their own goals and performance by a scriptural standard.

The decline of the Federalists was a measure of the potency of the new Secular-Democratic ideals; the older class attitudes were far from dead, though few presumed to express them. Chancellor James Kent, the author of *Commentaries on American Law*, was an exception. In the convention called in 1821 to recommend changes in the constitution of the state of New York, Kent drew a lurid picture of the dangers of universal suffrage. It was, in his opinion, "too mighty an excitement for the moral constitution of men to endure. The tendency of universal suffrage, is to jeopardize the rights of property, and the principles of liberty." It simply encouraged the "tendency of the poor to covet and to share the plunder of the rich . . . in the majority to tyrannize over the minority, and trample down their rights; in the indolent and profligate, to cast the whole burdens of society upon the industrious and virtuous. . . . However mischievous the precedent may be in its consequences, or however fatal in its effects, universal suffrage never can be recalled or checked, but by the strength of the bayonet. We stand, therefore, this moment, on the brink of fate, on the very edge of the precipice."

We have argued that, from the inception of the Republic, "equality" equaled "competition." It was an especially cruel competition at the top and bottom of American society. At the bottom, immigrants faced a desperate struggle to acquire land. Those who failed to do so were condemned, for the most part, to economically marginal lives. They constituted the major element in that depressed urban class that we have already encountered who suffered most acutely in good times and in bad times experienced that "distress which touches life," in Daniel Raymond's vivid phrase.

The United States has always been officially a classless society in which only two classes have been acknowledged—middle class and working class, or blue collar as we call it today. Nevertheless, the middle class and the upper class experienced the competitive character of American life in very different manners. As the American upper class did not have the protection of law and custom afforded to upper classes or aristocracies in other societies, its members were always in danger of falling out of their class, so to speak. While birth or "good breeding" was important, it was not enough, in itself, to insure one's permanent social standing. Although there were valuable if unofficial privileges and opportunities accorded to those fortunate enough to be born in the upper class, in the last analysis they had to make their own way in the world. There was not the complex system of "places" to provide sinecures of one kind or another for the less able or energetic sons of a traditional and legally defined aristocracy. The pressures on the upper class, especially on the sons, to succeed were thus severe. To fail financially was to drop into obscurity and to bear the irredeemable stigma of that failure.

The problem was complicated by the limited number of what we would call today "career opportunities" for upper- and middle-class males. These were essentially three: law, the ministry, and commerce or business. Law was by far the most preferred. While it did not convey the status of the ministry, its material rewards were usually substantially better. The ministry was an increasingly limited field. Manufacturing was in its infancy and could absorb only a handful of the unusually aggressive and enterprising from the middle and upper classes.

A successful business, on the other hand, had the advantage of being able to accommodate a number of male heirs of varying capacities, thus preventing them from falling out of the upper class. But business did not have the prestige of the law. Law and oratory were closely identified with each other, and law led, quite naturally, to politics. Since even the United States, notorious as the most litigious nation in the world, could absorb only a limited number of lawyers, the casualty rate was high. There were few prominent families in the post-Revolutionary era who did not count a number of such casualties among their offspring.

Many members of such families "fell out" of their privileged positions as a consequence of their lack of self-discipline. In the brutally competitive conditions of life in America there were, in every generation, young men who "failed." They took to drink most commonly or, in the Southern states, to gambling and general dissipation. They married too early or married women of inferior social status and simply dropped out of the charmed circle of the upper class. The family of John Adams is a case in point. Of John and Abigail's three sons only John Quincy sustained the tradition established by his father. Charles, married too young to a woman of lower social standing, found it impossible to make a living, took to drink, and drank himself to death in his late twenties. His brother, Thomas Boylston, a Harvard graduate and a lawyer, also married "beneath" him, in the words of his nephew, Charles Francis Adams, "an effably coarse" woman who was "cunning and deceitful, hypocritical . . . and malicious as a serpent." Thomas Boylston, like his brother Charles, was an intemperate drinker, and Charles Francis described him as "one of the most unpleasant characters in the world, in his present degradation, being a brute in manners and a bully in his family."

John Quincy Adams had three sons: John, George Washington,

and Charles Francis. George Washington Adams, the most brilliant and promising of the sons, embarked on a life of dissipation from which he never recovered. He got a serving girl pregnant, and this misadventure undoubtedly contributed to his suicide or, since the circumstances of his death are not entirely clear, to the emotional collapse that preceded his death at the age of twenty-eight.

John Adams, expelled from Harvard with the entire senior class for rioting and rebellion, determined to go to sea but never found his proper calling. His father put him in charge of a flour mill he had purchased in Washington, but the project was a failure and Adams went from one disaster to another, his physical and emotional health increasingly impaired. He died in 1834 at the age of thirty-one, after, as his brother put it, "a long declension."

After his death, Charles Francis, who had mourned the death of his other brother five years earlier, wrote in his diary: "Had my brother been more useful to himself and those about him, had he listened more to the dictates of prudence he might have been invaluable to his friends. It was not heaven's will. He plunged my father into pecuniary embarrassment, and himself into moral ruin. . . . And there remained to our view nothing but a dreary future which a merciful heaven cut off." The letters of the second John Adams were removed from the family's voluminous correspondence. The full nature of his shame should not be known.

Much the same story could be told in the Warren family, for many years the most intimate friends of the Adamses. Although Jefferson had no sons, in his "extended" family, among sons-in-law, nephews, and grandsons, the toll of failure and breakdown was a heavy one. Here America exacted a heavy price from her sons and daughters; it put a high premium on "self-control." Above everything else, one must control oneself, one's passions and emotions, one's indulgence and inattention, laziness or tendency toward procrastination.

When Charles Francis Adams, having "sowed his wild oats," decided to marry Abigail Brooks, a wellborn Boston girl, he recorded in his diary the awkwardness of having to tell his mistress that their relationship must come to an end. "In the evening," he noted under the date of April 24, 1827, "I went through one of those disagreeable scenes which occur sometimes in life. No man of sense will ever keep a Mistress. For if she is valuable, the separation when it comes is terrible, and if she is not, she is more plague than profit. Ever since my engagement I have been preparing for a close of my amorous intrigues, and this evening I cut the last cord which bound me. What a pity that experience is always to be learnt over and over by each succeeding generation."

What is perhaps most striking about the passage is its matter-of-factness; the clear implication that most upper-class young men keep mistresses and have to learn the hazards and complications by painful experience. Later he notes with satisfaction that he had never had any "voluptuous" feelings for his wife, Abby. As for Abby, perhaps not surprisingly, she lapsed almost at once into the kind of semi-invalidism that characterized many such marriages, and was given to periods of extreme gloom and morbidity.

Charles Francis had experienced passion and put it behind him as youthful excess. He now wished an orderly, agreeable life and a well-kept household, with as little overt display of emotion as possible. For men like Adams, men of unusual energy and ambition with the strong sexual drives that are characteristic of such types, the relative continence required by a marriage of the kind he describes so unselfconsciously in his diary was often a severe strain. Some took mistresses. More typically, they had recourse to prostitutes— prostitutes in elegant bawdy houses that catered to the wealthy.

The division into good women—upper-class young ladies whom one married and who were presumed to have only the mildest interest in, and often an active distaste for, sexual relations—and "other" women—bad women, or exciting and sexually stimulating women, almost invariably lower-class women—gave a social character to sex. More or less uninhibited sexuality was a characteristic of the lower classes. In the South, as we have noted, it was identified with the sexual prowess of slavewomen. The consequence of this division into good women with low sexual drives and bad (and usually lower-class) women with high sexual energy was to remain a deeply ingrained aspect of the American middle- and upper-class consciousness down to the so-called sexual revolution of the late 1960s and early 1970s.

Sexual anxiety thus became one of the most basic of those numerous anxieties (getting ahead, holding on, feeling threatened by "other races") that contributed so much to American nervousness. Men who sought sexual release with various categories of prostitutes ran a substantial risk of incurring venereal disease—and of infecting their wives on those relatively rare occasions when they had intercourse with them. So, for the wife, the secret knowledge that if her husband was like most other men he had probably had illicit sexual relations made the act of intercourse a potential danger to her health and to the health of children born of the union; and psychologically, marital sex was a kind of legalized rape. The association of sexual intercourse with disease and with the lower classes did nothing to improve the frame of mind of ladies who felt obliged to submit to their husband's attentions. Thus, the problem compounded itself; the more unpleasant the act of intercourse became to the wife, and the more ingenious the strategies she developed—headaches, debilitation, and a variety of essentially psychosomatic ailments—to avoid intercourse, the more disposed the husband was to seek solace in the arms of an experienced professional.

For an upper-class young male, the ultimate test of the disciplined will came in the matter of whom he married. To marry *beneath* one was, almost certainly, to fall out of the charmed circle of one's class. In a sense, it was the first test. If a man married beneath his social class, he might never have an opportunity to advance to test number two— whether he could earn enough money to maintain his place in that class. Charles Francis Adams spoke with contempt of a friend who had been so weak and foolish as to marry a lower-class woman. The reason such emphasis was placed on a proper marriage was that it was the severest test of self-control. To give way to "love," or sexual attraction (it was inconceivable that any other impulse could induce an upper-class youth to marry beneath him), was to reveal a dangerous and perhaps irreparable "weakness." Thus, to marry beneath one was to initiate a kind of self-fulfilling prophecy. Since such a marriage resulted in social discrimination and often in ostracism, it denied the culprit those helping hands that could otherwise be counted on to advance one's career if one were obedient to the canons of one's class.

The reader will recall Charles Francis Adams's admiration for his father's "Iron Mask." We could hardly find in the literature of American history a more compelling image of the upper-class ideal of the disciplined will. To be self-controlled was never to betray emotion or give way to "foolish" or "shallow" feelings—to loud laughter or, most deplorable of all, to tears. Such behavior was "weak" and "feminine" or "childish." Never to be able to express freely and openly sorrow, tenderness, fear, or exaltation was to cruelly deny the affective life and thereby to warp and distort it.

It was such self-control that made Americans appear to immigrants and visitors from countries where a more expressive emotional life prevailed as cold and unresponsive. It sometimes seems that the one emotion that Americans felt it was legitimate to express was anger. Anger was used in home and school (in school in the ritualized form of whippings) to instill in children the rudiments of that disciplined will that must become an essential part of their character if they were to succeed in life.

Anger, reinforced by the giving and withholding of love, was the means by which character—self-control—was shaped. For Jefferson, like Adams, indolence was the supreme vice. He wrote to his eleven-year-old daughter: "I expect you will write to me by every post. Inform me what books you read, what tunes you learn. . . . Take care that you never spell a word wrong. . . . I have placed my happiness on seeing you good and accomplished, and no distress which the world can now bring on me could equal that of your disappointing my hopes. If you love me then, strive to be good under every situation."

It was a theme constantly reiterated by Jefferson in his correspondence with his daughters: Work hard and learn your lessons or I will withhold my love. There are two ways to view such, to the modern mind (which is not, after all, the ultimate mind), severe means of "internalizing" values or creating modes of behavior in the younger members of "the rising generation." One is that they were, in essence, arbitrary deformations of the human personality that came to distinguish, in largely negative ways, the "American character." The other is that they were techniques for instilling in young men and women qualities that were, in practical fact, essential to survival in our society; that they must be understood primarily in terms of the psychic price paid, generation after generation, for the "complex destiny" of being an American. There is ample evidence that those upper-class young American males who failed to master their natural inclinations often came to very dismal ends.

In the older cities the upper class clung doggedly to its privileges and did its best to rebuff those newly rich pushing their way up from below. Benjamin Franklin had tried to reassure his English friend about the dangers of luxury in a republic by predicting that those who indulged themselves in material things would soon become bankrupt and drop to the lower levels of society. That proved to be only partially the case. William Manning's diagnosis proved the more accurate. The Massachusetts farmer's account of the strategies by which the upper class—the "few"—maintained its status can hardly be improved upon. But Manning, not surprisingly, had no notion of the high psychic cost of holding one's position in those exalted ranks.

48

Whatever Happened to the Founding Fathers?

W hen John Quincy Adams was chosen president by the House of Representatives in 1825, his father was in his eighty-ninth year and Jefferson was eighty-one. Madison was seventy-three. There were other relics of the Revolution, but they were fewer in number with every passing year. Thirty-eight years had passed since the delegates to the Federal Convention had put their names to the Constitution. In the intervening years, the "signers," the delegates to the Convention, and other lesser "Fathers" had watched the country that they, in a real sense, had created, grow and change in ways they could not possibly have imagined.

Most of the Founding Fathers were, by definition, Federalists, and the majority remained so, especially in the North. Changing social customs and political attitudes made them seem increasingly like anachronisms. Most of them had little sympathy with the crude and assertive democracy that was springing up around them, with the luxury so conspicuously displayed by an aggressive middle class, or with the fever of speculation in Western lands and canals (though, as we have noted, many of them were caught up in that same fever). They observed with dismay the course of events in Europe and pondered over their implications for the future of the American Republic. Most distressing of all were the signs of a growing chasm between the Slave States and the Free States.

Benjamin Rush lived to witness the beginning of the War of 1812, but his perpetual optimism had begun to wane well before that and more and more he found his consolations in religion. A few weeks before his death in 1813, he wrote to John Adams that he was worn out examining candidates for medical degrees and expected "to spend the same number of hours in the same dull, mechanical, and fatiguing business for more than a week to come." But such labors at least served to distract him from the misfortunes of his beloved country. "Oh! worse and worse—omnia in pejus ruunt [everything rushes to destruction]. The blunders, disasters, and disgraces of 1774 and 1775 and 1776 are poor apologies for similar events in 1812 and 1813."

The deaths of two signers of the Declaration of Independence— Benjamin Rush and, a few months later, George Clymer—moved John Adams to note that it was a document "which has too much Credit in the World." He especially lamented the death of Rush. Adams wrote to Mercy Otis Warren: "As a man of Science, Letters, Taste, Sense, Phylosophy, Patriotism, Religion, Moralty, Merit, Usefulness, taken all together Rush has not left his equal in America, nor than I know in the World. In him is taken away, in a manner most sudden and totally unexpected, a main Prop of my Life."

Mercy Warren had deeply offended John Adams by attributing monarchical notions to him in her history of the American Revolution, but by the last years of her life the two old friends had become reconciled. She was dismayed at the general decline in patriotism. "Am I mistaken," she wrote to Adams, "when I observe that the generations of men which have arisen since [the Revolution] have been too notoriously negligent in their enquiries relative to the principles and the foundation of the rights and liberties acquired by the labours and blood of their Ancestors, that with few exceptions they appear a very ignorant and narrow-minded people?"

John Dickinson, who had infuriated John Adams by dragging his feet on the issue of independence in the spring of 1775, later became a strong supporter of Jefferson and the Republicans, denouncing the Jay treaty for what appeared to him to be its anti-French bias. But Dickinson became disillusioned with the French Revolution much sooner than most of his fellow Republicans. In 1803 he wrote and printed anonymously an essay entitled "An Address to the Past,

Present, and Eventual Relations of the United States to France," in which he recanted. "It has become our painful office," he wrote, "to declare that these pleasing hopes have vanished. The virtues appear to be proscribed by ambition. A gigantic power seems animated by the devastating spirit of conquest, and glares with a fierce aspect all around." The only remedy against "the tragedy" of French aggression appeared to Dickinson to be "a conjunction of the naval powers of Britain and these States" to "seize every island [in the Caribbean] held by France and her associates."

Dickinson deplored slavery and opposed its introduction to the territories. In a letter to a Pennsylvania senator in 1804, he urged, "Let the pernicious project, the detestable precedent, never be sanctioned by votes of the sons of liberty."

Dickinson wrote to Mercy Otis Warren in 1806 expressing his gratitude for his good health and adding, "When I look at the State of the world, I see Cause, according to the apostolic Language, to be troubled on every Side, and perplexed; but not despairing. Great Changes have taken place; and as great, I presume, will succeed. Human Affairs are now flowing along in a vast Torrent. It will not continue. It does not appear to Me likely, that any of the Actors in the present Tragedies will establish the Jews in the Land of Canaan." The conversion of the Jews and the Second Coming of Christ, Dickinson suspected, was "an Event . . . two or three Centuries remote." But he took comfort in the belief that "the Sovereign of the Universe can deduce Good out of Evil; and that he is inclined so to do." Dickinson died two years later in his seventy-seventh year, expressing on his deathbed his wish for the "happiness of all mankind, and the blessings of peace to all the nations of the earth."

Tom Paine had not been a delegate to the Federal Convention, but his authorship of Common Sense was enough to qualify him as a Founding Father. Certainly he was, with the possible exception of Jefferson, the most radical member of the American Revolutionary generation. And he was unique in that he had made his way up from the lower levels of British society to play a conspicuous role in American politics. Yet he undoubtedly paid a price for his radicalism and perhaps even more for his lower-class origins. If there were, among the leading American patriots, some who, like Roger Sherman, had begun life in modest circumstances, most were definitely of the upper-middle class or the upper class. Paine was inescapably lower class;

and with his untidiness, his accent, and his tendency to drink too much, he never really became a member of the inner circle of Revolutionary leaders.

Paine shared with Jefferson a deep concern that those elements of a society dispossessed by the institution of private property be adequately compensated. One of his last essays was on the subject of agrarian justice. In primitive, tribal cultures, Paine argued, there was no conception of the private ownership of land—it belonged equally to everyone or to no one. With the coming of civilization and the institution of the private ownership of land, some were excluded from what had once been a common heritage. According to Paine (and Jefferson), the dispossessed should be provided for from general public funds created by a ground rent or fee on all "private" land. In Paine's words, "The first principle of civilization ought to have been, and ought still to be, that the condition of every person born into the world after a state of civilization commences, ought not to be worse than if he had been born before that period." But the fact was that "the conditions of millions in every country in Europe, is far worse than if they had been born before civilization began, or had been born among the Indians of North-America at the present day." Paine's proposal was to create a national fund, "out of which there shall be paid to every person, when arrived at the age of twenty-one years, the sum of fifteen pounds sterling, as a compensation in part, for the loss of his or her natural inheritance, by the introduction of landed property. . . . And also, the sum of ten pounds per annum, during life, to every person now living, at the age of fifty years, and to all others as they shall arrive at that age."

The last years of Paine's life were sad and lonely ones. He died in poverty in 1809 at the age of seventy-two in New Rochelle, New York, where the children of the town sang a bit of doggerel that went: "Poor Tom Paine, there he lies/Nobody weeps and nobody cries." Ten years later William Cobbett, the fierce editor of the Federalist newspaper, *Peter Porcupine's Gazette*, now a radical in British politics, dug up Paine's bones from his neglected grave and carried them back to England, intending to erect a monument to him; the bones were lost, however, and the most original and "common" figure of the Revolution has no burial place.

Charles Pinckney, who at thirty had been the youngest delegate to the Federal Convention and who had spoken so eloquently about the future of the United States and brilliantly analyzed the conflicting economic interests of the various sections of the country, the next year became the governor of South Carolina. He presided over the constitutional convention of that state and was again elected governor under the new constitution for three terms. In 1798 he was elected to the U.S. Senate as a Republican supporter of Thomas Jefferson; and after Jefferson's election he was appointed ambassador to Spain, where we have encountered him assisting substantially in the negotiations leading to the Louisiana Purchase. In 1806 he was elected governor for the fourth time. He supported the War of 1812 enthusiastically and was elected to Congress in 1819–20. He advocated free schools and was "the principal agent of the removal of the civil and religious disabilities" that had been imposed on Jews in South Carolina. Yet Pinckney owned seven plantations and innumerable slaves and was tireless in defense of the South's "peculiar institution." The slave uprising in Santo Domingo filled him with apprehensions about the dangers of a slave revolt in the South. In the debate over the Missouri Compromise, Pinckney fixed his attention especially on the rights of the states to exclude free blacks, and a few years later in his home state he supported the Seamen's Acts of 1822 and 1823, which, following Denmark Vesey's abortive rebellion, stipulated that free blacks on ships entering the port of Charleston must be placed in jail for the duration of their vessel's time in port, the cost of their room and board to be borne by the master of the ship. Nothing more was needed to complete the decline of Charleston as a port and fix its citizens' beleaguered state of mind. The duke of Saxe-Weimar, visiting German immigrants in Charleston in the 1820s, noted in his journal: "Charleston keeps in pay a company of police soldiers, who during the night occupy several posts. . . . This corps owes its support to the fear of the negroes. At nine o'clock in the evening a bell is sounded; and after this no negro can venture out without a written permission from his master, or he will immediately be thrown into prison. . . . Should the master refuse to pay [a] fine, then the slave receives twenty-five lashes."

When Charles Pinckney died in 1824 at the age of sixty-seven, his fears of a slave uprising had come to dominate his thinking on all political and social issues. His precocious talents had been expended in an increasingly shrill denunciation of every effort to improve the lot of the slave or the free black. His democratic ideals lay in ruins.

His cousin, Charles Cotesworth Pinckney, eleven years his senior and as dogged a Federalist as Charles was a Republican, died a year later at the age of seventy-nine. The older Pinckney, like John Jay,

John Dickinson, and Elias Boudinot, had found his principal consolation for the general disarray of the world and the agonizing paradoxes of slavery in the Christian religion; he was founder and president of the Charleston Bible Society.

Pinckney's fellow South Carolinian, Pierce Butler, had been a delegate from that state to the Constitutional Convention. Like Charles Lee and Horatio Gates, Butler was a Briton, a scion of the Irish aristocracy; descendant of the noble Ormond family, he so thoroughly drummed the fact into the citizens of his adopted land that a Democratic "poem" described him: "Pierce Butler next, a man of sterling *worth*/Because he justly claims a noble birth."

Butler had come to America in 1766 in the aftermath of the French and Indian Wars and had fallen in love with and married the Charleston heiress, Polly Middleton. When the war came, Butler, then thirty-one, cast his lot with the Americans. As a leading figure in Charleston social and political circles, Butler was chosen, along with the Pinckneys, to be a delegate to the Constitutional Convention. William Pierce noted of him that "as a politician or an Orator, he has no pretensions to either." It was, in Pierce's view, primarily as "a Gentleman of fortune" that he had been chosen as a delegate. Butler, nonetheless, was one of the most vocal of the delegates, favoring a strong executive but upholding the supremacy of the states over the federal government. It was undoubtedly as a champion of slavery that Butler made his principal mark in the Convention. He "insisted that the labour of a slave in S. Carolina was as productive & valuable as that of a freeman in Massachusetts, that as wealth was the great means of defence and utility to the Nation they were equally valuable to it as freemen; and that consequently an equal representation ought to be allowed for them in a Government that was instituted principally for the protection of property, and was itself to be supported by property." In the waning days of the debate he joined Charles Pinckney in a motion "to require fugitive slaves and servants to be delivered up like criminals."

Butler was elected to the first U.S. Senate from South Carolina. There he was a classic Southern firebrand, who, in Maclay's words, "flamed like a meteor," and charged his colleagues "with a design of oppressing South Carolina." He was against any trade whatever, he declared; against "encouraging. . . . Foreigners of every kind to come and take away our produce." Maclay judged him "the most local and partial creature I ever heard open a mouth." A few days later Butler "flamed away, and threatened a dissolution of the Union with regard to his State, *as sure as God was in the firmament!*" Butler soon identified himself with the Jeffersonian faction in the Senate and was an often rancorous opponent of the Federalists.

With the invention of the cotton gin, Butler, already wealthy, retired from politics, established plantations on several of the Georgia sea islands, and in that lush soil raised the long-fibered cotton that brought a premium price from British buyers. He invested the profits in Philadelphia real estate and in lands in western Pennsylvania, dividing his time between Philadelphia and his Southern plantations, so vividly described years later by the famous English actress Fanny Kemble, who married his grandson, Pierce Mease Butler.

Butler was the prototype of the successful exploiter of the burgeoning cotton economy, the absentee landowner whose unhappy slaves were left in the charge of an overseer, often a transplanted New Englander whose only responsibility was to make money for his employers. When he died in 1822 at the age of seventy-eight he, like Charles Pinckney, had come to measure every issue by its relation to slavery.

Although Elias Boudinot did not sign the Declaration of Independence or participate in the Federal debates, he was a leading patriot in New Jersey, twice president of the Continental Congress, and the first director of the mint. Like his friend John Dickinson, Boudinot, after his retirement from public life, became preoccupied with advancing the cause of Christianity and the particular issue of the millennium— Christ's Second Coming. As a philanthropist, a trustee of Princeton for almost fifty years, and a writer on theological issues, Boudinot was a model of republican "civic virtue" and an ardent defender of the Constitution. He had been alarmed at the Republican efforts to alter that document in the early years of the new government and wrote to Timothy Pickering: "Perhaps we old-fashioned folk may feel more keenly every innovation on the Constitution from former Experience of the evil Consequences of unrestrained power in Man of any description. I fear many of our mistakes arise from the fashionable mistake, that our Government is a Republican one. Altho' this may be true in a strict sense, it is certainly not so in the popular or democratic Idea of the term. Our Government was intended by its formers, and really is in fact, to be a mixed Government, properly balanced, partaking, in a wise proportion, of all the forms of Government, Monarchic, Aristocratic & Democratic. . . . In short I consider the Constitution, to be the foundation of all our political happiness, and when that is gone, I see nothing before us, but anarchy & Confusion. . . . If a Constitution is to be altered on the Spur of every occasional Event, there is an End to its usefulness."

Like most of the Founding Fathers, Boudinot was deeply concerned about the practical consequences of Christianity. A strong supporter of the Theological Seminary at Princeton, he wrote, "I have wished, among other improvements in Theological Studies, a Professorship of Common Sense & Prudence was established. . . . I really have known so many ruinous Errors in practice, among our pious & zealous Ministers, for want of this celestial quality."

Boudinot's interest in domestic and foreign missions prompted him to found one of the first Bible societies for the distribution of the Scriptures and the support of missionary work, and he became the first president of the American Bible Society in 1816.

Boudinot deplored the excesses of the French Revolution and saw Napoleon as a kind of Antichrist. The administrations of Jefferson and Madison, not surprisingly, seemed to him wrongheaded and misled. "The good folks at Washington are at their wits' end, and scarcely know how to get out of the Toils they have entangled themselves with," he wrote a friend early in Madison's administration. "Property is at a low Ebb. It must rise unless we are all ruined together, and then it matters not much."

Boudinot's principal philanthropic interest was in the Indians. His book, *Star in the West, or A Humble Attempt to Discover the Long Lost Ten Tribes of Israel Preparatory to Their Return to Their Beloved City, Jerusalem,* published in 1816, was part of that considerable literature that undertook to prove that the Indians were the Jews of the Diaspora. Boudinot's concern with the Indians was not limited to the theoretical. In his will he left 4,542 acres of land in Lycoming County, Pennsylvania, for philanthropies to the Indians, and an additional gift of five thousand dollars for missionary work among them.

Another five hundred dollars went to the Institution for Instructing and Educating the Heathen. A young Cherokee named Galagina came to the school in 1818 and took the name of Elias Boudinot. The Indian Boudinot returned to his tribe to become one of its leaders, publishing a weekly newspaper in English and Cherokee and translating a portion of the New Testament into his native language. At the time of the Cherokee removal, the red-skinned Elias Boudinot signed a treaty accepting the removal without tribal approval and was assassinated for his pains a few years later.

Boudinot also left money to buy spectacles for "poor old people so they could read the Bible in their declining years." The Public Hospital in Philadelphia was left 3,270 acres of land to help pay the hospital bills of indigent foreigners and 13,000 acres of woodland were left to the mayor and Corporation of Philadelphia to provide firewood for the poor.

Perhaps Boudinot's most unusual bequest was to "aid and assist in promoting the settlement of a body of Jews who have been represented . . . as desirous of removing from the continent of Europe to some asylum of safety . . . where they may be able to examine and judge for themselves into the great things of our divine religion without fear or terror." Each family, up to the number of fifteen, was to receive fifty acres of land. The concern for the Jews was also evidenced in Boudinot's organization of the American Society for Ameliorating the Condition of the Jews a year before his death at the age of eighty-one. It was Boudinot's hope that the conversion of the Jews and the Indians to Christianity would hasten the millennium.

Like so many of his colleagues, John Jay in retirement devoted himself to church activities; he was one of the founders and the first president of the Westchester Bible Society and later, in 1821, a successor to Boudinot as president of the American Bible Society. He professed to eschew current politics. "The post, once a week, brings me our newspapers," he wrote, "which furnish a history of the times. By this history, as well as by that of former times, we are taught the vanity of expecting, that from the perfectibility of human nature and the lights of philosophy the multitude will become virtuous or wise, or their demagogues candid and honest." Jay died in 1829 at the age of eighty-four.

Charles Carroll of Carrolton, a signer of the Declaration of Independence from Maryland, had the distinction of being the last surviving signer when he died at ninety-five in 1832. The last third of Carroll's life, after he left the U.S. Senate in 1800, was devoted to his land speculations and business enterprises. He was a prominent figure in the development of the Potomac Company and its successor, the Chesapeake and Ohio Canal Company, and was on the original board of directors of the Baltimore and Ohio Railroad, whose first tie he laid on July 4, 1828. By the time of his death he was reputed to be the richest man in the United States.

James Madison, who had made the awkward transition from constitutional theorist and intellectual to practical politician and had the unhappy role of presiding over a country engaged in a foreign war and torn by internal conflict, retired to Montpelier, not far from Monticello, where he spent nearly twenty years, in the words of a nineteenth-century biographer, "with books and friends" in a "sweet and tranquil old age." Madison's case is, in a way, the most interesting of all. In the Federal Convention and in *The Federalist Papers* he had given the archetypal statement of the philosophic assumptions of the Classical-Christian Consciousness. Then, as we have noted, he converted to Jeffersonian democracy. But, one wonders, with what reservations? Was he actually wooed and won over to the notion of the perfectibility of man and a progressive view of history, or did he simply suppress his misgivings and go along with his charismatic leader and fellow Virginian? How could the champion of a strong national government so readily switch to the heretical states' rights doctrines of the Virginia and Kentucky Resolutions?

In 1829, he emerged from retirement to participate in the convention called to revise the Virginia constitution of 1776. In it he restated his political philosophy. Government was instituted for "the rights of persons and the rights of property. . . . These rights cannot well be separated. . . . The essence of Government is power; and power, lodged as it must be in human hands, will ever be liable to abuse." In monarchies, "the interests and happiness of all may be sacrificed to the caprice and passions of a despot." In aristocracies, "the rights and welfare of the many may be sacrificed to the pride and cupidity of the few." In republics the great danger was that "the majority may not sufficiently respect the rights of the minority." Some of his colleagues seemed inclined to trust "social feelings," "respect for character," moral constraints. "But man," Madison continued, in tones similar to those he had used some forty-two years earlier in the Federal Convention, "is known to be a selfish as well as a social being. . . . We all know that conscience is not a sufficient safeguard; and besides, that conscience itself may be deluded; may be misled by an unconscious bias, into acts which an enlightened conscience would forbid." Madison's point was in reference to the rights of "the colored part of our populations." They had rights that must be protected, and proper measures were "due to justice; due to humanity; due to truth; to the sympathies of our nature; in fine to our character as a people, both abroad and at home." It was his conviction that the slaves should be viewed, "as much as possible, in the light of human beings, and not as mere property." Ironically, Madison's eloquence was expended in behalf of a state constitutional provision that would allow representation from Virginia counties on the basis of slave as well as free population in the lower house and free population alone in the upper house.

The Union itself seemed to Madison "a wonder; the harmonious establishment of a common Government over them all, a miracle." Another miracle would clearly be needed to preserve it, but he still dared to hope for one.

One of Madison's most interesting observations concerned the future rate of growth of the population at the United States. Based on the period since the Revolution, Madison projected a population of 192 million in a hundred years, or by 1929. Madison speculated that such a growth in population might have as a concomitant a scarcity of capital "for the expensive establishments which facilitate labour [presumably factories] and cheapen its products on the one hand, and, on the other, of the capacity to purchase the costly and ornamental articles consumed by the wealthy alone." The wealthy must then "cease to be idlers and become labourers."

One of Madison's last papers concerned the issue of sovereignty. In his rather convoluted argument upholding the notion of "divided sovereignty" and the rights of the states vis-à-vis the national government, Madison bespoke his own "dividedness" and that of his region. The power of the federal government was, he insisted, derived from a compact with the states. The Union had not deprived the states "of that corporate existence which would in the event of a dissolution, voluntary or violent, of the Constitution replace them in the separate communities, that being the condition in which they entered into the compact." While Madison was promulgating, with many evasions and qualifications, a doctrine of secession, it must be remembered that many New England Federalists had expounded the same doctrine during the period of the embargo and the War of 1812 and that as the slavery issue grew more bitter, many Northern abolitionists would advocate splitting the Union into Slave and Free States.

But if Madison allowed for, or was evasive on, the issue of secession, in his last public papers he specifically rejected the doctrine of nullification put forth by the legislature of South Carolina. "The true question," Madison wrote, "is whether a single state has a constitutional right to annul or suspend the operation of a law of the U.S. within its limits, the State remaining a member of the Union, and admitting the Constitution to be in force. . . . A plainer contradiction in terms, or a more fatal inlet to anarchy, cannot be imagined." Madison went on to denounce such a doctrine "in its naked and suicidal form."

After his death a sheet was found among Madison's papers that read, in part: "As this advice, if it ever sees the light will not do it till I am no more, it may be considered as coming from the tomb where the truth alone can be respected, and the happiness of man alone consulted." It came from one "who has served his Country in various stations through a period of forty years, who espoused in his youth and adhered through his life to the cause of its liberty and who has borne a part in most of the transactions which will constitute epochs of its destiny.

"The advice nearest to my heart and deepest in my convictions is that the Union of the States be cherished and perpetuated. Let the open enemy to it be regarded as a Pandora with her box opened; and the disguised one, as the Serpent creeping with his deadly wiles into Paradise."

In other words, disunionists were agents of the Devil himself, the fatal tempter, insinuating himself into the Garden. It is a measure of Madison's anguish that he, always so moderate and discreet in his public utterances, the model of the restrained and rational intelligence, should have turned, at the end of his life, to such grim mixed biblical and classical metaphors to express his anxiety about the future of his country.

Gouverneur Morris, the stylist of the Constitution, was, as we have suggested earlier, the most exotic of the Founding Fathers. He had a mordant wit and a gift for phrasemaking. A skeptic if not a cynic, he had little hope for the long life of the document he had played such an important role in framing. From the beginnings of the federal government he was, as we have noted on more than one occasion, a constant and invariably entertaining commentator on the progress (or decline) of the new nation.

Morris was, of course, thoroughly conservative in his politics, but he was by no means a doctrinaire conservative and his observations on people and politics are full of surprises. Certainly he had no notion that the Constitution was a perfect work. He shared, to a considerable degree, the views of his friend Hamilton who had acquiesced in the Constitution though he "disliked it" and "detested . . . democratical government." He attributed to Hamilton the conviction "that democracy, ending in tyranny, is, while it lasts, a cruel and oppressing domination." It was plain that the materials for creating a conventional aristocracy "do not exist in America; therefore taking the people as a mass in which there was nothing of family, wealth, prejudice, or habit to raise a permanent mound of distinction . . . he considered the fate of Rome . . . and that of Athens . . . as the portraits of our future fortune. Moreover the extent of the United States led [Hamilton] to fear a defect of national sentiment. That which, at the time our Constitution was formed, had been generated by friendship in the Revolutionary War, was sinking under the pressure of State interest, commercial rivalry, the pursuit of wealth, and those thousand giddy projects which the intoxication of independence, an extravagant idea of our own importance, a profound ignorance of other nations, the prostration of public credit and the paucity of our resources had engendered."

Morris felt that Hamilton believed that the aristocratic or modified monarchical form of government he desired could come about only "as the result of a civil war, and I suspect," Morris added, "that his belief in that which he called an impending crisis arose from a conviction that the kind of government most suitable, in his opinion, to this extensive country, could be established in no other way."

The reason Morris himself had concurred in the Constitution, imperfect as it was, was "that nothing human can be perfect . . . that the old Confederation was worse; and . . . that there was no reason, at that time, to suppose our public morals would be so soon and so entirely corrupted. . . . Surrounded by difficulties, we did the best we could, leaving it with those who should come after us to take counsel from experience, and exercise prudently the power of amendment which we had provided." The United States seemed to Morris an enigma beyond penetrating. He wrote to a friend: "I have told you that, with respect to this country, calculation outruns fancy, and still fact goes beyond calculation."

As to the future of the Republic, Morris's hopes rose and fell. While he shared Hamilton's skepticism about democracy, he differed from him in that he did not expect much better from other systems of government. "Those who expect to bring men right by reasoning," he wrote to a friend, "pay an unmerited compliment to human nature. A nation must suffer severely before it can be reformed. The Jewish history contains a clear explanation of that great riddle—man. Make him a slave, you make him humble and base—a scoundrel; make him a democrat, you make him proud, ungrateful, a rascal; make him subject to just laws and a wise administration, work hard and live moderately, you make him industrious, virtuous, happy, a good husband, a good father, a good citizen."

In Morris's view, history was the great teacher, and citizens of a democracy had little time or inclination to reflect upon its lessons; hence their shallowness and impatience. "Those," he wrote, "who will not trust the experience of history are incapable of political knowledge." "America," he noted to a friend, "will at length learn some of those things which an attentive study of the ancients long since taught you. The people of the United States will discover that every kind of government is liable to evil; that the best is that which has the fewest faults; that the excellence even of that best depends more on its fitness for the nation where it is established than on intrinsic perfection. . . . One thing is certain, democracy cannot last. It is . . . the natural death of republics . . . in reality, there are but two forms of government, monarchy and aristocracy . . . be the complexion of a government monarchic or aristocratic, it can do little when unsupported by public sentiment."

Morris was gloomy about the tendency of Congress to usurp the powers of the judiciary. Once the representatives had comprehended that "their power has no bound except their discretion . . . the more they feel their power the less will be their discretion. Authority so placed is liable as well to excess as to abuse, and this country, unless I am mistaken, will experience not a little of both." Even a mob, "a whimsical legislature and a wild tribunal . . . has, in the midst of its madness, some sense of national honor and some regard for justice." But a body of representatives, "when influenced by Faction, will do acts of cruelty and baseness which the most profligate among them would, in his personal character, be ashamed to avow."

"The dangerous doctrine" that the public will, "expressed by a numerical majority, is in all cases to be obeyed," was, to Morris, the essence of popular tyranny and what the Supreme Court had been fashioned to prevent. "That numerical majority not only may, but frequently does, *will* what is unwise and unjust."

To Morris, the crucial question became, increasingly, that of slavery. He had inveighed in the Federal Convention against slaves' being counted as part of the population for purposes of representation while being denied all human rights. Now he associated himself with those who began to call for a separation of the Free States from the Slave States. Yet his hopes for an enduring Union alternated with his pessimism, and in his last public utterance he called for his fellow citizens "to forget party and think of our country. . . . It has been the unvarying principle of my life, that the interest of our country must be preferred over every other interest."

Almost sixty years old, Morris scandalized many of his friends by marrying for the first time a woman half his age. Anne Cary had been involved in the most notorious scandal of the day. Living with her sister, Judith Cary Randolph, the wife of Richard Randolph, at the Randolph estate, Bizarre, in Virginia, Anne was accused of having had an affair with her brother-in-law. She apparently became pregnant by him and had a stillborn child that she tried to dispose of, hoping to keep the liaison a secret. She had been charged with murder, or infanticide, defended by Patrick Henry, and acquitted. She then returned to Bizarre with her sister and brother-in-law, Richard. When Richard died several years later under rather mysterious circumstances, his brother, John Randolph, was convinced that Anne Cary had killed him.

After Richard Randolph's death, Anne Cary moved to New York and met and married Gouverneur Morris, who wrote: "If I had married a rich woman of seventy the world might think it wiser than to take one of half my age without a farthing, and, if the world were to live with my wife, I should certainly have consulted its taste; but as that happens not to be the case, I thought I might, without offending others endeavor to suit myself, and look rather into the head and heart than into the pocket."

John Randolph did his best to bias Morris against his young bride by writing a letter denouncing her as a murderess and adulteress and warning Morris that she would poison him.

In the last year of his life Morris replied to a letter from Timothy Pickering, inquiring about his role in the Federal Convention. If he had it to do over again, he assured Pickering, he would do as he had done that famous summer—"What I should do now is what I did then, my sentiments and opinions having undergone no essential change in forty years." And to an old friend he wrote, "How large a portion of human life! How eventful a period in the history of mankind! . . . I lead a quiet and, more than most of my fellow-mortals, a happy life. The woman to whom I am married has much genius, is well-educated, and possesses, with an affectionate temper, industry and a love of order." He had not married earlier because he was determined to find "a fine woman who could love an old man."

Like so many of his age, he had some appropriate reflections on his deathbed. "Sixty-four years ago it pleased the Almighty to call me into existence—here, on this spot, in this very room; and now shall I complain that he is pleased to call me hence?" He asked about the weather outside, and being told the day was a bright and clear one, he replied: "A beautiful day, yes, but—

> Who, to dumb forgetfulness a prey,
>   This pleasing, anxious being yet resigned—
> Left the warm precincts of the cheerful day,
>   Nor cast one longing, lingering look behind?"

Besides the abundant elements of tragedy in history, there is an ineffable poignance in the simple passage of time as measured by individual lives. Many of the Founders, as we have seen, survived well into the new century. A few—Jefferson, Adams, Jay, Madison, and Carroll prominent among them—lived for a half century or more after the Declaration of American Independence and thus witnessed, in addition to the extraordinary growth of the United States itself, so far beyond their wildest dreams, the terrible convulsions of Europe during the Napoleonic wars, the most prolonged and devastating upheaval of modern times. Many, as we have seen, served their country as politicians and diplomats, especially the latter, and when they retired gave their attention to the advancement of Christianity through the encouragement of missionary activity. Their religious convictions, uncommonly strong, ranged from Calvinistic orthodoxy to the most eccentric heterodoxy; from Unitarianism to the wildest millennial expectations. A striking number took both a scholarly and a philanthropic interest in the American Indians. Almost without exception, they despaired in varying degrees, at one time or another, of the future of the Republic.

Most intriguing of all, in a time when men were "old" by their mid-fifties and often died in their sixties, most of the Founding Fathers lived well into their seventies and eighties. In other words, they seem to have defied the "actuarial tables" of their times—perhaps because they were so centrally involved in, and energized by, one of the great events of world history.

Here, of course, we have only a sampling of the subsequent lives of the Founders, but hopefully it is enough to give a sense of their response to the unfolding history of the Republic they had created and their reality as human beings rather than merely as figures in history. In addition, their reflections on the "enormities" of their times give us invaluable reference points for the early decades of the new age.

49

Lafayette in America

In France the restoration of the Bourbons in 1818 in the person of Louis XVIII, the brother of the monarch who had lost his head in the French Revolution, brought with it a strong reaction against the principles of the French Revolution. Lafayette, elected to Parliament with a handful of Liberals in 1822, served as an unwelcome reminder of the opening phases of the Revolution, when so much had been hoped for. Fearing him as a symbol of revolutionary idealism, the Royalists, while they dared not arrest him, had left no stone unturned to defeat him in the next parliamentary election, even to changing the election laws. His defeat and his consequent evocation of America as the only hope of freedom inspired Congress to invite the general, then in his sixty-seventh year, to visit the United States.

Although deeply in debt, in large part because of his generosity toward the hungry peasants of his estate at La Grange, Lafayette declined the offer of a United States frigate and took passage for America on a merchant vessel, the *Cadmus*. With him the general brought one of his sons, George Washington Lafayette, and a radical young Scotswoman, Frances Wright, an admirer of America and a constant though discreet companion of Lafayette on his journey.

Approaching the shoreline of New York, the Marquis—although

he had renounced his title before the Constituent Assembly of the Revolution in 1790, in the United States, so fond of titled foreigners, he was still the Marquis—stood at the rail of the *Cadmus* and wept. The ship dropped anchor, and soon a steamboat, evidence of the advance of science in the Republic, tied up alongside. It was Sunday, Lafayette was reminded, and since it would be unsuitable to receive him on the Lord's Day, the celebration welcoming him would be held on Monday. The next day a delegation from the board of aldermen of New York City steamed out on the *Chancellor Livingston* to conduct him to the city; aboard were a West Point band that played the *Marseillaise*, now outlawed in France, and a contingent of veterans of the Revolution. One of the veterans, eighty-five-year-old Colonel Willet, asked Lafayette if he remembered him from the Battle of Monmouth, when he had been an aide to General Charles Scott. "I saw you in the heat of battle. You were but a boy, but you were a serious and sedate lad. Ay, ay; I remember well. And on the Mohawk, I sent you fifty Indians and you wrote me that they set up such a yell that they frightened the British horses and they fled one way and the Indians another." Other reminiscences poured out while the aldermen watched in some embarrassment, and once more the Marquis wept.

As the *Chancellor Livingston* approached the Battery, Lafayette could see the shores lined with cheering crowds. At the dock, the militiamen assigned as his special guard wore on their chests portraits of the Marquis; the rest displayed ribbons proclaiming: "Welcome La Fayette." The shore forts and the warships in the harbor all fired salutes as Lafayette was carried in an open barouche along Broadway to New York City Hall, where he was met by the mayor and where the citizens of the city and its environs filed by to shake his hand. After two hours of this classic democratic ceremony Lafayette was granted a respite. Thereafter he allotted two hours every morning for five successive days to the ritual. People came in seemingly endless lines: veterans of the Revolution, women with children in arms, boys and girls who had read in their history books of the exploits of the hero. Tears were abundant. And memories. Every afternoon there was a fête, and every night a banquet. George Washington Lafayette, with that magic name, received almost as much attention as his father. Samuel Morse was commissioned to paint the general's portrait.

Finally, Lafayette had to leave New York, with thousands of hands still unshaken, and make his way to New England, riding through triumphal arches and greeting veterans along the way. At Putnam's

Hill on the Boston Post Road, he passed through an arch decorated with Republican symbols and was addressed by a survivor of the Revolution, who concluded his remarks by saying, "Sir, America loves you." "And Sir," Lafayette replied, "I truly love America."

On he went, through Stamford, Bridgeport, and New Haven, Connecticut, everywhere to the touching and tumultuous greetings of a people delirious at catching sight of this authentic reminder of the nation's birth. Benjamin Talmadge, who had been one of Washington's young aides and to whom we are indebted for the dramatic scene of Washington's parting with his officers—his "weeping children"—at Fraunces Tavern at the end of the Revolution, rode all night to see the Marquis, and although now an old man, "without introduction was recognized and embraced by him." Another old soldier said to Lafayette, "I saw you, General, dismount from your horse and at the head of your division ford the Schuylkill then four feet deep on two cold nights in succession!" With tears running down his cheeks, the old officer turned to those surrounding Lafayette and said, "Yes, he never shunned any fatigue or danger and always led the way!"

Some of the journey occurred, of necessity, after dark, and then the processions accompanying his carriage carried torches, and bonfires were built on the hills along the way. Bells were rung in the village churches and ancient bugles sounded. It was two o'clock in the morning when Lafayette reached Roxbury on the outskirts of Boston, but Governor William Eustis of Massachusetts was awaiting him with a crowd bearing torches and rockets, the latter discharged at the general's arrival. He spent the night at the governor's mansion, and when he awoke a few hours later what appeared to be his old Light Infantry was drawn up on the lawn with red-and-black plumes—the Marquis's colors—in their hats. Roused by the music of their band, he went to the window and called to his son, "My brave Light Infantry! It is exactly like that that they were uniformed! What courage! What resignation! And how I loved them!" Once more he was overcome by tears.

Boston was determined to outdo New York in its greeting. Lafayette was passed from the governor to the mayor of Boston— Josiah Quincy, five times reelected, as great a figure in the life of that city as De Witt Clinton was in New York. Progress was slow through the jammed streets, and at the entrance to the city the procession stopped while free punch was served to the crowd. Then Mayor Quincy delivered an official welcome, assuring the Marquis that the vast assemblage was "not the movement of a turbulent populace excited by the fresh laurels of some recent conqueror," but a free people displaying "a grave, moral, intellectual impulse."

On the Boston Common a battery of 101 guns fired round after round of salutes as the official party made its way under a series of arches along Boylston Street, one of which bore the words:

> The fathers in glory shall sleep
> Who gathered with thee to the fight;
> But the sons will eternally keep
> The tablet of gratitude bright.

> We bow not the neck
> And we bend not the knee
> But our hearts, La Fayette,
> We surrender to thee.

Three thousand schoolchildren dressed in the colors of France were gathered on Boston Common. One of them ran forward to place a wreath of immortelles on Lafayette's head. Assembled with the state and city dignitaries in Charles Bulfinch's noble State House, the Marquis was addressed by Governor Eustis, who was so overcome with emotion that he was forced to hand his speech to an aide to read. The Marquis's response was the epitome of Gallic graciousness. When he was later complimented on his fluency in English, he replied, "And why should I not, being an American just returned from a long visit to Europe?" On Sunday the general went to church at the Brattle Street meetinghouse and sat in John Hancock's pew as he had done almost a half century earlier.

After church, he rode out to Quincy to visit with John Adams, now in his eighty-ninth year. Adams's hands were too palsied to carry his food to his mouth; his grandchildren had to feed him, and if the plain New England meal was perhaps not much to the general's liking, there was a feast of conversation. After the general departed, Adams reported himself "highly delighted" with the visit but noted, "That was not the Lafayette I knew"; and the general, saddened by Adams's obvious infirmities, went off declaring, "That was not the John Adams I knew."

In the five days at Boston, the general attended a Harvard

commencement and heard young Edward Everett, who was reputed to have a great career ahead of him as an orator, deliver the principal address on "The Circumstances Favorable to the Progress of Literature in America." Then it was off to Portsmouth, New Hampshire, the trip interrupted by celebrations in every hamlet the general's party passed through, for another ecstatic welcome. Returning to Boston for a hasty lunch and a few quick farewell visits to old friends, Lafayette set out on the Lexington-Concord road west and south to New York. Ralph Waldo Emerson, standing on the steps of the First Parish Church, was among the citizens of the latter town who watched him go by.

At Hartford, Connecticut, he visited the splendid new Asylum for the Deaf and Dumb, the first such institution in the country, and then boarded a packet for New York. Finally he could sleep, although a band played on the deck above him and guns along the shore fired perpetual salutes.

Lafayette was back in New York on September 6, in time for an extravagent celebration in honor of his sixty-eighth birthday. Before the toasts that concluded the meal, a curtain was raised at the end of the hall unveiling a picture of Washington and Lafayette clasping hands in front of the altar of freedom. Even that was not enough. Another fête and ball were planned at Castle Garden, the largest hall in the city. There six thousand guests assembled to dine and dance. At two the next morning, while the party was still in full swing, Lafayette and his son were carried out to the *James Kent* and steamed up the Hudson to West Point, where the general, standing at the rail, told his son how Washington had discovered Benedict Arnold's plot to betray his commander in chief and the fort: how Washington, at breakfast, had read the dispatches that revealed Arnold's treachery without showing the slightest sign of emotion, left the dining room after finishing his meal, and then, in the hallway, had thrown his arms around Lafayette's neck and burst into tears.

The journey had not a few moments of democratic absurdity. At Albany an elaborate apparatus had been designed to lower a stuffed eagle, clutching a laurel wreath in its talons, from the ceiling above Lafayette's head. The eagle was to deposit the wreath on the general's brow as he dined, but things went awry and it descended precipitately, striking him a glancing blow and showering the table with feathers.

On and on it went—from Albany to Newark, to Philadelphia,

Baltimore, Washington, Charleston, and finally to New Orleans. He was like a national treasure, like the ark of the covenant that must be carried throughout the land to restore and heal all that was broken and divided. Perhaps his procession could serve to bind the country together once more, the tracks of his carriage laying down in the dusty roads over which it passed a thinly traced but magic cord of memory. What must he have thought of it all, this man who had seen so much history, who had been borne on its tides and tossed by its waves so that his life had been often in peril? He drew on remarkable emotional as well as physical resources to endure the endless evocations of the Revolutionary days by all those old soldiers who retrieved and burnished their memories, ancient talismanic images stored in the cabinets of their minds, and offered them to the Frenchman to be blessed by his remembering. "Yes, *mais oui*, of course I remember. Brandywine, Germantown, Monmouth. Yes, yes, of course, I remember."

One of the most poignant moments of Lafayette's visit was his meeting at Bordentown, New Jersey, with Joseph Bonaparte, Napoleon's brother. Joseph Bonaparte had been placed by Napoleon on the throne of Naples and then of Spain. Twice driven from the Spanish throne and twice restored, he had been defeated by Wellington at Vitoria, had fled Spain, and then, after his brother's defeat at Waterloo, had escaped to the United States under an assumed name, planning to meet Napoleon there. As one biographer wrote, "His benevolence and hospitality, his affable and courtly manners, and his knowledge and taste, made him a general favorite." Indeed, Bonaparte and his charming daughters were lionized by American society. In the mad swirlings of the French Revolution he and Lafayette had been, at various times, friends and coadjutors. Their meeting was full, one might say, of compressed history, and when they parted, Joseph said, "Permit me to leave you at my frontier, and to give you once again to the tenderness of Americans, who claim the happy right to pay you the honours of their country."

Philadelphia revived the ghost of the Grand Procession—bands and militia companies; Revolutionary veterans in carriages; floats representing, as they had on that July Fourth, thirty-six years before, the various crafts and trades of the city. After the parade, Lafayette stood for hours shaking hands with well-wishers in Independence Hall until his hand and arm were sore. In one of the official gatherings, Lafayette caught sight of old Charles Willson Peale. Poor and eccentric, Peale had not been included among the dignitaries. Lafayette, with characteristic tact, embraced the old man and took his place beside him.

In Washington, Lafayette found himself in the midst of the hectic election of 1824 with Clay, Adams, Crawford, and Jackson locked in a struggle for the presidency. An aide of Lafayette's, Auguste Levasseur, who also acted as chronicler of the journey, noted that President Monroe had a simple democratic manner and that he and his Cabinet all wore unpretentious swallow-tailed coats without decorations or any of "those puerile ornaments for which so many ninnies dance attendance in the ante-chambers of the palaces of Europe."

Since Lafayette was out of favor with the restored Bourbons, his visit gave his American hosts an opportunity to indulge in one of their favorite literary exercises—denouncing kings. During Lafayette's visit, Louis XVIII died in 1824 after ten years of uneasy and increasingly authoritarian rule and was succeeded by his brother, Charles X. In Baltimore, the editor of *Niles' Weekly Register* expressed his view that the "king-and-priest-ridden population of the European continent, the white slaves of Russia, Prussia and Austria, and the degraded people of France, with the miserable wretches . . . that inhabit Spain . . . cannot have anything more like a just conception of our feelings, as associated with the arrival of General La Fayette, than a Hottentot possesses of algebra."

Lafayette visited Mount Vernon and walked up the hill behind the house to the tomb of that other general to whom he had been so like a son. There he knelt alone by the marble sarcophagus, then came out in tears and took his son and Levasseur with him back into the tomb, where all three knelt and kissed the sarcophagus.

As they left the enclosure, George Washington Custis, Martha Washington's grandson by her first husband, a gentleman rather inclined to pomposity, advanced toward Lafayette holding up a ring and intoned: "Last of the generals of the Army of Independence! At this awful and impressive moment, when, forgetting the splendour of a triumph greater than the Roman consul ever had, you bend with reverence over the remains of Washington, the child of Mt. Vernon presents you with this token containing the hair of him whom while living you loved, and to whose honoured grave you now pay the manly and affecting tribute of a patriot's and a soldier's tear. The ring has ever been an emblem of the union of hearts . . . and this will unite the affections of all Americans to the person and posterity of La Fayette, now and hereafter. . . . Surely where liberty dwells, there must be the country of Lafayette."

Custis then offered the Marquis a final resting place beside Washington when the appointed hour should come. To which Lafayette gave thanks and replied, "I pay a silent homage to the tomb of the greatest and best of men, my paternal friend."

Custis then showed Lafayette around the house and pointed out the key to the Bastille, still hanging where Washington had placed it beside the letter the Marquis had sent him describing the first dramatic moment of the French Revolution.

From Mount Vernon the trail led on to Yorktown. Now the reenactment took on, if possible, an even more heavily symbolic character. The general spent the night in the house that had been Cornwallis's headquarters. The next day, shaded by Washington's tent, brought down from Mount Vernon for the occasion, Lafayette greeted the officers of regiments that had assembled in honor of the occasion and a handful of veterans who had come, some from considerable distances, to see the Marquis. Two fainted from the excitement. That night there was a grand dinner and a ball lit by Cornwallis's candles, found that morning in the cellar of his former headquarters.

But all the three-month-long procession, with its seemingly inexhaustible major and minor dramas and striking incidents, had been for many Americans simply a prelude to that moment when Lafayette and Jefferson would be reunited at Monticello. That meeting took place in early November. Before an awed and silent audience of friends, visitors, slaves, and Albemarle County officials, the two old friends who embodied more than half a hundred years of revolutionary experience and liberal dreams ran or tottered into each other's arms crying, "Ah, Jefferson!" and "Ah, Lafayette!" and weeping for the joy and sadness of meeting. "Of the 3 or 400 persons present," Lafayette wrote later, "not a sound escaped except an occasional supprest sob, there was not a dry eye in the crowd—altho invited into the house none would enter." So the two old men went arm in arm into the famous mansion, so many of whose furnishings were tangible reminders of Jefferson's happy days in Paris. They had a lifetime of things to talk over, doubtless most prominent among them the strange course of revolutions.

Of all the things they talked about, we have only one brief record. The slave Israel, who waited table and drove the carriage, recalled one conversation that made an indelible impression on him. Lafayette expressed his abhorrence of slavery. "No man could rightfully hold ownership in his brother man; that he gave his best services and spent his money in behalf of the Americans freely because he felt that they were fighting for a great and noble principle—the freedom of mankind; that instead of all being free a portion were held in bondage." They should at the very least be educated and thereby prepared for eventual freedom. "Mr. Jefferson replied that he thought the time would come when slaves would be free, but did not indicate," Israel noted, "when or in what manner they would get their freedom. He seemed to think that the time had not then arrived." As to teaching them, Jefferson asserted that he was willing to teach them to read, but "to teach them to write would enable them to forge papers, [then] they could no longer be kept in subjugation."

There can be no doubt that Lafayette's brilliant young mistress, Frances Wright, an ardent feminist and abolitionist who was making plans to establish a utopian interracial community somewhere in the South, joined forces with the Marquis to admonish Jefferson on the subject of slavery and to lecture him on the importance of cooperation between individuals rather than the often desperate competition that seemed to her to characterize American life. Not long after the Lafayette entourage had departed from Monticello, she sent Jefferson the plan of her mixed community of blacks and whites and solicited his criticisms. He replied sympathetically: "At the age of eighty-two, with one foot in the grave, and the other uplifted to follow it, I do not permit myself to take part in any new enterprises, even for bettering the condition of men, not even in the great one which is the subject of your letter, and which has been through life that of my greatest anxieties. . . . The abolition of the evil [slavery] is not impossible; it ought never therefore to be despaired of. Every plan should be adopted, every experiment tried, which may do something toward its ultimate object."

After his visits to Mount Vernon, Yorktown, and Monticello, the three great shrines or sacred places of the young Republic, the rest of Lafayette's extended American visit had about it something of the air of anticlimax. The season was rapidly growing too cold and blustery for travel. The Marquis decided to winter in Washington and established himself at Gadsby's Hotel there. He was invited to address a joint session of both houses of Congress, and at the Capitol on December 9, 1824, before a crowd of some two thousand persons, he was greeted by Henry Clay: "The vain wish has sometimes been indulged that Providence would allow the patriot, after death, to return to his country, and to contemplate the intermediate changes which had taken place. . . . General, your present visit to the United States is the realization of the consoling object of that wish. You are in the midst of posterity!"

Lafayette read his reply in his heavily accented English. The honors bestowed upon him he accepted as "one of the American veterans, to signify in his person their esteem to our joint services." He was "proud and happy to share those extraordinary favours with my dear Revolutionary companions."

For the raw, chaotic land, wracked at that moment by a hotly disputed election whose bitterness recalled the Jefferson–Burr conflict twenty-five years earlier, Lafayette had a cheering benediction. He had been called, as it were, "to witness the immense improvements, the admirable communications, the prodigious creations of which we find an example in this city, whose name itself is a venerated palladium; in a word, all the grandeur and prosperity of these happy United States, which, at the same time they nobly seem the complete assertion of American independence, reflect on every part of the world the light of a far superior political civilization." This was the kind of talk Americans liked.

The general's financial difficulties in France were common knowledge. Monroe had invited Congress to vote the Marquis "a donation worthy of the American people." The Senate and the House, the latter somewhat more hesitantly, voted the hero of the Revolution the sum of two hundred thousand dollars and a township of public land in gratitude for his services to the Republic. Congress gave a banquet in his honor on New Year's Day. The toast to Lafayette lauded "the great apostle of liberty whom the persecutions of tyranny could not defeat, whom the love of riches could not influence, whom popular applause could never seduce." To which the Marquis replied: "To the perpetual union of the United States. It has always saved us in times of storm, one day it will save the world."

The Washington winter gave the Marquis some respite from the continual adulation, though the cold and damp took its toll of his health. He longed to be home, but further chores awaited him. He had committed himself to visit the Carolinas and Georgia and New Orleans before starting his four-thousand-mile journey back to Boston, where he had promised to lay the cornerstone of the Bunker Hill Monument.

The triumphal tour had become a heavy labor—a campaign more arduous than any of the Revolution. He was too tactful, too gracious to show it, but he wrote from Fayetteville, North Carolina, named after him, to his children in France: "I feel at each instant an increasing need to be with you once more; the sensations of waking from sleep when one is sad weighs ceaselessly on the heart in the midst of brilliant and touching surroundings, in which nevertheless, one must give oneself over, with affection and gratitude."

Somehow he survived it all. In Georgia he visited Indians in their war paint lining the banks of the Chattahoochee. They did a war dance for him and played a game of lacrosse. An old chief addressed him as one sent by the Great Spirit. "The youngest among us will tell their grandchildren that they have touched your hand and seen your face; they will see you perhaps again, for you are the favorite of the Great Spirit and you never grow old." Most moving of all, groups of slaves, having heard of his fame as the champion of freedom and the enemy of black servitude, gathered whenever they could along the roadside to wave to him as he passed.

At New Orleans, with its French antecedents and tradition of hospitality, there was a veritable orgy of festivities. Then it was up the Mississippi River by steamboat to Nashville for more ceremonies and a visit to General Andrew Jackson, in whose famous collection of firearms the Marquis identified a brace of pistols he had given to Washington. "I feel a real satisfaction," he told Jackson, "in finding them in the hands of a man so worthy of such a heritage."

As the steamboat struggled up the Ohio River it struck a snag one night, listed heavily, and began to sink. Lafayette and the other passengers barely made it to shore before the craft capsized. They were rescued by another steamer the next day after spending the night in the rain in an improvised camp.

The next stop was Cincinnati, with more interminable speeches, and then overland to Uniontown and Friendship Hill, Albert Gallatin's remote, mosquito-infested plantation on the Virginia frontier. At Uniontown, Gallatin and the Marquis embraced. They had last met in the glittering chambers and hallways of Versailles and on the boulevards of Paris. Now they encountered each other in this odd rustic retreat, and here Lafayette was witness to a classic frontier gathering. As James Gallatin noted, "People came from miles away and camped out, bringing their tents." Lafayette spoke and Gallatin spoke. "The subject was the critical position of the Greeks" fighting for their independence from the Turks. James noted in his diary that after the speeches he had "never heard such an outburst of genuine enthusiasm and cheering; it lasted quite half an hour."

Arrived at last in Boston for the laying of the cornerstone, the general was faced with one last fling of patriotic oratory. Daniel Webster was inevitably the orator of the day. Fifteen thousand spectators were seated in hastily erected stands, and twice as many covered the hillside above Charlestown. A choir sang:

> O is not this a holy spot!
> 'Tis the high place of Freedom's birth
> God of our Fathers! Is it not
> The holiest spot of all the earth?

The aged and tremulous Reverend Thaxter, who had led prayers on that same hill before the battle, prayed once more. Just as Webster began his address a section of the stands collapsed, with resultant disorder and near panic. But Webster thundered on: "Fortunate, fortunate man! With what measure of devotion will you not thank God for the circumstances of your extraordinary life! You are connected with both hemispheres and with two generations. Heaven saw fit to ordain that the electric spark of liberty should be conducted through you, from the New World to the Old."

Was that the last? No, Lafayette had not yet visited Vermont or the new state of Maine. So there must be a final dash northward, with all the familiar rituals repeated a dozen times more. He laid the cornerstone of the University of Vermont and then turned back through Albany, arriving there, to the bliss of its citizens, on the eve of the Fourth of July. There, amid the fervid fanfare, the bands, the parades, the speeches, he was conducted to the excavation for a new library where a company of children had gathered to welcome him. Reaching down, the Marquis picked up a rosy-cheeked little six-year-old boy and gave him a kiss. The child's name was Walter Whitman. There were, to be sure, other memorable moments, more fêtes and celebrations still to come, but that is certainly a good one to end on.

Lafayette paid yet another visit to Jefferson. His sixty-ninth birthday on that September 6 was celebrated in the White House with the new "Clay" president, John Quincy Adams. The Marquis had been in the United States for more than a year and had celebrated two birthdays here. The next day he started home. The parting was the most emotional moment of all. Adams of the "Iron Mask" was observed to tremble, and his voice broke as he spoke. "We shall look upon you always as belonging to us, during the whole of our life, and as belonging to our children after us. You are ours by that more than patriotic self-devotion with which you flew to the aid of our fathers . . . ours by that tie of love, stronger than death, which has linked your name for the endless ages of time with the name of Washington."

For a moment Lafayette could not reply, but then he gave his blessing to "the American people, each of their States and the federal government!" He threw his arms around Adams and, both men weeping, they said their final farewells. Lafayette entered his carriage and was driven past silent throngs to the packet that would carry him down the bay to the new frigate, the *Brandywine*, which he had christened a few months before and which would carry him across the Atlantic to his other home.

There had never been and would never be in the Republic another episode like it. The visits to the shrines of freedom, the viewing of the sacred relics—the key to the Bastille, Washington's pistols, the battle flags—and the aged veterans touched the deepest levels of the national psyche. The symbolism seemed inexhaustible. The great continuous democratic festival sought to affirm that the Revolutionary ideals were not transitory, that they had endured and would endure against all the forces of tyranny and oppression, against all the kings and courts, all the despots and all the aristocrats who clung to their privileges with such tenacity. Lafayette had said it himself: America would one day save the world. The America that to many of its more thoughtful citizens seemed to be every year sliding deeper into the terrible morass of sectional conflict; the America that so often appeared to be excessively preoccupied with material concerns, with sharp bargaining, with getting ahead at the cost of civic duties; the America whose bitter political divisions were being displayed to the world in the presidential elections that so inopportunely coincided with Lafayette's visit, was strengthened and revitalized by Lafayette's remarkable odyssey. In his dogged determination to encompass the better part of the inhabited areas of the country, it was as though he was conscious that his role was more than that of a returning hero. He brought back the Revolution; made it vividly present to the minds and imaginations of a people for whom it had grown dim and remote; rekindled, if only for a moment, the unity of patriotic hearts.

50

Jefferson and Adams Correspond

A few years after Jefferson returned to Monticello, like "a prisoner released from his chains," Benjamin Rush managed to heal the breach between him and John Adams. That reconciliation, so typical of Rush's warm heart, may have been his greatest gift to the Republic he so loved. A young visitor to Adams reported to Jefferson that Adams had said, "I have always loved Jefferson, and still love him." When this comment was reported to Jefferson, he wrote in a letter to Rush, "This is enough for me. I only needed this knowledge to revive towards him all the affections of the most cordial moments of our lives."

At Rush's prompting, Adams opened the correspondence by sending Jefferson a book by John Quincy Adams, and Jefferson replied: "A letter from you calls up recollections very dear to my mind. It carries me back to the times when, beset with difficulties and dangers, we were fellow laborers in the same cause, struggling for what is most valuable to man, his right of self-government. Laboring always at the same oar, with some wave ever ahead threatening to overwhelm us and yet passing harmless under our bark, we knew not how, we rode through the storm with heart and hand, and made a happy port." Here was Jefferson at his most graceful and felicitous.

Rush was ecstatic at having been the agent of the reconciliation. "I rejoice in the correspondence," he wrote to Adams. "I consider you and him as the North and South Poles of the American Revolution. Some talked, some wrote and some fought to promote and establish it, but you and Mr. Jefferson *thought* for us all." It was true. We cannot find among the Founders two better exemplars of the Classical-Christian and the Secular-Democratic consciousnesses. They expressed the yin and yang of American political theory. "Never mind it, my dear Sir," Adams wrote to Jefferson, "if I write four letters to your one; your one is worth more than my four. . . . You and I ought not to die until we have explained ourselves to each other."

Adams was keenly aware that Jefferson's doctrines, shallow as they seemed to him, were far more in accord with the sentiments of the American people than were his own. "Your Character in History may be easily foreseen," he wrote. "Your Administration, will be quoted by Philosophers, as a model of profound Wisdom; by Politicians, as weak, superficial and short sighted. Mine, like Pope's Woman will have no Character at all." In Adams's view, Jefferson's "steady defence of democratical Principles, and . . . invariable favourable Opinion of the French Revolution laid the foundation of your Unbounded Popularity."

To Adams, man was a fallen creature, tainted with original sin, bearing ineradicable tendencies to self-love and self-aggrandizement. The foundation of any sound social order was the clear perception that power would be abused. Under the banner of reason one might assemble the most merciless and tyrannical armies of all. That had been the lesson of the French Revolution for Adams.

Jefferson's reply was oblique but pointed. There had been party and political differences since the beginning of recorded history. Everyone took sides in these controversies, "in favor of the many, or of the few, according to his constitution, and the circumstances in which he is placed." He and the Republicans had cast their lot with the many, and Adams and the Federalists with the few. Beyond that it was always a struggle between the defenders of the status quo, typically the few who profited unduly from it, and the many who wished for a better and more just society. Science held the key to that better society. "Science," Jefferson wrote, has "liberated the ideas of those who read and reflect. . . . An insurrection has consequently begun, of science, talents and courage, against rank and birth, which have fallen into contempt."

Adams was convinced that science notwithstanding, aristocracies of one kind or another would keep reasserting themselves in history. The aristocracy of talents of which Jefferson spoke so confidently would in time become a "hierarchial Despotism" as onerous as any that had appeared earlier. But, Adams wrote teasingly, "Our pure, virtuous public-spirited federative Republick will last for ever, govern the Globe and introduce the perfection of Man, his perfectibility being already proved by Price Priestly, Condorcet Rousseau Diderot and Godwin."

Jefferson's optimism about inevitable progress suffered a slight setback when he considered the tendency of the younger generation—what he called "our post-revolutionary youth"—to behave as though they had acquired all knowledge "in their mothers' wombs, and bring it into the world ready-made," with no need for books and teachers. "Every folly," he added, "must run its round; and so, I suppose, must that of self-learning, and self-sufficiency, of rejecting the knowlege acquired in past ages, and starting on the new ground of intuition." Was this the Jefferson who had been so confident that science and reason were sufficient as the basis of education who was now lamenting the disposition of the youth to reject "the knowledge acquired in past ages"?

Adams was willing, he wrote, to leave "those profound Phylosophers whose Sagacity perceives the Perfectibility of Human Nature, and those illuminated Theologians who expect the Apocalyptic Reign, to enjoy their transporting hopes, provided always that they will not engage Us in Crusades and French Revolutions, nor burn Us for doubting."

Adams was especially persistent in prodding Jefferson on the latter's belief in the perfectibility of man: "Let me now ask you, very seriously my Friend, Where are now in 1813, the Perfection and perfectibility of human Nature? Where is now, the progress of the human Mind? Where is the Amelioration of Society? Where the Augmentations of human Comforts? Where the diminutions of human Pains and Miseries. . . . When? Where? and how? is the present Chaos to be arranged into Order?"

In Adams's view, "This World is a mixture of the Sublime and the beautiful, the base and contemptible, the whimsical and ridiculous. . . . It is a Riddle and an Enigma. You need not be surprised then, if I should descend from these Heights, to an egregious Trifle. . . . An Aristocracy of Land jobbers and Stock jobbers is . . . irremediably entailed upon Us, to endless generations."

Each passing year of the young nineteenth century seemed to bring fresh horrors, and Adams was moved to comment that "the Eighteenth Century, notwithstanding all its Errors and Vices has been, of all that are past, the most honourable to human Nature. Knowledge and Virtues were increased and diffused, Arts, Sciences useful to Men, ameliorating their condition, were improved, more than in any former equal period. But, what are We to say now? Is the Nineteenth Century to be a Contrast to the Eighteenth? Is it to extinguish all the Lights of its Predecessor?"

While the course of the French Revolution, ending in a dictatorship more arbitrary than most monarchies, seemed to Adams to confirm his view of the tendency of men's passions to overcome their reason, Jefferson believed that Napoleon represented no more than a temporary setback to the march of progress. In his words, even in Europe, "an insurrection has taken place of science, talents and courage, against rank and birth. . . . It has failed in its first effort, because the mobs of the cities . . . debased by ignorance, poverty and vice, could not be restrained to rational action. But the world will recover from the panic of this first catastrophe. Science is progressive, and talents and enterprise on the alert."

Adams replied, in turn, that he had no doubt that "the horrors We have experienced for the last forty Years, will ultimately, terminate in the Advancement of civil and religious Liberty, and Ameliorations, in the condition of Mankind." But he could not accept the "Doctrine of the Perfectibility of the human Mind," and he warned Jefferson that "our hopes . . . of sudden tranquility ought not to be too sanguine. Fanaticism and Superstition will still be selfish, subtle, intriguing, and at times furious. Despotism will still struggle for domination; Monarchy will study to rival nobility in popularity; Aristocracy will continue to envy all above it, and despize and oppress all below it; Democracy will envy all, contend with all, endeavour to pull down all; and when by chance it gets the Upper hand for a short time, it will be revengeful, bloody and cruel. These and other Elements of Fanaticism and Anarchy will yet for a long time continue a Fermentation, which will excite alarms and require Vigilance."

The Congress of Vienna and the emergence of the Holy Alliance certainly were grounds for the gloomiest apprehensions, and Adams did not scruple to remind Jefferson repeatedly that his, Adams's, view of history and human nature was daily being vindicated, both at home and abroad. He wrung a reluctant concession from the Virginian: "Your prophecies [at the beginning of the French Revolution] . . . proved truer than mine," Jefferson wrote, "and yet fell short of the fact, for instead of a million, the destruction of 8. or 10. millions of human beings has probably been the effect of these convulsions. . . . But altho' your prophecy has proved true so far, I hope it does not preclude a better final result. . . . The idea of representative government has taken root and growth among them. . . . Opinion is power, and that opinion will come. Even France will yet attain representative government. . . . The idea then is rooted, and will be established, altho' rivers of blood may yet flow between them and their object."

Adams had a ready answer to Jefferson's query as to why the doctrine that "power made right" had come to govern European politics. "Power always sincerely, conscientiously . . . believes itself Right. Power always thinks it has a great Soul, and vast Views, beyond the Comprehension of the Weak; and that it is doing God Service when it is violating all his Laws. Our Passions, Ambition, Avarice, Love, Resentment etc possess so much metaphysical Subtilty and so much overpowering Eloquence, that they insinuate themselves into the Understanding and the Conscience and convert both to their Party. And I may be deceived as much as any of them, when I say, that Power must never be trusted without a Check."

Adams confessed that since he could not "contemplate human Affairs, without laughing or crying, I choose to laugh." Pleasure had far outweighed pain in his long life, and the essence of his philosophy was "Mind Your own Business! Do no Wrong! Do all the good You can! Eat Your Canvas back ducks, drink Your burgundy, sleep Your S[i]esta, when necessary, And *Trust in God!*"

As the years wore on, an increasing note of anxiety crept into the letters of Jefferson and Adams about the dangers to the Union posed by the slavery issue. The question of the admission of Missouri alarmed Jefferson, who termed it "a breaker on which we lose the Missouri country by revolt, and what more, God only knows. From the Battle of Bunker's Hill to the treaty of Paris we never had so momentous a question. . . . Thank God that I shall not live to witness its issue."

Jefferson was troubled by the conjunction of the Missouri question and the Holy Alliance. To him the Missouri issue could be reduced to a familiar and terrifyingly simple question: "Are our slaves to be presented with freedom and a dagger?" The wars of independence of the Spanish colonies of South America aroused the sympathy of both men, but Jefferson as well as Adams feared that the people of the newly proclaimed republics were not yet ready for self-government and that the consequence would be "military tyrannies, more or less numerous."

Jefferson favored a reuniting of the revolted colonies with the mother countries under constitutional guarantees, while Adams took the pessimistic view that Catholicism and a free government could not exist together and that "consequently . . . all projects for reconciling them in old Spain or new are Eutopian, Platonick and Chimerical."

As for the slavery issue, Adams had "seen it hanging over [this country] like a black cloud for half a Century." In his mind's eye he had envisioned "Armies of Negroes marching and counter-marching in the air, shining in Armour. I have been so terrified with this Phenomenon that I constantly said in former times to the Southern Gentlemen, I cannot comprehend this object; I must leave it to you. I will vote for forcing no measure against your judgements. What we are to see, *God* knows, and I leave it to him, and his agents in posterity."

The news of war in Europe between Russia and Turkey prompted Jefferson to write, "It seems that the Cannibals of Europe are going to be eating one another again. A war between Russia and Turkey is like the battle of the kite and snake. Whichever destroys the other, leaves a destroyer less for the world. This pugnacious humor of mankind seems to be the law of his nature, one of the obstacles to too great multiplication provided in the mechanism of the Universe. . . . I hope that we shall prove how much happier for man the Quaker policy is, and that the life of the feeder is better than that of the fighter."

As sight, hearing, and even the ability of the correspondents to write diminished, the letters between Adams and Jefferson dwindled to a trickle. Somehow, without perhaps even consciously willing it, they concentrated their enfeebled energies on surviving until the coming Fourth of July, 1826, which would mark the fiftieth anniversary of independence. By whatever amiable intervention of Providence, the two old friends both died on that hallowed day. John Adams had written to Abigail after the resolution approving independence had passed Congress that the day "will be the most memorable Epocha, in the History of America,—I am apt to believe that it will be celebrated, by succeeding Generations, as the great anniversary Festival. It ought to be commemorated, as the Day of Deliverance by solemn Acts of

Devotion to God Almighty, It ought to be solemnized with Pomp and Parade, with Shews, Games, Sports, Guns, Bells, Bonfires and Illuminations from one End of this Continent to the other from this Time forward forever more." Now, while their fellow citizens celebrated the day in every city and town, the two heroes of the Revolution died. Adams's last words were, "Jefferson still lives," but Jefferson had, in fact, died several hours earlier.

The two philosophers of the Revolution, so different in temperament, in background, in regional ties, in their own philosophies, were gone, and with their deaths an epoch was indeed over.

President John Quincy Adams, having heard that his father was sinking, had started for Quincy on July 8. He had traveled only a few miles when he received word that his father had died on the afternoon of the Fourth—"a strange and very striking coincidence," he noted in his journal. "My father had nearly closed the ninety-first year of his life—a life illustrious in the annals of his country and of the world. . . . He had served to the great and useful purpose of his age, and his God. . . . The time, the manner, the coincidence with the dicease of Jefferson has the visible and palpable marks of divine favor, for which I would humble myself in grateful adoration before the Ruler of the Universe. For myself, all that I care to ask is that I may live the remnant of my days in a manner worthy of him from whom I came and at the appointed hour of my Maker, dic as my father has died in peace with God and man, sped to the regions of futurity with the blessings of my fellow men."

John Adams's grandson, Charles Francis Adams, who had stayed behind in Washington, heard the news the same day and wrote in his diary, "My Grandfather John . . . and Jefferson died on the fourth of July, 1826. There is nothing more to be said, With all the volumes of Eulogies that have been published on these men, and the remarks that have been studied upon this coincidence, nothing has been produced so eloquent as the simple fact. There are occurrences sometimes in the course of Human affairs, too great for words. The mind is already so exalted that any attempt to shackle it by expression destroys the flight, and lets it down again to common place. The wonder, the awe, the feeling of indefinable grandeur which comes over one though they might earnestly seek an outlet in language, would vanish in the attempt. The greatest of all eloquence in the known world is the eloquence of *facts*."

Charles Francis Adams then added a characteristic and revealing paragraph. His grandfather, he felt, had died without that fame which his great achievements deserved. He was confident that his son, John Quincy, Charles Francis's father, would "redeem his fame." But should his father die before that task was complete, "the duty will fall on *us*, his grandchildren, those whom he looked upon with combined feelings of pride and high expectation. Should it so happen then, I trust that we shall not come unwilling to the task and I hope at least so far as it lies with *me*, that not an act shall be done, not a sacrifice shall be avoided, till my utmost efforts have been made to restore him to the place which is his justly due." In addition to his own distinguished career, Charles Francis Adams became the indefatigable editor of his grandfather's papers.

In their extended old age, their long time dying, the two old Revolutionaries achieved a substantial degree of detachment from the "horrors" of the times. Not only had they been present at the creation, they had been among the principal creators, and they had lived to observe and reflect upon the consequences of their Revolution at home and abroad. They had used the unanticipated gift of longevity well, exploring the intellectual terrain, "explaining themselves to each other," and, in a sense, the country to itself. They had compared notes on the pleasures and the pains of age, chief among the latter the inevitable waning of physical capacities and the growing dependency that was its consequence; speculated about the "uses" of grief and a future state of punishments or rewards. (Adams was even reconciled to encountering "old Tim Pic"—Timothy Pickering—and "Alec Hamilton" in the hereafter, especially if they gave some evidence of contrition for the harm they had done him.) Nothing, to be sure, had come out the way they had imagined it would (and Adams's philosophy was much better able to accommodate that fact than Jefferson's); they retained their quite different faiths in the "amelioration" of the human condition, however, although Jefferson confessed he had been forced to amend his timetable considerably.

The country was of course overwhelmed by what was generally considered to be an instance of divine intervention. It was as though God had, by this signal act of His favor, called the attention of a sometimes faithless people to the principles on which the nation had been founded.

We should not lose sight of the vast disparity between the public reputations of Jefferson and Adams at their death. Time has flattened that perspective and somewhat obscured their respective standing in the popular imagination. It was the fact that Jefferson towered over Adams in public reputation that prompted Charles Francis Adams's resolution not to rest until his grandfather's reputation had been vindicated. Indeed it is not too much to say that the restoration of John Adams to that eminence that, in the eyes of his loyal posterity, he so richly deserved became a kind of family obsession. Into the fourth and fifth generation, Adamses labored in the cause. Henry Adams did his bit by whittling Thomas Jefferson's reputation down to size in his great *History of the United States during the Administrations of Jefferson and Madison*, and more recently, his descendants of the present generation arranged for the publication of the family papers in one of those editions of countless volumes that appear as the most striking achievement of modern scholarly technology. Help has also come from an unexpected source. The novelist and critic Gore Vidal, a descendant of Aaron Burr, has written a widely read historical novel that elevates his ancestor and cuts up Thomas Jefferson. It would not have pleased John Adams, whose contempt for Burr was as profound as his love for Jefferson.

The fact is that Jefferson dominated the first quarter century of the nation's history as no other political figure of our past (with the possible exception of his mortal enemy, John Marshall). At the time of his death his reputation was at its height. He had, after all, founded the Republican party and established the so-called Virginia Dynasty: twenty-four years of rule by Jefferson and his disciples, Madison and Monroe. Where Adams had returned to Quincy, an embittered and ailing old man, ready to die, Jefferson had retired to Monticello to direct the fortunes of his party from that famous mountain. Madison was his hand-picked successor and seldom made an important move without consulting his master, who was especially interested in all appointments to the Supreme Court, hoping thereby to neutralize the influence of Marshall (but instead having to watch as Marshall turned good Republicans into solid Federalists).

Monroe was, likewise, a dutiful student and frequent solicitor of the Sage's counsel. Without Jefferson's support, the never very daring Monroe would hardly have had the nerve to proclaim his famous doctrine. As we have noted before, Jefferson's trinity of science, education, and progress became basic articles of faith for most Americans, supplementing, where they did not replace, the older Trinity.

This aristocratic, slaveholding democrat had an imperial imagination that reached to the redwood-covered slopes of the Pacific Coast; the West loved him for the Louisiana Purchase. As much as any individual he had formed the Secular-Democratic Consciousness that was to be the major element in the collective consciousness of his countrymen for generations to come. Millions of Americans regarded the Virginian with a reverence little short of that reserved for the Almighty. Only the hard-shelled Federalists of New England continued to hate him. (Some of his detractors spread the rumor that he had taken an overdose of laudanum, an opium-derived pain killer and hallucinogen, in order to die on the Fourth of July and thereby steal some of Adams's glory. He had, in fact, been taking it in increasing amounts in the last months of his life to help him sleep.)

The Jefferson-Adams reconciliation had such powerful symbolic significance because it gave the promise of a wider reconciliation. If these two ancient friends and then bitter adversaries, who had enacted in their own lives the devastating divisions of their countrymen, could be reconciled, all Americans might one day be reconciled. If, in their persons, the poles of the Classical-Christian and the Secular-Democratic consciousnesses could be reconciled, all ideological wounds might be healed. If the hero of New England could once again embrace the hero of Virginia, North and South might one day compose their differences. Adams and Jefferson stood for the relatively brief moment when it had seemed that the center might hold, that the Union might be, if not perfect, at least impregnable. As we have seen, that moment had passed all too swiftly. Anxieties of the most corrosive kind had possessed the Founders, driven them into the stony fastnesses of their respective philosophical predilections, and above all, had bound them by their regional loyalties. Jefferson and Adams, by making their friendship new, transcended those divisions; said, in effect, that love can triumph over ideology, that love is greater than "reason" or "science." They thereby demonstrated most dramatically the power of common memories. Of History.

51

The Nation Takes Shape

The era that came to such a dramatic end with the concurrent deaths of Jefferson and Adams is not easy to summarize or to understand. The greater part of it—from 1800 to 1825—was, politically at least, the age of Jefferson. The Virginian and the party he created dominated the first quarter of the nineteenth century. But so many other things were going on that were perhaps of more fundamental importance that it is misleading to attach to it the name of one particular individual. The period of time covered by this volume runs, after all, from 1783 to 1826, and the years from 1787 to 1800 are the crucially important years of Federalist hegemony; of the drafting of the Constitution, the most momentous political accomplishment in history; and the presidency of Washington, which, if it covered only seven years, nonetheless shaped the office and, in large measure, the entire structure of our government.

It is difficult this far removed in time to recover adequately the turmoil and disorder of the early days of the Republic. For most Americans the single most traumatic event between the end of the Revolution and the War of 1812 may well have been the revolt of the Massachusetts farmers, called, misleadingly, Shays' Rebellion. It alarmed patriots in every state and provided the principal incentive for calling the Federal Convention to devise some means of strengthening the union of the states. The establishment of the new government was followed by two more "rebellions" that had to be put down by force of arms—the Whiskey Rebellion and Fries' rebellion. Political rhetoric of the period was in what has been called recently, in connection with a quite different episode in our history, "the paranoid style."

Somewhat over half the citizens of the United States gave their undeviating loyalty to the French Revolution despite the bloody horrors that culminated in a military dictatorship. In the name of the French Revolution, which it must be assumed they hardly understood, they often seemed quite ready to tear their own country to shreds. Another substantial portion of the population was as unremitting in its devotion to the nation from whom we had just won independence after a long and bitter conflict. As we have suggested earlier, when the response is out of all proportion to the primary cause or provocation, we must assume a hidden pathology.

The relentlessly violent rhetoric that characterized American politics from 1789 to the end of the War of 1812 obsured a process that no one clearly understood and, indeed, at whose nature we can only guess. John Adams said of the American Revolution that it took place in the hearts and minds of Americans long before the first shot was fired. We might say of the post-Revolutionary period that another revolution was taking place in the hearts and minds of Americans that had little to do with the common "verbalization" or with what passed for intelligible political discourse. Americans, having torn up the old political and social maps, were trying to discover how to live together in some kind of coherent society. "Open" as colonial society had been, especially in contrast with the mother country, it had still been only a modest foreshadowing of the "openness" of post-Revolutionary society. In that later era all the ties and bonds of traditional societies since the beginning of historical man and woman had been cut asunder, vast new human energies released, and vast new problems generated. No adequate anthropology, sociology, or social psychology existed (or exists) to make the process comprehensible. And perhaps it was just as well.

It may be that the French Revolution was a blessing in disguise in that it provided a language and set of political propositions of considerable dubiety and, for many Americans, irresistible charm that drew attention away from the *real issues* the country had to resolve —issues such as the relation of what, in traditional societies, were called classes, to each other. Certainly it is hard to escape the feeling that while much of this rhetoric entered deeply and permanently into the complex of tenuous ideas and half-formed prejudices that constitute a substantial part of the American consciousness, much of it simply served as a lightning rod to collect and "ground" anxieties and hostilities that could not be articulated. Thus, when the War of 1812 cleared the air, it turned out that (the all-important issue of slavery aside) under the often shocking violence of the rhetoric, of the paranoid style, a kind of American temper or consciousness had taken a surprisingly well defined shape; indeed a nation had taken shape. All the essential elements were there: the westward migration; sectionalism—North, South, and West—with different and clearly defined interests; the American talent for improvising, for making tools and saving labor; the gross materialism and the infatuation with conspicuous display; the desire to "get ahead," to succeed in the world, along with the desire to redeem it; the boastfulness and the self-doubt it concealed; the crudity, the violence, the idealism, and the cynicism; the youth bias; the speculative mania; the anxieties—sexual, political, financial; the impulse to repress emotion; the conflict of classes; the merciless competitiveness of American life; the unrestrained growth of "capitalism"; the longing for the "true community"; the reckless exploitation of the natural resources of the land; the tragic confrontation with the Indian tribes who haunted the waking and sleeping visions of Americans; the endlessly repeated trauma of immigration; the conflict of country and town with the metropolis that mocked all dreams of innocence; the faith in science, reason, education, and progress; the wild outpourings of emotion in the periodic religious revivals that swept the country; and underlying it all, the terrible, irreconcilable fact of black slavery, the paranoid schizophrenia, a wound that could not be healed.

What was to come would be a kind of unfolding, an exploration of the implications of the beginning; a projection of those initial dreams and fears and fantasies. And always and always there was, obscuring all tragedies and failures, this evocation of the United States as the highest human accomplishment, the hope of the world.

These sentiments were eloquently expressed by Hugh Swinton Legaré, a Charleston lawyer and newspaper editor who delivered a classic Fourth of July oration in 1823 in which he touched many of the notes that the Reverend Samuel Thacher had sounded at Concord in 1798. Legaré began by comparing the achievements of Americans with those of other peoples. "What," he asked his listeners, "were the victories of Pompey—to the united achievements of our Washingtons and Montgomerys and Greens—our Franklins and Jeffersons and Adamses and Laurens—of the Senate of Sages whose wisdom conducted—of the band of warriors, whose valour accomplished—of the 'noble army of martyrs,' whose blood sealed and consecrated the Revolution of '76?"

With the possible exception of the Reformation, he continued, the United States had ushered in "by far the greatest era . . . that has occurred in the political history of modern times," an era "that has fixed forever the destinies of a whole quarter of the globe, with the numbers without number that are soon to inhabit it—and has already had, as it will probably continue to have, a visible influence upon the condition of society in all the rest."

But what had passed, glorious as it was, was only the prelude to "the scene of unmingled prosperity and happiness that is opening and spreading all around us." Americans could contemplate a "prospect as dazzling as it is vast . . . the uncircumscribed career of aggrandize-ment and improvement which we are beginning to run under such happy auspices. . . . Our triumphs are the triumphs of *reason*—of happiness—of human nature. Our rejoicings are greeted with the most cordial sympathy by the cosmopolite and the philanthropist: the good and the wise all round the globe give us back the echo of our acclamations."

It was not material achievements that Legaré was celebrating but "moral improvement." In that "race we have outstripped every competitor and have carried our institutions, 'in the sober certainty of waking bliss,' to a higher pitch of perfection than ever warmed the dreams of enthusiasm or the speculations of the theorist." Indeed it was as if the entire continent had been "set apart, as if it were holy ground, for the cultivation of pure truth—for the pursuit of happiness upon rational principles . . . for the development of all the sensibili-ties, and capacities, and powers of the human mind, without any artificial restraint of bias, in the broad daylight of modern science and political liberty."

What was perhaps the most important was that all these improve-ments were taking place "in a New World," a world untarnished and uncompromised, with "no grievances established by custom—no corruptions sanctified by their antiquity." Thus, "the human race began a new career in a new universe." What could be "more striking and sublime, than the idea of an Imperial Republic—spreading over an extent of territory, more immense than the empire of the Caesars . . . founded on the maxims of common sense—employing within itself no arms, but those of reason—and known to its subjects only by the blessings it bestows or perpetuates."

Depending only on "the strength of reason," the United States had before it "many ages of glory and freedom . . . many nations shall learn from our example, how to be free and great. The fortunes of the species, are thus, in some degree identified with those of THE REPUBLIC—and if our experiment fail, there is no hope for man on this side of the grave." Here, stated once again, was the now familiar theme that we found in Washington's address to the states after the Newburgh "revolt." The fate of the United States was the fate of the world.

Bibliographic Note

As in my earlier volumes on the American Revolution I have depended primarily on primary sources—letters, diaries, journals, official state papers, the accounts of visiting foreigners and newspapers. For the period from 1783 through the framing of the Constitution, I have made extensive use of Edmund Burnett's *Letters of Members of the Continental Congress* in eight volumes, and Max Farrand's *Record of the Federal Convention* in four. Jonathan Elliot's *Debates of the Adoption of the Federal Constitution* in five volumes was also an important source. Elsewhere I have usually indicated my source, e.g., William Maclay's *Journal* or the writings of Fisher Ames. James Richardson's *Messages and Papers of the Presidents* (available in various multivolume editions) was essential as was the *Congressional Globe*, a record of congressional proceedings.

Among the secondary works that were most useful were Walter Lord's history of the War of 1812, Kenneth Silverman's comprehensive *A Cultural History of the American Revolution* (New York, 1976), and Samuel Eliot Morison's *The Maritime History of Massachusetts* (Boston, 1941). Most useful of all was John Bach McMaster's inchoate but encyclopedic *History of the People of the United States from the American Revolution to the Civil War* in eight volumes. Written with a heavy emphasis on newspapers, the first volume published in 1883 and the last thirty years later, it is a commodious grab bag of historical facts with an emphasis on social history far ahead of its time.

About the Author

Page Smith was educated at Dartmouth College and Harvard University. He has served as research associate at the Institute of Early American History and Culture and has taught at the University of California at Los Angeles and at Santa Cruz, where he was Provost of Cowell College. He is now Professor Emeritus of that university as well as co-director of the William James Association. Dr. Smith is the author of *The Historian and History*; *Daughters of the Promised Land: Women in American History*; *As a City upon a Hill: The Town in American History*; the highly acclaimed two-volume biography *John Adams*, which was a selection of the Book-of-the-Month Club, a National Book Award Nominee, and a Bancroft winner; and *A New Age Now Begins*, a Main Selection of the Book-of-the-Month Club. Page Smith lives in Santa Cruz, California.

Acknowledgments

I wish to express my gratitude for the interest, the encouragement, and the assistance of David Stanford, Patty Nelson, and Ann Fabian in the preparation of this work. Frances Rydell, David Stanford, Carol English, and Charlotte Cassidy performed heroic labors in typing an often barely decipherable manuscript.

INDEX

Abolition movement, 760–765
  newspapers, 765
Adams, Abigail, 32, 218, 221, 262, 277, 370,
  390, 726
  bitterness toward Jefferson, 490–491
  on Hartford Convention, 641
  on John Randolph, 281
  religious beliefs, 324
  on uprising of Massachusetts farmers, 32
  on Washington, 251
Adams, Charles, 780
Adams, Charles Francis, 371, 376, 726, 729,
  780–781
  on achievements of John Adams, 821–823
Adams, George Washington, 781
Adams, Henry, 823
Adams, John, 24, 32
  administration, 297–298
  ambassador to England, 119
  on American Revolution, 826
  on Ames speech on Jay Treaty, 238–241
  attacks on, 281–284
    by Callender, 281–282, 490–492
    by Republicans, 281–284
  on British-American relations, 218
  on Burr, 506
  Cabinet plots against Adams, 282–283
  candidate for vice-president, 119–126
  capital moved to Washington, 293–294
  character, 252, 500–501

constitutional principles, 1–2, 119
"Convention of Peace, Commerce and
  Navigation" signed with France, 284
courtship of Abigail, 371
death of Jefferson and Adams on July 4,
  1826, 820–821
death of Washington, 279–280
*A Defence of the Constitutions of Government of
  the United States of America,* 119-120,
  252
direct property taxes, 272–274
Dwight's epic poem praised by, 420
election of 1800, 293–294
  defeat by Jefferson, 297–298, 307, 723
on education, 352, 358, 359, 360
on equality, 120, 146
family relationships, 371, 725–726,
  780–781
fast-day proclamation, 254, 263, 268, 287
father of John Quincy Adams, 725–726,
  729
fear of American aristocracy, 10–11, 299,
  777, 817–818
foreign policy, 250
on Fourth of July celebrations, 820–821
French Revolution, views on, 244
and Hamilton, 121–122, 248–249
on Jay Treaty, 221–222
Jefferson and, 244–245, 282–283, 577, 692,
  723

Adams, John (*cont.*):
    correspondence, 359, 368, 815–822
    reconciliation with, 815–824
  judges appointed by, 296
  Lafayette's visit with, 805–806
  leadership functions of "democratic
      aristocracy," 777
  and Madison, 121
  Marshall nominated Chief Justice, 296–297
  on monarchial form of government, 10–11,
      200, 244, 777, 786, 817–818
  on party platforms, 658
  Pinckney affair, 260–262
    threat of war, 260–262
  political views, 115, 146, 157, 816–822
  portraits, 401
  on "power made right," 819
  presidency, 250–271
    envoys sent to France, 254–255, 277–
        279
    inaugural address, 250–251
    observations on France, 250–251,
        262–263
    support for, 261–262
    threat of war with France, 253–266
  presidential candidate, 244–249
  on prohibition, 680
  public career and reputation, 119, 551,
      822–824
  on pursuit of luxury, 38–42
  religious beliefs, 315, 320–324
  on republican government, 41
  and Benjamin Rush, 786
  on slavery issue, 692, 761–762, 819–820
  Thoughts on Government, 32, 60, 119
  Treaty of Paris negotiations, 119
  vice-president, 119–126, 201
  at Washington's inaugural, 125–129
Adams, John (son of John Quincy Adams),
    780–781
Adams, John Quincy, 265, 275, 283,
    297–298, 370, 376, 691
  character and temperament, 725–726
  chosen president by House of
      Representatives in 1825, 726, 785
  Classical-Christian Consciousnesses of, 816,
      824
  and Clay, 721, 727–728
  electoral votes, 726
  embargo and, 568
  family relationships, 780–781
  inaugural address, 729–730
  influence on Monroe Doctrine, 714–717
  "Iron Mask," 726, 729, 783, 814
  Jackson's advocate, 666–667
  Jefferson-Adams reconciliation, 815
  Lafayette and, 813–814
  on Missouri Compromise, 693

    negotiations with Russia over rights on
        Northwest coast, 713
    negotiations with Spain, 711, 713–714, 717
    opposed European intervention in
        American affairs, 713–714
    peace negotiations, War of 1812, 638
    political views, 720–726, 729–731
    portraits (*illus.*) 407, 726
    presidency, 729–731
      candidate (1824), 721–723, 724
      qualifications for, 728–729
    recommended establishment of national
        university, 731
    secretary of state, 660
    on slavery, 696–697
    son of John Adams, 725–726, 729
Adams, Nabby, 281–282
Adams, Samuel, 8, 99, 224, 395
Adams, Thomas Boylston, 284, 780
"Adams and Liberty," 262
Admission of new states, 58–60, 690
  Federal debates, 58–60, 82, 84–85
  slave states and nonslave states, 17, 63
African Methodist Episcopal Church, 388
Age, negative attitude toward, 368
Agricultural Society, 111
Agriculture, 235, 351
  (*See also* Farmers)
Alabama, 466
  admission to the Union, 690
  land speculation, 736
Alaska, 510
Albion (frontier settlement), 739–741
Alcoholism (or intemperance), 677, 679
  national malady, 680–681
  prohibition and, 680
  (*See also* Drunkenness; Temperance
      Movement)
Alexander, Cosmo, 399
Algiers, attacks on American shipping, 552
  (*See also* Barbary War)
Algonquian family, 514–516, 531, 603
Alien and Sedition Acts, 266–267
  attempt to repeal, 281
  constitutionality of, 269–270
Alienation, modern society, 349
Allegheny River, 454
Allen, John, 605
Ambrister, Robert, 664–666, 668
L'Ambuscade (French frigate), 208–214
American Bible Society, 755, 792–793
American character, 425, 784
  coping with success and failure, 336
  people consider themselves chosen of God,
      425
  success in business enterprises, 342–343
American dreams, 48, 280
  equality and community, 48

American Philosophical Society, 37, 116, 387, 510
American Revolution:
  Adams views, 826
  historical paintings, 415
  historical treatment, 364
  mission of, 247
  postwar problems, 51
  radical vision of better human destiny, 300, 416
  young men involved in, 368
Ames, Fisher, 137, 163, 205, 217, 277, 495
  on election of John Adams, 249
  on Jacobin Clubs, 223
  supported Jay Treaty, 237
Ames, Dr. Nathaniel, 205, 225–226, 241–242, 280, 309
  on election of Jefferson and Burr, 294
Anarchiad, The, 32
Anarchy, 61
  dangers of, 32–35
André, John
  execution of, 668
Anger, and withholding of love, 784
Anglicans, 312
  (*See also* Episcopal Church)
Annapolis, British raid threatened, 628
Annapolis Convention, 50–52
Anti-Federalists, 95–97, 99, 147, 160
  and absence of bill of rights, 97
  adopted name "Republicans" and "Democrats," 145, 244
  attachment to French Revolution, 299–301
  fear of monarchial form of government, 131, 139–141, 207–208
  New York ratifying convention, 106
  opposition to Constitution, 95, 118, 131
  opposition to powers granted president, 118
  in Second Congress, 195–196
  (*See also* Republicans)
Antioch, Ohio, 735
Apalachicola River, Indian fort, 663
Appleseed, Johnny, 765
Appleton, Nathan, 766–767
Arabella, 14, 47
Arbuthnot, Alexander, 663–666, 668
Architects and architecture, 395, 424
  Bulfinch, 395
  Classical Revival, 395
  Federal style, 395
  Jefferson, 394–422
Arikara Indians, 517, 523, 542, 549
Aristocracy, 7–8, 10, 34, 60
  Adams views, 777, 817–818
  fear of, 10–11
  Jefferson's "a natural aristocracy," 7, 62, 106, 358, 360, 422–423, 777, 817

  role in democratic society, 777–784
Arkansas River, 466, 549
Arkwright, Richard, 349–350
Arminianism doctrine, 311
Armistead, George, 634, 636–637
Armstrong, John, secretary of war, 610
Army:
  Adam's policy, 264–265
  attempts to raise, 217, 220
  Congressional authorization, 592, 597
  forces, 43
  Indian fighters, 622
  lack of discipline and leadership, 622
  (*See also* Continental Army)
Arnold, Benedict, 195, 217, 597, 646, 652
  Washington's reaction to treason, 806
Art and literature, 394–425
  association with monarchy and aristocracy, 418
  building manuals, 395–396
  classical influences, 394
  literature, 419–424
  paintings, 396–418
  Protestant suspicion of, 418
Articles of Confederation, 1–3, 62–63, 95
  Annapolis Convention (1785), 50–52
  authority of Federal Convention to replace, 62–63
  failure to provide for chief executive, 18
  inadequacies of, 3, 18–19, 34, 50–52, 57
  ineptness of Congress, 3
  movement to reform, 40
  one-state, one-vote rule, 57
  Philadelphia convention to amend, 52–53
  (*See also* Constitutional convention)
Ashe, Thomas, 450
Assembly line technique, 348
Associations, Americans inclination to form, 116
Assumption of state debts, 147–148
  crisis over, 154–155, 157
Astronomical Observatory, 731
Aurora (newspaper), 211, 222, 254, 287, 488, 589
  on Adams, 263
  edited by William Duane, 273–274, 281, 297, 306, 556, 589
  on Jay Treaty, 242
  resentment against editor, 273–274
  on Washington's birthday, 236–237
Austin, Moses, 711–712
Austin, Stephen Fuller, 711–712

Bache, Benjamin Franklin, 211, 222, 242, 261, 306, 556
  on Adams' term in office, 254–255
Baily, Francis, 502, 546

Baily, Francis (*cont.*):
 travels on the Ohio and Mississippi Rivers,
  455–470
Bainbridge, William, 552, 618–619
Baldwin, Loammi, 330
Baltimore:
 antislavery meetings, 692
 British attack on, 628, 633–638
 defense of, 633–634
 desire for capital to be located in, 156
 famous families, 370
 Federal-Republican riots, 598–599, 603
 foreign commerce, 342
 population growth, 732
 War of 1812, 598–599
 yellow fever epidemic, 428–429
Baltimore and Ohio Railroad, 794
Bancroft, George, 36
Bank of the United States, 157–158
 Congressional debates on chartering,
  657–658
 rechartering of, 584–585, 588
 state banks and, 702–703
Bankruptcies and business failures, 13, 673
Banks and banking, 48
 chartering debates, 657–658
 democratic impulse behind the banks,
  672–673
 establishment of national bank, 157–158
 hostility to, 584
 paper currency, 657
 proliferation of banks, 657, 672–673
 speculation in, 158–159
Baptists, 289, 312–313, 324, 751
Bar associations, 116
Barbary War, 484, 552–553, 597, 613, 621,
  622
 American reaction to, 552
Barclay, British Capt. Robert Heriot,
  608–609
Barlow, Joel, 32, 420, 422, 459
 The Vision of Columbus, 420–421, 558
Barney, Joshua, 630–631
Barron, James, 552, 563–564
Barry, John, 266
Baton Rouge, 468
Battle of Bunker Hill (*see* Bunker Hill,
  Battle of)
Bayard, James A., 295–296, 638
Bear-hunting, 456, 526
Bedford, Gunning, 73, 81
Beecher, Harriet, 753
Beecher, Henry Ward, 753
Beecher, Lyman, 752–754
 family, 753
 opposition to Unitarianism, 752–754
Belknap, Jeremy, 318–319
Benjamin, Asher, 395

Benton, Thomas Hart, 645
Berkeley, British Admiral George Cranfield,
  563–565
Berlin and Milan decrees, 562, 565, 588–589,
  671
Bernard, John, 386, 439–441
Bible societies, 755, 792–793
Bill of rights, 91, 133
 adopted by French Assembly, 145
 adoption of, 165–167
 property rights, 674
Billy Bowlegs (trading post) on Suwannee
  River, 664
Birkbeck, Morris, 738–741
"Black codes," 584
Black consciousness, 442–443
Black Hills, 526
Black Rock camp, 601–602, 611
Blackfoot Indians, 542
Blacks:
 attitudes toward, 388–389
 crime and criminals, 676
 racial hostility and contempt toward, 490
 techniques of survival, 448–449
 treatment by whites in the North, 434–435
 (*See also* Slaves and slavery)
Blackston Canal, 333
Bladensburg rout, 630–631, 635
Blair, John, 138–139
Blennerhasset, Herman, 502–505, 507
Blockade:
 British paper blockade, 559
 (*See also* Embargo)
Bompard, French Citizen-Captain, 212
Bonaparte, Joseph, 807
Bonaparte, Napoleon (*see* Napoleon)
Bond, Dr. Thomas, 432
Book of Common Prayer, 313
Boone, Daniel, 459, 461–462
Boone's Lick, 691
Boston:
 antislavery meetings, 692
 celebration of adoption of Constitution,
  116
 celebration of French Revolution victories,
  203–204
 China trade, 337–340
 immigrants, 737
 Lafayette's visit, 804–805, 811–813
 Monroe's visit, 661
 old families, 370
 opposition to Jay Treaty, 222–224
 population growth, 732
 soup kitchens, 675
 statehouse designed by Bulfinch, 395
 War of 1812, 618, 620
 Washington's journey to, 165
Boston (British frigate), 212

Boston Centinel, 661
Boston Gazette, 99, 641
Boudinot, Elias, 109, 114–115, 125, 693, 791–793
  opposed altering Constitution, 791–792
  philanthropic interests, 792
  president of Continental Congress, 791
  writer on theological issues, 791
Bowdoin, James, 27, 29, 31, 98
Boyle, Thomas, 624
Brackenridge, Hugh Henry, 422–424
Bradford, David, 228, 230
Bradford, Rachel, 226
Brant, Joseph, 187
Braxton, Carter, 7
Bray, Thomas, 752–753
Breckinridge, John, 271, 477, 479
Bridges, construction of, 336
British-American relations:
  Adams' views, 297
  after War of 1812, 655–656
  attachment of Federalists to British, 278
  economical interdependence, 656
  effect of Monroe Doctrine, 714–717
  impressment policy, 221, 254
  Jefferson's views, 715
  nonintercourse bill, 218
  seizure of American ships on high seas, 215–217
  (*See also* Great Britain; War of 1812)
British East India Company, 758
Brock, British Gen. Isaac, 600–602
Brooke, British Col. Arthur, 634–636
Brougham, Henry, 716
Brown, Jacob, 611–612
Brown, Moses, 350
Brown University, 350, 353
Bryan, William Cullen, 573
Buchanan, James, 720
Buckmaster, Henrietta, 764–765
Buffalo, British attack, 600, 611
Buffalo hunts, 515, 518–519, 523
Bulfinch, Charles, 395, 805
Bunker Hill, Battle of, 25, 27, 187, 597
  monument to, 811, 813
Burnt Corn Spring, Alabama, 736
Burr, Aaron, 201, 248, 474, 823
  Clay and, 586
  conspiratorial activities, 502–509, 545
  enemy of Jefferson, 495–496
  exile and return to U.S., 507–508
  family background, 290–292
  Hamilton and, 290–291, 293, 308
    duel and death of Hamilton, 496, 498–501
  indicted for murder, 502
  insatiable appetite for fame, 508
  leadership qualities, 652

"machine politics," 292
New York elections of 1798, 290–293
New York gubernatorial contest of 1804, 498–499
political career, 290–291
relationship with daughter, 291–292, 367, 504, 508
treason charges, 504–507, 698
vice-presidential candidate (1800), 290, 293
Burr, Theodosia, 291–292, 367, 504, 508
Business enterprises, 326–351, 766–776
  failures and bankruptcies, 673
  Hamilton's influence, 500
  leaders, 422–424
  riskiness of, 671–672
  (*See also* Capitalism)
Butler, Frederick, 364–365
Butler, Pierce, 83–84, 118, 135, 155, 222, 790–791
  absentee landowner, 791
  champion of slavery, 790–791
  political career, 790–791
Byron, British Capt. Richard, 615

Cabot, George, 224, 277, 283
Caddoan family, 517
Cairo, 454
Calhoun, John Caldwell, 586–587
  advocate of public works, 685–686
  candidate for vice-president, 724
  Jackson and, 662, 665
  on Missouri Compromise, 693
  national bank chartering favored by, 658
  presidential candidate (1824), 721–723
  secretary of war, 660, 721
  sectional leader, 719–720
  slave interests represented by, 719
  support of War of 1812, 593–594, 721
  views of slavery, 696–697, 719
  visited Lowell mills, 768
Callender, James Thomas, 306, 556
  attack on Adams, 281–282, 490–492
  attack on Hamilton, 258
  attacks on Washington, 281–282, 490–491
  Jefferson and, 281, 297, 490–492, 556, 576
  Prospect Before Us, 281
Calvinism, 47, 310, 324, 752–753, 800
  effect of Enlightenment ideas, 320–321
  doctrine of predestination, 311
Cameahwait, Shoshone chief, 529–530
Canada, 488
  boundary with U.S., 714
  escape of slaves to, 762–764
  invasion of, 590, 599–604, 606, 609, 611, 654–655
Canal-building, 329–337
  benefits of, 335, 337
  canal boom, 335, 774–775

Canal-building (*cont.*):
  construction of locks, 329
  Erie Canal, 769–773
    feeder canals, 774
  locks, 329–330
  Middlesex Canal Company, 330–331
  stock speculation, 330–331
  technology for, 329
  use of Irish immigrant labor, 747–748
  (*See also* Internal improvements)
Canning, George (British prime-minister),
  563, 565, 581, 619, 628
Canning, Stratford, 714
Canton (China), trade with, 337–341
Capital punishment, 319
Capitalism, 326–351, 500
  American character and, 342–343
  canal-building, 329–337
  capacity to take initiative, 342
  foreign commerce, 337–344
  influence of Protestantism on, 310
  need for capital, 672–673
  risk-taking, 342
  toll roads, 335–337
Capital of United States
  location of permanent, 133–134, 141–142,
    154–156
  in New York City, 117
  in Philadelphia, 120, 133–134, 141–142,
    154–156, 274
  reconstructed, 694
  (*See also* Washington)
Caribbean, trade with, 559
Carlyle, Thomas, 391
Carolina (fourteen-gun), 649–650
Carolinas:
  land speculation, 4
  post-revolutionary tension and conflicts,
    15–16
  warfare between Loyalists and Patriots,
    4–7
  (*See also* North Carolina; South Carolina)
Carr, Dabney, 576
Carroll, Charles, 126
  signer of the Declaration of Independence,
    793–794
Carter, George, 398
Cary, Anne, 799
Cary, Matthew, 263, 267
Catherine the Great of Russia, 510
Catholicism, 748, 820
  (*See also* Roman Catholic Church)
Causes, American's espousal of, 300
Cayuga Indians, 603
Census, 198–199
  1810, 732
  1820, 732
Chamber of Commerce, 116

Channing, William Ellery, 752
Charbonneau, Toussaint, 525, 530, 540
Charitable organizations, 46, 116, 679
  controversy over, 677–678
  to help unemployed, 675
  soup kitchens, 675
Charles X, King of France, 808
Charleston, South Carolina:
  anti-British feelings, 217
  British blockade, 559
  free blacks on ships placed in jail, 789
  opposition to Jay Treaty, 224
  Seamen's Acts of 1822 and 1823, 789
  summer plantation residents, 439
Chase, Samuel, 16, 495–496
  impeachment trial, 495–496
Chauncey, Isaac, 607, 611
  naval engagement on Lake Champlain,
    613
Checks and balances, 61
Cherokee Indians, 198
  Elias Boudinot, 792–793
Chesapeake (American warship), 563–565, 567
Chesapeake and Ohio Canal Company, 334,
  793
Chesapeake Bay:
  British attacks, 629
  controversy over Potomac River and, 16
Chestnut, Mary, 444
Chew, Benjamin, 5
Chickasaw Bluffs, 465–466, 505, 545
Chickasaw tribe, 465–466
China trade, 337–339
  centered in Boston, 340
Chinook Indians, 534, 537
Chippewaa Indians, 548
Choctaw Indians, 198
Christianity:
  republican form of government and, 115
  utopian ideals and, 35–37
  (*See also* Protestant Christianity)
Cincinnati, Ohio, 185, 461
Cities, 376–377
  ambivalence about, 392
  urban life, 380–393
Citizen Genêt (French privateer), 208–209
Citizenship, duties of, 320–321
Clark, George Rogers, 487, 514, 546, 646,
  652
Clark, William, 511
  command of territorial militia, 544, 546
  governor of Missouri Territory, 546
  leadership ability, 543
  (*See also* Lewis and Clark Expedition)
Class differences, 42–46, 206–207, 777–784,
  827
  competitive character, 779–781
  entrepreneurial activities, 45

first families, 370, 778
hereditary privileges, 43
idealized Christian "type," 778
local elites, 370, 778
lower classes, 44, 779
middle class, 43, 45, 779
no official classes in U.S., 778
and right to make money, 43–44
upper class, 43, 64, 370, 778–784
  career opportunities for, 780
  effect of competitive conditions on, 780–781
  failure and breakdown, 781–782
  marriages, 781–783
  mistresses, 781–782
  pressures on sons to succeed, 779
  self-control and lack of emotion, 783–784
  sexual drives, 782–783
  working class or blue collar, 779
Classical-Christian Consciousness, 19–20, 54, 57, 68, 71, 116, 144, 252, 279, 479, 709, 759
  Madison and, 579
  represented by John Adams, 500–501, 816, 824
  supplanted by Secular-Democratic Consciousness, 310
  tragic view of history, 279, 319
Clatsop Indians, 537
Clay, Henry, 504, 585–590, 811
  Compromise of 1820, 656–657
  denunciation of Jackson's conduct in the Seminole wars, 666–668, 723, 727
  election of 1824, 719–723, 726–729
  electoral votes, 726
  favored chartering national bank, 658
  Missouri Compromise and, 694–696
  peace negotiations with British, 638
  popularity in Southwest, 719
  presidential candidate (1824), 721–723
  Speaker of the House, 694, 721
  supported John Quincy Adams, 727
  supported declaration of war, 593
Clinch, D.L., 663
Clinton, De Witt, 362, 724, 804
  Erie Canal and, 769–773
Clinton, George (Governor of New York), 124, 201, 210–211, 213
  and Burr, 291
  vice-presidential candidate (1804), 551–553
  vice-presidential candidate (1808), 574–575
Clothing and dress, 389–391
  Federalist and Republican influence, 389
  French versus American cockades, 223
  hats and plumes, 223, 390
  introduction of trousers, 389–390
  shoes, 390–391

Clymer, George, 155
  signer of the Declaration of Independence, 786
Cobbett, William, 277, 306, 749, 788
Cochrane, Vice Admiral Sir, 629–630, 632, 635–636
  attack on Baltimore, 633, 636, 639
  at New Orleans, 648
Cochrane, Sylvester, 735
Cockades, French vs. American, 223
Cockburn, Rear Admiral Sir George:
  attack on American coastal towns and cities, 628–629, 631, 633–634
Cockfighting, 440–441
Coffee from Arabia, 341
Cohens v. Virginia, 706
Colles, Christopher, 333
Columbia (merchant ship), 337–338
Columbia (Ohio), 460–461
Columbia River, 338, 527, 713
  Indians, 531–538
  Lewis and Clark Expedition, 530–531
Columbian Centinel, 641
Comanche Indians, 549
Commerce, 133, 235
  effect of Jay Treaty, 240
  imports and exports, 670–671
  trading rights of nonbelligerents in wartime, 558–559
  (*See also* Foreign commerce; Ships and shipping)
Committee of the States, 18
Common Sense (Paine), 8, 101–102, 207, 787
Communism, 286, 301, 349
Communities, 47–48, 376–379, 688
  boom-towns, 378
  celebrations and holidays, 378
  colonized, 686
  cooperative, 688–689
  congregations of families, 366
  covenanted, 377, 670, 688
  cooperative, 688–689
  cumulative, 377–378, 736
  makers, 733
  names given to, 391–392
  primacy over the individual, 47–49
  town life, 378–379
Competitive character of American life, 688, 779
Compromise of 1820, 656–657
Concord, Mass., 25–26
Confederation, 1–22
  Adams defense of, 120
  candidates for public office, 7–11
  critical period (1783–1789), 33–34
  economic conflicts, 11–18
  friction between debtor and creditor, 13–16

Confederation (*cont.*):
  inadequacies of, 34, 133
  Loyalists and, 4–7
  Massachusetts Farmers' Revolt, 23–34
  shortage of money, 12
  slavery issue, 16–17
Confederation Congress, 1, 3, 6–7, 18, 97
  Committee of the States, 18
  power to levy duties, 12
  powerlessness of, 6, 142
  redemption of certificates, 147
  resentment toward, 3, 9, 18
  sessions poorly attended, 18
  slavery problem, 16–17
  speculation in certificates of, 157–158
  trade regulations, 16
Congregationalists (the Puritans), 39, 40,
    288–289, 311–313, 759
Congress:
  amendments of the Constitution, 165–167
  authority to emancipate slaves, 163
  bill of rights, 133
  birth of, 131–133
  Confederate (*see* Confederation Congress)
  debate on Jackson's campaign in Florida,
    666–668
  First (1789), 117
    achievements, 142–143
    assumption of state debts, 147–148
    discussion of proper pay, 141
    import duties and protective tariffs,
      133–136, 142
    issues facing, 148
    Judiciary Act of 1789, 136–139
    location of permanent capital, 141–142,
      154–156
    Maclay's record of, 159–160
    redemption of old Confederate Congress
      certificates, 147
    relationship between executive branch
      and, 132–146
    Washington's influence, 160
    white-Indian relations, 183–184
  import duties on foreign goods, 133–136,
    142
  location of permanent capital, 133–134,
    141–142, 154–156, 198
  make-up of legislators, 132
  protective tariff issue, 134–136
  relations with executive branch, 132–146
  resentment of Continental Army veterans,
    9
  Second (1791), 195–196
Congress of Vienna, 718, 818
Connecticut, 453
  delegates to Constitutional Convention, 52
  old families, 370
  prisons, 13

  retirement age for judges, 368
  Western Reserve, 4
  Wyoming Valley controversy, 4
Connecticut River, canals, 331–332
Consciousness:
  Classical-Christian (*see* Classical-Christian
    Consciousness)
  historical, 415–416
  ideas and prejudices, 827
  postprimitive, 192
  Protestant Christianity and, 46–47
  radical democratic, 307–308
  Secular-Democratic (*see*
    Secular-Democratic Consciousness)
Constitution, 33
  admission of new states, 584
  adoption in less than ten months, 114
  Amendments to, 165–167
    proposed by Hartford Convention, 643
  Bill of Rights, 91, 133, 165–167
  conservative reaction to Declaration, 95–96
  executive branch, 66–69
    powers, 494
  expression of Classical-Christian
    Consciousness, 96
  First Amendment, 267–270
  framers, 96, 785–801
    (*See also* Constitutional Convention)
  interpretation of, 108
  modeled on constitutions of states, 21
  momentous political accomplishment, 825
  Ninth Amendment, 167
  object of, 699–700
  opposition to, 96–98
  opposition to altering, 791–792
  Philadelphia celebration of ratification,
    109–116
  powers granted Congress, 21
  ratification (*see* Ratification)
  right to bear arms, 349
  Secular-Democratic Consciousness,
    107–108
  separation of powers, 238
  signing, 785
    Franklin's comment on "rising sun," 93,
      110
  Tenth Amendment, 167
  Twelfth Amendment, 726
  Washington on, 33
Constitution (American warship), 618–620
  Guerrière vs., 615–620
Constitutional Convention (1787), 13, 50–94
  adjournment of July 16, 86–87
  admission of new states, 58–60, 82, 84–85
  amendments, 60
  authority to replace Articles of
    Confederation, 62–63
  bill of rights, 91, 133, 165–167

brilliant achievement, 54
British models and precedents, 62, 66, 76, 78, 94, 128
Committee of Detail to draft Constitution, 88–89
compromise proposed, 82–83
debates and oratory, 56–57
delegates to, 52–56, 788
equal vs. proportional representation, 57, 62–63, 79, 81, 83
  compromise proposed, 82–83
  large-state versus small state, 79–87
  rules for counting slaves, 83–89
executive branch, 66–67, 88, 494
  power to impeach executive, 68–69
  term in office, 66–67
historic importance, 54, 93–94, 108
impassé, 80–88
impeachment issue, 68, 88
import and export duties, 90
judicial branch, 58, 69
legislative branch, 57, 65–66, 88
  choice by state legislatures or by people directly, 69–70
  right to negate state laws, 57–58, 72–73
Madison's notes, 56
nation "talked into existence," 57, 588, 707
nationalists vs. powers of the states, 58, 69, 71–79
New Jersey Plan, 74–79
North-South differences, 63, 83–87
opposition to, 52
paper money issue, 72–73
popular elections, 70–71
provisions, 57–74
ratification of the Constitution, 92–93, 95–109
  (See also Ratification)
rule of secrecy, 53
signing of, 92–93, 110, 785
slave states and free states, 63
slavery question, 83–85, 89–91
small-state, large-state conflict, 79–88
state-federal relationships, 58, 69, 71–79
state sovereignty issue, 57–58
states vs. national government, 58, 69, 71–72
to strengthen union of the states, 826
suffrage issue, 63–65
Virginia Plan, 57–74, 76
  philosophical background, 60–61
Washington served as chairman, 52–53, 86, 101
Constitutions, states, 21, 62, 119
Continental Army, 7, 25
  devotion to Washington, 9–10
  recruits, 8
  resentment toward Congress, 9

Continental Congress:
  Boudinot president of, 791
  lacked power to govern, 50–51
Continental Divide, 530, 541
Contradictions and paradoxes in America, 742–746
Convict-servants, 178
Cooper, Charles, 499
Cooper, Thomas, 297, 306
Copenhagen, 565, 566
Copley, John Singleton, 396–401
  Death of Major Peirson, 416–417
  historical paintings, 399
  portrait of John Quincy Adams, (illus.) 407, 726
Corporations, chartered, 702
Cosway, Maria, 130, 493
Cottage industry, 767
Cotton:
  export of, 221
  Lowell cotton mills, 766–769
  manufacturing cloth, 350, 669–670, 766–769
  shipping to New Orleans, 468
  Southern trade with Great Britain, 560
Cotton-gin, invention of, 346–349
Couche's Fort, 228
Council Bluffs, 518
Counterrevolutions, 301
Courtney, Captain, 212
Crawford, William H., 585, 588, 659, 662, 665
  electoral votes, 726, 728
  illness, 723–724
  presidential candidate (1824), 721–724
  secretary of the treasury, 660, 721
Crazy Horse, Indian Chief, 520
Creditors, 11
  (See also Debtor-creditor conflicts)
Creek Nation, 148, 198, 466, 596
  Jackson's campaign against, 644–647
  treaty negotiations, 183–184, 198
Crèvecoeur, Hector St. John de, 169
Crime and punishments, 676
  frontier settlements, 178
  youth gangs, 678
Crockett, Davy, 768
Croghan, George, 607, 609
Crowninshield, Jacob, 341
Culture, American, 180
  politics and, 310
Cumberland Gap, 459
Currency, 657
  (See also Money)
Currie, Dr. William, 429
Curtis, George Ticknor, 707
Cushing, William, 139
Custis, George Washington, 808–809

Dacres, British Capt. James, 616–617
Dakotan Indians, 521
Dallas, Alexander, 212
Dallas, Alexander James, secretary of the treasury, 589, 670
Dana, Francis, 255
Dana, Richard Henry, 344, 363, 725
Dancing, 451
Dartmouth College, 197, 353, 755
Dartmouth College Case, 700–702
Daveiss, Joseph, 504
Davie, William, 277
Davis, John, 382, 448
    comments on yellow fever, 427–429, 435
    on contrast between Virginians and New Jerseyians, 452–453
    on Jefferson's inauguration, 472
    on plantation life, 435–439, 441
    tutor to Drayton family, 435
Dayton, Jonathan, 245, 297, 504
Dearborn, Henry, 477, 574, 597, 600, 611
    headquarters at Plattsburgh, 604
Death, preoccupation with, 368–369, 415, 418
Debtor-creditor conflicts, 11–16, 673–675
    belief friends and family would pay debt, 674–675
    flight from debt, 675
    incarceration for debt, 14
    savagery of laws, 673–674
Decatur, Stephen (the elder), 265
Decatur, Stephen (the younger), 552, 613, 618, 656
Declaration of Independence, 7–8, 9, 95
    celebration in Philadelphia, 109–110
    equality, 47
    expression of Secular-Democratic Consciousness, 96
    influences on, 36, 55, 96
    removed from Washington, 630
Declaration of Independence, historical painting by John Trumbull, 417
Declaration of the Rights of Man, 145, 309, 674
Delaware
    delegates to Constitutional Convention, 63
    ratification of Constitution, 98
Delaware (sloop of war), 265
Delaware and Hudson Canal, 747–748
Delaware Indians, 595
Democracy, 60–61, 785
    country's ills due to "excess of democracy," 51, 61, 63
    fears of, 34, 420
    Hamilton's skepticism about, 797–798
    leaderships and, 543–544

suspicion of power and wealth, 300–305
    vices of, 76
Democratic Societies, 205, 209
    anti-British feelings, 217–218
    opposition to Jay Treaty, 217, 223
Democrats, Jeffersonian, 107
de Neuville, Baron Hyde, 425
Dennie, Joseph, 422, 490, 493–494, 551, 556
Depression following War of 1812, 669–689
    effects in agricultural communities, 686–689
    side effects, 676–681
Descartes, René, 315
de Soto, Hernando, 466, 468
Detroit, 599–600
    British at, 609
    Hull's surrender, 600, 604
Dexter, Samuel, secretary of war, 283
Dickens, Charles, 775–776
Dickinson, John, 68–69, 71, 320
    Founding Father, 786–787
Dictatorships, 61
Diderot, Denis, 35
Diplomacy, frank and open, 225
Distribution system, 350
Disunion, threats of, 656, 796
    effect of Missouri question, 691–693
Divine Providence, 80
    and creation of United States, 127, 425
Doddridge, Rev. Dr. Joseph, 173–181, 470–471, 555
    Notes on Early Settlement and Indian Wars, 173–174
Douglass, Frederick, 763
Downie, British Capt. George, 613–614
Drayton, William Henry, 436
Drayton plantation, 435–436
Drewyer, George, 525, 529
Drummond, British General, 612–613
Drunkenness, 388, 431
    Indian problem, 462, 680
    temperance movement, 751
    upper class families, 780–781
    (*See also* Alcoholism)
Duane, William, 273–274, 281, 297, 306, 556, 589
Duels and dueling, 450, 452
    Hamilton and Burr, 499
    Philip Hamilton and Eaker, 475
Dunkards (religious sect), 313
Duponceau, Peter, 205, 209, 300
Du Pont de Nemours, 506
Duties on imported goods, 25, 592–593
    (*See also* Tariffs)
Dwight, Timothy, 171–172, 179, 183, 219, 342, 752–753

The Conquest of Canaan, 420
poetry, 419–420

Eaker, George, 474–475
Earle, Ralph, portrait of Roger Sherman, 399,
   (*illus.*) 409
Earthquakes, Mississippi River Valley, 591
East Indian trade, 220
Eastern Establishment, 123
Economic conditions:
  access to capital, 672–673
  economic remedies, 679
  moral remedies, 679
  public works to stimulate economy, 685
  side effects of depressed economy,
    676–681
Education, 352–365
  based on science and reason, 817
  classical vs. practical, 354–355
  exaltation of United States, 364–365
  family responsibilities, 369
  founding of Christian colleges, 352–353
  free public, 353, 356, 359–360, 362, 678
  of Indians, 197
  influence on mind and character, 353
  of an informed citizenry, 353, 358
  Jefferson's comprehensive plan, 357–359,
    361, 817
  Manning's views, 353–354, 687
  moral aspects, 355–356, 360–363
  physical punishments, 363
  plans for Federal University, 360–361, 731
  private tutors, 369
  Protestant emphasis on, 352–354, 360
  religious schools, 361–362
  schools for poor children, 362, 687
  state universities and community colleges,
    360
  study of history, 355, 358, 364
  views of John Adams, 352–353, 358–360
  views of Benjamin Franklin, 354–355
  views of Benjamin Rush, 353–355, 360–362
  views of Noah Webster, 355–357
  of women, 356–357
Edward, Jonathan, 195, 290
  descendants, 419
Edwards County (Illinois), English
  settlements, 738–741
Eisenhower, Dwight D., 116
Elections:
  of 1792, 200–201, 248
  of 1796, 244–249
  of 1800, 285–308
    Adams-Pinckney ticket, 290
    decided by House of Representatives,
      294–295
    electors, 290, 293–294

Jefferson-Burr ticket, 290, 294
  power transferred from one party to
    another, 298
  Republican issues, 289
  slavery and nonslavery issue, 305
of 1804, 551–553
  Jefferson-Clinton, Republican ticket, 551
  Pinckney-King, Federalist ticket, 551
of 1808, 574
  Madison-Clinton Republican ticket, 574
  Pinckney-King, Federalist ticket, 574
of 1816, 654–661
of 1820, 690
of 1824, 718–731
  Adams-Jackson ticket, 722, 724
  candidates, 721–728
  caucus method of nomination, 722, 724
  Crawford-Clay ticket, 724
  decided by House of Representatives,
    726–729
  first "modern" election, 720–721
  mudslinging and slander, 723
Electors and electoral votes, 67, 117, 121
  Adams-Jackson election in 1824, 726–727
  election of 1792, 248
  election of 1800, 290, 294–295, 726
    attempt to rob Jefferson of the election,
      295
  procedures for choosing, 293
Eliot, John, 754
Elliott, Jonathan, *Debates in the State Ratifying
  Convention,* 101
Ellsworth, Oliver, 130, 136–137, 282
  envoy to France, 277
  resignation of, 296
  Supreme Court justice, 195
Embargo, 551–574
  attacks on, 569
  consequences of, 566–572
  debates in Congress, 593
  disastrous economic effects, 573
  effect on Britain and France, 572–573
  enforcement of, 567, 570–571, 573–574
    Force Act, 573–574
  Nonimportation Act, 559–562
    signed by Jefferson, 560
  proclaimed by Washington, 216–217
  replaced by nonintercourse bill, 575–576
  smuggling and, 569–571
  third supplementary embargo bill, 570
Embargo Act, 566–567
Emerson, Ralph Waldo, 806
Emotional reactions of American men, 241
England (*see* Great Britain)
Enlightenment, 35–36, 107, 144, 286, 310,
  554
  effect on Calvinism, 311, 315

Enlightenment (cont.):
  effect on religious doctrines, 311, 315–316, 319–321
  philosophers, 35
  (See also Secular-Democratic Consciousness)
Entertainment, within families, 369
Episcopal church, 312, 751, 759
Eppes, John, 588–589
Equality, 45–46, 206
  American interpretation, 331
  class distinctions and, 42–43
  community and, 47–49
  early enthusiasm for, 687
  ethic of, 47
  Pinckney's speech on, 77–79
  right to make money and, 43–46
  views of John Adams, 120
"Era of good feelings," 661, 669
Erie Canal, 335, 747–748, 769–773
  Commission to survey, 770
  engineers, 770–771
  feeder canals, 774
  labor-saving methods, 771
  locks, 770–771
  official opening (1825), 772–773
  passengers and freight, 775–776
  success of, 774, 776
  symbol of American determination and ingenuity, 772–774
  traveling medicine shows, 776
Erie School of Engineering, 770
Erskie, David (British minister), 581–582
Establishment, 123
  New England ruling class, 312
  power in hands of, 720
European powers, effect on United States policies, 710–712, 717
Europeans, view of American people, 424, 449
Eustis, William, secretary of war, 581, 601, 604
Eustis, William (Governor of Massachusetts), 804–805
Everett, Edward, 806
Ewing, William, 547
Excise bill (1791), 161–163
Executive branch, 66–69, 699–700
  judicial branch and, 698
Expansionist spirit, 654
  (See also Westward migration)

Failure and success, coping with, 336, 681
Fallen Timbers, Battle of, 232, 514, 531, 595
Families and family life, 366–376
  affectional character, 370
  basic economic unit, 366
  communities and, 376–379
  educational responsibilities, 369

entertainment, 369
  extended families, 367–368
  food and shelter, 374–376
  need for large families, 376
  parent-child relationships, 367
  religious attitudes, 377
  role of elders, 368
  rural poor, 374–376
  sexual behavior, 370–374
  social life, 367–368
  Southern, 370–371, 435–441
    (See also Plantation life)
  upper-class, 370, 380–393, 426, 778–784
  urban life, 380–393
  wife's role, 372–373
  youth oriented, 368
  women's role, 366–367, 372–373
Farmers, 686–687
  petition for redress of grievances, 23–24
  relationship with plantation owners, 440–441
  Southern states, 440
  uprising of Massachusetts farmers, 23–24
Fauchet (Genêt's successor), 225
Fayal, neutral port, 624–625
Fayetteville, North Carolina, 812
Federal Convention (see Constitutional Convention)
Federal court system, 136–139
  relationship to state courts, 137
  (See also Supreme Court)
Federal government, 34
  ability to pay for internal improvements, 683
  attacks on Union, 641–642
  authority of, 237
  disunion, threats of, 328, 656, 796
  material achievements and moral improvement, 827–829
  nationhood and national unity, 656
  powers of, 795
Federal Republican (newspaper), 598
"Federalist" aristocracy, 671
Federalist newspapers, 32, 555–556
  Jefferson's opposition to, 555–556
Federalist Papers, 105, 146, 304, 424, 579
  debates on treaty-making power of the House, 237
  Madison's views, 71, 794
Federalists, 35, 95–97, 105, 122
  accomplishments, 304, 307
  Anti-Federalists versus, 117–118, 131
  anti-French feelings, 204–205, 278
  Congressional program, 160–163
  decline of party, 267, 551, 553, 778
  election of 1796, 244–249
  election of 1800, 299
  election of 1804, 551

election of 1816, 658–659
Hamilton and Adams wings, 275–279
Jay Treaty favored by, 237–242
Jefferson and, 555–557
leaders, 300
Marbury v. Madison, 476–483
objected to repeal of Judiciary Act, 477–483
opposition to Louisiana Purchase, 487–489, 648
party rupture, 283
philosophy of, 240–241
principles and policies, 304
pro-British feelings, 278
property tax law passed by, 272–274
reaction to French Revolution, 204–205
Secession Federalists, 639–640
supporters of Constitution, 95
Fenno, John, 154
Ferdinand VII, king of Spain, 710–712
Fillmore, Millard, 720
"Financial oligarchy," 305
Findley, William, 159, 195, 423
Finney, Charles, 751–752
Fire departments, 387
First Amendment, 267–270
Fitzsimmons, Thomas, 110
Five-Civilized Tribes, 663
Flags:
    at Fort McHenry, 634, 637
    star added for each new state, 625
Flathead Indians, 531
Fletcher v. Peck, 608, 700–701
Flint, Timothy, 690
Florida:
    Indians in East Florida, 662–663
    Jackson attacks on Seminole Indians, 662–665, 723
    refuge for runaway slaves, 662
    Spanish control, 484, 663–665
    West Florida, 486–487
Folger, Benjamin, 746
Food and shelter, 385
    frontier settlements, 174–176
    on plantations, 436
    rural poor, 374–375
Forbes, Robert Bennet, 340
Ford, Henry, 287
Foreign commerce, 11, 337–344
    American Revolution and, 337
    China trade, 337–339
    effect of British paper blockade, 559–560
    with Far East, 337–339
    (*See also* Embargo; Ships and shipping)
Foreign missionary activity, 756–758
    financial support, 756–757
    hospitals and clinics, 757–758
    schools and colleges, 757–758

Foreign policy:
    of John Adams, 250
    Washington's Inaugural Address and, 246–247
Forests, 328
Fort Clatsop, 537–539
Fort Defiance, 232
Fort Deposit, 646
Fort Erie, 612
Fort Gadsden, 665
Fort George (British), 601, 608, 611
Fort Hamilton, 188
Fort Jackson, 647
Fort Jefferson, 188–189
Fort McHenry, 633, 656
    British bombing of, 634–637
Fort Malden, 599–600, 605, 609
Fort Massac, 503, 505, 546
Fort Meigs, 606
Fort Miami, British post, 232
Fort Niagara, British driven from, 611
Fort Recovery, 231
Fort Stanwix Treaty, 184
Fort Stephenson, 607, 609
Fort Strother, 646
Fort Washington, 187, 630
Fort Wayne, 233, 595, 604
Forts, for protection from Indians, 176, 231–233
Foster, Augustus, 589–590
Founding Fathers, 785–801
    deplored obsession with money making, 45
    on education, 353
    Federalists, 785
    Madison, 580
    (*See also* Constitutional Convention)
Fourth of July celebrations, 681, 820–821
    death of Adams and Jefferson on July 4, 1826, 820–821
    Grand Procession in Philadelphia, 109–116
    Legaré's oration, 807–809
    Lewis and Clark Expedition, 515–516
Fox, Charles James (British prime minister), 562
France, 110
    Berlin and Milan decrees, 562, 565, 588–589, 671
    declared war against England, Holland, and Spain, 208
    defeat of Napoleon and peace with England, 627
    effect of embargo on, 572–573
    immigration from, 738
    occupied by Allied troops, 710
    sale of Louisiana territory to U.S., 486–487
Francis (Indian prophet), 663–664, 667
Franklin, Benjamin, 242, 306
    on ambition and avarice, 67–68

Franklin, Benjamin (*cont.*):
  colonial agent in London, 397
  comments on constitution & "rising sun,"
    92–93, 110
  death of, 155
  delegate to Constitutional Convention,
    54–55
  on divine guidance, 80
  on education, 354–355
  "First Principles" of religion, 316–317
  French Revolutionary song written by, 203
  on impeachment, 88
  interest in women, 371–372, 397
  inventions, 345
  land speculation, 4
  on love of power and money, 67–68
  on Loyalists, 5
  opposition to Cincinnati, 10
  religious beliefs, 315–317, 324
  on pursuit of luxury, 40–41, 64, 784
  on salary of executive, 67–68, 71
Franklin, William Temple, 371
  Tory son of Benjamin Franklin, 400
Fraunces Tavern, New York City:
  Washington's farewell to officers, 9–10, 125
Fredericktown, 629
Free enterprise, 48, 183, 422
  (*See also* Business enterprise)
Freedom of speech, 598–599
  First Amendment guarantees, 267–269
Freemasons, 286
French Alliance of 1788, 110
French-American relations:
  Adams and, 250–271, 297
  anti-Gallican faction, 255
  French-British war (1793), 208–214
  opposed by Federalists, 278
  Pinckney affair, 253–266
    demands for bribes and public apologies,
      259
    negotiations (1797–1798), 259–260
  pro-French sentiment in U.S., 264
  "quasi war," or undeclared war, 266,
    272–284, 486
  threat of war with France, 253–266
  Treaty of Commerce, 209
  (*See also* Lafayette, Marquis de)
French Directory, 276
  Adams' envoys to, 255, 259
  demands for bribes and apologies, 259
  Pinckney affair, 253–256, 259–264, 275
  relations with United States, 248, 253–265,
    269, 275
  threat to hang American sailors captured
    at sea, 254
  Washington's policy toward, 248
French immigrants, 380–382

French philosophers, 35, 320
French Revolution, 142–145, 202–214,
  229–300, 719, 826–827
  American support for, 202–214
  awesome and cataclysmic event, 299–300,
    308
  Battle of Valmy, 202–204
  celebrations of victories in Boston, 203–204
  compared to American Revolution,
    204–205, 300, 309
  Declaration of the Rights of Man, 145,
    309, 674
  dissillusionment with, 720, 755, 786–787
  émigrés to U.S. following, 380–382
  "Gallomania," 204–205, 301
  implications for Americans, 304–305
  infatuation of Americans with, 204–205,
    239, 241
  Jefferson-Adams correspondence, 816, 818
  philosophical doctrines, 286
French traders, 547
Frenchtown, occupation of, 605
Freneau, Philip, 36–37, 154, 211, 297, 420
  sponsored by Jefferson, 556
Fries, John, 272–274
Fries's rebellion, 272–274, 826
Frontier settlements, 168–194
  along rivers, 327
  bill for protection of, 199–200
  character of people, 343, 453
  colonization of wilderness, 171–172
  counterculture, 180
  crops, 170
  English settlements, 738–741
  failures and defeats, 741
  food supply, 174–176
  forts, 176, 231–233
  frontier life, 173–180
  gouging and biting, 449–450
  hardships and sacrifices, 174
  Indian ràids, 176–177, 181–183
  migration to, 732–737
  missionary activities, 754–755
  population, 732
  progress of "science and civilization," 179
  religious revivals, 314–315, 751–752
  settlers advice to those at home, 740–741
  Southern settlers, 441–442
  stages of, 169–171
  successful, 738–741
  (*See also* Westward migration)
Funerals and mourning, 369
  preoccupation with death, 368–369, 415,
    418
Fur trade, 182, 515, 713
  with China, 340–341
  Pacific coast, 338–339

Gadsden, Christopher, 298
Gaines, Gen. Edmund, 663
Gallatin, Albert, 230, 237, 261, 269, 292, 477, 571, 581, 589, 679
  Jefferson and, 700
  Lafayette and, 812–813
  opposed embargo, 566, 568
  peace negotiations with British, 638
  U.S. minister in Paris, 712
Gallatin, James, 812–813
Gallipolis, 459
Gallomania, 204–205, 301
Galveston (Spanish warship), 125
Gambling, 677, 746
  upper class families, 780
Garrison, William Lloyd, 194
Gates, Horatio, 790
Gazette of the United States, 154, 591
General Armstrong (American schooner), 624–625
General Intelligencer (newspaper), 704
Genêt, Edmond Charles Édouard, 208–214, 381
  denunciation of Washington, 210–211
  on the embargo, 574–575
  marriage to Clinton's daughter, 574
  public acclaim, 209–211
Genius of Universal Emancipation (abolitionist newspaper), 765
Geography of 18th-century America, 326–327, 363
  land and water, 326–328
Georgetown, British attacks, 629
Georgia, 453
  post-revolutionary conflicts, 15
  ratification of the Constitution, 98
  Yazoo Land fraud, 698–699
German immigrants, 738, 742
  worked building canals, 747–748
Gerry, Elbridge, 69–70, 83–84, 92–93, 165, 269
  Anti-Federalist opposition, 97
  country ills due to "excess of democracy," 61, 63, 95
  delegate to Constitutional Convention, 63, 66, 69, 87
  envoy to French Republic, 255, 275
  opposition to Constitution, 98
Ghent, Treaty of, peace negotiations, 638–639
Gibbons v. Ogden, 706–709
Gibbs, Gen. Sir Samuel, 651
Gilbert, Felix, 225
Giles, William, 496–497, 589, 686
Ginseng root, exported to China, 337
Girard, Stephen, 46, 128
Gladstone, William, 94

Gorham, Nathaniel, 11–12, 99
Gouging and biting, 449–450
Goulburn, Henry (British negotiator), 638
Government (*see* Federal Government)
Grant, William, 400
  The Skater, Portrait of William Grant by Gilbert Stuart, (*illus.*) 410
Gray, Capt. Robert, 337–339
Graydon, Alexander, 42, 272
Grayson, William, 130, 135, 138, 165
Great Britain:
  anti-British feelings, 217, 590, 654
  aristocracy, 777–778
  boundary between Canada and U.S., 714
  contempt for American fighting qualities, 651–652
  desire to chastise Americans, 627–628, 632
  effect of American naval victories, 619–620
  effect of embargo on, 572
  impressment of American seamen, 560–564
  Indian allies, 597
  Jay sent to London, 218
  manufacture of cotton cloth, 349
  mercantile system, 3
  merchant ships attacked by American privateers, 623–626
  as model for American Constitution, 62, 66, 76, 78, 94, 128
  Monroe Doctrine approved by, 716
  naval fleet on Great Lakes, 608–609
  negotiations over neutral trade and impressment, 561–565
  New Orleans expedition, 639, 647–653
  Old Northwest posts, 4, 168, 184, 217, 713
  orders in council, 558, 562, 566, 572, 600, 654, 671
    repeal of, 600
  "paper blockade," 559
  peace negotiations with Americans, 638–639
  raids launched against American coastal towns, 628–629
  seizure of American ships in Carribean, 215–216
  sentiment for war with, 216, 560, 564–565, 590
  trade interests in Northwest, 713
  War of 1812 (*see* War of 1812)
  war with France (1793), 208
    American neutrality, 208–214
  (*See also* British-American relations)
Great Lakes:
  American fleet, 607–608
  British fleet, 608–609
  War of 1812, 594, 597, 600–607
Great Plains, 465

Green Spring, Battle of, 189
Greene, Nathanael, 10–11, 15–16
Greene, Mrs. Nathanael, 346–347
Greenleaf, Colonel, 28–29
Greenville, Treaty of, negotiations, 231–234
Greenwood, John, 402
Griswold, Gov. Roger, 268, 498, 597
Gruber, Rev. John, 634, 762
Guerrière (British warship), 615–620
Guns:
   manufacturing, 348–349
   right to bear arms, 349
Gwinnett, Button, 15

"Hail Columbia!" 262
Haley, Alex, 441
Halifax, 615
Hamilton, Alexander, 19, 35, 80, 93, 381
   and Adams, 121–122, 248–249, 252, 275,
     822
   animosity between Burr and, 290–291,
     293, 308, 496, 498–501
   attempts to nullify Republican victory in
     1798, 293
   character, 499–501, 652
   death of son, 474–475, 499
   delegate to Constitutional Convention,
     75–76, 80
   denigration of, 501
   duel with Burr, 496, 499–501
   Federalist Paper author, 105
   Federalist Party leader, 121–122, 214,
     275–279
   financial plans, 147, 148
   funeral, 501–502
   "gladiators," 155–156, 160, 244
   ineligible for election to presidency, 121
   and Jefferson, 153–154, 499
   leadership qualities, 652
   Monroe's attempt to discredit, 257–258
   Morris and, 797
   on New Jersey Plan, 75–76
   pamphlet warfare, 211–212
   personal coterie, 155–156, 160, 244
   plan of government, 75–76
   plot against election of Adams, 248–249
   political views, 797
   pro-British feelings, 217–223
   ratification, supported by, 106–107
   on republican government, 102
   scandal involving Maria Reynolds,
     257–258, 371, 499
   secretary of treasury, 129, 208, 210
   Washington's advocacy of, 118–119,
     230–231, 474
Hamilton, Paul, 581
Hamilton, Philip, 475, 499

Hammond, George (British minister to U.S.),
   217, 220, 225
Hampton, Wade, 597, 611
Hampton, Virginia, British attack, 629
Hamtramck, Maj. John, 185
Hancock, John, 31, 165, 805
   governor of Mass., 31, 34
   voted for the Constitution, 99
Happiness, right to, 35–36
Harbah, Leonard, 346
Hardin, John, 185–187
Harmar, Josiah, 186–187, 190
Harper, William, 709
Harrison, William Henry, 505
   Battle of the Thames, 610–611
   commander in chief of army in the
     Northwest, 604, 610
   at Fort Meigs, 606
   governor of Indiana Territory, 595–596
   Kentucky volunteers, 610
   on Ontario peninsula, 610
   raid on Tippecanoe, 596
   treaty negotiations, 595–596
Hart, Lucretia, 586
Hartford (Conn.), Lafayette's visit, 806
Hartford Convention, 640–643
   opposed in the South, 641–642
   proposed amendments to Constitution, 643
Harvard College, 352–353, 420
   Lafayette's visit, 805–806
   Unitarianism stronghold, 754
Haswell, Anthony, 281
Havre de Grace, British attacks, 628–629
Hawkins, Benjamin, 644–645
Hawthorne, Nathaniel, 775
Hazard, Ebenezer, 318
Heard, Gerald, 193
Heighway (settler), 455–461
   new town, founded by, 460–461
Hemings, Easton, 577–578
Hemings, Madison, 492, 577–578
Hemings, Sally, 476, 490–493, 577
Henry, Patrick, 130, 207, 799
   land speculation, 4
   opposition to ratification, 101–104
Herrick, George, 369
Hewson, Mr. and Mrs., 111
Hibernian Society, 116
Hidalgo y Costilla, 711
Higginson, Stephen, 264
Historical consciousness, 415–416
Historical societies, 416
History:
   cyclical view of, 60–61
   study of, 355, 358, 364
Holland, seizure of neutral ships, 566
Holmes, John, 194, 691

Holmes, Isaac, 741
Holt, Charles, 281
Holy Alliance, 710–717, 818–819
  interference in Western Hemisphere
    affairs, 713
  opposed movements for independence in
    colonial possessions, 712
  reaction to Monroe Doctrine, 716–717
Hopkinson, Francis (poet, essayist), 109,
  262
Hopkinson, Joseph, 262, 703
Hornet (American warship), 618–619
Horses and horseracing, 440–441
  Indians and, 518, 521, 533, 540
  in Virginia, 441
House of Representatives:
  deadlocked presidential vote in 1824,
    726–727
  first session, 117
  organizational problems, 123–124
  treaty-making powers, 237–242
Housing, 375–376
  building manuals, 395–396
Houston, Samuel, 647
Howell, Richard (Governor of New Jersey),
  230
Hudson, David, 135
Hudson, Ohio, 734
Hudson's Bay Company, 524
Hull, Isaac, 616–618
Hull, William, 223, 597, 599–600
Human nature:
  classical view of, 19–20
  natural goodness and natural badness of
    man, 107
Humane Society, 673
Humphreys, David, 32, 118, 420
Hunting and fishing, importance in South,
  441–442
Huss, John, 313

Idleness, attitudes toward, 677–678, 784
Illinois:
  admission to Union, 690
  English settlements, 738–741
Illinois-Wabash Company, 4
Illuminati, doctrine of, 286–287
Immigration, 90, 149–150, 737–750
  adaptability and resilience needed by
    immigrants, 745–746
  from England, 732, 737–741
  experience of immigrants, 749–750
  following War of 1812, 737–750
  from Germany, 738, 742–746
  increase in, 732, 737–738
  from Ireland, 732, 737–738, 746–748
  Priestly on the advantages of America, 749

  resentment toward immigrants, 743–744
  from Switzerland, 738, 742–746
Impeachment powers, 68, 88
Imports and exports:
  British imports, 669
  duties, 553
  value of, 671
  (*See also* Tariffs)
Impost bill, 133–136, 142
Impressment of American sailors, 560–564,
  654
  British sailors encouraged to desert, 561
  campaign against, 561
  negotiations, 561–565
Indentured servants, 740–741, 746
  Irish immigrants, 748
Independent Chronicle (Boston newspaper),
  206, 263, 267, 274, 287
India, commercial ties to, 341
Indiana Territory, 595
  migration to, 733
  settlements, 741
Indians:
  allied with British, 4, 168, 603
  antagonisms between tribes, 532
  astronomers, 517
  attacks, 148, 159, 168–194, 199
  Battle of Fallen Timbers, 232, 514, 531,
    595
  Bible translated into Indian language, 754,
    793
  Big Bottom Massacre, 187–188
  buffalo hunts, 515, 518–519, 525
  burial mounds, 456, 461
  California tribes, 534
  canoes, 535
  clothing, 520
  Colombia River, 338–339, 531–538
    potlatch rituals, 339
  Constitutional guarantees, 59
  conversion to Christianity, 197, 754, 793
  corruption of innocence, 193
  culture, 182–183, 554–555
  diseases, 182, 519
  drunkenness problem, 462, 680
  in East Florida, 662–663
  education, 197
  forts, 231–233
  fur trade, 182, 515
  gambling, 536
  horses and horse-stealing, 518, 521, 533,
    540
  Jackson's campaign against Creeks,
    644–647
  Jefferson's views, 553–555
  languages, 194
  long lodges, 534

Indians (*cont.*):
military weaknesses, 232–233
Mississippi River Valley, 595–596
myths and legends, 193, 514–515
Northwest, 338–339
pipe of peace, 522
Plains Indians, 518–519, 531
religious beliefs, 524–525
salmon fishing, 531
scalps, 522
smallpox epidemics, 519
Southern Indians, 140
tepees, 520
trade with, 182, 465–466, 713
trading goods, 193
treatment of old Indians, 535–536
treatment of women and wives, 533, 535
treaty negotiations, 140, 181–185, 595–596, 647
Treaty of Greenville, 231–234
Treaty of 1796, 595–596
tribes, 194
Washington's policy, 196–200
Wayne's expedition to Indian Territory, 231–234
white-Indian relationship, 191–194
(*See also* under names of various tribes)
Individualism, 48–49, 183, 324–325, 342
alcoholism and, 680–681
Indolence, supreme vice, 677–678, 784
Industrialization, 41, 717
early ventures, 329–351
effect of tariff issue, 670
Lowell factories, 766–769
(*See also* Manufacturing industries)
Infidels, 755
Ingersol, Charles Jared, 49
Intemperance, 677
(*See also* Temperance movement)
"Interested parties," 147
Internal improvements:
Congressional debates, 683, 685
investments in, 671
need for public works, 676
sectional differences, 683–684
Inventions, 345–351
cotton-gin, 346–349
Washington's interest in, 333–334
Iredell, James (Supreme Court Justice), 139, 238
Irish Greens, 603
Irish immigrants, 334, 565, 737–738, 746–748
canal-building, 747–748
opposition to government, 266
Roman Catholic religion, 748
Iron industry, 134, 344
Iroquois Indians, 184

Irving, Washington, 172, 609–610
Isolationism, 247
Izard, George, 611, 613
Izard, Ralph, 132, 139–140, 155

Jackson, Andrew, 503, 505, 587, 589, 625
attack on Florida, 662–668, 711
Congressional debates on, 665–668
Battle of New Orleans, 647–653
Madison's instruction, 647–648
campaign against Creek Indians, 644–647
poorly trained and disciplined soldiers, 645–646
character and qualifications, 725
Clay's denunciation of his conduct in the Seminole Wars, 722, 723, 727
elected to Senate, 725
election of 1824, 719–720, 727–728, 808
electoral votes, 726
fight with Thomas Hart Benton, 645
hostility toward Indians, 725
Lafayette and, 812
leadership qualities, 645–646, 649, 652, 719–720
Monroe and, 660
popular support for, 719, 722
Seminole wars in Florida, 662–668
Clay's denunciation of Jackson, 666–668, 723, 727
destruction of Negro Fort, 663
Spanish protest, 665–668
slaveholder, 725
visited Lowell mills, 768
Jackson, James, 135, 184, 195, 196
"Jacobin Clubs," 205, 223
James, Henry, 773
James, William, 773
Janson, Charles, 45–46, 367, 438, 450
Jay, John, 23, 123, 201, 789–790
Chief Justice of Supreme Court, 138
church activities, 793
on deterioration of interstate relations, 19–22
elected governor of New York, 290
Federalist Papers author, 105
Genêt affair, 212–213
mentioned as presidential candidate, 244–245
mission to England, 218–219
Jay Treaty, 215–226, 562
Ames speech on behalf of, 238–241
anti-French bias, 786
debates in House, 237–242
led by Fisher Ames, 237
Federalist support, 221–226
indemnification for seizure of American ships, 219
ratification of, 222, 237

Republican opposition, 221–226
signed by Washington, 225–226
terms, 220–221
Jefferson, Martha Wayles, 576, 578
Jefferson, Thomas:
Adams and, 282–283, 359, 577, 692, 723
correspondence, 815–822
administration, 309, 472–483, 484–490
age of Jefferson, 825
ambassador to France, 10, 101, 130
on American Indians, 553–555
on Annapolis Convention, 51
appearance and temperament, 477–478
architectural interests, 394–395, 422
capital of Virginia designed by, 394
"aristocracy of talents," 7, 62, 106, 358,
360, 422–423, 777, 817
assaults on Supreme Court, 576, 642, 698,
700
attack on Barbary pirates, 552
belief in perfectibility of man, 817–818
and Burr conspiracy and trial, 504–509
campaign for presidency, 285–286
Cabinet, 477
character, 477–478, 501, 570, 576
charisma, 551–552
confrontation between Marshall and,
477–480, 700, 823
Burr's trial, 506–509
correspondence with Adams, 359, 815–822
correspondence with daughters, 784
Maria Cosway and, 130, 493
Dartmouth College Case, 701–702
death of Adams and Jefferson on July 4,
1826, 820–821
Declaration of Independence written by,
55
education, views on, 357–359, 361
election of 1800, 285–308
attack by Federalists, 285–286, 295
bloodless revolution, 298
charges of atheism, 311
platform, 285–286
embargo on American shipping, 566
family, 576–578
fear of slave insurrection, 692
Federalists removed from office, 477, 642
feelings toward Federalist newspapers, 371,
555–556
Force Act, 573–574
Genêt affair, 208–214
hostility toward banks and bankers, 157
hostility toward Hamilton, 153–154
inaugural address (1801), 296, 472–474
on interference of foreign powers in
affairs of the New World, 714–715
lack of sympathy with New England,
570–572, 643

Lafayette's visit, 809–810, 813
letter to Philip Mazzei, 256–257
Lewis and Clark Expedition authorized by,
510–512, 542, 544
on "little rebellions," 32, 144
Louisiana Purchase, 510, 552–553
Madison and, 574
on manufacturing, 392
on Missouri question, 691–692
Monroe and, 655, 659–661, 714–715
Monticello, 394, 576–578
mythology, 576
national debt, 553
navy dismantled by, 552, 592
nonimportation bill, 559–560
Notes on the State of Virginia, 144, 288
nullification doctrine, 270
opposition to Cincinnati, 10–11
patent legislation, 345
personal tragedies, 576–578
murder of young slave by nephews, 592
policy of peace at any price, 654
political enemies, 570
political views, 62, 143–144, 150, 256–257,
556–557, 816–822
limitation on executive powers, 494
redistribution of property, 301
on religious liberty, 285–289
presidential candidate, 244–249
on private ownership of land, 301, 788
on property rights, 143–145, 301
public reputation, 501, 552, 576, 823–824
on public works, 686
on pursuit of luxury, 43, 47–48
reconciliation with Adams, 815–824
symbolic significance, 824
on relations with Great Britain, 715
relationship with Sally Hemings, 371, 476,
490–493, 577–578
religious views, 285–289
attack on, 285–289, 311
represented Secular-Democratic
Consciousness, 816, 824
on republican government, 473
republican simplicity in White House,
476
retirement from public life, 574–576
revision of statutes of Virginia, 39
"revolutionary" doctrine, 270–271
on rural life, 392–393, 684
second term, 575–576
inaugural address, 553–557, 570
Secretary of State, 129–131, 152–153, 208,
214
Shays' Rebellion and, 33, 130
on slavery issue, 446–447, 577, 692, 761,
810, 819–820
trading rights of nonbelligerent in

Jefferson, Thomas (*cont.*):
  wartime, 558
  and Washington, 118, 200
Jefferson River, 527, 541
Jeffersonian Democrats, 107
Jeffersonian Republicans, 137, 207
Jews, 287, 313
  Boudinot's concern for, 793
Johnson, Gov. (of North Carolina), 155
Johnson, Richard, 610
Johnson, Dr. Samuel, 400
Jones, James, 269
Jones, John Paul, 608, 646, 652
Journal politique de Bruxelles, 94
Joy, Benjamin, 341
Joyce, James, 443
Judicial branch, 699–700
  executive branch and, 698
Judiciary Act of 1789, 136–139, 296, 495,
    699
  attempts to repeal, 477–483
Judson, Adoniram, 757–758
Juvenile crime, 678–679

Kalamath Indians, 534, 537
Kansas River, 515, 549
Kansas Tribe, 515–516
Kent, James, 779
Kentucky, 459–462
  admission to Union, 202
  frontier settlements, 172
  seige by Tecumseh, 604
  volunteers, 610
Kentucky and Virginia Resolutions, 271, 574,
    580, 705, 794
Key, Francis Scott, 634, 637
  "The Star-Spangled Banner," written by,
    637, 656
Kickapoo Indians, 233, 514, 595
King, Rufus, 52, 65, 81–82, 89, 93, 99, 568,
    659, 694–695
  Genêt affair, 212–213
  vice-presidential candidate, 551
Knox, Henry, 9–10, 131, 148, 214
  secretary of war, 131, 208
Kremer, George, 728

Labor-saving techniques, 743, 769
Lacrosse, played by Sioux warriors, 547, 812
Lafayette, George Washington, 802–803
Lafayette, Marquis de, 86, 94, 202, 802–814
  accompanied by son and Frances Wright,
    802–803
  Congressional invitation to visit U.S., 802
  financial condition, 802, 811
  French Revolution, 143
  meeting with Joseph Bonaparte, 807
  in New England, 803–806

  in New York, 803, 806
  portraits, 803, 806
  reunion with Revolutionary officers, 803
  role in French politics, 802
  title renounced by, 803
  urged Washington to accept Presidency,
    118
  visit to Mount Vernon, 808–809
  visit with John Adams, 805–806
  visit with Indians, 812
  visit with Jefferson, 809–810
  in Washington, 808–809
  on Washington's weeping at Benedict
    Arnold's treason, 806
Lake Borgne, destruction of American
    gunboats, 648–650
Lake Champlain, naval engagements, 607,
    613–614
  smuggling, 569–570
  use of Wellington's veterans, 613–614
Lake Erie, 600
  American naval engagements, 607–609
  War of 1812, 612–613
Lake Ontario, 600, 611, 660
  naval engagements, 607
Lamson, Zachary, 344
Lancaster, Pennsylvania, 742
Land:
  ambivalent view of, 327–328
  form of currency, 327
  Old World attitude, 327
  speculation, 4, 60, 327–328, 378, 671, 736,
    785
Land companies, 151–152
Land division, township plan for, 59
Langdon, John, 123
Lansing, Robert, 77, 92
La Rochefoucauld-Liancourt, 453
Latin America, trade with, 559
Lawrence, James, 619
Laws and lawyers, 426, 780
  debtors, 673–674
  property rights, 674
Leaders and leadership, 207, 777
  American navy, 620–623
  business and political, 422–424
  military leaders, 646, 652–653
  provided by "old families," 370
Leander (British warship), 560
Lear, Tobias, 190
Lechmere, Thomas, 341
Ledyard, John, 510
Lee, Charles, 790
Lee, Henry, 33, 52, 104
Lee, Henry "Light-Horse" Harry, 97,
    199–200, 599, 603
Lee, Richard Henry, 97, 126, 132, 133, 135,
    165, 440

Leech Lake, 547–548
Legaré, Hugh Swinton, 827–829
Legislative branch, 57, 65–66, 88, 699–700
  Federal debates, 57–58, 69–70, 72–73
Leiper, Thomas, 571
L'Enfant, Pierre, 122
Leopard (British frigate), 563–564
Levasseur, Auguste, 808
Levees, 468–469
Lewis, William, 605
Lewis, Lilurn and Isham, 592
Lewis, Meriwether, 511
  appointed Governor of Louisiana, 544–545
  death of, 545
  protégé of Jefferson, 545, 550
  leadership ability, 543–544
  (*See also* Lewis and Clark Expedition)
Lewis and Clark Expedition, 471, 510–538, 713
  articles sent back to Jefferson, 525
  cache of supplies, 541
  Columbia River explorations, 527, 539
  departure from Pittsburgh (1803), 515
  to explore route to Pacific, 511
  fame as doctors, 540–541
  at Fort Clatsop, 537–539
  Fourth of July celebration, 515–516
  Indians and, 511–524
    attacks, 541
    councils with, 515–524
    dealings with, 511–512
    food, clothing and domestic
      accommodations, 511
    gifts and speeches, 521, 523, 524, 528–529
    negotiations, 515–524, 543–544
    pipe of peace, 522
    possessions and relations with other
      tribes, 511
    studies of, 511–538
  interpreters, 525
  Jefferson authorized expedition, 510–512, 542, 544
  Missouri River trip, 511, 514, 530
  in Nez Percé area, 531, 534, 540
  notes and journals, 516, 543
  observations of flora and fauna, 512, 538
  Ohio River trip, 513
  portages, 539–540
  recommendations, 713
  return trip, 539–546
  Rocky Mountains passage, 526–527, 540
  Sacaqawea, Indian woman, 525, 527, 530, 540, 542, 546
  significance of, 542–544
  supplies and equipment, 513, 539
  Washington reception (1807), 544
  winter in Mandan villages, 524

York, slave belonging to Clark, 513, 523
Lewiston (Pennsylvania), British attack, 628
Lewiston on Niagara River, 601, 611
Liberal intellectuals, 300–301
Liberty, 419
  Southern evocation of, 289
  James Wilson on, 114
Liberty poles, 269
  symbol of defiance, 229–230
Licking River, 458
Light Infantry companies, 111, 114
Lincoln, Benjamin, 29–31, 34, 597
Lincoln, Levi, 477
Lingan, James, 599, 603
Literature, 419–424
  Hugh Henry Brackenridge, 422–424
  "how-to" books, 395
  (*See also* Arts and literature)
Little Belt (British warship), 589–590
Little Sally (British brig), 211
Little Turtle, chief of Miami Indians, 190, 232–233, 680
Little Warrior, Indian chief, 644–645
Liverpool, Lord, 639
Livingston, Brockholst, 269
Livingston, Edward, 648
Livingston, Robert, 106, 126, 486
Lloyd, James, 266–267
Lloyd's of London, 623–624
Logan, Dr. George, 159, 567, 572
Logan Act, 567
"Logrolling," 160
London Times, 620
Lotteries, 677, 706
  to build toll roads, 336
Louis Bonaparte, 566
Louis Philippe, 381
Louis XVIII, King of France, 710, 717, 802, 808
Louisiana Purchase, 484–497, 552–553
  Napoleon's reason for selling, 710
  negotiations with France, 486–487, 710
  opposition of Federalists, 487–489
  opposition of New England, 640, 648, 733
  territorial government, 489–490
Louisiana Territory, 151, 489–490
  admission as slave state, 584, 690
  Burr conspiracy, 545
  Lewis appointed governor, 544–545
  Pike's explorations of, 546–549
  prohibition against slavery, 695–696
Louisville, 459, 461–462
Loundes, William, 721–722
Lowell, Francis Cabot, 766–769
Lowell cotton mills, 766–769
  girls employed in, 767–769
  literary young ladies, 768–769
  visitors to, 768–769

Loyalists:
    attempts to reclaim property, 4–7, 17
    conservative element, 5
    Fishing Creek disaster, 16
    flight of, 4–5
    hostility toward, 6–7
    lands appropriated by patriots, 3
    New York City, 3
    symbolic significance, 6–7
    warfare between patriots and, 4–7
Ludwell, Philip, 442
Lundy, Benjamin, 765
Lutheran churches, 313
Luxury, 38–49
    attitudes toward, 38–49, 785
    as incentive to industry, 40–41
    money-making and equality, 43–46
    moral dilemma, 38–41
    obsession with, 38–49
Lyon, Matthew, 255, 268, 297

Macaulay, Thomas Babington, 348
Macdonough, Thomas, 613–614
    victory on Lake Champlain, 655–656
McGillvray (chief of Creek Nation), 196
MacGregor, Gregor, 663
Machine politics, 292
McIntosh, Lachlan, 15
McKean, Thomas, 110, 289
    elected governor of Pennsylvania, 274–275
McKeever, Lt. Isaac, 663–664
Maclay, William, 123–136, 139–141, 145, 195,
    423
    on Pierce Butler, 790–791
    on First Congress, 148–161
    political offices, 159–160
McMaster, John Bach, 553, 571, 647
McNemar, Richard, 314
McQueen, Peter (Indian prophet), 663
Madison, Dolley, 580–581, 630
    burning of Washington, 632
Madison, James, 16, 19, 32–33, 70, 101, 137
    and John Adams, 121
    appointments to Supreme Court, 823
    on Bill of Rights, 166
    British attack on Washington, 629–631
    Cabinet, 581
    conversion to Jeffersonian democracy, 794
    delegate to Constitutional Convention, 53,
        55–57, 579
    Federalist Papers author, 105
    on funding certificates, 149
    inaugural address, 580
    Jackson and, 647
    on Jay Treaty, 221–222
    and Jefferson, 130, 477–480, 579, 823
    militia called up for defense of city, 629
    and Monroe, 659

    on nature of social groups, 70, 304
    notes kept by, 93
    pamphlet warfare, 211–212
    political views, 304, 794–796
    presidency, 574, 579–590
    presidential candidate, 574–575
    proclamation of war with Great Britain,
        594
    proclamation renewing trade with France,
        588–589
    public life, 579
    reelection in 1812, 593
    Virginia Plan, 57
    warning sent to Great Britain, 593
    Washington's Farewell Address prepared
        by, 200, 245
Maine, 453
    admission to Union, 692, 694–695
    British invasion, 629
Mandan Indians, 519, 532, 542
Mandan villages, 523–524
"Manifest destiny," 654
Manning, William, 20, 301, 420
    on free education, 353–354
    "The Key of Liberty," 301–304, 687
    on political theory, 301–304
    on upper classes, 784
Manufacturing industries, 235, 344–350
    career opportunities, 780
    Congress passed act to encourage
        manufacturers, 350
    inventions and, 345–351
    labor-saving techniques, 769
    lack of capital, 351
    lacked distribution system, 350
    Lowell cotton mills, 766–769
    Society for the Encouragement of
        Manufacturers, 111
    war as stimulus to, 669
Marbois, Francois, 288
Marbury, William, 478–483
Marbury v. Madison, 472–483, 698
Marias River, 541
Marriages, 781–783
    beneath one's social class, 783
Marseillaise, 803
Marshall, John, 101, 138
    appearance and temperament, 477–478
    Chief Justice of Supreme Court, 296–297,
        476, 698
    envoy to France, 255, 264
    Jefferson and, 491–492, 700, 823
    Secretary of State, 283
    speech in Virginia ratifying convention,
        703
    on Supreme Court, 104
    Supreme Court opinions, 698–699,
        701–704

trial of Aaron Burr, 505–509
on Washington's death, 280
Martin, Luther, 92, 703
Marx, Karl, 286, 349
Maryland:
  British attacks, 628–639
    (*See also* Baltimore)
  controversy with Virginia over rights to
    Potomac River, 16
  convention to reform Articles, 50–51
  delegates to Constitutional Convention, 52
  slaves freed, 136
  states rights, 703
  Whiskey Rebellion, 229
Mason, George, 16, 63–64, 69, 83, 88, 90,
    92–93, 446
  Anti-Federalist opposition, 97
  author of Virginia Constitution and Bill of
    Rights, 55
  opposition to ratification, 97, 101–104
Masons, 116, 286
Mass production, 328
Massachusetts, 453
  commercial activities, 3
  danger of insurrection over embargo, 571
  debtor-creditor conflicts, 12–13
  delegates to Constitutional Convention, 52
  education, 353–354
  Great and General Court, 23–24, 28, 395
  Monroe's visit, 661
  post-war depression, 669
  prisons, 13
  ratification of Constitution, 98–100, 107
    opposition to, 99–100
  revolt of farmers (Shays' Rebellion), 23–37,
    90, 107, 825–826
  secession movement, 640–649
Massachusetts Bay Colony, education,
    353–354
Massachusetts Centinel, 399
Massachusetts Constitutional Society, 206
Materialism, 38–49
  critics of, 44
  following Revolution, 38–49
Matlack, Timothy, 37
Maumee River, 604–605
Maurer, Hermann, 376
Mazzei, Philip, 256–257
Medical associations, 116, 426
Medicine, 426–433
  bloodletting, 431–432
  common illnesses, 431–432
  folk remedies, 430
  opium used to kill pain, 431–432
  prestige of physicians, 426–427, 430–431
  remedies, 430–432
  yellow fever epidemics, 427–430
Melville, Herman, 344

Mennonites, 313, 764
Merry, Anthony, 502, 504
Methodists, 312–313, 751
Metternich, 718
Mexico, 488
  independence of, 712
  uprising against Spain, 711–712
Miami Indians, 184, 186, 190, 198–199, 595,
    680
  peace mission sent by Washington,
    198–199
  victory over St. Clair, 198
Miami River, settlements, 455
Michaux, André, 510
Michigan Territory, 597, 599
Middle States, 453
  diversified farming, 326
  population, 732
Middlebury College, 755
Middlesex Canal Company, 330–331
Middleton, Polly, 790
Mifflin, Thomas (Governor of Pennsylvania),
    124, 228, 230, 273, 381
Migration (*See* Westward migration)
Milan decrees (*See* Berlin and Milan decrees)
Millennium, 420, 756, 759, 800
  Christ's Second Coming, 791
Miller, Samuel:
  A Brief Retrospect of the Eighteenth Century,
    310
Mills, Samuel John, 754–756
Mims, Samuel, 645
Mingo Creek meeting, 228
Ministry, career opportunities, 780
Minitari (or Hidatsa) Indians, 527, 530, 532,
    541–542
Mint, establishment of, 202
Mirabeau, Count, 142–143
Mission to redeem the world, 35–37,
    717–718, 751–765
Missionary movement, 754–758, 800
  Bible societies, 755
  conversion of Indians, 754
  development of, 751–752
  foreign missionary activity, 756–758
  frontier settlements, 754–755
Mississippi River Valley, 454–471
  Francis Baily's travels, 455–470
  British desire to control, 639
  effect of Westward migration, 733
  floods, 591
  French settlers, 468
  Grand Gulf, 467
  hunting and fishing, 465
  Indian tribes, 595–596
    trade with, 465–466
  missionary movement, 754–755
  Pike's expedition to headwaters, 546–549

Mississippi River Valley (*cont.*):
  right to use, 151
  scenery, 464, 468
  "separatist" sentiment, 509
  settlements, 465–466
  Spanish control, 464, 484–485
Missouri Compromise, 690–697, 819
  admission of Maine and Missouri, 692
  amendment forbidding slavery, 691, 694
  Committee of Thirteen, 696
  Congressional debates, 692, 694–697
  effect on disunion, 691–692
  emancipation issue, 691, 693–695
  Missouri refused admittance, 696
  Pinckney-King debates, 694, 695
  proposed constitution, 695
  rights of states to exclude free blacks, 789
Missouri Indians, 515, 517
Missouri River, 471
  expedition to headwaters, 540–541
  Lewis and Clark Expedition, 511–519, 527, 530
Missouri Territory, 546
  request for statehood, 691
  Southern slaveholders in, 690–691
Mitchell, Stephen Mix, 18
Modern Chivalry (Brackenridge), 422–424
Monarchy and aristocracy, 60, 115, 139–141, 200, 714, 718
  Adams' views, 10–11, 299, 777, 817–818
  Anti-Federalist opposition, 131, 139–141, 206–208
  arts and, 418
  constitutional monarchy, 62
  fear of, 10–11, 131, 136, 202
  Republican paranoia about, 206–207
Money and currency, 657
  encouraged ingenuity and invention, 158
  redemption of Confederation Congress certificates, 147–148
  shortage of, 12
Money-making, 240–249
  American obsession with, 240–249, 488
  equality and right to make money, 43–44
  philanthropy and, 46
  preoccupation with, 42, 385–386
Monongahela River, 454
Monopolies, 708
Monroe, James, 137, 589, 808
  ambassador to Great Britain, 561–562
  British attack on Washington, 630
  election of 1816, 659
  Governor of Virginia, 444–445
  and Hamilton, 257–258
  inaugural address, 660–661
  Jackson's request to attack Spanish Florida, 663–665
  Jefferson and, 655, 659–661, 714–715, 823

  minister to France, 218, 258, 484–487
  minister to Spain, 484–487
  negotiation with British over neutral trade and impressment, 561–565
  recalled as ambassador to France, 252–253
  reelection in 1820, 691, 719
  triumphal tour of Middle and Northern states, 661
Monroe Doctrine, 710–718
  declaration of global independence, 717
  influence of John Quincy Adams, 714–717
  relationship of European powers and Western Hemisphere, 715–716
  statement to deter European intervention in American affairs, 713
Montesquieu, 62, 94
Montreal, 594, 605
Morals:
  decline in Christian piety, 679
  pursuit of luxury and, 38, 42
Moravians, 313
  opposed to slavery, 452
More, Hannah, 768
Morgan, Daniel, 230
Morgan, David, 650–651
Morison, Samuel Eliot, 340, 343
Morocco, 110
Morris, Gouverneur, 60, 82–84, 89–90, 475, 500, 598, 796–800
  on Adams' defeat, 297
  delegate to Constitutional Convention, 53–55, 796–797, 799
  embargo and, 568
  Erie Canal and, 769–770
  Hamilton and, 797
  marriage to Anne Cary, 799
  minister to France, 218, 381
  political views, 172, 796–799
  on repeal of Judiciary Bill, 481
  on secession, 640
  on slavery, 626
  supported Louisiana Purchase, 489
  on Washington's death, 280
Morris, Robert, 13, 132, 142
  in debtors' prison, 674
  speculation in Western lands, 150–151
Morse, Jedidiah, 206–207, 286–288
  Universal Geography, 363
Morse, Samuel F.B., 286, 803
  portrait of President John Adans, (*illus.*) 408
Mosquitoes, 526
Moultrie, Governor of South Carolina, 213
Mount Vernon, Lafayette's visit, 808–809
Muhlenberg, Frederick, 240, 257
Murray, William Vans, 275
  appointed ambassador to France, 277
Museums, Philadelphia, 387, 403

Name-giving, 543
  to communities, 391–392
Nantucket, Massachusetts, British occupation, 629
Napoleon, 259, 486–487, 581, 792, 807
  Berlin and Milan decrees, 562, 565, 588–589, 671
  defeat of, 627, 718
  effect of embargo on, 572–573
  return to Paris, 718
  wars and victories, 276, 565, 567, 572, 800
Nash, Thomas, 282
Natchez, 467–468, 504
Natchitoches (French town), 468, 549
National Gazette, 154, 211
National Intelligencer, 580–581, 631
Nationalists, 65, 95
  (*See also* Federalists)
Nationhood and national unity, 656
  formation of new nation, 1–22
  heightened sense of nationalism, 656–657
  "talked into existence," 57, 588, 707
Naturalization issue, 148–150, 266, 565
Naval engagements:
  with British ships, 560, 563–564
  classic naval encounters, 616–617
  contrast between performance of American sailors and soldiers, 620–623
  depredations of privateers and, 623–626
  epic of courage and endurance, 608–609
  on Great Lakes, 607–611
  on Lake Champlain, 607, 613–614
  on Lake Erie, 608–609, 612–613, 614
  on Lake Ontario, 611
  superior American seamanship, 618, 621–622
  War of 1812, 615–626
    Constitution vs. *Guèrriere,* 615–620
Navy, 264
  authorized by Congress, 216, 592
  building of, 263, 266
  effect of embargo on, 570
  funds voted for 10 gunboats, 220
  impressment and, 561
  Jefferson's policy, 552, 592
  War of 1812, 594, 615–626
Negro Fort, 663
Negroes (*see* Blacks; Slaves and slavery)
Nelson, Horatio, 552
Neutral trade, 558–565
  British restrictions, 558, 562–566, 572, 600, 654, 671
  Napoleon's decrees, 562, 565–566, 588–589, 671
  negotiations with British over impressment and, 561–565
Neutrality, proclamation of, 208–214
  authority of Washington to issue, 211–212

New England:
  anti-Western bias, 683
  canal-building, 330–333
  clergy opposed to Jefferson, 287–289
  commercial activities, 3
  Congregationalists, 288–289, 312–313
  cotton manufacturing, 766–769
  desired British victory at New Orleans, 648
  differences between states, 452–453
  education, 363
  effects of embargo, 568–569
  forests and streams, 326
  Hartford Convention, 640–643
  Lafayette's triumphal tour, 803–806, 813
  molasses, rum, and taxes, 134
  Ohio settlement, 377, 454, 734–735
  opposition to Louisiana Purchase, 733
  population, 732
  separatists movement, 568, 580, 639–640, 656, 705, 795
  states' rights and, 705
  tariff issue, 670
  town life, 733–734
  thrift and restraint, 39
  War of 1812 opposed by, 568–569, 594, 598, 639–640
  Washington's tour of, 163–165
  Westward migration, 733–735
New England Primer, 363
New Hampshire:
  Dartmouth College Case, 700–702
  delegates to Constitutional Convention, 52
  ratification of Constitution, 105
New Harmony (cooperative community), 688–689
New Haven, Monroe's visit, 661
New Jersey:
  character of citizens, 452
  delegates to Constitutional Convention, 73
  ratification of the Constitution, 98
New Jersey Blues, 230
New Jersey Plan, Constitutional Convention, 74–76
New Lights, 755
New Madrid, 464–465, 591
New Mexico, 549
New Orleans, 468–469, 625
  Battle of, 623, 644–653
    American forces, 650–651
    British forces, 639, 647–653
    destruction of American gunboats on Lake Borgne, 648–650
    devastating British losses, 651–652
    Jackson's great victory, 643, 662
    Morgan's battery, 650–651
  Burr's plan for rebellion, 502–503, 505
  inhabitants, 469–470
  Lafayette's visit to, 807, 812

New Orleans (*cont.*):
  Spanish control, 484–485
  territorial government, 489
New York, 453
  British occupation, 3
  Burr defeated for Governor (1804),
    498–499
  celebration of adoption of Constitution,
    116
  delegates to Constitutional Convention,
    75
  economic conditions, 11
  effects of embargo, 568–569
  election of 1798, 290
  election of 1800, 290
  election of 1824, 724–725
  Federalist vs. Anti-Federalists, 117–118
  first capital of U.S., 117
  foreign trade, 11, 342
  immigrants to, 737, 742
  Lafayette's triumphal tour, 803
  leaders, 370
  poor or pauperism, 677
  population growth, 732
  ratification of Constitution, 104–107
  rent riots, 12
  retirement age for judges, 368
  and Rhode Island, 4
  soup kitchens, 675
  visit of Monroe, 661
  Washington's reception, 125–126
  yellow fever epidemics, 428–429
New York Bible Society, 755
New York Independent Journal, 105
New York State Barge Canal, 776
Newspapers:
  abolitionist, 765
  attacks on the government, 306
  editors, 306, 422
  Federalist, 32, 422
    Jefferson's opposition to, 556
  first free press in history, 306
  free speech issue, 598–599
  invective and vituperation, 305–306
  Republican, 274, 285, 297, 306
  persecutions against, 281
Nez Percé ("Pierced Noses") Indians, 531,
    534, 540
Niagara River, attempt to drive British from,
    600–601, 611
Nicholas, George, 271
Nicholls, British Col. Edward, 663
Nichols, Thomas Low, 365
Nicholson, Joseph, 560
Niles, Hezekiah, 720
Niles' Weekly Register, 704, 720, 738
Nonimportation resolution, 559–560
Nonintercourse bill, 218–219, 575–576, 593

Norfolk, 563–564
North Carolina:
  Constitutional Convention, 87
  emigration from, 736–737
  ratification of Constitution, 148
North-South differences:
  appropriation to carry out Jay Treaty, 240
  Constitutional Convention, 83–85
  nonintercourse measure, 218–219
  slavery and, 305, 434, 448–449, 692
  tariff issue, 670
North West Company, 548
Northwest Ordinance (1785), 59–60, 377,
    595
  admission of new states, 58–60
Northwest Territories:
  British posts, 4, 168, 184, 217, 713
    to be relinquished under Jay Treaty,
      239–240
  Harrison appointed commander in chief,
    604
  Indian attacks, 185–189, 200–201
  St. Clair appointed governor, 185, 188–189
  St. Clair's defeat, 190–191
  War of 1812, 591–614
  Washington's Indian policy, 196
Nullification doctrine, 270, 796

Oberlin, Ohio, 735
Occom, Samson, 197
Ocfuskee Indian settlement, 646–647
Ogden, Aaron, 707
Ogden, Peter, 504–505
Ohio:
  Connecticut claims, 4
  settlers from New England, 377, 454,
    734–735
  states rights, 705
  underground railroad, 762–763
  war in the Northwest, 594–607
  westward migration to, 377, 454, 733–735
Ohio Company, 151
Ohio Resolutions, 705
Ohio River, 454–465
  barge travel, 455–457
  ice floes, 455–457
  scenery, 458, 464
Ohio Territory, 173
  frontier settlements, 187, 377, 454,
    734–735
  Indian attacks, 185, 594–607
Oligarchy, 61
Omaha Nation, 514, 519
Onis, Don Luis de (Spanish minister), 665
Ontario peninsula, 610
Orators, 587–588, 668
Orders in council (British), 558, 562, 566,
    572, 600, 654, 671

Oregon country:
  Britain's interest in, 714
  Russia's expansionist policies, 713–715
Oregon Territory, 338, 471
Osage Indians, 549
Otis, Harris Gray, 639–640
Otis, James, 8, 20, 91
Otis, Samuel, 249
Oto Indians, 517, 519
Ottawa Indians, 761
Otto, Louis-Guillaume, 51
Owen, Robert, 688–689
Owen, Robert Dale, 688
Oyster-houses, 680

Pacific coast:
  Russian settlements, 510, 639, 713–715
  trade with Indians, 338–339
Paine, Thomas, 8, 204, 493–494, 787–788
  Age of Reason, 493–494
  attack on Washington, 256
  Common Sense, 101–102, 207, 787
  death of, 788
  member of French National Convention,
    256
  radicalism, 787
  Rights of Man, 256
Paintings and portraits, 396–418
  Copley, John Singleton, 396–401, 407
  Earle, Ralph, 399, 409
  engravings, 415
  Greenwood, John, 402
  historical paintings, 399, 415–416
  miniatures on ivory, 402
  Peale, Charles Willson, 397, 401–404
  Stuart, Gilbert, 399–401
  Trumbull, John, 404, 414, 417–418, 511
  West, Benjamin, 396–401, 404, 414
Pakenham, Sir Edward, 625
  assault on New Orleans, 644, 650–652
Panikkar, Raimundo, 192
Paper blockade, 559
Paper industry, 134
Parades and celebrations:
  First Inaugural, 122, 128
  Grand Procession in Philadelphia
    (adoption of Constitution), 109–116
  Washington's Inaugural, 128
  (See also Fourth of July celebrations)
Parker, Isaac, 701
Parker, Josiah, 135
Parkinson Ferry, 230–231
  Whiskey Rebellion, 231
Parsons, Eli, 31
Party system:
  revolt against the "old politics," 719–720
  violence of party feelings, 599, 603
  (See also Federalists; Republicans)

Patent legislation, 345
Paterson, William, 85, 136–137, 296–297
  delegate from N.J., 73
Patowmack (Potomac) Company, 333–334
Patriotism, decline in, 38–39, 786
Patriots, 4–8
  warfare between Loyalists and, 4–7
Pawnbrokers, 677
Pawnee Indians, 517, 549
  astronomers, 517
Peabody, Joseph, 341–342
Peale, Charles Willson, 387, 401–404
  The Artist in His Museum, (illus.) 411
  Lafayette and, 807–808
  miniatures on ivory, 402
  "moving-picture" show, 402–403
  natural history museum, 403
  served as Continental soldier, 402
Pennsylvania:
  delegates to Constitutional Convention,
    54–55
  election of 1824, 723–724
  gubernatorial campaign of 1798, 274–275
  iron or steel imports, 134
  opposition to property tax, 272–274
  postrevolutionary war, 3
  postwar depression, 669
  ratification of Constitution, 98
  Whiskey Rebellion in western counties,
    227–231
  Wyoming Valley Controversy, 4
Pennsylvania Abolition Society, 388
Pepper trade, 341
Perry, Oliver Hazard, 607–611, 613, 646, 656
  naval engagement on Lake Erie, 608–609,
    614
  public reaction to victory, 609–610
Perry (American privateer), 623–624
Peter Porcupine's Gazette, 788
Philadelphia:
  antislavery meetings, 692
  associations, 116, 675
  black-white relations, 388, 434
  charitable organizations, 675
  commercial center, 385–386
  Constitutional Convention, 52–53
    (See also Constitutional Convention)
  famous families, 370
  foreign commerce, 342
  French refugees, 380–382, 427
  Genêt affair, 208–209
  Grand Procession to celebrate new
    Constitution, 109–116
    address by James Wilson, 114
    floats and spectators, 110–116
    foreign spectators, 110, 112
    patriotic emotions aroused by, 112–113
    symbolism of, 113–114

Philadelphia (*cont.*):
  immigrants to, 380–382, 427, 737
  Lafayette's visit, 807–808
  museums, 387, 403
  nation's interim capital, 274
  physicians, 426–427
  population growth, 732
  postwar depression, 669, 673
  sexual mores, 382–384
  soup kitchens, 675
  theaters, 386–387
  visit of Monroe, 661
  wanted to be permanent capital, 120,
    133–134, 141–142, 154–156, 274
  yellow fever epidemic, 427–430
Philadelphia (U.S. ship), 552
Philadelphia Convention (*see* Constitutional
  Convention)
Philadelphia's College of Physicians, 387
Philanthropic societies, 46, 116, 679
Philanthropist (antislavery newspaper), 692
Physic, Phillip, 426–427
Pickering, Timothy, 225, 791, 799, 822
  delegate to Federal Convention, 799
  Federalist leader, 498, 567–568, 648
  Secretary of War, 214, 252
  and separatist movement in N.E., 567–568
Pickersgill, Mary Young, 634, 637
Pierce, John, 560
Pierce, William, 54–56, 790
  sketches of delegates to Constitutional
    Convention, 54–56
Pigeon Creek, 462
Pike, Zebulon, 462, 611
  Arkansas and Red River expedition,
    549–550
  discovered Pike's Peak, 549
  expedition to explore headwaters of
    Mississippi, 546–549
  notes and journals, 548–549
Pinckney, Charles:
  analysis of American society, 77–79
  Founding Father, 788–789
  political career, 789
  youngest delegate to Federal Convention,
    788
Pinckney, Charles Cotesworth, 75, 83, 85, 87,
    89, 282, 481, 789–790
  presidential candidate (1804), 551
  presidential candidate (1808), 574
  rebuffed as ambassador to France,
    253–256, 259–264
Pinckney, Thomas, 597
  Directory's refusal to accept as ambassador,
    275
  vice-presidential candidate, 248–249
Pinckney, William, 589, 694–695, 703
  neutral trade negotiations, 562–565

Pinckney affair, 253–256, 259–264
Pirates of the Mediterranean, 235, 484,
    662
  preyed on American shipping, 484
  (*See also* Barbary War)
Pitt, William, 217
Pittsburgh, 454, 505
Pizarro, Don José, 666
Plantation life, 435–441, 451
  along the Mississippi, 468–469
  cuisine, 436
  elegance and crudity, 436–437
  owner-farmer relationships, 440
  planter's routine, 439–440
  relationship between slaves and masters
    and mistresses, 443–444
  summers spent in cooler country, 439
Platte River, 514, 517
Plattsburgh, 604, 613
  British debacle at, 639
Plumer, William, 498, 506
Pluralism, religious, 324
Poets and poetry, 419–422
Political offices, candidates for, 7–8
Political parties (*see* Party system)
Poor or paupers, 749
  causes of, 677
  charitable assistance, 677–678
  food and shelter, 374–376
  provisions for assisting, 676–677
  schools for children, 687
Population growth, 732
  Madison's views, 795
Port Folio (literary magazine), 422, 490,
    493–494, 551
Postal system, establishment of, 148, 202
Potawatomi Indians, 549, 595
Potlatch of Northwest Indians, 46
Potomac Company, 793
Potomac River, 16
  British attacks, 629
  permanent residence for the government,
    156, 198
Poverty, causes of, 677, 749
  (*See also* Poor or paupers)
Powder mills, 344
Power:
  Adams on "power made right," 819
  change of parties in election of 1800,
    243–271, 298, 307
Prebel, Edward, 552, 613
Presbyterians, 312–313, 751, 756, 759
  underground railroad, 762
Presidency:
  appointments and right of removal, 130
  Federal debates, 66–68, 71, 88, 118, 494
  nomination of candidates, 722, 724
  power to impeach, 68–69, 88

proposed title for, 132–133
term of office, 66–67, 243
President (American frigate), 589–590
Presidential electors, 117
(*See also* Electors)
Preston, William, 172–173, 373
Prevost, Sir George, 600, 611
governor general of Canada, 600
Price, Richard, 50, 318
Priestley, Joseph, 240, 748–749
Princeton College, 290, 420, 423, 791–792
portrait of Washington, 402
Prisons and prisoners, 13, 387
debtors, 673
Privateers, 3
attacks on British merchant ships, 623–626
French, 208
Proctor, British commander, 605–607, 610, 612
Progress, American faith in, 319
Property rights, 310, 674
Prosser, Uriah, 635
Prostitution, 383–384, 428–429, 677, 680, 782
Protective associations, 116
Protestant Christianity, 36, 46–47, 49, 310–325
Catholicism and, 748
influence on capitalism, 310
"Puritan" form of, 311–313, 758–759
sacredness of obligations, 14–15
Protestant Reformation, 401
property and money, 310, 674
Provincialism, 328
Prussia, 110
Public works, 553
employing unemployed on, 676
need for, 676
stimulant effect on economy, 684–685
Puritans (Congregationalists), 311–313, 758–759
compact or covenant, 14–15
treatment of debtors, 14–15
Putnam, Israel, 187, 332–333
Putnam, Rufus, 187–188

Quakers, 3, 289, 312–313, 383, 453, 764–765
appearance before Congress, 163
opposed to slavery, 163, 452
"Quasi War" with France, 266, 272–284, 486
"Convention of Peace, Commerce and Navigation" signed (1800), 284
Queenston, Canada, 601
Quincy, Josiah, 447–448, 584, 804

Radical universalism, 363
Raisin River, disaster at, 605–606, 644
Ramsey, David, 363–364

Rand, Ayn, 44
Randolph, Edmund, 16, 200
attorney general, 131, 200, 208
delegate to Constitutional Convention, 57, 62, 65, 75, 85, 92–93, 101
Jay Treaty, 222
resignation from office, 225
secretary of state, 214, 218
Randolph, John (of Roanoke), 506
Randolph, John, 370, 479, 588–589, 658, 695, 799
case against Samuel Chase, 496
character, 281
elected to Congress, 280–281
nonimportation resolution, 559–560
Randolph, Judith Cary, 799
Randolph, Richard, 799
Randolph, Thomas Mann, 576, 577, 589
Randolph family of Virginia, 370
Rapp, George, 688
Ratification of Constitution, 92–93, 95–108
delegates to state conventions, 107
Grand Procession in Philadelphia to celebrate, 109–116
by Massachusetts, 98–100, 103, 107
by New York, 105–107
by Virginia, 100–105, 109
Raymond, Daniel, 779
Thoughts on Political Economy, 676, 683–685
Read, George, 128
Read, William, 63, 71–72
Reason, age of, 554
Jefferson on rule of, 144
reliance on, 127
science and, 286, 416, 817
Rebellions:
Fries's rebellion, 272–274, 826
Jefferson on "little rebellions," 32, 144
Shays's Rebellion, 23–37, 825
Whiskey Rebellion, 227–231, 592, 826
Reconciliation, national, 661
Red Cedar Lake, 548
Red River, 466, 468, 549
Red Stick Creek Indians, 645–647, 662
in Florida, 662
Redemption of old Congress's certificates, 147–148
Redemptive mission of America, 34, 37, 247, 717–718, 751–765
isolationism versus, 247
Redstone Old Fort, 230
Reeve, Judge Tapping, 586
Reform and reformers, 319, 679, 687–688
Protestant passion for, 36, 324
"Regulators," 27–31
Reid, Samuel, 624–625
Religion, 309–325, 751–765
Arminianism, 311

Religion (*cont.*):
  Biblical interpretations, 321–322
  Book of Common Prayer, 313
  Calvinism, 47, 310–311, 324, 752–753, 800
    doctrine of predestination, 311
  Congregationalists (the Puritans), 39–40,
    288–289, 311–313, 758–759
    Great Awakening of 1740's, 312
    suspicion of worldly pleasures, 317
  diversity of sects and religions, 313, 755
  dogma and doctrine, 310–325
    divinity of Christ, 310
    duties of citizenship, 320–321
    human perfectibility, 320–321
    omnipotence of God, 311
    original sin, 320
    Trinitarian creed, 310, 315
  Enlightenment ideas and, 311, 315–316,
    319–321
  expansion 1800 to 1826, 751–765
  foreign missionary activity, 756–758
  freedom of, 59
  frontier revivals, 314–315, 379, 751–753
  German Pietist, 313
  individual responsibility, 324, 759–760
  influence of French Revolution, 309, 311
  missionary movement, 752–755
  pluralism, 324
  Protestant Christianity, 310–325
  "Puritan" form of American Protestantism,
    311–313, 758–759
  of reason and science, 286
  revived interest in, 755–756
  threat of "godless atheism," 286–287
  Unitarians, 324
  views of John Adams, 315, 320–324
  views of Benjamin Franklin, 315–317, 324
  views of Thomas Jefferson, 285–289
  views of Benjamin Rush, 315–321, 323–324
Religious revivals, 314–315, 379, 751–753
  in New England, 753
  preachers, 751–752
Representation:
  "equal" vs. proportional, 62–63, 79, 83–84
  Federal debates, 57, 62–63, 79–84
  slaves counted as three-fifths of all other
    persons, 641
Republican government, 2, 39, 115, 301–304
  based on confidence of the people, 64
  classical principles, 60
  Jefferson's views, 473–474
  poems and essays in praise of, 419
  and pursuit of material things, 39–41
Republican newspapers (*see* Newspapers,
  Republican)
Republican party, 107, 557
  adopted principles of Federalists, 553, 658,
    720

  Anti-Federalists adopted name, 145
  election of 1800, 299
  election of 1804, 551, 553
    Jefferson-Clinton ticket, 551–553
  election of 1816, 658–659
  enraged over Marbury decision, 480–483
  fear of Supreme Court, 700
  Jeffersonian, 137, 207
  principles and policies, 304, 307
Revere, Paul, 395
Revivals, religious, 314–315, 379, 751–753
Revolutionary leaders:
  deplored decline in moral fiber, 38–42
  on pursuit of luxury, 39
Revolutions in government:
  counterrevolutions, 301
  "Democratic Revolutions," 143–144
  Jefferson on, 32, 144, 270–271
  ways of preventing, 60–61
  (*See also* Rebellions)
Reynolds, Sir Joshua, 396, 398
Reynolds, Maria, 257–258, 371, 499
Rhode Island, 453
  commercial activities, 3
  debtors and creditors, 12
  did not send delegates to Constitutional
    Convention, 52
  and New York, 4
  postwar depression, 669
Riall, British Major Gen. Sir Phineas, 612
Richard (coastal sloop), 560
Richmond, Virginia:
  capital designed by Jefferson, 394
  fire, 591
Richmond Enquirer, 641, 706
Richmond Examiner, 492
Rights of Man, 145, 309, 674
Ripley, Eleazer Wheelock, 612
Rising Sun (ship), 110, 114
Rivers:
  hazards, 455
  settlements at junction, 377–378
  (*See also* under name of river)
Roads and highways, 148
  toll roads, 335–337
  (*See also* Internal improvements)
Robbins, Jonathan, 282
Roberts, Nathan, 771
Robespierre, Maximilien Marie Isidore,
  381
Rochambeau, French general, 110, 206
Rocky Mountains, 526–527, 540
Rodger, John, 589
  commander of naval fleet, 615, 633, 637
Rodney, Caesar, 481
Rollin, Charles, 418
Roman Catholic church, 48–49, 748, 820
  Roman Catholics in 1800, 313

Roosevelt, Franklin Delano, 576
New Deal, 684
Roots (Haley), 441
Rose, George Henry, 567
Rosenstock-Huessy, Eugen, 243
Ross, British Maj. Gen. Robert, 629, 632–634
attack on Baltimore, 633–634
Rousseau, Jean Jacques, 94, 153, 159
Rousseau, Pierre (French interpreter), 547
Royal Academy, London, 396, 398
Rumsey, James, 334
Rural areas, effect of hard times, 686–689
Rush, Benjamin, 50–51, 96, 279, 680, 759
John Adams and, 120–121
on Annapolis Convention, 50–51
on care of insane, 387–388
Founding Father, 96, 786
Jefferson-Adams reconciliation and, 815–816
medical accomplishments, 426–433
plans for a Federal University, 360–361
religious beliefs, 315–321, 323, 324
remedies for yellow fever, 429–430
on role of women, 373–374
views on education, 353–355, 360–362
on westward migration, 164, 171–172, 179, 181, 183, 187
Rush, Richard, 714
Russell, Jonathan, 638
Russia, 639
expansionist policies on Northwest coast, 510, 713–715
Napoleon's retreat from, 627
Russia-Turkey war, 820
Rutledge, John, 84, 91
Supreme Court justice, 139
Rütlinger, Jakob, 671–672, 742–746

Sac and Fox Indians, 515–516, 547
Sacaqawea, Indian woman, 525, 527, 530, 540, 542
legendary figure, 546
Sackett's Harbor, 571, 601, 611
Sailors, 343–344, 620–623
adventure and money, 344
British navy, 621
compared with American soldiers, 620–623
independence and self-reliance, 621
St. Andrews Society, 116
St. Charles, French settlement, 513–514
St. Clair, Arthur, 185, 188–191, 196
defeat by Miami, 190, 198
forts built by, 188–189
St. Lawrence River, 601
St. Louis, 471, 542
St. Mark's on Apalachee Bay, 663–665
St. Mery, Moreau de, 367, 379, 380–388, 424
Salaries for government officers, 148, 153

Salem, Mass., foreign commerce, 341
Salmon fishing, 531, 535
Salt licks, 515
Salt springs, 459
San Antonio, capture of, 711–712
San Domingo (Haiti), slave uprising, 427, 468, 789
Sandusky region, 606–607
Sandwich Islands, 341
Santa Fe, 549
Sauk Indians, 548
Savannah, welcome for Samuel Reid, 625
Schermerhorn, John, 755
Schizophrenia of American people, 207, 310–311
redemption of humanity vs. isolationism, 247
slavery, 434
of South, 17
Schools (*see* Education)
Schuyler, Philip, 291
Schuylkill and Susquehannah Canal, 333
Schweizer, Anna, 41
Schweizer, Johannes, 367, 374–376, 740, 742–746, 769
Science:
advancement of, 731, 803
and reason, 286, 416, 817
study of, 418
Scott, Charles, 803
Scott, John, 694
Scott, Sir Walter, 451
Scott, Winfield, 597, 611–612
Jackson and, 662
Scriptomania, 161
Seacoast towns and cities, 377
British raids against, 628–629
fortifications of harbors, 216
postwar depression, 671–689
Secession movement, 135, 270, 795
New England states, 639–641
Sectional differences, 134–135, 150, 161, 328
antagonisms between states, 142
import duties or tariffs, 134–135
internal improvements, 683–684
slavery, 805
tariffs, 670
(*See also* North-South differences)
Sectional leaders, 719–720
Secular-Democratic Consciousness, 36, 54, 102, 116, 144–145, 159, 225, 479–480, 653, 778
Constitution and, 107–108
Declaration of Independence and, 96
election of 1800, 305
Jefferson and, 501
Madison and, 579–580
manifesto of, 309–310

Secular-Democratic Consciousness (*cont.*):
  optimistic view of history, 279
  reason must rule, 554–555
  represented by Jefferson, 816, 824
  role of Indians, 555
  supplanted Classical-Christian
    Consciousness, 310
  themes, 421
Sedgwick, Theodore, 219, 261
Segur, Count, 449
Seminole Wars, 662–668
  Clay's denunciation of Jackson's conduct,
    666–668, 723, 727
  destruction of Negro Fort, 663
  Spanish protest, 665–668
Senate:
  advice and consent, 130, 140
  first session (1789), 117
Seneca Indians, 603
Separatist movements, 580
  in New England, 568, 639–640, 656, 705,
    795
  (*See also* Secession movement)
Settlements (*see* Frontier settlements)
Sevier, Nolachucky Jack, 503
Sexual mores, 382–384, 492–493
  family life and, 370–372
  slave women and white masters, 372–373,
    437–438, 443–444, 447–448, 782
  upper class society, 372–373, 782–783
  venereal disease, 372, 392, 782–783
Shattuck, Job, 26, 29
Shawnee Indians, 595–596
Shays, Daniel, 27–31, 34–35
Shays' Rebellion, 23–37, 63
  anti-Regulator army, 29–31
  causes, 23–24
  historical treatment, 34
  petition for relief from debt, 25
  Regulators, 27–34
  wore sprigs of evergreen in hat, 27, 29
  Worcester convention, 24–25
Shelby, Isaac, 610
Shepard, William, 27–28, 30
Sherman, Roger, 74, 79, 91, 95, 137, 195,
  787
  delegate to Constitutional Convention, 63,
    66
  portrait by Ralph Earle, 399, (*illus.*) 409
  on proportional vs. equal representation,
    80–81, 84
Shippen, William, 426–427
Ships and shipping:
  Boston-Canton trade, 337–340
  British blockade, 589
  British seizure of American ships, 215,
    558–565
  China trade, 337–339

Jefferson's embargo on, 566
  neutral trade, 558–565, 671
  nonimportation resolution, 559–560
  sailors, 343–344, 620–623
  trading empire of U.S., 558
  West Indian trade, 215
  (*See also* Foreign commerce)
Short, William, 130, 494
Shoshone Indians, 527–533
Sibley, John, 468
Singletary, Amos, 99
Siouan family, 514
Sioux Indians, 185, 515, 519–520, 522–523,
  525, 531–532, 542, 547
Sitting Bull, 520
Six Nations, 603, 612
Slater, Samuel, 349–350
Slave states and nonsalve states, 17, 63
Slaves and slavery:
  abolition movement, 692, 760–765
  John Quincy Adams' views, 696–697
  Calhoun's views on, 696–697
  Constitutional dilemma, 63, 83–85
    importation forbidden after 1808, 91
  corrupting effect on white masters, 446
  dominated American politics, 434–435, 720
  elections of 1800, 305
  emancipation, 163, 445, 693–694
  fear of uprisings, 444–447, 486, 692, 789
  field hands, 438, 442
  fugitive slaves, 443, 760–761
  gouging and biting, 449–450
  household slaves, 442
  Jefferson's views, 446–447, 492–493, 789
  laws relating to, 443
  love-hate relationship with whites, 434–449
  miscegenation, 447–448
  Missouri Compromise and, 690–697
  of mixed blood, 763
  nighttime bonfires, 442–443
  plantation life, 436–441
  prohibited north of 36°, 30', 695–696
  prohibitions against reading and writing,
    763
  proposed tax on imported slaves, 135–136
  punishments, 437–438
  relationship with masters and mistresses,
    443–444
  runaway slaves, 760–761
    pursuit and capture, 760–761
  sexual relations of slave women with white
    masters, 372–373, 437–438, 443–444,
    447–448, 782
  slave markets, 438
  threat to Union, 697, 819–820
  treatment of, 441–452
  underground railroad, 761–765
  value of, 761

(*See also* Blacks; North-South differences; South)
Smallpox epidemics, among Indians, 519
Smith, Josiah, 99–100
Smith, Margaret Bayard:
  on British burning of Washington, 631–632
  on Clay's speech attacking Jackson, 667
  on Madison's inauguration, 580–581
  on Robert Owen, 688
Smith, Melancton, 106
Smith, Robert, 572, 581, 589, 633
Smith, Samuel, 580, 589, 633–634
Smugglers and smuggling, 569, 571
Smyth, Alexander, 601–604
Smyth, J.F.D., 438
Snake (or Shoshone) Indians, 527
Snake River, 527, 531, 539
Social injustice, 35
Socialism, 286
Society, American:
  analysis of, 77–79
  character of, 342
  equality of rank, 78–79
  horse-shedding, 378
  Madison's view of, 70–71, 105
  "Openness" of, 826
  Pinckney's analysis of, 77–79
  sailors as subculture, 343–344
  structured on basis of making money, 44–45
  in urban centers, 384–388
  youth oriented, 368
Society for the Encouragement of Manufacturers, 111, 116
Society of the Cincinnati, 9–11, 111, 122, 185
Soldiers:
  contrast between sailors and, 620–623
  lack of discipline and leadership, 622
Songs and music, 262
Sons of Liberty, 8
South, 434–453
  aristocracy and yeoman farmers, 326
  basic split between North and South, 17
    (*See also* North-South differences)
  differences between states, 453–454
  dueling, 450
  effect of invention of cotton-gin on, 347–348
  effect of slavery, 434
  farmers, 326, 440
  feudal character of society, 451–452
  gouging and biting, 449–450
  horses and horsemanship, 440
  hunting and fishing, 436–437
  love-hate relationship with blacks, 434–449
  Missouri Compromise and state rights, 693
  paradoxes of Southern life, 437

plantation life, 435–441
  cuisine, 436
  political parties, 446
  population, 732
  schizophrenia and paranoia, 17, 103, 108
  sexual behavior, 372–373
    exploitation of female slaves by white masters, 447–448
  slave and antislave cultures, 764
  slavery question, 16–17, 108
  tensions and conflict, 15–16
  two classes of whites, 449
  (*See also* Blacks; North-South differences; Slaves and slavery)
South America:
  and Monroe Doctrine, 716
  Spanish colonies in, 820
  trade with, 558–559
South Carolina:
  character of people, 453
  delegates to Constitutional Convention, 84–85, 87, 89
  Loyalist killed at Fishing Creek, 6
  threat of secession, 135
South Hadley Falls Canal, 331–332
Southern Indians, 198–199
  Spanish influence, 208
  treaty with, 140
Southwest frontier, 719
  Indian attacks, 644–647
Spain:
  colonies in South America, 820
  control of Florida, 663–665
  decrees against American shipping, 565
  Ferdinand VII restored to throne, 710
  Genêt's plan to attack posts in Louisiana Territory, 212
  Louisiana Territory, 151, 208, 485
  Mississippi controlled by, 464–467
  Napoleonic wars, 572–573
  negotiations between John Quincy Adams and, 711, 713–714, 717
  protests Jackson's action in Florida, 665–668
  revolt of American colonies, 710
  tariffs on food passing through New Orleans, 212
Speculation in land, 327–328, 671, 785
  in Alabama, 736
  Western lands, 4, 60, 150–152, 180–181
Spiritualists, 755
  settlements of, 735
Springfield, Massachusetts and Shays' Rebellion, 26–28
  attacks on arsenal, 30
Stamp Act, 8, 24
Stansbury, Colonel, 630
"The Star-Spangled Banner" (Key), 637, 656

States:
  admission of new states, 58–59
  constitutions, 1–2, 21
    British models and precedents, 62
    influence of John Adams, 119
  democratic fever, 7–8
  deterioration of interstate relations, 19–22
  differences between citizens of, 452–453
  economic conflicts, 11–16
  "home-rule" controversy, 7
  legislative powers, 698–699
  limited ability to raise money by taxation, 683
  Supreme Court dominance over state courts and legislatures, 698–703
  "Unitedness" of, 1–2
States rights, 137, 453
  Bank of the United States case, 702–705
  Federal debates, 71–77
  Gibbons v. Ogden defining federal-state powers, 706–709
  Marshall's speech in Virginia ratifying convention, 138, 703
  Supreme Court decisions, 698–703
  Virginia and Kentucky Resolution, 271, 574, 705, 794
Steam engines, 345
Steamboats, 334, 803
  Gibbons v. Ogden defining federal-state powers, 706–709
Steuben, Baron Friedrich von, 216
Stocks and stock-jobbing, 158
  canal-building, 330
Stone, William, 772
Stony Point, Battle of, 597
Story, Joseph, 699–700, 703
Stricker, John, 634–635
Strong, Caleb, 641
Strutt, Jedediah, 350
Stuart, Gilbert, 399–401
  portrait of John Quincy Adams, 726
  portrait of Washington, 632
  The Skater. Portrait of William Grant, 400, (illus.) 410
Success-failure syndrome, 185, 215, 336, 681
Suffrage issue, 779
  Constitutional debates, 63–65
Sullivan, James (Governor of Massachusetts), 471
Supreme Court, 69, 73, 94, 136–139, 296, 698–709
  appeals from decisions of state courts, 137
  appointments to, 138–139, 823
  attacks on, 480–481, 576
  Bank of United States case, 702–705
  bastion of Federalism, 698
  Cohens v. Virginia, 706
  Dartmouth College Case, 700–702

  decisions on obligation of contracts, 698
  dominance over state courts and legislatures, 137, 698–703
  Fletcher v. Peck, 698, 700–701
  Gibbons v. Ogden, 706–709
  impeachment trial of Samuel Chase, 495–496
  issue of constitutionality, 483
  Judiciary Act of 1789, 136–139, 296, 495, 699
    attempts to repeal, 477–483
  Marbury v. Madison, 480–483, 706
  John Marshall, chief justice, 104, 476
  Martin v. Hunter's Lesee, 699
  opposition to, 709
  powers, 479, 700
    to hear criminal cases on appeal, 706
    of national government over the states, 705–708
  review of state court decisions, 699
  right of state to tax corporations chartered by Congress, 702–703
Swarthout, Samuel, 504–505
Sweden, 110
Swedenborgians, 755
Swiss immigrants, 738, 742–746

Talleyrand, 173, 259, 269, 275, 381, 486, 717
Talmadge, Benjamin, 804
Tammany Society, New York, 560, 746, 748
Taney, Robert, 762
Tangiers, 552
Tariffs, 151
  auction sales to circumvent, 670
  conflict in Congress, 134–136
  demand for protective, 134, 670, 673
  sectional differences, 134
Tawney, R.H., 96
Taxes and taxation:
  duties on distilled spirits, 197–198, 201–202, 227
  import duties, 592–593
  property taxes, 272–274
  War of 1812, 592–593
  whiskey tax, 161–163
Taylor, John, 694
Taylor, Zachary, 720
Tea trade with China, 337–339
Tecumseh, Shawnee warrior, 233, 595–596, 605
  Battle of the Thames, 610–611
  joined with British, 597
  military alliance of Indian tribes, 595–596
  visit to Creek Indians, 444, 596
Temperance movement, 115, 681, 751
  Christianity and, 753–754
  tracts, 753

Tennessee, supported Jackson's bid for
    presidency, 722
Tenskwatawa (the Prophet), 595
Territories:
    organization of, 58–59
    slavery prohibited in, 59
Teton Sioux, 521, 523, 532
Texas:
    raids and forays, 711
    reestablishment of Spanish rule, 711
    settlement by Americans, 711–712
    uprising in Mexico, 711
Textile industry:
    Arkwright's technology, 349–350
    cotton cloth, 669–670
    cotton mills, 350, 766–769
    invention of power loom, 766–767
Thacher, Rev. Samuel, 681–682, 813, 827
Thames, Battle of the, 610–611
Theaters, 386–387
Thomas, Jesse, 695
Threshing machine, invention of, 346
Time, attitudes toward, 376
Tippecanoe, Harrison's raid on Indians, 596
Tobacco, 367, 388, 468
    Connecticut grown, 332–333
Toll roads, 335–337
Tories (see Loyalists)
Torpedoes, invention of, 346
Toussaint L'Ouverture, 427, 486
Town life, 378, 380–393
    in New England, 733–734
    (See also Urban life)
Tracy, Uriah, 277, 498
Trading empire of U.S., 558–559
    (See also Foreign commerce; Ships and
    shipping)
Transmigration, 243–271
Transportation, 329–344
    canal building, 329–337
    foreign commerce, 337–344
    "internal improvements," 329
    ships and shipping, 337–344
    toll roads, 335–337
Treaty of Ghent, 643
    peace negotiations, 600–603
    signing of, 644
Treaty of 1795, between Spain and U.S., 666
Treaty of Paris (1783), 1, 168, 718
    provisions about Loyalists, 6
    resentment over terms, 17–19
    resistance of states, 4
    on slavery, 3
Trenton:
    antislavery meetings, 692
    visit of Monroe, 661
Tripolitan War, 552, 613
    (See also Barbary War)

Trollope, Anthony, 768, 776
Trollope, Frances, 776
Trotter, Col. James, 185–186
Trumbull, John (poet), 32, 404, 419–420
Trumbull, John (painter), 404, 414, 417–418,
    511
    Battle of Bunker Hill, (illus.) 412, 416–417
    The Death of General Montgomery, (illus.) 406,
    416–417
    The Declaration of Independence, 417
    historical paintings, 416–417
    in Capitol in Washington, D.C., 417
    portraits of George Washington, 417
    The Resignation of General Washington, at
    Annapolis, Maryland, 417
    Surrender of Cornwallis, (illus.) 413, 417
    The Surrender of General Burgoyne at
    Saratoga, 417
    Mrs. Sara Trumbull on Her Deathbed, (illus.)
    414
Trumbull, Jonathan (governor of
    Connecticut), 404, 574
Truxtun, Thomas, 266, 624
Tucker, Henry St. George, 496
Tuckerman, Henry, 173
Turkey-Russia war, 820
Tyler, John, 103, 720
"Tyranny and oppression," 36
    saving mankind from, 4–37
    (See also Redemptive mission of America)

Underground railroad, 761–765
    conductors, 762
    support system, 763–764
Unemployment, 669
    debate over public measures to ameliorate,
    675–676
    postwar, 671
    side effects of depressed economy,
    676–681
Union (federal ship), 111
Unitarianism, 324, 751, 800
    opposed by Lyman Beecher, 752–754
United Netherlands, 110
United States:
    exaltation of books, 364–365
    glory of Republic, 418–419
    idealization of, 34, 365
    ideas and prejudices, 827
    "talked into existence," 57, 588, 707
    (See also Federal government)
United States (American frigate), 254–255,
    266, 618, 620
"Unitedness" of states, 1–2
Universalists, 755
University, national, recommended by John
    Quincy Adams and Washington,
    360–361, 731

Upper classes (*see* Class differences)
Upward mobility, 43
Urban life, 378, 380–393
   clothing and dress, 389–391
   French influence, 380–382
   names given to communities, 391–392
   in New England, 733–734
   rural versus urban, 392–393, 686–689
   sexual mores, 382–384
   social life and entertainment, 384–388
Utopian ideals, 35–37

Valmy, Battle of, 202–204
Van Buren, Martin, 709, 720, 724
Vandalia Company, 151
Van Rensselaer, Solomon, 602
Van Rensselaer, Stephen, 601–602, 728
Vaughn, Benjamin, 40
Venable, Abraham, 257
Venereal disease, 372, 392, 782–783
Vermont, 453
   admission to Union, 202
   delegates to Constitutional Convention,
     52
   emigration from, 735–736
Vermont Gazette, 268, 281
Vermontville, Ohio, 736
Vesey, Denmark, 789
Vidal, Gore, 823
Villere, Gabriel, 649
Villere, Jacques, 649
Virginia:
   canals, 333–334
   capital designed by Jefferson, 394
   character of Virginians, 452–453
   Convention to reform Articles, 39, 50–51,
     794
   delegates to Constitutional Convention,
     55–56
   emigration from, 737
   Gabriel's slave insurrection, 444–445
   horseracing, 441
   influence on Old South, 719
   land disputes with Pennsylvania, 4
   opposition to Supreme Court decisions,
     704
   Potomac River controversy, 16
   presidents from, 659, 823
   ratification of Constitution, 97, 100–105,
     109, 579, 703
   slavery issue, 103
   state rights issues, 705–706
   Statute of Religious Liberty, 288
   tidewater economy, 327
   Whiskey Rebellion, 230
Virginia and Kentucky Resolutions, 271, 574,
     705, 794
   separatist doctrines, 580

Virginia Assembly, Annapolis Convention
   called by, 50–51
Virginia Dynasty, 659, 823
Virginia Plan, Constitutional Convention,
   57–74, 76
Vision of Columbus, The (Barlow), 420–421,
   558
Voighy, Henry, 346
Voltaire, 35
Vox populi, vox Dei (the voice of the people
   is the voice of God), 153, 159

Wabash Indians, 159, 183, 185–187
Wabash River, 462
Walker, Betsy, 493
Walker, John, 493, 576
Waltham (Mass.) cotton mills, 766–769
War of 1812, 590–643
   altered England's perception of Americans,
     655
   American naval victories, 615–626
     pursuit of British merchant ships, 615
   army and militia, 597, 601–604
   British desire to chastise Americans,
     627–628, 632
   British naval superiority, 594
   causes, 654
   declaration of, 592–594
   Indian allies of British, 603, 604
   invasion of Canada, 601–602
   military situation on Canadian-U.S. border,
     600–614
   Napoleon's defeat, effect of, 627
   naval engagements, 597–598, 655–656
     depredations of privateers, 623–626
     on Great Lakes, 607–611
     on Lake Champlain, 607, 613–614
     on Lake Erie, 607, 612–613
     on Lake Ontario, 607
     superior American seamanship, 618,
       621–622
   New England opposition, 598, 639–640
   in Northwest, 591–614
   on Ohio frontier, 599–600
   peace negotiations, 638–639
   pillaging and burning of Washington and
     Baltimore, 627–638
   postwar depression, 669–689
   raids against American coastal towns,
     628–629
   South in favor of, 598–599
   theater of operations, 594
   War Hawks, 590, 593–654
Ward, Artemas, 25, 27, 29, 195
Wareham (Mass.), British attacks, 629
Warren, James, 24, 38, 780
   on pursuit of material things, 38–39, 42,
     45–46

Warren, Joseph, 416
Warren, Mercy Otis, 38–39, 786–787
Warville, Brissot de, 386, 390
Washington, George:
  address after Newburgh revolt, 21–22, 829
  address to Congress, 148, 195–198, 201,
    235–236
  affairs with women, 493
  Anti-Federalists and, 164–165
  Benedict Arnold's treason, 806
  awesomeness of, 53
  birthday celebration, 236–237
  Cabinet, 129–131, 153–154, 214
  Callender's attack, 281–282, 490–491
  character of, 251, 493
  Constitutional Convention chaired by,
    52–53, 86, 101
  criticism from Republicans, 198, 200
  death of, 279–280
  defamed by Tom Paine, 493
  deification of, 9–10, 279
  denunciations of, 210–211, 224, 493
  on deterioration of interstate relations,
    19–22
  on duties on distilled spirits, 197–198,
    201–202
  election of 1792, 200–201
  embargo declared by, 216–217
  execution of Major André, 668
  Farewell Address, 245–247, 474, 643
    to avoid involvement in European
      politics, 717
    prepared by Madison, 200, 245–247
  farewell to officers at Fraunces Tavern,
    9–10, 125, 804
  fear of anarchy, 23, 33
  first President, 118–119, 121–122,
    124–127, 129–132, 138–141, 145, 825
    inauguration, 122, 125–126
    only president elected unanimously, 690
    reluctance to run for office, 118–119
  General of Continental Army, 9–10, 630
  Indian policy, 196–200
  interest in inventions, 333–334
  Jay Treaty, 217–218, 222, 224–226
  Lafayette and, 808–809, 812
  land speculation, 4
  learns of St. Clair's defeat, 190
  on Loyalists, 5
  Maclay invited to dinner with, 140–141
  monarchial charges against, 136
  New England tour, 163–165
  portraits, 394, 402, 417, 632
  president of canal-building company, 333
  problem of selecting successor to, 244–249
  Proclamation of Neutrality, 208–209
    authority to issue, 211–212
  rages and tears, 241, 668, 806
  reaction to uprising of farmers in Mass., 33
  recalled Monroe as ambassador to France,
    252–253
  retirement, 243–244
  second term, 200–202
  statues of, 394
  supporter of national university, 360
  Supreme Court justices selected by,
    138–139
  triumphal journey to New York, 124–125
  Whiskey Rebellion, 229–230
Washington, Martha, 141
Washington, D.C.:
  British attack and burning, 629–633
    burning of Capitol and White House,
      631–632
    effects on world opinion, 633
    removal of government documents, 630
  canals, 334
  defense of, 630
  Lafayette's visit, 808–809
    address to both houses of Congress,
      810–811
  new capital, 294–295
  presidential mansion, 294
Water power, 345, 766
Watson, John, 740
Wayne, "Mad" Anthony, 195, 514, 531, 652
  expedition against Northwest Indians,
    200–201
  victory at Fallen Timbers, 227, 231–234,
    595
Wealth, pursuit of, 158
  (See also Money-making)
Weber, Max, 310, 376
Webster, Daniel, 501, 641, 703, 707–708, 813
  Dartmouth College Case, 700–701, 703,
    707–708
  election of 1824, 719–720, 725, 728
  eloquence, 703
  New England represented by, 719
  opposed chartering of national bank, 658
  political career, 725
  sectional leader, 719–720
Webster, Noah, 319, 587
  spelling book, 356
  views on education, 355–357
Weehawken, New Jersey, 500
Weems, Parson Mason, 279, 363
Weights and measures, 731
  uniform system of, 148
Welfare state, 685
Wellington, defeated Napoleon at Waterloo,
  627, 710, 718
West, Benjamin, 396–401
  Death of General Wolfe on the Plains of
    Abraham, 396, (illus.) 405, 416
  Loyalist sympathizer, 397

West, Benjamin (cont.):
  The Parting of Hector and Andromache, 396
  young American painters studied with,
    396–397, 400–401, 404, 414
West Indian trade, 219, 558–559, 669
  British seizure of American ships, 215
  terms of Jay Treaty, 220–221
Weston, William, 330
Westward migration, 58–60, 79, 84, 151, 234,
    679, 732–737
  cumulative communities, 736
  depopulation of older states, 733
  failures and defeats, 741
  by families, groups, 733–734
  hardships and dangers, 169
  incentives to, 733–734
    to improve material condition, 736
  land speculators, 4, 16, 60, 150–152,
    180–181
  new towns, 733–734
    covenant or agreement, 734
  by religious congregations, 733–734
  settlers advice to those at home, 740–741,
    748–749
  settlers and Indians, 168–194
  settlers led by "founder," 735
  by Southerners, 736–737
  successful settlements, 738–741
  by unorthodox sects, 735
  vices and virtues of "democracy," 183
  (See also Frontier settlements)
Wheeling, Virginia, 456
Wheelock, Eleazar, 197, 700
"Whiskey Boys," 230–231
Whiskey Rebellion, 227–231, 592, 826
  causes, 227–228
  militia muster, 228–229
White, Canvass, 770–771
White House, 294
  set afire by British, 631–632
Whitman, Marcus, 191–193
Whitman, Narissa, 191–192
Whitman, Walter, 813
Whitney, Eli:
  developed assembly line technique, 348
  development of interchangeable parts,
    348–349
  gun factory, 348–349
  invention of cotton-gin, 346–349
Wilkinson, James, 198–199, 502–505, 508,
    546, 549, 550, 611
  negotiations with Miami Indians, 198–199
  War of 1812, 597
Willard, Emma, 682–683
Willet, Colonel, 803
William and Mary College, 353, 357
Williams College, 755
Williamson, Hugh, 80

Wilson, James, 13, 64–66, 79, 90, 92, 98, 114,
    371
  debts, 674–675
  delegate to Constitutional Convention, 55
  manufacturing ventures, 344–345
  Supreme Court Justice, 138–139
Wilson, Samuel, 364
Winchester, James, 604–605
Winder, William, 630–631
Windsor Locks Canal, 332–333
Windward Passage, 266
Winthrop, John, 35, 733
  "Model of Christian Charity," 14–15,
    35–36, 47–48, 80, 736
Wirt, William, 477–478, 703, 707–708
Witherspoon, Betsey, 444
Wolcott, Oliver, 206, 214, 219, 225, 245,
    252
  on Adams and Jefferson, 283
  secretary of treasury, 283–284
Women:
  attitudes toward feminine sexuality, 373
  education of, 356–357, 682–683
  financially dependent, 675
  freedom allowed young women, 383
  Indian treatment of, 533
  lacked equality, 43
  "land of daughterhood," 291–292
  political activities, 366–367
  reformers, 679
  role in family, 372–373
  sexual mores, 382–384
Woodmason, Charles, 313
Worcester, Noah, 313–314
Worcester convention, 24–25, 28–29
Work ethic, 369, 677
Workingman associations, 687
Wright, Frances, 802, 810
Wyandot Indians, 596
Wyoming Valley controversy, 4
Wythe, George, 101, 576–577, 585

XYZ affair, 263–266, 269, 275

Yale College, 352–353, 418–420, 755
"Yankee Doodle," 262
Yankton Sioux, 519–520
Yazoo Land Act, 698–699
Yazoo River, 466–467
Yellow fever epidemic of 1793, 427–429
Yellowstone River, 526, 541
Yeo, Sir James, 611
York, slave belonging to Clark, 513, 523
York (now Toronto), 611
Young, William, 390–391
Youth gangs, 678
Youth oriented society, 368
Yrujo, Marquis Casa, 504

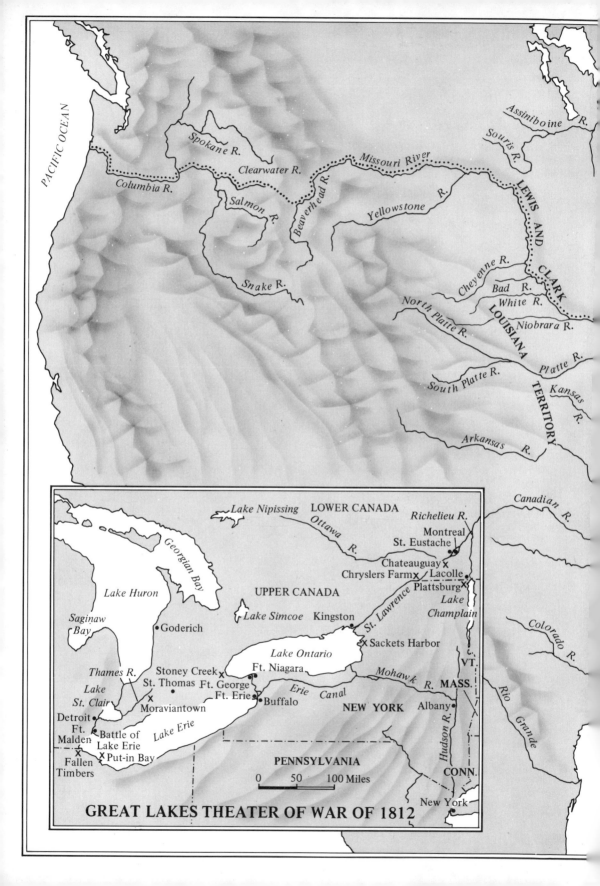

PACIFIC OCEAN

Spokane R.

Columbia R.

Clearwater R.

Salmon R.

Beaverhead R.

Snake R.

Missouri River

Yellowstone R.

Cheyenne R.

Bad R.

White R.

Niobrara R.

North Platte R.

South Platte R.

Platte R.

Kansas R.

Arkansas R.

Assiniboine R.

Souris R.

LEWIS AND CLARK

LOUISIANA TERRITORY

Canadian R.

Colorado R.

Rio Grande

GREAT LAKES THEATER OF WAR OF 1812

Lake Nipissing   LOWER CANADA

Ottawa R.

Richelieu R.

Montreal
St. Eustache
Chateauguay ✕
Chryslers Farm ✕   Lacolle ✕
Plattsburg ✕
Lake Champlain

Georgian Bay

Lake Huron

Saginaw Bay

UPPER CANADA

Lake Simcoe   Kingston

St. Lawrence R.

Sackets Harbor ✕

• Goderich

Lake Ontario

Ft. Niagara

VT.

Colorado R.

Thames R.

Stoney Creek ✕
St. Thomas •
Ft. George
Ft. Erie •
• Buffalo

Erie Canal

Mohawk R.   MASS.

Lake St. Clair

Detroit
Ft. Malden

Moraviantown ✕

Lake Erie

Battle of Lake Erie
✕ Put-in Bay

Fallen Timbers ✕

NEW YORK   Albany •

Hudson R.

PENNSYLVANIA

CONN.

0   50   100 Miles

New York